THE ROUTLEDGE COMPANION
TO TWENTIETH CENTURY PHILOSOPHY

The Routledge Companion to Twentieth Century Philosophy is an authoritative survey and assessment of the major figures, themes, and movements in twentieth-century philosophy. Featuring twenty-two chapters written by leading international scholars, this outstanding collection is divided into five clear parts and presents a comprehensive picture of the period for the first time:

Major Themes and Movements: The Birth of Analytic Philosophy; The Development of Analytic Philosophy: Wittgenstein and After; Hegelianism in the Twentieth Century; Kant in the Twentieth Century; American Philosophy in the Twentieth Century; Naturalism; Feminism in Philosophy

Logic, Language, Knowledge, and Metaphysics: Philosophical Logic; Philosophy of Language; Metaphysics; Epistemology in the Twentieth Century

Philosophy of Mind, Psychology, and Science: Philosophy of Mind; Philosophy of Psychology; Philosophy of Science

Phenomenology, Hermeneutics, Existentialism, and Critical Theory: Phenomenology; Twentieth-Century Hermeneutics; German Philosophy (Heidegger, Gadamer, Apel); Critical Theory; French Philosophy in the Twentieth Century

Politics, Ethics, and Aesthetics: Twentieth-Century Moral Philosophy; Twentieth-Century Political Philosophy; Twentieth-Century Aesthetics

The Routledge Companion to Twentieth Century Philosophy is essential reading for students of philosophy, and for anyone interested in the development of philosophy over the last one hundred years.

Dermot Moran holds the Chair of Philosophy at University College Dublin and is a Member of the Royal Irish Academy. He is the author of *The Philosophy of John Scottus Eriugena*, *Introduction to Phenomenology*, and *Edmund Husserl: Founder of Phenomenology*. He has co-edited *The Phenomenology Reader*, *Phenomenology: Critical Concepts in Philosophy*, and *Eriugena, Berkeley, and the Idealist Tradition*. He is the founding editor of *The International Journal of Philosophical Studies*.

Routledge Philosophy Companions

Routledge Philosophy Companions offer thorough, high quality surveys and assessments of the major topics and periods in philosophy. Covering key problems, themes and thinkers, all entries are specially commissioned for each volume and written by leading scholars in the field. Clear, accessible and carefully edited and organised, *Routledge Philosophy Companions* are indispensable for anyone coming to a major topic or period in philosophy, as well as for the more advanced reader.

The Routledge Companion to Aesthetics, Second Edition
Edited by Berys Gaut and Dominic Lopes

The Routledge Companion to Philosophy of Religion
Edited by Chad Meister and Paul Copan

The Routledge Companion to Philosophy of Science
Edited by Stathis Psillos and Martin Curd

The Routledge Companion to Twentieth Century Philosophy
Edited by Dermot Moran

Forthcoming:
The Routledge Companion to Nineteenth Century Philosophy
Edited by Dean Moyar

The Routledge Companion to Philosophy of Psychology
Edited by John Symons and Paco Calvo

The Routledge Companion to Philosophy of Film
Edited by Paisley Livingston and Carl Plantinga

The Routledge Companion to Ethics
Edited by John Skorupski

The Routledge Companion to Metaphysics
Edited by Robin Le Poidevin, Peter Simons, Andrew McGonigal, and Ross Cameron

The Routledge Companion to Epistemology
Edited by Sven Bernecker and Duncan Pritchard

The Routledge Companion to Seventeenth Century Philosophy
Edited by Dan Kaufman

The Routledge Companion to Eighteenth Century Philosophy
Edited by Aaron Garrett

THE
ROUTLEDGE COMPANION
TO TWENTIETH CENTURY
PHILOSOPHY

Edited by
Dermot Moran

Routledge
Taylor & Francis Group

LONDON AND NEW YORK

First published 2008
by Routledge
2 Park Square, Milton Park, Abingdon, OX14 4RN

Simultaneously published in the USA and Canada
by Routledge
270 Madison Ave, New York, NY 10016

Routledge is an imprint of the Taylor & Francis Group, an informa business

© 2008 Dermot Moran for selection and editorial matter; individual contributors for
their contributions

Typeset in Goudy Oldstyle Std 10.5/13pt by Fakenham Photosetting Ltd,
Fakenham, Norfolk
Printed and bound in Great Britain by TJ International Ltd, Padstow, Cornwall

British Library Cataloguing in Publication Data
A catalogue record for this book is available from the British Library

Library of Congress Cataloging in Publication Data
A catalog record for this book has been applied for

ISBN 10: 0–415–29936–5
ISBN 13: 978–0–415–29936–7

In Memory of my Mother Nora (O'Sullivan) Moran

(† 27 November 2006)

Ar dheis Dé go raibh a h-anam dhílis

CONTENTS

CONTENTS

CONTRIBUTORS

Karl-Otto Apel was born in Düsseldorf, Germany, in 1922 and studied at the universities of Bonn and Mainz. He is currently Professor Emeritus at the University of Frankfurt, having previously taught at Kiel and Saarbrucken. His publications in English include *Understanding and Explanation: A Transcendental-Pragmatic Perspective* (1984), *Towards a Transcendental Semiotics: Selected Essays of K.-O. Apel*, vol. 1 (1994), *Ethics and the Theory of Rationality: Selected Essays of K.-O. Apel*, vol. II (1996), *Charles S. Peirce: From Pragmatism to Pragmaticism* (1995), *From a Transcendental-Semiotic Point of View* (1998), and *Towards a Transformation of Philosophy* (1980, repr. 1998).

Nicholas Davey was educated at the Universities of York, Sussex, and Tübingen. He has lectured at the City University London, the University of Manchester, the University of Wales Institute, Cardiff (1981–96) and is presently Professor of Philosophy and Dean of Humanities at the University of Dundee, Scotland. His principal research interests are in aesthetics and hermeneutics. He has published widely in the field of Continental philosophy, aesthetics, and hermeneutic theory. His most recent book is *Unquiet Understanding, Gadamer's Philosophical Hermeneutics* (2006). He is currently working on a study of hermeneutics and aesthetics which will appear under the title *Seeing Otherwise*.

Hans-Johann Glock is Professor of Philosophy at the University of Zurich, Switzerland. He was previously Professor of Philosophy at the University of Reading, and has held research fellowships or visiting professorships at Oxford University, Queen's University (Canada), Bielefeld University, and Rhodes University (South Africa). He is the author of *A Wittgenstein Dictionary* (1996), which has been translated into several languages, *Quine and Davidson on Language, Thought and Reality* (2003), and *What is Analytic Philosophy?* (2008). He has edited or co-edited eight volumes, and published numerous articles on the philosophy of mind, the philosophy of language, Wittgenstein, and the history of analytic philosophy.

Gary Gutting holds the Notre Dame Endowed Chair in Philosophy at the University of Notre Dame, Indiana. He is the author of five books: *Religious Belief and Religious Skepticism* (1982), *Michel Foucault's Archaeology of Scientific Reason* (1989), *Pragmatic Liberalism and the Critique of Modernity* (1999), and *French Philosophy in the Twentieth Century* (2001), and *Michel Foucault: A Very Short Introduction* (2005). He has co-authored or edited another six volumes. He is founding editor of *Notre Dame Philosophical Reviews*, an electronic book review journal (http://ndpr.nd.edu/).

Paul Guyer is Professor of Philosophy and Florence R. C. Murray Professor in the Humanities at the University of Pennsylvania. He is the author, editor, or translator of eighteen books and numerous articles on Kant, the history of modern philosophy, and the history of aesthetics. Among his recent works are Kant's "Notes and Fragments" (2005), Kant (2006), The Cambridge Companion to Kant and Modern Philosophy (2006), Kant's Groundwork for the Metaphysics of Morals: A Reader's Guide (2007), and Knowledge, Reason, and Taste: Kant's Responses to Hume (2008). He is currently writing a history of modern aesthetics.

Robert Hanna is Professor of Philosophy at the University of Colorado, Boulder. He received his BA from the University of Toronto and his Ph.D. from Yale University. He is the author of Kant and the Foundations of Analytic Philosophy (2001), Kant, Science, and Human Nature (2006), Rationality and Logic (2006), and Embodied Minds in Action (co-authored with Michelle Maiese) (2008).

Axel Honneth was born in 1949 in Essen, Germany, and studied philosophy, sociology, and German literature at the universities of Bonn, Bochum, and Berlin. Currently he is Professor of Social Philosophy at the Johann Wolfgang Goethe University and Director of the Institute for Social Research in Frankfurt am Main. His publications in English include: Social Action and Human Nature (with Hans Joas) (1988), The Critique of Power: Reflective Stages in a Critical Social Theory (1990), The Struggle for Recognition: The Moral Grammar of Social Conflicts (1995), The Fragmented World of the Social: Essays in Social and Political Philosophy (1995), Suffering from Indeterminacy: Spinoza Lectures Amsterdam (1999), Redistribution or Recognition? A Political-Philosophical Exchange (together with Nancy Fraser) (2003), Disrespect: The Normative Foundations of Critical Theory (2007), and Reification and Recognition: A New Look at an Old Idea (2008).

Geert Keil holds a chair in philosophy at RWTH Aachen University, Germany. Born in 1963, he studied philosophy, linguistics, and German literature at the Universities of Bochum and Hamburg. In 1991, he received his Ph.D. from the University of Hamburg. From 1992 to 2004 he was Assistant Professor at the Humboldt University of Berlin and a visiting scholar in Norway, USA (Stanford), and Switzerland. His areas of specialization are the philosophy of mind and action, philosophy of language, metaphysics, and philosophy of science. He is the author of Kritik des Naturalismus (1993), Handeln und Verursachen,(2000), Quine zur Einführung (2002), and Willensfreiheit (2007), and the co-editor of six anthologies, including Fifty Years of Quine's "Two Dogmas" (2003). A list of publications is available at http://www.phil-inst.rwth-aachen.de.

E. J. Lowe is Professor of Philosophy at Durham University, specializing in metaphysics, philosophy of mind and action, philosophy of logic and language, and the philosophy of John Locke. His books include Kinds of Being (1989), Subjects of Experience (1996), The Possibility of Metaphysics (1998), Locke (2005), and The Four-Category Ontology (2006).

Kelby Mason is a graduate fellow in philosophy at Rutgers University. He received his BA and Master of Public Health from the University of Sydney.

Matt Matravers is Professor of Political Philosophy at the University of York, England. He has for many years been involved in the Morrell Studies in Toleration Programme. His current research focuses on dangerousness with particular reference to personality disorders. He is the author of *Justice and Punishment* (2000) and *Responsibility and Justice* (2007). In addition, he is the contributing editor of *Punishment and Political Theory* (1999), *Scanlon and Contractualism* (2003), and *Managing Modernity: Politics and the Culture of Control* (2005).

Dermot Moran is Professor of Philosophy at University College Dublin and a Member of the Royal Irish Academy. He has previously taught at Queen's University Belfast and Maynooth University, Ireland, and has held visiting positions at Yale University, Connecticut College, Rice University, and Northwestern University. He has published widely on medieval philosophy and contemporary European philosophy (especially phenomenology). His monographs include *The Philosophy of John Scottus Eriugena* (1989, reissued 2004), *Introduction to Phenomenology* (2000), *Edmund Husserl: Founder of Phenomenology* (2005). He has edited Edmund Husserl's *Logical Investigations* (2001), and *Edmund Husserl, The Shorter Logical Investigations* (2001), as well as co-editing (with Tim Mooney) *The Phenomenology Reader* (2002), and (with Lester E. Embree) *Phenomenology: Critical Concepts in Philosophy*, 5 vols. (2004). He is currently writing a critical commentary on Husserl's *Crisis of European Sciences* for Cambridge University Press.

Andrea Nye is Professor of Philosophy Emeritus at University of Wisconsin at Whitewater, USA, and currently Adjunct Professor in Liberal Arts at the Boston Conservatory in Boston. Her books include: *Feminist Theory and the Philosophies of Man* (1988), *Philosophy and Feminism: At the Border* (1990), *The Princess and the Philosopher* (1999), and *Feminism and Modern Philosophy* (2004).

James O'Shea is Senior Lecturer in philosophy at University College Dublin. In addition to a variety of articles on Hume, Kant, and William James, recent publications include *Wilfrid Sellars: Naturalism with a Normative Turn* (2007) and "Conceptual connections: Kant and the twentieth-century analytic tradition," in the *Blackwell Companion to Kant* (2006).

Sarah Patterson is Lecturer in Philosophy at Birkbeck College, University of London. She has published papers in philosophy of mind, philosophy of psychology, and early modern philosophy, and is working on a book on Descartes's theory of mind.

Terry Pinkard is currently a Professor of Philosophy at Georgetown University, where he also previously taught from 1975 to 2000. From 2000 to 2005 he was Professor of Philosophy at Northwestern University, Evanston, Illinois. Among his most recent publications are *Hegel's Phenomenology: The Sociality of Reason* (1994), *Hegel: A Biography* (2000), *German Philosophy 1760–1860: The Legacy of Idealism* (2002), and he is the editor of *Heinrich Heine: On the History of Religion and Philosophy in Germany and Other Texts* (2007). In 2003–4, he was the Humboldt Preisträger at the Humboldt University in Berlin. In 1998, he was made an "Honorary Professor" (*Ehrenprofessor*) and "Honorary Teacher" (*Ehrenlehrbeauftragte*) at Tübingen University, Germany.

Michael Potter is Reader in the Philosophy of Mathematics at Cambridge University and a Fellow of Fitzwilliam College. His books include *Reason's Nearest Kin* (2000), *Set Theory and its Philosophy* (2004), and *Wittgenstein's Notes on Logic* (2008).

Stathis Psillos is Associate Professor of Philosophy of Science in the University of Athens, Greece. He is the author of *Philosophy of Science A–Z* (2007), *Causation and Explanation* (2002) – which was awarded the British Society for the Philosophy of Science Past President's prize – and *Scientific Realism: How Science Tracks Truth* (1999). He is the editor (with Martin Curd) of the *Routledge Companion to the Philosophy of Science*. He has published over 50 articles in learned journals and edited collections.

R. M. Sainsbury was born in London in 1943. He is Professor of Philosophy at the University of Texas at Austin and Susan Stebbing Professor of Philosophy at King's College London. He is the author of *Russell* (1979, 1985), *Paradoxes* (1988, 2nd edn. 1995), *Logical Forms* (1991, 2nd edn. 2000), *Departing From Frege* (2002), and *Reference Without Referents* (2005). He is currently working on a book entitled *Fiction and Fictionalism*.

Chandra Sekhar Sripada is a resident in psychiatry and adjunct Assistant Professor in Philosophy at the University of Michigan Ann Arbor. He received his MD from the University of Texas Houston, his internship in psychiatry from the University of California San Francisco, and his Ph.D. in philosophy from Rutgers University.

Jason Stanley is Professor of Philosophy at Rutgers University. He specializes in the philosophy of language, epistemology, and the history of analytic philosophy. He has published two books, *Knowledge and Practical Interests* (2005) and *Language in Context* (2007).

Matthias Steup is Professor of Philosophy at St Cloud State University in Minnesota, USA. He is the author of *An Introduction to Contemporary Epistemology* (1996), and has edited *Knowledge, Truth and Duty* (2001), and, with Ernest Sosa, *Contemporary Debates in Epistemology* (2005). Currently, he is working on defending an evidentialist response to skepticism.

Stephen Stich is Board of Governors Professor of Philosophy and Cognitive Science at Rutgers University and Honorary Professor of Philosophy at the University of Sheffield. Stich received his BA from the University of Pennsylvania and his Ph.D. from Princeton University. In addition to Rutgers and Sheffield, he has taught at the

University of Michigan, the University of Maryland, and the University of California, San Diego and has held visiting appointments at universities in the United States, the UK, Australia, and New Zealand. His books include *From Folk Psychology to Cognitive Science* (1983), *The Fragmentation of Reason* (1990), *Deconstructing the Mind* (1996), and *Mindreading* (with Shaun Nichols) (2003). He received the Jean Nicod Prize in 2007.

Rowland Stout

Rowland Stout is Senior Lecturer in Philosophy at University College Dublin, having previously taught at Oxford University and Manchester University. He works on the nature of agency, rationality, and emotion. He is the author of *Things That Happen Because They Should* (1996), *Action* (2005), and *The Inner Life of a Rational Agent* (2006).

Dan Zahavi

Dan Zahavi, born 1967 in Copenhagen, studied philosophy in Copenhagen, Wuppertal, Leuven, and Boston. At present he is Professor of Philosophy at the University of Copenhagen and Director of the Danish National Research Foundation's Center for Subjectivity Research in Copenhagen. Selected publications in English include: *Self-Awareness and Alterity: A Phenomenological Investigation* (1999), *Husserl and Transcendental Intersubjectivity* (2001), *Husserl's Phenomenology* (2003), *Subjectivity and Selfhood: Investigating the First-Person Perspective* (2005), and *The Phenomenological Mind* (with Shaun Gallagher) (2007).

PREFACE AND ACKNOWLEDGMENTS

Editing and compiling this historical and critical review of twentieth-century philosophy has been extremely challenging, but ultimately it has been a rewarding task. The project was conceived in 2002 with the aim of drawing together experts in the various subject areas who could comment both authoritatively and critically on the current condition of their respective disciplines and on the nature of the problems still present today. Clearly, any account of the current status and problems of a philosophical subdiscipline needs also to be supplemented by some kind of historical survey of the development of philosophy over the course of the century. The chapters in this volume therefore do attempt to combine an historical sketch with a critical assessment.

On the other hand, although philosophy can never be completely disengaged and isolated from other scientific, cultural, and indeed social and political developments, the chapters in this volume focus primarily on the intrinsic philosophical issues, and external social and political developments are in general left to one side. One might say, then, that the chapters here offer an *internalist* vision of the development of twentieth-century philosophy.

Each chapter aims to provide a comprehensive introduction and overview, sketch the main stages in the development of the particular subject through the century and offer some reflective assessment of its current state. To assist the reader in working through the diverse contributions in this volume, I have grouped the twenty-two chapters under five more general headings: Major Themes and Movements; Logic, Language, Knowledge, and Metaphysics; Philosophy of Mind, Psychology, and Science; Phenomenology, Hermeneutics, Existentialism, and Critical Theory; and Politics, Ethics, and Aesthetics. Of course, more subject areas could have been added, but the book had to remain of finite size!

It is worth emphasizing at the outset that this collection of essays focuses exclusively on the development of philosophy in the West (which means primarily Europe, America, Australasia) during the twentieth century. As I shall attempt to explain in my Introduction, twentieth-century philosophy emerges first of all in Europe in the first half of the century and then subsequently continues, in a very powerful form, in the USA (and to a lesser extent in Canada and Australia) during the latter half of the century. Philosophical activity is South America, for instance, is primarily an extension of European or American philosophy of the same period. While there has been enormous growth in knowledge of, and interest in, non-western philosophies (primarily Chinese, Indian, African, Islamic) through the twentieth century, it is arguably the case that it is the scholarly methodology of western academic philosophy that has actually framed the debate, made the decisive contributions in terms of editions and so on, and, indeed, set the academic standards for the manner in which non-western philosophies have been investigated and evaluated. Indeed, although issues of multiculturalism, pluralism, identity and difference, cultural relativism, and so on, are now a lively part of the current philosophical scene, especially in social and political philosophy, these debates are primarily conducted in the technical languages and styles of argumentation of western academic philosophy. Whether this will continue in the twenty-first century is an open question, as diverse forms of human cultural experience and conceptions of the world come to be understood and included in philosophical discussion.

Despite the exclusive focus on western philosophy, the century, nevertheless, offers an extraordinary wide spread of different philosophical voices. On the one hand, the twentieth century is the century of Frege, Russell, Wittgenstein, Kripke, and Quine; on the other hand, it is the century of Husserl, Heidegger, Gadamer, Sartre, and Derrida. In quite another sense, judged by the scale of their transformative effects, it is also the century of Marx, Lenin, and Mao. It is the century of advances in logic and philosophy of science, but also the century in which poetic thinking and openness to mystery are advanced as ways of freeing thought from the domination of technological enframing. Various forms of naturalism, physicalism, and materialism (even of the "eliminative" kind) compete with non-reductive, hermeneutic, and transcendental approaches. New voices emerge also: specifically the voices of women who enter the academy early in the century and have contributed enormously to transforming many traditional debates as well as introducing new themes and forms of discourse. The elimination (due to the Communist Revolutions early in the century) and the subsequent re-emergence of traditional forms of philosophy in the former Communist countries of Eastern Europe is another major transformation of twentieth-century thought. I have tried in my Introduction to identify some of the main continuities and discontinuities in the manner in which philosophy has been pursued in the twentieth century. However, the main discussions concerning the individual movements, themes, and disciplines, are of course to be found in the chapters contained in this volume.

I believe that the chapters in this volume represent informed and vital contributions to their subjects and will offer readers an indispensable guide to twentieth-century philosophy. In general, the chapters collected here present critical overviews of their subject matters written as lucidly as possible, with the non-specialist in mind. Of course, there are many quite technical areas in philosophy (in all its sub-disciplines) and while the contributors have taken great care to clarify their central concepts and terminology, grasping the meaning of the issues involved may require some effort on the part of the reader. Thus, for example, readers may need to familiarize themselves with the basic symbols of formal logic in order to appreciate more fully the discussions in metaphysics, philosophy of logic, and philosophy of language, although the chapters can be understood at a reasonably advanced level without having mastered these symbols. Likewise, the chapters "German philosophy" and "Critical Theory" are written from the standpoint of eminent participants in those fields and will be somewhat challenging to those uninitiated in the style of reasoning of those particular strands of contemporary European thought. Readers, therefore, are encouraged to move selectively through the volume in order to familiarize themselves with the philosophical concepts and reasoning needed to address in an informed manner the more challenging topics. While the chapters aim to lead beginners to a mature understanding of the topic in question, there are also real philosophical challenges awaiting those more advanced in philosophical argumentation. I myself have learned an enormous amount in the course of reading and editing the chapters in this volume. I want therefore to thank all the contributors who have been extraordinarily generous with their time and impressive in the range and depth of their expertise. I want also to thank the many referees (who must remain anonymous) who were responsible for reading and critiquing each contribution very carefully, and who made excellent constructive suggestions, which, significantly, were, in the main, appreciated by the authors of the chapters.

I would like to thank the Irish Research Council for the Humanities and Social Sciences (IRCHSS) for a Senior Fellowship in the Humanities in 2002–3, and University College Dublin for the President's Fellowship for 2003–4. Thanks to Professor Steven Crowell and my colleagues at the Philosophy Department of Rice University who hosted me as Lynette S. Autry Visiting Professor in the Humanities for the Fall Semester 2003 and again for the Spring Semester 2006. Thanks to Ken Seeskin, Richard Krant, Cristina Lafont, Axel Mueller, Rachel Zuckert, and all my colleagues in the Philosophy Department at Northwestern University for welcoming me to Evanston as Visiting Professor there for the Winter Quarter 2007. Thanks also to my colleagues at UCD, in particular Maria Baghramian, Maeve Cooke, Jim O'Shea, and Rowland Stout. I would also like to give special thanks to my colleague Brian Elliott for his careful translations from the German of the chapters by Karl-Otto Apel and Axel Honneth. I am grateful to my graduate students at Northwestern University for their comments on draft chapters of this book, in particular Max Cherem, who provided helpful editorial assistance.

I would like here to record my thanks to those who have assisted me at Routledge. Special thanks must go to Tony Bruce, Philosophy Editor, for his good counsel, patience, and unflagging enthusiasm for the project. Thanks also to Amanda Lucas, Editorial Assistant at Routledge, for her practical help in the production of this volume. Special thanks must also be given to the copy editor, Mary Dortch, for her painstakingly detailed and patient work in preparing the text for printing.

Finally, I would like to thank my family for their support, especially my wife Loretta and our three children, Katie, Eoin, and Hannah.

Dermot Moran
University College Dublin, May 2007

INTRODUCTION: TOWARDS AN ASSESSMENT OF TWENTIETH-CENTURY PHILOSOPHY

Dermot Moran

The long twentieth century

What is the legacy of twentieth-century philosophy? Or, to adapt the question originally asked (in relation to Hegel) by the Italian philosopher Benedetto Croce (1866–1952):[1] What is living and what is dead in twentieth-century philosophy? The sheer range and diversity of the philosophical contribution is surely one of the century's most singular characteristics. As the century fades into memory, so many of the great philosophers associated with it have also passed away: Rudolf Carnap (d. 1970), Martin Heidegger (d. 1976), Jean-Paul Sartre (d. 1980), Simone de Beauvoir (d. 1986), A. J. Ayer (d. 1989), Emmanuel Levinas (d. 1995), Gilles Deleuze (d. 1995), Thomas Kuhn (d 1996), W. V. O. Quine (d. 2000), Elizabeth Anscombe (d. 2001), David Lewis (d. 2001), Hans-Georg Gadamer (d. 2002), John Rawls (d. 2002), Robert Nozick (d. 2002), Donald Davidson (d. 2003), Bernard Williams (d. 2003), and more recently Jacques Derrida (d. 2004), Peter Strawson (d. 2006), Jean Baudrillard (d. 2007) and Richard Rorty (d. 2007). When one thinks of the names that were current at the beginning of that century – Croce, Bradley, McTaggart, Pritchard, Joachim, Collingwood, Whitehead, Duhem, Husserl, Natorp, Dilthey, James, Dewey, Cassirer, Josiah Royce, George Santayana, Roy Wood Sellars, to name but a few[2] – one realizes just what a rich and varied legacy of philosophy the century has produced and how great is the span that separates those who opened the century from those who closed it.

How can we even begin to appreciate the philosophical heritage of that turbulent, terrifying, but enormously productive period? To review such a vast repertoire of philosophy is certainly challenging. Developing a critical assessment of twentieth-century philosophy, then, one that identifies accurately its main accomplishments (avoiding ideological distortion and clannishness) as well as the problems it bequeaths to current thinking, is a remarkably complex and demanding affair, but nonetheless it stands as an important, even urgent, task, one that calls for judgement and decision.[3]

Given that historians are apt to speak of "long" centuries, certainly the twentieth century must now seem one of the longest. This tumultuous period was characterized by world wars, the rise and fall of Communist, fascist, and totalitarian states, the invention of nuclear weapons and other weapons of mass destruction, genocide, famine, anti-colonial struggles, globalization and technologization on an enormous scale. Rapid scientific and technological advances were coupled with political catastrophes and dramatic events of a scale hitherto unimagined. But we are still too close and the century in many ways – not least in terms of its intellectual legacy – remains an undigested mass for us, we who are still living so completely in its shadow.

Thinking specifically of philosophy, there probably has never been a time when there have been so many professional philosophers at work in universities across the world. Yet what has been their contribution? Perhaps, for most of the century, one could say that the nineteenth-century Karl Marx and his twentieth-century followers, including Lenin and Mao, were the most influential philosophers in terms of the scale of their practical impact stretching over almost half the globe (including the countries of the USSR, China, North Korea, Cuba, as well as in Central and South America). In terms of impact, one can also name the great public intellectuals in the West: Jean-Paul Sartre ("*the* philosopher of the twentieth century,"[4] who turned down a Nobel Prize) and Bertrand Russell, united in their opposition to the Vietnam War; or, much earlier, John Dewey who campaigned for progressive education; or the displaced intellectual Hannah Arendt, reporting on the Eichmann trial in Jerusalem;[5] or the roles of Noam Chomsky (a prominent critic of US political engagements), Richard Rorty,[6] Bernard Henri-Lévy[7] or Slavoj Žižek today. There is undoubtedly a public appetite for philosophy in many countries; think of the public interest in the philosophical dissertations on happiness, such as that by Alain de Botton;[8] or perhaps an interest in philosophical *lives*, witness the popularity of Ray Monk's biography of Wittgenstein.[9] One cannot overestimate the extraordinary influence of A. J. Ayer's *Language, Truth and Logic*, especially the manner in which it was developed by those who wanted to argue that moral and religious statements were in fact literally meaningless. While, perhaps, Roger Scruton's defense of fox-hunting[10] in England is not momentous enough to be counted here, certainly Peter Singer's book *Animal Liberation* sparked enormous public debate about the ethical treatment of animals, for which he argued on utilitarian grounds on the basis of animal sentience.[11] Existentialism was perhaps the first great philosophical movement (since the ancient Greek movements such as Stoicism, Skepticism, or Epicureanism) to have had popular support among the masses and even to become a fashion for a time in the mid-century. There are philosophers who preached engagement and critique (for instance, Sartre, or the Frankfurt School), and those who recommended skeptical distance and irony (Rorty). On the other hand, many of the more exciting technical advances in philosophy have been produced by retiring figures working relatively unseen, absorbed in their research (one thinks of Wittgenstein, Kripke, Husserl, Levinas, or Rawls), who contributed little to public debate.

Continuities, discontinuities, novelties

Philosophy does seem to have undergone enormous changes in the course of the century, but it also has diversified into many different and competing forms. New disciplines have emerged: from mathematical logic and meta-ethics to philosophy of language, philosophy of mind, and philosophy of psychology: from philosophy of gender and embodiment to environmental philosophy (or "ecosophy" as founded by the Norwegian philosopher Arne Naess).[12] Unfortunately, to date, there have been remarkably few academic studies of twentieth-century philosophy in its inter-connections although there are some studies of specific traditions.[13] Indeed, it is noteworthy that even the ten-volume *Routledge Encyclopedia of Philosophy* contains no entry for "Twentieth-century philosophy,"[14] yet it is clear that the very meaning of philosophy changed in profound ways in that century, ways that are certainly not even documented, never mind fully understood. It is important, then, to document the commonalities and continuities; to identify the transformations, discontinuities, dead-ends and sheer novelties.

In terms of continuity, many aspects of philosophical *practice* in the twentieth century follow on directly from patterns set in the nineteenth century, e.g. the academic *professionalization* and *specialization* of the subject, begun in the nineteenth century, became all-pervasive during the twentieth, such that the independent, non-institutionally funded scholar contributing substantially to a discussion is now almost an extinct species (apart from some dissidents who emerged in the former USSR and elsewhere). Philosophy is now carried out, almost universally, in universities and higher research academies. Yet, a most important – and indeed novel – feature of the ongoing professionalization of philosophy has been the entrance of women into the philosophers' academy. Rosa Luxemburg emerged in Germany quite early in the century, and, partly because women were the majority of university students during the First World War in Germany, Edmund Husserl became one of the first major philosophers to attract a sizable number of women students and assistants in his Freiburg years. Hedwig Conrad Martius, Edith Stein, and Gerda Walther all studied with him, even if he was not always supportive of these women's desire to continue to professional careers in philosophy.[15] In fact, women philosophers in Germany were active in removing institutional constraints;[16] e.g. both Hannah Arendt and Edith Stein promoted equality of education between women and men. In England, Elizabeth Anscombe emerged as Wittgenstein's student at Cambridge in the 1940s, and acted as his editor, translator, and interpreter, before going on to develop her own path as an original and influential philosopher, especially in the area of philosophy of mind and action.[17] Anscombe also opposed the Second World War and was an active critic of the American President, Harry Truman, for his actions in relation to the dropping of atomic bombs on Japanese cities.

Following on from Simone de Beauvoir, a whole generation of women philosophers emerged in France, leading to a particular tradition which includes Julia Kristeva (born in Bulgaria but educated in a French school), Hélène Cixous, Luce Irigaray, Sarah Kofman, and Michèle Le Dœuff (see "Feminism in philosophy," Chapter 7). In

Britain, prominent women philosophers include: Philippa Foot, Onora O'Neill, Susan Stebbing, Sarah Waterlow Broadie; in the US: Ruth Barcan Marcus, Seyla Benhabib, Judith Butler, Christine Korsgaard, Martha Nussbaum, and Judith Jarvis Thomson; in Australia, Genevieve Lloyd.[18] Women not only entered the academy to work in traditional areas, but often transformed the debate in certain areas, introduced new topics, and made ground-breaking contributions (Ruth Marcus in logic; Judith Jarvis Thomson in the area of the ethics of abortion). Following on from the theme of feminism, new areas have emerged that include issues surrounding the philosophy of gender and lately "queer theory," which has overlapped the boundaries of philosophy and linked it more with disciplines of social criticism.

Thinking of technical breakthroughs, it is easy to point to the development of modern mathematical logic (with Frege, Russell, and Whitehead), modal logic (the logic of necessity and possibility, begun by Aristotle but formalized in the twentieth century by C. I. Lewis, Ruth Barcan Marcus, Saul Kripke, and others), temporal logic (A. N. Prior), the discovery of the incompleteness of formal systems (Gödel), and many more logical innovations. It is less easy to find solutions to perennial philosophical problems or revolutionary new approaches to ethical and political issues that have gained the status of scientific discoveries. As always, the human world is extremely complex and escapes the exact lawfulness found in the natural sciences, and there is no clearly identifiable progress in moral concepts. As the German Critical Theorist Theodor Adorno once put it, "No universal history leads from savagery to humanitarianism, but there is one leading from the slingshot to the atom bomb."[19] In moral philosophy, for instance, the argument continues to rage about whether statements such as: "slavery is and always has been wrong," is an objectively true proposition.

With respect to direct continuities in philosophy across the centuries, it is remarkable how many of the issues that were discussed so vitally at the start of twentieth century, e.g. the nature of consciousness, perception, space and time, the meaning of naturalism, the nature of the a priori, the proper methodology of the human sciences, and so on, continue to be vigorously debated at the century's end. The descriptive phenomenology of inner time consciousness is as much an issue now as it was one hundred years ago when Husserl was giving his 1905 lectures on time-consciousness, at a time when Bergson and James were also focusing on the temporal nature of consciousness. Time-consciousness certainly has been a major focus of discussion among European philosophers such as Jacques Derrida;[20] whereas, in the UK and USA, McTaggart's discussions of temporal flux, with his A- and B-series continue to provoke discussion concerning the unreality of time, by A. N. Prior, Richard Swinburne, Hilary Putnam, Sidney Shoemaker, and others.[21] Similarly, William James's interest in the existence and nature of consciousness[22] is surely replicated in the work of David Chalmers and others writing about the "hard problem" of consciousness.[23] It is hard to believe that the metaphysics of internal relations that so preoccupied the British Idealists should again be a matter of discussion among contemporary analytic metaphysics (see "Metaphysics," Chapter 10).

In some cases, the continuities are of a different kind: where a subject seems to appear and disappear only to reappear again some time later. The issue of embodiment is one such issue which gets a very full discussion by Husserl in his *Ideas* II (written between 1912 and 1918 but not published until 1952), is continued in Merleau-Ponty's *Phenomenology of Perception* (1945) and is again a hot topic among philosophers, including analytic philosophers of mind.[24] Essentialism is also a theme that surfaces and disappears at regular intervals across the century (Husserl, Wittgenstein, Kripke, et al.). Other kinds of continuities are of a more persistent kind. Thus, in "Moral Philosophy" (Chapter 20), Rowland Stout even suggests, somewhat paradoxically, that the great philosophers of twentieth-century moral philosophy continued to be Aristotle, Hume, and Kant! Continuities of this kind are also evident in the manner in which both epistemology and analytic philosophy of religion have managed to continue to talk, in ever more refined ways, about traditional problems such as the nature of knowledge, skepticism, and the meaning of faith. Arguments concerning the existence of God or the compatibility of the divine attributes continue in the work of Anthony Kenny, Richard Swinburne, Alvin Plantinga, Nelson Pike, and others, refining and sharpening debates to be found in Anselm, Aquinas, or Descartes. One could say the same for aesthetics, whose central task, as suggested by Paul Guyer (Chapter 22), has been to respond to Plato's questioning of the arts as a form of lie (*pseudos*).

The rise and rise of *naturalism* is surely one of the most important of the continuities to be acknowledged in philosophy over the course of the twentieth century. As Geert Keil has shown in "Naturalism" (Chapter 6), in 1922 Roy Wood Sellars (1880–1973) could confidently declare: "We are all naturalists now," and at the end of the century that claim would look quite accurate for large swathes of contemporary epistemology, ethics, philosophy of mind and philosophy of science, where naturalisms of varying kinds have flourished (see Geert Keil's nuanced discussion). In keeping with this recognition of the growth of naturalism, Edmund Husserl, in his 1911 essay "Philosophy as a rigorous science," diagnosed it as the greatest threat to the possibility of a genuinely scientific philosophy. Yet despite the popularity of naturalism, there has also been a constant counter-movement, and especially since the 1970s there has been a strong resurgence of transcendental philosophy and persistent arguments advanced that the normative cannot be naturalized (see "Kant in the twentieth century," Chapter 4).[25] Furthermore, following on from early twentieth-century neo-Kantians such as Rickert and Natorp, Husserlian phenomenology also adopted a resolutely post-Kantian transcendental position against naturalism, arguing that objectivity can only ever be objectivity-correlated-with-subjectivity and denying even the meaningfulness of talking about things in themselves independent of the subjective knower. Indeed, the manner in which Kant and Hegel continue to haunt twentieth-century discussions is reflected in this volume by two chapters devoted respectively to Kant and to Hegel (see Chapters 4 and 3). So much for the continuities.

In terms of novelties, some philosophical disciplines certainly seem to be new. In "Philosophy of Language" (Chapter 9), Jason Stanley makes a strong case for philosophy of language as making a unique twentieth-century contribution, although the precise nature of the contribution has to be carefully nuanced. As Jason Stanley contends,

The Twentieth Century was the century of "linguistic philosophy," not because all or even most philosophical problems have been resolved or dissolved by appeal to language, but because areas of philosophy that involved meaning and content became immeasurably more sophisticated.

Contemporary discussions of meaning, content, and reference, are indeed far more sophisticated than anything to be found in Bolzano, Mill, or even Frege. So there is certainly progress in philosophy in terms of increasing discriminations and disambiguations of complex concepts. Of course, technical refinements are not confined to one tradition. As Nicholas Davey shows in "Twentieth-century hermeneutics" (Chapter 16), the linguistic turn in twentieth-century thought owes as much to Heidegger and Gadamer, in their opposition to the Cartesian "philosophy of consciousness", as it does to Frege and Wittgenstein, and furthermore, evidence of a linguistic turn in German philosophy can be traced back to the Enlightenment with Hamann and others.[26] In particular, this tradition points up the holistic nature of the linguistic enterprise and the fact that the subject (speaker and hearer) cannot be disengaged from the practice of linguistic communication and miscommunication.

Along with philosophy of language, one could also argue that philosophy of science emerges decisively in twentieth-century philosophy as a distinct discipline. Indeed, there has been an explosion of interest in the logic and philosophy of science from the 1930s onwards, as Stathis Psillos documents in "Philosophy of science" (Chapter 14), and, especially as developed by members of the Vienna Circle and others, who put science at the centre of philosophy's concerns.[27] But even here there are continuities, especially in the vigorous debate over the nature of the a priori, which continues in the work of Reichenbach (and following him Putnam and others) with the puzzling notion of the revisable a priori.

The ongoing legacy of the nineteenth century

It is an obvious truism to assert that to understand the twentieth century one must begin in the nineteenth. Many different traditions in contemporary philosophy have a common origin in nineteenth-century problematics. For instance, in German philosophy during the latter half of the nineteenth century, there were serious efforts to resist the bewitchment of Hegel (who had dominated philosophy in the first half of the nineteenth century). The various schools of neo-Kantianism (Windelband, Cohen, et al.), with their war cry "back to Kant" (*zurück zu Kant*),[28] as well as those inspired by classic British empiricism (and its nineteenth-century representatives, e.g. J. S. Mill), sought to distance themselves from what they considered to be the excessive and ungrounded speculative nature of the Hegelian system.[29] Oddly, in Britain at the turn of the twentieth century, the situation was almost the reverse of that prevailing on the Continent, with neo-Hegelian Idealism in the ascendant with McTaggart at Cambridge; F. H. Bradley (1846–1924), T. H. Greene (1836–82), and Harold Henry Joachim (1868–1938) – all at Oxford, and Bernard Bosanquet (1848–1923), who translated Hegel's *Aesthetics*, and was for a time President of the Aristotelian Society, in London. Hegel also continued to have influence in the USA in the late nineteenth century owing to the St Louis Hegelians led by William Torrey Harris (1835–1909) and Henry Conrad Brokmeyer (1828–1906),[30] and was represented by Josiah Royce (1855-1916) at Harvard. Of course, it was against this Hegelian and Bradleyian system that Russell reacted so strongly (albeit that Russell's interest was focused on the logic of relations and defending their reality against Bradley). Similarly, on the European mainland, Kierkegaard too may be seen as leading a defense of the individual and singular against the sweeping universalism of the Hegelian system.

Notwithstanding the onslaught on idealism found in Russell, G. E. Moore,[31] and others, a critique that was foundational for the new analytic movement, idealism in various kinds continued to be found across twentieth-century philosophy. One of Sartre's early teachers at the École Normale Supérieure was Léon Brunschvicg (1869–1944), a neo-Cartesian idealist. In the latter part of the twentieth century (in Germany, partly inspired by Heidegger and Gadamer) there was a huge resurgence of (primarily scholarly) interest in Hegel (e.g. in the Hegel-Archiv in Bochum), but there was also somewhat earlier a strong resurgence of interest in Hegel in France (with Jean Wahl, Jean Hyppolite as well as through the astonishing lectures of Alexandre Kojève[32]), and in the UK and USA with works by J. N. Findlay and Charles Taylor, both movements aiming to restore Hegel's shaken credibility and to show the relevance of his dialectic to current concerns.[33] The rehabilitation of Hegel is now complete (see "Hegelianism in the twentieth century," Chapter 3) in that Hegel has now entered the canon of analytic philosophy, having once been its *bête noire*, in the work of McDowell, Brandom, and others. Whereas Wilfrid Sellars had once claimed that with Wittgenstein's *Philosophical Investigations*, analytic philosophy passed from its Humean to its Kantian phase, Rorty suggested that with Brandom, analytic philosophy has moved on to the Hegelian phase of analytic philosophy.[34] Furthermore, certain central Hegelian concerns run through the work of the Frankfurt School especially in the writings of Marcuse, Adorno, and even Habermas himself, as Axel Honneth has shown in "Critical Theory" (Chapter 18).

Certain philosophical subject areas seem to have developed in direct continuity from the nineteenth century onwards: ethics and epistemology are obvious examples here. Epistemology in the twentieth century, as Matthias Steup argues in Chapter 11, to a large extent remains a response to problems posed by the modern philosophical tradition stemming from Descartes, particularly with regard to the problem of our knowledge of the external world (e.g. Russell's *Our Knowledge of the External World*, 1914) and in defending the possibility of knowledge against skeptical arguments. The main developments of the twentieth century appear to be new problems (Gettier-type problems that challenge the conception of knowledge as justified true belief)[35] and new efforts at articulating non-foundationalist forms of epistemic justification, but much epistemology in the twentieth century is still based on forms of a priori reasoning familiar in traditional philosophy.

Scholarly interest in the history of philosophy and the production of critical editions of the great philosophers' works continues to develop in a steady stream from the nineteenth through the twentieth century. In terms of continuities, the main philosophical journals that were important at the turn of the twentieth century, e.g. *Mind* (founded 1876), *The Monist* (founded 1888), *Proceedings of the Aristotelian Society* (the Society was founded in 1880; the *Proceedings* began to be published from 1888), *Philosophical Review* (founded 1892), *Kant-Studien* (founded 1896), *Journal of Philosophy* (founded 1904), continue to flourish – and continue to remain significant – for the dissemination of peer-refereed professional philosophy research.

In the nineteenth century, the scholarly history of philosophy began to be practiced entirely for its own sake, independently of the ideological baggage of Hegelianism for instance, or, to give another example, neo-Thomism, whose advocates (e.g. Étienne Gilson, Jacques Maritain, even Frederick Copleston), wanted to revive the realism found in medieval philosophy, while downplaying the nominalist or even Neoplatonic traditions. This history of philosophy is now flourishing as an independent discipline in its own right and there are serious journals devoted to it (e.g. *Journal of the History of Philosophy* and the *British Journal of the History of Philosophy*), as well as to many of the individual figures (Locke, Hume, Kant, Hegel, and so on). The critical edition of Hegel's works is still being produced at the beginning of the twenty-first century, replacing earlier unsatisfactory editions. Similarly, the works of Plato and Aristotle continue to be edited, translated, and commented on; see the work of W. D. Ross (1877–1971), for instance; and new editions are being produced of classical philosophers and early medieval writers who were almost unknown in the nineteenth century. For example, the elegant nineteenth-century translations of Plato's dialogues by Benjamin Jowett (1817–1893),[36] or Aristotle's major works by W. D. Ross,[37] are gradually being replaced with more contemporary translations, but by no means have been made redundant and are still in common circulation among students. Similarly, the twentieth century has seen an extraordinary growth of knowledge of the later antique tradition, especially Plotinus, Proclus, Pseudo-Dionysius, and others, who were first "re-discovered" in the nineteenth century, primarily by students of German Idealism (e.g. F. A. Staudenmaier). The growth in interest in medieval theories of logic, semiotics, and semantics is another indication of a continuation and deepening of nineteenth-century scholarship.

In regard to the history of philosophy, it is important to recognize how recent are many of our historical discoveries; to realize, for example, that more has been learned about all aspects of medieval philosophy in the twentieth century (its figures, texts, sources, and influences) than in the whole period from the seventeenth to the nineteenth centuries. Similarly, thanks to the discovery of the 1844 manuscripts, a new version of Marx emerged in the twentieth century, that was highly influential on the thinking of the Frankfurt School (see "Critical Theory," Chapter 18).

Philosophy at the dawn of the twentieth century

In intellectual terms, one might consider the dawn of the twentieth century to be marked by a number of important events: there was the death of Friedrich Nietzsche (1844–1900), and the publication of two works that would transform European thought in very different ways: Sigmund Freud's *Traumdeutung* (*Interpretation of Dreams*, 1899), which inaugurated psychoanalysis, and Edmund Husserl's *Prolegomena zu reinen Logik* (*Prolegomena to Pure Logic*, 1900), which broke decisively with the prevailing *psychologism* in the understanding of logic and mathematics and led to the development of phenomenology. G. E. Moore's essay "The nature of judgment"[38] appeared in 1899 (for Moore on propositions, see also "The birth of analytic philosophy," Chapter 1) and is often seen as the first paper in analytic philosophy, because of its particular view of the nature of propositions as objective complex entities independent of minds and analyzable into component parts (which had a formative influence on Bertrand Russell).[39] The International Congress of Philosophy, held in Paris in 1900, was also an important event, and Russell later recorded that it represented a turning point in his life, because there he met Peano, whose precision impressed the young Englishman, and, as a result, Russell turned to mathematical logic as *the* methodology for his own philosophy.[40] He wrote a paper which he sent to Peano and even claimed: "Intellectually, the month of September 1900 was the highest point of my life,"[41] and this before any of his own major works had been published and while the *Principles of Mathematics* (1903) was being composed.

One might at first be tempted to see that self-proclaimed "posthumous" man, Friedrich Nietzsche, as the principal philosophical voice of the century. His writings seem to resonate with themes that became vital for the century – the nature of truth, the nature of power relations, the problem of the writing of *history*, the fragmentary nature of inheritance and tradition, the threat of relativism, the naturalization of values, the need for radical and creative critique and destruction – philosophizing with a hammer – in order to free up sedimented meanings, the integration of the human with the rest of nature (especially after Darwin), the exercise of hermeneutic suspicion, with "ears behind one's ears" in the interpretation of others, the ironic probing of dreams of mastery, the recognition of the hidden ties between reason and force. Michel Foucault is clearly one of Nietzsche's direct successors, but Bernard Williams, too, for instance, sees Nietzsche's repudiation of traditional conceptions of truth as crucial for defining contemporary thought. Yet, even Richard Rorty himself, a sympathetic reader of Nietzsche, believed that Nietzsche was really integrated into philosophy only through Heidegger, and before that was a figure of mainly literary inspiration, influencing George Bernard Shaw and others.

In similar fashion, initially Sigmund Freud had little impact on academic philosophy, particularly on the European mainland, in the first half of the twentieth century, apart from the work of Horkheimer and Adorno[42] and Herbert Marcuse[43] (see "Critical Theory," Chapter 18). Jean-Paul Sartre, for instance, was seen as having dismissed Freudian analysis in *Being and Nothing*ness (1943) with his demolition of the concept of an unconscious that is always unconscious to itself. The French philosopher Paul Ricoeur was important for reinscribing Freud into French philosophy in the latter half of the century.[44] It was not until the 1960s, however, that Freud fully entered the philosophical scene in Europe, with Jacques Lacan, Derrida, Foucault, Deleuze, and Guattari,[45] Kristeva, and others, and even later in the 1970s and 1980s in the UK, with Richard Wollheim, Juliet Mitchell, and others.[46] One reason that delayed the acceptance of psychoanalysis by philosophers was the extremely hostile approach taken by Karl Popper to the claims of psychoanalysis to be a genuine science (on the grounds of its supposed lack of falsifiability).[47] Indeed, Freud is still left somewhat in the background in academic philosophical discussion; philosophers who are interested in analyzing the emotions, for instance, may advert to his writings, but will quickly go on to develop their independent analyses that pay little more than lip service to the Master.

So, despite their inaugural moments at the turn of the century, perhaps Nietzsche and Freud are not in fact the most representative or archetypal philosophical figures for the twentieth century, certainly if one considers the nature of their respective influences on philosophy. In fact, the pair of names most often advanced (in the work of Richard Rorty among many others) as best representing twentieth-century philosophy are: Heidegger and Wittgenstein, especially after both had made the "linguistic turn" subsequent to their own early publications.[48] The influence of these two philosophers probably outweighs all other philosophers in the twentieth century.

Here, however, I would like to make a case for Edmund Husserl as one of the most influential European philosophers of the twentieth century, who, as Merleau-Ponty put it, casts a long shadow over his times.[49] Almost every European philosopher in the first half of the century had some contact direct or indirect with Husserl (e.g. Heidegger himself, but also Schutz, Levinas, Horkheimer, Adorno, Merleau-Ponty, and Derrida).

Husserl's "ground-breaking" work

Phenomenology was inaugurated with Husserl's ground-breaking *Logische Untersuch-ungen* (*Logical Investigations*, 1900/1901),[50] the second volume of which, appearing from the publisher Max Niemeyer in two parts in 1901, characterized phenomenology as the project of descriptively clarifying the "experiences of thinking and knowing." With this work, Husserl believed he had made a start in clarifying problems that were at the heart of contemporary science and philosophy, problems concerning the nature of the experience and determination of meaning in the broadest sense. In the First Edition, he used the term "phenomenology" to mean a kind of descriptive psychology (such as had been practiced by the school of Brentano, Stumpf, and Meinong). For Husserl, phenomenology was to be a way of describing what shows itself *as it shows itself* in its essential forms. It had to avoid speculation and remain true to the evidential situations, which Husserl somewhat misleadingly called "the things themselves" (*die Sachen selbst*) or "the matters themselves." Husserl's primary principle – a radical variant of empiricism – is to accept as evident only what shows itself to be so in intuition. Intuition is the keystone of his philosophy. Intuition refers to the primary grasp of the presence of entities.

As Husserl put it in the Foreword to the Second Edition, and as he would subse-quently stress, the *Investigations* was his "breakthrough work" (*Werk des Durchbruchs*, LU I 3; Hua XVIII 8). It certainly made his reputation as a philosopher, being praised by the foremost philosophers of his day in Germany, including Paul Natorp,[51] Wilhelm Wundt, who welcomed its anti-psychologism, and Wilhelm Dilthey, who saw it as providing the method to investigate lived experiences in their concreteness. In terms of its philosophical significance, the import of the *Investigations* is many-faceted. On the one hand, it abjured psychologism and defended a broadly Platonist account of numbers, logical forms, and other ideal entities. They are what they are independently of their being thought or known. On the other hand, Husserl recognized that ideal entities and meanings are only reached by consciousness through a set of determinate acts whose essential natures and interconnections can be specified. There are acts of intending meanings, acts of recognizing, judging, and so on. These acts can be understood as themselves making up a framework of idealities. Husserl's subsequent recognition that these idealities are themselves embedded in the transcendental ego moved his thought in a transcendental direction, renewing his links with the more dominant tradition of neo-Kantianism.

Husserl moved to Göttingen in 1901 and, through the influence of the *Investigations* on a group of philosophers in Germany, a phenomenological "movement" (*Bewegung*) began to emerge in the first decade of the century with Adolf Reinach, Alexander Pfänder, Johannes Daubert, Moritz Geiger, and subsequently, Max Scheler. Through the fascination which the *Logical Investigations* provoked, Husserl effectively revolutionized existing philosophy in Germany, changing the very way philosophy was practiced, shifting the focus from the history of ideas and from epistemology to an attempt to describe what he called "the things themselves" (*die Sachen selbst*). Until Husserl himself came to have a significant influence, German philosophy had been dominated by neo-Kantianism (divided into the so-called "South German" and "Marburg" schools), which accepted the fact of science and whose project was to specify the preconditions of objective scientific knowledge. Furthermore, united in opposition to Hegelian speculative idealism, various forms of positivism were on the rise in Germany, influenced by John Stuart Mill and the older British empiricist tradition, as well as by Comte. Husserl's teacher, Franz Brentano, for instance, was a strong advocate of this positivism and of the unity of exact philosophy and science. Husserl's phenomenology had a profound effect. Issues of knowledge had to be given a much deeper analysis. No longer could the study of the history of philosophy substitute for philosophy.

The next major transformation of phenomenology took place with the publication of Heidegger's *Being and Time* (*Sein und Zeit*) in 1927. Clearly, *Being and Time* had an extraordinary influence on a whole generation, as Hannah Arendt later reported.[52] Heidegger made thinking come alive again! As his student, Hans-Georg Gadamer also wrote with deliberate irony,

> Just as might have been the case in fifth-century Athens when the young, under the banners of the new sophistic and Socratic dialectic, vanquished all conventional forms of authority, law, and custom with radical new questions, so too the radicalism of Heidegger's inquiry produced in the German universities an intoxicating effect that left all moderation behind.[53]

As we know, Husserl himself was isolated and humiliated by the rising Nazi movement, a movement in which his successor Heidegger enthusiastically participated.

Any history of twentieth-century philosophy must face that great betrayal of Husserl and of the academy by Heidegger – a betrayal which might be interpreted as being a kind of Nietzschean philosophizing with a hammer. Heidegger hated the ensconced academic practice in the university and saw in Nazism a chance for university renewal and at the same time a vehicle for cultural renewal, or *Erneuerung*, the very term of Husserl's project in the Kaizo lectures of the 1920s.[54] Husserl had claimed that the First World War had exposed the "internal untruthfulness and senselessness" of contemporary culture. In response he sought intellectual renewal through radically self-critical reflection. Heidegger, on the other hand, in his Rectoral Address of 1933, demanded that the university dedicate itself to following the will of the Führer.[55] It would later fall to other German philosophers, notably Jaspers, Habermas, and Adorno, to seek to break Heidegger's spell and to show up his feet of clay. Nevertheless, it is indisputable that Heidegger continues to have enormous influence today, especially in the discussion concerning the meaning of art, poetry, and technology.

The revolutionary importance of Gottlob Frege

Just as one could advance the thesis that Husserl is more influential than Heidegger, one could also argue that Frege has been more radical and wide-reaching in his influence than Wittgenstein. Gottlob Frege's importance is undeniable, as many of the chapters in the present volume attest. Like Nietzsche, he too is something of a posthumous figure. Regarded primarily as a mathematician, he had little impact among philosophers in the nineteenth century, apart from on Edmund Husserl who discussed him in the first volume of his *Logical Investigations* (1900). Frege was enormously influential not just on Russell and Wittgenstein but subsequently on discussions in the philosophy of language (his context principle is important for the linguistic turn, as Michael Dummett has argued[56]) (see also "The development of analytic philosophy: Wittgenstein and after," Chapter 2), for philosophy of science (problems raised by the notion of analyticity), philosophy of mind (the meaning of logical, conceptual, and mental "content"), even metaphysics. As Jason Stanley points out, Frege had a particularly modern way of approaching the notion of content (see "The philosophy of language," Chapter 9). Furthermore, as Stanley argues, Frege's account of quantifiers had a lasting impact on the semantics of natural languages. And Frege's views have an important bearing on metaphysics, although he himself paid scant regard to that subject. As E. J. Lowe writes in "Metaphysics" (Chapter 10), first-order quantificational logic in its modern form, as developed by Frege, Russell, and Whitehead, has embedded within it certain important metaphysical assumptions of an ontological character, specifically, the notions of an *atomic proposition* and *quantification*. Frege operated with a rather restricted ontology of individuals and relations, but he set the stage for subsequent discussions in analytic metaphysics. Of course Frege cannot be said to have had universal influence on all areas of philosophy (he had little interest in epistemology or ethics, for instance) but nonetheless he has to be credited with giving twentieth-century analytic philosophy its particular sharpness and distinct style. Like Heidegger, Frege had a dark side. Frege's political beliefs were somewhat naive, to say the least. He allied himself with Bruno Bauch's right-wing Deutsche Philosophische Gesellschaft (German Philosophical Society), a group that supported Hitler's rise to power. Furthermore, Frege's diary contains anti-Catholic and anti-Semitic sentiments, including the view that Jews should be expelled from Germany.[57]

Two main traditions: analytic and Continental philosophy

Discussing the relative significance of Husserl or Frege, Heidegger or Wittgenstein, leads naturally to a consideration of a philosophical divide that became prominent from the 1930s onwards. It is generally recognized that one of the most notable features of twentieth-century philosophy is that there developed two dominant intellectual traditions, traditions that in that century began to be named as the "analytic" or "Anglo-American" or "Anglo-Saxon" on the one hand, and "Continental" or "European" on the other. These traditions are widely held to have developed separately, with opposing aspirations and methodologies, and, indeed, to be fundamentally hostile to one another.[58] More careful scrutiny actually shows that these traditions emerge from common sources in nineteenth-century philosophy and address many of the same problematics, albeit with differing emphases and conclusions (both, for instance, are sensitive to language and meaning, aware of the problem of multiple and competing interpretations, sensitive to the challenges of science and technology, and also to the challenges of skepticism and relativism, interested in the nature of intentionality, and so on).[59] Early twentieth-century philosophy in most of its forms was united in its hostility to German Idealism, and its broad suspicion of speculative systems and of ungrounded metaphysics. This suspicion can be found not only among empiricists (such as Mill and Brentano) and positivists (Comte), but also among the German neo-Kantians (who looked to philosophy to provide a kind of logic of science), as well as in Russell and Moore, after they had come to reject the late-flowering British and American neo-Hegelian idealism current in their philosophical youth.

I don't propose here to spend too much time discussing the merits of the labels "analytic" and "Continental," as there is now an enormous literature documenting this divide.[60] In short, Continental philosophers have never been comfortable with the label "Continental," since they see themselves as doing philosophy in the traditional sense – upholding the tradition of historical scholarship, for instance. They see "Continental" as a label imposed on them from without, often from a rather narrow – even Euro-skeptical – British perspective.[61] Philosophers in this tradition have begun to express a preference for describing their tradition as "European philosophy," a title that recognizes the long and unbroken European tradition from the Greeks through to German Idealism, hermeneutics and neo-Kantianism. The problem is that European philosophy includes, alongside Nietzsche, Foucault, Deleuze, and Lacan, such names as LaPlace, Comte, Frege, Carnap, Schlick, Popper, and Wittgenstein. Further it seems to be ceding too much to British Euro-skeptics to exclude such figures as Hume, Mill, Russell, and Ayer from the cast of acceptable "Europeans." On the other hand, the term "European" philosophy also seems unhelpful since it excludes all those in the USA who write about Heidegger, Derrida, and others (e.g. Richard Rorty, John

Sallis, Jack Caputo) in a "Continental" manner. A. P. Martinich and David Sosa are in a similar predicament with regard to the term "analytic" philosophy, which they believe most accurately characterizes the work of Moore and Russell and other British philosophers up to the mid-century.[62] To capture the subsequent development of this philosophy, they suggest the term "Anglo-German philosophy," to recognize the important contribution that Carnap, Feigl, Reichenbach, and others made after they emigrated to the United States.

The difficulty in handling the labels of these traditions is mirrored in a difficulty in distinguishing their respective methods. Both attempt to be rigorous, scientific, and to be sensitive to language. There have been suggestions that analytic philosophy is more problem-centered whereas Continental philosophy is more focused on *explication de texte*.[63] Often, however, both traditions circle around the same kinds of problematic. For instance, both traditions have had to grapple with *skepticism* and *relativism*. Relativism, the view that truth or rationality is relative to a particular group of people (a view as old as Protagoras) is a particularly strong tendency to be found across a range of twentieth-century thinkers[64] from John Dewey, Thomas Kuhn,[65] and Wittgenstein to Quine[66] and Putnam; from Nietzsche to Michel Foucault, Derrida and Richard Rorty; even Martin Heidegger has been accused of relativism.[67] Early in the century, Wilhelm Dilthey's philosophy of worldviews appeared to Husserl to be leading inevitably to relativism, whereas late in the century Hilary Putnam's espousal of conceptual relativity has also been interpreted as a kind of relativism, since "what there is" is considered to be relative to a particular conceptual scheme. Both traditions show radical shifting of ground and abandonment of their supposed "founding" or "foundationalist" methodologies. In the Continental tradition, Husserl's descriptive phenomenology soon gave rise to Heidegger's hermeneutical phenomenology and ultimately (partly in reaction to structuralism which itself was reacting to existentialism) to French deconstruction. Deconstruction challenged the notion of fixed, ideal meanings and espoused *différance* and *dissémination*, concepts that suggest the dispersal of significance and the impossibility of final closure in issue of meaning. In analytic philosophy, philosophical confidence in ordinary language was gradually eroded by the problems associated with radical translation (Quine), the recognition of the open plurality of conceptual schemes (Putnam), and the plurality and incommensurability of language-games (later Wittgenstein).

These two most prominent twentieth-century movements, namely, analytic philosophy and phenomenology (I shall leave aside for the time being two other extremely important movements, namely pragmatism and Marxism, which both are in effect reactions against German Idealism), both have their origins in a set of interrelated concerns, namely: the scientific status of logic (and its relation to mathematics); the nature and extent of the new science of psychology, which had been inaugurated in the final quarter of the nineteenth century by Wilhelm Wundt (1832–1920), his English student E. B. Titchener (1867–1927), and Franz Brentano (1838–1917), among others; and the challenge posed by reductive naturalism to the traditional philosophical enterprise. These problematics are interrelated: prominent philosophers in the nineteenth century (e.g. J. S. Mill) had explained logic in terms of psychology and the internal processes of the human mind (so-called "psychologism"), and twentieth-century philosophy begins with Frege, Russell, Husserl, and Wittgenstein all rejecting this explanation in order to defend the ideality and independence of logical truths. A kind of Platonic realism about logical entities (objects, propositions, states of affairs) and a rejection of psychologism are hallmarks of the beginning of twentieth-century philosophy, whether it be that of Moore or Russell or Frege or Husserl.

Bertrand Russell once characterized the nineteenth century as the age of mathematics. It is interesting that the major developments in mathematics and logic were of central interest to philosophers in the twentieth century also including: Husserl, Frege, Russell, Whitehead, and Wittgenstein. Quine and Putnam were both fascinated by mathematical logic. Russell and Husserl were both deeply influenced by the crisis of foundations in mathematics and by Cantor's work on infinite numbers. Russell's early work was in the philosophy of mathematics and his famous paradox was not only known to Husserl but may even have been anticipated by him. In the Husserl Archives at Leuven we have the works of Frege, which the author had sent to Husserl, heavily annotated by Husserl, and Husserl in particular makes comments on Frege's context principle, which Michael Dummett sees as one of the inaugural moments of analytic philosophy. In his book *Origins of Analytic Philosophy* Dummett locates the linguistic turn in Frege's 1884 *Die Grundlagen der Arithmetik*, where he articulates the context principle that only in the context of a sentence does a word have meaning.[68] Sentences express thought but the decomposition of thought into its components is achieved through the decomposition of sentences. Dummett sees it as crucial to the rise of analytic philosophy that thoughts were stripped of their subjective mental character, thought was "extruded from the mind" as he puts it. Yet this is precisely true also, as Dummett recognizes, of Husserl. The components of thoughts could be tracked through the composition of language once the "disguised" logic of language had been unmasked.

One way to distinguish the traditions is to look at the role played by logic in the analysis of philosophical concepts. Frege and Husserl – the founders of the analytic and Continental traditions – parted company in their evaluation of the role of mathematical formalization in logic. In 1918, when Russell was sent to jail, he took with him Husserl's *Logical Investigations* with the intention of reviewing it for *Mind*. But the review was never written. The failure to continue the development of symbolic logic was in part due to a deliberate decision by Husserl, who regarded it as a mere formal calculus of no philosophical importance. Husserl was interested in transcendental logic, reviving the Kantian problem of how it is that logical acts achieve objectivity. This issue of the nature of transcendental logic has only in the late twentieth century reappeared in analytic philosophy, inspired by contemporary forms of neo-Kantianism.

It may very well be that the distinction between analytic and Continental philosophy may in the end not prove to be a very useful tool for explicating the meaning of philosophy in the twentieth century. There is ample evidence that philosophers in the USA were unhappy with the distinction, especially as it appeared to be used primarily for political purposes to assert the validity of some particular approach to philosophy to the exclusion of all others. The sheer diversity of twentieth-century philosophy and its increasing internationalization need other ways of being described. But it is worth looking a little more in detail at the manner in which analytic philosophy evolved over the century.

The evolution of the tradition of analytic philosophy

Originally, analytic philosophy was presented simply as a method or indeed as *the* method of philosophy. It was primarily understood – by Russell and others – as a method of decompositional analysis. In his "Analytic realism," for instance, Russell wrote: "the philosophy I espouse is analytic, because it claims that one must discover the simple elements of which complexes are composed, and that complexes presuppose simples, whereas simples do not presuppose complexes." Morris Weitz, in his *Twentieth-Century Philosophy: The Analytic Tradition*,[69] lists a number of characteristics of analytic philosophy, including: the refutation of idealism (Russell, Moore), the defence of realism and common sense (Moore), logical analysis (Russell, Ryle), logical positivism (Carnap, Ayer), and a more generic kind of conceptual elucidation. Carnap offers a definition of logical analysis in his *Philosophy and Logical Syntax* (1935):

> The function of logical analysis is to analyse all knowledge, all assertions of science and of everyday life, in order to make clear the sense of each such assertion and the connections between them. One of the principal tasks of the logical analysis of a given statement is to find out the method of verification for that statement.[70]

Examples of the kind of logical analysis that developed in the tradition actually are of a much broader kind. Consider, for instance, Russell's theory of descriptions, and, building on that, Ryle's discussion of systematically misleading expressions.[71] Analytic philosophy was seen as offering a tool-kit for the identification, diagnosis and eventual solution of philosophical problems.

Only gradually was it recognized that analytic philosophy was in fact a historical movement or even a tradition, an idea that gained currency in the last decade of the twentieth century.[72] Certainly, there is a recognition that the nature of the analytic tradition has radically altered over the decades, even if the official ideology, as it were, has resolutely claimed that there has been no change. Indeed, it is now more or less a truism to state that analytic philosophy is a historical tradition which more or less spans the twentieth century itself (certainly from 1905). There is now even talk of "post-analytical philosophy"[73] (see also "The development of analytic philosophy: Wittgenstein and after," Chapter 2).

Although the older empirical tradition of Hume and Mill is clearly in the background (in the work of Bertrand Russell especially), Gottlob Frege, as we have seen, is usually regarded as the first analytic philosopher insofar as he developed a precise way of talking about logical form (in terms of *function* and *argument*) and managed to distinguish it from the *grammatical form* of a sentence. As Frege wrote, "Instead of following grammar blindly, the logician ought rather to see his task as that of freeing us from the fetters of language" (quoted in "Philosophical logic," Chapter 8). This allowed Frege to break free of psychologism (and the "psychological" conception of a judgment as the uniting of subject and predicate). Similarly, his distinction between "sense" (*Sinn*) and "reference" or "meaning" (*Bedeutung*) was seen as assisting the kind of clear analysis that would subsequently be favored by philosophers. As Michael Potter comments:

> there is nothing deep, of course, in the distinction between a sign and the thing it signifies, nor in the distinction between both of these and the ideas I attach to a sign when I use it. What goes deeper is the claim that if we are to have a satisfying account of language's ability to communicate thoughts from speaker to listener we must appeal to yet a fourth element – what Frege calls sense. (in "The birth of analytic philosophy," Chapter 1)

As early as 1905, Russell's article "On denoting,"[74] which also enshrined the difference between logical and grammatical form, became a model of its kind and the paradigm of analytic philosophy.[75] The task was to free logic of the enslavement in language. In part this would lead to the pressure to develop ideal languages; it also led to the recognition that many traditional philosophical problems were actually insoluble because their linguistic form was "systematically misleading" as Ryle would put it. Analytic philosophy – beginning with Carnap – now recognized the category of the "pseudo-problem" (*Scheinproblem*).

Bertrand Russell and G. E. Moore must also be given enormous credit for establishing the manner of analytic writing in philosophy that soon became current: writing crisply, identifying a thesis, addressing its merits, entirely independently of its historical context or location in the scheme of a philosopher's thinking. Thus, for example, idealism could be reduced to a single issue: the nature and possibility of internal relations.[76] Leibniz's philosophy could be reduced to a set of principles and the question was whether they were consistent with one another.[77] The form of writing became the lucid essay. But the will-to-system is also evident, from early on, in analytic philosophy. Russell himself was by nature a system builder, trying in his books to give clarification to the central scientific and metaphysical concepts of space, time, matter, causation, the nature of relations, classes, and so on. The most notable case of systematization in point here is Wittgenstein's *Tractatus* (see further in "The birth of analytic philosophy," Chapter 1). According to this book, the object of philosophy is the "logical clarification of thoughts" (*Tractatus* 4.112) and the *Tractatus* is surely an extraordinary edifice, a purely modernist construction. The *Tractatus* encouraged the early Vienna Circle members who were intent on promoting a "scientific conception of the world" (their phrase). Moritz Schlick, for instance, had studied physics and was struggling to find an appropriate philosophical vehicle to accommodate the insights of Einstein's Theory of Relativity and the new physics in general. The Vienna Circle was the most hardnosed set of analytic philosophers and, given their influence, and perhaps a residual institutional memory of their European roots, often Continental philosophers assume there is no other kind of analytic philosophy and dismiss it all as logic-chopping "positivism." Certainly the members of the Vienna Circle were hardnosed in their rejection of metaphysics and gave epistemic predominance to science and that too in a particularly stringent form. There is science and there is stamp collecting, as Quine would later put it, paraphrasing Ernest Rutherford. The human and cultural sciences were often passed over by the analytic tradition, a move that the Continental tradition regarded as disastrous for the very conception of what science is. Rorty saw this tension between a focus on the hard sciences and a softer focus on the humanities as encapsulating a traditional battle between poetry and philosophy (construed as a kind of superscience).[78]

Side by side with the hard, formalistic, systematic side of analytic philosophy, however, there was also a softer edge first typified by G. E. Moore and soon afterwards by Whitehead. Moore's "In defence of common sense" lists propositions which he claims he knows (that he has a body, that he once was younger than he is now, and so on), but many of these knowledge claims embody assumptions that belong to the background of what Husserl would call the life-world.[79]

Analytic philosophy as a tradition continued to be practiced even after many of its central theses were rejected. For example, Peter Strawson (1919–2006) was recognizably an analytic philosopher yet he rejected the Russellian analysis of definite descriptions. The central notion of analytic philosophy seems to be the clarification of concepts through the clarification of the linguistic forms in which those concepts appear. As Michael Dummett has written,

> What distinguishes analytical philosophy, in its diverse manifestations, from other schools is the belief, first, that a philosophical account of thought can be attained through a philosophical account of language, and secondly, that a comprehensive account can only be so attained.[80]

Central then to Dummett's characterization of analytical philosophy is the linguistic turn.

What is difficult to understand is how logical analysis and specifically the disambiguation of the logical from the grammatical form of sentences should end being coupled with a strong defense of ordinary language. This is precisely what happened in the emergence of Oxford ordinary language philosophy in the 1950s, with Austin and Ryle and, incidentally subsequently in the USA, with their two American followers, John Searle (1932–) and Daniel Dennett (1942–). Dennett, for example, applies Ryle's analysis of systematically misleading expressions to deny that there exist "sakes" (as in "I did it for John's sake") and to determine which if any of our nouns denoting mental items are in fact referential.[81]

It would be wrong to think that analytic philosophers are wedded to a fixed set of presuppositions which they do not critically analyze. Perhaps the next most paradigmatic revisionary article for analytic philosophy is W. V. O. Quine's 1951 paper, "Two dogmas of empiricism,"[82] which attacked the very basis of the analytic/synthetic distinction so beloved of neo-Kantians and Carnapians alike. This was a challenge to the very meaning of analysis, and an undermining of the theoretical assumptions that had given rise to analytic philosophy in the first place. Quine is not saying that the distinction between analytic and synthetic truths is badly drawn or vague or useless, rather that it is illusory. It is for Quine "an unempirical dogma of empiricists, a metaphysical article of faith."

Quine's article also included an explicit attack on the verificationist principle of meaning which had become, as Quine calls it, a "catchword" of twentieth-century empiricism. Against the "reductionist" claim that meaningful statements can be traced back to a statement about immediate experience, Quine wants to propose that our "statements about the external world face the tribunal of sense experience not individually but only as a corporate body."[83] What Quine wants to propose in that paper is an "empiricism without dogmas" and one that is holistic in that it sees the web of knowledge as a "man-made fabric which impinges on experience only at the edges".[84] Every statement is revisable, whether it be a statement about experience or the formulation of a logical law. Moreover, the positing of abstract entities such as classes is on a par with the positing of Homeric gods or physical objects. This positing is a matter of convenience, or as Quine puts it, "swelling ontology to simplify theory."[85]

The next step in this overhaul of the very meaning of classical empiricism and indeed classical analytic philosophy (as represented by Carnap or Ayer) is the attack on the scheme/content distinction in Davidson's famous "On the very idea of a conceptual scheme" (1974).[86] Indeed, this step is already prefigured in Quine's "Two dogmas" article. In that article, Quine already recognizes that some sentences look more like statements about our conceptual schemes (whether we admit classes or not) while others look more like statements about brute fact ("there are brick houses on Elm Street"). Quine wants to deny that there is a difference in kind between these two types of statement. They are on a continuum and the decision which to accept is "pragmatic" according to Quine. Davidson begins his article by recognizing that many philosophers speak of conceptual schemes and contrast them with experience and specifically "the data of sensation." Even those who think there is only one conceptual scheme still cling to the idea of there being such a "scheme." But in particular Davidson is interested in the idea (current in modern anthropology and elsewhere – he cites Whorf's work on the Hopi languages and their untranslatability, as well as Thomas Kuhn's work in the *Structure of Scientific Revolutions* on revolutions in science leading to different paradigms or "mindsets") that what makes one conceptual scheme different from another is that one is not translatable into the other. Davidson is explicit that he is seeking to build on Quine's exposure of two dogmas by himself exposing the third dogma of empiricism – that between scheme and content. As Davidson recognizes, to give up the third dogma is to abandon a principle that is at the very heart of empiricism:

> I want to urge that this second dualism of scheme and content, of organizing system and something waiting to be organized, cannot be made intelligible

and defensible. It is itself a dogma of empiricism, the third dogma. The third, and perhaps the last, for if we give it up it is not clear that there is anything distinctive left to call empiricism.[87]

These are paradigmatic moments in analytic philosophy, and there is evidence of a clear sense of tradition. Quine is utilizing but criticizing the approach of Carnap, and Davidson is moving to reject a new dualism that emerges after the analytic/synthetic dualism has been jettisoned. Davidson quotes closely from Quine's article, deliberately invoking phrases like "the tribunal of experience" and it is clear that the conception of a "conceptual scheme" he has in mind comes directly from Quine.

It is interesting that, despite the commitment to naturalism in analytic philosophy, there has been a progressive move *away* from empiricism through the century. Interestingly, as we have seen, both the early Russell and Moore began from the point of view (inherited from German Idealism and its British counterpart) that empiricism had been refuted. Nevertheless, for a long time, analytic philosophy was supposedly linked with empiricism. The essays of Quine and Davidson, then, may be seen as a corrective of the distorting empiricist interpretations of the Vienna School of the central tradition of analytic philosophy. The sheer multiplicity of forms of analytic philosophy in the twentieth century makes it difficult to provide a single account of its history and evolution through the century (but see "The birth of analytic philosophy," Chapter 1, "The development of analytic philosophy," Chapter 2, "Philosophy of language," Chapter 9, and "Philosophy of science," Chapter 14).

A suspicion of grand narratives

In trying to write the history of twentieth-century philosophy, then, one must be careful not to impose a "grand narrative," and indeed, one must resist being deceived by accepting one of the grand narratives which contemporary philosophers themselves espouse and tell. Analytic philosophers no less than Continental philosophers purport to have a suspicion of these grand narratives (whether they offer, to use Rorty's favorite terms, "upbeat" or "downbeat" stories about the development of philosophy). But while one must be wary of the veracity of grand narratives, one must also be aware of the many grand narratives that have been proposed even during the suspicious twentieth century (from Nietzsche and Freud, to Husserl and Heidegger, and even Rorty who had his own grand narrative of the clash between systematic and "edifying" philosophies).

As we have seen, Freud and Husserl both self-consciously sought to inscribe themselves into history as the founders of radically new disciplines: psychoanalysis and phenomenology respectively. But there were many other inaugural moments during the century, not just programmatic announcements such as the Manifesto of the Vienna Circle,[88] but also, for instance, Derrida's proclamation of the new science of grammatology. In typically ambiguous manner, in his *Of Grammatology*, Derrida announces a new science of grammatology (a call taken up by Julia Kristeva) while at the same time explaining how the metaphysical closure of the epoch would prevent this science from ever being established as such. In his *Of Grammatology* Derrida proclaims:

> By alluding to a science of writing reined in by metaphor, metaphysics and theology, this exergue must not only announce that the science of writing – *grammatology* – shows signs of liberation all over the world . . . I would like to suggest above all that, however fecund and necessary the undertaking might be . . . such a science of writing runs the risk of never being established as such and with that name. . . . For essential reasons: the unity of all that allows itself to be attempted today through the most diverse concepts of science and writing is, in principle, more or less covertly yet always, determined by an historico-metaphysical epoch of which we merely glimpse closure. I do not say the end.[89]

In other words, Derrida wants to participate in the grand gesture of the founding of a new science of writing ("grammatology") and at the same time to protect himself against the inevitable failure of such vaulted ambition. Manifestos are indeed a recurrent feature of contemporary philosophy, as they have been through the centuries (think of the 1848 *Communist Manifesto* of Marx and Engels).[90]

In terms of inaugural proclamations, Heidegger, too, is a curious case, both a "modern" and a "postmodern" in many ways, in that he wants both to advance and at the same time deconstruct grand narratives. He wants to speak of and diagnose the history of philosophy, indeed the "history of being" in terms of "epochs." Heidegger and Derrida want to see western philosophy in terms of an occlusion of the meaning of being, or the all-pervasive dominance of an understanding of being in terms of presence. In his narrative of "the history of Being," Heidegger claims apparently to be able to stand above time and history in order to diagnose essential tendencies (see also "German philosophy," Chapter 17). Thus he can, somewhat idiosyncratically, characterize Nietzsche as a metaphysician, albeit one who diagnoses nihilism as the contemporary meaning of Being.

There are many examples of the grand gesture in Heidegger: Consider his claims concerning the "end of philosophy." Heidegger sees the end of philosophy as coming with Nietzsche who "completed" metaphysics and gave "planetary thinking" the form it would have for decades to come. Philosophy has come to an end because a certain form of philosophy has been incorporated into this planetary thinking, Heidegger proclaims:

> With Nietzsche's metaphysics, philosophy is completed. That means: it has gone through the sphere of prefigured possibilities. Completed metaphysics, which is the ground for the planetary manner of thinking, gives the scaffolding for an order of the earth which will supposedly last for a long time. The order no longer needs philosophy because philosophy is already its foundation. But with the end of philosophy, thinking is not also at its end, but in transition to another beginning.[91]

The rhetoric of end is always correlated with the rhetoric of beginning. We have Michel Foucault claiming both that the concept of "man" is a philosophical, or cultural, invention of modernity and also that it will have an "end." As he writes in *The Order of Things*,

> One thing in any case is certain: man is neither the oldest nor the most constant problem that has been posed for human knowledge... As the archaeology of our thought easily shows, man is an invention of recent date. And one perhaps nearing its end.[92]

Analytic philosophy too at various times has proclaimed an end to philosophy as traditionally practiced and there has been considerable discussion about the transformation of philosophy in this tradition also.[93] Philosophy was supposed to be different in character from the history of philosophy. Carnap and Ayer and the Logical Positivists announced the elimination of metaphysics from philosophy.[94] Metaphysical statements have no literal meaning or "sense"; they are not subject to the criteria of truth or falsity, since they are incapable of verification. As Ayer proclaims in *Language, Truth and Logic*,

> We may accordingly define a metaphysical sentence as a sentence which purports to express a genuine proposition, but does, in fact, express neither a tautology nor an empirical hypothesis. And as tautologies and empirical hypotheses form the entire class of significant propositions, we are justified in concluding that all metaphysical assertions are nonsensical.[95]

Metaphysicians have been "duped by grammar" and philosophy must be distinguished from metaphysics, for Ayer. Ayer went further and denied that metaphysical statements can be cherished alongside poetic statements as statements of nonsense that still have emotive value. No, while poetry is rarely literal nonsense, metaphysics always is and is of no scientific value. Yet, in his autobiography, *A Part of My Life*, Ayer described his Oxford training in philosophy as primarily being a kind of critical engagement with the history of philosophy, including much traditional metaphysics, and the writing of essays on Aristotle, Leibniz, and others.[96] It is clear in his own work that he too practiced philosophy in a very traditional manner. Indeed he recommended the historical approach as the best way of introducing students to philosophy.

Both the early and the later Wittgenstein may be said to have contributed to the end of philosophy debate. The Wittgenstein of the *Tractatus* is already advocating silence on certain kinds of questions and the later "therapeutic" approach of the *Philosophical Investigations* may also be seen as a way of diffusing philosophical claims such that philosophical worries may be overcome. At the end of the *Tractatus* (1921), Wittgenstein claims (in a manner that would subsequently inspire the Vienna Circle),

> The correct method in philosophy would really be the following: to say nothing except what can be said, i.e. propositions of natural science – i.e.

something that has nothing to do with philosophy – and then, whenever someone else wanted to say something metaphysical, to demonstrate to him that he had failed to give a meaning to certain signs in his propositions.[97]

Later in the *Philosophical Investigations*[98] he will continue to maintain that philosophical problems arise because of misunderstandings of language (see "The development of analytic philosophy: Wittgenstein and after," Chapter 2)), but the resolution to the problem is to identify the right language-game to be playing:

> The real discovery is the one that makes me capable of stopping doing philosophy when I want to. – The one that gives philosophy peace, so that it is no longer tormented by questions which brings *itself* in question. – ... Problems are solved (difficulties eliminated), not a *single* problem.
>
> There is not a philosophical method, though there are indeed methods, like different therapies. (*Philosophical Investigations*, §133)

Evident in both Wittgenstein and Heidegger is a certain frustration with the manner in which philosophy has been traditionally practiced and an attempt to begin anew. Both the *Tractatus* and *Being and Time* (1927) are modernist documents, as Rorty recognized, in that there is an attempt to break new ground, to use an innovative style, to present *a form* of thinking. Heidegger is explicit about conducting an *Abbau* or *Destruktion* (deconstruction, destruction) which argues that even the history of philosophy, the way the tradition of philosophy itself appears to us, needs to be broken down, unpackaged, and thought again. There is a strong sense in Heidegger of the kind of dilemma that Samuel Beckett's characters find themselves in: "I can't go on; I must go on."

Heidegger's ambitious destructive attack on the possibility of philosophy was countered, however, by his own student Gadamer's more conservative interpretation of hermeneutics. As Karl-Otto Apel writes in Chapter 17,

> Instead Gadamer endeavors, in his founding of a "hermeneutical philosophy" (which appeared in a time of reconstruction after the German catastrophe), to utilize the structures of Heidegger's thought, presupposed in his approach, for what is on the whole a culturally conservative task of reintegrating contemporary philosophy into the European tradition. The classical Greek thinkers (Socrates, Plato, and Aristotle), who were, already for Heidegger, the founders of "metaphysics," thereby play a thoroughly positive role that Gadamer explicitly defends *against* Heidegger's "destruction."

Heideggerian revolution gives way to Gadamerian conservation of the tradition.

Of course, once a new tradition is inaugurated, there will always be those who claim it had prior incarnations and who will write the prehistory of that tradition. Thus, the "linguistic turn" in analytic philosophy (initiated by Frege but really developed by Russell and Wittgenstein) is also paralleled in Continental philosophy with the concern for language and interpretation of Heidegger, Gadamer, and others. There are differences, of course. In analytic philosophy, for instance, the linguistic turn is given specifically scientific garb, whereas the turn to language in eighteenth-century thought is an attempt to achieve universalization of thinking, freeing thinking from the peculiarities of local inscription in language. But even among analytic philosophers, a prehistory to what Austin calls "the way of words" is given, which recognizes specifically analytic philosophy in the work of Socrates, Plato, and Aristotle. Thus we get the emergence of another grand narrative – this time within analytic philosophy – according to which the best philosophy has always been analytic philosophy, whether in Plato's *Theaetetus* or Aristotle's analyses of the different senses of the term *ousia* in his *Metaphysics*. Once a new tradition is identified, it is easy for it to find its forbears.

Philosophical self-reflection

If the nineteenth century saw philosophy becoming thoroughly professionalized and academicized, it also saw, with Hegel, philosophy coming to produce a philosophical reflection on its own genesis. An increasing self-awareness about the nature – and limits – of philosophical practice (grown acute in Wittgenstein and Heidegger) is already evident in philosophy since the time of Immanuel Kant and his conception of *Kritik*. But it was in Hegel's lectures that, for the first time, the history of philosophy itself became self-consciously philosophical. Hegel saw the need for that side of philosophy which was to be "its time comprehended in thought" (*ihre Zeit in Gedanken gefasst*), as he put it. Incidentally, Richard Rorty interprets this Hegelian idea of philosophy (as the self-comprehension of an era) as freeing philosophy from the need to offer explanation and instead allowing it to take the form of celebration:

> I happily join with Charles Taylor in thinking that Hegel's importance lies chiefly in his historicism, and specifically in his redescription of philosophy as its time held in thought. One happy consequence of this redescription seems to me that it frees philosophers from the need to give explanations. It lets us relax and be frankly and openly celebratory (or in Heidegger's case, frankly and openly nostalgic).[99]

Indeed, not only Husserl and Heidegger but also Wittgenstein conceived of philosophy as description. Thus we have Wittgenstein say:

> Philosophy simply puts everything before us, and neither explains nor deduces anything. – Since everything lies open to view there is nothing to explain. (*Philosophical Investigations*, § 126)

Whether philosophy is able to comprehend the times in which it emerged and of which it is supposedly the rational representation, is an open question, but it is at least true that the effort to comprehend our philosophical time is itself a philosophical (rather than merely a sociological) challenge.

To think about the twentieth-century philosophical legacy, one has to be aware of the many hermeneutical challenges involved. Yet, in one sense, one must be resolutely Hegelian in that one has to see a certain sense in history and not just one damn thing after another. The historical developments of philosophy through the century must themselves have philosophical significance, but the recognition of that significance must not endanger the very understanding of the radical contingency and facticity which underlie human achievement. Hegel himself recognized the tension between concept and contingency, between the rationality which philosophy demands and the chaos of what happens, and claimed that "the only thought which philosophy brings with it is the simple idea of reason – the idea that reason governs the world, and that world history is therefore a rational process."[100]

But precisely this assumption of reality is what is in question in contemporary philosophy. On the other hand, any scientific enterprise, any enterprise of understanding surely begins from the assumption of rationality, that there is an identifiable order even in apparent chaos. Heidegger, for instance – and Gadamer here follows him – sees it as belonging to the meaning of philosophy to say something essential about "the spirit of the age"[101] (for further discussion of Gadamer see "Twentieth-century hermeneutics," Chapter 16). Heidegger, Gadamer, Blumenberg, Cassirer, and Arendt all want to characterize the essence of *modernity*, for instance. Foucault wants to diagnose contemporary civilization using the mirror of the history of madness. His employment of the Nietzschean figures of genealogy and diagnosis confirms that he too believes that it is possible to penetrate to the essence of a time or a period. This is a kind of phenomenological essentialism, one which needs much fuller study.

In any event, to write a history of twentieth-century philosophy is not, as Hegel correctly recognizes, merely to assemble a list of all the philosophical works and tendencies. It is also an attempt to seize *the rationale* at work in the processes. For example, Jean-François Lyotard is doing just that in diagnosing what he has termed the "postmodern condition." He writes: "Our working hypothesis is that the status of knowledge is altered as societies enter what is known as the post-industrial age and cultures enter what is known as the postmodern age."[102] Lyotard goes on to attempt (while disputing grand narratives) to diagnose the age in terms of a set of key characteristics. In precisely this sense, I believe that the history of philosophy is relevant to philosophy, in contrast to the way in which the history of physics or medicine is not relevant to the current practice of these disciplines. Concepts and problems have histories, and understanding those histories is important to understanding and contextualizing the concepts themselves. As Peter Hylton has written in his elegant *Russell, Idealism and the Emergence of Analytic Philosophy* (1990), "Philosophical problems, and the concepts in which they are formulated, and the assumptions on which they rest, have a history; and this history is surely a legitimate subject of study."[103] Moreover, Hylton argues it is not just a subject of interest in historical terms but it is of philosophical interest too. That is, it challenges our conceptual frameworks.

Twentieth-century philosophy and the meaning of Europe

One important hermeneutic scruple that has to be invoked in any writing of the history of twentieth-century philosophy concerns the meaning of the very terms in play in the description and categorization of that thought. As with the strictly philosophical concepts involved so too the supposedly cultural – or even geographical – terms are fraught with ambiguity. For instance, even if, in philosophy, the latter half of the twentieth century became very much the "American" century, no philosophical account of the first half of the century can ignore the vital contribution of Europe.[104] But immediately we have to ask: What do we mean by Europe?

The very notion of "Europe" itself has not remained static in the period in question, but has been the subject of intense analysis from Husserl and Jan Patočka to Jacques Derrida and Jürgen Habermas. Edmund Husserl in his *Crisis of the European Sciences* (1936) sought to overcome the dangerous slide of European culture into irrationalism by tracing the roots of modernity in the mathematicization of nature successfully begun by Galileo.[105] Modern science had literally split the world in two (into objective measurable properties and "subjective-relative" properties) and had separated fact from value to a degree that twentieth-century scientifically informed culture was left without means to analyze the incipient loss of meaning and value that threatened its very existence. Husserl actually proposes self-reflective meditative philosophy (*Besinnung*) as a cure for this malaise. But Husserl's concept of Europe was not without controversy. Critics point especially to Husserl's *Vienna Lecture* (1935) where he explicitly excluded nomadic gypsies from the concept of "Europe" as the center of scientific rationality.[106]

Jan Patočka also wrote urgently and incisively on the meaning of Europe and about the "problems of a post-European humanity," for which he developed the term "post-Europe" (*Nach-Europa*).[107] Like Husserl, he turns to the ancient Greeks, but he draws inspiration from the desire for justice which emerged there and in the idea of the need for "care of the soul." In one of his last articles, Jacques Derrida also wrote on the nature of Europe, speaking of a "Europe of hope," which would not be "Eurocentric" but a guardian of irreplaceable values, many of which stem from the Enlightenment:

> Caught between US hegemony and the rising power of China and Arab/ Muslim theocracy, Europe has a unique responsibility. I am hardly thought of as a Eurocentric intellectual; these past 40 years, I have more often been accused of the opposite. But I do believe, without the slightest sense of European nationalism or much confidence in the European Union as we currently know it, that we must fight for what the word Europe means today. This includes our Enlightenment heritage, and also an awareness and regretful acceptance of the totalitarian, genocidal and colonialist crimes of the past. Europe's heritage is irreplaceable and vital for the future of the world. We must fight to hold on to it. We should not allow Europe to be reduced to the status of a common market, or a common currency, or a neo-nationalist conglomerate, or a military power.[108]

The German Critical Theorist Jürgen Habermas, too, recognized the importance of the European contribution to world culture when he wrote:

> The main religion in Europe, Christianity, obeyed its missionary imperative and expanded all over the world. The global spread of modern science and technology, of Roman law and the Napoleonic Code, of human rights, democracy and the nation-state started from Europe as well.[109]

Habermas sees the critique of Eurocentrism emerging at the heart of Europe's own efforts to face up to its own history of struggles and disasters. He sees the possibility of encounter taking place as concepts of identity transcend the arbitrary boundaries of the old nation states.[110] The meaning of Europe, therefore, continues to demand philosophical discussion and critique.

For the first half of the century, Europe was at the center of western academic philosophy, especially if we include Britain as part of Europe. As in the later half of the nineteenth century, the most active centers of European philosophy continued to be found in Germany, Austria, France, and Britain. Philosophically significant cities included: Berlin (Dilthey, Simmel), Vienna (Wittgenstein), Marburg (Cassirer), Göttingen (Husserl), Freiburg (Rickert, Heidegger), Frankfurt (Adorno), Prague (Patočka), Paris (Bergson, Sartre, Merleau-Ponty), Cambridge (Russell, Moore, Wittgenstein), Oxford (Ryle, Grice, Austin, Dummett) and London (A. J. Ayer). But, especially since 1945, the axis has been moving persistently westward, specifically to the United States. Later, especially from the 1960s on, Australia too emerged with a distinctive kind of analytic philosophy of a materialist and realist variety (one thinks of Armstrong and Smart, among others).

The philosophical Europe in question for the first half of the century is a very small Europe; it does not contain Greece, Portugal, or Spain (apart from Unamuno at Salamanca and Ortega Y Gasset in Madrid; Santayana, for instance, was educated in the USA and wrote in English). If Wittgenstein went to Norway in 1913, it was because of his desire for darkness and to escape from life at Cambridge. He did not go there for its universities and the same is true of his sojourns in rural Ireland during the late 1940s. Europe continued to attract visiting international philosophers until the outbreak of the Second World War. Thus, in 1932 W. V. O. Quine thought it worthwhile to leave Harvard, where he had studied with C. I. Lewis and Whitehead, to visit Vienna, Prague (where he met Carnap), and Warsaw, to learn more about logic. Gilbert Ryle, who himself lectured in Oxford on Austrian philosophers (Bolzano, Brentano, Meinong, and Husserl), could recommended the young A. J. Ayer to study with Moritz Schlick in Vienna.[111] During the nineteenth century there had been significant developments in logic in Austria and Prague (Bolzano) and later in Poland, in the Lvov-Warsaw schools,[112] but by the mid-twentieth century, especially after 1945, western academic philosophy in general had forgotten Poland (Tarski, for example, was in the US) and indeed the whole Eastern bloc, with the possible exception of a small number of thinkers (such as Leszek Kolakowski who later emigrated to the UK), Georg Lukács in Hungary, Jan Patočka in Prague, and the Praxis group of Marxists in

Belgrade (Mihailo Marković) and Zagreb (Gajo Petrović) in the former Yugoslavia, some now discredited owing to their support for Serbian extremist nationalism during the Kosovo disputes.[113] This is not to say that the discoveries of Tarski, for example, were ignored. Indeed, the work of Tarski on truth is essential to understanding the work of Davidson and contemporary philosophy of logic and of language (see "Philosophical logic," Chapter 8, "Philosophy of language," Chapter 9). It is rather that Tarski became completely absorbed in the American context, whereas post-1945 Poland together with its philosophers remained locked in a Soviet cul-de-sac.[114]

Another hermeneutic scruple concerns the manner in which thinkers are either inscribed or inscribe themselves into a specific tradition in terms of the language and culture of a particular group. Often a tradition metamorphized when translated into another country. Thus, for instance, Sartre very quickly harnessed Husserlian phenomenology to the native tradition of Cartesianism in France, clearly spurred on by Husserl's own efforts to communicate with French philosophy in his Paris Lectures of 1929.[115] Similarly, in his essay on Husserl, Emmanuel Levinas links him with the native intuitionist tradition of Henri Bergson.[116] In like manner, Hegel – whom Husserl regarded as ungrounded speculative system-builder and hence the opposite of a true phenomenologist – was grafted onto the phenomenological tradition by Sartre, Merleau-Ponty, and others, who had all heard the lectures of Alexandre Kojève.[117] Sartre self-consciously developed existentialism but in the 1950s he deliberately reinscribed it as a moment within a larger conception of dialectical materialism, in his *Critique of Dialectical Reason* (1960).

Here again, it is important to bear in mind that each country – and certainly each language – has its own conversation going on and its own conception of tradition. Heidegger's *Being and Time* was not translated into English until 1962[118] and thus discussion of Heidegger in the Anglophone world really did not begin until the 1960s, whereas it had been continuing in Germany since 1927 and in France since the 1930s. Similarly, A. J. Ayer reminds us that although Wittgenstein's *Tractatus* had been published in 1922 and that he had been teaching at Cambridge since 1929, Wittgenstein's ideas had hardly penetrated Oxford (which was at that time deeply resistant to the mathematical logical approach being promoted at Cambridge) until introduced by Gilbert Ryle.[119] The Frankfurt School began in Germany; its members were forced to emigrate during the Nazi years and returned to Frankfurt after the war. Analytic philosophy of language, which emerged from the work of Wittgenstein and others, began to re-enter German philosophy only in the late 1950s, as Karl-Otto Apel relates, and it took him some time to understand it in relation to the existing tradition of hermeneutics practiced in Germany at that time by Heidegger, Gadamer, and others.[120]

In the analytic tradition similar insertions and reinscriptions into traditions occur but they are usually not explicitly trumpeted. David Pears, in his book on Russell,[121] argued that Russell was responding to the challenge of skepticism, and both Pears and A. J. Ayer paint Russell as an empiricist philosopher following in the footsteps of Hume. In fact, however, as Peter Hylton has shown, Russell was primarily influenced by the idealisms of Bradley and McTaggart, and was a practicing metaphysician, frequently introducing abstract metaphysical entities into his explanations as no empiricist would have done. Russell and Moore, influenced by Green and Bradley, both regarded empiricism as false and as having been effectively refuted by idealism.[122] Thus Russell could write in his *History of Western Philosophy*: "David Hume ... developed to its logical conclusion the empirical philosophy of Locke and Berkeley, and by making it self-consistent made it incredible."[123]

Mistaken inclusions of a philosopher into a particular tradition occur frequently and often with creative consequences. When Ryle advised Ayer to study with Schlick, it was because he thought the Vienna Circle were pursuing Wittgenstein's program in philosophy. Wittgenstein himself was soon to distance himself from the Circle and show that his philosophical interests were quite different. In *Being and Time*, Heidegger inscribed phenomenology into the older Greek tradition of philosophy, even claiming that the meaning of phenomenology was better understood by Aristotle than by his mentor Husserl! Derrida extracted the deconstructive moment from Husserlian *Abbau* and Heideggerian *Destruktion* and Nietzschean *Zerstörung* to make it into a kind of permanent principle of interpretative change. It is interesting to see that deconstruction will probably be reabsorbed into the longer tradition of hermeneutics.

The World Wars: fragmentation and dislocation

The single most important historical and sociological factor that had an impact on the meaning and practice of academic philosophy was the Second World War. The First World War was catastrophic in its human and political consequences, breaking up the old order and separating Russell and Wittgenstein, it did not threaten the very existence of philosophy as such. In fact, the First World War was seen by Gadamer and others (e.g. Hannah Arendt) as having loosened the grip of neo-Kantianism and other nineteenth-century traditions, and as providing an opportunity for students hungry for meaning and relevance to explore the new more "concrete" philosophies, such as phenomenology (Husserl), *Lebensphilosophie* (Simmel, Dilthey), existentialism (Kierkegaard and Nietzsche), and mysticism (inspired by the publication of Meister Eckhart's work as well as by the anti-materialist poetry of Stefan George). The First World War had similar important consequences for the nascent analytic philosophical tradition. It woke Bertrand Russell up from his detached mathematical and metaphysical concerns. Russell was horrified by the war fever gripping Britain in 1914 and argued against it, writing a number of articles on the ethics of war which, though they might not measure up to the politically correct standards of our day in that they defend the war of a more advanced civilization on a lesser, nevertheless demand serious reasons for war and were considered so shocking at the time that journals such as the *New Statesman* refused to publish them.[124] In effect, his opposition to the war and to conscription destroyed his academic career and led to his being jailed in 1918. In 1916 Russell was dismissed from Trinity College for publishing a pamphlet defending a conscientious objector. He was prevented from taking up a job in Harvard because Britain would not issue him a passport. Particularly shocking for Russell was that his friend and protégé Wittgenstein had enlisted in the

Austrian army and was effectively fighting for the other side. Russell wrote to his friend Ottoline Morrell, "It seems strange that of all the people in the war the one I care for much the most should be Wittgenstein, who is an 'enemy'."[125]

The First World War gave Russell a taste for activism (and Wittgenstein too served heroically on the opposing side), but otherwise it was more or less welcomed by other academics. In Germany, Max Scheler, who had lost his academic post because of various personal indiscretions, made a living writing patriotic pamphlets enthusing on the nature of war.[126] The classicist and socialist Paul Natorp also wrote some pamphlets related to the German war effort and later reflected on the meaning of war for the spirit of Germany.[127] Edmund Husserl was broadly supportive of Germany's claims, even though he lost a son and his second son was seriously injured, and he delivered some lectures on the political situation with reference to Fichte.[128] Heidegger was serving on the western front with the meteorological division.

The rise of European fascism (not just in Germany but in Italy and Spain) and the Second World War had a much more decisive impact on the academy. According to Jean-Paul Sartre, for instance, the war divided his life in two.[129] He went from bourgeois idealist to committed existential Marxist over the course of the 1940s and later became an apologist for the Russian Communist regime of Stalin (until the Soviet repression in Hungary in 1956).[130] Heidegger tied his academic career to the rise of the Nazis and, as a result, his teaching career lay in ruins along with the collapse of Germany in 1945, as a result of his being denounced to the occupying administration by another German philosopher and his former friend, Karl Jaspers. Jaspers regarded Heidegger's attempt to curry favor with the National Socialists as naive but its effect was to destroy German philosophy.[131]

The rise of the Nazis in Germany with their specific anti-Jewish policies led to the mass migration of intellectuals, with most members of the Vienna Circle and Frankfurt School being forced to leave Germany. The Vienna Circle members (including Carnap and Feigl) went primarily to the United States;[132] but Neurath went to England, as did Adorno initially. Later, Adorno also went to the United States, where he was joined by Horkheimer and Arendt. Others too, such as Reichenbach and Hempel, had to leave Germany. The war, and more specifically Nazism, cost the lives of philosophers such as Walter Benjamin, who died in 1940 on the border between France and Spain, while fleeing from the Nazis, and Edith Stein, who died in Auschwitz concentration camp in 1942. In France, the philosopher of mathematics Jean Cavaillès, a member of the French Resistance, was shot by the Gestapo in 1944. Many French philosophers, including Albert Camus, were members of the French Resistance. Others, such as Sartre and de Beauvoir, had more complicated relations with the Vichy regime (Sartre was not exactly the Resistance hero he later claimed to have been; and de Beauvoir made broadcasts on a radio station blacked by the Resistance), but there is no doubt that the war radically changed all their lives. The young W. V. O. Quine, who had studied in Vienna, was so horrified by the prospect of the rise of the Nazis that he enlisted in the navy and fought in Italy. He later wrote, "I felt that Western culture was on the verge of collapse and all I was doing was philosophy of logic."[133]

After the Second World War, as Adorno too has recognized in a different context, everything had changed. The second half of the century has seen a steady drift towards America and the recognition of a distinct voice emerging in the US, especially in the form of pragmatism. Arthur Danto, however, recognizes that a distinctive American academic philosophy emerged only in the 1960s (see "American philosophy in the twentieth century," Chapter 5). In reading accounts of the education of typical American philosophers such as Quine and Rorty one is struck by the fact that their orientation was entirely towards Europe. Quine had gone to Harvard to study logic with Whitehead but was disappointed and felt the need to move in a different direction. He spoke good German and traveled to Europe to study logic and became a member of the Vienna Circle. Richard Rorty was taught by Carnap at the University of Chicago; Hilary Putnam wrote his doctoral dissertation under Reichenbach at UCLA; Thomas Kuhn taught with Hempel at Princeton; Henry Allison studied with Gurwitsch at the New School for Social Research. The influence of European philosophy was dominant in American academe through the 1960s.

Given the political turmoil and cataclysms of the century, it seems rather strange that political philosophy did not really develop as a subject until the latter part of the century. Clearly the Russian Revolution appeared to justify the philosophy of Lenin and its interpretation of Marx, so thenceforth Communist countries embraced Marxist-Leninism. The so-called "western Marxism" of Georg Lukács and the Frankfurt School represented a different, less doctrinaire approach to Marxism, as did the work of Gramsci and other Italian Marxists. Hannah Arendt made a significant contribution to political philosophy with her *The Origins of Totalitarianism* (1951) and *The Human Condition* (1958), as did Karl Popper and Isaiah Berlin, both writing in the 1950s,[134] but the theoretical situation was transformed by the work of John Rawls, especially his *Theory of Justice* which circulated in manuscript during the 1960s before it was finally published in 1971 (see "Twentieth-century political philosophy," Chapter 21). In Europe, a new beginning in political philosophy was made by Maurice Merleau-Ponty and Jean-Paul Sartre with their journal *Temps Modernes* (begun 1945), which published interesting and engaged critiques of colonialism and imperialism. Sartre was active in criticizing the French adventure in Algeria and Merleau-Ponty wrote a stinging attack on the Russian system in his *Humanism and Terror*[135] and fell out with Sartre who at that time sought to maintain solidarity between the French working class and the Russian Communist Party.[136] Frantz Fanon's *The Wretched of the Earth*,[137] to which Jean-Paul Sartre wrote an important Preface, was an important contribution to the critique of colonialism and for its analysis of the French use of torture against Algerians. In the late 1960s the student and worker protests in France gave Sartre new prominence, whereas in the USA in the same period the work of Herbert Marcuse, with his analysis of a kind of "repressive-tolerance" that characterized advanced industrial society, also was popular among the student left.[138] Subsequently in Europe, political thought has continued to be predominantly leftist, whether it be in the form of the structuralist Marxism of Louis Althusser or his follower Alain Badiou, or the attempt to pursue the emancipation of society as advocated by Jürgen Habermas (see "Critical Theory," Chapter 18), or in the analysis of forms of hegemony in Ernesto Laclau and Chantal Mouffe.

Philosophy in the twenty-first century

How should the legacy of twentieth-century philosophy be characterized for the present day? Perhaps it will emerge that, just as Kant and Hegel emerged as the dominant figures in nineteenth-century philosophy, Heidegger and Wittgenstein will continue to be seen as the leading figures of the twentieth. But if that is so then there will need to be much more effort made to connect these two authors. After all, both Kant and Hegel were from the same intellectual stable, as it were, and Hegel's work addresses many issues initially raised by Kant. Wittgenstein and Heidegger, however, cannot easily be put in such close relation or in the same kind of terms. The century has many different philosophical voices and profound differences in style and content in doing philosophy. To paraphrase Mao, a hundred schools of thought contend. To illustrate the different styles and contents at work in contemporary philosophy, let us playfully indulge in a little thought-experiment. Imagine two books written by prominent philosophers. Both have the title "Identity and Discrimination." One is a European philosopher who is interested in the issue of shared identity, in terms of one's belonging to a family, a gender, a class, a culture, and so on. Her worry is how do we preserve and celebrate diversity. She is against discrimination in all forms and indeed regards all forms of monism as hegemonous. The other book is a careful study of the meaning of identity as expressed in Leibniz's law. Can one discriminate between identicals? What does logical identity mean and what are the epistemological criteria involved in any act of discrimination? One philosopher sees identity as follows:

> Anything whatsoever has the relation of identity to itself, and to nothing else. Things are identical if they are one thing, not two. We can refute the claim that they are identical if we can find a property of one that is not simultaneously a property of the other. The concept of identity is fundamental to logic. Without it, counting would be impossible, for we could not distinguish in principle between counting one thing twice and counting two different things. When we have acquired the concept, it can still be difficult to make this distinction in practice. Misjudgements of identity are possible because one thing can be presented in many guises. Identity judgments often involve assumptions about the nature of things. The identity of the present mature tree with the past sapling implies persistence through change. The non-identity of the actual child of one couple with the hypothetical child of a different couple is implied by the claim that ancestry is an essential property. Knowledge of what directions are involves knowledge that parallel lines have identical directions. Many controversies over identity concern the nature of the things in question. Others concern challenges to the orthodox conception just sketched of identity itself.[139]

On the other hand, our European philosopher is suspicious of the notion of identity, and is concerned to show that all claims of identity involve the suppression of some alterity and difference. As Peter Fenves has written:

the Cartesian attempt to secure the legitimacy of knowledge finds its principal point of reference in the identity of the self-conscious subject. This subject can serve as the source of legitimation to the extent that it can immediately identify itself and can treat its act of self-identification as knowledge. Postmodern theories of identity and alterity are concerned for the most part with the nature of self-identity and with the relation between the self and whatever presents itself as other than the self ... If modern philosophy rests on the principle of self-consciousness, then one criterion for a postmodern philosophy would be its contesting of this principle.[140]

One philosopher is suspicious of the hegemony of identity and argainst discrimi-nation, the other considers identity to be of absolutely paramount importance and that discrimination is the act of any mind that wants to understand anything. Not to be able to discriminate between elms and oak trees is a failure of knowledge. Clearly, there is a sense in which these contrasting accounts of identity could be integrated with one another. Indeed, there is an interesting collection of essays, *Identity*, edited by Henry Harris,[141] which consists of six essays addressing different aspects of the concept of identity, including numerical identity (what are the criteria for saying that two phenomena observed at different times are the *same* thing?), personal identity, sexual identity, national identity, and even fictional identity. The authors include Bernard Williams and Derek Parfit and draw on the work of Alasdair MacIntyre among others. The point, I think, is that analytic philosophy has, perhaps unknown to itself, expanded to become more inclusive of different standpoints and radically different metaphysical views and approaches. There is increasing recognition that concepts such as "identity" are fluid and many-sided. Besides Habermas, Ricoeur, and Apel, few Continental philosophers have been quite so expansive and accommodating in attempting to fuse their accounts with versions of problems imported from the analytic tradition. The hope of twenty-first-century philosophy is that there will be a true appreciation of the many-sidedness of philosophical problematics and of the multiplicity of modes of approach to them.

Philosophy will undoubtedly develop in unpredictable ways and it would be impossible to try to set out hard and fast tasks for the philosopher or to attempt to indicate where its future lies. As Merleau-Ponty, one of the philosophers most appreciated by all sides of contemporary philosophy, put it so perceptively in his *Éloge de la philosophie*, "The philosophical absolute does not have any permanent seat." In that same essay, he gives us an interesting portrait of the philosopher: "The philosopher is marked by the distinguishing trait that he possesses *inseparably* the taste for evidence and the feeling for ambiguity."[142] Certainly, Wittgenstein too, despite his logical focus, or perhaps indeed because of it, also had a "feeling for ambiguity." In his correspondence with Russell in early 1914, Wittgenstein at one point states that he hopes that Russell, in his forth-coming lectures in Harvard, will reveal something of his thinking and not just present "cut and dried results."[143] Wittgenstein had put his finger on something in the manner of Russell's way of writing; Russell favored the scientific manner of reporting results and discoveries. Wittgenstein, on the other hand, recognized that the *process* of philosophizing is the important thing, the showing, the revealing that is done in the very acts of questioning and probing. Both aspects of philosophy – the discovery of "results" and the unveiling of the very processes of philosophical thinking – will surely continue into the twenty-first century.

Notes

1 B. Croce, *What is Living and What is Dead in the Philosophy of Hegel*, trans. D. Ainslie (London: Macmillan, 1915).

2 For a full list of twentieth-century philosophers, see Stuart Brown, Diane Collinson, and Robert Wilkinson (eds.) *The Biographical Dictionary of Twentieth-Century Philosophers* (London and New York: Routledge, 1996).

3 An earlier version of this chapter was presented as a plenary address to the Society for European Philosophy conference, "European Philosophy and the Human Condition," held at University College Cork on September 14, 2002. See also Dermot Moran, "What is historical in the history of philosophy? Towards an assessment of twentieth-century European philosophy," in Peter Kemp (ed.) *History in Education, Proceedings from the conference "History in Education" held at the Danish University of Education March 24–5, 2004* (Copenhagen: Danish University of Education Press, 2005), pp. 53–82.

4 Bernard Henri-Lévy, *Sartre: The Philosopher of the Twentieth Century*, trans. Andrew Brown (Cambridge: Polity Press, 2003).

5 Hannah Arendt, *Eichmann in Jerusalem: A Report on the Banality of Evil*, 2nd rev. edn. (New York: Penguin, 1964).

6 See Richard Rorty, *Achieving Our Country: Leftist Thought in Twentieth-Century America* (Cambridge, MA: Harvard University Press, 1998).

7 Bernard-Henri Lévy, *War, Evil and End of History* (London: Duckworth, 2004).

8 See Alain de Botton, *The Consolation of Philosophy* (London: Hamish Hamilton, 2000).

9 Ray Monk, *Ludwig Wittgenstein: The Duty of Genius* (New York: Free Press, 1990).

10 Roger Scruton, *On Hunting: A Short Polemic* (London: Yellow Jersey Press, 1998).

11 See Peter Singer, *Animal Liberation: A New Ethics for our Treatment of Animals* (New York: Random House, 1975).

12 Naess defines ecosophy as follows: "By an ecosophy I mean a philosophy of ecological harmony or equilibrium. A philosophy as a kind of *sofia* or wisdom is openly normative, it contains both norms, rules, postulates, value priority announcements and hypotheses concerning the state of affairs in our universe. Wisdom is policy wisdom, prescription, not only scientific description and prediction. The details of an ecosophy will show many variations due to significant differences concerning not only the 'facts' of pollution, resources, population, etc. but also value priorities." Quoted in Alan Drengson and Yuichi Inoue (eds.) *The Deep Ecology Movement: An Introductory Anthology* (Berkeley, CA: North Atlantic Publishers, 1995), p. 8. Arne Naess more or less invented "deep ecology" in a ground-breaking article, "The shallow and the deep, long-range Ecology Movement: a summary," published in *Inquiry* 16 (1973), pp. 95–100.

13 See, for instance (to name but a few), John Passmore, *A Hundred Years of Philosophy* (Harmondsworth: Penguin, 1968); Dagobert D. Runes (ed.) *Twentieth Century Philosophy: Living Schools of Thought* (New York: Greenwood, 1968); Wolfgang Stegmüller, *Main Currents in Contemporary German, British and American Philosophy* (Dordrecht: Reidel, 1969); Gilbert Ryle (ed.) *Contemporary Aspects of Philosophy* (London: Oriel Press, 1976); J. Habermas, *The Philosophical Discourse of Modernity* (Cambridge, MA: MIT Press, 1987); A. Coffa, *The Semantic Tradition from Kant to Carnap* (Cambridge: Cambridge University Press, 1991); Peter Simons, *Philosophy and Logic in Central Europe from Bolzano to Tarski* (Dordrecht: Kluwer, 1992); Paul Gorner, *Twentieth Century German Philosophy* (Oxford: Oxford

University Press, 2000); Avrum Stroll, *Twentieth-Century Analytic Philosophy* (New York: Columbia University Press, 2000); Tom Baldwin, *Contemporary Philosophy: Philosophy in English since 1945* (Oxford: Oxford University Press, 2001); Christian Delacampagne, *A History of Philosophy in the Twentieth Century* (Baltimore, MD: Johns Hopkins University Press, 2001); Brian Shanley (ed.) *One Hundred Years of Philosophy* (Washington, DC: Catholic University of America Press, 2001); and Scott Soames, *Philosophical Analysis in the Twentieth Century*, vols. 1 and 2 (Princeton, NJ: Princeton University Press, 2003).

14 Routledge has devoted three volumes in its History of Philosophy series to the twentieth century. Two volumes deal with analytic philosophy (seen as the dominant tradition, including epistemology, metaphysics, philosophy of language, ethics, philosophy of science); see S. G. Shanker (ed.) *Philosophy of the English-Speaking World in the Twentieth Century 1: Science, Logic and Mathematics*, Routledge History of Philosophy vol. IX (London: Routledge, 1996) and John Canfield (ed.) *Philosophy of the English-Speaking World in the Twentieth Century 2: Meaning, Knowledge and Value*, Routledge History of Philosophy vol. X (London: Routledge, 1996); whereas one volume deals with Continental European philosophy: R. Kearney (ed.) *Continental Philosophy in the Twentieth Century*, Routledge History of Philosophy vol. VIII (London: Routledge, 1994).

15 See Dermot Moran, *Edmund Husserl: Founder of Phenomenology* (Cambridge: Polity Press, 2005), p. 34.

16 See Edith Glaser, "Emancipation or marginalisation: new research on women students in the German-speaking world," *Oxford Review of Education* 23/2: *Writing University History* (June, 1997), pp. 169–84.

17 See, e.g. G. E. M. Anscombe, *Intention* (Oxford: Blackwell, 1957); Cora Diamond and J. Teichman (eds.) *Intention and Intentionality: Essays in Honour of G. E. M. Anscombe* (Brighton: Harvester Press, 1979); and R. Teichmann (ed.) *Logic, Cause and Action: Essays in Honour of Elizabeth Anscombe*, Royal Institute of Philosophy, *Philosophy* Supplement 46 (Cambridge: Cambridge University Press, 2000).

18 See Jean Grimshaw, *Philosophy and Feminist Thinking* (Minneapolis: University of Minnesota Press, 1986) and Miranda Fricker and Jennifer Hornsby, *The Cambridge Companion to Feminism in Philosophy* (New York: Cambridge University Press, 2000). See also Mary Ellen Waithe (ed.) *A History of Women Philosophers*, vol. 4: *1900–Today* (Dordrecht and Boston: Kluwer, 1994).

19 Theodor W. Adorno, *Negative Dialectics*, trans. E. B. Ashton (New York: Continuum, 1992), p. 320.

20 Jacques Derrida, *Speech and Phenomena and Other Essays on Husserl's Theory of Signs*, trans. David B. Allison (Evanston, IL: Northwestern University Press, 1973).

21 J. E. McTaggart, "The unreality of time," *Mind* 17/4 (1908), pp. 457–74. For a discussion of time that revives McTaggart, see D. H. Mellor, *Real Time II* (London: Routledge, 1998).

22 See William James, "Does 'consciousness' exist?," *Journal of Philosophy, Psychology, and Scientific Methods 1* (1904), pp. 477–91.

23 David Chalmers, *The Conscious Mind* (Oxford: Oxford University Press, 1996).

24 See F. Varela, E. Thompson, and E. Rosch, *The Embodied Mind* (Cambridge, MA: MIT Press, 1991).

25 See, for instance, Robert Stern (ed.) *Transcendental Arguments: Problems and Prospects* (Oxford: Oxford University Press, 1999) and Mark Sacks, *Objectivity and Insight* (Oxford: Oxford University Press, 2000).

26 See also Cristina Lafont, *The Linguistic Turn in Hermeneutic Philosophy* (Cambridge, MA: MIT Press, 1999).

27 One should also acknowledge the many new journals that appeared in philosophy of science, especially in the 1930s, e.g. Erkenntnis (founded 1930), *Philosophy of Science* (founded 1934), Synthèse (founded 1936).

28 See Klaus Christian Köhnke, *The Rise of Neo-Kantianism: German Academic Philosophy between Idealism and Positivism*, trans. R. J. Hollingdale (Cambridge: Cambridge University Press, 1991).

29 See C. L. Ten (ed.) *The Routledge History of Philosophy*, vol. VII: *The Nineteenth Century* (London and New York: Routledge, 1994).

30 See William H. Goetzmann (ed.) *The American Hegelians: An Intellectual Episode in the History of Western America* (New York: Alfred A. Knopf, 1973).

31 G. E. Moore, "The refutation of idealism," *Mind* 12 (1903), pp. 433–53.

32 See A. Kojève, *Introduction to the Reading of Hegel: Lectures on the Phenomenology of Spirit*, trans. James H. Nichols, Jr. (Ithaca, NY: Cornell University Press, 1969).

33 See J. N. Findlay, *Hegel: A Re-Examination* (London: Allen & Unwin, 1958) and Charles Taylor, *Hegel* (Cambridge: Cambridge University Press, 1975). .

34 On Robert Brandom's appreciation of Hegel see his, "Holism and idealism in Hegel's phenomenology," in *Hegel Studien*, Band 36 (2001), pp. 57–92. Rorty made his remark regarding the Hegelian phase of analytic philosophy in his Introduction to Wilfrid Sellars, *Empiricism and the Philosophy of Mind* (Cambridge, MA: Harvard University Press 1997). Brandom endorsed Rorty's remark in his paper to the colloquium "Relation between Analytic and Continental Philosophy," which took place at the Twentieth World Congress of Philosophy held in Boston in 1998. For a discussion of Brandom's relation to Hegel, see Tom Rockmore, "Brandom, Hegel and inferentialism," *International Journal of Philosophical Studies* 10/ 4 (November 2002), pp. 429–47.

35 See Edmund Gettier's pithy three-page paper, "Is justified true belief knowledge?," *Analysis* 23 (1963), pp. 121–23.

36 Jowett's translations continue to feature prominently in a standard textbook, *The Collected Dialogues of Plato*, ed. Edith Hamilton and Huntington Cairns, Bollingen Series LXXI (Princeton, NJ: Princeton University Press, 1961).

37 See, for instance, W. D. Ross's translation of Aristotle's *Nicomachean Ethics* (Oxford: Clarendon Press, 1908). This translation was revised by J. Urmson and J. Ackrill for Oxford in 1980 and continues to be in use among students.

38 G. E. Moore, "The nature of judgment," *Mind* 8 (1899), pp. 176–93. .

39 See Ray Monk, *Bertrand Russell: The Spirit of Solitude* (London: Jonathan Cape, 1996), p. 117.

40 See Bertrand Russell, *The Autobiography of Bertrand Russell, 1872–1914* (Boston, MA: Little, Brown & Co., 1951), pp. 217–18.

41 Russell, *Autobiography*, pp. 218–19.

42 See M. Horkheimer and T. Adorno, *Dialectic of Enlightenment*, ed. Gunzelin Schmid Noerr, trans. Edmund Jephcott (Stanford: Stanford University Press, 2002).

43 See H. Marcuse, *Eros and Civilization: A Philosophical Inquiry into Freud* (Boston, MA: Beacon Press, 1974).

44 P. Ricoeur, *Freud and Philosophy: An Essay on Interpretation*, trans. Denis Savage (New Haven, CT and London: Yale University Press, 1972).

45 G. Deleuze and Felix Guattari, *Anti-Oedipus: Capitalism and Schizophrenia*, trans. Robert Hurley, Mark Seem, and Helen R. Lane (London and New York: Continuum, 2004).

46 See R. Wollheim (ed.) *Freud: A Collection of Critical Essays* (Garden City, NY: Anchor Press/ Doubleday, 1974) and his *Freud*, 2nd edn. (London: Fontana, 1991) and Juliet Mitchell, *Psychoanalysis and Feminism: A Radical Reassessment of Freudian Psychoanalysis* (Harmondsworth: Penguin, 1974).

47 See Karl Popper, "Philosophy of science: a personal report" (1957), reprinted in Karl Popper, *Conjectures and Refutations: The Growth of Scientific Knowledge* (London: Routledge & Kegan Paul, 1963; 2nd edn. 1965), pp. 33–65. See also Frank Cioffi, *Freud and the Question of Pseudoscience* (Chicago and La Salle, IL: Open Court, 1998).

48 See Richard Rorty, *Philosophy and the Mirror of Nature* (Oxford: Blackwell, 1980) and his *Essays on Heidegger and Others: Philosophical Papers II* (Cambridge: Cambridge University Press, 1991).

49 See M. Merleau-Ponty, "The philosopher and his shadow," in *Signs*, trans. Richard McCleary (Evanston, IL: Northwestern University Press, 1964).

50 Edmund Husserl, *Logische Untersuchungen*, vol. 1: *Prolegomena zur reinen Logik*, text of the 1st and 2nd edns., ed. E. Holenstein, *Husserliana* XVIII (The Hague: Nijhoff, 1975), and *Logische Untersuchungen*, vol. 2: *Untersuchungen zur Phänomenologie und Theorie der Erkenntnis*, in 2 vols., ed. Ursula Panzer, *Husserliana* XIX (Dordrecht: Kluwer, 1984), trans. by J. N. Findlay as *Logical Investigations*, 2 vols., revised with new introduction by Dermot Moran and new preface by Michael Dummett (London and New York: Routledge, 2001).

51 See Paul Natorp, "Zur Frage der logischen Methode. Mit Bezug auf Edm. Husserls Prolegomena zur reinen Logik," *Kantstudien* VI (1901), pp. 270–83.

52 See Hannah Arendt, "Martin Heidegger at eighty," repr. in M. Murray (ed.) *Martin Heidegger and Modern Philosophy* (New Haven, CT: Yale University Press, 1978).

53 See H.-G. Gadamer, "The phenomenological movement," repr. in D. Moran and L. Embree (eds.) *Phenomenology: Critical Concepts* (London and New York: Routledge, 2004), vol. 5, p. 12.

54 See E. Husserl, "Renewal: its problem and method," in Edmund Husserl, *Husser: Shorter Works*, trans. and ed. Frederick Elliston and Peter McCormick (Notre Dame, IN: University of Notre Dame Press, 1981), pp. 326–31.

55 See M. Heidegger, "The self-assertion of the German university," in R. Wolin (ed.) *The Heidegger Controversy: A Critical Reader* (Cambridge, MA: MIT Press, 1993), pp. 29–39 and M. Heidegger, "The Rectorate 1933/4: facts and thoughts," trans. K. Harries, *Review of Metaphysics* 38 (March 1985), pp. 481–502.

56 See Michael Dummett, *Origins of Analytic Philosophy* (London: Duckworth, 1993), p. 5.

57 See G. Frege, "Diary: written by Professor Dr Gottlob Frege in the time from 10 March to 9 April 1924," *Inquiry* 39 (1996), pp. 303–42.

58 See Dermot Moran, "The analytic and Continental divide: teaching philosophy in an age of pluralism," in D. Evans and I. Kuçuradi (eds.) *Teaching Philosophy on the Eve of the Twenty-First Century* (Ankara: International Federation of Philosophical Societies, 1998), pp. 119–54.

59 See Dermot Moran, "Analytic philosophy and phenomenology," in *The Reach of Reflection: Issues for Phenomenology's Second Century*, 3 vols., Proceedings of Center for Advanced Research in Phenomenology Symposium, Florida Atlantic University, 2001, ed. Lester Embree, Samuel J. Julian, and Steve Crowell (West Hartford, CT: Electron Press, 2001), vol. 3, pp. 409–33; and Dermot Moran, "A case for pluralism: the problem of intentionality," in *Philosophy, Royal Institute of Philosophy Supplementary Volume*, ed. David Archard (Cambridge: Cambridge University Press, 1996), pp. 19–32.

60 See for instance, C. G. Prado (ed.) *A House Divided: Comparing Analytic and Continental Philosophy* (New York: Humanity Books, 2003); and William Egginton and Mike Sandbothe (eds.) *The Pragmatic Turn in Philosophy: Contemporary Engagements between Analytic and Continental Thought* (Albany, NY: State University of New York Press, 2004), to name but two collections. See also David Cooper, "The presidential address: analytical and Continental philosophy," *Proceedings of the Aristotelian Society* 94 (1994), pp. 1–18.

61 See Tom Baldwin, "Two approaches to Sartre," *European Journal of Philosophy* 4/ 1 (April 1996), pp. 81–2.

62 A. P. Martinich and David Sosa (eds.) *Analytic Philosophy: An Anthology* (Oxford: Blackwell, 2001).

63 See, for instance, Barry Smith, "German philosophy: language and style," *Topoi* 10 (1991), pp. 155–61.

64 See Maria Baghramian, *Relativism* (London: Routledge, 2004). Hilary Putnam defines relativism as follows: "Reason is whatever the norms of the local culture believe it to be"; see Hilary Putnam, *Realism and Reason: Philosophical Papers*, vol. 3 (Cambridge: Cambridge University Press, 1983), p. 235. See also Richard Rorty, "Relativism — finding and making," in Josef Niznik and John T. Sanders (eds.) *Debating the State of Philosophy: Habermas, Rorty and Kolakowski* (Westport, CT: Praeger, 1996), pp. 31–47. Rorty writes; "We have given up the idea that there are unconditional, transcultural moral obligations, obligations rooted in an unchanging, ahistorical, human nature" (p. 31).

65 See Thomas S. Kuhn, *The Structure of Scientific Revolutions*, 2nd edn. (Chicago: University of Chicago Press, 1970).

66 See Willard Van Orman Quine, *Ontological Relativity and Other Essays* (New York: Columbia University Press, 1969).

67 See Cristina Lafont, *Heidegger, Language and World-Disclosure* (Cambridge: Cambridge University Press, 2000).

68 Dummett, *Origins of Analytic Philosophy*, p. 5.

69 M. Weitz (ed.) *Twentieth-Century Philosophy: The Analytic Tradition* (London: Collier-Macmillan, 1966).

70 See R. Carnap, "The rejection of metaphysics," in Morris Weitz (ed.) *Twentieth-Century Philosophy: The Analytic Tradition* (London: Collier-Macmillan, 1966), p. 207.

71 For a collection of classical analytical texts, see Robert Ammerman, *Classics of Analytic Philosophy* (Indianapolis: Hackett, 1990).

72 See, e.g. Peter Hylton, *Russell, Idealism and the Emergence of Analytic Philosophy*. (Oxford: Clarendon

Press, 1990) and Dummett, *Origins of Analytic Philosophy*). See also Anat Biletzki and Anat Matar (eds.) *The Story of Analytic Philosophy: Plot and Heroes* (London and New York: Routledge, 1998).

73 J. Rajchman and C. West (eds.) *Post-Analytic Philosophy* (New York: Columbia University Press, 1985).

74 Bertrand Russell, "On denoting," *Mind* 14 (1905), pp. 479–93, repr. in Bertrand Russell, *Essays in Analysis* (London: Allen & Unwin, 1973), pp. 103–19.

75 See the essays, especially Peter Hylton, " 'On denoting' and the idea of a logically perfect language," in Michael Beaney (ed.) *The Analytic Turn: Analysis in Early Analytic Philosophy and Phenomenology* (London and New York: Routledge, 2007).

76 See also G. E. Moore, "External and internal relations," *Proceedings of the Aristotelian Society* 20 (1919–20), pp. 40–62, repr. in G. E. Moore, *Philosophical Studies* (London: Kegan Paul, Trench, Trubner, 1922).

77 Bertrand Russell, *A Critical Exposition of the Philosophy of Leibniz* (1900; repr. London: Routledge, 1993).

78 See R. Rorty, *Philosophy and the Mirror of Nature* (Oxford: Blackwell, 1980), p. 359 n. 4.

79 See Stanley Rosen, "Moore on common sense," in *The Elusiveness of the Ordinary: Studies in the Possibility of Philosophy* (New Haven, CT: Yale University Press, 2002), p. 174.

80 Dummett, *Origins of Analytic Philosophy*, p. 4.

81 See D. Dennett, *Content and Consciousness* (London: Routledge & Kegan Paul, 1969; repr. Routledge, 1993), pp. 6–18.

82 See *Philosophical Review* 60 (1951) and Martinich and Sosa, *Analytic Philosophy*, pp. 450–62.

83 Martinich and Sosa, *Analytic Philosophy*, p. 459.

84 Ibid., p. 460.

85 Ibid., p. 461.

86 See D. Davidson, "On the very idea of a conceptual scheme," repr. in *Inquiries into Truth and Interpretation* (Oxford: Oxford University Press, 1984), pp. 184–98.

87 Ibid., p. 189.

88 In 1929, the Vienna Circle published its manifesto entitled *Wissenschaftliche Weltauffassung. Der Wiener Kreis*, written by Rudolf Carnap, Hans Hahn, and Otto Carnap. An abridged English translation, "The scientific conception of the world: the Vienna Circle," can be found in Marie Neurath and Robert S. Cohen (eds.) *Empiricism and Sociology* (Dordrecht and Boston: Reidel, 1973), pp. 299–318.

89 J. Derrida, *Of Grammatology*, trans. G. C. Spivak (Baltimore, MD: Johns Hopkins University Press, 1976), p. 4.

90 For a recent example see Alain Badiou, *Manifesto for Philosophy*, trans., ed., and with an Introduction by Norman Madarasz (Albany, NY: State University of New York Press, 1999).

91 M. Heidegger, "Überwindung der Metaphysik," in *Vorträge und Aufsätze* (Pfullingen: Neske, 1954), trans. as "Overcoming metaphysics," in J. Stambaugh (ed.) *The End of Philosophy* (New York: Harper & Row, 1973), pp. 95–6.

92 See Michel Foucault, *The Order of Things* (New York: Random House, 1973), pp. 386–7. See also Jacques Derrida, "The ends of man," in *Margins of Philosophy*, trans. Alan Bass (Chicago: University of Chicago Press, 1982).

93 See the contributions by Dummett, Davidson, Apel, and others in Kenneth Baynes, James Bohman, and Thomas McCarthy (eds.) *After Philosophy: End or Transformation* (Cambridge, MA: MIT Press, 1986).

94 See Carnap, "Rejection of metaphysics," pp. 206–19.

95 A. J. Ayer, *Language, Truth and Logic* (New York: Dover, 1952), p. 41.

96 A. J. Ayer, *A Part of My Life* (New York and London: Harcourt Brace Jovanovich, 1977), p. 78.

97 L. Wittgenstein, *Tractatus Logico-Philosophicus*, trans. D. F. Pears and B. F. McGuinness (London and New York: Routledge & Kegan Paul, 1961), §6.53.

98 L. Wittgenstein, *Philosophical Investigations*, ed. G. E. M. Anscombe and R. Rhees, trans G. E. M. Anscombe (Oxford: Blackwell, 1953).

99 Richard Rorty, "Comment on Robert Pippin's 'Naturalism and mindedness: Hegel's compatibilism'," *European Journal of Philosophy* 7/ 2 (August 1999), p. 215.

100 G. W. F. Hegel, *Lectures on the Philosophy of World History: Introduction*, trans. H. B. Nisbet (Cambridge: Cambridge University Press, 1975), p. 27.

101 Mill already uses this phrase as a title to one of his own works, see J. S. Mill, *The Spirit of the Age* (1831).

102 Jean-François Lyotard, *The Postmodern Condition: A Report on Knowledge*, trans. Geoff Bennington and Brian Massumi (Manchester: Manchester University Press, 1984).

103 Peter Hylton, *Russell, Idealism and the Emergence of Analytic Philosophy* (Oxford: Clarendon Press, 1990), p. 13.

104 Both Dewey and Russell gave lectures in Peking University in China in the period 1919–21, but in general there was little contact between Europe and China over the course of the century. Japanese philosophers studied with Husserl and Heidegger from the 1920s onwards. See Graham Parkes (ed.) *Heidegger and Asian Thought* (Honolulu: University of Hawaii Press, 1987) and Harmut Buchner et al., *Japan und Heidegger: Gedenkschrift der Stadt Messkirch zum 100. Geburtstag Martin Heideggers* (Sigmaringen: Jan Thorbecke, 1989). German Idealism and British empiricism both had an influence in India during the nineteenth century, but Indian philosophy itself remained stagnant during the period in question.

105 E. Husserl, *The Crisis of European Sciences and Transcendental Phenomenology: An Introduction to Phenomenological Philosophy*, trans. David Carr (Evanston, IL: Northwestern University Press, 1970).

106 See for instance, William Casement, "Husserl and the philosophy of history," *History and Theory* 27/ 3 (October 1988), pp. 229–40. See also Seyla Benhabib, "Another universalism: on the unity and diversity of human rights," APA presidential address for the Eastern Division of the American Philosophical Association on December 29, 2006.

107 See J. Patočka, "Réflexion sur l'Europe," in *Liberté et sacrifice: Écrits politiques*, trans. from the Czech into French by Erika Abrams (Grenoble: Millon, 1990) and *Plato and Europe*, trans. Peter Lom (Stanford: Stanford University Press, 2002).

108 See Jacques Derrida, "Une Europe de l'espoir," *Le Monde diplomatique* (November 2004), p. 3. See also his *Specters of Marx: The State of the Debt, the Work of Mourning, and the New International*, trans. Peggy Kamuf (New York: Routledge, 1994); *Politics of Friendship*, trans. George Collins (New York: Verso, 1997); and "On cosmopolitanism," trans. Mark Dooley, in *On Cosmopolitanism and Forgiveness* (New York: Routledge, 2001)

109 J. Habermas, "Why Europe needs a constitution," *New Left Review* 11 (September–October 2001).

110 See also J. Habermas, "February 15, or, What binds Europeans together: plea for a common foreign policy, beginning in core Europe," in *Old Europe, New Europe, Core Europe: Transatlantic Relations After the Iraq War*, ed. Daniel Levy, Max Pensky, and John Torpey (London: Verso, 2005).

111 See Ayer, *Part of My Life*, pp. 80 and 121.

112 See Peter Simons, *Philosophy and Logic in Central Europe from Bolzano to Tarski* (Dordrecht: Kluwer, 1992).

113 See Laura Secor, "Testaments betrayed: Yugoslavian intellectuals and the road to war," *Lingua Franca* (September 1999).

114 In 1939 Tarski set out for a lecture tour of the USA but could not return to Poland because of the outbreak of the Second World War. He subsequently held positions at Harvard University, the City College of New York, and the Institute for Advanced Study at Princeton. In 1942 he was appointed to the mathematics department of the University of California at Berkeley, where he remained until his retirement in 1968.

115 E. Husserl, *The Paris Lectures*, trans. P. Koestenaum (The Hague: Nijhoff, 1970).

116 See E. Levinas, *The Theory of Intuition in Husserl's Phenomenology*, trans. A. Orianne (Evanston, IL: Northwestern University Press, 1973).

117 A. Kojève, *Introduction to the Reading of Hegel*, trans. James H. Nichols Jr. (Ithaca, NY: Cornell U.P., 1980).

118 Martin Heidegger, *Being and Time*, trans. John Macquarrie and E. Robinson (New York: Harper & Row, 1962).

119 Ayer, *Part of My Life*, p. 115 (see also p. 77 on Pritchard's efforts to resist the spread of Russell's and Moore's ideas to Oxford).

120 See Karl-Otto Apel, "The impact of analytic philosophy on my intellectual biography," in K.-O.

Apel, *From a Transcendental-Semiotic Point of View*, ed. Marianna Papastephanou (Manchester: Manchester University Press, 1998), pp. 9–42.

121 David Pears, *Bertrand Russell and the British Tradition in Philosophy* (London: Fontana, 1967).

122 Hylton, *Russell, Idealism and the Emergence of Analytic Philosophy*, p. 22.

123 Bertrand Russell, *A History of Western Philosophy*, 2nd edn. (London: Allen & Unwin, 1961), p. 634.

124 Monk, *Bertrand Russell*, pp. 383ff.

125 Ibid., p. 374.

126 Max Scheler, *Der Genius des Krieges und der deutschen Krieg* (Leipzig: Verlag der Weissen Bücher, 1915) and *Krieg und Aufbau* (1916). Scheler, at least at the outbreak of the First World War, welcomed the war as an activity whereby the individual subordinates himself to the state and thus creates a higher-order community. His "Genius of war" book is enthusiastic for the struggle and is dedicated to his "friends in the field." Later he moved more to embrace Christian socialism and toned down his enthusiasm for war. For an interesting discussion, see Sebastian Luft, "Germany's metaphysical war: reflections on war by two representatives of German philosophy: Max Scheler and Paul Natorp," Paper presented to the conference "An Improbable War? The Outbreak of World War I Reconsidered," Emory University, October 16, 2004.

127 See Paul Natorp, *Der Tag des Deutschen. Vier Kriegsaufsätze* (Hagen: O. Rippel, 1915).

128 See E. Husserl, "Fichte's ideal of humanity (Three lectures)," trans. James G. Hart, *Husserl Studies* 12 (1995), pp. 111–33.

129 See Jean-Paul Sartre, *The War Diaries*, trans. Quintin Hoare (London: Verso, 1984).

130 See Jean-Paul Sartre, *The Communists and Peace with a Reply to George Lefort*, trans. Martha H. Fletcher and J. R. Kleinschmidt (New York: Braziller, 1968).

131 See Karl Jaspers, "Letter to the Freiburg University Denazification Committee," trans. R. Wolin, in Richard Wolin (ed.) *The Heidegger Controversy: A Critical Reader* (Cambridge, MA: MIT Press, 1993), pp. 147–51.

132 For an interesting discussion of the social and political circumstances surrounding the development of philosophy of science in the USA after the war, see George A. Reisch, *How the Cold War Transformed Philosophy of Science: To the Icy Slopes of Logic* (Cambridge: Cambridge University Press, 2005).

133 In conversation with Giovanna Borradori; see her *The American Philosopher: Conversations with Quine, Davidson, Putnam, Nozick, Danto, Rorty, Cavell, MacIntyre and Kuhn*, trans. Rosanna Crocitto (Chicago: University of Chicago Press, 1994), p. 33.

134 Isaiah Berlin originally delivered his famous paper "Two concepts of liberty" as his inaugural lecture as Chichele Professor of Social and Political Theory at Oxford in 1958.

135 M. Merleau-Ponty, *Humanism and Terror: An Essay on the Communist Problem*, trans. John O'Neill (Boston: Beacon Press, 1969).

136 M. Merleau-Ponty, *Adventures of the Dialectic*, trans. J. Bien (Evanston, IL: Northwestern University Press, 1973).

137 F. Fanon, *The Wretched of the Earth*, trans. Constance Farrington (New York: Grove Weidenfeld, 1963).

138 See especially Herbert Marcuse's *One-Dimensional Man: Studies in the Ideology of Advanced Industrial Society* (Boston: Beacon Press, 1964).

139 Tim Williamson, "Identity," in E. Craig (ed.) *Routledge Encyclopedia of Philosophy* (London: Routledge, 1998).

140 Peter Fenves, "Alterity and identity," in E. Craig (ed.) *Routledge Encyclopedia of Philosophy* (London: Routledge, 1998).

141 Henry Harris (ed.) *Identity: Essays Based on Herbert Spencer Lectures Given in the University of Oxford* (Oxford: Clarendon Press, 1995).

142 M. Merleau-Ponty, *In Praise of Philosophy*, trans. J. Wild and J. M. Edie (Evanston, IL: Northwestern University Press, 1963).

143 Monk, *Bertrand Russell*, p. 340.

Part I

MAJOR THEMES AND MOVEMENTS

1

THE BIRTH OF ANALYTIC PHILOSOPHY

Michael Potter

Analytic philosophy was, at its birth, an attempt to escape from an earlier tradition, that of Immanuel Kant (1724–1804), and the first battleground was mathematics. Kant had claimed that mathematics is grounded neither in experience nor in logic but in the spatio-temporal structure which we ourselves impose on experience. First Frege tried to refute Kant's account in the case of arithmetic by showing that it could be derived from logic; then Russell extended the project to the whole of mathematics. Both failed, but in addressing the problems which the project generated they founded what is nowadays known as analytic philosophy or, perhaps more appropriately, as the analytic method in philosophy. What this brief summary masks, however, is that it is far from easy to say what the analytic method in philosophy amounts to. By tracing the outlines of the moment when it was born we shall here try to identify some of its distinctive features.

Frege

Begriffsschrift

In 1879 Gottlob Frege (1848–1925) published a short book called *Begriffsschrift* (*Concept Script*). What this book contains might nowadays be described as a formalization of the predicate calculus, the part of logic dealing with quantification. Frege's aim in trying to formalize logic was to codify the laws not of thought but of truth. He was commendably clear from the start, that is to say, that logic is not a branch of psychology. Logic consists of the laws to which our reasoning ought to adhere if it is to aim at the truth, not of those to which our reasoning does in fact adhere. There are certainly errors in reasoning which most people are inclined to make, but Frege's point is that it is indeed appropriate to describe these as *errors*. He regarded it as possible for there to be a form of reasoning which all of us have always been inclined to accept but which is, in some way not yet detected by any of us, a mistake.

Frege was certainly not the first to formalize part of logic: that was Aristotle. And 200 years before Frege Gottfried Wilhelm Leibniz (1646–1716) had even had the ambition of developing a formal system that would reduce reasoning to a mechanical process like arithmetic. But there is nothing in Leibniz's surviving writings to show that he carried forward this project very far. More recently, however, nineteenth-century British logicians such as George Boole (1815–64), William Stanley Jevons (1835–82) and John Venn (1834–1923) had made significant progress: Boole had invented a notation for expressing the logical operations of negation, conjunction, and (exclusive) disjunction, and he had discovered that the logical rules which propositions involving these operations obey are strikingly similar to those of elementary arithmetic; Jevons had designed a "logical piano," a machine which could solve problems in Boolean logic with impressive speed and accuracy.

This work can thus be seen as a working out, for one part of logic, of Leibniz's ambition. Once a proposition has been expressed in Boolean notation, it can be transformed by means of quasi-arithmetical rules into a simpler but logically equivalent form, in a manner that is quite analogous to the algebraic manipulations of elementary arithmetic. Boole's method has turned out to have widespread practical applications: it can be used, for instance, to simplify electrical circuits and computer programs.

Nonetheless, what Boole was doing was to develop a technique within the scope of logic in the sense in which it had been understood since the time of Aristotle. What distinguishes Frege's work from Boole's is that he advanced into quite new territory by inventing a notation for quantifiers and variables. There is no doubt a sense in which the idea of quantifiers and variables was already "in the air" in 1879. It is at any rate striking that Charles Sanders Peirce (1839–1914) invented his own notation for quantifiers and variables independently at almost exactly the same time as Frege (see Peirce 1885). But it was for Peirce only a notational device, not in itself a tool for reasoning, and he did not develop the idea with anything like Frege's philosophical subtlety. One reason for this, no doubt, is that Peirce was working much more in the algebraic tradition of Boole and Jevons. It did eventually turn out that Boole's idea of treating reasoning as a form of algebraic manipulation could be generalized to encompass reasoning that involves quantifiers: the notion that plays the analogous role to that of a Boolean algebra is called a "cylindric algebra." But when this idea was explored in the 1950s by Alfred Tarski (1902–83), it quickly became apparent why no one had thought of it before: the theory is, at least by comparison to the method involving rules of inference, inelegant and unintuitive.

What is important about Frege's work, in comparison to Boole's, is thus that it enlarged the scope of formal logic decisively. It would be an exaggeration to say that Frege's was the first major advance in logic since Aristotle, but it would not be wholly wrong either. The medievals had been aware that what can be shoe-horned into the form of the Aristotelian syllogism by no means exhausts the forms of reasoning that are to be counted as valid, and they had therefore striven to extend the scope of formal logic accordingly. But they had done so piecemeal: the decisive advance had always eluded them.

The reason Frege's invention of polyadic predicate calculus counts as decisive is one that received precise expression only half a century later, when Alonzo Church (1903–95) and Alan Turing (1912–54) showed in 1936 (independently of one another) that it is not mechanically decidable which arguments involving polyadic quantification are logically valid. By contrast the corresponding problem for arguments involving only monadic quantification (or, indeed, for the Aristotelian syllogistic) *is* mechanically decidable. Church's and Turing's discovery marks a major step in logic, since by showing for the first time that there are problems in logic which cannot be solved mechanically it demonstrated a disanalogy between logic and elementary arithmetic, and hence showed that there must be some limits to Leibniz's dream of a mechanical calculus to take over the task of reasoning.

Although Frege never knew of this limitative result, he seems to have had a sense from the outset of the remarkable power of the method he had invented:

> Pure thought, irrespective of any content given by the senses or even by an intuition a priori, can, solely from the content that results from its own constitution, bring forth judgments that at first sight appear to be possible only on the basis of some intuition. (Frege 1879: §23)

This remark of Frege's about the power of reasoning that involves polyadic quantification is in marked contrast to what earlier philosophers had said about Aristotelian logic and its mediaeval accretions. When Descartes, for example, said of logic that "its syllogisms and most of its other instructions serve to explain to others what one already knows" (*Discourse on Method*, part 2), it was syllogistic – therefore decidable – logic he had in mind. And Kant, in presenting the central task of the first *Critique* as that of explaining how synthetic a priori knowledge is possible, had taken arithmetic as his first and best example of a domain of synthetic truths. If what he meant by an analytic truth was anything that can be deduced from explicit definitions by syllogistic logic, then what is analytic is in an important sense trivial. If, on the other hand, we enlarge the scope of the analytic to include what can be deduced by means of polyadic logic, what then remains of Kant's claim that arithmetic is synthetic (and hence, according to Kant, dependent in some way on the spatio-temporal structure of the world as we experience it)?

Grundlagen

Frege was not the only person interested in this question. J. W. Richard Dedekind (1831–1916), in his beautiful treatise *What are Numbers and What Should They Be?* (*Was sind und was sollen die Zahlen?*, 1888), also attempts to show, contrary to Kant, that arithmetic is independent of space and time. There are three stages involved in establishing this claim. The first is to characterize the natural numbers in axiomatic terms and show that the familiar arithmetical properties follow logically from these axioms. The second is to show that there exists a structure satisfying these axioms. The third is to abstract from the particular properties of the structure used in the second stage, so as to identify the natural numbers as a new structure satisfying the axioms. Dedekind's execution of the first of these three stages may be counted a complete success: the axioms he identified (which are nowadays called Peano's axioms) do have as (second order) logical consequences all of the truths of arithmetic. But the second and third stages are more problematic. In order to achieve the second part of the program Dedekind found that he needed what is now called the axiom of infinity, which asserts that there exist infinitely many objects. Dedekind thought he could prove this axiom, but for his proof to be regarded as correct we would at the very least have to widen the scope of logic even further than Frege had done, since what he proves is at best that the realm of thoughts that are available to us as reasoning beings is infinite. And for the third stage of the program Dedekind appealed to a sort of creative abstraction that has seemed obscure to many later writers.

Frege's aim in *Die Grundlagen der Arithmetik*, 1884 (*The Foundations of Arithmetic*) was the same as Dedekind's – to show that arithmetic is independent of space and time – and the shape of his approach was also the same. First he identified an axiomatic base from which the properties of the natural numbers could be deduced, then he tried to show logically that there exist objects satisfying these axioms, and finally he needed a principled reason to ignore whatever properties the objects chosen in the second stage may have that do not follow from the axiomatic characterization of them identified in the first stage.

But although the three stages of the program were the same for Frege as for Dedekind, how he executed them differed significantly. In the first place Frege's axiomatic characterization of the natural numbers treated them as finite cardinal numbers and characterized cardinal numbers by means of the principle that the cardinals of two concepts F and G are equal if and only if there exists a one-to-one correlation of the Fs with the Gs (or, as is sometimes said, if F and G are "equinumerous"). This equivalence, known in modern literature on the topic (with tenuous historical license) as "Hume's Principle," can be used to derive the properties of the natural numbers in much the same way as Peano's axioms can. For the second stage of the program, showing that there are objects satisfying Hume's Principle, Frege made use of the notion of the extension of a concept, i.e. a sort of logical object associated with a concept in such a way that two concepts have the same extension just in case they have the same objects falling under them. Frege defined the number of Fs to be the extension of the (second-order) concept under which fall all those concepts equinumerous with the given concept F.

Having defined numbers in terms of extensions in this way, Frege needed some account of why the extra properties numbers acquire accidentally as a consequence of the definition can be ignored. But what Frege's account was is somewhat hazy. It is plain that he thought some role was played by the "context principle," the methodological principle that it is only in the context of a sentence that words mean anything. The importance he placed on this principle is shown by the fact that he mentioned it in both the introduction and the conclusion to the *Grundlagen* as well as in the text, but it is less easy to see what this importance amounts to.

It sometimes seems, indeed, as if the importance of the context principle may lie not so much in Frege's use of it but in the significance it has been given subsequently by Frege's most noted commentator, Michael Dummett (1925–). According to Dummett, Frege's enunciation of the context principle marks a fundamental shift in philosophy, the so-called "linguistic turn," of comparable significance to Kant's Copernican turn a century earlier.

The puzzle, though, is to see what role the context principle is supposed to play in Frege's account of numbers. If he had sought to treat Hume's Principle as a contextual definition of numbers, that role would be clear enough: the context principle seems designed precisely to allay any concern one might have that a contextual definition does not say what the term it introduces refers to but only gives us the meaning of whole sentences in which the term occurs. But Frege rejects the idea of treating Hume's Principle as a contextual definition of numbers because, while it settles the truth conditions of some of the identity statements in which number terms can occur, it does not settle them all. (Most famously, to use Frege's "crude example," it does not settle whether Julius Caesar is a natural number.) Instead, as we have seen, Frege treats Hume's Principle only as a contextual *constraint* – a condition, that is to say, that any definition of natural numbers must satisfy if it is to be regarded as correct. But if we end up giving an explicit definition of numbers and then showing that numbers so defined do indeed satisfy the constraint, it is not at all clear what role is left for the context principle to play.

A further (and, as it was to turn out, much worse) problem for Frege was that the explicit definition of numbers that he settled on defined them in terms of the notion of the extension of a concept. But what is that? The best that he could be said to have achieved by the end of the *Grundlagen* was to reduce the problem he started with, of explaining how numbers are given to us, to the rather similar question of how extensions of concepts are given to us.

The similarity between the problems, as Frege thought of them, is indeed rather more than superficial. For Hume's Principle, the contextual specification of the identity conditions for numbers, has the form of an abstraction principle, which is to say that it asserts the logical equivalence of, on the one hand, an identity between two terms (in this case number terms) and, on the other, the holding of an equivalence relation (in this case equinumerosity) between the relevant concepts. But note now that the explanation we gave of the notion of the extension of a concept – that concepts have the same extension just in case the same objects fall under them – is an abstraction principle too. If the Julius Caesar problem puts paid to the idea of introducing numbers by means of the first abstraction principle, does it not also put paid to the idea of introducing extensions by means of the second?

This is a question Frege never satisfactorily answered. In the *Grundlagen* he did not even address it, mentioning only (in a footnote) that he would "assume it is known what the extension of a concept is" (§68). Plainly a little more needs to be said, but when he came to say it, in *Grundgesetze der Arithmetik*, 1893–1903 (*The Basic Laws of Arithmetic*), he confined himself to treating the notion of an extension within the formal language of the *Begriffsschrift*. In that language he does indeed introduce extensions by means of the abstraction principle just mentioned (which he calls "Basic Law V"),[1] but he does not have to address the Julius Caesar problem because the formal language he is dealing with does not have terms for referring to Roman emperors.

It is plain that this is only a deferral of the problem, not a solution. Frege was clear, after all, that any satisfactory account of arithmetic would have to explain its applicability to the world, and he was scathing about the failure of formalism to deal with just this point. So at some point he would have to expand the formal language to encompass terms for Roman emperors, so that they could be counted, and he would have to do so in such a way as to settle the question whether Julius Caesar is a natural number (or, indeed, the extension of a concept).

Sense and reference

What was appealing to Frege about abstraction principles such as Hume's Principle or Basic Law V lay partly, as we have seen, in the validation which he somehow thought they receive from the context principle. But it also lay in his belief that they are in some weak sense logical. Just what that weak sense is, however, Frege was never able to say precisely. Indeed he granted that Basic Law V was more open to doubt than the other axioms of his theory. Nonetheless, he remained attracted to the thought, first enunciated in the *Grundlagen*, that the left hand side of an abstraction principle, which expresses an identity between the objects the principle seeks to introduce, is somehow a recarving of the content of the relation of equivalence between concepts which occurs on the right hand side.

The difficulty, then, is to say what the notion of content is which can give substance to this metaphor of recarving. When he wrote the *Grundlagen*, Frege had only a very coarse-grained theory of content to offer, according to which any two logically equivalent propositions have the same content. By the time of *Grundgesetze*, however, Frege had elaborated the theory of sense and reference for which he is now famous.

There is nothing deep, of course, in the distinction between a sign and the thing it signifies, nor in the distinction between both of these and the ideas I attach to a sign when I use it. What goes deeper is the claim that if we are to have a satisfying account of language's ability to communicate thoughts from speaker to listener we must appeal to yet a fourth element – what Frege calls sense.

The interest of Frege's notion of sense lies in two features of it. First, senses are abstract. Since the sense of an expression is what it is that is communicated from speaker to hearer, it must be possible for each of us to grasp it and it cannot, therefore, be something private to either of us, as an idea is. So a sense is not a mental entity. But neither, plainly, is it physical. It therefore inhabits what Frege calls a third realm,[2] defined negatively, of elements that are neither physical nor mental. (This alone, of course, has been enough to make many twentieth-century philosophers treat the notion with deep suspicion.)

Second, it is not just names like "Hesperus" and "Phosphorus" that have sense. The thought expressed by a whole sentence is a sense for Frege, and it is somehow composed out of the senses of the subsentential expressions that make up the sentence.[3] The theory is, that is to say, *uniform* in attributing sense to the meaningful elements of language: no linguistic item, for Frege, latches onto the world directly, but the reference of each is mediated by its sense, which is the mode by which the linguistic item presents the object it is supposed to refer to.

Both these aspects of Frege's theory are problematic. Quite apart from any suspicion some might have of abstract entities, it is hard to get a stable grasp of the notion of sense Frege required: a notion, namely, that is finely grained enough to distinguish the sense of "Hesperus" from that of "Phosphorus" (which it must if it is to explain why I can learn something about astronomy when you tell me that Hesperus = Phosphorus); and yet not so fine that it distinguishes the sense I, ignorant of astronomy, attach to the word "Hesperus" from the sense you, who know much more about the planets, do (since if it does, the sense cannot be what is communicated when you tell me). And the compositionality of sense is puzzling too. It is certainly puzzling what sort of compositionality could make it the case that the two sides of an abstraction principle have the same sense. But even if we prescind from that and agree not to regard Frege's notion of sense as an attempt to legitimate this aspect of his project of using an abstraction principle to ground arithmetic, it remains puzzling what sort of composition is supposed to be at work.

Moore and Russell

Objective propositions

The second strand in the birth of analytic philosophy began in 1898. Bertrand Russell (1872–1970) later described it as having been born in conversations between him and George Edward Moore (1873–1958). What is clear at any rate is that the first publications that bear witness to it are Moore's articles, "The nature of judgment" and "The refutation of idealism."

The overall shape of the revolution is clear: Moore thought that by conceiving of propositions as objective complex entities he could resist the temptations of idealism. In a dictionary entry, "Truth," Moore wrote:

> Once it is definitely recognized that the proposition is to denote not a belief (in the psychological sense), it seems plain that it differs in no respect from the reality to which it is supposed merely to correspond, i.e. the truth that *I exist* differs in no respect from the corresponding reality *my existence*. (Moore 1901–2)

At the center of the project, in other words, was what would now be called an identity theory of truth. But if the overall shape of the project is clear, the details are not. Although "The nature of judgment" is written in a crisp style that is in marked contrast to the narcoleptic pedantry of some of Moore's later work, it is nonetheless difficult to determine exactly what its arguments are. The targets of Moore's criticism are broadly spread: although it is Bradley's post-Hegelian denial that absolute truth is ever attainable which is the principal target, at times Berkeley's view that *esse est percipi* ("to be is to be perceived") or Kant's view that the relations the objects of experience bear to one another are supplied by the mind are also attacked.

Moore's conception of a proposition is embodied in two central doctrines. The first is that the entities of which a proposition is composed (which he calls "concepts") are themselves the items the proposition is about. He opposes this to F. H. Bradley's view that when I have an idea of something, that thing is itself part of the idea. This opposition is plainly not exhaustive of the possibilities, but once he had disposed (no doubt rightly) of Bradley's view, Moore seems to have seen no need of an argument for his own. Nonetheless, the doctrine is central to the refutation of idealism as Moore conceives of it. Propositions are the objects of judgment, and the concepts that make up the proposition are therefore part of what we judge, but the view is nonetheless realist because this is "no definition of them"; "it is indifferent to their nature," he says, "whether anyone thinks them or not" (Moore 1899: 4). Concepts are, that is to say, objective entities.

The second central doctrine is that there are no internal relations between concepts – no relations between concepts that are part of the nature of the concepts related. What it is for a proposition to be true is just for the concepts it is composed of to be externally related to each other in a certain way. Once again, the main target is Bradley (1846–1924), who had denied that external relations are ever real. If knowledge is conceived of as an internal relation between the knower and the proposition known, the mere act of coming to know a proposition will alter it, since the property it now has of being known is internal to it and therefore makes it different from what it was before I knew it. For Bradley, therefore, no judgment is ever wholly true: judgment is inherently distorting. For Moore, on the other hand, the act of judgment relates a proposition to the judging subject only externally and does not thereby alter what is judged. But it is much less clear why in opposing Bradley's view Moore should have gone to the opposite extreme and said that there are *no* internal relations between concepts at all. And, as in the case of the first doctrine, Moore seems (at this stage at least) to have been oblivious to the need for an argument.

The Principles of Mathematics

The doctrine that there are no internal relations between concepts runs into an obvious difficulty in the case of identity statements. If the identity "$a = a$" expresses anything about a, a relation between a and itself, it seems clear that this must be internal. So if there are no internal relations, we are forced to conclude that it does not express anything at all. This is perhaps not so bad in itself, but we shall need to say something about the identity "Hesperus = Phosphorus," which expresses genuine astronomical information. And a lot more will have to be said about arithmetic, in which apparently informative identity statements (such as "$7 + 5 = 12$") play such a central role.

The work in which this was attempted was Russell's *Principles of Mathematics* (1903). To modern readers (of whom there are not as many as one might expect, given its place in the history of the subject) this comes across as a transitional work: it contains extended passages which we can recognize as analytical philosophy in quite the modern sense, but these are juxtaposed to passages written in a style that strikes us as wholly antiquated, introducing for no apparent reason bizarrely elaborate classifications that develop into an architectonic of almost Kantian complexity. In this regard

Russell's book stands in interesting contrast to Frege's *Grundlagen*: there are indeed occasional *longueurs* in this book, arising in the main when Frege targets errors that we are no longer tempted to make, but the arguments Frege uses to dispose of them do not strike us as obsolete.

Russell's main purpose in writing the *Principles* was to make plausible a version of what is now called "logicism": he wished to generalize to the whole of mathematics Frege's more limited claim that arithmetic is part of logic. Central to this project, as Russell now conceived it, was his adoption of Moore's conception of a proposition as containing the parts of the world it is about. But Russell now amended this conception by adding to it the notion of a denoting concept. A denoting concept is what one might call an "aboutness shifter" (Makin 1995); its task is to enable a proposition to be about something else that is not itself part of the proposition. On Moore's view the proposition expressed by the sentence "I met John" contains me, John and the universal *meeting*. What is expressed by "I met a man" similarly contains me, meeting, and a third element expressed by the phrase "a man." But what is this third element? It cannot be any particular man, since it is just the same proposition whichever man it was that I actually met.

> The proposition is not about *a man*: this is a concept which does not walk the streets, but lives in the shadowy limbo of the logic-books. What I met was a thing, not a concept, an actual man with a tailor and a bank-account or a public-house and a drunken wife. (Russell 1903: §56)

Yet there must be *some* connection between the man with the bank account and the propositional component in question. In the *Principles* Russell calls the propositional component a "denoting concept" and the relation it has to the man that of "denoting." "A concept *denotes* when, if it occurs in a proposition, the proposition is not *about* the concept but about a term connected in a certain peculiar way with the concept" (ibid.).

Russell seizes on denoting as the central element in his account of mathematics.

> The concept *all numbers*, though not itself infinitely complex, yet denotes an infinitely complex object. This is the inmost secret of our power to deal with infinity. An infinitely complex concept, though there may be such, can certainly not be manipulated by the human intelligence; but infinite collections, owing to the notion of denoting, can be manipulated without introducing any concepts of infinite complexity. (ibid.: §72)

A proposition about all numbers therefore does not itself contain all the (infinitely many) numbers but only a (finite) concept which denotes all numbers.

"On denoting"

In 1901, when Russell already had a complete draft of *The Principles of Mathematics*, he discovered the famous paradox which bears his name. He showed, that is to say, that the denoting concept, the class of all classes which do not belong to themselves, does not denote anything (since if it did, the class it denoted would belong to itself if and only if it did not belong to itself, which is absurd).

The paradox had already been discovered by the mathematician Ernst Zermelo (1871–1953) at Göttingen a couple of years earlier (and other somewhat similar paradoxes were known to Cantor). What is significant about its rediscovery by Russell is the manner in which the problem it raised now affected philosophy. The most immediate effect of the paradox on Russell was that it made him focus his attention on those denoting concepts (such as, most famously, that of the present king of France) which do not denote anything. The point, of course, is not that he had until then been unaware that according to his theory there would have to be such concepts, but only that the paradox showed him the need to gain a better understanding of how they function. He had said that a proposition in which a denoting concept occurs "is not about the concept but about a term connected in a certain peculiar way with the concept." If the term in question does not exist, the way in which it is connected with the concept will indeed be peculiar.

But the moment of revelation for Russell came when he saw that the relationship is peculiar even when the term *does* exist. For if there is a relationship between the concept and the thing it denotes, there will be a true proposition expressing that relationship, and this true proposition will be about the concept. But a denoting concept, let us recall, is defined as one whose job is to occur in a proposition but to point at something else which the proposition is about. So how can *any* proposition be about the denoting concept itself? What sort of entity should occur in a proposition in order for the proposition to be about, say, the denoting concept expressed by the phrase "the first line of Gray's Elegy"? Not, certainly, the denoting concept itself, since if it is doing its aboutness-shifting job properly, it will ensure that the proposition ends up being not about the concept but about what it denotes, i.e. about the sentence "The curfew tolls the knell of parting day." Nor, clearly, is it any use to put in the proposition the denoting concept "the meaning of the first line of Gray's Elegy," since that would make the proposition be about the meaning of the sentence "The curfew tolls the knell of parting day," which again is not what we want.

Up to this point there is something that is apt to strike the reader as puzzling. The argument is supposed to show that there can be no informative proposition about the concept expressed by the phrase "the first line of Gray's Elegy." Yet this last sentence seems to express a proposition that is about just this concept. Russell has to say that it is not what he wants. Why? At this point he introduces a further constraint. The relationship between a concept and its denotation (if any) is not, he says, "linguistic through the phrase." Concepts exist, he evidently thinks, whether or not we choose to devise means to express them in language. So the relationship between the concept and its denotation exists independent of language and hence so does the proposition expressing it. So any sentence in which a linguistic item, such as the phrase "the first line of Gray's Elegy," is mentioned (rather than used) cannot be what we are after, since the proposition it expresses will be about language whereas the proposition we are trying to express would, if it existed, be independent of language.

It is a staple of undergraduate essays on Russell's theory of descriptions to point out that it deals with the case of definite descriptions which do not refer to anything, but this, while true, was only ever part of the point. Russell's earlier theory of denoting had of course recognized that there are denoting phrases which do not denote anything. There is certainly in such cases a puzzle about the role of the corresponding denoting concept: if a denoting concept is thought of as a sort of pointer, a denoting concept that does not denote anything is a pointer pointing at nothing. But Russell's objection to the theory applies just as much in the case of denoting concepts that do denote something.

The argument we have just described (which is always known as the Gray's Elegy argument because of the example he uses to make the point) led Russell to reject the theory of denoting he had put forward in the *Principles*. What he replaced it with was an account according to which the true structure of the proposition a sentence expresses is to be revealed by translating it into the predicate calculus with identity. The sentence "I met a man," for instance, might be translated as $(\exists x)(Mx \,\&\, Rax)$, where "$\exists x$" means there exists at least one x, "Mx" means that x has the property of manhood, "Rxy" means that x met y and "a" denotes me. (In words: there is someone I met who has the property of manhood.) The denoting phrase "a man" has disappeared, to be replaced by the notation of quantifier and variable. And, as undergraduates learn in their elementary logic course, "The present king of France is bald" can be translated as $(\exists x)(Kx \,\&\, (\forall y)(Ky \supset x = y) \,\&\, Bx)$, where "$\forall y$" means "for all y," "$\supset$" means "implies," "$Bx$" means that x is bald and "Kx" means that x is currently a king of France. (In words: There is currently a bald king of France such that every current king of France is equal to him.) Once again, the denoting phrase has disappeared in the translation, to be replaced with quantified variables.

Logicism

What was significant about this method of translation was that it showed how the grammatical form of a sentence might differ from the logical form of the proposition the sentence expresses. Thus in the standard example, "The present king of France is bald," the sentence has a subject, "The present king of France," which does not correspond to any single component of the proposition it expresses. The theory thus avoids the need to appeal to a shadowy realm of nonexistent objects – often called "Meinongian" although this is unfair to Alexius Meinong (1853–1920; see Oliver 1999) – to explain the meaning of the sentence.

This is a general method of considerable power. Wherever in philosophy we come across linguistic items which appear to refer to entities which are in some way problematic, the possibility now arises that the terms in question may be what Russell soon called "incomplete symbols," that is to say expressions which have no meaning on their own but which are such that any sentence in which the expression occurs can be translated into another in which it does not. By this means we eliminate reference to the problematic entities without rendering meaningless the sentences which apparently refer to them.

The first application Russell made of this idea was to the case which had originally prompted him to examine the problem of the present king of France, namely that of classes. In *Principia Mathematica* (1910–13), written jointly with Alfred North Whitehead (1861–1947), he developed a theory in which terms apparently referring to classes are incomplete symbols which disappear on analysis. The solution to the paradox Russell had discovered was to be that any sentence in which the term "the class of all classes which do not belong to themselves" occurs would resist rewriting according to the translation rules and would therefore turn out not to express a proposition at all.

This solution does not just drop out all by itself, however. It is easy enough to formulate rewriting rules for eliminating class terms (so that, for instance, a proposition that appears to be about the class of all men turns out really to be about the property of manhood), but if that is all we do, we simply transfer the focus of attention to the corresponding paradox for properties (in Russell's terminology, propositional functions): we consider, that is to say, the property which holds of just those properties which do not hold of themselves. In order to avoid such paradoxes as this, Russell found it necessary to stratify propositional functions into types. Russell's theory is said to be "ramified" because it stratifies propositional functions in two ways, once according to the types of the free variables they contain and then again according to the types of the bound variables.

As we noted earlier, Whitehead and Russell's aim in *Principia Mathematica* was an extension of Frege's. They wanted to embed not just arithmetic but the whole of mathematics in logic. If they had succeeded, they would perhaps not quite have solved the epistemological problem of how we come to know mathematical truths, but they would at least have made it subsidiary to the corresponding problem for logic. However, they did not succeed. Their principal difficulty was that the paradox-avoidance measures they had to take do too much. In order to embed traditional mathematics in the theory of classes, we need to be able to count as legitimate many class terms that are *impredicative*, which is to say that the properties which define them somehow involve the classes themselves and are thus ineliminably circular. In order that such class terms should count as legitimate it was necessary to assume the axiom of reducibility, which asserts that every such circular propositional function can be replaced by a logically equivalent non-circular one. But if *Principia Mathematica* was to be taken as showing that mathematics is part of logic, Whitehead and Russell had to maintain not only that the axiom of reducibility is true but that it is a truth of logic. And the reasons they gave for thinking that it is were unconvincing. A further difficulty was that in order to derive higher mathematics they had to assume the axiom of infinity, which asserts that there are infinitely many objects. Since they did not share Dedekind's conception of thoughts as objects, they could not adopt his "proof" of this axiom. Their view therefore seemed to make the truth of higher mathematics depend on an unverified physical hypothesis.

Because of these difficulties over the axioms of reducibility and infinity, therefore, Whitehead and Russell's attempted reduction of mathematics to logic is generally regarded as a failure. Far more influential in philosophy, however, was the method of logical analysis of which it was an instance. The aim of this method, in application to any sphere of discourse, is to find the true logical form of the propositions expressed in the discourse. In the background, no doubt, was the hope that this would in turn, because of the conception of a proposition as made up of the things it is about, reveal the entities acquaintance with which the discourse requires. It was thus an assumption of the process, which Russell most of the time scarcely thought worthy of argument, that there *is* in this sense a determinate epistemological base to the discourse. In 1911 he coined the phrase "logical atomism" to describe this assumption.

Sense-data

What, on this view, is the ultimate subject matter of ordinary discourse about the physical world? To answer this question we need to examine how Russell dealt with non-referring expressions. Russell analyzed "The present king of France does not exist" as $\sim(\exists x)(Kx\ \&\ (\forall y)(Ky \supset x = y))$. (In words: it is not the case that there is exactly one present king of France.) And an analysis of the same form is to be used in any case where we say that something does not exist. Thus, for instance, if we say that Homer did not exist, we should be taken to mean that no one person wrote both the *Odyssey* and the *Iliad*. Thus, Russell thought, we avoid the difficulties involved in supposing there to be a person, Homer, with the awkward property of nonexistence. "Homer" is thus for Russell an example of a term that is grammatically a proper name, but not logically so, since the correct logical analysis of "Homer does not exist" reveals "Homer" to be really a definite description in disguise. And in the same sort of way "Sherlock Holmes does not exist" might be analyzed by replacing "Sherlock Holmes" with a definite description such as "the detective who lived at 221b Baker Street."

Russell used the term "logically proper name" for any proper name which functions as such not just grammatically but logically – for any name, that is to say, which logical analysis does not reveal to be really a disguised definite description. But in ordinary language logically proper names are the exception rather than the rule. For it is not just words for spurious classical poets and fictional detectives that turn out to be disguised descriptions. The eliminative doctrine applies in any case where I can say intelligibly, even if falsely, that someone does not exist: since I can wonder whether Plato existed, "Plato" is (at least in my idiolect) a disguised definite description. The same will apply to anything whatever of whose existence I can coherently entertain a doubt: the term referring to it must on this view be a disguised definite description.

It follows that a term "*a*" in my language can be a logically proper name only if the sentence "*a* does not exist" is not merely false but unintelligible: the object *a* must be something of whose existence I am so certain that I cannot intelligibly doubt it. This is a very demanding criterion: even tables, chairs, and pens do not fulfill it since they might be holograms, tricks of the light, or hallucinations. The only things in the physical realm that do fulfill the criterion, according to Russell, are sense-data. Even if the green table on the other side of the room were an illusion, the patch of green at the center of my visual field when I (as I think) look at it would certainly exist. It follows that if I say something about the table (that it is oblong, for example), the proposition that I express does not contain the table itself but instead contains various sense-data that I have experienced, such as the green patch just mentioned.

Where does this leave the table? At first Russell was inclined to infer its existence as the best explanation for the sense-data. (If I look away or leave the room and come back in, the various sense-data I experience have a regularity which is best explained by positing a table which causes them.) But later Russell was less inclined to ascribe any independent existence to the table and preferred to regard it as *constructed* out of the sense-data. "Whenever possible, substitute constructions out of known entities for inferences to unknown entities" (Russell 1924).

By taking items of experience as building blocks in this way Russell showed evident sympathy with a central strand of empiricism, but he was very far from being a classical empiricist in Locke's mold, since he certainly did not think that sense-data are the only constituents of propositions. He maintained a liberal ontology of universals such as love or meeting, which he thought were constituents of propositions such as "John met Mary and fell in love with her." Universals, he somewhat over-exuberantly claimed, are "unchangeable, rigid, exact, delightful to the mathematician, the logician, the builder of metaphysical systems, and all who love perfection more than life." (Russell 1912: ch. 9)

Difficulties with the theory

One curious side effect of Russell's theory is that it forced him to abandon the notion that modalities of possibility and necessity may be applied to propositions. The reason is as follows. Recall Russell's argument for the identification of the simple entities as those things whose existence it would be incoherent to doubt. The argument was that if a is a simple entity then the sentence "I doubt whether a exists" cannot be intelligible, since if it is intelligible, the Russellian analysis will reveal "a" to be not a logically proper name but a disguised description, in which case a is not simple. We concluded, therefore, that simples are things whose existence is indubitable. But we can evidently run an exactly analogous argument in the case of the sentence "it is possible that a does not exist": if this is intelligible, the Russellian analysis will reveal "a" to be a disguised description once more.

But if we simply use the second argument to place a further constraint on the simples, the theory collapses, since we now need the simples to be entities whose existence is not only indubitable but necessary, and even sense-data do not fulfill this criterion: I may be sure that there is a patch of green in the center of my visual field, but can I not also represent to myself the possibility that it might not have been (if, for instance, I had painted the wall a different color)?

The only way out for Russell if there are to be any simples in the world at all is to say that despite appearances to the contrary I cannot in fact represent the possibility of there not having been that sense-datum. If talking of propositions as possible is to be legitimate, it will have to be explained as a way of saying something not about how the world could have been but about how it actually is. If I say that I could have been killed cycling to work this morning, for instance, I am really saying something about how busy the traffic was on the main road or how carelessly I was steering.

Frege, we have seen, made explaining communication one of the central tasks of his theory of meaning; that is why he had to insist that the sense of an expression is not simply an idea in my mind but a distinct, inter-subjectively available entity. For Russell, on the other hand, it was not really part of the task he was engaged in to explain communication; on his view the fact that we communicate at all emerges as a strange kind of miracle. For the sense-data experienced by me are not the same as those experienced by anyone else. Even if you are in the room with me, the angle at which you look at the table, and hence the exact sense-data you obtain from it, will be different. As a consequence the logically proper names in my language do not mean the same as those in yours (see Russell 1918: §II). The only entities the propositions you and I express have in common are universals. Since the propositions of mathematics and logic, Russell thought, have no components that are not universals, there is the prospect that we can genuinely communicate them, but in all other cases some degree of failure seems inevitable.

Russell's theory is thus at risk of a kind of solipsism. At first sight it might also be thought to flirt with idealism. The sense-datum I experience is private in the sense that no one else but me has experienced it. It seems a short step from there to the claim that the sense-datum is an idea in my mind. But if we say that, then the world is constructed out of ideas, and this is idealism.

So at any rate a casual reader of Russell's *The Problems of Philosophy* (1912) might think. But it is not Russell's view (or Moore's). Something is not a sense-datum unless it is experienced, but saying that does not commit us to identifying the sense-datum with the experience. Russell and Moore both conceived of sense-data as objective entities to which we may bear a relation of acquaintance (Russell) or direct apprehension (Moore). Sense-data may, they came to think, exist when they are not being experienced; and among the things of the same sort as sense-data – Russell called them "sensibilia" – there may be some that no one ever has experienced or ever will experience. To say that no sensibile is a sense-datum unless someone is sensing it is thus on their view much like saying that no man is a husband unless there is someone he is married to.

The multiple relation theory of judgment

A proposition, according to Russell and Moore, is a sort of complex made up out of entities of various sorts: sensibilia, ideas, or universals. If I give two sense-data that I am experiencing the names "a" and "b," for instance, the sentence "a is above b" might express a proposition which consists of a, b and a certain spatial relation (a universal) of aboveness. But what it is for a actually to be above b is just that there should be a complex consisting of a, b and this spatial relation. The proposition may be thought of as asserting the existence of a certain fact. So in the case where the proposition is true, it is identical with the fact whose existence it asserts. But what of the case where the proposition is false? In that case there is no fact, as there is when the proposition is true. It is hard to see how there can be a complex consisting of *a*, *b* and aboveness if *a* is not in fact above *b*, since what it would be for *a* to be above *b* is just that there should be such a complex.

The solution to this problem, Russell came to think, was to eliminate propositions from the account of what it is to make a judgment. And Russell's logical method apparently gave him the means to achieve this. In "A judges that *p*," the expression apparently referring to a proposition *p* was to be treated as an incomplete symbol to be eliminated on analysis, in much the same manner as the present king of France, so that the judgment would turn out to consist not in a binary relation between the person A who makes the judgment and the proposition that is judged, but in a multiple relation between A and the various components of the erstwhile proposition. So, for instance, "Othello judges that Desdemona loves Cassio" will turn out on analysis to express a relationship between four entities: Othello, Desdemona, Cassio, and love.

Now one might think that this theory is at risk of a regress: it eliminates the proposition *p* from the analysis of "A judges that *p*," to be sure, but is not "A judges that *p*" itself another proposition requiring analysis in turn? Presumably, though, Russell was proposing an analysis not of the proposition "A judges that *p*," but only of the judgment itself, i.e. of the fact (when it is fact) that A judges that *p*. Since the difficulty that led him to adopt the theory was only a difficulty with false propositions and not with facts, there is no problematic regress at this point.

There is, however, a different problem. If I say "Othello judges that Desdemona loves Cassio", I do not thereby commit myself to believing about Desdemona what Othello believes, but I do at least express it. Now what is essential to expressing a judgement is the verb. Yet in my presentation of Russell's theory a moment ago, I was compelled by grammar to turn the verb "loves" into the noun "love". The analysis therefore no longer expresses what it is that Othello judges. The judgement relation, as Russell conceived it, has nouns in its argument places rather than verbs, and is therefore powerless to explain why I cannot judge, for instance, that the table penholders the book.

Ludwig Wittgenstein (1889–1951), who was at that time still officially Russell's student at Cambridge, pointed out this difficulty to him in the summer of 1913. "Every right theory of judgment," he said in his *Notes on Logic*, "must make it impossible for me to judge that this table penholders the book. Russell's theory does not satisfy this requirement" (Wittgenstein 1979: 103) Moreover, since the objection depends not on detailed features of Russell's theory but only on its overall shape, it is presumably devastating. At any rate it devastated Russell, who abandoned forthwith a book he was writing (*Theory of Knowledge*) in which the theory played a central role.

The *Tractatus*

Propositions

But if Wittgenstein had disposed of Russell's theory, he had not disposed of the need which it was intended to fill. What was needed, he repeatedly urged, was "a correct theory of propositions." The problem of false propositions which Russell tried to solve by means of the multiple relation theory had arisen from Russell's conception of propositions as complexes. He had started, that is to say, from the view that "The book is on the table" and "the book" both refer to complex entities, and had tried to analyze these entities in similar ways. Wittgenstein's starting point was the realization that there is a fundamental error in Russell's way of conceiving the matter. Sentences are not like names, and the reason they are not like names lies precisely in the feature which had led to Russell's puzzlement, namely that they are capable of truth and falsity.

Wittgenstein called this the bipolarity of the proposition. He was especially struck by the symmetry that exists between a proposition and its negation, a symmetry which Russell's conception of propositions as complexes did not account for. Wittgenstein thought of p and $\sim p$ as being two sides of the same coin, and hence rid himself of the temptation to think of one of them as essentially more complex than the other. There is no more reason to think that negation is in some way a constituent of $\sim p$ than that it is a constituent of p, and hence no reason to think that it is a constituent of either. "My fundamental thought," he said, "is that the 'logical constants' do not represent" (1922: 4.0312).

How, then, is the bipolarity of the proposition achieved? Wittgenstein's answer to this question is famously known as the picture theory: a proposition pictures how the world would have to be for the proposition to be true; the proposition is true if things are as it pictures them to be. Wittgenstein's theory avoids Russell's difficulty over false propositions because the entities which make up the proposition are not the real-world objects but only linguistic proxies for them – names. Wittgenstein's was nonetheless an identity theory, as Moore's had been, and not a correspondence theory. For the names are arranged in the proposition (picture) in the *same* way as their real-world correlates, the objects, are arranged if the proposition is true. The theory thus nicely sidesteps Frege's powerful objection to correspondence theories, that correspondences come in degrees but truth does not. "What is only half true is untrue," as Frege (1918: 60) succinctly puts it.

So far, though, picturing is only a vague metaphor. Plainly much more would have to be said if we wanted it to amount to a semantic theory, and it is far from clear, to me at least, whether it can be said in such a way as to make the theory coherent. Lying behind the picture theory, however, there is what seems to me to be a genuine insight, of which there are glimmerings in Frege, but which Wittgenstein was the first to bring fully to light: it is an essential component of what enables a sentence to express something about the world that the complexity of the proposition the sentence expresses should track the complexity of the possibilities of arrangement of the world which it represents.

Wittgenstein's way of cashing out this insight is to conceive of a proposition not merely as saying how the world is but as contrasting how it says the world is with other ways the world could have been but isn't. The role of a proposition, we might say, is to divide all the possible worlds into two classes: if the actual world is in one class, the proposition is true; if it is in the other, the proposition is false. The bipolarity noted earlier is explained by the fact that the negation of the proposition divides the world into exactly the same two classes: what is reversed is only which class is to count as true and which false. (Wittgenstein calls the division of possible worlds which a proposition effects its *sense*.) A *tautology* is a proposition which is true in all possible worlds; dually, a *contradiction* is one which is true in none. Wittgenstein called these two extreme cases "senseless" because, placing all the possible worlds in one class or the other, they cannot really be said to divide them at all.

Notice, then, that the notion of possibility is built into the expressive nature of propositions from the start. This fact makes vivid how different Wittgenstein's conception was from Russell's. Russell's conception had forced him to abandon the notion that propositions may be possible or necessary at all, whereas for Wittgenstein it is precisely this that makes them expressive. For Russell an entity can be simple only if its existence is indubitable, whereas for Wittgenstein the simple entities (which in the *Tractatus* are just called "objects") are just those that are necessarily existent. The role of propositions, on Wittgenstein's view, is to express possible configurations of the world; the role of objects is to be the hinges around which these possibilities turn. What varies between possible worlds, that is to say, is not what objects there are but only how they are combined with one another to form states of affairs. What makes language expressive is that the substitutional possibilities of the linguistic elements which it allows for match precisely – are identical with – the combinatorial possibilities of the objects these elements represent. That "John" and "Adam" are words of the same grammatical category is the linguistic correlate of the fact that John and Adam themselves are capable of getting into just the same situations.

Mathematics

We saw earlier that Wittgenstein's conception of the sense of propositions gave him an elegant criterion of logical truth: a proposition is a logical truth (tautology) just in case it is true in all possible worlds. Using this criterion Wittgenstein showed that Russell's axiom of reducibility is not a logical truth. So much the worse, Wittgenstein thought, for mathematics. Rather than try to repair Russell's system so that mathematics would consist of tautologies, he simply ditched it, or most of it: the only part of mathematics he kept was simple arithmetic, equations such as $7 + 5 = 12$. Equations, he held, do not express genuine senseful propositions, but nor are they logical truths (i.e. tautologies). Instead, they have the same form as general claims that certain sorts of symbols express tautologies.

We need not go into the details of Wittgenstein's account of mathematics here (see Potter 2000: ch. 6). What is important here is to note that Wittgenstein opposed the idea that mathematics consists of tautologies, and yet went out of his way to emphasize in the *Tractatus* how *similar* the equations of mathematics are to tautologies: "The logic of the world, which the propositions of logic show in tautologies, mathematics shows in equations" (Wittgenstein 1922: 6.22). If this is the similarity, then, what is the difference? The fundamental difference between tautologies and equations lies in how they can be applied. A tautology, such as $p \vee \sim p$, can be seen as a sort of limiting case of a genuine proposition. (For more on this see the following section.) Its component parts, such as p, have sense, and the ways in which those parts are combined to form the whole are ways in which propositions with sense can be formed. It is just that in this case the sense so formed turns out to be empty. What happens when we try to form a parallel explanation of the equation $7 + 5 = 12$? The intended application is that this equation allows us to infer such facts as that if there are 7 apples and 5 oranges then there are 12 pieces of fruit. The general principle the equation encodes is thus:

> (A) If the number of Fs is 7, the number of Gs is 5 and nothing is both an F and a G, then the number of things that are either Fs or Gs is 12.

But this is now plainly not parallel to the tautology case. For no one instance of (A) carries the import of the equation $7 + 5 = 12$. If we try to treat the equation as meaning the universal generalization of (A), we run into a technical difficulty connected with the theory of types, namely that we can only generalize over one level in the hierarchy at a time, which is not what we want; we ought to be able to count first-level properties by just the same means as we count apples. But even if we prescind from this difficulty and focus only on the case where what we are trying to count are Wittgensteinian objects, we still do not get what we want; it is possible that no first-level property has just five instances, and in that case the equation $7 + 5 = 13$, interpreted according to the current proposal, would come out true, as would every other equation with the number 5 on the left hand side (because the antecedent of the conditional would be uninstantiated). This sort of accidental truth is plainly not what we were aiming for, so the only thing left to us is to interpret $7 + 5 = 12$ as meaning that (A) is not merely always *true* but always *tautological*. This, though, cannot *itself* be a tautology since it is at the wrong semantic level for that: as we are about to see, nothing which expresses that something is a tautology is, according to the *Tractatus*, itself a tautology.

Saying and showing

Wittgenstein's logic was truth-functional: the truth-value of a compound proposition is always a function of the truth-values of its component propositions. But propositional attitudes are not truth-functional. There are truths I do not believe and falsehoods I do, so "I believe that p" is not a truth-function of p. Wittgenstein therefore had to reject the view that "A believes that p" and "A doubts whether p" and their ilk are really propositions.

But if they are not propositions, what are they? Wittgenstein's gnomic utterance on the matter tells us only that they are of the same form as " 'p' says that p" (1922: 5.542).

His idea was that for A to believe that p is for A to have in mind a symbol of an appropriate sort which says that p. The key element in the holding of a belief is thus the ascription of sense to a certain symbol. But this ascription is *not* a proposition. More generally, nothing can be a proposition that attempts to express the expressiveness of a symbol. So, for instance, we cannot say that the name "a" refers to a.

To see why Wittgenstein made this claim, we need to contrast it carefully with another that is superficially similar. Wittgenstein distinguished between a sign, which is an arrangement of words (or, in the degenerate case, a single word), and a symbol, which is what the sign becomes when I read it as saying something. That the *sign* "Snow is white" says that snow is white is plainly a contingent fact about English: the word "white" might have meant black, for instance. But anyone who is fluent in English will, on seeing the sentence, immediately read it as saying what it says in English: they will, as Wittgenstein would put it, see in the sign a particular symbol. And it is not contingent that that *symbol* says that snow is white: if it said something else, it simply wouldn't be the same symbol.

This shows readily enough, I think, that

The symbol "p" says that p

is not a proposition with sense, i.e. something that is true in some possible worlds and false in others. And in the same way we can understand why

The name "a" refers to a

is not a proposition with sense either.

What is harder to see is why they cannot be tautologies. To see this let us compare them with

Either it is raining or it isn't.

This does not express a sense: it does not, in Wittgenstein's terms, divide the possible worlds into two classes. But this is only because it puts all the worlds into one class: it has the right general shape to be a proposition with sense, but its parts cancel one another out and end up saying nothing. We can see this by noting that we can approximate what it says (i.e. nothing) by means of propositions that do have sense. For instance:

Either it is raining or it is snowing.
Either it is raining or it is snowing or it is overcast.
Either it is raining or it is snowing or it is overcast or it is sunny.
...

If we carry on like this, eventually we list all the ways the weather could be, and the resulting disjunction says nothing about the weather at all, i.e. it is a tautology.

Return now to our earlier example, "The name '*a*' refers to *a*." It is not hard to convince oneself that there is nothing analogous we can do to approximate this by means of propositions with sense. Hence we are forced to conclude that it is not senseless but *nonsense*: it is not something of the right shape to have a sense which ends up cancelling out and saying nothing – not a limiting case of senseful proposi-tions – as "Either it is raining or it isn't" was; rather is it something which is not of the right shape to have a sense at all.

The examples of nonsense which we have considered so far are what might broadly be called semantic: they attempt to say what it is that some symbol expresses. But once Wittgenstein had identified the category, there were many other sorts of discourse that he realized should be put in it. Consider, for example, an ethical claim such as "Killing babies is wrong." It is easy to see that this is not a tautology: not only is it fairly obviously not a matter of logic, but it does not have the sort of triviality that "Either it is raining or it isn't" has: it cannot be approximated in the same manner by senseful propositions. What is harder in this case, in contrast to the semantic examples considered earlier, is to see why it is not a contingent truth. But if it were contingent, there would be some possible worlds where killing babies is wrong and others where it is not. What if the actual world happened to be one of those in which killing babies is not wrong? One might be tempted to say then that that would be a worse *world* than one in which killing babies is wrong. But if one said that, then it would really be this last claim that was doing the ethical work, not the original claim that killing babies is wrong. Either way, therefore, the claim which carries the ethical content is not a contingent truth. Since there are in Wittgenstein's system only three categories – senseful, senseless, and nonsensical – we must conclude that sentences making ethical claims are nonsense.

The same goes for almost all the spheres of discourse which philosophy has traditionally found problematic: aesthetics, religion, scientific laws, the relationship between mind and body. In all these cases, and others, Wittgenstein held that the solution to our philosophical difficulties is, properly speaking, their *dissolution*. Our mistake was to treat as senseful propositions linguistic expressions which turn out to be nonsense.

Important nonsense?

What is most important here is to see what the scope of Wittgenstein's argument for nonsense is. Notice, in particular, that the argument does not depend on some of the features of Wittgenstein's system that have subsequently been rejected, such as his atomism or his assumption that elementary propositions are logically independent of one another. Notice, too, that it cannot simply be assimilated to arguments such as the liar paradox, which depend on diagonalization arguments. Indeed the conclusions of these diagonalization arguments are typically weaker than Wittgenstein's because they demonstrate only the *relative* inexpressibility of the notions in question (in the case of the liar paradox, truth). The liar paradox shows, that is to say, only that the truth predicate for a language cannot consistently belong to the language itself. But the now-familiar Tarskian resolution of the paradox simply recognizes a hierarchy of languages: the notion of truth for any language in this hierarchy is expressible in the next language up.

There is of course nothing remotely surprising about the fact that for each language there are notions which that language cannot express. (Unsurprisingly, for example, classical Latin has no word for a mobile phone.) All that was ever surprising about the liar paradox was that truth turned out to be such a notion. The inexpressibility which Wittgenstein demonstrates, on the other hand, is of a radically different kind, since what he shows is that what we are trying to say simply does not have the right shape to be said in *any* language, however extended, provided only that the language obeys the fundamental Tractarian constraint that it aims to distinguish between ways the world could be. So in any case of Tractarian inexpressibility moving to a meta-language will not do the trick.

Part of what is powerful about Wittgenstein's inexpressibility argument, then, is its generality. But notice also, on the other hand, how restricted its conclusion is. "Nonsense" in the *Tractatus* is, as we have seen, a technical term defined in contrast to "sense." Even if we accept the Tractarian picture according to which the *primary* purpose of any functioning language is the expression of sense, it does not follow that that is its only purpose; we would need a further argument if we wanted to conclude that any linguistic item which does not succeed in expressing sense is simply gibberish. Not only does the *Tractatus* not supply such an argument; it is plain that Wittgenstein himself did not believe the conclusion. There is ample testimony to the importance he placed on ethics and religion (not only then but throughout his later life).

Even if we ignore ethics and religion, moreover, it would be hard to hold resolutely to the view that in the *Tractatus* all nonsense is gibberish, given that what is there characterized as nonsense includes not only such mundane items as ascriptions of belief but also arithmetical equations such as $7 + 5 = 12$.

There is a danger, therefore, that the emphasis recent work has placed on a contrast between so-called "old" and "new" (or irresolute and resolute) readings of the *Tractatus* (see, for example, McCarthy and Stidd 2001) may create a polarized debate between two equally implausible extremes. If the old, irresolute reader is supposed to be someone who thinks that nonsense can be appropriately expressed by moving to a meta-language, then it is hard to find a respected commentator on the book who counts as irresolute. (The nearest, perhaps, is Russell, who briefly canvassed the idea in his introduction to the *Tractatus*, but even he immediately noted that this was not Wittgenstein's own view.) And nonsense, on the other hand, is no doubt nonsense; but a resolute reader who steadfastly maintains that nonsense is simple gibberish misses the subtlety of Wittgenstein's view.

The challenge to all readers of the *Tractatus*, whether they choose to label themselves new or old, is to explore the constraints there plainly are on which nonsense we may utter in which circumstances – constraints which do not apply to gibberish. The *Tractatus* offers us a reason why logic does not apply to nonsense, a reason whose attraction is that it contrives in a recognizable sense not to threaten the universality of logic. That, if it is right, is an important conclusion. It is equally striking, however, how much nonsensical sentences have in common grammatically with senseful ones. The same observation, of course, could be made about Lewis Carroll's nonsense verse, "Twas brilling, and the slithy toves / Did gyre and gimble in the wabe." Much more would have to be said, however, before we could derive from the *Tractatus* the suggestion that the psychological effects of the sentence "7 + 5 = 12" are importantly analogous to those of nonsense verse, or that the constraints on correct mathematics are anything like those on good poetry.

One does well to remember that when Wittgenstein said that he believed himself to have found the final solution to the problems of philosophy, he meant what he said. In particular, he intended the doctrine of saying and showing to solve (or more properly, once again, to dissolve) the problem of the relationship between the self and the world – the problem, that is to say, to which realism and idealism represent contrasting solutions. His thought was that the things which cannot be said but only shown – symbolic expressiveness, ethics, aesthetics, God – are all different aspects of this relationship. And their absolute unsayability was for him a way of coming to see that what this is is not really a *relationship* at all. The traditional philosophical picture, let us recall, sees a problematic gap between the self and the world, which realism attempts to bridge. Idealism obviates the need for a bridge by removing the world from the picture. What Wittgenstein does, by contrast, is in a certain sense to remove the self. Or, more accurately, he conceives of my self as constituted by the process of representing the world in which I am engaged. And what we are showing when we speak nonsense is always an aspect of this process.

If this is right, then the consequences for philosophy are far-reaching indeed. All the "big" questions of philosophy are, according to the *Tractatus*, not really questions at all and cannot be answered by the application of logical reasoning in anything like the manner that Russell and others were attempting. For logical reasoning applies only to propositions, and the sentences which occur in "big" philosophy do not express propositions. Wittgenstein's closing admonition, "Whereof one cannot speak, thereof one must be silent" (1922: 7), therefore enjoins us not to try to discuss these questions. It certainly does not follow, however, that we should dismiss them as worthless. There may well be other processes – of more or less conscious reflection, perhaps, or of prayer – which may lead us to awareness that killing babies is wrong, that a painting is beautiful, or that God exists.

Reactions to the Tractatus

There is certainly something very mystical about Wittgenstein's view of the unsayable, and it is unsurprising that neither Cambridge atheists such as Russell nor scientistic positivists in Vienna such as Carnap were inclined to take much notice of it. What they took much more seriously at first was Wittgenstein's dismissal of the logicist reduction of mathematics to the theory of classes. He rejected it because, as he put it, "The theory of classes is altogether superfluous in mathematics. This is connected with the fact that the generality which we need in mathematics is not the *accidental* one" (1922: 6.031).

According to Wittgenstein, let us recall, mathematical theorems (to the extent that he granted them house room at all) are not themselves tautologies but have the form of claims that various other symbols are tautologies. There seemed to be little prospect of giving an account of any more than elementary arithmetic in accordance with this view.

What was needed if Wittgenstein's view was to be refuted, therefore, was a demonstration that the theorems of the theory of classes were indeed simply more elaborate tautologies. The person who attempted this was Frank P. Ramsey (1903-30), in his paper on "The foundations of mathematics" (1926). What he argued was that the theory of classes could indeed be regarded as part of logic because of a logical notion that he called a "propositional function in extension." On Wittgenstein's understanding, a propositional function is what we obtain if we take a proposition and replace some symbolic element in it with a variable. Thus, for instance, the proposition "Socrates is dead" gives rise to the propositional function "x is dead." If we now replace the variable in this propositional function with another name, "Plato" for example, we obtain the proposition "Plato is dead," which in an immediately recognizable sense says the same thing about Plato as the previous proposition did about Socrates. Ramsey's new notion, by contrast, is simply a function (in the mathematical sense) taking objects to propositions: we might, for instance, define a propositional function in extension φ so that

φ (Socrates) = Queen Anne is dead.
φ (Plato) = Einstein is a great man.

The difficulty Ramsey's notion was designed to overcome is that if we combine Wittgenstein's understanding, according to which φa must say the same about a as φb says about b, with Whitehead and Russell's idea that talk about classes is to be reduced to talk about propositional functions, we obtain the result that the only sort of class we can talk about is, in Wittgenstein's terminology, *accidental*, i.e. a class of things having some property in common. We cannot talk about the *essential* classes which we need in mathematics, e.g. classes defined by enumeration such as {a,b}. Another usage would be to call the first notion *de dicto* and the second *de re*, since they differ in how they vary across possible worlds. In a world in which a and b happen to hold all their properties in common, the *de dicto* notion is unable to retrieve the *de re* class {a,b}. With Ramsey's notion, by contrast, we can talk about the class {a,b} by defining a propositional function in extension which expresses tautology if $x = a$ or $x = b$ and expresses contradiction otherwise.

If Ramsey's notion of propositional function in extension were indeed, as he claimed, an "intelligible notation," we would therefore be well on the way to resurrecting Russell's logicist program. Unfortunately, however, it is not. If we wish to claim that mathematics consists of tautologies, it is no use treating equations as merely abbreviated embodiments of their intended applications; the only course is to treat them as tautologies in their own right, their tautologousness not being seen as derived from their applications. Ramsey's account is evidently an instance of this general strategy. But if we do this, we shall eventually have to explain how these tautologies nevertheless do get applied: we shall have to establish a connection between the new ways of expressing senses thus introduced and the old ones. But now our difficulty is that we have broken the link with a crucial aspect of Wittgenstein's account of tautologies described earlier, namely that they can be seen as limiting cases of genuine propositions, i.e. as trivial cases of forms capable of expressing non-trivial senses. Without that link mathematics floats free of the rest of language and the account lapses into a version of formalism.

That is the philosophical reason for Ramsey's failure: for the details consult Potter 2000 (ch. 8). There is also a technical reason, which was discovered by Kurt Gödel (1906–78) just after Ramsey's premature death in 1930. One way of expressing what Gödel's incompleteness theorems demonstrate is that arithmetic (and mathematics more generally) have a complexity that tautologies do not have. This shows that mathematics cannot simply be regarded as consisting of more complicated tautologies: the difference is one of kind, not degree. The incompleteness theorems, in other words, force us to recognize a distinctively mathematical notion of necessity distinct from the logical notion of tautology picked out by Wittgenstein.

The claim that there is only one kind of necessity, namely logical necessity, was in fact the first of the Tractarian doctrines that Wittgenstein himself retracted, but his reason was not mathematical. In the *Tractatus* he had admitted it as necessary that nothing is both red and green simultaneously. Since he then held that the only sort of necessity is logical necessity, he was forced to conclude that red and green are not simples but have some analysis from which the incompatibility emerges as tautological. But he did not trouble to supply the required analysis, or even sketch how it might go.

When he resumed philosophy in the late 1920s, he began to meet members of the Vienna Circle such as Friedrich Schlick (1882–1936), Friedrich Waismann (1896–1959) and (for a time) Rudolf Carnap (1891–1970). Their approach to philosophy, heavily influenced as it was by scientific method, was certainly not to Wittgenstein's taste. Nonetheless, it may well have been their influence that led him to wonder how the analysis of color words is actually supposed to proceed. Moreover, it is not just color incompatibilities that have to be dealt with. If I look at a lamp, a patch in my visual field is filled with light of a certain intensity: the same patch cannot simultaneously be filled with light of another intensity. This incompatibility, too, would according to the *Tractatus* have to be analyzable in some way. When Wittgenstein came to realize that it cannot (Wittgenstein 1929), he abandoned the doctrine that elementary propositions are logically independent. In other words, he came to hold that there are internal relations – necessary relationships – between atomic facts.

This is not perhaps such a major retraction. In the *Tractatus* he simply asserted the doctrine of the logical independence of elementary propositions without argument, and one might even wonder whether he had simply taken it over from Moore. More significant, however, is the problem of identifying the simple entities which logical atomism presupposes. We have seen that Russell took them to be sense-data.

Wittgenstein did not, but made only one remark in the *Tractatus* about what else they might be: "Space, time and colour (colouredness) are forms of objects" (1922: 2.0251). Points in space, moments in time[4] and coloredness (but not, as we have just seen, the various colors such as red and green) are therefore Tractarian objects. It might be thought surprising that he said so little about such an apparently central question, but in a way what is more surprising is that he said even this much. For there is a sustained passage in his wartime notebooks (June 1915) in which he lays out the difficulties there are in supposing that we have *any* stable conception of what is simple in the world.

What he evidently recognized in 1915, but chose in the finished book simply to ignore, was that what we take to be simple is highly sensitive to context, shifting not just from one conversation to another, but even from sentence to sentence. In his later philosophy Wittgenstein tried to capture something of this sensitivity to context by means of the notion of a "language-game": our language is to be thought of not, as in the *Tractatus*, as a single unit, but as an overlapping patchwork of sub-languages (games) in which different (and sometimes conflicting) notions of simplicity may be at work.

It is a truism of modern Wittgenstein scholarship that the *Philosophical Investigations* do not represent the clean break from the *Tractatus* that was once supposed: the similarities between early and late are as significant as the differences. One example of this is the continuing importance in his later work of the idea that the expressiveness of a proposition is inherently contrastive, so that something can make sense only if its negation also makes sense. It is, for example, a repeatedly exploited thought in his later work that in order for us to count something we do as correct we must have an account of what it would be for it to be a mistake.

This continuity in thought between early and late is especially apparent in the notion of the unsayable. The perplexity which the later Wittgenstein encourages in us about what it is to follow a rule cannot be dissolved by means of a further rule, since the new rule would merely inherit the same perplexity. Yet Wittgenstein does not intend our perplexity to be permanent: we do indeed apply rules correctly all the time. When he invokes what he calls "our form of life" as a solution to the problem, he intends it to play much the same role as the metaphysical subject plays in the *Tractatus*. The point of the rule-following considerations is to free us of a conception he takes to be misleading – the conception, that is to say, according to which there can be any further question as to whether our application of the rule is *really* correct if we take it to be so. And this is just the same picture whose abandonment Wittgenstein recommended in the *Tractatus* as a way of dissolving the dispute between realism and idealism.

This has been a recurring theme in twentieth-century philosophy, taken up with considerable sensitivity by Hilary Putnam (1926–) (see Putnam 1981), for example. His use of the so-called permutation argument has much in common with Wittgenstein's use of the rule-following considerations; he aims not to question whether "cat" really refers to cats but to reject the idea, central to what he calls metaphysical realism, that there is a perspective from which we can coherently ask whether it does or not.

Analytic philosophy

What it is not

The survey we have given of themes in the birth of analytic philosophy is certainly selective, as is inevitable in a volume of this kind. Nonetheless, there would, I think, be widespread agreement that what I have described are at any rate *some* of the origins of analytic philosophy. The fact of this agreement is itself quite remarkable: not all intellectual movements have such clearly identifiable births, nor ones so localized. But when one tries to identify philosophical views that characterize analytic philosophy, the picture becomes murkier: it is surprisingly hard to find a coherent cluster of views that would be subscribed to by all those twentieth-century philosophers who have been taken to belong to the analytic tradition.

The idea which gave the tradition its name, that an analysis of sentences could reveal the true structure of the propositions they express and hence the true nature of the world, has re-emerged in various forms, and is not yet quite dead, but it certainly is not universally accepted. Followers of Willard Van Orman Quine (1908–2000), for example, have held that no sentence-by-sentence analysis can hope to explain what we are saying. The correct way to understand the relationship between language and the world was not even a point of agreement between the founders of the tradition, let alone their inheritors. And the assumption, prominent in philosophy since ancient times, that there is anything we might term the *given*, an unanalyzable substance of which the world is composed, seems to be believed by hardly anyone in the analytic tradition nowadays.

One thing that analytic philosophers have certainly had in common has been a belief that natural science, as it has been practiced since the early nineteenth century, has conformed very largely to the norms of rationality, and that its evident success owes much to its employment of these norms. That, however, is scarcely enough to distinguish analytic philosophers from anyone else. Many of them have also been tempted to argue in the other direction – to use the practice of natural science as an aid to identifying these norms, and its success as a justification for them. But it is a further step, on which they have certainly not all agreed, to claim that the norms exemplified in the practice of natural science are the only rational norms we have.

I mentioned earlier Frege's "linguistic turn." Part, at least, of what this involved was his realization that if we are to analyze the structure of thought, we have no choice but to engage in an analysis of language, for the straightforward reason that, except perhaps in the first-personal case, language is our primary means of access to thought. Whether it is also constitutive of the linguistic turn to claim that language is our only means of access is more controversial, however. This stronger claim has been repeatedly urged by Dummett, who has even asserted (1993) that an acceptance of it is a necessary condition for anyone to count as an analytic philosopher.

It is of course unsurprising that a precise delineation of a hitherto vaguely under-stood boundary should place a couple of cases on unexpected sides of the fence, so Dummett is no doubt right to be unperturbed that Gareth Evans (1946–1980) and Christopher Peacocke (1950–), for example, do not count according to his definition as analytic philosophers. But what about Russell? In the great phase of his work we have been discussing here (between 1898 and 1914) Russell always conceived of the subject matter of philosophy as consisting of abstract configurations of parts of the world. He changed his mind, as we have seen, about what these configurations are (facts, propositions, judgments); and it was a profound insight for him when his discovery of the theory of descriptions led him to the idea that the surface grammar of a sentence can mislead us significantly about the structure of the part of reality to which it corresponds. But although this insight led him to be somewhat more careful than before about the distinct structure of language, it did not lead him to the linguistic turn in Dummett's sense. It was only after 1918 that Russell abandoned the view that logic is transparent (see Russell 1959: 145) and became interested in the relationship between language and fact.

Even in his later philosophy, however, Russell would still not count on Dummett's view as an analytic philosopher, because taking up the study of meaning led him directly to abandon the form of anti-psychologism which Dummett takes to be another essential characteristic of analytic philosophy. Russell abandoned, that is to say, the view that "the study of *thought* is to be sharply distinguished from the study of the psychological process of *thinking*" (Dummett 1978: p. 458).

In Frege's hands anti-psychologism was a thesis about logic with normative content: logic is the study not of the laws by which we in fact think but of those by which we ought to think; and the normativity of the "ought" here was not, Frege thought, simply to be resolved into an account of the benefits that accrue if we reason according to these rules rather than others.

This normativity is something Carnap explicitly renounced, at least for a time. "In logic," he said in (1934), " there are no morals," because what counts as a logical truth depends on the linguistic framework we adopt and this choice is determined only by pragmatic, not normative, constraints. Carnap did not hold this ruthlessly pragmatic line for very long, but even while he did, he did not thereby rid logic wholly of normativity: it remained the case, he believed, that once we have adopted a framework, what follows from what within the framework is a determinate matter that admits of right and wrong.

Something similar applies to the later Russell. During his most psychologistic phase, he thought that "the non-mental world can theoretically be completely described without the use of ... logical words" (1938: 43). Concepts like disjunction and negation are required, he thought, only because of "such mental phenomena as doubt or hesitation." He did not say, and it does not follow, however, that once we have acquired these concepts their properties are up to us to settle.

Most extreme of all was the later Wittgenstein, whose endeavors to expose what the normativity of logical reasoning amounts to led him to deconstruct it completely. Even in his case, however, the aim was to reject an inappropriate picture of normativity rather than to give us a license, when arguing, to say whatever we like.

Another feature which has been offered as distinctive of analytic philosophy is what one might call the one-level view of language – the view, that is to say, that all cognitive content is factual content (see Skorupski 1997). The discussion of the

Tractatus earlier will have made plain how little sympathy I have with this view or, therefore, with the idea that it might be essential for an analytic philosopher to hold it. It was no doubt an influential strand in logical positivism, and many Quineans seem to take naturalism to be somehow an endorsement of something very like it, but Wittgenstein did not share it, early or late, and it is not widely held today outside Quinean circles.

That the view was ever influential is indeed attributable to a failure by its proponents to appreciate the role of the metaphysical subject in Wittgenstein's philosophy. That my language is *mine* makes it normative in a way that a simple listing of its rules does not capture. The point is quite general: if we identify any process as constitutive of our rationality, we must recognize that a bare description of that process will inevitably fall short of representing what is involved, since it will leave out the further fact that the process is ours. The error that consists in failing to realize this is one that has been made not only by positivists. It may be traced too, for example, in a kind of argument for physicalism that has found favor more recently. Even if modern physics were all that our best theory of the world came to, there would be a further fact, not contained in the theory itself, namely that it was indeed our best theory.

One might be tempted, therefore, to conclude that the analytic tradition is no more than that – a tradition; to conclude, that is to say, that what unites its practitioners is only that they agree on the historical origins from which their disparate approaches to philosophy have stemmed. This is no doubt helpful, but it is in the end too coarse-grained, not so much because there have been philosophers outside this historical tradition (such as Bernard Bolzano, 1781–1848) whom we would nevertheless wish to describe as analytic, but rather because there have been many in the twentieth century who took inspiration from the authors I have discussed here but who would generally be considered to lie outside this tradition.

Another method that is tempting is to define analytic philosophy by what it is not. And no doubt this too has its point. Just as Protestantism has, historically and to some extent theologically, been defined by its opposition to Roman Catholicism, analytic philosophy has undoubtedly acquired its identity partly by its oppositions, first to what is unhelpfully described as Continental philosophy (Hegel, Nietzsche, Heidegger, Sartre) and then more recently to postmodernism. But these oppositions, although they tell us something about the nature of analytic philosophy, do not tell us very much, if only because neither Continental philosophy nor postmodernism is much easier to characterize than it is.

What it is

Nonetheless, even if none of these ideas picks out analytic philosophy precisely, each has some truth in it. There is at the very least a cluster, if not of beliefs, then of working methods which very many of those who regard themselves as analytic philosophers have held in common and which serve, when taken together, to illuminate something distinctive in their approach. We can insist first of all, I think, that the term "analytic philosophy" is not wholly inappropriate: although there is no general agreement about what is analyzed and why it is being analyzed, the analytic method does nonetheless involve analysis.

The most prominent debate here concerns the holism of Quine, which has substituted the theory for the sentence as the appropriate unit on which surgery is to be performed. According to Quine, that is to say, it is misleading to attempt the analysis sentence-by-sentence. In explaining this idea Quine (1960: 3) famously adopted a metaphor of Neurath's according to which our theory is a ship which we must rebuild while staying afloat. (Quine himself called it a raft, perhaps to emphasize its fragility.)

Another leading idea has been the importance of rational argument in philosophy, not just as a tool but also as something which it is one of our primary tasks reflexively to critique and explain. I alluded earlier to the view, characteristic of a sort of naturalism, that rational norms just are scientific norms. A rather similar view, namely that rational argument just is logical argument, is nowadays even more widespread. I am not wholly convinced that this identification is correct, but what is at any rate clear is that it was only the developments in logic which began with Frege's invention of quantifier-variable notation in 1879 that made it even plausible. It is no accident, in other words, that analytic philosophy was born shortly thereafter.

Analytic philosophy may thus be seen as the inheritor of the eighteenth-century debate between the rationalist and empiricist traditions. For part of the twentieth century, indeed, analytic philosophers hoped that modern logic would close the gap between these two: rationalists, on this view, had appealed to reason as a source of knowledge distinct from sense experience only because they had thought of logic as essentially trivial; the power of modern logic reawakened, for a time at least, the hope that some version of empiricism might give us, if not all we want, then at least all we need by way of knowledge.

Another common element in the analytic method has something to do with the ineluctability, when one argues from within a perspective, of the structural features of that perspective. But it is hard to formulate what this comes to in a way that all analytic philosophers would agree on. Perhaps the best formulation is Wittgenstein's: we must grant what he called the hardness of the logical "must" (1953: §437).

The underlying point here goes well beyond logic. What is fundamental, not just in logic, is that there is a distinction between being true and being taken to be true. What exactly this distinction comes to has certainly not met with agreement among analytic philosophers. Nor is it even agreed whether it makes sense to suppose that our best theory of the world might be wrong: one sort of anti-realism consists precisely in denying this. Nonetheless, what analytic philosophers who present matters in terms of theory choice share is the view that there are criteria for the acceptance or rejection of a theory that are not wholly internal to the theory itself.

It is at the very least disputable, that is to say, whether it makes sense to suppose that we might all be wrong about everything; but it is not disputable that some of us may be wrong about something. Views which make errors impossible have surfaced from time to time, but only as proposals for dealing with specific problematic spheres of discourse (Wittgenstein in his middle period held such a view about arithmetic, for example) and certainly without much acclaim.

The final belief that many analytic philosophers hold in common is the one that Russell and Moore came to in their escape from Hegelianism, namely that the content of a judgment is not changed by the mere act of judging it. Not only is there a difference between being true and being taken to be true, but the latter does not change the former. (It is important, incidentally, to distinguish this from the superficially similar claim that coming to know something to be true does not change what is true. This last claim may well be false, as quantum mechanics tells us.) By means of their insistence on this point analytic philosophers aim to resist a sort of wholly general pessimism, prominent in the Continental tradition, which concludes that we can never accurately represent anything about the world because the very act of representing ensures that we thereby miss our target. This no doubt contributes to the fact that hostility to postmodernism has been especially strong among analytic philosophers.

Why it is

If we now have a sense of the dominant features that characterize the analytic movement, the further question then presses of why it has arisen. There are two facts to be explained here. On the one hand, the analytic tradition has achieved a dominance in English-speaking philosophy departments that is, in its way, astonishing; in some departments, indeed, authors in other traditions (Sartre, Derrida) are mentioned so rarely that undergraduates presume their works to be a sort of pornography. On the other hand, the dominance is limited in both respects – only to philosophy depart-ments, and largely (although this is now changing) to the English-speaking world.

As with other intellectual movements, some of the reasons for acceptance and rejection lie outside the discipline itself, in a jumble of historical, cultural, and linguistic facts. An important factor contributing to the influence in America of logical positivism, for example, was the flight of (mainly Jewish) philosophers from Nazi Europe in the 1930s. The lack of influence of some Continental writers in Britain may have been partly a consequence of British linguistic incompetence. The approach to historical texts popular among analytic philosophers, of arguing with their authors on equal terms, and ignoring the awkward fact that Kant is not available to answer back, will from some cultural perspectives seem unduly disrespectful. The popularity of ordinary-language philosophy in Oxford after the Second World War was no doubt due partly to the fact that, unlike other approaches to philosophy then current, it could at least be practiced competently by a "Greats"[5] man without the least knowledge of modern science and mathematics.

One rather more internal factor in the acceptance of the analytic approach was undoubtedly its success: analytic philosophy made enormous progress in the fifty years after its birth, especially in the philosophy of mathematics, but also in the philoso-phies of language, mind, and science. Once again, though, we cannot easily exclude external factors completely. The articles which Russell and Moore published in *Mind* during the 1900s are evidently more interesting and more illuminating than almost all of what surrounds them, but is that because of the power of the philosophical methods they had hit on or simply because they were able and inventive thinkers?

The analytic virtues of conceptual clarification and rational argument are no doubt applicable to problems that are not distinctively philosophical. (That, at any rate, is what we tell prospective philosophy students.) But the benefits the study of analytic philosophy is supposed to confer, of freeing the mind from prejudice and enabling it to see what is important in a problem, have their limits, as anyone who has attended a staff meeting in a philosophy department will attest. Moreover, it is noticeable that the successes of the method are much more prominent in some areas of philosophy than in others: analytic philosophy has told us much more since the early twentieth century about the nature of mathematics and science than it has about art. For that reason it is perhaps no great surprise that literary critics have not on the whole been very interested in it.

The more general point lying in the background is this. Analytic thinking – thinking in accordance with the norms of analytic philosophy – may seem, to someone embedded in it, simply to be the same as clear thinking. The difficulty we have had in character-izing what analytic thinking involves might encourage the suspicion that this is not quite right. What I have tried to emphasize here is how the analytic method was developed at a particular time, in particular places, in response to particular problems. It may well be that some of what postmodernists say about the nature of the reader's response to a literary text is horribly confused, but it does not follow that anything analytic philosophy has to say about the matter, by being less confused, is thereby more illuminating.

Notes

1 Basic Law V is actually somewhat more general, but the extra generality is irrelevant to the point under discussion here.
2 The expression "*ein drittes Reich*" did not when Frege used it in (1918) have all the connotations which it later acquired.
3 Frege also thought that the notion of reference could, parallel with sense, be given a treatment that is uniform for sentences and the expressions that make them up, so that a sentence has a reference, namely its truth value, in just the way that a name has a reference, namely the object it names. This element of Frege's theory is clearly wrong, as Wittgenstein (1922: 4.063) showed.
4 Or perhaps regions of space and intervals of time – Wittgenstein does not say which.
5 "Greats" refers to the Oxford University undergraduate classics course, from which until quite recently most Oxford philosophers were drawn.

References

Baldwin, J. (ed.) (1901) *Dictionary of Philosophy and Psychology*. London: Macmillan.

Carnap, R. (1934) *Logische Syntax der Sprache*. Vienna: Springer. Translated as *The Logical Syntax of Language*. London: Routledge & Kegan Paul, 1937.

Dedekind, R. (1888) *Was sind und was sollen die Zahlen?* Braunschweig: Vieweg. Translated as "What are numbers and what should they be?" in W. B. Ewald (ed.) *From Kant to Hilbert: A Source Book in the Foundations of Mathematics*, 2 vols., Oxford: Oxford University Press, vol. 2, pp. 787–832.

Dummett, M. (1978) *Truth and Other Enigmas*. London: Duckworth.

—— (1993) *Origins of Analytical Philosophy*. London: Duckworth.

Frege, G. (1879) *Begriffsschrift, eine der arithmetischen nachgebildete Formelsprache des reinen Denkens*. Halle: Nebert. Translated as "Concept script," in J. van Heijenoort (ed.) *From Frege to Gödel: A Source Book in Mathematical Logic 1879–1931*, Cambridge, MA: Harvard University Press, 1967.

—— (1884) *Die Grundlagen der Arithmetik*. Breslau: Koebner. Translated as *The Foundations of Arithmetic*, rev. edn. 1953.

—— (1893–1903) *Grundgesetze der Arithmetik, begriffsschriftlich abgeleitet*. Jena: Pohle. Partially translated as *Basic Laws of Arithmetic*, Berkeley: University of California Press, 1967.

—— (1918) "Der Gedanke," *Beiträge zur Philosophie des deutschen Idealismus* 1: 58–77. Translated as "The Thought" in G. Frege, *Collected Papers*, ed. B. McGuinness. Oxford: Blackwell, 1984.

—— (1953) *The Foundations of Arithmetic: A Logico-Mathematical Enquiry into the Concept of Number*, trans. J. L. Austin, 2nd rev. edn., Oxford: Blackwell. Repr. Evanston, IL: Northwestern University Press, 1980.

—— (1964) *The Basic Laws of Arithmetic: Exposition of the System, Volume 1*, trans. and ed. M. Furth. Los Angeles: University of California Press.

—— (1972) *Conceptual Notation and Related Articles*, trans. and ed. T. W. Bynum. Oxford: Clarendon Press.

McCarthy, T. and S. C. Stidd (2001) *Wittgenstein in America*. Oxford: Oxford University Press.

Makin, G. (1995). "Making sense of "On denoting." *Synthèse* 102: 383–412.

Moore, G. E. (1899) "The nature of judgment." *Mind* 8: 176–93.

—— (1901–2) "Truth." In J. Baldwin (ed.) *Dictionary of Philosophy and Psychology*, London: Macmillan. Repr. in *G. E. Moore: Selected Writings*, ed. T. Baldwin, London: Routledge, 1993, pp. 20–2.

Oliver, A. (1999) "A few more remarks on logical form." *Proceedings of the Aristotelian Society* 99: 247–72.

Peirce, C. S. (1885) "On the algebra of logic: a contribution to the philosophy of notation." *American Journal of Mathematics* 7: 180–202.

Potter, M. (2000) *Reason's Nearest Kin: Philosophies of Arithmetic from Kant to Carnap*. Oxford: Oxford University Press.

Putnam, H. (1981) *Reason, Truth and History*. Cambridge: Cambridge University Press.

Quine, W. V. O. (1960) *Word and Object*. Cambridge, MA: MIT Press.

Ramsey, F. P. (1926) "The foundations of mathematics." *Proceedings of the London Mathematical Society* 25: 338–84.

Russell, B. (1903) *The Principles of Mathematics*. London: Allen & Unwin.

—— (1912) *The Problems of Philosophy*. Oxford: Oxford University Press.

—— (1918) "The philosophy of logical atomism." *The Monist* 28: 495–527.

—— (1924) "Logical atomism." *Contemporary British Philosophy, Personal Statements* (first series), ed. J. H. Muirhead. London: Allen & Unwin, pp. 365–83.

—— (1938) "The relation of psychology to logic." *Proceedings of the Aristotelian Society, Supplementary Volume* 17: 42–53.

—— (1959) *My Philosophical Development*. London: Allen & Unwin.

Skorupski, J. (1997) "Why did language matter to analytic philosophy?" In H.-J. Glock (ed.) *The Rise of Analytic Philosophy*. Oxford: Blackwell, pp. 77–91.

Whitehead, A. N. and B. Russell (1910–13) *Principia Mathematica*. Cambridge: Cambridge University Press.

Wittgenstein, L. (1922) *Tractatus Logico-Philosophicus*. London: Kegan Paul & Trubner.

—— (1929)"Someremarksonlogicalform."*ProceedingsoftheAristotelianSociety,SupplementaryVolume9*:162–71.

—— (1953) *Philosophical Investigations*. Oxford: Blackwell.

—— (1979) *Notebooks, 1914–1916*, ed. G. H. Von Wright and G. E. M. Anscombe (includes "Notes on Logic," 1913). Oxford: Blackwell; Chicago: University of Chicago Press.

Further reading

Ayer, A. J. (1982) *Philosophy in the Twentieth Century*. London: Weidenfeld & Nicolson. (A clear and engaging account which covers in detail much of the material mentioned here but also emphasizes other figures such as Collingwood and Lewis).

Dummett, M. (1993) *Origins of Analytical Philosophy*. London: Duckworth. (A delightfully thought-provoking and opinionated perspective on the historical origins of analytic philosophy).

Kenny, A. (2005) *Wittgenstein*, rev. edn. Oxford: Blackwell. (The best single introduction to Wittgenstein's thought, both in the *Tractatus* and subsequently).

Noonan, H. (2000) *Frege*. Cambridge: Polity Press. (A lucid treatment of Frege's philosophy of logic).

Potter, M. (2000) *Reason's Nearest Kin: Philosophies of Arithmetic from Kant to Carnap*. Oxford: Oxford University Press. (More detail on much of the material discussed in this chapter).

2
THE DEVELOPMENT OF ANALYTIC PHILOSOPHY: WITTGENSTEIN AND AFTER

Hans-Johann Glock

My aim is to chart and critically assess the development of analytic philosophy from roughly the 1930s onwards. The most striking feature is the transformation of the self-assured (if distinct) programs of logical atomism and logical positivism into highly diverse strands which come to question and undermine the very idea of analysis and finally of analytic philosophy itself. To begin with, I recount the linguistic turn of the early Wittgenstein and the logical positivists, and then turn to the emergence of two branches of analytic philosophy: logical construction ("ideal language philosophy") led by Carnap and conceptual analysis ("ordinary language philosophy") inspired by the later Wittgenstein. Next I describe the collapse of positivism under the impact of Quine and Kuhn, and after that the rehabilitation of metaphysics through Strawson, Quine, and Kripke. The subsequent sections look first at the reversal of the linguistic turn in the philosophy of language and mind in the 1970s and after, and then at the conception of moral and political philosophy within the analytic movement.

In the remainder, I consider some more recent issues that are important to the self-image and to the practice of analytic philosophy. I defend conceptual analysis against the accusation of indulging in a cult of common sense and ordinary use, and I insist, against naturalism, that it is both feasible and necessary to distinguish between factual, conceptual, and moral issues. The next sections favorably contrast the pragmatist approach to language epitomized by Wittgenstein with the mentalist and Platonist alternatives, and then explore the connections between meaning, use, and rules. I end by asking whether at the beginning of the twenty-first century there is still a distinctive analytic movement, by pronouncing on its philosophical legacy and by speculating about its future.

The linguistic turn

To some commentators, anyone who addresses philosophical problems in a discursive and rational fashion qualifies as an analytic philosopher. On this construal, the vast majority of philosophers have been analytic. But on a more discerning and fruitful construal analytic philosophy is a distinctive historical movement that flourished in the twentieth century (see Glock 2008). This movement had two interconnected roots. One was the interaction between logic and mathematics. The foundational crisis of mathematics in the nineteenth century spawned Frege's and Russell's logicist project of setting mathematics on secure logical foundations (see "The birth of analytic philosophy," Chapter 1). This first led to the technical development of the new function-theoretic logic, next to the application of logical analysis for the purposes of avoiding ontological commitment to *entia non grata* in Russell's theory of descriptions, and finally to the philosophical reflections on the nature of logic in Wittgenstein's *Tractatus*. The other root is Moore's and Russell's revolt against the idealism and monism of the British neo-Hegelians. On the one hand this led to Moore's attempt to break down concepts into their ultimate constituents. On the other it led to reflections on the nature of propositions, concepts, and facts that culminated in Wittgenstein's picture-theory.

Certain ideas in Frege, Russell, and Moore implied that language plays a more important role in philosophy than it had been accorded since John Locke's *Essay Concerning Human Understanding* (1690). Frege's context-principle suggested that the way to understand certain concepts lies in analyzing the sentences in which they occur. Similarly, Russell's theory of descriptions suggested how traditional philosophical problems concerning existence and intentionality might be solved by paraphrasing sentences in the idiom of formal logic. And Moore's program of conceptual analysis breathed new life into the Socratic ambition of defining terms like "good" or "knowledge" that give rise to philosophical problems. Nevertheless, all three early pioneers of analytic philosophy explicitly stated that philosophy is essentially concerned with reality rather than either thought or language. Both logical and conceptual analysis were attempts to parse abstract entities – thoughts, propositions, facts, or concepts – which were treated as non-linguistic in character (see Hacker 1996: chs. 1–2).

It was the *Tractatus* which took the linguistic turn for which analytic philosophy remains famous – or notorious – in many quarters. Whereas his predecessors were largely inspired by Platonist ideas – in Russell's case combined with a hefty dose of empiricism – Wittgenstein pursued a Kantian project (see "Kant in the twentieth century," Chapter 4). Echoing Kant's ambition to draw the bounds between possible knowledge and illegitimate speculation, the *Tractatus* aimed to "draw a limit to thought." At the same time, Wittgenstein gave a linguistic twist to the Kantian tale. Language is not just a secondary manifestation of something non-linguistic. For thoughts are neither mental processes nor abstract entities, but themselves propositions, sentences which have been projected onto reality. Thoughts can be completely expressed in language, and philosophy can establish the limits and preconditions of thought by establishing the limits and preconditions of the linguistic expression of thought. Indeed, these limits *must* be drawn in language. They cannot be drawn by propositions talking about both sides of the limit. By definition, such propositions would have to be about things that cannot be thought about and thereby transcend the limits of thought. These limits can only be drawn *from the inside*, namely by delineating the "rules of logical grammar" or "logical syntax" (*Tractatus* 3.32–3.325). These rules determine whether a combination of signs has sense, whether it is capable of expressing a thought and hence of representing reality either truly or falsely. What lies beyond these limits is not unknowable things in themselves, as in Kant, but only nonsensical combinations of signs, e.g. "The concert-tone A is red."

Many philosophers of the past have disparaged the theories of their predecessors as false, unfounded, or pointless. But according to Wittgenstein metaphysical theories suffer from a more basic defect, namely that of being "nonsensical" in the sense of being meaningless or unintelligible. It is not just that they provide wrong answers, but that the questions they address are misguided questions to begin with (what the logical positivists later called "pseudo-questions"). They are based on a misunderstanding or distortion of the rules of logical syntax, and must hence be rejected. Legitimate philosophy is not a *doctrine* but an *activity*, namely a "critique of language" to be pursued through *logical analysis*. Without propounding any propositions of its own, it brings to light the logical form of meaningful propositions which, according to the *Tractatus*, are confined to the propositions of empirical science. This positive task is complemented by the negative task of demonstrating that the statements of metaphysics are nonsensical, since they violate the rules of logical syntax.

With engaging modesty, Wittgenstein felt that the *Tractatus* had solved the fundamental problems of philosophy and abandoned the subject after its publication in 1921. Meanwhile, the book had come to the attention of the logical positivists of the Vienna Circle. The logical positivists aimed to develop a "consistent empiricism." They agreed with British empiricism and Ernst Mach (1838–1916) that all of human knowledge is based on experience, but tried to defend this position in a more cogent way, with the help of modern logic, a point they stressed by using the label "logical empiricism." Inspired by Frege, Russell, and Wittgenstein they employed logical rather than psychological analysis to identify the elements of experience, reality, and language (Carnap et al. 1929: 8). Moreover, they invoked the *Tractatus* to account for the propositions of logic and mathematics, without reducing them to inductive generalizations (Mill), lapsing into Platonism (Frege), or admitting synthetic a priori truths (Kant). Logic and mathematics, they conceded, are necessary and a priori; but they do not amount to knowledge about the world. For all a priori truths are analytic, that is, true solely in virtue of the meanings of their constituent words. *Logical* truths are tautologies which are true in virtue of the meaning of the logical constants alone, and *analytical* truths can be reduced to tautologies by substituting synonyms for synonyms. Thus

(1) All bachelors are unmarried

is transformed into

(1') All unmarried men are unmarried

a tautology of the form "$\forall x\ ((Fx\ \&\ Gx) \rightarrow Gx)$," or in words: "for all x, if x is a man and if x is unmarried, then x is unmarried." Necessary propositions, far from mirroring the essence of reality or the structure of pure reason, are true by virtue of the conventional rules governing our use of words (e.g. Ayer 1936: 21–4 and ch. 4). Nowadays the logical positivists are best known for verificationism, the view that the meaning of a proposition is its method of verification (the "principle of verification"), and that only those propositions are meaningful which are capable of being verified or falsified (the verificationist "criterion of meaningfulness"). On the basis of this criterion, they condemned metaphysics as meaningless, because it is neither a posteriori – by contrast to empirical science – nor analytic – by contrast to logic and mathematics. Metaphysical pronouncements are vacuous: they neither make statements of fact that can ultimately be verified by sensory experience, nor do they explicate the meaning of words or propositions

Legitimate philosophy boils down to what Rudolf Carnap (1891–1970) called "the logic of science" (1937: 279). Its task is the logico-linguistic analysis of those propositions which alone are strictly speaking meaningful, namely those of science. To complete this linguistic turn, Carnap reformulated philosophical problems and propositions from the traditional "material mode" – concerning the nature or essence of objects – into the formal mode – concerning linguistic expressions, their syntax and semantics.

The logical positivists took over the analytic methods of logical atomism while repudiating the (diverse) metaphysical rationales given for them by Russell and Wittgenstein. From the latter they inherited the linguistic turn, from the former the ambition to vindicate empiricism by means of reductive analysis. They were committed to the "unity of science," the idea that all scientific disciplines, including the social sciences, can be unified in a single system with physics as its foundation. The theoretical terms of science are defined through a more primitive observational vocabulary and this makes it possible to break down all significant propositions into propositions about what is "given" in experience.

These so-called "protocol-sentences" or "observation-sentences" occasioned the first major split within the positivist movement. According to the "phenomenalists," led by Moritz Schlick (1882–1936), these sentences are about subjective sense-experiences; according to the physicalists, led by Otto Neurath (1882–1945) and later joined by Carnap, they are about physical objects rather than mental episodes. The physicalist option does justice to the fact that the objects of science must be intersubjectively accessible. The price to be paid is that even the propositions which constitute the empirical foundations of science are fallible, a view which was also supported by Karl Popper (1902–94), an associate of the Vienna Circle.

Another controversy arose over the status of philosophy *vis-à-vis* science. All logical positivists believed that philosophy should emulate not just the rigor of the formal and empirical sciences but also their cooperative and technological spirit. But whereas Schlick and Carnap held fast to a qualitative distinction between the empirical investigation of reality and the philosophical analysis of the propositions and methods of science, Neurath adopted a naturalistic stance according to which philosophy itself dissolves into a unified physicalist science.

Carnap had originally been impressed by Wittgenstein's strictures against any attempt to talk about the relation between language and reality, and he had therefore restricted the analysis of language to logical *syntax*, the intra-linguistic rules for the combination of signs. In 1935, however, Alfred Tarski (1902–83) published a seminal paper that defined the central semantic notion of truth in a way that avoids semantic paradoxes like that of the liar. This persuaded Carnap to drop the restriction to syntax, and his subsequent attempts to explicate semantic notions have had a profound influence on analytic philosophy of language.

Verificationism also came under pressure. The principle of verification was attacked by conceptual analysts influenced by Wittgenstein and Austin, who pointed out that linguistic meaning attaches not just to declarative sentences capable of being true or false and hence of being verified or falsified, but also, for example, to interrogative, imperative, and performative sentences. In response, logical positivists restricted the principle to what they called "cognitive" as opposed to emotive (for example) meaning (Carnap 1963: 45; see Stroll 2000: 84–6).

This concession deprives the principle of verification of its central semantic role, unless it can be shown that even non-declarative sentences must have a truth-apt and hence verifiable component (see below). It does not threaten the verificationist critique of metaphysics, since metaphysics purports to provide descriptions of reality with cognitive content. But traditional metaphysicians objected that the criterion of meaningfulness is self-refuting, since it is neither empirical nor analytic, and hence meaningless by its own light (e.g. Ewing 1937). In response, some logical positivists presented it as a heuristic maxim on how to use the term "cognitively meaningful," which is justified by its usefulness (Carnap 1937: 51). Alas, its usefulness lies mainly in serving as a stick with which to beat metaphysics, which leaves open the crucial question of whether the latter deserves such punishment. A more promising response is to present the criterion as a non-trivial analytic proposition, a consequence of the term "meaning" (Ayer 1936: 20–1). The trouble is that plenty of sentences which competent speakers count as perfectly meaningful do not allow of conclusive verification. As logical positivists such as Carl Hempel (1905–97) came to realize (see Hempel 1950), the verificationist critique of metaphysics faces a dilemma. If it insists on conclusive verifiability or falsifiablity, it rules out sentences which are part of science ("All quasars are radioactive" cannot be conclusively verified and "There are unicorns" cannot be conclusively falsified). If it insists merely that a statement should allow of some kind of confirmation or disconfirmation, it is too liberal, in that it allows back in metaphysical sentences like "Only the Absolute is perfect."

Logical construction vs. logical analysis

Meanwhile in Cambridge there emerged a new generation of logical analysts, Ramsey pre-eminent among them. The Cambridge analysts shared neither the anti-metaphysical fervor of the logical positivists nor their verificationism. They did, however, share with them Wittgenstein's "thesis of extensionality" (simple propositions occur in complex ones only in such a way that the truth-value of the latter depends solely on those of the former) and Russell's empiricist aspiration of analyzing propositions and concepts into constructions referring exclusively to the contents of experience. Alas, their attempts to reduce all meaningful propositions to truth-functional constructions out of elementary propositions referring to sense-data were no more successful than Russell's fledgling attempts and Carnap's heroic effort in *Der logische Aufbau der Welt*, 1928 (*The Logical Structure of the World*).

Analysis worked well enough when it came to showing that – grammatical appearances notwithstanding – we are not committed to the existence of the present king of France, the round square or the average Briton. Such "logical" or "same-level analysis" aims to present the actual logical form of a proposition and thereby its logical implications or inferential role. It contrasts with "new-level" or "metaphysical analysis," a reductionist procedure supposed to eliminate things of one kind in favor of things of an ontologically more basic kind (Stebbing 1932; Wisdom 1934). The flipside of new-level analysis was *logical construction*. This procedure can be pursued in the material mode, as in Russell's elimination of allegedly fictional entities like numbers in favor of classes of classes and propositional functions. Or it can be pursued in the formal mode. Thus Carnap and Quine sought to replace linguistic constructions that refer to problematic entities by constructions that refer only to entities of a less problematic kind. New-level analysis seemed to have succeeded in mathematics, by reducing numbers to sets.[1] However, it failed in other areas. Even the prima facie undemanding analysis of propositions about nation-states into propositions about individuals and their actions proved tricky. When it came to the phenomenalist reduction of propositions about material objects to propositions about sense-data, the difficulties were insuperable. The occurrence of sense-data is neither necessary for the presence of a material object, since we may fail to perceive objects even under favorable conditions, nor sufficient, because of the possibility of illusion and hallucination. Other stumbling blocks included attributions of belief: the truth-value of "Sarah believes that Blair is honest" is not determined simply by that of the sentence expressing the belief, contrary to the thesis of extensionality (Urmson 1956: 60–74, 146–62).

As regards the analysis of *concepts*, an additional hurdle was the so-called "paradox of analysis" (Langford 1942). Suppose that "brother" is analysed as "male sibling". Either the analysandum has the same meaning as the analysans, in which case the analysis is trivial and nothing is learned by it; or the two are not synonymous, in which case the analysis is incorrect.

It is tempting to blame the failure of reductive analysis on the vagaries of ordinary language: the proposed analysis fails to say precisely the same thing as the analysandum simply because the analysandum does not say anything precise to begin with. This was the attitude of a strand within analytic philosophy that is known as "ideal language philosophy" and comprises Frege, Russell, Tarski, the logical positivists, and Quine. It holds that owing to their logical shortcomings (ambiguity, vagueness, referential failure, category-confusions), natural languages need to be replaced by an ideal language – an interpreted logical calculus – at least for the purposes of science and "scientific philosophy."

According to Carnap, the attempt to reveal the underlying logical form of sentences in the vernacular is futile; analysis should instead take the form of logical construction, not just in the sense that eliminated phrases are reconstructed out of acceptable ones, but in the sense of devising *entirely new artificial languages*. "The logical analysis of a particular expression consists in the setting-up of a linguistic system and the placing of that expression in this system." (1936: 143). Carnap's procedure of "rational reconstruction" or "logical explication" bypasses the paradox of analysis (1928: §100; 1956: 7–9). The objective is not to provide a synonym of the analysandum, but to replace it by an alternative expression or construction, one which serves the cognitive purposes of the original equally well while avoiding drawbacks such as obscurity, philosophical puzzlement, and undesirable ontological commitments. In the same vein, Quine regards it as a "philosophical paradigm" that "whatever good had been accomplished by talking of an ordered pair <x, y> could be accomplished by talking instead of the class {{x}, {x, y}}," without claiming that these expressions carry the same meaning (1960: §53; see also the section "The rehabilitation of metaphysics," below).

Emboldened by the emergence of Brouwer's intuitionist logic, which denies the law of the excluded middle recognized by the bivalent logic of Frege and Russell, Carnap espoused a "principle of tolerance" in logic (1937: §17). We are at liberty to construct novel calculi, constrained only by the demand for consistency and considerations like ease of explanation and avoidance of puzzlement. This pragmatist attitude puts him at odds with the *Tractatus*, for which there is a single "logical syntax," a logico-metaphysical structure which *all* meaningful languages – including natural languages – must have in common, since it is only by sharing this structure with reality that a sign system is capable of representing reality. It also puts him at loggerheads with Frege, Russell, and Quine, who insist that an ideal formal language should uniquely mirror the metaphysical structure of reality.

An alternative to both reductive analysis and logical constructionism emerged from 1929 onwards, when Wittgenstein returned to Cambridge and subjected his own earlier work to a withering critique. The eventual result was his second masterpiece, *Philosophical Investigations*, 1953 (*Philosophische Untersuchungen*).

The color-exclusion problem forced Wittgenstein to realize that nothing could possibly fit the bill of logically independent elementary propositions (see "The birth of analytic philosophy," Chapter 1). This had the further consequence that there are logical relations between propositions which do not result from the truth-functional combination of such elementary propositions. Ordinary language is not "a calculus according to definite rules" (1953: §81), as the *Tractatus* had assumed. Its rules are more diverse, diffuse, and subject to change than those of artificial calculi. The atomistic idea of unanalyzable names and indecomposable objects is a chimera. The distinction between simple and complex is not absolute but relative to one's analytic tools and even to one's philosophical purposes.

The collapse of logical atomism also undermines the picture theory of the proposition. If there are no ultimate constituents of facts – objects – which are simple in an absolute metaphysical sense, then there are no corresponding constituents of propositions which are simple in an absolute semantic sense. Wittgenstein also jettisoned the idea that a proposition must have a logical form which it shares with what it depicts. The spell of this idea was broken by an exchange with the economist Sraffa, who presented him with a Neapolitan gesture of contempt and asked "What is the logical form of *that?*" The explanation of how propositions represent possible facts cannot be that they are arrangements of logical atoms which share a logical form with an arrangement of metaphysical atoms.

Moreover, the possibility of linguistic representation does not presuppose a one-to-one correlation between words and things. Fundamentally, Frege, Russell, and the early Wittgenstein all shared a referential conception of meaning, according to which the meaning of an expression is an object for which it stands. This conception is doubly wrong. Not all meaningful words are names that refer to objects. The referential conception is modeled solely on proper names, mass nouns, and sortal nouns. It ignores verbs, adjectives, adverbs, connectives, prepositions, indexicals, and exclamations (Wittgenstein 1958: 77; 1953: §§1–27). Moreover, even in the case of referring expressions, their meaning is not the object they stand for. "The word 'meaning' is being used illicitly if it is used to signify the thing that 'corresponds' to the word."

"When Mr. N.N. dies one says that the bearer of the name dies, not that the meaning dies" (1953: §40). There are two parts to this objection. First, if the meaning of a word were an object it stands for, referential failure would have to render a proposition like "Mr. N.N. died" senseless. Secondly, identifying the meaning of a word with its referent is what Gilbert Ryle (1900–76) called a category mistake, namely of confusing what a word stands for with its meaning: the referent of "Mr. N.N." can die, but not its meaning. Wittgenstein also presented an alternative to the referential conception: the linguistic meaning of an expression is its "use in the language." The meaning of a word is not an entity of any kind – whether physical, mental, or abstract, but its use according to linguistic rules (see below).

Both the picture theory and verificationism restrict meaningful propositions to statements of fact. Wittgenstein now rejects the idea, epitomized in the *Tractatus* notion of the general propositional form, that the sole function of language is to describe reality. In addition to statements of fact there are not just questions and commands but "countless" other "language-games," linguistic activities such as telling jokes, thanking, cursing, greeting, praying, etc. Furthermore, the logical and semantic rules that constitute a language – Wittgenstein calls them "grammatical rules" – do not have to mirror the structure of reality but are "autonomous." They are not responsible either to physical reality or to a Platonic realm of "meanings." Language is not the self-sufficient abstract system which it appears in Frege, Russell and the *Tractatus*. Rather, it is a human practice which in turn is embedded in a social "form of life" (1953: §23).

Wittgenstein still held that philosophical problems are rooted in misunderstandings of language. But he rejected both logical analysis and logical construction as means of resolving these confusions. There are no logically independent elementary propositions or indefinable names for analysis to terminate with. Indeed, not all legitimate concepts can be sharply defined by reference to necessary and sufficient conditions for their application. Such *analytic definition* is only one form of explanation among others. Many philosophically contested concepts are united by "family-resemblances," overlapping similarities rather than by a common characteristic mark. In particular, propositions do not share a common essence, the single propositional form detected by the *Tractatus*. Finally, the idea that analysis can make unexpected discoveries about what ordinary expressions *really mean* is misguided. The rules of language cannot be "hidden" beneath the surface and await discovery by logicians and linguists. Rather, competent speakers must be capable of recognizing them, since they are the normative standards which guide their utterances. To fight the "bewitchment of our understanding through the means of our language" we need neither the construction of artificial languages nor the uncovering of logical forms beneath the surface of ordinary language. Instead, we need a description of our public linguistic practices which constitute a motley of language-games (1953: §§65–88, 108, 23).

Wittgenstein's new ideas, combined with Moore's defence of common sense against both idealism and skepticism, had a profound impact on a movement which dominated British philosophy between the 1930s and the 1960s. Its opponents called it "ordinary language" or "Oxford philosophy," since its most eminent proponents – Ryle, Austin, and Peter Strawson (1919–2006) – were based there. They themselves preferred labels such as "conceptual analysis" or "linguistic philosophy." For they took a linguistic turn by regarding philosophical problems as conceptual and concepts as embodied in language. To possess a concept is to know the meaning of certain expressions; and concepts are neither mental occurrences nor entities beyond space and time, but abstractions from our use of words.

Initially, Ryle upheld the view that ordinary language creates philosophical confusion because its surface conceals its underlying logical form. Later he denied that there is a logical form to be discovered underneath the surface of ordinary language (see Rorty 1967: 305). Strawson (1952) argued at length that the predicate calculus – the weapon of choice for previous logical analysts – does not reveal the true structure of ordinary discourse. The gulf between the truth-functional connectives and their vernacular correlates is wider than commonly accepted. Similarly, by paraphrasing away singular referring expressions, Russell's theory of descriptions misconstrues their distinctive role, which is to pick out the things we talk about. According to Strawson, the subtlety and variety of natural languages is mangled by the Procrustean bed of formal logic. No matter whether it stands in the service of reductive analysis or of logical construction, formal logic is not a sufficient instrument for revealing all the logical and conceptual features that have a bearing on philosophical problems and philosophical argument.

What survives is conceptual analysis and linguistic paraphrase. Philosophical problems are resolved by explaining expressions and by establishing the status and inferential powers of the statements in which they occur. The structure of "I have a pain" is the same as that of "I have a pin"; yet Wittgenstein maintained that these statements are disanalogous moves in the language-game (1953: §§572–3). Similarly, Ryle advocated that philosophy should chart the "logical geography" of our concepts.

In *The Concept of Mind* he argued that the Cartesian dualism of mind and body results from "category mistakes": it treats mental concepts which signify behavioral dispositions as if they referred to processes that are just like physical ones, only more ethereal. Ryle accepted that philosophy is a meta-discipline which does not "talk sense with concepts" but tries to "talk sense about concepts" (1949: 9-10). Yet he rejected Wittgenstein's therapeutic simile according to which "the philosopher treats a question like a disease" (1953: §255).

J. L. Austin (1911–60) exemplified linguistic philosophy, especially to its enemies, since he was a master of observing minutiae of linguistic use: "*what we should say when, and so why and what we should mean by it.*" For example, he carefully contrasted apparently equivalent terms such as "appear," "look," and "seem" by looking at the different situations that license their application. But his interest in language was not motivated solely by the desire of rectifying confusions, and he even toyed with the idea that linguistic analysis might turn into a branch of linguistics (1970: 181, 231–2). By a similar token, whereas Wittgenstein and his disciples regarded the quest for systematic theories as a misguided intrusion of scientific methods into philosophy, Austin founded a systematic approach to language, namely speech act theory. At the same time, even Austin was suspicious of the craving for uniformity that logical positivism shared with traditional philosophy. Thus he condemned as a "descriptive fallacy" the dogma that language has just a single function, namely to describe.

The collapse of logical positivism

The rise of Nazism forced most logical positivists to emigrate, mainly to the USA. By the 1940s their views had achieved the status of orthodoxy, partly aided by the existence of an indigenous form of empiricism derived from American pragmatism. It is probably no more than mild hyperbole when Donald Davidson (1917–2003) states that he got through graduate school by reading Feigl's and Sellars' anthology of positivist writings (1980: 261).

Labels such as "logical analysis," "philosophical analysis," and "conceptual analysis" had been rife since Russell and Moore, and they were soon joined by "linguistic philosophy" and "the analysis of language." But pertinent uses of "analytic(al) philosophy" came relatively late. One of the first occurs in Ernest Nagel (1901–85) (see Nagel 1936). But the label caught on only after the war, perhaps through Arthur Pap (von Wright 1993: 41n; Hacker 1996: 275–6n). Later it was extended from logical positivism to conceptual analysis (Beck 1962; Montefiori and Williams 1966).

Thus, between the 1930s and 1950s, analytic philosophy established itself as a self-conscious philosophical movement or tendency, albeit one splitting into two distinct branches: logical construction and conceptual analysis. At the same time, however, some assumptions uniting these two branches came to be questioned. The main protagonist of this development was the Harvard logician W. V. O. Quine (1908–2000). Quine was heavily indebted to the logical positivists. He shared their predilection for artificial languages, the conviction that natural science constitutes the paradigm of human knowledge, their vision of a unified science, their suspicion of abstract entities, and the empiricist credo that sensory experience not only provides the evidence on which our beliefs rest (doctrinal empiricism), but also endows our language with its meaning (conceptual empiricism), "Whatever evidence there *is* for science *is* sensory evidence," and "all inculcation of meaning of words must rest ultimately on sensory evidence" (1969: 75). But just as the logical positivists had tried to improve on Hume and Mach, Quine tried to improve on them, replacing their logical empiricism by a more pragmatist variety.

Quine first came to fame in 1951 through "Two dogmas of empiricism" (reprinted in 1953). The article vigorously attacked the two pillars of the logical positivists' conception of philosophy, namely the distinction between analytic and synthetic propositions and the project of reductive analysis. The linguistic turn promised a *distinctive role for philosophy*, without dubious appeals to a Platonic realm of abstract entities, Aristotelian essences, or Kantian pure reason. While science results in empirical propositions that describe reality – and are hence synthetic – philosophy results in analytic propositions which unfold the meaning of the terms employed by science or common sense.

A similar line was taken by Wittgenstein and linguistic philosophers. In spite of their considerable disagreements, these philosophers accepted that there is a qualitative difference between science, which is concerned with factual issues and hence a posteriori, and philosophy, which is concerned with conceptual issues, and hence a priori. Quine overturned this picture by vigorously denying that there is a significant qualitative difference between apparently a priori disciplines like mathematics, logic, and philosophy on the one hand, and empirical science on the other. Unlike John Stuart Mill (1806–73), Quine did not simply assimilate necessary propositions to empirical generalizations. Instead, he questioned the distinctions that had traditionally been used to set philosophy and science apart, in particular the analytic/synthetic distinction. He thereby challenged the idea that there is a distinct type of proposition which articulates logical and conceptual connections rather than empirical facts, and reinvigorated radical empiricism, according to which even apparently a priori disciplines are ultimately based on experience.

Quine's attack on the analytic/synthetic distinction involved two lines of reasoning, one concerning epistemology and scientific method, the other concerning semantics and ontology. The impetus of the first line is that the analytic/synthetic distinction presupposes a second dogma of empiricism, namely "reductionism," the view that every meaningful statement is translatable into a statement about the immediate experiences that confirm it. Reductionism would allow one to define analytic statements as those which are confirmed come what experience may. However, Quine argues, it is at odds with the *holistic* nature of scientific belief-formation, the fact that our beliefs form a "web" in which each belief is linked to all others, and ultimately to experience. This means that it is impossible to specify confirming evidence for individual statements. It also means that any belief can be abandoned for the sake of preserving other parts of the web, and hence that there are no a priori statements immune to empirical revision.

Quine's semantic argument is that analyticity is part of a circle of *intensional* notions – notions concerning what expressions mean or say – that cannot be reduced to purely *extensional* notions – notions like reference, concerning what expressions stand for or apply to. But, he insisted, all these notions are obscure, because there are no criteria of identity for "intensions": while we know what it is for two expressions to have the same extension, we do not know what it is for them to have the same intension or meaning. In *Word and Object* Quine supported this contention by focusing on "radical translation," the translation of a completely foreign language from scratch (1960: ch. 2). Because such translation cannot assume any prior understanding, it helps to appreciate that translation is "indeterminate": there is no fact of the matter as to whether two expressions are synonymous, and hence no criteria of identity for intensions. For this reason, scientific philosophy should eliminate them from its ontology.

The result of Quine's assimilation of the analytic and the synthetic, the a priori and the empirical, is a thoroughgoing naturalism. For Quine, philosophy is a branch of or continuous with natural science (meta-philosophical naturalism). There is no genuine knowledge outside natural science (epistemological naturalism), and the latter provides the sole standard for what is real (ontological naturalism). This naturalistic conception of knowledge in turn requires a new, "naturalized epistemology." Like traditional epistemology, this novel discipline investigates the relationship between our beliefs and the empirical evidence for them. Yet it does so not by providing an a priori "rational reconstruction" (à la Carnap) of the *reasons* we have for accepting scientific theories, but through a *scientific* investigation – behaviorist psychology or neurophysiology – of what *causes* us to adopt them. In the wake of Quine, this naturalistic conception of philosophy has achieved the status of orthodoxy, especially in the USA. Few analytic philosophers these days would dare to publish a book in the philosophy of mind without at least professing their allegiance to some form of naturalism in the preface, however implausible such professions may ultimately be.

Reductionism and verificationism proved to be an Achilles' heel of logical positivism not just in the philosophy of language, but also in the philosophy of science. Their failure undermined *logical* empiricism, but other versions soon came to the fore. Close to Quine's *holistic* empiricism is Karl Popper's *fallibilism* (1934). Popper rejected the verificationist criterion of meaningfulness on several grounds. First, separating meaningful science from nonsensical metaphysics is not just unfeasible but also undesirable, since metaphysical speculation provides an invaluable stimulus to scientific research. Second, what is needed is a demarcation not between sense and nonsense, but between empirical science and other disciplines. Finally, the criterion for that demarcation cannot be verifiability. Science depends on universal laws, and these can never be conclusively verified, since they cover an infinite number of cases. Instead, it is *falsifiability*. A theory is scientific if it allows for the derivation of predictions that can be falsified by empirical data. Science proceeds not by fine-tuning inductive generalizations, but by bold conjectures, the logical deduction of predictions from these conjectures, and their ruthless refutation in the light of novel data.

For the logical positivists, scientific theory-formation was an *ahistorical* activity, namely of constructing theoretical frameworks to fit the available empirical evidence. Popper introduced a historical element, because a novel scientific theory is judged largely by the extent to which it can explain the observations that refuted its predecessors. He nevertheless retained the image of scientific progress as a linear and rational process in which theories are conclusively falsified and replaced by new ones which increasingly approximate the truth. This image was questioned by Thomas Kuhn (1922–96) (see Kuhn 1970), and Paul Feyerabend (1924–94) (see Feyerabend 1975). They maintained that the history of science does not consist of rational shifts from inferior to superior theories, but of "paradigm-shifts" that are partly dictated by non-cognitive factors (social, aesthetic, etc.). There is no universal scientific rationality which would allow us to maintain that more recent theories are objectively better than their predecessors. They also questioned the Kantian distinction between the "context of discovery" and the "context of justification," which had allowed the logical positivists to keep the rational reconstruction and defense of scientific theories apart from an explanation of their origins, whether it be physiological or sociological.

Although few analytic philosophers have swallowed their relativistic conclusions, Kuhn and Feyerabend turned philosophy of science from ahistorical methodological questions to the history and, to a lesser extent, the sociology of science. Since the 1970s, the preoccupation with methodology also came under pressure from metaphysics. Casting off what they regarded as positivistic shackles, philosophers of science maintained that unobservable theoretical entities and the laws of nature are mind-independent features of reality rather than merely linguistic expedients for the explanation and prediction of experience (see "Philosophy of science," Chapter 14).

The rehabilitation of metaphysics

In this respect, post-positivist philosophy of science was part of a more general trend. The ground for this rehabilitation of metaphysics had been cleared by the aforementioned withdrawal of the verificationist criterion of meaningfulness. Into this ground analytic philosophers planted three distinct metaphysical seeds.

The first was Quine's naturalistic approach to ontology. For Carnap, the only genuine questions of existence are scientific questions like "Are there neutrinos?" or "Are there prime numbers greater than 10^{10}?"; they concern particular groups of entities and can be solved within a specific "linguistic framework." By contrast, philosophical questions like "Are there material objects?" or "Do numbers exist?" concerning whole categories of entities are either meaningless or "practical" in nature. They boil down to the pragmatic question of whether for scientific purposes it is convenient to adopt a linguistic framework like that of the natural numbers.

By contrast, Quine's naturalism resulted in a "blurring of the boundary between speculative metaphysics and natural science" (Quine 1953: 20). Philosophy is concerned with the "limning of the most general traits of reality." It investigates the fundamental "furniture of our universe," and differs from science only quantitatively, in the generality and breadth of its questions. Quine declares himself to be "no champion of traditional metaphysics." He denies that a priori philosophical reflection can establish what kinds of things there are. Nevertheless, he finds a place for ontology (1966: 203–4). Like traditional ontology, Quine's naturalistic variety seeks to establish what kinds of things there are. But it does not pursue this aspiration directly or in isolation. Instead, it helps science in drawing up an inventory of the world. It translates our scientific theories into an ideal formal language – Quine calls it "canonical notation" – and thereby clarifies and, where possible, reduces their "ontological commitments," the types of entities the existence of which these theories presuppose. A canonical notation displays our ontological commitments and allows us to paraphrase them in order to keep them at a minimum. While

(2) Red is a color

contains a name for a property, and thereby seems to commit us to the existence of an intensional entity, the paraphrase

(2') $\forall x \, (x \text{ is red} \rightarrow x \text{ is a color})$

avoids any such commitment. Decisions on whether to admit entities that cannot be paraphrased away are guided by a pragmatic trade-off between the systematic efficacy (explanatory power) attained by admitting them and the ontological economy achieved by excluding them.

Like Carnap, Quine does not analyze our existing notions but explicates them, i.e. replaces them by analogues deemed to be scientifically more respectable. But whereas the logical positivists aspired to an ideal language that avoids metaphysical problems, Quine's ideal language aims to reveal *the metaphysics of science*. This has become a guiding principle of contemporary naturalists. By exploring what things our best current scientific theories *take* to exist, they also purport to provide the best account of what things *actually* exist.

A contrasting rehabilitation of metaphysics was provided by Strawson. His early writings criticized orthodoxies of logical construction by appeal to ordinary use. But in *Individuals* (1959) Strawson's concern shifted to "descriptive metaphysics." This Kantian enterprise differs from previous conceptual analysis in its greater scope and generality, since it seeks to "lay bare the most general features of our conceptual structure." These are not discernible in the motley of ordinary use, but in fundamental functions of discourse, notably those of *reference* – picking out an individual item – and *predication* – saying something about it. Descriptive metaphysics "is content to describe the actual structure of our thought about the world," by contrast to *revisionary metaphysics*, which aspires "to produce a better structure" based either on a priori insights, as in traditional metaphysics, or on the perceived demands of science, as in naturalism. It also differs from both in that it elucidates not the most abstract features of the *world*, but the preconditions of our *thought* about the world, of our "conceptual scheme" (1959: 9).

This idea is also central to Strawson's epistemology, which revived the idea of *transcendental arguments*. Such arguments aim to show that skeptical doubts are incoherent or self-refuting, because they question preconditions of any meaningful discourse, the skeptic's own doubts included. The skeptic saws off the branch on which he is sitting, because his doubts employ concepts which make sense only on the tacit assumption of conceptual connections he explicitly rejects.

Critics have protested that transcendental arguments establish at best that we must *employ* concepts like those of a mind-independent object, not that they are *actually* satisfied by anything in reality (Stroud 1968; cf. Glock 2003c). Nevertheless, the idea of establishing the preconditions of experience, thought, or discourse continues to inspire philosophers, including Davidson. It promises to avoid both the Scylla of skepticism and the Charybdis of naturalized epistemology, which bypasses the question of whether our beliefs are justified in favor of causal explanations of their origins. The same goes for descriptive metaphysics, the attempt to make explicit the fundamental notions and assumptions of our conceptual scheme (e.g. Jackson 1998: 31–3).

The final source of contemporary analytic metaphysics has two interrelated roots. The first is the thriving of modal logic, in particular the idea that the logic of terms like "necessarily" and "possibly" can be explicated in terms of Leibniz's notion of a possible world. The second is the rise of theories of "direct reference," according to which many expressions, notably proper names and natural kind terms, refer to their denotata directly, without the mediation of Fregean senses, i.e. of properties which the denotata uniquely possess. Quine had followed the logical positivists in treating the necessary, the analytic, and the a priori as equivalent. This is at odds not just with Kant's endorsement of synthetic a priori truths, but also with contemporary essentialism. For Saul Kripke (1940–), the a priori is an epistemological category, necessity a metaphysical one, and analyticity a logical one (see Kripke 1980: 34–9). In the wake of Kripke, the following definitions have found favor: a truth is *a priori* if and only if (abbreviated to "iff") it can be known independently of experience; it is *necessary* iff it is true in all possible worlds; it is *analytic* iff it is true by virtue of meaning. According to Kripke's and Putnam's "realist semantics," these categories differ not just in their intension, but also in their extension. Theoretical identifications like

(3) Water is H_2O

are both a posteriori, because they are discovered by science, and necessary. For natural kind terms (like proper names) are "rigid designators." In all possible worlds in which they pick out anything at all, they pick out the same thing, namely a substance with a particular microstructure (H_2O in our case), and that microstructure constitutes the *essence* of the natural kind.

With characteristic foresight, Quine had anticipated the essentialist implications of modal logic, yet he ridiculed the idea that philosophers can get essences into the hair-crosses of their intellectual periscopes. Ironically, instead of undermining modal logic, his warnings led to a revival of essentialism. What is more, this revival can appeal to Quine's own naturalism. Quine holds that philosophy must eschew necessity and essences because it is continuous with empirical science. But if some necessary truths – truths about the essence of things – are a posteriori, philosophy can be continuous with science precisely because it scrutinizes such essences.

This presupposes, however, that sense can be made of modal notions like that of possible worlds. In line with his general attack on intensions, Quine complained that there are no criteria for trans-world identity. The essential features of an individual are those which it possesses in all possible worlds in which it exists. But what determines who is who in different possible worlds? Another issue is the ontological status of possible worlds. According to the hyper-realism of David Lewis (1941–2001), possible worlds are just as real as the actual one. Each world is a self-contained space-time with no connection to any other world. According to Kripke's, by contrast, a possible world is a way this world might have been, it is something real yet abstract. And according to fictionalism, a possible world is a fiction, a totality of consistent representations. To say that it is possible that p is to say that there is a consistent description of a world according to which p. Reality attaches not to the unactualized possibilities themselves, but rather to our representations of them (see Baldwin 2001: ch. 6).

Irrespective of these difficulties, essentialism has led to a new genre, one in which metaphysical questions are answered by appeal to modal intuitions, intuitions about whether there is a possible world satisfying certain conditions. For instance, the question whether the mind is identical with the body is tackled by contemplating whether there is a possible world with "zombies," creatures physically identical to us but without any kind of mental life (Chalmers 1996).

Their metaphysical ambitions notwithstanding, all three projects remain faithful to the linguistic turn, insofar as they proceed through reflections on language. Quine's contribution to the investigation of reality lies in devising a canonical notation and in providing ontologically parsimonious formulations of scientific theories. For Strawson, the metaphysically fundamental categories are those that play a central role in our conceptual scheme as embodied in language. And although essentialism seeks to establish necessities which concern reality rather than our conceptual scheme, it identifies these through the workings of language, notably the rigid fashion in which proper names and natural kind terms designate. This is why Kripke and Putnam (1975) frequently appeal to "what we would say" about certain counterfactual situations, e.g. a "Twin Earth" on which a substance which shares all the surface properties of water turns out to have a chemical composition other than H_2O.

From language to mind

For logical positivism, Wittgenstein and linguistic philosophy language mattered because it provided a means of resolving philosophical problems. For logical atomism as well as for Quine and essentialism it matters because it provides a guide to the ontological constitution of reality. But the linguistic turn also encouraged an interest in language as a topic in its own right. From the 1960s onwards, *linguistic philosophy* was contrasted unfavorably with the *philosophy of language* (Searle 1969: 3–4; Dummett 1978: 441–3). Two differences were diagnosed. First, whereas philosophy of language is a *discipline* just like the philosophy of law or of religion, linguistic philosophy is a *method*, namely for the resolution of problems from all areas of philosophy. Second, linguistic philosophy was said to proceed by the piecemeal investigation of particular expressions or constructions, whereas proper philosophy of language was deemed to require a *systematic* account of language. Even among those eager to utilize linguistic analyses for the resolution of philosophical problems, many felt that without such an account these analyses lack a proper foundation.

The rise of philosophy of language thus understood reveals that the received contrast between ideal and ordinary language philosophy actually comprises two distinct conflicts. The first is between two different *aims*: while logical construction seeks to replace natural languages by artificial alternatives, both conceptual analysis and the new philosophies of language explore the workings of actual languages. The second is between two different *techniques* (which in turn are connected to different *perspectives on language*, see below): while formal approaches define terms and paraphrase sentences by translating them into an interpreted logical calculus, non-formal approaches explain words and paraphrase sentences by describing their role and their connections with other expressions from the vernacular.

Formal approaches are not confined to logical construction. For it is possible and indeed popular to treat formal calculi not as ideal languages which avoid the shortcomings of ordinary language, but as indicating the underlying "logical form" that sentences in the vernacular possessed all along. Thus Strawson (1971: 171–2) highlighted the "Homeric struggle" between formal semanticists, who treat language – natural languages included – as an abstract system of complex formal rules, and those who regard it primarily as a kind of human activity. Yet some figures straddle even this divide. This holds for Quine and his pupil Donald Davidson (1984). Both combine formal semantics with a pragmatist emphasis on language as a form of social human behavior. Whereas Quine is ultimately interested in artificial languages, however, Davidson has been the most eminent champion of a *theory of meaning for natural languages*. Before him, a theory of meaning was supposed to provide an analysis – in a suitably loose sense – of the concept of meaning (as in referential, verificationist and use theories of meaning). By contrast to such analytic theories, Davidson envisages a *constructive* theory which does not explain directly what meaning is. Instead, it generates for each sentence of a natural language a theorem that specifies its meaning. Such a theory is empirical; and actually to construct it is a task for linguistics. The philosopher's brief is to establish the requirements that such theories must fulfill. This is done by *Tractatus*-like reflections on the essential preconditions of language. Thus it is argued that speakers can produce and understand a potentially infinite number of sentences, and that this "semantic productivity" requires a "compositional" theory, one which displays the meaning of each sentence as determined by that of its components (drawn from a finite lexicon) and the mode of their composition.

Just as the *Tractatus* maintained that the hidden depth-structure of ordinary language is given by Russellian logic, Davidson maintains that it is given by Tarski's formal theory of truth. According to Davidson, a Tarskian truth-theory satisfies these requirements, because with a finite number of axioms it permits for each sentence of a language the derivation of a "T-sentence." For instance, a theory for German delivers

(4) "Schnee ist weiss" is true iff snow is white

Whereas Tarski tried to define *truth*, Davidson employs T-sentences to state the *meaning* of sentences by specifying the *conditions under which they are true*. Unlike

Tarski, Davidson is optimistic that such theories can be devised not just for formal but also for natural languages. He argues that they allow of empirical confirmation under conditions of "radical interpretation" (a variant of radical translation), namely, if one ascertains the conditions under which alien speakers assent to their own sentences.

According to Davidson's "principle of charity," it is a precondition of radical interpretation, and hence of linguistic understanding in general, that the interpretees hold beliefs which are by-and-large correct. On this assumption, a theory of meaning can answer questions about reality, since any interpretable language must have a logical form that mirrors the structure of reality. Thus Davidson seeks to demonstrate the existence of events by showing that certain inferential patterns of ordinary discourse ontologically commit us to events (1980: ch. 7). Michael Dummett's "anti-realism" (1978) also regards theories of meaning as a guide to metaphysical insights. Against Davidson's truth-conditional semantics, however, he maintains that the meaning of sentences is determined not by the conditions under which sentences are true, which are independent of our ability to decide whether they obtain, but by the conditions "which warrant their assertion."[2]

In another respect, Davidson and Dummett (1925–) are on the same side. Like many icons of mid-century analytic philosophy (Wittgenstein, linguistic philosophy, Quine, Sellars) they adopt a *third-person perspective* on language, holding that the meaning of words and sentences is determined by observable behavior. All of the aforementioned also tend to assign priority to language over thought. Both claims conflict with a powerful recent trend. The slogan that meaning is use came under scrutiny by Grice's theory of conversational implicatures. Paul Grice (1913–88) maintained that many of the patterns of linguistic use highlighted by conceptual analysts are semantically irrelevant, since they are due not to the meaning of specific expressions, but to pragmatic principles governing discourse in general (Grice 1989). Furthermore, a common theme in linguistic philosophy is that language is a form of intentional behavior. This suggested to Austin that the philosophy of language is a branch of the philosophy of action. Taking this proposal one step further, Grice and John Searle (1932–) turned it into a sub-domain of the philosophy of mind, by trying to reduce semantic notions to psychological ones like intention.

Gricean theories still hold that expressions derive their meaning from the use to which speakers put them. Approaches influenced by Noam Chomsky's "revolution in linguistics" shed any vestige of the commonsense idea that meaning and language are rooted in communication. Thus Jerry Fodor (1935–) argued that both the meaning of public languages and the intentionality of thought can be explained by a "language of thought" (Fodor 1975). *External* sentences are meaningful because they are correlated with *internal* symbols, sentence-like representations in the brain which also constitute our thoughts.

This reversal of the linguistic turn has turned the philosophy of mind into the perceived foundation of philosophy (see "Philosophy of mind," Chapter 12). Nevertheless the postwar flourishing of the subject received its initial impetus from Wittgenstein and Ryle. Running through the mainstream of modern philosophy is the idea that a person can be certain about his inner world of subjective experiences, but can at best infer how things are outside him. Subjective experience was conceived not only as the foundation of empirical knowledge, but also as the foundation of language: the meaning of words seems fixed by naming subjective experiences (impressions, sense-data, qualia, preconceptual contents), for example through inner ostension ("'pain' means *this*"). Wittgenstein's famous private-language argument undermines this assumption (1953: §§243–314). A ceremony of naming can only lay down standards for distinguishing between correct and incorrect uses of a term "S," and hence provide the latter with meaning, if it *can* be explained to and understood by others.

Wittgenstein explicitly does not exclude the possibility of a language spoken or even invented by a single speaker, but only of a language which cannot be understood by others because its "meanings" are private in principle. The fulcrum of his argument is neither a stipulation according to which the term "language" is confined to systems of communication, nor skepticism about memory. At issue is not whether the private linguist can remember what he means by "S," but whether he has managed to endow "S" with meaning in the first place. To this end, the putative naming ceremony would have to lay down a rule for the correct use of "S." But there is no such thing as a non-operational rule, one which cannot even in principle be used to distinguish between correct and incorrect applications. Yet the putative definition of the private linguist is non-operational. The private linguist's application of "S" at t_1 is incorrigible not just at t_1, it cannot even be corrected by him at t_2. For at t_2 nothing distinguishes the private linguist's rectifying a mistake by reference to a prior rule from his adopting a new rule. Justification consists in "appealing to something independent," and this is *ab initio* precluded in the case of a private language (1953: §265). Hence there can be no private ostensive definition in which a private impression functions as a sample.

Wittgenstein's attack on the Cartesian picture of mind and meaning was reinforced by Ryle's assault on the myth of the "ghost in the machine," the idea that perception and action are cases of an immaterial soul interacting with the physical world. Both of them distinguished between establishing the causal preconditions of mental phenomena, such as the firing of neurons, and the analysis of mental concepts, which specifies features that are *constitutive* of mental phenomena. Quinean naturalism fueled an opposing outlook, according to which the philosophy of mind is either continuous with or a branch of psychology, biology, or neuroscience. The widely accepted task is to *naturalize* mental phenomena, i.e. to show that they are fully explicable in the terms of physical science.

Wittgenstein's and Ryle's attacks on Cartesian dualism found favor. But their denial that mental terms refer to inner states which cause our outward behavior was repudiated, especially by "Australian materialists" such as U. T. Place (1924–2000), John Jamieson Carswell Smart (1920–), and David Armstrong (1926–) (see Baldwin 2001: 47–52, 201–3). And if these inner states are not irreducibly mental, they must be physical. The result was the mind/brain identity theory: the mind is identical with the brain and mental properties are identical with neurophysiological properties. The identity theory was not presented as a *semantic* or *analytic* reduction showing that mental concepts mean the same as terms referring to neurophysiological phenomena. Instead, it was put forward as a *scientific* or *synthetic* reduction based on a posteriori hypotheses. The identity of the mind with the brain is supposed to be a scientific discovery on a par with that of the identity of water with H_2O. In effect, however, the identity theory combined the conceptual claim that mental terms refer to inner states that cause behavior with the scientific claim that this causal role is played by certain neural states.

This combination soon came a cropper. As Putnam (1975: chs. 18–21) and Fodor (1974) pointed out, mental phenomena are *multiply realizable* through physiochemical phenomena, not just in principle (Martians, computers) but in fact, and not just across species. When different test persons solve one and the same problem, slightly different parts of the brain are activated. This led to a novel form of materialism. According to *functionalism*, mental states are functional states of a machine. What is constitutive of a mental phenomenon is not the particular physical process but the *causal role* or *function* that it performs, a role which could be realized or implemented in diverse physical states. Pain, for instance, can only be identified with the function of correlating a stimulatory input (e.g. injury) with a behavioral output (e.g. crying), not with the firing of specific neurons.

The mind/brain identity theory maintained that types of mental states are identical with *types* of neurophysiological states. Davidson's "anomalous monism" (1980) abandons this "type/type" identity: But it retains the idea that each "token," each instance of a mental state or event occurring in an individual, is identical with a particular neurophysiological event or state. Like functionalism, it also holds on to the idea that mental properties *supervene* on physical properties. While there can be a physical difference between individuals without *any* mental difference, there cannot be a mental difference without a physical difference.

Though hugely popular, functionalism faced objections on two fronts. At one end it was castigated for failing to do justice to the indelibly subjective nature of the mind. Thus Thomas Nagel (1974) and Frank Jackson (1986) argued that materialism in general and functionalism in particular cannot account for "qualia," the private feel of mental phenomena. At the other end, it was alleged that functionalism cannot explain intentionality, and in particular the content of our thoughts. Searle's Chinese room argument (1980) uses a thought-experiment in the style of conceptual analysis to show that the mere "syntactic" ability to produce an appropriate output of symbols in response to an input does not amount to genuine understanding or thought about the world, since it is present even in a system that merely simulates these achievements. Furthermore, so-called externalists denied that the content of an individual A's thoughts is exclusively determined by her intrinsic (mental or physiological) properties. Instead, what A thinks depends at least partly on facts "external" to, and often unknown to, A, facts about A's physical (Putnam 1975) or social (Burge 1979) environment. Two physically identical individuals might have different thoughts. When a physical duplicate of mine on Twin Earth thinks about the transparent, odorless, and potable liquid surrounding him, the content of his thoughts differs from mine: he cannot be thinking about water, since he is surrounded by XYZ rather than H_2O.

A radical, some would say desperate, reaction to the travails of existing variants of materialism is *eliminative materialism* (Churchland 1981). It treats our ordinary psychological beliefs and concepts as part of a theory – "folk psychology" – which is simply wrong and does not refer to real phenomena. Therefore folk psychology should be replaced by a more scientific, purely neurophysiological theory. Like Quine's nihilism about meaning, this is a form of *eliminative* naturalism. Statements which involve concepts that cannot be accommodated within natural science – notably about thought and meaning – are not *analyzed*, not even in the weaker sense of scientific reduction. Instead, they are simply *replaced* by naturalistically acceptable statements and notions.

Matters of value

For Moore, the question of how "good" is to be defined was the most fundamental problem of ethics. But his famous "open question" argument drove him to the conclusion that "good" is indefinable, since goodness is a simple quality which has no parts. Consider any definition of the form:

(5) Good is X.

(Candidates for "X" include "that which causes pleasure".) For any substitution for "X" – other than "good" itself – it is always an intelligible and in that sense "open" question whether (5) is true. Therefore, even if things which are X are in fact good, "X" cannot *mean* the same as "good" and hence cannot be used to define it. In particular, any attempt to define "good" in terms of natural properties is bound to fail, the contrary view being dubbed by Moore the "naturalistic fallacy" (1903: 10–16). Good is a non-natural simple property, to which we have access by a kind of rational *intuition*. Nevertheless, this property supervenes on natural properties: any two things with exactly the same natural properties would also have to be equally good.

Later analytic philosophers tended to accept Moore's conclusion that moral properties cannot be analytically defined in terms of natural ones, while rejecting his intuitionism. This led many to the conclusion that moral judgments are not descriptive and hence not strictly speaking truth-apt at all. According to the logical positivists, cognitively significant propositions are either analytic or a priori. But moral statements fit neither category. They concluded that moral statements are not cognitively significant, and that their real function is not to make factual claims but rather to express our emotions, in particular of approval or disapproval (Ayer 1936: ch. 6). This emotivism was supported by C. L. Stevenson (1908–79) on independent grounds (Stevenson 1944). According to him, it accounted for the fact that whereas descriptions of fact seem to be motivationally neutral, moral statements are intrinsically action-guiding: it would be odd to say "Φ-ing is the right thing to do, but I am in no way in favor of Φ-ing."

Emotivism runs the risk of reducing moral statements to interjections like "boo" and "hurrah," and to ignore the role that reason plays in moral argument. This shortcoming was addressed by R. M. Hare (1919–2002), the most influential moral philosopher among the Oxford conceptual analysts. According to Hare, moral statements are closer to imperatives than to avowals of emotions: their purpose is to guide action. But unlike imperatives they are universalizable: if one morally condemns a lie, one is committed to condemning all lies in circumstances of a similar kind. The question of whether the person making a moral statement can consistently desire this kind of universalization provides scope for reasoned argument, even though there are no moral facts.

Because of this last point, and in spite of its Kantian provenance, universal prescriptivism came to be lumped with emotivism under the heading of "non-cognitivism." Hare's work set the scene for the subsequent debate. In line with the linguistic turn, he initially restricted moral philosophy to "meta-ethics" – a second-order discipline which does not issue any moral claims but instead analyses moral concepts, examines the status of moral judgments and delineates the structure of moral argument. "Ethics, as I conceive it, is the logical study of the language of morals" (1952: v). H. L. A. Hart (1907–92) provided a comparable stimulus to legal and political theory (Hart 1962). He tried to avoid futile metaphysical disputes about the nature of obligations and rights through conceptual analysis. But under the influence of Wittgensteinian ideas he rejected the search for analytic definitions in favor of a more contextual elucidation of the role such concepts play in legal discourse.

Non-cognitivism was challenged in the first instance by conceptual analysts who cast doubt on its picture of moral discourse. Peter Geach (1916–) argued that it cannot do justice to the occurrence of moral statements in inferences, because the latter requires propositions that can be truth-apt. Later cognitivists set store by the fact that we ordinarily call moral judgments true or false and that moral discourse displays the full grammar and logic of assertions. Philippa Foot (1920–) and Mary Warnock (1924–) maintained that the sharp distinction between descriptive and prescriptive uses of language is untenable (on Foot, see "Twentieth-century moral philosophy," Chapter 20). Among the most pervasive moral concepts are "thick concepts" such as rudeness, concepts which include both descriptive and prescriptive elements. And Searle argued that by appeal to institutional facts it is after all possible to derive prescriptive from descriptive statements, an "ought" from an "is."

Putnam (1981) pointed in a similar direction when he insisted that the philosophy of science no longer supports the fact/value distinction, since scientific inquiry itself rests on norms. And John McDowell (1942–) and David Wiggins (1933–) urged a rethink of the non-cognitivist dichotomy of the subjective (expression, prescription) and the objective (description), by exploring the analogy between values and secondary qualities. Similarities between moral and perceptual judgments were also explored through a revival of intuitionism, especially in Britain under the label "particularism" (Dancy 2004).

At the same time, both non-cognitivism and intuitionism had to face a novel, methodological challenge. Can meta-ethical issues about the logic of moral discourse really be kept separate from substantive moral questions? For one thing, Hare himself moved from an allegedly neutral meta-ethics to a position which tries to draw substantive ethical conclusions from the nature of our moral concepts. For another, there were Quinean animadversions against distinguishing the analysis of concepts from the discovery of matters of fact (Harman 1977). Third, the 1960s and 1970s brought to the fore issues such as war, nuclear deterrence, abortion, civil disobedience, and the destruction of the natural environment. Many philosophers realized that these issues raise substantive moral questions that cannot be left to either religious dogma or political ideologies like Marxism. "Applied ethics" became the name of the attempt to deal with such specific moral issues in a cogent rational manner. Finally, the rebirth of normative ethics was completed by the realization that grand normative theory beyond conceptual analysis remained possible. John Rawls's A *Theory of Justice* (1971) was a compelling trend-setter (see "Twentieth-century political philosophy," Chapter 21). It marked the rise of political theory, hitherto neglected, within the analytic tradition. Rawls (1921–2002) argued that a principle of distributive justice can be justified by considering the kind of rules which agents ignorant of their future place within society should rationally opt for. Rawls also inspired a revival of the Kantian idea that there is such a thing as objective practical reasons for action, over and beyond the means–ends rationality stressed by Hume and also explored by decision theory, yet independent of any contentious ontology of moral facts.

These developments did not spell the end for meta-ethics, but instead led to an intertwining of meta-ethical and ethical discussions. Furthermore, the focus altered from specific moral notions to investigations into the nature of moral justification and the metaphysical status of values. Naturalism also reasserted itself at this level. One variant maintains that moral concepts can be accommodated within naturalism once we give up the misguided ambition of analyzing them. Moral predicates meet naturalistic demands because the properties they attribute – e.g. contributing to human flourishing – play a role in the best explanatory theories of empirical science (Boyd, Sturgeon), or because they are idealizations of psychological properties (Lewis, Harman). But there is also a contrasting, eliminative version of naturalism. According to Mackie's "error theory" (1977), moral concepts and judgments are indeed descriptive or factual. The trouble, according to Mackie, is that nothing corresponds to moral concepts in reality, which is purely physical, and that hence our moral judgments – all and sundry – are mistaken.

An equally iconoclastic attack on the very terms of moral debate was launched by neo-Nietzscheans such as Alasdair MacIntyre (1929–) and Bernard Williams (1929–2003). They suggested that philosophy is impotent to fill the moral gap left by the decline of religion. The demand for objective, rational, and impersonal validation unites all major positions in normative ethics. But, the neo-Nietzscheans urged, it is of dubious origins, unfeasible, and lacks sufficient credibility to sustain the project of a philosophical ethics. Although the neo-Nietzscheans are less infatuated with science than the naturalists, in one respect they point in a similar direction. Even as regards matters of value, the story goes, philosophy is not an autonomous discipline; rather, it needs to be supplemented by other modes of discourse, whether they be natural science, the social and historical sciences, or even art and religion.

The end of analysis?

Analytic philosophy has undergone a sea-change since its inception by Frege, Moore, and Russell. The major development has no doubt been the linguistic turn and its subsequent reversal, notably through the rise of naturalism and of subjectivist/mentalist approaches to mind and language. To many contemporary philosophers, conceptual analysis is out of date and out of touch with cutting-edge scientific philosophy. On closer inspection, however, the objections to it are far from conclusive.

The struggle between conceptual analysis and logical construction was originally fought on a common ground, namely the assumption that philosophical problems are rooted in conceptual/linguistic confusions. Conceptual analysts tried to resolve these problems not through substituting artificial terms and constructions for the idioms of natural languages, but by clarifying the latter. To logical constructionists, this appeared as a philistine cult of common sense and ordinary use, at the expense of scientific insights and terminology. Similarly, present-day cognitive and neuro-scientists complain that conceptual analysts like Searle and Hacker who criticize their philosophical conclusions prefer thought-experiments to real experiments, and that they set themselves up as "guardians of semantic inertia" (Gregory 1987: 242–3).

These complaints ignore that the term "ordinary use" is ambiguous (*mutatis mutandis* for "ordinary language"). It can either mean the *everyday use* of a term; or it can mean its *established use*, whether it be in common parlance or in technical forms of discourse with a tightly regimented vocabulary (Ryle 1971: ch. 23). Conceptual analysis does not extol the virtues of the mundane everyday over the sophisticated specialized employment of a term. Nor does it prohibit the introduction of technical terminology in either science or philosophy, as the case of Austin makes patently clear. Persistent misinterpretations notwithstanding, conceptual analysts have *refrained explicitly* from criticizing philosophical positions merely for employing novel terms or familiar words in ways that differ from the established patterns of use.

Rather, they insist that such novel terms or uses need to be adequately explained by laying down clear rules. They further allege that many metaphysical questions and theories – no matter whether propounded by philosophers or scientists – get off the ground only because they employ terms in a way which is at odds with their official explanations, and that they trade on deviant rules along with the ordinary ones. Thus Ryle insisted that linguistic philosophy is interested less in language as a system, than in the often slippery and equivocal uses to which it is put in the course of philosophical argument. Conceptual analysis is not linguistics masquerading as philosophy: it is a tool of critical thinking and a way of dealing with the quest for the essences of things that have been central to philosophy since Plato. In a similar vein, Wittgenstein tried to confront metaphysicians with a "trilemma": either their novel uses of terms remain unexplained (unintelligibility), or it is revealed that they use expressions according to incompatible rules (inconsistency), or their consistent employment of new concepts simply passes by the ordinary use – including the standard use of technical terms – and hence the concepts in terms of which the philosophical problems were phrased.

"If we are using the word 'to know' as it is normally used (and how else are we to use it?), then other people very often know when I am in pain" (Wittgenstein 1953: §246). According to the established rules, it makes perfectly good sense to say that I know that others are in pain. This suggests that the skeptic about other minds is like someone who claims that there are no physicians in London, since by "physician" he understands someone who can cure any disease within twenty minutes. His doubts either amount to an *ignoratio elenchi*, since they employ "knowledge" according to other rules than the knowledge-claims which these doubts purport to attack, or they simply manifest his repudiation of those rules (1958: 55ff.). But how could such a repudiation be justified? The established rules are unmistakably superior to those implicit in the skeptic's position, since they draw important distinctions – e.g. between more or less well-established beliefs or between more or less trustworthy informants – which he obliterates (see Glock 1996: 258–64, 336–41).

However, isn't the simplest way of avoiding such equivocations to abandon the old concepts altogether? Logical constructionists reasoned as follows: since philosophical confusions originate in natural languages, the recipe for avoiding them is to replace natural languages by artificial alternatives. Conceptual analysts replied that precisely because the problems originate in our actual conceptual framework, as ideal language philosophers granted, the introduction of a novel framework will merely sweep these problems under the carpet, *unless* its relation to the old concepts is properly understood (Strawson 1963).

One rejoinder to this last point is Quine's suggestion that clarity about *our actual* linguistic framework is best achieved by translating its constructions into a formal language. The "familiarity" of our ordinary idiom, Quine opines, "carries no presumption of clarity. It merely breeds contentment" (Hahn and Schilpp 1986: 228). This line is uncompelling. There is no reason whatever why the mere introduction of novel concepts could shed light on the old ones. One cannot understand how birds fly simply by constructing an airplane (Hacker 1996: 310n). Furthermore, if we can successfully apply and explain the terms of natural languages, this certainly creates a presumption of clarity.

It is more plausible to insist that this presumption is defeated by the fact that the ordinary use of terms like "true" leads to antinomies and paradoxes like that of the liar. The moot question, however, is whether the philosophical difficulties arise out of ordinary language as such, or out of its distortion and misunderstanding in the course of philosophical theorizing. Furthermore, it is downright mysterious how clarity might be achieved through the introduction of artificial alternatives, *if* natural languages were indeed irredeemably obscure or incoherent. For as Wittgenstein, Austin, and Quine himself have pointed out, ordinary language is the ultimate medium of explanation. In Austin's words, while "ordinary language is *not* the last word ... it *is* the *first* word" (1970: 185). All neologisms, those of science included, need to be explained. By pain of regress, this can ultimately be done only in terms of ordinary expressions which are already understood. These expressions we acquire not through explanation in terms of another language, but through training in basic linguistic skills. With respect to many purposes ordinary language is inferior to technical idioms. But it is *semantic bedrock*. It is only by acquiring ordinary language that we acquire the ability to learn and explain new and technical terms.

Science can and must develop its own terminology and conceptual apparatus. The explanation of perception, for instance, cannot be couched exclusively in everyday concepts, but must employ technical concepts from a variety of areas, ranging from psychology to biochemistry. Yet it is arguable that in presenting and interpreting the results of empirical research into perception, both philosophers and scientists do not stick to that technical terminology. Instead, they often employ everyday terms like "representation," "symbol," "map," "image," "information," or "language" in ways which either remain unexplained or illicitly combine their ordinary uses with technical ones (Bennett and Hacker 2003; Glock 2003a). This is no coincidence, moreover. Everyday statements like "Maria saw that Frank had put on weight," "Sarah listens to the *Eroica*," "One can smell the wild strawberries," "The sense of taste is not affected by old age," etc. pick out the *phenomena that the science of perception seeks to explain*.

Consider another philosophical problem that is hotly debated at present and intimately connected to thriving scientific research: Can non-human animals have a mind? The answer to this question depends not just on empirical findings about animal behavior, its physiological causes or its evolutionary emergence (no matter whether these stem from field studies in the wild or experiments in laboratories). It also depends on *what counts* as having a mind (as thinking, behaving intelligently, etc.), and on the circumstances under which mental properties can be ascribed to an organism. Even in these cases, which prima facie favor a hardnosed methodological naturalism, the distinctively philosophical task does not consist in collecting novel data, but in clarifying contested concepts and in spelling out their implications for the methods and results of scientific research. This is not to say that one needs a watertight definition of mental properties before cognitive ethology can begin to devise empirical theories. But such theory-formation inevitably presupposes a certain understanding of its subject area. Consequently it stands in need of being accompanied by reflections on the concepts which *determine* this subject area, concepts which are presupposed in specific research projects, methods, or conclusions from the special sciences. For these reasons it is a precondition of any sober approach to philosophical problems that it should pay attention to the established use of philosophically contested notions within their normal surroundings.

Whether such investigations will terminate in analytic definitions of concepts, i.e. definitions in terms of necessary and sufficient conditions, is another matter. Certain contemporary opponents of conceptual analysis have devoted themselves to a pastime invented by Wittgenstein. They take delight in pointing out that ever since Plato, philosophers have failed spectacularly to come up with convincing definitions of any but the most trivial concepts. Thus Fodor opines hyperbolically though not without some justice that "the number of concepts whose analyses have thus far been determined continues to hover stubbornly around none" (2003: 6; similarly Davidson 1996).

Nevertheless, we need not share such extreme pessimism. For one thing, it appears that even some central philosophical concepts allow of definitions, once one bids farewell to unjustified assumptions, e.g. that truth must be a relation between a truth-bearer and a truth-maker or that knowledge must be belief plus something else (Hyman 1999; Künne 2003). Other cases may indeed defy analytic definition. This does not mean, however, that it is either impossible or unnecessary to elucidate them. There are other perfectly respectable ways of explaining concepts. Nor are these confined to contextual definitions like the ones Frege gave for numerals or Russell for definite descriptions. In this context, Strawson has distinguished between "reductive" and "connective analysis" (1992: ch. 2). The former seeks to break down concepts and propositions into ultimate components. But the developments in the wake of the later Wittgenstein and of Quine cast doubt on the idea of ultimate components and a definite structure. Connective analysis, by contrast, abandons the analogy to chemical analysis. It is simply the description of the rule-governed use of expressions, and of their connections with other expressions by way of implication, presupposition, and exclusion. Connective analysis need not result in definitions, it can rest content with elucidating features which are constitutive of the concepts under consideration, and how they bear on philosophical problems and arguments. It is this kind of connective analysis which plays a role both in contemporary conceptual role semantics and in recent attempts to tackle metaphysical issues by way of conceptual analysis (Jackson 1998).

Meeting the naturalistic challenge

Even connective analysis, however, separates conceptual from factual issues, and the explanation of expressions from the investigation of reality. Until quite recently, most analytic philosophers have rejected such separations out of hand, by appeal to Quine's metaphilosophical naturalism. The naturalistic assimilation of philosophy to science is widely regarded as up-to-date and inevitable, a philosophical analogue to globalization. But Quine's actual arguments against the analytic/synthetic distinction are less compelling than commonly assumed.

As regards the semantic prong of his attack, the initial circularity charge merely shows that intensional notions like analyticity or meaning can only be explained by using other intensional notions, and hence cannot be reduced to purely extensional ones. It does not show that they are in any way obscure or illegitimate to begin with. To that end Quine maintains that "intensions" lack clear criteria of identity: there is no objective way of telling whether two expressions mean the same. Yet he himself grants that criteria of identity for intensions *could* be provided, *if* we could appeal to notions like analyticity, necessity, or synonymy: two predicates mean the same attribute, for example, if they are synonymous. Quine rejects that solution precisely because he repudiates these notions as unclear (1953: 4, 152; 1969: 19–23).

An argument that doesn't simply beg the question is in the offing only if Quine succeeds in establishing that meaning is indeterminate, *without* assuming from the outset that intensional notions are obscure. This is the task of the thesis of indeterminacy of translation. That thesis, however, is widely resisted by most contemporary naturalists, who are realists about meaning and intentionality and recoil from the nihilistic conclusion that there is no such thing as meaning. What is more, they are right to do so, since Quine's indeterminacy thesis relies on behavioristic and holistic assumptions about meaning which are unconvincing (see Glock 2003b: chs. 3, 7).

The epistemological prong of Quine's attack suggests that within scientific revolutions even definitions and analytic propositions can be abandoned. In Newtonian physics, for instance, "momentum" was defined as "mass times velocity." It soon turned out, moreover, that momentum is conserved in elastic collision. But with the acceptance of Einstein's Special Theory of Relativity a problem emerged. If momentum was to remain a conserved quantity, it could not be exactly equal to rest-mass times velocity. Consequently it was not only possible but rational for Einstein to revise the statement that momentum is equal to mass times velocity, in spite of the fact that this statement was originally a definition.

This case turns on the fact that before Einstein both "equals mass times velocity" and "is preserved in elastic collision" could be regarded as constitutive of the meaning of "momentum." Since the two seemed to coincide invariably, there was no need to decide which one of them should have an analytic status and which one should be regarded as empirical. When it was discovered that mass times velocity is not strictly preserved in elastic collision, Einstein accorded analytic status exclusively to "preserved in elastic collision," which amounts to partially redefining the term "momentum." Scientific revolutions of this kind illustrate that scientific concepts are frequently held in place by more than one connection (analytic proposition), and that both concepts and the analytic propositions that define them are subject to change rather than being immutable. It does not show that there is no dynamic distinction between conceptual and factual connections. For once the question of status arises, it is possible to distinguish between those connections which are then adopted as constitutive of meaning (conservation) and those which are abandoned (mass times velocity). With respect to specific scientific experiments or lines of reasoning, it is often possible to decide whether or not particular sentences are used empirically or as a definition.

The same goes for specific philosophical problems or arguments. Precisely *because* at present many of these are intertwined with scientific issues, it is imperative to disentangle the factual issues ascertained by empirical science from issues of a different kind. These include not just conceptual issues, but also fundamental moral and aesthetic convictions. It would be futile to pretend, for instance, that rational debate in medical ethics can proceed without distinguishing between conceptual questions (e.g. What should count as a person?), factual questions (e.g. What happens in cloning?), and moral questions (e.g. Can it be legitimate to design a person?). Behind the backs of their Quinean super-egos, even conscientious naturalists constantly need to draw distinctions of a kind which their official positions prohibit or at least cannot account for.

Though often derided at present, the image of philosophy promoted by conceptual analysts squares well with the actual practice of philosophers, naturalists included. Ironically, Quine himself is a case in point. Although he is fêted for having liberated the subject from the scourge of "armchair philosophy" (e.g. in Churchland 1986: 2-3), he was in practice himself of the armchair variety. He did not claim that philosophy is empirical because he had discovered scientific evidence which solves philosophical problems. Instead, his line of argument was purely a priori. He maintained that from a *logical* point of view there is no qualitative difference between empirical propositions and the allegedly necessary propositions of logic, mathematics, and philosophy. And in support of this claim he employed thought-experiments – notably in his argument for the indeterminacy of translation – which are totally removed from empirical evidence. In fact, his arguments are much closer to Descartes's hyperbolical doubts than to scientific research. This is no coincidence, moreover, since naturalism is itself a philosophical rather than a purely scientific thesis (see "Naturalism," Chapter 6).

Quine even came to recognize that there is a legitimate dichotomy between the analytic and the synthetic: "a sentence is analytic if *everybody* learns that it is true by learning its words" (1974: 79). According to Quine, this approximates the layperson's intuitive conception of analyticity. Yet he also insists that this conception does not have the epistemological and meta-philosophical importance traditionally accorded to it, and that, in fact, it lacks "explanatory value." The reason is that the distinction concerns only the acceptance of the sentences in question and hence does not capture an "enduring" trait of the truths thus "created" (1966: 113, 119–21).

Fortunately, this defect can be remedied by jettisoning the genetic element of Quine's definition. Whether a sentence counts as analytic should not depend on how it came to be accepted (whether it was accepted as part of language acquisition). Rather, it should depend on its *subsequent* status. What counts is whether in a linguistic community rejecting the sentence is generally regarded as a criterion of having failed to understand it.

Contrast the following two propositions:

(6) My five-year-old daughter understands Russell's theory of types.
(7) My five-year-old daughter is an adult.

To (6) we would typically react with *disbelief* and by demanding evidence. By contrast, we *fail to understand* (7) and will demand an explanation of what, if anything, the speaker means by an adult (Grice and Strawson 1956: 150–1). Our typical reaction to (6) is "I don't believe what you say" (provided that we take the statement to be in earnest), whereas our typical reaction to (7) is "I don't understand what you mean" (provided that we do not take it as shorthand for "My five-year-old daughter *behaves* like an adult"). This contrast is firmly established in our conceptual scheme. It is evident in the difference between terms like "doubt" and "incredible" on the one hand, terms like "misunderstanding" and "unintelligible" on the other, terms that have an established and clear use.

The sincere refusal to acknowledge an analytic proposition is a criterion *either* for not understanding at least one of its constituents, *or* for deliberately employing that constituent in a new sense. On this basis, one can define a class of propositions that one can label *analytic* or *conceptual*. A sentence s expresses an analytic proposition:

if a speaker x sincerely denies or rejects s, this shows *either* that x has failed to understand s, *or* that x is deliberately employing s in a novel sense.

Whether the resulting distinction has the significance traditionally bestowed upon it depends on what that significance is supposed to be. No workable distinction will accommodate all the disparate claims made by the various proponents of an analytic/synthetic distinction (see Bealer 1998). Nevertheless, the distinction introduced here is a legitimate and useful instrument of sober philosophizing.

Language revisited

Ironically, even the widespread repudiation of linguistic philosophy has done little to dampen analytic philosophy's preoccupation with language and semiotic (syntactic and semantic) themes. The reason is threefold. For one thing, the linguistic turn – especially as taken by the *Tractatus* – placed the nature of representation or intentionality at the center of philosophy. It thereby set the agenda for current theories of meaning and content. Furthermore, even the linguistic approach to this agenda remains pertinent. Whether or not it is prior to thought, language provides the paradigmatic and clearest case of intentionality, and willy-nilly shapes the discussion of the latter. Fodor's "language of thought hypothesis" is indicative of this schizophrenic situation. It extols the priority of private minds over public languages, while retaining the machinery and vocabulary (meaning, content) of logico-linguistic analysis, because it regards thought as a process of logical computations on internal sentences.

Even those who do not regard thoughts as sentences of a mental language continue to operate in a linguistic vein, by discussing the relation between thought/language and reality in semantic terms such as truth, reference, and meaning. When it comes to the philosophical elucidation of thought, moreover, not even the most ardent subjectivist can abstain from considering sentences. For it is through their linguistic expression alone that thoughts are amenable to intersubjective paraphrase and analysis into components. Finally, at least in practice most analytic philosophers not only concede that the analysis of concepts and the paraphrase of propositions constitutes an important *part* of philosophy (if only a propaedeutic one); they also accept the connection between concepts and propositions on the one hand, and the meaning of words and sentences on the other.

For these reasons, language, meaning, and concepts remain on the analytic menu, even outside the burgeoning fields of philosophy of language and of mind. One can distinguish three general approaches to these topics, which might be termed mentalism, Platonism, and pragmatism (all in a wide sense), since they place emphasis on, respectively, individual psychic/neurophysiological phenomena, abstract entities and systems, and intersubjective practices.

Mentalist approaches adopt an individualistic perspective on language. The fundamental linguistic phenomenon is the idiolect, the language of an individual rather than a shared public language. Furthermore, they play down or repudiate the commonsensical idea that language is a means of communication.

According to Noam Chomsky (1928–), a language is a "system of knowledge," a "state of the language faculty," which itself is an internal "component of the mind/

brain" of individuals (1988: 60). He calls languages in this sense "I-languages," and contrasts them with languages in the everyday sense, which he calls "E-languages." Note that this model is not just individualistic but psychologistic. An I-language is not the idiolect of an individual speaker; it is an internal state of the "mind/brain" which causally underlies that idiolect.

Chomsky's psychologistic conception entails that language has no essential connection with communication, and even less with shared norms of communication. It has the unpalatable (if openly acknowledged) consequence that English and Xhosa, for example, are not languages, and strictly speaking do not exist. Unfortunately, this deprives the study of language of its ultimate topic, which consists in patterns of inter-subjective linguistic behavior. To explain this behavior we may have to regard it as the exercise of a specific language faculty, and that faculty may depend on specific areas in the brain. But the faculty itself is a set of complex abilities possessed by speakers. To identify it with either the brain or a state of the brain is to confuse an ability with its vehicle, the physical mechanism or structure in virtue of which an individual has an ability (Kenny 1989: ch. 5). And to deny the existence of the exercise of the ability by appeal to the vehicle is to saw off the branch on which anyone talking about faculties, capacities, or abilities must be sitting.

Unsurprisingly, Chomsky's denial of any substantial link between language and communication has stretched the credulity even of admirers (e.g. Jackendoff 2002). It creates insurmountable difficulties for explaining the origins of language. There is no conceivable evolutionary explanation of why our hominid ancestors should have developed biologically costly neural structures simply in order to soliloquize or to run through the tree diagrams of a Chomskian phrase-structure grammar in silence. This point is all the more acute since these ancestors were social primates like us, with an immediate and pressing need for media of communication and coordination (see Greenspan and Shanker 2004). Furthermore, Chomsky describes "the language faculty" as an organ. But an organ, especially one that is not a physiological unit, had better have a function. Chomsky seems to acknowledge this point, since he describes language as a means for expressing thoughts. Yet it is difficult to see what principal purpose the expression of thoughts could serve, if not that of communicating.

Platonists for their part treat language as an abstract system that exists eternally in a realm beyond space, time, and causation, independently of either individual speakers or intersubjective practices. Thus for Lewis a language is an abstract entity that maps (sequences of) signs onto abstract meanings (1983: ch. 11). This has the equally unpalatable consequence that languages cannot emerge, undergo change. or die out (and *mutatis mutandis* for language per se). Neither mentalism nor Platonism conform to the established use of "language" that prevails both in ordinary parlance and in the linguistic sciences. Both introduce a new and entirely stipulative use of "language." Unfortunately, they are rarely explicit about this fact. Furthermore, even if the theoretical enterprises that motivate the introduction of a novel concept are legitimate, it is confusing to express that concept through a familiar term, one that serves the distinct and indispensable function of identifying the very topic of any study of language – whether scientific or philosophical.

Mentalist approaches to concepts suffer from similar shortcomings. They treat concepts as phenomena in the minds of individuals, entities or goings-on "in the head." Thus according to Fodor's high-profile representational theory of mind, concepts constitute a kind of "mental representation" and hence a "kind of mental particular" (Fodor 1998: 7, 22), "objects in the mind" of individuals that have causes and effects in the physical world (Fodor 2003: 13n). Representationalism comes in two versions. According to the traditional dualist one, these representations are mental images or words occurring in a private non-material realm. According to the contemporary physicalist version, they are ultimately neurophysiological phenomena, for instance patterns of neural firings that instantiate a computer program, as in Fodor.

The dualist version falls prey to criticisms by Frege and Wittgenstein: no mental images or words need cross my mind when I engage in conceptual thought, and those that do fail to determine the content of my thoughts. The physicalist version avoids some of these criticisms, since the representations it postulates are neurophysiological phenomena of which normal subjects cannot be aware. It inherits another difficulty, however. Both mental and neurophysiological particulars occur in different heads and are hence specific to individuals. Yet even Fodor accepts as one of the "non-negotiable conditions on a theory of concepts" that "concepts are *public*; they're the sorts of things people can, and do, *share*" (1998: 22, 28). For instance, different individuals may operate with the same concept of a dog. Fodor tries to overcome the difficulty by appealing to the distinction between type and token signs. According to Fodor, concepts are symbols of the language of thought; and what is shared between individuals are abstract concept-*types*, of which the neural particulars are *tokens*, i.e. concrete occurrences. When Sue and Joe both believe that dogs bark, Fodor maintains, in both brains there occur tokenings of the word-type "dog," i.e. neural word-tokens with the meaning "dog."

But this solution amounts to nothing other than a surreptitious recantation of the central mentalist claim about concepts, namely that they are particulars which form part of the causal order. For that claim applies *only* to the neural tokens, which are not shareable. At the same time, the non-negotiable constraint of shareability is satisfied *only* by the abstract types, which are not particulars. By Fodor's own lights, concepts cannot be particulars, whether mental or neural:

P_1 Concepts must satisfy the non-negotiable constraint of shareability.
P_2 Mental particulars cannot satisfy this constraint.
C   Concepts are *not* particulars.

Echoing Putnam's externalism about meanings we might say: "Any way you cut up the pie, concepts ain't in the head!" Even if patterns of neural firing could be symbolic representations (cf. Bennett and Hacker 2003: ch. 3.1; Glock 2003a), concepts cannot themselves be such representations, since they are among the kinds of things which representations represent or express. Like Chomsky's I-languages at a more general level, Fodor's token-concepts are charitably seen as phenomena that provide the *causal basis* for the possession and operation of concepts (the understanding and use of words); but such phenomena must be distinguished both from the *concepts themselves* and from their *possession*.

Such considerations carry no weight against Platonist accounts, since the latter treat concepts and meanings as abstract entities independent of goings-on in the minds or brains of individuals. Well-known arguments by Wittgenstein, Ryle, and Quine demonstrate that the meaning of an expression is neither the object it stands for, nor any kind of physical object. For one thing, failure to stand for an object does not render referring expressions meaningless; if it did, expressions like "Kant's first wife" could not make sense. For another, two expressions may refer to the same thing without having the same meaning. Finally, to identify the meaning of a word with its referent is to commit a category mistake – of reification. The referent of "Prince Charles's first wife" can die or weigh 60 kilos, yet its meaning cannot.

These arguments do not preclude, for example, the Fregean option that the meaning of an expression might be a sense, an abstract entity associated with it which is not its referent but a "mode of presenting" the referent. Unfortunately, the idea of a separate realm of abstract entities is contentious, and the question of how we can have access to such a realm remains shrouded in mystery. By a similar token, while Platonism does justice to the fact that concepts can be shared, it has difficulty in accounting for the role they play in the thought and action of flesh-and-blood creatures like ourselves. At a more specific level, it can be shown that *knowledge* of meaning is not acquaintance with an object, whether referent or sense. Whereas "A knows Willy Brandt" and "Willy Brandt is identical with Karl Frahm" jointly entail "A knows Karl Frahm," "A knows the meaning of 'superfluous'" and "The meaning of 'superfluous' is identical with the meaning of 'redundant'" do not entail, even jointly, "A knows the meaning of 'redundant'." Nor do they entail that there is an entity x such that "superfluous" means x and A knows x. "The meaning of s_1" does not designate a genuine object; it is equivalent to "what s_1 means." The "what" here is not a *relative* pronoun, as in "what s_1 is written on," but an *interrogative* pronoun (Latin *quid* rather than *quod*). It indirectly introduces a question, namely: "What does s_1 mean?" That s_1 has a meaning means that there is an answer to this question; that A knows the meaning of s_1 means that she can answer it; and that s_1 has the same meaning as s_2 means that the same answer can be given for both (see Austin 1970: 96–7).

Meaning, use, and rules

These ruminations lend credence to the pragmatist alternative. Its most striking manifestation has been Wittgenstein's dictum that the meaning of a word is "its use in the language" (1953: §43). The idea that meaning is use not only unites Wittgensteinians and Ordinary Language philosophers, it has also been accepted by some of their opponents, notably Quine, Davidson, and Dummett; furthermore, it informs the work of field-linguists and lexicographers. What is more, there are obvious arguments in its favor:

> *whether* an expression like "sesquipedalian" means something in a given language depends on whether it has an established use in a linguistic community;

what an expression means depends on *how* it can be used within that community;

we *learn* what an expression means by learning how to use it, just as we learn how to play chess not by associating the pieces with objects, but by learning how they can be moved.

In spite of its prima facie plausibility, however, the identification of meaning with use is problematic. Ironically, one reason is that while the uses of "meaning" and "use" overlap, they also diverge in important respects (Rundle 1990: chs. 1, 9–10). First, there are expressions which have a use, but no meaning, such as "tally-ho" and "abracadabra." Second, unlike its meaning, the use of a word can be unjustified, accompanied by gestures and reveal something about the speaker, etc., and even a *way of using* a word can be fashionable or die out. Third, two expressions may have the same meaning without having the same use, e.g. "cop" and "policeman." "Cop" does not mean "nasty policeman," it is explained in the same way as "policeman," and applied on the same grounds. Nor does it necessarily express hostility towards law-enforcement agents; it merely indicates that the word is employed in a certain social context.

This last difference indicates that not all aspects of the use of a term are relevant to its meaning. This leaves open a more modest pragmatist claim, however. Meaning does not determine use, yet use *determines* meaning, not causally, but logically, just as for Frege sense determines reference. While sameness of meaning coexists with difference of use, every difference in meaning is a difference in use. Given the use of a word, we can infer its meaning without further evidence, but not vice versa. One cannot tell from a dictionary explanation of "cop" whether the term is frequently used by British academics. By contrast, one can write the dictionary entry on the basis of a full description of the term's employment.

If use determines meaning, we can learn from the use of a word everything there is to its meaning; use remains the guide to meaning, and conceptual analysis a matter of investigating linguistic use. Some critics have protested that far from being determined by use, meaning antecedes use: speakers use expressions in a particular way *because* they have a particular meaning which is independent of that use. But we must distinguish between the use an individual speaker *a* makes of *e*, and the use that the linguistic community C makes of it. While *individual* use is *responsible* to meaning, *communal* use *constitutes* meaning. For expressions do not have an intrinsic meaning. Rather, human beings give them a meaning by explaining and applying them in a certain way (Wittgenstein 1958: 28).

A related complaint is that meaning cannot depend on use, since people often use words incorrectly. But the pragmatist contention is that the meaning of *e* is determined by its established use, not by its *misuse*. In this connection, Wittgenstein and Oxford conceptual analysts have emphasized the normative aspects of both meaning and use. This normative dimension is absent from behaviorist and causal theories of meaning; they also explain the meaning of an expression by reference to its use, yet their conception of use is purely causal. Leaving aside various complications, the meaning of a word is equated either with the conditions which *cause* a speaker to utter it, or with the *effects* which such an utterance has on hearers.

From different angles, Wittgenstein and Chomsky have subjected these theories to decisive criticism. The causes and effects of uttering an expression determine neither whether the expression has meaning, nor what meaning it has. The meaning of an expression is not identical with the conditions that determine whether or not it is uttered in specific situations, since that depends not just on its meaning, but on extrinsic factors. That few people would dare to call the Pope a "liar" is due not to the meaning of the term, but to social norms.

Similarly, whether an expression is meaningful and what meaning it has does not depend on either its actual or intended effect, whether on a particular occasion or in general. If I say "Milk me sugar!" this may well have the result that my hearers stare at me and gape. But it does not follow that this combination of words means "Stare at me and gape!" It doesn't even follow if this entertaining effect can be repeated. Indeed, it does not even follow if I utter these words with the *intention* of bringing about this reaction (Wittgenstein 1953: §§493–8).

The meaning of an utterance depends not on how it is actually used and understood, but on how it *ought* to be used and understood by members of a linguistic community. What is semantically relevant about the use of an expression is neither the causes nor the effects of its utterance, nor the intentions with which speakers utter it, but its *correct* use. According to normativists, the linguistic meaning of an expression is determined by semantic rules which lay down how it can be meaningfully used.

This idea also promises a middle way between the Scylla of epistemic naturalism and the Charybdis of ontological supernaturalism. Wittgenstein famously compared language to a game like chess. On the one hand, a chess-piece is a piece of wood that can be described by physics. On the other hand, one cannot explain what a chess-piece or what the game of chess is in purely physical terms. But the difference between a chess-piece and a simple piece of wood is not that the former is associated with an abstract entity or with a process in a separate mental realm. Rather, it is that there are rules for its use (see 1953: §108). The chess-piece has a role in a rule-guided practice. That practice in turn presupposes agents with special and distinctively human capacities. But while these capacities cannot be adequately characterized in physical terms, they do not transcend the natural world. They are perfectly intelligible features of animals of a unique kind; and their causal prerequisites and evolutionary emergence can be explained by science.

The view that language is governed by rules has been a commonplace at least since Aristotle observed that words have their meaning by convention. It is enshrined in disciplines like grammar (irrespective of whether it be prescriptive, descriptive, or generative), logic (irrespective of whether Aristotelian or Fregean), and formal semantics. It is central to speech-act theorists and Wittgensteinians who regard language as a form of behavior. Thus John Searle writes: "speaking a language is to engage in a rule-guided form of behavior. To put it more briskly, talking is performing acts according to rules" (1969: 22). It is equally shared by philosophers who regard language primarily as a formal system. According to David Lewis, it is a "platitude – something only a philosopher would dream of denying" that language is governed by conventions (1983: 166).

For all that, individualists such as Chomsky and Davidson have attacked the very idea that language is rule-governed, including the idea of semantic or lexical rules that determine the meaning of words. Thus Davidson contends that "the yearning for [linguistic] norms is a nostalgic hangover from the dependence on a Platonic conception of meaning" (1994: 145).

There is a straightforward normative dimension to meaning, however. Because of what words mean, some of their applications are correct while others are incorrect. It is correct to call an unmarried, unwidowed, adult male a bachelor, a male duck a drake, or the Kremlin red; it is incorrect to call a married man a bachelor, a female duck a drake, or the Taj Mahal red, because of what the terms "bachelor," "drake," and "red," respectively, mean. Meaningful expressions possess conditions of correct application or of correct use (see Glock 2005).

There are three individualist objections against normativism. The first is that we are dealing here merely with "descriptive facts" concerning linguistic behavior (Davidson 1994: 146). Now, it is true that a proposition like

(8) In English, it is correct to apply "drake" to an object x iff x is a male duck

states a fact about the behavior of Anglophones. But it does so only because the Anglophone speech community accepts a certain norm, a standard of correctness. We must distinguish between (8), which is an empirical proposition to the effect that a community follows a norm, what von Wright calls a "norm-proposition" (1963: viii), from the expression of the norm itself, as in:

(9) It is correct to apply "drake" to an object x iff x is a male duck.

Like a definition of "drake," (9) can be used to explain what the term "drake" means, and it does so by laying down *conditions* for its correct application (whether it *actually applies* depends on whether x satisfies these conditions).

Correctness is a normative notion par excellence, since it signifies that something is in accordance with an acknowledged standard. However, the individualist has a second objection in store. Even if (9) is normative, it is not a rule, since it does not guide behavior (Glüer and Pagin 1999). It does not oblige or even entreat us to apply the term "drake" to an object in a particular situation.

This second complaint is based on an unduly narrow conception of what counts as a rule. For one thing, it ignores the "definitory aspect of rules" (Baker and Hacker 1984: 259). Some rules do not prescribe a certain form of behavior, but instead lay down what a thing must be like to satisfy a certain description. Prime examples are the beloved EU norms concerning, for instance, what counts as a sausage. This point is connected to a well-known distinction between regulative and constitutive rules (Searle 1969: ch. 2.5). The former specify how one should optimally pursue an activity that can be specified independently of the rule; the latter are partly definitive of the activity in question. What goes on at dinner parties can be described as eating independently of the rules of etiquette. By contrast, what goes on when people move certain pieces across a board cannot be described as castling, checking, mating, or, more generally, as playing chess, independently of rules such as "The king cannot castle out of a check" or "The king is mated if it is in check in such a way that no move will remove it from being in check." This contrasts with a regulative rule of chess like "Do not relinquish control of the center." Even someone who disregards all of these regulative rules does not cease to play chess; he will just play chess badly.

It can hardly be in doubt that constitutive rules form a paradigmatic type of rule or norm. Furthermore, the fact that they do not prescribe the use of a word does not entail that they play no role in guiding behavior. We can appeal to norms like (9) in justifying or criticizing a particular use of an expression. If I am challenged why I call Donald Duck a drake I can defend myself by saying that Donald is a male duck and that male ducks are called drakes. For another, they function as transformation or inference rules. Thus (9) licenses the inference from, e.g., "Donald is a male duck" to "Donald is a drake" and vice versa.

One of the main arguments in favor of a normativist conception of language is that linguistic utterances are subject to both regulative and constitutive rules in the same way as chess moves. Someone who calls his superior an "idiot," or who provides lengthy explanations when he requires urgent help is imprudent, but he does not commit a linguistic mistake. By contrast, someone who violates rules of syntax, e.g. by failing to conjugate properly, or lexical rules, e.g. by calling an ambiguous statement ambidextrous, commits a linguistic mistake.

It might be thought that the analogy with games fails, on the grounds that someone who violates a constitutive rule of chess is no longer playing chess, while someone who violates the alleged constitutive rules of English, for example, is still speaking English. But this objection is dubious on both grounds. It is implausible to insist that a game involving a single incorrect move no longer counts as chess, just as it is implausible to insist that the medieval board game was not really chess because the pawns could not move two squares at a time in their first move. Conversely, although someone who commits a mistake may still be said to be speaking English, the mistake itself does not count as English. It is quite common to react to a serious mistake by saying "That's not English!" And someone who commits too many such mistakes won't be speaking English. What is true is that the margins of tolerance are wider and looser in the case of natural languages than in the case of chess, for the simple but important reason that the constitutive rules of natural languages do not form a precise and stable system.

Failure to appreciate this fact underlies a final individualist objection. Followers of Davidson and Chomsky rightly note that "if no two speakers ever share the very same vocabulary items or observe exactly the same rules of grammar there will be no formally precise, syntactic and semantic characterization of the language spoken by a given community" (Smith 1998). And from this they conclude that no two individuals ever share a language and that all there is are different idiolects. The crucial assumption of this reasoning is that languages are individuated by such formally precise characterizations. But this is clearly not how natural languages such as Basque or Mandarin are actually individuated. Not every divergence in linguistic use amounts to a difference in idiolects. Someone who persistently says that it is raining whenever it is raining diverges from the common pattern of speech. But he does not speak an idiolect, he is simply an idiot. Similarly, the fact that Americans do not use the sentence "God save the Queen!" does not show that their language is impoverished, since the rules of American English allow for the construction of that sentence no less than those of British English; it shows rather that their political system differs from the British. Nor did the British alter their language when they stopped using "God save the King!" in 1952. The current anti-normativist vogue in analytic philosophy is symptomatic of a reluctance to come to terms with social and historical practices that go beyond individual behavior as well as individual brains.

Whither analytic philosophy?

When it comes to recognizing language as an intersubjective and historical practice, the hermeneutic tradition has the edge over analytic philosophy. To their credit, quite a few contemporary practitioners are both willing and capable of learning from so-called "Continental philosophy." There have also been a handful of thinkers who have tried to synthesize the two in a more sustained manner, such as Georg Henrik von Wright (1916–2003), Robert Brandom (1950–), Dagfinn Føllesdal (1932–), Ernst Tugendhat (1930–), and Hubert Dreyfus (1929–). Furthermore, in the course of graduating from a revolutionary movement into the philosophical establishment, analytic philosophy has become so diverse as to lose its distinctive profile (von Wright 1993: 25). As a result of rapprochement on the one hand and diversification on the other, the very idea of analytic philosophy has come under fire. There have been persistent rumors about analytic philosophy being in crisis or even defunct (e.g. Biletzki and Matar 1998: xi; Leiter 2004: 1). A sense of crisis is palpable not only among commentators but also among some leading protagonists. Thus both Putnam and Jaakko Hintikka (1929–) have called for a revitalization and renewal of analytic philosophy. Small wonder that those more hostile to analytic philosophy, notably Richard Rorty (1931–2007) (see Rorty 1979), for some time clamored for its replacement by a "post-analytic philosophy" (Rajchman and West 1985).

At the same time, in terms of the sociology of science analytic philosophy has become the dominant force within western philosophy (Searle 1996: 1–2). It has prevailed for several decades in the English-speaking world and in Scandinavia; it is in the ascendancy in Germanophone countries; and it has made significant inroads even in places once regarded as hostile, such as France. For better or worse, the threat facing analytic philosophy is not defeat by a new philosophical paradigm, but turning into an ill-defined mainstream without serious competitors.

Even this threat should not be overestimated, however. The division of western philosophy into analytic and Continental streams has been deplored by leading analytic philosophers such as Dummett and Putnam, and may indeed be deplorable. For all that, it remains real. The labels "analytic" and "Continental" philosophy continue to be widely used. This holds even when it is suggested that the distinction is not a hard and fast one. In reviews, for instance it is absolutely standard to read not only that a book or author is typical of either the analytic or Continental movement, but also that X is unusually sensitive or open minded "for an analytic philosopher" or that Y uncharacteristically clear or cogent "for a Continental thinker." What Grice and Strawson (1956) pointed out decades ago about the term "analytic proposition" holds equally of the terms "analytic philosophy." Although there may not be a clear and compelling explanation, we by-and-large agree in our application of these terms. Furthermore, we agree not just on what the clear cases are, but also on what count as borderline cases. Finally, the agreement is not based on a list but can be extended to an open class of new cases. There is no gainsaying the fact that the idea of a distinct analytic philosophy continues to shape the institutional practice of philosophy, whether it be through distinct journals, societies, job advertisements, or institutes.

Contemporary analytic philosophy is in danger of turning into an increasingly scholastic academic industry. This shows itself in, among other things, the focus on a very narrow range of issues and authors in what are regarded as the leading journals, a general disinclination to explain why these issues and authors are important, the tendency to treat many fundamental issues as settled once and for all, and a predilection for technicalities irrespective of their usefulness. Finally, there is a general attitude that those who do not conform to these various standards and preconceptions, those who dissent from the naturalistic orthodoxy or demand explanations of an established jargon, for example, are simply unprofessional.

In my view, however, the remedy for these defects does not lie in turning towards Continental or post-analytic philosophy. Instead, it lies in recovering some of the virtues of twentieth-century analytic philosophy. A cherished self-image of analytic philosophy notwithstanding, the inspirational figures from its past have not bequeathed us a series of indisputable demonstrations. But they have shown us how one can question deep-seated assumptions and resolve tempting confusions in a way that is striking, innovative, and illuminating; they have also shown us how one can broach complex problems in a manner that is clear, profound, and honest. At its best, analytic philosophy conforms to Russell's ideal of "cold steel in the hand of passion" (Monk 1996: 262). At a time when economic dogmas and conflicting religious ideologies are ruling the planet with devastating effects, analytic philosophy might even have beneficial effects in a wider sphere, provided that it is used to slay a few intellectual monsters.

Notes

1 But whether there is an ultimately satisfactory way of blocking the logical and set-theoretic paradoxes remains a contentious issue. The feasibility of reducing numbers to sets is questioned in Paul Benaceraf's influential article of 1965.

2 They further disagree on how to deal with a problem confronting any explanation of sentence-meaning in terms of truth, verification, or assertion, namely non-declarative sentences. Dummett, in accordance with the mainstream of formal semantics, distinguishes in each utterance a "sense-conveying component" or "propositional content clause" and a "force-indicator" or "mood indicator." The former is common, e.g. to the assertion "The door is open," the command "Open the door," and the question "Is the door open?" and it has truth-conditions. The latter determines that the three utterances have different illocutionary force. Davidson, by contrast, tries to account for non-declarative sentences without distinguishing between reference, sense, and force (see Glock 2003a: 159–65; and "Philosophy of Language," Chapter 9).

References

Austin, J. L. (1970) *Philosophical Papers*. Oxford: Oxford University Press.

Ayer, A. J. (1936) *Language, Truth and Logic*. Harmondsworth: Penguin, 1971).

Baker, G. and P. M. S. Hacker (1984) *Language, Sense and Nonsense*. Oxford: Blackwell.

Baldwin, T. (2001) *Contemporary Philosophy: Philosophy in English since 1945*. Oxford: Oxford University Press.

Bealer, G. 1998 "Analyticity." In E. Craig (ed.) *The Routledge Encyclopedia of Philosophy*, London: Routledge, vol. 1, pp. 234–39.

Beck, L. (ed.) (1962) *La Philosophie analytique : Cahiers de Royaumont IV*. Paris: Éditions de Minuit.

Benacerraf, P. (1965) "What numbers could not be." *Philosophical Review* 74: 47–73.

Bennett, M. and P. M. S. Hacker (2003) *Philosophical Foundations of Neuroscience*. Oxford: Blackwell.

Biletzki, A. and A. Matar (eds.) (1998) *The Story of Analytic Philosophy*. London: Routledge.

Burge, T. (1979) "Individualism and the mental." *Midwest Studies in Philosophy* 4: 73–121.

Carnap, R. (1928) *Der logische Aufbau der Welt*. Translated by R. A. George as: *The Logical Structure of the World and Pseudoproblems in Philosophy*, Berkeley: University of California Press, 1969.

—— (1936) "Die Methode der logischen Analyse." In *Actes du huitième Congrès international de philosophie* (Conference in Prague, September 2—7, 1934). Prague: Orbis, pp. 142–5.

—— (1937) *The Logical Syntax of Language*. London: Routledge & Kegan Paul.

—— (1956) *Meaning and Necessity*. Chicago: Chicago University Press.

—— (1963) "Intellectual autobiography." In P. Schilpp (ed.) *The Philosophy of Rudolf Carnap*, La Salle, IL: Open Court, pp. 1–84.

Carnap, R., H. Hahn and O. Neurath (1929) *Wissenschaftliche Weltauffassung: der Wiener Kreis*. Translated as: *The Scientific Conception of the World: The Vienna Circle*, Dordrecht: Reidel, 1973.

Chalmers, D. (1996) *The Conscious Mind*. Oxford: Oxford University Press.

Chomsky, N. (1988) *Language and Problems of Knowledge*. Cambridge, MA: MIT Press.

Churchland, P. M. (1981) "Eliminative materialism and the propositional attitudes." *Journal of Philosophy* 78: 67–90.

Churchland, P. (1986) *Neurophilosophy*. Cambridge, MA: MIT Press.

Dancy, J. (2004) *Ethics without Principles*. Oxford: Oxford University Press.

Davidson, D. (1980) *Essays on Actions and Events*. Oxford: Oxford University Press.

—— (1984) *Inquiries into Truth and Interpretation*. Oxford: Oxford University Press.

—— (1994) "The social aspect of language." In B. McGuinness and G. Oliveri (eds.) *The Philosophy of Michael Dummett*, Dordrecht: Kluwer, pp. 1–16.

—— (1996) "The folly of trying to define truth." *Journal of Philosophy* 93: 263–78.

Dummett, M. A. E. (1978) *Truth and Other Enigmas*. London: Duckworth.

Ewing, A. C. (1937) "Meaninglessness." *Mind* 46: 347–64.

Feyerabend, P. (1975) *Against Method*. London: Verso.

Fodor, J. (1974) "Special sciences." *Synthèse* 28: 77–115.

—— (1975) *The Language of Thought*. New York: Crowell.

—— (1998) *Concepts: Where Cognitive Science Went Wrong*. Oxford: Oxford University Press.

—— (2003) *Hume Variations*. Oxford: Oxford University Press.

Glock, H. J. (1996) *A Wittgenstein Dictionary*. Oxford: Blackwell.

—— (2003a) "Neural representationalism." *Facta Philosophica* 5: 147–71.

—— (2003b) *Quine and Davidson on Language, Thought and Reality*. Cambridge: Cambridge University Press.

—— (2003c) "Strawson and analytic Kantianism." In *Strawson and Kant*, Oxford: Clarendon Press, pp. 15–42.

—— (2005) "The normativity of meaning made simple." *Proceedings of GAP 5*, Paderborn: Mentis.

—— (2008) *What is Analytic Philosophy?* Cambridge: Cambridge University Press.

Glüer, K. and P. Pagin (1999) "Rules of meaning and practical reasoning." *Synthèse* 118: 207–27.

Greenspan, S. I. and S. G. Shanker (2004) *The First Idea*. Cambridge, MA: Da Capo Press.

Gregory, R. L. (1987) "In defense of artificial intelligence – a reply to John Searle." In C. Blakemore and S. Greenfield (eds.) *Mindwaves*, Oxford: Blackwell, pp. 235–44.

Grice, H. P. (1989) *Studies in the Way of Words*. Cambridge, MA: Harvard University Press.

Grice, H. P. and P. F. Strawson (1956) "In defense of a dogma." *Philosophical Review* 65: 141–58.

Hacker, P. M. S. (1996) *Wittgenstein's Place in Twentieth-Century Analytic Philosophy*. Oxford: Blackwell.

Hahn, L. E. and P. A. Schilpp (eds.) (1986) *The Philosophy of W. V. Quine*. La Salle, IL: Open Court.

Hare, R. M. (1952) *The Language of Morals*. Oxford: Oxford University Press.

Harman, G. (1977) *The Nature of Morality*. Oxford: Oxford University Press.

Hart, H. L. A. (1962) *The Concept of Law*. Oxford: Oxford University Press.

Hempel, C. G. (1950) "The empiricist criterion of meaning." In A. J. Ayer (ed.) *Logical Positivism*, New York: Free Press, 1959, pp. 108–29.

Hyman, J. (1999) "How knowledge works." *Philosophical Quarterly* 49: 433–51.

Jackendoff, R. (2002) *Foundations of Language*. Oxford: Oxford University Press.

Jackson, F. (1986) "What Mary didn't know." *Journal of Philosophy* 83: 291–5

—— (1998) From Metaphysics to Ethics: A Defence of Conceptual Analysis. Oxford: Clarendon Press.

Kenny, A. J. P (1989) *The Metaphysics of Mind*. Oxford: Oxford University Press.

Kripke, S. A. (1980) *Naming and Necessity*. Oxford: Blackwell.

Kuhn, T. (1970) [1962] *The Structure of Scientific Revolutions*. Chicago: University of Chicago Press.

Künne, W. (2003) *Conceptions of Truth*. Oxford: Oxford University Press.

Langford, C. H. (1942) "The notion of analysis in Moore's philosophy." In P. A. Schilpp (ed.) *The Philosophy of G. E. Moore*. La Salle, IL: Open Court, pp. 321–42.

Leiter, B. (ed.) (2004) *The Future for Philosophy*. Oxford: Oxford University Press.

Lewis, D. (1983) *Philosophical Papers*, vol. 1. Oxford: Oxford University Press.

Mackie, J. (1977) *Ethics: Inventing Right and Wrong*. Harmondsworth: Penguin.

Monk, R. (1996) *Bertrand Russell: The Spirit of Solitude*. New York: Free Press.

Montefiori, A. and B. Williams (1966) *British Analytical Philosophy*. London: Routledge & Kegan Paul.

Moore, G. E. (1903) *Principia Ethica*. Cambridge: Cambridge University Press.

Nagel, E. (1936) "Impressions and appraisals of analytic philosophy in Europe." *Journal of Philosophy* 33: 5–24, 29–53.

Nagel, T. (1974) "What is it like to be a bat." *Philosophical Review* 83: 435–50.

Popper, K. R. (1934) *Die Logik der Forschung*. Tübingen: Mohr. Translated as: *The Logic of Scientific Discovery*, London: Hutchinson, 1959.

Putnam, H. (1975) *Mind, Language and Reality: Philosophical Papers*, vol. 2. Cambridge: Cambridge University Press.

—— (1981) *Reason, Truth and History*. Cambridge: Cambridge University Press.

Quine, W. V. O. (1953) *From a Logical Point of View*. Cambridge, MA: Harvard University Press, 1980.

—— (1960) *Word and Object*. Cambridge, MA: MIT Press.

—— (1966) *Ways of Paradox and Other Essays*. Cambridge, MA: Harvard University Press, 1976.

—— (1969) *Ontological Relativity and Other Essays*. New York: Columbia University Press.

—— (1974) *The Roots of Reference*. La Salle, IL: Open Court.

Rajchman, J. and C. West (eds.) (1985) *Post-Analytic Philosophy*. New York: Columbia University Press.

Rawls, J. (1973) *A Theory of Justice*. Oxford: Clarendon Press.

Rorty, R. (1979) *Philosophy and the Mirror of Nature*. Princeton, NJ: Princeton University Press.

—— (ed.) (1967) *The Linguistic Turn*. Chicago: University of Chicago Press.

Rundle, B. (1990) *Wittgenstein and Contemporary Philosophy of Language*. Oxford: Blackwell.

Ryle, G. (1949) *The Concept of Mind*. London: Hutchinson.

—— (1971) *Collected Essays*, vol. 2 London: Hutchinson.

Searle, J. (1969) *Speech Acts*. Cambridge: Cambridge University Press.

—— (1980) "Minds, brains and programmes." *Behaviour and Brain* 3: 450–6.

—— (1996) "Contemporary philosophy in the United States." In N. Bunnin and E. P. Tsui-James (eds.) *The Blackwell Companion to Philosophy*, Oxford: Blackwell, pp. 1–24.

Smith, B. (1998) "Language, conventionality of." in E. Craig (ed.) *The Routledge Encyclopedia of Philosophy*, London: Routledge, vol. 5, pp. 368–71.

Stebbing, L. S. (1932–3) "The method of analysis in metaphysics." *Proceedings of the Aristotelian Society* 33: 65–94.

Stevenson, C. L. (1944) *Ethics and Language*. New Haven, CT: Yale University Press.

Strawson, P. F. (1952) *Introduction to Logical Theory*. London: Methuen.

—— (1959) *Individuals*. London: Methuen.

—— (1963) "Carnap's views on constructed systems vs. natural languages in analytic philosophy." in P. Schilpp (ed.) *The Philosophy of Rudolf Carnap*, La Salle, IL: Open Court, pp. 503–18.

—— (1971) *Logico-Linguistic Papers*. London: Methuen.

—— (1992) *Analysis and Metaphysics*. Oxford: Oxford University Press.

Stroll, A. (2000) *Twentieth-Century Analytic Philosophy*. New York: Columbia University Press.

Stroud, B. (1968) "Transcendental arguments." *Journal of Philosophy* 65: 241–56.

Urmson, J. O. (1956) *Philosophical Analysis: Its Development between the Wars*. Oxford: Oxford University Press.

von Wright, G. H. (1963) *Norm and Action*. London: Routledge & Kegan Paul.

—— (1993) *The Tree of Knowledge*. Leiden: Brill.

Wisdom, J. (1934) "Is analysis a useful method in philosophy?" *Proceedings of the Aristotelian Society, Supplementary Volume 13*: 65–89. Repr. in *Philosophy and Psycho-Analysis*, Oxford: Blackwell, 1953, pp. 16–35.

Wittgenstein, L. (1922) *Tractatus Logico-Philosophicus*. London: Routledge & Kegan Paul, 1961.

—— (1953) *Philosophical Investigations*, trans. G. E. M. Anscombe. Oxford: Blackwell. Repr. 1967.

—— (1958) *Blue and Brown Books*. Oxford: Blackwell.

Further reading

Beaney, M. (2003) "Analysis." In *The Stanford Encyclopedia of Philosophy (Summer 2003 Edition)*, ed. E. N. Zalta. <http://plato.stanford.edu/archives/sum2003/entries/analysis/>. (A very good survey of different conceptions and styles of analysis both inside and outside the analytic tradition).

Biletzki, A. and A. Matar (eds.) (1998) *The Story of Analytic Philosophy*. London: Routledge. (Essays from very diverse angles on the history, the character and the future of analytic philosophy).

Dummett, M. A. E. (1993) *The Origins of Analytic Philosophy*. London: Duckworth. (An important starting point of recent debates about analytic philosophy. Dummett stresses the non-Anglophone roots, and argues that analytic philosophy started with Frege and is characterized by taking a linguistic turn).

Glock, H. J. (2008) *What is Analytic Philosophy?* Cambridge: Cambridge University Press. (The book looks not just at the historical roots, but also at what analytic philosophy and the analytic/Continental divide currently amount to. It considers the pros and cons of various definitions of analytic philosophy, and tackles the methodological, historiographical, philosophical, and cultural issues raised by the issue).

Hacker, P. M. S. (1996) *Wittgenstein's Place in Twentieth-Century Analytic Philosophy*. Oxford: Blackwell. (Illuminates Wittgenstein's central role in the development of analytic philosophy. But it also discusses the origins, the nature and the contours of the analytic tradition).

Preston, A. (2007) *Analytic Philosophy: The History of an Illusion*. London: Continuum. (Argues that analytic philosophy is not a proper philosophical movement, since it is not held together by shared doctrines).

Soames, S. (2003) *Philosophical Analysis in the Twentieth Century*, 2 vols. Princeton, NJ: Princeton University Press. (Places special emphasis on the philosophy of language and the contribution of American authors such as Quine and Kripke).

Stroll, A. (2000) *Twentieth-Century Analytic Philosophy*. New York: Columbia University Press. (A sympathetic historical survey of analytic philosophy, with special emphasis on Moore).

Urmson, J. O. (1956) *Philosophical Analysis: Its Development between the Wars*. Oxford: Oxford University Press. (The first survey of the analytic movement).

von Wright, G. H. (1993) *The Tree of Knowledge*. Leiden: Brill. (Includes very knowledgeable essays about the nature of analytic philosophy by one of its prime practitioners).

3

HEGELIANISM IN THE TWENTIETH CENTURY

Terry Pinkard

At his rather sudden death in 1831, Georg Wilhelm Friedrich Hegel (1770–1831) occupied the heights of fame and authority in German philosophy; however, within only a few years, that authority had almost entirely dissipated, and for the remainder of the nineteenth century Hegelianism settled into being a minor strand in the development of German philosophy. Hegelianism started to make a comeback at the very beginning of the twentieth century when new critical editions of his work began to be prepared and when important figures such as Wilhelm Dilthey (1833–1911) produced studies on Hegel's intellectual development, partly to serve as exemplars of their own views about what was at stake in the humanities (by then called the *Geisteswissenschaften*). In Britain, there was a flowering of the "British Idealists" at the end of the century — some called them "British Hegelians" — and virtually all of those British Idealists saw themselves as engaged in something like a common project with Hegel and the Hegelians. In the United States, figures such as Josiah Royce (1855–1916) at Harvard championed a form of idealism that also saw itself related to Hegelianism. In almost all other European countries in the nineteenth century, Hegelianism had its defenders, and its influence was felt, even if it did not enjoy in those other places the high status enjoyed by Hegel's exponents among the British Idealists.

By the early years of the twentieth century, however, Hegelianism's authority evaporated once again, with almost the same rapidity as the first time. After the withering attacks launched by Bertrand Russell and G. E. Moore on "Hegelianism," very little of the Hegelian edifice was left standing, and there was even less desire on the part of virtually anybody to rebuild it. Although there continued to be Hegelians of a sort teaching in Britain after that, for the most part of the twentieth century, they did not produce work that was taken up by the leading developments in twentieth century Anglophone philosophy.

Benedetto Croce's 1906 book on Hegel thus prefigured all the succeeding Hegel debates of the century, if by nothing else than its title: *What is Living and What is Dead of the Philosophy of Hegel?* Given Hegel's low reputation by that point, one would have thought that the answer was: not much at all living, almost all dead. The powerful neo-Kantian movement in Germany in the last quarter of the nineteenth century had reacted with a mixture of contempt, horror, and indifference to Hegel. By the 1870s Hegel had been charged with just about every philosophical crime that could be committed; as his first biographer, Karl Rosenkranz (1805–79), put it (in his belated attempt in 1870 — *Hegel als deutscher Nationalphilosoph* — to rescue Hegel as a philosopher suited for the new German nationalism of the latter part of the century), Hegel had been accused variously of being a spiritualist, a pantheist, an atheist, a rationalist, a reactionary, and a revolutionary. He was also felt to have been an excessive metaphysician, to have sinned against all philosophical method, and, of course, to have corrupted the young. More than anything else, though, he was charged with being completely out of touch with the *scientific* spirit as it was coming to be formulated by intellectual heroes such as Hermann von Helmholz (1821–94); the explosive developments in mathematics, the rapid progress in the sciences of chemistry and biology (which now challenged physics for supremacy in the university), and the increased interest in empirically oriented and naturalistic explanations made Hegel seem all the less relevant and certainly all the less interesting.

Croce (1866–1952) distinguished his own investigation from that of Hegel's few remaining defenders. As Croce pointed out, they of course admitted that Hegel made mistakes, but for them, the core of his method and approach was still valid, and he needed only to be brought up to date, not to be fundamentally reformed. Croce disagreed: for Croce, what was vital was Hegel's discovery of a way of thinking dialectically so that one had the "concrete universal" as the object of philosophical thought; philosophy could thereby deal with something approaching the richness of the experienced world instead of reducing it to bloodless abstractions. Part of this was Hegel's far-reaching historicism, something that before Hegel, only Giambattista Vico (1668–1744) had rivaled. To grasp that, Croce claimed, one must understand the way in which Hegel took over Schelling's conception of the various potencies (*Potenzen*) of reality — what Croce calls a theory of "degrees" — and gave it his own twist. For philosophical thought, Hegel rejected all theories of philosophy as classification, of philosophy as category-theory, of philosophy as the activity of putting things into pigeonholes; instead, Hegel substituted a conception of how these concrete universals (such as art, religion, and philosophy) are both distinct from and related to each other in various stages of "degree." Thus, art and philosophy, so Croce argued, are not two distinct members of the same species but different "degrees" of activity of spirit; or, as Croce put it, "Art does not include philosophy, but philosophy directly includes art" (1915: 56), and one can move from one to the other depending on spirit's interests at the time. For Croce, it was this Schelling-inspired theory of "degrees" of forms of spirit that remained most vibrant and living in Hegel's philosophy.

Where then did Hegel go wrong? Unfortunately, Hegel conflated this idea of distinct realms of spirit that are related in terms of "degree" with his theory of opposites. Instead of seeing certain concepts as distinct but related in terms of "degree" (such as art and philosophy), Hegel was led to see these concepts as logical opposites. Thus, Hegel was led to think, for example, that art and philosophy had to be opposites, and one of them therefore had to be the truth of the other. But if that were the case, then any return to art from philosophy would be a return from something true to something false and would thus be a degeneration rather than a mere shift of focus — and "who could ever persuade himself that religion is the not-being of art, and that art and religion are two abstractions which possess truth only in philosophy, the synthesis of both?" (1915: 60). The objectionable and almost mechanical use of the triadic form, which Hegel explicitly condemned in other places, has, so Croce argued, its roots in this conflation. This conflation accounts for all that is "dead" in Hegel's philosophy, since it leads directly to the "panlogicism" (the identification of the real with the rational) of which so many of Hegel's early critics complained. Everything from nature to mentality to social life to history itself seemed to be swallowed into the Hegelian "logic" in a way that did violence to the very concrete nature of Hegel's own thought. One sees this in all the spheres of Hegel's system, from his logic to his philosophy of nature, and one sees it most clearly in his philosophy of history. With regard to the philosophy of history, for example, Hegel conceded that it was not necessary to use his logic to deduce all the contingent facts of history; instead (in a formulation that Croce attributes to Eduard Gans), "its function was to demonstrate the necessity ... only of the great epochs of history of great groups of people, and to leave the rest to merely narrative history" (1915: 82). However, even on Hegel's own account, that does not work since surely the contingent facts about the Eighteenth Brumaire, Waterloo, Napoleon, etc., are crucial to understanding what Hegel took to be the modern epoch, and if those had been different, the epoch itself would have been different.

Hegel's own characterization of philosophy as a "circle" more adequately captures what is "living" in it, since "a circle can be entered at any point; and so it is with philosophy" (Croce 1915: 67). Philosophy seeks to understand all the ways in which spirit manifests itself in terms of the "concrete universal" and the theory of "degrees of reality." On the other hand, these tools should be used "to refute ... all panlogism and every speculative construction of the individual and of the empirical, of history and of nature" (p. 109).

In effect, Croce's characterization of what was still of use in Hegelianism set the stage (or perhaps just expressed the emerging consensus) that Hegel's *logic* was dead, but something like Hegel's *phenomenology* was still alive. In the same year that Croce's book appeared in Italian, the American idealist, Josiah Royce, gave his famous series of lectures at Johns Hopkins University, later published as *Lectures on Modern Idealism*. In his own philosophy, Royce himself exemplified (as did most of the group called the "British Idealists") a kind of vaguely Neoplatonist idealism that was responding to the issues and problems raised by the rapid industrialization and its attendant social chaos of the late nineteenth century, the second of the great revolutions of modernity (the first being the political upheavals of the American and the French revolutions in the late eighteenth century); one could make sense of the order of nature, history, and the new post-revolutionary life of the West by seeing individual life as a "fragment" of a larger, "absolute" life of which individuals were expressions or emanations of some sort. These "Neoplatonist" idealists took their lead from two things: first, Spinoza's doctrine that there was only one substance of which both thought and extension were attributes — or, put more colloquially, the idea that what seemed like irreconcilable aspects of the way things appeared were only different manifestations of the same underlying "stuff"; second, the interpretation of Hegel's claim that "substance must become subject" as a call to transform Spinoza's substance into something like an absolute subject, God, of which individual lives were fragments or parts.

In his lectures, Royce interpreted Hegel along similar lines to Croce's views (although there was no apparent influence going in either direction). For Royce, Hegel's masterwork was the Jena *Phenomenology*, whose greatness consisted in its being a "study of human nature as it is expressed in various individual and social types" which describes "in serial order, some varieties of experience . . . types of character . . . [and] social development," the choice of which is "for us today somewhat arbitrary" (Royce 1919: 139.) What Croce finds still "living" in Hegelianism, Royce finds at work in the *Phenomenology* itself: instead of "by means of a false translation of real life into the abstract categories of logic," the *Phenomenology* operates by "illustrating the way in which men live as well as the way in which men must think" (p. 145), with the "ideal hero" of the *Phenomenology* being the "*Weltgeist*, or call him by a more familiar name, *Everyman*" (1919: 188). Thus, when Royce actually explicates the *Phenomenology*, he finds more or less what Croce thought was the crucial and living part: "The use of historical types as illustrations of stages of evolution of a rational consciousness. It finds the illustrations empirically. It analyzes them logically" (p. 164). Royce in fact follows through on this interpretation, seeing, for example, the "unhappy consciousness" in the *Phenomenology* as "expressly what William James [1842–1910] would call a variety of religious experience; it is not a concrete form of religion" (p. 181). Purged of Hegel's mania for system and the ensuing panlogism it brought with it, Hegel's philosophy approaches, so Royce thought, the more experientially based theory of the absolute that Royce himself defended, such that when we reason, we do so in light of a "conscious rational ideal, which, when it becomes conscious, must appear as the ideal of our own intelligence, of the self that speaks through us, of the reason of which we are the embodiment" (p. 240). Royce's "absolute" was an outgrowth of the quasi-Neoplatonist approach to Hegel: an attempt to find a conception of the link between God and man that understood man not to be a part of God but to be some kind of fragment of God, a way in which the divine nature spoke to itself and participated with itself.

At roughly the same time as Royce was giving what amounted to his last sustained effort to trace out the relation between Hegel and his own form of idealism, the idealist establishment in Britain, as was mentioned, was coming under the devastating attacks led by Bertrand Russell and G. E. Moore (see "The birth of analytic philosophy," Chapter 1). In some ways, their criticisms of idealism in general and of Hegel and Hegelianism in particular mirrored the general dissatisfaction that as Edwardians they felt with all things they identified as Victorian For them, Hegel was the equivalent of the mutton-chopped, overfed, stuffy, repressed, and arrogant Victorians (at least as they took shape in their own picture of them) against whom they were rebelling. Whereas Croce thought that the panlogism in Hegel was objectionable, Russell thought that everything making a claim to philosophical importance in Hegel was not only dead but was never living in the first place; for Russell, the obscurity of

Hegel's terminology (something virtually nobody has ever denied) was only a cover for Hegel's meaningless or virtually meaningless assertions. In a clever move, Russell described his own new approach to philosophy in terms of an older characterization of the difference between British and Continental mathematics, in which the British followers of Newton's calculus were characterized as "synthetic" (loose, lacking in strict proof) whereas the Continental followers of Leibniz were described as "analytical" (strict and in possession of a much more rigorous symbolism). Reversing that, Russell called the new philosophy based on the path-breaking developments in logic by Frege and then by Russell himself (together with Alfred North Whitehead) "analytical" to distinguish it from the allegedly trumped-up "synthetic" system-building that he thought went on in German philosophy in particular and Continental philosophy in general. The result for Hegelianism in Britain (and later in the United States) was devastating; Russell's development of analytical philosophy was the metaphorical asteroid whose impact came close to wiping out Hegelian life on the Anglo-American planet. After the outbreak World War I and the intense anti-German feelings that were stirred up in Britain and the United States by the Kaiser's reckless adventure, Hegelianism's fate seemed sealed. Russell had denounced Hegel as a charlatan; now he also seemed to be some kind of philosophical cousin to the Kaiser, and who therefore bore partial blame for the slaughter that had almost ripped Europe apart. Even Royce got into the act and spent some of the last few years of his life engaged in anti-German diatribes.

Hegelianism continued, however, to lead at least a furtive existence in Germany. There was much attention to philological issues, and starting in 1927, Hegel's complete works were republished in a very expensive photomechanical reproduction of the original edition of the complete works first published in the 1840s. (In fact, it was not until 1971 that an alternative edition of Hegel's collected works was published; the critical edition is still not fully done.)

A European revival of Hegel began, oddly enough, in the development of what came to be called "western Marxism" and sometimes "Hegelian Marxism" (to distinguish it from the "eastern," Soviet style of Marxism). In 1923, the Hungarian philosopher and Marxist, Georg Lukács (1885–1971), published *History and Class Consciousness*. He did this, moreover, more than a decade before the publication of Karl Marx's "1844 Manuscripts," which brought out the Marx–Hegel link much more clearly than before. In his book, Lukács did not specifically argue for the primacy of the *Phenomenology* over other works by Hegel, but he might as well have. As was the case with the French Hegelians, for him the true importance of Hegel lay in his having historicized everything, including his own system, while at the same time having supposedly discovered a logic to that history which was somehow internal to history itself and not imported into it from outside. Lukács set himself a hard task: as a self-described orthodox Marxist, he wished to show just how Hegelian the orthodox conception of Marxist historical materialism really was. Marx had, of course, insisted that Hegel was an idealist in that Hegel thought that the moving force of history had to do with changes in self-consciousness, whereas he, Marx, insisted on his own "materialism," which held that changes in self-consciousness were to be explained by changes in the economic relations in society (which, roughly, consisted in the forces of production and the existing relations of ownership of the means of production). To "Hegelianize" Marx thus looked, from the orthodox Marxist perspective, like a step backwards.

Hegel had famously claimed in his 1820 *Philosophy of Right* that the civil servants were the "universal estate" of modern life since, as civil servants, their own ethos consisted in acting in the interest of the state as a whole, not in the interest of any other particular estate. Marx had jettisoned Hegel's already old-fashioned idea of modern society as consisting of estates and had substituted for that the more contemporary notion of "class" (where a class, for Marx, was defined by its relation to the means of production). The proletariat supposedly was to be the new "universal class," since in overthrowing what went against its interests (the arrangements of capitalist society), it was acting in the name of humanity, in the name of a future order where there would be no exploitation of man by man. Lukács wanted to show how Hegel's notion of self-consciousness and Hegel's own idea that the "truth is the whole" (as Hegel put it in the preface to the *Phenomenology*) were the correct conceptions to put to work to understand what Marx was really trying to say.

To grasp society correctly, Lukács claimed, we must grasp it in its totality. To do that, however, was not just to add up all the facts about a given society; it was instead to grasp it in its essence as a "whole." The essence of "bourgeois society" was, of course, the dominant power of capital which, according to what came to be called "dialectical materialism" in Soviet style Marxism, determined the consciousness a society had of itself. Such consciousness, however, so Lukács argued, should not be understood in psychological terms, or even in the terms in which people (such as proletarians or bourgeois) actually spoke about themselves. Fusing Hegel with Max Weber (1864–1920), Lukács argued that it was to be taken in a *normative* sense, as the kind of commitments one assumes by virtue of having a place in the social space that constituted that "totality." As he put it,

> By relating consciousness to the whole of society it became possible to infer the thoughts and feelings which men would have in a particular situation if they were able to assess both it and the interests arising from it in their impact on immediate action and on the whole structure of society. (1968: 51)

One looks at how the people actually, for example, speak about themselves and, using the best theory, one infers what *other* commitments they would be obligated to undertake if they were to remain consistent with their current beliefs (which is not to say that as a matter of fact they *actually* make those further commitments or are willing to do so). Class consciousness therefore is not a matter of psychological introspection or of getting a time slice of current opinion but, for the proletariat, it is the "sense, become conscious, of the historical role of the class" (1968: 73).

Using that as his point of departure, Lukács effectively argued for redoing historical materialism in the terms of Hegel's philosophy of history, particularly as that philosophy played out in the *Phenomenology*. Hegel had in effect argued in that book and in his later Berlin lectures that the meaning of history was to be construed as a succession of "shapes of spirit," that is, of entire ways of life structured around the self-consciousness of that way of life, a set of authoritative conceptions about what constituted knowledge, what constituted the divine — in short, a set of specific conceptions that constituted that way of life's more general and overall conception of what it meant to be human and what counted as authoritative for that conception of what it meant to be human. What distinguished that kind of history from being a mere succession was Hegel's contention that each of these "shapes of spirit" comes to a historical end because of the contradictions inherent in that way of life, so that as its participants become more self-conscious about what it is that holds them together, it becomes impossible for them to *be* those people, such that eventually the irrationalities within their collective self-conceptions lead to a breakdown of the way of life itself. The historical sense that becomes established in the West, however, forces each of the succeeding ways of life to understand its own self-conception as a rational successor to what came before it and to have somehow solved the problems that beset its predecessors. Modern European life, on the other hand, has come to a full self-consciousness about what is at stake in this historical progression and to a consciousness therefore that it is humanity itself, taken as a whole, which is the author of the normative laws to which it is subject, For Hegel, that amounted to the claim that neither god, nor nature, nor biblical words, nor tradition can count as authoritative without submitting to the test of reason, and, after Kant's destruction of all prior metaphysics, modern European humanity realized that even reason itself is a product of human activity and spontaneity, not a feature of the cosmos itself. (This was in distinction to Royce's idea that the absolute was a kind of Neoplatonic reason – a version of the Neoplatonic god – of which we were the embodiment.) Modern life thus effectively assumes responsibility for itself in light of this new, epochal form of self-consciousness. This has the implication that the meaning of history consists in mankind's progressive attempt to construct an adequate sense of what it is to be a human being, and the answer turns out, in the abstract, to be a *free* agent, to be self-determining.

In his other writings, Hegel argued that this kind of self-responsibility could be carried out only within modern practices which embody commitment to universal rights to life, liberty, and property, and an equal commitment to the limited but crucial importance of morality in life. This morality, although making a place for the valid appeal to individual conscience, is fundamentally structured in terms of universally valid moral demands. Those two practices themselves, however, can only be effectively carried out if they are embedded in a larger set of practices and institutions consisting of nuclear families based on love and free consent, modern market societies based on careers open to talent and effective mediating institutions (such as associations of professionals, among others), and a state based on a constitutional monarchy and structured around a representative (although for Hegel decidedly not democratic) government. For Lukács, as for all Marxists, this showed that however brilliant Hegel might have been, he remained a "bourgeois" thinker who could not rise beyond the standpoint of capitalist, bourgeois society and who thus had no place in his system for the coming proletarian revolution.

The problem was how to use Hegel to get out of Hegel, and Lukács thus argued that historical materialism had to take over Hegel's philosophy of history without its bourgeois character. This in effect meant reinterpreting Hegel's succession of "shapes of spirit" as a succession of shapes of life structured around determinate forms of production. In turn, that meant that in order to reframe the Hegelian discussion in a Marxist way, one needed to explain how it was that only in the period of advanced capitalism had it become possible to have a self-consciousness about history itself as a totality. So Lukács argued, it was by reframing the Marxist doctrines in that way that one could finally and comprehensively understand how the true motor of history had to do with how the revolutionary ruptures in a whole way of life were brought on by the contradictions between the forces of production and the relations of production, as that way of life developed its economy over time. Those contradictions, however, could trigger such breakdowns only if they became *self-conscious* in the right way, and it was only in Marxist historical materialism that a *full* self-consciousness about the movement of history as a totality was possible. Everything else until then had been only "ideology," a succession of mythologies about human life that effectively articulated what was at stake in a way of life (a historical epoch defined by a type of economic productive activity) while at the same time obscuring what was really going on. Modern Marxist theory, on the other hand, decisively shows that it is the proletarian revolution and the establishment of socialism, not Hegel's constitutional monarchy, that is the stage at which history had become fully conscious of itself in and through certain modern agents (the philosophers) themselves becoming self-conscious about it.

Taking Marx's celebrated chapter in *Capital* on the "Fetishism of commodities" as his jumping off point, Lukács argued that as the worker becomes conscious of himself as a commodity, as an entity subject to the laws of the market, his own individual self-consciousness becomes effectively the consciousness of the "totality" of modern bourgeois society and consciousness of its essential structure, and he thereby becomes conscious not of a causal force at work in history but of a kind of inner *logic* of capitalist society that commits him, independently of whether *he* endorses that commitment, to the proletarian revolution; it is this new self-consciousness that is crucial for the development of capitalism to its final breakdown and replacement by Marxist socialism. The worker's own *alienation* is his consciousness of the contradictions at work in the logic of capitalism.

Lukács argued therefore for an immanent logic to history that conditions *all* claims to knowledge, not just those about the economy, and he realized that for that claim to be valid, he had to argue for the stronger view that the true grasp of reality as a whole could only emerge at the end of the capitalist period. As he put it,

> only if, as a result the subject moved in a self-created world of which it is the conscious form and only if the world imposed itself upon it in full objectivity, only then can the problem of dialectics, and with it the abolition of the antitheses of subject and object, thought and existence, freedom and necessity, be held to be solved. (1968: 142)

Even nature itself had to be understood as a social, historical category which can be grasped in its full objectivity only from within the terms of historical materialism. Italicizing the words to drive home his point, Lukács claimed that the "*developing tendencies of history*" were therefore "*a higher reality than the empirical 'facts'*" (1968: 181) and therefore the class that had a grasp on the meaning of history by virtue of who it was (the proletariat) grasped for the first time the "absolute" at work in history. Indeed, only the proletariat was in a position to understand the significance of various contemporary facts (such as the refusal of many of the workers actually to accept the leadership of the party). Lukács also concluded that the Leninist conception of the Communist Party as the vanguard party of the revolution had to be correct, since the party was only the self-consciousness of the proletariat brought to its fullest and most clear expression.

Unfortunately for Lukács, the actual, existing Leninist party was less than enthused about the book; the party condemned it, a judgment that Lukács himself, as a loyal Marxist, dutifully accepted. In the official view of the party, the book was only a relapse into "idealism," and therefore an expression of "bourgeois" thought. The book nonetheless continued to play a role in the development of western Marxism, which maintained an overtly Hegelian element to itself.

About a decade after the publication of Lukács's book, Hegelianism experienced a renaissance in France. The interest in Hegel in France in the 1930s was based in a generational experience that bore some very general similarities to the experiences of Royce's generation. Royce was born in 1855 and came to maturity in the years after the trauma of the American Civil War and the onset of industrialism had thrown into question many of the views held by the generations preceding him. In the United States, Hegel's appeal after the Civil War had to do with his offering a way of binding up differences into a unity (a pressing issue in the post–war period), of reconciling a secular state with religion, and, in a post-Darwinian world, of reconciling religion with science (this was despite the fact that Hegel was a pre-Darwinian anti-evolutionist). Likewise, although France had been one of the victors in World War I, France had been left exhausted and devastated, and it found itself to be having a difficult time with the process of industrialization. There was no small amount of brooding about the unity of France (which was fragmenting itself into a variety of political parties and groups) and the future of the French nation, especially in light of the threats emanating at the time from Germany. Hegelian philosophy seemed to offer a way of thinking through how a unity might be produced from the energy latent in all those internal differences, and of how the secular state (one of the main legacies of the original revolutionary republic) and religion might be combined. For both these generations (the post-Civil War American, the post-World War I French), there was also the question of the sense of history. Given the recent slaughter still vivid in the memories of both, and given the revolutionary past of both countries, there was a felt need for a way to interpret that past in order to see where history, as it were, was going. Moreover, in France there was also a lively left-wing movement that promised change for the better through some form of revolutionary (or at least avowedly political) action, and the question of the revolutionary "movement" of history was clearly in the air.

The turn to Hegel in France in the 1930s thus focused more on the experiential bases of Hegel's thought, and the key text was, as it had been for Croce and for Royce, the 1807 *Phenomenology*. The beginning of the Hegelian revival in France can be marked with the publication of Jean Wahl's (1888–1974) path-breaking *Le Malheur de la Conscience* [*The Unhappy Consciousness*] in 1929. The book took one early chapter from Hegel's *Phenomenology* ("das unglückliche Bewußtsein") and interpreted it as the key to understanding the whole work. What might seem in a more "historicist" reading of the book to be a chapter on medieval Christianity, the yearning for the savior who has not returned, along with a yearning for a unity with god, was taken by Wahl to bear a more universal human theme, that of *alienation*. The kind of alienation experienced by the "unhappy consciousness" as being that between man and god (or man and the "unchangeable") is the driving force of all human history, as people individually and collectively strive to overcome what separates them from what they long for (basically, the idea of a non-fragmented personal life and a fulfilling, non-fragmented cultural life). But what history teaches is that although such unity is always promised, it is never achieved, since any semblance of having overcome alienation only serves as the starting point for a new breakup, new separation, and a new search for unity. Wahl's somewhat romantic reading of Hegel's work was the precursor to the French existentialist philosophy that was to follow. Alienation is our lot, and it is the motor of all progress in history. For Wahl, whatever "logic" there is in Hegel's *Phenomenology*, it is not the apparently all too rigid logic of Hegel's *Logic*, and it is also certainly not the logic of Marxian class struggle. It is rather the inevitable way in which humans seek to secure some kind of fulfilling, non-fragmented life for themselves, only to find that whatever they have achieved in order to do so itself produces a new kind of fragmentation that leaves them dissatisfied and propels them to new attempts at seeking reconciliation.

In the early 1930s Marx's early manuscripts (the "1844 Manuscripts") were published. Just as Wahl was coming out with his existential reading of Hegel (and Lukács with his Hegelian Marxism), the manuscripts revealed a younger, more "Hegelian" Marx. This Marx was concerned with alienation, and the overcoming of it through the creation of a new socialist order, and was at odds with what seemed like the "scientific" Marx of *Capital* (and the Marx who was the official philosopher of the Soviet revolution). Earlier in the century, in 1907, Hegel's youthful writings had also been published for the first time, bearing the slightly misleading title, *Hegels Theologische Jugendschriften* [*Hegel's Early Theological Writings*]; this had been preceded by Wilhelm Dilthey's very important work, *Die Jugendgeschichte Hegels* [*The History of Hegel's Youth*] in 1905, which attempted to show how Hegel's mature works were best understood as an outgrowth of the life experiences of the young Hegel. For the younger generation in France who were interested in philosophy, those new findings about both the young Hegel and the young Marx were revealing: The fact that the young Hegel and the young Marx were both interested in alienation (and in Hegel's case, in trying to think through how a modern religion might be crucial in the personal and collective overcoming of this alienation), and that both went on in their maturity to produce "scientific" systems (although the sense of "science" in each was slightly different) pointed to the way in which one's sense of what is really at work in life can become covered over by theory and ideology. The conclusion to be drawn was that if philosophy was to be true to experience and to what was really at work in the modern world, it had to retain that sense of the concrete and not let, for example, academic careerism take it away from that basis. Jean Wahl's book thus found a receptive audience, and it further cemented the role of the *Phenomenology* as *the* work of Hegel's that was crucial; it came to be seen as the last work of the "young" Hegel, who in turn came to be seen as an early existentialist or even an early revolutionary, and to be distinguished from the system-crazy, stuffy old professor he supposedly later became. Croce's claim that what was living in Hegel was his lively sense of the individual and the "concrete" found a new expression in the early French reappropriation of Hegel.

In the course of the 1930s, however, another reading of Hegel established itself in French philosophy. The Russian émigré, Alexandre Kojève (1902–68), was asked in 1933 to take over the course at the École Pratique des Hautes Études from another Russian émigré, Alexandre Koyré (1892–1964), who was moving to the French embassy in Cairo. Kojève taught a seminar on Hegel there from 1933 to 1939, and a great many of the later postwar luminaries of French philosophy and letters were in attendance at the course. His interpretation of Hegel, while completely idiosyncratic, influenced several generations of Hegel scholars in France and elsewhere, and it effectively set the stage for the confrontation between Hegelianism, Marxism, phenomenology, Heideggerianism, existentialism, and Nietzschean thought that made French philosophy in that period so fecund and exciting. Kojève in effect proposed a reading of Hegel that fully meshed together Hegel, Heidegger and some themes from Marx. From Heidegger, he took the notion that the being of human being (*Dasein*, in Heidegger's terminology) is time; from Marx, he took the idea that history is a story of revolutionary struggle that has an end-point; and he then read all of these into the text of the *Phenomenology* itself. There is also some apparent influence of Friedrich Nietzsche (1844–1900) on Kojève's early thought, although Kojève himself gives no indication of that; he seemed to take from Nietzsche the story of the "slave revolt" in morality, which Kojève interpreted in terms of Hegel's famous dialectic of master and slave, as the key to understanding the historical move from the ancient to the modern world (and a way of understanding why the ancient world had to fail on its own terms).

Thus, instead of seeing the "unhappy consciousness" as the key to the *Phenomenology*, as Wahl had done, Kojève proposed that one look at the "master/slave" dialectic of the chapter on self-consciousness as the key to the whole book. He read the section as explaining the origin of self-consciousness itself: we become self-conscious agents by recognizing each other as agents. This arises out of our desire for objects (such as food) being overruled by our desire for another's desire, which comes about in two ways: one can desire an object simply because another desires it (Kojève gives as examples a medal or "the enemy's flag"), or, more importantly, "to desire a desire is to want to substitute oneself for the value desired by this desire ... I want him to 'recognize' my value as his value" (1969: 7) To do this, however, is to engage in a fight for "pure prestige," to demand of the other person that he recognize my desire as binding on him and to be willing to stake my life on the outcome. When in the thick of such a life and death struggle between two such people, one of them (out of the fear of death) surrenders, then the relationship of "master" and "slave" is established. The slave remains at the level of animal desire, wanting only to stay alive; but the master shows he lives the truly *human* life because he was willing to risk death, to triumph over the merely "animal" desire to preserve his life. He was willing to die, that is, for an idea, even if it is an idea of "pure prestige." Each is thus, on Kojève's reading, self-conscious only as having been given some form of recognition by the other. However, in a dialectical reversal, as the slave works on things for the master, the master becomes the idle, "animal" member of the relationship, whereas the slave, in working and transforming the world to serve the master, becomes the active participant in the relationship. As the slave gradually becomes conscious of the master's dependence on him (instead of the other way around), he becomes ready for revolution. The master, whose passion for recognition made him stake his life on acquiring it, becomes an idle creature, and the revolutionary slave becomes the man of passion.

What for Wahl was the key — the "unhappy consciousness" — became for Kojève just another tale of mastery and slavery, this time one about how in the reign of Christianity, everybody was enslaved to the "absolute master," God. Moreover, rather then being the key to the book, it is instead a particularly poignant chapter, since, on Kojève's interpretation, it is only the account of how the world of "slaves" creates the fiction of an absolute master (God) before whom all (including the earthly, the "real" masters) are slaves, and, as such a fiction, it provides a resolution to the problem of mastery and servitude only in thought and not in reality. However, Christianity sets the stage for the final "slave revolt" in history, which involves the rejection of the fictional heavenly master and the struggle to institute full and equal mutual recognition.

According to Kojève, the struggle for mastery thus emerges as the moving force of all history, and it is the history of these kinds of confrontations between people seeking recognition as "masters" that drives the story told by Hegel in the *Phenomenology*. History is the movement whose motor consists in people seeking recognition (or "glory") through great deeds that involve violence and forcing others to submit to their rule and their judgment. Those who are forced to submit ("the slaves"), however, eventually revolt and in pursuit of recognition for themselves, overthrow their masters and establish a new order with themselves as the masters. This process has a natural end to it in that if a form of social life were to be created in which everyone (somehow) received equal recognition, there would be no more dichotomy between master and slave (or, rather, each would be both master and slave to each other). The achievement of such a state would be, Kojève said, the "end of history." The "end of history," however, would consist in a social and political order in which there is no longer any reason to strive for glory, any reason to become a "master," since all are now equally master *and* slave. This is in fact the modern "homogeneous" state since all are equal in it. The "end of history" does not mean that nothing more will happen; but it does mean that the impulse to creativity and great historical events will be gone. Indeed, the "end of history" looks rather like Nietzsche's image of the "last man," living a life of "pitiable comfort."

Kojève's seminar ended in 1939 at the outbreak of World War II, and after the end of the war (and after he himself had become a French bureaucrat at the Ministry of Finance), Kojève noted that he had been too pessimistic about the "end of history." In a note added to the second edition of the book several years later, he claimed that in fact there was still a struggle for glory at the end of history, but it took the form of snobbism, of doing things or acquiring things simply because they were hard to do or hard to get. "Glory," as it were, consists in acquiring the right wristwatch or knowing how to perform some otherwise meaningless but terribly difficult task, such as the Japanese tea ceremony.

Kojève's reading of Hegel was contentious and often at odds with the text, but its brilliance and originality were right for the time. His Hegel was not a philosopher telling the story of the reconciliation of man and god; nor was it a story of individuals finding their unity in an "absolute" that was a form of Neoplatonic reason coursing throughout the world. It was instead a social account of history and humanity that rested on the concept of recognition (in that human animals become self-conscious agents only through recognition), and it also stressed that history was ultimately led by the force of "slaves" revolting against their "masters" for recognition, a struggle which was bloody, violent, and which only had its natural end in a state involving full and mutual recognition. To those looking for a meaning to the harsh realities of World War I and the problems that set in afterwards, Kojève's Hegel thus seemed to offer a kind of map through the maze, and, just as important, it held out the hope for a progressive political change for the better. After the allied victory in World War II, Kojève's way of being a Hegelian became one of the key elements in the debate among Marxists and phenomenologists. When Lukács's book became more widely known in France and elsewhere, Kojève's Hegelianism and Lukács's Hegelian-Marxism pulled interest back into understanding what was at work in Hegel's system. Kojève and Lukács went at the project of Hegelianizing Marx, however, in different directions: Kojève worked on pulling Marx back into Hegel's scheme (in such a way that Marxism in Kojève's account appeared only as an offshoot of the grander Hegelian theory), whereas Lukács worked at pulling Hegel up to Marx's standpoint. Nonetheless, both ended up providing grist for a "revolutionary" and "social" as opposed to a religious-metaphysical reading of Hegel.

There was, however, around the same time in France a competing, although in some ways similar reading of Hegel offered by an older contemporary of Kojève's, Jean Hyppolite (1907–68). Hyppolite both translated the *Phenomenology* into French (with superb elegance), and wrote what remained for a long time the standard commentary on the book, *Genesis and Structure of the Phenomenology of Spirit*. In some ways, Hyppolite's Hegel stood at a kind of mid-point between Wahl's proto-existentialist reading and Kojève's Marxist-Heideggerian reading. The "unhappy consciousness" in Hyppolite's understanding becomes the figure of what happens after the battle to the death that results in the relationship of mastery and servitude. The "unhappy consciousness" experiences a profound gap between his subjective, or personal, individual grasp of the world and what he takes to be the objective, or impersonal grasp of the world (as exemplified by what Hegel calls the "unchangeable" in that section). The "unhappy consciousness" longs for union with the objective point of view, which in the course of the *Phenomenology* comes to be seen as the point of view of the human community as such, but it cannot accomplish this except through a long period of historical struggle and pain. However, in the last analysis Hyppolite came down more on the side of Wahl, taking issue with Hegelianism about whether there could be an "end" to history; for Hyppolite, the "unhappy consciousness" necessarily appears in each stage of the historical process described in the *Phenomenology*, which moves from integration, or unity, to loss (that is, disintegration of unity, fragmentation) to a partial recovery of the unity, only to experience that loss again (although in a new way). For Hyppolite, it went against the very dynamic of the Hegelian dialectic itself to hold that there could ever be an end-point to that process; it was simply presumptuous of Hegel to think that there could be a unity that was "strong" enough to preserve the individuality of individuals while uniting them in a community without any kind of tension or loss of individuality. For such a complete (or "absolute") unity to be established, it would have to dissolve the individuals into itself, and that possibility (which sounds like totalitarianism) is itself surely at odds with everything else that goes on in the Hegelian dialectic.

To this end, Hyppolite read the chapter on forgiveness and reconciliation (the final section in the long chapter on "spirit" that precedes the transition into the equally long chapter titled, "religion") as something other than *recognition*. For Kojève, that chapter played little to no role in his interpretation; reading all of the *Phenomenology* as an account of the history of struggles over mastery and servitude, Kojève could only see that section in terms of his earlier accounts of how Napoleon completed the revolution in practice and how Hegel had then completed Napoleon's efforts in thought: As Kojève put it, "This dyad, formed by Napoleon and Hegel, is the perfect Man, fully and definitively 'satisfied' by what he *is* and by what he *knows* himself to be," and that dyad, as Kojève says in the very next sentence, is the "revealed God" (Kojève 1969: 70). For Hyppolite, writing a few years after Kojève but after the war had already broken out, the moment of forgiveness is definitively not a struggle over mastery and servitude but a way of getting *beyond* that struggle to a reconciliation that binds up and heals the wounds left in the wake of all the past battles over mastery. In Hegel's own words, in the moment of reconciliation, "the wounds of the spirit heal, leaving no scars behind" (*Phenomenology*, §671). Hyppolite insightfully argued that the reconciliation in that chapter occurs between the political man of historical action, such as Napoleon, and the thinker, such as Hegel (or himself), and not the secularization of the Christian God. Nonetheless, Hyppolite seemed to come down somewhere nearer to Kojève in his interpretation of the status of religion in Hegel's dialectic. While granting that Hegel wanted to have religion amount to more than the atheism Kojève attributed to Hegel, Hyppolite did not endorse a fully theistic interpretation of the *Phenomenology*. He seemed both to be saying that the standards for judging the progress of history are somehow immanent within the historical process itself, which implied that no Hegelian can accept the idea of a transcendent standard of rightness that goes beyond the development of the human community to that point, and to be insisting that this is nonetheless not relativism, a claim that came very close to Kojève's own reading. If anything, the Kojève–Hyppolite reading of Hegel in France seemed to be better at identifying the problem than in offering a clear-cut answer to it: How do we reconcile accepting that we are finite, historical beings (whose standards for judging things themselves develop and change historically and are therefore relative) with the necessary and rational demand to *justify* our practices and judgments, which seems to push us in the direction of non-contingent standards of judgment?

In the 1960s and afterwards in France, the response to Hegel seemed to be more or less what Hyppolite (who after the war eventually turned to a form of Heideggerian thought) had apparently been hinting at all along: first, that Hegel was an all-important crucial figure whose basic lesson was negative; second, that pushing thought in any genuinely Hegelian direction inevitably led one to some version of the "absolute" and the end of history as pronounced by a particular person or party (Hegel at his lectern in one case, the Communist Party at the head of the army in another); and third, that such a pronouncement was not only philosophically dubious but politically and existentially dangerous. Maurice Merleau-Ponty (1907–1961), in his 1955 book, *The Adventures of the Dialectic*, argued for a more open-ended, non-totalizing notion of historical development, something that steered between a non-normative, purely factual account of history and a moralist, or millenarian conception of historical progress. However, Merleau-Ponty did not do much more than issue a call to develop such a view, and he died before he could do anything to flesh it out. Nonetheless, the issue quickly went beyond the confines of discussions of Hegelian philosophy and became part of the stock in trade of the ensuing structuralist versus post-structuralist debate in French philosophy from the late 1960s onward.

In Germany after 1945 (in the western part at least), there was a gradual and renewed interest in Hegel, although there were few "Hegelians" to be found. In the Federal Republic, the Hegel Archives were established at the university in Bochum, and these became the center of crucial and lively research into Hegel's thought, his life, the formation of his texts, and so on — in short, it gave new life to the interpretation of Hegel. There were also a series of important reinterpretations of Hegel as German philosophers sought to come to terms with the horrible legacy of Hitler's failed Reich. In light of these reinterpretations, the rather exclusive interest in the historicism of the *Phenomenology* as the key to Hegel's thought (so prominent in Lukács, Kojève, and Hyppolite) was replaced by a revived concern with Hegel's system, in particular his *Science of Logic* and the system outlined in Hegel's own *Encyclopedia of the Philosophical Sciences*.

The reappropriation of Hegel into German philosophy was in part initiated by Hans-Georg Gadamer (1900–2002), a sometime student and associate of Martin Heidegger (1889–1976); in the postwar period, Gadamer developed his own original conceptions of philosophy as "hermeneutics" (as an overall theory of interpretation not only of philosophical texts but also of human communication and social life, resulting in a conception of philosophy as intrinsically historical in character), and he turned a good bit of his interest into rehabilitating Hegel as a kind of forerunner to his hermeneutical philosophy (Gadamer 1976). Gadamer quite explicitly read

Hegel, not as a forerunner of Marx, but as the last step in the development of German Idealism, in which the attempt was made to finish and perfect the project in transcendental philosophy that Kant had begun. In Gadamer's reconstruction of Hegel's thought, Hegel completed in his own fashion the move begun in Fichte's critique of Kant's division of our epistemic capacities into two groups. These groups were "receptivity" (which was structured around the pure, i.e. non-empirical forms of space and time) and "spontaneity" (from which come the pure, non-empirical categories of the understanding). What Fichte (1762–1814) in effect saw was that the same reasons Kant had for detaching reason (or "spontaneity") from receptivity in practical philosophy, and for arguing that in morality we therefore can be subject only to those laws of which we could regard ourselves as the authors, extended to all of Kant's philosophy, once one abandoned Kant's contentious conception of pure, a priori forms of intuition. If there was no "given" from sensibility that could function as an epistemic, normative check on our conceptual spontaneity, then we had a new problem on our hands, so Fichte thought, namely, that of showing how from within the spontaneity of the "I think" itself, we can generate enough "contact" with the world to guarantee that we can really be said to know something about it. Fichte was thus led into the verbal acrobatics of his *Wissenschaftslehre*, in which the "I" is said to posit the "Not-I" as a "check" on itself. As Gadamer understood Hegel's objection to Fichte, this reliance on the "I" as the starting point was itself unjustified since it did not give us any understanding of the mediation by which the "I" itself is generated; and Hegel thus substituted a "we" (spirit) for Fichte's "I," and the truth of that "we" in the *Phenomenology* turned out to be "pure thought," the starting point of the *Logic*. The *Logic* in turn is the true explication of what it means to be subject only to norms that one can regard as having been authored by oneself, and the model for that is the dialectical form of conversation found in Plato in which there are a series of stages of claims to knowledge that are modified or abandoned in the course of the Socratic dialogue. Hegel's own innovation was to transform this Platonic, "dialogical" form of dialectic into a more systematic, logical method. Hegel's mistake, however, was to think that this transformation put him in the position of being able to assert an "absolute" standpoint (that is, a standpoint completely grounded within itself and not requiring any relation to anything outside of itself to vouch for its justification). Human finitude and the very language in which Hegel had to formulate this view, so Gadamer argued, shows that Hegel's dialectic, rather than being absolute, was itself part of the always partial, never completed process of understanding that Gadamer called the object of hermeneutics.

Gadamer's student, Dieter Henrich (1927–), also helped to push Hegel back into the scene in a way that did not privilege the *Phenomenology* and the philosophy of history over the *Logic* and the *Encyclopedia*'s "system." Henrich put front and center Hegel's claims that his philosophy was to be *wissenschaftlich* (or "scientific") and was to lead to a reconciliation, a *Versöhnung*, of modern agents with their lives, so that it would, *as philosophy*, perform something like the function that Christian religion had taken upon itself. The starting point was that which Hegel, Hölderlin (1770–1843), and Schelling (1775–1854) all shared together at the Tübingen Seminary: a commitment to a kind of "monism," the idea that despite all the differentiation among the various things of the world, there is at bottom a unity, the "one-in-all" (as their Spinozistic phrase at the time expressed it) (Henrich 1971). But whereas Schelling came to take that "all-in-one" as a kind of "identity" among all the elements while at the same time being the "all," the totality in his construction was also nonetheless supposedly both self-moving and possessing the structure of an "I." Schelling, however, could not show how the absolute's supposed self-movement was to come about or how this "identity" did not obliterate all difference. In light of that, Hegel came to see the absolute as "spirit," *Geist*, which, in his newly developed dialectical terminology, posits *itself* as an *other*. (Both Schelling and Hegel called this "all" the "absolute.") To arrive at that, so Henrich argued, Hegel had to develop a new logic of what it meant to be something finite, something whose "being" is determined and bounded by an "other." In Hegel's conceptualization, what is "finite" cancels, abolishes, and raises itself up to a higher level (using Hegel's notion of the German verb, *aufheben*, as incorporating all three meanings), and this movement of the finite's self-cancellation constitutes the absolute's own process of coming-to-be. "For the absolute is, however, 'at work' itself in the finite to the extent that the finite abolishes itself" (Henrich 1982: 158). Employing the dark terms of Hegel's *Logic* itself, Henrich argued that by seeing the self-negation of the "finite" as the "absolute" itself, Hegel had shown how the absolute's negativity (its being the "other of itself") puts the absolute into a self-relation so that the absolute posits the finite as the other of itself, and the finite itself comes to be thought as the "other" of itself. The self-relation of the "finite" to itself is thus the process of the finite's becoming an other to itself, and the very self-relation of the absolute is thus to be (or, to generate) the other of itself (the finite) in and through a process that Henrich sometimes called "autonomous negation." In that way, Henrich tried to give some precise content to just what the alleged "logic" of Hegel's *Logic* really was (or, to put it differently, that it really was a *logic* of sorts and not just a metaphor for historical movement or something else) and to argue that it made sense for Hegel to think of this logic as also a *metaphysics* of the absolute.

Indeed, it was this metaphysics which drove Hegel to conceive of the absolute as *spirit*, since only in the concept of spirit is there an adequate conception of the absolute as relating itself to an other since it stands in a self-relation in its relation to the other (or, to put it somewhat more colloquially, spirit exists only in relating itself both to a world other than itself and to other "spirits" different from itself). Thus, the very metaphysics of the absolute (inaugurated by Schelling) ultimately drives one to understand it as spirit and to understand it as involving an epistemic relation (as being the absolute only as a form of "knowing" (*Wissen*)). As a form of monism, though, it is driven to the thought of the "all" as being a form of self-conscious spirit; the absolute as spirit (Hegel's reinterpretation of God) relates itself to itself in positing a finite natural world and a finite world of self-conscious agents as both identical with itself and nonetheless other than itself. This dialectical metaphysics of Hegelianism cannot therefore be taken out of Hegel or omitted in some form of "reconstructing" Hegel's thought (as any number of people since Croce have proposed to do) since the quasi-paradoxical form of his thought makes sense only in terms of such an distinctive fusion of logic and metaphysics.

Thus, while Croce declared Hegel's *Logic* dead and his historicism and philosophy of spirit alive, Henrich declared that if Hegel's *Logic* was dead, so was Hegelianism. Nonetheless, as Henrich worked out his own thoughts on the successes and failures of German Idealism, he ultimately came to the view that Hegel had failed, although in the most instructive way possible, namely, by pointing to the need for a conception of self-consciousness as the "other of itself" while also showing where a certain view of that conception logically takes us. Over a number of years, Henrich's work in Hegel and Kant thus developed into a new project: that of reconstructing the kinds of conversations that went on in, among other places, Jena during Hegel's time there with the idea that such a reconstruction would bring out the hidden impulses behind the explosive development of post-Kantian German philosophy over such a short period of time. As Henrich sharpened his thoughts on the matter, he came to argue that the truth of the idealist line of thought lay, so to speak, prior to Hegel's capstone achievement, in the different but much more defensible line that Hegel's old friend, Friedrich Hölderlin, had started to take it (before he became finally uninterested in a philosophical development of those themes). Hölderlin had begun to work out a view in which the "absolute" origin of self-consciousness is both a necessary accompaniment to all self-conscious life while at the same time being radically "withdrawn" (*entzogen*) from our conscious life. Hegel's great mistake, as it were, was to think of it as being fully manifested in the so-called self-development of reason. In Henrich's formulation, Hegel's development of the absolute was logical, consistent, but ultimately myopic about the realities of self-conscious life, even if it contained within itself one of the most insightful accounts of it.

At the same time in Germany, Klaus Hartmann was defending Hegelianism through his controversial reinterpretation of Hegel's dialectic. Hartmann's influence, although negligible in Germany, was most widely felt in the United States (and to some extent in Britain as well). Hartmann's interpretation was broadly neo-Kantian in inspiration (drawing heavily on the work of the southwest neo-Kantians, such as Heinrich Rickert, although drawing hardly at all on the work of the Marburg neo-Kantians). In some ways, Hartmann was trying to perform the act of "completion" for German neo-Kantianism that Hegel had himself performed for orthodox Kantianism. In doing so, Hartmann developed his own rather singular jargon. His starting point was the familiar Kantian claims that the basic categories of experience are those presupposed by the kinds of ordinary experiences and claims we make. Those categories express our *ontology* of the world (our commitments to what we must ultimately presuppose as being) and not a "metaphysics" (that is, a postulation of supersensible entities that are invoked as explanations for experience) (Hartman 1972). However, the categories can be given only a partial and not a full or "absolute" justification by virtue of being shown to be presupposed by experience; to be fully justified (or "grounded"), they must be shown a priori within their own terms to be justified. Hartmann called this the "transcendental turn," attributing it to Kant for its origins and attributing to Hegel the completion of the transcendental project begun by Kant. What is most characteristic about such arguments, Hartmann noted, is their necessary circularity, since they cannot be shown to be justified by virtue of the items that presuppose them, and only Hegel, with his dialectical version of the transcendental turn, understood fully that the circle in which they are justified must somehow be self-validating. Hegel's solution was to think of a logic that began with a category which both expressed something about the world and which was also a point of zero-determinateness (the category of "pure indeterminate being" that begins the *Logic*) and then to show that the contradictoriness of such a conception compels one to introduce new categories until one arrives at the category of "thought thinking itself" (the "absolute Idea," the final category of the *Logic*) as what supposedly explains the whole dialectical movement and explains itself as the necessary result of the dialectical movement. The *Phenomenology*, on Hartmann's view, should be taken as the introduction to the system (as Hegel explicitly titled it), a way of motivating the reader to leave the realm of "representational thinking" (thinking in terms of representations that presuppose certain categories and seeing the categories as justified in the work they do in making those representations possible) and then to move to the "categorial" level, as Hartmann called it (which was equivalent to what he also called the transcendental level). The *Phenomenology's* complex structure of historical and conceptual argument was thus a mere propaedeutic, a kind of way in which Hegel, like Wittgenstein, offered us a ladder to the system, only to have us throw it away once we arrive at the transcendental level.

Hartmann thus referred to his version of Hegelianism as categorial philosophy, and he liked to speak of the *categoriality* of this aspect of Hegelian philosophy. (Given the roots of his interpretation as lying in southwestern neo-Kantianism, he could just as well have called it "normativity," but he did not.) He extended this idea to the rest of Hegel's *Encyclopedia*, seeing it all as one large, self-moving transcendental argument (in Hartmann's sense) which advances by showing that each new category introduced has its normativity (its "categoriality") only in terms of its being the unity of a prior set of categories that does away with the contradictions that those categories contained before being conceived as lying within that new unity. (He called this the system's necessary "linearity.") Hegel's political philosophy, in Hartmann's view, thus became reinterpreted as a theory of *social* categories, unities of persons (such as "abstract right," or, most famously, family, civil society, and state) whose normativity is the same as all other such categories. Unfortunately, in political philosophy in general, one is usually not content with merely showing that *in theory* such and such a category (such as that of the state) is normative for other categories (e.g. the family and civil society) *simply* because it is the unity in which the contradictions of the prior social categories are to be conceived and done away with; one also typically wants to show how civil society influences the state and vice versa. However, the kind of linear, transcendental theory favored by Hegel (on Hartmann's interpretation) cannot show that, and all attempts to do so are versions of "transcendental illusion" (a term Hartmann took over from Kant, although it was used by Kant in a different sense). So Hartmann controversially argued: when Hegel himself made his move into the philosophy of history, he went beyond the limits of his own theory and tried to show how a development in time (in the empirical world) mirrored the kind of development in theory of the categories, and thus even Hegel himself fell prey to "transcendental illusion." That the Roman empire succeeded Periclean Athens in time was true; but that Rome was thereby the "categorial unity" of the contradictions of Athenian life such that it *had* to come on the scene at a later point in historical time and then had to be supplanted in turn by "Europe" was the kind of assertion that could only be made under the spell of transcendental illusion.

With the discarding of Hegel's philosophy of history, Hartmann discarded a good portion of what had been most valued in Hegel (the lectures on the philosophy of religion, on art, and on the history of philosophy) as not true to the basic impulses of the Hegelian system. Thus, in Hartmann's own self-proclaimed Hegelianism, what was supposed to be dead in Hegel (the *Logic* and the overarching systematic aspirations as a whole) was instead what was really alive, and what was supposed to be still alive in Hegel was effectively dead – supposedly on Hegel's own terms! Hartmann's Hegel emerged as an austere neo-Kantian who still had to be constrained from engaging in the excesses that had originally made him famous. Hartmann controversially called this the "non-metaphysical interpretation" of Hegel, a label which drew a lot of fire from critics. The charge against this interpretation was not only the obvious one (that this was not really "Hegel"), but that he had, at best, only saved Hegel by banning all that was most interesting in his thought — something Hartmann's followers, of course, vehemently denied.

From the 1960s onward, there continued to be a virtual explosion of new and interesting work in Germany on Hegel. The group of people assembled around the Hegel Archive in Bochum turned out an astonishing amount of new and historically informed studies on Hegel's development, on receptions of his thought, and on his relations to a variety of other historical figures (and they continue to do so). Very important studies on various aspects of Hegel's metaphysics, his "logic," his practical philosophy, and his aesthetics were produced by Hans Friedrich Fulda, Rüdiger Bubner (1941–2007), Ludwig Siep, Rolf-Peter Horstmann, and several others.

The other development in German thought in which Hegel played a role, although a fairly negative one, had to do with the development of what came to be known as the "Frankfurt School," particularly in the works of Theodor Adorno (1903–69) and Jürgen Habermas (1929–). Neither could be called "Hegelian," except that Hegelianism continued to play a large role in the background position of each thinker. Adorno's book, co-authored with Max Horkheimer (1895–1973), called *The Dialectic of the Enlightenment* had a Hegelian "look and feel" to it in its description of one supposedly liberating social movement turning into a new form of domination. In Adorno's and Horkheimer's story, the Enlightenment conception of rationality, which as instrumentalist in its conception has initially played a liberating role, had undergone a development in which it turned into its opposite by virtue of the way that the development of modern technological rationality as liberation had instead turned into yet another, even more rigid form of social control and domination of nature than the system it displaced. In his other works, Adorno often returned to Hegel, and in his major theoretical statement of his position, *Negative Dialectics* (1966), he tried to show that Hegelian dialectic, like all contemporary academic philosophy, had to be dethroned; it should be replaced with a form of thought that was critical but that nonetheless would eschew any attempt to tell a reconciliatory story or render the tensions and contradictions of modern life into some kind of consistent form (since that would be falsifying the very persistence and existence of those tensions themselves). Instead of the dangerous, all-subsuming force of the Hegelian dialectic, truly critical dialectics (so Adorno argued) had to be – somehow – open to the particularity and individuality of things (in nature but especially in social relations). In a manner similar to the charges leveled against Hegel by post-1960 French thinkers, Adorno claimed that the all-encompassing "totality" sought by Hegel was only a step away from the genuinely and really dangerous "totalitarianism" at work in the modern world. Hegel (like almost all modern philosophies) represented, in Adorno's odd jargon, "identity thinking," a phrase which for Adorno designated all the ways in which we fall prey to thinking that we have got a final, homogeneous, comprehensive, and true view of the world, which in turn leads to a kind of "violence" in forcing the great variety of individual things into the pigeonholes of the theory that claims to comprehend them.

Against such "identity thinking" (which has little if anything to do with the concept of "identity" at work in logic), Adorno defended the "non-identical," by which he meant the radically individual, the "other" of such totalizing (or "identity" oriented) thought and the way in which what is radically individual contains more or less within itself the seeds of what it would mean to be a better instantiation of itself. Adorno's "negative dialectic" was constructed as part of the antidote to the increasing homogeneity of modern commercial society, itself brought on by the dynamic of a society that rests on rational self-interest as its social glue and which therefore continues to develop a variety of mechanisms to produce a homogeneity of interests among its citizenry. Whereas Kojève had seen Hegel as foretelling the inevitably of the "homogeneous" state, Adorno saw him as instead *contributing* to the "homogeneous" state, and therefore as someone to be resisted, a task which Adorno's own conception of "negative dialectic" was supposed to help to carry out.

Habermas's appropriation of Hegel in turn used some of Hegel's criticisms of Kant (particularly of Kant's ethics as being too rigoristic and formalistic) to fashion a post-Kantian conception of social and political life that met all of Hegel's criticisms head-on, incorporated them, and produced something that looked very different from Kant but which nonetheless remained very Kantian. Habermas's own designation for this was his theory of "communicative action." In this theory, he developed, first, a demonstration of the conditions of possibility for full, unhindered communication between rational agents; second, a theory of how those communications can become distorted by class, race, power, and the like; and third, how we had to understand the status of our claims to rights, liberties, and the like in terms of a historical "learning process"; in this process we should come to understand how certain modes of social interaction had failed because of the internal pressures they generated within their own resources and thus that these modes cannot be repeated. Habermas's conception of the "learning process" thus replaced the Hegelian conception of a teleology of history while retaining the idea of there being progress in history by virtue of what we have learned about what works and does not work in human life. In later developments of this theory, he stressed the way in which speaking a language involves accepting a minimal set of normative commitments that are rich enough, when combined with the proper empirical social theory, to maintain a "critical" edge on existing social developments (Habermas 1996). Like Kant, Habermas sought to derive the principles of his social theory from the minimal conditions necessary for successful agency; like Hegel, he stressed that this agency was social in character, and like Hegel, he stressed that there was an element of "negativity," which he called a "surplus of validity claims" at work in the intersubjective relations among agents. His successor at Frankfurt, Axel Honneth, has attempted (see Honneth 1995) to carry this forward by showing how the minimal conditions for successful recognition among socially constituted agents provide the key to a "critical" theory (see "Critical Theory," Chapter 18).

On the other side of the great postwar philosophical divide — in postwar Anglophone philosophy — Hegel had pretty well become a dead duck. He continued to be taught in some courses in the history of philosophy, in the theory sections of political science departments, and there were a few universities that were holdouts to the overarching wave of analytical philosophy that was so dramatically transforming the shape of Anglo-American philosophy (and later philosophy everywhere) in which Hegel continued at least to be taught. That changed in the 1960s and 1970s because of two separate developments. The first was the great Kant revival which began in the 1960s. Peter F. Strawson's 1959 book, *Individuals: An Essay in Descriptive Metaphysics*, was a sensation when it was published: The very idea that a leading British analytical philosopher had put the term, "metaphysics," into the title of his book carried its own philosophical *frisson* — it is now difficult to comprehend just how shocking that was, appearing as it did in the heyday of the positivist rejection of metaphysics — and it extolled Kant as paving the way for solutions to the problems surfacing in analytical philosophy at the time. Strawson's own book on Kant, *The Bounds of Sense*, in 1966, effectively put Kant back on the philosophical map. When Jonathan Bennett published *Kant's Analytic* around the same time, the Bennett–Strawson debates on "transcendental arguments" as answers to skepticism helped to create a new Kant industry in Anglo-American scholarship. A few years later, John Rawls's highly original, magisterial, *A Theory of Justice*, published in 1971, which styled itself as a Kantian conception of political philosophy and which revived political philosophy in the Anglo-American arena, firmly established Kant in another area of contemporary thought. What few saw at the time, though, was that the revival of Kant was opening the door, even if only ever so slightly, to a reconsideration of what followed from Kant, namely, Hegel.

The second development had to do with the publication of two new large studies of Hegel at the end of the 1950s and the 1970s. The first was John Niemeyer Findlay's *Hegel: A Re-examination* (originally published in 1958, one year before Strawson's revival of Kant). Although Findlay (1903–87) was not originally a Hegelian (being at first more attracted to analytical philosophy), he found himself drawn to Hegelianism as he began the project of writing a book on him. However, unlike the earlier French and German versions of Hegel, Findlay's version downplayed the political and historical elements in Hegel and instead highlighted certain aspects of his philosophy of mind and of language, especially those that played into his philosophy of art and of religion. Thus Findlay stressed Hegel's relation to Wittgenstein: just as Wittgenstein had argued that philosophy is the result of our intellect being bewitched by language (and acquiring various bumps by running up against the limits of language), Findlay claimed that Hegel's own distinction between the hard-and-fast "understanding" (or "intellect," *der Verstand*) and the more fluid "reason" expressed much the same thought. On Findlay's telling, both Hegel and Wittgenstein thought that some, if not all, traditional problems of philosophy were merely illusory and brought on by the seductions of language (Wittgenstein) or by relying too heavily on the rigid intellect (Hegel). Hegel did not, of course, think that this showed that the "intellect" was merely illusory or misleading, only that it *can* be misled by its own fixity and that it then requires the therapeutic care of "reason" to set it aright again. Likewise, on Findlay's reading, Hegel was as much opposed to transcendent metaphysics — the metaphysics of the supersensible — as the most hard-headed positivist. Indeed, Findlay claims that Hegel's system "is one of the most anti-metaphysical of philosophical systems" (1962: 353); Hegel's conception of spirit was very much a this-worldly kind of thing, indeed was just the collective and individual activity of humanity "universalizing" its encounters with itself and the world. Hegel's striking thesis was that we gain a more interesting picture of the world if we see all things in terms of their contribution to the emergence of self-conscious spirit (again, with "spirit" as equivalent to human agency, taken both collectively and individually), a demand that comes from within the dynamics of "spirit" itself.

In Findlay's novel reading, this movement of going beyond the rigidities of the intellect to see the deeper and novel connections among thoughts and things constitutes the Hegelian dialectic. Findlay granted that Hegel's dialectic was not the entirely self-generating method that he claims even Hegel took it to be. For Findlay, there are too many ad hoc measures brought in from experience to make it work, and indeed, like Croce and so many others who followed him, Findlay thought that Hegel's structuring of his system into triadic forms was *the* great defect of it. As much as anybody else, Findlay thought that Hegel's triadic "logic" was dead and deserved no resuscitation. However, that did not constitute an argument against the way Hegel *actually* deployed his dialectic in his works; in Hegel's actual usage, the dialectic is not a series of lock-step moves whereby a contradiction supposedly impels one to move to a higher stage that, according to his notoriously difficult concept of *Aufhebung* (usually translated as "sublation") supposedly abolishes it while preserving it. Rather, it describes a set of *tendencies* of thought which, if each tendency were to be carried out completely, would set those ways of thought and life at odds with each other (or even in contradiction to each other). The move to the next "stage" in the dialectic sometimes involves avoiding a contradiction, but more often involves simply making something more explicit, or completing a thought that would otherwise remain incomplete, and it sometimes involves a passage from rule-based uses of language to meta-linguistic commentaries on those rule-based usages. "Dialectic" is thus the name for a loose procedure that aims to throw light on the fuzzier aspects of our experience, such as the way in which certain concepts have a natural affinity and tend to favor other concepts, ways that cannot be precisely pinned down by more analytical methods; and, as Hegel himself insists, these favoring relations are not in our power to alter but are features of the "things themselves." For Findlay, Hegelian dialectic *illuminates* but does not *demonstrate* anything.

Thus, Findlay did not think that the vaunted necessity of the dialectic in the *Phenomenology* was really there at all. Instead, the *Phenomenology* consists in a variety of illuminating discussions of various shapes of human experience, and any attempt to see one of them as *the* basic pattern for all the others (such Kojève did with the master/slave dialectic or Wahl did with the "unhappy consciousness") misses the point. The point is not to *argue* or to progress "logically" from one stage to another but instead to throw light on how certain ways of conceiving human life in relation to itself and to the world naturally favor certain other modes of living and thinking, and on how those other modes can be shown to have shortcomings (although not necessarily contradictions) within themselves that make them unstable — indeed, whose instability and shortcomings can only properly be appreciated from another standpoint that has gone beyond them. Thus the transitions from one stage to another often proceed not by logical necessity but, in Findlay's words, by a "wave of the dialectical wand" (1962: 107).

Like the French readers of Hegel, Findlay found support in Hegel's texts to argue that he should not be taken to be any kind of theist, although Findlay makes it clear that Hegel's thought is nonetheless thoroughly Christian in its inspiration. The images of God as redeemer, as creator of the world, etc. are for Hegel nothing more than "misleading pictorial expressions" of the "saving forces *intrinsic* to self-conscious Spirit" (1962: 142). Nonetheless, Findlay's Hegel is not Kojève's humanist Hegel. What plays the role of God in (Findlay's version of) Hegel's thought is the "impersonal, reasonable element in him" (p. 143), which is the self's consciousness of the tendency within itself to "universalize" everything; such divine self-consciousness is "simply the consciousness of this universalizing activity (which is also an *exercise* of this activity)" (p. 144). In this respect, Findlay's version was very much like Royce's. In this way, so Findlay claims, Hegel "may therefore fitly be regarded as the father of 'modernism,' that ever assailed but unsuppressible, and authentic expression of Christian belief" (p. 138).

For Findlay, the crucial texts for Hegelianism (for what is still alive in them) are the 1807 *Phenomenology*, the 1812–16 *Logic*, and the "phenomenologically" oriented Berlin lectures on art, religion, and philosophy. On the other hand, Hegel's work on political philosophy (such as the *Philosophy of Right*) was not really important: in Findlay's words, "At its worst it is small-minded and provincial, at its best it achieves the level of inspiration of an average British back-bench conservatism" (1962: 331). For Findlay, Hegel the anti-metaphysician, whose philosophy, Findlay mused, "perhaps ... is in its outcome an aesthetic philosophy" (p. 346), is a welcome antidote to the more finely tuned, naturalist tendencies of contemporary analytical thought. (Both Findlay and Klaus Hartmann taught at the University of Texas at Austin in the 1960s, making it the home of Anglophone "anti-metaphysical" readings of Hegel at the time, even as Findlay himself gradually moved to a more religious and metaphysical philosophical stance.)

Although Findlay's work was a step in the reawakening of interest in Hegel, it at first did little to interest analytical philosophers in exploring Hegel further. The Hegel revival came into fuller swing when in 1975, the Oxford philosopher, Charles Taylor (1931–), published his ground-breaking *Hegel*, which, like Findlay's book, attempted to survey the whole of Hegel's system to see what was living and what was dead in it. Like Findlay, Taylor saw Hegel as a quintessential "modernist," but unlike Findlay, Taylor argued that we should understand Hegel as responding to a deeper philosophical problem in western modernity. Indeed, for Taylor, it is *because* Hegel turns out to be so at odds with the dominant trends of contemporary philosophy (rather than as being continuous with, say, Wittgenstein or some other contemporary figure) that he is all the more interesting. The deeper problem to which Hegel was responding, so Taylor claimed, was the difficulty of reconciling two different demands that modern life made on itself: On the one hand, after the scientific revolution, nature was "disenchanted," devoid of meaning; on the other hand, the new conception of the human agent (the modern "subject") that had emerged out of the scientific revolution and the political and cultural upheavals of modernity claimed a certain rational and even radical autonomy for itself. The problem was how to unite these two — self-determining subjectivity and objective, disenchanted nature — into one comprehensive view, and, this formed, in a sense, *the* philosophical problem for modernity, which although deeply philosophical, was nonetheless not just "academic." The response to this was at first that of "expressivism" (a term of art Taylor introduced to capture the sense of what was at work in the late eighteenth and early nineteenth centuries). Rather than understanding meaning as the link between two types of objective things (for example, signs and states of affairs), many of the figures in early Romanticism and the prelude to it — Johann Gottfried Herder (1744–1803) in particular — sought to understand meaning as the expression of some kind of order, not as a link between two types of "things." In expression, we *clarify* something about ourselves that otherwise remains indeterminate (such as a feeling), and we realize some aspiration (thus making the aspiration more determinate). Expressivism revived a key element of the Aristotelian tradition, namely, Aristotle's "hylomorphism," the union of form and matter. However, expressivism differed from that tradition in holding that the form that is realized in matter (or embodiment) is not something that is determinate prior to its embodiment and then is only actualized; rather, it *acquires* its determinateness *in its being expressed.*

The Romantics extended this further to push for a conception of the unity of self-determining subjectivity and nature, which they saw as possible only if nature were to be seen as the expression of, in Taylor's terms, a "cosmic subjectivity." In the hands of some Romantics, such as Schelling, nature as the expression of cosmic subjectivity was to be united with radical freedom by seeing nature itself as finding its ultimate expression in free human agency. The Romantic synthesis, however, foundered on its inability to show that there was any real autonomy present in the union of "cosmic subjectivity" and human agency, so the Romantics, in the end, found themselves making the age-old recommendation to learn to submit to one's fate (or to see that to be free is to learn to bow to necessity).

On Taylor's reading, Hegel's entire program was best understood in terms of the three major influences on it: Aristotle, Kant, and Christianity; with these three influences in mind, Hegel took the Romantic synthesis further and pushed it through to its logical conclusion. Thus Hegel was led to see *Geist*, spirit, as having one aim: "That rational subjectivity be" (Taylor 1975: 93), and that there was a kind of conceptual necessity involved in that basic aim such that for spirit to realize its inherent teleology, certain kinds of conditions necessarily had to be met. The account of those conditions in turn constitutes the structure of Hegel's system. Thus, given the general "expressivist" demand for unity and the Aristotelian view that form always be embodied in matter, spirit requires an embodiment, and Hegel took his dialectic to show how the general structure of nature (although not its details) is conceptually required if spirit is to express itself. Furthermore, for spirit to achieve its aim, it must posit the existence of finite subjects (human agents), and the dialectic is supposed to go on to show that human agents can come to a full self-consciousness about themselves and thus express their nature as free, rational agents only through an agonistic historical process that gradually emancipates them from purely natural determination, all the while being an expression of the same "cosmic subjectivity" of which nature itself is an expression. It is this way that man both *clarifies* who he is and *achieves* his ultimate purpose, that of uniting his rational, free subjectivity with the larger life of nature, thus rounding out the expressivist picture of agency.

However, spirit *must* accomplish not just the conditions for the existence of human agency; it must also accomplish the conditions under which human agency can make some claim to being radically *autonomous*. It can do this only if the structure of this "cosmic subjectivity" is at one with the nature of human agency; and, thus, in coming to see themselves as "moments" of this "cosmic subjectivity," modern agents achieve a kind of reconciliation with it since they come to see that what otherwise would have looked like an external, deterministic fate (or just cruel bad luck or a lucky roll of the dice) is in fact what is conceptually necessary for them to achieve their highest goal, freedom. In the social world, that amounted to a demand for a demonstration of "how to combine the fullness of moral autonomy with the recovery of that community which was expressive of its members and whose paradigm was the Greek polis" (Taylor 1975: 365).

Thus, echoing Karl Rosenkranz's complaint in 1870, Taylor argued that the older labels for Hegel's political and philosophical thought — that he was a liberal *manqué*, a conservative, a reactionary apologist for Prussia, a forerunner of totalitarianism, a theocrat thinly disguised — were all wide of the mark. Hegel's philosophy, on Taylor's reading, is something different, practically *sui generis*, whose importance lies in the way he (in a sense) made it part of his own project to critique all of those labels as themselves fully inadequate comprehensions of spirit's grasp of itself in the modern world. In outlining Hegel's ambitious attempt to describe the progress of history as having its culmination in the modern European state, Taylor argued (by explicating both the historical context in which Hegel operated and the general tendencies of his line of thought) that Hegel's conception of modern life as fully articulated in the institutions of the family, civil society, the estates, the representation of estates in the state, the constitutional monarchy, and the like, was both interesting, still relevant, and irremediably flawed in a way that carried an important lesson within itself. Hegel fully understood, first, the Romantic protest about modern life, that it had made nature into something valueless and only to be exploited by humanity; and, second, he understood that the model of liberal society, which claimed to hold the "whole" together only out of a concatenation of rational calculations of self-interest, was inevitably headed in the direction of "homogenization." Hegel's entire system in fact was structured around the idea of providing a reconciliation, as it were, *within* the Romantic synthesis rather than providing a utopian revolutionary overthrow of modern conditions or a reactionary yearning for an imagined golden past. Indeed, Hegel understood better than almost all others the great tendency of liberal, commercial society to *homogenize* itself as a way of maintaining its fragile unity and stability, even though he underestimated the power of the modern institutions he recommended to keep that tendency in check.

Like almost all the other interpreters of Hegel during this period, Taylor declared that however brilliant Hegel's thought was, its major role in contemporary thought was mostly negative; it taught us a lesson about what kind of solution did not work. Hegel's solution to the problem of reconciling modern autonomy with disenchanted nature — resting as it did on a conception of "cosmic subjectivity" — turned out to be the wrong solution to the right problem. Hegel's vision of history as a progress guided by the "cunning of reason" is simply impossible to believe in our own times because the explosive growth of the natural sciences since Hegel's day has made his aspiration for an all-encompassing "absolute science" unbelievable. Moreover, his belief that the homogenizing, atomizing forces of modern industrial life would be kept in check by what he thought to be the newly instituted form of communal ethical life — the Hegelian combination of a universal commitment to very general human rights and a commitment to a universalizing morality that still has room for individual appeal to conscience, both of which were possible only in a social and political order structured around nuclear families, market societies, and constitutional monarchies — turned out to be terribly mistaken. However, even though it turned out to be so wrong, Taylor concluded that Hegel's philosophy remains a live option simply because the problems it so effectively put forth are still with us and still call out for a solution, and some of the Hegelian "instincts" about this — such as the conviction that "nature must still figure in it in some fashion" (1975: 546) — mean that the study of Hegel is a call to deal with these problems in a new way, not to declare that the problems have gone away simply because the flawed solution to them failed.

The success of Taylor's other work — for example, in the debates in the 1980s and 1990s about "communitarianism" versus "liberalism" — along with the growing interest in other forms of German philosophy helped to spur more interest in Hegel even though Taylor himself was obviously no Hegelian. The wave of interest in Kant spurred on by people such as Strawson and Rawls also helped to soften up the ongoing resistance in Anglophone philosophy to any kind of reception of Hegel.

In 1989, Robert Pippin (1948–) published *Hegel's Idealism: The Satisfactions of Self-Consciousness*, a defense and reinterpretation of Hegel's general philosophical outlook. That book took the line that some of the German commentators had taken, namely, that Hegel's philosophy was best read as an attempt to complete what Kant had left undone; the barely spoken premise of the book was, of course, that if Kant was still of great contemporary interest, then the later post-Kantian solutions to the notorious problems in Kantian philosophy might be of more than just historical interest. For Pippin, the Kantian stress on "spontaneity" and "autonomy" played out in Hegel's dialectic, and like the French commentators before him, Pippin placed more stress on the historical and social aspects of Hegel's work (in other words, the *Phenomenology*) than on the more purely systematic works (although the book included a long section on the *Logic*). Once one abandoned all appeals to any kind of "given" in empirical knowledge (a vibrant theme in the analytical philosophy of the day coming out of the influential writings of Wilfrid Sellars (1912–89) and W. V. O. Quine; see "American philosophy in the twentieth century," Chapter 5), the problem of providing an account of both conceptual content and justification was clearly on the horizon; and once one gave up on Kant's own theory of pure intuition, the problem was acute for the newly minted Kantians among the analytical philosophers. Hegel's own solution was seen by Pippin as an extended form of Kantian transcendental philosophy (that is, as a way of arguing for the necessity and objective validity of certain key concepts by showing that they were the conditions of the possibility of any kind of self-consciousness at all); it showed that Hegel, even given a rather orthodox interpretation, provided a promising avenue of thought. Like some of the other Anglophone interpreters, Pippin's Hegel was also a "non-metaphysical" Hegel, at least in the sense that in Pippin's interpretation, Hegel should not be seen as attempting to resuscitate the sort of metaphysical appeal to the "supersensible" that Kant had so devastatingly argued against. Instead, Hegel showed how one could be a Kantian without appealing to pure intuitions and how one could have a dynamic, historicized conception of the a priori status of basic categories. Pippin's Hegel was thus a Hegel who was not only responding to Kant, Fichte, and Schelling but also to Strawson, Sellars, and Rawls. In the 1990s and into the new century, Pippin continued to publish essays and books articulating and refining this interpretation of Hegel, which has inspired a number of new studies about the ongoing relevance of Hegel's thought.

Near the end of the century, the circle had come around almost fully. The demise of Hegelianism in the Anglophone world had to do in large part with the devastating attacks by Russell and Moore and the success of analytical philosophy in attracting some of the best minds to itself, a process that led analytical philosophy to exercise an almost complete hegemony in Anglophone philosophy after the Second World War (and which now seems to be beginning the same process in European philosophy). In 1994, Robert Brandom (1950–) published a long-awaited work, *Making It Explicit*, in which he defended and articulated a robust form of inferentialist semantics (that is, very roughly, the idea that the meaning of terms, at least in the sense that is of interest to philosophy, could be satisfactorily explained by their inferential links to each other; or, still very roughly, a theory that claims that to know what a term means is to know what inferences one can make with it, to what other positions in the conceptual firmament one is entitled to move by virtue of undertaking the commitments that term brings with it). Brandom's breathtaking treatment of the technical issues in such a program alone would have made it an important and indispensable work; his ability to show how those solutions to issues in inferentialist semantics also underpinned other controversial and interesting views in the philosophy of mind and theory of knowledge helped to cement it as a contender for one of the basic modern classics of the century. What was even more startling to Brandom's readers, however, was his unapologetic claim that this was in fact a *Hegelian* view of things (not just in a loose metaphorical sense but in a deeper sense grounded in the Hegelian texts), and that Hegel's *Phenomenology* and his *Logic*, for example, are best understood as a careful working out of an internally inferentialist position in philosophy. Unlike, for example, Henrich's explicitly metaphysical reading of the "self-movement" of the absolute, Brandom saw Hegel's dialectic, particularly in the *Phenomenology*, as a *social* account of how agents reciprocally undertake commitments (to claims and what follows from those claims) and issue entitlements to each other (that is, judge the other to be entitled to what they are claiming), with the result that as each "keeps score" (in Brandom's terminology) of what the other is doing, they collectively build up a sense of the whole, that is, what Hegel called the "absolute," as the totality of all such inference licenses. By the end of the century, Brandom began to publish some essays on Hegel which have helped to flesh out his claim that he is a Hegelian — an act which, like Strawson's claim almost thirty-five years earlier, was received with a shock that future generations will probably find it difficult to grasp (Brandom 2002). The end of the century found him at work on a book on Hegel's *Phenomenology* which will probably see the light of day sometime in the first decade of the twenty-first century.

Likewise, his colleague, John McDowell, another analytic philosopher, has turned to writing about the affinity between his own influential views and those of Hegel (McDowell 1994). McDowell claims to have been inspired in this by both Brandom's and Pippin's work, although the line he takes is far more sympathetic to Pippin's approach than it is to Brandom's. For McDowell, Hegel is best understood as showing, in a manner similar to Wittgenstein, how the ordinary problems in philosophy, particularly those of skepticism, can be dissolved through a kind of therapeutic approach. In Hegel's case this involves showing how the standpoint of the "understanding" generates problems that from the standpoint of "reason" are not there; only by taking Hegel's radicalization of Kant seriously can we get a hold on what it would mean to say that we have direct access to an empirically accessible reality independent of us while preserving the Kantian-Hegelian sense of the "spontaneity" of our intellects.

The close of the twentieth century thus saw Hegelianism, at least on the metaphorical level, mirroring the Hegelian move of "turning into its opposite." From starting out at the high point of new interest at the beginning of the century, Hegelianism suffered a variety of distressing setbacks; in the Anglophone philosophical world, the analytic attack on Hegelianism seemed to have killed it off for good or at least to have rendered it into an item of only antiquarian interest. From its inception, analytical philosophy had distinguished itself in many ways, but one of its key self-understandings was that it was *not Hegelian*. However, by the end of the century, some leading analytical philosophers were proclaiming themselves in fact to be Hegelians, and some Hegelians were proclaiming themselves to be the successors to the problems of analytical philosophy. Likewise, for many on the European continent, Hegel was originally of interest as a way of making his own successor, Marx, more intelligible and humanistic; but after the demise of Marxism, Hegel appeared as a philosopher worthy of study in his own right. In the wake of Findlay, Taylor, and Pippin, new and interesting work on Hegel was starting to appear more and more frequently in Anglophone studies. (Some pieces by the author of this essay also played some role in the Hegelian revival.) At the beginning of the twenty-first century, the jury is still out on what is alive and what is dead in Hegel's thought; but, against the odds, the philosophical figure, "Hegel," is once again still very much alive and as controversial as he has ever been.

References

Adorno, T. (1973) *Negative dialectics*, trans. E. B. Ashton. New York: Seabury Press.

Brandom, R. (1994) *Making It Explicit*. Cambridge, MA: Harvard University Press.

_____ (2002) *Tales of the Mighty Dead: Historical Essays in the Metaphysics of Intentionality*. Cambridge, MA: Harvard University Press.

Croce, B. (1915) *What is Living and What is Dead in the Philosophy of Hegel?*, trans. D. Ainslie. London: Macmillan.

Findlay, J. N. (1962) [1958] *Hegel: A Re-examination*. New York: Collier Books.

Gadamer, H.-G. (1976) *Hegel's Dialectic: Five Hermeneutical Studies*, trans. P. C. Smith. New Haven, CT: Yale University Press.

Habermas, J. (1996) [1994] *Between Facts and Norms: Contributions to a Discourse Theory of Law and Democracy*, trans. W. Rehg. Cambridge, MA: MIT Press.

Hartmann, K. (1972) "Hegel: a non-metaphysical view." In A. MacIntyre (ed.) *Hegel: A Collection of Critical Essays*, Notre Dame, IN: University of Notre Dame Press, pp. 101–24.

Henrich, D. (1971) *Hegel im Kontext*. Frankfurt am Main: Suhrkamp.

_____ (1982) "Andersheit und Absolutheit des Geistes." In *Selbstverhältnisse*, Stuttgart: Philipp Reklam, pp. 142–72.

Honneth, A. (1995) [1992] *The Struggle for Recognition: The Moral Grammar of Social Conflicts*, trans. J. Anderson. Cambridge, MA: MIT Press.

Hyppolite, J. (1974) [1946] *Genesis and Structure of the Phenomenology of Spirit*, trans. S. Cherniak and J. Heckman. Evanston, IL: Northwestern University Press.

Kojève, A. (1969) *Introduction to the Reading of Hegel: Lectures on the Phenomenology of Spirit*, trans. J. H. Nichols, Jr. Ithaca, NY: Cornell University Press.

Lukács, G. (1968) [1923] *History and Class Consciousness*, trans. R. Livingstone. London: Merlin Press.

McDowell, J. (1994) *Mind and World*. Cambridge, MA: Harvard University Press.

Merleau-Ponty, M. (1973) [1955] *The Adventures of the Dialectic*, trans. J. Bien. Evanston, IL: Northwestern University Press.

Pippin, R. (1989) *Hegel's Idealism: The Satisfactions of Self-Consciousness*. Cambridge: Cambridge University Press.

Rosenkranz, J. K. F. (1870) *Hegel als deutscher Nationalphilosoph*. Leipzig: Duncker & Humblot.

Royce, J. (1919) *Lectures on Modern Idealism*. New Haven, CT: Yale University Press.

Taylor, C. (1975) *Hegel*. Cambridge: Cambridge University Press.

Wahl, J. (1951) [1929] *Le Malheur de la conscience dans la philosophie de Hegel*, 2nd edn. Paris: Presses Universitaires de France.

Further reading

For a comprehensive bibliography of nineteenth- and twentieth-century works on Hegel that span all the European languages, see the article by R. Stern and N. Walker, "Hegelianism" in the *Routledge Encyclopedia of Philosophy*. Stern's and Walker's account is a magisterial overview of all the literature on the subject.

Habermas, J. (1984) [1981] *The Theory of Communicative Action*, vols. 1–2, trans. T. McCarthy. Boston: Beacon Press.

Hartmann, K. (1966) "On taking the transcendental turn." *Review of Metaphysics* 20/2 (December): 223–49.

Houlgate, S. (2005) *An Introduction to Hegel: Freedom, Truth and History*. London: Wiley-Blackwell.

Malabou, C. (2005) *The Future of Hegel: Plasticity, Temporality and Dialectic*, trans. L. During. London: Routledge.

Pinkard, T. (1994) *Hegel's Phenomenology: The Sociality of Reason*. Cambridge: Cambridge University Press.

_____ (2000) *Hegel: A Biography*. Cambridge: Cambridge University Press.

Pippin, R. (1997) *Idealism as Modernism: Hegelian Variations*. Cambridge: Cambridge University Press.

Rockmore, T. (1995) "Hegel as a French master thinker." In *Heidegger and French Philosophy: Humanism, Anti-Humanism, and Being*, London: Routledge, pp. 27–39.

_____ (2003) *Before and After Hegel: A Historical Introduction to Hegel's Thought*. Indianapolis: Hackett.

Stern, R. (2002) *Hegel and the 'Phenomenology of Spirit'*. London: Routledge.

4
KANT IN THE TWENTIETH CENTURY

Robert Hanna

Introduction

Alfred North Whitehead (1861–1947) quotably wrote in 1929 that "the safest general characterization of the European philosophical tradition is that it consists of a series of footnotes to Plato."[1] The same could be said, perhaps with even greater accuracy, of the twentieth-century Euro-American philosophical tradition and Immanuel Kant (1724–1804).[2] In this sense the twentieth century was the post-Kantian century.

Twentieth-century philosophy in Europe and the USA was dominated by two distinctive and (after 1945) officially opposed traditions: the *analytic tradition* and the *phenomenological tradition*. Very simply put, the analytic tradition was all about logic and analyticity,[3] and the phenomenological tradition was all about consciousness and intentionality.[4] (See also "The birth of analytic philosophy," Chapter 1; "The development of analytic philosophy: Wittgenstein and after," Chapter 2; "American philosophy in the twentieth century," Chapter 5; and "Phenomenology," Chapter 15.) Ironically enough however, despite their official Great Divide, both the analytic and the phenomenological traditions were essentially continuous and parallel critical developments from an earlier dominant neo-Kantian tradition. This, by the end of the nineteenth century had vigorously reasserted the claims of Kant's transcendental idealism against Hegel's absolute idealism and the other major systems of post-Kantian German Idealism, under the unifying slogan "Back to Kant!" So again ironically enough, both the analytic and phenomenological traditions were alike founded on, and natural outgrowths from, Kant's Critical Philosophy.

By the end of the twentieth century however, and this time sadly rather than ironically, both the analytic and phenomenological traditions had not only explicitly rejected their own Kantian foundations and roots but also had effectively undermined themselves philosophically, even if by no means institutionally. On the one hand the analytic tradition did so by abandoning its basic methodological conception of analysis as the process of logically decomposing propositions[5] into conceptual or metaphysical "simples," as the necessary preliminary to a logical reconstruction of the same propositions, and by also jettisoning the corresponding idea of a sharp, exhaustive, and significant "analytic-synthetic" distinction. The phenomenological tradition on the other hand abandoned its basic methodological conception of phenomenology as "seeing essences" with a priori certainty under a "transcendental-phenomenological reduction," and also jettisoned the corresponding idea of a "transcendental ego" as the metaphysical ground of consciousness and intentionality.

One way of interpreting these sad facts is to say that just insofar as analytic philosophy and phenomenology alienated themselves from their Kantian origins, they stultified themselves. This is the first unifying thought behind this chapter, and it is a downbeat one. The second unifying thought, which however is contrastively upbeat, is that both the analytic and phenomenological traditions, now in conjunction instead of opposition, could rationally renew themselves in the twenty-first century by critically recovering their Kantian origins and by seriously re-thinking and re-building their foundations in the light of this critical recovery. Or in other words: *Forward to Kant*.

A sketch of Kant's Critical Philosophy

What the Critical Philosophy is

Not surprisingly, Kant's Critical Philosophy is to be found primarily in his three *Critiques*: the *Critique of Pure Reason* (1781–7), the *Critique of Practical Reason* (1788), and the *Critique of the Power of Judgment* (1790). But the Critical Philosophy is not exhausted by the *Critiques*. Kant's *Prolegomena to Any Future Metaphysics* (1783), *Metaphysical Foundations of Natural Science* (1786), and *Jäsche Logic* (1800) all complement and supplement the first *Critique*; his *Grounding for the Metaphysics of Morals* (1785), *Religion within the Limits of Reason Alone* (1793), and *Metaphysics of Morals* (1797), similarly complement and supplement the second *Critique*; and his *Anthropology from a Pragmatic Point of View* (1798) and the unfinished and posthumously published *Transition from the Metaphysical Foundations of Natural Science to Physics* (also known as the *Opus postumum*) together make up his final Critical reflections on human reason and physical nature.

But what *is* the Critical Philosophy? In a word, *it's all about us*. Less telegraphically put, the Critical Philosophy is a comprehensive theory of human nature, carried out by means of detailed analyses of human "cognition" (*Erkenntnis*), human volition or "the power of choice" (*Willkür*), and human "reason" (*Vernunft*). Cognition, volition, and reason are all "faculties" (*Vermögen*), which in turn are innate, spontaneous mental "capacities" (*Fähigkeiten*) or "powers" (*Kräfte*). The innateness of a mental capacity means that the capacity is intrinsic to the mind, and not the acquired result of experiences, habituation, or learning. Correspondingly, the spontaneity of a mental capacity implies that the acts or operations of the capacity are

1   causally and temporally unprecedented, in that (a) those specific sorts of act or operation have never actually happened before, and (b) antecedent events do not provide fully sufficient conditions for the existence or effects of those acts or operations,

2 underdetermined by external sensory informational inputs and also by prior desires, even though it may have been triggered by those very inputs or motivated by those very desires,

3 creative in the sense of being recursively constructive, or able to generate infinitely complex outputs from finite resources, and also

4 self-guiding.

Cognition is a faculty for the conscious mental representation of objects (*CPR* A320/376–7). Volition, or the power of choice, is a faculty for causing actions by means of conscious desires (*MM* 6: 213). And reason is a faculty for cognizing or choosing according to "principles" (*Principien*) (*CPR* A405, A836/B864 and *CPrR* 5: 32), which are necessary and strictly normative rules of the human mind or human action, and constitute either theoretical laws or practical laws. Theoretical reason is cognizing that is aimed at the *truth of judgments*, according to necessary and strictly normative rules of logic and in particular according to the Law of Non-Contradiction, which says that only those propositions that are not both true and false, can be true. Practical reason by contrast is choosing that is aimed at either *the instrumental good of actions* or *the non-instrumental good of actions*. The latter arises according to strictly normative rules of morality and in particular according to the unconditional universal moral law or Categorical Imperative, which says that only those chosen acts whose act-intentions, when generalized to every possible rational agent and to every possible context of intentional action, are internally consistent and also coherent with the general aims of rational agents as such, can be morally good.

What makes the Critical Philosophy a specifically *critical* philosophy, however, is Kant's striking and substantive thesis – which amounts to a mitigated form of rationalism – to the effect that the human faculty of reason, whether theoretical or practical, is inherently constrained by the brute fact of human finitude, or our animality. Otherwise put, Kantian critique is the philosophical story of how our reason, which initially aims to occupy the standpoint of God through theoretical speculation and practical aspiration alone, rationally reconciles itself to cognitive and moral life in a messy material world. More precisely, this is to say that our capacity of reason finds itself inherently constrained by the special contingent conditions of all human animal embodiment: the faculties of "sensibility" (*Sinnlichkeit*), and "desire" (*Begehren*) or "drive" (*Trieb*). In what ways constrained? The answer is that human sensibility strictly limits our theoretical reason to the cognition of sensory appearances or phenomena, and that human desire or drive strictly limits our practical reason to choices that are bound up with our psychophysical and psychosocial well-being, or "happiness" (*Glückseligkeit*). So rational creatures like us are nevertheless *inherently human*, and indeed *all-too-human*:

> Human reason has this peculiar fate in one species of its cognition that is is burdened with questions which it cannot dismiss, since they are given to it as problems by the nature of reason itself, but which it also cannot answer, since they transcend every capacity of human reason. (*CPR* Avii)

Out of the crooked timber of humanity, nothing straight can ever be made.
(IUH 8: 23)

By sharp contrast, the theoretical reason of a divine cognizer, or "intellectual intuition" (CPR B72), is (barely) conceivable by us; and such a being would know "things-in-themselves" or objective "noumena," that is, supersensible Really Real objects whose essences are constituted by mind-independent intrinsic non-relational properties (CPR A42–9/B59–72, B306–7), directly and infallibly by thinking alone. Similarly, the practical reason of a divine agent or "holy will" (GMM 4: 439), which is a *subjective* noumenon, is also (again, barely) conceivable by us; and such a being would do the right thing directly and infallibly by intending alone. Kant thinks that we cannot help being able to conceive such beings, and that an essential part of our rational intellectual and moral make-up is the fact that we are finite embodied beings who burden ourselves with invidious comparative thoughts about these non-finite non-embodied beings. We crave a transcendent, superhuman justification for our finite embodied thoughts and actions. So for Kant, to be human is not only *to be* finite and embodied, and also *to know* that we are finite and embodied, but most importantly of all, *to wish that we weren't.*

Kant's metaphysics

On the theoretical side of the rational human condition, this inherent anthropo-centric limitation specifically means that human cognition is sharply constrained by three special conditions of sensibility: two formal conditions, namely the necessary a priori representations of space and time (CPR A38–9/B55–6); and one material condition, namely affection, or the triggering of cognitive processes by the direct givenness of something existing outside the human cognitive faculty (CPR A19/B33). The basic consequence of these constraints is *transcendental idealism*. Transcendental idealism, as the name obviously suggests, is the conjunction of two sub-theses: (1) *the transcendentalism thesis*, and (2) *the idealism thesis*.

(1) The transcendentalism thesis says that all the representational contents of cognition are strictly determined in their underlying forms or structures by a set of primitive or underived universal a priori innate spontaneous human cognitive capacities, also known as "cognitive faculties" (*Erkenntnisvermögen*). These cognitive faculties include (i) the "sensibility" (*Sinnlichkeit*), or the capacity for spatial and temporal representation via sensory "intuition" (*Anschauung*) (CPR A22/B36), (ii) the "understanding" (*Verstand*), or the capacity for conceptualization or "thinking "(*Denken*) (CPR A51/B75), (iii) the power of "imagination" (*Einbildungskraft*), which on the one hand comprehends the specific powers of "memory" (*Gedächtnis, Erinnerung*) (A 7: 182–5), "imaging" (*Bildung*), and "schematizing" (CPR A137–42/B176–81), but also on the other hand includes the synthesizing or mental-processing power of the mind more generally (CPR A78/B103), (iv) "self-consciousness" (*Selbstbewußtsein*) (CPR B132) or the capacity for "apperception," which is the ground of unity for all conceptualizing and judging (CPR B406), and finally (v) reason, which as we have

already seen is the capacity for logical inference and practical decision-making. The whole system of cognitive capacities is constrained in its operations by both "pure general logic," the topic-neutral or ontically uncommitted, a priori, universal, and categorically normative science of the laws of thought, and also by "transcendental logic," which is pure general logic that is semantically and modally restricted by an explicit ontic commitment to the proper objects of human cognition (CPR A50–7/ B74–82).

(2) The idealism thesis says that the proper objects of human cognition are nothing but objects of our sensory experience – appearances or phenomena – and not things-in-themselves or noumena, owing to fact that space and time are nothing but necessary a priori subjective forms of sensory intuition (Kant calls this "the ideality of space and time"), together with the assumption (which I will call *the intrinsicness of space and time*) that space and time are intrinsic relational properties of every object in space and time (CPR A19–49/B33–73, A369 and P 4: 293). Appearances, in turn, are token-identical with the intersubjectively communicable contents of sensory or experiential representations (PC 11: 314). Correspondingly, the essential forms or structures of the appearances are type-identical with the representational forms or structures that are generated by our universal a priori mental faculties: "objects must conform (*richten*) to our cognition" (CPR Bxvi), and "the object (as an object of the senses) conforms to the constitution of our faculty of intuition" (CPR Bxvii).

Putting transcendentalism and idealism together, we now have the complex conjunctive Kantian metaphysical thesis of transcendental idealism:

> Human beings can cognize and know only either sensory appearances or the forms or structures of those appearances – such that sensory appearances are token-identical with the contents of our objective sensory cognitions, and such that the essential forms and structures of the appearances are type-identical with the representational forms or structures generated by our own cognitive faculties, especially the intuitional representations of space and time – and therefore we can neither cognize, nor scientifically know,[6] nor ever empirically meaningfully assert or deny, anything about things-in-themselves. (CPR A369, B310–11)

This is of course is a highly controversial and substantive metaphysical thesis. But Kant both mitigates the sting and enriches the substance of his idealism by also defending *empirical realism*:[7]

> [The] empirical realist grants to matter, as appearance, a reality which need not be inferred, but is immediately perceived (*unmittelbar wahrgenommen*). (CPR A371)

> Every outer perception ... immediately proves (*beweiset unmittelbar*) something real in space, or rather [what is represented through outer perception] is itself the real; to that extent, empirical realism is beyond doubt, i.e., to our outer intuitions there corresponds something real in space. (CPR A375)

In other words, he is saying that when we eliminate things-in-themselves as possible objects of human sensible cognition (although we remain capable of *thinking* about them abstractly), focus exclusively on appearances instead, and then identify *them* with the real material objects in space, it follows that we perceive real material objects in space through our senses without any further intermediary (let us call this Kant's *direct perceptual realism*), and also that all the essential properties of real material objects in space are macrophysical directly perceivable or observable properties (let us call this Kant's *manifest realism*). In other words, for Kant the classical "veil of mere appearances" becomes *the field of authentic appearances*, in which all things are precisely what they seem to be. In this sense, his idealism is also paradoxically the most robust realism imaginable.

But what is the *point* of transcendental idealism? Kant's immensely brilliant answer, worked out in rich (and occasionally stupefying) detail in the *Critique of Pure Reason*, is that transcendental idealism alone adequately explains how synthetic a priori propositions – that is, non-logically necessary, substantively meaningful, experience-independent truths – are semantically possible or objectively valid (CPR B19), and also how human freedom of the will is both logically and metaphysically possible (CPR Bxxv–xxx, A530–58/559–86). His two-part thought in a nutshell is this:

(1) The *synthetic apriority thesis* says that all and only empirically meaningful synthetic a priori propositions express one or more of the transcendental conditions for the possibility of our human experience of objective appearances.

(2) The *transcendental freedom thesis* says that the synthetic a priori proposition (call it "*F*") – which says that human noumenal (a.k.a. "transcendental") freedom of the will exists – *cannot be scientifically known to be true*. Yet (a) F is logically consistent with the true synthetic a priori proposition (call it "*G*"), which says that the total mechanical system of inert macrophysical material bodies in phenomenal nature – bodies that are in fact constituted by fundamental attractive and repulsive forces under natural laws – have deterministic temporally antecedent nomologically sufficient causes; (b) the actual truth of G underdetermines the truth value of *F*; (c) both the metaphysical possibility and the actual truth of *F* are presuppositions of human morality.

If the synthetic apriority thesis is true, it follows that there are two irreducibly different kinds of necessary truth, namely analytic or *logical* necessities and synthetic or *non-logical* necessities (which I will call Kant's *modal dualism*), and that the first principles of metaphysics are among those synthetic or non-logical necessities. It also follows that the set of first principles of metaphysics, and the set of truths about how our transcendental cognitive faculties make a priori contributions to the formal structures of sensory representations, are one and the same. And if the transcendental freedom thesis is true, it follows that the law-governed mechanism of nature is not only *consistent* with human freedom of the will, but also implies the *necessary possibility* of human freedom in nature.

This shows us that the ultimate upshot of Kant's metaphysics is thoroughly anthropocentric and practical.[8] Otherwise put, Kant fully rejects scientific or reductive naturalism, which says that science – more precisely, *exact science*, or mathematics-plus-physics – is, as Wilfrid Sellars famously formulates it, "the measure of all things."[9]

On the contrary, for Kant scientific reductionism leads directly to both epistemic and moral skepticism (*CPR* xxix). Moreover, for Kant, by a fundamental explanatory inversion or "Copernican Revolution," exact science is grounded on the transcendental metaphysics of rational human nature. But it gets even better than this. In order to allow for the possibility of human freedom, he also holds that we must sharply *limit* the epistemic and metaphysical scope of exact science: "I have therefore found it necessary to deny *scientific knowing* (*Wissen*) in order to make room for [moral] *faith* (*Glauben*)" (*CPR* Bxxx). Indeed, practical reason has both explanatory and ontological *priority* over theoretical reason (*CPrR* 5: 120–1). So, perhaps surprisingly, the key to Kant's metaphysics is his ethics.

Kant's ethics

On the practical side of the rational human condition, the intrinsic constraints on human volition are in certain ways highly analogous, but also in other ways sharply disanalogous, to the intrinsic constraints on human cognition. Like human cognition, whose proper objects are restricted to sensory appearances, so too the proper objects of human volition are *desiderative appearances*, or *things that seem desirable or good to the rational human animal*, and thus are bound up with its individual and social well-being or happiness. For Kant, this directly implies that rational human animals are *radically evil* (*Rel* 6: 32–3). Despite our being *fallible* or error-prone creatures however, this does not mean that rational human beings are *fallen* creatures, whether in the theological (Christian) sense of original sin, or in the secular (Rousseauian) sense of an inevitable corruption by socialization.[10] What it means instead is the much more prosaic fact that in the developmental order of time rational humans are *human animals* long before they are able to actualize their capacity for reason (*Rel* 6: 26–7), and are therefore subject to the thousand natural shocks that flesh is heir to; and even once human beings do finally become mature adults and actualize their rational capacity, nevertheless in order to survive and flourish as animals in an often unfriendly and dangerous world that they did not create and did not ask to be born into, they must as a matter of contingent fact *almost* inevitably think and act prudentially. Therefore rational humans will – not necessarily but as a matter of contingent fact *almost* inevitably, given their profound vulnerability to sheer luck and their partially constitutive animality – freely choose things, by virtue of the power of choice inherent in their animal nature (*MM* 6: 213), in violation of the moral law (*CPrR* 5: 100).[11]

The moral law, or Categorical Imperative – that is, an unconditional universal rational command – is our duty or strict obligation as rational animal beings or persons, and says that we ought to do only those acts whose "maxims" or act-intentions (1) can be consistently universalized, (2) always involve treating other persons as "ends-in-themselves," or as having *intrinsic value*, and never merely as means to the satisfaction of our own desires, (3) inherently express our pure rational volitional nature as free or causally spontaneous and also autonomous or self-legislating agents, and (4) directly imply our belonging to an indefinitely large ideal community of persons and free and autonomous agents, "the kingdom of ends," the card-carrying members of which can self-legislate the moral law only insofar as they *also* legislate for every other member of the self-same ideal moral community (GMM 4: 406–45).

Now according to Kant the Categorical Imperative provides a universal unconditional non-instrumental reason for human action (as specified in particular unconditional non-instrumental reasons, constructed by us in particular act-contexts) in the form of a rational command, and is to be sharply contrasted with *hypothetical* imperatives either of "skill" or "prudence," which are conditional instrumental rational commands and thereby provide conditional instrumental reasons for human action: such as that I ought to flip the light switch in order to turn on the light (imperative of skill), or that I ought to bring the glass up to my lips if want to drink my tot of Jack Daniel's (imperative of prudence). But the Categorical Imperative, in and of itself, does not tell us *which* maxims or act-intentions to form but rather but rather only *how* we must form maxims in order to be morally good. So the Categorical Imperative is a purely *procedural* or *constructive* principle of human volition and action (exactly analogous to the Law of Non-Contradiction in relation to the truth of theoretical judgments and the soundness of arguments), and not a *substantive* or material principle that in and of itself yields maxims. This means that practical reasoning must always begin with actual human desires and hypothetical imperatives as inputs or data, and then, if the moral law is to be heeded, suitably constrain intentional animal action by choosing to act only on those maxims that satisfy the four formulations of the Categorical Imperative. The recognition of our obligation and ability to constrain intentional animal action appropriately, when concretely realized and non-cognitively consciously experienced via some characteristically moral feelings such as self-respect, self-denying concern for others, moral disgust, or righteous anger, is what Kant calls the "Fact of Reason" (CPrR 5: 31). Most crucially, the Fact of Reason yields direct affective, non-conceptual, and non-propositional (hence non-cognitive, non-scientific, and non-theoretical) *compelling empirical evidence* for the actual existence of transcendental freedom and practical freedom (CPR A802/B830).

So, unlike empirically meaningful human cognition, which can never even in principle transcend the bounds of sensibility (CPR A42–3/B59–60), the rational human animal still *does* possess the capacity for practical freedom or autonomy, which is a spontaneous causally efficacious capacity for self-legislative choosing in a way that is underdetermined by all alien causes and prudential concerns, and in self-conscious conformity with the Categorical Imperative (CPrR 5: 28–33). In other words, autonomy is rational freedom of the pure "will" (*Wille*) (MM 6: 213–14). No matter how infrequent such choices are, to exercise rational freedom of the will is to realize the rational practical aspect of our human nature, and to that extent, transcend the intrinsic constraints on human volition, or our animality. So, paradoxically, we rationally transcend ourselves only when we fully come to terms with our animality. We are immediately conscious of the fact that (or in any case *we must act under the idea that*) autonomy or practical freedom of the will actually exists, because (1) freedom of the will is (as an online capacity) a necessary and (as an implemented capacity) sufficient condition of moral responsibility and (2) rational human animals are, as a social matter of fact, held morally responsible for their right and wrong intentional actions alike (GMM 4: 446–63). Or more succinctly put: the *ought* and *ought not* of morality alike entail the *can* of rational volitional human agency, or the autonomously and practically free will.

This power of autonomy is to be sharply contrasted with the "power of choice" (*Willkür*) (*CPR* A802/B830 and *CPrR* 5: 97), shared by human animals and non-human animals alike, which is *not necessarily* autonomous and therefore has no sufficient connection with moral responsibility. Yet, whenever the power of choice is realized in a rational animal, this implies at least a transcendentally free causal responsibility and thus remains a necessary condition of autonomy and moral responsibility. No rational human animal can be practically free and operate independently of all alien causes and sensuous motivations unless it can *also*, just like any other conscious animal, move itself by means of its desires in a way that is strictly underdetermined by the universal mechanism of the causal laws of inert material nature – or in other words, move itself *animately, purposefully, and freely*. And in this way, according to Kant, the *inertial* causal dynamics of mechanical matter is radically extended by the *vital* causal dynamics of embodied moral persons.

Neo-Kantian openings

What neo-Kantianism is

Neo-Kantianism[12] in all its forms was a German philosophical movement that ran its course from roughly 1870 to roughly 1945. It consisted in the close study and passionate promulgation of Kant's Critical Philosophy plus some editorial changes and critical updates, whereby certain troublesome concepts and doctrines (for example, things-in-themselves and their metaphysical status) were omitted or finessed, and whereby certain themes (for example, Kant's psychology, his idealism, or his philosophy of the exact sciences) were specially emphasized and further developed. The unifying slogan "Back to Kant!" was the motto of Otto Liebmann (1840–1912) in his *Kant und die Epigonen* (1865). Other leading neo-Kantians included Alois Riehl (1844–1924), Hermann Cohen (1842–1918), Paul Natorp (1854-1924), Heinrich Rickert (1863–1936), and Ernst Cassirer (1874–1945).

Neo-Kantianism and the emergence of analytic philosophy

Neo-Kantianism carried over into the early twentieth century in three significantly different versions: (1) a *science-oriented* neo-Kantianism (mainly centered in Marburg) that was fueled by contemporary developments in the exact sciences, together with classical empiricism in the tradition of David Hume (1711–76) and John Stuart Mill (1806–73); (2) a *psychologistic* neo-Kantianism (mainly centered in Göttingen) that reacted against science-oriented neo-Kantianism and fused with empirical psychology; and (3) an *idealistic* neo-Kantianism (mainly centered in Heidelberg) that merged with elements of the dominant Hegelian tradition. Psychologistic neo-Kantianism led to *phenomenology*. Idealistic neo-Kantianism led to *neo-Hegelianism*. And science-oriented neo-Kantianism led to *logical positivism*.

By the end of the twentieth century, analytic philosophy comfortably dominated the Anglo-American philosophical scene, and analytic philosophers were the Establishment.[13] But at the beginning of the century things were very different: the dominant philosophies in English-speaking countries and Europe alike were neo-Kantianism or neo-Hegelianism, and analytic philosophers were the Young Turks. Analytic philosophy emerged in the period from the *fin de siècle* to the mid-1930s by means of, on the one hand, a sharp reaction against neo-Kantianism and neo-Hegelianism, which pulled it in the direction of Platonism and radical realism, and on the other hand, the anti-metaphysical impetus provided by logical positivism, which, rather confusingly, also pulled analytic philosophy simultaneously in the opposite direction of conventionalism and anti-realism. This inner conflict in the foundations of analytic philosophy between Platonism and realism on the one side, and conventionalism and anti-realism on the other, later worked itself out in the historical-philosophical careers of the paired concepts of *the analytic proposition* (a necessary a priori truth by virtue of logical laws and logical definitions – or perhaps "meanings" – alone) and *analysis* (the process of knowing an analytic proposition). There will be more to say about these important notions below. The crucial point at the moment is that they make sense only in relation to a neo-Kantian and thereby Kantian backdrop. Without Kant's Critical Philosophy, *there would have been no such thing as analytic philosophy*.[14]

Now back to exploring the influence of psychologistic neo-Kantianism, and the emergence of phenomenology.

Kantian themes in the early phenomenological tradition

Kant, Brentano, and the foundations of phenomenology

Phenomenology, according to its founder Franz Brentano (1838–1917) in his *Psychology from an Empirical Standpoint* (1874), is "descriptive psychology."[15] This contrastively refers back to Kant's Paralogisms, where he thoroughly criticizes *rational psychology*, which claims that the mind is a simple substantial immortal Cartesian soul, or a subjective thing-in-itself (*CPR* 341–405/B399–432). In other words, rational psychology is the a priori science of *mental noumena*. By sharp contrast, descriptive psychology in Brentano's sense is the a posteriori science of *mental phenomena*. Brentano's mental phenomena are essentially the same as the contents of what Kant called "inner sense," and what William James (1842–1910) later called "the stream of consciousness" or "stream of thought."[16] More precisely, mental phenomena are occurrent apparent facts about the human activity of consciously representing objects, which Brentano dubbed (following the Scholastics) *intentionality*. Intentionality is a necessary and sufficient condition of mental phenomena.[17] Another necessary and sufficient condition of mental phenomena is *inner perception*, which is an immediate, infallible, self-evident knowledge about intentional facts.[18] Brentano's notion of inner perception in turn corresponds to what Kant called "empirical apperception" (*CPR* B132), with the crucial difference that unlike Brentano he does not suppose that empirical apperception is either immediate (because for Kant it is always mediated by concepts), infallible (because for Kant it is merely contingent cognition), or certain (because for Kant it is merely empirical cognition).

According to Brentano, every act of intentionality – every mental phenomenon – has an intentional object or "immanent objectivity." Intentional objects in turn have the ontological property of "inexistence" or *existence-in*, which means that their being necessarily depends on the being of the act of intentionality itself. So for Brentano the act of intentionality literally *contains* its intentional objects as intrinsic contents. Consequently, an intentional object cannot also exist outside the mind, as a thing-in-itself. It is therefore equivalent to what Kant called an "appearance" (*Erscheinung*).[19] When an intentional object is represented spatially or by means of what Kant called "outer sense," whether or not it is presented as actually extended in space (as, for example, in the case of the visual experience of color, which sometimes is directed proximally to phosphenes – the tiny phenomenal fireworks you experience when you close your eyes and press your fingers on your eyelids – and not distally to colored surfaces), then it is what Brentano calls a "physical phenomenon."[20]

Brentano's notion of phenomenology is therefore, with one crucial exception, the same as Kant's notion of empirical psychology, The crucial exception is that whereas for Kant empirical psychology can never be a genuine science – that is, an a priori discipline whose basic claims are necessarily true, law-governed, and known with certainty – owing to the non-mathematizable and idiosyncratically subjective character of its subject matter (*MFNS* 4: 470–1), by contrast for Brentano phenomenology is a genuine empirical science founded on first-person epistemic self-evidence and certainty. This lingering Cartesian assumption of a "privileged access" to mental phenomena implies, in effect, their intrinsic non-relationality, logical privacy, infallibility, ineffability, and immediate apprehensibility[21] in Brentano's phenomenology – something that would have been thoroughly rejected by Kant. The assumption of privileged access has fundamental significance for the phenomenological tradition. For to the extent that it is retained, it entails that *phenomenology* is always teetering on the edge of *phenomenalism*.

Kant, Husserl, phenomenology, and philosophical logic

Husserlian phenomenology began as philosophical logic. Edmund Husserl (1859–1938), in his first book, *Philosophy of Arithmetic: Psychological and Logical Investigations*, Vol. I (1891), applied Brentano's phenomenology to arithmetic cognition. But unfortunately he also committed the cardinal sin of *logical psychologism*: the explanatory reduction of the necessary, a priori, and universal subject matter of logic to the contingent, a posteriori, and relativized subject matter of empirical psychology. This sin was very helpfully pointed out to him in a devastating book review by Gottlob Frege.[22] Husserl too quickly came to doubt his own approach and, as a result, the second volume of the *Philosophy of Arithmetic* never appeared.

In the first volume entitled *Prolegomena to Pure Logic* (1900) of his second book (*Logical Investigations*, 1900/1), Husserl expiated his sin and also indirectly obtained a suitable revenge against Frege. He did this by working out a lengthy, rigorous, and radical critique of logical psychologism in the context of a strongly rationalistic – and officially anti-Kantian – conception of pure logic, thereby becoming the leading German philosopher of logic, and completely outshining Frege on the contemporary scene. Husserl's official anti-Kantianism – "for even transcendental psychology *also* is psychology"[23] – is misleading, however. This is because Kant in actual fact explicitly rejected logical psychologism in the first *Critique* (CPR A52–5/B77–9). So the real issue between Kant and Husserl about logic has to do with whether pure logic has a "transcendental" foundation in Kant's sense (that is, whether pure logic fundamentally depends on the spontaneous mental processing abilities of our innate a priori cognitive capacities), or not. This was not resolved until Husserl decisively opted for the Kantian doctrine in his later *Formal and Transcendental Logic* (1929).

In any case the *Prolegomena* was published as the first volume of an even bigger book, *Logical Investigations*, in which, equally brilliantly and remarkably, Husserl directly applied Brentano's phenomenology to foundational topics in philosophical logic: meaning, pure logical grammar or syntax, mereology (the logic of parts and wholes, closely related to both property-theory and set-theory), the nature of intentional content of all sorts, propositions and judgment-acts, truth, and propositional knowledge. Nevertheless Brentano was not the only or even the primary influence on Husserl's approach to philosophical logic. In the first (1901) edition of *Logical Investigations*, as Husserl explicitly admitted in the second (1913) edition, "I spoke of 'pure grammar', a name conceived and expressly devised to be analogous to Kant's 'pure science of nature'."[24] Husserl also introduced an importantly new idea about intentionality that was a significant advance over Brentano's doctrine: namely, a sharp and explicit distinction between (1) the subjectively conscious "lived experience" (*Erlebnis*) or act (*Akt*) of intentionality (2) the objectively existing and intersubjectively shareable logical or semantic *content* (*Inhalt*) of intentionality, and (3) the mind-independent *objective reference* (*objektive Beziehung*) of intentionality. More precisely Husserl showed how, while each of these is an intrinsic feature of every intentional mental state, each component can nevertheless vary logically independently of the other. Ironically enough, in contemporary writings Frege also systematically developed essentially the same distinction[25] between what he calls (1*) the subjective "idea" (*Vorstellung*) or attitudinal "coloration" (*Farbung*), (2*) "sense" (*Sinn*), and (3*) "reference" (*Bedeutung*). Nevertheless, if the truth be told, both Husserl and Frege were merely recurring to Kant's threefold distinction, made explicitly in and throughout the first *Critique*, between (1**) the phenomenal "matter" (*Materie*) of inner sense (its subjectively experienced attitudes, desires, feelings, sensations, and images), (2**) the "intension" (*Inhalt*) of concepts (their "sense" or *Sinn*) and judgments (their propositional content or *Satz*), and (3**) the "reference" (*Beziehung*) of intuitions (their individual objects) and concepts (their "comprehension" or *Umfang*).

There is however a fundamental meta-philosophical tension in *Logical Investigations*. This tension is that Brentano's phenomenology, as a descendant of Kant's empirical psychology, is at bottom factual and empirical, while Husserl's phenomenology is irreducibly modal, non-empirical, and non-logical. Husserl's response to this tension is to reinterpret Brentano's notion of self-evident inner perception as a priori *insight* (*Einsicht*) or a priori *self-evidence* (*Evidenz*).[26] So for Husserl phenomenology has an a priori foundation, and its basic truths are synthetically necessary and a priori.

It may then seem that Husserl is back safely in the Kantian fold of transcendental psychology. Nevertheless there is another problem. Brentano's phenomenology has no rational soul as a subjective foundation, but instead only a functional unity of human intentional activities, and Husserl had explicitly adopted this conception of the phenomenological ego in the first edition of *Logical Investigations*: "I must frankly confess, however, that I am quite unable to find this ego, this primitive, necessary centre of relations [to the contents of experience]."[27] But by the second edition, Husserl explicitly realized that this would not suffice for an epistemic foundation of his apriorist version of phenomenology, and that he had to upgrade to a higher-order ego: "I have since managed to find [this ego], i.e., have learnt not to be led astray from a pure grasp of the given through corrupt forms of the ego-metaphysic."[28] In other words, he managed to find a Kant-style *transcendental ego* to ground his logical epistemology.

Kant, Husserl, and transcendental phenomenology

According to Husserl in his *Idea of Phenomenology* (1907), *Ideas I* (1913), and *Cartesian Meditations* (1931), finding a transcendental ego requires a special philosophical effort, or more precisely a series of such efforts.[29] Recall that the function of a transcendental ego for Husserl is to ground his a priori rationalist phenomenological epistemology. And a transcendental ego in the Kantian sense is not a Cartesian mental substance, but instead an innate spontaneous non-empirical cognitive capacity for self-consciousness. So the nature of a transcendental ego must be such that the act of self-conscious reflection suffices for the knowledge of the propositional content of intentionality. This in turn requires (1) that this propositional content be guaranteed to be true, and (2) that this content be grasped by the thinking subject with self-evidence. And *that* in turn requires (1*) that this propositional content be materially identical with the truth-making object of the proposition, and also (2*) that the form of this propositional content be immediately and infallibly apprehended by the thinking subject.

Husserl secures condition (1*) by means of what he calls "the transcendental-phenomenological reduction." This treats the logical or semantic content of intentionality (now dubbed the "noema," as opposed to the "noesis," which is the intentional act) as *identical to* the objective reference of intentionality, and is therefore broadly equivalent to Kant's breathtaking fusion of transcendental idealism and empirical realism. But there is a subtle difference. Whereas Kant had argued for both his transcendental idealism and empirical realism theses via his thesis of the transcendental ideality of space and time, Husserl takes a different route, which he rather unhelpfully calls by the Greek term *epoché*, and only slightly more helpfully calls "abstention" (*Enthaltung*), "bracketing" (*Einklammerung*), and "putting out of play" (*außer spiel zu setzen*). The basic idea goes back to Brentano's idea of an intentional "presentation" of an object and to Husserl's own corresponding notion of a "mere presentation" in the Fifth Logical Investigation: it is one thing to represent an object or state-of-affairs *as actually existing*, and another thing altogether to represent it merely *as possibly not existing*. Given Cartesian skeptical doubts, the object possibly does not exist. Assuming that this possibility obtains in the actual world, then all that remains for the thinking subject of intentionality is the logico-semantic *presentational content* which represents the object in a certain way. So this logico-semantic presentational content becomes the new or indirect object of intentionality. Frege discusses essentially the same idea under the rubric of the "indirect reference" of meaningful expressions in "opaque" contexts – that is, ordinary referring expressions falling within the scope of certain psychological verbs followed by propositional complements, such as "believes that" or "wonders whether," and so-on – although without the Cartesian and Kantian metaphysical backdrops assumed by Husserl. What the parallel with Frege shows is that transcendental idealism and empirical realism do not automatically *follow* from the transcendental-phenomenological reduction, but must in fact be a further metaphysical hypothesis added by Husserl in order to guarantee the truth of the propositional content to which the truth-making object has been "reduced."

Correspondingly, Husserl secures condition (2*) by means of what he calls "seeing essences" (*Wesensschau, Wesenserschauung*) and "eidetic intuition." Despite the allusion to the Platonic *eidos* however, seeing essences is not supposed by Husserl to be Platonic insight, or a mysterious infallible grasp of mind-independent, non-spatio-temporal, causally inert, universal, ideal objects; nor is it supposed to be Leibnizian insight, or the infallible, certain, clear and distinct awareness of innate ideas. Instead it is *Kantian* insight, which is a reflective awareness of just those formal elements of representational content that express the spontaneous transcendental activity of the subject in synthesizing that content: "reason has insight only into what it itself produces according to its own design" (*CPR* Bxiii). So Kantian insight is a special form of self-knowledge. More specifically, Kantian insight includes elements of conceptual "decomposition" (*Zergliederung*), of pure "formal intuition" (*formale Anschauung*), and also of the "figurative synthesis" or "transcendental synthesis of the imagination" or "*synthesis speciosa*" (*CPR* A5/B9, B151, B160 n.).

The crucial point of contrast with Husserl's eidetic insight however, is Kant's fallibilistic thesis that insight yields at best only a subjective sufficiency of belief or "conviction" (*Überzeugung*), but not, in and of itself, objective "certainty" (*Gewißheit*) (*CPR* A820–2/ B848–50). The world must independently contribute a "given" element, the manifold of sensory content, in order for knowledge to be possible (*CPR* B145). Husserl, by sharp contrast, takes eidetic insight to be infallible and certain, which again shows his troublesome tendency to run together Kantian transcendental idealism/empirical realism, which is explicitly anti-Cartesian, and Cartesian epistemology, which entails a corresponding Cartesian metaphysics of substance dualism. Descartes's epistemology is forever haunted by skepticism, and Descartes's dualism of mental substance (whose essence is *thinking*) and physical substance (whose essence is *extension*) is forever haunted by the unintelligibility of mind–body interconnection and interaction. The phenomenological tradition would have been much better off if *Cartesian Meditations* had been *Kantian Reflections*.

Kant, Heidegger, and the analytic of Dasein

But phenomenology did not end with Husserl. The reactionary Cartesian elements of Husserl's transcendental phenomenology were arrested and sent to the wall by his revolutionary student Martin Heidegger (1889–1976), in his groundbreakingly brilliant and occasionally bumptious book *Being and Time* (1927). The result is a transcendental phenomenology of direct intentionality, in which the human being – now somewhat unhelpfully dubbed Dasein or "being-there" – finds that the intentional content of her intentional mental acts is no longer locked up inside her pineal gland but instead literally spread out into her local spatial environment and into her larger social and historical world, and either wholly or at least partially dynamically determined in time by her skillful practical engagement with that environment and that world. From our vantage point, it is easy enough to see how Heidegger's new conception of human intentionality and his corresponding "analytic of Dasein" is essentially Kant's theory of spatio-temporal intuition in the Transcendental Aesthetic and of empirical judgment in the Transcendental Analytic, now ingeniously turned inside out so that the representation of time essentially spreads itself onto the representation of space, *plus* Kant's conception of an embodied human practical reasoner. The Kantian grounds of Heidegger's phenomenology are explicitly worked out in his *Phenomenological Interpretation of Kant's Critique of Pure Reason* (1927–8).[30]

In short, Heidegger is a *radical Kantian externalist* about intentional content. But he is also an *existential Kantian pragmatist* about intentional content. For he posits an irreducibly non-conceptual practical element in perceptual intentionality by treating it as the directly engaged and attentively absorbed skillful manipulation of a fundamentally usable commonsense world. Correspondingly he treats propositional linguistic intentionality as a form of "interpretation" (*Auslegung*) or worldly hermeneutics based on a projective "understanding" (construed now in the gerundive form of *Verstehen*, as opposed to Kant's noun-substantive *Verstand*) whereby meaning is essentially contextually determined.[31]

This in turn implies that the classical accounts of perception and empirical judgment, as the sense-datum-mediated and logically mediated quasi-pictorial representations of a microphysically real material thing-in-itself of modern natural science, are both deeply misleading. Perception and judgment for Heidegger are worldly human performances in a world of self-manifesting or cognitively accessible, fundamentally usable appearances, and *not* passive mirrorings of a set of colorless, valueless, intrinsic non-relational, essentially hidden or cognitively inaccessible, fundamentally physical properties.[32]

Heidegger's other deeply important Kant-inspired phenomenological innovation was to emphasize spontaneous affect, feeling, and volitional action over passive sensation and sensa (or phenomenal qualia) in intentionality, and thereby to construe consciousness and cognition alike as irreducibly emotive, active, and normative. For this reason he calls object-directed intentionality "concern" (*Bekümmerung*). This revolutionary Kant-driven Heideggerian re-working of the mind/world relation is, in turn, deeply similar in many ways to John Dewey's contemporary and independent development of radical externalist pragmatism in *Experience and Nature* (1929).

It is significant that like Husserlian phenomenology, Heideggerian phenomenology also began as philosophical logic. In his 1913 doctoral thesis, *The Theory of Judgment in Psychologism*, Heidegger isolated the logico-semantic question, "What is the sense (or point) of sense?" ("*Was is der Sinn des Sinnes?*") as a fundamental philosophical problem. The other fundamental philosophical problem animating Heidegger in the years prior to *Being and Time* was the question, "What is the being (or essence) of being?," something which had obsessed him ever since he had read Brentano's *On the Several Senses of Being in Aristotle* as a precocious Gymnasium student in 1907. From 1909 to 1911 he closely studied Husserl's *Logical Investigations*, and began to identify logico-semantic issues with ontological issues. So, first philosophy for early Heidegger was the phenomenological analysis of *logic, meaning, and the world*. This is clearly a recurrence to the basic themes of Kant's transcendental logic in the Metaphysical Deduction of the Pure Concepts of the Understanding (CPR A66–83/B91–116). It is also precisely where the twentieth-century analytic tradition begins. Indeed, Heidegger's second published work in philosophy was *Neuere Forschungen über Logik* [*New Investigations in Logic*] (1912), a sympathetic survey of contemporary logical theory, including the first volume of Bertrand Russell's and A. N. Whitehead's *Principia Mathematica* (1910). As we saw above, analytic philosophy and phenomenology alike were the natural progeny of the Kantian tradition; and as we will see below, they did not have a genuine falling-out until *after* 1945. Like most fallings-out between siblings, the inside story is interestingly complicated.

Kantian themes in the early analytic tradition

What analytic philosophy is

The analytic tradition is based on two core ideas: (1) that all necessary truth is logical truth, which is the same as analytic a priori truth, and that there are no non-logical or non-analytic necessary truths (the thesis of *modal monism*), and (2) that all a priori knowledge is knowledge of analytic truths and follows directly from the process of (2.1) logically decomposing analytic propositions into conceptual or metaphysical simples which are mind-independently real yet immediately and infallibly apprehended with self-evidence, and then (2.2) rigorously logically reconstructing those propositions by formal deduction from (a) general logical laws and (b) premises that express logical definitional knowledge in terms of the simple constituents (the thesis of *a priori knowledge as decompositional analysis*).[33]

Both core ideas are explicitly anti-Kantian. For Kant holds (1*) that there are two irreducibly different kinds of necessary a priori truth, namely (a) logically or analytically necessary a priori truths, and (b) non-logically or synthetically necessary a priori truths (the thesis of *modal dualism*), and (2*) that a priori knowledge can be directed to either analytically or synthetically necessary a priori truths, but in either case (as we have seen already above) this knowledge stems essentially from a reflective awareness of just those formal elements of representational content that express the spontaneous transcendental activity of the subject in cognitively synthesizing or mentally processing that content (the thesis of *a priori knowledge as self-knowledge*).

So what *is* analytic philosophy? The simple answer is that analytic philosophy is what Frege, G. E. Moore, Russell, and Rudolf Carnap did for a living after they rejected Kant. The subtler answer – because it includes the major contribution of Ludwig Wittgenstein – is that analytic philosophy is *the rise and fall of the concept of analyticity* (see "The development of analytic philosophy: Wittgenstein and after," Chapter 2).

Frege was undoubtedly the founding grandfather of analytic philosophy, by virtue of his bold and brilliant attempt to reduce arithmetic systematically to pure logic, whose theorems are all analytic,[34] and thereby demonstrate (1) that Kant was miserably mistaken in holding that all arithmetic truth and knowledge is synthetic a priori, and (2) that arithmetic proof is a fully rigorous and scientific enterprise. This is the beginning of the project of *logicism*, which Russell, Whitehead, Wittgenstein, and Carnap all pursued in the first three decades of the twentieth century. Logicism provides the first half of modal monism. The second half of modal monism is provided by the rejection of the very idea of a synthetic a priori proposition. This was the unique contribution of Wittgenstein and Carnap, via the Vienna Circle (*Wiener Kreis*) and logical positivism, in the third and fourth decades of the twentieth century. Frege himself held, like Kant, that geometry is synthetic a priori.[35]

Kant, Moore, and the nature of judgment

In view of Frege's partial Kantianism, G. E. Moore (1873–1958) was in fact the founding father of philosophical analysis. Paradoxically however, Moore invented analysis not so much by writing about it, as instead by *living it*, that is, by virtue of his passionately and relentlessly deploying the method of of decompositional analysis in his early philosophical writings,[36] and by the powerful influence of his charismatic philosophical personality on Russell and Wittgenstein.[37]

Moore began his philosophical career as a psychologistic neo-Kantian, and wrote his fellowship dissertation on Kant for Trinity College, Cambridge, under the direction of the equally neo-Kantian and Brentano-inspired philosophical psychologist James Ward (1843–1925),[38] who had previously been Moore's undergraduate supervisor and mentor at Trinity. But like other young philosophers with minds of their own – and, ironically enough, quite like the early Husserl in relation to Brentano – Moore vigorously rejected the teachings of his teacher. Moore's specific act of rebellion against his mentor Ward was to develop a sharply anti-psychologistic, anti-idealistic, and radically realistic critique of Kant's theory of judgment. Correspondingly, he also developed a sharply anti-psychologistic and radically realistic (and in particular, moral-intuitionist) extension of Kant's ethics, although in this respect Moore quite explicitly *followed* Brentano's *Origin of Our Knowledge of Right and Wrong*.[39] In any case, Moore's critique of Kant's theory of judgment was later published in his remarkable papers "The nature of judgment" (1899) and "The refutation of idealism" (1903). And in the same year as "Refutation," Moore also published his radical extension of Kant's ethics in *Principia Ethica* (for some details, see the section below, "Kant, Moore again, and the naturalistic fallacy").

Moore's ostensible target in "The nature of judgment" is the neo-Hegelian F. H. Bradley (1846–1924), specifically his theory of judgment in his *Principles of Logic* (1883). But the real target is Kant.[40] Moore's basic objection is that Bradley's (read: Kant's) theory of judgment involves a psychologistic confusion between two senses of the "content" of a cognition: (1) content as that which literally belongs to the phenomenally conscious mental act of cognizing (the psychologically immanent content, or intentional act-content); and (2) content as that at which the mental act is directed, or "about" (the psychologically transcendent content, or objective intentional content). The communicable meaning and truth-or-falsity of the judgment belong strictly to objective intentional content. According to Moore, the Bradley–Kant theory of judgment assimilates the objective intentional content of judgment – that is, the proposition – to the act-content of judging. This is what, in the Preface to *Principia Ethica*, Moore glosses as

> the fundamental contradiction of modern Epistemology – the contradiction involved in both distinguishing and identifying the *object* and the *act* of Thought, 'truth' itself and its supposed *criterion*.[41]

Given this "contradiction," the communicable meaning and the truth-or-falsity of cognition are both reduced to the point of view of a single phenomenally conscious subject. The unpalatable consequences are that meaning becomes unshareably private (semantic solipsism) and that truth turns into mere personal belief (cognitive relativism).

For Moore himself by contrast, judgments are essentially truth-bearing or falsity-bearing connections of mind-independent Platonic universals called "concepts." So concepts are decidedly not, as they were for Kant, simple or complex unities of mental content under the analytic and synthetic unities of self-consciousness. Nor do Moorean concepts and judgments relate to objects in the world, as concepts and judgments alike had for Kant, via directly referential, singular, existential, non-conceptual sensory mental representations, or intuitions (*Anschauungen*). On the contrary and in explicit rejection of Kant's theory of judgment, for Moore complex concepts and judgments alike are mind-independent logically unified semantic complexes built up out of simple concepts grasped by direct Platonic insight. But not only that: according to Moore the world itself is nothing but a nexus of simple or complex concepts insofar as they enter into true propositions.[42] No wonder then that, as his fellow Cambridge Apostle and philosophical sparring partner the logician and economist John Maynard Keynes (1883–1946) later wrily reported, Moore once had a nightmare in which he could not distinguish propositions from tables.[43]

Moore's "Refutation of idealism" and his corresponding Aristotelian Society paper "Kant's idealism" (1904) are even more explicitly anti-Kantian. Here Moore ingeniously doubly assimilates Kant's transcendental idealism to Brentano and to Berkeley by interpreting Kantian appearances as sensory intentional objects that "in-exist" or are nothing but immanent contents of phenomenal consciousness. This of course completely overlooks Kant's crucial distinction between inner sense and outer sense, not to mention his equally crucial doctrine of empirical realism, and his Refutation of Idealism (*CPR* B274–9). And it also incidentally ushered in another hundred years of phenomenalistic interpretations of Kant's theory of appearances.[44]

By vivid contrast to Kant's supposed phenomenalism however, Moore's radical realism is the thesis that every object exists as the external relatum of the intentionality of a sheer transparent subjective consciousness. But this implies, in an odd reversal of Brentano's doctrine of mental phenomena – whereby intentional objects reduce to "immanent objectivities" – that all intentional contents are now external intentional objects, and that therefore there will be as many mind-independently real objects as there are fine-grained differences between intentional contents. So Moore uses the transparency of consciousness to escape Brentano's conception of narrowly ideal phenomenal content enclosed within the mental intention, only to lose himself in a Platonic looking-glass world of unrestrictedly many real intentional objects, one for every possible act of thought – presumably even including the impossible ones that the White Queen boasted of having before breakfast.[45] Brentano's student, the radical phenomenological ontologist Alexius Meinong (1853–1928), had gone through precisely the same looking-glass.[46] Russell's great task as an analytic philosopher was to bring them all back alive.

Kant, Russell, and logicism

Russell, like Moore, began his philosophical career as a psychologistic neo-Kantian, in an early treatise on the nature of geometry, *An Essay on the Foundations of Geometry* (1897), which was also based on *his* Trinity fellowship dissertation. The basic point of the *Essay* was to determine what could be preserved of Kant's Euclid-oriented theories of space and geometry after the discovery and development of non-Euclidean geometries. Russell had been supervised by Ward too, and by Whitehead. At the same time there was also a significant Hegelian element in Russell's early thought, inspired by his close study of Bradley's *Logic* and discussions with another Trinity man and fellow Apostle, the imposingly-named Scottish Hegelian metaphysician John McTaggart Ellis McTaggart (1866-1925).[47] Despite being a close friend of Russell's, Moore wrote a sternly critical review of the *Essay* which was comparable in its both its philosophical content and its impact on Russell to Frege's review of Husserl's *Philosophy of Arithmetic*, in that it accused Russell of committing the "Kantian fallacy" of grounding a priori modal claims on psychological facts.[48] Moore's stinging criticism seems to have almost instantly liberated Russell from his neo-Kantian and Hegelian beliefs. This, combined with the close study of Meinong's writings, led him to a radically realistic Moorean see-through epistemology and a correspondingly rich looking-glass ontology of concrete and abstract real individuals, although he prudently stopped well short of accepting the existence or subsistence of Meinongian impossibilia.[49]

In any case, powered up by strong shots of Moore and Meinong, Russell's titanically brilliant, restless, and obsessive intellect[50] was now focused exclusively on the logical foundations of mathematics, and deeply engaged with the works of George Boole (1815–64), Frege, and the Italian logician Giuseppe Peano (1858–1932). By

1903 Russell had produced the massive *Principles of Mathematics*, and then by 1910, in collaboration with Whitehead, the even more massive *Principia Mathematica*. Above all however, on the collective basis of his intellectual encounters with Kant, Bradley, Boole, Frege, Peano, Whitehead, Moore, and Meinong, he developed a fundamental conception of *pure or symbolic logic*.

Pure or symbolic logic as Russell understood it, is the non-psychological, universal, necessary, and a priori science of deductive consequence, expressed in a bivalent propositional and polyadic predicate calculus with identity as well as quantification over an infinity of individuals, properties, and various kinds of functions. Pure or symbolic logic in this heavy-duty sense has direct metaphysical implications. But most importantly for our purposes here, Russell's logic expresses the direct avoidance of Kant's appeal to intuition in the constitution of mathematical propositions and reasoning:

> [T]he Kantian view ... asserted that mathematical reasoning is not strictly formal, but always uses intuitions, *i.e.* the *à priori* knowledge of space and time. Thanks to the progress of Symbolic Logic, especially as treated by Professor Peano, this part of the Kantian philosophy is now capable of a final and irrevocable refutation.[51]

The result of all these influences, together with Russell's maniacally creative intellectual drive in the period from 1900 to 1913, was a seminal conception of philosophical analysis based on a radically platonistic, atomistic, and logicistic realism, according to which (1) not merely arithmetic but all of mathematics including geometry reduces to pure or symbolic logic, (2) propositions literally contain the simple concrete particulars (instantaneous sense-data) and simple abstract universals (properties or relations) that populate the mind-independently real world,[52] and (3) both the simple concrete particulars and abstract universals are known directly and individually by cognitive acts of self-evident and infallible acquaintance.[53] In autobiographical retrospect, Russell explicitly identified his conception of analysis with his complete rejection of Kant's metaphysics:

> Ever since I abandoned the philosophy of Kant ... I have sought solutions of philosophical problems by means of analysis; and I remain firmly persuaded ... that only by analysing is progress possible.[54]

But that tells only *part* of the story about Russellian analysis. In fact Russell's program of philosophical analysis had fundamentally collapsed by 1914, mainly as the result of his tumultuous personal and philosophical encounters with the young Wittgenstein:

> [Wittgenstein] had a kind of purity which I have never known equalled except by G. E. Moore. ... He used to come to see me every evening at midnight, and pace up and down my room like a wild beast for three hours in agitated silence. Once I said to him: "Are you thinking about logic or about your sins?"

"Both," he replied, and continued his pacing. I did not like to suggest that it was time for bed, as it seemed probable both to him and me that on leaving me he would commit suicide.[55]

From 1912 onwards Wittgenstein was ostensibly Russell's research student, working with him on the philosophy of logic and the logical foundations of mathematics, and supposedly becoming Russell's philosophical successor. But the student, who was as personally difficult as he was philosophically brilliant, soon very helpfully pointed out to his teacher the irreversible philosophical errors in his work-in-progress, *Theory of Knowledge*.[56] This criticism changed Russell's philosophical life, and he abandoned *Theory of Knowledge* shortly thereafter:

> I wrote a lot of stuff about Theory of Knowledge, which Wittgenstein criticised with the greatest severity[.] His criticism ... was an event of first-rate importance in my life, and affected everything I have done since. I saw he was right, and I saw that I could not hope ever again to do fundamental work in philosophy. My impulse was shattered, like a wave dashed to pieces against a breakwater. ... I *had* to produce lectures for America, but I took a metaphysical subject although I was and am convinced that all fundamental work in philosophy is logical. My reason was that Wittgenstein persuaded me that what wanted doing in logic was too difficult for me. So there was really no vital satisfaction of my philosophical impulse in that work, and philosophy lost its hold on me. That was due to Wittgenstein more than to the war.[57]

Despite being shattered to pieces against a breakwater, nevertheless in typical Russellian fashion he promptly sat down and wrote *Our Knowledge of the External World* (1914) for his Lowell Lectures at Harvard. And leaving aside Russell's characteristic self-dramatization, the simple facts of the matter are (1) that Wittgenstein had seriously challenged four fundamental elements of Russell's seminal conception of analysis, and (2) that he had no effective reply to Wittgenstein's challenges.

Recall that Russell's notion of analysis in the period from 1900 to 1913 is logicistic, platonistic, radically realistic, and grounded epistemically on a series of self-evident infallible acquaintances with the simple concrete or abstract constituents of propositions. One problem with this notion is that Russell never provides an adequate explanation of how a human mind in real time and space can be directly related to causally inert non-spatio-temporal universals (the problem of *non-empirical knowledge*). Another problem is how propositions construed as ordered complexes of individuals, properties, and relations, along with logical connectives or constants such as *all, some, and, or, not*, and *if–then*, can ever be formally or materially unified into coherent, semantically unambiguous truth-bearers (the problem of *the unity of the proposition*). A third problem is that the notion of a direct self-evident infallible acquaintance with logical constants, as if they were regular objects alongside real individuals, properties, and relations, seems absurd (the problem of *the nature of the logical constant*). And a fourth and final problem is that Russell never adequately clarifies the nature or status of logical necessity, and in particular whether logical truths are analytic a priori, synthetic a priori, or something else (the problem of *the nature of necessity*). To be sure, all four problems had already been handled by Kant by means of his transcendental idealism: non-empirical knowledge is based on transcendental reflection or self-knowledge; the unity of the proposition is based on the transcendental unity of apperception; logical constants are nothing universal functions of thought, corresponding to pure concepts of the understanding; and logical necessity is irreducibly analytic necessity, not synthetic necessity. But it was precisely the Kantian approach that Russell was completely rejecting. So these possible solutions to his problems were already ruled out, and he was thereby driven into a theoretical cul de sac.

Russell and Wittgenstein were personally divided by World War I. Russell very bravely professed pacifism in a nation hell-bent on smashing the Germans, and was imprisoned by the British government and lost his Trinity fellowship – a bellicose and by now philosophically alienated McTaggart working hard to bring this about – for his troubles. Wittgenstein went back to Austria and very bravely fought on the German side, and was imprisoned by the Allies in Italy after the German surrender for *his* troubles. Back in England however, by the end of the Great War Russell had completely capitulated to Wittgenstein's conception of philosophical analysis. He officially recorded this conversion in his long essay, "The philosophy of logical atomism":

> The following is the text of a course of eight lectures delivered in Gordon Square London, in the first months of 1918, which are very largely concerned with explaining certain ideas which I learned from my friend and former pupil, Ludwig Wittgenstein. I have had no opportunity of knowing his views since August, 1914, and I do not even know whether he is alive or dead.[58]

Kant, Wittgenstein, and the Tractatus

The "certain ideas" that Russell spoke of were elaborately worked out by Wittgenstein in a stunningly unorthodox masterpiece written from 1913 to 1918 and published in 1921, the *Tractatus Logico-Philosophicus*. This "logico-philosophical treatise" (*Logisch-philosophische Abhandlung*) offers a radically new conception of philosophical analysis, according to which

1 not only mathematics but also metaphysics reduces to the propositions of logic (including both the truth-functional tautologies and the logico-philosophical truths of the *Tractatus* itself) together with factual propositions;
2 factual propositions and facts alike reduce to logically-structured complexes of ontologically neutral "objects," which can variously play the structural roles of both particulars and universals (including both properties and relations);
3 factual propositions are nothing but linguistic facts that "picture" other facts according to one-to-one isomorphic correspondence relations;
4 all non-factual propositions are either (a) "senseless" (*sinnlos*) truth-functional tautologies expressing nothing but the formal meanings and deductive implications

of the logical constants, (b) the logico-philosophical propositions of the *Tractatus* itself, or (c) "nonsensical" (*unsinnig*) pseudo-propositions that violate logico-syntactic rules and logico-semantic categories, especially including all the synthetic a priori claims of traditional metaphysics;

5 the logical constants do not represent facts or refer to objects of any sort (prop. 4.0312) but instead merely "display" (*darstellen*) the a priori logical "scaffolding of the world" (prop. 6.124), which is also "the limits of my language" (prop. 5.6), and can only be "shown" or non-propositionally indicated, *not* "said" or propositionally described;

6 the logical form of the world is therefore "transcendental" (prop. 6.13), and finally

7 the logical form of the world reduces to the language-using metaphysical subject or ego, who is not in any way part of the world but in fact solipsistically identical to the world itself.

Looking at theses (5), (6), and (7), we can clearly see that Wittgenstein's new "transcendental" conception of analysis is radically ontologically ascetic, since everything logically reduces to one simple thing: the language-using metaphysical subject or ego. Indeed, it is by means of theses (5) and (6) that Wittgenstein directly expresses the surprising and often-overlooked but quite indisputable fact that the *Tractatus* is every bit as much a neo-Kantian idealistic metaphysical treatise directly inspired by Arthur Schopenhauer's *World as Will and Representation* (1819, 1844, 1859),[59] and thereby mediately inspired by Kant's first *Critique*, as it is a logico-philosophical treatise inspired by Frege's *Begriffsschrift* and Russell's and Whitehead's *Principia*. Whereas Russell *abandoned* Kant's epistemology and metaphysics, Wittgenstein *sublimated* them. And from this standpoint, we can see that the *Tractatus* is fundamentally an essay in *transcendental logic*:

> The limit of language is shown by its being impossible to describe the fact which corresponds to (is the translation of) a sentence, without simply repeating the sentence. (This has to do with the Kantian solution of the problem of philosophy.)[60]

The *Tractatus* ends with the strangely moving proposition, "Wovon man nicht sprechen kann, darüber muss mann schweigen": "Whereof one cannot speak, thereof one must be silent" (prop. 7). What on earth does this mean? One possible interpretation, now known as the "resolute" reading, is that proposition 7 is saying that the *Tractatus* itself – except for the Preface and proposition 7 – is literally nonsense.[61] But against a Schopenhauerian and Kantian backdrop, this extreme and implausible reading can be neatly avoided, because proposition 7 is then instead saying:

1 that traditional metaphysics has been destroyed by the philosophical logic of the *Tractatus* just as Kant's first *Critique* had destroyed traditional metaphysics;

2 that the logico-philosophical propositions of the *Tractatus* itself *would have* counted as literally nonsensical because they are neither factual propositions nor truth-functional logical truths, *were it not for* the much deeper fact

3 that these Tractarian propositions are *self-manifesting transcendental truths in the Kantian sense* about the nature of logic, and thus have the basic function of constituting a logical stairway or "ladder" (*Leiter*) between the factual natural sciences and ethics, and finally

4 that ethics consists exclusively in mystical feeling and noncognitive volitions (props. 6.4–6.522), not propositional thoughts.

So at the end of the *Tractatus* Wittgenstein logically transcends scientific knowledge in order to reach the ethical standpoint. And this is precisely why in 1919 – perhaps not entirely coincidentally, shortly after he had studied the *Critique of Pure Reason* carefully for the first time[62] – he told the journal editor Ludwig von Ficker that "the [*Tractatus*]'s point is an ethical one."[63] As we have already seen, Kant makes essentially the same radical move in the B edition Preface to the first *Critique*: "I had to deny *scientific knowing* (*Wissen*) in order to make room for [moral] *faith* (*Glauben*)" (CPR Bxxx).

Kant, Carnap, and logical positivism

Wittgenstein's actions conformed to his written words, and he gave up philosophy for roughly ten years after the publication of the *Tractatus*. During Wittgenstein's "silent decade" – equally but oppositely, Kant's own silent decade had immediately *preceded* the publication of the first *Critique*[64] – Rudolf Carnap (1891–1970) was discovering his own voice. Falling into what will by now no doubt seem like a familiar pattern, and indeed very like Russell, Carnap started his philosophical career as a neo-Kantian philosopher of the foundations of geometry:

> I studied Kant's philosophy with Bruno Baum in Jena. In his seminar, the *Critique of Pure Reason* was discussed in detail for an entire year. I was strongly impressed by Kant's conception that the geometrical structure of space is determined by our forms of intuition. The after-effects of this influence were still noticeable in the chapter on the space of intuition in my dissertation, *Der Raum* [published in 1922]. ... Knowledge of intuitive space I regarded at the time, under the influence of Kant and the neo-Kantians, especially Natorp and Cassirer, as based on "pure intuition," and independent of contingent experience.[65]

Carnap's progress away from Kant's metaphysics also followed the familiar dual pattern of (1) treating post-Kantian developments in the exact sciences as refutations of basic Kantian theses, and (2) replacing transcendental idealism with philosophical logic. By the end of the 1920s and into the early parts of the 1930s, Carnap had been heavily influenced by the Theory of Relativity and by the close study of Frege's writings, along with the Russell's and Whitehead's *Principia*, Russell's *Our Knowledge of the External World*, and above all the *Tractatus*. Carnap's intellectual ferment was expressed in two important books, *The Logical Structure of the World* (*Der logische Aufbau der Welt*, 1928), and *The Logical Syntax of Language* (1934).

The *Aufbau* played a crucial variation on Russell's platonistic conception of philosophical analysis by turning it into *constructive empiricism*, which can be glossed as follows:

> The natural world as a whole is the object of analysis. But the simples out of which the world is logically constructed are not Really Real mind-independent substances but instead nothing but subjective streams of experience and a single fundamental relation, *the recollection of similarity*.

Correspondingly, *Logical Syntax* converts Wittgenstein's transcendental conception of analysis into *logico-linguistic conventionalism*, which can be glossed this way:

> There is no One True Logic, just as there is no One True Natural Language, but instead there as many distinct logical languages as there are formal symbolic calculi constructed on the models of the *Begriffsschrift* and *Principia*, plus distinct axiom-systems, or distinct sets of logical constants, or distinct notions of logical consequence; and the choice of precisely which logical language is to be adopted as the basis of the exact sciences is purely a pragmatic matter (whether voluntaristic or social) having nothing to do with logic itself.

The overall result is that Kant's "transcendental turn" from the apparent world to a set of a priori world-structures that are imposed on phenomenal appearances by our innate spontaneous cognitive capacities, is replaced by Carnap with a "linguistic turn"[66] from the apparent world to a set of a priori world-structures that are imposed on those phenomenal appearances by the syntax and semantics of our logical and natural languages. Needless to say however, even *after* the linguistic turn, the gambit of imposing a priori logico-linguistic structures on phenomenal appearances remains basically a neo-Kantian and thereby Kantian move.[67] Indeed, the very same Carnapian fusion of pure logic and epistemological neo-Kantianism is vividly evident in C. I. Lewis's *Mind and the World Order* (1929) and Nelson Goodman's *The Structure of Appearance* (1951).

In any case, Carnap's *Aufbau* and *Logical Syntax*, together with the basic writings of Frege, Russell, and Wittgenstein, and also Moritz Schlick's *General Theory of Knowledge* (1925), became the philosophical basis of the Vienna Circle,[68] which flourished throughout most of the 1930s, until the coming-to-power of the Nazis in Germany caused the diaspora of its core membership to Britain and the USA. The political leanings of the inner circle of the Circle were radical socialist, universalist, egalitarian, and Communist. So staying in Austro-Germany would have most certainly meant their cultural and intellectual deaths, and very probably their actual deaths too.

The Circle philosophically professed logical positivism or logical empiricism, which is essentially the fusion of Carnap's constructive empiricism and logical conventionalism, plus the explicit rejection of Kant's notion of the synthetic a priori. According to Carnap, synthetic a priori propositions are meaningless because they violate rules of the logical syntax of language.[69] And according to Moritz Schlick (1882–1936), the official founder and leader of the Circle, synthetic a priori propositions are meaningless because they are neither tautological logical truths (analytic truths) nor verifiable factual empirical truths, and analyticity and verifiability exhaust the possible sources of cognitive significance.[70] The Carnap–Schlick attack on the synthetic a priori, plus constructive empiricism, plus logico-linguistic conventionalism, plus the general semantic thesis that all and only meaningful propositions are either analytic logical truths or else verifiable empirical factual propositions (the Verifiability Principle or VP), were all crisply formulated and beautifully written up for English-speaking philosophers in Alfred Jules Ayer's *Language, Truth, and Logic* (1936).

It is however a notorious and serious problem for Ayer (1910–89) in particular, and for the Vienna Circle more generally, that the VP itself is neither an analytic proposition nor a factual proposition. Looked at with a wide lens, the problem of the logico-semantic status of the VP is merely a special case of Wittgenstein's earlier worry about the logico-semantic status of his Tractarian logico-philosophical propositions. A standard "solution" to the special worry is to say that the VP is a *meta-linguistic* or *meta-logical* proposition: the VP is nothing but a further bit of language and logic that also happens to be about language and logic. But unfortunately that in turn only invokes an even more general and intractable worry about the logico-semantic status of meta-languages and meta-logics: *the logocentric predicament*, which says that *logic is epistemically circular*, in the sense that any attempt to explain or justify logic must itself presuppose and use some or all of the very logical principles and concepts that it aims to explain or justify.[71] The obvious way out of these problems would be to return to Kantian modal dualism and say that the VP is non-logically necessary or synthetic a priori. But of course this violates the official positivist ban on the synthetic a priori.

A parting of the ways? Kant, the Davos conference, and the Great Divide

In Davos, Switzerland, from 17 March to 6 April 1929, an "International University Course," sponsored by the Swiss, French, and German governments, brought together the leading neo-Kantian Ernst Cassirer, famous author of the multi-volume *Philosophy of Symbolic Forms* (1925, 1927, 1929),[72] and the soon-to-be leading phenomenologist Martin Heidegger, famous author of *Being and Time* (1927), in an official and more or less explicit attempt to bring about a philosophical reconciliation between Marburg (or science-oriented) neo-Kantianism and phenomenology.[73] The soon-to-be leading logical positivist Rudolf Carnap was there too, along with many other professors and students from across Europe. And a good time was had by all: "It appears that the Davos encounter itself took place in atmosphere of extraordinarily friendly collegiality."[74]

The key sessions at Davos were two lecture series by Cassirer and Heidegger, followed by a public disputation between them. Strikingly, both the lectures and the disputation dealt with the question of how to interpret the *Critique of Pure Reason* correctly.[75] In other words, it was all about Kant and the neo-Kantian origins of phenomenology.

Now for this reason it can be argued, and indeed has been argued, that the Davos conference was emblematic of the death-by-mitosis of the neo-Kantian tradition, during the 1930s, into two fundamentally distinct and irreconcilable philosophical traditions: the analytic tradition (whose paradigm case was logical positivism), and the phenomenological tradition (whose paradigm case was existential phenomenology).[76] According to this historical reconstruction, the basic disagreements between analysis and phenomenology were latent in the period 1900–30, during which – as we have seen above – Moore, Russell, and Carnap all started their philosophical careers as neo-Kantians, went on to reject neo-Kantianism and Kant by means of foundational work in philosophical logic and the influence of the contemporary exact sciences, and then correspondingly worked out various new logically-driven conceptions of a priori analysis. And then, so the story goes, the latent eventually became manifest, and the post-Kantian stream of philosophical influence consisting of Brentano → Husserl/ Meinong → Heidegger was officially divided from the other post-Kantian stream consisting of Moore → Russell → Wittgenstein → Carnap, basically because the phenomenologists rejected the Frege–Russell conception of pure logic while contrariwise the analysts affirmed pure logic.[77] And never the twain shall meet.

But although this makes a conveniently neat story, it is at least arguably not quite true to the historico-philosophical facts. The highly collegial atmosphere at Davos was no polite put-on. Obviously there were some important differences and disagreements between logical positivism and existential phenomenology. Nevertheless Heidegger took Carnap very seriously as a philosopher well into the 1930s, and Carnap also took Heidegger very seriously as a philosopher well into the 1930s.[78] (As did Wittgstenstein,[79] and as also did Gilbert Ryle at Oxford[80] – who, according to Michael Dummett, "began his career as an exponent of Husserl for British audiences and used to lecture on Bolzano, Brentano, Frege, Meinong, and Husserl"[81] throughout the 1920s and 1930s.) For his part, Heidegger was every bit as dismissive of traditional metaphysics as Carnap was.[82] And while it is quite true that Heidegger significantly criticized the Fregean and Russellian pure logic of the *Begriffsschrift* and *Principia Mathematica,* and challenged its metaphysical commitments, so too did Carnap; after all, that is the main point of the *Logical Syntax of Language.* Furthermore, objectively considered, Heidegger's existential phenomenology is not essentially *more* different from or opposed to pure logic, or logical positivism for that matter, than is Dewey's pragmatism, which despite its radical critical philosophical implications (see "American philosophy in the twentieth century," Chapter 5),[83] cohabited very comfortably with mainstream analytic philosophy in the USA after 1945. Nor, objectively speaking, is Heidegger's existential phenomenology essentially *more* different from or opposed to either pure logic, or logical positivism, than is Wittgenstein's later philosophy as expressed in his *Philosophical Investigations* (1953), which despite its equally radical critical philosophical implications,[84] also cohabited very comfortably with mainstream analytic philosophy in the USA and England after 1945.

So it appears that the Great Divide between analytic philosophy and phenomenology did not actually happen in the 1930s. And it also appears that the Divide is not the consequence of any fundamental philosophical disagreements between analysts and phenomenologists about pure logic. On the contrary, it *appears* that the Divide happened almost entirely after 1945, and that it was the joint result of the three following factors:

1 The sharply divisive cultural politics of anti-fascism and anti-Communism in Anglo-American countries after World War II: Heidegger publicly and notoriously supported the Nazis in the mid-thirties;[85] Vienna Circle exiles in the USA were understandably very eager to avoid being persecuted during the McCarthy Communist-trials era for their pre-war radical-socialist and Communist sympathies, so were generally playing it safe (Carnap however being a notable exception[86]) by not rocking the boat;[87] and the leading French phenomenologists Jean-Paul Sartre and Maurice Merleau-Ponty were both closely politically associated with the radical Left.[88]
2 The sharply divisive debate about the cultural-political significance and philosophical implications of the exact sciences after World War II; taking his cue from Heidegger's *Being and Time*, but also reflecting on the worsening cultural-political situation in Europe, Husserl had seriously criticized the epistemological and metaphysical foundations of the exact sciences in his *Crisis of European Sciences*; and then taking his cue directly from Husserl, Merleau-Ponty further deepened and developed this critique in his *Phenomenology of Perception* (1945).
3 The sharply divisive struggle for control of the major Anglo-American philosophy departments after World War II: given the aging and retirement of historically-trained philosophers, neo-Kantians, and neo-Hegelians, it was going to be either the analysts or the phenomenologists who took over, but not both.[89]

In other words, I am suggesting that although the Great Divide between analytic philosophy and phenomenology is real enough, *nevertheless it didn't happen until after 1945*, and *was essentially the result of cultural-political factors, together with one serious philosophical disagreement about the foundations of the exact sciences*. To be sure, this is only one possible explanation of the historical facts. But in any case the serious philosophical disagreement was itself definitely of Kantian origin, for as we saw at the end of the section "Kant's metaphysics," Kant explicitly rejects scientific or reductive naturalism.

Kantian themes in the middle and later analytic tradition

Kant, Quine, and the analytic/synthetic distinction

Although the official or institutional acceptance of the basic tenets of logical positivism by the leading Anglo-American philosophy departments did not fully occur until the end of the 1950s, by 1945 all that actually remained of Kant's metaphysical legacy for philosophers in the analytic tradition were (1) the analytic/synthetic distinction, and (2) the notion of the a priori, including the idea that apriority and necessity entail each other. It is to be particularly noted, however, that both doctrines are intrinsic parts of the original foundations of analytic philosophy.

Yet these doctrines were repeatedly attacked from 1950 onwards until the end of the century by Carnap's protégé and greatest critic, W. V. O. Quine (1908–2000). In fact, Quine's "Two dogmas of empiricism" (1951) effectively destroyed logical empiricism or positivism and the philosophical basis of the analytic tradition along with it. So the analytic tradition quietly committed cognitive suicide by undermining its own Kantian foundations. Reflecting on this striking fact, it will perhaps seem to be a very puzzling thing that the *institution* of analytic philosophy has been able to get along so well since 1950 without any philosophical foundations. A possible solution to this puzzle will be proposed in the section "The end of the a priori: Kant, Sellars, and scientific naturalism," below.

The two dogmas of logical empiricism attacked by Quine are (1) the thesis that there is a sharp and significant distinction between analytic and synthetic truths, and (2) the thesis of "reductionism," which says that every empirically meaningful proposition has a unique translation into a determinate set of logically independent atomic propositions in a sense-datum language. Now any proposition that expresses the unique translation of an empirically meaningful proposition into a determinate set of logically independent propositions in a sense-datum language is itself going to be an analytic proposition. So if (1) goes down, then (2) also goes down. Therefore the crucial dogma is the analytic/synthetic distinction.

Quine's argument against the analytic/synthetic distinction in "Two dogmas"[90] is famously crisp, and proceeds like the basic steps of a dance. He starts by defining analyticity as the truth of a statement by virtue of meanings alone, independently of fact. Then he discards *intensional* meanings – that is, meanings that (1) are essentially descriptive in character, (2) are underdetermined by reference, (3) uniquely determine cross-possible-worlds extensions of terms, and (4) directly entail the modal concepts of necessity and possibility – on the grounds that intensions are nothing but "obscure intermediary entities" unhelpfully inserted between words and their Fregean reference or *Bedeutung*. Then he distinguishes between two types of analytic truth: (1) the truths of classical bivalent first-order predicate logic with identity, and (2) analytic statements that are not truths of class (1), but that can be systematically translated into truths of class (1) by systematically replacing synonyms with synonyms. Then he accepts the analytic truths of class (1) as provisionally unproblematic, and focuses on the analytic truths of class (2). Then he considers, case by case, three attempts to give a clear and determinate account of synonymy: definition, interchangeability, and semantic rules. Then he shows that each attempt ends in circularity by employing various notions that presuppose or entail the unreduced concept of intensional identity, and rejects them all. And then finally he concludes that without the provision of a non-circular account of synonymy,

> a boundary between analytic and synthetic statements simply has not been found. That there is such a distinction to be drawn at all is an unempirical dogma, a metaphysical article of faith.[91]

This argument changed the face of twentieth-century philosophy. Yet it is a *very* bad argument. The many problems with it can be sorted into two sorts: (1), those having to do with whether his argument actually applies to *Kant's* analytic/synthetic distinction, and (2) those having to do with the soundness of his argument against the logical positivists' analytic/synthetic distinction.

(1) Quine's argument clearly does not apply to Kant's analytic/synthetic distinction, for two reasons. First, Quine says that a statement is analytic if and only if it is true by virtue of meanings independently of fact. But for Kant, this gloss would also hold of synthetic a priori propositions, because (a) "meanings" for him include both concepts and *intuitions*, (b) synthetic apriority is defined in terms of a proposition's semantic dependence on pure intuitions, and (c) Quine presupposes without argument that there are no such things as synthetic a priori propositions.[92] Kant would therefore reject the "if" part of Quine's definition of analyticity. Second, according to Kant, a proposition is analytic if and only if it is necessarily true by virtue of intrinsic structural semantic relations between conceptual intensions.[93] Since Quine will not countenance intrinsically structured intensions as meanings, this implies that Kant would also reject the "only if" part of Quine's definition of analyticity. Indeed, since Quine rejects all semantic appeals to intensions from the outset, his attack on analyticity simply cannot apply to Kant's theory.

(2) Furthermore Quine's argument is clearly unsound, for four reasons. First, since he explicitly *accepts* analytic propositions of class (1), it is false to say that no sharp boundary can be found between analytic and synthetic statements. For there *is* by Quine's own reckoning a sharp boundary between analytic truths of class (1) and all other truths. Second, as J. J. Katz points out, even if we focus exclusively on analytic truths of class (2), those based on synonymy, the argument against the intelligibility of such truths is based entirely on an argument by cases, and Quine never gives an argument to show that his set of cases is exhaustive.[94] Third, as H. P. Grice (1913–88) and P. F. Strawson (1919–2006) argue, even if we grant that Quine has shown that *every possible* attempt to define analyticity in terms of synonymy for cases of class (2) ends in circularity with respect to the notion of intensional identity, he still has not shown that an explanation of analyticity in terms of a circular network of irreducibly intensional notions is a philosophically *bad* thing: philosophical analysis can be a semantically *non-reductive* and *holistic* enterprise.[95] Fourth and perhaps most damningly of all, Quine's arguments for the rejection of intensions are both insufficient and self-stultifying, because he himself covertly presupposes intensions in order to explain the analytic truths of class (1).[96]

So Quine's attack on the analytic/synthetic distinction does not actually apply to Kant, and is based on an unsound argument to boot. Still, the attack almost universally convinced analytic philosophers. For example, in a 40-year survey article on the philosophy of language and mind published in the *Philosophical Review* in 1992, Tyler Burge (1946–) asserted:

> no clear reasonable support has been devised for a distinction between truths that depend for their truth on meaning alone and truths that depend for their

truth on their meaning together with (perhaps necessary) features of their subject-matter.[97]

This seems astounding when it is recalled that to reject the analytic/synthetic distinction is to undermine the foundations of philosophical analysis itself.[98] Fortunately there was at least one prominent analytic philosopher after 1945 who was willing to challenge Quine's apostasy: Peter Frederick Strawson.

Kant, Strawson, and transcendental arguments

At this point there is an important twist in the plot of our historical narrative: Strawson, the primary *defender* of philosophical analysis after Quine, was also a *Kantian* philosopher. But as we will see, Strawson's highly influential version of Kantian philosophy nevertheless leaves twenty-first century Kantians with a fundamental leftover problem to solve.

Strawson initially worked in philosophical logic, was strongly influenced by the *Critique of Pure Reason*, and also wrote an important treatise in transcendental metaphysics. Trained at Oxford before World War II by neo-Kantians and British Hegelians, and – along with his Oxford contemporaries J. L. Austin, A. J. Ayer, Michael Dummett, Paul Grice, and Gilbert Ryle – heavily influenced by the logico-linguistic tradition stemming from Frege, Russell, and Wittgenstein, Strawson was arguably the most important British philosopher from 1945 to the end of the century.

We have already seen that along with Grice, Strawson defended the analytic/synthetic distinction against Quine by developing a non-reductive and holistic conception of philosophical analysis.[99] This in turn is intimately connected with Strawson's vigorous defense of irreducible conceptual intensionality in both logic and semantics, in *Introduction to Logical Theory* (1952), *Logico-Linguistic Papers* (1971), and *Subject and Predicate in Logic and Grammar* (1974). Here it is obvious that Strawson's line of thinking runs strongly parallel to Kant's theory of judgment, analyticity, and logic, which is also explicitly based on irreducible conceptual intensionality.[100]

Irreducible conceptual intensionality is also a basic theme of Strawson's immensely influential book on Kant, *The Bounds of Sense* (1966). *Bounds* not only made it respectable for analytic philosophers to write books on topics in the history of philosophy; it also developed a highly original and still controversial interpretation of the first *Critique* that is at once semantically oriented (Strawson treats Kant as a verificationist), anti-psychologistic (he rejects Kant's transcendental psychology), and anti-idealistic (he accuses Kant of Berkeleyanism).

The crucial move in *Bounds*, however, is to connect Kant's seminal idea of a "transcendental deduction" or "transcendental proof" (CPR A84–92/B116–24, B274–9, A734–8/B762–66) directly with the logico-semantic concept of a *presupposition* that Strawson had developed in *Introduction to Logical Theory*. The result is the more-or-less Kantian notion of a *transcendental argument*. Now a presupposition can be contextually defined as follows: A proposition *Q* presupposes a proposition *P* if and only if the truth of *P* is a necessary condition of the truth of *Q* and also a necessary condition of the falsity of Q. Thus P is a necessary condition of the meaningfulness and truth-valuedness of Q. So what then is a transcendental argument? In its general form it looks like this:

1 Assume either the truth or the falsity of the proposition Q, where Q is a contingent claim about the world of human experience.
2 Show that the proposition P is a (or the) presupposition of Q, where P is a claim that is necessarily true and priori if it is true at all.
3 Derive the truth, and thus also the necessity and apriority, of P. [101]

A transcendental argument is also an *anti-skeptical* argument when P states the logical denial of some skeptical thesis such as the Cartesian dream-skeptic's "Possibly nothing exists outside my own phenomenally conscious states" (which is what Kant calls the thesis of "problematic idealism" at *CPR* B274) and Q states a proposition that the skeptic herself also rationally accepts, such as "I am conscious of my existence as determined in time" (*CPR* B275).[102]

Strawson made explicit and liberal use of transcendental arguments in his ground-breaking book *Individuals: An Essay in Descriptive Metaphysics*.[103] So *Individuals* is a work firmly embedded in the Kantian tradition. Kant of course held that his transcendental deductions and proofs entailed transcendental psychology, idealism, and the synthetic apriority of P. And Strawson rejects idealism and modal dualism alike in favor of a thoroughly anti-psychologistic, non-reductive, holistic, analytical realism about individual universals, individual material objects, and individual persons.[104] But leaving all that aside, it remains only a very slight exaggeration to say that Strawson's "descriptive metaphysics" is Kant's transcendental metaphysics *minus* Kant's mentalism.

Nevertheless there is a serious worry about Strawson's key notion of a transcendental argument. It is arguable that step (2) will never work unless semantic verificationism is true, and further that verificationism is true only if transcendental idealism is true and P is synthetic a priori.[105] If this criticism is correct, then either verificationism and transcendental idealism are true and P is synthetic a priori, or else transcendental arguments are invalid. Alternatively, if this criticism is not correct, then it must be shown how step (2) can still work without verificationism, transcendental idealism, or the synthetic a priori. This is an unsolved problem that all Kantian philosophers after Strawson must face up to.

The end of the a priori: Kant, Sellars, and scientific naturalism

In *The Rise of Scientific Philosophy* (1951), the logical positivist and Vienna Circle insider Hans Reichenbach (1891–1953) sketched an influential and widely accepted history of the progress of modern philosophy that culminates with analytic philosophy and merges it ineluctably with the progress of the exact sciences. The basic idea is that philosophy is legitimate precisely to the extent that (1) it is analysis, and (2) it works on fundamental problems arising from mathematics and physics. This is an important historical thesis, not only because it resuscitates Locke's seventeenth-century conception of philosophy as an "underlabourer" for the flagship sciences of the scientific revolution, but also, and indeed primarily because, its unabashed scientism was the engine that drove analytic philosophy in the second half of the twentieth century.

Now it is plausibly arguable, and has indeed been compellingly argued by, for example, Hilary Putnam (1926–) and John McDowell (1942–),[106] that the basic problem of European and Anglo-American analytic philosophy after 1950 – and perhaps also *the* fundamental problem of modern philosophy – is how it is possible to reconcile two sharply different, seemingly incommensurable, and apparently even mutually exclusive metaphysical conceptions, or "pictures," of the world. On the one hand, there is the objective, non-phenomenal, perspectiveless, mechanistic, value-neutral, impersonal, and amoral metaphysical picture of the world delivered by pure mathematics and the fundamental natural sciences. And on the other hand there is the subjective, phenomenal, perspectival, teleological, value-laden, person-oriented, and moral metaphysical picture of the world yielded by the conscious experience of rational human beings. In 1963 Wilfrid Sellars (1912–89) evocatively dubbed these two sharply opposed world-conceptions "the scientific image" and "the manifest image."[107] (For further discussion of Sellars see "American philosophy in the twentieth century," Chapter 5.) So I will call the profound difficulty raised by their mutual incommensurability and inconsistency the "two images problem."

From the 1950s onwards, a possible complete solution to the two images problem gradually emerged, in the form of scientific or reductive naturalism.[108] As we saw in the section "Kant's metaphysics," scientific or reductive naturalism asserts, in Sellars's crisp phrase, that "science is the measure of all things." More generally, scientific naturalism includes four basic theses:

1 *anti-supernaturalism*, or the rejection of any sort of explanatory appeal to non-physical, non-spatio-temporal entities or causal powers,
2 *scientism*, or the thesis that the exact sciences are the paradigms of reasoning and rationality, as regards both their methodology and their content,
3 *physicalist metaphysics*, or the thesis that all the facts are reducible to basic micro-physical facts, and
4 *radical empiricist epistemology*, or the thesis that all knowledge and truths are a posteriori.

Each of the theses of scientific naturalism is flagrantly anti-Kantian, in that it is the direct contradictory of some basic Kantian doctrine. Thus thesis (1) directly contradicts Kant's theory of transcendental freedom. Thesis (2) directly contradicts Kant's doctrine that logic and ethics are the paradigms of theoretical and practical reasoning. Thesis (3) directly contradicts Kant's transcendental idealism. And thesis (4) directly contradicts Kant's theory of the a priori.

There are two basic ways of holding the thesis that all knowledge and truths are a posteriori. One ways asserts the existence of *necessary a posteriori* truths and attempts to substitute them for all necessary a priori truths, and this is the doctrine of *scientific essentialism*, which will be discussed shortly. The other way asserts that all truths are *contingent a posteriori*, and this is the doctrine of *modal skepticism*, as defended by Quine.[109] So, in other words, corresponding to scientific essentialism and Quine's modal skepticism there are two ways of contradicting Kant's theory of the a priori. The first way breaks the entailment from necessity to apriority. And the second way rejects the existence of necessity and apriority alike.

At this point there is another important historical twist in our narrative. This is the striking fact that Sellars was both the father of scientific naturalism[110] *and* a leading Kantian.[111] Wearing the latter hat, Sellars first formulated and defended the highly influential idea, later promoted by Donald Davidson (1917–2003)[112] and John McDowell,[113] that inner or outer sensory experience has no independent cognitive significance, semantic implications, or logical force apart from conceptualization and thought. Thus *percepts without concepts are rationally meaningless, or outside the logical space of reasons* (cf. CPR A51/B76), and to hold otherwise is to fall fallaciously under the siren spell of "the Myth of the Given."[114]

In McDowell's hands, this Sellarsian doctrine becomes the widely-held contemporary thesis of *conceptualism about mental content*, which says (1) that all cognitive capacities are fully determined by conceptual capacities, and (2) that none of the cognitive capacities of rational human animals can also be possessed by non-rational animals, whether human or non-human.[115] Now McDowell is not a scientific or reductive naturalist.[116] And McDowell's conceptualism is arguably more a *Hegelian* thesis than it is a Kantian thesis.[117] But looked at from *Sellars's* point of view, the deep connection between (a) conceptualism about mental content, (b) scientific naturalism, and (c) the two images problem, is this: *if* scientific naturalism is true, and *if* we also fully reject the Myth of the Given, *then* our best exact scientific theories will ultimately determine the structure, content, and objects of inner and outer sensory experience. And in that way, the scientific image both assimilates and also eliminates the manifest image.[118]

Oddly enough, although Sellars was the true father of scientific naturalism, Quine was the leading scientific naturalist in the latter half of the twentieth century even despite the presence of some important non-naturalistic strands in his work.[119] But the combined Sellars–Quine doctrine of scientific naturalism still would not, perhaps, have convinced most mainstream analytic philosophers of its truth without the additional support of the highly influential doctrine of *scientific essentialism* that was developed by Saul Kripke (1940–) and Hilary Putnam in the 1970s.[120] According to scientific essentialism,

1 natural kinds like gold and water have microphysical essences,
2 these essences are either known or are at least in principle knowable by contemporary natural science,
3 propositions stating these essences, such as "Water is H_2O," are necessarily true because statements of identity are necessarily true if true at all, and
4 essentialist necessary truths about natural kinds are knowable only a posteriori.

Unlike Quine, who was an anti-realist and a severe critic of modal logic, the scientific essentialists are both scientific realists and also strong proponents of the idea that modal logic is the analytic philosopher's fundamental analytical tool. So for essentialists, exact science and modal logic are *really deep*. If scientific essentialism is correct, then not all necessary truths are a priori, and perhaps even *all* necessary truths are a posteriori – and in that case, the very last substantive Kantian epistemological and metaphysical thesis in the analytic tradition, the existence of the a priori, again goes the way of all flesh.

We now have in place the means to offer a possible solution to the historico-philosophical puzzle described in the section "Kant, Quine, and the analytic/synthetic distinction," above. This puzzle was: How has analytic philosophy managed to get on so well institutionally since 1950 despite the fact that its Kantian foundations were undermined by Quine's attack on the analytic/synthetic distinction? And the possible solution I am proposing is: despite its foundational crisis, the analytic tradition has flourished since the middle of the twentieth century by affirming the Sellars–Quine doctrine of scientific naturalism, and by widely embracing scientific essentialism, and thus by latching itself for dear life onto the high speed train of the exact sciences.

Kantian themes in the middle and later phenomenological tradition

Kant, Husserl, and the crisis of European sciences

But is this high-speed train actually heading straight for a big smash-up? In 1947, Wittgenstein had precisely that thought:

> The truly apocalyptic view of the world is that things do not repeat themselves. It isn't absurd, e.g., to believe that the age of science and technology is the beginning of the end for humanity; the idea of great progress is a delusion, along with the idea that the truth will ultimately be known; that there is nothing good or desirable about scientific knowledge and that mankind, in seeking it, is falling into a trap. It is by no means obvious that this is not how things are.[121]

Husserl had also seriously considered the same sobering idea in the early 1930s, in conjunction with a close reading of his former student Heidegger's *Being and Time*. The result was a series of manuscripts composed between 1934 and 1938 and posthumously published as *The Crisis of European Sciences* (1954).

In the *Crisis*, Husserl attempts to combine his transcendental phenomenology with the profound existential-phenomenological thesis that the conscious, intentional, cognizing, and knowing rational human subject is necessarily embodied as a living animal, and also necessarily situated in and actively engaged with an integrated network of spatio-temporal, macrophysical, practical, intersubjective or social, and historical contexts. He called this total network the "lifeworld" (*Lebenswelt*). By sharp contrast, the classical conception of the rational human subject and its world which is offered by the exact sciences, either (1) converts the rational human subject into an alienated, fundamentally non-physical, causally-isolated, or even epiphenomenal phenomenally conscious Cartesian ego over against a fundamentally physical world of causally efficacious microphysical entities and forces (= Cartesian substance dualism plus Boyle's and Locke's microphysicalism), or else (2) explanatorily and ontologically reduces the human subject to nothing but fundamentally physical properties and facts (= reductive materialism). In either case we are in serious philosophical trouble because, as Kant had explicitly pointed out in the first *Critique*, both human knowledge and freedom are thereby rendered respectively impossible by the Cartesian skepticism entailed by (1)[122] and the "hard" or incompatibilist determinism entailed by (2).[123] But as Husserl makes very clear, since the exact sciences *themselves* are rational human enterprises seemingly based on the presuppositions of human knowledge and freedom, this means that the sciences themselves are in serious trouble too: hence their foundational "crisis."

The only way out of the crisis, according to Husserl, is to invert the epistemic and metaphysical foundations, and show how exact science is in fact explanatorily and ontologically founded *on the lifeworld*, which is then in turn intentionally "constituted" by *the transcendental ego*. This if course is a classically Kantian move. But will Husserl's lifeworld-constituting "transcendental-phenomenological turn" be able to avoid falling back into Cartesian substance dualism?

The end of phenomenology: Kant, Derrida, and deconstructionism

According to the highly influential French philosopher Jacques Derrida (1930–2004), the answer was a resounding *no*. Derrida started his career as a Husserlian phenomenologist; his thesis at the École Normale Supérieure was a general study of Husserl's phenomenology, *The Problem of Genesis in Husserl's Philosophy*, but he critically broke away from the phenomenological tradition, and more famously and influentially set up shop as a *deconstructionist*.

Derrida's deconstructionism consists, at bottom, in a great many subtle variations on the following fairly straightforward five-step argument: [124]

1 Traditional metaphysics in general and Kant's metaphysics in particular is essentially the "metaphysics of presence," or the attempt to find objects, properties, facts, or principles that are directly, self-evidently, and infallibly given to the cognitive subject.
2 The metaphysics of presence in turn presupposes "logocentrism," or the assumption of a unitary logic, syntax, and semantics underlying all languages and at the basis of all rationality.
3 But cognitive access to objects, properties, facts, and principles is necessarily mediated by language-in-use, which is also essentially open to multiple interpretations, some of which are inconsistent with other interpretations.
4 So the metaphysics of presence and logocentrism are both false, and rationality is inherently self-undermining or "undecidable" in roughly Kurt Gödel's sense of a proposition that is logically true if and only if it is logically false.

5 Therefore, traditional metaphysics in general and Kant's metaphysics in particular are impossible.

There are significant parallels between Derrida's deconstructionist argument against traditional metaphysics, and Quine's argument against the analytic/synthetic distinction from "the indeterminacy of translation."[125] But the crucial point for our purposes is that in *Edmund Husserl's Origin of Geometry: An Introduction* (1962) and in *Speech and Phenomena* (1967), in reverse order, Derrida applied the deconstructionist argument directly to Husserl's early logico-semantic phenomenology in *Logical Investigations* and to his later transcendental phenomenology in *Crisis*.

The basic thesis linking together both Derridean studies is that while phenomenology purports to criticize and replace traditional metaphysics in general and Kant's metaphysics in particular, it falls directly back into the metaphysics of presence and logocentrism. And then just like both traditional metaphysics and Kant's metaphysics, phenomenology for that reason is ultimately impossible. As a consequence of this deconstructionist worry, together with a more sympathetic but in fact philosophically far more rigorous critique of Husserl's epistemology in 1974 by the Marxist philosopher Leszek Kolakowski (1927–) ironically enough, delivered as the Cassirer Lectures at Yale),[126] by the end of the 1970s phenomenology was widely regarded as a philosophical program that had come to an end. It survived only in the substantially downsized form of the exegetical historical-philosophical study of Husserl's texts and the texts of those significantly influenced by Husserl – in particular, the early Heidegger, early Sartre, and Merleau-Ponty. And unlike analytic philosophy, which closely linked its fate to that of the massively successful and culturally dominant exact sciences, phenomenology firmly rejected scientific or reductive naturalism at about mid-century, and so institutionally had largely withered away by the end of the twentieth century as well.[127]

Kantian themes in ethics

Kant, Moore again, and the naturalistic fallacy

Thus far we have been following the direct and indirect protean influences of Kant's Critical Philosophy on the mainstream of twentieth-century philosophy running from neo-Kantianism up through the European and Anglo-American analytic and phenomenological traditions. But this story concerns almost exclusively the role of Kant's metaphysics. What about the role of Kant's ethics?

One crucial difference between the role of Kant's metaphysics and the role of his ethics in twentieth-century philosophy is that whereas Kant's metaphysics is *the* original foundation of analytic philosophy and phenomenology alike, his ethics by sharp contrast always was (and still is) in direct competition with two other equally important moral traditions: (1) the *utilitarian consequentialist* tradition, which runs backwards through J. S. Mill and Jeremy Bentham to Hume's *Treatise of Human Nature* and second *Enquiry*, and (2) the *contractualist* tradition, which runs backwards through

Rousseau and Locke to Hobbes's *Leviathan*. Adequately narrating and then critically analyzing the philosophical story of the interplay between Kantian ethics, utilitarian consequentialism, and contractualism in the twentieth century would easily use up another chapter at least as long as this one. Nevertheless, two scenes from that story are directly relevant to the present account.

The first scene comes from the first decade of the century, and concerns Moore's seminal treatise in moral theory, *Principia Ethica* (see also "Twentieth-century moral philosophy," Chapter 20). The *Principia* is a characteristically ingenious and intensely passionate attempt to combine various elements of Henry Sidgwick's and J. S. Mill's utilitarian consequentialist (that is, hedonic, instrumentalist, and results-oriented) ethics with Kant's deontological (that is, duty-based, non-instrumentalist, and intentions-oriented) ethics. Moore does this by way of a radical critique of what he calls ethical "naturalism":

> [Naturalism] consists in substituting for "good" some one property of a natural object or of a collection of natural objects; and in thus replacing Ethics by some one of the natural sciences. In general, the science thus substituted is one of the sciences specially concerned with man. ... In general, Psychology has been the science substituted, as by J. S. Mill.[128]

And his objection centers on the "naturalistic fallacy":

> [T]he naturalistic fallacy ... [is] the fallacy which consists in identifying the simple notion which we mean by "good" with some other notion.[129]

> [The naturalistic] fallacy, I explained, consists in the contention that good *means* nothing but some simple or complex notion, that can defined in terms of natural qualities.[130]

In other words, according to Moore ethical naturalism is the claim that the property[131] of being good is identical with some simple or complex natural property (i.e. either a first-order physical property or a sensory experiential property); and the naturalistic fallacy consists precisely in accepting such an identification of properties. So far, so good – awful pun intended. Here Moore has clearly assimilated and further refined Kant's sharp and irreducible distinctions between the categorically normative *ought* and the factual *is*, and between the categorical norm of *altruism* and the empirical psychology of *self-interest*. And virtually all post-Moorean analytic ethicists have accepted Moore's characterization of ethical naturalism as well as his anti-naturalistic conclusions. So in this way, Kantian ethics covertly belongs to the foundations of all twentieth-century moral theories, of any conceivable stripe. But now for the sad part of the story.

Moore's basic argument in support of the putative fallaciousness of the naturalistic fallacy – the "open question argument" – is generally held to be a notorious failure. Here is his argument:

The hypothesis that disagreement about the meaning of good is disagreement with regard to the correct analysis of a given whole, may be most plainly seen to be incorrect by consideration of the fact that, whatever definition be offered, it may always be asked, with significance, of the complex so defined, whether it is itself good.[132]

We must not, therefore, be frightened by the assertion that a thing is natural into the admission that it is good: good does not, by definition, mean anything that is natural; and it is always an open question whether what is natural is good.[133]

For convenience, I will call the fundamental ethical property of being good, "the Good." The open question argument says that any attempt to explain the Good solely in terms of some corresponding natural property N (say, the property of being a pleasurable state of mind), automatically falls prey to the decisive objection that even if X is an instance of N it can still be significantly asked whether X is good: that is, it can be significantly postulated that X is an instance of N but X is not good. Moore's rationale for this is that the only case in which it would be altogether nonsensical to postulate that X is an instance of N but X is not good, is the case in which it is strictly impossible or contradictory to hold that X is not good, that is, when X is, precisely, good. So if it is significant to ask whether X is N but not good, then N is not identical to the Good. And Moore finds it to be invariably the case that it is significant to ask whether X is N but not good, hence invariably the case that N is not identical to the Good. He concludes that the Good is an indefinable or unanalyzable non-natural property, and that it is a fallacy to try to identify the Good with any natural property.

The open question argument is doomed because of a mistake Moore has made about the individuation of properties. The problem is that the argument implies a criterion of property-identity that is absurdly strict.[134] Familiar criteria of identity for two properties include equivalence of analytic definition, synonymy of their corresponding predicates, and identity of their cross-possible-worlds extensions. But Moore's criterion is importantly different:

[W]hoever will attentively consider with himself what is actually before his mind when he asks the question "Is pleasure (or whatever it may be) after all good?" can easily satisfy himself that he is not merely wondering whether pleasure is pleasant. And if he will try this experiment with each suggested definition in succession, he may become expert enough to recognise that in every case he has before his mind a unique object, with regard to the connection of which with any other object, a distinct question can be asked. Everyone does in fact understand the question "Is this good?" When he thinks of it, his state of mind is different from what it would be, were he asked "Is this pleasant, or desired, or approved?" It has a distinct meaning for him, even though he may not recognize in what respect it is distinct. Whenever he thinks of "intrinsic value," or "intrinsic worth," or says that a thing "ought to exist," he has before his mind the unique object – the unique property of things – which I mean by "good". ... "Good," then is indefinable.[135]

Moore's criterion is that two properties are identical if and only if the intentional contents of the states of mind in which the properties are recognized, are phenomenally indistinguishable. Moore seems to have inherited the phenomenal criterion of the identity of properties from his teacher Ward, who in turn inherited it from Brentano, thus by an ironic twist returning us full-circle to psychologism. Consequently, even two properties that are by hypothesis definitionally equivalent – for example, the property of being a bachelor, and the property of being an adult unmarried male – will come out non-identical according to this test. The intentional content of the state of mind of someone who says or thinks that X is a bachelor is clearly phenomenally distinguishable from that of the same person when she says or thinks that X is an adult unmarried male. I might not wonder even for a split second whether a bachelor is a bachelor, yet find myself mentally double-clutching as to whether a bachelor is an unmarried adult male. But then according to that test it is not nonsensical to ask whether X is an unmarried adult male but not a bachelor – from which we must conclude by Moorean reasoning that the property of being a bachelor is indefinable, and that it is a fallacy to try to identify any property with any other property, *including the property which expresses its definition*. Obviously this cannot be correct: it is patently absurd to constrain property identity so very, very tightly.[136] Moore has clearly confused what Kant carefully separated: (1) the phenomenal content of inner sense and (2) the intensional content of concepts.[137] (See also the section "Kant, Husserl, phenomenology, and philosophical logic," above.)

From the standpoint of Kantian ethics however the result is far more dire, since Moore's mistake seems to cast doubt on the fundamental Kantian ought/is and altruism/self-interest distinctions that had originally motivated Moore's attack on the naturalistic fallacy. Yet we must not confuse the messenger with the message. For Kant, as we saw in the section "Kant's ethics," above, these distinctions have an independent foundation in our innate spontaneous mental capacity of pure practical reason.

Kantian ethics after Rawls

The second scene from the story of Kant's ethics in twentieth-century philosophy comes from the period after 1950. The dominant figure in moral philosophy during this period was the Harvard philosopher John Rawls (1921–2002), whose *Theory of Justice* (1971) had an impact on post-World War II moral and political theory fully comparable to that of his departmental colleague Quine's earlier paper "Two dogmas" on postwar semantics, epistemology, and metaphysics. (For further discussion of Rawls, see "Twentieth-century political philosophy," Chapter 21.)

But unlike "Two dogmas," yet very like Strawson's *Individuals*, and again also very like the influential theory of "communicative ethics" developed in the same period by Jürgen Habermas (1929–),[138] Rawls's *Theory of Justice* is in fundamental ways a work firmly embedded in the Kantian tradition.[139] Just as Moore had attempted to combine utilitarian consequentialism with Kant's ethics, so Rawls's project was to combine contractualism with Kant's ethics. This lead Rawls to two basic ideas. The first basic idea is that the first principles of morality are indeed categorical or unconditional and non-instrumental just as Kant had argued, but also essentially *procedural* or *constructive*, not substantive (more on this in a moment). The second basic idea is that Kantian moral principles are not grasped either by Kantian pure practical reason or by a Moorean intuition of the Good, but instead are to be generated by a contractualist methodology which asks what a group of rational human participants in a social contract *would* agree to, by way of a set of procedural principles of justice-as-fairness, on the purely hypothetical assumption (called "the veil of ignorance") that the actual identities and worldly circumstances of the participants in the contract-forming assembly are not known.

Rawls's veil-of-ignorance methodology is not dissimilar to Husserl's *epoché*, although in an intersubjective rather than a solipsistic context. But the crucial point for our purposes is the idea that the Kantian first principles of morality are essentially procedural or constructive, and not substantive. This important Rawlsian idea has been further developed by several of Rawls's students, most notably Thomas Hill,[140] Christine Korsgaard (1952–),[141] and Onora O'Neill (1941–),[142] both as a way of interpreting Kant's Categorical Imperative (which I have also adopted in the section "Kant's metaphysics") and as a way of doing Kantian ethics.

According to O'Neill, it is a great mistake to think of the Categorical Imperative (CI) as a superstrong first-order principle for action or a super-maxim, that is, as an all-purpose practical decision-procedure or algorithm. On the contrary, the CI is a second-order procedural principle applying universally to first-order maxims. Negatively described, the CI is a filter for screening out bad maxims; positively described, the CI is a constructive protocol for correctly generating maxims, given the multifarious array of concrete input-materials to practical reasoning, that is, beliefs, desires, habits, personal situation, social-historical context, and so on. Thus the CI says, roughly:

> Act *only* according to those maxims that every rational human being could adopt, and that thereby remain consistent with our innate rational capacity for constructing and acting upon maxims.

The crucial point here is that we cannot say in advance of actual practical reasoning processes just *which* maxims will turn out to be permissible or obligatory, but we can know a priori that any maxim that will count as action-guiding *must* have a format or structure that is determined by the CI.

When it is construed in this way as essentially procedural or constructive, the CI functions not only as a categorically normative first principle of moral reasoning, but also as a categorically normative first principle of logical reasoning:

> The Categorical Imperative is the supreme principle of reasoning not because it is an algorithm either for thought or for action, but because it

is an indispensable strategy for disciplining thinking or action in ways that are not contingent on specific and variable circumstances. The Categorical Imperative is a fundamental strategy, not an algorithm; it is the fundamental strategy not just of morality but *of all activity that counts as reasoned*. The supreme principle of reason is merely the principle of thinking and acting on principles that can (not "do") hold for all.[143]

O'Neill is saying that the basis for the construction of any rational scheme of principles, whether that scheme is to be thought-guiding (logic) or intentional-action-guiding (morality), is the CI. As applied to intentional action, the CI says that any first-order action-guiding principle must be universalizable, non-exploitative, and so on. But when it is applied to thought, the CI says that every reasoning process must satisfy some minimal principle of logical consistency. For example, let us consider what I will call "the Weak Law of Non-Contradiction," which says that *not every proposition is both true and false*. [144] The CI as applied to logical reasoning then says:

> Think *only* according to those processes of logical reasoning every rational human being could adopt, and that thereby satisfy the Weak Law of Non-Contradiction.

But Kantian moral constructivism does not exhaust Kantian ethics. According to Hill, these are its main theoretical commitments:

1 "Kantian ethics is primarily *addressed to concerns we have as rational moral agents*, as we deliberate conscientiously about what we ought to do."
2 "Moral 'oughts' purport to express categorical imperatives or judgments based on these … [and] these express *rational constraints on choice* that are not grounded in either the need to take necessary means to one's particular contingent ends or one's general desire for happiness."
3 "Categorical imperatives and the moral judgments derived from them express rational prescriptions in a vocabulary of constraint ('must', 'bound', 'obligatory', 'duty', 'Do it!') that reflects how recognizing a rational moral requirement is experienced by those ('imperfect wills') who know that they can satisfy the requirement but also know that they can and might violate the requirement and choose instead to pursue some conflicting desire-based end."
4 "Moral 'oughts' express a deep, self-identifying, and inescapable disposition of moral agents, who have reason and autonomy of will, to acknowledge certain considerations as overridingly authoritative and so internally binding."
5 "It is a fundamental moral principle that humanity in each person is to be regarded as an end in itself."
6 "We can think of the policies and acts that would be acceptable for everyone, in the relevant sense, as just those policies and acts that would conform to the 'universal laws' that moral legislators would accept if trying to work out a reasonable system of moral principles under certain ideal conditions ('the kingdom/realm of ends')."

7 "These general principles are supposed to establish a strong presumption against willful deception and manipulation."

8 "When thinking from a practical moral perspective rather than an empirical scientific perspective, we conceive typical human actions as done intentionally – for reasons – by agents presumed capable of choosing to act differently."

9 "In human beings, practical judgments and feelings are not usually separable."[145]

It is obvious enough how this set of commitments both refines and extends Kant's ethics (see "Kant's ethics," above). There is, however, in this connection a fairly serious problem with the eighth theoretical commitment. What would Kant himself say about it? Presumably something like this: The fact that from a practical perspective, as opposed to a scientific perspective, we must *conceive* of ourselves as acting intentionally for reasons, in such a way that we could also have acted differently if we had recognized that we morally ought to, is of course perfectly consistent with our being *falsely* so conceived. If that conception is false, then there really is no such thing as practical freedom or autonomy. Yet in that case our everyday lives as lived from the inside are nothing but a tragic metaphysical hoax, for every sane person is a "phenomenal libertarian" for whom it at least *feels as if* ordinary choices are such that she could have willed or done otherwise. Furthermore, our autonomy or practical freedom and along with it our noumenal ability to will or do otherwise are both required by the very nature of morality to be *real*, not merely self-conceptions that we have to believe in. In this way it appears that the thesis of "soft determinism," or *compatibilism*, which says that "internal" or "agent-centered" freedom of the will and moral responsibility are consistent with a complete actual inability to will or do otherwise in view of the universal deterministic or indeterministic mechanism of the natural world, *cannot* be the metaphysical basis of a truly Kantian ethics. The free will must have real causal efficacy, or else we are not the persons we seem to be.

Conclusion

Despite the sobering fact that the two major philosophical traditions of the twentieth century – as someone wittily wrote about the history of the nineteenth century – began with *Great Expectations* but ended with *Lost Illusions*, a positive moral can nevertheless be extracted from this otherwise downbeat story. Both analytic philosophy and phenomenology *could* renew themselves in the twenty-first century by critically recovering their Kantian origins, and by rethinking and rebuilding their own foundations in the light of this critical recovery.

What I mean is this. Analytic philosophers *could* directly engage with Kant's two revolutionary ideas (1) that natural science is ultimately all about the intrinsic structures and causal functions of a directly humanly perceivable macrophysical empirical reality, not about microphysical noumena and their humanly unobservable non-relational essences (this is what I called Kant's *manifest realism*), and (2) that the exact sciences presuppose and are inherently constrained by rational human nature, and all theoretical reasoning including pure logic and mathematics is categorically normative at its basis, because practical rationality is explanatorily and ontologically prior to theoretical rationality (let us call this *the priority of practical reason over theoretical reason*).[146] Correspondingly, phenomenologists *could* also directly engage with Kant's equally revolutionary ideas (a) that inner sense (temporal phenomenal consciousness) and outer sense (spatial embodied consciousness) are necessarily interdependent, and (b) that the intentionality of the mind is continuous with biological life. So phenomenologists could face up to the thoughts that there is no such thing as an ontologically independent, epistemically infallible, world-constituting Cartesian/Kantian transcendental ego, and that the rational human mind is nothing more and nothing less than the activating form of the living human animal fully embedded in its worldly environment and fully engaged in all its ordinary practices.[147]

In these ways, it seems at least possible that the seemingly unbridgeable explanatory and ontological gaps that opened up in mid- and late-twentieth century philosophy between the basic subject matters of post-Quinean analysis (that is, the noumenal micro-world described by mathematical physics) and classical phenomenology (that is, consciousness or subjective experience, and intentionality)[148] could ultimately close themselves up and become a single integrated set of facts about rational human animals and their macrophysical world. If so, this would in effect solve the two images problem without in any way reducing or eliminating the manifest image.

Kant dealt with essentially the same clash of fundamental philosophical images under the rubrics of *nature* and *freedom*.[149] And in this way a partial anticipation of Kant's strategy for integrating the two images can be found in Kantian ethics.[150] Here the indissoluble fusion of the concepts of (1) mind as the embodied locus of cognitive, affective, and volitional capacities, (2) intentional action, (3) basic human practices (including language and exact science), (4) the sharp modal distinction between instrumental or hypothetical normativity and non-instrumental or categorical normativity, (5) logic as the non-instrumentally or categorically normative science of theoretical rationality, and (6) constructivist moral theory as the non-instrumentally or categorically normative science of practical rationality, aptly captures the sense in which the analytic and phenomenological traditions could together rejoin, reformulate, and recover Kant's notion of philosophy as a self-critical *rational anthropology* (JL 9:25–6).

So it appears – to echo the famous opening lines of the first *Critique* – that twenty-first century philosophy *has the peculiar fate*, that either it will eventually achieve genuine autonomy as a form of rational anthropology in the Kantian sense, more or less along the lines projected by Kantian ethics, or else it will inwardly perish and become no more than a subdepartment of the exact sciences. But the choice of which it is to be, is entirely up to us.

Notes

1 Whitehead, *Process and Reality*, p. 39.
2 For convenience, I cite Kant's works infratextually in parentheses. The citations include both an abbreviation of the English title and the corresponding volume and page numbers in the standard "Akademie"

edition of Kant's works: *Kants gesammelte Schriften*, edited by the Königlich Preussischen (now Deutschen) Akademie der Wissenschaften (Berlin: G. Reimer (now de Gruyter), 1902–). I generally follow the standard English translations, but have occasionally modified them where appropriate. For references to the first *Critique*, I follow the common practice of giving page numbers from the A (1781) and B (1787) German editions only. Here is a list of the relevant abbreviations and English translations.

A   *Anthropology from a Pragmatic Point of View*, trans. M. Gregor. The Hague: Nijhoff, 1974.

CPJ   *Critique of the Power of Judgment*, trans. P. Guyer and E. Matthews. Cambridge: Cambridge University Press, 2000.

CPR   *Critique of Pure Reason*, trans. P. Guyer and A. Wood. Cambridge: Cambridge University Press, 1997.

CPrR   *Critique of Practical Reason*, trans. L. W. Beck. Indianapolis: Bobbs-Merrill, 1956.

CPrR   *Critique of Practical Reason*, trans. M. Gregor. In *Immanuel Kant: Practical Philosophy*, Cambridge: Cambridge University Press, 1996, pp. 133–272.

GMM   *Groundwork of the Metaphysics of Morals* trans. M. Gregor. In *Immanuel Kant: Practical Philosophy*, Cambridge: Cambridge University Press, pp. 37–108.

IUH   "Idea of a universal history of mankind from a cosmopolitan point of view." In *Kant on History*, trans. L. W. Beck, New York: Bobbs-Merrill, 1963, pp. 11–26.

JL   "The Jäsche logic." In *Immanuel Kant: Lectures on Logic*, trans. J. M. Young, Cambridge: Cambridge University Press, 1992, pp. 519–640.

LE   *Lectures on Ethics*, trans. P. Heath. Cambridge: Cambridge University Press, 1997.

MFNS   *Metaphysical Foundations of Natural Science*, trans. J. Ellington. Indianapolis: Bobbs-Merrill, 1970.

MM   *Metaphysics of Morals*, trans. M. Gregor. In *Immanuel Kant: Practical Philosophy*, Cambridge: Cambridge University Press, 1996, pp. 353–604.

OP   *Opus postumum*, trans. E. Förster and M. Rosen. Cambridge: Cambridge University Press, 1993. P *Prolegomena to Any Future Metaphysics*, trans. J. Ellington. Indianapolis: Hackett, 1977.

PC   *Immanuel Kant: Philosophical Correspondence, 1759–99*, trans. A. Zweig. Chicago: University of Chicago Press, 1967.

Rel   *Religion within the Boundaries of Mere Reason*, trans. A. Wood and G. Di Giovanni. Cambridge: Cambridge University Press, 1998.

3   See, e.g., Hanna, *Kant and the Foundations of Analytic Philosophy*, esp. ch. 3; Proust, *Questions of Form: Logic and the Analytic Proposition*; and Soames, *Philosophical Analysis in the Twentieth Century*, esp. vol. 1.

4   See, e.g., Moran, *Introduction to Phenomenology*; and Spiegelberg (with Schuhmann), *The Phenomenological Movement*.

5   In this chapter for simplicity's sake I am using the notions of a proposition, an assertoric judgment, an indicative sentence, and a statement interchangeably.

6   Kant distinguishes carefully between (1) "cognition" (*Erkenntnis*), or the conscious mental representation of objects (CPR A320/B376), which does *not* strictly imply either belief, truth, or justification (CPR A58–9/B83), and (2) "scientific knowing" (*Wissen*), which *does* strictly implies belief, truth, and justification (CPR A820–31/B848–59). From this simple terminological point, however, it follows that to the considerable extent that the first *Critique* is all about the nature, scope, and limits of human *Erkenntnis*, then it is fundamentally a treatise in cognitive semantics, and *not* fundamentally a treatise in epistemology. See Hanna, *Kant and the Foundations of Analytic Philosophy*, esp. pp. 18 and 30.

7   See Abela, *Kant's Empirical Realism*; and Hanna, *Kant, Science, and Human Nature*, chs. 1–4.

8   See Hanna, *Kant, Science, and Human Nature*, chs. 5–8.

9   Sellars, "Empiricism and the philosophy of mind," p. 173.

10   But see Wood, *Kant's Ethical Thought*, p. 288.

11   See Grimm, "Kant's argument for radical evil."

12   See Beck, "Neo-Kantianism"; and Köhnke, *The Rise of Neo-Kantianism*.

13   See Soames, *Philosophical Analysis in the Twentieth Century*, esp. vol. 2, pp. 461–76.

14   See, e.g., Coffa, *The Semantic Tradition from Kant to Carnap*; and Hanna, *Kant and the Foundations of Analytic Philosophy*.

15 Brentano, *Psychology from an Empirical Standpoint*, book I.
16 James, *Principles of Psychology*, vol. 1, ch. ix.
17 Brentano, *Psychology from an Empirical Standpoint*, pp. 88–91.
18 Ibid., p. 91.
19 Ibid., p. 81.
20 Ibid., pp. 83–5.
21 In other words, mental phenomena in Brentano's sense are *phenomenal qualia*. See Dennett, "Quining qualia."
22 Frege, "Review of E. G. Husserl, *Philosophie der Arithmetik I*."
23 Husserl, *Logical Investigations*, vol. 1, p. 122n.
24 Ibid., vol. 2, p. 527.
25 Unlike Husserl, Frege does not think it is possible to hold the sense of a linguistic expression fixed, and vary the reference. But this is only a superficial difference, since Husserl's examples exploit either the semantic phenomenon of multiple applications of the same predicate ("is a dog" can be multiply applied to Asta, Bullet, or Lassie) or the semantic phenomenon of multiple reference under the same indexical ("I" can multiply refer to Tom, Dick, or Harriet as token-reflexively uttered by each), neither of which, presumably, Frege would upon reflection really want to reject.
26 This is made clear in the second edition version of the Introduction to vol. 2 of the *Logical Investigations*, which was published in 1913.
27 Husserl, *Logical Investigations*, vol. 2, p. 549.
28 Ibid., p. 549, n. 1.
29 See Moran, "Making sense: Husserl's phenomenology as transcendental idealism."
30 See Weatherston, *Heidegger's Interpretation of Kant*.
31 This idea heavily influenced Hans-Georg Gadamer's philosophical hermeneutics in *Truth and Method*; see Moran, *Introduction to Phenomenology*, ch. 8.
32 See Rorty, *Philosophy and the Mirror of Nature*, part two.
33 See, e.g., Bell and Cooper, *The Analytic Tradition*; Dummett, *Origins of Analytical Philosophy*; French et al., *The Foundations of Analytic Philosophy*; Hanna, *Kant and the Foundations of Analytic Philosophy*; Pap, *Elements of Analytic Philosophy*; Soames, *Philosophical Analysis in the Twentieth Century*; and Tugendhat, *Traditional and Analytical Philosophy*, esp. part I.
34 See Frege, *Begriffschrift*; Frege, *Foundations of Arithmetic* and *Basic Laws of Arithmetic*. According to Frege in the *Foundations*, a proposition is analytic if and only if it is either provable from a general law of logic alone, or else provable from general laws of logic plus "logical definitions." One problem with this account is that unless general laws of logic are provable from themselves, they do not strictly speaking count as analytic. Another and more serious problem is that the precise semantic and epistemic status of logical definitions was never adequately clarified or settled by Frege; see Benacerraf, "Frege: the last logicist." But the most serious problem is that Frege's set theory contains an apparently insoluble contradiction discovered by Russell in 1901, as a direct consequence of the unrestricted set-formation axiom in Frege's *Basic Laws of Arithmetic*: *Russell's Paradox*, which says that the set of all sets not members of themselves is a member of itself if and only if it is not a member of itself.
35 See Frege, *Foundations of Arithmetic*, pp. 101–2; and Frege, "Foundations of geometry," pp. 22–6.
36 See Langford, "The notion of analysis in Moore's philosophy." Moorean analysis is best examplified in *Principia Ethica* and the essays later collected in his *Philosophical Studies* (1922).
37 See Levy, *Moore: G. E. Moore and the Cambridge Apostles*.
38 See Ward, "Psychology."
39 Moore, *Principia Ethica*, pp. x–xi.
40 See Hanna, *Kant and the Foundations of Analytic Philosophy*, pp. 55–6.
41 Moore, *Principia Ethica*, p. xx.
42 See Baldwin, *G. E. Moore*, chs. I–II.
43 Keynes, "My early beliefs," p. 94. The Cambridge Apostles were (and still are) a highly-selective Cambridge secret debating society. See also Levy, *G. E. Moore and the Cambridge Apostles*.
44 Phenomenalistic interpretations of Kant's idealism have been around, and possibly even dominant, from at least the time of the Christian Garve–Johann Feder review of the first *Critique* in 1782. See

also, e.g., Strawson, *The Bounds of Sense*; and Van Cleve, *Problems from Kant*. Most of the many changes made by Kant in the B edition of 1987 were directed against this interpretation.

45 See Carroll, *Through the Looking-Glass*. Carroll was really Charles Lutwidge Dodgson, an Oxford logician and contemporary of Moore and Russell.

46 See Meinong, "The theory of objects."

47 See Hylton, *Russell, Idealism, and the Emergence of Analytic Philosophy*.

48 Moore, "Review of Russell's *Essay on the Foundations of Geometry*."

49 See Russell, *Introduction to Mathematical Philosophy*, pp. 169–70.

50 See Monk, *Bertrand Russell*, part I.

51 Russell, *Principles of Mathematics*, p. 4.

52 See Russell, "Knowledge by acquaintance and knowledge by description."

53 See Russell, *The Problems of Philosophy*, ch. 5.

54 Russell, *My Philosophical Development*, pp. 14–15.

55 Russell, *Autobiography*, p. 330.

56 See Eames, "Introduction," in Russell, *Theory of Knowledge*, pp. xiv–xx.

57 Russell, *Autobiography*, p. 282.

58 See Russell, "The philosophy of logical atomism."

59 Wittgenstein told G. H. von Wright that "he had read Schopenhauer's *Die Welt as Wille und Vorstellung* in his youth and that his first philosophy was Schopenhauerian epistemological idealism" (von Wright, "Biographical sketch of Wittgenstein," p. 6). This is also fully explicit in Wittgenstein's *Notebooks 1914–1916*. See also Brockhaus, *Pulling Up the Ladder: The Metaphysical Roots of Wittgenstein's* Tractatus Logico-Philosophicus.

60 Wittgenstein, *Culture and Value*, p. 10e.

61 See, e.g., Diamond, *The Realistic Spirit: Wittgenstein, Philosophy, and the Mind*.

62 Wittgenstein read the *Critique of Pure Reason* in 1919 while interned as a POW at Como in Italy. See Monk, *Ludwig Wittgenstein: The Duty of Genius*, p. 158.

63 As quoted in Brockhaus, *Pulling Up the Ladder: The Metaphysical Roots of Wittgenstein's* Tractatus Logico-Philosophicus, p. 296.

64 See Kuehn, *Kant: A Biography*, ch. 5.

65 Carnap, "Intellectual autobiography," pp. 4 and 12.

66 See Rorty, *The Linguistic Turn*, esp. the editor's Introduction.

67 See Richardson, *Carnap and the Construction of the World*.

68 See Friedman, *Reconsidering Logical Positivism*; Passmore, "Logical positivism"; and Waismann, *Wittgenstein and the Vienna Circle*.

69 Carnap, "The elimination of metaphysics through the logical analysis of language."

70 Schlick, "Is there a factual a priori?"

71 See Hanna, *Rationality and Logic*, ch. 3; and Ricketts, "Frege, the *Tractatus*, and the logocentric predicament."

72 Cassirer's version of neo-Kantianism is both science-oriented and neo-Hegelian, and later had an important impact on American philosophy when Cassirer taught at Yale during the Nazi period.

73 See Friedman, *A Parting of the Ways: Carnap, Cassirer, and Heidegger*.

74 Friedman, *A Parting of the Ways*, p. 5.

75 See Cassirer, "Kant and the problem of metaphysics"; and Heidegger, *Kant and the Problem of Metaphysics*.

76 See Friedman, *A Parting of the Ways*, esp. ch. 9.

77 Ibid., chs. 7–8.

78 Ibid., ch. 2.

79 See Wittgenstein, "On Heidegger on being and dread."

80 See Ryle, "Heidegger's *Sein und Zeit*."

81 Dummett, *Origins of Analytical Philosophy*, p. ix.

82 See Carnap, "The elimination of metaphysics through the logical analysis of language" (1932) and *Pseudoproblems in Philosophy* (1928); Heidegger, *Kant and the Problem of Metaphysics* (1929) and "What is metaphysics?" (1929).

83 See Rorty, *Consequences of Pragmatism*.

84 See Hacker, *Wittgenstein's Place in Twentieth-Century Philosophy*, ch. 5; and Hanna, "Kant, Wittgenstein, and the fate of analysis."

85 See Sluga, *Heidegger's Crisis: Philosophy and Politics in Nazi Germany*.

86 Carnap refused to sign an oath of allegiance, which was required of all faculty at UCLA in the wake of McCarthyism. See also Carnap, "Intellectual autobiobraphy," pp. 81–4.

87 See McCumber, *Time in the Ditch: American Philosophy and the McCarthy Era*.

88 See Judt, *Past Imperfect: French Intellectuals 1944–1956*.

89 See Wilshire, *Fashionable Nihilism: A Critique of Analytic Philosophy*, chs. 1–4.

90 Quine also offers another argument against the analytic/synthetic distinction, from the indeterminacy of translation, in *Word and Object*, ch. II. For a critique of this argument, see Katz, *The Metaphysics of Meaning*, ch. 5.

91 Quine, "Two dogmas of empiricism," p. 37.

92 See Hanna, *Kant and the Foundations of Analytic Philosophy*, ch. 5.

93 See ibid., ch. 3.

94 Katz, *Cogitations*, pp. 28–32.

95 Grice and Strawson, "In defense of a dogma."

96 See Hanna, *Kant and the Foundations of Analytic Philosophy*, pp. 175–80; and Strawson, "Propositions, concepts, and logical truths."

97 Burge, "Philosophy of language and mind: 1950–1990," pp. 9–10.

98 See Hacker, *Wittgenstein's Place in Twentieth-Century Philosophy*, ch. 7.

99 See Strawson, *Analysis and Metaphysics*.

100 See Hanna, *Kant and the Foundations of Analytic Philosophy*, ch. 3 and "Kant's theory of judgment."

101 This is my own formulation. For other versions, see Stern, *Transcendental Arguments: Problems and Prospects*.

102 See Stern, *Transcendental Arguments and Skepticism*. See also Hanna, "The inner and the outer: Kant's 'Refutation' reconstructed."

103 See Strawson, *Individuals*, p. 40.

104 See Strawson, *Analysis and Metaphysics*.

105 See Stroud, *The Significance of Philosophical Skepticism*, ch. 4 and "Transcendental arguments."

106 See Putnam, *The Many Faces of Realism*; and McDowell, *Mind and World*.

107 Sellars, "Philosophy and the scientific image of man."

108 See, e.g., Danto, "Naturalism"; Friedman, "Philosophical naturalism"; McDowell, "Two sorts of naturalism"; Maddy, "Naturalism and the a priori"; Papineau, *Philosophical Naturalism*; and Stroud, "The charm of naturalism."

109 See Quine, "Two dogmas of empiricism" and *Word and Object*, esp. chs. 2 and 6.

110 See Sellars, *Science, Perception, and Reality*.

111 See Sellars, *Science and Metaphysics: Variations on Kantian Themes*. The primary influence on twentieth-century Kantian epistemology and metaphysics in North America was C. I. Lewis at Harvard, both through his own writings and those of his best Ph.D. students, especially Lewis White Beck and Sellars. (In the latter half of the century John Rawls, also at Harvard, exerted a similar influence on Kantian ethics. See the section "Kantian ethics after Rawls.") In 1929 Lewis published his highly influential neo-Kantian epistemological treatise, *Mind and the World Order*. In 1936, *Mind and the World Order* was the first contemporary philosophical text ever to be taught at Oxford, in a seminar run by J. L. Austin and Isaiah Berlin. Sellars attended this Oxford seminar, started a D.Phil. dissertation on Kant with T. D. Weldon the same year, and then later transferred to Harvard, where he wrote his Ph.D dissertation on Kant with Lewis.

112 Davidson, "On the very idea of a conceptual scheme."

113 See McDowell, "Having the world in view: Sellars, Kant, and intentionality" and *Mind and World*.

114 See Sellars, "Empiricism and the philosophy of mind."

115 See Hanna, "Kant and nonconceptual content."

116 See McDowell, "Two sorts of naturalism."

117 See Sedgwick, "McDowell's Hegelianism."

118 See Churchland, *Scientific Realism and the Plasticity of Mind*.

119 See Fogelin, "Quine's limited naturalism"; Johnsen, "How to read 'Epistemology naturalized'"; and Quine, "Epistemology naturalized."

120 See Hanna, "A Kantian critique of scientific essentialism"; Kripke, "Identity and necessity" and *Naming and Necessity*; Putnam, "Explanation and reference," "Is semantics possible?" and "The meaning of 'meaning'"; and Soames, *Philosophical Analysis in the Twentieth Century*, vol. 2, chs. 14–17.

121 Wittgenstein, *Culture and Value*, p. 56e.

122 As Kant notes in the Fourth Paralogism, Cartesian skepticism is the direct consequence of "transcendental" or noumenal realism (CPR A366–80).

123 Hard or incompatibilist determinism, which says that "there is no freedom, but everything in the world happens solely in accordance with laws of nature," is spelled out by Kant in the Antithesis of the Third Antinomy (CPR A445–51/B473–9).

124 See Derrida, *Of Grammatology*, pp. 97–8; and Moran, *Introduction to Phenomenology*, pp. 444–53.

125 See Quine, *Word and Object*, ch. II.

126 See Kolakowski, *Husserl and the Search for Certitude*.

127 See, e.g., Wilshire, *Fashionable Nihilism: A Critique of Analytic Philosophy*.

128 Moore, *Principia Ethica*, p. 40.

129 Ibid., p. 58.

130 Ibid., p. 73.

131 Moore fails to distinguish between concepts and properties, and again between properties and predicates. See Bealer, *Quality and Concept*; Oliver, "The metaphysics of properties"; and Putnam, "On properties." This is of course controversial territory. For my purposes here I will make the fairly standard assumptions that concepts are intersubjectively-accessible psychological intensional entities whose identity criterion is definitional equivalence; that predicates are linguistic intensional entities whose identity criterion is synonymy; and that properties are non-psychological, non-linguistic intensional entities whose identity criterion is sharing cross-possible-worlds extensions. Predicates express concepts as their meanings, and concepts pick out corresponding properties in the world. For convenience, however, in the following discussion of Moore's argument against ethical naturalism I will allow "property" to range over all three sorts of intensional entity. The flaws in his argument will persist no matter which sort of intensional entity is at issue.

132 Moore, *Principia Ethica*, p. 15.

133 Ibid., p. 44.

134 Indeed Moore adopts Bishop Butler's Monty-Pythonesque dictum, "everything is what it is and not another thing," as the motto of *Principia Ethica*, and also uses it repeatedly as an axiom in his arguments.

135 Moore, *Principia Ethica*, pp. 16–17.

136 Moreover the phenomenal criterion of property identity leads directly to the paradox of analysis: If only *phenomenal* identity will suffice for property identity, and property identity is a necessary condition of a correct analysis, then every correct analysis must be epistemically trivial. See Langford, "The notion of analysis in Moore's philosophy"; and Moore's reply to Langford, "Analysis."

137 See also Hanna, "How do we know necessary truths? Kant's answer."

138 See McCarthy, *The Critical Theory of Jürgen Habermas*, esp. pp. 325–7.

139 See Rawls, "A Kantian conception of equality," "Kantian constructivism in moral theory," and "Themes in Kant's moral theory."

140 See Hill, *Autonomy and Self-Respect, Dignity and Practical Reason in Kant's Moral Theory*, "Kantian constructivism in ethics," *Human Welfare and Moral Worth*, and *Respect, Pluralism, and Justice*.

141 See Korsgaard, *Creating the Kingdom of Ends* and *The Sources of Normativity*.

142 See O'Neill (Nell), *Acting on Principle*; and O'Neill, *Constructions of Reason*, ch. 11.

143 O'Neill, *Constructions of Reason*, pp. 58–9, emphasis added.

144 See Hanna, *Rationality and Logic*, ch. 7; and Putnam, "There is at least one a priori truth."

145 See Hill, *Human Welfare and Moral Worth*, pp. 367–70, numbering slightly altered.

146 See Hanna, *Kant, Science, and Human Nature*.

147 The later Husserl in fact sketched a view quite similar to this in *Ideas II* and the *Crisis*. See Smith, "Mind and body."

148 See, e.g., Nagel, "What is it like to be a bat?"; and Chalmers, *The Conscious Mind*.
149 See Ameriks, *Kant and the Fate of Autonomy* and "Kant on science and common knowledge"; and Guyer, *Kant's System of Nature and Freedom*.
150 Another partial anticipation of rational anthropology in the Kantian sense can be found in the philosophy of the later Wittgenstein; see Hanna, "Kant, Wittgenstein, and the fate of analysis."

References

Abela, P., *Kant's Empirical Realism*. Oxford: Oxford University Press, 2002.
Ameriks, K., *Kant and the Fate of Autonomy*. Cambridge: Cambridge University Press, 2000.
—— "Kant on science and common knowledge." In E. Watkins (ed.) *Kant and the Sciences*, New York: Oxford University Press, 2001, pp. 31–52.
Ayer, A. J., *Language, Truth, and Logic*, 2nd edn. New York: Dover, 1952.
Baldwin, T., *G. E. Moore*. London: Routledge, 1990.
Bealer, G., *Quality and Concept*. Oxford: Oxford University Press, 1982.
Beck, L. W., "Neo-Kantianism." In P. Edwards (ed.) *The Encyclopedia of Philosophy*, vol. 5, New York: Macmillan, 1967, pp. 468–73.
Bell, D. and N. Cooper (eds.) *The Analytic Tradition*. Oxford: Blackwell, 1990.
Benacerraf, P., "Frege: the last logicist." In P. French et al. (eds.) *The Foundations of Analytic Philosophy*, Midwest Studies in Philosophy 6, Minneapolis: University of Minnesota Press, 1981, pp. 17–35.
Bradley, F. H., *Principles of Logic*. London: G. E. Stechert, 1883.
Brentano, F., *On the Several Senses of Being in Aristotle*, trans. R. George. Berkeley: University of California Press, 1975.
—— *Psychology from an Empirical Standpoint*, trans. A. C. Rancurello et al. London: Routledge & Kegan Paul, 1973.
—— *The Origin of Our Knowledge of Right and Wrong*, trans. R. Chisholm and E. Schneewind. London: Routledge & Kegan Paul, 1969.
Brockhaus, R., *Pulling Up the Ladder: The Metaphysical Roots of Wittgenstein's* Tractatus Logico-Philosophicus. La Salle, IL: Open Court, 1991.
Burge, T., "Philosophy of language and mind: 1950–1990." *Philosophical Review* 101 (1992): 3–51.
Carnap, R., "Intellectual autobiography." In P. Schilpp (ed.) *The Philosophy of Rudolf Carnap*, La Salle, IL: Open Court, 1963, pp. 3–84.
—— *Pseudoproblems in Philosophy*, trans. R. George. Berkeley: University of California Press, 1967.
—— "The elimination of metaphysics through logical analysis of language." In A. J. Ayer (ed.) *Logical Positivism*, New York: Free Press, 1959, pp. 60–81.
—— *The Logical Structure of the World*, trans. R. George. Berkeley: University of California Press, 1967.
—— *The Logical Syntax of Language*. London: Kegan, Paul, Trench, Trubner, 1937.
Carroll, L., *Through the Looking-Glass*. New York: Dial, 1988.
Cassirer, E., "Kant and the problem of metaphysics." In M. Gram (ed.) *Kant: Disputed Questions*, Chicago: Quadrangle, 1967.
—— *Philosophy of Symbolic Forms*, 3 vols, trans. R. Manheim. New Haven, CT: Yale University Press, 1955, 1957.
Chalmers, D., *The Conscious Mind*. New York: Oxford University Press, 1996.
Churchland, P. M., *Scientific Realism and the Plasticity of Mind*. Cambridge: Cambridge University Press, 1979.
Coffa, A., *The Semantic Tradition from Kant to Carnap*. Cambridge: Cambridge University Press, 1991.
Danto, A., "Naturalism." In P. Edwards (ed.) *Encyclopedia of Philosophy*, 8 vols., New York: Macmillan, 1967, vol. 5, pp. 448–50.
Davidson, D., "On the very idea of a conceptual scheme." In *Inquiries into Truth and Interpretation*. Oxford: Clarendon Press, 1984, pp. 183–98.
Dennett, D., "Quining qualia." In D. Chalmers (ed.) *Philosophy of Mind: Classical and Contemporary Readings*, New York: Oxford University Press, 2002, pp. 226–46.
Derrida, J., *Edmund Husserl's Origin of Geometry: An Introduction*, trans. J. Leavey. Stony Brook, NY: Nicholas Hays, 1978.

—— *Of Grammatology*, trans. G. C. Spivak. Baltimore: Johns Hopkins University Press, 1974.

—— *Speech and Phenomena*, trans. D. Allison. Evanston, IL: Northwestern University Press, 1973.

—— *The Problem of Genesis in Husserl's Philosophy*, published as: *La Problème de la genèse dans la philosophie de Husserl*. Paris: Presses Universitaires de France, 1990.

Dewey, J., *Experience and Nature*. New York: Dover, 1929, 1958.

Diamond, C., *The Realistic Spirit: Wittgenstein, Philosophy, and the Mind*. Cambridge, MA: MIT Press, 1991.

Dummett, M., *Origins of Analytical Philosophy*. Cambridge, MA: Harvard University Press, 1993.

Eames, E. R., "Introduction." In B. Russell, *Theory of Knowledge*, London: Routledge, 1992, pp. vii–xxxvii.

Edwards, P. (ed.) *The Encyclopedia of Philosophy*, 7 vols. New York: Macmillan, 1967.

Fogelin, R., "Quine's limited naturalism." *Journal of Philosophy* 94 (1997): 543–63.

Frege, G., *Basic Laws of Arithmetic*, trans. M. Furth. Berkeley: University of California Press, 1964.

—— *Begriffsschrift*. Halle: a/S, 1879.

—— *Foundations of Arithmetic*, trans. J. L. Austin, 2nd edn. Evanston, IL: Northwestern University Press, 1953.

—— "On the foundations of geometry." In *On the Foundations of Geometry and Formal Theories of Arithmetic*, trans. E.-H. Kluge, New Haven, CT: Yale University Press, 1971, pp. 22–37, 49–112.

—— "Review of E. G. Husserl, *Philosophie der Arithmetik I*." In *Collected Papers on Mathematics, Logic, and Philosophy*, trans. M. Black et al., Oxford: Blackwell, 1984.

Friedman, M., *A Parting of the Ways: Carnap, Cassirer, and Heidegger*. La Salle, IL: Open Court, 2000.

—— "Philosophical naturalism." *Proceedings and Addresses of the American Philosophical Association* 71 (1997): 7—21.

—— *Reconsidering Logical Positivism*. Cambridge: Cambridge University Press, 1999.

French, P. et al. (eds.) *The Foundations of Analytic Philosophy*. Midwest Studies in Philosophy 6, Minneapolis: University of Minnesota Press, 1981.

Gadamer, H.-G., *Truth and Method*. New York: Crossroad, 1982.

Goodman, N., *The Structure of Appearance*, 2nd edn. Indianapolis: Bobbs-Merrill, 1966.

Grimm, S., "Kant's argument for radical evil." *European Journal of Philosophy* 10 (2002): 160–77.

Grice, H. P. and P. F. Strawson, "In defense of a dogma." *Philosophical Review* 65 (1956): 141–58.

Guyer, P. (ed.) *Kant's System of Nature and Freedom*. Oxford: Clarendon Press, 2005.

—— *The Cambridge Companion to Kant*. Cambridge: Cambridge University Press, 1992.

Hacker, P., *Wittgenstein's Place in Twentieth-Century Philosophy*. Oxford: Blackwell, 1996.

Hanna, R., "A Kantian critique of scientific essentialism." *Philosophy and Phenomenological Research* 58 (1998): 497–528.

—— "How do we know necessary truths? Kant's answer." *European Journal of Philosophy* 6 (1998): 115–45.

—— "Kant and nonconceptual content." *European Journal of Philosophy* 13 (2005): 247–90.

—— *Kant and the Foundations of Analytic Philosophy*. Oxford: Clarendon Press, 2001.

—— *Kant, Science, and Human Nature*. Oxford: Oxford University Press, forthcoming.

—— "Kant's theory of judgment." *The Stanford Encyclopedia of Philosophy* (Fall 2004 Edition), ed. E. Zalta. http://plato.stanford.edu/archivesfall2004/entries/kant-judgment/.

—— "Kant, Wittgenstein, and the fate of analysis." In M. Beaney (ed.) *The Analytic Turn*, London: Routledge, 2007.

—— *Rationality and Logic*. Cambridge, MA: MIT Press, 2006.

—— "The inner and the outer: Kant's 'Refutation' reconstructed." *Ratio* 13 (2000): 146–74.

Heidegger, M., *Being and Time*, trans. J. Macquarrie and E. Robinson. New York: Harper & Row, 1962.

—— *Kant and the Problem of Metaphysics*, trans. R.Taft, 4th edn. Bloomington: Indiana University Press, 1990.

—— *Phenomenological Interpretation of Kant's* Critique of Pure Reason, trans. P. Emad and K. Maly. Bloomington: Indiana University Press, 1997.

—— *The Theory of Judgment in Psychologism*, published as: *Die Lehre vom Urteil in Psychologismus*. Leipzig: Barth, 1914.

—— "What is metaphysics?" In D. Farrell Knell (ed.) *Martin Heidegger: Basic Writings*, New York: Harper & Row, 1977, pp. 95–112.

Hill, T., *Autonomy and Self-Respect*. Cambridge: Cambridge University Press, 1991.

—— *Dignity and Practical Reason in Kant's Moral Theory*. Ithaca, NY: Cornell University Press, 1992.

—— *Human Welfare and Moral Worth: Kantian Perspectives*. Oxford: Clarendon Press, 2002.

—— "Kantian constructivism in ethics." *Ethics* 99 (1989): 752–70.

—— *Respect, Pluralism, and Justice: Kantian Perspectives*. Oxford: Oxford University Press, 2000.

Husserl, E., *Cartesian Meditations*, trans. D. Cairns. The Hague: Nijhoff, 1960.

—— *Crisis of European Sciences and Transcendental Phenomenology*, trans. D. Carr. Evanston, IL: Northwestern University Press, 1970.

—— *Formal and Transcendental Logic*, trans. D. Cairns. The Hague: Nijhoff, 1969.

—— *Idea of Phenomenology*, trans. W. P. Alston and G. Nahnikian. The Hague: Nijhoff, 1964.

—— *Ideas: A General Introduction to Pure Phenomenology*, trans. W. R. Boyce Gibson. London: Allen & Unwin, 1931.

—— *Logical Investigations*, 2 vols., trans. J. N. Findlay. London: Routledge, 1970.

—— *Philosophy of Arithmetic: Psychological and Logical Investigations*, vol. I, published as: *Philosophie der Arithmetik*, vol. 1. Halle: C. M. Pfeffer, 1891.

—— *Prolegomena to Pure Logic*. In *Logical Investigations*, vol. 1, trans. J. N. Findlay, London: Routledge: 1970.

Hylton, P., *Russell, Idealism, and the Emergence of Analytic Philosophy*. Oxford: Oxford University Press, 1990.

James, W., *Principles of Psychology*, 2 vols. New York: Dover, 1950.

Johnsen, B., "How to read 'Epistemology naturalized'." *Journal of Philosophy* 102 (2005): 78–93.

Judt, T., *Past Imperfect: French Intellectuals 1944–1956*. Berkeley: University of California Press, 1992.

Katz, J., *Cogitations*. New York: Oxford University Press, 1986.

—— *The Metaphysics of Meaning*. Cambridge, MA: MIT Press, 1990.

Keynes, J. M., "My early beliefs." In *Two Memoirs*, London: R. Hart-Davis, 1949, pp. 78–103.

Köhnke, K., *The Rise of Neo-Kantianism*, trans. R. Hollingdale. Cambridge: Cambridge University Press, 1991.

Kolakowski, L., *Husserl and the Search for Certitude*. New Haven, CT: Yale University Press, 1975.

Korsgaard, K., *Creating the Kingdom of Ends*. Cambridge: Cambridge University Press, 1996.

—— *The Sources of Normativity*. Cambridge: Cambridge University Press, 1996.

Kripke, S., "Identity and necessity." In A. W. Moore (ed.) *Meaning and Reference*, Oxford: Oxford University Press, 1993, pp. 162–91.

—— *Naming and Necessity*, 2nd edn. Cambridge, MA: Harvard University Press, 1980.

Kuehn, M., *Kant: A Biography*. Cambridge: Cambridge University Press, 2001.

Langford, C. H., "The notion of analysis in Moore's philosophy." In P. Schilpp (ed.) *The Philosophy of G. E. Moore*, 2nd edn., New York: Tudor, 1952, pp. 321–42.

Liebmann, O. *Kant und die Epigonen*. Canstatt: Emil Geiger, 1865.

Levy, P., *Moore: G. E. Moore and the Cambridge Apostles*. New York: Holt, Rinehart & Winston, 1980.

Lewis, C. I., *Mind and the World Order*. New York: Dover, 1929, 1956.

McCarthy, T., *The Critical Theory of Jürgen Habermas*. Cambridge, MA: MIT Press, 1978.

McCumber, J., *Time in the Ditch: American Philosophy and the McCarthy Era*. Evanston, IL: Northwestern University Press, 2001.

McDowell, J., "Having the world in view: Sellars, Kant, and intentionality." *Journal of Philosophy* 95 (1998): 431–91.

—— *Mind and World*. Cambridge, MA: Harvard University Press, 1994.

—— "Two sorts of naturalism." In R. Hursthouse et al. (eds.) *Virtues and Reasons,* Oxford: Clarendon Press, 1995, pp. 149–79.

Maddy, P., "Naturalism and the a priori." In P. Boghossian and C. Peacocke (eds.) *New Essays on the a priori*, Oxford: Oxford University Press, 2000, pp. 92–116.

Meinong, A., "The theory of objects," trans. R. Chisholm. In *Realism and the Background of Phenomenology*, Glencoe, IL: Free Press, 1960.

Monk, R., *Bertrand Russell*. London: Jonathan Cape, 1996.

—— *Ludwig Wittgenstein: The Duty of Genius*. London: Jonathan Cape, 1990.

Moore, G. E. "Analysis." In P. Schilpp (ed.) *The Philosophy of G. E. Moore*, 2nd edn., New York: Tudor, 1952, pp. 660–7.

—— *Philosophical Studies*. London: Kegan Paul, Trench, Trubner, 1922.

—— *Principia Ethica*. Cambridge: Cambridge University Press, 1903.

—— "Review of Russell's *Essay on the Foundations of Geometry*." *Mind* 8 (1899): 397–405.

Moran, D., *Introduction to Phenomenology*. London: Routledge, 2000.

—— "Making sense: Husserl's phenomenology as transcendental idealism." In J. Malpas (ed.) *From Kant to Davidson: Philosophy and the Idea of the Transcendental*, London: Routledge, 2003, pp. 48–74.

Nagel, T., "What is it like to be a bat?" In *Mortal Questions*, Cambridge: Cambridge University Press, 1979, pp. 165–80.

Neiman, S., *The Unity of Reason*. New York: Oxford University Press, 1994.

Nell, O. [= O'Neill, Onora], *Acting on Principle*. New York: Cambridge University Press, 1975.

O'Neill, O., *Constructions of Reason*. Cambridge: Cambridge University Press, 1989.

Oliver, A., "The metaphysics of properties." *Mind* 105 (1996): 1–80.

Pap, A., *Elements of Analytic Philosophy*, 2nd edn. New York: Hafner, 1972.

Papineau, D., *Philosophical Naturalism*. Oxford: Blackwell, 1993.

Passmore, J., "Logical positivism." In P. Edwards (ed.) *The Encyclopedia of Philosophy*, vol. 5, New York: Macmillan, 1967, pp. 52–7.

Proust, J., *Questions of Form: Logic and the Analytic Proposition*, trans. A. Brenner. Minneapolis: University of Minnesota Press, 1989.

Putnam, H., "Explanation and reference." In *Mind, Language, and Reality: Philosophical Papers, Vol. 2*, Cambridge: Cambridge University Press, 1975, pp. 196–214.

—— "Is semantics possible?" In *Mind, Language, and Reality: Philosophical Papers, Vol. 2*, Cambridge: Cambridge University Press, 1975, pp. 139–52.

—— *Mind, Language, and Reality: Philosophical Papers, Vol. 2*. Cambridge: Cambridge University Press, 1975.

—— "On properties." In *Mathematics, Matter, and Method: Philosophical Papers, Vol. 1*, 2nd edn., Cambridge: Cambridge University Press, 1979, pp. 305–22.

—— *The Many Faces of Realism*. La Salle, IL: Open Court, 1987.

—— "The meaning of 'meaning'." In *Mind, Language, and Reality: Philosophical Papers, Vol. 2*, Cambridge: Cambridge University Press, 1975, pp. 215–71.

—— "There is at least one a priori truth." In *Realism and Reason: Philosophical Papers, Vol. 3*. Cambridge: Cambridge University Press, 1983, pp. 98–114.

Quine, W. V. O. "Epistemology naturalized." In *Ontological Relativity*, New York: Columbia University Press, 1969, pp. 69–90.

—— "Two dogmas of empiricism." In *From a Logical Point of View*, 2nd edn., New York: Harper & Row, 1961, pp. 20–46.

—— *Word and Object*. Cambridge, MA: MIT Press, 1960.

Rawls, J., "A Kantian conception of equality." *Cambridge Review* 96 (1975): 94–9.

—— *A Theory of Justice*. Cambridge, MA: Harvard University Press, 1971.

—— "Kantian constructivism in moral theory." *Journal of Philosophy* 77 (1980): 515–72.

—— "Themes in Kant's moral philosophy." In E. Förster (ed.) *Kant's Transcendental Deductions*, Stanford, CA: Stanford University Press, 1989, pp. 81–113.

Reichenbach, H., *The Rise of Scientific Philosophy*. Berkeley: University of California Press, 1951.

Richardson, A., *Carnap and the Construction of the World*. Cambridge: Cambridge University Press, 1998.

Ricketts, T., "Frege, the *Tractatus*, and the logocentric predicament." *Philosophers' Annual* 8 (1985): 247–59.

Rorty, R., *Consequences of Pragmatism*. Minneapolis: University of Minnesota Press, 1982.

—— (ed.) *The Linguistic Turn*. Chicago: University of Chicago Press, 1967.

—— *Philosophy and the Mirror of Nature*. Princeton, NJ: Princeton University Press, 1979.

Russell, B., *Autobiography*. London: Unwin, 1975.

—— *Introduction to Mathematical Philosophy*. London: Routledge, 1993.

—— "Knowledge by acquaintance and knowledge by description." In *Mysticism and Logic*, Totowa, NJ: Barnes & Noble, 1981, pp. 152–67.

—— *My Philosophical Development*. London: Allen & Unwin, 1959.

—— "The philosophy of logical atomism." In *Logic and Knowledge*, London: Unwin Hyman, 1956, pp. 177–281.

—— *Principles of Mathematics*, 2nd edn. New York: W. W. Norton, 1996.

—— *The Problems of Philosophy*. Indianapolis: Hackett, 1995.

—— *Theory of Knowledge*. London: Routledge, 1992.

Ryle, G., "Heidegger's *Sein und Zeit*." In M. Murray (ed.) *Heidegger and Modern Philosophy*, New Haven, CT: Yale University Press, 1978, pp. 53–64.

Schilpp, P. (ed.) *The Philosophy of G. E. Moore*, 2nd edn. New York: Tudor, 1952.

Schlick, M., *General Theory of Knowledge*, trans. A Blumberg. La Salle, IL: Open Court, 1985.

—— "Is there a factual a priori?" In H. Feigl and W. Sellars (eds.) *Readings in Philosophical Analysis*, New York: Appleton-Century-Crofts, 1949, pp. 277–85.

Schopenhauer, A., *World as Will and Representation*, 2 vols., trans. E. F. J. Payne. New York: Open Court, 1969.

Sedgwick, S., "McDowell's Hegelianism." *European Journal of Philosophy* 5 (1997): 21–38.

Sellars, W., "Empiricism and the philosophy of mind." In *Science, Perception and Reality*, New York: Humanities Press, 1963, pp. 127–96.

—— "Philosophy and the scientific image of man." In *Science, Perception and Reality*, New York: Humanities Press, 1963, pp. 1–40.

—— *Science and Metaphysics: Variations on Kantian Themes*. London: Routledge & Kegan Paul, 1968.

—— *Science, Perception and Reality*. New York: Humanities Press, 1963.

Sluga, H., *Heidegger's Crisis: Philosophy and Politics in Nazi Germany*. Cambridge, MA: Harvard University Press, 1993.

Smith, D. W., "Mind and body." In B. Smith and D. W. Smith (eds.) *The Cambridge Companion to Husserl*, Cambridge: Cambridge University Press, 1995, pp. 323–93.

Soames, S., *Philosophical Analysis in the Twentieth Century*, 2 vols. Princeton, NJ: Princeton University Press, 2003.

Spiegelberg, H. (with K. Schuhmann), *The Phenomenological Movement*, 3rd edn. Dordrecht: Kluwer, 1994.

Strawson, P. F., *Analysis and Metaphysics*. New York: Oxford University Press, 1992.

—— *The Bounds of Sense*. London: Methuen, 1966.

—— *Individuals: An Essay in Descriptive Metaphysics*. London: Methuen, 1959.

—— *Introduction to Logical Theory*. London: Methuen, 1952.

—— *Logico-Linguistic Papers*. London: Methuen, 1971.

—— "Propositions, concepts, and logical truths." *Philosophical Quarterly* 7 (1957): 15–25.

—— *Subject and Predicate in Logic and Grammar*. London: Methuen, 1974.

Stern, R. (ed.) *Transcendental Arguments: Problems and Prospects*. Oxford: Oxford University Press, 1999.

—— *Transcendental Arguments and Skepticism*. Oxford: Oxford University Press, 2000.

Stroud, B., "The charm of naturalism." *Proceedings and Addresses of the American Philosophical Association* 7 (1996): 43–55.

—— *The Significance of Philosophical Skepticism*. Oxford: Oxford University Press, 1984.

—— "Transcendental arguments." *Journal of Philosophy* 65 (1968): 241–56.

Tugendhat, E., *Traditional and Analytical Philosophy*, trans. P. A. Gorner. Cambridge: Cambridge University Press, 1982.

Van Cleve, J., *Problems from Kant*. New York: Oxford University Press, 1999.

von Wright, G. H., "Biographical sketch of Wittgenstein." In N. Malcolm, *Ludwig Wittgenstein: A Memoir, with a Biographical Sketch by G. H. von Wright*, Oxford: Oxford University Press, 1984.

Waismann, F., *Wittgenstein and the Vienna Circle*, trans. J. Schulte and B. McGuinness. New York: Harper & Row, 1979.

Ward, J., "Psychology." In *Encyclopedia Britannica*, 11th edn., 29 vols. New York: Encyclopedia Britannica Co., 1911, vol. XXII, pp. 547–604.

Weatherston, M., *Heidegger's Interpretation of Kant*. New York: Palgrave Macmillan, 2002.

Whitehead, A. N., *Process and Reality*. Cambridge: Cambridge University Press, 1929.

Whitehead, A. N. and B. Russell, *Principia Mathematica to *56*. Cambridge: Cambridge University Press, 1962.

Wilshire, B., *Fashionable Nihilism: A Critique of Analytic Philosophy*. Albany: State University of New York Press, 2002.

Wittgenstein, L., *Culture and Value*, trans. P. Winch. Chicago: University of Chicago Press, 1980.

—— *Notebooks 1914–1916*, trans. G. E. M. Anscombe, 2nd edn. Oxford: Blackwell, 1979.

—— "On Heidegger on being and dread." In M. Murray (ed.) *Heidegger and Modern Philosophy*, New Haven, CT: Yale University Press, 1978, pp. 80–1.

—— *Philosophical Investigations*, trans. G. E. M. Anscombe. New York: Macmillan, 1953.

—— *Tractatus Logico-Philosophicus*, trans. C. K. Ogden. London: Routledge & Kegan Paul, 1981.

Wood, A., *Kant's Ethical Thought*. New York: Cambridge University Press, 1999.

Further reading

Beaney, M., (ed.) *The Analytic Turn*. London: Routledge, 2007. (A helpful collection of essays on the central topics of this chapter from a broadly analytic perspective).

Malpas, J., (ed.) *From Kant to Davidson: Philosophy and the Idea of the Transcendental*. London: Routledge, 2003. (A helpful collection of essays on the central topics of this chapter from a broadly Continental perspective).

5

AMERICAN PHILOSOPHY IN THE TWENTIETH CENTURY

James R. O'Shea

Introduction

Any brief portrait of American philosophy in the twentieth century will inevitably illustrate at least one fundamental principle of William James's (1842–1910) psychology and his pragmatist philosophy: namely, the idea that all cognition is *selective*, for "without selective interest, experience is an utter chaos" (James 1983: I, 402).[1] "Hence, even in the field of sensation," wrote James in 1907 in his classic work *Pragmatism*,

> our minds exert a certain arbitrary choice. By our inclusions and omissions we trace the field's extent; by our emphasis we mark its foreground and its background; by our order we read it in this direction or in that. We receive in short the block of marble, but we carve the statue ourselves. (James 1978a: 119)

It follows according to James's pragmatic *pluralism* that there are typically alternative, often conflicting ways of carving up any given object or domain. Each resulting conceptual "statue" may nonetheless be useful (and for the Jamesian pragmatist, so far true) relative to the purposes and constructions of that particular working framework.[2]

This essay will itself be highly selective, one statue among many others that might have been carved.[3] The account that follows will place in the foreground just one central story concerning the relative dominance of *analytic philosophy* in America in the decades following World War II as this style of philosophizing developed in distinctive ways, with initial stimulation from European sources, out of its earlier roots in *American pragmatism*, *realism*, and *naturalism*.[4] There are many other important movements and topics that will not be covered in this selective overview, most of which, however, are addressed under other headings in this volume.

I shall begin by taking some time to lay out as a relatively comprehensive interpretive framework certain enduring themes that were developed by the two main founders of classical American pragmatism, Charles Sanders Peirce (1839–1914) and William James. Against the background of the pervasive influence of Kantian and Hegelian idealism in America in the decades surrounding the turn of the century, pragmatism and related philosophical outlooks emphasizing naturalism and realism were dominant during the first three decades of the century. Beginning in the 1930s and 1940s, however, the middle third of the century witnessed the rising influence in America of what would become known as "analytic philosophy," with its primary roots in Europe: in the Cambridge philosophical analysis of Moore, Russell, and Wittgenstein; logical empiricism and positivism on the Continent; and linguistic analysis and ordinary-language philosophy at Oxford.

The particular story of philosophy in America during the twentieth century to be told here, then, will be a story of the persistence of pragmatist themes throughout much of the century, while emphasizing the mid-century transformations that resulted from developments primarily in analytic philosophy. These combined influences resulted at the turn of the millennium in the flourishing, among other developments, of distinctively analytic styles of pragmatism and naturalism.

Lasting themes in American philosophy from Charles Sanders Peirce

American pragmatist philosophy finds its most important conceptual and epistemological origins in a series of essays of extraordinary depth and originality by Charles Sanders Peirce, beginning in the 1860s and 1870s. With the ever-increasing influence of his works, Peirce is now justifiably regarded by many as the most original systematic philosopher that America has produced.

There were essential connections for Peirce between his groundbreaking investigations in pure logic, his experimental work as a practicing scientist for over thirty years with the US Coast and Geodetic Survey, and his intense philosophical and historical investigations. For what Peirce sought most fundamentally to understand was the *logic of experimental inquiry* in general. This concern with *method*, however, must be understood in a very broad sense. According to Peirce it is the particular "method of reasoning . . . that is always the most important element in every system of philosophy" (1992: 236). In what follows we shall very briefly highlight the following interrelated themes from Peirce's thought, themes which will frequently resurface in our discussion of twentieth-century philosophy in America:

- a *critique of foundationalism* in epistemology and metaphysics
- a focus on the *logic and methods of science* ("experimentalist" methods)
- a *fallibilist* approach to knowledge and inquiry
- an *anti-skeptical* emphasis on real doubt vs. Cartesian "hyperbolic" doubt
- epistemological *holism* (and an "inferentialist" view of cognition)
- the epistemic priority of the "outer" and social over the "inner" and private
- "all thought must necessarily be in signs" (compare the "linguistic turn")

- the *pragmatic maxim* concerning conceptual meaning
- a rejection of much traditional metaphysics, but not of metaphysics itself
- a pragmatist conception of *truth* (belief-fixation and ideals of inquiry)
- methodological and Darwinian evolutionary *naturalism*
- a complex mixture of epistemological realism and metaphysical idealism

Let us see how these enduring themes arguably arise out of Peirce's conception of our basic cognitive powers, working up gradually to his pragmatism.

The predominant theories of knowledge throughout much of western philosophy prior to the nineteenth century tended to share certain basic *foundationalist* assumptions in epistemology and metaphysics. On pain of infinite regress or vicious circularity, it was commonly argued, we must be in possession of some knowledge that is self-evident, direct, immediate, or given – or to use the traditional term Peirce picks up on, *intuitive* knowledge. In "Questions concerning certain faculties claimed for man" and "Some consequences of four incapacities" (in Peirce 1992), published in 1868 in the *Journal of Speculative Philosophy* (a journal which had been founded by the St Louis Hegelian idealist, W. T. Harris), Peirce launched a series of powerful broadsides against the very idea of intuitive cognition and against the entire foundationalist picture of the proper method for philosophy. It is striking the degree to which Peirce in these articles of 1868 managed to anticipate both the style and substance of so much of the practice of philosophy in America in the twentieth century.

Peirce defines an *intuition* in the sense he wants to reject as "a cognition not determined by a previous cognition of the same object, and therefore so determined by something out of the consciousness" (1992: 11). The idea is that an intuitive cognition allegedly directly reveals the nature or character of an object "independently of any previous knowledge and without reasoning from signs" (ibid.). Against this foundationalist picture Peirce begins by arguing that it is at least an open philosophical question whether or not we possess any such self-evident or intuitive knowledge (ibid.: 12). That is, it does not seem to be simply directly or intuitively evident *that we have such direct or intuitive knowledge*. It is invariably a heated subject of dispute, for instance, just how much or what aspects of any given cognition is contributed by the knower rather than by the object or fact known. To insist that it just seems self-evident that we possess such self-evident knowledge begs the question at issue.

So the question whether or not we know by self-evident intuition that we possess any intuitive cognitions is one that has to be settled by argument and evidence. As far as historical and factual evidence is concerned, Peirce points out that many "external" authorities such as sacred texts and oracles, and even the authority of Aristotle in logic, were at one time taken by intelligent inquirers to have an *intrinsic* authority that was later recognized to be inconsistent with their proven fallibility. "Now, what if our *internal* authority," Peirce suggests with reference to the philosophical assumption that the mind is capable of directly intuitive cognitions (1992: 13), "should meet the same fate, in the history of opinions, as that external authority has met? Can that be said to be absolutely certain which many sane, well-informed, and thoughtful men already doubt?" After considering a variety of more sophisticated examples in detail, Peirce concludes:

We have, therefore, a variety of facts, all of which are most readily explained on the supposition that we have no intuitive faculty of distinguishing intuitive from mediate cognitions. Some arbitrary hypothesis may otherwise explain any one of these facts; this is the only theory which brings them to support one another. Moreover, no facts require the supposition of the faculty in question. Whoever has studied the nature of proof will see, then, that there are here very strong reasons for disbelieving the existence of this faculty. These will become still stronger when the consequences of rejecting it have ... been more fully traced out. (1992: 18)

Here we can see already how Peirce has subtly interwoven higher-level questions concerning the *proper method for philosophy* into what seemed at first to be simply a first-order dispute about whether or not we possess a faculty of direct apprehension or intuitive cognition. The philosopher, like the scientific experimentalist, must offer hypotheses to explain the apparent facts – "apparent," for *any* supposed fact is open to further scrutiny and possible rejection if doubt arises concerning it (this is Peirce's *fallibilism*). If a given hypothesis would explain all the relevant facts and is seen to entail further consequences that are judged to provide additional confirmation of the hypothesis, then the given explanatory hypothesis is so far "proved" in the tentative, fallibilist sense that is common to both empirical science and philosophy. That is, we have the best available hypothesis sufficient to explain the phenomena (this is Peirce's method of hypothesis or *abduction*), subject always to reassessment and potential rejection in the light of further experience and argument. Peirce's meta-hypothesis, as it were, that the *method of hypothesis* is the proper fallibilist method for philosophy has itself just received its own tentative confirmation. The fallibilist methodological blood running throughout Peirce's philosophy was subsequently to be one of the most distinctive traits of American philosophy throughout the twentieth century.

Having shown it to be at least questionable whether we possess any foundational faculty of intuitive cognition, Peirce proceeds to offer alternative hypotheses concerning the sources of our most basic conceptions. Surely the facts, for example, suggest that conscious subjects at the very least have direct, intuitive knowledge of their private *selves*, in their own "immediate" self-consciousness? Peirce argues to the contrary that empirical self-awareness probably presupposes a set of learned associations or primitive "inferences" on the part of the child (1992: 18–21). Our cognitions are at first primarily outward-looking sensations, and the most likely hypothesis is that *self*-awareness ("me," "I") develops only as part of a package that involves associations between sounds, including parents' utterances, and movements of bodies, including the child's own body. The facts suggest that the crucial element is the resulting learned distinction and frequent divergence between how things *are* (for example as the child experiences them to be reliably testified by the parent) as opposed to how they might *seem* or feel to the child, or to how the child *wants* them to be. As Peirce sums up what he takes to be the best available hypothesis: "In short, *error* appears, and it can be explained only by supposing a *self* which is fallible." A tentative hypothesis of this kind is superior to one that supposes a faculty of the direct apprehension of the empirical self, for the former supposes only "known faculties, acting under conditions known to exist" (1992: 20).

The Cartesian turn in modern philosophy had prioritized the "inner light" of natural reason and the direct apprehension of one's own clear and distinct ideas and states of consciousness. Peirce argues, however, that in case after case what might seem to be apprehended by a simple act of consciousness, whether as object of intellect or of sensation, is inevitably better explained as the product of association or as presupposing a background of learned inferences in the broadest sense. Consequently, understanding the nature of any cognition, for Peirce, requires theorizing concerning the particular patterns of *inference*, whether habitual or also reasoned and critical, which make it the sort of cognition that it is. The key to philosophy as a whole, therefore, turns out to be *logic* broadly construed as the study of valid patterns of inference embodied objectively in living systems of signs and in particular in increasingly refined forms of scientific inquiry.

It is important not to misunderstand Peirce when, for example, he questions whether "we have any power of introspection" and when he argues that "our whole knowledge of the internal world is derived from the observation of external facts" (1992: 22). Peirce is not denying that there are distinct subjective elements of consciousness, nor that in a suitably understood and derivative sense we can each reliably report our own mental states in a way in which others cannot. What he *is* arguing is that all our "knowledge of the internal world" of these kinds is ultimately and essentially "derived from external observation" (ibid.).

Peirce proceeds to draw the important further consequence that when the nature of thought is thus properly viewed in "the light of external facts, the only cases of thought which we can find are of thought in signs," which suggests the hypothesis that all "thought, therefore, must necessarily be in signs" (1992: 24). Not all sign-systems are spoken natural languages, of course, but with regard to the nature of human conceptual thinking Peirce is anticipating key aspects of the later "linguistic turn" that would transform twentieth-century Anglo-American philosophy in particular. Crudely put, to understand what thinking is one must view thoughts as themselves being signs in the way that spoken and written words, for instance, are signs; and a sign has the *meaning* or signification it does owing to the role that the sign plays within a wider system of signs, and in particular as caught up in our perceptual responses, inferences, and actions. Ultimately the consequence for Peirce is that all intelligible conceptions, being of the nature of signs, derive their meaning from the *difference they make*, so to speak, within our habitual patterns of perceptual response, inference, and action.

This last consequence can now be seen to be closely related to what Peirce was the first philosopher to call the maxim or principle of *pragmatism*, conceived as a method for clarifying the conceptual meaning of any term or idea (see also on William James, below). American pragmatism, strictly speaking, had its primary origin in Peirce's attempt to discover a method for clarifying with precision the conceptual content of any given intellectual conception. In "How to make our ideas clear" (1878) Peirce characterized what came to be called *the pragmatic maxim* as follows:[5] "Consider what effects, which might conceivably have practical bearings, we conceive the object of our conception to have. Then, our conception of these effects is the whole of our conception of the object." "To say that a body is heavy," Peirce explains with a deceptively simple example, "means simply that, in the absence of opposing force, it will fall" (1992: 132, 133). Peirce offered many examples to illustrate the pragmatic maxim, and over the years he also attempted several different characterizations of the maxim itself. For present purposes we may take the core of the pragmatic maxim to be a theory of conceptual content that runs roughly as follows.

Concepts pick out general kinds and properties of things, such as what it is for anything to be *heavy* or to be a *dog*, thus enabling us to successfully re-encounter particular things as instances of those general properties or kinds. The first step towards the pragmatic maxim is the idea that the *generality* achieved by concepts consists in certain lawful consequences, predictions, and inferential entailments that follow from assertions involving those concepts. To grasp some portion of one's experience as an encounter with a dog, for instance, is to rule out certain past and future courses of experience and reasoning as impossible or unlikely, and to rule in certain others as necessary or probable. The generality of conceptual meaning is not "seen" in an act of direct apprehension, however carefully the "inspection" might be made. Rather, conceptualization is a matter of one's gradually acquired and disciplined habits of response, inference, and expectation coming to reflect the "habitudes" of things in the perceptual and intellectual world that surrounds one. For some mental or linguistic sign to lawfully function in this way in perception, reasoning, and action is precisely what makes it a *sign* and endows it with the entire conceptual meaning that it has; as the above version of the pragmatic maxim has it, "our conception of these effects is the whole of our conception of the object." Or as Peirce put it more loosely in 1902, "the spirit of the maxim itself . . . is that we must look to the upshot of our concepts in order rightly to apprehend them" (in Thayer 1982: 49).

Peirce's pragmatism thus argues that there is a necessary connection between conceptual meaning and *practice*: the relevant effects, as indicated in the "maxim" above, are ones with conceivably "practical bearings." We have seen Peirce argue that there is no foundation or origin for conceptual meanings in direct intuitive apprehension. The pragmatic maxim has brought out the ultimate consequence that "there is no distinction of meaning so fine as to consist in anything but a possible difference of practice" (1992: 131); or again later in 1903, "as pragmatism teaches us, what we think is to be interpreted in terms of what we are prepared to do" (1998: 142). For if two alleged conceptions entailed no real difference in how someone would respond or act or infer in some generally specifiable circumstance (as Peirce thinks is the case with many traditional metaphysical disputes; e.g. 1998: 338–9), the question arises of how such a difference in meaning could conceivably be cognized. Given what Peirce has already argued concerning cognition in general, however, such a cognition cannot itself be directly intuitive but rather must depend essentially upon some "prior" relations among cognitions; but the latter, as we also saw, must ultimately take the form of some "external" or publicly ascertainable modes of reasoning or association. On this way of understanding what Peirce was up to, the pragmatic maxim, which seeks to clarify conceptual meaning in terms of public inferential practices and ongoing fallible inquiry, is itself grounded in a philosophical theory or best available explanation of the nature of our most basic cognitive capacities.

Let us consider, finally, some central features of scientific and philosophical inquiry as conceived by Peirce in light of the above account of our cognitive capacities and of the pragmatic maxim. As we have seen, the epistemic status of any cognition is always that of a fallible hypothesis subject to the test of further experience, strengthened by its explanatory ties to other such hypotheses. Consequently, inquiry always takes place *in media res*, in the middle of things, setting out from our *actual* doubts and our actual beliefs. As Peirce puts it, a person "doubts because he has a positive reason for it, and not on account of the Cartesian maxim [of universal doubt]. Let us not pretend to doubt in philosophy what we do not doubt in our hearts" (1992: 29). This, too, would become an important theme in later twentieth-century American philosophy.

Peirce further applied the pragmatic maxim to the nature of inquiry in the brilliant essay of 1877, "The fixation of belief." Peirce contends that the real goal of all inquiry is the *fixation of belief* and the cessation of doubt. One might object that *truth* is the object of inquiry, but practically, Peirce argues, we regard as true any of our beliefs to which we do not attach any real doubt; and furthermore our only access to reality is always through the testing and readjustment of our network of beliefs. But if Peirce is thus right in holding that "the settlement of opinion is the sole object of inquiry" (1992: 115), it becomes a matter of the highest importance what *method* is judged to be appropriate to that end. Peirce considers and ultimately rejects three general methods of settling opinion: (1) by individual "tenacity" in belief, (2) by communal imposition of belief through social "authority" (e.g. church or state), and (3) through the dialectical examination of what is "agreeable to reason (*a priori*)" itself. Peirce argues that each of these methods is likely, eventually, to give rise to doubts about whether (respectively) (1) *my* protected beliefs, or (2) the beliefs of the communal authorities I accept, or (3) the beliefs arrived at by my favorite systematic metaphysician, might rather be based on accidents of birth, or passing philosophical tastes, or on various other grounds that I myself am likely to question when I encounter reasonable persons holding beliefs that are opposed to my own. If the goal of inquiry is to satisfy our doubts, Peirce concludes, a different kind of method for settling belief is required: what he calls the *method of science*.

> To satisfy our doubts, therefore, it is necessary that a method be found by which our beliefs may be caused by nothing human, but by some external permanency – by something upon which our thinking has no effect. . . . Such is the method of science. Its fundamental hypothesis ... is this: There are real things, whose characters are entirely independent of our opinions about them; those realities affect our senses according to regular laws, and, though our sensations are as different as our relations to the objects, yet, by taking advantage of the laws of perception, we can ascertain by reasoning how things really are, and any man, if he have sufficient experience and reason enough about it, will be led to the one true conclusion. The new conception here involved is that of reality. (Peirce 1992: 120)

The relevant modes of reasoning here will be those of the "experimentalist" using the tentative methods that involve the testing of explanatory hypotheses, which we have already seen to characterize not only science and common sense but also philosophy as it ought to be practiced according to Peirce.

Below we shall encounter much dispute concerning this conception of the primacy of scientific methods for philosophy, both within and outside of the pragmatist tradition. It represents, however, a robust defense of one important dimension of philosophical *naturalism* – and in fact in Peirce, it is an *evolutionary* naturalism, both Darwinian and metaphysical – and naturalism, too, will be a dominant theme distinguishing so much of twentieth-century philosophy in America. For on one important construal, philosophical naturalism is the idea that there is no general method of inquiry in philosophy that is prior to, or foundational in relation to, the fallible but self-correcting explanatory methods that are characteristic of the empirical sciences.

It is crucial to note, however, that in Peirce's hands this scientific naturalist outlook is seen as consistent with (in fact, to entail) various *metaphysical* hypotheses concerning the nature of reality, which for Peirce includes a defense of the reality of "scholastic" universals in the form of evolving general laws in nature; in fact it includes the defense of an entire systematic evolutionary metaphysics. Furthermore, the "realist" hypothesis that formed the basis of Peirce's scientific method above – an *über*hypothesis which he sees can admit of only an indirect justification (1992: 120–1) – is combined in Peirce with a variety of fundamentally *idealist* themes. And this, too, will be a recurring theme (in some cases, an accusation to be overcome) in pragmatist outlooks throughout the twentieth century. For given the pragmatic maxim that meaning, as we might put it, is exhaustively constituted by functional and practical roles within evolving inferential frameworks, Peirce draws out the (apparent) consequence that the meaning of *truth* and of *reality* themselves must admit of definition in those pragmatic terms as well:

> The opinion which is fated to be ultimately agreed to by all who investigate, is what we mean by the truth, and the object represented in this opinion is the real. That is the way I would explain reality. (1992: 139)

This famous Peircean conception of truth in terms of an ideal convergence of opinion in the long run among responsible inquirers was also to make various reappearances during the twentieth century.

On the whole, then, Peirce attempted to rigorously combine in a unique and comprehensive vision elements of both realism and idealism; of speculative metaphysics and scientific empiricism; of naturalistic experimentalism and pure categorial ontology; of a new, forward-looking, fallibilist method for philosophy, and a deep awareness of the evolving, historical patterns of reasoning and action that shape our most basic conceptions and values. It is also certainly a mark of their merit that the themes from Peirce's philosophy highlighted above provide a useful framework for understanding a complex century of philosophy in America that was to follow.

William James, John Dewey, and other classical American pragmatists

Peirce originated the idea of pragmatism, but it was his famous friend and supporter William James (1842–1910) at Harvard who brought pragmatism into prominence. In an address to the Philosophical Union of the University of California in 1898 entitled "Philosophical conceptions and practical results" (published in part in 1904 as "The pragmatic method") James credited Peirce with having developed the pragmatic maxim:

> … Mr. Charles S. Peirce, with whose very existence as a philosopher I dare say many of you are unacquainted … is one of the most original of contemporary thinkers; and the principle of practicalism – or pragmatism, as he called it, when I first heard him enunciate it at Cambridge in the early '70's – is the clue or compass by following which I find myself more and more confirmed in believing we may keep our feet upon the proper trail. (James 1898: 347–8)

James indicates that he would express "Peirce's principle by saying that the effective meaning of any philosophic proposition can always be brought down to some particular consequence, in our future practical experience, whether active or passive" (1898: 349).[6]

James argued that the pragmatic maxim had the effect of reconciling the fundamentally opposed "philosophical temperaments" that he suggests are evident, in varying mixtures and degrees, not only in the great philosophers but in every thinking person. Both of these tendencies were certainly present most strikingly in James himself. On the one hand, there is what James calls the *tender-minded* temperament: rationalistic, "going by principles," intellectualistic, idealistic, optimistic, religious, free-willist, monistic, dogmatical; and on the other hand there is the *tough-minded* temperament: empiricist, "going by facts," sensationalistic (i.e. prioritizing sensations), materialistic, pessimistic, non-religious, fatalistic, pluralistic, skeptical (James 1978a: 13). Most people, James suggests, want both to respect empirical evidence and to indulge in a spiritual metaphysics. The "layman's dilemma," however, is that tough traditional empiricist and tender metaphysical idealist philosophies have tended to render such a synthesis impossible. For James the pragmatic maxim, both as a method for ascertaining the meaning of concepts and as a general "humanist" conception of truth, enables just such a philosophical reconciliation.

Here we may fruitfully appeal to some of the theses discussed in the previous section which were broadly shared by Peirce and James. On the one hand, the fallibilist, naturalistic, and open-ended nature of inquiry on the pragmatist and experimentalist picture can plausibly be taken fully to respect the scientific temperament and the empiricist's methodological restriction to hypotheses that allow of experiential testing. On the other hand, the same anti-foundationalist, anti-reductionist, and holistic outlook characteristic of pragmatism also encourages an openness to consider any sort of hypothesis concerning the nature of reality, however value-laden or speculative it may be – including the "religious hypothesis" – provided that the supposition of its truth can be shown to have genuine experiential consequences or practical import. In some respects traditional metaphysical and religious doctrines will fail this pragmatic test, but in others – particularly, according to James, in those decisive, "forced," ultimate questions that really matter to us and which are not ruled out by the facts – they will survive in clarified form as live hypotheses and predictions concerning the overall character of future experienced reality as a whole. (Essentially it is this idea that was carefully defended in James's famous and philosophically controversial doctrine of "*the will* (or the right) *to believe*.")

James held a broadly functionalist theory of conceptual cognition along the lines sketched earlier, as part of a rich phenomenological account of the interplay between percepts and concepts in our cognitive carving of objects and relations out of the flux of sensory experience (O'Shea 2000). From his earliest writings in psychology to his last writings concerning *radical empiricism* and *pure experience*, James argued that while a concept may be "incarnate" in a word or a mental image, what makes it the conceptual cognition that it is – whatever its "structural" or material aspects might be – are its instrumental or functional "leadings" in bringing the knower into eventual successful engagement with relevant portions of the future experienced world, both inner and outer. Conceptual thinking for James is essentially teleological – adaptive and purposeful – in that our conceptual schemes function as cognitive maps enabling successful reference and lawful prediction across experiences. What James especially stressed, as we saw at the very outset, was the variety of selective interests and purposes that such experiential cognitions can serve, whether concerning practical, theoretical, aesthetic, or emotional ends. As he had put it early on in "The sentiment of rationality" in 1879,

> Every way of classifying a thing is but a way of handling it for some particular purpose. Conceptions, "kinds," are teleological instruments. No abstract concept can be a valid substitute for a concrete reality except with reference to a particular interest in the conceiver. The interest of theoretic rationality, the relief of identification, is but one of a thousand human purposes. When others rear their heads, it must pack up its little bundle and retire till its turn recurs. (1978b: 62)

It is these views concerning the purpose-relative and selective nature of all cognition that underpin both the philosophical *pluralism* and the pragmatist account of *truth* for which James is most famous.

James's respected Harvard colleague and friend Josiah Royce (1855–1916), in highly influential works including *The Religious Aspect of Philosophy* (1885), *The World and the Individual* (1900–1), and *The Philosophy of Loyalty* (1908), had been developing a sophisticated version of absolute idealism that reflected, in the very different Hegelian style of philosophizing, many of the themes concerning logic and experience, the primacy of the will and the deep importance of community, that likewise animated the thought of Peirce, James, and Dewey.[7] James, however, used his theory of conceptual cognition to object to the monistic Hegelian theories of the Absolute in favor of a thoroughgoing pluralism. In particular, the arguments of the monists (as well as of atomistic empiricists such as Hume) covertly rely upon what James dubbed the fallacy of *vicious abstractionism*. Both the monist and the empirical atomist, James argues, in effect detach conceptual abstractions from the context of their legitimate instrumental role in lawfully mapping the "insuperable" richness of given experiences, and then (illegitimately) regard any property not explicitly contained in the abstract definition of the concept as excluded from those rich experiences themselves (see James 1978a: 300ff.). Ultimately this misconception leads to the view that all real connections and relations among things would have to be *necessary*, in the way in which abstract conceptual connections are necessary – and we are on the road either to Humean skepticism or to the Absolute. By contrast, James argues that all proposed conceptual connections whatsoever, insofar as they are taken to be applicable to the world, have the status of fallible hypotheses of varying scope and usefulness. On this basis he defends a radically pluralist empiricism in which there is, and might forever be, no overarching, compulsory system of conceptual classification that takes in all the manifold aspects of ordinary commonsense reality. (Aspects of this outlook will later resurface in the neo-pragmatist views of Goodman, Putnam, Quine, and Rorty, discussed below.)

On these bases James developed what might be called a *conceptual scheme pluralism*, along with a corresponding pragmatist conception of truth. In *Pragmatism* James outlined four basic conceptual schemes: those of common sense, realist science, instrumentalist science, and idealist philosophy. Each of these global conceptual frameworks is useful or functionally adaptive (in the senses described above) relative to certain purposes and not others; yet each scheme portrays reality under categories that in various ways ostensibly conflict with the others. Which of them, then, is *true*? For James, this is a deep and difficult question:

> The whole notion of truth, which naturally and without reflexion we assume to mean the simple duplication by the mind of a ready-made and given reality, proves hard to understand clearly. There is no simple test available for adjudicating offhand between the divers types of thought that claim to possess it. ... [The four schemes] all seem insufficiently true in some regard and leave some dissatisfaction. It is evident that the conflict of these so widely differing systems obliges us to overhaul the very idea of truth ...
> (James 1978a: 93–4)

James's resulting pragmatist overhaul of the idea of truth will look to some to be implausible on the surface, but it was to prove a far more subtle conception than many of his early opponents would recognize. The basic conception is this:

> *"The true,"* to put it very briefly, *is only the expedient in the way of our thinking, just as "the right" is only the expedient in the way of our behaving.* Expedient in almost any fashion; and expedient in the long run and on the whole of course.
> ...

> The "absolutely" true ... is that ideal vanishing-point towards which we imagine that all our temporary truths will some day converge. (1978a: 106–7)

How can truth consist in utility or expedience, it will be asked, when it is obvious that useful theories are often false? The classical *correspondence* or "copy theory" of truth holds that an idea or belief is true only if it *agrees with reality*. James argues, however, that when we actually attempt to spell out what such agreement consists in, in any given case of a belief accepted as true, we find that the actual relations to or "agreements with" reality are as many and various as the different kinds of substantive, functional adaptations to reality of the sort described earlier (among which "copying" or representing is only one, defeasible such relation). The *satisfactoriness* of our beliefs, in which truth consists for James, is to be measured by a variety of sometimes conflicting standards that must themselves be evaluated against the totality of the community's evolving beliefs through time, including highly refined theoretical beliefs, and must be tested for overall coherence against the repository of past and projected experience on the whole. The fallibilist and regulative conception of a *more* satisfactory system of belief not yet attained, along with the fact of earlier such schemes having been corrected, is sufficient to preserve the ideal objectivity of truth as *overall* satisfactoriness of belief.

Even while embracing that regulative ideal, however, for James in the end we ought finally to recognize the validity of the hypothesis of radical pluralism concerning reality:

> There is nothing improbable in the supposition that analysis of the world may yield a number of formulae, all consistent with the facts. In physical science different formulae may explain the phenomena equally well, – the one-fluid and the two-fluid theories of electricity, for example. Why may it not be so with the world? Why may there not be different points of view for surveying it, within each of which all data harmonize, and which the observer may therefore either choose between, or simply cumulate one upon another? A Beethoven string-quartet is truly, as some one has said, a scraping of horses' tails on cats' bowels, and may be exhaustively described in such terms; but the application of this description in no way precludes the simultaneous applicability of an entirely different description. (1978b: 66)

Finally, in his later so-called "Bergsonian" phase (named after the French philosopher Henri Bergson, and particularly evident in James's 1909 collection, A *Pluralistic Universe*), James contended that there was a deeper, metaphysical truth to be revealed in the flux of immediate experience: the "pulse" of reality itself, which cannot be adequately "mapped" by concepts but rather must be experienced or felt directly, or non-conceptually. This opened up for James the possibility of further bold cosmological hypotheses and metaphysical speculations of a broadly pantheistic or panpsychist kind (though arguably at the cost of embracing highly problematic doctrines involving ineffability and givenness; O'Shea 2000).

The views of Peirce, James, and Royce were reflected in later thinkers in the classical American pragmatist tradition, most notably by the eminent figure of John Dewey (1859–1952) and by George Herbert Mead (1863–1931) in what became known as the "Chicago School" of pragmatism (in 1904 Dewey moved to Columbia University), as well as in the works of the Harvard philosopher Clarence Irving Lewis (1883–1964). Mead's theories concerning significant communication and symbolic interaction, particularly in relation to the social origins of mind and selfhood, were subsequently highly influential in social psychology and sociology. Here I shall focus briefly on Dewey's important outlook, and further below on C. I. Lewis as well.

Dewey's early influences, similar in many respects to Peirce and James, included a mixture of Kantian and Hegelian idealism, empirical psychology, and (in some important respects) Darwinian scientific naturalism. Increasingly the pragmatist themes highlighted above came to the fore in Dewey's thought: fallibilism, naturalism, holistic empiricism, meaning as functionally anticipated experience, and the overall *instrumentalist* or experimentalist outlook on the logic of inquiry, including the view of truth as satisfactory, purposeful engagement with one's concretely experienced environment. For much of the first half of the twentieth century Dewey was by name if not always by detailed acquaintance with his writings the most widely known philosopher in America. The title of one of his classic works, *Democracy and Education* (1916), indicates two of his deepest philosophical concerns throughout his career, and also reflects the socially and politically engaged character of his thinking; and the title *Art as Experience* (1934) indicates another rich area of inquiry for Dewey. Among his many other important books are *Experience and Nature* (1925), *The Quest for Certainty* (1929), and *Logic: The Theory of Inquiry* (1938).[8]

For present purposes I will highlight one especially pervasive theme that reoccurs throughout Dewey's wide-ranging philosophy: namely, his questioning of the deep-seated dichotomies in philosophy that have prevented what he sees as the required *Reconstruction in Philosophy* (1920 and 1948) that needs to take place. Like James on the pragmatic method, Dewey saw his own broadly instrumentalist logic of inquiry as the way toward reconciling or overcoming the traditionally divisive philosophical contrasts between the eternal or essential and the merely mutable or in process; between facts and values; between the subjective and the objective; between nature and human experience; and between abstract theory and concrete practice. (Some of these contrasts, on Dewey's account, have legitimate counterparts when interpreted *instrumentally* in terms of contextually specified, behavioral problem-solving situations.) We have already witnessed in the case of the empirical sciences, according to Dewey, the overcoming of many such traditional dichotomies, but they have yet to be overcome in culture or experience as a whole:

> Science as conducted, science in practice, has completely repudiated these separations and isolations. Scientific inquiry has raised activities, materials, tools, of the type once regarded as practical (in a low utilitarian sense) into itself; it has incorporated them into its own being. ... Theories have passed into hypotheses. It remains for philosophy to point out in particular and in

general the untold significance of this fact for morals. For in what is now taken to be morals the fixed, the immutable, still reign, even though moral theorists and moral institutional dogmatists are at complete odds with one another ... In science the order of fixities has already passed irretrievably into an order of connections *in process*. One of the most immediate duties of philosophical reconstruction with respect to the development of viable instruments for inquiry into human or moral facts is to deal systematically with *human* processes. (Dewey 1948: xxxix–xl)

The "secularization" that has accompanied the rise of instrumentalist science, but which remains in tension with traditional religious attitudes, must be *humanized*, as it were, "in terms of ends and standards so distinctively human as to constitute a new moral order" (1948: xxxviii–ix). Dewey's thoroughgoing *naturalism* is thus one in which the experiences to be successfully accommodated in inquiry, unlike either the "sense-data" of traditional empiricism or the intellectually intuited, ready-made natural kinds of classical essentialism, are contextualized, biological experience-situations which are saturated with values and in process of change.

We shall return to further developments within the pragmatist tradition later, including the considerable influence of Dewey upon recent neo-pragmatists such as Putnam, Quine, and Rorty. Let us now turn, however, to consider some of the other influential movements in philosophy in America during the first half of the twentieth century that developed alongside the classical pragmatist tradition.

Varieties of realism, naturalism, and positivism from 1900 to 1950

The new realism

During the first two decades of the twentieth century there was a semi-cooperative philosophical movement in America that came to call itself the *new realism* or neo-realism. In 1910 there appeared in the *Journal of Philosophy, Psychology and Scientific Methods* "The program and first platform of six realists," containing short summary theses of aspects of the new realism by E. B. Holt (Harvard), W. T. Marvin (Rutgers), W. P. Montague (Columbia), R. B. Perry (Harvard), W. B. Pitkin (Columbia), and E. G. Spaulding (Princeton).[9] This platform contended that the perpetual disagreements characteristic of philosophy, while due in part to its subject matter, are due "chiefly to the lack of precision and uniformity in the use of words and to the lack of deliberate cooperation in research. In having these failings philosophy still differs widely from such sciences as physics and chemistry. They tend to make it seem mere opinion" (Holt et al. 1910: 393). This was followed by a collaborative book in 1912, *The New Realism: Cooperative Studies in Philosophy*. The proximate targets of the new realists were the widespread doctrines of the neo-Hegelian idealists, especially the much admired works of Royce, who along with James had been one of Ralph Barton Perry's teachers at Harvard. (Royce dubbed the collaborators "the six little realists.") As Montague put it in the platform article: "Realism is opposed to subjectivism or epistemological idealism which denies that things can exist apart from an experience of them, or independently of the cognitive relation" (Holt et al. 1910: 396).

R. B. Perry (1876–1957) in particular criticized the many arguments supporting ontological idealism that implicitly appealed to what he called the *egocentric predicament* (Perry 1910). According to Perry, idealists of various stripes in effect argue that any existing object has a necessary (intentional) relationship or "internal relation" to some mind that knows or conceives that object. The egocentric predicament is basically the idea that any attempt by a critic to falsify this idealist claim by considering a case in which an object exists apart from any such relationship to some mind, will necessarily be unsuccessful, since this very consideration of the object will itself be an instance of that internal relation. But if alternatively I try to subtract all such intentional or cognitive relations, I am in that case *unable to know* whether the object has thereby been eliminated or not. Perry pointed out, however, that pervasive appeals to this predicament do not in the end entail any idealist conclusions. They entail only that the realist's thesis of the independence of objects from the mind, and hence of cognition as an "external relation" that neither modifies nor creates the object, cannot be established or justified by those comparative methods. Perry suggests, however, that a contrary realist *analysis* of the cognitive relation is left quite untouched by any of these considerations (Perry 1910: 14).

Perry's realist analysis of cognition may be regarded as taking in one possible direction some of his teacher William James's highly sophisticated suggestions in essays from 1904–6 collected posthumously (by Perry himself) in James's *Essays in Radical Empiricism* in 1912 (James 1976). James's own distinctive "radical empiricism," for its part, had involved the conception of "A world of pure experience," which Russell later indicated had influenced his own development of a *neutral monism*. According to Russell's neutral monism, minds and physical bodies are alike logical constructions out of (James would say "functional leadings to," or "experienced relations between") neutral given contents, or "sensibilia" for Russell ("pure experiences" on James's conception). Perry's more behavioristic realism differed in crucial respects from James's phenomenologically rich radical empiricism, but there is some common ground evident in the following remarks from Perry's contribution to the neo-realist platform (compare in particular James's essay in *Essays in Radical Empiricism*, "Does consciousness exist?"):

> [T]he difference between subject and object of consciousness is not a difference of quality or substance, but a difference of office or place in a configuration.
>
> [...] The same entity possesses both immanence, by virtue of its membership in one class, and also transcendence, by virtue of the fact that it may belong also to indefinitely many other classes. ... [T]his implies the falsity of the subjectivistic argument from the ego-centric predicament, *i.e.*, the argument that because entities are content of consciousness they can not also transcend consciousness ... (Perry in Holt et al. 1910: 397–8)

For the new realists in general, there is an act of cognition and an object or datum directly cognized, without any intermediary ideas or perceptions of the sort proposed by traditional representational or indirect realists (Descartes, Locke), and without the object of cognition being itself dependent upon or modified by the act of cognizing that object (in contrast to certain idealist arguments attributed to Berkeley, Kant, and Hegel). The objects of such acts of consciousness, for the new realists, are (typically) *non-mental* objects of many different kinds, including for some of the new realists the abstract objects treated in logic and mathematics. It is a matter of ongoing scientific inquiry rather than a priori theorizing, for many of the new realists, to determine just what kinds of objects there are. *Methodological naturalism* and *ontological pluralism* were thus taken to be plausible corollaries of the new realism.

The basic non-representationalist direct realism in the neo-realist account of cognition was susceptible to many different lines of interpretation and development. Several characteristic problems tended to plague all versions of the new realism, however. Serious epistemological and ontological puzzles arose in relation to the ineffable (or quasi-ineffable) immediately given "datum," which on some versions looked to be neither physical nor mental. Furthermore, the hypothetical or relational constructions of ordinary objects out of those elusive "data" more often than not resembled just the sort of phenomenalistic idealism that the new realism had been designed to replace. On the other hand, those act/object versions of the new realism that sought to avoid such constructions in favor of straightforwardly admitting the non-mental, independent existence (or perhaps the *subsistence*, or Being) of nearly all objects of thought, including fictional objects, perceptual illusions, Platonic entities, and so on, faced continual problems of ontological crowd control and population explosion. The *problem of error* was thus another deep difficulty for neo-realism, given its apparent identification of the *content* of experiences with the *objects* experienced.

Critical realism

In America all of these objections, and others, were raised in particular by a second important group of collaborative researchers: the *critical realists*. In 1916 Roy Wood Sellars (1880–1973), born in Canada and later a professor at Michigan, published his book *Critical Realism: A Study of the Nature and Conditions of Knowledge*. This was followed in 1920 by a second collaborative work by American philosophers: *Essays in Critical Realism: A Cooperative Study of the Problem of Knowledge*, by D. Drake (Vassar), A. O. Lovejoy (Johns Hopkins), J. B. Pratt (Williams), A. K. Rogers (Chicago and Yale), George Santayana (Harvard, active retirement in Europe from 1912), Sellars himself, and C. A. Strong (Chicago) (Drake et al. 1920). Lovejoy was a brilliant philosophical critic and historian of ideas, whose book *The Revolt Against Dualism* (1930) continued the critical realists' defense of the epistemological dualism of inner mental contents and external realities, as opposed to the monistic identification of these in neo-realism (and to some extent in pragmatism and idealism, too). Santayana (1863–1952, born in Spain) has been a figure in American philosophical literature of a stature to rival James or Dewey. His developing thought idiosyncratically combined elements of pragmatism, a Platonic realism of essences (hence the so-called "essence wing" of critical realism), and a comprehensive materialism, expressed in a rich literary style.

For present purposes, however, let us focus on the systematic critical realist episte-mology and evolutionary naturalist metaphysics of Roy Wood Sellars. His thought illustrates the kind of philosophical naturalism that was becoming predominant in America, and will also afford an interesting view of the changes that took place in philosophy in America across a generation when we come to consider the currently much discussed views of his son, Wilfrid Sellars (1912–89).[10]

R. W. Sellars's anti-skeptical stance insisted that we should start from a presumption in favor of our ordinary and reflective scientific knowledge of the world. Two of his most important books, *Evolutionary Naturalism* (1922) and *The Philosophy of Physical Realism* (1932), outline a conception of the human being as a complex product of organic evolution, resulting in a dynamic and multi-leveled cognitive and causal relationship to its environment. Dewey's more influential pragmatist instrumentalism had emphasized these outlooks as well, but Sellars argues that Dewey insufficiently accounted for the role of the contents of subjective consciousness in cognition, and that he prematurely abandoned the traditional projects of epistemology.[11] The neo-realists were correct in rejecting idealism and Locke's representative or indirect realism, but Sellars judged their direct or naive realism and their alternative construc-tivist approaches to knowledge to fail primarily for the reasons discussed earlier.

"Critical realism," as Sellars put it in 1929 in "A re-examination of critical realism," "is a direct realism which examines very carefully the nature and mechanism of knowing and shows that it harmonizes with all the facts of the causal theory of the conditions of the perceptual act" (1929: 455). The perceptual act itself is a direct cognition, in an interpretive judgment, of the independent physical object itself. Such cognitions are causally mediated, however, by the sorts of sensory data and meaningful predicates that naive realism and neo-realism mistakenly assume constitute an *intuitive* appre-hension or acquaintance with the object itself. Scientific and philosophical reflection indicate that we judge the characters of the object itself *by means of* the mind's sensory and "logical" contents, as Sellars puts it, but the physical object itself that is thereby directly cognized is not directly intuited or "existentially" given in consciousness. Perceptual errors and illusions are now explainable without either losing contact with or overpopulating reality. "It is the claim of the critical realist that all the valid insights of realist, idealist, and pragmatist, will be found in this position" (1929: 455).

In conjunction with critical realism Sellars developed what he called a "double knowledge approach" to the mind-problem, along with an account of the evolutionary emergence of higher levels of complexity and organization. With respect to the former position, we have knowledge of the biological brain-mind from the "inside," as it were, directly in terms of the contents of qualitative consciousness; but we know the same brain-mind from the outside, scientifically, as a functionally adaptive cognitive mechanism or structure that is geared to its environment. Sellars's non-reductively materialist naturalism also extended to a frank atheism in which he called for a reori-entation of religious values in the direction of what he called a "religious humanism," based essentially on humanistic moral values. (Sellars was in fact the author of the first draft of the well-known "Humanist Manifesto" of 1933, which was signed by many leading intellectuals, John Dewey most prominent among them.)

We saw earlier that Peirce, James, and Dewey were all to varying degrees influenced by Darwinian naturalism, but it ought to be emphasized that naturalism as a philosophical outlook is open to multiple interpretations (see Kitcher 1992 and Kim 2003). For example, Peirce, James, and some of the neo-realists and critical realists (e.g. Strong, Drake) took themselves to be naturalists while also entertaining or developing various versions of *panpsychism*, according to which something akin to mind is considered to be the fundamental stuff of the universe. (Peirce once described matter as "effete mind.") Dewey's robustly Darwinian experientialism was also developed under the banner of naturalism by philosophers influenced by him at Columbia and New York Universities, such as F. J. E. Woodbridge (1867–1940), John Herman Randall (1899–1980), Ernest Nagel (1901–85), Sidney Hook (1902–89), and Morris Cohen (1880–1947). The pragmatists and the various cooperative efforts of the new and critical realists all certainly tended to champion what has often been called *methodological naturalism* in philosophy. Again, this is roughly the idea that the fallibilist, observationally data-based, inductively testable and hence self-correcting methods of the successful natural sciences represent the only reliable means of obtaining knowledge about reality; hence philosophy ought to exhibit the same modes of inquiry conducted at the most general and comprehensive level.

Some naturalists, however, such as Roy Wood Sellars himself, came to think that the "merely methodological" naturalism characteristic of the flexible Columbia naturalists and of Dewey's philosophy of "experience" was no longer an ontologically *substantive naturalism* of the sort Sellars was committed to in his physical realism and his evolutionary naturalism. In this spirit, R. W. Sellars, V. J. McGill (1897–1977), and Marvin Farber (1901–80), as editors of the 1949 collection *Philosophy for the Future: The Quest of Modern Materialism* (once again another "cooperative book in which scientists and philosophers collaborate," p. v) remarked in their Foreword that whereas the methodological or procedural "type of naturalism is reluctant to commit itself to a positive theory of the world, materialism endeavors to set forth a synoptic view of man and the universe implicit in the sciences at their present stage of development" (pp. ix–x). Debates concerning the nature and commitments of naturalism and materialism would intensify again later in the century (and never more so than at the present time).

The revolution in logic and the conceptual pragmatism of C. I. Lewis

The character of philosophy as practiced in America underwent an important sea-change that became increasingly evident from the late 1920s through the 1930s and 1940s. These changes resulted, first, from the increasing interest in America in the sorts of logical and linguistic analyses that Russell and others were bringing to bear on traditional philosophical problems in the light of Russell and Whitehead's monumental transformation of logic in their *Principia Mathematica* (1910–13), as well as Wittgenstein's elusive but revolutionary work, the *Tractatus Logico-Philosophicus* (1922); and second, from the influx (resulting from the rise of the Nazis) of logical positivist and logical empiricist philosophers from the Vienna Circle and from Berlin who had been strongly influenced by the developments in logic just mentioned and by other revolutionary developments in science (see "The birth of analytic philosophy," Chapter 1 and "The development of analytic philosophy: Wittgenstein and after," Chapter 2). The twin influences of early Cambridge analysis and what Russell called "logical atomism" on the one hand, and logical empiricism or positivism on the other, were to form the first stage of the dominance in America and Britain of what would later be known as "analytic philosophy."

In America, however, one of the first philosophers to do important work both in logic itself and in putting the new logical methods to philosophical use was C. I. Lewis, who was nurtured in the Harvard pragmatist tradition. Lewis was influenced by both of his teachers Royce and James, as well as by his study of Kant and Peirce.[12] In his classic book, *Mind and the World Order* (1929) Lewis put to work the new methods of logical analysis in ways that in some (but certainly not all) respects parallel, within his own distinctive "conceptual pragmatism," many of the characteristic moves of both Russell and the logical empiricists. In his Preface Lewis lays out his view that the new logical methods would have revolutionary consequences:

> Whoever has followed the developments in logistic and mathematical theory in the last quarter-century can hardly fail to be convinced that the consequences must be revolutionary. It has demonstrated, with a degree of precision and finality seldom attained, that the certitude of mathematics results from its purely analytic character and its independence of any necessary connection with empirical fact. Its first premises are ... definitions and postulates which exhibit abstract concepts more or less arbitrarily chosen for the purposes of the system in question. Intrinsic connection with experience is tenuous or lacking. (1929: viii)

Furthermore, the development of non-Euclidean geometries and their successful use in Einstein's relativity physics had suggested that the principles of Euclidean geometry and Newtonian mechanics do not have the indispensable "synthetic a priori" status which Kant had claimed for them. Lewis and other philosophers argued that either of the Euclidean or non-Euclidean geometries could in principle be held true by convention and still successfully accommodate the data of experience. The choice as to which of the alternative a priori analytic conceptual systems to apply to empirical reality is for Lewis a matter that goes beyond the given data and must always rest on overall systematic explanatory and pragmatic grounds.

The pragmatic pluralism of conceptual schemes stressed by James had now found a rigorous logical formulation in Lewis's conceptual pragmatism. His *pragmatic conception of the a priori* extended to all human cognition this basic distinction between analytic a priori definitional truths laid down by the mind, and probable empirical hypotheses that meet the test of the "given" in sensory experience:

> While the delineation of concepts is a priori, the application of any particular concept to particular given experience is hypothetical; the choice

of conceptual systems for such application is instrumental or pragmatic, and empirical truth is never more than probable. (Lewis 1929: x)

All our empirical knowledge is thus a matter of "if–then" predictions concerning given perceptual experiences, in conjunction with an ongoing pragmatic evaluation of possible alternative a priori frameworks and categorizations of experience. The mind-independence of the object of experience, for Lewis, primarily consists in its not being up to us whether the given will in fact comport with our free conceptualizations, or not.

> If the idealist should find that there is nothing in such "independence" which is incompatible with his thesis, then it may be that between a sufficiently critical idealism and a sufficiently critical realism, there are no issues save false issues which arise from the insidious fallacies of the [representationalist or] copy-theory of knowledge. (Lewis 1929: 194; compare this with the later neo-pragmatist views of Goodman and Putnam, below)

To Roy Wood Sellars the physical realist, however, it is not surprising that Lewis's view looked suspiciously like yet another, albeit more sophisticated version of phenomenalistic empiricism or even idealism, insofar as for Lewis all knowledge is reducible either to analytic truths-by-definition or to hypothetical "if–then" predictions concerning the directly "given element" in qualitative sensory experience. Whatever we should hold is ultimately the correct interpretation of Lewis's subtle, modified Kantian epistemology, it was the logical empiricists or positivists who would come to formulate the most influential versions of the basic methodological dichotomy, "either analytic a priori, or empirical," as a general philosophical outlook.

Logical positivism

Among the many logical empiricists or positivists who emigrated from Europe and made a strong impact at universities in America was the following impressive group of thinkers: Rudolf Carnap (1891–1970) emigrated to Chicago in 1935, where with the help of Charles Morris (1903–79) the *Encyclopedia of Unified Science* was produced. Hans Reichenbach (1891–1953) was at the University of California, Los Angeles in 1938 until his death in 1953, where he was succeeded by Carnap. Herbert Feigl (1902–88) went to Iowa in 1933, and then to Minnesota in 1940 and was the founder of the influential Minnesota Center for the Philosophy of Science from 1953. Feigl was joined in Iowa in 1938 by Gustav Bergmann (1906–87), who kept a form of metaphysics alive while using the formal methods of his anti-metaphysical positivist colleagues. Carl Hempel (1905-97) moved to Chicago in 1935, and was later at Yale, Queens College, Princeton, and Pittsburgh. Two of the greatest mathematical logicians of the century also arrived, namely Alfred Tarski (1902–83), who was fortunate to be visiting Harvard when the Nazis invaded his native Poland and remained in the USA at Berkeley from 1942; and Kurt Gödel (1906–78), who was at the Institute for Advanced Study in Princeton from 1940.

If there was indeed to be a philosophical revolution inspired by the new logical methods in philosophy as applied to the exact sciences and to human knowledge generally, as C. I. Lewis had anticipated, then in one form or another this impressive group of mathematically and scientifically trained philosophical thinkers looked likely to bring it about. It was once customary among philosophers and historians to look back on logical positivism after its decline in the 1950s as a regrettable case of anti-philosophical and myopic scientism, doomed from the start by its own impossibly strict *verifiability criterion* of meaningfulness. Roughly speaking, on most versions of the positivist verifiability criterion all meaningful or cognitively significant statements are only of two kinds: they are either analytic propositions pertaining to logic and linguistic conventions, or they are testable empirical hypotheses about the world. One crippling problem, unfortunately, was that this verification principle did not *itself* seem to be either a merely analytic proposition or an empirical hypothesis. Some positivists responded by suggesting that the verification principle is merely a proposal for language reform or for what should be taken to be properly scientific epistemology; but in that case it became difficult to distinguish such a proposal from a merely dogmatic scientism. However, the admitted difficulties with positivism should not blind us to the fact that in many respects the logical empiricists helped to raise the level of sophistication of philosophical analysis in America in ways that most philosophers now routinely take for granted.

There were, of course, important disagreements and changes of view within logical empiricism – as with any diverse and developing philosophical outlook – but as an example of a mature positivist standpoint on philosophical method in general one turns naturally to Rudolf Carnap's widely discussed article at mid-century, "Empiricism, semantics, and ontology" (1950 reprinted 1956). Central to Carnap's philosophy since early in his career was the general idea of *alternative linguistic frameworks*. We have already seen William James and C. I. Lewis emphasize the ever-present plurality of conceptual frameworks in terms of which reality may be interpreted, with the choice between them to be made on essentially pragmatic grounds. Carnap's position is similar to theirs in those respects, but with more emphasis on linguistic or semantical rules than one finds in Lewis's theory of a priori concepts, and with more of an anti-metaphysical outlook than one finds in James's pluralist pragmatism. According to Carnap, philosophical questions, insofar as they are cognitively meaningful and are not mere pseudo-questions, are primarily questions concerning the formal-analytic features of various linguistic frameworks.

To adapt an example of Carnap's, consider a philosophical realist concerning the existence of physical objects, such as John Locke, an idealist such as Bishop Berkeley (or a "sense-datum" phenomenalist), and a skeptic such as David Hume; and suppose each of these philosophers to make the same empirical observation of a certain red apple. The philosophical realist and the philosophical idealist will vehemently disagree about whether the apple is *really* a mind-independent material thing or whether, to the contrary, the apple is *really* just a certain complex collection of mind-dependent perceptual contents or sense-data. And the skeptic, for his part, will take the dispute between the other two philosophers to be a meaningful one, but one that is incapable of any rational solution. Carnap argued, however, that in such a case no possible empirical observation (e.g. "here is a red apple") could provide support for one of those three philosophical positions against the others. Unlike ordinary empirical hypotheses, the alternative philosophical statements are thus neither verifiable nor falsifiable. If they are mistakenly construed as cognitive statements concerning the nature of reality, they show themselves to be meaningless pseudo-statements.

Carnap suggests that the resulting philosophical impasse may be due to the fact that what the idealist and the realist take to be a dispute about reality is really a dispute concerning possible alternative linguistic frameworks. It is indeed worthwhile for the scientific philosopher to investigate whether a rigorous *sense-datum language* might be constructed in which, for example, the basic terms would designate only the qualities of immediate and remembered perceptual experiences, and in which the empirical truths of common sense and science would be logically constructed out of the former sense-datum sentences using the pioneering methods of Russell and of Carnap himself. (Carnap had attempted a similar reconstruction in his earlier *Der logische Aufbau der Welt* in 1928, translated as *The Logical Structure of the World* in 1967.) The choice between (1) such a comprehensive sense-datum language, (2) an ordinary "physical thing" language, and (3) a possible comprehensive scientific language referring only to four-dimensional space-time manifolds (i.e. referring neither to sense-data nor to ordinary physical objects), depends on the pragmatic purposes for which the language is being constructed.

If we are using a physical thing language, then what Carnap calls an *internal question* such as, "Is there a red apple on the table?" will admit of a straightforward answer in terms of the logical and semantic rules of empirical investigation and confirmation within that framework. However, from "these questions we must distinguish the external question of the reality of the thing world itself. In contrast to the former questions, this question is raised neither by the man in the street nor by scientists, but only by philosophers" (1956: 207). If philosophers have thought *external questions* of the latter kind are genuine theoretical questions concerning the nature of things, they have been deluded, "and the controversy goes on for centuries without ever being solved."

A genuinely scientific epistemology, as Carnap sees it, thus recognizes that all meaningful questions are either: (1) questions internal to some particular linguistic framework of syntactic and semantic rules, in which case they are either straightforward empirical hypotheses subject to verification, or else they point to propositions that are merely analytically true-by-definition according to the rules of that framework; or (2) they are external *pragmatic* questions concerning whether or not to accept some particular or proposed linguistic framework itself, given whatever purposes or ends in view the investigator or the agent may have. (The positivist also recognizes the non-cognitive expression of attitudes, feelings, and emotions, in morality, aesthetics, and religion.) Apart from these questions pertaining to the analytic framework-rules, empirical hypotheses, and pragmatic choices between frameworks, there are also external questions concerning linguistic frameworks that have been mistakenly treated by the traditional metaphysician as genuine theoretical propositions, resulting in the sorts of pseudo-questions which Carnap's version of *the linguistic turn* in philosophy is designed to avoid.

Carnap was without doubt one of the most important philosophers working in America throughout the middle third of the twentieth century. Many of his technical analyses, constructions, and proposals concerning the language of science in the broadest sense – whether concerning the nature of probability, induction, and laws; the problem of reduction and the unity of science; the analysis of meaning and modal logic; the problem of abstract entities, of the propositional attitudes, or of observational knowledge – would subsequently shape the form and matter of much philosophical work in the analytic tradition long after the decline of logical positivism.

Positivism itself, however, was by the end of the 1950s taken to have died by the double-edged sword by which it had lived: the strict verifiability criterion that all cognitively meaningful statements are analytic a priori linguistic conventions or empirically verifiable hypotheses. Some of the reasons for this decline and the transition to a new style of philosophizing are the subject of the next section.

Mid-century developments: from positivism to ordinary-language philosophy

In 1950 Willard Van Orman Quine (1908–2000) read a paper to the Eastern Division of the American Philosophical Association entitled "Two dogmas of empiricism." This was to become the most famous of a variety of attacks on the analytic a priori versus synthetic a posteriori dichotomy that lies at the heart of logical positivism. Quine had already initiated his critique in "Truth by convention" in 1936, discussing among other things Carnap's conventionalist account of logical and mathematical truths. On the one hand, Quine's overall view that the most predictively efficient and economical language of science (as canonically reconstructed in a purely extensional logic) is the last arbiter in matters of ontology and epistemology clearly marks him out as in many ways "The Greatest Logical Positivist," as Putnam has characterized him (Putnam 1990: ch. 20). On the other hand, Quine's twin attack on the notion of analyticity (basically, truth or falsity in virtue of conventional or conceptual meanings) and on reductionist empiricism in "Two dogmas" rendered problematic the central logical empiricist contention that some sentences are determinable as true or false a priori, by convention or solely in virtue of the meanings of the terms involved, while other "protocol" or observation sentences are strictly determinable as true or false in isolation by direct comparison with features of sense experience. Quine would later conclude his article "Carnap on logical truth" by painting a picture of his own holistic and pragmatic naturalism, which from the 1960s onwards was to have considerable influence among analytic philosophers in America:

> The lore of our fathers is a fabric of sentences. In our hands it develops and changes, through more or less arbitrary and deliberate revisions and additions of our own, more or less directly occasioned by the continuing stimulation of our sense organs. It is a pale gray lore, black with fact and white with convention. But I have found no substantial reasons for concluding that there are any quite black threads in it, or any white ones. (1966: 132)

We shall return to Quine's own philosophical views later on.[13]

A significant and weighty internal criticism of positivism additional to Quine's was Carl Hempel's "Problems and changes in the empiricist criterion of meaning" published in the *Revue Internationale de Philosophie* (Hempel 1950). Hempel's characteristically careful and incisive analysis displayed by its own impressive example the philosophical virtues of logical empiricism and of analytic philosophy at their best. One ultimate effect of its content, however, was to suggest that the various verificationist criteria that had been continually proposed as requirements on empirical meaningfulness or cognitive significance by the positivists were highly problematic indeed. Many such reductive empiricist proposals would in fact rule out clearly significant aspects of scientific theories themselves; other proposals would allow in, as meaningful, statements that the positivists clearly wished to exclude; and finally, the status of the verification principle itself as an unverifiable linguistic proposal remained highly suspect by its own lights. Hempel was laboring tirelessly to keep the logical empiricist ship afloat, but it would not be long before he and others would take the philosophy of science in directions leading away from positivistic empiricism (owing to the influence, among others, of Quine, Wilfrid Sellars, Hilary Putnam, and especially Thomas Kuhn; more on these thinkers below).

The most visible transformation in philosophy in America at mid-century, however, came as a result of a new style of linguistic analysis that was beginning to make its presence felt on the American scene after World War II. Let us continue to focus on the years surrounding 1950 for evidence of this change.

In 1949 Herbert Feigl and Wilfrid Sellars of the University of Minnesota had put together an important anthology of articles entitled *Readings in Philosophical Analysis*. In 1950 the two of them also co-founded the journal *Philosophical Studies* as the first periodical in America explicitly dedicated to publishing articles in the style of what was now coming to self-consciousness as "analytic philosophy." The selections in the Feigl–Sellars *Readings* for the most part reflected the various streams of influence in pragmatism, positivism, and analytic philosophy which have been discussed up to this point. As Feigl and Sellars put it in their preface to the volume:

> The conception of philosophical analysis underlying our selections springs from two major traditions in recent thought, the Cambridge movement deriving from Moore and Russell, and the Logical Positivism of the Vienna Circle (Wittgenstein, Schlick, Carnap) together with the Scientific Empiricism of the Berlin group (led by Reichenbach). These, together with related developments in America stemming from Realism and Pragmatism, and the relatively independent contributions of the Polish logicians have increasingly merged to create an approach to philosophical problems which we frankly consider a decisive turn in the history of philosophy. (Feigl and Sellars 1949: vi)

Feigl and Sellars were correct in their assessment that there had been developing in twentieth-century analytic philosophy a new way of practicing the discipline that would prove to be tremendously influential in the coming decades, and remains so today. A large part of that influence in the 1950s and 1960s, however, would in fact be due to a further influx of philosophical ideas and methods from Britain not represented in that volume, and in particular from Wittgenstein's later philosophical work (which had been circulating by word of mouth and in transcribed conversations and lecture notes since the 1930s). One year after Feigl and Sellars's *Readings in Philosophical Analysis* there appeared in 1950 another anthology of essays, with the similar title *Philosophical Analysis: A Collection of Essays*, edited by Max Black (1909–88) of Cornell University. This collection, both in its preface by Black and in many of its selections, evinces the emergence of a noticeably different philosophical emphasis and style from what was represented in the Feigl and Sellars volume.

In the preface to his collection Black confines himself to "some informal comments upon the work of Russell, Moore, and Wittgenstein; these may serve to recall the complexity of the recent historical background and act as a deterrent against treating 'Philosophical Analysis' as a 'School' having well defined articles of association" (Black 1950: 2). Black calls attention to Russell's conception of philosophical method as "*the application of scientific methods to philosophy*" (ibid.). As we have seen, this view of philosophy as a cooperative, most general scientific endeavor was also stressed by many of the thinkers associated with pragmatism, realism, naturalism, and positivism in the first half of the century in America, as it would later be vigorously endorsed again by Quine and other philosophical naturalists in the analytic tradition. Significantly, however, Black suggests that "these hopes [are] no longer so widely held" and that they were in fact based on "a radical misconstruction of the relations between philosophy and science" (Black 1950: 5). Referring "to some (though not all) of the writers of the essays which follow" – among the American and British authors he has in mind are Alice Ambrose, G. E. M. Anscombe, O. K. Bouwsma, Norman Malcolm, Gilbert Ryle, and John Wisdom – Black suggests that it may seem to them,

> as it seems to me, that Russell has systematically, though unwittingly, *misused* such crucial terms as "doubt," "evidence," and "inference"; that no "philo-sophical" evidence can be superior to the evidence acceptable in a court of law or in other everyday contexts; and that Russell's pursuit of the indubitable is a jack-o'-lantern hunt for mathematical demonstration of matters of fact. (1950: 5–6, italics added)

It is when Black finally turns to the work of Ludwig Wittgenstein that a very different conception of the nature of philosophical *analysis* begins to emerge.[14]

Wittgenstein had published his *Tractatus* back in 1921–2. Aspects of this enigmatic and brilliant work had been appropriated both by Russell in his logical atomism and in the logical positivism of the Vienna Circle. During the 1930s, however, Wittgenstein's lectures at Cambridge were being transcribed and were showing evidence of a funda-mental shift in his thinking away from the doctrines of the *Tractatus*. In 1936 Ernest Nagel, in "Impressions and appraisals of analytic philosophy in Europe" (a title that represents a very early use of the label "analytic philosophy"), reported back to America as follows:

While I was at Cambridge a letter from a friend in Vienna assured me that in certain circles the existence of Wittgenstein is debated with as much ingenuity as the historicity of Christ has been disputed in others. I have seen Wittgenstein, though only casually, and therefore feel competent to decide that question. But since I did not receive his permission to attend his lectures, and since except to small, exclusive groups at Cambridge and Vienna his present views are not accessible, I feel extraordinarily hesitant in reporting on the doctrines he holds. For various reasons Wittgenstein refuses to publish; and even among his students of years' standing there is considerable doubt as to what his beliefs are on crucial issues. My information about Wittgenstein's views depends upon certain notes on his lectures which are in circulation and upon conversations with students and disciples both at Cambridge and Vienna. Mystery and a queerly warped personality lend charm to many a philosophy which otherwise is not very significant; but in spite of the esoteric atmosphere which surrounds Wittgenstein, I think his views are both interesting and important. (Nagel 1936: 16–17)

Although Nagel could not gain entrance into the exclusive Wittgensteinian club, his reconnaissance work evidenced in the succeeding pages successfully brought out much of the spirit of the thinking of the later Wittgenstein, which would not appear in published form until the appearance of his *Philosophical Investigations* in 1953 (Wittgenstein died in 1951), but which would soon become highly influential in American philosophy.

"The original sin committed in discussing meanings, according to Wittgenstein," Nagel reports, "is to suppose that meanings are *things* of some sort" (1936: 18), as Frege, Meinong, Bolzano, and others had arguably done. Wittgenstein's view, as Nagel was able to reconstruct fairly accurately from his rummaging in Cambridge, is that

the meaning of *all* expressions must be determined by discovering the usages which govern them. The usage to which an expression is subject is called by Wittgenstein its *grammar*, so that philosophy is an activity of clarifying the meaning of expressions by making explicit their grammar. Sentences obtain their significance from the system of signs or language to which they belong; the meaning, "the life of signs," lies in their use. (1936: 18)

This is not to say, however, that there are explicit rules for every occasion of use of a given linguistic expression. At best "there is what Wittgenstein calls a 'family resemblance' between the different grammatical rules exemplified in each of these occasions; intellectual confusions result in supposing that the vague resemblances between them merge into identity" (1936: 19). On Wittgenstein's view, Nagel writes, "the philosophic function is not to *legislate* meanings, but to note and describe the various meanings which expressions have. It is in this way that the philosopher can become the physician to some of the ills besetting mankind" (ibid.).

By the time of Max Black's edited collection in 1950 there had been other American philosophers who, unlike Nagel, had found actual entrance into the exclusive inner sanctum of Wittgenstein's Cambridge seminars and were bringing his new "thera-peutic" philosophy to bear on the American scene. One such philosopher was Alice Ambrose (1906–2001) of Smith College also known as Alice Ambrose Lazerowitz after marrying her colleague and frequent co-author, the philosopher Morris Lazerowitz in 1938. Ambrose received her BA from Millikin University in Illinois in 1928 and her Ph.D. from Wisconsin in 1932. She received a second doctoral degree at Cambridge during the crucial period in the 1930s when Wittgenstein chose a select few, herself among them, to transcribe the lectures known as the "Blue Book" (1933–4) and the "Brown Book" (1934–5). Ambrose's contribution to the Max Black volume in 1950 was "The problem of linguistic adequacy," and at one point she notes that she is "indebted to lectures at Cambridge University by Dr. L. Wittgenstein" (Ambrose Lazerowitz 1950: 32). Ambrose argues in the manner of the later Wittgenstein that if we *look to the actual functions and uses* of words as they are employed in ordinary language, we shall find that, for example, the vagueness so much complained of by formal logicians is not an inadequacy of ordinary language to be "corrected" on the basis of some "perfectionist ideal." Rather, "vagueness resides in our language and precision in what it inexactly designates" (Ambrose Lazerowitz 1950: 33). "What would it be like," she asks in a manner characteristic of the Wittgensteinian philosophers of the period, "for language to be free from vagueness? Does 'having no possible borderline cases' describe a possible situation? I think it does not and that we have only the pretense of a standard in the demand that words be applicable in such a way as always to set off things having ϕ from those not having it" (1950: 34). The philosophical analysis of the multifarious forms of living language is now understood in a very different sense from the earlier ideal of the analysis of language into its rock-bottom logical atoms on a supposed "ideal language" account or "logical reconstruction."

Norman Malcolm (1911–90) was perhaps the most well-known of the American philosophers who during this period introduced the ideas of the later Wittgenstein to an American audience. Malcolm was born in Kansas and received his Ph.D. from Harvard. He taught at Princeton in 1940 after having studied at Cambridge in the late 1930s with Wittgenstein, with whom he maintained a close relationship thereafter. He was at Cornell University from 1947 to 1979, after which he emigrated to Britain. Malcolm is perhaps best known for his anti-skeptical arguments against the coherence of Descartes's dream argument, as well as for his attempt to strengthen the "ontological argument" for God's existence. In 1942 Malcolm published an important article in the Schilpp-edited *Library of Living Philosophers* volume on *The Philosophy of G. E. Moore*, entitled "Moore and ordinary language" (Malcolm 1942).[15] In the Max Black volume in 1950 Malcolm has a long piece, "The verification argument" examining the form this argument takes among authors such as C. I. Lewis and Carnap, for whom in principle, owing to the potentially infinite number of hypothetical statements taken to be implied, *no complete verification* of any empirical proposition or hypothesis is possible. Malcolm uses ordinary examples to argue, to the contrary, that there are clear cases in which I can fully adequately verify some humdrum empirical fact (e.g. that Milton's *Paradise Lost* begins with the words "Of Man's first disobedience …"), where this verification is in no intelligible sense "incomplete." According to Malcolm it "is *not* possible that I should continue the verification of that fact because, in those circumstances, we should not describe *anything* as 'further verification' of it. The verification *comes to an end*" (Malcolm 1950: 277). (Related views on the part of Wittgenstein himself would later be published posthumously in 1969 in his important work, *On Certainty*.) This type of linguistic analysis was very influential in America well into the 1960s, and was exhibited in such works as A. I. Melden's *Free Action* (1961) and Stanley Cavell's *Must We Mean What We Say? A Book of Essays* (1969).[16]

So-called "ordinary-language" views of this kind do not entail, of course, that *every* concept embodied in some ordinary linguistic practice or other is true, or that every criterial or "grammatical" distinction reflected in our everyday linguistic practices is valid. What they do suggest is that attention to the conceptual distinctions embodied in actual usage, as well as in the "language-games" incarnate in various "forms of life" or social practices, might show that distinctively *philosophical* puzzles about mind, free will, knowledge, morals, and so on are themselves typically generated by dubious generalizations and doubtful contrasts. Consequently such puzzles would require dissolution or philosophical therapy rather than solution on their own confused terms. From the perspective of this variety of linguistic philosophical analysis, the widespread goal (characteristic of logical atomism and positivism) of constructing "ideal languages" is misguided if it is taken to be anything other than an exercise in formal logic. The usual philosophical analyses, translations, and paraphrases into a putatively ideal logical form – insofar as the attempt was made to extrapolate beyond specialized formal contexts – would typically be viewed by these post-World War II "Oxford School" and Wittgensteinian philosophers as importing just the sorts of conceptual or grammatical confusions highlighted above.[17]

There were many important criticisms leveled against the strategies of linguistic analysis employed by the ordinary-language philosophers, the most important of which are well represented in Richard Rorty's anthology, *The Linguistic Turn* (1967). In general many American philosophers within the analytic tradition came increasingly to believe that the insights of the conceptual-linguistic analysts could be combined with more bold attempts at naturalistic or metaphysical philosophical theorizing of the sort that the ordinary-language philosophers had wanted to resist. One example of such a philosopher was Wilfrid Sellars, and the comparison of his views with those of his father Roy Wood Sellars will make for an interesting case study of two different generations of American philosophy spanning the twentieth century.

One case study in philosophical continuity and change across two generations

Wilfrid Sellars (1912–87) of the universities of Iowa, Minnesota, Yale, and from 1962 to 1987 at the University of Pittsburgh, was one American philosopher who internalized insights from all of the main European influences which, as we have seen, eventually came under the rubric of "analytic philosophy" over the first two-thirds of the century. Yet Sellars's philosophy also developed in new philosophical guises many of the positions that had been articulated by his father Roy Wood Sellars in the distinctively American milieu of the debates between the Hegelian idealists, the pragmatists, the realists (both neo- and critical), and the naturalists, of the first three or four decades of the twentieth century. Both Roy Wood and Wilfrid defended versions of physical realism and evolutionary naturalism in metaphysics, critical realism in epistemology, and subtle versions of non-reductive materialism in the philosophy of mind. Both also stressed the vital importance of the history of philosophy as well as the idea that philosophy should strive to be thoroughly systematic and synoptic in its speculative vision. Both were atheistic humanists who defended the priority of science in telling us how things are, but also the priority of rational, communal reflection on human welfare in our deliberations concerning how things *ought* to be.

However, as we have seen, much had changed in philosophy in America by the time Wilfrid began writing in the post-World War II scene, and these changes are interestingly reflected in the differing fabrics of the philosophical works of father and son. To an elderly Roy Wood, looking back at it all across the century in his *Reflections on American Philosophy from Within* (1969), it seemed as if American philosophy had lost some of its native vitality as a result of the influence of the various imported philosophies from Britain and Germany surveyed above:

> It is not surprising that the next generation after mine of American thinkers turned to Great Britain with its cultural prestige, and what seemed to me, as an onlooker, its immersion in debate between Oxford and Cambridge. I do not want to oversimplify. But since I could not agree with either Russell or Moore on fundamental points … it seemed to me that the so-called *analytic philosophy* which got quite a vogue was ambivalent. In one sense, I liked its emphasis. In another sense, it did not seem to me very creative in either epistemology or ontology. American addiction to it and disregard of its own momentum struck me as a form of neo-colonialism.
>
> [...] Analysis was a word to conjure with and then came the movement called that of "ordinary language." But all this was, in effect, a clearing of the ground. Philosophy in partnership with science could not be made that easy, as Bertrand Russell pointed out. And with increased communication at work something of the nature of interplay between the United States and Great Britain is occurring. I hope much from it. (R. W. Sellars 1969: ch. 1, "The nature of the project")

Roy Wood Sellars thought there were systematic questions concerning the nature of mind, perception, and organic "levels of reality" that had been addressed with more insight by the American pragmatists, realists, and naturalists (including, of course, himself) than by the mathematical logicians, logical positivists, and ordinary-language philosophers of more recent vogue. As noted earlier, there is a group of philosophers and historians in America who would emphatically agree with many of the historical sentiments expressed by Roy Wood Sellars above. These thinkers call for a renewal of the sort of engaged, comparatively non-technical, culturally and socially conscious philosophical reflections that characterized much of the work of classical American philosophy, with its roots in Emerson, Peirce, James, Royce, Dewey, Mead, Santayana, Whitehead, and others. This is sometimes contrasted with what is portrayed as the comparatively spiritless, socially detached, stultified and professionalized academic discipline that resulted from the successive trends in analytic and linguistic philosophy outlined above.

It is arguable to the contrary, however, that it was in large part due to his immersion in the works of such thinkers as Russell, Carnap, Ryle, and Wittgenstein that his son Wilfrid Sellars was able to give his philosophical naturalism an argumentative depth and conceptual sophistication that is generally not achieved in the more discursive, non-technical and highly readable works of his father. Whereas Roy Wood tended systematically to sketch desired philosophical results (admittedly often with significant originality and insight), Wilfrid was able to produce detailed philosophical theories. For example, Roy Wood was reaching in perceptive but often largely metaphorical ways for an ontological nominalism that might "do justice," as he would put it, to our grasp of meanings and to the intentional directedness of thought. He remarked, for instance, that "it is merely *as if* there were universals because meanings have the capacity to disclose the characteristics of similar things" (R. W. Sellars 1932: 156). However, it is not clear that we are ever given a detailed account by Roy Wood of what such "disclosure" consists in or of how it is possible. Wilfrid, on the other hand, was able to adapt and transform Carnap's conceptions of logical syntax, meaning rules, and linguistic frameworks to develop in the 1950s what amounted to the first detailed *functional role semantics*. In a nutshell, the latter view was a robust normative and causal account of meaning-as-use, and upon that basis Sellars constructed a theory of thoughts as inner episodes in a functionally conceived "mentalese." The examples of this sort of contrast between the two thinkers and the two generations could be multiplied.

The non-reductive materialism that was being sketched in original ways by Roy Wood Sellars should certainly be credited, as noted by Jaegwon Kim (1934–) earlier, with anticipating many developments later in the century. But it was the tools provided by the various phases of the logical and linguistic turn in the analytic tradition that enabled Wilfrid Sellars to develop more powerful and substantive theories on just how (as he frames the central issues) the perceptual, conceptual, and normative dimensions of the perceptually experienced world or *manifest image* of persons-in-the-world are to be successfully integrated with the comprehensively causal and naturalistic picture of physical nature that is projected in our ongoing *scientific image* of that same world.

Somewhat ironically, then, it might plausibly be argued in relation to this "test case" that the so-called "neo-colonial" philosophical influences of which the 87–year-old Roy Wood Sellars complained in 1967 were in point of fact the indispensable enabling factors for the various cutting edge and – currently in the twenty-first century – much discussed theories that his son had been developing in defense of their shared naturalistic outlook since the late 1940s.

The specific mid-century "analytic" contributions highlighted in the previous sections may also be seen from this case study to have sharpened the overall systematic naturalism that Wilfrid Sellars effectively inherited from his father. For example, Wilfrid did indeed put to use the insights into the "logic" or "grammar" of our ordinary rule-governed concepts by such thinkers as Ryle, Austin, and the later Wittgenstein. But he also departed sharply from those thinkers and embraced his father's and Russell's view, quoted above, that "philosophy in partnership with science" ought to have more ambitious theoretical, explanatory, and systematic aspirations than many philosophers (in both the "analytic" and "Continental" traditions) were inclined to entertain in the middle decades of the century. Malcolm, for instance, in company with the three British thinkers just mentioned, would from Sellars's perspective be right to stress that, for example, the language we learn, and therefore the concepts we acquire, are governed by implicit norms according to which our ordinary perceptual judgments in standard circumstances will generally be *correct* (other things being equal). And as such these judgments will indeed constitute instances of reliable perceptual knowledge of ordinary physical objects, rather than such knowledge having to be inferred from an allegedly more basic acquaintance with the character of one's own sensations or sense-data. This is part of Sellars's famous rejection in his "Empiricism and the philosophy of mind" (1956) of the *myth of the given* and his account of knowledge as a standing within the *logical space of reasons*.[18] But all four of those thinkers, Sellars believes, were wrong to simply leave the matter there, satisfied with their correct ordinary-language diagnosis of the confusion of the normative (or conceptual) with the natural (or causal) dimensions of discourse that lies at the heart of classical sense-datum views such as Russell's. For according to Sellars, in the spirit of his father's generation of American philosophers, we can and must push further and attempt a systematic theoretical or metaphysical account of the phenomena (in this particular case, an account of the constraining and representational role played by non-conceptual sensations in our various perceptual experiences).

In short, the conceptual insights of the ordinary-language philosophers must, on Sellars's view, be combined with speculative theorizing concerning the ultimate nature of mind, meaning, and matter, if the philosophical and scientific quest for a truly adequate understanding of "man-in-the-world" is to be brought closer to completion. The trademark Wittgensteinian emphasis on the public and communal nature of all meaning and hence of all conceptualization, as normatively rule-governed, was essentially correct. However, it is only in light of just the sort of substantive, naturalistic theorizing in philosophy that would typically be abjured by the more "quietist" Wittgensteinian philosophers, that such conceptual insights can really be put to use in providing an overall satisfactory philosophical and explanatory account of the nature of the human being within the physical world. On Sellars's meta-philosophical outlook, then, the boldly systematic and naturalistic philosophical theorizing of the sort often practiced by pre-1950 American pragmatists, realists, and naturalists (including, of course, his father) as well as by the great figures in the history of philosophy from Plato and Aristotle to Kant and Hegel, must be rejuvenated within the new technical medium if the truly revolutionary insights of the analytic movement, as Sellars did indeed view them, were to bear their proper philosophical fruit.

Once again with some historical irony, then, it seemed that what was needed in order to fulfill the promise of the methods introduced by the vigorously anti-metaphysical European imports of positivism and linguistic analysis was an equally vigorous rebirth of metaphysical speculation and epistemological reflection using those same sharpened analytical tools. And indeed it was the distinctive combination of analytical, logical, and linguistic precision with richly metaphysical, naturalistic, causal theorizing that was arguably to make America the most productive and creative site of philosophical activity in the world in the last third of the twentieth century.

However, philosophers' attitudes toward the theory of meaning in the second half of the twentieth century in America were soon to undergo more radical changes than in the case of Wilfrid Sellars, whose views on meaning and conceptual analysis, rules and normativity, in many respects shared certain fundamental assumptions with the views on meaning and rules that had been developed by Carnap, Ryle, and Wittgenstein. Although broadly Wittgensteinian views on meaning of this kind have since about the 1980s once again become the center of lively philosophical discussion (see for example Robert Brandom (1994) and in certain respects the British philosopher John McDowell (1994), both at the University of Pittsburgh), the impressive hive of activity in analytic philosophy in America from the 1960s through the 1990s was based to a large extent on new ways of thinking about mind, language, and meaning that were developed within the American analytic and neo-pragmatist traditions. It is to these particular developments that we shall now turn in the final two sections.

Analytic philosophy in the naturalistic American style comes of age

For many American analytic philosophers from the 1960s to the end of the century the various publications of W. V. O. Quine represented an important turning point for the discipline, from "Two dogmas of empiricism" and other articles in the 1950s to *Word and Object* and his other books in the 1960s. The various notions of *conceptual analysis* that had been articulated throughout the major developments in analytic philosophy discussed above had sought to bequeath to philosophers the primary task of conceptual clarification. Quine charted a different path, however, by arguing that philosophers should not take themselves to be in the business of conceptual analysis or meaning analysis at all, at least not in the various senses in which those enterprises have typically been understood by philosophers.

In "Two dogmas," as we saw briefly earlier, Quine argued that there is no principled, non-circular way of distinguishing the class of statements that are analytic (or necessary, or a priori) from those that are synthetic or have empirical content. The belief in the analytic/synthetic distinction is an unsupported "dogma" of empiricism, for Quine. Furthermore, he argued, the flipside of that same dogma is the reductive empiricist idea that there are particular empirical propositions or observation statements that may be directly verified or falsified in isolation from one's wider system of beliefs and assumptions, thus allegedly providing foundational evidence for the latter. To the contrary, Quine argues, the "unit of empirical significance is the whole of science" (Quine 1953: 42). In the following famous passage from "Two dogmas" Quine sums up his holistic and anti-foundationalist picture of human knowledge in metaphorical terms:

The totality of our so-called knowledge or beliefs, from the most casual matters of geography and history to the profoundest laws of atomic physics or even of pure mathematics and logic, is a man-made fabric which impinges on experience only along the edges. Or, to change the figure, total science is like a field of force whose boundary conditions are experience. A conflict with experience at the periphery occasions readjustments in the interior of the field. ... But the total field is so underdetermined by its boundary conditions, experience, that there is much latitude of choice as to what statements to reëvaluate in the light of any single contrary experience.

[...] Any statement can be held true come what may, if we make drastic enough adjustments elsewhere in the system. Even a statement very close to the periphery can be held true in the face of recalcitrant experience by pleading hallucination or by amending certain statements of the kind called logical laws. Conversely, by the same token, no statement is immune to revision. (1953: 42–3)

The slogan, "there is no First Philosophy" epitomizes Quine's anti-foundationalist point that there are no items of knowledge, whether a priori or observational, that are somehow justifiable independently of questions concerning the *pragmatic* virtues (of simplicity, predictiveness, conservatism, etc.) of the overall system of beliefs or conceptual scheme concerned. At the outset we saw that Peirce's critique of the idea of "intuitive" knowledge had made many of these same points (and indeed, Peirce also anticipated many aspects of Wilfrid Sellars's critique of the myth of the given mentioned above as well). Quine in fact presents his resulting position as a pragmatism that is more thoroughgoing and naturalistic than that of his immediate predecessors:

Carnap, Lewis, and others take a pragmatic stand on the question of choosing between language forms, scientific frameworks; but their pragmatism leaves off at the imagined boundary between the analytic and the synthetic. In repudiating such a boundary I espouse a more thorough pragmatism. Each man is given a scientific heritage plus a continuing barrage of sensory stimulation; and the considerations which guide him in warping his scientific heritage to fit his continuing sensory promptings are, where rational, pragmatic. (1953: 46)

Reminiscent of Carnap's "tolerance" in relation to the development of alternative linguistic frameworks as well as of James's pragmatic pluralism, in choosing between alternative conceptual schemes Quine's "counsel is tolerance and an experimental spirit" ("On what there is," in Quine 1953: 19). If our interest is in epistemology, for instance, a particularly strict "phenomenalistic" language *might* be appropriate (see the discussion of Goodman below). But this "point of view is one among various, corresponding to one among our various interests and purposes" (1953: 19). For purposes of prediction and simplicity of theory, the "physicalistic" conceptual scheme will have priority.

In his now classic book *Word and Object* (1960, dedicated "To Rudolf Carnap: Teacher and Friend"), Quine developed a comprehensive philosophical outlook based on the rejection of analytic a priori "truths of meaning" and carrying through the anti-foundationalist, holistic empiricism outlined above, along methodologically behaviorist lines. Since there is no First Philosophy our knowledge is best pictured, not on Descartes's metaphor of a house built on a firm foundation, but rather on the logical positivist Otto Neurath's metaphor of sailors having to repair a ship while at sea: "Neurath has likened science to a boat which, if we are to rebuild it, we must rebuild plank by plank while staying afloat in it. The philosopher and the scientist are in the same boat" (Quine 1960: 3). We have no choice but the productive one of accepting our best ongoing, revisable scientific theories about the nature of the world and of ourselves. Against that inherited background the philosopher or the reflective scientist can practice what Quine called "Epistemology naturalized" (in Quine 1969). This is essentially the attempt to formulate causal-explanatory (and for Quine, largely behavioristic) hypotheses about how human beings have been able to generate predictively successful beliefs, theories, and conceptual schemes from the relatively meager sensory inputs which enter through the sense organs. "The stimulation of his sensory receptors is all the evidence anybody has had to go on, ultimately, in arriving at his picture of the world. Why not just see how this construction really proceeds? Why not settle for psychology?" (Quine 1969: 75). In further spelling out the ways in which, as he contends, our "theories and beliefs in general are under-determined by the totality of possible sensory evidence time without end" (1960: 78), Quine developed his controversial theses of the *indeterminacy of translation* ("rival systems" of interpretation, he contends, "can fit the totality of speech dispositions to perfection" and yet "still specify mutually incompatible translations of countless sentences," 1960: 72) and *ontological relativity* or the indeterminacy of reference (diverse ontologies can preserve the same repository of evidence, which consists in observation sentences considered as wholes).

It is perhaps fair to say that Quine's widespread influence on analytic philosophers in America since the 1960s has had more to do with his naturalistic conception of philosophical method and his skeptical challenges to traditional views than with his own conclusions concerning mind and knowledge, meaning and necessity – conclusions which to many have appeared to be largely negative in import. Many philosophers came to share Quine's emphasis on the importance to future philosophy of naturalistic inquiries into psychological processes and causal mechanisms, in contrast to the frequent dismissal of such inquiries as irrelevant during the heyday of linguistic and conceptual analysis. After Quine the idea of philosophy as engaged primarily in the analysis of concepts or meanings was certainly put on the defensive. The naturalistic, fallibilist and non-foundationalist conception of the nature of philosophy, which as we have seen had in many ways already been championed by the American pragmatists, realists, and naturalists during the first half of the century, had once again returned to the fore, now practiced with significantly sharpened analytical tools.

In point of fact, however, most naturalistically inclined analytic philosophers soon advanced beyond Quine's strictures and offered causal theories attempting to illuminate rather than merely set aside questions concerning the sources and nature of the intentionality of thought and belief, the intensionality of meaning and necessity, and the normativity of knowledge and of value claims themselves.[19] In America from the 1960s through to the end of the century such branches of philosophy as the philosophy of mind, philosophy of language, epistemology, logic, philosophy of science, metaphysics, and moral philosophy have witnessed a rebirth of vigorous theorizing conducted primarily in the manner of what might be called *analytic naturalism*. The predominant style of philosophizing among American philosophers has continued to make use of the powerful tools of analysis and the new philosophical problems inherited from Frege, Russell, Wittgenstein, Carnap, Austin, Quine, and the other analytic philosophers, but more often than not without the previously dominant view that the classical problems of philosophy had somehow to be dissolved or diagnosed as confusions rather than being tackled head on. There was an open-ended, speculative quality to the more recent bouts of philosophical theorizing that was made possible, in large part, by the neo-pragmatist, fallibilist and naturalist critiques of positivism and other foundationalist conceptions of analysis that had been carried out by Quine and Sellars among others. Of course, equally vigorous critics of naturalism, as well as proponents of various alternative views on the significance of the decline of foundationalist analytic philosophy have been continual participants in these various dialogues, which – philosophy being what it is – have been the richer for it.

It is outside the limited scope of this essay to attempt to survey the various technical approaches that have been developed over the last three decades within the branches of analytic philosophy just mentioned, most of which are at any rate covered in adequate detail within the appropriate chapters of the present volume. Analytic philosophy of mind and philosophy of language underwent particularly productive changes during the 1960s and 1970s, however, and a brief note of some of the more notable of these developments will serve to illustrate both the analytic style of naturalism that continues to be practiced by many American philosophers, as well as a robust revival of *metaphysics* within the analytic tradition.

The development of *functionalism* in the philosophy of mind, associated in particular with the American philosophers Hilary Putnam (see the Putnam 1975 collection), David Lewis (1941–2001, Lewis 1983 collection), Daniel Dennett (1969, 1978), and Jerry Fodor (1968, 1975), made more plausible than heretofore the naturalistic hypothesis that our thoughts and other mental processes are in fact, ontologically, nothing over and above certain postulated or a posteriori discoverable neurophysiological processes. The various conceptual distinctions between the mental and the physical, it was argued in a variety of ways, are in principle consistent with mental happenings *turning out to be* certain highly complex goings-on in the central nervous system.[20] Interesting new problems and challenges continue to arise for any such materialist account of consciousness and intentionality, functionalist or otherwise. In itself, however, the development of detailed and plausible naturalistic accounts of the mind since the 1960s has arguably represented one of the most significant philosophical developments in the history of metaphysics, successfully opening up new conceptual and explanatory possibilities and marking a genuine advance on previously more crude materialist speculations.

In both philosophy of mind and philosophy of language Noam Chomsky's work on innate, representational "depth grammars" in theoretical linguistics provided an additional impetus for functionalist (e.g. computationalist) theories of mind, particularly influencing the work of Jerry Fodor (1935–). For example, this passage from Chomsky's major 1965 work, *Aspects of a Theory of Syntax*, illustrates the dominant "top-down" approach characteristic of the new cognitive theories in philosophy and psychology that were gradually replacing more behavioristic outlooks (such as Quine's):

> The mentalist … need make no assumptions about the possible physiological basis for the mental reality that he studies. In particular, he need not deny that there is such a basis. One would guess, rather, that it is the mentalistic studies that will ultimately be of greatest value for the investigations of neurophysiological mechanisms, since they alone are concerned with determining abstractly the properties that such mechanisms must exhibit and the functions they must perform. (Chomsky 1965: 193)

Fodor's work has been influential in attempting to develop a non-reductive, cognitive symbol-processing conception of the mind along these lines in a series of books from *Psychological Explanation* (1968) and *The Language of Thought* (1975) to many other works over the last three decades of the century. In these areas interdisciplinary programs specializing in cognitive studies have become part of a productive tendency to cross the traditional university borders between the arts and humanities on the one side and the sciences on the other. These developments have found particularly fertile ground in the various strains of scientific naturalism that we have seen to be a pervasive feature of American philosophy generally, and which to a significant degree distinguished the American style of analytic philosophy from its British counterparts throughout the century.

The views on mind of Daniel Dennett (1942–) and Donald Davidson (1917–2003) represent two further influential attempts since the 1970s to explain the predictive efficacy of our higher-level interpretations of human beings as rational, intentional agents within a broadly physicalist ontology (Dennett 1978; Davidson 2001a). Dennett introduced the notion of the *intentional stance*, according to which attributions of coherent beliefs and desires to complex systems are often indispensable for predicting their behavior. And Davidson articulated what he called *anomalous monism*, according to which interpretations of human agents as governed by rationality assumptions do not uncover any strict psychological laws (hence, "anomalous"), yet such mental events are also causally efficacious in virtue of being "token identical" with certain physical events (hence, "monism"). Whether such attributional and interpretationist accounts of the nature of mind in a physical world are able to provide sufficiently realist accounts of *mental causation* continues to be a vigorous topic of debate.

In the philosophy of language, in addition to mentalist linguistic theories inspired by Chomsky and various versions of conceptual role semantics along functionalist lines, there were certain other developments in the theory of meaning that inspired what might be called the *neo-metaphysical* turn that took place in analytic philosophy during the final three decades of the twentieth century. Three key thinkers in this regard were Saul Kripke, Hilary Putnam, and David Lewis. The connection between the philosophy of language and the new metaphysical turn may be brought out by briefly considering some lines of thinking from two groundbreaking publications from the 1970s: Hilary Putnam's "The meaning of 'meaning' " (1975) and Saul Kripke's *Naming and Necessity* (1980, from three lectures given in 1970 at Princeton). Kripke's work may be taken as the clearest example of a style of analytic philosophy that broke sharply with the pragmatic, verificationist, and meaning-analysis approaches discussed above, and which remains among the most widely practiced ways of approaching philosophical problems in America today (see Soames 2003).[21]

Saul Kripke was born in Omaha, Nebraska in 1940, and he developed a ground-breaking semantics for quantified modal logic (the formal logic of necessity and possibility) at the age of 15, and a proof of its completeness by age 18. His watershed work *Naming and Necessity* consists of three lectures from the early 1970s that were apparently delivered without notes and which are highly readable despite their conceptual and technical sophistication.

The lectures begin with familiar problems in the philosophy of language concerning the reference of proper names, but Kripke's rejection of the reigning *descriptivist* approaches, according to which the reference of a name is determined by associated descriptions or senses (for example, "Aristotle was the student of Plato") quickly develops in the lectures into a full-blooded metaphysical *essentialism*. This is the view that some properties of an object or kind are necessary or essential to it, and hence are possessed by that object in all possible circumstances or "possible worlds" in which it exists (hence the link with his technical works in modal logic and possible worlds semantics). For example, *being H_2O* might be essential to water, assuming the correctness of our a posteriori discovery that water is in fact H_2O. This leads to Kripke's crucial idea that there are a posteriori discoverable *necessities*, which is in pointed contrast to the traditional Kantian, pragmatist, conventionalist, and analytic equation of the a priori and the conceptually necessary. Necessity is now viewed as a feature of reality, as a metaphysical matter of truth in all (or all relevant) possible worlds, rather than being an artifact of our thought or of language.

The bridge between the philosophy of language and the new metaphysical essentialism was made by what came to be called (if not by Kripke himself) the new *causal theory of reference*. In *Naming and Necessity*, crudely put, the treatment of reference was built upon the consideration that it is not the descriptions which, as far as we know, Aristotle happens to satisfy that make the name "Aristotle" refer to that particular human being, since many of these descriptions might conceivably be false. Rather, it is the causal or (for Kripke) historical chain from an "initial baptism" that links the name "Aristotle" directly with a certain human being, whatever descriptions turn out to be true of him; and it is this causal-historical chain that constitutes the real word/world relation of reference. Putnam (1975) developed similar notions into an influential conception of the meaning of *natural kind* terms, according to which the meaning of such terms as "water" is partly a matter of what the real essential nature of water turns out to be (e.g. H_2O), no matter how it is "internally," mentally, or descriptively taken to be by us at any given time. Hence, our meanings and the contents of our thoughts turn out to be determined in large part not by how things seem internal to some descriptive scheme, but rather by external natures and facts pertaining to mind-independent reality; and so in this and related senses *externalism* was often conceived to be central to the new *metaphysical realism*.

David Lewis (1941–2001) and others also appealed to the idea of possible worlds to address a host of traditional philosophical problems in epistemology, philosophy of language, and metaphysics (see Lewis 1986). The development of a wide variety of externalist conceptions of mind, knowledge, and meaning also grew out of Donald Davidson's truth-conditional theory of meaning (Davidson 2001b), and from various causal-*reliabilist* theories of knowledge that had been developed in the wake of the famous "Gettier" problem in epistemology (Gettier 1963, "Is justified true belief knowledge?"; and, e.g., Alvin Goldman 1967, 1986). These are just a few of the most well-known ways in which analytic philosophers from the 1970s to the turn of the century shifted, in a spirit broadly similar to Kripke's groundbreaking work, toward the development of technical approaches to traditional problems that build on metaphysical realist, modal realist, or causal-naturalistic starting points.

Quine, as we have seen, had raised problems for classical analytic conceptions of meaning-analysis and had urged an abandonment of those notions in favor of a scientifically naturalized epistemology or psychology. The rise of the new metaphysical realism and essentialism, however, had now given analytic philosophers a way of resuscitating and exploring the problems of philosophy in novel ways, which are still in the process of being worked out and evaluated. Furthermore, many of the enduring pragmatist themes that we have been tracing from Peirce through much of the analytic tradition in America, such as holistic empiricism, naturalism, verificationism, and the primacy of language and action, would in varying degrees be challenged by analytic philosophers who now took themselves to be liberated from many of those allegedly misguided epistemological and meaning constraints. For example, while it is true that many of the new realists and externalists were also naturalists and materialists, Kripke, for example, was neither of the latter. The only constraints on philosophical theorizing were now thought to consist in judgments of overall intuitive plausibility, technical adequacy, and explanatory fecundity. Again with some historical irony, Quine's anti-foundationalist methodological clarion call of "no First Philosophy" was now being enthusiastically embraced by philosophers attracted more to the tropical rainforests of traditional metaphysics and epistemology than to the behaviorist, verificationist, and nominalist desert landscapes preferred by Quine himself.

Not all analytic philosophers embraced the new metaphysical turn, however, and there has in fact been a revival of varieties of *neo-pragmatism* from the 1950s through the turn of the century. (It is interesting to note that Jerry Fodor, writing from the broad perspective of the new metaphysical realism, has characterized these neo-pragmatist tendencies as "the defining catastrophe of analytic philosophy of language and philosophy of mind in the last half of the twentieth century", Fodor 2004: 73–4.)

Some of these neo-pragmatist thinkers consider themselves to be broadly analytic philosophers, while others take themselves to be already in a "post-analytic" period in which the divisions between pragmatism, analytic philosophy, and Continental philosophy are viewed as merely superficial artifacts of the discipline. It will be appropriate to close with some brief remarks on these neo-pragmatist developments.

Neo-pragmatism and other recent developments

In the second half of the twentieth century there was a revival of pragmatism in American philosophy. We have seen this already in the case of Quine and Sellars, who in their different ways embraced many of the lasting themes from Peirce discussed at the outset: fallibilism, holism, non-foundationalist empiricism, naturalism, realism, and the priority of the "outer" over the "inner." The views of Quine and Sellars in fundamental ways also resembled those of Peirce in arguing for the primacy of *scientific* method and explanation in epistemology and ontology. Other neo-pragmatist thinkers in the analytic tradition, however, such as Nelson Goodman (1906–98), Hilary Putnam (since the mid-1970s), and Richard Rorty (1931– 2007), made use of pragmatist ideas from James and Dewey in a more pluralistic manner, reflecting a more thoroughgoing rejection or reworking of the traditional distinctions: fact versus value, the subjective versus the objective, what "depends on us" as opposed to what "depends on the world." According to these thinkers, there is – contrary to what the "metaphysical realists" contend – no one, unique way of representing how the world really is in itself. Rather, there are multiple versions or approaches within any given domain of inquiry or action, and there are no neutral or overarching criteria of rightness or truth apart from considerations internal to those various perspectives. This is not, however, taken to entail an implausible relativism according to which any perspective or conceptual scheme is as good or as true as any other. (Putnam, Kuhn, and Rorty reject the attribution of relativism, while Goodman by contrast defends what he calls a "radical relativism under rigorous constraints, that eventuates in something akin to irrealism," Goodman 1978: x.)

Nelson Goodman received his Ph.D. from Harvard in 1941 and taught at the University of Pennsylvania (1946–64), Brandeis (1964–7), and then Harvard (1968–77). Prior to his professional academic career he was Director of the Walker-Goodman Art Gallery in Boston from 1929 to 1941. Goodman believed that our understandings of the world, whether in the arts or the sciences, whether literal or metaphorical, are achieved by means of symbol systems of various kinds, the complex nature and diversity of which was the primary object of his philosophical investigations. Different symbol systems may be useful and yield understanding while carving up their worlds of objects in different, sometimes incompatible ways. It follows, for Goodman, that the presumption that there must ultimately be one fundamental classification of the world "as it is in itself" is groundless. We should rather speak of *many worlds* (if any), corresponding to the plurality of *versions* of reality that are presented in our various symbolic representations and renderings. Hence the title of Goodman's engaging yet subtle little book in 1978, *Ways of Worldmaking*.

These themes were already in evidence in 1951 in *The Structure of Appearance*, in which Goodman sympathetically criticized Carnap's logical reconstruction of the empirical world in the *Aufbau* and developed his own complex mereological, nominalistic construction of concrete things out of repeatable qualia taken as the basic elements. There is no absolute epistemic priority accorded by Goodman to phenomenal qualia, however; he insists that an alternative physicalistic basis for the constructions could have been chosen instead. The work is pluralist in spirit but rigorously formal in its design and execution. In *Fact, Fiction, and Forecast* Goodman presented his famous *grue paradox* concerning induction: the evidence up to a given future time t that all emeralds are green is also evidence that all emeralds are *grue*, where x is *grue* if and only if x is examined before future time t and is found to be green, or x is not so examined and is blue. Goodman's solution to this puzzle meshes with the pragmatist tradition: we continue to "project" the predicate *green* into the future rather than *grue* because the former has as a matter of fact become entrenched in our linguistic practices. This reflects the fact that what kinds of things there are in a world is a matter of the symbolic system in accordance with which the things of that world are constructed, rendered, and remade. Goodman is better known to many, however, for his important contribution to aesthetics in *The Languages of Art* (1968, with the pluralist theme again to the forefront). Here Goodman's technical sophistication in logic and the philosophy of language combined with his knowledge of the various worlds of art were put to use in applying his general investigations into the various modes of symbolic understanding to the syntactic and semantic structures which, he argues, are embodied in aesthetic representations. The metaphorical and other truths exhibited in the arts, on Goodman's view, are not less objective or otherwise cognitively inferior to the truths articulated in the sciences. Furthermore, not all *rightness* of representation is the stating of truths, and denotation and exemplification (e.g. of emotions) is achieved in the arts in ways that may be assessed as objectively better or worse in a given context.

On a general methodological level Goodman's writings were also important for articulating and exemplifying a form of anti-foundationalist rational justification that John Rawls (1921–2002) of Harvard University – one of the most important moral and political philosophers of the century – called, in his groundbreaking work *A Theory of Justice* (1971), the *method of reflective equilibrium* (see "Twentieth-century political philosophy," Chapter 21). Rawls duly noted that Goodman in *Fact, Fiction, and Forecast* had already emphasized the "process of mutual adjustment of principles and considered judgments" in which the method consists, noting in particular Goodman's "remarks concerning the justification of the principles of deductive and inductive inference" (Rawls 1971: 20).[22] As Goodman had put it, the "point is that rules and particular inferences alike are justified by being brought into agreement with each other" through delicate mutual adjustments, and "in the agreement achieved lies the only justification needed for either" (Goodman 1954: 64). Overall rightness of fit is the goal, within any given working version of reality.

Partly under the influence of Goodman, Hilary Putnam's thought has taken a strong neo-pragmatist turn since the mid-1970s, articulated in what he has called his *internal realism* (or later his "pragmatic," "commonsense," "human" realism, as he has variously characterized it) in contrast to the "God's eye point of view" allegedly characteristic of metaphysical realism. Central to Putnam's later thought is his critique of the correspondence theory of truth (which he sees as a descendent of James's pragmatist criticisms of the "copy theory" of truth), as well as his defense of what he calls *conceptual relativity*; this is a scheme-relative ontological pluralism that is in some ways similar to Goodman's views about multiple incompatible world-versions each of which may nonetheless be true. "That there are ways of describing what are (in some way) the 'same facts' which are (in some way) 'equivalent' but also (in some way) 'incompatible' is a strikingly non-classical phenomenon" (Putnam 1987: 29). It is a phenomenon that Putnam, like James, wants to celebrate without losing touch with commonsense realism and objectivity, and without endorsing either relativism or subjectivism. Putnam's book *The Many Faces of Realism* of 1987 is a clear example of these later trends in his thinking, and his 1995 book *Pragmatism: An Open Question* makes explicit the connections with the pragmatism of James, Dewey, and the later Wittgenstein. As Putnam himself described the former lectures (which explore many of the pragmatist and neo-pragmatist themes discussed above):

> in the present lectures I stress the *pluralism* and thoroughgoing *holism* which are ubiquitous in Pragmatist writing. If the vision of fact, theory, value and interpretation as interpenetrating undermines a certain sort of metaphysical realism, it equally, I believe, undermines fashionable versions of antirealism and "postmodernism." (1987: xii)

One main source of the "fashionable" views that Putnam is concerned to distance himself from are the views of his fellow neo-pragmatist Richard Rorty. Rorty mobilized resources from analytic philosophy, pragmatism, and Continental philosophy to stake out a historicist and in certain ways postmodernist philosophical perspective, one which also exhibited affinities with the intellectual currents of the time in literary criticism, cultural theory, feminist theory, and a variety of emancipatory political philosophies.[23]

From 1946 to 1952 Rorty completed his BA and MA at the University of Chicago, studying under Rudolf Carnap, Charles Hartshorne (1897–2000), and Richard McKeon (1900–85), and then he received his Ph.D. at Yale with the thesis "The concept of potentiality" under the metaphysician Paul Weiss (1901–2002). His combined training both in the history of philosophy and in technical analytic philosophy would serve Rorty well as he moved gradually from his more analytic phase as an "eliminative materialist" in the philosophy of mind in the 1960s, toward his now famous break with the traditional epistemological tasks of modern philosophy in *Philosophy and the Mirror of Nature* (1979), *Consequences of Pragmatism* (1982), and later works. Broadly put, Rorty attacked the traditional foundationalist picture of knowledge from Descartes, Locke, and Kant through Husserl's phenomenology and Russell's analytic philosophy, according to which "to know is to represent accurately what is outside the mind; so to understand the possibility and nature of knowledge is to understand the way in which the mind is able to construct such representations" (Rorty 1979: 3). On this traditional outlook, according to Rorty:

> Philosophy's central concern is to be a general theory of representation, a theory which will divide culture up into the areas which represent reality well, those which represent it less well, and those which do not represent it at all (despite their pretense of doing so). (1979: 3)

The heroes in Rorty's account are the later, revolutionary stages in the thought of Wittgenstein, Heidegger, and Dewey. These "therapeutic" thinkers, Rorty thought, sought to liberate us from the traditional dead-ends of epistemology by questioning the entire framework in which the traditional problems of philosophy could seem to be pressing and to require a forever elusive, systematic theoretical resolution.

The centerpiece of Rorty's argument in 1979 was his combined use of Quine's attack on the analytic/synthetic distinction and Sellars's attack on the myth of the given, in order to argue beyond Sellars and Quine for the incoherence of the main twentieth-century analytic-epistemological projects of empiricism and meaning analysis in the philosophy of science and the philosophy of language. Thomas Kuhn's massively influential book, *The Structure of Scientific Revolutions* (1962), had shown convincingly, according to Rorty, that there is no neutral or timelessly rational methodology that is common across the revolutionary shifts between incommensurable "paradigms" (to use Kuhn's famous term) that characterize progress in scientific problem-solving.[24] In general, for Rorty, there is no a priori foundation for knowledge to be derived from principles pertaining to mind, meaning, or method that may be unearthed by the philosopher. Rather, truth and knowledge are changing social phenomena that concern the ability to justify one's beliefs to one's peers, with no constraints foreseeable in advance of the contingencies of history and conversation (this is one respect in which Rorty sees Dewey as a precursor); language is a tool for satisfying our interests rather than a representational medium that "mirrors" reality (here Rorty appeals to the later Wittgenstein in particular); and the idea of the knower as a source of necessary truths is (as Rorty credits Heidegger with pointing out) just "one more self-deceptive attempt to substitute a 'technical' and determinate question for that openness to strangeness which initially tempted us to begin thinking" (Rorty 1979: 9). Philosophy, Rorty suggests, should cease attempting to emulate the sciences by portraying itself as an ahistorical tribunal of knowledge, and should rather become more like the arts and humanities in cultivating edifying conversations and developing new, more fruitful vocabularies for coping with the world.[25]

With Rorty's brand of neo-pragmatism we are now certainly very far away from anything that Peirce, the originator of pragmatism, would have recognized as a desirable direction for philosophical inquiry to take (see Haack 2004). Even Putnam in his most "internalist" phases rejects Rorty's identification of truth with intersubjective agreement or the compliments and consensus of one's peers. Putnam wants to hold that there are rational warrants beyond what the majority of one's peers believe, but the basis for Putnam's normative distinction in this regard, given his other philosophical commitments, has not always been clear. Robert Brandom's 1994 book, *Making it Explicit: Reasoning, Representing, and Discursive Commitment*, is the most rigorous recent attempt to outline a thoroughgoing neo-pragmatist outlook that owes much to the later Wittgenstein, Sellars, and Rorty.

At the beginning of the new millennium, philosophy in America is in a state of fruitful turbulence. The various strains and developments of analytic philosophy along the naturalist, neo-metaphysical, and neo-pragmatist lines described above remain the most visible styles of philosophical inquiry in most of the leading journals and graduate departments of philosophy in America. However, increasing numbers of philosophers now argue that the distinctions between analytic, Continental, and pragmatist approaches are, or ought to be, losing their significance. The fallibilism, anti-foundationalism, naturalism, holism, pluralism, and social perspective that we have seen to be characteristic themes in the classical American pragmatist and analytic traditions from Peirce and James to Quine and Putnam remain pervasive, though certainly not universal methodological features across the current philosophical divides. Those themes taken as a whole do go some way toward marking out much of twentieth-century philosophy in America as distinctive in relation to the various prevailing modes of approach taken by philosophers in periods prior to the twentieth century. Perhaps it is the open-ended nature of philosophy as practiced in America in the twentieth century that also makes it difficult to predict what lies in store in the rest of the twenty-first century.[26]

Notes

1 See the entire concluding section of the chapter entitled "The stream of thought" in James's *Principles of Psychology* for a striking discussion of the selectivity that he argues is operative throughout all levels of cognition.

2 As pertains to James in what follows I have drawn freely from the more detailed discussion to be found in my "Sources of pluralism in William James" (O'Shea 2000).

3 For reasons of space, this chapter will refer primarily to philosophers working at universities in the United States, with no attempt being made to cover the important developments in twentieth-century philosophy taking place in the rest of North America, Central America, and South America, which merit separate treatment. Furthermore, the discussion will generally be limited to topics concerning the nature of philosophical method and the theory of knowledge broadly construed; crucial developments in moral and political philosophy in America, among many other subject matters, are adequately covered elsewhere in this volume. Important issues concerning social, cultural, and biographical context will also generally be sacrificed in order to highlight conceptual and epistemological themes.

There are many other respects in which the range of this essay has been restricted. In particular, in this survey of the most influential movements of the period I have not attempted to canvass a variety of important speculative/metaphysical, religious/theological, and existential/phenomenological traditions in twentieth-century American thought. Bruce Kuklick's *A History of Philosophy in America: 1720–2000* (2001) will provide an excellent starting point for anyone interested in further pursuing a more comprehensive historical survey of the variety of philosophical influences and streams in twentieth-century American philosophy.

4 Many American philosophical and cultural historians stress a distinction between an indigenous or classical "American Philosophy" and "Philosophy in America." The former had its roots in the Founders (e.g. Franklin, Jefferson), Native American philosophy (on which in general, see Wilshire 2000, Pratt 2002), Whitman, Emerson, the classical pragmatists (Peirce, James, Dewey, Mead), and

such other figures as Royce, Santayana, Whitehead, the Columbia naturalists, and the more recent revival of pragmatist thinking in general. The latter term ("Philosophy in America") is thought to be especially useful for characterizing the period after World War II in particular, which was dominated by analytic philosophy with its sources in large part stemming from British analysis and Vienna positivism. For a recent statement of the distinction and an explicit championing of the former outlook, see *The Blackwell Guide to American Philosophy*, which the editors begin as follows:

> This book is a guide to American philosophy, not to philosophy in America. The distinction is an important one. Beginning roughly after the end of the Second World War . . . American philosophers turned to various European philosophical movements then current for their inspiration. [. . .] But American philosophy . . . is something else. [. . .] The point is that there is a continuous story of the development of American philosophy from its Puritan origins through the classical period of the pragmatists and naturalists, to contemporary writings by a number of philosophers who work in the broadly defined pragmatist and naturalist traditions. The chapters in this volume tell that story. (Marsoobian and Ryder 2004: xv, xvi; see also the helpful Epilogue by John J. McDermott, "The renascence of classical American philosophy").

In a similar spirit, for a stimulating collection of essays examining the changes from classical or "progressivist" pragmatism, through mid-century "positivist and linguistic" pragmatism, to recent "postmodernist" pragmatism, see Hollinger and Depew (1995).

In what follows I do not insist on this distinction, since I regard the contributions of analytic philosophy to have been vital to the progressive development in the twentieth century of "American Philosophy" on any plausible understanding of that subject matter, and since I will be emphasizing the ways in which analytic philosophy itself took a particular shape in America precisely because of the pragmatism and naturalism that permeated classical American philosophy.

5 For a close examination of Peirce's various formulations of the pragmatic maxim, see Christopher Hookway 2004, "The principle of pragmatism: Peirce's formulations and examples."

6 James 1977, edited by John McDermott, is a useful selection of James's writings, but the definitive edition is *The Works of William James* published in multiple volumes by Harvard University Press.

It should be noted that Peirce objected to certain aspects of James's version of pragmatism, including James's nominalistic emphasis on *particular* experiences, as in the quote from James on p. 212. In 1905 Peirce announced for his own view "the birth of the word 'pragmaticism', which is ugly enough to be safe from kidnappers" (Peirce 1998: 335).

7 For a useful selection of Royce's writings, see Royce 2005, edited by John McDermott.

8 For representative selections from the works of Dewey, see Dewey 1981 and 1998.

9 The title of this leading journal of American philosophy was shortened to *The Journal of Philosophy* in 1921. It was intended to cover "the whole field of scientific philosophy, psychology, ethics and logic," and was founded by Frederick J. E. Woodbridge at Columbia University in 1904.

10 Jaegwon Kim has remarked in an excellent historical and conceptual examination of the nature of philosophical naturalism that to "see that American naturalists held substantive doctrines in metaphysics and epistemology as constitutive of their naturalism, it is useful to go back to earlier naturalists, in particular, Roy Wood Sellars, a philosopher whose work, in my view, has been unjustly neglected" (2003: 88). For a comprehensive overview of philosophical naturalism in the second half of the twentieth century, see Kitcher 1992.

11 Richard Rorty would later use Dewey to portray Roy Wood's son Wilfrid Sellars's rejection of "the given" as likewise recommending an abandonment of the traditional tasks of epistemology, whereas in fact Wilfrid Sellars is philosophically far closer to the views of his father than he is to those of Rorty's Dewey.

12 For more on the "golden age" at Harvard, see Kuklick 1977 and 2001.

13 It should be noted that in 1950 Morton White had also published his article, "The analytic and the synthetic: an untenable dualism" (reprinted in White 2005, *From a Philosophical Point of View* – a title in pointed contrast to Quine's 1953 collection, *From a Logical Point of View*). While Quine pursued his holistic rejection of the analytic/synthetic distinction in the direction of a scientific naturalism having clear roots in Carnap's positivism and in formal logical concerns, White over the years developed what he calls a *holistic pragmatism* that has its origins in Dewey's broader philosophy of culture and experience (see also White 1956).

Another example of just one of the many other important streams of American philosophy outside the positivist and analytic traditions may be noted in the occurrence, also in 1950, of the first meeting of the Metaphysical Society of America. This society was founded by the metaphysician Paul Weiss of Yale (1901–2002). Although logical empiricism, as we shall now see, would at mid-century gradually be eclipsed in America by what is usually referred to as "linguistic philosophy" or "ordinary-language philosophy," it is important to recognize that there were always throughout the century many other currents of thought in American philosophy that kept alive, contributed to, and transformed the classical, metaphysical, and speculative traditions of philosophy. I regret that I have not been able to explore these other developments in this selective overview.

14 See Nelson 1965 for an overview of Wittgenstein's influence in America covering the period from the 1930s to 1964.

15 See also Richard Rorty's book, *The Linguistic Turn: Recent Essays in Philosophical Method* (1967) for an excellent anthology that includes Malcolm's article and many other articles pertaining to both the earlier so-called "ideal-language philosophy" and the later "ordinary-language philosophy." The 1942 Schilpp volume on Moore was a watershed publication, including essays by C. D. Broad, C. L. Stevenson, W. K. Frankena, O. K. Bouwsma, C. J. Ducasse, Norman Malcolm, M. Lazerowitz, Alice Ambrose, John Wisdom, L. Susan Stebbing, and others.

16 Stanley Cavell has taught at Harvard since 1963, where he became the Walter M. Cabot Professor of Aesthetics and the General Theory of Value, and then Professor Emeritus since 1997. In wide-ranging and cross-disciplinary works since the 1960s he has explored issues concerning ordinary-language philosophy, the interpretation of Wittgenstein, skepticism, aesthetics (film studies, Shakespeare, modernism, opera, art history), American studies (Emerson, transcendentalism), romanticism, philosophy of language, and ethics.

17 Wittgenstein, of course, was at Cambridge rather than Oxford, and there were differences of emphasis between the two strains of linguistic philosophy. For further details see J. O. Urmson, "The history of philosophical analysis" in Rorty 1967, as well as Geoffrey Warnock's entry in *The Routledge Encyclopedia of Philosophy* (Craig 1998–2005), "Ordinary-language philosophy, school of."

18 For further commentary on Wilfrid Sellars on these and other themes, see deVries and Triplett 2000 and O'Shea 2007.

19 See, for example, Jaegwon Kim's widely cited response to Quine, "What is 'naturalized epistemology'?" (Kim 1988). For more on naturalized epistemology, see Hilary Kornblith 1985 and Philip Kitcher 1992.

20 Crucial problem areas in this connection have been how to account for intentionality or representational content (John Searle's (1980) "Chinese room" thought-experiment was an early, much discussed critique of computationalist accounts of intentionality); how to accommodate the nature of qualitative consciousness and subjective experience (Thomas Nagel's (1974) "What is it like to be a bat?" was an equally influential critique of materialist accounts of consciousness); and ontologically, how to explain the relationship between the "higher" levels of mind and the "lower" biological and physical levels on which they supervene (see Kim 2004 for an overview).

21 Ruth Barcan Marcus (born 1921, Ph.D. Yale 1946 and later Professor at Yale) wrote important articles in the area of modal logic and identity from the late 1940s on, including in particular Marcus 1961. Marcus had put forward the idea that identities between names are necessary, and a debate has subsequently ensued about the originality of some of Kripke's basic ideas in *Naming and Necessity*. For this debate, and on the "new theory of reference" generally, see Fetzer and Humphreys 1998.

22 In fact, however, Rawls had already outlined an earlier version of what was in many ways the same method in 1951 ("Outline of a decision procedure for ethics"). Rawls deserves a prominent place in any history of American philosophy, but since the present brief overview is restricted to general methodological issues primarily in epistemology and metaphysics I shall not attempt to convey his views here. Charles L. Stevenson, William Frankena, Robert Nozick, and many other notable American moral and political philosophers have regrettably had to be omitted as well.

23 Two recent anthologies of pragmatism that include emphases on the Rortyean, literary, political activist, and postmodernist strains of neo-pragmatism are those edited by Russell B. Goodman (1995) and Louis Menand (1997). For trenchant criticism of some of those recent tendencies from the perspective of an analytic, Peircean pragmatist, see Susan Haack's "Pragmatism, old and new" (2004),

as well as her criticism of Menand's anthology in "Vulgar Rortyism" (*The New Criterion*, vol. 16, available online at http://www.newcriterion.com/archive/16/nov97/menand.htm). Another Peircean pragmatist outlook of note is the conceptual idealism of Nicholas Rescher of Pittsburgh (see his 1992 book, among his many others).

24 The influence of Kuhn's conception of paradigm shifts and of incommensurability in scientific revolutions has been extraordinary, both within philosophy and in the humanities and social sciences generally. The very brief reference to Kuhn here should be supplemented with the discussion of his views in "Philosophy of Science," Chapter 14.

25 Rorty contends that we can be deeply committed to promoting and reshaping our western democratic ideals without having to see our ideals as corresponding to a culture-transcendent, ahistoricist reality or reason. On this basis Rorty sees pragmatism as a useful outlook for feminist thinkers:

> We pragmatists see universalism and realism as committed to the idea of a reality-tracking faculty called "reason" and an unchanging moral reality to be tracked, and thus unable to make sense of the claim that a new voice is needed. So we commend ourselves to feminists on the ground that we can fit that claim into *our* view of moral progress with relative ease. (Rorty in Goodman 1995: 129)

For an in-depth discussion of feminist philosophy in the twentieth century, see "Feminism in philosophy," Chapter 7. The Goodman collection (1995) is useful for containing a selection of recent neo-pragmatist thinkers who are active in the social and political domains of thought, including Cornel West (1953–), Professor of Religion and African American Studies at Princeton University. West is an example of a politically conscious neo-pragmatist philosopher whose "prophetic pragmatism" is influenced by Rorty but who suggests (unlike Rorty) that a blend of Marxist and Christian perspectives might be put to use in transforming cultural traditions in more free and democratic ways (see, for example, West 1989).

26 I would like to thank Dermot Moran and the publisher's anonymous readers for their comments on an earlier (and longer) version of this chapter.

References

Ambrose Lazerowitz, A. (1950) "The problem of linguistic adequacy." In M. Black (ed.) *Philosophical Analysis: A Collection of Essays*, Ithaca, NY: Cornell University Press, pp. 14–35.

Black, M. (ed.) (1950) *Philosophical Analysis: A Collection of Essays*. Ithaca, NY: Cornell University Press.

Brandom, R. (1994) *Making it Explicit: Reasoning, Representing, and Discursive Commitment*. Cambridge, MA and London: Harvard University Press.

Carnap, R. (1928) *Der Logische Aufbau der Welt*. Leipzig: Felix Meiner Verlag. English translation: *The Logical Structure of the World: Pseudoproblems in Philosophy*, Berkeley: University of California Press, 1967.

_____ (1950) "Empiricism, semantics, and ontology." *Revue Internationale de Philosophie* 4: 20–40. Repr. in *Meaning and Necessity: A Study in Semantics and Modal Logic*, Chicago: University of Chicago Press, 1956, pp. 203–21.

Cavell, S. (1969) *Must We Mean What We Say? A Book of Essays*. New York: Charles Scribner's Sons.

Chomsky, N. (1965) *Aspects of the Theory of Syntax*. Cambridge, MA: MIT Press.

Craig, E. (1998–2005). *The Routledge Encyclopedia of Philosophy*. London: Routledge. Also available online by subscription at www.rep.routledge.com.

Davidson, D. (2001a). *Essays on Actions and Events*, 2nd edn. Oxford: Clarendon Press.

_____ (2001b). *Inquiries into Truth and Interpretation*, 2nd edn. Oxford: Clarendon Press.

Dennett, D. (1969) *Content and Consciousness*. London: Routledge & Kegan Paul.

_____ (1978) *Brainstorms*. Montgomery, VT: Bradford Books. Reissued by Penguin, 1997.

DeVries, W. and T. Triplett (eds.) (2000) *Knowledge, Mind, and the Given: Reading Wilfrid Sellars's 'Empiricism and the philosophy of mind'* (including the complete text of Sellars's essay). Indianapolis and Cambridge: Hackett.

Dewey, J. (1920, 1948) *Reconstruction in Philosophy*, with a new introduction 1948. Boston: Beacon Press. Repr. 1948.

_____ (1981) [1973] *The Philosophy of John Dewey*, ed. J. J. McDermott. Chicago and London: University of Chicago Press.

_____ (1998) *The Essential Dewey*, 2 vols., ed. L. A. Hickman and T. M. Alexander. Bloomington, IN: Indiana University Press.

Drake, D. et al. (1920) *Essays in Critical Realism: A Cooperative Study of the Problem of Knowledge*. London: Macmillan.

Feigl, H. and W. Sellars (eds.) (1949) *Readings in Philosophical Analysis*. New York: Appleton-Century-Crofts.

Fodor, J. (1968) *Psychological Explanation*. New York: Random House.

_____ (1975) *The Language of Thought*. Cambridge, MA: Harvard University Press.

_____ (2004) *Hume Variations*. Oxford: Oxford University Press.

French, P. A. and H. K. Wettstein (eds.) (2004) *The American Philosophers*, Midwest Studies in Philosophy 28. Oxford: Blackwell.

Gettier, E. L. (1963) "Is justified true belief knowledge?" *Analysis* 23: 121–3.

Goldman, A. (1967) "A causal theory of knowing." *Journal of Philosophy* 64: 335–72.

_____ (1986) *Epistemology and Cognition*. Cambridge, MA: Harvard University Press.

Goodman, N. (1951) *The Structure of Appearance*. Boston, MA: Reidel. 3rd edn. 1977.

_____ (1954) *Fact, Fiction, and Forecast*. Cambridge, MA: Harvard University Press. 4th edn. 1984.

_____ (1968) *Languages of Art*. Indianapolis: Hackett.

_____ (1978) *Ways of Worldmaking*. Indianapolis: Hackett.

Goodman, R. B. (ed.) (1995) *Pragmatism: A Contemporary Reader*. New York and London: Routledge.

Haack, S. (2004) "Pragmatism, old and new." *Contemporary Pragmatism* 1/1: 3–39.

Hempel, C. (1950) "Problems and changes in the empiricist criterion of meaning." *Revue Internationale de Philosophie* 4: 41–63. Repr. in L. Linsky (ed.) *Semantics and the Philosophy of Language*, Urbana, IL: University of Illinois Press, 1952, pp. 163–85.

Hollinger, R. and D. Depew (eds.) (1995) *Pragmatism: From Progressivism to Postmodernism*. Westport, CT and London: Praeger.

Holt, E. B., W. T. Marvin, W. P. Montague, R. B. Perry, W. B. Pitkin, and E. G. Spaulding (1910) "The program and first platform of six realists." *Journal of Philosophy, Psychology and Scientific Methods* 7: 393–401.

Holt, E. B., W. T. Marvin, W. P. Montague, R. B. Perry, W. B. Pitkin, and E. G. Spaulding (1912) *The New Realism: Cooperative Studies in Philosophy*. New York: Macmillan.

Hookway, C. (2004) "The principle of pragmatism: Peirce's formulations and examples." In P. A. French and H. K. Wettstein (eds.) *The American Philosophers*, Midwest Studies in Philosophy 28, Oxford: Blackwell, pp. 119–36.

Humphreys, P. and J. Fetzer (eds.) (1998) *The New Theory of Reference: Kripke, Marcus and its Origins*, Synthèse Library Series. Dordrecht and Boston: Kluwer.

James, W. (1977) [1898] "Philosophical conceptions and practical results." In J. McDermott (ed.) *The Writings of William James: A Comprehensive Edition*, Chicago and London: University of Chicago Press, pp. 342–62.

_____ (1976) *Essays in Radical Empiricism*. Cambridge, MA: Harvard University Press.

_____ (1977) *The Writings of William James: A Comprehensive Edition*, ed. J. J. McDermott, Chicago and London: University of Chicago Press.

_____ (1978a) *Pragmatism: A New Name for Some Old Ways of Thinking* and *The Meaning of Truth: A Sequel to 'Pragmatism'*. Cambridge, MA: Harvard University Press.

_____ (1978b) *The Will to Believe*. Cambridge, MA: Harvard University Press.

_____ (1983) *The Principles of Psychology*. Cambridge, MA: Harvard University Press.

Kim, J. (1988) "What is 'naturalized epistemology'?" In J. E. Tomberlin (ed.) *Philosophical Perspectives 2: Epistemology*, Atascadero, CA: Ridgeview, pp. 381–405. Repr. in S. Bernecker and F. Dretske (eds.) *Knowledge: Readings in Contemporary Epistemology*, Oxford: Oxford University Press, 2000, ch. 21.

_____ (2003) "The American origins of philosophical naturalism." *Philosophy in America at the Turn of the Century*, APA Centennial Supplement, *Journal of Philosophical Research*. Charlottesville, VA: Philosophy Documentation Center, pp. 129–53.

_____ (2004) "The mind/body problem at century's turn." In B. Leiter (ed.) *The Future for Philosophy*, Oxford: Clarendon Press, pp. 83–98.

Kitcher, P. (1992) "The naturalists return." *Philosophical Review* 101: 53–114.

Kornblith, H. (ed.) (1985) *Naturalizing Epistemology*. Cambridge, MA: MIT Press.

Kripke, S. (1980) *Naming and Necessity*. Cambridge, MA: Harvard University Press. From lectures in 1970; originally published in G. Harman and D. Davidson (eds.) *The Semantics of Natural Language*, Dordrecht: Reidel, 1972.

Kuhn, T. (1962) *The Structure of Scientific Revolutions*, Chicago: University of Chicago Press. 2nd edn., with postscript, 1970.

Kuklick, B. (1977) *The Rise of American Philosophy: Cambridge, Massachusetts 1860–1930*. New Haven, CT and London: Yale University Press.

_____ (2001) *A History of Philosophy in America: 1720–2000*. Oxford: Clarendon Press.

Lewis, C. I. (1929) *Mind and the World Order*. New York: Dover. Repr. 1956.

_____ (1968) "Autobiography." In P. A. Schilpp (ed.) *The Philosophy of C. I. Lewis*, The Library of Philosophers, vol. 13, La Salle, IL: Open Court, pp. 1–21.

Lewis, D. (1983) *Philosophical Papers*, vol. I. Oxford: Oxford University Press.

_____ (1986) *On the Plurality of Worlds*. Oxford: Blackwell.

Lovejoy, A. O. (1930) *The Revolt against Dualism*. Chicago: Open Court.

McDowell, J. (1994) *Mind and World*. Cambridge, MA: Harvard University Press. Paperback edition with a new introduction by the author, 1996.

Malcolm, N. (1942) "Moore and ordinary language." In P. A. Schilpp (ed.) *The Philosophy of G. E. Moore*, La Salle, IL: Open Court, pp. 345–68.

_____ (1950) "The verification argument." In M. Black (ed.) *Philosophical Analysis: A Collection of Essays*, Ithaca, NY: Cornell University Press.

Marcus, R. B. (1961) "Modalities and intensional languages." *Synthèse* 13: 303–22. Discussion with Quine, Kripke, and others in *Synthèse* 14/ 2–3 (1962): 132–43.

Marsoobian, A. T. and J. Ryder (eds.) (2004) *The Blackwell Guide to American Philosophy*. Oxford: Blackwell.

Melden, A. I. (1961) *Free Action*. London: Routledge & Kegan Paul.

Menand, L. (ed.) (1997) *Pragmatism: A Reader*. New York: Random House.

Nagel, E. (1936) "Impressions and appraisals of analytic philosophy in Europe: I & II." *Journal of Philosophy* 33: 5–24.

Nagel, T. (1974) "What is it like to be a bat?" *Philosophical Review* 83: 435–50.

Nelson, J. O. (1965) "The influence of the later Wittgenstein on American philosophy." In F. H. Donnell, Jr. (ed.) *Aspects of Contemporary American Philosophy*, Würzburg and Vienna: Physica-Verlag.

O'Shea, J. R. (2000) "Sources of pluralism in William James." In M. Baghramian and A. Ingram (eds.) *Pluralism: The Philosophy and Politics of Diversity*, London: Routledge, pp. 17–43.

_____ (2007) *Wilfrid Sellars: Naturalism with a Normative Turn*, Key Contemporary Thinkers series. Cambridge: Blackwell/ Polity Press.

Peirce, C. S. (1992 and 1998) *The Essential Peirce*, vols. 1 and 2, ed. N. Houser and C. Kloesel. Bloomington, IN: Indiana University Press.

Perry, R. B. (1910) "The ego-centric predicament." *Journal of Philosophy, Psychology and Scientific Methods* 7: 5–14.

Pratt, S. L. (2002) *Native Pragmatism: Rethinking the Roots of American Philosophy*. Bloomington, IN: Indiana University Press.

Putnam, H. (1975) *Mind, Language and Reality*, Philosophical Papers, vol. 2. Cambridge: Cambridge University Press.

_____ (1987) *The Many Faces of Realism*. LaSalle, IL: Open Court.

_____ (1990) *Realism with a Human Face*. Cambridge, MA and London: Harvard University Press.

_____ (1995) *Pragmatism: An Open Question*. Oxford: Blackwell.

Quine, W. V. O. (1953) *From a Logical Point of View: Logico-Philosophical Essays*. New York: Harper & Row. Page references are to the revised 2nd edn., 1961.

_____ (1960) *Word and Object*. Cambridge, MA: MIT Press.

_____ (1966) "Carnap and logical truth." In *The Ways of Paradox and Other Essays*, Cambridge, MA: Harvard University Press, pp. 107–32.

_____ (1969) *Ontological Relativity and Other Essays*. New York and London: Columbia University Press.

Rawls, J. (1971) *A Theory of Justice*. Cambridge, MA: Harvard University Press.

Rescher, N. (1992) *A System of Pragmatic Idealism*, 3 vols. Princeton, NJ: Princeton University Press.

Rorty, R. (ed.) (1967) *The Linguistic Turn: Recent Essays in Philosophical Method*. Chicago: University of Chicago Press. Midway Reprint edn., 1988.

_____ (1979) *Philosophy and the Mirror of Nature*. Princeton, NJ: Princeton University Press.

_____ (1982) *Consequences of Pragmatism*. Minneapolis: University of Minnesota Press.

Royce, J. (2005) [1969]. *The Basic Writings of Josiah Royce*, 2 vols., ed. J. J. McDermott. New York: Fordham University Press.

Schilpp, P. A. (ed.) (1963) *The Philosophy of Rudolf Carnap*, The Library of Living Philosophers, vol. 11. La Salle, IL: Open Court.

Searle, J. (1980) "Minds, brains, and programs." *Behavioral and Brain Sciences* 3: 417–24.

Sellars, R. W. (1916) *Critical Realism: A Study of the Nature and Conditions of Knowledge*. Chicago: Rand-McNally.

_____ (1922) *Evolutionary Naturalism*. New York: Russell & Russell. Repr. 1969.

_____ (1929) "A re-examination of Critical Realism." *Philosophical Review* 38: 439–55.

_____ (1932) *The Philosophy of Physical Realism*. New York: Macmillan.

_____ (1969) *Reflections on American Philosophy from Within*. Notre Dame, IN: University of Notre Dame Press.

Sellars, R. W., V. J. McGill, and M. Farber (eds.) (1949) *Philosophy for the Future: The Quest of Modern Materialism*. New York: Macmillan.

Sellars, W. (1956) "Empiricism and the philosophy of mind." In *Science, Perception and Reality*, London: Routledge & Kegan Paul, 1963, pp. 127–96. Reissued by Atascadero, CA: Ridgeview, 1991.

Thayer, H. S. (ed.) (1982) *Pragmatism: The Classic Writings*. Indianapolis: Hackett.

West, C. (1989) *The American Evasion of Philosophy: A Genealogy of Pragmatism*. Madison: University of Wisconsin Press.

White, M. (1956) *Toward Reunion in Philosophy*. Cambridge, MA: Harvard University Press.

_____ (2005) *From a Philosophical Point of View: Selected Studies*. Princeton, NJ and Oxford: Princeton University Press.

Wilshire, B. (2000) *The Primal Roots of American Philosophy: Pragmatism, Phenomenology, and Native American Thought*. University Park: Pennsylvania State University Press.

Wittgenstein, L. (1922) *Tractatus Logico-Philosophicus*, trans. C. K. Ogden. Repr. London: Routledge & Kegan Paul, 1983.

_____ (1953) *Philosophical Investigations*, ed. G. E. M. Anscombe and R. Rhees, trans. G. E. M. Anscombe. Oxford: Blackwell.

Further reading

Anderson, D., C. Hausman, and S. Rosenthal (eds.) (1999) *Classical American Philosophy: Its Contemporary Vitality*. Urbana: University of Illinois Press. (A collection of essays on the relevance today of American thinkers from Peirce and James to Dewey and Mead).

Chisholm, R. M. (ed.) (1960) *Realism and the Background of Phenomenology*. Atascadero, CA: Ridgeview. (An excellent resource on late nineteenth- and early twentieth-century issues concerning realism, edited by a leading American analytic epistemologist).

Egginton, W. and M. Sandbothe (eds.) (2004) *The Pragmatic Turn in Philosophy: Contemporary Engagements between Analytic and Continental Thought*. Albany, NY: State University of New York Press. (Current philosophers seeking to bridge the divide between analytic and Continental philosophy, with pragmatism new and old as mediating).

Flower, E. and M. Murphey (1977) *A History of Philosophy in America*. New York: G. P. Putnam's Sons. (A comprehensive, two-volume history of American philosophy from the Puritans to C. I. Lewis).

MacKinnon, B. (ed.) (1985) *American Philosophy: A Historical Anthology*. Albany, NY: State University of New York Press. (An excellent collection of writings from all the main traditions of American philosophy, with introductions).

McDermott, J. J. (1986). *Streams of Experience: Reflections on the History and Philosophy of American Culture*. Amherst: University of Massachusetts Press. (A passionate and eloquent articulation of the aesthetic, experiential, and cultural dimensions of American pragmatism as a philosophy of experience).

Shook, J. R. and J. Margolis (eds.) (2006) *A Companion to Pragmatism*. Oxford: Blackwell. (A comprehensive collection of essays exploring the continuing philosophical significance of both classical pragmatist and neo-pragmatist philosophers).

Smith, J. E. (ed.) (1970) *Contemporary American Philosophy*, 2nd series. New York: Humanities Press. (Essays by many leading American philosophers prior to 1970 who are not discussed in the chapter above, such as Blanshard, Randall, Weiss, Frankena, Northrop, Hook, Bernstein, and Harris).

—— (1978) *Purpose and Thought: The Meaning of Pragmatism*. New Haven, CT: Yale University Press. (Examines fundamental conceptions from classical pragmatism).

—— (1992) *America's Philosophical Vision*. Chicago and London: University of Chicago Press. (A collection of essays by one of the leading scholars of American philosophy, emphasizing the enduring philosophical significance of the classical pragmatists Peirce, Royce, and Dewey).

Soames, S. (2003) *Philosophical Analysis in the Twentieth Century*, vol. 1: *The Dawn of Analysis*; vol. 2: *The Age of Meaning*. Princeton, NJ: Princeton University Press. (A philosophically rigorous, if inevitably selective, history of analytic philosophy from 1900 to 1975, analyzing the central arguments of some of the main figures in the analytic tradition).

Thayer, H. S. (1968) *Meaning and Action: A Critical History of Pragmatism*. Indianapolis: Bobbs-Merrill. (A history and analysis of themes from the classical pragmatists).

6

NATURALISM

Geert Keil

Introduction

"We are all naturalists now," declared Roy Wood Sellars (1880–1973) in 1922.[1] A bold assertion then, it had come closer to the truth by the end of the century. During the course of the twentieth century, "naturalism" seems to have become a synonym for a respectable philosophical methodology. On the other hand, there are a number of distinguished philosophers who advise against paying too much attention to what they view as a long series of unsuccessful naturalistic endeavors. As Peter Geach (1916–) has written:

> When we hear of some new attempt to explain reasoning or language or choice naturalistically, we ought to react as if we were told someone had squared the circle or proved $\sqrt{2}$ to be rational: only the mildest curiosity is in order – how well has the fallacy been concealed?[2]

This clash of opinions is remarkable. For Geach, it goes without saying that the series of naturalistic approaches is a series of failures, whereas Sellars takes it for granted that we are all naturalists now.

It appears that the parties are not talking about the same thing. Sellars described naturalism as "less a philosophical system than a recognition of the impressive implications of the physical and biological sciences."[3] This characterization is typical for naturalists from the first half of the century. John Dewey (1859–1952) described a naturalist as "one who has respect for the conclusions of natural science."[4] If this kind of respect suffices to be converted to naturalism, then one can easily accept Sellars's view. It seems silly to deny or belittle the unprecedented success of the natural sciences since the Enlightenment. Or, in the words of Bouwsma, "Who then would not accept scientific method, and prefer to go to Babylon by candlelight? Scientific method is successful."[5] If the only alternatives to naturalism are obscurantism, superstition, and supernaturalism, then naturalism seems to be the only game in town in our scientific culture. Although there still exist enclaves of religiously motivated supernaturalism, particularly in the United States, naturalism has become the most forceful metaphilosophical trend of the twentieth century.

When Geach takes any "new attempt to explain reasoning or language or choice naturalistically" to be doomed to failure, he has more specific and demanding tasks in mind. Sellars and Dewey give general vindications for the natural sciences, whereas Geach refers to specific projects of naturalization. Now, having respect for the natural sciences and their methods does not yet guarantee the success of specific naturalistic projects. When it comes to these projects, naturalism does not compete with obscurantism and supernaturalism, but rather with well-established philosophical theories that purport to explain phenomena with the use of non-empirical methods. Some naturalists hold that non-empirical methods are unscientific. But if this were true, then, not only philosophy but also neither mathematics nor logic could contribute to our scientific picture of the world.

The attractiveness of philosophical naturalism crucially hinges on the available alternatives. As long as naturalists confine themselves to selling their position as a bulwark against irrationality, obscurantism, and superstition, they insinuate that any kind of philosophy not committed to naturalism must be obscurantist.[6]

So let us take a step back. The *Oxford English Dictionary* defines a naturalist as "one who studies natural, in contrast to spiritual, things," or as "one who studies, or is versed in, natural science."[7] This non-philosophical meaning can be traced back to the medieval Latin expression *naturalista*. Secondly, a naturalist is someone who believes in philosophical naturalism, which is characterized by the *OED* as "a view of the world, and of man's relation to it, in which only the operation of natural (as opposed to supernatural or spiritual) laws and forces is admitted or assumed." Finally, in literary theory and the history of art, "naturalism" is a term for a certain style or epoch. Zola was a naturalist in the third sense of the word, Quine in the second, and Darwin in the first. Only naturalism in the second sense is a philosophical position. It is this second sense that this chapter addresses.

Naturalism in the first half of the century

As a philosophical trend, naturalism has played a prominent role since the late nineteenth century. Of course, the term is older. Christian apologetics from the seventeenth century used it in a pejorative sense. Naturalists were labeled with the epithets "blasphemous" and "atheistic," where a naturalist was simply someone who refused Christian supernaturalism. As quoted above from the *OED*, naturalists aimed to explain all phenomena with "the operation of natural (as opposed to supernatural or spiritual) laws and forces." Philosophical naturalism in the present sense of the word has been characterized thus: "The closest thing to a common core of meaning is probably the view that the methods of natural science provide the only avenue to truth."[8] Understood in this sense, the term has been in use on a larger scale since the late nineteenth century. Unquestionably, Hobbes and Hume would today call themselves "naturalists," and so would Holbach and LaMettrie. We have to keep in mind, however, that the geography of those debates was described in different terms. Throughout the nineteenth century, other -isms covered what is subsumed under "naturalism" today: materialism, mechanism, positivism, empiricism, and monism.

For clarity's sake, naturalism should not have the same meaning as one of the related expressions. It should also be distinguished from physicalism, biologism, psychologism, and behaviorism. This task is complicated by the fact that many declared naturalists – Quine being a classic example – also hold some of the other positions.

In programmatic declarations of naturalists, demarcations from nineteenth-century predecessor positions are the order of the day. Many naturalists are reluctant to adhere to materialism and mechanism – physics has changed after all. Ernest Nagel (1901–85) states representatively:

> Naturalism does not maintain that only what is material exists ... What naturalism does assert as a truth about nature is that though *forms* of behavior or *functions* of material systems are indefeasibly parts of nature, forms and functions are not themselves agents in their own realization or in the realization of anything else.[9]

Within mid-century American naturalism, the question whether naturalism entails materialism was discussed at length.[10] The phrasing "the methods of natural science provide the only avenue to truth" has the advantage that it does not commit naturalism to a specific leading science. Contrary to physicalists, biologists, and behaviorists, a naturalist has a right to relate to all sciences. However, the claim by Dewey, Hook, and Nagel that scientific naturalism is ontologically neutral was called into question, for they counted only spatio-temporally extended bodies with causal powers as scientifically researchable entities. Hence: "Their naturalism is just materialism over again under a softer name."[11]

The two eminent figures of early American naturalism were John Dewey and George Santayana (1863–1952). They will not be discussed here in detail, because their views were interwoven with other ideas in such a way that they contain no distinctive naturalistic program. In *Scepticism and Animal Faith*, Santayana proposed a biologically inspired, anti-rationalist, pragmatist epistemology, according to which knowledge consists of inescapable belief essential for action ("animal faith mediated by symbols"). Correspondingly, Dewey's naturalism cannot be easily told apart from his pragmatism. (For the connection between American naturalism and pragmatism, see "American philosophy in the twentieth century," Chapter 5.) A recurrent theme in Dewey's thinking was a refutation of all kinds of dualisms. He wished to bridge the gaps between morals and science, between mind and body, man and nature, knowledge and the world. Besides, Dewey refused the idea of perception as passive observation and operated with an extended concept of *experience* instead. He also favored a pragmatic notion of truth and advocated fallibilism. In the 1920s, Santayana and Dewey conducted what seems today a scarcely comprehensible debate about the "right" naturalism.[12] Santayana accused Dewey of being only a "half-hearted naturalist," and Dewey retorted that Santayana's naturalism "reduces itself to a vague gesture of adoring faith in some all-comprehensive unknowable," while he himself has "tried to bring together on a naturalistic basis the mind and matter that Santayana keeps worlds apart."[13]

In the first half of the century, American naturalism, as advocated by Dewey, Santayana, Woodbridge, Roy Sellars, and Sidney Hook (1902–89), was not a particularly well-defined view. Some decades later Sellars's son, himself an eminent philosopher, remembers:

> As for Naturalism. That, too, had negative overtones at home. It was as wishy-washy and ambiguous as Pragmatism. One could believe *almost* everything about the world and even *some* things about God, and yet be a Naturalist. What was needed was a new, nonreductive materialism.[14]

Only when Quine bound naturalism to the definite superiority of scientific method did a distinct program emerge, more specific than the broad-churched naturalisms from the first half of the century.

In German-speaking countries, the situation toward the end of the nineteenth century was marked by the methodological emancipation of the *Geisteswissenschaften* (humanities).[15] In the work of Ranke, Droysen, Jacob Burckhardt, and Wilhelm Dilthey (1833–1911), naturalism was opposed to *historicism*. Historicism included the claim that scientific method necessarily fails to capture the historical and thus the specific human aspects of civilization. By proposing a "Critique of Historical Reason," Dilthey tried to rid the historic sciences of their metaphysical presuppositions about the subjects of history and nature. He thus turned a metaphysical dispute into a methodological debate about the relation between natural sciences and humanities. This was later called the *explanation/understanding* (*Erklären/Verstehen*) controversy.[16] Dilthey put it bluntly: "We explain nature, but we understand mental life."[17] In this debate, naturalists demanded a unified scientific methodology, i.e. a methodological monism.[18] The "historical," and later "culturalist" or "hermeneutic" counterparty proposed a dualistic, or at least a complementary relationship between the natural sciences and the humanities. In the explanation/understanding controversy, adherents of the humanities party at first defended a historicist position, since the humanities viewed themselves as an essentially historical discipline, particularly in Germany. This turned out to be insufficient, because philology and systematic linguistics did not fit into the picture. The new catchword in defending the independence of the humanities was "culture." The proponents of Southwest German neo-Kantianism (Windelband, Rickert), in particular, laid out a methodological foundation of cultural sciences, which was taken to be independent of ontological premises.

The term "culturalism," though, is not yet in general use; the major dictionaries show no respective entry. In western universities, however, "cultural studies" are flourishing. It is not easy to see how the constituent fields of study are bound together methodologically. At any rate, they are *not* naturalistic, given their methodological pluralism. Those who emphasize the culturally and historically shaped character of human existence typically refuse to accept scientific method as the only avenue to truth.

Three eminent figures

Among the three most influential twentieth-century philosophers, two were moderate anti-naturalists; the third was a convinced naturalist.

Edmund Husserl (1859–1938)

In his earlier works Husserl dealt with naturalism in the form of psychologism. Psychologism was prefigured in British empiricism and widespread in the late nineteenth century. It equated the laws of logic with the psychological laws of thought. Frege, Husserl, and the neo-Kantian Paul Natorp (1854–1924) were all eminent critics of psychologism. Husserl's objections to psychologism were not original; indeed, the essential arguments from volume one of his *Logical Investigations* (1900) can already be found in Frege. Frege summarized his views as follows: "an explanation of a mental process that ends in taking something to be true, can never take the place of proving what is taken to be true."[19] Anti-psychologism insists that questions of validity are independent from questions of the actual acquisition of knowledge; the *quaestio facti* can never replace the *quaestio iuris*. Husserl followed this idea. The ongoing debates about naturalizing epistemology are partly a resumption of the psychologism controversy.

The most important source for Husserl's critique of naturalism, however, is his later essay *Philosophy as a Rigorous Science* (1911). In this work, Husserl argues against a "naturalization of reason," which he criticizes as "countersense."[20] He points out in particular that experimental psychology, as a science of facts, can never account for the *justification* of rational claims.[21] The natural scientist advances arguments and adduces evidence, but he cannot explain, according to Husserl, the normative force of the laws of logic he presupposes. Empirical science fails to face the phenomenon of *normativity*, as it is later termed.

Husserl adds that the empirical sciences are essentially naive. They take their objects of research as given, and hence they cannot develop a critical stance towards their own presuppositions and assumptions.[22] For Husserl, to expect natural science to provide the solution for a genuine epistemological problem "would mean to move in a countersensical circle."[23] Natural science is bound to miss the epistemological problem, for it cannot answer the *quaestio iuris*.[24]

Husserl characterizes naturalism by its totalization of the experimental method.[25] He complains that nowhere in experimental psychology has the necessary methodological work of acquiring rigorous concepts been carried out: "We look for it in vain in the vast literature" of "'exact' psychology."[26] Within empirical psychology, this shortcoming cannot be remedied, for the attempt "to obtain the rigorous concepts that alone can give scientific value to the characterization of the psychical [...] by psychophysical experiments [...] would be the pinnacle of absurdity."[27] Two decades later, Wittgenstein snidely noted in a similar fashion: "For in psychology, there are experimental methods *and conceptual confusion.*"[28]

Arguably, pivotal to Husserl's critique of naturalism is his objection that it is viciously circular. Experimental philosophy takes for granted the possibility of knowledge and experience, but it never isolates phenomenal experience. It "unavoidably carries out analyses of the contents of these [psychological] concepts" which are "a priori," while it does not recognize that "presuppositions of experimental methods cannot be justified through themselves."[29] It is this alleged circularity of a naturalized episte-mology that Quine later countered with the following move: "such scruples against circularity have little point once we have stopped dreaming of deducing science from observations."[30]

Finally, it is characteristic of Husserl's critique of naturalism in *Philosophy as a Rigorous Science* that he criticizes the presumptuousness of an empirical science that does not know its own boundaries in the name of a *better* and *more profound* science. Far from being opposed to the scientific pursuit of truth, phenomenological philosophy claims to be a more rigorous science that reflects and compensates for the shortcomings of empirical psychology. Husserl has also envisaged the cultural reverberations of scientific naturalism. He is especially annoyed at "that kind of sham philosophical literature … that grows so rampantly today and that offers us, with the pretension to the most serious scientific character," to renew all philosophical theories "on a natural scientific and above all 'experimental-psychological basis'." In view of that literature, Husserl adds, "one can only be astonished at the decline of the sense for the profound problems and difficulties to which the greatest minds of mankind have devoted their life's work."[31]

Ludwig Wittgenstein (1889–1951)

The most important characteristic of Wittgenstein's critique of naturalism is his strict demarcation between philosophy and the natural sciences. Wittgenstein drew this line in the *Tractatus*: "Philosophy is not one of the natural sciences" (4.111). The task of natural science is to determine "the totality of true propositions" (4.11), whereas philosophy aims at "the logical clarification of thoughts." Hence, the result of the philosophical enterprise is "not a number of 'philosophical propositions', but to make propositions clear" (4.112).

In Wittgenstein's demarcation between philosophy and the natural sciences, the former pays a high price. Philosophy is deprived of participating in the pursuit of truth. This consequence is due to the peculiar theory of meaning in the *Tractatus*, according to which philosophical sentences, including the sentences of the *Tractatus* itself, lack truth values. According to Wittgenstein, there are no logical and philosophical truths, for only those sentences have sense that are a picture of reality (4.021). If one does not share Wittgenstein's curious theory of meaning, it is hard to see why the logical clari-fication of thoughts to which Wittgenstein restricts philosophy should not contribute to the pursuit of truth, namely by yielding *conceptual* truths.

Wittgenstein held on to the methodological confrontation between philosophy and the natural sciences, even when his picture of philosophical practice had changed in his later work. In his middle period, Wittgenstein used to say things such as:

> Philosophers constantly see the method of science before their eyes, and are
> irresistibly tempted to ask and answer questions in the way science does. This

tendency is the real source of metaphysics, and leads the philosopher into complete darkness.[32]

In this respect, Wittgenstein was the natural antipode to Quine, who assumed a continuum between philosophy and the other sciences. While Wittgenstein was tremendously interested in determining what is *distinctive* about philosophical investigations, for Quine, this concern was a matter of indifference. The Oxford philosopher Peter Hacker (1939–) put the disagreement bluntly: "If Quine is right, then philosophy is an extension of science ... If Wittgenstein is right, then philosophy is *sui generis*."[33]

An important element of Wittgenstein's skepticism towards naturalization projects was the conceptual conservativism inherent in his ordinary-language approach. The following, much-debated remark is typical: "Only of a human being and what resembles (behaves like) a living human being can one say: it has sensations; it sees, is blind; hears, is deaf; is conscious or unconscious."[34] A few decades later, cognitive scientists and philosophers of mind began to attribute mental states to computers, to robots and to brains, and some even to thermostats. Wittgensteinians take the quoted remark as a significant insight, which anticipates the objection to the widespread *homunculus fallacy* in the cognitive sciences, namely "the reckless application of human-being predicates to insufficiently human-like objects," which is "tantamount to the postulation of a little man within a man to explain human experience and behaviour."[35] Cognitive scientists have countered Wittgenstein's verdict by claiming that answering the question whether computational or neural processes can be described with mental predicates goes astray, if the answer is simply stipulated with reference to ordinary usage of language. The *functionalist* view of the mental assumes that mental states are abstract and multiply realizable. From this viewpoint, it appears to be dogmatic to assert that living human beings are the only bearers of mental predicates.[36]

As quoted above, Wittgenstein occasionally criticized conceptual confusions within experimental psychology. However, he never developed a thorough methodological and conceptual criticism of theories in the empirical sciences of mind and language. His main focus was always on unmasking bad philosophy, rather than on unmasking bad science.

I have called Wittgenstein a *moderate* anti-naturalist, for while he emphasized the autonomy of philosophy with respect to the natural sciences, he took the subjects of his philosophical endeavor – language and mind – as situated in the natural and social world. Some of his doctrines have been interpreted in the spirit of a non-reductive naturalism (among others, by Peter Strawson), particularly, his idea of the connection between language-games and forms of life, his behavioristic references to "trained" or "inculcated" rule-following, and his occasional appeals to the "natural history" of our species.[37] Arguably, this assessment is based on an equivocation in the notion of nature. The late Wittgenstein repeatedly points out that changing certain beliefs and language-games is not on offer to us. The only notion of nature, however, that could support these remarks is the *topos* of the nature of things. But the reference to an unalterable human nature does not by itself render a position a naturalistic one (see the section "Naturalism and human nature," below). For Wittgenstein, the reason why we cannot change at will our language-games and forms of life is not grounded in our physical or biological nature, but rather in the quasi-transcendental condition that the game of doubting presupposes a frame, or background, of unquestioned certainty.[38] Wittgenstein does not entertain the idea of naturalizing this background; at most he suggests its socialization. The relevant kind of stability and inertia is explicable by social, or cultural, reasons. This is why Strawson suggests the label "social naturalism" for Wittgenstein's later views.[39]

Willard Van Orman Quine (1908–2000)

If there was a prototypical naturalist of the twentieth century, it was W. V. O. Quine. For Quine, naturalism plays a twofold role. On the one hand, he is the inventor of the label "naturalized epistemology" (see below). On the other, the term "naturalism" gives a general characterization of Quine's philosophy. Quine's epistemological and meta-philosophical naturalism have a common root that comes out in the following:

> I hold that knowledge, mind, and meaning are part of the same world that they have to do with, and that they are to be studied in the same empirical spirit that animates natural science. There is no place for a prior philosophy.[40]

Quine's meta-philosophical naturalism consists in the "abandonment of the goal of a first philosophy prior to natural science."[41] The natural sciences require no philosophical foundation. They are "not answerable to any supra-scientific tribunal."[42] They need not justify themselves at the "court of reason," as Kant demanded. Formulated positively, Quine's meta-philosophical naturalism comprises his *thesis of continuity* between philosophy and science: "I see philosophy not as an *a priori* propaedeutic or groundwork for science, but as continuous with science."[43]

The continuity thesis is only understandable in the light of Quine's unusually broad notion of "science." Unlike Wittgenstein, who equates "science" with "the sum total of the natural sciences," Quine finds it "awkward that 'science', unlike *scientia* and *Wissenschaft*, so strongly connotes natural science nowadays."[44] Quine's notion of "total science" encompasses "the totality of our so-called knowledge or beliefs" which constitutes "a man-made fabric which impinges on experience only along the edges."[45] In Quine's view, all sciences interlock to some extent, and his main reason for this view is that all sciences "share a common logic and generally some common part of mathematics, even when nothing else."[46]

Quine's sweeping notion of science includes a second continuity thesis, namely, the view that "science is a continuation of common sense."[47] Both the scientist and the common man are engaged in the pursuit of truth, and we may safely reckon that the majority of truths ever discovered was not discovered by professional scientists. Commonsense investigations have a scientific or proto-scientific character insofar as both the scientist and the common man care about empirical evidence:

> The scientist is indistinguishable from the common man in his sense of evidence, except that the scientist is more careful. This increased care is not a revision of evidential standards, but only the more patient and systematic collection and use of what anyone would deem to be evidence.[48]

While Quine's views about the continuity between philosophy and natural science are characteristic of his naturalism, his view that science is a continuation of common sense is very much in the spirit of American *pragmatism*.

An important building block of Quine's critique of a priori philosophy is his famous attack on the analytic/synthetic distinction (see "Kant in the twentieth century," Chapter 4).[49] Logical empiricism defined analytical sentences as those that are true by virtue of the meanings of their constituent words, while synthetic sentences are true depending on how the world is. In "Two dogmas of empiricism," Quine argues that no clear line can be drawn between analytic and synthetic sentences, more precisely: all attempts to define analyticity are circular. The expressions *analytical*, *synonymous*, *necessarily true*, *true by definition*, and *true in virtue of a semantical rule* form a definitional circle that cannot be broken by means of a scientifically respectable extensional language. Quine concludes: "That there is such a distinction to be drawn at all [between analytic and synthetic statements] is an unempirical dogma of empiricists, a metaphysical article of faith."[50] The connection with naturalism arises from the fact that for Quine one effect of abandoning this dogma is "a blurring of the supposed boundary between speculative metaphysics and natural science."[51]

Let us return to Quine's definition of naturalism as the "abandonment of the goal of a first philosophy prior to natural science," and as "the recognition that it is within science itself, and not in some prior philosophy, that reality is to be identified and described."[52] Late in his career, Quine acknowledged "these characterizations convey the right mood, but they would fare poorly in a debate. How much qualifies as 'science itself' and not 'some prior philosophy'? [...] What then *have* I banned under the name of prior philosophy?"[53] These are good questions to ask. Quine seems eventually to have had an inkling of how vaguely he had always described his naturalism. Unfortunately, he refrained from answering these questions, reiterating instead "demarcation is not my purpose."[54] This declaration will not do, since the very intelligibility of his naturalism hinges on such a demarcation. The question of how much qualifies as "science itself" and not "some prior philosophy" will have to be addressed.

The nature of naturalism

Naturalism was too multifarious a philosophical trend in the twentieth century to confine oneself to three eminent figures. So let us complement this with a second approach. Some expressions are *motivated*, as linguists say; that is, they contain morphemes that hint at the meaning of the whole. "Naturalism" contains the morpheme "nature." So, one should be able to tell how this came about.

The concept of nature is an iridescent concept in philosophy. Hume and Mill already regarded it as "vague" and "indeterminate," the chemist and natural philosopher Robert Boyle (1627–91) even suggested banning it from philosophical usage. It is helpful to situate ambiguous terms in the logical space of their counter-concepts, which is the way the concept of nature has always had its contours established. The classical dichotomies are: *physis* versus *nomos*, *physis* versus *technē*, and *physis* versus *thesis* in Greek philosophy; nature versus the supernatural in the Judeo-Christian tradition, nature versus freedom in Kant, nature versus mind, nature versus culture, and nature versus society in the modern age. In the self-characterization of naturalistic positions in the second half of the century, these antitheses play a gradually diminishing role. Although "naturalism" contains the morpheme "nature," only a few naturalists explain their position by means of the concept of nature. Now it seems only fair to demand that someone who refuses to speak about nature should be silent about naturalism. However, the connection could be weaker than the word "naturalism" suggests. Being defined by the superiority of scientific method, naturalism refers to *natural science* rather than to *nature*.

Under modernity, nature has lost many of its former attributes, with the effect that the concept of nature has gradually became paler. In the triumphant advance of modern natural sciences, animistic and teleological views about nature have receded, as well as the conception of a divine natural order in which everything has its predestined place. For Kant, "nature" was nothing more than the epitome of appearances falling under strict laws. In the same way, for naturalists today, nature is essentially anything that is the subject of natural sciences and in the realm of the laws of nature. In this sense, the concept of natural sciences appears to be more basic than that of nature itself.[55] Besides, naturalists have little to say about the *extension* of the concept of nature. The realm of nature is taken to be identical with the realm of all being. Nature is simply what there is: "Naturalism … can be defined negatively as the refusal to take 'nature' or 'the natural' as a term of distinction. … For present-day naturalists 'Nature' serves rather as the all-inclusive category."[56] In other words, everything counts as nature, except for supernatural phenomena, and these do not exist anyway.

The demise of the qualitative concept of nature cannot be blamed on any single philosophical school or tradition. However, even if it should be possible to explain the concept of naturalism without the concept of nature, a successor problem emerges: a naturalism worth its name should be able to say something about what distinguishes the natural sciences from the other sciences. This shift of investigation marks a transition from *metaphysical* to *methodological* naturalism.

A classification of naturalisms

According to Ernest Nagel, "the number of distinguishable doctrines for which the word 'naturalism' has been a counter in the history of philosophy is notorious."[57] Neil Roughley adds: "The term can be used to designate anything from a broad commitment to keep the 'supernatural' out of philosophy to a methodologically highly specific conception of how that has to be done."[58]

It has become customary to distinguish different kinds of naturalism. Nevertheless, this custom has its dangers. The cheerful pluralism of attribute-naturalisms, as can be found in recent literature on naturalizing epistemology,[59] does not absolve one from saying what all these positions have in common *qua* naturalisms. The following depiction is led by the idea that many explications of the concept of naturalism only seemingly compete; in fact, they represent *different levels of elaboration of the same basic idea*. I will distinguish three levels of elaboration: metaphysical, methodological, and semantic naturalism. This tripartite classification is not novel. It should be added that especially in the field of methodological naturalism, finer grained differentiations have been suggested.

Metaphysical naturalism

Naturalism as an ontological or metaphysical position is a thesis about what there is, or, how the world is structured. Metaphysical naturalism can be described by the sayings "Nature includes everything," "everything is natural," or "Everything is part of the natural world." These phrases leave open many questions, in particular what exactly is meant by "nature" or the "natural world." If nature is simply equated with everything that exists,[60] then such an universalization jeopardizes the requirement for naturalism to be a definable position. Some naturalists have noticed the danger of trivializing the concept of nature by universalization.[61] Metaphysical naturalism has to give criteria apt to *disqualify* entities as parts of nature, *omnis determinatio* being *negatio* (every determination is a negation). However, the fuzzy concept of nature employed in metaphysical naturalism is not an accident. As described above, the modern concept of nature looks back over a long history of loss of semantic value. Yet before equating "nature" with "reality" or with "the existing," one should keep in mind that this loss of semantic value was closely tied to the development of a scientific worldview. Metaphysical naturalism was modeled on physical science as the last arbiter of questions about the structure of the world. The Australian materialist David Armstrong (1926–) defines "naturalism" as follows:

> Naturalism I define as the view that nothing else exists except the single, spatio-temporal world, the world studied by physics, chemistry, cosmology, and so on.[62]

> Naturalism … is the contention that the world, the totality of entities, is nothing more than the spacetime system.[63]

Here "Nature" is equated with "the spatio-temporal world," and naturalism is the view that nothing exists outside the spatio-temporal world. Interpreted in this fashion, the slogan "Everything is natural" amounts to a defense of ontological physicalism. However, Armstrong draws a more subtle distinction and regards physicalism as the additional thesis "that the only particulars that the spacetime system contains are physical entities governed by nothing more than the laws of physics."[64] I shall return to physicalism below.

Ontological or metaphysical naturalism may as well be formulated in terms of *facts* instead of objects. The American philosopher Gilbert Harman (1938–), for example, claims: "Naturalism as a general view is the sensible thesis that *all* facts are facts of nature."[65] Yet other naturalists propose that all *properties* are natural properties. This variant can be found especially in the debate following G. E. Moore's objection to ethical naturalism, namely that "good" is not a natural property. (For further discussion of Moore, see "Twentieth-century moral philosophy," Chapter 20.)

Methodological, or scientific, naturalism

Many declared naturalists are reluctant to restrict metaphysical naturalism to a physicalistic position. They rather attempt to specify the indistinct dictum "everything is natural" methodologically. The metaphysical thesis that all things, facts, or properties are natural is turned into a methodologically grounded thesis about the privileged status of scientific knowledge, namely the thesis of the explanatory superiority of scientific method. A few examples: Sidney Hook writes:

> Despite the variety of specific doctrines which naturalists have professed from Democritus to Dewey, what unites them all is the wholehearted acceptance of scientific method as the only reliable way of reaching truths about the world of nature, society, and man.[66]

And Arthur Danto:

> Naturalism ... is a species of philosophical monism according to which whatever exists or happens is natural in the sense of being susceptible to explanation through methods which, although paradigmatically exemplified in the natural sciences, are continuous from domain to domain of objects and events.[67]

David Armstrong:

> [I]t is natural science that gives us whatever detailed knowledge we have of the world.[68]

Manley Thompson:

> The closest thing to a common core of meaning is probably the view that the methods of natural science provide the only avenue to truth.[69]

W. V. O. Quine:

> We naturalists say that science is the highest path to truth.[70]

The quoted passages clearly exceed general demonstrations of respect for the natural sciences (remember Dewey's definition of a naturalist as "one who has respect for the conclusions of natural science"). For one thing, the natural sciences are distinguished by their *methods*: solely in following scientific methods are the sciences "the only avenue" or "the highest path" to truth. Secondly, a twofold *universalization* is bred: scientific method yields knowledge about everything that can be known, and it is the only reliable way to this knowledge. These universal claims are not optional ingredients of naturalism, rather they are part of the program's inner logic. One can surely admit that *areas* exist in which scientific method is unrivalled without being a naturalist. It lies in the logic of naturalism to tolerate no enclaves. This kind of naturalism is well put by Sellars:

> In the dimension of describing and explaining the world, science is the measure of all things, of what is that it is, and of what is not that it is not.[71]

I will call this the *scientia mensura* principle. A similar version can be found in Quine: "The world is as natural science says it is."[72] I shall use the three expressions "methodological naturalism," "scientific naturalism," and "*scientia mensura* naturalism" interchangeably to describe this view.

Another expression for this position is *scientism*. Because of its pejorative ring, however, hardly any naturalist uses this expression for self-characterization. Besides, often scientism is regarded less a theoretical, but rather a practical view about the *role* of science in society. All problem-solving shall be done by scientific methods, which answer to no higher authority. According to this kind of scientism, science is the only avenue not only to truth, but also to the solution of social and political problems. To avoid this connotation, I will not use the term "scientism."

The naturalist's talk of the only avenue to truth involves an emphasis that could lead to confusion. Hence two clarifications: first, "truth" simply stands for "the set of all true propositions." Second, part of the program's inner logic is universality, but not *infallibilism*. Superiority of scientific method does not imply that it inevitably leads to true propositions. Occasionally this latter claim was employed as defining attribute of naturalism,[73] yet on closer examination it is hard see why the *scientia mensura* principle should incorporate certainty or infallibilism.[74] The naturalist who rejected this inclusion most decidedly was Quine. According to him, scientific methods lead to assertions that are claimed to be true, yet always revisable. Even what is held to be true on the best scientific grounds, can in turn be proved wrong by science. For this reason, Quine adds to his credo that "the world is as natural science says it is" the proviso "insofar as natural science is right."[75] For him, it is part of the concept of science that it cannot guarantee truth. Skeptical doubts are part of science and they are answerable within science. Skepticism against science as a whole, however, is ill placed. In any period of scientific development, arguably there are more things in heaven and earth than are dreamt of in our philosophy. By way of compensation, as Lichtenberg has retorted to Prince Hamlet, there are many things in our science books which can be found neither in heaven nor on earth. But science books can be corrected. This is a permanent occupation of the sciences. A naturalist in the spirit of Quine takes science to be a self-correcting process of a methodologically controlled pursuit for truth, "fallible and corrigible but not answerable to any supra-scientific tribunal."[76]

The above quoted definitions make it clear that scientific naturalism is not a scientific theory (arguably not even a family of theories), but rather a meta-philosophical thesis, or, in practice, a *program*. A program cannot be evaluated in the same way as a fully-fledged scientific theory, for it does not claim to have explained anything. The naturalistic program rather makes a claim about *explainability*. Now, since this claim itself needs to have a definable content, naturalism should not escape assessment owing to its vagueness. I said above that for scientific naturalism, the concept of the natural sciences is more basic than the concept of nature. On closer inspection, this view appears to be implausible. "Naturalism" contains "nature" as a morphological constituent, and arguably, there is a semantic connection as well. Thus a transformation of the problem takes place: a methodological naturalist, who is reluctant to speak of nature, has to answer the question, What distinguishes the *natural* sciences from the other sciences? The answer can no longer appeal to the fact that they are the sciences of nature. Criteria are needed, since it is not the usage of the word "scientific" that makes a discipline, theory, explanation, or vocabulary naturalistically respectable. All the above-quoted definitions of the naturalistic program appeal to "the scientific method(s)." In order to pinpoint the content of the program, one needs to know which methods exactly are meant by it, or *not* meant by it.

So, let us ask which methods the naturalistic program excludes. Here opinions diverge. Methodological naturalists formulate their position either with respect to a *leading science*, or without.

Naturalism with a leading science

The two main approaches of twentieth-century naturalisms with a leading science were physicalism and biologism. For some reason, no prominent naturalist has yet declared chemistry as a leading science. Sociologism cannot count as naturalism, as sociology is not a natural science. The case of psychologism is more intricate, since in the twentieth century, psychology was taught as a discipline in the humanities as well as in the empirical sciences. Frege's and Husserl's critique of psychologism is often understood as a critique of naturalism, yet the psychologism they criticized had little to do with scientific psychology. Their anti-psychologism rather insisted that questions of justification cannot be turned into descriptive questions. In today's terminology, scientifically refined positions of psychologism would count as *naturalistic epistemologies* (see the section "Naturalizing epistemology," below). So we are left with physicalism and biologism.

Physicalism: Physicalism is a refined version of materialism with reference to physics. Thus understood, physicalism is an ontological thesis. According to this view, the world consists of only those entities acknowledged by physics. Some physicalists refer to an *ideal* physics instead. Philip Pettit has categorized ontological physicalism into four partial theses:

1   There are microphysical entities.
2   Microphysical entities constitute everything.
3   There are microphysical regularities.
4   Microphysical regularities govern everything.[77]

In Pettit's fourfold claim, ordinary materialism is enriched first by reference to physical laws or regularities, and second by reference to the thesis of the primacy of a micro-level. On this thesis, there are only elementary particles, and everything else is composed of these elementary particles.

Ontological physicalism is a variety of *metaphysical* naturalism. Members of the Vienna Circle proposed a different variant of physicalism. Carnap (1891–1970) and Neurath (1882–1945) did not take "physicalism" to be an ontological position, but rather the thesis that all meaningful sentences are translatable into a universal language of science. Carnap deemed ontological claims about what there is to be senseless. His physicalism is defined methodologically, in defending a primacy of explanation by a science that is distinguished by a certain linguistic form. Carnap's version of the translatability thesis is: "*physical language is a universal language*, that is, a language into which every sentence may be translated [...]. This is the thesis of physicalism."[78]

This kind of physicalism was closely related to the Viennese program of a *unity of science*. In the words of Carnap: "If the physical language, on the grounds of its universality, were adopted as the system language of science, all science would become physics."[79] For Carnap, physical language does not coincide with the language of current physics. Physics keeps its status as a leading science, yet Carnap specifies it in a rather idiosyncratic fashion:

> [P]sychology is a part of the domain of unified science based on physics. By "physics" we wish to mean, not the system of currently known physical laws, but rather the science characterized by a mode of concept formation which traces every concept back to state-coordinates, that is, to systematic assign-ments of numbers to space-time points.[80]

Subsequently, the main impediments to pursuing the program of translation into a universal language of science were dispositional predicates and the intensional idiom (modality and intentional attitudes). The early Carnap (as well as his student Quine) defended a *principle of extensionality*; that is, he excluded intensional ("opaque") contexts from scientific language. In intensional contexts, constancy of truth-values cannot be guaranteed in cases of substitution of co-referring singular terms and in cases of existential generalization. While Carnap's version of physicalism cannot count as a variety of metaphysical naturalism, his demand to eliminate or reductively analyze the intensional idiom brings him close to a semantic-analytic naturalism, of which more below. Even today, the thesis of "the eliminability of intensionality at all levels of description or explanation" is sometimes taken to be the defining character-istic of physicalism.[81]

Quine denied his teacher's physicalism as well as logical empiricism in general the honorary title "naturalistic." Once the dream of deducing science from sense-data is over, he claimed, Carnap's method of rational reconstruction loses "the last remaining advantage ... over straight psychology; namely, the advantage of translational reduction." "Why not just see how this construction really proceeds? Why not settle for psychology? [...] Better to discover how science is in fact developed and learned than to fabricate a fictitious structure to a similar effect."[82]

Further issues discussed in the context of physicalism were as follows: Is the physical world causally closed? Is determinism true? Which kinds of reduction must be distinguished? Can mental and social properties be understood as supervenient properties of physical systems? Could token physicalism be true when type physicalism is not?

Biologism and evolutionary naturalism: Discussing both physicalism and biologism under the heading "naturalism with a leading science" admittedly blurs a significant disanalogy. While physicalism says, more or less, that everything is physics, almost no one says that everything is biology. Biologism is not such a broad metaphysical view as physicalism is, since it has nothing to say about the realm of inanimate nature. But it has much to say about man and his abilities, and this is what matters for naturalism. Naturalistic theories purport to explain those phenomena scientifically that do not belong to the proper study of natural science beyond dispute (see the section "Analytic, or semantic, naturalism," below pp. 274–77).

The starting point of biological naturalism is the fact that *Homo sapiens* is a species of mammal that has come about through natural evolution. For some philosophers, the recognition of this fact already marks a naturalistic position: "A philosophical approach is naturalist iff its procedures are consistent with the assumption that its subject matter has come into being as a result of evolutionary processes."[83] This condition is extraordinarily weak. Holding views that are "consistent with" the insights of evolutionary theory hardly suffices to be a naturalist. Also weak, but assuredly more poetic, is the following: "To be a naturalist is to see human beings as frail complexes of perishable tissue, and so part of the natural order."[84]

The term "evolutionary naturalism" was already in use at the beginning of the twentieth century (see also "American philosophy in the twentieth century," Chapter 5).[85] In the second half of the century, various theories were developed which widened the area of what was amenable to evolutionary explanations. Sociobiology, evolutionary epistemology, evolutionary psychology, and evolutionary ethics make the claim to explain cognitive, cultural, social, and moral accomplishments of humankind in the light of evolutionary history. These theories are more appropriately called "naturalistic," while the mere insight that human beings are mammals that evolved through history should not count as a distinctive feature of naturalism. It is true that creationists deny this claim, yet aside from these religiously motivated supernaturalists there are no serious opponents. Naturalists and non-naturalists battle over the question of which explanatory claims are associated with this insight. Many evolutionary naturalists, though, try to get by with quite weak assumptions about the natural history of *Homo sapiens*. They stress the fact *that* our physical makeup and our abilities are the result of a contingent evolutionary history, and leave it open *how* this history has taken course in detail, and what precisely appeals to evolutionary history do explain. A popular philosophical comment on views of this level of generality is that they are either trivial or false. This comment seems appropriate in this case. The claim that the abilities of human beings are the result of natural history in the sense that we would lack them, had evolution taken a different tack, is a claim with only a smidgen of empirical content. Short of supernaturalism or creationism, it is hard to see what this view is arguing against. But this view might also have a more robust reading. Yet the more challenging the claim about evolutionary naturalism, the harder it is to corroborate.

Let us look at the "evolution of the mental." Some creatures that wander over today's earth have intentional states. This is a contingent fact, in the sense in which the existence of oxygen or the value of the gravitational constant are contingent facts. If one kept on asking on what this fact depends, or, how it could enter the world, one would have to tell two long stories, namely, the natural history of *Homo sapiens* followed by its cultural history. Since the mind did not come into being immediately with the Big Bang, it must have evolved. There must have been proto-phenomena and intermediary steps. Now it is notoriously difficult to characterize these steps, for we literally have no words for it. Our intentional idiom is tailor-made for the description of fully-fledged cognitive capacities. Some of us can even compose, play chess, estimate spring tides, or write philosophical essays. It is a hard fact that we human beings can do these things. However, it is not a natural or biological fact, since these abilities emerged over the history of mankind on the basis of a largely unchanged genetic constitution. It is a *cultural* fact, since the emergence of these features required that the *animal symbolicum* passed on acquired abilities to the next generation.

Culture has occasionally been called the "second nature" of human beings, but this parlance cannot seriously be used to buttress a *biological* naturalism. According to Arnold Gehlen (1904–76), it is part of human nature to be a cultural creature. Man, he taught, is a deficient being (*Mängelwesen*), its instincts reduced, stepmotherly treated by Mother Nature, and therefore in need of culture and institutions. In the German tradition of philosophical anthropology, reference to a second nature of human beings was widespread. It played on the ambiguity within the notion of nature. In talk of second nature, "nature" is understood in the sense of "characteristic" or "real essence," but not in the biological sense. Hence, this reference is not an expression of a naturalistic orientation of philosophical anthropology, rather the opposite. Even if human beings are by nature reliant on culture, their culturally developed abilities are not part of their natural biological endowment. Besides, it is hard to understand why many naturalists accept only those explanations in which human traits are explained with reference to sub-humane conditions.[86]

Evolutionary naturalism is the main target of attacks by creationism. Creationism is incompatible with many naturalistic theories, but it predominantly rejects Darwin's theory of natural selection. The Christian philosopher Alvin Plantinga (1932–) is an important figure in these debates. Plantinga takes naturalism simply as the negation of theism,[87] and he has developed an "evolutionary argument against naturalism," according to which one cannot at the same time adhere to evolutionary theory and deny that there is supernatural influence on the history of the world. His evolutionary argument against naturalism goes as follows: Only a form of evolution guided and orchestrated by God can explain why our cognitive system produces mostly true beliefs. If evolution proceeded blindly and randomly, as atheistic evolutionism claims, it would be highly unlikely that our beliefs are largely true, including the belief in evolutionary theory itself. But proponents of evolutionary theories of course claim those theories to be true. Thus, evolutionary naturalism is self-defeating. It cannot explain its own pretence of truth.[88]

The late twentieth century was a good era for biological naturalism, since owing to rapid developments in the life sciences it could renew its scientific foundations. Further issues discussed in the context of biological naturalism are as follows: Are there strict laws of biology? Do our genes determine our behavior? How can biology explain purposeful behavior? What is the relation between intentional, teleological, and functional explanations? Can biology do without what Daniel Dennett has called "the design stance"?

Naturalism without a leading science

Methodological or scientific naturalism takes scientific method as the only avenue to truth. However, methodological naturalists have to indicate what makes scientific method a method of the *natural* sciences, even if they formulate their position without reference to a leading science. In order to give their naturalistic credo a determinate content, they have to demarcate the endeavor "natural sciences" from other cognitive enterprises.

Quine famously holds that "[t]he world is as natural science says it is, insofar as natural science is right."[89] Clearly, this declaration does not contribute to distinguishing science from non-science, but rather presupposes such a distinction. One needs a positive characterization of the notion of natural science invoked in Quine's naturalism. Simply declaring, as Quine does, that "demarcation is not my purpose"[90] does not suffice, since his notion of naturalism cannot have sharper contours than his notion of the natural sciences.

Many methodological naturalists who reject a leading science refrain deliberately from specifying which scientific methods distinguish science from non-science, or good science from bad science. The reason is that they do not want to domineer over the sciences. Neither can the material findings of scientific research be identified *a priori*, they maintain, nor can the *methods* of science. Methodological naturalists do not want to anticipate what the sciences will acknowledge and develop as a methodological standard. Standards are revisable, after all. One can boil down this attitude to the maxim: *Wherever science leads, I will follow*.

This kind of naturalism appears to be attractive in that it does not commit itself to any scientific branch, theory, or program. Thus, for example Quine declared Carnap's physicalism to be unfruitful and remote from science. In turn, it has been argued that Quine's own theory of language acquisition bet on the wrong horse by relying on behavioristic psychology.[91] In the course of the "cognitive turn," behaviorism lost a large part of its reputation to the cognitive sciences. (For a description of the turn from behaviorism to cognitivism, see "Philosophy of psychology," Chapter 13.) To put it bluntly: scientific programs come and go, paradigms are exhausted; what remains is methodological naturalism, as long as it does not commit itself to any leading science. The *scientia mensura* naturalist does not bind his fate with a particular scientific theory or paradigm, but declares his solidarity with the course of science itself. Hence Quine's favored phrase: "Science itself tells us that …"[92]

But what *is* science itself? Who exactly is allowed to care of himself in matters of method? Arguing that the natural sciences are sciences of nature does not help, for *scientia mensura* naturalism replaced reference to nature by reference to the natural sciences. Now if naturalists reject a narrower specification of scientific methods, an unsatisfactory situation results, a situation already bewailed in the debates of postwar American naturalism: "naturalism stands for scientific method; whatever rules out scientific method – that is supernatural. We are back where we were. 'Nature' means that which is open to scientific method."[93] Even more succinctly: "Naturalism excludes what is not scientifically investigable, and calls the domain of possible investigation 'nature'."[94]

Two contemporary methodological naturalists who refuse to give any definition of the enterprise of the natural sciences are the American philosophers of science Arthur Fine (1937–) and Stephen P. Stich (1943–). Fine holds that science will take care of itself in every respect. He advocates a "natural ontological attitude" which abstains from any "essentialist premises about the 'nature' of science."[95] He recommends that science is taken at its face value, rejecting "the mistaken idea that one must add distinctively philosophical overlays to science in order to make sense of it."[96] This anti-essentialist scientism indeed boils down to the maxim mentioned above: *Wherever science leads, I will follow.* Now, it is not easy to distinguish between scorn for "essentialist premises about the 'nature' of science" and the refusal to explain what one is talking about. Fine would surely not accept as science just any cognitive endeavor that anyone has ever *called* science. His maxim, "follow good science as far as science goes but do not demand that science do more"[97] at least indicates that he feels able to tell apart good science from bad science. Presumably, he would advise us to ask the good scientists about what good science is. But a charlatan or a fraud, passing himself off as a scientist, is unlikely to shy away from passing himself off as a good scientist. We may hope that, in the long term, he will not be accepted by the scientific community, but if he is clever enough in faking and cheating, it may take some time until he gets unmasked. What about his status up until then? Is he a good scientist just as long as the majority of his colleagues accepts him as a peer? Or worse yet: what if one of the next "science wars" is won by the united social constructivists and relativists, so that the good scientists Fine relies on find themselves in a minority?

For a naturalist, it is not advisable to regard membership in the scientific community as a brute sociological or institutional fact. The truth is that the peer group has *reasons* for accepting or not accepting somebody as a member. And such reasons will be needed as soon as the charlatan takes the university to court over his dismissal.

Fine's defeatism regarding the definability of the science game would simply leave the scientific community empty-handed in such quarrels.

Another methodological naturalist who seems to resort to the maxim *Wherever science leads, I will follow* is Stephen Stich. Stich takes exception to a widespread "puritanical naturalism" in the philosophy of mind. The search for a naturalistic criterion of acceptable properties or predicates, as carried out in the various armchair projects of naturalizing the intentional, he says, is "misunderstanding the way that science works."[98] According to Stich, there is no way of identifying naturalistically acceptable predicates in advance, i.e. independently of the role they play in science as practiced:

> What "legitimates" certain properties (or predicates, if you prefer) and makes others scientifically suspect is that the former, but not the latter, are invoked in successful scientific theories. ... [B]eing invoked in a successful science is all that it takes to render a property scientifically legitimate.[99]

Just as Fine speaks of "good" science, Stich speaks of "successful" science. And just like Fine, Stich becomes quite taciturn when pressed for an explanation of what successful science amounts to. He says "I don't claim to have an account of what it takes to be a successful scientific theory. Indeed, I suspect that that, too, is a pluralistic, open-ended, and evolving notion." And as to "the question of whether successful science can be constructed using intentional categories ... it is working scientists ... who will resolve this question, not philosophers of the puritan persuasion."[100]

Again, this result is disappointing. Whatever the philosophical merits of anti-apriorism and anti-essentialism are, the advice "Ask the working scientists!" cannot by itself settle the question of what counts as good or successful science. Abstaining from setting any methodological standards or criteria that distinguish science from humbug and charlatanism leaves us with nothing but a sociological notion of science: *Everything that can be studied at a university is a science.* Or, *science is what professors are paid for.* Or, *science is what you can get money for from the National Science Foundation.* But, as is well known, weird things are taught at universities, for example that science is just another genre of literature, or that reality is but a social construction. Naturalism cannot be so liberal as to embrace all these claims as *scientific* doctrines, just because they are taught at universities by tenured professors. Affiliation to the sciences cannot only be a matter of the respective doorplate. Suppose that all professors of physics defect to a spiritualist sect overnight while keeping their chairs. Would Fine and Stich still hold that the world is just as these so-called physicists say? No, they would – one hopes – call them *former* physicists, irrespective of their doorplate. And they would campaign to re-advertise their posts. Naturalists should not only defend "the natural sciences," but they should also find something *about* science defensible.[101] If a naturalist did not dare to propose what is estimable about the sciences, he has nothing to counter an ideological redefinition of the concept of science that successfully infiltrated scientific institutions.

A final misgiving about my examination of scientific naturalism must be addressed. Why, one might ask, could not naturalism be more pluralistic? Why does it have to rely on *natural* science exclusively, instead of including the social sciences? Philosophers such as Fine and Stich despair of spelling out a set of necessary and jointly sufficient conditions that define the science game. Why not, in the face of this difficulty, adopt a broadly Wittgensteinian view, according to which the different branches of the scientific enterprise are held together by family resemblances? Why not base scientific naturalism on a pluralistic notion of science?

This alternative view confounds two questions that are better kept apart. It is one thing to determine which views about science are worth being held, it is quite another thing to determine which views are worth being called "naturalism." Reference to the *natural* sciences is the last remaining link between naturalism and its morphological and semantical constituent "nature." Surely there are good reasons to dispute the claim that natural science is the only avenue to the truth. But these reasons are not at the same time good reasons for calling more pluralistic alternatives "naturalistic" as well.

Analytic, or semantic, naturalism

On the one hand, *scientia mensura* naturalists are anxious to delineate the scientific enter-prise from other cognitive endeavors. On the other hand, they have to draw a dividing line between the natural sciences and other sciences. This is an intricate business. They must be neither too restrictive, in excluding respectable natural sciences, nor too liberal, in including just any discipline in the humanities or social sciences. From this situation, one could infer that *scientia mensura* naturalism is a hopelessly vague program. At the end of the day this assessment may be correct. This assessment would, however, ignore a project known as "analytic" or "semantic" naturalism, which is put forth in philosophy of mind. Analytic naturalism takes the view that a scientific discipline is largely distin-guished by its concepts or predicates, and that the project of naturalizing is an endeavor in conceptual analysis. Instead of favoring a class of scientific disciplines, it privileges a class of naturalistically acceptable predicates. Other predicates must be analyzable as predi-cates of this reference class. Thus the method of analytic naturalism is reductive analysis.

As regards the reference class, it is common to favor predicates that designate physical properties of concrete objects. In fact, analytic naturalists mostly proceed in reverse order: they indicate the predicates that must *not* occur. In analytic naturalism, the view is widespread that the only criterion for naturalistic acceptability is a ban on intentional language: only those sciences, explanations, and theories are natural-istically acceptable that avoid the idiom of intentional psychology. The background for this criterion is the estimation that ascriptions of propositional attitudes (beliefs, desires, intentions, and so forth) and the associated practice of explanation, if inter-preted realistically, form a serious hindrance to science. The intentional idiom of belief-desire psychology is not readily connectable to scientific theory, because any ascription of an intentional attitude can only be justified or explained in a circular way by further intentional ascriptions. Owing to this failure of connectability, belief-desire psychology does not take part in scientific progress. From the royal road to truth it has forked off into a dead-end street. Paul Churchland (1942–) formulated this position vividly. The natural sciences, he says, explore the world in a division of labor and thus contribute to the growth of our empirical knowledge. Folk psychology is the only thing that "is no part of this growing synthesis. Its intentional categories stand magnificently alone." It is "a stagnant or degenerating research program, and has been for millennia."[102] In his *eliminative materialism*, Paul Churchland draws the ontological conclusion that no entities correspond to the intentional categories of folk psychology, that is, that *there are no such things as* beliefs, desires, and intentions. Dennett and Fodor phrase it more cautiously:

> Beliefs have a less secure position in a critical scientific ontology than, say, electrons or genes, and a less robust presence in the everyday world than, say, toothaches or haircuts.[103]

> The worry about representation is above all that the semantic (and/or the intentional) will prove permanently recalcitrant to integration in the natural order ... [104]

> I suppose that sooner or later the physicists will complete the catalogue they've been compiling of the ultimate and irreducible properties of things. When they do, the likes of *spin*, *charm*, and *charge* will perhaps appear upon their list. But *aboutness* surely won't; intentionality simply doesn't go that deep. It's hard to see, in face of this consideration, how one can be a Realist about intentionality without also being, to some extent or other, a Reductionist. ... If aboutness is real, it must be something else. ... [T]here is no place for intentional categories in a physicalistic view of the world.[105]

There are three possible avenues for those who do not accept the autonomy of intentional psychology: analytical naturalization, eliminativism, and instrumentalism. Intentional terms should be either (a) analyzed reductively, i.e. reduced to non-intentional terms via analytic definition, or (b) eliminated and replaced by others, or (c) treated as useful fictions. Only the first option has direct bearings on naturalism. In Churchland's eliminativism and Dennett's instrumentalism, there is nothing to be naturalized, since strictly speaking the intentional realm does not exist. The program of analytic naturalization of the intentional idiom (i.e. the attempt to give necessary and sufficient conditions for applying intentional predicates) will be described in more detail below in the section "Naturalizing intentionality."

In the 1980s, many philosophers engaged in the project of naturalizing intentionality (e.g. Fodor, Dretske, Millikan, Sterelny, Lycan, Schiffer, Loar, Block, Devitt, Stalnaker, Stampe). In the 1990s, some authors argued that the significance of analytic or semantic naturalism had been overrated.[106] Stephen Stich objected that the criterion for naturalistic acceptability was both too strong and too vague. He compared the search for such a criterion with the search in logical empiricism for a general criterion of meaning. In both cases, a relation R is being searched, which a predicate or a property must have with respect to a basic vocabulary or a specifiable empirical base, in order to be acceptable. Stich holds that in both cases one cannot state such a criterion that separates the good from the bad. All proposed criteria are either too restrictive or too liberal. They either throw out the baby with the bath water, or leave much foul water in the tub.

However, there is a blind spot in Stich's view that the recommended criteria are not apt to distinguish good from bad. This view already presupposes the idea of what counts as good and bad. Stich confines himself to the note that all that counts is that the predicates or properties in question are applied in "successful scientific theories."[107] This move is familiar now, and so is the rejoinder: A naturalist must be able to indicate what he takes to be successful science and why he does so. Moreover, the sought-after criterion does not necessarily consist in specifying a legitimizing relation R, in which intentional predicates must stand to a privileged vocabulary, as Stich assumes. Stich overlooks a crucial disanalogy between the ban on intentional concepts and the criterion of meaning in logical empiricism. The ban on intentionality has the form of a *condition of exclusion*. No basic vocabulary is privileged; the naturalist rather pledges to abstain from using certain resources. In view of this fact, the terms "semantic" or "analytic naturalism" can lead to confusion by suggesting sameness of meaning between *analysans* and *analysandum*. However, the program proposed by Fodor, Fred Dretske (1932–), Ruth Millikan (1933–), and others is not committed to such a claim, since it is possible to take the relation at hand in the sense of an extensional definition: A given intentional phenomenon, say a belief of type *p*, *is present if* certain empirical conditions are fulfilled. These conditions need not be understood as semantic components of the intentional concept. The semantic aspect of analytic naturalism consists only in the restriction for the vocabulary in which sufficient conditions are phrased.

Besides, Stich has objected to analytic naturalism on the grounds that the requirement for giving necessary and sufficient conditions for applying intentional terms is unachievably strong. Insofar as this objection targets a specific kind of conceptual analysis, it cannot be settled here. (For a rehabilitation of conceptual analysis, see "The development of analytic philosophy: Wittgenstein and after," Chapter 2.) However, let us suppose that Stich is right in arguing that one cannot pursue any interesting enterprise in the cognitive sciences under such severe restrictions. But why should this count against the criterion of naturalistic acceptability? Stich bases his rejection of the criterion on the claim that it does not separate the good from the bad. From the outset, he assumes that the criterion will reveal intentional naturalism as a good or promising project. Maybe this is asking too much. One contentious issue between naturalists and non-naturalists is precisely the question of how much good science is left if one abandons intentional terms. Consider again the parallel to the empiricist criterion of meaning: According to Stich, it speaks against logical empiricism that all proposed versions of the criterion of meaning lead to intuitively implausible demarcations between what is meaningful and what is not. Stich does not conclude that logical empiricism must have had something different in mind. In the case of the naturalistic criterion, he prefers to reject the criterion, while his own concept of naturalism remains diffuse.

Stich is a representative of the large group of philosophers whose *rhetorical* solidarity with naturalism is stronger than their willingness to commit themselves to a defining characteristic. These philosophers have misgivings against attaching much weight to semantic or analytic reductions, and they complain that the notion of analytic naturalism forces them into a position that they are not committed to qua naturalists. In a similar vein, one might ask why the philosophy of mind should be the discipline that decides the fate of naturalism, and not for example ontology, philosophy of science, or epistemology. Now, let us recall by which path the debate arrived at analytic naturalism: alternative definitions of naturalism were debunked as insufficient. It is widely accepted that naturalism is under-specified as an ontological thesis about what kinds of objects exist. In the philosophy of science, all attempts at a definition only reach the question of what distinguishes approved from pseudo-sciences. Now, an answer suggests itself. In particular, those disciplines that stick to the unanalyzable intentional idiom count as inferior and explanatorily weak. Analytical naturalism gives a criterion of naturalistic acceptability for philosophical theories and explanations. Can this demarcating criterion be seen as a specification of the *scientia mensura* maxim of methodological naturalism? On closer look, the criterion is at best only part of the answer. Analytic naturalism purports to provide a sufficient condition for *bad* science. Its criterion, though, is not a sufficient criterion for good science, since astrology or phrenology might very well be free from intentional language.

Now, a pivotal characteristic of analytic naturalism is the dynamical aspect of naturali*zation*. One cannot in general consider the label "naturalistic theory" as synonymous with a "theory that contains no intentional terms." Otherwise, we could speak of a naturalistic mineralogy, for example. The fact that mineralogy is pursued without intentional ascriptions, however, does not count among those things over which naturalists and non-naturalists are at odds. The conditions of analytic naturalism have no application where *explananda* are given in non-intentional terms. Therefore, a science of mineralogy that is free of intentional language does not *confirm* naturalism. Converse views rest on a confusion between the terms "naturalistic" and "scientific." A theory in the natural sciences is not per se naturalistic; whether it is, depends on its area of application, among other things. Naturalistic theories purport to extend the area of application of the natural sciences to those phenomena that are not already covered beyond dispute.

If one attempts to give naturalism a more global meaning beyond single naturalization projects, then the following suggests itself: naturalism is the programmatic thesis *that naturalization is possible everywhere*. Analytic naturalism does not render metaphysical or methodological naturalism obsolete. It can be understood as a further step in elaborating upon these programs. Just because naturalists "regard human beings and mental phenomena as part of the natural order," it is their duty "to explain intentional relations in naturalistic terms."[108] At the bottom of the program of naturalizing intentionality lies the opposition of mind and nature, which can hardly be called idiosyncratic.

Three fields of naturalization

Naturalizing epistemology

The distinction into fields of naturalization – epistemology, intentionality, normativity – cuts across the above-mentioned triple classification of naturalisms. Naturalizing epistemology is not creating a new *kind* of naturalism; rather it relates naturalism to a specific *subject matter*.

In 1969, Quine entitled a programmatic essay "Epistemology naturalized." This is the succinct title of a whole bunch of epistemological theories, which occupy a peculiar intermediate position between natural science and philosophical analysis (see "Epistemology in the twentieth century," Chapter 11, pp. 508–09).[109] All these theories have in common that they reject aprioristic methods in epistemology. They highlight the role of empirical knowledge and challenge the authority of conceptual analysis, Cartesian knowledge, and introspective methods. In this spirit, Quine calls for "abandonment of the goal of a first philosophy prior to natural science." Quine's statement and several similar ones are hard to evaluate, however, for he says little about the rejected counter-positions. He never specifies systematically or histori-cally what exactly epistemological apriorism is, except for a few notes on Descartes's foundationalism or Carnap's *The Logical Structure of the World*. It is, for instance, not clear whether the philosophical projects of Kant or Husserl fall under his notion of "first philosophy."

The central passage from Quine's programmatic essay reads as follows:

> Epistemology, or something like it, simply falls into place as a chapter of psychology and hence of natural science. It studies a natural phenomenon, viz., a physical human subject. This human subject is accorded a certain experimen-tally controlled input – certain patterns of irradiation in assorted frequencies, for instance – and in the fullness of time the subject delivers as output a description of the three-dimensional external world and its history.[110]

Quine's talk of experimentally controlled irradiation patterns is deliberately outlandish. In fact, he does not discuss the main question of epistemology "how evidence relates to theory",[111] in terms of laboratory experiments. As a starting point, he prefers everyday situations of observation, as in his scenario of radical translation. The alienated parlance of irradiation patterns on the surface of our bodies is intended to highlight the fact that any observation or perceptual judgment is based on the triggering of our sensory receptors: "Our only source of information about the external world is through the impact of light rays and molecules upon our sensory surfaces";[112] in short "whatever evidence there *is* for science *is* sensory evidence."[113] Thus Quine takes up and varies the rationale of classical empiricism, namely that there is nothing in the mind that was not first in the senses (*nihil est in intellectu quod non prius fuerit in sensu*).

A central topic of the debate about naturalistic epistemology is the question of how traditional and naturalized epistemology are related. In Quine's own, often-cited view, there is a certain continuity in subject matter:

The relation between the meager input and the torrential output is a relation that we are prompted to study for somewhat the same reasons that always prompted epistemology; namely, in order to see how evidence relates to theory, and in what ways one's theory of nature transcends any available evidence.[114]

Now Quine describes input on the one hand in terms of stimuli, on the other hand in terms of "evidence" and "information." Various critics have objected that he thus levels the difference between a question of fact and a question of justification, a difference that was important to traditional epistemology (*quid facti* versus *quid iuris*). In particular, the objection reads that Quine uses the term "evidence" equivocally. Take the first sentence of *The Roots of Reference*: "Given only the evidence of our senses, how do we arrive at our theory of the world?"[115] Here, the expression "evidence of our senses" is in need of explanation. What exactly do the senses transfer, or what do they present us for evaluation? In other phrasings of the main question of epistemology, Quine replaces "evidence" by "source of information." Both terms suggest a relation of epistemic support or justification. Elsewhere, however, Quine notes: "By sensory evidence I mean stimulation of sensory receptors."[116] But how can stimulations of sensory receptors be pieces of "information," or "evidence for" our beliefs and theories? Quine often characterizes the relation at stake with pale verbs such as "depend on" or "is due to".[117] Such formulations, however, leave open the nature of the relation: is it a causal relation or rather one of epistemic support or justification?

Among others, Donald Davidson (1917–2003) criticized this ambiguity: "No doubt meaning and knowledge depend on experience, and experience ultimately on sensation. But this is the 'depend' of causality, not of evidence or justification."[118] Davidson insists that sensory stimuli or external factors in the face of which something is uttered, can never be the kind of entities that justify or ground an assertion. Otherwise, the cognitive subject would need to be able to compare the stimulations of his sensory receptors with the resulting beliefs, in order to decide whether the former support the latter. Yet for this, sensory stimulations would have to be epistemically accessible. This requires an epistemic subject that can observe the perceptual process again, a sort of *homunculus* whose working would in turn be subject to epistemological analysis. In order to avoid these absurdities, one has to distinguish the causal and the justificatory relation. Both relations cannot hold between the same relata. Davidson insists "nothing can count as a reason for holding a belief except another belief."[119]

Apparently there are two readings of the main epistemological question of how we get from stimulus to science. Quine prefers the causal reading, yet irritates the reader by using justificatory vocabulary. The causal reading, namely to "view perception squarely as causal transaction between external bodies and talking people, with no curtain to screen them",[120] does not preclude that at the same time rational relations hold between perceptual *beliefs* and theoretical beliefs. But the relata are different then, and Quine's critics point out that instead of two readings of a single question, we deal with two entirely different questions.

Quine influentially replied to the objection that naturalistic epistemologies are circular. The circularity charge, as known from Husserl's critique of psychologism, goes as follows: Naturalistic epistemologies cannot solve the problem of skepticism, for they rely on scientific beliefs, the reliability of which is under consideration. According to Quine, any reasonable skepticism is part of science itself and motivated through science. "Scepticism is an offshoot of science," and "sceptical doubts are scientific doubts.".[121] Skepticism towards science as a whole, on the other hand, is misguided, since it is based on a misconception of the relation between philosophy and science: the misconception that philosophy has a justificatory function towards the sciences. In this vein Quine rejects the objection that he uses Darwin's evolutionary theory in order to justify induction:

> I am not appealing to Darwinian biology to justify induction. This would be circular, since biological knowledge depends on induction. Rather I am granting the efficacy of induction, and then observing that Darwinian biology, if true, helps explain why induction is as efficacious as it is.[122]

More generally, his answer to the charge of circularity is this:

> The reason I shall not be impressed by this is that my position is a naturalistic one; I see philosophy not as an *a priori* propaedeutic or groundwork for science, but as continuous with science. I see philosophy and science as in the same boat – a boat which, to revert to Neurath's figure as I so often do, we can rebuild only at sea while staying afloat in it.[123]

By turning away from *foundationalism*, Quine steals the thunder of the objection. Skepticism against science as a whole has a point only if one could expect philosophy *to provide a justification for* scientific knowledge. Once this pretension is given up, the complaint vanishes that it cannot be fulfilled.

It is also possible that Quine uses the term "sensory evidence" exclusively in a causal reading without wishing to profit from the above-mentioned ambiguity. In this case, Quine would turn out to be an epistemological *eliminativist*, as Hilary Putnam (1926–) has diagnosed:

> Taken at face value, Quine's position is sheer epistemological Eliminationism: we should just abandon the notions of justification, good reason, warranted assertion, etc., and reconstrue the notion of "evidence" (so that "evidence" becomes the sensory stimulations that cause us to have the scientific beliefs we have).[124]

In this reading, Quine's naturalized epistemology constitutes a change in topic with respect to what is traditionally called epistemology. This alternative has strongly influenced the subsequent debate about naturalizing epistemology. The eliminative variant was called "replacement naturalism," whereas the idea of holding on to old questions, which should be answered jointly with the sciences, was called "cooperative naturalism."[125] The latter, weaker view is more widespread.

Stephen Stich opts for a "weak naturalism" that states "there are some legitimate epistemological questions that are *not* scientific questions and cannot be resolved by scientific research."[126] It is questionable why such a position should still be called naturalistic.

Alvin Goldman, Larry Laudan, Philip Kitcher, Jane Duran, and Hilary Kornblith have called an epistemology naturalistic if it "considers" or "makes use of" empirical knowledge.[127] This can mean different things. An epistemologist could claim to have *considered* empirical knowledge already if nothing he says *contradicts* empirical knowledge. This requirement is too weak, of course. Even Descartes, Leibniz, and Kant appear to be naturalists then, for they too "sought to show that their ideas comported well with the best available science of their times."[128] Kitcher notably accepts this consequence.[129] However, there is a stronger version of the requirement to consider empirical knowledge. Often it means that certain *rationalistic idealizations* of traditional epistemology be revoked in favor of how epistemic subjects really function and acquire knowledge:

> [A]dvice in matters intellectual, as in other matters, should take account of the agent's capacities. There is no point in recommending procedures that cognizers cannot follow or recommending results that cognizers cannot attain. As in the ethical sphere, "ought" implies "can."[130]

This demand certainly marks a difference between theories that can be right and those that must be wrong. For if an epistemology binds the acquisition of knowledge to conditions that cannot by fulfilled by epistemic subjects like us, it is descriptively inadequate. We were not searching, however, for the difference between right and false theories, but between naturalistic and non-naturalistic ones.

Empirical research into epistemic processes, especially in the cognitive sciences, has led to surprising results. In the last two decades of the century, these results made a strong impact on philosophical epistemology. The insights into the amount of irrationality in our everyday reasoning are particularly impressive (for an overview, see "Philosophy of psychology," Chapter 13, pp. 598–604). In the face of these results, it seems wise to rethink the idealized concept of rationality that was used in decision theory and game theory, and instead focus on rationality as it is embodied in finite, imperfect beings like us. However, criticism of apriorism and idealization is barely relevant for the question of where the exact difference is between naturalistic and non-naturalistic epistemologies. In the philosophical tradition, one can always find epistemological theories in which certain empirical constraints were overlooked or neglected. Quine's behavioristic theory of language acquisition is among them. The requirement to include empirical knowledge, however, is insufficient for defining epistemological naturalism. *Disregarding* empirical knowledge was never a programmatic point in non-naturalistic epistemologies. Even Kant, the arch-apriorist, invoked a good deal of empirical psychology in his analyses; today, his psychology of faculties is criticized as being inadequate. The demand for empirical knowledge is at best distinctive if one confines it to *particular* empirical knowledge. This is a common and tacit practice, if, for instance, findings from the cognitive sciences count as empirical, whereas Austin's linguistic phenomenology does not. But the actual uses of words in a speech community do constitute empirical evidence, possibly the only empirical clues available to conceptual analysis.[131] Without further qualification, almost everyone will subscribe to the demand for including empirical knowledge. Thus this demand cannot be a defining characteristic of epistemological naturalism. The "pure apriorism" naturalistic epistemologies warn of is only a straw man. If on the other hand only particular knowledge is meant, one is thrown back to the question of which disciplines count as the reference class. This was an open question above. Answering it is two-edged even for the *scientia mensura* naturalist. In general, it will always be rewarding for philosophers to have non-philosophical knowledge at their disposal. However, there is no reason to favor, say, cosmological or physiological knowledge over the knowledge of linguistics, law, or art history.

Scientifically minded epistemology is most interesting if instead of favoring particular bits of knowledge, it rather specifies how to *use* such knowledge, in other words, if proposals are put forth about how epistemological cooperation between philosophy and the empirical sciences should look. Scientific epistemology is valuable where it determines what *role* empirical knowledge can play in formulating worthwhile epistemic aims or virtues, for example in the framework of the *meliorative project*, which seeks to "specify strategies through whose use human beings can improve their cognitive states."[132] An important differentiation of cooperative naturalism is *reliabilism* (see pp. 474 and 482–84, in "Epistemology in the twentieth century," Chapter 11). Reliabilism identifies reliable cognitive processes, namely those that lead to knowledge with high probability. It is based on an *externalist* approach to justification, according to which a subject can be justified in his beliefs even if he is not aware of the justifying reasons or facts. Bringing such "external reasons" into play constitutes a sharp break with traditional theories of justification, which confined themselves to "internal" reasons that are accessible to the epistemic subject.

Naturalizing intentionality

The project of naturalizing intentionality is a specification of analytical naturalism. The motivation for this project – as presented by Paul Churchland above – is the view that the intentional idiom of folk psychology (the unanalyzed parlance of beliefs, desires, intentions and other intentional attitudes) is out of place in the theories of natural sciences and thus an obstinate hindrance to science. In the final quarter of the century, naturalizing intentionality was the most discussed project of naturalization. The main reason for this was the immense success of cognitive sciences in the wake of the "cognitive turn." "The development of the cognitive sciences has ... made the mind the most intensely hunted game in the philosophical jungle."[133] In the philosophy of mind, philosophers such as Roderick Chisholm (1916–99), Fodor, and John Searle (1932–) rehabilitated mentalism, turning away from a behavioristic philosophy of mind. The rehabilitation of mentalism went hand in hand with developments outside philosophy, namely, "the revival of cognitivism in psychology and the advent of the computer model of the mind" (see "Philosophy of mind," Chapter 12).

A statement from Fred Dretske can serve as a first approach to the project of naturalizing the mental. Dretske describes his information theoretic based semantics as "an exercise in naturalism . . . Can you bake a mental cake using only physical yeast and flour? The argument is that you can."[134] According to this view, the mental is made up of physical ingredients, which are themselves not mental. Dretske's metaphorical formulation leaves open what kind of production or constitution is strived for (or reduction, being the converse of constitution). An *ontological* reduction of the mental to the physical is not distinctive for a naturalization of the mental. Such a reduction secures the ontological primacy of the physical, but this is compatible with quite weak conceptual and nomological relations between the physical and the mental, for example with a global supervenience thesis, which does not even presuppose token–token identities. As explained above, ontological physicalism or materialism does not in itself support specific programs of scientific investigation of the mind. Ontological physicalism is even compatible with a critical attitude toward a science of the mind, for instance with the "New Dualism" of the Oxford School. A naturalist in the spirit of Dretske searches rather for a *conceptual* reduction of intentionality. Stalnaker exemplifies this further approach: "The challenge represented to the philosopher who wants to regard human beings and mental phenomena as part of the natural order is to explain intentional relations in naturalistic terms."[135] This formulation explicitly links the project of naturalizing intentionality to metaphysical naturalism, which considers human beings and the mental as "part of the natural order."

It remains to specify what it means "to explain intentional relations in naturalistic terms." According to Fodor, naturalizing intentional phenomena means providing a set of sufficient conditions for those "in nonintentional, nonsemantical, nonteleological, and, in general, non-question-begging vocabulary."[136] Fodor and other authors entertain unsettled beliefs about whether this requires only sufficient or rather sufficient *and necessary* conditions. The latter option conforms to classical conceptual analysis. Those who confine themselves to sufficient conditions argue as follows: intentional concepts must be applicable to hitherto unknown, intelligent creatures, which crucially differ from our species, and they must be applicable to human beings under bizarre science fiction scenarios.[137]

Fodor's conjunction "nonintentional, nonsemantical, nonteleological" has a long history in the philosophy of mind. Declared naturalists often come up with analyses of intentional phenomena without immediate reference to mental entities, yet these analyses rely on intentional *presuppositions*, i.e. they depend upon the fact that other intentional phenomena remained unanalyzed. Putnam explains: "From the fact that a statement is not explicitly about anything mental it does not follow that none of its presuppositions make any reference to our cognitive interests, our way of regarding different contexts, or our intentional powers."[138] An indicator for such indirect dependence is the usage of semantical or teleological concepts. One way of reacting to the problem of intentional presuppositions is to employ a wider concept of the intentional in the first place. It is mostly non-naturalists who embark on this strategy: "Say that a property is intentional if and only if either it is a propositional-attitude property – for example, the property of believing that such and such – or its instantiation presupposes instantiation of propositional-attitude properties."[139]

Fodor prohibits semantical and teleological concepts, in addition to intentional ones. As a further caveat, he adds the clause "and, in general, [in] non-question-begging vocabulary."[140] The ban on semantical expressions implies that "meaning" or "representation" must not be used unanalyzed. Notably Quine has highlighted the close relation between the semantical and the mentalistic idiom. The reason for this is that propositional attitudes as the paradigm cases of the mental have semantical identity conditions. We ascribe to two speakers the same belief, if the linguistic expressions of their beliefs are translatable into one another. It is not surprising then that for Quine meanings are just as suspect as mental entities.

The ban on teleological expressions implies that *aims, purposes, intentions,* and *functions* must not be used unanalyzed. The ban on teleology is more contentious than the ban on the semantical. This is evident in cases where teleological characterizations are explicitly or implicitly used for a purportedly naturalistic introduction of semantic concepts. Ruth Millikan, David Papineau (1947–), Fodor, and Dretske have devised "teleofunctionalist," or "biosemantical" theories of meaning and representation. Teleofunctionalists justify their use of teleological concepts by referring to the fact that biology as a respectable science "is already shot through with ascriptions of natural teleology and that such ascriptions are not going to go away, for without them we would lose valuable generalizations."[141] This view considers the naturalistic acceptability of biology as already agreed. It gets into difficulties, however, if biology is criticized as anthropomorphic for its use of teleological concepts, as for instance an eliminative materialist, who restricts himself to a physicalist concept of nature, would not hesitate to do.

There are recurring patterns in the debates about naturalizing intentionality. In these debates, the intentional presuppositions of proposed analyses are passed around like a hot potato. The following discussion between Nat(uralist) and Nonnat(uralist) is typical: Nonnat starts off considering intentionality as the defining and exclusive mark of the mental (Brentano's thesis). Nat readily ascribes intentional states to thermostats, robots, and ants. Nonnat avows himself a species chauvinist and adduces that intentional states have semantic identity conditions, whereas artifacts and lower animals have no linguistic capacities. Nat replies with a semantics of "natural indication" (Dretske). Nonnat objects that such a semantics cannot explain misrepresentation, hence is not a correct theory of meaning for a natural language. Nat denies this by means of relativizing representational content to normal conditions, or to biological "proper functions" (Millikan). Nonnat points out that teleological concepts are forbidden. Nat appeals to biology as a respectable science. Nonnat is not impressed and quotes from Kant's *Critique of Judgement,* that purpose must remain a "stranger in natural science" (B 320/§72). Nat now distinguishes between purposes and functions; evolutionary theory, he claims, gets along with the latter. Nonnat is still not impressed, functions are no less teleological than purposes. Besides, he claims that, after dropping anthropomorphic connotations, the concept of selection is unintelligible. (Typically, the debate stagnates at this point, for both opponents insist on their position.)

After this see-saw debate, Nat may try disposing of intentional presuppositions of teleological explanation by resorting to "homuncular functionalism" and its strategy of "recursive decomposition" (Dennett, Lycan): functions to fulfill, or problems to solve, must be decomposed into partial tasks, until the postulated agents are so dumb that they can be replaced by a mechanism. Nonnat objects that the gap to mechanistic descriptions cannot be closed this way, for even dumb homunculi remain homunculi, as long as they are the addressees of instructions. Nat may introduce the "robot reply," according to which intentional predicates can only be applied literally to machines if these machines have receptors and effectors. Nonnat considers the abilities to perceive and act as requiring intentionality, thus again defending species chauvinism plus supporting a thesis of linguistic dependency of intentional states, perhaps through a Davidsonian semantic holism. Nat either reintroduces "natural signs," which delimit semantic holism, or he loses his patience and resorts to Dennett's instrumentalism, denying a difference between "real" and "only ascribed" intentionality.

Debates about naturalizing intentionality typically go round in circles. They may take shortcuts or detours, but no matter where one starts, eventually one reaches the point where the journey began. It is the well-known *circle of intentional concepts*, according to which

> it is not possible to give a logical analysis of the intentionality of the mental in terms of simpler notions, since intentionality is, so to speak, a ground floor property of the mind ... Any explanation of intentionality, therefore, takes place within the circle of intentional concepts.[142]

Eventually, the point of disagreement comes into sharp focus: *The program of naturalizing intentionality is committed to the view that the intentional circle can be broken.* Were it possible to formulate sufficient non-intentional conditions for any intentional phenomenon, the naturalist could count on the domino effect. This is Fodor's conclusion: "Given any ... suitably naturalistic break of the intentional circle, it would be reasonable to claim that the main *philosophical* problem about intentionality had been solved."[143]

The non-naturalist does not have to maintain positive theses in such debates. His task is simply to prevent the naturalist from eating the forbidden fruit. Sure, forbidden fruit is sweetest, but sooner or later, the naturalist will have to give an analysis of an intentional phenomenon in non-intentional and in non-question-begging vocabulary. The insight that such debates yield is not *that* intentional concepts form a closed circle. Many philosophers have discovered this before. What we gain is a new insight into the *size* of the intentional circle, into the *amount* of phenomena circumscribed by it. Quine and Churchland maintain that the intentional idiom stands "magnificently alone"[144] in the face of natural science, which alone describes the "true and ultimate structure of reality."[145] If once the debate about analytical naturalization of intentionality has become history, it will probably have emerged, *pace* Quine and Churchland, that the attempt to isolate the intentional idiom rested on a misconception. Intentionality is more pervasive than naturalists and eliminativists think. Dramatic book titles such as *Intentionality in a Non-Intentional World* (Jacob), *Reasons in a World of Causes* (Dretske), or *Mind in a Physical World* (Kim) express this misconception.

Not the smaller part of our knowledge, but most likely the larger is riddled with, or presupposes, intentional notions. This is a conclusion drawn by some contemporary non-naturalists, such as Hilary Putnam and Lynne Rudder Baker (1944–):

> It does not look as if the intentional can simply be reduced to the non-intentional; rather, it begins to look as if the intentional intrudes even into our description of the non-intentional, as if the intentional (or, better, the cognitive) is to some extent ubiquitous.[146]

> Intentionality abounds, and the significance of the distinction between what is intentional and what is not intentional has been overblown: The fact that being a carburetor has intentional presuppositions has no bearing on the objectivity of carburetors ... *Pace* Quine, there is no a priori reason to be suspicious of a science whose domain is defined in part by intentional properties.[147]

The project of naturalizing intentionality takes an exceptional position among other projects of naturalization. This holds even with respect to the project of naturalizing epistemology. In order to discuss questions of acquisition and justification of beliefs, we have to suppose that beliefs *exist* in the first place. Beliefs, however, are individuated by their semantic contents. This implies that the decision relevant for naturalism is pre-positioned. Whether epistemology deals with naturalistically respectable phenomena is not settled in epistemology, but depends on success or failure of naturalizing intentionality. In short: epistemology presupposes intentionality on pain of changing the subject.[148] It is because inquiries into the possibility of naturalization should rather explain than presuppose intentional phenomena, that the real battleground is the philosophy of mind, rather than epistemology.

Naturalistic theories of *meaning* and of *representation* and of *action* are not alternatives to the project of naturalizing intentionality, but partial projects of this overarching endeavor. Linguistic meaning and intentional action are themselves intentional phenomena, and projects of naturalization aim at the very intentional dimension of these phenomena. Intentionality is the common denominator of mind, meaning, and action.

Naturalizing normativity

Normativity divides into moral and non-moral normativity. The projects of naturalizing normativity are divided accordingly.

Ethical naturalism is concerned with naturalizing moral normativity. This kind of naturalism is known from the debate about the *naturalistic fallacy*. Ethical naturalists hold that moral judgments can be deduced from non-moral facts, or that moral properties can be defined by non-moral properties. They believe that in this enterprise, the naturalistic fallacy can be avoided; or alternatively, that for some reasons it is no fallacy at all.[149]

The meta-ethical discussion of the twentieth century was particularly influenced by G. E. Moore's *Principia Ethica* (1903) (see "Kant in the twentieth century," Chapter 4 and "Twentieth-century moral philosophy," Chapter 20). Up to the second half of the century, it was widely accepted that Moore had struck a blow against ethical naturalism, strong enough to prevent recovery. Moore warned against "the fallacy which consists in identifying the simple notion which we mean by 'good' with some other notion."[150] He tried to show that any reductive definition of "good" in terms of natural properties is doomed to fail. For this purpose he introduced his "open question argument," according to which "good does not, by definition, mean anything that is natural; and it is therefore always an open question whether anything that is natural is good."[151] "[W]hatever definition be offered, it may always be asked, with significance, of the complex so defined, whether it is itself good."[152]

Moore's view that the meaning of "good" is unique and non-definable should be distinguished from the more general view that the moral *ought* is by no means reducible to the factual *is*, as stressed by Hume and Kant. The meta-ethical debate after Moore has concentrated on the question of whether moral properties are natural properties or not. If non-naturalism is framed in terms of the is–ought gap instead, one is not committed to locating the essence of morality in *properties* of anything, an idea that Kantians would reject.

Post-Moorean ethical naturalism is a meta-ethical position. It can be expressed without using the concept of nature. Now, unlike methodological naturalism, which replaces "nature" with the natural sciences in the spirit of the *scientia mensura* maxim, in ethical naturalism the notion of nature gets replaced with *descriptively ascertainable facts* or *properties*. The pivotal antitheses are *descriptive* versus *prescriptive*, *facts* versus *norms*, and *is* versus *ought*. Accordingly, Hare (1919–2002) suggested replacing the term "naturalistic fallacy" (already considered unfortunate by Moore) by the term "descriptivistic fallacy."[153]

Yet the parlance of descriptively ascertainable facts has never superseded the familiar terminology. Many ethical naturalists continue to speak of "natural facts" or "natural properties," so that the question about the meaning of the epithet "natural" resurfaces. What exactly does the naturalness of a natural property or fact consist in? Moore himself took natural properties as properties "with which it is the business of the natural sciences or psychology to deal."[154] This explanation is not very illuminating, and it raises the question of what sciences count as natural sciences. Many professed ethical naturalists argue for including the social sciences. There are good reasons for acknowledging social properties and facts, but as indicated above, these reasons are at the same time good reasons against calling the respective enterprise naturalistic. Elsewhere, Moore gave another explanation: "A property is natural if it does not depend on the existence of its object."[155] The problem with this view is that given an Aristotelian (as opposed to Platonist) view of universals and their instantiations, no properties come out as natural.

The question of which properties or facts count as natural leads to problems of demarcation, which already troubled naturalism in theoretical philosophy. Those who prefer not to answer this question are better off with *moral realism* than with naturalism. According to moral realism, moral facts exist that are independent of our beliefs. Unlike ethical naturalism, realism does not insist that those facts are natural facts. The opponents of moral realism are the whole array of *non-cognitivist* ethical theories: subjectivism, intuitionism, emotivism, expressivism, and prescriptivism.

The second key figure in the discussion about ethical naturalism is Richard Mervyn Hare. Hare drops all reference to the natural sciences and what it is their business to deal with. Instead, he assumes that all genuine properties are natural, insofar as they belong to the causal, empirically accessible order of things. Ethical naturalism he frames as the view that normative and evaluative concepts are definable entirely in terms of non-evaluative concepts.[156] Like Moore, he considers ethical naturalism as a failed enterprise.

John Mackie's "argument from queerness" is a further anti-naturalistic consideration. Mackie (1917–81) states that values "are not part of the fabric of the world,"[157] insofar as they possess imperative force and guide our actions. He argues that a property with "to-be-doneness" built into it would be "utterly different from anything else in the universe"; in a nutshell: "queer."[158]

Post-Moorean ethical naturalism being a meta-ethical position, it is important to distinguish it from the phenomenon of an immediate *appeal to nature* for the purposes of moral justification. In such appeals, the concept of nature does play a role. Nature or the natural are taken as the guideline for moral conduct, or source of moral norms. Such views are subsumed under "ethical naturalism" as well. Historically, they are older than meta-ethical naturalism (the Stoics propagated the slogan *naturam sequi*). Appeals to nature, the natural, or naturalness for moral instruction did not disappear with the rise of meta-ethical naturalism alias descriptivism.

Since ethical naturalism is already discussed in "Twentieth-century moral philosophy," Chapter 20 and "Kant in the twentieth century," Chapter 4, I will restrict myself to the following tangential issues: (1) the issue of non-moral normativity, and (2) the surprisingly scarcely discussed question of how ethical naturalism relates to naturalism in theoretical philosophy.

(1) The phenomenon of non-moral normativity appears to be less clear-cut than the ethical *ought*, for its place in nature is not necessarily specified with reference to human action. Those who advocate non-moral normativity and situate it in nature typically invoke an Aristotelian conception of nature, according to which natural substances (*ousiai*) exhibit a kind of built-in teleology. A representative figure is Philippa Foot, who attributes "natural goodness" to all living beings. Natural goodness, she holds, is an "intrinsic" and "autonomous" form of goodness "in that it depends directly on the relation of an individual to the 'life form' of the species. [...] The way an individual *should be* is determined by what is needed for development, self-maintenance, and reproduction."[159] This reference to species-relative biological needs is supposed to explain why "Aristotelian categoricals" such as "Cats are four-legged" are "able to describe norms rather than statistical normalities."[160] The antonym to "natural goodness" is not "evil," but "defect."

Aristotelians do not consider themselves hit by the naturalistic fallacy charge, for they exploit a normatively meaty, teleological concept of nature in the first place. Not considering oneself to be hit and not being hit are two separate things, though. Even an Aristotelian concept of nature is in need of justification and defense against objections. In particular, the worry needs to be addressed that in modernity, the Aristotelian springs of natural teleology have run dry.

One can try to establish that the alleged naturalistic fallacy is not fallacious in various ways. For one thing, there might be no fallacy because the *missing link* between *is* and *ought* has been discovered. Many philosophers have worked on constructing a traceable inference from descriptive to normative sentences. One example is Searle's account of institutional facts with built-in commitments. Other authors have introduced facts about basic needs or vital interests as sources of normativity.

Many accounts of non-moral normativity are not based on a teleological concept of nature, but retain instead the close connection to human actions and evaluations. These accounts still deny that all norms, standards, and rules have a *moral* content, but they do not hold that the phenomenon of normativity can be understood without any reference to human agency, i.e. to sentient beings who can understand and comply with requests. Normativity need not be grounded in morality, but at least beings seem to be needed who can follow *prudential* norms. Various philosophers have talked about the normativity of *meaning, language, mind,* and *rationality*. For Davidson, intentionality and rationality are essentially normative, insofar as intentional predicates sort their entities according to the principles of coherence and rationality, which have "no counterpart in the world of physics."[161] Intentional behavior of persons, he claims, is holistically embedded in a comprehensive pattern of interlocking attitudes. Its interpretation is constrained by normative considerations. In interpreting the utterances and other actions of persons, revisions might be necessary in the light of later evidence. This kind of reinterpretation guided by considerations of overall cogency has no counterpart in scientific theories, since "in the natural sciences, reasons and propositional attitudes are out of place, and blind causality rules."[162]

A hotly debated issue is the alleged normativity of *meaning*. This debate originates from a phenomenon in need of explanation, namely that there are right and wrong uses of expressions. Now "right" and "wrong" are clearly normative notions, as are "sense" and "nonsense." Classifying a parlance as wrong or nonsensical presupposes some norm or standard. The *locus classicus* of the slogan "meaning is normative" is Kripke's interpretation of Wittgenstein's considerations on rule-following.[163] Yet what exactly is meant by "using a word incorrectly," i.e. by producing a linguistic error? According to Wittgenstein's influential approach, it simply means to infringe upon a linguistic norm or convention. For Wittgenstein, analytic sentences are best viewed as *rules* not as assertions. Their normative status explains why they cannot be refuted empirically. The later Wittgenstein even holds that what he calls "grammatical sentences" are devoid of truth-value. Furthermore, he demands that there must be a difference between following a rule and just *believing* that one is following a rule. This difference would collapse if someone could follow a rule *privatim*. Linguistic rules need to be stabilized by public use, hence the very notion of a private language is incoherent. Wittgenstein's way of anchoring rule-following in a shared practice or form of life, however, corresponds rather to socializing than to naturalizing the normativity of meaning.

On closer examination it is far from clear what the alleged normativity of linguistic rules or meaning postulates consists in. Suppose norms and rules are always directions for action. Directions, or imperatives, may either be categorical or hypothetical (conditional), i.e. of the type "If you want to achieve p, you must do q." The difficulty lies in the fact that one cannot ask a speaker to mean a certain thing with his words. According to Wittgenstein, it is impossible to say "green" and mean "blue," for only within a language can one mean anything. It is not up to individual speakers what their words mean (the opposite view is sometimes called a *Humpty Dumpty* theory of meaning). Rules of meaning are, in other words, *constitutive* rules, not regulative ones. Constitutive rules *define* what counts as a particular linguistic or non-linguistic activity. They resemble game rules in this respect. If someone does not play by the rules, we might say "You may move your castle diagonally, but then we are no longer playing chess." Of course, one can refuse to play chess. It seems, however, pointless to question the rules of chess. Wittgenstein remarks "it has no meaning to say that a game has always been played wrong."[164] The claim that no one has ever played chess correctly would be hard to understand. Chess is so *called* as a game arranged in a certain way. And we have played according to these rules, even if we revise them one day. As constitutive rules they cannot be "false."

There is the question of whether constitutive rules can be simultaneously normative, i.e. prompt us to do something. If it is not up to the speakers to endow their words with certain meanings, then it does not make sense to ask them to do so. In this respect, the only sensible advice is the following: "If you want to be understood, you should use your words according to the convention of your speech community. For example, you should call only green objects 'green'." This piece of advice can hardly be called a rule of meaning. It is rather a *prudential* norm, as such connected with the expectation that in pursuing their goals, human beings are well advised to proceed rationally. Some say that the normativity of meaning consists in the fact that a speaker's use of words is always subject to criticism by the relevant linguistic community. Now it is certainly *possible* to use "green" to refer to non-green objects, but it is unwise. If this is the correct view, then the normativity of meaning is grounded in the normativity of rationality.

It is hardly surprising that the question of whether a naturalistic account can be given of non-moral normativity has not yet found any consensus. The very phenomenon of non-moral normativity seems to be more elusive than the moral *ought*. Only the latter is clearly tied to imperatives, either hypothetical or categorical. There is another unsettled question, namely how moral and non-moral normativity are related. On the one hand, the moral *ought* appears to be a partial problem of normativity. On the other hand, from a Kantian perspective it is the explicative basis for normativity as such. Seeing things this way, one would have to lay out the explicative primacy of moral *ought* in two steps. First, it would be necessary to show that norms directly or indirectly constitute directions to do or say something. Second, it would be necessary to show that "you ought" cannot be elucidated from hypothetical imperatives alone, but only from categorical ones.

Within naturalistic *epistemology*, there is a discussion on the phenomenon of normativity and the naturalistic fallacy, too. This is not surprising, if epistemology is concerned with questions of justification, not only with questions of fact. The naturalistic epistemologist Laudan has developed a "normative naturalism," according to which epistemic norms are to be understood as instrumental norms, which give the appropriate means for reaching certain goals.[165] Quine proposes a similar account of epistemic norms. In case we are forced to revise our web of belief in the face of recalcitrant experience, Quine appeals to the principles of *simplicity* and *conservativism*. Both are normative principles, which cannot be read off from the descriptive content of scientific theories. Quine holds that "normative epistemology gets naturalized as a chapter of engineering: the technology of anticipating sensory stimulation."[166] As a comment on the prospects of bridging the is–ought gap, this account misses the point, for it does not answer the crucial question of where on earth the normative "ought" is to be taken from. Some desirable aim of scientific practice must be justified first, such that the means can be considered instrumental or technological rules.

(2) Scarcely discussed in the literature is the question of how ethical naturalism is related to projects of naturalization in theoretical philosophy. The assumption seems only natural that a thoroughly naturalized account of human beings and their abilities should *comprise* ethical naturalism. On second thoughts, however, this assumption is less plausible. Why should a completely naturalized anthropology include the possibility of deducing normative from descriptive sentences? The assumption seems more plausible that in a completely naturalized anthropology the phenomena of morality and normativity would vanish altogether. In his *Anthropology from a Pragmatic Point of View*, Kant distinguished between "what nature makes of [man]" and "what *man* as a free agent makes, or can and should make, of himself."[167] A thoroughly naturalistic view of human beings might have the effect that Kant's second question merges in the first, insofar as under naturalistic assumptions there is nothing left for human beings to make of themselves.

Kant's condensed formulation is very precise. He says that a human being is a *free* agent, that he *can do* something (has certain abilities), and that he *ought to*. Naturalizing these properties and abilities is a task for theoretical naturalism, not for ethical naturalism. This also holds for the third characteristic, moral ability. Naturalizing this ability is not the same as deducing normative claims from anthropological insights into the nature of humans.

Now the logical autonomy of normative matters does not exclude less tight connections between theoretical and ethical naturalism. Even if naturalizing human capacities does not bridge the is–ought gap, something akin could be the case. Anthropological naturalism could have implications for ethics, implications concerning the necessary conditions of morality, rather than the content of moral rules. A successful naturalization of mind, reason, culture, freedom, or human abilities might eliminate the presuppositions on which the alleged autonomy of ought-sentences is grounded. Presumably, theoretical and ethical naturalism are related in this indirect way. Suppose a naturalistic anthropology proves those traits of human beings illusionary which are the *prerequisites of moral accountability of actions* or *necessary conditions for the development of normative practice*. This would not bridge the is–ought gap, but it would make the phenomenon of morality homeless. A thoroughly naturalistic anthropology would render the fact inexplicable that something *ought to* be the case in the first place. Recall that "'ought' expresses a kind of necessity and of connection with grounds which is found nowhere else in the whole of nature. [...] When we have the course of nature alone in view, '*ought*' has no meaning whatsoever."[168] An *ought* cannot be found in non-human nature, for there is neither an addressee for ought claims, nor a claiming subject. Ought claims may be logically autonomous, in not being deducible from descriptive statements, yet their *existence* is not unconditional. For Kant, human beings are committed to the moral law without ifs and buts, but only qua rational creatures who can choose their actions. Morality needs a *bearer*. In a world without beings who understand claims of ought and who can act for reasons, there would be no phenomenon of moral ought.

So even if moral facts should exist independently of our beliefs, as both ethical naturalism and ethical realism hold, they are not independent of the existence of rational beings who can act for reasons. In this respect, the phenomenon of morality has been compared to *secondary qualities*.[169] Morality presupposes abilities and characteristics of acting subjects. It would be deprived of its *ratio essendi*, if these presuppositions were regarded as illusionary. Such a position would not be ethical naturalism, but rather *deontic nihilism*. Deontic nihilists cannot understand what it means that something *ought* to be the case at all, either in moral or non-moral matters.[170] They adhere to Wittgenstein's dictum that the world is everything that *is* the case, being blind to the phenomenon of ought.

Therefore the conjunction of theoretical and ethical naturalism is presumably not a consistent position. A full-blown naturalism in theoretical philosophy amounts to deontic nihilism, for it cannot reconstrue the anthropological presupposition of the accountability of actions, which are a fortiori the condition of the possibility of morality. Ethical naturalism, on the other hand, has to hold on to those presuppositions, in particular on to the freedom of choice, as long as it understands the appeal to natural facts as the request that one ought to act in a certain way. Ought-sentences would be pointless, if it were not up to us to follow them or reject them. By the same token, praise and blame would be pointless if the agent could not have acted otherwise.

Naturalism and human nature

For some naturalists, appeals to human nature play an eminent role. But not any kind of reference to human nature indicates a naturalistic position.

In his book *Skepticism and Naturalism*, Peter Strawson distinguishes "two species of naturalism." In addition to strict scientific naturalism, he says, there is a second, liberal, and non-reductive naturalism of *human* nature.[171] As an example of this non-reductive naturalism, Strawson refers to David Hume's view that our very nature leaves us no choice but to believe in the existence of the external world. We are naturally disposed towards realism rather than towards skepticism about the external world. Strawson generalizes this view, holding that it is "simply not in our nature" to give up certain beliefs, attitudes, and convictions.[172] From this perspective, even the late Wittgenstein appears to be a naturalist, insofar as he holds the view that some assumptions which underlie all questions and all thinking are exempt from doubt, and that certain language-games are such that we cannot help but play them.[173]

Similarly, Jennifer Hornsby (1951–) defends a position in the philosophy of mind that she labels "naive naturalism."[174] She is concerned with justifying the ascription of beliefs, desires and intentions in view of the fact that these concepts have no place in scientific theories. Hornsby maintains that it is simply in the nature of human beings to entertain mental attitudes. According to "naive naturalism," human nature gets not only described in scientific theories, but is also reflected in commonsense insights.

In the field of ethics, Martha Nussbaum (1947–) appeals to human nature in the context of her neo-Aristotelian "capabilities approach." She explicates this appeal as a reference to deeply enrooted self-interpretations of human beings: "beliefs that are so firmly a part of our conception of ourselves that they will affect our assessment of questions of identity and persistence".[175]

In Strawson, Hornsby, and Nussbaum, the concept of nature plays a different role than in metaphysical or scientific naturalism. In talk of human nature, the concept of nature is used in the sense of "essence" or "real character." This second meaning of the word "nature" can already be found in ancient Greek. It deals with the nature of things, while the first deals with things of nature.

It is questionable to what extent an appeal to a human nature can be called "naturalistic." Strawson and Hornsby use this term, yet arguably they exploit the ambiguity of the word "nature." My argument against their use of "naturalism" is simple. Even non-natural objects can have a nature in the sense of essential properties. A soccer ball is round and a match lasts 90 minutes – that lies in the nature of the things, namely the nature of the ball and of the soccer match. However, it does not make ball and match objects of nature (as a designation of a certain domain). If reference to the nature of things would suffice to constitute naturalism, then every *essentialist*, i.e. anyone who ascribes essential properties to things, would count as a naturalist. Yet there are good reasons for not using the notion of naturalism that way. After all, human beings have not only a species-specific *physis* in the sense of a biological nature, but also other essential properties. The absurdity of the view that appeals to human nature amount to naturalism is particularly conspicuous in philosophical anthropology. According to Arnold Gehlen and many others, it is in the nature of human beings to have to rely on culture and civilization, being deficient beings with limited instincts and poorly equipped by nature. Gehlen's thesis of compensation, prefigured in Plato's *Protagoras*, culminates in the jargon about culture as "second nature" of human beings. Again, appeals to a second nature of human beings play on the ambiguity of the word "nature." Talk of second nature does not reveal a naturalistic orientation of philosophical anthropology, quite the contrary. Even if it is in the nature of human beings to be dependent on culture, culturally developed abilities are not part of their natural, biological endowment.[176]

Hence, talk about "nature" in the sense of "essence or real character" does not – *pace* Strawson and Hornsby – render an account naturalistic. Appeals to the nature of human beings are often decidedly non-naturalistic in spirit, even if they make extended use of the word "nature."

Scientific naturalism *quo vadis?*

Scientia mensura and the disunity of the special sciences

Above I distinguished two continuity theses in Quine. The thesis about a methodological continuity between philosophy and natural sciences is characteristic of Quine's naturalism. The thesis about continuity between philosophy and common sense shows his indebtedness to American pragmatism. Some writers, however, regard the latter continuity thesis as a defining feature of naturalism as well. For instance, Sidney Hook writes: "Naturalism, as a philosophy, is a systematic reflection upon, and elaboration of, the procedures man employs in the successful resolution of the problems and difficulties of human experience."[177] This use of "naturalism" is infelicitous. Plausibly, the naturalist's distinguishing trait is his reaction in the case of *conflict* between common sense and science. Since the Quinean naturalist holds that science is the highest path to truth, scientific investigations must in some way be superior to commonsense ways of determining truths about the world. As Arthur Danto (1924–) saliently points out:

> Science reflects while it refines upon the very methods primitively exemplified in common life and practice. [...] Should there be a conflict between common sense and science, it must be decided in favor of science, inasmuch as it employs, but more rigorously, the same method that common sense does and cannot, therefore, be repudiated without repudiating common sense itself.[178]

For the naturalist, science is not only a continual extension of common sense, but at the same time its better half. Everything that common sense can find out science can find out as well, but science is more reliable and more accurate, and it has special methods and tools at its disposal when things get complicated. This is why science has the last word in cases of conflict.

Accordingly, there is a certain tension between the pragmatistic thesis of continuity and *scientia mensura* naturalism. The continuity thesis is a fair weather thesis that is of little help if common sense and science come into conflict. There is a further tension within scientific naturalism, insofar as the commitment to scientific method presupposes homogeneity between the special sciences, which is a counterfactual assumption. Among the scientific disciplines, we find not only cooperation and division of labor, but also boundary disputes – for instance between psychological and physiological explanations of mental disorders; or between nativist and non-nativist theories about the relative importance of socialization and genetic dispositions. If no scientific discipline is privileged, such conflicts cannot be solved by naturalistic arguments in favor of the "harder" discipline, whatever the naturalist may mean by "harder." If the scientific caravan splits, then *Wherever science leads, I will follow* is not a maxim one can follow. A *scientia mensura* naturalist is then left with the following options. (1) He could present a list of approved scientific disciplines; (2) He could privilege a leading science; (3) He could commit himself to a unified science program or to some shrunken version of it; (4) He could refrain from appealing to *natural* science and use the concept of science liberally, thus including the humanities and social sciences as well.

The fourth option is not reasonably related to the naturalistic program. Ironically, (4) could fall under the concept of *scientism*. If we take seriously the lament of Quine, who finds it "awkward that 'science', unlike *scientia* and *Wissenschaft*, so strongly connotes natural science nowadays,"[179] then it should be possible to advocate scientism without advocating naturalism. Such a position would accept the *scientia mensura* maxim without identifying science with the natural sciences.[180] Admittedly this would be an unorthodox use of "scientism."

The problem of the third option is that the unity of science is not a fact, but a project. Jerry Fodor submitted a now classical argument for the "disunity of the special sciences": generalizations may be explanatory powerful in one discipline, but not in the other. Sometimes they cannot even be expressed in the vocabulary of both disciplines. The special sciences *cross-classify* their natural kinds.[181] In addition to classificatory differences, there are also those in methodology. Denying or explaining away the actual differentiation of the special sciences is hardly a promising enterprise: *Hell is paved with failed unified theories.* Simply *stipulating* the unity of science instead goes against the spirit of scientific naturalism. It is unnaturalistic to customize science to a certain philosophy of science, rather than vice versa. The resulting tension for scientific naturalism has been described thus:

> A tension which has been ignored by the proponents of naturalized philosophy of science has been introduced into their program. On the one hand, naturalism demands unified method. On the other hand, naturalism also demands that the philosophy of science be true to science as practiced, and, *pace* the positivists, science itself has been shown not to be unified in its method.[182]

So only the first two options are left, that is, presenting a list of approved scientific disciplines, or privileging a leading science. Quine serves as a good example for discussing both options. In explicating his version of naturalism, Quine advises us to make use of scientific knowledge of any kind: "[M]y position is a naturalistic one ... All scientific findings, all scientific conjectures that are at present plausible, are therefore in my view as welcome for use in philosophy as elsewhere."[183] Yet what does Quine mean by "all" scientific findings? Apparently, not findings from all subjects taught at university. Although he never presented a list of approved sciences, his practice is telling. He refers to half a dozen disciplines, and never mentions others. In particular, he refers to behavioristic psychology, physics, evolutionary biology, parts of linguistics, logic, and mathematics. This list is longer than that of many other naturalists, but it is still biased. Besides, *offering* a list of approved sciences is not enough, one has to argue for it. In some programmatic passages, Quine's liberality finally goes astray. While logic and mathematics are related to all disciplines, he arranges the empirical sciences into a hierarchy, at the top of which is physics. "Physics investigates the nature of the world," whereas biology is only concerned with a local "bump," and psychology with a "bump on a bump."[184] Explanations that employ linguistic and behavioral dispositions are taken only as a substitute for physical explanations;[185] mental entities are hypothetical posits, standing in for still unknown physiological mechanisms.[186] When it comes to limning "the true and ultimate structure of reality,"[187] there is no place for intentionality and the propositional attitudes. Brentano's insight into the peculiarity of the intentional shows "the baselessness of intentional idioms and the emptiness of a science of intention."[188]

Hence, Quine is by no means as large-hearted as suggested by his sweeping notion of a "total science." When push comes to shove, he tends towards physics chauvinism, rather than readily using "all scientific findings" from all disciplines. In Quine's work, there is an unsolved tension between a general scientism that preserves neutrality and a physicalism plus extensionality thesis, which bans intentionality and intensionality from the sciences.

It is hard to see how the naturalist should answer from his own resources the question of which scientific disciplines exemplify scientific method(s) best or paradigmatically. In any event, Quine's refrain "science itself tells us" or Sellars's *scientia mensura* maxim cannot answer it. If the sciences are methodologically manifold, those maxims lose their radiance. In the end, the two options "naturalism with a leading science" and "naturalism without a leading science" are not so far apart. In the first event, arguments are needed for privileging the leading science. In the other event, arguments are needed in favor of a continuity relation between the sciences strong enough for *scientia mensura* naturalism.

The business of philosophy

A final challenge for scientific naturalism is the question which role, if any, is assigned to philosophy. If we accept Quine's dictum that for the questions "what there is" and "how we know what there is, … the last arbiter is so-called scientific method,"[189] then it becomes doubtful what is left for philosophy to do in this enterprise. The scientific naturalist has to explain what role he envisages for a naturalistic *philosophy*, *after* he has given his commitment to the explanatory privilege of the natural sciences. Programmatic naturalistic texts, often flavored with polemics, rather cloud the issue,

> the chief divisions being not so much between naturalists and antinaturalists [...] but between competing views of what *philosophy* is. And here the critics of naturalism are not necessarily antinaturalistic in the comfortable sense of being unhappy with science, in proposing that there are nonnatural entities, etc., but rather in the sense of supposing philosophy has its own problems and techniques.[190]

The suspicion that for philosophy there is nothing to do in the project of scientific naturalism can be hardened into an objection: the credo of naturalists that the methods of natural science provide the only avenue to truth is precisely *not* a finding of any natural science.[191] This implies that the truth of scientific naturalism cannot be established by those means that allegedly provide the only avenue to truth! Critics of naturalism have turned the knife in this wound: "Methodological naturalism is a claim about best method; yet the methods employed to arrive at methodological naturalism are not those of natural science but of philosophy of science."[192] A similar objection was already put forth in the debate about mid-century American naturalism, namely that the "apparent main thesis of naturalism" is no thesis at all, but "strictly an enunciation of policy. In effect they say: 'Let us be scientific'. ... What causes the difficulty is that having said: 'We are going to do science', they do not do science."[193]

Given that Quine was the prototypical philosophical naturalist of the twentieth century, it seems only fair to conclude with his own job description for naturalistic philosophy. "Naturalistic philosophy," Quine submits, "undertakes to clarify, organize and simplify the broadest and most basic concepts, and to analyze scientific method and evidence within the framework of science itself."[194] With suitable omissions, the passage reads: "Naturalistic philosophy clarifies concepts and analyzes scientific method." This job description is remarkably traditional, and it does not fit well with Quine's naturalistic avowals. Naturalistic philosophy seems to be, in a word, conceptual analysis, though "within the framework of science itself." What precisely this addition means is anything but obvious. And while Quine's naturalistic avowals had a huge impact on the scientific community in the second half of the century, his celebrated blurring of the boundary between philosophy and natural science had little effect on the way he himself actually philosophized. His own writings clearly belong to philosophy and logic, and not to some other scientific discipline. Even if names of disciplines should be nothing but "technical aids in the organization of libraries,"[195] librarians know pretty well on which shelf Quine's books are to be placed. "Quine offered a new job description for philosophy," Steve Stich stated in his obituary.[196] One can agree with this only with the qualification that changing a job description is one thing, while providing somebody with a new job is quite another.[197]

Notes

1 R. W. Sellars 1922: i.
2 Geach 1977: 52.
3 R. W. Sellars 1922: i.
4 Dewey 1944: 2.
5 Bouwsma 1948: 13.
6 This has been acknowledged quite early on, for instance by Ralph Perry: "The attacks upon the method of science have tended to create the supposition that the only alternative to naturalism is inexactness or unreason. [. . .] As the only alternative to supernaturalism, obscurantism, irrationalism, agnosticism, mysticism, and subjectivism, – naturalism has acquired a place of intellectual distinction which it does not in fact merit" (Perry 1925: 109).
7 "Naturalist." In *The Oxford English Dictionary*, vol. VII, Oxford 1933, repr. 1961, p. 38.
8 Thompson 1964: 183.

9 Nagel 1954: 7.
10 See for instance Dewey 1944; Dewey et al. 1945; Sheldon 1946; Garnett 1948; Oliver 1949. An overview of mid-century American naturalism is given in an anthology, Krikorian 1944.
11 Sheldon 1945: 254.
12 See Santayana 1925; Dewey 1927.
13 Dewey 1927: 81 and 79.
14 W. Sellars 1979: 2.
15 For an overview, see Schnädelbach 1984.
16 See von Wright 1971; Maninnen/Tuomela 1976.
17 "Die Natur erklären wir, das Seelenleben verstehen wir." Dilthey 1894: 144.
18 Within logical empiricism, the advocates of a unified science did not use the expression "naturalism" to mark their position. Carnap and Neurath talked of "physicalism" and proposed in their 1929 manifesto a general "scientific worldview" (Carnap et al. 1929).
19 Frege 1918: 326.
20 Husserl 2002: 255 (1911: 295–6).
21 Ibid.: 254–8 (1911: 295–8).
22 Ibid.: 257–8 (1911: 298–9).
23 Ibid.: 259 (1911: 300).
24 Ibid.: 259–61 (1911: 300–2).
25 Ibid.: 266–7 (1911: 309).
26 Ibid.: 265 (1911: 307).
27 Ibid.: 276 (1911: 320).
28 Wittgenstein 1953: 232.
29 Husserl 2002: 266 (1911: 308–9).
30 Quine 1969: 76.
31 Husserl 2002: 277 (1911: 321).
32 Wittgenstein 1958: 18.
33 Hacker 1996: 33.
34 Wittgenstein 1953: §281.
35 Kenny 1971: 155.
36 For a wide-ranging, Wittgenstein-inspired critique of the conceptual confusions of neuroscientific theories, see Bennett and Hacker 2003.
37 See for example Wittgenstein 1953: §25.
38 See Wittgenstein's late remarks in *On Certainty* (1969).
39 Strawson 1985: 24.
40 Quine 1969: 26.
41 Quine 1981: 67.
42 Ibid.: 72.
43 Quine 1969: 126.
44 Quine 2000: 411.
45 Quine 1953: 42.
46 Quine 1981: 71.
47 Quine 1953: 45.
48 Quine 1966: 233.
49 See Glock et al. 2003.
50 Quine 1953: 37.
51 Ibid.: 20.
52 Quine 1981: 67 and 21.
53 Quine 1995b: 251–2.
54 Ibid.
55 Ecological naturalism is an exception, for it is based on a distinct concept of nature, namely that of a well-ordered household (*oikos*).
56 Randall 1944: 357.
57 Nagel 1954: 3.

58 Roughley 2004: 48.

59 In two recent texts, for instance, the following kinds of naturalism are distinguished: aposteriorical, cooperative, eliminative, expansive, integrative, metaphysical, methodological, moderate, ontological, radical, reformist, restricted, reductive, revolutionary, scientific, scientist, and unrestricted naturalism (Haack 1993; Koppelberg 1996).

60 "By definition nature is singular and all-inclusive. Unnatural things do not exist." (Schneider 1944: 122)

61 "Now naturalism . . . can be defined negatively as the refusal to take 'nature' or 'the natural' as a term of distinction. . . . For present-day naturalists 'Nature' serves rather as the all-inclusive category, corresponding to the role played by 'Being' in Greek thought, or by 'Reality' for the idealists. In this sense . . . naturalism, in becoming all-inclusive, ceases to be a distinctive 'ism'. It regards as 'natural' whatever man encounters in whatever way" (Randall 1944: 357–8).

62 Armstrong 1983: 82.

63 Armstrong 1997: 5.

64 Ibid.: 6.

65 Harman 1977: 17.

66 Hook 1944: 45.

67 Danto 1967: 448.

68 Armstrong 1997: 7.

69 Thompson 1964: 183.

70 Quine 1995b: 261.

71 W. Sellars 1956: 173.

72 Quine 1992b: 9.

73 Perry (1925: 85) defined naturalism as "the claim that physical science is unqualifiedly and exclusively true."

74 In his two-volume work *Naturalism and Agnosticism* (1899), James Ward criticized naturalism for its alleged infallibilism. He argued from the incomplete success of science, from the hypothetical status of scientific knowledge, and suggested contradictions within the body of scientific findings. In short, he brought to bear the fact of human fallibility against the pretensions of scientific naturalism.

75 Quine 1992b: 9.

76 Quine 1981: 72.

77 Pettit 1993: 214–17.

78 Carnap 1932: 165–6.

79 Ibid.: 166.

80 Ibid.: 197.

81 Wilkes 1978: 18.

82 Quine 1969: 75 and 78.

83 Roughley 2004: 51.

84 Blackburn 1998: 48.

85 See R. W. Sellars 1922; see also Ruse 1995.

86 Ryle comments acidly: "But the influence of the bogy of mechanism has for a century been dwindling because, among other reasons, during this period the biological sciences have established their title of 'sciences'. The Newtonian system is no longer the sole paradigm of natural science. Man need not be degraded to a machine by being denied to be a ghost in a machine. He might, after all, be a sort of animal, namely, a higher mammal. There has yet to be ventured the hazardous leap to the hypothesis that perhaps he is a man" (Ryle 1949: 328).

87 This equation was widespread in the first half of the century: "Naturalism, or the claim that physical science is unqualifiedly and exclusively true, is equivalent to the denial of optimistic religion" (Perry 1925: 85).

88 See Plantinga 1993. For objections to Plantinga's argument see the volume edited by Beilby (2002).

89 Quine 1992b: 9.

90 Quine 1995a: 252.

91 "[H]ere is the irony – both of them [Quine and Descartes] bet on the wrong horse in the scientific sweepstakes of their day: Quine's contributions to psychology and psycholinguistics, in *Word and*

Object and elsewhere, were very much embedded in the Behaviorist tradition, and that tradition, it has become increasingly clear, is not a productive one" (Stich 2001).

92 For a discussion of this phrase of Quine's, see Keil 2003.
93 Sheldon 1945: 263.
94 Randall and Buchler 1942: 183.
95 Fine 1996: 175.
96 Ibid.: 188.
97 Ibid.: 184.
98 Stich 1996: 198.
99 Ibid.: 199.
100 Ibid. Another author claims that scientific naturalism "need not presuppose a solution to the so-called 'demarcation problem' – i.e., the problem of what demarcates genuine science from pseudo-science – as long as there remain clear, paradigmatic cases of successful sciences" (Leiter 2002: 2). I submit that Leiter's appeal to "clear, paradigmatic cases" has all the advantages that theft has over honest labor, if I may borrow a phrase from Russell.
101 Quine, in his later work, defends the hypothetic-deductive method and regards testability of scientific hypotheses by means of observable consequences as a *defining* characteristic of scientificality (see Quine 1992a: 20). Thus Quine would avoid the objection of employing a sociologistic science criterion.
102 Churchland 1981: 75.
103 Dennett 1987: 117.
104 Fodor 1984: 232.
105 Fodor 1987: 97.
106 See for example Tye 1994 and Stich 1996.
107 Stich 1996: 199.
108 Stalnaker 1984: 6.
109 For an overview see Kornblith 1985; Maffie 1990; Kitcher 1992; Rosenberg 1996; Giere 1998.
110 Quine 1969: 82–3.
111 Ibid.: 83.
112 Quine 1975b: 68.
113 Quine 1969: 75.
114 Ibid.: 83.
115 Quine 1974: 1.
116 Quine 1981: 24.
117 "All I am or ever hope to be is due to irritations of my surface"; "our knowledge must depend thus solely on surface irritation" (Quine 1966: 228 and 229).
118 Davidson 1983: 431. Similar objections were brought up by Putnam, Kim, and Rorty.
119 Davidson 1983: 426.
120 Quine 1981: 178.
121 Quine 1975b: 67 and 68.
122 Ibid.: 70.
123 Quine 1969: 126–7.
124 Putnam 1982: 19.
125 See Feldman 2001.
126 Stich 1993: 2.
127 For an overview see Kitcher 1992.
128 Kornblith 1994: 49.
129 See Kitcher 1992: 54.
130 Goldman 1978: 510.
131 "Questions about the actual structure of our concepts are *in principle* as empirical as questions about the actual structure of iron" (Bishop 1992: 269).
132 Kitcher 1992: 74.
133 Roughley 2004: 49.
134 Dretske 1981: xi.

135 Stalnaker 1984: 6.
136 Fodor 1987: 126, cf. 98; Fodor 1984: 232.
137 It should be mentioned that outside of the project of naturalizing intentionality, the broadly Wittgensteinian view has gained ground that definition via necessary or sufficient conditions is neither possible nor necessary to explain the meaning of a concept.
138 Putnam 1992: 57.
139 Baker 1995: 193.
140 Fodor 1987: 126. It is disputed whether there is a reliable linguistic test for Fodor's non-intentional, non-semantical and non-teleological conditions, whether for example semantic intensionality is a criterion for it. In this case, one may ask how intentionality and *modality* are related, for modal claims create intensional contexts as well.
141 Lycan 1991: 264.
142 Searle 1983: 26.
143 Fodor 1990: 52.
144 Churchland 1981: 75.
145 Quine 1960: 221.
146 Putnam 1992: 59.
147 Baker 1995: 208–9.
148 By "changing the subject," I understand with Davidson: "deciding not to accept the criterion of the mental in terms of the vocabulary of the propositional attitudes" (Davidson 1980: 216).
149 For overviews see Hudson 1969; Villanueva 1993; Crisp 1996; Dancy 2000; Copp 2003.
150 Moore 1903: 58.
151 Ibid.: 44.
152 Ibid.: 15.
153 See Hare 1972: 55.
154 Moore 1993: 13. Note the disjunction "natural sciences *or* psychology." In other places (e.g. 1903: 92), Moore chooses a conjunctive formulation, thus counting psychology among the natural sciences.
155 Moore 1903: 41.
156 See Hare 1952: 82.
157 Mackie 1977: 15.
158 Ibid.: 38–42.
159 Foot 2001: 27 and 33. In the philosophy of biology the concept of *function* is often explicated with reference to what is good or beneficial for individual living beings. This view is called "the welfare view of biological function."
160 Ibid.
161 Davidson 1980: 230, cf. 223.
162 Davidson 1982: 292.
163 See Kripke 1982.
164 Wittgenstein 1969: §496.
165 See Laudan 1987.
166 Quine 1992a: 19.
167 Kant [1798] 1974: 3.
168 Kant 1781: B575/A547.
169 Wiggins, McDowell, and other have drawn the parallel between moral facts and values and secondary qualities, which – according to Locke – cannot be defined without reference to human perceptual capacities.
170 Deontic nihilism can be viewed as generalization of moral nihilism. Moral nihilists like Nietzsche, de Sade, and the Sophists accept no moral rules which constrain the right of the stronger or the pleasure principle.
171 Strawson 1985: esp. 1–3, 10–21, 37–42, 51–3.
172 Ibid.: 41. Accordingly, in research on Hume there is a discussion on the relation between Hume's naturalism and his empiricism. With respect to Hume's view on causality, Mounce notes: "What appears in sense experience as constant conjunction is turned by the mind into the form of causality. But the

workings of the mind are instinctive or natural. They are not based on any rational insight into the objective nature of the causal process. On a matter of this importance, nature has not trusted to our fallible reasonings and speculations. . . . It follows that our understanding of the world is based on relations which arise from the workings of nature, not from those of our own understanding" (Mounce 1999: 4).

173 See Strawson 1985: 15 and 41. Strawson also calls the Wittgensteinian view "social naturalism" (ibid.: 24).

174 See Hornsby 1997. Michael Tye has argued in the same vein that the mental is part of the natural world, without indispensably being reducible to anything (Tye 1992).

175 Nussbaum 2001: 366.

176 See my remarks above on cultural and natural facts (in the section "Naturalism with a leading science," pp. 276–71). A further attempt to employ the notion of a "second nature" for a more liberal naturalism stems from John McDowell. According to McDowell, the natural world is "in the space of *logos*," so that even autonomous normative facts about reasons, values, and meanings count as constituents of (second) nature (cf. McDowell 1995). The fact that McDowell labels this view a "naturalism of second nature" only shows the extraordinary prestige of the concept of naturalism, which attempts to mark even naturalistically remote positions with this name.

177 Hook 1961: 195.

178 Danto 1967: 448.

179 Quine 2000: 411.

180 Here is a relevant comment: "It is the argument of this book that though, because social objects are irreducible to . . . natural objects . . . they cannot be studied in the same way as them, they can be studied 'scientifically'." "[I]t is not their similarities with, but precisely their differences from, natural objects that makes scientific knowledge possible" (Bhaskar 1979: 26 and viii).

181 See Fodor 1974.

182 Stump 1992: 457.

183 Quine 1969: 126–7.

184 Quine 1981: 93.

185 Quine 1975a: 95.

186 Quine 1974: 33–4.

187 Quine 1960: 221.

188 Ibid.

189 Quine 1960: 22–3.

190 Danto 1967: 450.

191 "Naturalism, as we have seen, is not science, but an assertion about science. More specifically, it is the assertion that scientific knowledge is final, leaving no room for extra-scientific or philosophical knowledge" (Perry 1925: 63).

192 Schmitt 1995: 344.

193 Bouwsma 1948: 20–1.

194 Quine 1995b: 256–7.

195 Quine 1981: 88.

196 Stich 2001.

197 The chapter was translated from the German original by Philipp Hübl and the translation was revised by Rory Domm.

References

Armstrong, D. M. (1983) *What Is a Law of Nature?* Cambridge: Cambridge University Press.

_____ (1997) *A World of States of Affairs*. Cambridge: Cambridge University Press.

Baker, L. R. (1995) *Explaining Attitudes*. Cambridge and New York: Cambridge University Press.

Beilby, J. K. (ed.) (2002) *Naturalism Defeated? Essays on Plantinga's Evolutionary Argument Against Naturalism*. Ithaca, NY: Cornell University Press.

Bennett, M. and P. Hacker (2003) *Philosophical Foundations of Neuroscience*. Oxford: Blackwell.

Bhaskar, R. (1979) *The Possibility of Naturalism: A Philosophical Critique of the Contemporary Human Sciences*. Brighton: Harvester Press.

Bishop, M. (1992) "The possibility of conceptual clarity in philosophy." *American Philosophical Quarterly* 29: 267–77.

Blackburn, S. (1998) *Ruling Passions: A Theory of Practical Reasoning.* Oxford: Oxford University Press.

Bouwsma, O. K. (1948) "Naturalism." *Journal of Philosophy* 45: 12–22.

Carnap, R. (1932) "Psychology in physical language," trans. G. Schick. In A. J. Ayer (ed.) *Logical Positivism.* New York: Free Press, 1959, pp. 165–198.

Carnap, R., H. Hahn, and O. Neurath (1929) *Wissenschaftliche Weltauffassung – Der Wiener Kreis.* Vienna: Artur Wolf.

Churchland, P. M. (1981) "Eliminative materialism and propositional attitudes." *Journal of Philosophy* 78: 67–90.

Copp, D. (2003) "Why naturalism?" *Ethical Theory and Moral Practice* 2: 179–200.

Crisp, R. (1996) "Naturalism and non-naturalism in ethics." In S. Lovibond and S. G. Williams (eds.) *Essays for David Wiggins: Identity, Truth and Value.* Aristotelian Society Series. Oxford: Blackwell, pp. 113–29.

Dancy, J. (ed.) (2000) *Normativity.* Oxford: Blackwell.

Danto, A. C. (1967) "Naturalism." In P. Edwards (ed.) *The Encyclopedia of Philosophy.* Vol. 5, New York and London: Macmillan, pp. 448–50.

Davidson, D. (1980) *Essays on Actions and Events.* Oxford: Oxford University Press.

_____ (1982) "Paradoxes of irrationality." In R. Wollheim and J. Hopkins (eds.) *Philosophical Essays on Freud.* Cambridge: Cambridge University Press, pp. 289–305.

_____ (1983) "A coherence theory of truth and knowledge." In D. Henrich (ed.) *Kant oder Hegel? Stuttgarter Hegel-Kongreß 1981,* Stuttgart: Klett-Cotta, pp. 423–38.

Dennett, D. C. (1987) *The Intentional Stance.* Cambridge, MA and London: MIT Press.

Dewey, J. (1927) "Half-hearted naturalism." In *The Later Works.* Vol. 3, Carbondale, IL: Southern Illinois University Press, 1984, pp. 73–81.

_____ (1944) "Antinaturalism in extremis." In Y. H. Krikorian (ed.) *Naturalism and the Human Spirit,* New York: Columbia University Press, pp. 1–16.

Dewey, J., S. Hook, and E. Nagel (1945) "Are naturalists materialists?" *Journal of Philosophy* 42: 515–30.

Dilthey, W. (1894) *Ideen über eine beschreibende und zergliedernde Psychologie.* In *Gesammelte Schriften.* Band 5. Stuttgart: Teubner; Göttingen: Vandenhoeck & Ruprecht, 1961.

Dretske, F. I. (1981) *Knowledge and the Flow of Information.* Oxford: Oxford University Press.

Feldman, R. (2001) "Naturalized epistemology." In *The Stanford Encyclopedia of Philosophy* (Fall 2001 edn.). URL = *http://plato.stanford.edu/entries/epistemology-naturalized/.*

Fine, A. (1996) *The Shaky Game.* 2nd edn. Chicago and London: University of Chicago Press.

Fodor, J. A. (1974) "Special sciences, or the disunity of science as a working hypothesis." In N. Block (ed.) *Readings in the Philosophy of Psychology,* vol. 1, Cambridge, MA: Harvard University Press, 1980, pp. 120–33.

_____ (1984) "Semantics, Wisconsin style". *Synthèse* 59: 231–50.

_____ (1987) *Psychosemantics: The Problem of Meaning in the Philosophy of Mind.* Cambridge, MA: MIT Press.

_____ (1990) *A Theory of Content and Other Essays.* Cambridge, MA: MIT Press.

Foot, P. (2001) *Natural Goodness.* Oxford: Oxford University Press.

Frege, G. (1918) "Thought," trans. P. Geach and R. H. Stoothoff. In M. Beaney (ed.) *The Frege Reader.* Oxford: Blackwell, 1997, pp. 325–45.

French, P. A., T. E. Uehling, Jr., and H. K. Wettstein (eds.) (1994) *Philosophical Naturalism.* Midwest Studies in Philosophy 19. Notre Dame, IN: University of Notre Dame Press.

Garnett, A. C. (1948) "Naturalism and the concept of matter." *Journal of Philosophy* 45: 477–89.

Geach, P. (1977) *The Virtues.* Cambridge: Cambridge University Press.

Giere, R. N. (1998) "Naturalized philosophy of science." In E. Craig (ed.) *Routledge Encyclopedia of Philosophy,* vol. 6, London and New York: Routledge, pp. 728–31.

Glock, H.-J., K. Glüer, and G. Keil (eds.) (2003) *Fifty Years of Quine's "Two Dogmas."* Amsterdam, Atlanta, and New York: Rodopi.

Goldman, A. I. (1978) "Epistemics: the regulative theory of cognition." *Journal of Philosophy* 75: 509–23.

Haack, S. (1993) "Naturalism disambiguated." In *Evidence and Inquiry,* Oxford: Blackwell, pp. 118–38.

Hacker, P. M. S. (1996) "Wittgenstein and Quine: proximity at great distance." In R. L. Arrington and H.-J. Glock (eds.) *Wittgenstein and Quine.* London and New York: Routledge, pp. 1–38.

Hare, R. M. (1952) *The Language of Morals.* Oxford: Oxford University Press.

_____ (1972) *Essays on the Moral Concepts.* London and Basingstoke: Macmillan; Berkeley: University of California Press.

Harman, G. (1977) *Thought.* Princeton, NJ: Princeton University Press.

Hook, S. (1944) "Naturalism and democracy." In Y. H. Krikorian (ed.) *Naturalism and the Human Spirit.* New York: Columbia University Press, pp. 40–64.

_____ (1961) *The Quest for Being (and Other Studies in Naturalism and Humanism).* London: St Martin's Press.

Hornsby, J. (1997) *Simple-Mindedness: In Defense of Naïve Naturalism in the Philosophy of Mind.* Cambridge, MA and London: Harvard University Press.

Hudson, W. D. (ed.) (1969) *The Is–Ought Question.* London: Macmillan.

Husserl, E. (2002) *Philosophy as a Rigorous Science,* trans. M. Brainard, *The New Yearbook for Phenomenology and Phenomenological Philosophy* II, Madison: University of Wisconsin Press, pp. 249–95. Orig. edn., *Logos* 1 (1910–11), pp. 289–341.

Kant, I. (1781) *Critique of Pure Reason.* Trans. N. K. Smith. London: Macmillan, 1929.

_____ (1798) *Anthropology from a Pragmatic Point of View.* Trans. M. J. Gregor. The Hague: Springer Netherland, 1974.

Keil, G. (2003) "'Science itself teaches.' A fresh look at Quine's naturalistic metaphilosophy." *Grazer Philosophische Studien* 66, pp. 253–80.

Kenny, A. (1971) "The homunculus fallacy." In: J. Hyman (ed.) *Investigating Psychology: Sciences of the Mind after Wittgenstein.* London: Routledge, 1991, pp. 155–65.

Kitcher, P. (1992) "The naturalists return." *Philosophical Review* 101: 53-114.

Koppelberg, D. (1996) "Was macht eine Erkenntnistheorie naturalistisch?" *Journal for the General Philosophy of Science* 27: 71–90.

Kornblith, H. (ed.) (1985) *Naturalizing Epistemology.* Cambridge, MA and London: MIT Press. 2nd edn. 1994.

_____ (1994) "Naturalism: both metaphysical and epistemological." In P. A. French, T. E. Uehling, and H. K. Wettstein (eds.) *Philosophical Naturalism.* Midwest Studies in Philosophy 19. Notre Dame, IN: University of Notre Dame Press, pp. 39–52.

Krikorian, Y. H. (ed.) (1944) *Naturalism and the Human Spirit.* New York: Columbia University Press.

Kripke, S. (1982) *Wittgenstein on Rules and Private Language.* Cambridge, MA: Harvard University Press.

Laudan, L. (1987) "Progress or rationality? The prospects for normative naturalism." *American Philosophical Quarterly* 24: 19–31.

Leiter, B. (2002) "Naturalism in legal philosophy." In *The Stanford Encyclopedia of Philosophy* (Fall 2002 edn.), http://plato.stanford.edu/entries/lawphil-naturalism.

Lycan, W. (1991) "Homuncular functionalism meets PDP." In W. Ramsey, S. P. Stich, and D. Rumelhart (eds.) *Philosophy and Connectionist Theory,* Hillsdale, NJ: Lawrence Erlbaum, pp. 259–86.

Mackie, J. L. (1977) *Ethics: Inventing Right and Wrong.* Harmondsworth: Penguin.

Maffie, J. (1990) "Recent work on naturalized epistemology." *American Philosophical Quarterly* 27: 281–93.

Manninen, J. and R. Tuomela (eds.) (1976) *Essays on Explanation and Understanding.* Dordrecht: Springer.

McDowell, J. (1995) "Two sorts of naturalism." In R. Hursthouse et al. (eds.) *Virtues and Reasons.* Oxford: Oxford University Press, pp. 150–79.

Moore, G. E. (1903) *Principia Ethica.* Cambridge: Cambridge University Press.

_____ (1993) Preface to *Principia Ethica.* 2nd edn. Cambridge: Cambridge University Press, pp. 1–32.

Mounce, H. O. (1999) *Hume's Naturalism.* London: Routledge.

Nagel, E. (1954) "Naturalism reconsidered." In *Logic Without Metaphysics.* Glencoe, IL: Free Press, 1956, pp. 3–18.

Nussbaum, M. (2001) *The Fragility of Goodness: Luck and Ethics in Greek Tragedy and Philosophy.* Rev. edn. Cambridge: Cambridge University Press.

Oliver, W. D. (1949) "Can naturalism be materialistic?" *Journal of Philosophy* 46: 608–15.

Perry, R. B. (1925) [1912] "Naturalism." In *Present Philosophical Tendencies*, New York and London: Longmans Green, pp. 45–109.

Pettit, P. (1993) "A definition of physicalism." *Analysis* 53: 213–23.

Plantinga, A. (1993) "Is naturalism irrational?" In *Warrant and Proper Function*, Oxford: Oxford University Press, pp. 216–38.

Putnam, H. (1982) "Why reason can't be naturalized." *Synthèse* 52: 3–23.

_____ (1992) *Renewing Philosophy*. Cambridge, MA and London: Harvard University Press.

Quine, W. V. O. (1953) *From a Logical Point of View*. Cambridge, MA: Harvard University Press.

_____ (1960) *Word and Object*. Cambridge, MA: MIT Press.

_____ (1966) *The Ways of Paradox and Other Essays*. New York: Random House. Repr. Cambridge, MA: Harvard University Press, 1976.

_____ (1969) *Ontological Relativity and Other Essays*. New York: Columbia University Press.

_____ (1974) *The Roots of Reference*. La Salle, IL: Open Court.

_____ (1975a) "Mind and verbal dispositions." In: S. Guttenplan (ed.) *Mind and Language*. Oxford: Clarendon Press, pp. 83–95.

_____ (1975b) "The nature of natural knowledge." In S. Guttenplan (ed.) *Mind and Language*. Oxford: Clarendon Press, pp. 67–81.

_____ (1981) *Theories and Things*. Cambridge, MA and London: Harvard University Press.

_____ (1992a) *Pursuit of Truth*. Cambridge, MA: Harvard University Press.

_____ (1992b) "Structure and nature." *Journal of Philosophy* 89: 5–9.

_____ (1995a) *From Stimulus to Science*. Cambridge, MA: Harvard University Press.

_____ (1995b) "Naturalism; or, Living within one's means." *Dialectica* 49: 251–61.

_____ (2000) "Quine's responses." In A. Orenstein and P. Kotatko (eds.) *Knowledge, Language and Logic: Questions for Quine*. Dordrecht, Boston, London: Springer, pp. 407–30.

Randall, J. H., Jr. (1944) "Epilogue: the nature of naturalism." In Y. H. Krikorian (ed.) *Naturalism and the Human Spirit*. New York: Columbia University Press, pp. 354–82.

Randall, J. H., Jr. and J. Buchler (1942) *Philosophy: An Introduction*, New York: Barnes & Noble.

Rosenberg, A. (1996) "A field guide to recent species of naturalism." *British Journal for the Philosophy of Science* 47: 1–29.

Roughley, N. (2004) "Naturalism and expressivism: on the 'natural' stuff of moral normativity and problems with its 'naturalisation'." In P. Schaber et al. (eds.) *Normativity and Naturalism*. Heusenstamm and Frankfurt am Main: Ontos, pp. 47–86.

Ruse, M. (1995) *Evolutionary Naturalism: Selected Essays*. London and New York: Routledge.

Ryle, G. (1949) *The Concept of Mind*. London: Hutchinson.

Santayana, G. (1925) "Dewey's naturalistic metaphysics." *Journal of Philosophy* 22: 673–88.

Schmitt, F. F. (1995) "Naturalism." In J. Kim and E. Sosa (eds.) *A Companion to Metaphysics*. Oxford: Blackwell, pp. 343–5.

Schnädelbach, H. (1984) *Philosophy in Germany: 1831–1933*. Trans. E. Matthews. Cambridge: Cambridge University Press.

Schneider, H. W. (1944) "The unnatural." In Y. H. Krikorian (ed.) *Naturalism and the Human Spirit*, New York: Columbia University Press, pp. 121–32.

Searle, J. R. (1983) *Intentionality: An Essay in the Philosophy of Mind*. Cambridge: Cambridge University Press.

Sellars, R. W. (1922) *Evolutionary Naturalism*. New York: Russell & Russell.

Sellars, W. (1956) "Empiricism and the philosophy of mind." In *Science, Perception and Reality*. New York: Humanities Press, 1963, pp. 127–96.

_____ (1979) *Naturalism and Ontology*. Reseda, CA: Ridgeview.

Sheldon, W. H. (1945) "Critique of naturalism." *Journal of Philosophy* 42: 253–70.

_____ (1946) "Are naturalists materialists? Reply to Professors Dewey, Hook, Nagel." *Journal of Philosophy* 43: 197–209.

Stalnaker, R. C. (1984) *Inquiry*. Cambridge, MA: MIT Press.

Stich, S. P. (1993) "Naturalizing epistemology: Quine, Simon and the prospects for pragmatism." In C. Hookway and D. Peterson (eds.) *Philosophy and Cognitive Science*. Cambridge: Cambridge University Press, pp. 1–17.

_____ (1996) *Deconstructing the Mind*. New York and Oxford: Oxford University Press.

_____ (2001) "Remarks for the memorial celebration of the life and philosophy of W. V. O. Quine, April 14, 2001." http://wvquine.org/wvq-obit5.html#PPSSl.

Strawson, P. F. (1985) *Skepticism and Naturalism: Some Varieties*. London: Routledge.

Stump, D. (1992) "Naturalized philosophy of science with a plurality of methods." *Philosophy of Science* 59: 456–60.

Thompson, M. (1964) "Naturalistic metaphysics." In R. M. Chisholm et al. (eds.) *Philosophy*, Englewood Cliffs, NJ: Prentice-Hall, pp. 183–204.

Tye, M. (1992) "Naturalism and the mental." *Mind* 101: 421–41.

_____ (1994) "Naturalism and the problem of intentionality." In P. A. French, T. E. Uehling, and H. K. Wettstein (eds.) *Philosophical Naturalism*. Midwest Studies in Philosophy 19, Notre Dame, IN: University of Notre Dame Press, pp. 122–42.

Villanueva, E. (ed.) (1993) *Naturalism and Normativity*, Philosophical Issues 4. Atascadero, CA: Ridgeview.

Ward, J. (1899) *Naturalism and Agnosticism*. 2 vols. London and New York: Macmillan.

Wilkes, K. (1978) *Physicalism*. London: Routledge & Kegan Paul.

Wittgenstein, L. (1922) *Tractatus Logico-Philosophicus*. Trans. C. K. Ogden. London: Routledge & Kegan Paul. Repr. 2002.

_____ (1953) *Philosophical Investigations*. Trans. G. E. M. Anscombe. Oxford: Blackwell.

_____ (1958) *The Blue and Brown Books*. Oxford: Blackwell.

_____ (1969) *On Certainty*. Ed. G. E. M. Anscombe and G. H. von Wright. Oxford: Blackwell.

von Wright, G. H. (1971) *Explanation and Understanding*. Ithaca, NY: Cornell University Press.

Further reading

Anthologies

de Caro, M. and D. MacArthur (eds.) (2004) *Naturalism in Question*. Cambridge, MA: Harvard University Press.

Craig, W. L. and J. P. Morland (eds.) (2000) *Naturalism: A Critical Analysis*. London: Routledge.

Keil, G. and H. Schnädelbach (eds.) (2000) *Naturalismus: Philosophische Beiträge*. Frankfurt am Main: Suhrkamp.

Ryder, J. (ed.) (1994) *American Philosophical Naturalism in the Twentieth Century*. Amherst, MA: Prometheus Books.

Schaber, P. et al. (eds.) (2004) *Normativity and Naturalism*. Heusenstamm and Frankfurt am Main: Ontos.

Shimony, A. and D. Nails (eds.) (1987) *Naturalistic Epistemology: A Symposium of Two Decades*. Boston Studies in the Philosophy of Science 100. Dordrecht, Boston, Lancaster, and Tokyo: Springer.

Wagner, S. J. and R. Warner (eds.) (1993) *Naturalism: A Critical Appraisal*. Notre Dame, IN: University of Notre Dame Press.

Walsh, D. M. (ed.) (2001) *Naturalism, Evolution and Mind*. Cambridge: Cambridge University Press.

Monographs

Almeder, R. F. (1998) *Harmless Naturalism: The Limits of Science and the Nature of Philosophy*. La Salle, IL: Open Court.

Baker, L. R. (1987) *Saving Belief: A Critique of Physicalism*. Princeton, NJ: Princeton University Press.

Churchland, P. M. (1979) *Scientific Realism and the Plasticity of Mind*. Cambridge: Cambridge University Press.

Keil, G. (1993) *Kritik des Naturalismus*. Berlin and New York: de Gruyter.

Millikan, R. G. (1984) *Language, Thought, and Other Biological Categories: New Foundations for Realism*. Cambridge, MA and London: MIT Press.

Papineau, D. (1993) *Philosophical Naturalism*. Oxford: Blackwell.

Pratt, J. B. (1939) *Naturalism*. New Haven, CT and London: Yale University Press.

Stich, S. P. (1983) *From Folk Psychology to Cognitive Science: The Case against Belief*. Cambridge, MA and London: Bradford Books.

Survey articles

Feigl, H. (1953) [1949] "The scientific outlook: naturalism and humanism." In H. Feigl and M. Brodbeck (eds.) *Readings in the Philosophy of Science*, New York: Appleton-Century-Crofts, pp. 8–18.

Friedman, M. (1997) "Philosophical naturalism." *Proceedings and Addresses of the American Philosophical Association* 71: 7–23.

Hylton, P. (1994) "Quine's naturalism." In: P. A. French, T. E. Uehling, and H. K. Wettstein (eds.) *Philosophical Naturalism*. Midwest Studies in Philosophy 19. Notre Dame, IN: University of Notre Dame Press, pp. 261–82.

Kim, J. (1988) "What is naturalized epistemology?" In J. Tomberlin (ed.) *Epistemology*. Philosophical Perspectives 2. Atascadero, CA: Ridgeview, pp. 382–406.

Kornblith, H. (1999) "In defense of a naturalized epistemology." In J. Greco and E. Sosa (eds.) *The Blackwell Guide to Epistemology*. Malden, MA: Blackwell, pp. 158–69.

Lenman, J. (2006) "Moral Naturalism." In *The Stanford Encyclopedia of Philosophy* (Fall 2006 edn.). http://plato.stanford.edu/entries/naturalism-moral/.

Papineau, D. (2007) "Naturalism." In *The Stanford Encyclopedia of Philosophy* (Spring 2007 edn.). http://plato.stanford.edu/entries/naturalism.

Schiffer, S. (1990) "Physicalism." In J. Tomberlin (ed.) *Action Theory and Philosophy of Mind*. Philosophical Perspectives 4. Atascadero, CA: Ridgeview, pp. 153–85.

Sellars, W. (1963) [1962] "Philosophy and the scientific image of man." In *Science, Perception, and Reality*, New York: Humanities Press, pp. 1–40.

Stroud, B. (2004) "The Claim of Naturalism." In M. de Caro and D. MacArthur (eds.) *Naturalism in Question*. Cambridge, MA: Harvard University Press, pp. 21–35.

Williams, B. (2000) "Naturalism and genealogy." In E. Harcourt (ed.) *Morality, Reflection, and Ideology*, Oxford: Oxford University Press.

7

FEMINISM IN PHILOSOPHY

Andrea Nye

From margin to center

The lack of references to feminist philosophy or feminist philosophers in other articles in the present volume (apart from a section on feminist epistemology in Matthias Steup's "Epistemology in the twentieth century," Chapter 11, and a section of feminism in Matt Matravers's "Twentieth-century political philosophy," Chapter 21) might be taken as indicating that feminism played little or no role in twentieth-century philosophy. Certainly this might have seemed true at mid-century when a standard reference work, the Macmillan *Encyclopedia of Philosophy*, was published with no entry under feminist philosophy and virtually no reference to feminism throughout its many volumes. Although feminists were challenging methods and findings in many fields of knowledge, philosophy might seem to be exempt. Philosophers had worked hard to eliminate the last vestiges of unscientific idealism from philosophy. They reinvented a discipline free from the taint of theology or politics. They developed methods of logical, linguistic, and phenomenological analysis that transcended personal and group interests, or so it seemed. Institutional barriers to women's participation had been removed, as proven by the success of notable woman philosophers such as Elisabeth Anscombe (1919–2001) and Philippa Foot (1920–). If women did not enter into the field, it might be assumed to be a result of choice and ability, not sexual discrimination.

Academic respectability in an age of science had been hard won. In Britain and North America a major concern was to reshape theories of knowledge and reality for a scientific age. Philosophy's identification with religion and the preaching of morality was cast aside, its role defined as a discipline with accredited methods and standards. The American Philosophical Association provided a venue where philosophers could meet, share ideas, correct errors, make progress in solving problems, just as problems were put to rest in science. Pragmatic lack of rigor and dabbling in politics was to be left behind. Logical atomism, Wittgenstein's *Tractatus*, the positivist's principle of verification, all reflected a conviction that the tools provided by modern mathematical logic philosophy could insulate philosophers from variable opinion and allow solid achievement to be rewarded (see "The birth of analytic philosophy," Chapter 1). Philosophers might have personal political interests – Russell himself was a self-declared feminist and libertarian – but there was to be no place in the new analytic philosophy for pleading of any kind.

In Europe, Edmund Husserl proposed phenomenology as a foundation for philosophical insight and a method that would prove that philosophers were not redundant in an age of science. A philosopher could "bracket" away ordinary and occasional experience and reveal the logical grammar of thought. He could uncover "essences" and form a substratum for all knowledge, and so mark off a field of specifically philosophical research. As phenomenology evolved with Heidegger's "Being" in time, and Sartre's "being and nothingness," gender difference was seldom discussed. Were not women, like men, mortal human beings living in time? If so, they needed no special voice or treatment.

Outside academic philosophy, powerful feminist voices were heard. Early in the century, Charlotte Perkins Gilman (1860–1935) traced the effects of "androcentric culture" on economics, observing that masculine bias had wrongly made assumptions of scarcity and competition a basis for theorizing (1898; 1911). Emma Goldman (1869–1940) launched a critique against the liberal philosophies of the woman's suffrage movement, arguing that there was no guarantee that women, restricted to traditional roles in the family, in awe of religious authorities, and unable to express their sexuality, would vote progressively or intelligently. A woman's enemies, argued Goldman, were not only external but also internal in the form of social and sexual conventions that block intellectual development (see Goldman 1970).

Clara Zetkin (1857–1933) pointed out inconsistencies in Marxian philosophy and Marxist practice in matters of family and sexual relations. Although no argument consistent with Marxist theory could be made for women's inferiority or special roles, women were not included in socialist leadership, nor were arrangements to free women from domestic labor given priority. Zetkin challenged Lenin's reluctance to endorse issues of sex and marriage as topics for serious socialist debate. She pressed for radical reforms in family life. In Russia Alexandra Kollontai (1872–1952) insisted that the abuse and exploitation of women be addressed. The bourgeois family, analyzed by Marx as an economic institution, was linked to capital and unworkable in a socialist society. Logic, said Kolontai, dictated new forms of domestic and reproductive labor that would allow women as well as men self-realization in work and personal relations.

Rosa Luxemburg (1871–1919), leader in the Social Democratic movement in Germany in the early years of the century, worked closely with Zetkin to negotiate philosophical and tactical relations between liberal movements for women's suffrage and socialist class struggles. In a 1914 article, "Proletarian women" written for International Women's Day, Luxemburg paid particular attention to the condition of women in Africa and Latin America whose interests were poorly served by both liberal democratic philosophies and socialist philosophies framed within the male-dominated European worker's movement.

Hannah Arendt (1906–75), a student of Heidegger as the Nazis came to power in Germany, produced along with her academic thesis on the ethics of St Augustine, a philosophical critique in a novel form. Her innovative biography of Rahel Varnagen (1974) traced the misfortunes of a woman and a Jew poorly served by Enlightenment philosophies. Liberal theories of equality and freedom had not enabled Varnagen, and by implication others of subordinated groups, to construct viable selves or live coherent and happy lives. Although Arendt never formally identified herself as a feminist, or participated significantly in women's movements, her later treatment of the nature of thought and human society gave feminist philosophers new ways to think about the nature of mind, knowledge, and political commitment.

At mid-century, came a turning point. In 1949, as the effect of World War II's dislocation of gender roles began to be most painfully felt, Simone de Beauvoir (1908–86) published a ground-breaking application of existentialist philosophy to the condition of women. What is it to be man? This had been the core question of philosophers from Husserl to Heidegger and Sartre. In *The Second Sex* (1949) de Beauvoir asked another question, "What is it to be a woman?" The same? Or are women radically different and "other" than man? Using arguments and examples from sociology, psychology, literary criticism, as well as from philosophy, de Beauvoir marked out a line of inquiry that feminist philosophers would vigorously and inventively pursue throughout the rest of the century. If to be human has been defined by men in canonical texts of western philosophy, and if those texts have often declared or assumed women to be less than fully human, what should women do? De Beauvoir's answer was clear. A liberated woman must reject the stereotype of "universal femininity;" she must overcome the disabilities she experiences in reproduction and sex. She must refuse the role of passive object and lay claim to existential freedom.

In the next fifty years feminist philosophers debated de Beauvoir's answer with increasing energy, in the process calling into question core assumptions of western epistemology, ethics, and metaphysics. Who am I? What do I know? What should I do? What can I hope for? These were Kant's questions at the close of the eighteenth century, and they were revived by feminist philosophers at the midpoint of the twentieth. They had often been lost sight of: in neo-Kantian speculation, in phenomenological reduction, and in logical analysis. Now they were asked in new forms. What is it to be a woman philosopher? What is it to be a philosopher? Are gender, race, or class relevant to a philosopher's views? Will diverse human natures and experiences result in concepts and positions different from any in the history of philosophy written by men of European descent? Technological developments were creating a global marketplace; old-style colonialisms were dying away; religious and ethnic tensions festered. The questions were asked not only by women, but also by postcolonial peoples and growing immigrant communities in industrialized countries.

A first impulse of reflection on the part of feminist philosophers was historical. Analytic philosophers tended to mute the importance of historical studies in favor of ahistorical logical and linguistic analysis. At the same time they took for granted a steady progress of modern philosophical thought culminating in the mathematical logics and naturalized epistemologies of the postwar period. Now critical feminist readings of Descartes, Kant, and others began to challenge that lineage. Was it the natural rights of propertied men that had been defended by the father of democratic theory, John Locke (1632–1704), and not the rights of all men? Was it men's reason that the founder of modern epistemology, Descartes, had championed against Aristotelian dogma? Were western philosophies of mind, idealist or naturalistic, theories of the male mind, or even the white European male mind? Feminist studies appeared, claiming that epistemologies based on existing methods and on concepts in the natural sciences were theories of masculine methods and procedures, that the deontological and utilitarian paradigms that had dominated ethics for a century gave voice to a man's but not a woman's moral sense, that logicist theories of language reflected masculine but not necessarily feminine styles of speaking.

Philosophers, pursuing a shrinking number of jobs in philosophy in the second half of the century, could find such questioning unnecessary and perverse. A growing movement for pluralism in organizations such as the American Philosophical Society was demanding and promoting greater diversity in conferences and professional journals. Feminist philosophy, along with other "special" interests, was finding a voice in splinter organizations such as the Society for Women in Philosophy and the Society for the Study of Women Philosophers. Courses in feminist philosophy were added to curricula in many university departments. A reading or two by feminist philosophers were included in at least some social and political philosophy texts, and some academic publishers were profiting from a brisk trade in feminist publications. Was this not enough? Feminist philosophy was in a peculiar position. Not just a new topic of philosophical interest such as "philosophy of the social sciences," not the philosophy of a particular school of thought such as Marxian philosophy or existential philosophy, not the use of existing methods and principles to promote a specific political agenda, feminism was a counter-movement "within" philosophy. As such it could seem to threaten the very existence of philosophy, and undermine the success of the few women who had achieved prominence as professional philosophers.

Friends and enemies

Not all feminist philosophers saw irresolvable conflict between mainstream lines of twentieth-century philosophy and feminism. De Beauvoir in *The Second Sex* found existentialism a powerful tool with which to rethink the condition of women. Throughout the suffrage and equal rights movements, feminists called on liberal political philosophies – utilitarianism, social contract theory, democratic theory – to justify claims that women should be granted equal rights and economic opportunity. Democratic philosophies might begin with arguments based on the nature of "man," but if "man" were understood as generic, the natural right of women to self-governance and property and wealth might follow as a matter of course.

Other feminists drew on mainstream socialist philosophies, supplementing Marxist class oppression with analyses of gender and race. Friedrich Engels (1820–95) had asserted that the downfall of women came with the institution of private property. Did it not follow that once private property was abolished in a socialist state, nothing would stand in the way of the equality of the sexes? The power of men, able to dominate women because they controlled the means of production, should wither away. In the 1960s and 1970s lively discussions among feminist philosophers echoed debates between liberals and socialists in establishment political philosophy, weighing the relative merits of free enterprise and nationalization, property rights and social welfare, individualism and communitarianism.

It was not only among political philosophers that feminists found friends. In Britain and the United States in the 1950s and 1960s, women philosophers used established analytic methods of logical analysis and conceptual elucidation on questions not previously considered worthy of philosophical notice. Philosophy had wrongly "relinquished the field of sex to the poets" said Baker and Elliston, the editors of a 1975 collection of articles, *Philosophy and Sex*. Love and marriage, important aspects of human life, should also be "examined" along with justice and knowledge. Papers began to appear sporadically in journals and edited volumes on promiscuity, monogamy, gay rights, and abortion. A popular model was a much anthologized 1971 paper by Judith Jarvis Thomson (1929–), "A defense of abortion," reprinted in the Baker and Elliston collection. To defuse the emotions and religious views surrounding abortion and restore words to their ordinary usage, Thomson used the method of imaginative counterexample popular in post-Wittgensteinian linguistic analysis. She constructed an elaborate hypothesis – what if a famous violinist were hooked up to a woman's kidneys without her consent – and then asked the classic question of ordinary-language philosophy: "What would we say then?" Is the woman obligated to sustain the life of the violinist? The answer, argued Thomson, must be no. Because the situation is analogous with unwanted pregnancy, it follows that a woman should not be forced to sustain a child for nine months either.

Marilyn Frye (1983) made feminist use of tools of "linguistic analysis" to elucidate the terms "male chauvinism" and "sexism." The precision of Frye's analyses had a purpose beyond demystifying philosophical problems. Clear concepts are essential, argued Frye, if feminists are to get men to see the nature of their "offenses." Her aim was not to leave "everything as it is," but to clarify and sharpen usage so as cogently and precisely to name the wrongs done to women. Mixing politics with ontology, Frye teased apart and wove together strands of meaning and fact to delineate complex phenomena of oppression. If the aim of orthodox linguistic analysis was to put to rest vexing philosophical problems like the status of mental objects or the existence of the external world, Frye's purpose was different. Careful description of possible occasions of use, sensitivity to root meanings, consideration of the reasons why an experience is singled out as an object of interest gave feminist critics a more secure grasp on reality and therefore a greater ability to challenge that reality.

Linguistic analysis and ordinary-language philosophy passed out of vogue in the 1970s and 1980s in favor of truth-functional semantics and naturalized epistemologies, and feminists found new inspiration in the neo-empiricisms of W. V. O. Quine and Donald Davidson. Lynn Nelson (1990) urged feminists to accept what philosophers had learned about knowledge in forty years of analytic philosophical inquiry, namely: theory is underdetermined by evidence, several theories might always be found to accommodate existing evidence, there is no reason to think that sensory observation can finally detect a best of all possible theories. Background assumptions shaped by race, gender, and culture can never be completely filtered out of science. Argued Nelson, this is no reason to give up on empiricism or lapse into relativism. Evidence matters whether or not it is ever finally decisive. Quinian holism allows feminist intuitions to figure in knowledge claims based on feminist experience. Knowledge, Nelson concluded, is a makeshift business, in constant repair as science struggles to predict painful and maximize pleasurable stimulations, and feminist insights can be part of that process. If Quine's underdetermined "web of belief" is extended to include a wider net of political, moral, and social feminist experience, if it is understood that data is collected by communities of researchers not by individuals whose sensory receptors are innocent of social conditioning, empiricist epistemology can become feminist empiricist epistemology (1990).

In a collection of articles meant to show that analytic philosophers and twentieth-century feminists have much in common, Sharyn Clough recommended use of Donald Davidson's neo-Quinian semantics to help feminist philosophers escape a self-defeating relativism of male and female conceptual schemes ("A hasty retreat from evidence," in Clough 2003: 85–114). Given the mechanics of reference as understood in Davidson's application of truth-theoretic semantics, argued Clough, there can be no question of competing conceptual schemes. Understanding a language, whether it is a foreign language or the language of a new theory, requires the assumption that the user of the language is truthful for the most part. Ultimately feminists, like everyone, are "radical interpreters," dependent on occasion sentences and shared environmental stimuli to establish true and false propositions that, joined by truth-functional connectives, constitute meaning. There is no private inner world of feminine belief from which to issue forth bold new representations of reality. Feminist theory, like any other theory, must be grounded in occasion sentences that point to one world of facts shared with men. Again the lesson was both humbling and hopeful; feminist philosophers who envisioned a separatist break with establishment philosophy had misunderstood the nature of knowledge, but on the bright side late analytic theories of meaning left room for feminist intervention.

Richard Rorty's neo-pragmatism offered another friendly basis for feminist philosophizing. In a postmodern era, said Rorty, truth could finally be given up, along with the philosopher's illusion that there is a foundation of knowledge or a reflecting "mirror" that can be held up to nature. Once the illusion is cast off of an "overseer" of knowledge, philosophy will be open to "abnormal" discourses like feminism. Philosophers will give up the pretension to discover essences or first principles. They will leave material and practical matters to economics and politics. They will enjoy the freedom to try on ideas, sample ways of thinking, pursue divergent lines of thought like feminism (Rorty 1991).

Rorty's "pragmatism" and call for openness was not wholeheartedly embraced by all feminists (see Fraser 1991). Many were unwilling to give up politics and economics for light-hearted conversation, nor were they always satisfied with tolerance at the margins of the philosophical establishment. In the United States and other English-speaking countries, regardless of calls for pluralism, a hard core of "real" philosophy prevailed. Proponents held jobs at important universities and set standards for publication in leading journals. In this inner circle, the mark of a philosopher was not tolerance of diversity and willingness to experiment with abnormal discourses, but rationality and respect for logic. Here the relation between feminist philosophers and the profession could be less than amicable. One of the first unfriendly attacks came from Janice Moulton (1983), who pointed out deficiencies in the adversarial style of much professional philosophizing, using Thomson's model paper on abortion as an example of these deficiencies. Thomson limited her argument to what might persuade her opponents, said Moulton. She accepted her adversary's premise that a fetus is analogous to a person. She restricted her treatment to refuting the arguments of her opponents. The result was a superficial analytic treatment of abortion that glossed over substantive questions about bodily identity and family relations. In emulation of science, philosophy tried to develop a distinctive method, but, said Moulton, different paradigms might be more fruitful and insightful. Moulton did not describe what a different feminist style of philosophical reasoning might be like, but feminist philosophers were already experimenting with philosophical styles far from the dry dialectic of much analytic debate. Going one step further, some began to weave together psychoanalysis, myth, personal history, blurring the line between philosophy and literature, philosophy and psychology, philosophy and memoir. The French philosopher Michele Le Dœuff (1948–) argued that a submerged metaphorical "philosophical imaginary" was at work in texts cited as models of philosophical reason such as Kant's *Critique of Pure Reason* (Le Dœuff 1989). Susan Griffin (1980) explored matter and bodily existence in a mix of poetry and critique, weaving together a variety of voices: the parodied voice of objective philosophical or scientific authority, the voices of victimized and assaulted women, the voice of the author's own tentative vision of another future. Hispanic philosopher Maria Lugones and Anglo Elizabeth Spelman paired their different voices in dialogue in an attempt at cross-cultural understanding (1986). In these writings, the movement was not from claim to proof and rebuttal, but from claim to response and revision.

Non-adversarial exchange of divergent views was a goal pursued by feminist philosophers not only in print, but in energetic and sometimes painful confrontations at meetings of the new Society for Women in Philosophy. Decisive as the refutation of an opponent might be as philosophers competed as adversaries, wounds inflicted in gentlemanly debate tended to be superficial; the loser went home, constructed a new position, and sallied forth to better defend himself. In feminist discussions emotionally charged issues surfaced, and cool and calm were harder to maintain. Discussion was often passionate and sometimes angry as lesbian and straight philosophers, philosophers of color and white philosophers struggled to find common ground. Trampled under foot, said some critics, was reason, the very defining characteristic of philosophy.

Reason had been singled out since Plato as the mark of a philosopher. Reason could take different forms – intuition of Platonic Form, Aristotelian syllogisms, medieval arguments from essence, contemporary mathematical logic – but one thing remained. Reason was dispassionate and unemotional. A philosopher's job was not to feel, but to think. Now, reflecting on the history of philosophical reason, some feminist philosophers indicted rationality itself as masculine illusion. Reason had been defined in hierarchical opposition to body, feeling, emotion, and, by extension, to femininity. In classical philosophy a superior reason ruled body, emotion, and women, making reason, some feminist charged, the mark of tyranny as men became masters of irrational women in the household and masters of primitive, less rational races abroad.

An early critique of modern reason came from the Australian philosopher and feminist Genevieve Lloyd (1984). On its face, Lloyd argued, Cartesian rationalism might seem to be sexless, not contaminated as was Aristotelian reason by a faulty biology and politics. Descartes himself declared his method available to anyone, including women. He paid due respect to the intellect of his female correspondent and patroness, Princess Elisabeth (Nye 1999). Later, in aristocratic salons in which Cartesianism was discussed, women played prominent roles. But, said Lloyd, Cartesian reason was defined against the bodily feeling ordinarily associated with femininity. That association and the fact that women continued to be expected to do the majority of reproductive, affective, and domestic work in families, meant that women were effectively barred from participating in rational Cartesian science. The separation of reason from sensual, emotional, bodily existence had ratified a sexual division of labor and separate roles for men and women.

Susan Bordo (1956–) went further in her indictment of modernist reason (Bordo 1987). It was not only that Cartesian reason ratified existing distinctions between masculinity and femininity. Rational method constituted, said Bordo, a virtual "flight" from the feminine sensibility of the Middle Ages to a new era of science devoted to mastering and ruling the natural world. Bordo used developmental psychology to analyze what she read as the paranoid anxiety-ridden tone of Descartes's arguments in the *Meditations*. What if all that I think has been put into my head not by a good God but an evil demon? What if everything my senses tell me is illusion and all that I think I see is a dream? A masculine pathology in these questions, said Bordo, continues to infect twentieth-century philosophy as philosophers return again and again to Descartes as founding father of modernism. Although she did not describe possible alternatives in detail, Bordo pointed to future styles of philosophizing, less alienated, less abstract, and friendlier to women.

Psychology was another popular basis for critiques of masculine reason. In an influential account, *The Reproduction of Mothering* (1978), psychologist Nancy Chodorow (1944–) argued that boy children, brought up exclusively by mothers with whom boys can never identify, have a masculine identity that is inevitably fragile. A boy cannot learn to be a man, because he has no early model of masculinity. He learns only how not to be, specifically how not to be a woman. As a result, a man establishes rigid ego boundaries, a barricaded sense of self, and sharp distinctions between masculinity and femininity. Feminist philosophers were quick to see a connection with the attributes of philosophical reason. On the Continent the French psychoanalyst Jacques Lacan (1901–81) in similar ways described a boy's entrance into the social world by way of language necessarily structured around an illusory male presence. In any ordered semantic system, said Lacan, the phallus is the master signifier of rational order, the guarantee of sanity and the key to mastery and stability, and also the strenuously defended fragile delusory byproduct of a split subject.

Lacan did not theorize any overcoming of masculine reason, but French feminist Luce Irigaray (1930–) took Lacanian psychoanalysis a step further (1985). If reason as well as sexual difference is anchored in universal symbolic structures, it explains the seeming intractability of the association of masculinity and reason, and the failure of women to participate effectively in fields like philosophy and science. Instead women should find their own native thought and style, argued Irigaray, explore alternatives to the rigid logic of hierarchical opposition within which the feminine will always be subordinate to the masculine. Along with other French feminists, Irigaray looked forward to an *écriture féminine* that would express a woman's nature. Her call elicited an outpouring of innovative readings and creative explorations of philosophical themes, at times densely theoretical but also lyrical, autobiographical, and imaginative.

English-speaking feminist philosophers read the bold new French feminisms with excitement, but some had doubts about the war on philosophic reason. How were feminist critiques to be grounded or feminist claims validated without rationally ordered concepts and logical arguments? If feminists gave up claims to truth as illegitimate assertions of cognitive authority, did they not also give up the hope of changing attitudes or practices prejudicial to women? Much of the new feminist writing depended on substrata of erudite and sometimes questionable psychoanalytic and linguistic theory inaccessible to many women and without clear reference to material existence. Intoxicating and seductive as were new French styles, by the 1980s there was the sense among many feminists that it was time to return to more orthodox and accessible methods of analysis and less global indictments of philosophical reason.

Philosophical reason, even in the rigidly codified form of a logic, could take a variety of historically conditioned forms that related in different ways to exercises of institutional power. If some of those forms had been implicated in silencing divergent voices, the possibility of reasoning aimed at understanding and integration rather than silencing and domination might not be ruled out. If the purpose of some forms of logic was to barricade what is said against critique, other forms of inference might leave room for response and intersubjective understanding. The search for such an idiom and the alternative theories of subjectivity, knowledge, and morality it might reflect would be a priority for feminist philosophers in the latter decades of the century.

Feminism in philosophy of mind

The metaphysical self of Wittgenstein's *Tractatus* represents a problematic beginning for twentieth-century philosophy of mind. "Not a human being, not the human body, or the human soul," Wittgenstein's subject occupied the insubstantial point of self-awareness from which a rational being surveys the world. All ghostly Cartesian substance was expunged from that consciousness, but its continued and seemingly necessary presence in a world understood in terms of a logically ordered materialist science had to be anomalous. Where *in* such a world could such a subject be found? The dilemma was laid out by Kant. If the knowable world is an ensemble of causally determined physical events and physical processes in space and time, as is the presupposition of empirical science, how can I think of myself as freely reflecting, judging, and acting in that world? How is it that I can hold myself and others morally responsible for thoughts and actions?

In Britain and the United States, Kant's question was deferred. The aim of Russell and transplanted positivists such as Carnap was to insure that philosophy fostered, supported the natural sciences, and removed impediments to progress in them. To that end, the task of "philosophy of mind" was not to negotiate Kant's antinomy but to account for commonsense beliefs and ordinary talk about minds and what goes on in minds, without recourse to non-natural souls or spiritual processes. Claims about mental objects and events, insofar as those claims are meaningful or true, were taken as referring to physical or neurological events, or to dispositions to behavior. Talk about what goes on in minds could be dismissed as naive "folk psychology" of no interest to philosophers or to scientists. What goes on in the mind could be seen as "functional," comparable to computer programming requiring no ghostly "hardware." Related, but mostly ignored, were clinical practices that the new theories of mind reflected and to some degree ratified. Should psychology concern itself with conditioning undesirable behavior, or should internal "cognitive" reconfiguring be its main concern? Should "talk therapy" be abandoned, and mental dysfunction due to faulty neural wiring be repaired with drugs or surgery? But of less importance than practical effects of theories of mind was the perceived need for philosophy to explain away as efficiently as possible any residue of unscientific spirituality.

Feminist philosophers approached philosophy of mind with interests closer to Kant's. Throughout the century, feminist research in history, linguistics, sociology, psychology, biology, and anthropology uncovered complex and diverse causes of women's lack of power. So successful and compelling was the growing body of research on the depth and ubiquity of sexism, that prospects could seem dim for any substantial change in women's situations. At the same time, a necessary element in feminist thought is the image of women as conscious beings with critical understanding, potentially free agents capable of acting according to freely formed beliefs and ideals. For feminists, the antimony between material causality on the one hand, and freedom of thought and action on the other cannot be so easily sidestepped in analyses of neural pathways or cognitive processing. In question is the very possibility of feminist reflective critical insight and progressive action.

Preliminary questions about analytic philosophies of mind were posed by Naomi Scheman in a paper, "Individualism and the objects of psychology," reprinted in Sandra Harding and Merrill Hintikka's *Discovering Reality* (1983), the first of many collections of essays critiquing mainstream epistemology and metaphysics from feminist perspectives. Scheman endorsed an "anti-individualist" approach to mental objects. Talk about beliefs and desires, she said, cannot be understood as talk about existing interior objects in individual minds. She went on to ask a further question: why did the assumption of individualism in contemporary philosophical analyses of the mind persist? Why the attempt to equate mental objects with neural events or functions in an individual's brain even after Ryle and Wittgenstein exposed the category mistake in thinking so? Was this an accidental glitch in logic to be cleared up with counter-arguments? The assumption of individualism in philosophical psychology, Scheman argued, is no simple mistake, but has roots in wider currents of political thought. Individualism is ideology, part of a ruling complex of attitudes about society, government, and family. The economics and politics of capitalism, related techniques in education and psychology, and conservative family values hold in place a mistaken view of the mind, even after its theoretical inadequacy is pointed out.

Scheman's genealogical and ideological interpretation of philosophies of mind undermined the objective professionalism that was the pride of analytic philosophy, but feminists came to philosophy with existential as well as theoretical concerns. If elements in a given mind stand alone ready to be identified and categorized like other objects of scientific research, then a woman must either take her mind as she finds it or submit to remedial "treatment." But twentieth-century women were not ready to accept those alternatives. Their minds were in a state of disorder as they reconsidered beliefs, hopes, and desires in the wake of a growing feminist consciousness, but it was not a disorder that they were ready to disown as dysfunctional or pathological. What feminists thought and felt was not neural or representational fact, but painful and confusing processes of rethinking and reinterpretation as beliefs and feelings both challenged and reshaped experience. Reworking beliefs and feelings meant reworking what beliefs and feelings are about: namely twentieth-century working life, family life, and politics. Scheman's observations of the ideological roots of philosophies of mind were not only relevant for feminists. In a changing global environment, people of color, subject ethnicities, gays and lesbians were experiencing similar unsettled states of mind.

In a complementary analysis, Jennifer Hornsby (1951–) pointed out some of the unacceptable implications of eliminating ordinary talk of beliefs, fears, and hopes, as "folk psychology" (Hornsby 1997). If what we ordinarily say about thinking, hoping, and fearing as we attempt to understand why we and others act is radically mistaken and eliminated, social life falls apart. What results is "nihilism," sustained by bizarre counter-factual examples featuring doppelgangers and body transfers that make life as we know it unintelligible. The alternative Hornsby prescribed was not a return to ghostly mental substance, but a "naive naturalism" that assumes "minded" human beings potentially conscious of their circumstances. The actions of a "minded" person cannot be understood from a purely extensional, impersonal point of view, as a predetermined causal sequence from neural event, to bodily movement, to physical consequences. Human life depends on the ability to understand action as a person's action, an aspect of coherent patterns in attitudes and beliefs governed by ideals. Behind attempts to eliminate mental talk in favor of descriptions of neural events, Hornsby saw faulty ontology. If naturalism means that there is nothing in the world except individual bits of matter and conglomerates of bits of matter, then there are no persons, actions, or subjects. If, however, naturalism means that not all aspects of reality are reducible to fusions of atomic bits, then persons and actions, as well as possible understanding of persons and actions, reappear.

Hornsby's conclusion left open the possibility of a style of philosophizing rooted in concern for social consequences. The quantitative logic taken as definitive of rationality had cast a restrictive and distorting grid on reality. Philosophical questions are not all about objects that can be ordered into sets or equated with a fusion of simpler components. "A belief that *p*," "a desire for *q*" might be anonymous tokens in logical games played by philosophers, but a person's beliefs and desires concern dynamic objects not reducible to elementary particles or elementary propositions. How are a woman's or man's beliefs and desires formed? In what ways does desire permeate judgment? Should the goal of thought be a coherent web of belief that maximizes pleasurable sensations and promotes survival? Or should a person strive for other kinds of thinking, related to the material world in different ways?

If feminism was at work in currents of analytic thought, it also was at work in Continental philosophies of subjectivity. Here the other side of the Kantian dilemma took precedence: not how to explain away the mind given scientific determinism and materialism but how to understand the subject who is the source of knowledge. The problem was not what to do with the mind, but what to do with reality outside the mind. Immediate material existence had been bracketed out by Husserl in transcendental reflection. Instrumental reason and its technological products were condemned by Heidegger as dehumanizing. Material circumstance was denied as the determinant of personality in Sartre's existentialism. The body disappeared, was tentatively revived by Merleau-Ponty, disappeared again in Derrida's linguistic reworking of Husserlian phenomenology (see "Phenomenology," Chapter 15). In the end what was left were systems of meaning, "representations" cast up by language. The subject remained, not as a physical brain or cognitive function, but as a subject place fixed in grammar, given substance in an ensemble of signifiers that identify that place as male or female, white or of color, straight or gay. "Women" figured, not as minded persons or embodied subjects, but as an idea or concept of "woman" different from and in subordination to "man." A primal gender opposition at the center of an inescapable matrix of oppositional meaning – nature/culture, passion/reason, woman/man, slave/master, body/mind – held in place women's subordinate identity.

As interest in Continental structuralism, post-structuralism and postmodernism grew, feminists responded to the new structural semantics of gender in different ways. Some were energized by post-structuralist and postmodern critiques of delusive unity of the Kantian or Husserlian "subject." Drawing on the neo-Freudian psychoanalytic theories of Lacan and on Derrida's critique of presence as the basis for meaning, feminists attacked the philosophical subject as a fraud, an attempt to manufacture substance and presence. "Any theory of the subject has already been appropriated "au masculine," wrote Irigaray (1985). If a woman attempts to assert herself as a rational subject – becomes a philosopher for example – she only buys into her own objectification. She becomes the truth-telling, logic-wielding theorizing subject, placing herself, given the symbolic identification of woman with nature, matter, earth, body, as an object to be worked, owned, grasped, penetrated.

For feminists it was a chastening diagnosis. If beliefs, desires, and ideals are not individual events within an individual, and not the fruit of dynamic interactions with reality either, but "constituted" within systems of representation organized around the "name of the father," whether those systems are ordered or disordered hardly matters. Feminist freedom to think, and to act creatively and constructively disappears. The would-be feminist activist is caught in a web of belief with the only recourse a self-defeating refusal to speak in intelligible terms. Given that reality is a linguistic construction not of anyone's making, there would seem to be no way to escape oppressive either/or identities. Much feminist philosophizing in the 1980s and 1990s was concerned with negotiating this Continental challenge. Techniques of "writing the feminine" were examined and analyzed. Michel Foucault (1926–84) was studied for ways temporarily and locally to elude the power of reason and science on physical bodies. Deconstruction was adopted as a technique to expose inconsistencies and incoherence in any attempt to establish stable logical sequences. Some left philosophy altogether for activist work, redressing in practical ways the violence done to women.

A sustained and complex treatment of the problem of the postmodern subject came from Judith Butler (1993; 1997). Butler (1956–) reviewed several decades of feminist attempts to rethink agency and consciousness within the context of Continental post-structuralism. Not only were women defined as "not men," said Butler, the oppositional structure of structural semantics is itself oppressive. Either/or logic makes it necessary to be either a man or a woman, enforces heterosexuality, and bans homosexuality. To be someone, a subject must take on an identity, male or female, white or colored, father or mother. Like a straitjacket, discourse traps subjects in preconstructed identities and behaviors. How – by what power – is an inferiorized psyche formed? asked Butler. The standard answer is that certain attitudes and beliefs are "internalized." This assumes that there are pre-existing minds into which ideas are transplanted and from which they might be expunged. But if one's very existence as a subject depends upon a place in a system of signs, there would seem to be only two alternatives: resignation to the fact that radical consciousness and action are impossible, or search for a stance outside established linguistic and social forms, a quest doomed to failure as subjects only further entangle themselves in compromised meanings. "Woman" produces "real" women, subjects with given identities, not by reference to any pre-existing unifying natural presence but by ruling out what real women are not (not masculine, not queer, not androgynous …). Because the list of identifying features is never complete, warned Butler, identity politics based on "natural kinds" such as "woman" or "black" or "gay" inevitably dissolve into factional dispute. There is a progressive alternative, argued Butler. Once the myth of rigid designation to natural kind is dissolved, names like "woman" and "queer" can be reinhabited and resignified. Refusing illusory utopian remedies, Butler cited the potential for liberation potential in "speech acts," in conscious citation and "performance" of stigmatized identities.

Another move was to attempt to resurrect the body. Subjects, feminist philosophers pointed out, have bodies marked by sex, race, and other physical determinants, a fact that Continental philosophies of subjectivity ignored. Moira Gatens (1996) turned to the non-dualist philosophy of Spinoza for inspiration. There was no twentieth-century philosophy of the body, noted Gatens, that feminists could draw on to understand the power politics of abortion, contraception, and sexual assault. The body was seen in physicalist terms as a mechanism or in idealist terms as a conception of the mind, all of which perpetuated dualist illusion. In Spinoza, Gatens found a philosophy of the person as a dynamic being with two expressions of thought and extension, in inter-action with others and with the world, constantly changing and striving. The result of thinking of the body in non-dualist terms, rather than terms of a male "imagining" based on a man's bodily relations with women, Gatens suggested, might be ways of thinking about sociality, ethics, and politics that take into consideration women's bodily experience. Further analyses of embodiment came from Rosa Braidotti (1991) and Elizabeth Grosz (1995).

It was not only the masculine identity of disembodied subjects that was in question but a subject's race, class, and ethnic identity. Theories of the subject, embodied or disembodied, are a product of white minds, said Hispanic philosopher Maria Lugones in a pair of influential essays (Lugones and Spelman 1986; Lugones 1987). What characterizes the subjectivity of Hispanic and other women of color, argued Lugones, is neither physiology nor entrapment in a conceptual scheme, but experience in a real borderland between dominant and exploited cultures. Forced to travel between "worlds of sense," a woman of mixed or mestizo identity understands mechanisms of oppression and possible escapes from that oppression in ways that monolingual and monocultural subjects cannot.

A complementary treatment of non-white subjects came from Patricia Hill Collins (1990). Black woman's subjectivity, said Hill Collins, is necessarily "dual." They see themselves in the symbolic terms of dominant white culture as "mammy," "welfare mother," "matriarch," and "whore," but given the degrading nature of these identities they also see themselves as themselves. The result is that they can look at semantic categories from a distance, and understand that the ideology in which those categories are embedded is not uniform or cohesive. So negative are white discourse's images for black women that there can be no doubt that they distort reality, and black women are able to develop a resistant internal sense of self.

"Who am I?" was not only a theoretical question for women like Hill Collins and Lugones, but part of an ongoing project of reworking feminine identities. Once a female "subject" turned and considered herself in a move seemingly essential to moral freedom and responsible agency, another subject appeared that might also have to be critically examined and overcome. Without reliable knowledge and realistic social categories the thinking feminine subject could seem trapped in an endless round of self-questioning. Theories of man's knowledge were readily available, but no theory of a woman's knowledge. The question remained: Is there any way to achieve knowledge of self and world certain enough to stop the process of self-reflection and become the basis for "minded" responsible action consistent with feminist ideals?

Feminism in epistemology

In philosophy, the question "who is it who claims to know?" is typically eclipsed by the supposedly more fundamental question: not "who" but "how" is knowledge properly acquired and justified? In an age of science, if any question remained for philosophy to answer it was this. Natural philosophy was now the province of the physical sciences.

The nature of man was determined by the human sciences. Normative ethics and aesthetics were delegated to moralists and art critics. The ultimate justification of methods in science was left for the philosophers, who offered a variety of positivist, constructionist, holistic answers to the question of how knowledge is possible. The very purpose of these accounts was removal of "who" of personality and perspective, a removal seen as necessary for science's objectivity and truth. When proper methods and procedures were identified, it would not matter who produced knowledge or why. Biases, prejudices, and preconceived ideas held by the producers of knowledge would be ruled out. This ideal, of a personality-free knowledge and its attendant projection of authority and universality, marked twentieth-century theories of knowledge in both the analytic and Continental traditions. The essential structures of subjectivity that Husserl's phenomenology mapped had no sexual, gender, or racial identity. Frege's "thoughts," ultimate building blocks of meaning in constructing the logic of science, were the thoughts of "everyone," man or woman, western or non-western, gay or straight. The sensory events and occasion sentences that grounded empiricist theories of knowledge from Russell to Carnap were not observed or spoken by individuals with identities, but were anonymous, experienced by any normal "observer."

Feminist philosophers were not the only ones to express doubt about this ideal of objectivity in knowledge. As the century wore on, Kuhn's incommensurable paradigms, Feyerabend's relativity, sociological science studies, Quine's ontological relativity and inscrutability of reference, all clouded the possibility of complete objectivity. But in few of these critiques of certainty was knowledge understood as personal motivated action in the Hornsby sense, or in any way shaped by the bodies or imaginations of scientists of specific genders, incomes, nationalities, or cultural identifications. If scientists and the philosophers who theorized about science happened to be predominately men or white or of a particular ethnicity resident in a particular geographical location, or involved in particular social or political relationships, this was not considered relevant to the cognitive status of the theories they produced. To think otherwise, went the standard wisdom, was to misunderstand the difference between accidents surrounding the discovery of a theory and a theory's justification. The methods of justification used in the various sciences might not be infallible or even commensurable, but their purpose was to transcend bias and personal interest.

Women philosophers, whose inferiority as women had often been the subject of scientific research, were less inclined to accept scientific methods without question. Feminist critical studies documented bias and distortion in many scientific fields: in anthropological theories of man the hunter, in brain studies that showed weakness in women's mathematical skills, in psychological studies that proved women's inferior moral sense, in biology texts that pictured "passive" female eggs invaded by "active" male sperm. Given the many examples, it was hard not to think that "who" conducted research might have made a difference.

A first response was a call for an alternate paradigm that would validate knowledge in traditionally female-dominated fields like nursing and teaching. "Women's ways of knowing" would include emotion, be empathic rather than analytic, come from feelings of oneness with nature, interact with rather than dominate nature, understand natural processes as organic rather than mechanistic. Immediately, a first surge of enthusiasm was checked by second thoughts. To aspiring women scientists, "women's ways of knowing" could seem a reversion to pre-modern superstition, producing enclaves to which feminist research could be safely consigned while well-funded mainstream science continued on unchallenged. To speak of "women's knowledge" might imprison women in feminine essence. It might wrongly imply that women subjects are all the same, a presumption vigorously protested by vocal constituencies of women of color, gay women, working-class women.

A scientist might be male, but he was also probably white, and either of North American or European descent, identities that colored his thinking as much as his gender or sex. "Ways of knowing" proliferated, not just "women's ways" but lesbian, Africanist, mestizo knowledges. The conclusion that knowledge is relative to many different perspectives seemed inevitable, prompting a deeper worry. If reality is constructed out of various incommensurable conceptual schemes, the truth of competing theories can never be established. Feminist science or Africanist science is no better than masculinist western science. There is no way to decide between them except by fiat or arbitrary choice. As a result, whatever faction is in power will have to dictate what is to count as knowledge.

Feminist philosophers energetically debated the dangers of relativism throughout the 1980s and 1990s. One response was to return to scientific empiricism, but with renewed diligence as to the possibility of bias. Repeatability of experiments, insistence that contrary evidence not be discounted, well-formed hypotheses, and logical clarity would lead to objective results. Faith in the reliability of empirical methods, however, was undermined by a growing consensus among mainstream philosophers that theory is underdetermined by evidence, that scientific ontologies are relative, and references ultimately inscrutable. If it is always possible that another theory might just as well account for empirical evidence, male or other bias can never be completely ruled out. In mainstream theory of knowledge two positions were popular: a "naturalized" epistemology that eschewed normativity for descriptive accounts of evolved ways of dealing with the world as exemplified in contemporary science, and a scientific realism that left it to scientific experts to identify the objects of scientific research. Neither approach, it seemed to many feminists, provided sufficient protection against flaws in thinking that were targets of feminist critique.

A second "feminist standpoint" approach borrowed from Marxism. Nancy Hartstock acknowledged the importance of perspective and at the same time hoped to avoid self-defeating relativism (1984). Marx had argued that science in western countries was "bourgeois" science, science from the standpoint of a ruling capitalist class; classical economics and functional sociology served capitalist and colonial interests even as they pretended to present a neutral and objective worldview. Similarly, argued Hartstock, western science is male science tailored to men's interests in controlling wealth and exercising power. Marx posited a "universal" working class, whose perspective would prevail. The challenge for feminist standpoint theorists was to show that women had a similarly privileged viewpoint. If male workers understand capitalism better than capitalist owners who have vested interests to defend, women, less privileged, with less to lose, and less ego to defend, might be in an even better position. The work of Nobel Prize-winning microbiologist Barbara McClintock (1902–92) was often cited as an example. At first ignored by her colleagues, McClintock used intuitive methods and models and eventually changed the way genes and genetic processes are understood. Male scientists had failed to understand genetic processes, feminist philosophers of science such as Evelyn Fox Keller (1936–) charged, because they came to biology with flawed masculinist conceptions of natural "law," master molecules, and linear causation (Keller 1983; 1985).

The choice between objectivity according to standard empiricist logic on the one hand and the possibly relativistic acceptance of different conceptual schemes on the other was uncomfortable for many feminist philosophers. Sandra Harding (1935–), reviewing the successes and failures of feminist empiricist and standpoint epistemologies, suggested several ways to negotiate the dilemma. A "strong objectivity" could be demanded in which critical scrutiny is given not just to theory but also to methods used to establish theory, relations in the community of scientists that produced it, and the presuppositions and interests that motivate research programs (1991). The credentials of "local" ways of knowing, better suited to different cultures and environments than western science, might be validated in their own settings with due attention to the needs and methods of non-western peoples (1993).

If feminist epistemologists were at work in analytic philosophy, they were also active in Continental philosophy. At the beginning of the century, Husserl addressed some of the same questions as Russell and Carnap. If scientific theories – and even the mathematical idioms in which those theories are expressed – change, can there be any noncontingent grounding for science? Even more important, if science alone decides on its methods, what is the role of philosophy? Russell and Carnap bowed to science's authority, reserving the right for philosophy to reconstruct the logic that best accounted for science's obvious success. Husserl, focusing on the subjectivity that produces logic, was less willing to leave the first or final word to science. Science claimed to describe the world, but its theories would be empty formulae with no roots in thought. A philosopher can uncover essences that are the very conditions for intelligibility and the beginning point of any knowledge. Science, grounded in philosophy, will have to return to the philosopher's intuited life-world conceptions to be understood.

By the 1960s Husserl's phenomenological attack on the independence of science was replaced by more radical claims. In a climate of counter-culture rebellion, Michel Foucault claimed to show in a series of historical/philosophical studies that the modern "episteme" that generates objective knowledge is not rooted in essential structures of subjectivity, but is a historically specific mix of discourses, logics, and practices that mandate non-judicial and impersonal exercises of power over physical bodies in prisons, institutions, medical facilities. (For further discussion of Foucault, see "French philosophy in the twentieth century," Chapter 19.) It was only a small step to apply Foucault's argument to women, whose bodies had so often been the object of scrutiny and control. Sciences of cosmetology, weight control, plastic surgery, argued Sandra Bartky (1990) exert a violent discipline on female bodies.

Jacques Derrida (1930–2004) presented another model for radical feminist doubt about truth in science. Tracing Husserl's generative studies of the emergence of essences from nature, body, psychology, Derrida traced the breakup of the phenomenological project to ground objectivity in subjectivity. Only language, and specifically writing, stabilizes meaning, argued Derrida, and it must do so on its own. There are no essential presences that words name, only a primal twist of "difference," a trace that generates fragile, always contradictory systems of oppositions that support linguistic meaning. As a result, no sharp line between knowledge claims in science and imaginative literature can be drawn, no line between fiction and truth. Postmodern critiques like Derrida's, argued theorists like Jane Flax (1990), had a natural affinity with feminism. To undermine the unitary subject, the transcendence of reason, and the idea that history is progressive is to question patriarchy. Nancy Fraser (1947–) and Linda Nicholson agreed – postmodernism could be a useful corrective to ethnocentricity and essentialism – but added a caveat: space has to be left for situated social criticism (Fraser and Nicholson 1990).

The question remained about the grounding for critique. If knowledge, and objects of knowledge, are constituted – or worse, constituted for purposes of domination – then the knowing subject who claims universality for his or her beliefs is not only a fraud but a tyrant. The claim to know with objectivity and truth is an imposition of authority that forbids alternative thought. To posit in addition to masculinist science an alternative feminist science is to mimic the master, a move that inevitably creates new "abject" objects of knowledge. Was this to give up any hope of realizing feminist hopes for the future? Was it to answer Kant's question "What can we know?" with the nihilist response, "Nothing, nothing unless one tyrannizes over and dominates others, nothing if one does not want to look out at the world with arrogant male eyes"? But critique was no more exempt from such doubt than positive theorizing. If there is no solid ground on which to base a truth claim, how is critique possible? How can a theory be said to be false if there is no basis for the judgment? As dangers and merits of postmodern and post-structuralist theory were vigorously debated by feminists in the last decades of the century, several new strains of feminist epistemology emerged.

One emphasis in much feminist epistemology was on relations, relations between producers of knowledge, and relations between producers and the objects of knowledge. There was general agreement that the assumption of a lone (probably male) scientist recording data innocent of preconception and constructing logically consistent theory was imaginary. Actual scientific research goes on in communities within which methods of experimentation and theoretical models and metaphors evolve. Nor are researchers independent of wider society. Relations by funding and affiliation with political, cultural, and commercial interests shape scientific interests and commitments. One hope was that with feminist insight critical thought could be fostered within such communities. One way to accomplish this was by simple inclusion. If women and men with diverse identities and affiliations were encouraged to become scientists, fresh perspectives, interest, concerns in science would naturally be voiced and addressed. From European critical theory came a further consideration. If truth is not transcendent but a result of rational discourse open to differing opinions, discourse requires a certain kind of speaking community. Divergent viewpoints must be not only articulated but also heard and understood. Critical theorist Seyla Benhabib (1950–) called attention to the radical institutional and funding changes necessary for a speaking situation in which women's and diverse voices enter into debate on an equal basis (1992).

A second emphasis was on the relation between scientists and the objects of scientific study. Inspired by critiques of mainstream epistemology, feminist researchers in psychology and sociology experimented with interactive research involving human subjects. Research models were developed in which battered women assisted in isolating causes for violence against women and in developing remedies for that violence. Women physicians forced male physicians to consider new kinds of cooperative relations in which patients were not passive followers of doctor's orders but active participants in their cures. Even in "hard" sciences like physics, Keller and others argued that intuitive interactive understanding of organisms as dynamic systems rather than as mechanisms subject to linear causation and manipulative control increased understanding.

Helen Longino (1944–) proposed standards of "epistemic virtue." Rules of method and foundational truths, she said, cannot guarantee results. Values are an integral part of good science, nor can any sharp line be drawn between cognitive and non-cognitive values. Empirical adequacy and originality are only a beginning requirement for understanding. As important are recognition of "ontological heterogeneity," complexity of relationship, applicability to human need, and the diffusion of power among producers of knowledge, virtues that refer not to logical adequacy of theory, but to relations between researchers, between researchers and objects of research, and between the scientific establishment and the greater community (Longino 1994).

Feminists from non-western traditions foresaw further changes. Foucault described in detail the discipline that western sciences like criminology and psychology had forced on western bodies; women from "developing" countries saw even more destructive discipline exerted by western science and epistemology on non-western environments. Vandana Shiva (1952–) drew from the experience of rural Indian women (1996). The foundationalist empiricist paradigm, argued Shiva, went hand in hand with interests in accumulating capital wealth at the expense of colonized "underdeveloped" regions. The result was not only an erasure of local cultures and "maldevelopment" that brought poverty to many peoples, but incipient ecological disaster due to deforestation, global warming, depletion of water reserves, desertification, and loss of diversity. Nor, Shiva charged, is this due to a wrong "use" of objective science. The philosophical notion that reality is solely describable as bits of matter, fused together to make bigger bits, provides a metaphysical foundation for exploitation that ignores dynamic systems, equilibrium between aspects of nature, and reciprocity between humans and the natural world.

In a review of twentieth-century coherentist epistemologies, Linda Alcoff (1996) looked forward to the abandonment of epistemologies generated historically in an age of Anglo-European economic and social dominance. Methods, she said, suited to new relations between men and women, and between different races and cultures, have to be developed that constantly negotiate multicultural values. Not only will new sciences be necessary in the twenty-first century, but also new epistemological and ontological paradigms. Alcoff's mixing of critical diagnosis and normative prescription was characteristic of much feminist epistemology at the end of the century. Given the fact that science had not always promoted human well-being, given the realization that no unmediated description of nature is possible, the choice between a naturalized epistemology that refuses normative judgment and a nihilist denial of science's authority might seem inevitable. Feminists, however, were unwilling to give up hope for a non-foundational global science of the future that would serve diverse human needs.

Feminism in ethics

In the early twentieth-century struggle for voting rights, feminist activists drew freely on utilitarian and democratic philosophies for arguments to justify their demands. They cited the beneficial "utility" of women's education and contribution to the work force. They pointed out the "greatest happiness of the greatest number" that would result when universal suffrage allowed women to register their preferences. They argued that women have the same "essential nature" as men, and the same "natural right" to political representation. Kantian principle was invoked; acting according to a law one can will to be universal requires that women be taken into account.

In the aftermath of World War II, with women forced back into prewar domesticity, came doubts that liberal standards of morality and justice were sufficient to bring about liberation. Women now worked, but remained clustered in low-paying service jobs while at home they continued to do the majority of unpaid childcare and housework. Women voted, but, as Emma Goldman warned, often they voted on principles that were socially conservative and protective of private interest. More important, the "right" to vote, attend college, apply for jobs was for many a right in name only, unexercised by women conditioned to think of themselves as inferior, burdened by childcare and domestic responsibilities, subject to rape and assault.

Socialist women had not fared much better. In Communist countries, constitutions guaranteed women full equality, but in public women continued to be marginalized and exploited while in private they did the major share of domestic labor and were subject to abuse. In western countries, women enlisted in radical civil rights and anti-war movements of the 1960s, but soon found that they were unlikely to rise to leadership positions. Western socialism gave lip service to women's liberation; in practice male socialists were no more willing than liberals to cede power to women. Lingering in the background was the assumption, seldom voiced, but with a long philosophical history, that women are less moral than men, less focused on principle, less rational when it comes to determining ultimate value, too concerned with personal relations and emotions to be impartial in ethical matters or resolute in matters of justice.

At this point of frustration came two catalysts that led to a flowering of feminist ethical theory in the latter decades of the century. The first was social psychologist Carol Gilligan's studies of women's moral thinking (1982). Standard psychological tests for moral development, on which women often scored lower than men, used philosophical ethics as guideline. The lowest level of moral development was taken to be egoistic self-interest; an advance was made when general utility was calculated. At the highest level of moral development a moral agent acted on Kantian principle regardless of consequences. At all levels of decision-making, autonomy and reason were the mark of moral agency, whether as objective calculation of private or group interests, or as rational grasp of universalizable principle. Gilligan's conclusions were provocative.

Women, said Gilligan, did not approach an abortion decision either as utilitarians or Kantians. They were not objective calculators of pleasure nor did they adopt principle and act on principle regardless of consequences. Emotionally involved, aware and protective of complex relations with others, they struggled to find courses of action that would prevent harm and preserve relationships. Gilligan's conclusion was not that women are less moral than men. It was that women think differently from men in moral matters, in ways that are complementary, or even superior to a man's sense of justice.

Feminist ethical theory, freed from the confining alternatives of utility and principle, was revitalized. Not only, it seemed, were there "women's ways of knowing" to explore, but also "women's ways" of virtue and goodness. Women's traditional care-giving and teaching of young children was used as a basis for "ethics of care." Nel Noddings (1929–) was a leading proponent. Values, Noddings argued, cannot be located in reason or rules, which are not a reliable protection against evil, but in concern for and responses to others (1984). She described in detail subtle and demanding exchanges between teacher and student, care-giver and patient, parent and child that allow both to grow and to prosper. Sara Ruddick proposed "maternal thinking" as the basis for a feminine ethics, in her book of that title (1989). The evil of war and genocide can be justified by appeals to utility or principle. In their place, Ruddick proposed a practicalist ethics rooted in responsible parenting. Mothers, as they care for children, develop a distinctive metaphysics, cognitive style, and matrix of values. Maternal virtue, claimed Ruddick, can be extended to governance and international relations to advance global peace and prosperity.

In these and other versions of distinctively feminine moral practice, an alternative paradigm emerged of virtue. To be good was not to stand off from personal involvement, to fight down instincts and emotions, to refuse partisan interests, and reason dispassionately from utility or principle. A virtuous woman looked at the unique context of a moral decision rather than abstracted features. She fostered empathetic concern for others so that she would know how to prevent harm. She engaged in collaborative discussion and tried to reach moral consensus. Instead of refusing emotion, she fostered in herself good feelings of love and care for others. She did not act as a lone individual but as a daughter, mother, care-giver, and friend. She did not pretend to bring about a utopia that could easily lapse into dystopia, but envisioned realistic and complex particular goods. Acting from calculations of utility or on principle absolves guilt; when good faith calculation from available information, or from principled action, turns out badly one escapes blame. An emerging feminine virtue ethics imposed a greater burden of responsibility. Not only ruptured personal relations, but poverty in developing countries, environmental collapse, causalities in war were potential objects of feminine care and maternal thinking.

Again there were second thoughts. Was this to essentialize women? To suggest that all women have the same moral sense? If so, it was a claim that offended women of different backgrounds and cultures. Did feminine "ethics of care" and "maternal ethics" assign women to the same care-giving self-sacrificial roles that traditionally restricted their autonomy and agency? Did care and maternity lay on women a crippling burden of guilt given that there was no final absolution, no way to limit the sphere of a responsibility for others? At the same time, there was little enthusiasm for a return to calculated utility or Kantian reason, ideals that for many feminist thinkers were associated with the illusions of masculinity.

A second catalyst came from Continental postmodernism and post-structuralism. If, in postmodern accounts of knowledge, truth claims were forms of authoritarian violence, to proclaim an action good or just could seem an even greater imposition. It is possible to remain unmoved by truth, but value judgments have imperative force. If postmodern accounts of knowledge denied the existence of pre-linguistic facts, even more suspect were non-natural or intrinsic qualities of goodness. Pleasure, good will, happiness, all had been claimed as guiding presences, standards of value that statements of moral obligation should reflect. Throughout the history of philosophy, the relative merits of standards had been contested and debated. Now that long history of debate was put on a different footing. In question, it seemed, was not moral truth – care rather than justice, mothering rather than war – but contested bids for power. In the new postmodernism, there was no founding presence of masculine or feminine goodness to be intuited in the depth of a subject's soul, grasped as an objective template, recognized as a universal value. "Good," like everything else, was a function of *différance*, "bad" turned back against itself in twisting oppositional matrixes of value whose pretense to stability and order is the mark of oppressive authority.

Again there were second thoughts. If feminists had to limit themselves to the deconstruction of moral authority, if no claim to positive justice could be made without the claimant becoming an oppressor, how was feminist critique, or any social critique, to be grounded? French theorists – Lyotard, Derrida, Foucault – all attempted to absolve postmodernism and post-structuralism of political quietism with limited success. For feminists there was much at stake. Could moral autonomy, seemingly necessary for moral agency and moral justification, be rescued from the postmodern claim that subjects and values are constituted in language? Could moral justification be reconceptualized in ways that accommodate postmodern critiques but also take account of women's moral experience? If autonomy was important for feminist agency, it had to be autonomy that acknowledged ties of relationship and societal positioning. If standards of evaluation were available by which to condemn the wrongs done to women, they would have to be standards that assumed no totalizing and oppressive principles.

In response to these questions came detailed studies, some avowedly feminist and some not, which, in the words of one editor of a collection of essays by women ethicists, "reset the moral compass" (Calhoun 2004). Abandoning the high ground of universal theories of right or justice, women philosophers examined the nuances and ambiguities of concrete moral life. In the place of fictitious and hyper-real examples they described commonplace dilemmas that arise in daily life. Moral decisions were realistically depicted as made by dependent and vulnerable women and men in relation with others. Women philosophers drew not only on standard examples in utilitarian or deontological ethics, but also on literature, psychoanalysis, and sociology to describe homely virtues such as diligence, decency, trust. They emphasized the element of moral luck and the importance of narration in moral deliberation and evaluation. A reworked conception of autonomy was of particular interest. Women ethicists worked to describe a realistic personal identity, shaped in interaction with others, but at the same time supporting choice based on reflection. A woman finds herself as daughter, wife, mother, lover, friend, but somehow out of these diverse relations she must achieve a stable sense of self so as to act in coherent ways. With no universal principle to make decisions automatic, she must acquire Hornsby's agency and be able to give reasons that refer back to her own ideals.

Annette Baier (1929–) championed trust as a way to straddle the choice between relational dependency and rational autonomy (2004). Trust, she argued, is the fabric of moral life, crucial in ethical relations as response to the human condition of mutual vulnerability. Trust requires not rational objectivity but a repertoire of interpersonal virtues such as thoughtfulness, considerateness, courtesy, patience, responsibility, respect. But trust, said Baier, must always be tempered with anti-trust. There is no easy categorical answer to the question: "Whom should women trust?" No mark of sex, race, or occupation guarantees trustworthiness. Nurses, mothers, care-givers, all on occasion harm those under their care. The key to responsible agency, argued Baier, is not so much in the corrective logic of moral calculation as it is in careful attentive distinctions between lesser and greater risks. Judgment is needed, judgment that takes one's own dependency into account.

Christine Korsgaard's neo-Kantian ethics, although not explicitly feminist, addressed similar questions. Investigating the "source of normativity" (1996), Korsgaard (1952–) rejected the bugbear of a scientific worldview in which free will is impossible. Like Hornsby, she focused on a person's ability to reflect on beliefs and desires and decide whether to act on them. The decision should be based on principle, said Korsgaard, but not on the empty formalism of a Kantian "categorical imperative." More is required than reason. A moral agent must think of herself as human, as part of family, friendship, national communities, and ultimately as a member of a possible human kingdom of ends. This requires a self in the world in actual and potential community with others.

Also renegotiated by feminist ethicists was moral justification. Foundationalism based on non-natural intuited properties of goodness, or the supposed intrinsic good of rational principle or utility was no longer possible, but the alternative of relativism in ethics was equally unappealing given the feminist sense of wrongs done to women and other oppressed groups. To escape the either/or of foundationalism or relativism, some feminists drew on procedural accounts of justice popular in the 1970s and 1980s. The hypothetical contractualism of John Rawls (1921–2002) dominated much mainstream analytic ethics in that period, but made little reference to gender inequities. An imagined social contract between heads of households left relations in the family outside the reach of justice. Susan Okin (1946–2004) in a 1989 feminist critique of Rawlsian justice suggested remedial additions. Justice and fairness have to prevail in "private" family relations as well as public life; any man devising standards of justice has to be able to put himself in the place of a woman.

Even when justice as fairness was extended to internal family matters, the demand that a theorist put himself or herself in the position of least advantaged others raised additional questions. Can a privileged male philosopher or policy-maker put himself in a woman's situation so as to come up with just arrangements that are to her advantage? Can he place his sex and race behind a "veil of ignorance," and imagine that he is a disadvantaged African-American unwed mother? There was doubt among some feminist philosophers whether imaginative empathy with the situation of oppressed others is possible and whether private hypothetical reflection can ever result in universally applicable standards of morality or justice. Should not the disadvantaged speak for themselves in real and not simulated dialogue?

For critical theorists such as Seyla Benhabib, Jürgen Habermas's rational discourse provided a better procedural model, requiring actual public discussion to determine right and wrong (Benhabib 1992). In "ideal speech situations," when diverse viewpoints are heard and debated, rational debate determines what is right. Again there were doubts and revisions. Habermas's distinction between private and public matters, said Benhabib, had to be overcome so that women's abuse and disadvantage in the family were not removed from discussion. In addition, rational adversarial debate had to be supplemented with empathic understanding. Social theorist Nancy Fraser (1947–) went further, questioning whether disadvantaged groups like welfare mothers would be able to articulate their needs "rationally" in public forums and be heard (1986). Iris Young (1990) questioned the very possibility of the empathetic understanding that was a prerequisite for a hypothetical "justice as fairness" or Benhabib's ideal speech situation. To claim to put oneself in the position of oppressed others, Young argued, is not only impossible but also disrespectful.

Doubts about procedural accounts of justice raised larger questions about the moral value of counterfactual visions of imagined social contracts or ideal speech situations. Rawlsian justice required the impossible exercise of forgetting one's own identity. Habermas required that debaters lay aside personal interests and listen to others with open minds. Both required domination-free discourse in which oppressed viewpoints can be expressed. In reality there are formidable barriers to the expression and under-standing of long-standing unvoiced wrongs, wrongs that often have no names and are not easily talked about. Public discourse, suited to rules of order and well-established principles, can be a poor venue for the moral work of isolating and describing evils not yet clearly delineated. Alison Jaggar reviewing the history of feminist ethics pointed to the philosophical importance of separatist groups – women, black women, lesbian women, Hispanic women – meeting to share narratives and experiences and do the conceptual work of describing and defining wrongs (2000a). She pointed to the importance of such groups in the history of philosophy, citing as examples the Vienna Circle and the Frankfurt School, where relatively closed circles of like-minded thinkers worked to develop new terms and new principles of analysis. In such groups the adversarial style of argumentative rational debate was suspended in favor of active listening and an attempt to develop common understanding. Out of separatist women's groups came new moral concepts: "heterosexism," "sexual harassment," "date rape," "objectification." Jaggar added a caveat: private enclaves formed to escape the dangers of dogmatism and exclusion must eventually return to public discourse and open discussion.

One source of feminist philosophical concepts was discussions between women from different constituencies. Martha Nussbaum gestured to the important conceptual work of cross-cultural understanding as contributor to a 2001 collection, *What is Philosophy?* Philosophers, said Nussbaum, have an important role to play redefining concepts like "development" that are the basis for economic policy-making. "Development" measured by gains in GNP may be an ultimate value only for western philosophers and policy-makers. From the perspective of women in "developing" countries, gains in GNP can be useless or harmful if men continue to control the wealth, social welfare is neglected, education unfunded, and public health neglected. But, said Nussbaum, postmodern relativism – the view that neoliberal western worldviews and traditional non-western cultures are incommensurable – is not the only alternative. Philosophy offers systematic and rigorous debate that can generate clearer concepts, but not necessarily when the debate is only between western academics. She noted that in meetings convened between philosophers and international economists, philosophers committed to various versions of epistemological theory made little attempt to communicate with economists who themselves continued to operate from prior assumptions and arguments. In contrast, in discussions with women in rural India, Nussbaum reached new understanding of the importance of property rights, work outside the home, and women's friendships, and was able to revise and strengthen an alternative "capabilities" approach to development.

At the end of the century, with ethnic wars in many parts of the world, with racial tensions growing in western countries, with growing conflict between rich and poor nations, there was a sense among feminists that values and ideals could no longer be western exports. Philosophers who move back and forth between professional philosophy and life in a variety of non-western cultures might be in a better position to develop global standards of right and justice than the privileged few who travel on the university lecture circuit or as members of international task forces. If it was a modernist fantasy to think that the knowing or moral self is autonomous, it might be a postmodern fantasy to think that values are constructed in the one hermetically sealed world of western semantics.

Feminism in philosophy of language

At mid-century, studies in socio-linguistics brought new insight into linguistic sources of gender inequality. Grammatical gender divides the world of persons into masculine and feminine. The generic use of "he" along with the species name "man" makes the subject of discourse male except in cases of feminine-identified roles like nurse or mother. Women are not "actors" or "stewards," but diminutive and sexually charged "actresses" or "stewardesses." Obligatory titles – Mr, Mrs, Miss – ignore a man's marital status but make it a woman's primal identity. Lexicons contain many more derogative sexual words for women than for men. Feminine speech styles – tag-on questions, avoidance of the assertive use of "I" – mark a woman's relative hesitancy and lack of authority in speech. These and other revelations resulted in a call for language reform. By the last decades of the century, "inclusive language" was required in academic writing and in publishers' guidelines.

Other more radical linguistic revisions were proposed. Feminist theologian Mary Daly (1928–) used creative etymologies to convert insults like "hag" and "slut" to emblems of feminist power (1978). In France, Julia Kristeva (1941–) called for a "revolution in poetic language" that would release the passionate maternal semiotic underlying the symbolic order of rationally ordered discourse (1974). Marilyn Frye looked for positive constructions of female difference generated as women relate to other women in separatist collective projects (1992). Rejecting both masculine assertiveness training for women and what she called a "vegetal blossoming" of passionate expression, Luce Irigaray called for a new "syntax" to support communication between men and women (1996, 1997). In Italy, Adriana Cavarero (1993) urged feminists to find a "fissure" by which finally to escape the whole ensemble of man-made concepts and begin to conceptualize from the women's situation outside the categories of man-made discourse.

There was a sense, however, that a deeper semantics of gender difference was not so easily dislodged. Philosopher of law Catherine MacKinnon pointed out the role of male dominance in the formation of linguistic meaning (1987). Men in positions of power, said MacKinnon, name reality on their own terms, in ways adequate to their experience and reflecting reality as they see it. But words can be made to respond to women's experience as well as men's, and must be, if there is to be a rule of law to which both men and women are subject. At the center of any feminist movement, she said, must be the ability to participate in defining terms that create public norms and standards: words such as "rape," "sexual assault," "pornography." The emergence of the legal term "sexual harassment" was of particular importance. Here was a phenomenon that had been an indistinguishable part of a neutral background of unnamed fact. The work of defining sexual harassment as a legal action singled out that phenomenon, marked it as important, and even more important, as wrong. A name, said MacKinnon does not create or construct an event; it allows events to be seen and judged.

A recurring theme in much feminist theorizing about language was the damaging effect of "dichotomy" as a deep structure of meaning. De Beauvoir had been one of the first but hardly the last to point out woman's status as "unmarked other" defined as what is *not*, "not male," "not rational," "not quite human." Post-Saussurean structural semantics only deepened a conviction among feminists that "hierarchical oppositions" – mind over body, civilized over native, man over woman, white over black, etc. – shape meaning in theoretical discourses that disadvantage women or minorities. The status of any logic that required negation as a core operator was called into question, along with a deeper question about logic's relations to natural language. If logical form requiring oppositional meaning is built into all language – or into all Indo-European languages or into any language in which rational thought can be expressed – there is little point of talking about feminist reform. If a semantics of plus and minus features constitutes only an ideal template restricting and regularizing the messy ungrammatical business of everyday expression, the result is not very different. Feminist critics can speak, but not speak rationally in a way that carries authority. If on the other hand, dichotomous categories are the reflection of a possibly false or overly restricted concept of reason, or worse the reflection of an ideology of dominance, then it might be possible to develop logics and languages that restructure discourses of gender and race and, more speculatively, change relations between sexes and races. To this end, various non-standard feminist logics were proposed, including "relevant" logic, neo-Aristotelian term logic, John Dewey's instrumental logic, and a revival of aspects of Stoic logic (Falmagne and Hass 2002).

Beyond both reforms and revolutions in logic and language lingered what is perhaps the core question in philosophy of language. Does language construct the real, or is reality parceled out and individuated, ready to be noticed and correctly named? More specifically, whether they naturally occur or are imposed by standards of logic and rationality, do gender inequalities and gender asymmetries in semantic and grammatical structure reflect and represent the fact of women's inferior nature or lesser social status? Or do linguistic devices construct and maintain that inferior status? If language constructs the world, linguistic reform can change reality by reconfiguring semantic categories or by rescinding grammatical rules that privilege masculinity. If, on the other hand, language names pre-linguistic qualities and relations, the effect of reform is uncertain. Demands for inclusive language or new logics may result only in awkwardness, artificiality, and lack of meaning. Proposed non-sexist titles like "Ms" can become terms of humorous derision. Acquiescence to the demand for inclusive language can become sardonic adherence to political correctness. "Deviant" logics can be theoretical constructions with no effect on actual discourse.

Inevitably, feminist philosophers turned to ontology and metaphysics. How does language relate to the world? Are the things we talk about manufactured by language? Or is the role of language to designate and describe pre-linguistic natural kinds? The traditional philosophical framework for answering the question is triangular. Three elements must be put into proper relation: real objects and events, subjective concepts of ideas about those objects and events, and lastly language itself. Seventeenth- and eighteenth-century empiricist philosophy focused on ideas and the correspondence of ideas with real qualities, treating language as secondary representation of ideas formed from sensory impressions. In the twentieth century attention shifted, away from psychology to language's structure, reference, and possible reform. Mathematical logic, reluctantly applied by Frege to natural language, was adopted by philosophers in English-speaking countries as the necessary structure of truth-stating language. Reference and meaning were reworked accordingly. Either meaning was "reduced" to references to sense-data, or sensory experience was bypassed as uncertain and subjective and words made to refer directly to physical elements. Or language could be seen as a logically structured matrix that touches down on reality only at certain anchor points. As theoretical disputes continued about the nature of meaning and reference in a logically structured empirically based language, the technical work of translating the idioms of natural language into forms of modern mathematical logic was ongoing and considered in establishment circles to be the hard core of "real philosophy." The logical ideal of a purely externalist language of science purged of ambiguity and subjectivity closed to citizen debate and questions of value troubled many feminists. Frege's stated aim was to fashion a system by which thought could be mechanized, in which the ambiguities and nuances of natural language were eliminated (Nye 1990). A science that adopted such an idiom would be true, barricaded against misunderstanding or equivocation, free from subjective coloring and the taint of values. Relations between subjects and predicates would be governed by existential and universal quantifiers that eliminated both singular and qualitative reference. Sentences would state facts. They would be true if they matched up with fact, false if they did not. True and false propositions could be assembled in logical order according to truth-functional rules governing the use of logical connectives like "and" and "or."

From a feminist point of view, however, this claim that science is or could be a "truth-machine" might block scrutiny of background assumptions, political motifs, metaphors, and images that shape objects and methods of scientific research that are responsible for biased research. If individuation of objects is informed by non-scientific concepts, values, experiences, and beliefs, if the relation of scientific language to physical reality is multidimensional and complex, truth in and out of science cannot be a simple matter of propositions in truth functional order, or countable objects gathered into sets. Even more important, a surface showing of logical inference might be used to paper over deep flaws in the identification and choice of facts and objects.

A beginning in clarifying feminist distrust of contemporary mathematical logic's authority was made by Merrill and Jaakko Hintikka, in their 1983 paper "How can language be sexist?" The prevailing truth-theoretic semantics, said the Hintikkas, deals with structure but neglects reference. Unspoken interests that determine the kind of objects that are subject to quantification and the kind of propositions that are put in truth-functional order are not addressed. In fact, said the Hintikkas, ways in which objects are individuated can differ, depending on who is doing the individuating. Men, focused on individual objects, might devise logics with reference to objects identifiable across possible worlds; women with a different approach might sort objects according to relations in this world. The implications were far-reaching. Throughout the history of philosophy a reason given for women's exclusion from rational pursuits had been a supposed failure to be logical. If, however, logic begins from a man-made domain of objects, the accusation that women are illogical says no more than that, for better or for worse, women do not talk and reason about the same things as men.

Both logic's defenders and its feminist critics tended to speak of logic in the singular, as if one Logic took more or less perspicacious surface forms. Taking into account the Hintikkas' suggestion of diversity, I looked at selected moments in the history of logic to give a critical account of the genealogy of differing forms of classical, medieval, and modern truth-functional logic (Nye 1990). In my "reading," logics were diverse human products, shaped by context, interest, and desire, subject, like any other form of expression, to quasi-hermeneutic interpretation and understanding. Given that a primary interest in developing a logic is often to place a discourse, practice, or institution beyond criticism, my interpretation of logic as codification of different styles of barricaded and authoritative speech could be seen as perverse. At the close of the century, for some, logic was still "the last word," to be vigorously defended if all knowledge was not to collapse into meaningless contingency and postmodern relativism. Even though there was talk of jettisoning once sacred laws like that of the excluded middle in the light of new findings in physics, the truth of *modens ponens* and the law of non-contradiction were often claimed to mark a last dividing line between respectable doubt and rabid postmodern or politically motivated irrationality.

On the Continent, language theory tended to begin not with Frege but with structural linguistics. Words, said the structuralists, have meaning not "externally" because they refer to facts or objects, but "internally" because of relations between words. There was agreement on the need to bypass psychology – concepts and ideas cannot be individuated without language – but neither can terms refer directly to objects and events. Structural meaning is differential. "Woman" means woman not because it designates an identifiable natural kind, but because "woman" is an element in interlocking patterns of plus and minus features that define features of reality. Again there was cause for feminist concern. If direct reference to objects is eliminated and linguistic meaning is seen as internal to language, if there is no extra-linguistic presence or experience in the name of which masculine power and feminine inferiority can be questioned, critical feminism theory would seem to be impossible. Language change may occur, but not as a result of consciously directed reform. If male presence and female absence are organizing principles of language and at the very core of linguistic meaning, the name and power of the father is written into language and inescapable.

Some hope was given to French feminist linguists by "deconstruction." Derrida's exposure of the fragility of oppositional semantic structures inspired readings to break down the rigidity and the hierarchical order of any language with pretensions to logical order. Irigaray's readings of canoncal figures in philosophy such as Plato, Kant, and Descartes were models of transgressive exposure of a delusive masculine imaginary as it pretended to model a neutral and universal truth. Judith Butler's proposed "performative" derailment of elements of semantic structure was another alternative. Once the myth of rigid designation to natural kind is dissolved, names like "woman" or "queer" can be reinhabited and resignified. No reality unmediated by language allows a reformer to stand back from language and dictate new usage consistent with reality; any attempt to do so only entangles the reformer in old categories. But language is not a static system. Meanings are perpetuated as words are repeatedly used, and when unconscious "use" is replaced by conscious citation, said Butler, both meaning and reality can change (Butler 1990).

Powerful as postmodern and post-structuralist critiques were in exposing the ways gender forms and deforms linguistic meaning, most feminists were unwilling to abandon the possibility of referring to something other than language itself. In a postmodern climate, reference could no longer be taken for granted, either as established in one-to-one correlation between pre-linguistic essences and designated terms or as reduction to sense-data or some class of privileged physical element. But the feminist sense of otherness, of critical difference in perspective, of distorted masculine views on reality was too strong to accept confinement in what some critics called the "prison house of language." For some analytic feminists Quine's behaviorism provided a possible basis for translatability if not for certain reference. Others, myself included, questioned the ethnocentricity that Quine's radical translator embodied, as well as set theory's elision of the problem of concept formation (Nye 1998). The inclusion of an object in a designated set says nothing about how that set is formed and how the objects that make it up are individuated. If the formation of categories and identification of objects is the real groundwork of science, it is groundwork which set-theoretic logic ignores, ruling out critical scrutiny of ontological and epistemological commitments that predate logical inference. As a result, condoned by logic, indexes of development tracked in economics, diagnoses of mental illness in psychiatry, the identification of "non-democratic" forms of government as candidates for "regime change," go unchallenged. A dangerous illusion is created of an ideal language in which preformed facts rigorously deployed guarantee truth.

The subject matter of philosophical semantics was never language as used by actual speakers and researchers. The aim of Russell and of those who came after him was not to describe speakers' or writers' meanings in science or elsewhere, but to lay out what could be "legitimately" meant by users of assertive language. Indeterminacy and personality that introduce subjectivity and so give rise to skepticism were to be eliminated as conceptual residue unworthy of philosophical attention. In contrast, the tendency among feminist philosophers was to return to actual spoken and written language in which there is no binary true or false. In natural language, truth is gradual, evidenced by infinite nuance expressible in prepositional attitudes (I think, believe, am certain, know, etc.), in extensive evaluative vocabularies (sure, probably, possible, inevitable, etc.), in subtle linguistic moves from personal experience to objective claim (I feel cold ... in my view it's cold ... it is cold, etc.), and emergent as a linguistic effect of communicative trust and intersubjective agreement. This is not to eliminate reasoning or inference, but to insist that reason takes a diversity of forms that may not be automatable or subject to one system of validation, and recognize that the reliability of inference ultimately depends on the referential adequacy of the terms in which that inference is expressed.

Conclusion

Reviewing a closely argued treatise on Saul Kripke's scientific realism at the turn of the twentieth century, a leading proponent of a functional approach to the philosophy of mind and knowledge confessed that he could not "shake off the sense that something has gone awfully wrong." The "laity," he commented, "seems to have lost interest" in philosophy, and indeed, he went on to confess, "there seems to be a lot of earnest discussion of questions that strike my ear as frivolous" (Fodor 2004). Fodor noted the relative popularity of Continental philosophers such as Foucault – "I wish I had his royalties," he quipped – but he offered no insight into why the equally dense and inaccessible prose of the postmodernists should have more appeal than the logical lucidity of Anglophone analysis.

One question posed by philosophy identified as feminist at the close of the twentieth century is whether it is possible to envision "non-frivolous" philosophies of the future with interest to those who are not professional philosophers. Certainly there was a sense among many feminists that more was needed than academic critique. It was important to answer the last of Kant's existential questions: What can we hope for? In what way can the mathematical formulas of the sciences be made to serve human aspirations to peace and prosperity? How can people of diverse identities establish common cause and values that transcend group interest? Can language be found to communicate changing and multicultural realities? Two twentieth-century philosophical visions stood in the way. One was the logician's vision of a purely extensional idiom in which "I think" is replaced by statements of fact arranged in truth-functional order. Such a language can lead, as Luce Irigaray charged, to "a sclerosis of discourse, a hardening of language and a repetitiveness that makes nonsense of established meaning" (1984: 135–6). Equally unhelpful in answering Kant's question was the deconstructed vision of the same language detached from reference to material reality, unregulated by coherent lines of thought, endlessly open to stylistic intervention. The problem for twenty-first-century philosophers would be to find a way between these two alternatives, to rethink the relation between words and objects, facts and propositions, reality and theoretical constructions of reality in ways that preserve truth and at the same time allow room for a continual reworking of both knowledge and reality.

One characteristic of feminist philosophizing of possible value in the new postmodern age of globalism and postcolonial consciousness was the tendency for feminists to accept the fact that all thought, including philosophical and feminist thought, is situated. No matter how it is structured, no matter how it clothes itself in certainty, thought is always the thought of thinkers with familial, cultural, ethical identities who speak from a location in space and time. The realization was not specific to feminism, but was particularly strong among feminist philosophers given the shock of discovering that most of the twentieth-century intellectual traditions available to women reflected the limited thinking of men whose view of the world was colored not only by their masculinity but also by class, ethnicity, and race. Feminist philosophy, energized by this discovery, had a richness of texture, an openness, and experiential reference lacking in both the technical virtuosity of philosophical analysis and the theoretic sophistication of Continental structuralism and deconstruction.

The problem was not that race, class, or gender shaped methods and styles of twentieth-century philosophies as they had philosophies in the past and would continue to shape philosophies of the future, but rather the hubris that allowed limited and interested viewpoints to be projected as absolute, universal, and complete. At the end of the century, given a global world economy, instant communication of information, and an irreversible mixing of cultures and ethnicities, that hubris was more and more untenable. Vestiges of the absolute remained, in projects of worldwide democratization, in evangelical and extremist religions, even in some versions of feminism, but globalization and emigration made a fully dominant imperial culture or a homogeneous racial or religious state increasingly difficult to conceive in reality.

The challenge for philosophers of the twenty-first century would be to avoid the dilemma of choosing between epistemological relativity that precludes any critical judgment on the one hand, and claims to truth that are inevitably ideological on the other. Feminist philosophers showed little liking for either alternative: for complacent tolerance of "diverse" views all equally true, or for claims to unassailable necessary truth. Instead the tendency was to dialogue, cross-cultural collaboration, and global understanding. The emerging image of philosophy among feminists was not a closely-knit group of professionals insulated from politics making progress in solving carefully delineated "theoretical problems," but a free-wheeling discussion energized by social concerns, open to insights from many disciplines and the participation of many kinds of thinkers.

Critique has always been the forte of philosophers. In the late twentieth century much critique turned away from the real, natural, and social world to philosophy itself. The targets for postmodern critiques were philosophers' universals and absolute values. The targets for analytic critiques were the formulations of rival analytic philosophers on issues whose original importance had often receded far out of consciousness. Tools of philosophical analysis were used by a few "applied" ethicists on clearly marked out "moral issues" like animal rights and stem cell research, but larger questions of public policy and political ideology were often left aside by philosophers as too large, too value-laden, too potentially charged with political favoritism. For many feminist philosophers, commitment to social change overcame such scruples. Issues such as gay marriage and abortion rights were debated not as opportunities to exercise techniques of refutation, but as ways to penetrate to deeply felt and strongly rooted social presumptions – heterosexuality, compulsory motherhood, the sanctity of marriage – that generated social inequality and whose disruption threatened long-standing social and conceptual structures.

Philosophy in this critical dialogic role does not pretend to be a science, or even the overseer or handmaiden of science. Nor is its job the naturalistic description of thought processes innate in the wiring of the brain or evolved by natural selection. Cognitive science may have an important role to play in diagnosing and treating developmental problems or in the invention of artificial intelligence. Naturalized epistemology might describe how some people reason. But feminist philosophers did not restrict themselves to statements of empirical fact, nor did they endorse the erasure of subjectivity and normativity assumed in externalist theories of meaning. In this they identified with philosophers of the past who often spoke out of a personal sense of outrage or puzzlement, and also from a conviction that legitimate puzzlement and outrage could not be a private affair but should be shared by others. Plato spoke for the educated few who deplored the excesses of democratic mob rule. Descartes spoke for scientists who dared to challenge the Aristotelian academic establishment; Locke spoke for entrepreneurs and colonists who opposed autocratic monarchies. Much feminist historical work has gone to show the limitations of these constituencies: classical refusal to acknowledge the point of view of slaves, women, and non-Greeks; Cartesian neglect of the social and political underpinnings of science; Locke's refusal to see the claim of native peoples to ancestral tribal lands. The question would be whether feminist philosophy's own inevitable narrowness of vision, if never finally overcome, could still be constantly redressed. Would it be possible to sustain both the admission of subjectivity and the claim to a normativity open to critique from outside the circle of its own certainty?

References

Alcoff, L. (1996) *Real Knowing: New Versions of the Coherence Theory*. Ithaca, NY: Cornell University Press.

Arendt, H. (1974) *Rahel Varnhagen: The Life of a Jewess*. New York: Harcourt Brace Jovanovich.

Baier, A. (1985) *Postures of the Mind*. Minneapolis: University of Minnesota Press.

—— (2004) "Demoralization, trust, and the virtues." In C. Calhoun (ed.) *Setting the Moral Compass: Essays by Women Philosophers*. Oxford: Oxford University Press, pp. 176–90.

Baker R. and F. Elliston (eds.) (1975) *Philosophy and Sex*. Buffalo, NY: Prometheus Books.

Bartky, S. (1990) *Femininity and Domination: Studies in the Phenomenology of Oppression*. New York: Routledge.

Beauvoir, S. de (1949) *Le Deuxième Sexe (The Second Sex)*. Paris: Gallimard.

Benhabib, S. (1992) *Situating the Self: Gender, Community, and Postmodernism in Contemporary Ethics*. New York: Routledge.

Bordo, S. (1987) *The Flight to Objectivity: Essays on Cartesianism and Culture*. Albany: State University of New York Press.

Braidotti, R. (1991) *Patterns of Dissonance: A Study of Women in Contemporary Philosophy*. New York: Routledge.

Butler, J. (1990) *Gender Trouble: Feminism and the Subversion of Identity*. New York: Routledge.

—— (1993) *Bodies that Matter: On the Discursive Limits of Sex*. New York and London: Routledge.

—— (1997) *The Psychic Life of Power*. Stanford, CA: Stanford University Press.

Calhoun, C. (ed.) (2004) *Setting the Moral Compass: Essays by Women Philosophers*. Oxford: Oxford University Press.

Cavarero, A. (1993) "Toward a theory of sexual difference." In S. Kemp and P. Bono (eds.) *The Lonely Mirror: Italian Perspectives on Feminist Theory*, New York: Routledge, pp. 189–221.

Chodorow, N. (1978) *The Reproduction of Mothering*. Berkeley: University of California Press.

Clough, S. (ed.) (2003) *Siblings under the Skin: Feminism, Social Justice and Analytic Philosophy*. Aurora, CO: Davies Group.

Code, L. (1987) *Epistemic Responsibility*. Hanover, NH and London: Brown University Press.

—— (1991) *What Can She Know? Feminist Theory and the Construction of Knowledge*, Ithaca, NY: Cornell University Press.

Daly, M. (1978) *Gyn/Ecology: The Metaethics of Radical Feminism*. Boston: Beacon Press.

Edwards, P. (ed.) (1967) *The Encyclopedia of Philosophy*. New York: Macmillan.

Falmagne, R. J. and M. Hass (eds.) (2002) *Representing Reason: Feminist Theory and Logic*. Lanham, MD: Rowman & Littlefield.

Flax, J. (1990) "Postmodern and gender relations in feminist theory." In L. Nicholson (ed.) *Feminism/Postmodernism*, New York: Routledge, pp. 39–62.

Fodor, J. (2004) "Water's water everywhere." *London Review of Books* 26/20 (October 21): 17–19.

Fraser, N. (1986) "Toward a discourse ethic of solidarity." *Praxis International* 5/4: 425–9.

—— (1989) *Unruly Practices: Power, Discourse, and Gender in Contemporary Social Theory*. Minneapolis: University of Minnesota Press.

—— (1991) "From irony to prophecy to politics: a response to Richard Rorty." *Michigan Quarterly Review* 30/2 (spring): 259–66.

—— and L. Nicholson (1990) "Social criticism without philosophy." In L. Nicholson (ed.) *Feminism/ Postmodernism*, New York: Routledge, pp. 19–38.

Frye, M. (1983) *The Politics of Reality*. Trumansburg, NY: Crossing Press.

—— (1992) *The Wilful Virgin: Essays in Feminism*. Freedom, CA: Crossing Press.

Gatens, M. (1996) *Imaginary Bodies: Ethics, Power, and Corporeality*. London and New York: Routledge

Gilligan, C. (1982) *In a Different Voice: Psychological Theory and Women's Development*. Cambridge, MA: Harvard University Press.

Gilman, C. P. (1898) *Women and Economics*. Boston: Small, Maynard.

—— (1911) *The Man-made World; or, Androcentric Culture*. New York: Charlton.

Goldman, E. (1970) *The Traffic in Women and Other Essays on Feminism*, ed. A. Shulman. Washington, DC: Times Change Press.

Griffin, S. (1980) *Woman and Nature: The Roaring Inside Her*. New York: Harper Colophon Books.

Grosz, E. (1995) *Space, Time, and Perversion: Essays on the Politics of Bodies*. New York: Routledge.

Harding, S. (1991) *Whose Science? Whose Knowledge? Thinking from Women's Lives*. Ithaca, NY: Cornell University Press.

—— (1993) *The "Racial" Economy of Science*. Bloomington: Indiana University Press.

Harding, S. and M. Hintikka (eds.) (1983) *Discovering Reality*. Dordrecht: Reidel.

Hartstock, N. (1984) *Money, Sex, and Power: Toward a Feminist Historical Materialism*. Amherst: University of Massachusetts Press.

Hill Collins, P. (1990) *Black Feminist Thought: Knowledge, Consciousness, and the Politics of Empowerment*. Boston: Unwin Hyman.

Hintikka, M. and J. Hintikka (1983) "How can language be sexist?" In S. Harding and M. Hintikka (eds.) *Discovering Reality*, Dordrecht: Reidel, pp. 139–48.

Hornsby, J. (1997) *Simple Mindedness: Naïve Naturalism in the Philosophy of Mind*. Cambridge, MA: Harvard University Press.

Irigaray, L. (1984) *Ethics of Sexual Difference*. Ithaca, NY: Cornell University Press.

—— (1985) "Any theory of the subject has already been appropriated by the masculine." In *Speculum of the Other Woman*, trans. G. Gill, Ithaca, NY: Cornell University Press, pp. 133–46.

—— (1996) *I Love to You*, trans. A. Martin. New York: Routledge.

—— (1997) *Sexes and Genres through Languages: Elements of Communication*. New York: Routledge.

Jaggar, A. (2000a) "Feminism in ethics." In M. Fricker and J. Hornsby (eds.) *The Cambridge Companion to Feminism in Philosophy*, Cambridge: Cambridge University Press, pp. 225–44.

—— (2000b)"Globalizing feminist ethics." In C. Calhoun (ed.) *Setting the Moral Compass: Essays by Women Philosophers*, Oxford: Oxford University Press, pp. 233–55.

Keller, E. F. (1983) *A Feeling for the Organism: The Life and Work of Barbara McClintock*. New York: W. H. Freeman.

—— (1985) *Reflections on Gender and Science*. New Haven, CT: Yale University Press.

Korsgaard, C. (1996) *The Source of Normativity*. Oxford: Oxford University Press.

Kristeva, J. (1974) *La Révolution du langage poétique*. Paris: Éditions du Seuil.

—— (1980) *Les Pouvoirs de l'horreur*. Paris: Éditions du Seuil.

Le Dœuff, M. (1989) *The Philosophical Imaginary*, trans. C. Gordon. London: Athlone Press.

Lloyd, G. (1984) *The Man of Reason*. Minneapolis: University of Minnesota Press.

Longino, H. (1994) *Science as Social Knowledge: Values and Objectivity in Scientific Inquiry*. Princeton, NJ: Princeton University Press.

Lugones, M. (1987) "Playfulness, 'world' traveling, and loving perception." *Hypatia* 2 (summer): 3–19.

Lugones, M. and E. Spelman (1986) "'Have we got a theory for you': feminist theory, cultural imperialism and the demand for the woman's voice." In M. Pearsall (ed.) *Women and Values*, Belmont, CA: Wadsworth, pp. 19–31.

Luxemburg, R. (2004) "The proletarian woman." In P. Hudis and K. Anderson (eds.) *The Rosa Luxemburg Reader*, New York: Monthly Review Press, pp. 242–7.

MacKinnon, C. (1987) *Feminism Unmodified*. Cambridge, MA: Harvard University Press.

Moulton, J. (1983) "The adversary method." In S. Harding and M. Hinitikka (eds.) *Discovering Reality*, Dordrecht: Reidel, pp. 149–64.

Nelson, L. H. (1990) *Who Knows: From Quine to a Feminist Empiricism*. Philadelphia: Temple University Press.

Noddings, N. (1984) *Caring, a Feminine Approach to Ethics and Moral Education*. Berkeley: University of California Press.

Nussbaum, M. (2001) "Public philosophy and international feminism." In C. P. Ragland and S. Heidt (eds.) *What is Philosophy?*, New Haven, CT: Yale University Press, pp. 121–51.

Nye, A. (1990) *Words of Power: A Feminist Reading of the History of Logic*. New York: Routledge, Chapman, Hall.

—— (1998) "Semantics in a new key." In J. Kourany (ed.) *Philosophy in a Feminist Voice*, Princeton, NJ: Princeton University Press, pp. 263–95.

—— (1999) *The Princess and the Philosopher: The Letters of Elisabeth Palatine to René Descartes*. Latham, MD: Rowman & Littlefield.

—— (2004) *Feminism and Modern Philosophy*. New York and London: Routledge.

Okin, S. (1989) *Justice, Gender and the Family*. Princeton, NJ: Princeton University Press.

Rorty, R. (1991) "Feminism and pragmatism." *Michigan Quarterly Review* 30/2 (spring): 231–58.

Ruddick, S. (1989) *Maternal Thinking: Toward a Politics of Peace*. Boston: Beacon Press.

Scheman, N. (1983) "Individualism and the objects of psychology." In S. Harding and M. Hintikka (eds.) *Discovering Reality*, Dordrecht: Reidel.

Shiva, V. (1996) "Science, nature, and gender." In A. Garry and M. Pearsall (eds.) *Women, Knowledge and Reality: Explorations in Feminist Philosophy*, New York and London: Routledge.

Young, I. M. (1990) *Justice and the Politics of Difference*. Princeton, NJ: Princeton University Press.

Further reading

General

Fricker, M. and J. Hornsby (eds.) (2000) *The Cambridge Companion to Feminism in Philosophy*. Cambridge: Cambridge University Press. (Critical treatments of feminist work in various areas of philosophy).

Kourany, J. (ed.) (1998) *Philosophy in a Feminist Voice: Critiques and Reconstructions*. Princeton, NJ: Princeton University Press. (In-depth reviews of feminist work by well-known feminist philosophers).

Le Doeuff, M. (1991) *Hipparchia's Choice: An Essay concerning Women, Philosophy, etc.*, trans. T. Selous. Oxford: Blackwell. (A meditation on relations between women and philosophy, both theoretical and personal)

Nye, A. (1988) *Feminist Theory and the Philosophies of Man*. London: Croom Helm. (A critical look at feminist use of Marxism, existentialism, psychoanalysis, and structural linguistics to ground feminist theory).

—— (1995) *Philosophy and Feminism: At the Border*. New York: Twayne Publishers. (An overview of the impact of feminist theory on mainstream philosophy).

Spelman, E. (1988) *Inessential Woman: Problems of Exclusion in Feminist Thought*. Boston: Beacon Press. (A critical examination of feminist essentialism and its effect on theory).

Philosophy of mind

Anzaldua, G. (1990) *Making Face, Making Soul*. San Francisco: Aunt Lute Foundation. (An exploration of Hispanic and mestizo subjectivity).

Wittig, M. (1992) *The Straight Mind and Other Essays*. Boston: Beacon Press. (An examination of the category "woman" and the oppressive ways it structures identity).

Hypatia 8/1 (Winter 1993) Special issue on feminine subjectivity.

Epistemology

Alcoff, L. and E. Potter (eds.) (1993) *Feminist Epistemologies*. New York: Routledge. (A representative collection including a variety of perspectives in feminist theory of knowledge).

Anthony, L. and C. Witt (eds.) (1993) *A Mind of One's Own*. Boulder, CO: Westview Press. (A collection of essays defending feminist versions of mainstream epistemology).

Code, L. (1987) *Epistemic Responsibility*. Hanover, NH and London: Brown University Press. (A study of the role that morality plays in scientific reasoning).

—— (1991) *What Can She Know? Feminist Theory and the Construction of Knowledge*, Ithaca, NY: Cornell University Press. (A critical account of feminist approaches to epistemology).

Longino, H. (1990) *Science and Social Knowledge: Values and Objectivity in Science*. (A classic feminist treatment of the role of values in science).

Smith, D. (1987) *The Everyday World as Problematic*. Boston: Northeastern University Press. (An approach to sociology rooted in women's experience).

Tuana, N. (1993) *The Less Noble Sex: Scientific, Religious, and Philosophical Conceptions of Women's Nature*. Bloomington, IN: Indiana University Press. (A critique of science studies dealing with women).

Ethics

Card, C. (ed.) (1991) *Feminist Ethics*. Lawrence, KS: University Press of Kansas. (A representative collection of essays in feminist ethical theory).

Cole, E. B. and S. Coultrap-McQuinn (eds.) (1992) *Explorations in Feminist Ethics: Theory and Practice*, Bloomington, IN: Indiana University Press. (A collection of essays that pays special attention to relations between ethics of care and ethics of justice).

Elshtain, J. B. (1981) *Public Man, Private Woman*. Princeton, NJ: Princeton University Press. (A hermeneutic reading of social philosophy inspired in part by Hannah Arendt).

Held, V. (1993) *Feminist Morality: Transforming Culture, Society, and Politics*. Chicago: University of Chicago Press. (A critique of contractualism and foundationalism in ethics).

Pateman, C. (1988) *The Sexual Contract*. Stanford, CA: Stanford University Press. (Pateman argues that there is an understood sexual contract that sets the terms for relations between the sexes prior to any social contract).

Philosophy of language

Cixous, H. (1976) "The laugh of the Medusa," trans. K. Cohen and P. Cohen. In *Signs* 1/4: 875–93. (Classic description of feminist writing as escaping logical syntax).

Kress, G. and R. Hodge (1979) *Language and Ideology*. New York: Routledge. (Kress and Hodge argue that an underlying semantic scheme constructs gender difference).

Lakoff, R. (1975) *Language and Women's Place*. New York: Harper & Row. (A review of systematic gender difference in language).

Nye, A. (1987) "The inequalities of semantic structure." *Metaphilosophy* 18: 222–40. (A review of gender inequalities inherent in systems of meaning).

—— (1989) "The voice of the serpent: French feminism and the philosophy of language." In A. Garry and M. Pearsall (eds.) *Women, Knowledge and Reality*, New York: Unwin Hyman, pp. 233–50. (An analysis of French feminist challenges to traditional philosophies of language).

Part II

LOGIC, LANGUAGE, KNOWLEDGE, AND METAPHYSICS

8

PHILOSOPHICAL LOGIC

R. M. Sainsbury

Instead of following grammar blindly, the logician ought rather to see his task as that of freeing us from the fetters of language.

Frege (1979: 143)

The old logic put thought in fetters, while the new logic gives it wings.

Russell (1914: 68)

Introduction

The first use of the phrase "philosophical logic" known to me is in a semi-popular essay by Bertrand Russell (1872–1970) called "Logic as the essence of philosophy" (1914). Russell and others had been practicing philosophical logic for years, but it was not until this essay that Russell identified and labeled what he considered to be a distinctive approach to philosophy as a whole. Philosophical logic, as Russell conceived it, was the program of resolving traditional philosophical problems by discovering and classifying logical forms, and this concern with logical form became a central and distinctive feature of analytic philosophy in the twentieth century. Analytic philosophers do things other than philosophical logic; but those willing to regard their work as contributions to philosophical logic are analytic philosophers.

The most famous contribution to the program was Russell's own theory of descriptions, whose first published version was given in "On denoting" (1905) (see also "The birth of analytic philosophy," Chapter 1). The apparent or grammatical form of, for example, *The present King of France is bald* is subject–predicate, but Russell argued that its logical form is very different, expressible as: *Something is a King of France, not more than one thing is a King of France, and whatever is a King of France is bald.* In Russell's opinion, being right about logical form has instrumental as well as intrinsic value: it prevents unsatisfactory metaphysics, for example a Meinongian ontology driven by a supposed need to postulate a being corresponding to "the King of France," and it makes possible plausible epistemology, since one can know that there are things with certain properties without being acquainted with any examples. In Russell's opinion, philosophical logic was not some especially important area of philosophy but the core of all serious philosophizing:

> Every philosophical problem, when it is subjected to the necessary analysis and purification, is found either not to be really philosophical at all, or else to be, in the sense in which we are using the word, logical. (Russell 1914: 42)

Later in the essay, the sense in question is identified precisely as "philosophical logic."

Russell applied the philosophical logic program to a wide range of problems, most centrally in the philosophy of mathematics. His logicism is the claim that mathematical truths are logical truths, provable by logical means (if provable at all), and so knowable in the same way as logic. The core of the position can be represented as a claim about logical form: we get closer to the logical form of, say, "2 + 2 = 4" by seeing it as about relations between classes of classes, and closer still when we appreciate that the apparent reference to classes is inessential (the "no class" theory of classes). This leads to his draconian view that there are no mathematical objects, neither numbers nor classes, or rather, more cautiously and correctly, to the view that there is no reason to suppose that there are any. In the Russellian tradition, logical form proposals are never far removed from often dramatic metaphysical or epistemological claims.

Other applications of the program of philosophical logic were to belief and judgment, truth, existence (including the ontological argument for the existence of God), and the epistemologically motivated program of replacing "inferred entities" by "logical constructions," applied to the external world and to minds.

Russell's influence is at work in any philosopher who is willing to make a contrast between grammatical form and logical form. We find a clear statement, and an acknowledgment to Russell, in Wittgenstein's *Tractatus*:

> 4.002: Language disguises thought. So much so, that from the outward form of the clothing it is impossible to infer the form of the thought beneath it, because the outward form of the clothing is not designed to reveal the form of the body, but for entirely different purposes.

> 4.0031: It was Russell who performed the service of showing that the apparent logical form of a proposition need not be its real one.

Russell's influence is also at work in many of those who pepper their text with logical symbols purportedly in the service of paraphrasing some idiom of ordinary speech. These philosophers may not be explicitly soldiering under the banner of the philosophical logical program, but they reveal that they have absorbed its influence, perhaps barely consciously, if they hold that the symbolic paraphrases reveal something that would otherwise be concealed in what they paraphrase. The upshot is that a fully detailed history of philosophical logic in the twentieth century would embrace a very large part of analytic philosophy. Rather than attempt this, I will in the following section indicate some major events in the development of philosophical logic, and will consider its methodology, and the justification for the conception of logical form which philosophical logic requires. I will subsequently discuss an aspect of the concept of truth which belongs to philosophical logic: the paradoxes to which it gives rise, and how these are related to some other paradoxes. I conclude with a prognosis concerning the future of philosophical logic.

"Logical form": the holy grail of philosophical logic

The Russell–Quine–Davidson tradition

Russell thought that the language of his *Principia Mathematica* (1910–13), co-written with A. N. Whitehead, was the language of logical forms; in this language, there is no distinction between logical form and grammatical form, no ambiguity, and no lack of clarity. A major philosopher to inherit this view, fully explicitly, was W. V. O. Quine, whose "On what there is" (1948) was a milestone in the application of logical form to ontology. The main claim of that paper was that a theory's ontological commitments are to be judged by first regimenting it into the language of first-order logic (a proper part of the language of *Principia Mathematica*) and then seeing what must exist for the existential quantifications to be true: "To be is, purely and simply, to be the value of a variable" (Quine 1948: 32).[1] The regimentation is essential to prevent us, for example, from supposing that commitment to the view that a person acted for another's sake is thereby commitment to an ontology of *sakes*; such false appearances would disappear once the claim is regimented in first-order logic.

Although a distinction between grammatical and logical form was freely used in the analytic tradition, for many decades the methodology of the distinction was relatively little discussed. In "On referring" (1950a), Peter Strawson (1919–2006) raised some doubts, deriving from his sense of the plasticity and context-dependence of ordinary language compared to the rigidity of formal languages. He suggested that there was no adequate program of finding logical forms, for "ordinary language has no exact logic" (1950a: 27). He was vividly aware that the same words can be used in different contexts to say different things ("I am hungry," said by me, says that I am hungry, but said by you it says that you are), and this precludes an exact description of language that pays no attention to how it is used. By contrast, formal languages are generally devised in such a way that there is no context dependence; what might in some ways resemble context dependence will be brought under the thumb of model-theoretic precision, for example, the fact that a variable can be assigned different objects on different interpretations.

The fullest defense of the Russell–Quine approach to logical form is due to Donald Davidson (1917–2003). He made free use of the contrast between logical and grammatical form in "The logical form of action sentences" (1967), proposing that sentences like "Shem kicked Shaun" are "really" (that is, at the level of logical form) existential quantifications over events (kicks), and that "kicked" is, despite being apparently two-place, in reality three-place. The logical form is something like: there is a kick which Shem kicked to Shaun. James Cargile (1970: 137–8) protested that, look as he might, he could not see the existential quantifier, and could not imagine a basis for supposing that "kicked," as it occurs in the sentence in question, has more than two places. More generally, he stressed that a claim of logical form should amount to more than a claim of logical equivalence, even if one of the equivalents is in some sense more perspicuous than the other. This elicited from Davidson historically the first full account of criteria for selecting logical forms (Davidson 1970), and a justification of their interest. At the same time, Davidson was explicit that finding logical forms is not, as Russell thought, the end of the story, but only the beginning; after that, and only after that, the substantive job of philosophical analysis can begin.

Davidson's views have been developed (for example, by Lycan 1984), but in the purely philosophical tradition there is no radically distinct paradigm in sight. A notion of logical form has led a somewhat different life in the hands of linguists, where it is often referred to as a level of syntactic description called "LF." As early as 1957, Noam Chomsky (1928–) suggested that a proper description or representation of a sentence, from the grammatical point of view, would have many layers, and this paved the way for the idea, developed subsequently, that LF would be one such layer. A standard view is that LF is the level of linguistic representation at which all grammatical structure relevant to semantic interpretation is specified (see Hornstein 1995). Although there is no doubt that the motivations for introducing LF typically differ from the motivations which led philosophers to introduce logical form, the question whether the LF of linguists and the logical form of philosophers are or are not essentially the same under the skin is a vexed one, which we will not explore (see Neale 1993). Instead, I will examine in more detail some of the methodological issues raised by the conception of logical form that has been dominant in the philosophical as opposed to the linguistic literature (though the distinction is by no means hermetic).

Russell

We know what Russell's kind of philosophical logic is if we know what logical form is, for philosophical logic is the program of finding logical forms. Here is Russell's earliest explicit formulation:

> Form is not another constituent [of propositions], but is the way the constituents are put together. It is forms, in this sense, that are the proper object of philosophical logic. (Russell 1914: 52)

The basic form is the atomic form, exemplified by a sentence composed of an n-place predicate conjoined with n names. Although this may now strike us as scarcely worthy of comment, this conception of the basic form was innovative and controversial. As Russell made explicit, the notion of an atomic sentence is designed to supersede the older notion of subject–predicate form, which Russell believed was defective for two reasons. One explicit reason is that it does not do justice to relations. Treated as subject–predicate, "Mary loves John" and "John loves Mary" share neither a subject nor a predicate (for "loves John" is a different predicate from "loves Mary"). Regarded as a two-place relation, there is a relation in common and two common names, and the only difference is order. The second description is superior from the point of view of developing a logic of relations.

The other reason for dissatisfaction with the notion of subject–predicate as opposed to atomic sentences was implicit. In the kind of languages with which Russell was concerned, there is a finite stock of names and predicates and hence a finite stock of atomic sentences. In the traditional conception, subject–predicate sentences are in infinite supply, for subject expressions can be complex without upper limit. For example, definite descriptions like "The Queen of England" are counted as subject expressions, which means that one must also count as subject expressions the following: "The Queen of the country which colonized India," "The Queen of the country which colonized the country in which alone tigers are indigenous," and so on. It was important to Russell that language or thought should start with a finite number of elements, and this is ensured by the conception of an atomic sentence or atomic judgment; the conception of a subject–predicate judgment cannot play the same role.

Russell's enthusiasm for Frege's insistence upon the notion of the atomic sentence[2] was in part based on his appreciation of the way in which it enabled the provision of the truth conditions of quantified sentences in terms of quantifications over the truth conditions of atomic sentences. As Michael Dummett (1925–) describes this aspect of Frege's work:

> "everybody envies somebody" is true just in case each of the sentences "Peter envies somebody," "James envies somebody," … is true; and "Peter envies somebody" is, in turn, true just in case at least one of the sentences "Peter envies John," "Peter envies James," is true. (Dummett 1973a: 11)

We find an account of quantification along these lines in Russell's "On denoting," as a precursor to his classification of definite descriptions as quantifier phrases. This contrasts with the traditional approach, found for example in Leibniz, according to which the inferential role of sentences like "Socrates is mortal" is explained in part by their equivalence to "Some-or-every Socrates is mortal" (see Sommers: 1982: 15–21).

The constituents of an atomic proposition or judgment are (1) the bearers of the names and (2) the property or relation introduced by the predicate; the logical form is not a constituent, but is, rather, the connection which holds between the constituents in virtue of which the sentence manages to say something. Russell struggled with this fundamental notion, labeling the problem that of the "unity of the proposition." Take an atomic sentence like "Desdemona loves Cassio," and suppose that it belongs to the world of fact rather than fiction.[3] The three constituents are Desdemona, Cassio, and love, three real entities (a woman, a man, and a relation). But the sentence is more than just a list of these things. It "combines" the things in such a way that the sentence says (truly or falsely, and in fact falsely) that Desdemona loves Cassio; in this it achieves something which no mere list can achieve. Russell chose an example of a falsehood to bring home the difficulty: in the case of a truth, this process of combination could be held to result in a fact, a complex entity consisting of Desdemona's love for Cassio. But as the sentence is false, there is no such fact, no such complex entity. The problem was to understand how the combining of the constituents could result in an entity which made the sentence more than a list without resulting in a fact, and so, absurdly, precluding the possibility of falsehood. At various points, Russell appealed to logical form to answer this question, though he never arrived at a formulation which satisfied him (see Russell 1913). The constituents of, say, a one-place atom are welded together through the unary atomic form. This form could not itself be a constituent on pain of regress (how is the form bound to the other constituents?); but it seemed puzzling to Russell that it could do any work in the proposition without being a constituent. And indeed it seemed puzzling to him how anything could combine the constituents in a way which made them say something without also combining them in a way which made what they said true, and so precluded falsehood. As he puts it, we need the relation to "really relate" the terms if we are to have more than a list; but if it really relates the terms then the proposition is true.

Russell's difficulty is not much discussed nowadays outside Russell scholarship, but it seems to me that it touches many contemporary theories. To take just one example: some identify propositions with sets of possible worlds, and say that a proposition is true at a world just in case that world belongs to it. This leaves unanswered the question of how a set can say something. Not all sets do so; only those which are propositions. What additional features do such sets possess? I do not say that the question is unanswerable, but only that it remains a genuine question.[4]

Three strands in the conception of logical form

Russell's conception of logical form thus had a shaky foundation in the account of atomic sentences and propositions. It was supposed to constitute the cement that bound the constituents of a proposition together in such a way that they said something, formed a content that could be judged, but Russell never felt he had satisfactorily explained how this could be so. Despite this, the remainder of the account proceeded fairly smoothly, thanks to a shift of focus. The standard sentence connectives bind atoms together in a way that can be explained through their truth functionality: they are pure cement and do not themselves introduce further constituents. The early Wittgenstein (1889–1951) advertised this as a central tenet of the *Tractatus*: "4.0312: My fundamental idea is that the 'logical constants' are not representatives; that there can be no representatives of the logic of facts." Logical constants, like "and" and "if" (or "&" and "→"), Wittgenstein says, are not representatives, that is, they do not stand for anything, do not introduce a further constituent but play a purely cementing role.[5]

Given that the role of the truth functional connectives is explained in terms of the truth functional dependence of the truth-values of complexes upon that of their sentential parts, why should not Russell, or the early Wittgenstein, have regarded them as referring to truth functions? On the face of it, this would have shown how a constituent could also function as cement, for a function binds its arguments together. Though I am not aware of an explicit discussion in Russell, I think his motivation was probably ontological. Consider the fact that Plato was Greek and Napoleon was

French. How must the world be for this to obtain? It is necessary and sufficient that two simpler facts exist: that Plato was Greek, that Napoleon was French. On the face of it, there is no need for a third thing to exist, namely the conjunction truth function. So there is no ground for supposing that there is such a function, and we do better to explain the truth or falsehood of conjunctive sentences without appeal to these doubtful entities.

Logical form as cement: that is one strand in its nature. It goes with the idea that logical vocabulary or the logical constants serve to introduce just cement, and not constituents, and we will see that this is one strand of which much is made in more recent writing, especially by Davidson. Another strand is logical form as revelatory of ontological commitment, the strand which Quine most famously exploited. The third strand is logical form as revelatory of the features of a judgment most relevant to inference. For example, Russell thought that Plato's problem of non-being will simply not arise if the problematic sentences are accorded their proper logical form, for then the paradoxical inferences are unavailable. The problem is to explain how can one truly say that something does not exist, given that if one says this of something one says something false, whereas if one says it of nothing one says nothing at all. The first horn of the dilemma presupposes that the logical form of a statement of non-existence is "not (Exists (a))." This does indeed classically entail that a exists (i.e. that there is something identical to a). According to Russell, a statement of non-existence does not have this form, but rather something along the lines: "not (there are so-and-sos)." This neither supports the unwanted inference, nor can it be regarded, as the second horn suggests, as "saying nothing." So "Unicorns don't exist" has the unproblematic logical form "not (there are unicorns)," and "Vulcan does not exist" has the unprob- lematic logical form "not (there is a unique planet between Mercury and the sun which is responsible for the perturbations in Mercury's orbit)" (see also "The birth of analytic philosophy," Chapter 1).[6] Can the three strands we have identified in logical form be seen as part of a single phenomenon? Cement provides structure, binding the bricks together, and valid inference, or at least logically valid inference, is inference in virtue of form or structure, independent of the specific features of the constituents. "Fido barks, therefore something barks" is valid in virtue of its form, which is shared by countless other arguments ("Plato thinks, therefore something thinks," "Napoleon commands, therefore something commands," and so on). So the logical vocabulary both binds and also shows the features relevant to inference; this connects two of our three strands. Since existential generalization is a mechanical matter once the premises are presented in their correct logical form, there is evidently a close connection with ontology, thus securing our third strand. Whereas we might think we could apply existential generalization to "The present King of France does not exist" to yield the undesirable "Something does not exist," no such inference is available once the true form of the premise is appreciated ("Nothing is uniquely king of France").

Davidson

This was how logical form was considered for about half a century from before World War I. Donald Davidson redeveloped the notion, first in his philosophical practice (Davidson 1967: "The logical form of action sentences"), and shortly thereafter in an explicit statement of the methodology (Davidson 1970: "Action and reaction"). He begins with what I regard as a fully accurate statement of the issue:

> logical form was invented to contrast with something else that is held to be apparent but mere: the form we are led to assign to sentences by superficial analogy or traditional grammar. What meets the eye or ear in language has the charm, complexity, convenience and deceit of other conventions of the market place, but underlying it is the solid currency of a plainer, duller structure, without wit but also without pretence. This true coin, the deep structure, need never feature directly in the transactions of real life. As long as we know how to redeem our paper we can enjoy the benefits of credit. ... The image may help to explain why the distinction between logical form and surface grammar can flourish without anyone ever quite explaining it. (Davidson 1970: 137)

In considering how the distinction could be justified, Davidson begins by locating the connection between logical form and inference: "Part of the answer – the part with which we are most familiar – is that inference is simplified and mechanized when we rewrite sentences in some standardized notation" (1970: 138). But the desire to simplify and mechanize inference does not in itself underwrite the contrast between logical and merely surface form. If simplifying inference was all that was at stake, one could as well say: "Let's recast our thoughts in this simple language, good for revealing inferential relations," without pretending that the recasting provided a better account of the shape of the original molds.

Davidson's final position is that the logical form of a sentence in natural language is the result of doing to it whatever is necessary to produce something accessible to systematic semantic theory: "To give the logical form of a sentence is, then, for me, to describe it in terms that bring it within the scope of a semantic theory" (1970: 144). This re-description may involve no change: perhaps "Fido barks" is the logical form of this sentence. Or the re-description may involve just "one small point". According to Davidson's paratactic account of the logical form of sentences ascribing propositional attitudes, the logical form of "Plato said that Hesperus is visible in the evening" is "Plato said that. Hesperus is visible in the evening". The only difference is the full stop (the small point) after "that", this last being construed as a demonstrative pronoun referring forward to the utterance of "Hesperus is visible in the evening". Or the change may be considerable. In the early paper (Davidson 1967) he suggested that the logical form of "Shem kicked Shaun" is something like "There was a kicking, x of Shaun by Shem"; in (roughly) first-order notation:

$\exists x$(kick (x) & kicked (Shem, x, Shaun)).

Ultimately, the justification for a logical form proposal, within Davidson's approach, is that it presents the original sentence, or its content, in a way which makes it accessible to systematic semantic theory. On the assumption that such a theory will be cast somewhat in the style of a first-order truth theory, and so will be extensional, the seemingly non-extensional idioms of belief-ascription are not directly accessible to semantic theory. The paratactic account is a dazzling solution to this problem: the seeming non-extensionality is an illusion of grammatical form, a result merely of the missing point after "that". A sentence is non-extensional iff (if and only if) substitution of co-extensive expressions within it does not preserve truth-value. If we think of the original belief attribution as a single sentence, "Plato said that Hesperus is visible in the evening," it is possible that substituting the co-extensive "Phosphorus" for "Hesperus" would alter the truth-value. It might be that "Plato said that Hesperus is visible in the evening" is true, but "Plato said that Phosphorus is visible in the evening" is false. Once we see that there are really two sentences, the illusion of non-extensionality is dispersed. In the first sentence – "Plato said that" – "that" will refer to different entities according to what utterance immediately follows; and replacing "Hesperus" by "Phosphorus" will not change the truth-value of the second sentence ("Hesperus is visible in the evening"). There is no shift of truth-value, within any one sentence, so long as there is no shift in the extension of any of that sentence's parts.

Accessibility to semantic theory is the ultimate justification. For Davidson, this is intimately connected with inference, as this way of putting the point illustrates:

> By saying exactly what the role [of a verb] is, and what the roles of the other significant features of the sentences are, we will have a deep explanation of why one sentence entails the other, an explanation that draws on a systematic account of how the meaning of each sentence is a function of its structure. (Davidson 1970: 142)

For example, appreciating the extra argument place in the logical form of sentences containing verbs of action permits an understanding of inferential relations in antecedently familiar terms. Intuitively, Davidson says, the following inference is not merely valid, but valid in virtue of form:

John buttered the toast in the bathroom, therefore John buttered the toast.

On many views of the logical form of the premise, the validity of this inference has to be accepted as a brute and inexplicable fact. Perhaps there are two verbs "buttered," one three-place (and used in the premise) and one two-place (and used in the conclusion) and a "meaning postulate" tells us that we can always infer from a sentence dominated by the three-place predicate to a corresponding sentence dominated by the two-place one. Apart from the fact that such an approach would have to postulate an indefinite series of predicates "buttered" (a four-place one for "John buttered the toast in the bathroom with a knife," a five-place one for "John buttered the toast in the bathroom with a knife at midnight," and so on), it is also explanatorily weak compared to Davidson's proposal, which is that the argument has the form:

$\exists x(\text{Buttered}(\text{John, the toast, } x) \text{ \& In}(\text{the bathroom, } x)) \vdash \exists x(\text{Buttered}(\text{John, the toast, } x))$

The validity of the argument is subsumed under a familiar first-order case: dropping a conjunct under existential quantification; this provides a serious explanation of its validity.

Russell and Davidson compared

Russell would no doubt have been pleased with this result. But Davidson's view differs significantly from Russell's. First, Davidson's concern is with the logical form of sentences, whereas Russell's is with the logical form of facts, judgments, or propositions (regarded as non-linguistic things). This connects with the second difference, that whereas for Russell the primary constraint on logical form is imposed by the need to do justice to inferential relations between judgments or propositions, for Davidson the primary constraint is imposed by the need to do justice to the semantics of sentences. Third, whereas Russell claimed (perhaps exaggerating his real view) that philosophical logic was the whole of philosophy, Davidson said that finding logical forms was just the beginning; after that there remained the serious business of philosophical analysis.

Davidson aimed to derive the relation between logical form and logical inference from the way in which semantic obligations determine logical form. A semantic theory is a theory of truth, with theorems like "'Snow is white' is true iff snow is white," which Davidson calls "T-sentences." One sentence entails another if the truth of the first guarantees the truth of the second, and this is formal (a matter of form) if this is so in virtue of the structure of the sentences. Semantic theory will reveal this structure and so underwrite formal entailments.

The connection between truth theoretical semantics and logical entailment emerges in Davidson's account of the logical constants. He said that these are expressions which receive a recursive rather than a basis clause within a semantic theory. "And," for example, will have a semantic axiom like the following:

for all sentences, "p", "q", "p and q" is true iff "p" is true and "q" is true.

This is recursive in the sense that it specifies a condition for the truth of a conjunction in terms of the truth of its components, so it is only one step on the way to the goal of a specification of a truth condition in truth-independent terms. If we want to reach a "pure" truth condition for, e.g., "Plato thinks and Napoleon commands" we may first apply the axiom for "and" to get:

"Plato thinks and Napoleon commands" is true iff "Plato thinks" is true and "Napoleon commands" is true but we will also have to find truth conditions for the components "Plato thinks" and "Napoleon commands" so that we can use the equivalences

"Plato thinks" is true iff Plato thinks

"Napoleon commands" is true iff Napoleon commands

to derive the target T-sentence

"Plato thinks and Napoleon commands" is true iff Plato thinks and Napoleon commands.

By contrast a semantic axiom for an expression like "Plato" or "thinks" will be a "basis" clause, one which does not involve the notion of truth on the right hand side, for example:

"Plato" refers to something iff that thing is Plato

"thinks" is true of something iff that thing thinks.

The contrast between the logical constants (with their recursive clauses) and other expressions (with their basis clauses) mirrors at the linguistic level Russell's contrast between cement (logical constants) and bricks (non-logical expressions). The contrast will be written into logical forms. To the extent that the validity of inference is grounded entirely in structure and independently of the bricks that compose it, identifying logical forms will be the same as identifying inferential properties. Hence Davidson's use of facts about inference to test for the correctness of logical form proposals:

> my only reasons for "rendering" or "paraphrasing" event sentences into quantificational form was as a way of giving the truth conditions for those sentences within a going theory of truth. We have a clear semantics for first-order quantificational languages, and so if we can see how to paraphrase sentences in a natural language into quantificational form, we see how to extend a theory of truth to those sentences. Since the entailments that depend on quantificational form can be completely formalized, it is an easy test of our success in capturing logical form within a theory of truth to see whether our paraphrases articulate the entailments we independently recognize as due to form. (1970: 144)

Whereas for Russell, the connection between logical form and inference was basic and primitive, Davidson seeks to derive it via the connections between logical form and semantics, and between semantics and entailment.

A further difference between Russell's and Davidson's perspective on logical form relates to identity. For Russell, whose logic involved quantification over predicates of every type and order, "=" is introduced as a defined logical connective:

*13.01 $x = y =_{df} \forall\varphi(\varphi!x \leftrightarrow \varphi!y).$ [7]

This is not available within Davidson's predominantly first order perspective. "=" will receive a basis clause and not a recursive clause in semantic theory and so should not be counted as a logical constant. This has further consequences. Whereas Russell can regard a purely numerical sentence like "There are exactly two entities" as composed wholly of logical vocabulary (a formalization is: $\exists x \exists y[x \neq y \ \& \ \forall z(x = z \lor y = z)]$), Davidson cannot. This precludes Davidson from thinking of standard numerical quantifiers (of the form "there are exactly n so-and-sos") as belonging to logic.

Inference and logical form

We have seen that Russell thought that logical form was the form of a judgment, not of a sentence. This explains his subsequent view of his work in the period up to the end of World War I as work that ignored language (Russell 1959: 145). This opinion surprises those who anachronistically see the early Russell, for example in his Theory of Descriptions, as engaged in an account of the semantics of definite descriptions in natural language. Even if we agree that the Theory of Descriptions, regarded as an account of natural language, involves "the butchering of surface structure" (Evans 1982: 57), this is no criticism of Russell, who was not concerned with surface structure but only with giving the most revealing account of judgment, of what is before the mind of a thinker using a sentence containing a definite description.

Up to now, I have drawn a veil over how precisely Davidson understands the relation between a sentence of natural language, s, and its logical form, s_{LF}. There are two options. He can say that s has as its logical form s_{LF} iff the T-sentence for s simply is " 's' is true iff s_{LF}." Or he can say that s has as its logical form s_{LF} iff as a preliminary to applying a semantic theory to s it is translated as s_{LF} and then the T-sentence is " 's_{LF}' is true iff s_{LF}" (the T-sentence is, as Davidson calls it, "homophonic"). The first option, as Davidson suggests in the following quotation, makes good sense of such claims as that an action sentence "really" contains an existential quantifier:

> all I mean by saying that "Jones buttered the toast" has the logical form of an existentially quantified sentence, and that "buttered" is a three-piece [sic] predicate, is that a theory of truth meeting Tarski's criteria would entail that this sentence is true if and only if there exists . . . . etc. (1970: 143)

However, this first option is precluded by the methodology. If there is to be any chance of deriving a T-sentence for "Jones buttered the toast" whose right hand side is as Davidson envisages, then the axiom for "buttered" must treat this as a three-place predicate, in which case the T-sentence must refer, on its left hand side, not to the unchanged English sentence but to its "logical form": "there exists an x such that (Buttered (Jones, the toast, x))." So Davidson has to adopt the second option, on which it is the natural language sentence's logical form, which will often be a sentence rather different from the natural language sentence itself, that is addressed by the semantic theory. This raises the question of how the semantics for s_{LF}, which we can accept are impeccably specified by the truth theory, transfer to the distinct sentence s. The English sentence and its logical form may agree in their truth conditions, yet achieve them through different semantic mechanisms. Cargile's question appears still to require an answer.

It would be appropriate for Davidson to reaffirm the role of inference. The original sentence and its logical form agree on all "formal" entailments (as well as on truth conditions), and this suggests that they stand in an intimate relationship, say R. R needs to be so intimate that, if it holds between two sentences, a semantic story told for the one is also correct for the other (even though just one of the sentences can be the target of a T-sentence). In my opinion, it remains for the Davidsonian method-ology of logical form to specify an R which both justifies the claim that if $R(s_1, s_2)$ then correct semantics for s_2 are thereby correct semantics for s_1, and also relates "John buttered the toast" and "there exists an x such that (Buttered (Jones, the toast, x))".

As I said above, Davidson is explicit that logical form is at most the beginning of philosophy. Once we have found the logical form, we can go on to do the philosophical analysis and metaphysics. In the case of action sentences, logical form considerations tell us that they quantify over events, but are silent on the nature of events, on the criteria for their existence and identity. In the case of sentences ascribing propositional attitudes, logical form considerations tell us that these involve a relation between a person and an utterance, but they do not tell us what this relation is. Davidson suggests that if I truly utter a sentence like "Plato said that Hesperus is visible in the evening," then Plato said something which makes him and me samesayers in virtue of my utterance of "Hesperus is visible in the evening." This claim belongs to analysis, not to logical form, and as Davidson says, "samesaying" itself marks a place where further analysis is needed (though he is optimistic that his conception of semantic theory can play a useful role).

In the course of a century, the conception of philosophical logic has changed from a panacea for philosophical problems to an aspect of semantics. In addition, a new usage has sprung up, according to which philosophical logic is the investigation of logical concepts and problems that are of special relevance to philosophers, truth being a prominent example (as we will see in the next section). Some insist on marking the divergent streams with distinct terms: keep "philosophical logic" for the logical form program, understood on Russellian or Davidsonian lines, and "philosophy of logic" for philosophical discussion of the notions special or central to logic, like truth, entailment, and form. There is a natural tendency to blur the boundaries, for philosophical logic (in the first sense) makes essential use of the notions of truth, entailment, and form, as we have seen, and it is in the nature of philosophy constantly to question the very tools it uses. Among these tools, nothing would seem more important than the notion of truth; and in the twentieth century, this has been a rich source of puzzlement, paradox, and imaginative and challenging theorizing.

Truth

Some approaches to truth

The concept of truth has played a central role in most philosophical traditions, and very conspicuously so in analytic philosophy in the twentieth century. Whatever their central interests, philosophers cannot ignore truth, and it has played an especially important part within philosophical logic on account of the paradoxes with which it is associated, and the theoretical work arising from reflection on these paradoxes. Whatever else one may demand of logic, consistency would seem to be an overriding requirement; yet the notion of truth has appeared to lead swiftly to contradictions. These are the topic of subsequent subsections.

One view of truth, which has informed many and disparate theories, goes back to Aristotle:

> To say of what is that it is not, or of what is not that it is, is false, while to say of what is that it is, or of what is not that it is not, is true. (*Metaphysics* Γ7, 27)

One can classify a variety of opinions about truth in terms of how they react to this Aristotelian view. Among those who agree with Aristotle, there are those who think that it shows that the nature of truth consists in some kind of correspondence with reality, and those who think that it shows that truth has no "nature" but is some kind of eliminable or at most very "thin" notion, expressing no substantive property. Those who disagree with Aristotle think that an account of truth should be sought in quite different terms. Non-Aristotelian notions which have been used in explicating truth include coherence, convergence, and assertibility. Some have held that to be true is to be consistent with what we believe; or that the truth is that upon which best opinion will in the long run converge; or that what is true coincides with what, under the most favorable conditions, we would be justified in asserting. Important as these approaches are, the following remarks relate just to the Aristotelian conception.

Some philosophers see Aristotle as advancing a correspondence theory of truth: what is true is what corresponds to the facts. One cannot dispute that in ordinary parlance there is little to choose between calling something true and saying that it corresponds to the facts. This as such does not give correspondence any special role to play in explaining truth: one could as well say that the notion of correspondence is to be explained in terms of truth. For a correspondence theory to make a significant contribution, it needs to offer more than just the verbal equivalence noted; it needs to show that the notions of correspondence and fact are somehow more basic than that of truth, and one way to achieve this is to give an independent account of the relation of correspondence itself, and of the terms between which the relation is supposed to hold, the truth-bearer on the one side and the truth-maker on the other. Sentences or beliefs are standard candidates for truth-bearers, and facts, states of affairs, or simply reality are candidates for truth-makers.

Russell (1912) suggested that truth-bearers are beliefs, analyzed as relations holding between believers and various things in the world. If Othello believes that Desdemona loves Cassio, the belief consists in a relation between Othello, Desdemona, love, and Cassio. This belief is true if there is a fact whose constituents are Desdemona, love, and Cassio (in that order). This provides an atomistic version of the correspondence theory. Truth consists not in correspondence with reality construed in an undifferentiated way, for example, simply as the way things are, but in a kind of isomorphism between parts of the belief and specific parts of reality.

Russell himself was never satisfied with this account, on the grounds that it did not do proper justice to love. In Othello's belief, this features as a term in a relation; but if there is a corresponding fact, love needs to feature in a quite different way, as a binder together of terms rather than as itself a term. Here we encounter an aspect of the problem, already noted above, of the "unity of the proposition."

The problem of giving an adequate characterization of the truth-maker was at the center of a famous debate between John Austin (1911–60) and Peter Strawson. Strawson claimed, reasonably enough, that a serious correspondence theory should be able to give a general specification of truth-makers without invoking the concept of truth, and in which they were clearly independent of truth-bearers. Austin's truth-makers were facts, but Strawson claimed that these were really linguistic entities, and not suitably distinct from truth-bearers (which both parties referred to as statements): "facts are what statements (when true) state. ... If you prize the statements off the world you prize the facts off it too; but the world would be none the poorer" (1950b: 38–9).

In developing the details of his theory of truth, Austin (1950) gave a quite theoretical account of how the correspondence was supposed to work.[8] He argued that a sentence is linked to two kinds of thing in the world, by two different sets of conventions. The descriptive conventions link it to a state of affairs, something which may or may not obtain. The demonstrative conventions link it to a particular situation. Thus (to use Austin's example) an utterance of the sentence "The cat is on the mat" is linked by the descriptive conventions to the state of affairs of the cat being on the mat, and by the demonstrative conventions to some particular situation in some region of the world. (Austin is rather unclear about just what particular situation is involved, as Strawson stresses.) The utterance of the sentence is true just if the particular situation is of a kind with (that is, instantiates) the state of affairs. For many years after this theory was advanced, it was widely thought to have been refuted by Strawson. (Strawson objected that Austin had made truth purely conventional, but this criticism seems to have been based on a misunderstanding of Austin's theory.) However, Austin's theory has received a new lease of life in the hands of Barwise and Etchemendy (1987), who claim that it can provide an account of truth for which the Liar paradox does not arise (this paradox is discussed below, starting on p. 365).

One of the most famous and important approaches to truth within the Aristotelian framework is Alfred Tarski's (1902–83) semantic conception of truth, of which he says that it certainly conforms with Aristotle's conception (Tarski 1944: 72). In an attempt to make Aristotle's definition more precise, he gives an example of how it might apply to the sentence "snow is white," suggesting that "the sentence is true if snow is white, and ... false if snow is not white," in summary:

The sentence "snow is white" is true if, and only if, snow is white. (1944: 63)

Tarski goes on to suggest that a correct definition of truth will entail every equivalence of this kind. The general form of the crucial equivalences is given by:

(T) X is true if, and only if, p

where "X" marks the place for some expression which refers to a sentence in a way which makes manifest how the sentence is built up of words,[9] and "p" marks a position occupied by that very sentence (the one referred to by the expression in "X"-position).[10]

> we wish to use the term "true" in such a way that all equivalences of the form (T) can be asserted, and *we shall call a definition of* truth *"adequate" if all these equivalences follow from it.* (Tarski 1944: 63)

For a formalized language, he was able to provide a precise definition of truth which is adequate by this standard, set in a forbiddingly technical theory (Tarski 1933). No one disputes his success in this respect, but there is widespread dispute about the significance of the result. I mention four debated points.

(1) Why is not (T) itself already a definition of truth? Tarski's answer was that it is not a definition because it is not even a sentence, but only the schema of a sentence. "X" has no specific reference, and there is no sentence that we are supposed to substitute for "p". Obvious attempts to turn (T) into a sentence lead to nonsense. For example, "for every sentence X, and every sentence p, X is true iff p" is strictly nonsense, because quantifiers, as Tarski conceived them, are associated with individual variables, expressions which occupy the position of names, but the position marked by "p" is not such a position (it is a position to be filled by a sentence, not by a name). Even if we could understand this attempted generalization, it seems to point in an absurd direction, suggesting that for any pair of sentences, one gives a necessary and sufficient condition for the truth of the other.

(2) The T-equivalences seem trivial, so how could it be enough for a definition of truth to be correct that it entail them all? On Tarski's side, it must be said that his criterion of correctness ensures that "true" will apply to all and only true sentences; this is so whatever we think about the triviality or significance of T-equivalences. On the other hand, one might want more from a definition, or at any rate from a philosophical account, than that it get the extension of "true" right. One might, not unreasonably, want an informal account of how truth relates to other interesting philosophical notions like reality, objectivity, warrant, and assertion, and an explication of why truth is of value and why we should strive for it. I imagine that Tarski would accept this observation, while insisting that these other tasks can be best performed only once one has provided a correct definition, in his narrower sense of something which precisely determines the extension of "true."

(3) The T-equivalences relate sentences to reality (for example, to snow's being or not being white) and so the semantic conception "finds itself involved in a most uncritical realism" (Tarski 1944: 75). Thus put, the objection is silly, and Tarski deals with it briskly: the semantic conception has nothing to say about what it is for snow to be white, and so a fortiori says nothing that is specially realist, irrealist, empiricist, or anything else:

> we may accept the semantic conception of truth without giving up any epistemological attitude we may have had; we may remain naïve realists, critical realists or idealists, empiricists or metaphysicians – whatever we were before. The semantic conception is completely neutral toward all these issues. (Tarski 1944: 75)

However, the objection can be urged from a different quarter. Michael Dummett has suggested that to accept the Law of Excluded Middle for a given subject matter (the law that for every sentence, either it or its negation is true) is to adopt realism with respect to that subject matter. For one is then committed to the view that even if we have no conceivable means of finding out which if either of a sentence and its negation is true, nonetheless one of them is: reality may go beyond what we can conceivably know. (See for example Dummett 1973b; 1978: Preface.)

(4) Don't the T-equivalences show that truth is redundant? Instead of saying "'Snow is white' is true" we can just say "Snow is white"; we can do just as well without the predicate "true." Tarski responds by giving two kinds of case which cause trouble for this view. One is where we ascribe truth without knowing the content of that to which we ascribe it, for example:

> The first sentence written by Plato is true. (Tarski 1944: 73)

Since we do not know what Plato's first written sentence was, we cannot affirm it instead; but the displayed claim seems intelligible and, indeed, mildly interesting. The other problematic kind of case involves generalizations like

> All consequences of true sentences are true. (Tarski 1944: 73)

The task of specifying every case in which the relation of consequence obtains is too long to be completed, whereas the displayed sentence says something important. It might seem we could get rid of "true" in such cases by a device along these lines:

> for all s, p, if s, and p is a consequence of s, then p.

If these quantifiers ("for all s, p") are of the kind Tarski recognized, this is nonsense for a reason already noted: the variables should mark a position for a name, whereas in the above the relevant position is one to be filled by a sentence. There may be other kinds of quantification. Perhaps one could introduce a sentence-quantifier, whose variables are to be filled by sentences. But one should not assume that this is coherent, or that it can be done without explicit use of the notion of truth. For example, one natural way to specify how a quantifier along these lines works in a sentence of the form "for all s, ... s ..." is to say that it claims that whatever sentence you put in the position marked by s, the result is a truth.[11]

Paul Horwich (1990) has used T-equivalences (or more exactly ones of the form "the proposition that p is true iff p") to suggest that this is all one needs to say about truth, which is therefore a "non-substantive" property. Such minimalist or deflationary views dominated discussions of truth in the 1990s. (The debate is well represented in Blackburn and Simmons 1999; see also Wright 1992.) Supposedly, all the things we think are important about truth, its relation to objectivity, its value, the fact that we should aim for it, can be derived from reflection on the equivalences.

One well-known reason for thinking that this needs some qualification is that (T) as it stands leads to paradox: far from being trivial, T-equivalence threatens to generate contradictions (see the following subsection). Threat of paradox was at the heart of Tarski's work, which constituted the inauguration of formal semantic theorizing, and has cast its shadow over all subsequent serious discussion of truth.

These truth-related paradoxes have a long history. They were known in antiquity, were studied in the Middle Ages by philosophers such as John Buridan (c.1300–c.1358), and have been the subject of intensive research within philosophical logic since the early twentieth century. An early development of this recent phase dates back to Russell, who linked the truth-related paradoxes closely to the Class paradox that he discovered in the very early years of the twentieth century and which bears his name (see pp. 371–73).[12] He reported what we now call Russell's paradox in a letter to Frege, who replied in a letter dated June 22, 1902: "Your discovery of the contradiction has surprised me beyond words and, I should almost like to say, has left me thunderstruck, because it has rocked the ground on which I meant to build arithmetic"(Frege 1980: 152). Both Frege and Russell espoused the logicist thesis that mathematical concepts can be defined in purely logical terms, using in particular the theory of classes, and mathematical truths proved from purely logical axioms. This thesis becomes unattractive if the supposedly purely logical theory of classes generates paradoxes, for then one would be reducing apparently unparadoxical mathematics to a paradox-ridden basis.

Russell (1908) provided what he took to be a unified solution to both Russell's paradox and the truth-related ones, in the form of his Ramified Theory of Types, which is designed to make certain kinds of circularity and self-reference impossible, and self-reference and/or circularity were cast as the main villains for most of the first half of the twentieth century. More recently the role of context (see pp. 369–71) has become increasingly significant in this area of philosophy, as it has in others.

The "new logic" was supposed to give thought wings, so it must have been distressing for the founder of philosophical logic to discover that it was a breeding ground for paradox. Russell no doubt found comfort in the view that the Class paradox and the truth-related paradoxes are at bottom the same, for then the new logic did not, after all, breed a new species of monster, but merely allowed existing monsters to don new colors, unless due hierarchical precautions are taken. Whether or not he was right to make that assimilation is considered below, pp. 371–73.

The Liar: levels

One version of the Liar is

(L) L is not true.

Here a sentence, called L, is supposed to say of itself that it is not true. Suppose it is true; then it is as it says it is, that is, not true. Suppose that it is not true. This is just what it says it is, and a sentence that correctly says how things are is true, so it is true. To sum up: if it is true it is not true, and if it is not true it is true. This is tantamount to a contradiction.

Using Tarski's schema (T) (X is true if, and only if, p), the contradiction can be derived by using the name "L" in place of "X" and "L is not true" in place of "p" yielding:

(*) L is true iff L is not true.

By our stipulations, "L" meets the condition (imposed by Tarski on the relation between "X" and "p" in instances of (T)) of being a name of "L is not true." So the Liar shows that the apparently platitudinous (T) leads by apparently correct reasoning to the contradictory (*).

Early systematic attempts to deal with such contradictions involved hierarchies of levels. Russell's, as we saw, was a dual-purpose hierarchy which also controlled Russell's paradox. Because of the complexity of Russell's ramified hierarchy, we do better to consider the idea as it was used by Tarski (1933) nearly thirty years later.

Tarski's response was that a precise account of truth can only be given for formalized languages (ones with a precisely specified grammar, or, to keep closer to Tarski's own formulation, one whose construction ensures that the sense of every expression is uniquely determined by its form), and that Liar-like paradoxes make it mandatory that the meta-language (the one in which "true" is defined) should be essentially richer than the object language (the one containing the sentences to which the predicate "true" is to be applied).

Suppose some language λ_0 contains a predicate "Tr_1" that applies to all and only the true sentences of λ_0. Suppose also that λ_0 contains a sentence σ that says of itself that it is not Tr_1. Then, granting T, we have a version of the Liar: if Tr_1 applies to σ, then σ says truly that Tr_1 does not apply to it; but if Tr_1 does not apply to it, then, since this is what it says, it is true, and so Tr_1 does apply to it. Tarski took the contradiction to refute the supposition that σ belongs to λ_0. The natural explanation of how this could be is that Tr_1 is not an expression of λ_0. Hence, no sentence belongs to λ_0 if it contains Tr_1. This blocks the paradox in the following sense: the proposed language, since it does not contain a predicate true just of its true sentences, is one in which the paradoxical sentence cannot be formulated. One can write down the words, but they will be devoid of significance: they are semantically wholly defective.

We can enlarge a language by adding new expressions. In particular, we could enlarge λ_0, taken to contain no occurrence of "Tr_1," by adding "Tr_1." We could call the newly formed language λ_1: it contains all the sentences of λ_0, together with all sentences which can be formed from these by using "Tr_1"; so it contains σ. Paradox is still avoided: σ does not belong to λ_0, and since Tr_1 is defined only for λ_0 sentences, there is no question of Tr_1 applying to σ. The expression σ (= "σ is not Tr_1") does not belong to λ_0, and so it is not one of which "Tr_1" can be significantly affirmed or denied.

The construction can continue. There is a predicate, call it "Tr_2," true of just the sentences of λ_1, but it cannot belong to λ_1. In general, a predicate T_m cannot belong to a language λ_{n-1} but only to a language of level at least n.

No paradoxical Liar sentence can be formulated in any of the languages in Tarski's hierarchy. How is this supposed to provide a "solution" to the paradox? The paradox arises in our language, so a proper defusing of it must say something about our language, and not merely offer a replacement. In earlier work, Tarski (1933: 153) seems to suggest that the Liar shows that our ordinary language is incoherent. Later, he says that "the semantic conception does conform to a very considerable extent with the commonsense usage" (Tarski 1944: 74). In any case, he is firmly committed to the following: ordinary language is not "semantically closed," where a semantically closed language is one which contains a genuine truth predicate and which can refer to any of its sentences. Yet it seems that our ordinary language is, in this sense, semantically closed. There is no doubt that Tarski's position involves some departure from what we are intuitively inclined to think.

Wherever we encounter paradox, some such departure from intuitive ways of thinking is mandatory. Even so, it is tempting to see how small one can make the departure. One idea in the present connection is that our ordinary language is implicitly a hierarchy of languages, none of which is semantically closed. The plethora of distinct unclosed languages generates an illusion of a single closed one.

A difficulty with this suggestion is that there would appear to be nothing in our usage that reflects the appropriate sensitivity to Tarski-style, fixed-in-advance levels. For example, suppose I say:

What you said just now is not true.

On the face of it, anyone, including myself, could quite well know what I have said without knowing what you have said. (Imagine a game on the lines of paper, stone, and scissors, in which two players have to make a simultaneous declaration. The task of one is to say whether the other has declared something true. Normally things work well: you declare "Snow is white" and I declare "Not true!" and you win. But what happens when I declare "Not true" and you declare "You win"? My declaration is intelligible in advance of knowing the content of yours.) On a hierarchical view in which levels are fixed in advance, something in my use of this sentence determines an association between "true" and some level. Presumably the normal (default) level would be 1. If you have said "Snow is white," there is no problem. But suppose you have said "What MS will say is true." On the present theory, the intelligibility of my utterance requires my "true" to be on a higher level than yours; but if my utterance can be understood without knowing what you have said, its level of truth must get fixed independently of the content of what you have said. This suggests that we cannot successfully apply this kind of hierarchy response to natural language in this way. (However, compare Burge 1979.)

Semantical defects: self-reference, circularity, revenge

Responses to the Liar in terms of levels entail that L is semantically defective, that is, does not say anything, true or false, because it does not respect the syntactical constraints which the levels impose. The idea that L is semantically defective can be implemented in other ways. For example, many philosophers in the twentieth century claimed that what is wrong with L is that it refers to itself. This idea, at least in any simple form, is incorrect and inadequate.

It is incorrect because a sentence can refer to itself, as for example this very sentence does, without leading to any kind of semantic defect or paradox. Sentential self-reference cannot be the whole source of Liar paradoxes (see Barwise and Etchemendy 1987: 15–16). It is inadequate because one can construct Liar paradoxes without using any sentence which refers to itself. One example of this phenomenon involves Liar cycles like the following.

(A) (said by α on Monday): Everything β will say on Tuesday is true.
(B) (said by β on Tuesday): Nothing α said on Monday is true.

If α and β said nothing other than, respectively, (A) and (B) on, respectively, Monday and Tuesday, we have a paradox of essentially the Liar type. Suppose (B) is true; then (A) is not true, and β will say something not true on Tuesday. Since β only says (B), (B) is not true. So if (B) is true, then it is not true. Suppose (B) is not true; then α said something true on Monday. Since α only said (A), (A) is true, that is, everything β will say on Tuesday is true. This includes (B), so (B) is true. Thus if (B) is not true, it is true.

Neither of the sentences in the story literally refers to itself. Rather, there is a kind of circle, so perhaps we should talk of "circular reference" rather than self-reference. As the circularity doesn't strictly involve reference at all, but rather quantification, it might be safer still just to speak of circularity. Many have seen some kind of circularity at the root of the paradoxes (including Russell); but what kind, exactly?

Russell's idea was that both truth-related and class-related paradoxes arise through infringing what he called the "vicious circle principle" (VCP), one formulation of which is:

(VCP) No totality can contain members fully specifiable only in terms of itself.

(See Russell 1908: 75, 63; Russell and Whitehead 1910–13: 37.[13]) This is intended as a general metaphysical principle, applicable to classes as well as everything else, and thus also applicable to propositions. The application to classes is straightforward. The Russell class, R, of classes which are not members of themselves, is defined as follows (see also pp. 371–73):

for anything y, y ε R iff ¬ (y ε y).

In Russell's eyes, the quantification "for anything, y" introduces a totality, the totality of things which are values of the variable. Suppose this totality contains R. Since the only proper specification of R is the displayed sentence just given, this means that the totality would contain a member, R, fully specifiable only in terms of the totality itself, and this is forbidden by VCP. So the totality introduced by "anything" does not contain R, and in that case the instantiation step to the contradictory "R ε R iff ¬ (R ε R)" does not follow.

The application to propositions is less straightforward, but is supposed to work along these lines. Consider the totality whose only member is L. How can we fully specify L? Only by identifying it as "L is not true." So this totality can be fully specified only in terms of itself, so there is no such totality. In this argument, we have to think of L not as a sentence, for that clearly exists and is before our eyes, but rather as the proposition the sentence labeled "L" expresses. In effect, VCP is supposed to entail that the sentence in question expresses no proposition.

From the1970s there was a revival of interest in trying to justify VCP and to show that it rules out all and only the things we want ruled out. One difficulty for it is the apparent consistency of non-foundational set-theory, which allows a class to be a member of itself, in defiance of VCP.[14] Another difficulty is that there appear to be Liar-like paradoxes which do not even involve circularity, let alone self-reference (see Yablo 1993; Sorensen 1998).

Another important line of thought about the Liar springs from the idea that truth must depend upon something outside itself: it needs to be "grounded."[15] If "snow is white" is true, this is because snow is white. The fact that snow is white, or that it is not white, is one that does not involve truth. Our applications of truth and falsehood are intelligible only to the extent that we can find a matter not involving truth (for example, whether or not snow is white) upon which truth can depend. We cannot do this with Liar-paradoxical sentences, and this explains their semantic defectiveness.

Although work inspired by the thought that Liar-sentences are semantically defective has been important philosophically and technically, any view of this kind faces the problem that anything which is semantically defective is not true. On such views, this means that L, being semantically defective, is not true; in short, it means that L is not true. But we have just used a supposedly semantically defective sentence, L itself, to say something we believe to be true. This argument, sometimes called the Liar's Revenge, or Revenge reasoning, needs to be addressed by any adequate treatment of Liar-paradoxes.

Indexicality and circularity

We must distinguish between sentences, regarded as things which can be uttered by different people and on different occasions, and the things which people can say or express by using sentences, which I will call statements (following Strawson's (1950a) usage). One reason to make the distinction is the "indexicality" of language: the fact that the same words may, without ambiguity, be used on different occasions to make different contributions to what is stated, pronouns being a conspicuous example. If you utter the sentence "I am hungry" you make the statement that you are hungry, whereas if I utter the same sentence I make the different statement that I am hungry. The different statements may have different truth values.

Indexicality is at least sometimes at work in Liar-paradoxes. We could expand the story of (A) and (B) by imagining a third utterance:

(C) (said by γ on Tuesday): Nothing α said on Monday is true.

The fact that β and γ use the very same sentence, yet only one of them is circular in the relevant way, shows that paradox-relevant circularity is not a property of sentences as such. Being meaningful or meaningless is a property of sentences. Since there is nothing paradoxical about (C), there is no reason to say it is other than meaningful, and since (B) is the same sentence, it follows that the property which circularity prevents is not that of being meaningful. We need a more refined notion, one sensitive to the use to which a sentence is put on a specific occasion.

Let us assume that bivalence holds for statements: every statement is either true or false. A sentence can be meaningful, yet on a specific occasion be used in such a way as to fail to make a statement (for example, "That elephant is about to charge," said when no elephant is present). Although sentences can be self-referential, or more generally can have the kind of circularity associated with paradox, it may be that statements cannot. Thus, reverting to the example in the previous section, we might be able to justify the claim that whereas both β and γ use the same sentence, only γ thereby succeeds in making a statement. To suppose that β made a statement would be to suppose that some statements are circular in the exemplified way, and the idea is that no statement can be that.

Once we have the distinction between sentence and statement, we need to recast the Liar paradox. Previously, "L" was supposed to label a sentence, but on the present view, "true" cannot be meaningfully applied to a sentence (as opposed to a statement). This means that there is no intelligible supposition that L is true, and this part of the argument to contradiction would break down. We can revive the paradox in the form:

(L*) L* does not express a true statement.

Following the original reasoning, suppose L* does express a true statement. Then things are as it says, so L* does not express a true statement. Suppose it does not express a true statement. Since this is just what it expresses, it does express a true statement. If we say that L* is semantically defective, we immediately generate Revenge reasoning. Since what is semantically defective does not express a statement at all, a fortiori it does not express a true statement; so L* does not express a true statement. We find ourselves trying to use a sentence which, according to our theory, does not express a true statement, in an attempt to express something we take to be true.

By working on the distinction between sentence and statement it may be possible to make sense of this, for a sentence may in one context not be capable of being used to make a statement at all ("that elephant is about to charge," said in the absence of any elephant), even though in another context it can be used to make a true statement. If this applies to the relevant uses of L*, Revenge reasoning will be neutralized.

The general feasibility of such an approach is suggested by cases like the following. Suppose that the following sentence is the only sentence written on the board in room 101:

> The sentence written on the board in room 101 does not express a true statement.

It appears perfectly consistent for me to write on this page that, because of some semantic defect, the sentence written on the board in room 101 does not express a true statement. I use the words which, as written on the board in room 101, are defective, in circumstances in which there is nothing defective about their use. This suggests that the same words, used to refer to the same thing, and applying the same predicate to it, do not necessarily make the same statement. The sentence written on the board in room 101 makes no statement, in its use in room 101; whereas I use those words, on this page, to make a true statement. I did not have to use the same words. Under suitable circumstances I could simply have said "That sentence does not express a true statement." That there are special circumstances under which I can re-use the same words is an accident of our use of language, and does not affect the truth of the statement I wish to make.

After consideration of the paradox generated by L*, the theorist wishes to say that it is semantically defective and so say that *L* does not express a true statement*. The theorist must hold that his use of the italicized words does express a statement, and a true one, and thus differs from the original use of these words. He could have made his point by using the non-paradoxical words "The sentence displayed above does not express a true statement." It is an accident of our labeling conventions that the very words to be condemned can be used to condemn them. In its defective use, L* calls for the impossible, the existence of a self-referential statement; in its non-defective use it does not.

Could the ingenious opponent not devise Liar sentences for which this response is ruled out? (For example, what should be said about "No use of this very sentence makes a true statement"?) Even if the answer is No, the theorist clearly owes some more details about exactly what features of the shift in context render a sentence which expresses no statement in the first context express a truth in the second.

Tyler Burge (1979) has contributed to this last problem, suggesting that there are different levels of truth, and which level is at issue is fixed not by the meaning of the sentence, but by the statement it is used to make on a given occasion. This approach based on indexical levels avoids many of the difficulties associated with Tarski's hierarchy, which attaches to sentences rather than to statements.

Russell's paradox: a close cousin?

Are the class-related and truth-related paradoxes totally different, or essentially the same? This is a paradigm of a philosophical logical question. Although Russell, as we have seen, thought of them as variations on a single theme, Frank Ramsey (1925: 183–4) urged that the paradoxes are different in kind, and his view has been dominant through most of the century. He based the distinction on their different subject matter: the logical paradoxes, under which heading he included Russell's paradox, arise from logical notions, like that of class; the semantic paradoxes, under which he included the Liar, arise from semantic notions, like that of truth. Before discussing the disagreement between Ramsey and Russell, let me briefly reconstruct Russell's paradox.

Because we are inclined to think that every intelligible condition determines a class, we are inclined to think that there is a class, R, whose members are just those classes which are not members of themselves. This is the Russell class, and the paradox consists in the combination of the demonstration that there can be no such class with the intuitions which support principles entailing that there is such a class. The basic intuition is something along these lines:

(CE) For every intelligible condition F, there is a class x, such that: for anything y, $y \, \varepsilon \, x$ if and only if y satisfies F.

This entails that there is such a class as R if there is the intelligible condition *being a class that is not a member of itself*, for then

There is a class, R, such that for anything y, $y \, \varepsilon \, R$ iff $\neg \, (y \, \varepsilon \, y)$

and by instantiation we get the absurd

(RP) There is a class, R, such that $R \, \varepsilon \, R$ iff $\neg \, (R \, \varepsilon \, R)$.

In addition to Ramsey's basis for claiming that Russell's paradox and the Liar are different in kind (the fact that they turn upon different concepts), there are other differences: there is no analogue in Russell's paradox of Revenge reasoning. There is an immediate problem with the idea that there is no statement expressed by L*, namely that it seems to follow that L* does not express a true statement. No such twist is consequent on the assertion that there is no class R. For the class paradox, there is quite widespread agreement on what we need to say: that there is no class R. What is unclear is how this can be justified. For the Liar, it is not clear even what ought to be said, let alone how to justify it.

So there are certainly some differences between the paradoxes. There are also similarities, and I enumerate five.

(1) The Class paradox resembles a paradox about properties, and the Property paradox in turn resembles the Liar. If we think that every intelligible condition determines a property, then there is a property, P, of being a non-self-applicable property (e.g. the property of being a man is non-self-applicable, since no property is a man). But this property, P, is self-applicable iff it is not self-applicable. One dimension of resemblance is with Russell's paradox, and another is with the contradiction that L truly predicates truth of itself if and only if it does not. Where the Property contradiction uses the notion of *not true of*, embedded in the notion of non-self-applicability, the Liar contradiction uses the notion of *not true*, a property that a sentence or statement may possess.

(2) Both the Class paradox and the Liar seem to involve self-reference, or some similar circularity.

(3) The principles appealed to in the derivation of the two paradoxes (CE: For every intelligible condition F, there is a class x, such that: for any object y, $y \, \varepsilon \, x$ if and only if y satisfies F; and (T): X is true iff p) are structurally similar, and appear to play similarly constitutive roles with respect to the intuitive notions of class and truth.

On the side of derivation, the comparison is that the schema

for any object y, $y \, \varepsilon \, x$ iff y is F

yields a contradiction when x is replaced by a name, say R, for the Russell class, and F by the condition, expressed in terms of this name, that supposedly defines membership for that class, " $\neg \ldots \varepsilon$ R." Similarly, the schema

X is true iff p

yields a contradiction when X is replaced by a name, say L, for the Liar sentence, and p by the condition, expressed in terms of this name, that supposedly defines truth for that sentence, "L is not true."

On the side of roles, the comparison is that just as (CE) appears constitutive of our pre-theoretical notion of a class, so (T) appears constitutive of our pre-theoretical notion of truth. (CE) determines what it is for a class to exist; (T) determines what it is for a truth condition to exist.

(4) Hierarchies have been used in response to both kinds of paradox, beginning with one of the earliest systematic treatments (Russell 1908). It is natural to suppose that we should think of classes as initially constructed out of non-classes, with each constructional step drawing only upon entities which have already been constructed. Likewise, it is natural to suppose that we should think of statements ascribing truth as initially applied to statements free of the notion of truth, with each constructional step drawing only upon statements which have already been constructed.

(5) Russell's classification of the Class paradox and the Liar as of a common kind is based on the claim that they both derive from an infringement of the vicious circle principle.

A formal vindication of Russell's claim that the paradoxes belong to a significant common kind has been provided by Priest (1994). This claim, as I have just expressed it, is consistent with these paradoxes also belonging to significantly different kinds.

The Class and Liar paradoxes, like most things, are similar in some respects, dissimilar in others. Classification matters here because of the constraints it imposes on proper responses to the paradoxes. (Many other paradoxes need to find their place in a classification; see Priest 1994.) If two paradoxes are essentially similar, similar in what really matters, then it is proper to respond in essentially similar ways. For example, if the Class paradox calls for a hierarchy of levels, and the Liar is essentially similar, then it too calls for a hierarchy of levels. If an adequate conception of classes should allow non-well-founded classes, e.g. the class α whose only member is α, and the Liar is essentially similar, then our response to it should allow for analogous circularity. Russell's allegedly common solution to the two paradoxes, his Ramified Theory of Types, has a somewhat specious uniformity, since some of its more complex features are motivated by matters relating to the Liar rather than the Class paradox.

To infer that the paradoxes require a uniform solution, we must show more than that there is a single kind to which they belong. (Unless we have some principled way of restricting kinds, for any two things there is a kind to which both belong.) We need in addition to show that this common kind reveals their common essential nature. I doubt, however, whether this can be done quite independently of views about what response is appropriate to each.

The future

Philosophical logic played a central role in analytic philosophy in the twentieth century. Was this a passing phase, or is its influence here to stay? A proper answer involves the distinction, noted towards the end of an earlier section '"Logical form": the holy grail of philosophical logic,' between philosophical logic understood as the Russell–Quine–Davidson program, and philosophical logic understood as the philosophical investigation of the central concepts of logic, like truth, validity, and entailment. Investigations of the latter kind have a long history, stretching back to Aristotle and beyond. There is every reason to think that they will continue to play an important part in any future work in philosophy. The Russell–Quine–Davidson program, by contrast, has had a much shorter history, arising as it did in the twentieth century. I suspect that its fading is already discernible. Philosophers may well resort to logical formalizations in order to clarify claims couched in natural language sentences and arguments. They are increasingly reluctant to affirm that such clarifications reveal something otherwise hidden in the nature of natural language sentences or ordinary thoughts. At the same time, the systematic study of language has developed in ways which make the kind of approach which Davidson championed seem both unnecessary and distorting. The hypothesis that ordinary speakers translate natural language sentences into the formulae of first-order logic has low initial plausibility. As Strawson presciently stressed (1950a), there is something about the rigidity of logical formulae which makes them a poor match for so flexible an instrument as natural language. I will illustrate with the example of the anaphoric dependence of pronouns.

Consider the following exchange:

A: We have a new neighbor.
B: I know. I saw her moving her stuff in yesterday.
A: She looks nice.

Given just the resources of classical logic, how should one understand the occurrences of the feminine pronouns "her," "she"? The only option is to see them as variables bound by an existential quantifier introduced by "a new neighbor." In classical logic, only closed formulae can be properly evaluated as true or false: a formula with a free variable can be true or false of objects, but not true or false absolutely.[16] Applied to the example, this means that either A's first utterance or B's utterance is not truth evaluable, since it will not be represented as corresponding to a closed formula. Suppose that A's utterance is so represented. Then the "her" in B's utterance will be represented by an unbound variable, so the utterance is represented as not truth evaluable. Suppose B's utterance is represented as closed. If this is possible at all (and the possibility would involve some changes in the standard definitions of closure), it is by representing A's utterance as open, and so as not truth evaluable: it will have a missing right-hand parenthesis, to enable the scope of its existential quantifier to reach to B's "her." This is a completely implausible upshot. In any case, as A's second utterance shows, the conversation may go on indefinitely, and no one could know when to insert that final right-hand parenthesis. Classical notions of variable binding are quite inadequate to represent this kind of anaphoric dependence in natural language.

This observation was, historically, the point of departure for a new approach to language, Discourse Representation Theory or DRT (see Kamp 1981; Kamp and Reyle 1993), which explicitly included the aim of doing more justice than could be done classically to the psychological reality of language processing. It is an example of the kind of approach to language in which the dynamics of discourse are not idealized away, but are treated as central (perhaps "dynamic semantics" might be a suitable phrase for the general nature of the approach, though some also use it in a narrower way); such approaches seem to me likely to make the notion of logical form, as exploited in the Russell–Davidson tradition, obsolete. Whereas in the Russellian tradition truth and reference are essential to an explanation of "meaning," dynamic theories describe meaning in terms of the way it forces or permits changes in the informational states of an interpreter as interpretation proceeds.

The structures whereby DRT represents natural language (these include nested boxes, arrows, and first-order formulae) are not identical with natural language sentences, and there is nothing in the methodology which requires that all interpretively valuable features can be introspectively identified in a way fitted to systematic theory; there is nothing to preclude "null" or "unsounded" elements" as theoretical posits. So are not DRT structures party to the original program of logical form, the only difference being that these more sophisticated structures replace first-order formulae? Should we not see the same methodology at work, but with a change in what is to count as the "logic" in "logical form"? Can it be right to see anything more radical than an improvement of detail?

A difference between Russell's approach and the approach exemplified by DRT and other dynamic semantical theories is this: whereas Russell began with the assumption that the structures of thought are the very structures found in first-order logic (or, more exactly, in the higher-order logic of *Principia Mathematica*), the new approach makes no assumptions of this kind, and introduces its theoretical structures with no aim other than to provide a revealing description of the data of language use. This transformation of aim, and the consequent weakening of the influence of first-order logic as a basis upon which to describe natural language, constitutes a definitive movement away from the program of logical form as implemented by Russell, Quine, and Davidson.

Turning to the other interpretation of "philosophical logic," according to which it is the philosophical study of the concepts important to logic (truth, validity, entailment, consistency, and so): no decline in the importance of this theoretical activity can be envisaged, so long as philosophy itself continues to be practiced. It is in the nature of philosophy to reflect on its aims and tools, attempting to free itself of impossible or worthless goals and of ineffective or distorting tools. The assessment of its arguments as valid or otherwise, its claims as true or otherwise, its propositions as related or not related by entailment: these invite reflection on the nature of the assessment itself. What is it for an argument to be valid, a belief to be true, or for propositions to be related by entailment? So long as philosophy is practiced, in the tradition we inherit from Plato and Aristotle, these questions will not go away.[17]

Notes

Acknowledgment: This essay is based upon an earlier publication in Italian: "Logica filosofica," in N. Vassallo and F. D'Agostini (eds.) *Storia della filosofia analitica*, © Giulio Einaudi editore, 2002. My thanks to the editors and publisher for allowing me to publish this English version.

1 When Quine reprinted this article, he replaced this famous sentence by a more nuanced one: "To be assumed as an entity is, purely and simply, to be reckoned as the value of a variable" (1961: 13).

2 "Traditional logic regarded the two propositions 'Socrates is mortal' and 'All men are mortal' as being of the same form; Peano and Frege showed that they are utterly different in form. ... the philosophical importance of the advance which they made is impossible to exaggerate" (Russell 1914: 50).

3 We must also pretend that "Desdemona" and "Cassio" are proper names in the logical sense, that is, are not to be analyzed as really definite descriptions.

4 The way in which I attempt to answer it (Sainsbury 2002: essay v) on Russell's behalf could be adapted to a range of views about the nature of propositions.

5 Wittgenstein writes as if he thought that Russell disagreed and regarded logical constants as non-linguistic entities: "it becomes manifest that there are no 'logical objects' or 'logical constants' (in Frege's and Russell's sense)" (1921: 5.4).

6 The claim that proper names like "Vulcan" have as their logical forms definite descriptions like "the planet between Mercury and the sun which is responsible for the perturbations in Mercury's orbit" has been much disputed within the philosophical logic tradition.

7 The "!" serves to restrict the quantifier to "predicative functions," ones which do not infringe the vicious circle principle (see below).

8 Perhaps it was unfair of Strawson to claim that Austin had given no truth-free specification of the nature of facts; see Austin 1961.

9 There is no need for a correct definition of truth to entail, for example, that the first sentence of the third section of Sainsbury's essay on philosophical logic is true iff the concept of truth has played a central role in most philosophical traditions.

10 This is a narrower condition than the one earlier used by Tarski (1933), which required only that the sentence in the position of "p" translate the sentence named by the expression in "X"-position. The earlier position is more liberal in that identity is presumably not the only form of correct translation.

11 Drawing on work by Prior, some recent discussions suggest alternative approaches to sentence quantifiers: see Williamson 1999; Künne 2003.

12 Class-theoretic paradoxes were known to Cantor as early as 1895 (see Kneale and Kneale 1962: 652). Russell's first published account of his paradox is in 1903.

13 Russell may have borrowed the idea of a vicious circle from Poincaré: see Russell and Whitehead 1910–13: 37n).

14 In non-foundational set-theory, sets are thought of in terms of membership diagrams. The set consisting just of London and the set whose members are the number 7 and Mount Everest (conventionally written: {London, {7, Everest}}) can be represented by the diagram:

$$\text{London} \qquad \qquad$$
$$7 \qquad \text{Everest}$$

Here each blob represents a set, and the branches beneath it represent its members. The following diagram would then represent the set α whose only member is α:

α

The theory of such diagrams is demonstrably consistent relative to classical set theory. A general account of the evils of circularity, like Russell's VCP, would do well to try to break the link between the diagrams and sets.

Non-foundational set theory owes a great deal to Aczel (1987). A good account, well adapted to present concerns, is by Barwise and Etchemendy (1987: ch. 3).

15 Classic texts are by Hertzberger (1970) and Kripke (1975).

16 There is an overall relativization to a model; it leaves the essence of the point unaffected.

17 Many thanks to two anonymous referees for this volume, who provided helpful comments.

References

Aczel, P. (1987) *Lectures on Nonwellfounded Sets*. Stanford, CA: CSLI Lecture Notes, No. 9.

Austin, J. L. (1950) "Truth." *Proceedings of the Aristotelian Society, Supplementary Volume 24*: 111–28.

_____ (1961) "Unfair to facts." In *Philosophical Papers*, Oxford: Clarendon Press, pp. 154–74.

Barwise, J. and J. Etchemendy (1987) *The Liar: An Essay in Truth and Circularity*. New York and Oxford: Oxford University Press.

Blackburn, S. and K. Simmons (1999) *Truth*. Oxford: Oxford University Press.

Burge, T. (1978) "Buridan and epistemic paradox." *Philosophical Studies 34*: 21–35.

_____ (1979) "Semantic paradox." *Journal of Philosophy* 76: 169–98. Repr. in R. L. Martin (ed.) *Recent Essays on Truth and the Liar Paradox*, Oxford: Oxford University Press, 1984, pp. 83–117.

Cargile, J. (1970) "Davidson's notion of logical form." *Inquiry* 13: 129–39.

Chomsky, N. (1957) *Syntactic Structures*. The Hague: Mouton.

Davidson, D (1967) "The logical form of action sentences." In N. Rescher (ed.) *The Logic of Decision and Action*, Pittsburgh: University of Pittsburgh Press, pp. 81–95, 115–20. Repr. in *Essays on Actions and Events*, Oxford: Oxford University Press, 1980, pp. 105–22.

_____ (1970) "Action and reaction." *Inquiry* 13: 140–8. Repr. as "Reply to Cargile" in *Essays on Actions and Events*, Oxford: Clarendon Press, 1984, pp. 137–48. (Page references are to the 1984 reprint.)

Dummett, M. (1973a) *Frege: Philosophy of Language*. London: Duckworth.

_____ (1973b) "The philosophical basis of intuitionistic logic." In H. E. Rose and J. C. Shepherdson (eds.) *Logical Colloquium '73*, Amsterdam: North Holland, pp. 5–40. Repr. in *Truth and Other Enigmas*, London: Duckworth, 1978: 215–47.

_____ (1978) "Preface." In *Truth and Other Enigmas*, London: Duckworth.

Evans, G. (1982) *The Varieties of Reference*. Oxford: Clarendon Press.

Frege, G. (1980) [1902] "Letter to Russell (22 June)." In *Philosophical and Mathematical Correspondence*, ed. G. Gabriel et al., Oxford: Blackwell, pp. 152–4.

_____ (1979) [1897] "Logic." In *Gottlob Frege: Posthumous Writings*, ed. H. Hermes, F. Kambartel, and F. Kaulbach, trans. P. Long and R. White, Chicago: University of Chicago Press, pp. 126–51.

Hertzberger, H. (1970) "Paradoxes of grounding in semantics." *Journal of Philosophy* 67: 145–67.

Hornstein, N. (1995) *Logical Form*. Cambridge, MA: Blackwell.

Horwich, P. (1990) *Truth*. Oxford: Blackwell.

Kamp, H. (1981). "A theory of truth and semantic representation." In J. A. G. Groenendijk, T. M. V. Janssen, and M. B. J. Stockhof (eds.) *Formal Methods in the Study of Language*, Amsterdam: Mathematisch Centrum, vol. 1: 277–322.

Kamp, H. and U. Reyle (1993) *From Discourse to Logic*. Dordrecht: Kluwer.

Kneale, W. and M. Kneale (1962) *The Development of Logic*. Oxford: Clarendon Press.

Kripke, S. (1975) "Outline of a theory of truth." *Journal of Philosophy* 72: 690–716. Repr. in R. L. Martin, *Recent Essays on Truth and the Liar Paradox*, Oxford: Oxford University Press, 1984, pp. 53–81.

Künne, W. (2003) *Conceptions of Truth*. Oxford: Oxford University Press.

Lycan, W. G. (1984) *Logical Form in Natural Language*. Cambridge, MA: MIT Press.

Martin, R. L. (ed.) (1984) *Recent Essays on Truth and the Liar Paradox*. Oxford: Oxford University Press.

Neale, S. (1993) "Logical form and LF." In C. Otero (ed.) *Noam Chomsky: Critical Assessments*, London: Routledge, pp. 788–838.

Priest, G. (1994) "The structure of the paradoxes of self-reference." *Mind* 103: 25–34.

Quine, W. V. O. (1948) "On what there is." *Review of Metaphysics* 2: 21–38. Repr. in *From a Logical Point of View*, 2nd edn., Cambridge, MA: Harvard University Press, 1961, pp. 1–19.

Ramsey, F. (1925) "The foundations of mathematics." *Proceedings of the London Mathematical Society* 25: 338–84. Repr. in D. H. Mellor (ed.) *F. P. Ramsey: Philosophical Papers*, Cambridge: Cambridge University Press, 1990, pp. 174–224. (Page references are to the 1990 reprint.)

Russell, B. (1903) *The Principles of Mathematics*. Cambridge: Cambridge University Press.

_____ (1905) "On denoting." *Mind* 14: 79–93. Repr. in R. C. Marsh (ed.) *Logic and Knowledge*, London: Allen & Unwin, 1956, pp. 41–56.

_____ (1908) "Mathematical logic as based on the theory of types." *American Journal of Mathematics* 30: 222–62. Repr. in R. C. Marsh (ed.) *Logic and Knowledge*, London: Allen & Unwin, 1956, pp. 59–102. (Page references are to the 1956 reprint.)

_____ (1912). *The Problems of Philosophy*. Since 1959 published by Oxford University Press (Oxford and New York).

_____ [1913] *Theory of Knowledge*. First published in E. R. Eames and K. Blackwell (eds.) *The Collected Papers of Bertrand Russell*, vol. 7: *Theory of Knowledge, The 1913 Manuscript*, London: Allen & Unwin, 1984.

_____ (1914) "Logic as the essence of philosophy." In *Our Knowledge of the External World*, London: Allen & Unwin, pp. 42–69.

_____ (1959) *My Philosophical Development*. London: Allen & Unwin.

Russell, B. and A. N. Whitehead (1910–13) *Principia Mathematica*. Cambridge: Cambridge University Press.

Sainsbury, R. M. (2002) "How can some thing mean something?" In *Departing From Frege*, London: Routledge.

Sommers, F. (1982) *The Logic of Natural Language*. Oxford: Clarendon Press.

Sorensen, R. (1998) "Yablo's paradox and kindred infinite Liars." *Mind* 107: 137–55.

Strawson, P. (1950a) "On referring." *Mind* 59: 269–86. Repr. in *Logico-Linguistic Papers*, London: Methuen, 1971, pp. 1–27.

_____ (1950b) "Truth." *Proceedings of the Aristotelian Society, Supplementary Volume 24*: 129–56. Repr. in G. Pitcher (ed.) *Truth*, Englewood Cliffs, NJ: Prentice-Hall, 1964, pp. 32–53. (Page references are to the 1964 reprint.)

Tarski, A. (1933) "The concept of truth in formalized languages." Repr. in *Logic, Semantics, Metamathematics*, Oxford and New York: Clarendon Press, 1956, pp. 152–278. (Page references are to the 1956 reprint.)

_____ (1944) "The semantic conception of truth and the foundations of semantics." *Philosophy and Phenomenological Research* 4: 341–75. Repr. in H. Feigel and W. Sellars (eds.) *Readings in Philosophical Analysis*, New York: Appleton-Century-Crofts, 1949: 52–94. (Page references are to the 1949 reprint.)

Williamson, T. (1999) "Truthmakers and the converse Barcan formula." *Dialectica* 53: 253–70.

Wittgenstein, L. (1921) *Tractatus Logico-Philosophicus*. London: Routledge & Kegan Paul.

Wright, C. (1992) *Truth and Objectivity*. Cambridge, MA: Harvard University Press.

Yablo, S. (1993) "Paradox without self-reference." *Analysis* 53: 251–2.

Further reading

A good starting point for work in philosophical logic is Bertrand Russell's "On denoting" (*Mind* 144: 79–93, reprinted in R. C. Marsh (ed.) *Logic and Knowledge*, London: Routledge & Kegan Paul, 1956, pp. 41–56), or alternatively his later and more accessible expression of essentially the same view in chapter 16 of his *Introduction to Mathematical Philosophy* (London: Allen & Unwin, 1919). This is a paradigm of a contribution to philosophical logic, and even though it does not make explicit mention of the idea of logical form, the theory can be rightly thought of as a proposal about the logical form of judgments expressible with definite descriptions. If one's main interest were in the theory of descriptions, one would consult Stephen Neale's excellent *Descriptions* (Cambridge, MA: MIT Press, 1990) and the collection edited by Gary Ostertag, *Definite Descriptions: A Reader* (Cambridge, MA: MIT Press, 1998). If one's main interest is in pursuing the idea of philosophical logic and logical form, one might move forwards in time to Russell's explicit introduction of the term "philosophical logic" in "Logic as the essence of philosophy," in *Our Knowledge of the External World* (London: George Allen and Unwin, 1914, pp. 42–69); and also, in order to improve the historical perspective, backwards to his *Principles of Mathematics* (Cambridge: Cambridge University Press, 1903) which, though designed to establish the logicist thesis that mathematics is part of logic, contains some detailed and often agonized discussions of such philosophical logical topics as proper names and denoting expressions. It also contains the first published explicit formulation of Russell's paradox.

Russell's conception of logical form almost certainly influenced Rudolph Carnap, who certainly influenced Quine and, thereby, Davidson. In, for example, Carnap's *The Logical Syntax of Language* (London: Routledge & Kegan Paul, 1937) we find a highly Russellian vision of the dissolution of philosophy into either empirical science or logic: "we shall here maintain that all these remaining philosophical questions [all those which remain once all empirical questions have been assigned to the appropriate special science] are logical questions. ... once philosophy is purified of all unscientific elements, only the logic of science remains. ... *the logic of science takes the place of the inextricable tangle of problems which is known as philosophy*" (p. 279). Carnap's "logic of science" is quite close to Russell's "philosophical logic."

For many years Russell's conception of logical form, and his program in philosophical logic, escaped explicit challenge (although there was plenty of philosophical activity, even within the Anglo-Saxon tradition, that did not conform to it). A serious attack on many Russellian preconceptions is found in Peter Strawson's "On referring" (*Mind* 59 (1950): 269–86, reprinted in his *Logico-Linguistic Papers*, London: Methuen, 1971, pp. 1–27). The main target is Russell's theory of descriptions, but in the course of the attack the very idea of straitjacketing ordinary language into "logical forms" is challenged, along with the thought that one can do justice to the relevant facts of meaning without taking context of use into account.

By the late 1960s, the methodology of logical form was receiving explicit and not always complimentary attention both from philosophers and from linguists. Donald Davidson's papers "The logical form of action sentences" (in N. Rescher (ed.) *The Logic of Decision and Action*, Pittsburgh: University of Pittsburgh Press, 1967, reprinted in his *Essays on Actions and Events*, Oxford: Oxford University Press, 1980, pp. 105–22) and "Action and reaction" (*Inquiry* 13: 140–8, 1970, reprinted as "Reply to Cargile" in his *Essays on Actions and Events*, Oxford: Clarendon Press, 1984, pp. 137–48) are essential reading, as is also the article by James Cargile which prompted the second one ("Davidson's notion of logical form," *Inquiry* 13 (1970): 129–39). Davidsonian approaches have been developed by others, for example William Lycan (*Logical Form in Natural Language*, Cambridge, MA: MIT Press, 1984), which includes a useful summary sketch of relevant historical developments at pp. 4–9. The doctrine that logical form should reveal all the logically significant features of a sentence has been attacked by John Etchemendy ("The doctrine of logic as form," *Linguistics and Philosophy* 6 (1983): 319–34), who states this aspect of the logical form program as follows: "sentences with different logical properties [must] be assigned different logical structures" (p. 319). In the mainstream logical form tradition, set by Russell, Quine, and Davidson, it was argued, or more often taken for granted, that logical forms would be, or be represented by, formulae of familiar languages (first-order languages or their extensions). There is no reason in principle why one should not combine the quest for formal rigor and the supposition that logical forms and surface forms may differ with a very different conception of the underlying logic. This possibility is impressively fleshed out by Fred Sommers in his *The Logic of Natural Language* (Oxford: Clarendon Press, 1982).

Linguists introduced the notion of logical form, or the LF level of representation, with rather different motivations, and it is a controversial question to what extent linguists' LF coincides with philosophers' logical form. Showing the linguists' notion in use, a classic text is R. May's *Logical Form: Its Structure and Derivation* (Cambridge, MA: MIT Press, 1985), and a more recent one is Norbert Hornstein's *Logical Form* (Cambridge, MA: Blackwell, 1995). Some linguists, like Greg Carlson in "Logical form: types of evidence" (*Linguistics and Philosophy* 6 (1983): 295–317) are disposed to start with some skepticism about the necessity for LF in a complete account of language. For an assessment of the relation between logical form and LF see Stephen Neale ("Logical form and LF," in C. Otero (ed.) *Noam Chomsky: Critical Assessments*, London: Routledge, 1993, pp. 788–838), who concludes that logical form in the philosophers' sense coincides with the linguists' LF, the upshot being that "Chomsky's work on the syntax of natural language has application well beyond theoretical linguistics" (p. 827). On the other hand, Daniel Sperber and Deirdre Wilson (*Relevance: Communication and Cognition*, Oxford: Blackwell 1995) use the notion of logical form for the semantic aspects of an utterance which are recovered in utterance interpretation by an automatic process of decoding. They claim that the logical form may not have complete truth conditions and typically underdetermines the proposition expressed. This usage is in clear conflict with most philosophical conceptions of logical form, which apply to sentences rather than to utterances, and are assumed unambiguously to express a complete truth condition.

The use of the notion of logical form to derive ontological conclusions faces the difficulty that the original sentence and its logical form are usually supposed to be equivalent in a way that should ensure that they have the same ontology (that is, that the same things need to exist for the one to be true as for the other). If "Shem kicked Shaun" and "There is a kick which Shem gave Shaun" are equivalent, should we say that since the former apparently does not require the existence of kicks, nor does the latter? Or should we say, rather, as Davidson urges, that since the latter does require the existence of kicks, so does the former? W. V. O. Quine tries to resolve the problem by denying that the equivalence is tight enough to preserve ontology, saying that it is enough that the preferred sentence, the paraphrase, be usable for more or less the same purposes as the one with the dubious ontology (see his *Word and Object*, New York: Technology Press of MIT and John Wiley & Sons, 1960, p. 214). This has not convinced all commentators: see, for example, William Alston ("Ontological commitment," *Philosophical Studies* 9 (1958): 8–17), and for a clear statement of the problem and an unusual solution, Stephen Yablo ("A paradox of existence," in Anthony Everett and Thomas Hofweber (eds.) *Empty Names, Fiction and the Puzzles of Non-Existence*, Stanford, CA: CSLI Publications, 2000, pp. 275–312, esp. Appendix A).

Possible starting points for work on truth include the following: Susan Haack's *The Philosophy of Logics* (Cambridge: Cambridge University Press, 1978), a book which also provides a good treatment of a number of other themes in philosophical logic; John Mackie's *Truth, Probability and Paradox* (Oxford: Oxford University Press, 1973); Paul Horwich's *Truth* (Oxford: Blackwell, 1990); Crispin Wright's *Truth and Objectivity* (Cambridge, MA: Harvard University Press, 1992); the collection of essays edited by Simon Blackburn and Keith Simmons, *Truth* (Oxford: Oxford University Press, 1999), which reprints some of the most important papers on this topic since the early 1900s; Scott Soames's *Understanding Truth* (Oxford: Oxford University Press, 1999); Wolfgang Künne's *Conceptions of Truth* (Oxford: Oxford University Press, 2003); and Aladdin M. Yaqūb's *The Liar Speaks the Truth: A Defense of the Revision Theory of Truth* (New York: Oxford University Press, 1993), which stresses the significance of the Tarski-equivalences. Horwich offers a deflationist account of truth, according to which it does not amount to a "substantive" property: all we need to know about it is given by equivalences similar to Tarski-equivalences; he also gives useful summary statements and criticisms of other positions. Wright pursues a modified anti-realist line, in which truth in many areas is applicable in a way which fails to guarantee objectivity of the subject matter. Blackburn and Simmons give a useful overview of deflationary or minimalist positions in their editorial introduction, and many of the essays they collect pursue that theme. David Wiggins provides a valuable sketch of connections between truth, meaning, assertion, and convergence in his "What would be a substantial theory of truth?" (in Z. van Straaten (ed.) *Philosophical Subjects: Essays Presented to P. F. Strawson*, Oxford: Oxford University Press, 1980, pp. 187–221). A different approach is taken by Julian Dodd in *An Identity Theory of Truth* (Basingstoke: Macmillan, 2000), who argues that a correspondence theory cannot give an appropriate account of facts which, as Strawson earlier suggested, are nothing but true thoughts, and this leads Dodd to his ingeniously defended version of an identity theory: to be true is to be identical with a fact.

It is often said that St Paul provides a version of the Liar (Epistle to Titus 1: 12–13):

12. One of themselves, even a prophet of their own, said, The Cretans are always liars, evil beasts, slow bellies.

13. This witness is true. Wherefore rebuke them sharply, that they may be sound in the faith.

It is not clear that the saint sees any logical as opposed to moral problem. For a thirteenth-century discussion of many Liar-like paradoxes see John Buridan's *Sophismata* (translated and edited by G. E. Hughes under the title *John Buridan on Self-Reference*, Cambridge: Cambridge University Press, 1982). Russell's account of truth-related paradoxes and their relation to class paradoxes can be found in his "Mathematical logic as based on the theory of types" (reprinted in R. L. Marsh (ed.) *Logic and Knowledge*, London: Allen & Unwin, 1956, pp. 59–102) and in the Introduction to his and Whitehead's *Principia Mathematica* (Cambridge: Cambridge University Press, 1910–13).

A starting point for contemporary discussions of Liar-like paradoxes is Mackie's *Truth, Probability and Paradox* and the essays in R. M. Martin's collection, *Recent Essays on Truth and the Liar Paradox* (Oxford: Oxford University Press, 1984). For an intriguing monograph, which begins with a very clear overview of the problem, see Jon Barwise and John Etchemendy's *The Liar: An Essay in Truth and Circularity* (New York and Oxford: Oxford University Press, 1987). (This work also contains an accessible introduction to Aczels's theory of non-wellfounded sets.) Alfred Tarski's "The concept of truth in formalized languages" (first published in Polish in 1933 and reprinted in his *Logic, Semantics, Metamathematics*, Oxford and New York: Clarendon Press, 1956, pp. 152–278) fairly quickly becomes dauntingly technical, but the early pages set out clearly the main philosophical motivations. In this paper he asserts: "In [colloquial] language it seems to be impossible to define the notion of truth or even to use this notion in a consistent manner and in agreement with the laws of logic" (p. 153). In the more popular version of some of his ideas in "The semantic conception of truth and the foundations of semantics" (reprinted in A. P. Martinich (ed.) *The Philosophy of Language*, 3rd edn., Oxford: Oxford University Press, 1996, pp. 61–84), he seems to take a more gentle line with ordinary language: "I happen to believe that the semantic conception does conform to a very considerable extent with the commonsense usage" (p. 74). He offers a later popular account in the *Scientific American* article "Truth and proof" (194 (1969): 63–77). Anil Gupta and Nuel Belnap provide (Section II) a careful statement of Tarski's precise premises, together with a challenge to the full generality of the conclusion Tarski drew, in their *The Revision Theory of Truth* (Cambridge, MA: MIT Press, 1993). For an excellent and accurate account of Tarski's work, stressing in particular the route Tarski saw from the semantic conception of truth to the Gödelian incompleteness of proofs in languages with reasonable expressive resources, see Jeff Ketland's "Deflationism and Tarski's paradise" (*Mind* 108 (1999): 69–94). Ketland suggests that the fact that Tarski's theory is in a certain sense non-conservative poses a difficulty for those who see in Tarski's work support for a deflationary or minimalist view of truth.

This conclusion needs to be set alongside Yaqūb's claim that a deflationary *conception* of truth suggests that a proper *theory* of truth will be non-deflationary (*The Liar Speaks the Truth*, p. 42).

For a post-Tarskian attempt to work out a suitable notion of circularity, see Charles Chihara's *Ontology and the Vicious Circle Principle* (Ithaca, NY: Cornell University Press, 1973). Jørgen Jørgensen, in "Some reflections on reflexivity" (*Mind* 62 (1953): 289–300, reprinted in Steven Bartlett (ed.) *Reflexivity: A Source-Book in Self-Reference*, Amsterdam and London: North-Holland, 1992), gives an account of the supposed horrors of self-reference. An early source of the notion of grounding is given by Hans Herzberger, "Paradoxes of grounding in semantics" (*Journal of Philosophy* 67 (1970): 145–67) and this idea also features in Saul Kripke's "Outline of a theory of truth" (*Journal of Philosophy* 72 (1975): 690–716, reprinted in R. L. Martin (ed.) *Recent Essays on Truth and the Liar Paradox*, Oxford: Oxford University Press, 1984, pp. 53–81). Kripke's paper presents a precise theory of truth for a language which both allows circular reference and contains its own truth predicate, a combination which Tarski had supposedly demonstrated was impossible. One alleged difficulty with Kripke's approach is that it is vulnerable to Revenge reasoning. This can be brought out either by considering a Liar-like sentence which purports to say of itself that it is either false or ungrounded, or by the reflection that what is not grounded is, presumably, not true.

Targeting self-reference or circularity as the villains of Liar paradoxes has become less popular in recent years. Among the causes are the appreciation that something like self-reference is used in the construction of various meta-mathematical proofs, for example Gödel's proof of the incompleteness of arithmetic; a growing appreciation of the need to do justice to our actual language, in which self-reference seems a clear possibility; and the emergence of paradoxes, like those invented by Stephen Yablo in "Paradox without self-reference" (*Analysis* 53 (1993): 251–2), which support his conclusion that "self-reference is neither necessary nor sufficient for Liar-like paradox" (p. 252).

The use of indexicality in dealing with Liar paradoxes goes back at least to Haim Gaifman's "Paradoxes of infinity and self-application, I" (*Erkenntnis* 20 (1983): 131–55). A more recent contribution on these lines is offered by Laurence Goldstein in his paper "'This statement is not true' is not true" (*Analysis* 52/1 (1992): 1–5). Tyler Burge suggests that what indexicality should do is generate context-sensitive levels; see his "Semantical paradox" (*Journal of Philosophy* 76 (1979): 169–98, reprinted in R. L. Martin (ed.) *Recent Essays on Truth and the Liar Paradox*, Oxford: Oxford University Press, 1984, pp. 83–117).

Graham Priest's *In Contradiction* (Dordrecht: Nijhof, 1987) has a clear introduction to both semantic paradoxes (chapter 1) and paradoxes involving classes (chapter 2). It also offers an unusual solution: some contradictions are true, and examples may include the Liar and the claim that Russell's class exists. For an introductory text on type theory, see Irving Copi's *The Theory of Logical Types* (London: Routledge & Kegan Paul, 1981).

Comparing the Liar and Russell's paradoxes requires noting Frank Ramsey's opinion that "It is not sufficiently remarked, and the fact is entirely neglected in *Principia Mathematica*, that these contradictions fall into two fundamentally distinct groups" ("The foundations of mathematics," *Proceedings of the London Mathematical Society* 25 (1925): 338–84, reprinted in D. H. Mellor (ed.) *F. P. Ramsey: Philosophical Papers*, Cambridge: Cambridge University Press, 1990, pp. 174–224, at p. 183). Russell's alleged neglect is manifest in the Introduction to his and Alfred Whitehead's *Principia Mathematica* (Cambridge: Cambridge University Press, 1910–13; the early parts are now reprinted in paperback). The most significant recent contribution is Graham Priest's "The structure of the paradoxes of self-reference" (*Mind* 103 (1994): 25–34).

Discourse Representation Theory dates to Hans Kamp's "A theory of truth and semantic representation," in J. A. G. Groenendijk, T. M. V. Janssen, and M. B. J. Stockhof (eds.) *Formal Methods in the Study of Language* (Amsterdam: Mathematisch Centrum, 1981, vol. 1, pp. 277–322). A more detailed source (the "blue bible") is H. Kamp and U. Reyle's *From Discourse to Logic* (Dordrecht: Kluwer, 1993). An approach with some similarities to Kamp's was developed independently by Irene Heim (1982, 1988): *The Semantics of Definite and Indefinite Noun Phrases* (Ann Arbor, MI: University Microfilms International).

For an impression of the richness of the topics that can be properly counted as belonging to philosophical logic, see a collection by David Lewis (1941–2001), one of the outstanding philosophers of the twentieth century. His *Papers in Philosophical Logic* (Cambridge: Cambridge University Press, 1998) discuss, among other things, adverbs, context, conditionals and probabilities, intensional logic, verificationism, set theory, and mereology.

9
PHILOSOPHY OF LANGUAGE

Jason Stanley

In the twentieth century, logic and philosophy of language were two of the few areas of philosophy in which philosophers made indisputable progress. For example, even now many of the foremost living ethicists present their theories as somewhat more explicit versions of the ideas of Kant, Mill, or Aristotle. In contrast, it would be patently absurd for a contemporary philosopher of language or logician to think of herself as working in the shadow of any figure who died before the twentieth century began. Advances in these disciplines make even the most unaccomplished of its practitioners vastly more sophisticated than Kant. There were previous periods in which the problems of language and logic were studied extensively (e.g. the medieval period). But from the perspective of the progress made since the late nineteenth century, previous work is at most a source of interesting data or occasional insight. All systematic theorizing about content that meets contemporary standards of rigor has been done subsequently.

The advances philosophy of language has made in the twentieth century are of course the result of the remarkable progress made in logic. Few other philosophical disciplines gained as much from the developments in logic as the philosophy of language. In the course of presenting the first formal system in the *Begriffsscrift* (Concept Notation), Gottlob Frege (1848–1925) developed a formal language. Subsequently, logicians provided rigorous semantics for formal languages, in order to define truth in a model, and thereby characterize logical consequence. Such rigor was required in order to enable logicians to carry out semantic proofs about formal systems in a formal system, thereby providing semantics with the same benefits as increased formalization had provided for other branches of mathematics. It was but a short step to treating natural languages as more complex versions of formal languages, and then applying to the study of natural language the techniques developed by logicians interested in proving semantic results about formal theories. Increased formalization has yielded dividends in the philosophy of language similar to those in mathematics. It has enabled philosophers to provide better and more fruitful definitions and distinctions.

Progress in philosophy of language and logic has positively affected neighboring disciplines such as metaphysics and meta-ethics. Because of this, some philosophers have thought that philosophy of language was some kind of "first philosophy," as

Descartes viewed what we would now call "epistemology." But the fact that philosophy of language has progressed significantly does not mean that it provides us with a first philosophy. One can recognize that a discipline has advanced more than others without thinking that it holds the key to all advancement. The twentieth century was the century of "linguistic philosophy," not because all or even most philosophical problems have been resolved or dissolved by appeal to language, but because areas of philosophy that involved meaning and content became immeasurably more sophisticated.

My purpose in this chapter is to explain some of the key developments in the philosophy of language. Discussions of content in other fields, such as philosophy of mind or meta-ethics, are reflections of the distinctions drawn and categories developed in thinking about languages, both formal and natural.

Frege

It is difficult to write about the development of the philosophy of language in the twentieth century without reaching back to the latter parts of the nineteenth, for the story of the revolution in logic and philosophy of language that occurred in the last century begins with the work of Gottlob Frege. Frege's project was not principally directed at language; it was rather primarily epistemological (see "The birth of analytic philosophy," Chapter 1). Frege set out to show that the truths of arithmetic were analytic in nature, by deriving them from the axioms and definitions of logic. In order to carry out this project, Frege needed to show that the theorems of arithmetic could be derived from the theorems of logic without appeal to any synthetic (non-analytic) step. To show that his deductions achieved this goal, Frege devised a formal language for carrying out his proofs. The formal language allowed for the characterization of a set of precise syntactic transformations, each of which was an instance of a purely logical inference rule. Frege's concern with using natural language to carry out his proofs was that natural language was too vague and imprecise to allow the characterization of precise syntactic transformations that expressed instances of purely logical inference rules.

In the *Begriffsschrift*, Frege says remarkably little about how his formal language is to be interpreted. In contrast to the sophistication of the syntax, Frege's few remarks about content are typical of the pre-modern era. Indeed, it is easy to think of Frege's naive conception of content as being principally about signs, rather than an extra-linguistic reality. First, Frege notoriously takes the identity relation to be a relation between signs (Section 8). Second, Frege's later ontological distinction between function and argument is presented as a distinction between *expressions* (see Section 9). However, an expression may be viewed either as the function or the argument of a sentence, so that what later is an ontological distinction now reflects merely how we apprehend either the content or the presentation of the content (Section 9). Frege does speak in rather contorted terms of *Begriffliche Inhalt* ("conceptual content"), but here too there is much confusion and obscurity. We are never told what an *Inhalt* (content) of any expression is, and Frege only hints at when two sentences have the same *Inhalt* (when they have the same "possible consequences," *möglichen Folgerungen*). Some contemporary philosophers (e.g. Brandom 1994: 94) have tried to read back into Frege's confused remarks about *Begriffliche Inhalt* some controversial modern doctrine about inferential semantics. But Frege did not at this time have sophisticated thoughts about content; indeed, no settled doctrine about content that met Fregean standards of clarity and rigor was to emerge until the early 1890s.

It is instructive to reflect upon what led Frege to an essentially modern way of thinking about content. As Frege started to develop the logicist project, he adopted the Platonist position that arithmetic is about an independently existing domain of abstract objects, namely numbers, and rejected the formalist view that arithmetic is about signs. There are two parts to the logicist task: deriving the theorems of arithmetic from logical principles, and showing that the concepts of arithmetic are logical concepts. Frege took the fact that numerical terms function as singular terms in arithmetic to be conclusive evidence that numbers are objects. His logicism thereby impels him to identify logical objects that are the numbers. The first part of the logicist project also requires that the syntactic transformations on expressions of the *Begriffsscrift* express inference rules that are indisputably logical. So Frege is led to the project of giving a rigorous interpretation to his formal system for two reasons. First, he is proving facts about numbers, not facts about signs. This position forces Frege to be more specific about the relation between signs and what they are about, since he denies the formalist view that arithmetic is simply about signs. Second, he needs to ensure that the syntactic transformations express transitions that are instances of genuinely logical inferences. This in turn forces him to develop a theory of content for his formal language.[1]

Frege's remarkable syntactic achievement in the *Begriffsschrift* of 1879 was to arrive at a notation that represented reasoning with quantifiers and variables (see "The birth of analytic philosophy," Chapter 1). Frege's remarkable semantic achievements occurred later. Frege (1966: Part I) provided a compositional semantics for the *Begriffsschrift* notation. In his seminal paper "On sense and meaning" (1993), he also isolated a series of puzzles and topics that provided much of the groundwork for twentieth-century philosophy of language.

Here is not the place to delve into all the details of Frege's mature theory of content. But it is important to sketch it, because Frege laid down the elements upon which all subsequent investigations of content are predicated. Frege's ontology is divided into two kinds of entities, *objects* and *functions* (for further discussion see "Metaphysics," Chapter 10). Although the distinction between object and function is fundamentally ontological, Frege explains it by appeal to language. For Frege, an object is the kind of thing that is named by a "complete expression," or proper name, such as "Bill Clinton," and a function is the kind of thing that is named by an "incomplete expression," for example a predicate such as "is running" or a one-place functional expression, such as "x^2." Frege took the category of complete expressions or proper names to include sentences, and so he took the reference of sentences to be objects, in particular *truth-values*. Since Frege took one-place predicates to denote a kind of function, and sentences to denote truth-values, he treated the referents of one-place predicates as functions from objects to truth-values. He called functions whose values are truth-values, *concepts*. So a predicate such as "is red" denotes a concept that takes an object to the truth-value True if and only if that object is red; otherwise, it takes that object to the truth-value False. The sentence "That apple is red" denotes the truth-value True if and only if the concept denoted by "is red" takes the object denoted by "that apple" to the truth-value True; otherwise, the sentence denotes the truth-value False. Frege also provided an account of the semantics of quantifiers. According to this account (1966: sect. 20), the expression for the universal quantifier denotes a "second-level function," one which takes a first-level function to the True if and only if the first-level function maps every object onto the True. So the occurrence of "everything" in "everything is red" denotes a function from concepts to truth-values. It takes a function, such as that denoted by "is red," to the true if and only the function denoted by "is red" yields the True as value for every argument. Frege's account of quantifiers as second-level functions has proved to have lasting impact in natural language semantics, as it is a standard way quantifiers are treated in Montague Grammar, the dominant contemporary tradition in natural language semantics.

Frege's ontology gave him the resources to provide a particularly elegant characterization of the conditions under which a sentence of his formal language was true. Indeed, he uses it to provide just such a characterization in Part I of the *Grundgesetze der Arithmetik* [*Basic Laws of Arithmetic*]. As he writes: "Every name of a truth-value expresses a sense, a thought. Through our stipulations it is determined under what conditions it denotes the True" (1966: sect. 32, my translation). So, not only did Frege provide a number of technical suggestions that were to affect the development of semantics, he also had a clear conception of the semantic project of giving a recursive characterization of the truth-conditions of sentences of a language, via assignment of semantic contents to the basic meaningful parts.

Frege's seminal paper "On sense and meaning" (*Über Sinn und Bedeutung*, sometimes translated "On sense and reference") raises topics that are even more germane for the study of natural languages than they are for the study of formal languages. The paper is famous for the modern statement of *the problem of cognitive significance*: how can two expressions that denote the same object in the world (such as "Hesperus" and "Phosphorus," or "Cicero" and "Tully") nevertheless have differing cognitive significance? Why is it that "Hesperus is Phosphorus" and "Cicero is Tully" are cognitively significant, but "Hesperus is Hesperus" and "Cicero is Cicero" are not? Frege's solution involves the introduction of yet another element in his theory of meaning, the notion of *sense* (*Sinn*). The sense of a term is (roughly) the way that term presents its referent. So "Hesperus" and "Phosphorus" both refer to the same object, namely Venus, but present this referent in different ways, and therefore have different senses.[2]

Frege uses the notion of sense to give an account of the meaning of *propositional attitude ascriptions*, which are sentences involving propositional attitude verbs such as "believes," "doubts," and "knows." A propositional attitude ascription, such as "John believes that Hesperus is a planet" appears to relate an agent to a thought (or proposition); in the case of this sentence, it appears to relate John to the thought that Hesperus is a planet. According to Frege, while the *referent* of a sentence is a truth-value, the *sense* of a sentence – the way it presents its referent – is a thought. Within the scope of a propositional attitude verb, an expression denotes, not its ordinary referent, but rather its ordinary sense. So propositional attitude verbs (such as "believes") create what are called *opaque contexts*, linguistic contexts in which substitution of co-referring expressions fails.[3] The claim that propositional attitude verbs create opaque contexts accords with our intuition that "John believes that Hesperus is a planet" may be true, whereas "John believes that Phosphorus is a planet" is false, even though "Hesperus" and "Phosphorus" refer to the same object, namely the planet Venus. "Hesperus" and "Phosphorus" cannot be substituted for one another in the scope of a propositional attitude verb, despite the fact that they have the same referent. Frege's account of the meaning of propositional attitude constructions explains this, because according to this account, "Hesperus" and "Phosphorus," within the scope of a propositional attitude verb, refer to their ordinary senses, rather than the object Venus. Therefore, within the scope of a propositional attitude verb, "Hesperus" and "Phosphorus" do not after all have the same referent.

Frege's reflections on natural language are not limited to propositional attitude ascriptions. "On sense and meaning" contains important and influential discussions of a number of other topics, including the topic that linguists now discuss under the rubric of *presupposition*. Frege's discussions of natural language reflect a great deal of insight about language, especially for someone whose primary interest was mathematics. For example, in addition to his contributions to the study of quantification, propositional attitude constructions, presupposition, Frege had important insights on the topics of plural reference and mass terms (in the course of discussing whether number was a property of objects, in Frege 1980b). Frege's late paper "The thought" (*Der Gedanke*) contains a remarkably lucid discussion of indexicals and demonstratives, expressions such as "I," "now," "today," "this," and "that." An indexical expression changes its referent from context to context; when Bill Clinton uses "I," it denotes a different object than when Hillary Clinton uses "I," despite the fact that the two uses of "I" have the same linguistic meaning. The context-sensitivity of indexicals raises certain difficulties for Frege's notion of sense and for characterizations of linguistic meaning generally, about which Frege showed clear awareness.[4] The sophistication of Frege's reflections about natural language was no doubt due to the fact that, despite his mistrust of its vagueness and context-sensitivity, Frege nevertheless took ordinary linguistic categories to reflect ontological ones.

Russell

In Frege's theory of meaning, each expression is associated with at least two semantic values, its ordinary referent (*Bedeutung*) and its ordinary sense (*Sinn*).[5] The semantic theory Frege provided for his formal language does not, however, involve the assignment of senses to any expressions. Partly, this is due to the absence of opacity-inducing expressions in his formal language, such as propositional attitude verbs.[6] The compositional semantic theory Frege provides in Part I of *Die Grundgesetz der Arithmetik* (1892) does not explicitly involve assigning thoughts (the senses of sentences) directly to senses. In some sense, Frege seemed to think that giving the truth-conditions of *Begriffsschrift* sentences was enough to represent the thoughts they expressed.[7]

In Britain, a somewhat different conception of meaning was emerging from the pages of the journal *Mind*, one that was to have an equally large impact on subsequent thought about content. G. E. Moore (1899) argued that in judgment, we are related to contents which he called *propositions*. Moore's conception of propositions was not exactly contemporary; for example, he thought each object was in fact an existential proposition (for more discussion, see "The birth of analytic philosophy," Chapter 1). But the idea of judgment as expressing a relation between an agent and a complex of existing entities that formed a distinctive kind of content, a proposition, was taken up by Bertrand Russell. In Russell's seminal 1905 paper "On denoting," he provided a rather modern characterization of propositions. On Frege's view, the contents of judgments were *Gedanken* (thoughts), the senses of sentences, which were themselves composed out of ways of thinking of objects and properties. In contrast, Russell's propositions contained actual objects and properties. As Russell wrote to Frege in his famous letter of December 12, 1904 (Frege 1980: 98–9):

> I believe that Mont Blanc itself, despite all of its snowfields, is a constituent of what would be asserted by the sentence 'Mont Blanc is higher than 4000 meters'. One does not assert the thought, which is a psychologically private matter: one asserts the object of the thought, and this is according to my conception a certain complex (an objective sentence, one might say) of which Mont Blanc itself is a constituent.[8]

Russell's motivation for developing his theory of propositions was also distinct from Frege's. Russell, like Frege, thought that mathematics posed certain epistemological problems that could be solved by resting it upon a logical foundation. But the episte-mological problems Russell thought were posed by mathematics were slightly different from the ones that exercised Frege.

Russell's theory of meaning emerged from his desire to account for our ability (most obvious in the mathematical domain) to think about an infinite class of objects, despite our inability to survey an infinite domain. According to Russell's 1903 theory (Russell 1996: ch. 5), what accounts for our ability to grasp propositions that are about an infinite class of objects is the fact that such propositions contain *denoting concepts*. As Russell writes (1996: 53):

> A concept *denotes* when, if it occurs in a proposition, the proposition is not *about* the concept, but about a term connected in a certain peculiar way with the concept. If I say 'I met a man', the proposition is not about *a man*; this is a concept which does not walk the streets, but lives in the shadowy limbo of the logic-books. What I met was a thing, not a concept, an actual man with a tailor and a bank-account or a public-house and a drunken wife.

When we grasp a proposition that is about an infinite domain of objects, it is because the proposition contains a denoting concept that is about that infinite domain of objects (Russell 1996: 73; see also "The birth of analytic philosophy," Chapter 1). A finite mind can grasp a concept that denotes an infinite class, but not the infinite class itself. Russell developed his theory of meaning to explain the essentially epistemological problem, so evident in mathematical thought about unsurveyable domains, of how we could grasp the proposition expressed by an occurrence of a sentence, despite the fact that we did not have the ability to grasp all the things the proposition was about.

The story of Russell's dissatisfaction with his 1903 theory of denoting, and his 1905 development of the theory of descriptions is told at some length elsewhere in this volume (see "The birth of analytic philosophy, Chapter 1). Here, I shall just briefly summarize some of the main differences between Russell's 1905 theory of meaning and its subsequent development and Frege's mature theory of meaning, differences that will be important in our discussion of subsequent developments.

For Russell, sentences express propositions, which are the ultimate objects of truth and falsity. Propositions are non-linguistic entities that contain as constituents objects and properties. Grasping a proposition requires bearing a privileged epistemological relation to each of its constituents (which relation, as we have seen, Russell does not think we can bear to an infinite class).[9] A *logically proper name* is an expression that contributes the object to which it refers to the proposition expressed by a sentence containing it. Thus, if "Jason Stanley" is a logically proper name, grasp of the proposition expressed by "Jason Stanley is a philosopher" would require bearing this epistemologically special relationship to the object Jason Stanley. Following Russell, we shall use the term *acquaintance* for the epistemologically special relationship one must have to the constituents of a proposition in order to grasp that proposition. Russell changed his mind throughout his career about what is required to have acquaintance with an object; soon after 1905 he came to the view that the only objects one could be acquainted with are sense-data and perhaps oneself.[10] Since we clearly do grasp many propositions that are not about objects that Russell thought we had acquaintance with (e.g. objects in the distant past, or people we have never met), Russell did not think that most ordinary proper names were logically proper names. For example, we clearly do grasp the proposition expressed by an occurrence of "Bismarck was a clever man," although we do not (according to Russell) have acquaintance with Bismarck. Therefore, the proposition expressed by this occurrence of "Bismarck was a clever man" does not contain Bismarck as a constituent (else we would not grasp it). Thus, "Bismarck," the ordinary proper name, is not a *logically* proper name.

According to Russell, most ordinary proper names were *disguised definite descriptions*. Since (according to Russell's theory of descriptions, see "The birth of analytic philosophy," Chapter 1) definite descriptions contribute only universals (i.e. properties) to the propositions expressed by sentences containing them, and since Russell was fairly liberal about acquaintance with universals, the propositions expressed by sentences containing ordinary proper names are capable of being grasped by ordinary people. For example, the ordinary proper name "Bill Clinton" would be, for Russell, a disguised definite description, perhaps the definite description "the President of the United States of America between 1992 and 2000" (although the proper name "the United States of America" is also presumably a disguised definite description). The proposition expressed by "Bill Clinton is a Democrat" would then contain as constituents only universals. Hence, it could be grasped by someone with no acquaintance with Bill Clinton.

Frege's "thoughts," or propositions, were composed of ways of thinking of objects and properties; the thought that Jason Stanley is a philosopher, on this view, consists of a way of thinking of Jason Stanley and a way of thinking of the property of being a philosopher. Russell's 1905 theory of meaning differs from Frege's in that it involves no notion of sense, no "ways of thinking" about things. Russell's propositions are composed of objects and properties (universals), not ways of thinking of them. Russell also had epistemological motivations for certain of his views that are absent in Frege. Russell thought we were not acquainted with many objects, but nevertheless could grasp propositions that seemed to be about them. So, for epistemological reasons, Russell took ordinary proper names to be disguised definite descriptions, and analyzed definite descriptions away using the apparatus of quantificational logic (see "The birth of analytic philosophy," Chapter 1).

Although Russell's motivation was primarily epistemological, his description theory of ordinary proper names, coupled with his account of the semantics of sentences containing definite descriptions, also allowed him to resolve certain philosophical puzzles. According to Russell, a sentence of the form "The F is G" expressed a proposition whose logical form was more complex than the grammatical form of "The F is G". In particular, "The F is G" expresses the proposition that there exists an x which is F, there is only one F, and x is G.[11] So a sentence containing a definite description expresses an existentially quantified proposition, together with a *uniqueness* condition, to the effect that the nominal complement of "the F" (which is the instance of 'F') is satisfied by one and only one object.[12]

Russell applied his description theory of ordinary proper names, together with his semantic account of sentences containing definite descriptions, to a number of problems. Most famously, Russell applied his views to *the problem of negative existentials*. The problem of negative existentials is raised by sentences such as "Pegasus does not exist," which clearly express truths, despite the fact that they contain non-referring terms (in this case, "Pegasus"). If "Pegasus does not exist" expresses a true proposition, then "Pegasus" must refer to something that lacks the property of existence. But if "Pegasus" refers to something that does not exist, then there are things that do not exist. This argument in favor of a realm of shadowy non-existents is the problem of negative existentials.

To solve the problem of negative existentials, Russell first applied his description theory of ordinary proper names to conclude that "Pegasus does not exist" expresses the same proposition as (say) "The winged horse of mythology does not exist." The proposition expressed by "The winged horse of mythology does not exist," according to Russell's theory of descriptions, has a true reading, one in which the denoting phrase "the winged horse of mythology" has a *secondary occurrence* (takes narrow-scope) with respect to the negation "not." According to this reading, the sentence expresses the proposition that it is not the case that there exists an x, x is a winged horse of mythology, and for all y, if y is a winged horse of mythology, then $y = x$, and x exists. This proposition is clearly true, and its truth does not commit us to a mysterious ontology of nonexistent things. Russell's dissolution of the problem of negative existentials is the paradigm example of using linguistic analysis to resolve metaphysical quandaries.

Russell also repeatedly applies his theory of descriptions to the problem of cognitive significance. The reason that "Scott is the author of *Waverley*" is cognitively significant, while "Scott is Scott" is not, is that "Scott is the author of *Waverley*" expresses the proposition that there exists an author of *Waverley*, and only one author of *Waverley*, and he is Scott, whereas "Scott is Scott" (taking "Scott" to be a logically proper name) expresses a trivial proposition of the form $a = a$ (Russell and Whitehead 1910: ch. 3 of Introduction). Using his description theory of ordinary proper names, Russell also can explain why a sentence containing an "is" of identity between two distinct ordinary proper names (such as "Hesperus is Phosphorus" or "Cicero is Tully") is cognitively significant, whereas a sentence containing an "is" of identity between two occurrences of the same name (such as "Hesperus is Hesperus") is not cognitively significant. For distinct ordinary proper names are treated, by Russell, as standing in for distinct definite descriptions. So, "Hesperus is Phosphorus" expresses the same proposition as "The morning star is the evening star," or perhaps "The planet called 'Hesperus' is the planet called 'Phosphorus'" (as in ch. 16 of Russell 1919). So, where Frege appealed to distinct senses associated with distinct proper names to resolve the problem of cognitive significance, Russell maintained that distinct ordinary proper names corresponded to distinct definite descriptions.

From Frege and Russell to Tarski

Frege, Moore, and Russell had several doctrines in common that have since become widely accepted, yet were not clearly adopted or even understood in previous philosophical work.[13] First, all three philosophers clearly distinguished the *act* of judging from the *object* of the judgment (and similarly the *relation* of believing from the contents of particular beliefs). Second, all three philosophers thought of the object of judgment as being a complex, mind-independent entity that was the object of knowledge and belief (although, as we have seen, they differed amongst one another about the nature of this mind-independent entity). Third, all three philosophers thought of these entities as the primary bearers of truth and falsity.

Frege, Moore, and Russell were not the only philosophers at the time to clearly make these distinctions and adopt these views. For example, Alexius Meinong (1853–1920) clearly thought of the objects of judgment as complex, mind-independent entities that we are related to in knowledge and belief, and provided sophisticated arguments for this conclusion (see Meinong 1910: ch. 3). Nor were all three of these founding fathers of analytic philosophy entirely consistent in retaining these positions. Moore and Russell abandoned their belief in the existence of propositions soon after they developed them, because of the concern that positing false propositions was ontologically profligate (see, e.g., Russell 1994). Indeed, after 1910, Russell used "proposition" as a way to talk about sentences, and went so far as to abandon the act-object conception of judgment, with the *multiple-relation theory of judgment* (see "The birth of analytic philosophy," Chapter 1). Nevertheless, the clarity and cogency of these views withstood even their abandonment by some of their chief proponents, and survive as presumptions of virtually all contemporary discussions of content.

The twenty years of philosophy that followed Frege and Russell's greatest accomplishments were relatively unimportant to subsequent work in the philosophy of language. Russell spent the years between 1910 and 1920 developing an idiosyncratic version of phenomenalism, according to which ordinary objects were "logical fictions," and names for them were to be treated as "incomplete symbols" to be analyzed away, so that we are left just with reference to sense-data and universals (see "The birth of analytic philosophy," Chapter 1). Ludwig Wittgenstein's *Tractatus Logico-Philosophicus* was also devoted to rather large-scale metaphysical endeavors, and was not written with the level of clarity that is so characteristic of the writings of Frege and early Russell. However, unlike Frege and Russell, Wittgenstein took seriously the modal notions of *possibility* and *necessity*.[14] For Wittgenstein, a meaningful content divided the space of possibilities. For a proposition to be meaningful, both it and its negation had to be possible; otherwise the proposition did not *divide* the space of possibilities into those in which the proposition is true and those in which it was false.

One way in which the *Tractatus* impeded progress in philosophy is that it led philosophers (in particular the logical positivists) to expend their energies in the pursuit of developing and honing a criterion of meaningfulness, and using the criterion to argue that traditional philosophical theses failed to satisfy it, and were hence meaningless (see "The development of analytic philosophy, Wittgenstein and after," Chapter 2). This project has been moribund for decades. It is nevertheless the quest of a criterion of meaningfulness that can be put to anti-metaphysical use that the many humanists outside of philosophy unfortunately most clearly associate with analytic philosophy.

However, the influence of the *Tractatus* has not been uniformly negative. As we shall see, other philosophers took up some of the metaphysical apparatus developed in the *Tractatus* and applied it to the study of content. As we shall also see, this research program has turned out to be extraordinarily fruitful, not just in subsequent investigations in the philosophy of language, but also in metaphysics. So Wittgenstein's belief that modality and meaningfulness were intimately related has, somewhat ironically, fueled something of a revolution in just the kind of philosophy he wanted to use it to undermine.

Tarski's theory of truth

As we have seen (Frege 1966: Part I), Frege provides a semantic theory for his formal language: a set of "stipulations" (*Festsetzungen*) that determines under what conditions an arbitrary sentence of the *Begriffsschrift* is true. Frege also provides semantic proofs about the formal theory of the *Grundgesetze*, including, rather notoriously, an attempted semantic consistency proof.[15] As Saul Kripke (1940–) has emphasized (2005: 1013–14), semantical proofs also occur in Russell's *Principia*. Furthermore, Frege proves some model-theoretic results about his formal system of arithmetic within the naive set-theoretical framework of the *Grundgesetze*; for example, it is plausible to take the proof of theorem 263 to be a categoricity theorem for his axioms of arithmetic (see Heck 1993: sect. 7). However, Frege and Russell's concern was ultimately to place mathematics on the secure foundations of logic, and they appealed to semantics chiefly in the service of this project. In contrast, the focus of the Polish logician Alfred Tarski (born Alfred Teitelbaum, 1901–83) was on the discipline of semantics itself. Tarski set himself the task of setting *semantics* on the secure foundations of mathematics, by providing mathematical definitions of semantical concepts such as *truth* and *logical consequence*.

Tarski's motivation for setting semantical concepts on secure foundations was distinct from Frege and Russell's motivations for logicism, although related to the reasons for its failure. The logicist program of reducing mathematics to logic was undermined by the fact that the systems that were powerful enough to provide a foundation for mathematics were not plausibly regarded as logical. First, Frege's system of naive set-theory turned out to be inconsistent, as Russell's paradox demonstrated. Second, Russell's system involved axioms that were too controversial to be regarded as logical (see "The birth of analytic philosophy," Chapter 1). But the fate of naive set-theory was to have repercussions in many areas of mathematics. In particular, it focused attention on the fact that intuitive principles governing a fundamental concept (such as that of an aggregation of objects) could lead to paradox, and that the paradox could be evaded by greater mathematical subtlety.

As in the case of naive principles governing the aggregation of objects, some of the most obvious principles governing semantical concepts lead quickly to paradoxes. For example, restricting ourselves only to sentences that contain no context-sensitive vocabulary, the following claim seems to be an obvious truism, one that follows from the meaning of the word "true":

(1) "S" is a true sentence if and only if S.

To illustrate this point (using *quotation-names* as names of sentences) consider the obviousness of the following:

(2) "Snow is white" is a true sentence if and only if snow is white.
(3) "Grass is green" is a true sentence if and only if grass is green.

Few claims are as uncontroversial as (2) and (3). Yet schema (1) seems to lead fairly directly to a contradiction. Consider the following:

(4) (4) is not a true sentence.

Sentence (4) contains no context-sensitive vocabulary. So it should be unproblematic to substitute it for "S" in schema (1). But if we plug in "(4) is not a true sentence" for "S" in the right-hand side of (1), together with a name of it on the left-hand side, we obtain:

(5) (4) is a true sentence if and only if (4) is not a true sentence

Since (5) is a contradiction, the intuitive principle about truth that the schema in (1) exemplifies is false.

So much the worse for truth, one might think. After all, the concept of truth is one that seems to belong to metaphysics, which is not the most reputable of disciplines. However, by 1930, it had become clear that the use of semantical concepts such as truth and logical consequence was of genuine mathematical use in describing desirable properties of formal systems. For example, one desirable property of a formal theory of a given subject matter is *completeness*, which is the question of whether that formal system is adequate to proving every sentence that is true in virtue of the subject matter in question. Another desirable property is satisfiability: is it possible for the axioms of the formal system all to express truths, or do some axioms result in contradictions (it is this that Frege was trying to demonstrate in sections 29–32 of the *Grundgesetze*)? There are a number of other semantical properties of formal systems that are defined in terms of semantical notions, and much work in the foundations of mathematics in the 1920s was in the service of proving semantical claims about formal systems. So as the century progressed, it became clear the semantical concepts were not just the philosopher's concern, but the mathematician's as well.[16]

In his landmark paper, "The concept of truth in formalized languages," Tarski set out to show that, for many languages, one could consistently define a truth-predicate for that language, although this definition must be given in a language that is expressively richer than the original language. Moreover, given the right theoretical resources, one can derive all the instances of (1), for sentences of the original language, from this definition. Thus, Tarski shows how to define the relative concept of Truth-in-L, for a specific language L.

Tarski's method of defining truth for the language L involves inductively defining the notion of *a sequence satisfying an open formula of L*, and truth is defined in terms of thus defined notion of satisfaction (a true sentence is one that is satisfied by all sequences).[17] In his original paper, Tarski focused on defining what he called "the absolute concept of truth" (1983b: 199). But the more important notion is the notion of truth for a language L *relative to a model*, of which Tarski's absolute notion is a special case (ibid.). A model is, intuitively, an interpretation of the language, relative to a domain of objects – the "universe" of that model. The reason to define the more general notion of truth for a language relative to a model (and not just truth for a language) is that the notion of truth in a model is what is required to capture fundamental semantic notions such as *logical validity* and *logical consequence*.[18] A sentence S is a *logical consequence* of sentences $\alpha_1 \ldots \alpha_n$ if and only if S is true in every model M in which $\alpha_1 \ldots \alpha_n$ are true; S is *logically valid* if and only if S is true in every model (logical validity is the limiting case of logical consequence; a logically valid sentence is a logical consequence of the empty set of sentences). The motivation behind these definitions is that a sentence S is logically valid if and only if it is true no matter how one interprets the non-logical vocabulary in S and no matter what objects there are in the domain. Models therefore serve the dual function of providing alternative interpretations of the non-logical vocabulary in the sentence, and varying the objects quantified over by the quantifiers. With the model-theoretic definition of logical consequence, one can give mathematical perspicuity to some of the fundamental notions in, for example, the completeness theorem for first-order logic. Since the ultimate goal was to give a mathematical characterization of the fundamental semantic notions of validity and consequence, defining truth in a model, rather than truth, should be the desired goal of the meta-mathematician seeking to legitimize the semantical notions most useful for logic.

To illustrate the Tarskian method of defining truth for a language relative to a model, it is instructive to look at a simple example in detail. In what follows, I will define a simple language L, and show how, with the use of Tarski's notion of satisfaction, to give a definition of truth for that language (readers who wish to avoid these details may skip the next few pages without loss).

The language L

Alphabet of L:

A, B, . . ., E	Name letters (constants)
F^n, G^n, . . ., Z^n	n-place predicate letters
P, Q, . . ., Z	Sentence letters
a, b, c, . . ., w, x, y, z	Variables
~, →, ↔, v, &	Sentential connectives
∀, ∃	Quantifiers (universal, existential)

Grammar of L:

Termhood of L:

(i) All name letters and variables are terms.

(ii) Nothing else is a term.

Well-formed formulae (wff) of L:

(i) 0-place predicate letters are wffs.

(ii) $\phi\alpha_1 \ldots \alpha_n$ is a wff if ϕ is an n-place predicate letter, and each of $\alpha_1 \ldots \alpha_n$ is a term.

(iii) ~ϕ is a wff if ϕ is a wff.

(iv) $(\phi \rightarrow \psi)$ is a wff if ϕ is a wff and ψ is a wff.

(v) $(\phi \leftrightarrow \psi)$ is a wff if ϕ is a wff and ψ is a wff.

(vi) $(\phi \text{ v } \psi)$ is a wff if ϕ is a wff and ψ is a wff.

(vii) $(\phi \text{ \& } \psi)$ is a wff if ϕ is a wff and ψ is a wff.

(viii) $\forall \alpha \phi$ is a wff if ϕ is a wff and α is a variable.
(ix) $\exists \alpha \phi$ is a wff if ϕ is a wff and α is a variable.
(x) Nothing else is a wff.

So, some well-formed formulae of L are:

R^2xy

$\exists x H^2 Ayx$

$\exists x((F^1x \ \& \ G^0) \rightarrow \forall z J^3 xzA)$

We shall define *truth relative to a model*, where a model consists of a *domain of discourse* (intuitively, the things spoken of, or quantified over) and an assignment of values to (an interpretation of) the non-logical expressions (the name letters and predicate letters). More formally, a model M for L consists of an ordered pair of sets, $<D, \Im>$. D is a set of objects, called the *universe*, or *domain*, of M, and $\Im$ is a function which (1) assigns to each name letter of L a member of D, (2) assigns to each 0-place predicate letter a truth-value (either the true or the false), and (3) assigns to each n-place predicate letter (n > 0), a set of n-tuples of members of D. So, $\Im$ "interprets" the non-logical constants (name letters, sentence letters, and predicate letters) of L.

Notice that we have yet to give a method for interpreting variables. For that, we will need Tarski's notion of *satisfaction*, which enters in below, in the definition of truth-in-a-model. The ultimate goal is to characterize what it is for an arbitrary sentence (a sentence is a well-formed formula with no free variables) to be true in a model. For this, we appeal to the notion of satisfaction. A sentence is true in a model if and only if it is satisfied by all sequences of that model. With the use of standard notation:

$|=_M \phi$ read: ϕ is true in (model) M.

$|=_{M,s} \phi$ read: ϕ is *satisfied* by (sequence) s in M.

Df.: $|=_M \phi$ iff for all sequences s of M, $|=_{M,s} \phi$.

A sequence s of a model M is a function which assigns, to each variable of the language of L, a member of D. In other words, sequences assign values to variables, and the values they assign are members of the domain of discourse of the model M.

Since a sentence is true in a model M if and only if it is satisfied by all sequences of that model M, we have now reduced the problem of defining truth in a model to that of defining satisfaction in a model of a sentence by a sequence.[19] We now turn to the inductive definition of satisfaction in a model. For this we will need two additional definitions. First, we will need the concept of *denotation relative to a sequence*:

Df.: Where t is a term, and s a sequence, $Den(t,s) = \Im(t)$ if t is a name letter, and $Den(t,s) = s(t)$ if t is a variable.

The denotation function is defined with the use of the interpretation function $\Im$ of the model, and is used to interpret the terms. We will also require the concept of an *s' variant of a sequence s*, which will help us in giving the interpretation clauses for the quantifiers (clauses (viii) and (ix) below)

Df.: $s' \approx_x s$ read: s' is identical to s except at most in assigning something different to the variable "x" than s does (so, for every variable $y \neq x$ of L, $s'(y) = s(y)$, and possibly, $s'(x) \neq s(x)$).

With the use of these notions, we may now turn to the inductive definition of satisfaction (for "sats" read "satisfies," and I have suppressed, for convenience's sake, the reference to the model M):

(i) If ϕ is a 0-place predicate letter, s sats ϕ iff $\Im(\phi)$ = the true.

(ii) If ϕ is an n-place predicate letter, and $\alpha_1 \ldots \alpha_n$ are terms, s sats $\phi\alpha_1 \ldots \alpha_n$ iff $<\mathrm{Den}(\alpha_1,s), \ldots, \mathrm{Den}(\alpha_n,s)>$ is in $\Im(\phi)$.

(iii) If ϕ is of the form «~ψ,» then s sats ϕ iff s does not sat ψ.

(iv) If ϕ is of the form «$(\psi \rightarrow \chi)$,» then s sats ϕ iff either s does not sat ψ or s sats χ.

(v) clause for "&"

(vi) clause for "v" (clauses for "&," "v," and "$\leftrightarrow$" are left to the reader)

(vii) clause for "$\leftrightarrow$"

(viii) If ϕ is of the form «$\exists x\psi$,» then s sats ϕ iff for some $s' \approx_x s$, s' sats ψ.

(ix) If ϕ is of the form «$\forall x\psi$,» then s sats ϕ iff for every $s' \approx_x s$, s' sats ψ.

With the use of these definitions, one may derive theorems that give the conditions under which an arbitrary sentence S of the language L is satisfied by a sequence in a model. For example, one can prove that:

(6) A sequence s of a model M satisfies "$\exists x(F^1 x \ \& \ G^1 x)$" if and only if for some sequence $s' \approx_x s$, $s'(x)$ is in $\Im(F^1)$ and in $\Im(G^1)$.

The sentence "$\exists x(F^1 x \ \& \ G^1 x)$" is a sentence of the object-language. The meta-language is the language in which the truth-conditions of this sentence are given. For example, the expressions occurring on the right-hand side of "if and only if" are in the meta-language. The meta-language is a combination of English together with some set-theoretical and logical vocabulary. Intuitively, what (6) says is that "$\exists x(F^1 x \ \& \ G^1 x)$" is satisfied by a sequence s of a model M if and only if there is something in the domain of discourse of M that falls within the extension of both the predicate F and the predicate G. Since "$\exists x(F^1 x \ \& \ G^1 x)$" contains no free variables, if one sequence satisfies it, then all sequences will satisfy it. So "$\exists x(F^1 x \ \& \ G^1 x)$" is true in a model M if and only if it is satisfied by at least one sequence of M, and (6) states the conditions under which "$\exists x(F^1 x \ \& \ G^1 x)$" is satisfied by an arbitrary sequence of M. So, with the use of the inductive definition of satisfaction, together with the definition of truth in a model in terms of satisfaction, we can derive the conditions under which an arbitrary sentence L is true in a model M.

So, a definition of truth for the language principally takes the form of an inductive assignment of satisfaction conditions to sentences of that language, couched in an appropriate meta-theory. Finally, Tarski had a condition of adequacy for a definition of truth for a language. A definition of truth for a language was *materially adequate* if and only if the definition has, as consequences, all instances of the following schema (where "S" is replaced by structural-descriptive names of sentences of the language, and "p" is replaced by meta-language translations of the sentence named):

S is true if and only if *p*

So, a definition of truth is materially adequate if and only if it produces, as theorems, for each sentence S of the language under consideration, a statement in the meta-language of the truth-conditions of S (if the meta-language contains the object-language, this statement can simply be the object-language sentence, as in (1) above). For example, I pointed out above that the definition of truth I provided for the language L produces (6) as a theorem, which adequately gives (on the right-hand side of "if and only if") the satisfaction conditions for "∃x(F¹x & G¹x)" in the meta-language (which is English plus some set-theory and logic). The above definition of truth for the language L is adequate according to convention T if and only if it produces theorems where the right-hand side of "if and only if" is a genuine translation into the meta-language of the intended interpretation of L. Since Tarski's condition of adequacy contains reference to the notion of translation, it is often said that Tarski defined truth by assuming translation.

So, Tarski shows how to define truth for a language, in an expressively richer meta-language. He also provides a famous negative result. His negative result concerns the impossibility of defining truth for a language that is sufficiently "rich" as to allow for "all concepts and all grammatical forms of the metalanguage" (Tarski (1983b: 254)) to be interpreted in that language. Tarski's particular example of a language that has this character is what he calls the "general theory of classes," which contains variables ranging over entities of any order (e.g. classes, classes of classes, etc.). Tarski proves that, on pain of contradiction, one cannot define a one-place predicate of that language that is true of all and only the true sentences of the general theory of classes.[20] The negative result places a limit on the positive results of the paper.

Tarski shared Frege's suspicion of natural language, but had additional reasons for so doing. He thought that natural language shared a feature with languages of powerful theories, such as the general theory of the calculus of classes. Both languages have a "universal character" that allows for the formulation of the "structural-descriptive concepts" of the meta-language within them. It is this "universal character" that allows for self-reference, and thereby leads to the formulation of the paradox, precluding the possibility of providing a consistent definition of truth. In other words, there is no meta-language for a natural language such as English or German, the resources of which cannot be appropriated within English or German (since natural languages are "universal"). Since there is no expressively richer language than such languages, there is no possibility of consistently defining truth for these languages. Since Tarski thought natural language, unlike the language of the general theory of classes, did contain its own truth-predicate, he rather puzzlingly (see Putnam 1975: 73) declared natural languages to be *inconsistent*.[21]

Tarski's theory of truth has come in for some serious criticism as a contribution to an understanding of the nature of truth (as opposed to a piece of meta-mathematics).

First, Tarski seemed to think he had "reduced" the semantical concept of truth to non-semantical concepts. In the opening remarks of "The concept of truth in formalized languages," he famously declares "I shall not make use of any semantical concept if I am not able previously to reduce it to other concepts" (1983b: 153). In his paper "The establishment of scientific semantics," he writes that in an adequate definition of truth, "the semantical concepts are defined in terms of the usual concepts of the metalanguage and are thus reduced to purely logical concepts, the concepts of the language being investigated, and the specific concepts of the morphology of language" (1983c: 406). However, Tarski either failed to recognize, or was ignoring for rhetorical purposes, the fact that a definition of truth appeals to primitive *interpretive* semantic notions. A definition of truth presupposes an assignment of semantic values to primitive expressions of the language. As one can see from clause (ii) of the inductive definition of satisfaction, and the definition of the denotation relation, the interpretation function ℑ of the model M is what interprets the predicates and name letters of the language. But the characterization of the interpretation function ℑ does not follow from some general account of denotation. It is simply provided as a mapping from expressions to values. This is not a reduction of denotation to non-semantical notions, or indeed an explanation of denotation at all (Field 1972).

Perhaps Tarski wished to maintain that ℑ is not a presupposed list of expressions and their semantic values (and so masks appeal to a primitive notion in need of a theoretical explanation), but simply the product of a stipulative mathematical definition. But then the theorems of Tarskian truth-definitions for languages (or fragments of languages) would be necessary truths, since they would follow from stipulative definitions and logic. However, intuitively an instance of Tarski's schema T such as (7) is not a necessary truth at all:

(7) "Bill Clinton is smart" is true if and only if Bill Clinton is smart.

(7) is not a necessary truth, because the sentence "Bill Clinton is smart" could have meant something other than it does. For example, "is smart" could have expressed the property of being from Mars, in which case (7) would be false. (7) is therefore a contingent truth, rather than a necessary truth. So if Tarski intends ℑ to be the result of a stipulative mathematical definition, then what his truth-definition produces will be necessary truths of mathematics, not contingent truths of semantics. In short, if Tarski's purpose was to reduce semantical concepts to non-semantical ones, he certainly did not succeed.

Tarski's purpose was not to use his theory of truth to give an account of the meaning of natural language sentences. It was rather to place semantics, construed as a branch of meta-mathematics, on a scientific grounding by showing that one could give a consistent definition of truth for a language of a theory, and perhaps (unsuccessfully) reduce the semantical concepts to non-semantical ones (either mathematical or physical). Within philosophy, Tarski's work is notable for the lively industry on the Liar paradox to which it has given birth (see "Philosophical logic," Chapter 8, pp. 365–67). But Tarski's work has also had much broader influence. For as a number of philosophers recognized (most famously Davidson 1967), a Tarskian definition of truth appears to give us a tractable form for a theory of meaning. If, instead of defining truth by appeal to translation, one takes truth as a primitive notion in the system, a recursion on truth provides a statement of the truth-conditions of sentences in the language in question (as we have seen, this much actually seems to have been recognized by Frege).[22] As subsequent decades showed, the idea that the proper form of a theory of meaning for a natural language is a recursive characterization of the conditions under which a sentence is true has been extraordinarily fruitful, perhaps the most fruitful insight in the long history of the study of meaning. In other words, perhaps unintentionally, Tarski discovered the proper *form* of a theory of meaning. Tarski's work, in addition to being a contribution to meta-mathematics, indeed gave birth to a science of semantics, but on a very different understanding of that science from that which Tarski intended.

Necessity and analyticity in Carnap and Quine

Tarski's work on truth was taken very much in the vein in which it was intended, as rehabilitating the scientific respectability of the semantic notions. Rudolf Carnap (1891–1970), one of the principal members of the Vienna School of logical positivists, was particularly influenced by Tarski in this regard. In his early work, Carnap had shunned semantics (or "semasiology" as he called it), and "intensional logic" in particular. As Carnap (1949: 259) wrote:

> All questions in the field of logic can be formally expressed and are then resolved into syntactical questions. A *special logic of meaning is superfluous*; "non-formal logic" is a *contradiction in adjecto*. *Logic is syntax*.

However, Tarski's work convinced him that semantics was worthy of scientific study. In his *Meaning and Necessity* (1958b, first published 1947), Carnap turned to the project of using semantics in the service of advancing his positivist program.

He sought to show how one could, with the use of semantical rules, set up *linguistic frameworks*. According to Carnap, the linguistic framework one decides to employ is not a factual question; it is simply a question of how to talk. The decision to adopt a linguistic framework is

> a practical, not a theoretical question ... The acceptance cannot be judged as being either true or false because it is not an assertion. It can only be judged as being more or less expedient, fruitful, conducive to the aim for which the language is intended. (1958a: 214)

Once one has decided upon a linguistic framework, then a number of factual questions may be formulated with the use of that linguistic framework. Philosophical (and in particular, metaphysical) disputes arise because people confuse questions about which framework to adopt (what Carnap called *external questions*) with questions that arise within the framework, either of a factual or an analytic nature (what Carnap called *internal questions*). The metaphysical question of whether there are properties or universals is either the external question of whether to accept a linguistic framework that assigns properties as semantic values of predicates, or is the internal question of whether there are properties, which has only a trivial answer. In a linguistic framework in which properties are assigned to predicates, it is analytically true that there are properties. So many philosophical questions are either pseudo-questions (that is, without cognitive content), or have only trivial analytically true or false answers.

Carnap's concern with necessity comes from his desire to make a distinction between two kinds of internal questions: questions whose answers are analytically true (true in virtue of the semantical stipulations of the framework), on the one hand, and questions that are "factual" in nature, on the other (that is, questions whose answer is not determined by the semantic rules of the language). So Carnap's purpose in *Meaning and Necessity* is to continue central features of the program of logical positivism. Nevertheless, within this work, Carnap presented the sort of intensional semantic account of an idealized language (one that nevertheless represents a fragment of natural language in crucial respects) that is recognizably contemporary in character. As a result, Carnap's work was to have resounding influence in the decades to come, long after its central philosophical task had been abandoned as hopeless.

As we have seen, Frege and Russell contributed much of importance and interest to our understanding of the semantics of non-extensional contexts, such as the linguistic contexts created by propositional attitude verbs like "believes" and "doubts." But in their formal semantic work, they focused on formal languages lacking expressions that created non-extensional contexts. Furthermore, though Frege and Russell attempted to address the thorny problem of propositional attitude contexts, they did not take the modal notions of necessity and possibility seriously. Carnap, in contrast, provided both a semantic theory for sentences containing modals expressions such as "necessary" and "possible," as well as propositional attitude verbs.

To treat the problem of giving a semantic theory adequate to giving the truth-conditions of sentences containing "necessary" and "possible," Carnap introduced the notion of a *state-description*, which is intended to be a representation of the metaphysical notion of a *possible world*, or *way in which the world could be* (1958b: 9–10). A state-description is a set of sentences that is supposed to give a complete description of a possible state of the universe. A sentence S is necessarily true if and only if that sentence is true in every state description, that is, true in every possible world. However, given the philosophical project discussed above, Carnap viewed necessity as *analyticity*, namely truth in virtue of the semantical rules of the linguistic framework (or, more briefly, *truth in virtue of meaning*). Indeed, Carnap laid down as a condition of adequacy of any definition of necessary truth that the necessary truths are all and only those sentences whose truth can be established on the basis of the semantical rules of the language alone (1958b: 10).[23]

In *Meaning and Necessity*, Carnap made various semantic distinctions that have since become standard. Every term has an *intension* and an *extension*; the intension of an expression is a function from possible worlds (state-descriptions) to its extension at that world. The intension of a term was what Carnap called an *individual concept*, which is a function from possible worlds to objects. The intension of a one-place predicate is a function from possible worlds to classes; the intension of a sentence is a proposition, which is a function from possible worlds to truth-values (the truth-value of that sentence at that world). These identifications have since become part of the basic landscape of the study of content.

Carnap's identification of intensions of terms with individual concepts, functions from possible worlds to objects, allowed him to give a distinct account of the problem of cognitive significance than Frege and Russell. According to Frege, "Scott is the author of *Waverley*" is cognitively significant, whereas "Scott is Scott" is not, because "the author of *Waverley*" has a different sense from "Scott." Russell employs his theory of descriptions to explain why "Scott is the author of *Waverley*" is significant and "Scott is Scott" is not. For Carnap, "Scott is the author of *Waverley*" is cognitively significant, because it is *factual*; it is neither a necessary truth nor a necessary falsehood. There are some state-descriptions with respect to which the extension of "the author of *Waverley*" is not the same as the extension of "Scott." In contrast, "Scott is Scott" is necessarily true, and so is not factual. In short, "Scott is the author of *Waverley*" is cognitively significant because it is *contingent*, whereas "Scott is Scott" is not informative, because it is *necessary*.

We saw in the discussion of Frege that propositional attitude verbs create *opaque linguistic contexts*, that is, contexts in which substitution of co-referential terms may change the truth-value of the sentence containing them. Using the notions of intension and extension, Carnap was also able to provide more rigorous distinctions between types of linguistic contexts in which expressions may occur. Abstracting from extra-linguistic context-sensitivity, which Carnap never considered, we may say that an occurrence of an expression *e* is within an *extensional context* in a sentence S if and only if one can substitute for that occurrence of *e* any expression with the same extension as *e*, without changing the truth-value of S. An occurrence of an expression *e* is within an *intensional context* in a sentence S if and only if that occurrence of *e* is not within an extensional context, and one can substitute for that occurrence of *e* any expression having the same intension, without changing the truth-value of S. If an occurrence of an expression in a sentence is not extensional and not intensional, then Carnap said that the occurrence of that expression in that sentence was *neither extensional nor intensional* (in contemporary vernacular, we would call that occurrence *hyper-intensional*).

As Carnap recognized, an occurrence of an expression within the scope of the modal expressions "necessarily" and "possibly" is within an intensional context. For example, from the fact that the President of the United States of America in 2005 is the youngest son of George H. W. Bush, and the fact that necessarily, if there is a unique President of the United States of America in 2005, the President of the United States of America in 2005 is a president, it does not follow that necessarily, if there is a unique President of the United States of America in 2005, the youngest son of George H. W. Bush is a president. So, substitution of co-extensional terms is not generally permitted within the scope of a modal operator such as "necessarily." But substitution of expressions with the same intension is permitted within the scope of "necessarily."

The fact that modal expressions create intensional contexts raises *the problem of de re modality*. A *de re* modal sentence is a sentence that contains a free variable in the scope of a modal operator, such as "∃x ℑ Fx," or in English, a sentence like "There is something such that necessarily it is rational" (a *de dicto* modal sentence is a sentence that contains a modal operator with no free variables in its scope). In *de re* modal sentences, a quantifier such as "something" or "everything" binds a variable within the scope of a modal operator, such as "necessarily" or "possibly." Since expressions occurring within the scope of modal operators occur in intensional contexts, this raises the worry that quantification into such positions is somehow illegitimate. After all, the quantifier that occurs outside the scope of the modal operator (to its left) presumably ranges over ordinary objects, extensions of singular terms. Yet, because the expressions occurring within the scope of the modal operator occur in intensional contexts, what is relevant for the truth of the sentence containing them are intensions, rather than extensions. In a series of influential papers, W. V. O. Quine tried to make this worry for the coherence of *de re* modal attributions more precise (Quine 1943; 1947; 1953).[24]

Over the years, considerable effort has been expended in laying out these arguments in detail (see in particular David Kaplan's masterful paper (1986); Fine 2005a; 2005b; and Neale 2000). The core of Quine's objection involves the following kind of contrast:

(1) (the number of planets $\geq$ 7)
(2) (9 $\geq$ 7)

As Quine points out, (1) is false, and (2) is true. Yet (3) of course is also true:

(3) the number of planets = 9

Thus it appears that two co-extensional terms (such as "the number of planets" and "9") cannot be substituted for one another *salva veritate* (without change in truth-value) under the scope of a modal operator. According to Quine, this shows that objectual quantification into modal operators is not permissible. Somewhat less enthymematically, Quine argues that failure of substitutivity of co-extensional expressions in a linguistic context entails that the context is not "purely designative," where "[a]n occurrence of the name in which the name simply refers to the object designated" is a purely designative occurrence of that name (Quine 1943: 114). He then proceeds to argue that the coherence of quantification into a position requires that expressions occurring in that position are purely designative (pp. 116–18).[25] Behind all of these arguments is the thought that the semantically relevant value of a variable in a non-extensional context is not just the object that is the value of that variable, but also how that object is thought of or named, and that this fact undermines the coherence of objectual quantification into that position.[26]

Carnap's own response to the problem of *de re* modality involved his "method of extension and intension," which involved simultaneously assigning to each expression, including variables, both an intension and an extension (1958b: 42–6).

When a variable occurs within the scope of a modal operator, the value that is relevant is the intension, rather than the extension. But nevertheless, even when the relevant value of an occurrence of an expression is its intension, that occurrence still has an extension as one of its semantic values. Carnap contrasted his "method of extension and intension" with what he called *the method of the name relation* (1958b: ch. 3). According to the method of the name relation, each occurrence of an expression has only one semantic value. The method employed by Frege and the influential developer of Frege's method, Alonzo Church (1903–95) (Church 1951) is a special case of the method of the name relation. Frege took each occurrence of an expression in a sentence to have only one semantic value. If the occurrence is within a non-extensional context, then the occurrence has as its semantic value something other than its ordinary reference; if the occurrence is embedded under only one intensional operator, then it has its ordinary sense as its referent. Carnap objected to Frege's method on the ground that it led to the *problem of the hierarchy of senses*. Frege takes an opaque context to shift the references of the expressions in its scope to the senses of those referents. So it looks as if Frege is fundamentally committed to the thesis that an expression embedded under two propositional attitude verbs (such as the occurrence of "Hesperus" in "John believes that Mary believes that Hesperus is a planet") must have, as its referent, its "indirect" sense, that is, a way of thinking of its ordinary sense. A Fregean semantic theory therefore involves the assignment of an infinite number of semantic values to each expression type.[27] Carnap's method of extension and intension does not suffer from this defect.[28]

From a contemporary perspective both the Frege–Church method and Carnap's method of treating the problem of *de re* modality are species of the same genus. Both treat variables occurring in modal contexts as special in some way, as not *simply* contributing ordinary referents, relative to an assignment function, to the semantic value of the sentence in which they occur. For both Church and Carnap, the semantically relevant value of an occurrence of a variable occurring in a non-extensional context, relative to an assignment function, is not an extension of a singular term, but something like an intension.[29]

In contrast to modal expressions, propositional attitude verbs, according to Carnap, do not create intensional contexts. Rather, positions within the scope of propositional attitude verbs are *neither intensional nor extensional*. Recall that for Carnap the intension of a sentence is a proposition, and two sentences express the same proposition if and only if those sentences have the same truth-value with respect to every possible world (are "L-equivalent," in Carnap's terminology). Suppose that John believes that 2 + 2 = 4. But John disbelieves that Peano arithmetic is incomplete (say he has been misinformed). But "2 + 2 = 4" and "Peano arithmetic is incomplete" express the same proposition, according to Carnap's criterion of identity for propositions. Both sentences are necessarily true, and according to Carnap's criterion of identity for propositions, there is only one necessarily true proposition. So "believes" does not create an intensional context, because one can substitute expressions with the same intension into its scope, and alter the truth-value of the whole sentence.

According to Carnap's criterion of identity for propositions, "2 + 2 = 4" and "Peano arithmetic is incomplete" express the same proposition, despite having very different structure. Indeed, unlike Frege's thoughts and Russell's propositions, there is no reason to think that Carnap's propositions have structure at all. We could take a Carnapian proposition to be a function from possible worlds to truth-values, or alternatively to be the set of possible worlds in which the proposition is true. But Carnap's account of the semantics of sentences containing propositional attitude verbs does involve the recognition that their truth-values do depend upon structure. Since his propositions were not structured, he made the truth-value of sentences containing propositional attitude verbs depend upon the structure of the *sentences* that occur within their scope. Two sentences are "intensionally isomorphic" if and only if "they are built in the same way out of designators such that any two corresponding designators are L-equivalent [have the same intension]" (1958b: 56). Carnap employed the notion of intensional isomorphism in his account of the truth-conditions of a propositional attitude ascription such as "John believes that D." According to this account, "John believes that D" is true if and only if there is a sentence S in a language understood by John that is intensionally isomorphic to D, and John is disposed to an affirmative answer to S. Carnap's analysis of propositional attitude constructions is a model for subsequent analyses that take the objects of propositional attitudes to be sentences, rather than extra-linguistic entities such as propositions.[30]

There is a similar problem to the problem of *de re* modality facing any account of the semantics of sentences containing propositional attitude verbs. A *de re attitude ascription* is a sentence containing a free variable in the scope of a propositional attitude verb, such as "∃x(N believes that x is F)," or in English, a sentence like "Some mayor is such that John believes he is not in politics." Since propositional attitude verbs at the very least create intensional contexts, *de re* attitude ascriptions should be at least as puzzling as *de re* modal sentences. In both cases, one has a quantifier that seemingly ranges over objects (extensions of terms) binding a variable that occurs within a context in which individual concepts, rather than their extensions, are semantically relevant. Interestingly, however, at least for a time, Quine's belief in the impossibility of regimenting *de re* modal statements into an acceptable formalism did not extend to *de re* attitude ascriptions; with regards to the latter Quine (1955: 188) notes, "we are scarcely prepared to sacrifice the relational construction." In that paper, Quine proposes a way of rescuing the truth of *de re* attitude ascriptions, by regimenting them into a formalism in which one is not quantifying into a non-extensional context after all (Kaplan (1986) in fact shows that one can use the same mechanism to regiment *de re* modal claims). The distinction Quine made between the problem of *de re* modality and the problem of *de re* propositional attitude ascriptions was no doubt due to his belief that making sense out of *de re* modality ultimately involved accepting the coherence of dubious metaphysical notions, such as *essentiality*, whereas making sense out of *de re* attitude ascriptions involved no such metaphysical commitments.

However, Quine (1976b; 1977) eventually came around to the same distrust of the possibility of regimenting *de re* attitude ascriptions as he always had in the case of modality *de re*. In particular, Quine concluded that *de re* attitude ascriptions were subject to the same inconstancies as *de re* modal ascriptions. One and the same *de re* attitude ascription could be true in one context (with the object thought of one way) and false in another (with the object thought of in another way). Following Hintikka (1962: 153), with whose influential work on epistemic logic Quine was engaging, Quine took the *de re* propositional attitude ascription "∃x(N knows (b = x))" to be synonymous with the claim that N *knows who b is*. And as Quine notes, "It is very ordinary language indeed to speak of knowing who or what something is. However, ordinarity notwithstanding, I make no sense of the idiom apart from context. It is essentially indexical" (1976b: 863). Quine concludes that the inconstancy of *de re* attitude ascriptions makes them no more susceptible to regimentation than *de re* modal ascriptions. As Quine writes, "I do not see the makings here of a proper annex to austere scientific language" (ibid.).

Quine's criticism of Carnap's semantical system did not just involve suspicions with quantified modal logic. Recall that Carnap set as an adequacy condition on any definition of necessary truth that the necessary truths are all and only the analytic truths. Within the semantics described by Carnap, the way this condition of adequacy was implemented was via *meaning-postulates*. For Carnap, a possible world is, in the first instance, a maximally consistent set of sentences. Though no such set can contain a logical contradiction, such as "S" and "~S," nothing prevents such a set from containing a sentence such as "Bachelors are married." Given the semantics, it would then come out as possible that bachelors are married, and "Bachelors are unmarried" therefore would not be a necessary truth (see Quine 1961). To prevent this, each term is associated with an analytic definition (or "meaning postulate"), and state-descriptions are constrained to make all such analytic definitions true (Carnap 1958c). So, in the case of "bachelor," the meaning postulate is that "bachelor" means the same as "unmarried man," and any possible state-description must be one that contains the sentence "bachelors are unmarried men." Thus, meaning postulates eliminate state-descriptions containing "bachelors are married men" (since this sentence is logically inconsistent with the meaning postulate that "bachelors are unmarried men"), and "bachelors are unmarried men" comes out necessarily true (and hence analytic and non-factual) after all.

The notion of analyticity is at the core of Carnap's semantical system. In Quine's seminal 1951 paper "Two dogmas of empiricism" (Quine 1961) he launched his influential attack on the coherence of the notion of analyticity. (See also the discussion of Quine in "The development of analytic philosophy: Wittgenstein and after," Chapter 2 and "American philosophy in the twentieth century," Chapter 5.) According to Quine, there is no coherent way of making a distinction between synthetic truths and analytic truths; that is, there is no way of forging Carnap's distinction between *factual* and *non-factual* internal questions. The majority of Quine's arguments take the form of showing that explanations of analytic truth always appeal to notions that are equally problematic. For example, Carnap attempts to ground the notion of analyticity by stating that analytic truths are those that are true in virtue of the semantical rules of the language. But as Quine points out, the notion of a semantical rule is no more lucid than that of an analytic truth; nothing demarcates the statements that are semantical rules from the statements that are not semantical rules besides "appearing on a page under the heading 'Semantical Rules' " (1961: 34). After finding no notion that can explicate the notion of analyticity, Quine then rejects it as ill-founded.[31] If it is ill-founded, then the project of dividing the genuinely empirical claims of science from the non-factual claims of metaphysics, a project that was at the heart of Carnap's semantics, is doomed.

The precise forms of Quine's arguments against analyticity have been a subject of continual debate ever since the publication of "Two dogmas" and I cannot provide a lengthy discussion of them here. It suffices to say that although Quine's grounds remain somewhat murky, his rejection of analyticity is widely (though certainly not universally) accepted.[32] But whatever one thinks of Quine's attack on analyticity, Carnap had developed and refined the tools of intensional semantics to such a degree that one could employ them independently of his intended interpretation of necessity. So as we shall see later, while Carnap's own motivation for his semantic project became bogged down in debates over the coherence of its central notion, and the popularity of his anti-metaphysical philosophical project waned, a number of logicians and philosophers took up the tools developed by Carnap and applied them to some of the traditional questions in the theory of meaning.

Strawson and the challenge from ordinary-language philosophy

All of the philosophers we have been discussing were suspicious of the possibility of using logical tools to investigate natural language. Frege regarded natural language as too vague and context-sensitive to conduct scientific investigation, and Tarski thought that the "universal character" of natural languages rendered them inconsistent. Carnap's semantical systems were intended to be systems of analytic stipulations governing the meanings of the terms in the language; he had no interest in applying his formal tools to the project of empirical semantics.[33] The uneasiness these philosophers felt about applying the tools of logic to natural language was mirrored by philosophers who focused mainly on natural language, the so-called "ordinary language" school of philosophy, whose work is best exemplified in the writings of J. L. Austin and Peter Strawson; I will focus on the latter in explaining the doctrines.

The semantical tools developed by Frege, Russell, Tarski, and Carnap involved giving a characterization of the conditions under which sentences of a given language were true (perhaps relative to a model). As we have seen, such a characterization involves assignment of reference to terms and satisfaction conditions to predicates. Central to the ordinary-language philosopher's view is the thesis that properties such as truth and reference do not apply to linguistic expressions but are rather properties of what people *do* with linguistic expressions. It is a *use* of a singular term by a person that refers, and it is an assertion of a sentence that has a truth-value; one cannot speak of a *term* having reference, or a *sentence* having a truth-value. In short: words do not refer, people do. If reference and truth are not properties of linguistic expressions, then giving an account of linguistic meaning in terms of reference and truth is fundamentally misguided. Carnap and Tarski were right to focus their attention on formal languages, because the kind of account of meaning they were trying to give (in terms of reference and truth) was inapplicable to natural languages.

Since truth and reference are not properties of linguistic expressions, and linguistic meanings are properties of linguistic expressions, ordinary-language philosophers sought an alternative account of linguistic meaning. According to it, the linguistic meaning of an expression is a *rule for its proper use*. As Strawson writes in his classic 1950 paper, "On referring" (1996: 219–20)):

> To give the meaning of an expression (in the sense in which I am using the word) is to give *general directions* for its use to refer to or mention particular objects or persons; to give the meaning of a sentence is to give general directions for its use in making true or false assertions ... The meaning of an expression cannot be identified with the object it is used, on a particular occasion, to refer to. The meaning of a sentence cannot be identified with the assertion it is used, on a particular occasion, to make. For to talk about the meaning of an expression or sentence is not to talk about its use on a particular occasion, but about the rules, habits, conventions governing its correct use, on all occasions, to refer or to assert.

In "On referring," Strawson does not just state that meaning is use. He shows by a detailed example that two sentences can be used to express the same truth-conditions, yet differ on their use-conditions, and that this difference is a matter of the conventional meaning of the words used. He thus shows, by detailed consideration of a particular case, that giving the truth-conditions of an occurrence of a sentence, or giving the proposition it expresses, is to miss something about the conventional meaning of that expression. Unsurprisingly, the example Strawson uses is the case of *definite descriptions*.

For Russell, sentences containing definite descriptions express existential propositions. A sentence such as "The shortest spy is nice" expresses, for Russell, a proposition whose initial quantifier is existential in force (the proposition that there is a shortest spy, that everything that is a shortest spy is identical to her, and that she is nice). But construing sentences containing definite descriptions as expressing the same proposition as a sentence that contains only existential and universal quantifiers is to miss a crucial distinction in use-conditions between definite and indefinite descriptions. Furthermore, these use-conditions are clearly part of the conventional meanings of definite and indefinite descriptions. As Strawson (1996: 228) writes:

> The difference between the use of definite and indefinite articles is, very roughly, as follows. We use "the" either when a previous reference has been made, and when "the" signalizes that the same reference is being made; or when, in the absence of a previous indefinite reference, the context (including the hearer's assumed knowledge) is expected to enable the hearer to tell *what* reference is being made. We use "a" either when these conditions are not fulfilled, or when, although a definite reference *could* be made, we wish to keep dark the identity of the individual to whom, or to which, we are referring.

So even if we grant to Russell the thesis that "The shortest spy is nice" expresses the same proposition as that expressed by "There is a shortest spy, and everything that is a shortest spy is her, and she is nice," it does not follow that the two sentences have the same *meaning*. There are very different conditions of use associated with the two sentences, despite the agreement in truth-condition. Furthermore, these distinctions in use clearly have something to do with conventional properties of definite and indefinite descriptions. As Strawson notes, definite descriptions are typically used to refer to entities already introduced (familiar entities), and indefinite descriptions are typically used to introduce novel entities into the discourse. Strawson's objection here to Russell's theory of descriptions is that, by ignoring non-truth-conditional features of use, it ignores crucial differences in conventional meaning between definite and indefinite descriptions.[34]

Strawson's famous concluding sentence (1996: 230) in "On referring" is that "[n]either Aristotelian nor Russellian rules give the exact logic of any expression of ordinary language; for ordinary language has no exact logic." This claim is best seen in the light of the discussions in Strawson (1952) of the differences between the truth-tables analyses of the logical connectives of propositional logic, and the ordinary words "and," "or," "if .. then", and "if and only if." In each case, Strawson argued that there was a large gulf between the logical connective and its alleged ordinary language counterpart. For example, Strawson (1952: 80) objects to the truth-table meaning as a suitable characterization of the meaning of the English "and" that occurs between sentences as follows (I use "&" to denote the connective defined by the truth-tables):

> It might be conceded that 'and' has functions that '&' has not … and yet claimed that the rules that hold for 'and', where it is used to couple clauses, are the same as the rules that hold for '&'. Even this is not true. [By the truth-table for '&'], 'p & q' is logically equivalent to 'q & p'; but 'They got married and had a child' or 'He set out to work and found a job' are by no means logically equivalent to 'They had a child and got married' or 'He found a job and set out to work'.

Strawson also rejected any kind of meaning equivalence between the material conditional "→" and the "if … then" of ordinary language. As he says about the latter (1952: 37), "in general its employment in linking two clauses indicates that a statement made by the use of the first would be a ground or a reason for a statement made by the use of the second." More explicitly, he writes (p. 88):

> I have spoken of a 'primary or standard' use of 'if … then ..y.', or 'if', of which the main characteristics were: that for each hypothetical statement made by the use of 'if', there could be made just *one* statement which would be the antecedent of the hypothetical and just *one* statement which would be its consequent; that the hypothetical statement is acceptable (true, reasonable) if the antecedent statement, if made or accepted, would be a good ground or

reason for accepting the consequent statement; and that the making of the hypothetical statement carries the implication either of uncertainty about, or of disbelief in, the fulfilment of both antecedent and consequent.

Certainly, none of these facts about the primary or standard use of "if … then" in English are captured by the truth-table for the material conditional.

Similar points apply to the "standard use" of disjunctive statements in English, instances of the schema "P or Q." It is reasonable to assert an instance of "P or Q" only if one is unsure about the truth-value of both disjuncts. For example, it is odd for someone fully aware of the political facts to utter, in 2006, "Either George Bush is President now or Bill Clinton is President now." The fact that it is not reasonable to assert an instance of "P or Q" unless one is unsure of the truth-value of both disjuncts is clearly a fact about the standard use of sentences containing "or," and not captured by the truth-table for the logical connective for disjunction. A further difference between the truth-table for disjunction and the English word "or" is "that in certain verbal contexts, 'either … or …' plainly carries the implication 'and not both … and …', whereas in other contexts it does not" (Strawson 1952: 92). So there are two distinct uses of the English word "or," and hence apparently two distinct meanings: one corresponding to the truth-table, or inclusive sense of "or," and the other corresponding to the "exclusive" sense of "or" (the "and not both" reading indicated by Strawson). So "or" is ambiguous, whereas the logical connective for disjunction is not (though both distinct meanings are of course characterizable with the use of truth-tables).

The central challenge of ordinary-language philosophy is that reference and truth are inappropriate notions to employ in explicating linguistic meaning for a language with pervasive context-sensitivity mediating the relation between word and world. Instead, we need the notion of a rule of proper use. Reference and truth do not help in the analysis of most rules of use; the rules of proper use governing words are not subject to rigorous semantic analysis. For example, truth-tables are clearly hopeless in explaining both the connection between the antecedent and the consequent of a natural language hypothetical statement, and the fact that a statement of this kind is assertible only if the speaker disbelieves the antecedent and consequent; they are equally useless in explaining the similar facts pertaining to natural language disjunctions.

Grice and the semantics/pragmatics distinction

In his extraordinarily influential paper "Logic and conversation" (1989c), Herbert Paul Grice (1913–88) set out to defend the truth-table analysis of the meaning of the natural language logical particles from the ordinary-language onslaught. Recall that when Strawson spoke of the connection between antecedent and consequent that is part of the "primary use" of an English conditional statement, he spoke of the *acceptability*, *truth*, or *reasonability* of a use of a conditional statement. This suggests that Strawson did not distinguish the *truth* of an utterance from the *acceptability* of that utterance. The key to Grice's defense of the truth-table analysis of the meanings of "and," "or" and "if ... not" is that these notions can (and often do) come apart. A given utterance can be true, even though uttering it is not acceptable, because it violates conversational norms. In explaining this distinction, Grice provided the foundations for a theory of conversational norms. The theory Grice gives clearly explains how an utterance may be true, although unacceptable as an assertion owing to specific facts about the conversation and its participants. He then used the distinction between the truth of a statement and its conversational acceptability in a defense of the thesis that the connectives of propositional logic were correct explications of their natural language counterparts. More specifically, Grice assumed that the natural language logical particles have the truth-table meanings of their logical counterparts, and argued that features of the uses of these expressions that are not explicable by the truth-tables are due to facts about the norms governing conversation, rather than the meanings of the words.

According to Grice, conversation is a cooperative rational activity; each conversation has a purpose. This fact about conversations imposes as a norm what Grice (1989c: 26) calls the *Cooperative Principle*, which is "Make your conversational contribution such as is required, at the stage at which it occurs, by the accepted purpose or direction of the talk exchange in which you are engaged." The Cooperative Principle is the overarching principle guiding conversation. Following it imposes a number of more specific norms on conversational participants. For example, lying involves one kind of uncooperative conversational behavior, being purposely irrelevant involves another, and not being sufficiently informative is yet a third kind of uncooperative behavior. Following the Cooperative Principle isn't always a matter of saying something true, relevant, and maximally informative; it is also a matter of how one says what one says. According to the maxim of *manner*, one should try to list events in the order in which they occur, and to cite causes before effects.

Using these conversational principles, Grice attempts to explain many of the facts about standard use cited by Strawson without giving up the thesis that the same truth-table analysis for the logical connectives also gives the meanings of their natural language counterparts. Consider Strawson's point that "or" in ordinary language is ambiguous between an *exclusive* use ("but not both") and an *inclusive* use. Assuming that "or" unambiguously means inclusive "or" (the meaning of the logical connective for disjunction), one can explain the fact that "or" is often used exclusively by general conversational principles. Suppose Hannah uttered an instance of "P or Q," but in fact believed that both P and Q were true. Then Hannah would not be maximally informative; she would be violating Grice's conversational maxim of *quantity*. So if someone believes that P and Q, and if they wish to follow conversational norms, they should say the more informative "P and Q," rather than the less informative "P or Q" (which is compatible with the truth of only one of P and Q). So, when someone utters an instance of "P or Q," they convey (without asserting, as part of the linguistically determined content) that they do not know that P and Q. The fact that this is part of what is conveyed by following conversational principles, rather than what is asserted as part of the linguistically determined content, can be ascertained by appeal to Grice's central criterion for distinguishing what is part of what is said (the linguistically determined asserted content) from what is merely conversationally conveyed, which is the test of *cancellability*. One can *cancel* the implication conveyed by an utterance of "P or Q" (which is that one doesn't know both P and Q) by saying "P or Q; in fact, both P and Q are true," as in "John is with Bill or he is with Frank; in fact he is with both." So, consistently with the assumption that "or" unambiguously *means* inclusive "or," one can explain why "or" is often *used* as if it meant exclusive "or."

One can use the very same kind of explanation to dissolve the sense that it is part of the meaning of a disjunctive statement that the speaker is unaware of the truth of either disjunct. If Hannah knows that John was at the party, it would be a violation of the maxim of quantity for her to assert that either John was at the party or he was at home. She would not be being maximally informative by asserting the disjunctive statement, and hence would be violating the maxim of quantity. Furthermore, the implication that the speaker is unaware of the truth of either disjunct can be cancelled, as in Grice's example (1989a: 44–5) "The prize is either in the garden or in the attic. I know that because I know where I put it, but I'm not going to tell you." Thus, one can explain the fact that a disjunctive statement is usually only proper if the speaker is unaware of the truth of either disjunct, without making that fact part of the conventional meanings of any words.

Grice also attempted to provide pragmatic explanations (that is, explanations from general principles governing conversation) for the divergences between the truth-table meaning for the conditional and ordinary indicative conditionals (1989b). (For the distinction between indicative and subjunctive conditionals, see the section "Conditionals," below.) In attempting to account for the connection thesis, the thesis that a conditional is only assertible if the antecedent provides a ground or good reason to accept the consequent, Grice (1989b: 61–2) appealed to the conversational maxims, in particular that of quantity, which directs interlocutors always to assert the strongest claim consistent with their evidence, and that of quality, which directs them to have adequate evidence for their assertions. If the indicative conditional is the material conditional, then it is true if and only if the antecedent is false or the consequent is true. If the speaker knows that the antecedent is false, adherence to the maxim of quantity requires that the speaker simply assert the negation of the antecedent, rather than the whole conditional; *mutatis mutandis* for the truth of the consequent. So a conditional is only assertible if the speaker is unaware of the truth values of the antecedent and consequent. But the maxim of quality requires anyone who asserts a conditional to have evidence for the truth of the material conditional. Since, for the reasons just given, the evidence cannot be truth-functional (that is, the speaker's grounds cannot be knowledge of the truth-values of the antecedent or consequent), the speaker must have non-truth-functional grounds for her assertion of the material conditional, if she is adhering to the maxims of quantity and quality. So, asserting an indicative conditional, on the supposition that it has the meaning of the material conditional, requires the speaker to have non-truth-functional grounds for her assertion. More specifically, it requires the speaker to know or believe that the antecedent would be a good ground for the consequent.

As we shall see, there are a number of problems with Grice's defense of the material conditional analysis of indicative conditionals. But Grice's defense of the thesis that the meaning of "or" is exhausted by the truth-table for inclusive "or" has been widely accepted, as have a number of other Gricean explanations of use-facts. The moral of Grice's work is that the facts of linguistic use are a product of two factors, meaning and conversational norms. Failure to absorb this fact undermines many of the main theses of ordinary-language philosophy.

However, recall that there were two aspects of the ordinary-language philosopher's position. The first involved emphasizing the divergences in use between the logical terms and their ordinary-language counterparts. The second involved the fact that natural languages involve context-sensitive words (e.g. "I," "here," and "now"), and that many words only have reference relative to a context of use, and many sentences only have truth-values relative to a context of use. Since reference and truth-value are only properties of *uses* of expressions, they are inappropriate notions to use in the analysis of the linguistic meanings of expressions. In general, expression types in natural language do not have references or truth-values, only uses of them do. So employing the apparatus of semantic theory, which crucially avails itself of notions such as reference and truth, is not the right way to give a theory of meaning for natural language; the meaning of expression types is given by rules of use. Grice's response to the ordinary-language philosopher speaks only to the first of these aspects of the ordinary-language philosopher's position. But a response to the second aspect of the ordinary-language philosopher's position was to emerge from the work of those who developed and refined intensional semantics.

The development of intensional semantics: from Montague to Kaplan

As we saw earlier, Carnap's semantic theory crucially exploits the notion of a possible world in defining semantic values of expressions. Each expression has, as its primary semantic value, an intension, which is a function from a possible world to the extension of that expression at that world. In the case of sentences, the intension of a sentence is a function from possible worlds to truth-values. Carnap's semantic theory has, as its "central notion" (in Michael Dummett's sense), the notion of *truth with respect to a possible world*. The logician Richard Montague (1930–71), a student of Tarski's, argued that a theory of meaning should take the more general form of *truth with respect to a context of use*, where possible worlds are but one feature of a context of use (Montague 1974c: 96). Montague treated a context of use as an *index*, a collection of semantically relevant aspects of the context of use. If the language in question contained tenses and modal operators, then the indices involved in the semantic interpretation of that language would contain times and worlds. If the language also contained the indexical terms "I" and "here," the indices would also have persons and places as aspects. Montague then generalized Carnap's notion of intension; instead of an intension being a function from possible worlds to extensions, an intension, for Montague, was a function from indices to extensions. For example, the intension of a sentence such as "I am tired" would be a function from indices to truth-values; it would take an index whose aspects were times, worlds, and persons to the truth if and only if the person at the index was tired at the time and world of the index.

The interpretation of modal operators in Montague's system was also a generalization from their interpretation in modal semantics. In Carnap's system, the function of modal operators was to *shift* the evaluation of a proposition from one possible world to another; a modal operator took an intension, and evaluated that intension at other possible worlds. On this account, a sentence such as "possibly S" is true relative to a world w if and only if the intension of S is true in some (possibly distinct) world w'. So the function of "possible," for Carnap, is to shift the evaluation of the intension of S from w to w'; "possibly S" is true in w if and only if S is true in w' (and the function of "necessarily" is to shift the evaluation of the content of the embedded sentence to all possible worlds). In Montague's system, modal and tense operators evaluate intensions at *indices* rather than just possible worlds. On this account, a sentence such as "possibly S" is true at an index i if and only if the intension of S is true at i', where i' differs from i at most in its world feature. So rather than truth with respect to a possible world being the fundamental notion, truth with respect to an index is Montague's fundamental notion, with worlds being one element of an index.[35] This apparatus allowed Montague to generalize the apparatus of intensional semantics to treat *context-sensitivity* in natural language, without sacrificing the elegant treatment of modal and tense operators. As we shall see below, this leads to a different kind of response to the challenge from ordinary-language philosophy from the one developed by Grice.

Montague's contributions to the systematic study of language went well beyond generalizing intensional semantics to capture tense and context-sensitivity. His most influential papers focused on intensional constructions in natural language. In one of them (1974b), he gave an account of a number of intensional constructions other than the classic cases of propositional attitude verbs and modal and temporal contexts. For example, he provided a semantic analysis of *intensional transitive verbs*, such as "seek" and "worship". The difference between intensional transitive verbs and extensional transitive verbs (such as "kick" and "meet") is that, while one cannot meet a unicorn or kick a unicorn (since there are no unicorns), one can nevertheless *seek* a unicorn. So, whereas satisfying an instance of the predicate "meeting N" requires that there is some existent entity that one meets, satisfying an instance of the predicate "seeking N" does not require that there is some existent entity that one seeks.

Intensional transitive verbs had generally been ignored in the literature, from Frege and Russell on, largely because of the influence of Russell's theory of descriptions, the standard method of dissolving apparent reference to non-existent entities. Russell's theory involves providing a contextual definition of definite descriptions; meanings are assigned only to sentences containing definite descriptions, rather than the definite descriptions themselves. Russell's theory helps us analyze away apparent reference to non-existent entities in a construction such as "John believes that the fountain of youth is in Peru," since we can apply the theory to the sentence "the fountain of youth is in Peru," and arrive at an object of John's belief, without there being a fountain of youth. In contrast, one cannot use Russell's theory to arrive at an object of seeking for a construction such as "Pizarro sought the fountain of youth," since that theory gives us no way of treating the definite description "the fountain of youth" in isolation. For this reason, Quine (1960: sect. 32) regimented intensional transitive verbs away in favor of propositional attitude verbs (so the intensional transitive construction "*x* looks for *y*" becomes the propositional attitude construction "*x* endeavors that *x* finds *y*").[36] The fact that analytic philosophers had not produced a successful analysis of intensional transitive verbs must be viewed as a bit of an embarrassment. The problem of intensional transitive verbs is one of the original motivations for twentieth-century discussions of content. For example, it was salient in the minds of Franz Brentano and his students, who sought to render consistent the thesis that the characteristic feature of mental states was that they were about things, with the fact that one could have a mental state the object of which did not exist. Montague's discussion of intensional transitive verbs was thus a watershed moment in the theory of meaning. It has subsequently given rise to a lively literature in semantics and philosophy of language on the topic (e.g. Partee 1974; Zimmerman 1993; Forbes 2000; Richard 2001).

Montague's semantic theory was not just distinctive for its focus on intensional constructions in natural language. He also returned philosophers of language and semanticists to a tradition that was lost or at the very least obscured in the kind of semantic theory favored by Tarski (and Davidson). Recall that Frege treated the traditional relation between the subject of a sentence and its predicate as that of an *argument* to a *function*. That is, Frege regarded the fundamental relationship between the semantic values of expressions in a sentence to be one of *functional application*. Although quantifiers, for Frege, had the function of binding variables within their scope, they also had determinate semantic values, namely *second-level functions*.[37] For example, as we saw above, "everything" denoted a function from first-level functions to truth-values. The denotation of "everything" is a function that takes any first-level function that takes every object to the true, to the true, and takes every other entity to the false. Similarly, the denotation of "something" takes to the true any first-level function that had the true for at least one value, and everything else to the false. So Frege operated with an ontology that was stratified into *types*; there were objects, then functions from objects to truth-values (first-level functions), then functions from first-level functions to truth-values (second-level functions), and on up. In Tarski's work, by contrast, no use is made of functional application as a relation between semantic values. Quantifiers are not assigned functions of various kinds; an object-language universal quantifier over objects is interpreted via the use of a meta-language quantifier over sequences. Montague's semantics returned philosophers of language to the Fregean tradition of treating semantic values as functions from arguments to values, with functional application as the primary mode of semantic composition. There are lively foundational debates between advocates of Montague's *type-theoretic* approach to semantics and advocates of the more Tarskian approach, such as James Higginbotham.

Montague's marriage of intensional semantics with type-theory was extraordinarily fruitful, and led (with the help of the work of his distinguished student Barbara Partee) to the emergence of *semantics* as a new discipline within linguistic theory. But that is not to say that the generalization of intensional semantics that was at the heart of his program has been universally accepted; in fact, the majority of philosophers of language today regard it as incorrect. The mistake made by Montague was to think that the study of modality was a branch of *pragmatics*, the study of context-sensitivity in natural language.

Recall that Montague's generalization of intensional semantics consisted of treating possible worlds as features of the more general notion of a *context of use*. He then generalized the treatment of operators as shifting the evaluation of the truth of a content from one world to the next, to shifting the evaluation of the truth of a content from one context of use (or index) to the next. It is this generalization that is widely (but not universally) regarded as an error.

The first hint that something was amiss in the assimilation of modal and temporal operators to the general study of truth relative to a context of use came from Hans Kamp's work on the temporal indexical "now." Kamp, a student of Montague's, established several theses about temporal logic. The first is there are certain natural language sentences that have readings that are most perspicuously captured via the postulation of more than just past and future tense operators. For example, consider the sentence in (1) (from Kamp 1971: 231):

A child was born that will become the ruler of the world.

Sentence (1) means something like "In the past, a child was born who, in the future of the present moment, becomes the ruler of the world." In order to supply (1) with its natural reading, one needs to have at one's disposal an operator with the meaning of the English word "now," whose function is to evaluate its embedded content *at the present moment*.[38] Kamp then established that a satisfactory semantics for "now" requires having two times in the Montagovian "index" that is supposed to represent a context of use. One of the times would be shifted by temporal operators such as "it was the case that" and "it will be the case that." The other time would be intuitively the time of the utterance, and would never be shifted by any operators. Its function would be to allow for the interpretation of any occurrences of "now" in the sentence. The present moment feature of the Montagovian index could not be shifted by any operators, because otherwise, in interpreting any embedded occurrences of "now" (that is, embedded inside other temporal operators), one could no longer access the present moment, and thereby successfully interpret "now."

Kamp's insights about "now" carry over directly to the modal indexical "actual." In order to provide a successful interpretation of embedded occurrences of "actual" (that is, occurrences of "actual" inside other modal operators), each Montagovian index must contain two worlds, one that would be shifted by modal operators, and the other that would be the world of utterance. Interpreting an embedded occurrence of "actual" (that is, one that occurs within the scope of other modal operators) requires keeping track of the world of utterance. For the function of the initial modal operator is to shift the evaluation of the content of the embedded sentence to another possible world, and one needs to retain the information about the actual world of utterance, in order to interpret any occurrences of "actual" within that embedded sentence. So Montague's indices each would contain two kinds of features. First, they would contain features (worlds and times) that were shifted by operators. Second, to interpret indexical operators such as "now" and "actual," the indices would contain features that were not capable of being shifted by operators, but would always represent features of the actual context of use of the sentence being uttered.

So Kamp's work suggests that within a single Montagovian index there are two quite different sorts of features. First, there are features that are shifted by operators, such as "necessarily" and "possible" (and the past and future tense, assuming that they are operators). Second, there are features that intuitively represent features of the actual context of use. These include the moment at which the utterance was made, and the world at which the utterance was made, which are required, respectively, to interpret indexical operators such as "now" and "actual." Furthermore, these features are not capable of being shifted by operators, or else one could not interpret embedded occurrences of indexical operators. So, for example, in evaluating the truth of the intension of say "Necessarily S" with respect to an index i, one would evaluate the intension of S at all indices i' that differed from i at most in their world index, and shared with i all the features relevant for interpreting indexical operators; that is, all those features that represent aspects of the context of use in which "Necessarily S" was uttered. This suggests that Montague's indices are not natural kinds. Each index contains two kinds of information: information relevant for interpreting modal and temporal operators, on the one hand, and information that represents features of the context of use, which are relevant for interpreting indexical expressions such as "now," "actual," "I," and "here."

There were also other reasons to be suspicious of Montague's index-theoretic approach. In 1970, Robert Stalnaker pointed out (1999b: 36ff.) that Montague's semantics (or as Stalnaker calls it, Montague's "semantics-pragmatics") did not allow for the representation of *propositions*. For Montague, there is only one semantic content of an utterance (or occurrence) of the sentence "I am tired," and that is a function from contexts of use to truth-values. If Hannah utters "I am tired," and John utters "I am tired," the only difference there is between the contents of their utterances is that one may be true and the other may be false (that is, the value of the semantic content of "I am tired" may be different, because it is being evaluated relative to distinct indices). But, as Stalnaker emphasizes, there are additional differences between their utterances. Intuitively, *what Hannah said* when she uttered "I am tired" is distinct from *what John said* when he uttered "I am tired"; they expressed different propositions. But there is no semantic value in Montague's system that represents the different propositions in question. There is just a function from indices to truth-values associated with "I am tired," and this is not the proposition expressed by either of these utterances of "I am tired" (since they express *different* propositions).

Kamp's work clearly shows the need for "double indexing." The first kind of index is required to interpret indexical expressions occurring within a sentence. The second kind of index is required to give the proper semantics for operators on content, such as "necessarily" and "possible" (and the tenses, if they are operators). But it took another student of Montague's, David Kaplan (1933–), to draw out the real moral behind the need for double indexing. In his seminal work "Demonstratives" (1989), Kaplan argues that the two kinds of indices correspond to two kinds of semantic values.[39] The first kind of index represents the dependence of semantic value upon context. The semantic content of a context-dependent sentence such as "I am tired" depends upon features of the context of use. If John is the speaker in the context of use, then "I am tired" expresses the proposition that John is tired; if Hannah is the speaker in the context of use, then it expresses the proposition that Hannah is tired. The second kind of index represents the dependence of truth of a semantic content on a *circumstance of evaluation* (such as a possible world, or a time if tenses are operators on contents), and is required to give a satisfactory semantics for sentence-operators. A proposition may be true at one possible world, but false at another.

Accordingly, expressions are associated with two kinds of semantic values, which Kaplan called *character* and *content* respectively. The character of an expression is a function from a context of use to the content of that expression relative to that context. According to Kaplan, the character of an expression is also the linguistic meaning of that expression. So, the linguistic meaning of the first-person pronoun "I" is a function from contexts of use to persons (intuitively, the speakers of those contexts). Any use of "I" has the same meaning as any other use, though a possibly distinct semantic content. Kaplan took the semantic contents of singular terms, such as proper names and indexicals such as "I" to be their referents, in Frege's sense, and he took the semantic contents of sentences relative to contexts to be propositions. Sentence operators such as "necessarily" and "possibly" shifted the world feature of the index that represented the circumstance of evaluation. The index that represented the context of use did not contain any features that were shifted by operators in the language (Kaplan 1989: 510ff.).

By dividing features of indices into contexts of use and circumstances of evaluation, Kaplan's semantic theory represents a clear advance over Montague's. It explains why only certain features are shiftable by operators and, more importantly, it gives a semantic representation of *propositions* (the values of the characters of sentences).[40] As a result, Kaplan's distinctions have been widely adopted in philosophy of language since the mid-1970s. In particular, most philosophers have come to accept that context-dependent expressions show that there are two levels of semantic value; first, linguistic meaning, and second, the content of an occurrence of an expression on an occasion. Different occurrences of an expression might have different semantic contents, despite sharing a linguistic meaning, as is so clearly the case with the first-person pronoun "I" and other indexicals.

The work done by Montague and then Kaplan allows for another kind of reply to the ordinary-language philosopher's skepticism about the possibility of giving a rigorous semantics for a natural language than the one provided by Grice. Recall that the ordinary-language philosopher's skepticism arose from the conviction that truth and reference were properties of *uses* of expressions, rather than properties of expressions, and meanings were rules for using those expressions. Kaplan's semantic theory undermines these considerations. It does make perfect sense to speak of singular terms having reference, albeit *relative to a context*, and it makes perfect sense to speak of sentences having truth-values, also relative to a context. So it makes perfect sense to attribute reference and truth to expression types, once contextual relativity is factored into the semantic theory. Whereas the notion of a rule of use is vague and mystical, Kaplan's notion of the character of an expression is not only clear, but set theoretically explicable in terms of fundamental semantic notions; the character of an expression is a function from a context to the reference of that expression in that context. Far from context-sensitivity being an impediment to giving a proper account of linguistic meaning in terms of reference and truth, appeal to these semantic notions allows us to give a considerably more explicit characterization of linguistic meaning than the ordinary-language philosophers were capable of providing.

Necessity regained

Although Montague and his descendents refined and extended the intensional semantic framework developed by Carnap, they did not at all share with him the interpretation of necessity as analyticity. Instead, a growing consensus developed around the idea that *metaphysical* necessity was a legitimate interpretation of modality. However, the consensus built up slowly, and in large part as a reaction to Quine's influential criticisms of *de re* modality.

Recall that Carnap's solution to the problem of *de re* modality involved assigning a dual interpretation to each expression; every occurrence of an expression had both an intension and an extension, including variables. What mattered for the truth of an open sentence embedded inside a modal operator were the value-intensions of the variables occurring within it. The Frege–Church method, by contrast, involved taking expressions occurring inside modal contexts as denoting intensions rather than extensions. Variables occurring within modal contexts, according to this approach, ranged only over intensions. Both of these approaches treated the semantically relevant values of variables occurring within modal contexts as intensions, and in the case of individual-level variables, *individual concepts* (functions from possible worlds to objects).

The individual concept approach to *de re* modal quantification concedes that quantification into modal contexts is special in some way. The insight that led to the current consensus about modality lies in recognizing that quantification into modal contexts is not special in any way; quantification into modal contexts should be treated just like quantification into extensional contexts. In other words, on this *objectual* conceptual of quantification, the semantically relevant values of variables in modal contexts are just the same as the semantically relevant values of variables in extensional contexts, namely normal objects.

Let us return to Quine's worry, and in particular, the distinction in truth-value between (1) and (2):

(1) (the number of planets ≥ 7)
(2) (9 ≥ 7)

Quine's concern is that objectual quantification into the position of the variable "x" in the open modal sentence "(x ≥ 7)" is incoherent, because whether or not a sequence satisfies "(x ≥ 7)" will depend not just upon the object that sequence assigns to the variable "x," but also on how we *describe* that object (as "9" or as "the number of planets"). The objectual conception involves rejecting the thought that in quantifying into a modal context one needs to have any description at all of the objects that are the values of the variables. The value of a variable is simply the object it designates, and so variables, no matter where they occur, are *purely designative* in Quine's sense, and hence permitted to be bound by quantifiers even when they occur in the scope of a modal operator.

But recall Quine's argument (see pp. 402–405), for the incoherence of quantifying into modal contexts. Quine inferred from the fact that co-extensive terms such as "the number of planets" and "9" could not be substituted for one another inside the scope of a modal operator without change in truth-value, to the conclusion that the position of the variable "x" in the open modal sentence "(x ≥ 7)" is not a purely designative position. So how is it possible to hold, in the face of the facts in (1) and (2), that the variable "x" in "(x ≥ 7)", is purely designative?

From the perspective of the advocate of objectual quantification, Quine's mistake was to infer from the premise that the two co-extensional terms "9" and "the number of planets" could not be substituted for one another in "(x ≥ 7)," to the conclusion that the position occupied by the variable "x" is not purely designative. As Kaplan (1986: 235) has clearly emphasized, all that follows from the premise is that at least one of the two occurrences of "9" and "the number of planets" in (1) and (2) is not purely designative. Nothing whatever follows about the *position* that these terms occupy. In particular, it may be that "the number of planets" does not have a purely designative occurrence in (1), whereas "9" has a purely designative occurrence in (2), and the variable "x" has a purely designative occurrence in "∃x (x ≥ 7)."

According to the advocate of objectual quantification, the function of any occurrence of a variable is simply to be purely designative. So the advocate of objectual quantification endorses substitutivity of identity in the form:

(3) ∀x ∀y(x = y → (φ(x) ↔ φ(y))).

The fact that (1) is false and (2) is true does not in the least threaten the truth of (3). For according to the advocate of objectual quantification, although not all occurrences of terms are purely designative, variables are always purely designative. The fact that (1) and (2) differ in truth-value demonstrates that at least one of the terms "the number of planets" and "9" has a non-purely designative occurrence in "(x ≥ 7)." But it does not show that (3) is false. Given the objectual interpretation of variables, what (3) expresses is *Leibniz's Law*, which, as Cartwright (1971) clearly shows, is an obviously true metaphysical principle not to be confused with the false principle that any two co-extensional terms (including descriptive terms) can be substituted *salva veritate* in modal contexts.

Another way of thinking of the failure of Quine's argument, emphasized in Stanley (1997a: 561), is that the failure of the substitutivity of identity with variables as stated in (3) only follows from the failure of substitutivity with terms (as in (1) and (2)) if we think of the quantifiers *substitutionally*, as allowing for arbitrary substitution of singular terms (including descriptions) for variables. The advocate of objectual quantification rejects this construal of quantification. The reason Quine construed quantification into modal contexts substitutionally is that his targets interpreted necessity as analyticity (as we have seen with Carnap). Since analyticity is fundamentally a property of sentences, it is natural to construe quantification into an open modal sentence in terms of the analyticity of a sentence with no free variables (Neale 2000: 302–3). But the advocate of objectual quantification rejects this interpretation of necessity and with it the corresponding non-objectual account of quantification. The natural interpretation of "□" on the objectual construal of quantification is as *metaphysical* necessity; on this interpretation, an object satisfies "□Fx" if and only if that object has F as an essential property. Thus Quine's charge (1953) that objectually quantifying into modal contexts involves "Aristotelian essentialism" is partially vindicated; at the very least, the *coherence* of essentialist attributions is presupposed by this construal of quantification into a necessity operator interpreted metaphysically.[41]

What, then, of the failure of substitution in pairs such as (1) and (2)? Quite early on, philosophers had started to recognize that Quine's argument seemed to play upon some feature peculiar to definite descriptions as opposed to proper names. In a review of Quine's 1947 paper, Arthur Smullyan wrote, with reference to the claim that it is not necessary that the evening star is identical to the morning star:

> We now may ask what sense of the word "constant" is needed in order to justify application of the principle of existential quantification. It is possible that by "constant" is meant what is commonly understood by "proper name." Under this interpretation it appears evident to this reviewer that the principle of existential generalization is true. However, we observe that if "Evening Star" and "Morning Star" proper-name the same individual they are *synonymous* and therefore [the claim is false]. (Smullyan 1947: 140)

So Smullyan claims that co-extensional terms *used as proper names* are substitutable for one another *salva veritate* in modal contexts (and in particular, if "Evening Star" and "Morning Star" are used as proper names, it is necessary that the evening star is the morning star). So it was because Quine was using the terms as descriptions rather than proper names that they were not substitutable for one another in modal contexts.[42] In a similar vein, some years later, Ruth Barcan Marcus (1921–) wrote in her classic 1961 paper "Modalities and intensional languages":

> Now, suppose we come upon a statement like (15) Scott is the author of *Waverley* and we have a decision to make … If we decide that 'the evening star' and 'the morning star' are proper names for the same thing, and that 'Scott' and 'the author of *Waverley*' are proper names for the same thing, then they must be intersubstitutable in every context. (Barcan Marcus 1993: 10)

Indeed, Barcan Marcus concludes that, "What I have been arguing is that to say truly of an identity (in the strongest sense of the word) that it is true, it must be tauto-logically true or analytically true (1993: 12). So she maintains that when "a" and "b" are being used as names (presumably logically proper names, in Russell's sense), as opposed to being used as descriptions (pp. 10–12), then "a = b" is analytically true, if true at all.[43]

What emerges from the suggestions of Smullyan and Barcan Marcus is that there is a distinction between *using terms as proper names* and *using terms as descriptions*. If one uses two terms as names, and they refer to the same object, then the two terms are synonymous, and the identity is analytically true. As a result, substitution is permitted even in modal contexts. So, if "the number of planets" is being used as a proper name of 9, then (1) and (2) are both true and one of Quine's premises (the falsity of (1)) is undermined. On the other hand, if (1) is false, then "the number of planets" is being used as a description and not a name, and (1) is not a genuine identity after all.

The problem with Smullyan and Barcan Marcus's suggestions is that it is quite implausible to take a sentence such as Barcan Marcus's (15) to be analytically true, and it is equally implausible to take "the evening star" and "the morning star" to be synonymous (and hence "The evening star is the morning star" to be analytically true). By not clearly disassociating the metaphysical notion of necessity from its epistemic cousins such as analyticity and a priority, Smullyan and Barcan Marcus failed to make plausible the thesis that true identities were necessary.

In 1972, Saul Kripke published *Naming and Necessity*, which transformed what had been certain abstract formal possibilities essentially into common sense and eventual philosophical orthodoxy. First, he clearly distinguished the metaphysical notions of necessity and contingency from the epistemic notions of a priority and a posteriority (1980: 34ff.). As he points out, the notion of a priority is a concept from episte-mology, and means roughly that a statement is knowable independently of experience. Though "necessary" can express an epistemic concept (and indeed, as Kripke points out, can sometimes be used to express the property of a priority), it can also be used to express *metaphysical necessity*, which is a concept that has nothing whatever to do with epistemology, but rather is a concept of *metaphysics*. Again very roughly, a truth is metaphysically necessary if and only if the world could not have been different in such a way as to make that proposition false. There is no prima facie reason to think that a priority, the concept from epistemology, coincides with metaphysical necessity, the concept from metaphysics, and indeed Kripke produces examples of metaphysical necessities that are not a priori and metaphysical contingencies that are a priori.

For example, Kripke (1980: 100–3, 108–9) argues that Barcan Marcus and Smullyan were correct to maintain that true identity statements involving names, such as "Hesperus is Phosphorus" and "Cicero is Tully," are necessarily true. However, Kripke (pp. 103–4) rejects Barcan Marcus's thesis that the statement that Hesperus is Phosphorus and the statement that Cicero is Tully are analytic, since he rejects that they are a priori, and construes "analytic statement" to entail that a statement is necessary and a priori.[44] So true identity statements involving ordinary proper names are, for Kripke, instances of statements that are both necessary and (as Frege pointed out) a posteriori.[45] He also gives other examples of statements that are both necessary and a posteriori besides identity sentences such as "Hesperus is Phosphorus" and "Cicero is Tully." For example, he argues that we have intuitions about the essential properties of things and among the essential properties of such things are their *origins*. A person essentially is the product of the sperm and egg that actually produced her; it makes no sense to think of *the same person* being produced by a different sperm or egg (p. 113). If a table is made from a hunk of wood, then it is essentially made from that hunk of wood; it could not be the very same table and be made from, for example, metal. Since it is not a priori what a thing's origins are, such necessities as are expressed by sentences such as "Elizabeth originated from this sperm and this egg" or "This table is made out of this hunk of wood" are both necessary and a posteriori. Finally, Kripke also argues that *theoretical identification statements*, such as "Heat is mean molecular motion," "Water is H_2O," and "Gold is the element with atomic number 79" are necessary a posteriori. However, his arguments here are more controversial, involving the topic of the "rigidity" of general terms (for an excellent introduction to the difficulties here, see Soames 2002: ch. 9). Kripke also produces examples of statements that are both contingent and a priori. For example, consider the "standard meter" (henceforth "stick S") in Paris, which is used to fix the reference of the expression "one meter." Stick S could have been slightly longer or slightly shorter (suppose, for example, that heat had been applied to it). However, "for someone who has fixed the metric system by reference to Stick S" (Kripke 1980: 56), the statement "Stick S is one meter long" is a priori. So the statement "Stick S is one meter long," for a person who has fixed the metric system by reference to stick S, is both contingent and a priori.[46]

Kripke also provides what are widely accepted as conclusive arguments against Russell's description theory of ordinary proper names. Since Nathan Salmon's (1951–) discussion in *Reference and Essence* (Salmon 1981: 23ff.) it has been standard to distinguish between three sorts of arguments provided by Kripke against the description theory of ordinary proper names; the *modal* argument, the *epistemological* argument, and the *semantic* argument. According to the modal argument against the description theory of proper names, proper names are *rigid designators*, where a designator N of an object *o* is rigid if and only if N designates *o* in all possible worlds w in which *o* exists, and N designates nothing other than *o* in all possible worlds in which *o* does not exist. In contrast, the descriptions that plausibly give the meaning of ordinary proper names are not rigid designators. For example, "the last great philosopher of antiquity" plausibly gives the meaning of the name "Aristotle," if any description does. But an utterance of the sentence "Aristotle is the last great philosopher of antiquity" expresses a contingent proposition. The designator "the last great philosopher of antiquity" designates other people than Aristotle relative to some possible worlds in which Aristotle exists; for example, relative to a possible world in which Aristotle did not write any philosophy at all, it designates Plato. So "the last great philosopher of antiquity" is not a rigid designator of Aristotle, while "Aristotle" is a rigid designator of Aristotle (for a detailed account of the empirical argument for the thesis that names are rigid designators, see Stanley 1997a: 565ff.).[47] According to the *epistemological argument* against the description theory of names, sentences containing names and the descriptions that supposedly give their meaning are not a priori true, which they should be if the descriptions are synonymous with those names. For example, "Aristotle is the last great philosopher of antiquity" is not an a priori truth, which it should be if "Aristotle" was really the covert definite description "the last great philosopher of antiquity." Finally, according to the *semantic argument* against the description theory of names, someone can still use a name to refer to an object, even if they are completely unaware of the reference-fixing description.[48]

So, according to Kripke, names are not covert definite descriptions. Kripke argues (1980: 78) that names are not just rigid designators, but are (in the vocabulary of Salmon 1981), *obstinate* rigid designators, in the sense that a name refers to the same object relative to every possible world, including worlds in which that object does not exist. If so, then names behave under modal operators *exactly as variables relative to an assignment* according to the objectual interpretation of quantification into modal contexts. On this interpretation of *de re* modal quantification, relative to a sequence, the occurrence of the variable "x" in the open modal formula "Fx" has the same value relative to any possible world. Where the sequence s assigns the object *o* to "x", the value of "x" relative to any possible world is just *o*. We are to think of "Fx" being satisfied by an assignment s that assigns the object *o* to the variable "x" if and only if the object *o* is F in every possible world. Kripke's point is that names behave in just the same way under modal operators, *whereas definite descriptions do not*. Quine's logical argument against the coherence of *de re* modal attributions fails, because (like co-extensional variables relative to an assignment) co-extensional names are substitutable in modal contexts. The fact that a definite description such as "the number of planets" cannot be substituted for a co-extensional expression within the scope of a modal operator does not entail that the *position* in which that definite description occurs blocks substitution. It has rather to do with a feature of *definite descriptions*, namely that definite descriptions (unlike names and variables with respect to an assignment) are not rigid designators.

According to Quine, our intuitions about *de re* modal statements are inconstant, fluctuating depending upon the way we think of an object. If we think of 9 as the number of planets, then it is not necessarily odd, whereas if we think of 9 as the number 9, it is necessarily odd. Kripke argues that our intuitions about *de re* modal statements are not context-sensitive. A genuine *de re* modal attribution attributes a property to an object essentially (an even clearer proponent of this position is Plantinga 1974). Quine's arguments for the inconstancy of *de re* modal attributions result from not clearly distinguishing *de dicto* modal statements with definite descriptions from *de dicto* modal statements with names.[49]

David Lewis (1941–2001) presented a very different response to Quine's objections to quantified modal logic. Lewis was a realist about different possible worlds, and believed that no object existed in more than one possible world. Lewis's metaphysical view about possible worlds prevented him from accepting the objectual interpretation of *de re* modal quantification, because the objectual interpretation requires making sense of an object in the actual world existing and having properties at other possible worlds. Instead, Lewis (1968) proposed what he called a *counterpart theoretic* interpretation of quantified modal logic.[50] According to counterpart theory, a *de re* modal sentence is true in virtue of *counterparts* of actual objects having properties in other possible worlds. Unlike Kripke, Lewis agrees with Quine's premise that our intuitions about *de re* modal attributions were inconstant, that is, fluctuated with context.[51] In fact, Lewis thought that this feature of *de re* modal attributions was the key to solving a number of classical metaphysical problems. But Lewis took the inconstancy of *de re* modal attributions as evidence that they called for a *context-sensitive semantic theory*. More specifically, Lewis thought that there were distinct *counterpart relations*. An open modal formula, such as "Fx" is satisfied by an object *o* if and only if each counterpart *c* of *o* in any world *w* has the property F. Since there are distinct counterpart relations, "Fx" may be true of an object relative to one counterpart relation and false of an object relative to another counterpart relation (since different sets of counterparts are determined by the different counterpart relations evoked in different contexts). So Lewis accepts Quine's claim that *de re* modal attributions are inconstant. But he does not think that this shows that quantified modal logic is not formally intractable. Instead, Lewis incorporates the contextual relativity into the formal semantics itself.

Lewis's account of quantified modal logic is an instructive example to consider in light of Quine's skepticism about the possibility of regimenting *de re* modal statements. Quine's skepticism about formalizing *de re* modal statements (and *de re* attitude ascriptions) arises in part from his belief that our intuitions about these constructions are context-sensitive, and this context-sensitivity is an impediment to regimentation. However, Lewis's reaction to the apparent context-sensitivity of *de re* modal sentences is to incorporate the context-sensitivity into the regimentation. What this shows is that the alleged context-sensitivity of a kind of discourse, far from serving as an impediment to regimentation, is simply further fodder for it.[52]

Conditionals

Paul Grice's response to the ordinary-language philosopher involved defending the material conditional analysis of the indicative conditional. By providing a pragmatic account of the conflicting data, he hoped to dispel the challenge to giving a truth-functional analysis of the indicative conditional. But his defense of the material conditional analysis is deeply problematic. For example, Grice's analysis predicts that if one has a high degree of credence in either the negation of the antecedent or the truth of the consequent, the conditional is not assertible. But, as Frank Jackson has emphasized (1987: 20), there are many conditionals that are highly assertible even though we have a high degree of credence in the falsity of the antecedent or the truth of the consequent, such as "If the sun goes out of existence in ten minutes' time, the earth will be plunged into darkness in about eighteen minutes' time," or, if we are convinced that Bekele will win the race, "If Webb runs, Bekele will win the race, and if Webb doesn't run, Bekele will win the race." In the former case, we are as certain of the falsity of the antecedent as we are of the truth of the conditional, yet it is highly assertible; in the latter case, we are certain of the truth of the consequent, yet the conditional remains assertible. Finally, Grice's theory of the indicative conditional predicts that logically equivalent statements to the material conditional have the same truth-conditions, and are equally assertible. For example, Grice's theory predicts that "If A then B" should have the same truth conditions and be equally assertible as "If not B, then not A." But this prediction is not borne out (Bennett 2003: 32). Grice's defense of the conditional postulates a large gap between standard use of conditionals and their meanings, a gap that he tries to cover with explanations from general conversational principles. Unfortunately, the conversational principles do not succeed in explaining the gap between indicative conditionals, construed as material conditionals, and their standard uses. Another theory is required.

Grice's focus was on indicative conditionals in natural language. In the 1960s, philosophers influenced by theories of meaning for modal languages turned their attention to subjunctive conditionals in natural language. Characterizing precisely the distinction between indicative and subjunctive conditionals is a thorny matter. But the basic contrast between the two classes of conditionals is brought out in the classic pair:

(a) If Oswald didn't shoot Kennedy, someone else did.
(b) If Oswald hadn't shot Kennedy, someone else would have.

The indicative conditional in (a) is true, but the subjunctive conditional in (b) is probably not true. Subjunctive conditionals generally (or always) contain modal terms in their consequents.

The first published account of a modal semantics for subjunctive conditionals was presented in Stalnaker 1968. According to Stalnaker, a subjunctive conditional "If A were the case, then B would be the case" is true at a possible world w if and only if B is true at the closest possible world to w at which A is true. Stalnaker's original analysis is both simple and elegant. But it also has some dramatic consequences. Call an "A-world" a world in which the proposition A is true. According to Stalnaker's theory, whenever a subjunctive conditional "If A were the case, then B would be the case" has a truth-value, there is always a unique closest A-world to the world of evaluation. As a consequence, Stalnaker's theory also validates *conditional excluded middle* (CEM), the principle that "Either if A were the case, then B would be the case, or if A were the case, ~B would be the case." Both of these consequences have been widely held to be problematic (according to David Lewis (1973: 79), the validation of CEM is "The principal virtue and the principal vice of Stalnaker's theory"). David Lewis (1973) presented a somewhat more complicated theory of subjunctive conditionals that does not involve the hypothesis of a closest A-world in evaluating the truth of a subjunctive conditional, and does not validate CEM.

Stalnaker's 1968 theory of conditionals, despite being "constructed primarily to account for counterfactual conditionals" (Stalnaker 1999a: 68), was "intended to fit conditional sentences generally, without regard to the attitude taken by the speaker to the antecedent or consequent or his purpose in uttering them, and without regard to the grammatical mood in which the conditional is expressed" (ibid.). According to this analysis, a conditional "If A, then B" is true if and only if B is true in the most similar A-worlds. In the case of indicative conditionals, there is a pragmatic principle governing the context-dependent notion of similarity; worlds that are assumed to be live epistemic possibilities are most similar. Of course, the actual world is always the most similar world to itself, so if the antecedent of a conditional is true, the conditional is true if and only if its consequent is true. But if the antecedent is false, then the truth of the conditional will depend upon the truth of the consequent in the most similar epistemically possible world in which the antecedent is true. Thus Stalnaker's analysis of conditionals elegantly explains the fact that natural languages employ the same expression to formulate indicative and subjunctive conditionals. Furthermore, the analysis predicts that indicative conditionals are context-sensitive constructions, since they depend for their truth-value on a parameter that shifts with context, namely the metric of similarity. Stalnaker's theory gives a *semantic* explanation for some of the distinctions that Grice's theory was powerless to explain. For example, Stalnaker's theory predicts that "If A, then B" does not have the same truth-conditions as "If ~B, then ~A." It also explains much of the contextual variability in our intuitions about the truth-values of indicative conditionals.

Grice attempted to give a simple semantic analysis of the indicative conditional, and a pragmatic explanation of the divergence between the ordinary uses of conditional sentences and their actual truth-conditions. However, Grice's explanation left an implausibly large gap between our intuitions about the truth-conditions of indicative conditionals and their semantic content, a gap that developments of similar views have arguably also failed to bridge (see Jackson 1987, and the criticism of Jackson in Bennett 2003: 38ff.). Stalnaker, in contrast, exploits the tools of intensional logic to provide a context-sensitive semantic theory for indicative conditionals, one that exploits more complex logical mechanisms to bring the semantic content closer to what it intuitively seems to be. The topic of conditionals is another area in which the central dispute is between sophisticated semantic theories that capture intuitive data by incorporating context-sensitivity, and semantic theories that eschew more complex mechanisms and context-sensitivity in favor of attempted pragmatic explanations of the intuitions.

The debate on conditionals has rightfully attracted more attention than other debates in the philosophy of language since the mid-1970s, not just because of the centrality of the construction to so many areas of thought, but also because the issues have been complicated by several surprising facts about them. The goal of Stalnaker's semantics for indicative conditionals was to bring the truth-conditions of these constructions closer to what they intuitively seem to be. One arguably intuitive claim about the use of indicative conditionals concerns their *probability*. Generally, people wish to assert propositions that they believe are very likely to be true, which suggests the general thesis that something is assertible for a speaker at a time if and only if it has a high subjective probability for that person. If so, then a conditional is assertible if and only if it has a high subjective probability. It is quite intuitive to take the probability of the indicative conditional "if A, then C" to be the conditional probability of C given A. This suggests that a semantic theory for indicative conditionals that accords with their use conditions should have as a consequence that the probability of an indicative conditional "if A, then C" for a person at a time should be equivalent to the conditional probability of C given A. But David Lewis (1976) proved the surprising result that no connective O that links propositions could have the property that the probability of O(A, C) is the conditional probability of C given A, and simultaneously yield a satisfactory (or even close to satisfactory) account of our ordinary intuitions about the probabilities of various conditionals. If having an account of the meaning of indicative conditionals that matches intuitive judgments about their content requires such a connective, then the search is futile. A second fact about indicative conditionals, emphasized by Gibbard (1981), is that they are extremely context-sensitive; one speaker can assert "if A, then C," and intuitively be correct, and another speaker can assert "if A, then ~C" to describe the same situation, and also intuitively be correct. Another fact about indicative conditionals (also emphasized in Gibbard 1981) is that it is not easy to embed indicative conditionals inside other conditionals. A number of distinguished philosophers have used these considerations, along with others, to motivate the view that indicative conditionals lack truth-conditions altogether.[53] On this view of their meaning, indicative conditionals are an example of one kind of non-normative sentence for which something like the model of meaning endorsed by expressivists about moral discourse is correct.[54]

Conclusion

In the 1960s and 1970s, philosophers started to exploit the resources of semantic theories for formal languages in the analysis of natural language meaning. A formal language differs from a natural language in having a simple, clearly defined syntax. To avoid the complexities of natural language grammar, many of these philosophers gave semantic theories for fragments of natural language regimented in various extensions of the language of first-order predicate logic (such as the language of quantified modal logic, or the language of intensional logic). But of course what we interpret when we understand sentences of natural language are the structures of those sentences, not the sentences of some regimented formal language. So the relevance for the project of giving a theory of meaning for natural languages of semantic theories for various extensions of the language of first-order logic is not completely clear.

However, in the 1960s, work by linguists, in particular the linguist Noam Chomsky (1928–), began to show that natural languages, like formal languages, had grammars that could be described formally. Chomsky's work made the project of transferring the tools of the logician to the analysis of meaning considerably more tractable. If natural languages have a systematic syntax, then there is no obstacle to mimicking the formal semantic project directly for natural languages. Using the research of contemporary syntax, one could represent what the objects of natural language interpretation were, using the tools of semantics one could interpret them, and using the norms of discourse described by Grice, one could explain divergences between use and meaning. It took a number of years for philosophers to absorb the lessons of syntax. But since an apparent fact about meaning may be due either to the syntax of a given sentence, its semantics, or general facts about language use, the contemporary philosopher of language must master all three branches of investigation.

The discovery that the notions of reference and truth could be used to give a theory of meaning for natural language, together with the twin developments of syntax and pragmatics, have resolved many of the foundational disputes of mid-twentieth-century philosophy of language. It is difficult to argue that context-sensitivity undermines the project of giving a systematic theory of reference and truth for natural language when the best models of context-sensitivity appeal to reference in giving the meanings of context-sensitive expressions (as in Kaplan's notion of character). It is difficult to argue that vagueness undermines this project, when sophisticated semantic theories for vague expressions have been developed (e.g. the supervaluational semantics for vagueness developed in Fine 1975). The very features that are used to cast doubt on the possibility of formalization are always the next challenge for the project of formalization. As a result, attention has shifted to giving the meaning of particular philosophically interesting constructions in natural language (of which the conditionals literature is but one especially interesting example). To be sure, in some of these literatures, philosophers frustrated with the intractability of the problems posed by the relevant constructions have tried to draw broader morals, and sometimes within this framework pleas to return to the pessimistic attitudes towards the prospect of a systematic theory of meaning have been advanced (e.g. Schiffer 1987). Nevertheless, cries of frustration with the difficulty of particular constructions have not been met with widespread defeatism, and the program of giving a systematic account of the theory of meaning has continued.

Once many of the foundational issues were settled, a vast amount of work was produced in philosophy of language and (especially) its close relative in linguistics, the field of semantics. It is impossible even to provide a road map to the wealth of work that has been done since the mid-1970s on adverbs, anaphora, determiners, mass terms, plurals, adjectives and gradability, modals, tense, aspect, and other topics. In terms of details, since the 1970s much of that sub-part of the investigation of natural language meaning that has been conducted by philosophers has been devoted to detailed arguments on various constructions about whether a Gricean response can account for the phenomena that go beyond a simple semantic analysis, or whether a more complex semantic theory that incorporates context-sensitivity semantically (as in Stalnaker's analysis of conditionals) is plausible. For every construction we have discussed, there are advocates of each view. Predictably, some of these disputes take place on a meta-level, with advocates of a non-semantic account of the phenomena arguing that a Gricean or quasi-Gricean apparatus does much more explaining than is ordinarily recognized, and advocates of semantic accounts arguing for greater attentiveness to the nuances of natural language meaning and form. But there is an overarching agreement even between most disputants at this meta-level; the overarching agreement is meaning and use should never be conflated, and that any adequate account of meaning fundamentally employs the notions of reference and truth.

Notes

1 I have discussed this topic at length in "Truth and metatheory in Frege" (1996); see especially section IV.

2 The problem of cognitive significance is not specifically a problem about identity sentences, although it is often misleadingly presented as such. Another version of the same problem can be raised by the difference in cognitive significance between "Hesperus is a planet" and "Phosphorus is a planet."

3 As we shall see below in the discussion of Carnap, there are two kinds of opaque contexts, contexts that are intensional and contexts that are neither intensional nor extensional.

4 These difficulties are described in some detail in Perry 1977. For an influential reply to Perry on behalf of (a somewhat psychologized version of) Frege, see Evans 1981.

5 I say "at least two," because of the problem of the "hierarchy of senses," which will be discussed below.

6 This is presumably not accidental. One way of thinking of Frege's treatment of propositional attitude verbs is that they induce a kind of systematic ambiguity, in which a term has one referent in one context (not under the scope of a propositional attitude verb), and another referent in another context (under the scope of a propositional attitude verb). Since Frege regards ambiguity as a defect of natural languages, there is little wonder that he would want to minimize the appearance of ambiguity-inducing operators into his formal language (if he did, he would also have to modify the language to include names of senses, so as to avoid ambiguity; see Frege's letter to Russell of December 28, 2002, reprinted in Frege 1980a: 82–5, especially p. 84).

7 As Dummett (1981: 227) writes, in explaining this methodology "even when Frege is purporting to give the sense of a word or symbol, what he actually states is what its reference is ... The sense of an expression is the mode of presentation of the referent: in saying what the referent is, we have to choose a particular way of saying this ... In a case in which we are concerned to convey, or stipulate, the sense of the expression, we shall choose that means of stating what the referent is which displays the sense: we might here borrow a famous pair of terms from the *Tractatus* and say that, for Frege, we *say* what the referent of a word is, and thereby *show* what its sense is."

8 This is my translation. Russell originally wrote: "Ich glaube dass der Mont Blanc selbst, trotz aller seiner Schneefelder, Bestandtheil desses ist was eigentlich behauptet wird im Satze 'Der Mont Blanc ist mehr also 4000 meter hoch.' Man behauptet nicht den Gedanken, der ja psychologische Privatsache ist: man behauptet das Objekt des Gedankens, und dies ist meines Erachtens ein gewisser Complex (ein objektiver Satz, koennte man sagen) worin der Mont Blanc selber ein Bestandtheil ist." Frege would of course dispute Russell's contention that thoughts are "psychologically private matters", since Frege takes senses (including thoughts, the senses of sentences) to be objective, mind-independent entities.

9 A distant relative of this claim survives in contemporary philosophy of language and mind, under the name "Russell's Principle." See Evans 1982 for discussion.

10 However, Russell remained rather liberal about acquaintance with universals (see Russell 1988: ch. X).

11 In Russell 1905, Russell was not yet fully fluent with the apparatus of quantifiers, and employed the primitive predicate of propositional functions, "is always true." The major modern defense of Russell's account of definite descriptions is Neale 1990. One influential criticism of Russell (Graff 2001) involves the topic of predicative uses of definite descriptions, as in "Napoleon was the greatest French general," which pose certain problems for Russell's theory.

12 There is a large literature challenging the uniqueness clause involved in Russell's theory. The classical attack on Russell's claim that descriptions involve uniqueness is Strawson 1996; Strawson argues that an utterance of "The table is covered with books" can be true even though we are perfectly aware that there is more than one table in the universe, and so Russell's uniqueness clause fails. Influential challenges to Russell's claim that descriptions involve uniqueness include Lewis 1979: example 3 and Szabo 2000.

13 Brentano (1995) rejects the view that judgment differs from presentation in that the former always has complex entities (like propositions) as objects, and the latter can have simple entities as objects. For example, he argues (ch. 7, sect. 5) that some judgments have simple entities as objects: in particular,

denials and affirmations of existence. Interestingly, as we have seen, the theory of Moore (1899) also has as a consequence that the judgment that A exists only has A as its object, because the object A is identified with the existential proposition that A exists.

14 Frege and Russell never took the modal concepts of possibility and necessity to be very central; see for example Russell's discussion of "possible" in Russell 1985: ch. 7.

15 This occurs in sections 29–32 of the *Grundgesetze* (see Heck 1998). As Frege writes about this attempted proof in his famous letter to Russell of June 22, 1902 (Frege 1980a: 61), "Es scheint danach [after the discovery of the paradoxes], dass die Umwandlung der Allgemeinheit einer Gleichheit in eine Werthverlaufsgleichheit … nicht immer erlaubt ist, dass mein Gesetz V … falsch ist und dass meine Ausfuehrungen im section 31 nicht genuegen, in allen Faellen meinen Zeichenverbindungen eine Bedeutung zu sichern." ("It appears after this, that the transformation of a generality of an identity into an identity of courses-of-value is not always allowed, that my Basic Law V is false, and that my explanations in section 31 are not sufficient, to secure a reference for my expressions in all cases." (my translation).) In other words, Frege's initial reaction to the paradox is to observe that his attempted consistency proof in section 31 fails.

16 As Tarski summarizes the situation (1983c: 401): "Concepts from the domain of semantics have traditionally played a prominent part in the discussions of philosophers, logicians, and philologists. Nevertheless, they have long been regarded with a certain skepticism. From the historical point of view, this skepticism is well-founded; for although the content of the semantical concepts, as they occur in colloquial language, is clear enough, yet all attempts to characterize this content more precisely have failed, and various discussions in which these concepts appeared and which were based on quite plausible and seemingly evident premises, have often led to paradoxes and antinomies."

17 Tarski transforms the recursive definition into an explicit one, with the use of Frege's ancestral (Tarski 1983b: 193 n. 1).

18 The above mentioned-property of *satisfiability* is also elegantly defined with the use of models; a set of sentences $\alpha 1 \ldots \alpha n$ is satisfiable if and only if there is some model in which they are all true.

19 It is worth noting that the following two definitions of truth in a model for sentences, that is, well-formed formula with no free variables, are equivalent:

(1) $\models_M \phi$ iff for all sequences s of M, $\models_M s \phi$

(2) $\models_M \phi$ iff for some sequence s of M, $\models_M s \phi$

It is clear, intuitively, that the equivalence holds. If ϕ has no free variables, then it won't depend at all for its truth on what s assigns to any variables. However, the proof of the equivalence of these two definitions is somewhat subtle, and I won't attempt it here.

Essentially, the trickiness seems to be due to the following. What one might set out to prove is that where s and s' are assignments of M, then, if $FV(\phi) = \varnothing$, then $\models_{M,s} \phi$ iff $\models_{M,s'} \phi$. However, there is a difficulty with proving this directly, since the induction hypothesis will be ineffectual in the interesting case, where ϕ is a quantified formula. So one must prove a stronger theorem, to the effect that, if s and s' are assignments of M such that for every variable v that is free in ϕ, $s(v) = s'(v)$, then s sats ϕ in M iff s' sats ϕ in M. The equivalence of (1) and (2) is an immediate consequence of this fact.

20 Tarski's method of establishing this theorem is very similar to Gödel's method of establishing his first incompleteness theorem, and there are important questions of relative priority (see Tarski 1983b: 247 n. 1).

21 Although some philosophers have recently come to the defense of Tarski's claim (e.g. Eklund 2002; Azzouni 2006: 98ff.).

22 The relative notion of truth in a model is far less important for this kind of project, that is, for the project of giving a theory of meaning for natural language. In the case of meta-mathematics, truth in a model is the fundamental notion, since it is required in the definition of notions such as logical consequence. But the semantics of natural language does not concern itself with, for example, completeness theorems; the purpose of the semantics of a natural language is to give a successful account of the meanings of natural language sentences, not to prove desirable semantic properties of formal systems. For another discussion of why the appeal to truth in a model is not central for natural language semantics, see Lepore's classic work (1982) and Higginbotham 1988: sect. 3.

23 Given Tarski's influence on Carnap, it is ironic that Carnap's semantic system depended so heavily upon the concept of analyticity. Tarski was deeply suspicious of this notion, and had voiced his concerns in print as early as 1936 (Tarski 1983a: 418–20).

24 The fact that Carnap interpreted necessity in terms of analyticity is important to bear in mind when assessing Quine's criticisms of the problem of *de re* modality. Quine is often criticized for treating quantifying into modal contexts as similar to quantifying into quotation marks. But Quine was writing for an audience that shared his assumption that a metaphysical interpretation of necessity was incoherent. Since analyticity is fundamentally a property of sentences, the view that necessity is another way of talking of analyticity makes necessity fundamentally a property of sentences as well. From this perspective, it is clear why Quine thought of the problem of *de re* modality as akin to quantifying into quotation marks; what "necessarily" appended to, on this view, is a quote-name of a sentence.

25 It is fair to say that the transition in Quine's argument that has received the most criticism is the transition from the premise of failure of substitution of co-designative expressions in a syntactic position in a sentence to the conclusion that that position is not purely designative. As Kaplan (1986: 235) rightly points out, all that follows from the premise is that at least one occurrence of the two expressions is not purely designative; it does *not* follow that the position itself is "opaque" (that is, it does not follow that *every* occurrence of an expression in that position is a not purely designative occurrence of that expression). For a different sort of criticism of the transition, see Fine 2005b: 89–90 and 2005a: 113–15.

26 If one construes this claim as ruling out the possibility of writing a satisfaction clause for quantifiers where the truth of the embedded formula depends upon more than just the object that is assigned to the embedded variable, then there are apparently clear counterexamples. As Mark Richard (1987) points out, it is simple to write up a clause for a quantifier that depends not only upon what object is quantified over, but also what the embedded variable is. For instance, suppose the variables in the object-language come with numerical subscripts, and consider the following satisfaction clause for the existential quantifier:
(1) If ϕ is of the form "$\exists x_n \psi$," then s sats ϕ iff for some $s' \approx_{x\text{-}n} s$, s' sats ψ and n is odd.
According to (1), an existentially quantified formula is satisfied by a sequence only if the variable in the object-language sentence has an odd-numbered numerical subscript. This is formally a perfectly coherent satisfaction clause for quantified sentences (although of course it doesn't correspond to any intuitively natural interpretation of the quantifiers).

27 As Carnap (1958b: 131) puts the point: "The fact that, according to Frege's method, the same name may have different nominata [references] in different contexts has already been mentioned as a disadvantage. But the multiplication of entities goes far beyond Frege's initial distinction between the ordinary and the oblique nominatum of a name. Actually, these two nominata constitute only the beginning of an infinite sequence of nominata for the same name. If we apply Frege's method to sentences with multiple obliqueness, then we have to distinguish the ordinary nominatum of the name, its first oblique nominatum, its second oblique nominatum, and so forth."
There is now a large literature devoted to the evaluation of this objection to Frege. Classic contributions include Church 1951; Burge 1979; Dummett 1981: 267ff.; Parsons 1981; and Davidson 1990.

28 As Jeffrey King has pointed out to me (personal communication), Carnap's method also evades some classic objections to the Frege–Church approach. For example, one classic objection to the Frege–Church version of the "method of the name relation" involves examples in which a single quantifier binds occurrences of variables both inside and outside non-extensional contexts, as in "Every teacher$_i$ John met x$_i$ John believed x$_i$ was a doctor." The first occurrence of "x" is in an extensional context, and the second occurrence is in a non-extensional context. Carnap would have no problem with this sort of example, since both occurrences of "x" have the same semantic values – an intension and an extension. In contrast, it is not clear how the Fregean method would treat this sort of example (although see Kaplan 1968: sect. 5 for one suggested solution on behalf of the Fregean).

29 Quine (1947: 47) criticizes this account as involving "queer ontological consequences." Essentially, Quine interprets individual concepts as strange sorts of objects, with the justification that "the ontology of a logic is nothing other than the range of admissible values of the variables of quantification."

30 Carnap's analysis has also been subject to powerful criticism (Church 1950); in particular, problems arise when considering iterated attitude ascriptions. When one says that John believes that Hans believes that snow is white, one does not attribute to John a belief about a particular language.

31 Although as Boghossian (1997: 340–1) emphasizes, from a contemporary perspective, it is unclear whether Quine thinks that the predicate "is analytic" fails to have any determinate meaning at all, or whether it has a determinate meaning, but has no instances.

32 In contrast, Quine's arguments (e.g. Quine 1960: ch. 2) for skepticism about meaning facts are generally not accepted. The literature here too is far too extensive to cite. But many philosophers accept Chomsky's famous charge (1969; 1975: 179ff.) that the problem with Quine's arguments for meaning skepticism is that the premise of his argument is just a standard instance of under-determination of theory by evidence, and that it raises no issue specific to the case of meaning.

33 As Carnap (1958c: 223–5) writes, "Suppose that the author of a system wishes the predicates 'B' and 'M' to designate the properties Bachelor and Married, respectively. How does he know that these properties are incompatible and that therefore he has to lay down [the relevant meaning postulate]? This is not a matter of knowledge but of decision. His knowledge or belief that the English words 'bachelor' and 'married' are always or usually understood in such a way that they are incompatible may influence his decision if he has the intention to reflect in his system some of the meaning relations of English words."

34 The contemporary advocate of a broadly Russellian view of definite descriptions can evade this criticism of Strawson by treating "the" as having a meaning in isolation, for example a two-place relation between sets. The structured proposition expressed by an occurrence of a sentence containing a definite description is not, on this more contemporary view, the same proposition as the proposition expressed by an occurrence in that same context of a sentence containing the Russellian expansion of that definite description, and may not even share its truth-conditions (Stanley and Williamson 1995: 294).

35 It is clear that Montague was influenced by Carnap. But, as Jeffrey King has emphasized to me, Montague repeatedly acknowledges a debt to Kripke's classic 1963 article. The fact that Kripke provides an elegant semantics for modal logics whose interpretations involve restricted accessibility relations is obviously important for Montague, since such semantics are important for the sort of applications Montague had in mind. But Montague attributes a greater debt than this to Kripke. Montague (1974b: 153) criticizes Carnap's treatment of possible worlds as what Montague calls *models* (presumably, he means state-descriptions, i.e. sets of sentences), and attributes to Kripke the discovery that possible worlds are not models, but rather primitive "points of reference" (Montague 1974c: 109).

36 In recent years, some more empirically minded philosophers and linguists have suggested that Quine's analysis does not need to be taken in the revisionary spirit in which it is intended, because there is some evidence that it is in fact correct as an analysis of natural language (see Larson et al. forthcoming).

37 In the standard treatment of quantifiers within the Montague tradition, quantified noun phrases are just treated as denoting second-level functions, although they are taken to introduce lambda abstracts that function to bind variables within their scope. In other words, the two aspects of quantification are formally distinguished (see, e.g., Heim and Kratzer 1998: ch. 7).

38 There are alternative regimentations that would give the sentence its natural interpretation, e.g. by placing the past-tense operator between "a" and "child" in the quantified noun phrase "a child," effectively rendering the sentence as "$\exists x[\text{Past}(\text{Child}(x)\ \&\ \text{Future}(\text{King}(x)))]$." But the problem is not to give the meaning of a sentence in the language of first-order logic. Rather, it is to give the meaning of the English sentence in (1). The proposed analysis would require defending the view that the past-tense operator takes intermediate scope between the determiner "a" and the common "child," and I am not sure how one could argue for this syntactic structure.

39 Kaplan's paper was only published in 1989, but had been widely circulated since the mid-1970s, as "UCLA mimeograph #2."

40 But for a dissenting view, see Lewis 1981. Because Kaplan regards tenses and place expressions such as "somewhere" as operators on contents, he is forced to treat sentence contents as true relative to several different kinds of features of circumstances of evaluation. So, the content of an occurrence of "It is raining," for Kaplan, is neutral as to time and place (Kaplan 1989: 504). But classic propositions are not neutral with regard to place or time. For example, the proposition expressed by an utterance of "It's raining" is intuitively about a particular time and place, for example New York City on December 16, 2005. As a result, Kaplan's contents do not "exactly correspond to the classical conception of a proposition" (ibid.). Continuing this line of reasoning, Lewis argues that, given the number of sentence

operators in the language, Kaplan's sentence contents are going to be no closer to propositions than Montague's index theoretic semantic values. Jeffrey King (2003) has persuasively argued that Kaplan and Lewis are wrong to take basic tenses as sentence operators. Following the tradition of Partee (1973), he argues that they are instead predicates of syntactically represented times. If locational expressions such as "somewhere" are also not operators (but rather, say, quantifiers over location variables in the sentence) then modal sentential operators are the only genuine content operators, and sentence contents are genuinely classical propositions.

41 Parsons (1969: sect. VI) maintains that quantified modal logic is not even committed to the *meaning-fulness* of essentialism. But what Parsons has in mind here is that one could provide an *alternative* interpretation of the language of quantified modal logic, "some *other* truth-conditions" than the Kripkean ones. Parsons does not supply such an alternative interpretation in his paper (although see Stalnaker 2003a for a suggestion).

42 Smullyan (1948) raises the point that substitution of co-extensional descriptions is permitted when the descriptions take wide-scope with respect to a modal operator. Neale (2000: 308ff.) argues convincingly that this merely obfuscates the debate.

43 In her 1947 paper Barcan proved that if an identity is true, then it is necessarily true, albeit in a language with only variables as singular terms.

44 One could raise quibbles about Kripke's definition of "analytic statement," since he defines it in such a way that an analytic statement is both a priori and necessary. Certain truths in virtue of meaning, such as any utterance of "I am here now" seem to be both a priori and contingent. However, Kripke repeatedly emphasizes that his definition of "analytic statement" is intended to be stipulative. Furthermore, this is independent of the genuine issue, which concerns his disagreement with Barcan Marcus. All agree that analytic statements are a priori, so Barcan Marcus is committed to the thesis that true identity statements involving expressions used as names are a priori.

45 I have here followed Kripke in using the unclear term "statement" to describe the thing that is both necessary and a priori. It is clear that Kripke takes the proposition expressed by an utterance of a sentence to be what is necessary. In contrast, it is not so clear *what* Kripke takes to be a priori or a posteriori. For example, it is not clear that he takes the proposition expressed by an utterance of a sentence to be what is a priori or a posteriori. Perhaps it is the sentence itself or its utterance rather than what it expresses on an occasion that is the bearer of epistemic properties. So perhaps Kripke would deny that there is one thing – a proposition – that is both a posteriori and necessary. I am not certain about the answer to this interpretative question.

46 However, it must be said the notion of a priority with which Kripke operates is somewhat non-standard, in that it seems to be relativized to a *person*. Kripke also speaks of *stage*-relative a priori truth in 1980: 79 n. 33, but this is equally unfamiliar.

47 For a classic response to Kripke's modal argument, see Dummett 1981: ch. 5, appendix. For more recent responses, see Stanley 1997a: sect. 7; 1997b; 2002; and Sosa 2001.

48 For a response to the semantic argument, see Stanley 1999.

49 An interestingly distinct response to the problems is given in Stalnaker 2003b. Stalnaker does not locate the difficulty with interpreting quantified modal logic in the distinction between names and definite descriptions; according to him, both are singular terms. Instead, he thinks that the substitution schema is properly formulated in terms of *predications*, and "one cannot treat sentences generally as predications" (2003b: 148). To forge the required distinction between sentences and predications, he employs a language with complex-predicate forming devices. For criticism of Stalnaker's view, see Williamson 2006.

50 Lewis in fact does not provide an interpretation of quantified modal logic, in the sense of a model-theoretic semantics for it, as in Kripke 1963. Rather, Lewis (1968) proposes a *translation* of quantified modal logic into the language of counterpart theory. The success of Lewis's translation schema (in particular, for the language of quantified modal logic augmented with an operator with the meaning of "actually") is challenged in Hazen 1979 and Fara and Williamson 2005

51 Lewis's agreement with Quine on this point is obscured by two facts. First, in his discussion of Quine in his original paper on counterpart theory (Lewis 1968: sect. 3), he writes as if there is no inconstancy in *de re* modal attributions, and indeed in this paper Lewis just talks as if there is one counterpart relation. Second, he surely does not agree with Quine's views about the *degree* of inconstancy of *de re*

modal attributions. Nevertheless, the inconstancy of *de re* modal attributions, which is explicated by the availability of multiple distinct counterpart relations, is crucial to Lewis's metaphysical applications of counterpart theory (Lewis 1971).

52 Very similar moves to Lewis's occurred in the literature on *de re* propositional ascriptions, in response to Quine's inconstancy worries about such constructions. That is, as we have seen, Quine's later suspicions about regimenting *de re* propositional ascriptions were due to his belief that our intuitions about them were too context-sensitive. Certain philosophers (in particular Richard (1990)) proposed a context-sensitive semantics for propositional attitude sentences, where the contextual relativity of our intuitions is reflected in a formal semantics that incorporates context-sensitivity.

53 In addition to Gibbard, Adams (1975) and Edgington (1986) have provided arguments for this view of indicative conditionals. I should say that I think a context-sensitive semantics, of the sort given by Stalnaker, provides an elegant explanation of the data presented by Gibbard; see Stalnaker 1984: 108ff.

54 Presumably, it is no accident that Gibbard is both a moral expressivist and denies that indicative conditionals have truth-conditions.

References

Adams, E. (1975) *The Logic of Conditionals*. Dordrecht: Reidel.

Azzouni, J. (2006) *Tracking Reason: Proof, Consequence, and Truth*. Oxford: Oxford University Press.

Barcan, R. (1947) "The identity of individuals in a strict functional calculus of second order." *The Journal of Symbolic Logic* 12/1: 12–15.

Barcan Marcus, R. (1993) [1961] "Modalities and intensional languages." In *Modalities: Philosophical Essays*, Oxford: Oxford University Press, pp. 5–23.

Bennett, J. (2003) *A Philosophical Guide to Conditionals*. Oxford: Oxford University Press.

Boghossian, P. (1997) "Analyticity." In B. Hale and C Wright (eds.) *A Companion to the Philosophy of Language*, Oxford: Blackwell, pp. 331–68.

Brandom, R. (1994) *Making it Explicit*. Cambridge, MA: Harvard University Press.

Brentano, F. (1995) [1874] *Psychology from an Empirical Standpoint*. London: Routledge.

Burge, T. (1979) "Frege and the hierarchy." *Synthèse* 40: 265–81.

Carnap, R. (1949) [1937] *The Logical Syntax of Language*. London: Routledge & Kegan Paul.

—— (1958a) [1947] "Empiricism, semantics, and ontology." In *Meaning and Necessity: A Study in Semantics and Modal Logic*, Chicago: University of Chicago Press, pp. 205–21.

—— (1958b) [1947] *Meaning and Necessity: A Study in Semantics and Modal Logic*. Chicago: University of Chicago Press.

—— (1958c) [1947] "Meaning postulates." In *Meaning and Necessity: A Study in Semantics and Modal Logic*, Chicago: University of Chicago Press, pp. 222–9.

Cartwright, R. (1971) "Identity and substitutivity." In M. K. Munitz (ed.) *Identity and Individuation*, New York: New York University Press, pp. 119–33.

Chomsky, N. (1969) "Quine's empirical assumptions." In D. Davidson and J. Hintikka (eds.) *Words and Objections: Essays on the Work of W. V. Quine*, Dordrecht: Reidel, pp. 53–68.

—— (1975) *Reflections on Language*. New York: Pantheon Books.

Church, A. (1950) "On Carnap's analysis of statements of assertion and belief." *Analysis* 10: 97–9.

—— (1951) "A formulation of the logic of sense and denotation." In P. Henle, H. M. Kallen, and S. K. Langer (eds.) *Structure, Method, and Meaning: Essays in Honor of H. M. Sheffer*, New York: Liberal Arts Press.

Davidson, D. (1967): "Truth and meaning." *Synthèse* 17: 304–23. Repr. in *Inquiries into Truth and Interpretation*, Oxford: Clarendon Press, 1990.

—— (1990) "Theories of meaning and learnable languages." In *Inquiries into Truth and Interpretation*, Oxford: Clarendon Press, pp. 3–15.

Dummett, M. (1981) *Frege: Philosophy of Language*. London: Duckworth.

Edgington, D. (1986) "Do conditionals have truth-conditions?" *Critica* 18: 3–30.

Eklund, M. (2002) "Inconsistent languages." *Philosophy and Phenomenological Research* 64: 251–75.

Evans, G. (1981) "Understanding demonstratives." In H. Parret and J. Bouveresse (eds.) *Meaning and Understanding*, Berlin: de Gruyter.

—— (1982) *The Varieties of Reference*. Oxford: Clarendon Press.

Fara, M. and T. Williamson (2005) "Counterparts and actuality." *Mind* 114: 1–30.

Field, H. (1972) "Tarski's theory of truth." *Journal of Philosophy* 69: 347–75.

Fine, K. (1975) "Vagueness, truth and logic." *Synthèse* 54: 235–59.

—— (2005a) "Quine on quantifying in." In *Modality and Tense*, Oxford: Oxford University Press, pp. 105–30.

—— (2005b) "The problem of de re modality." In *Modality and Tense*, Oxford: Oxford University Press, pp. 40–104.

Forbes, G. (2000) "Objectual attitudes." *Linguistics and Philosophy* 23/2: 141–83.

Frege, G. (1879) *Begriffsschrift*. In G. Frege, *Begriffsschrift und andere Aufsaetze*, ed. I. Angelelli, Hildesheim: Georg Olms, 1988.

—— (1966) [1892] *Grundgesetze der Arithmetik*. Hildesheim: Georg Olms.

—— (1980a) *Gottlob Freges Briefwechsel*, ed. G. Gabriel, F. Kambartel, and C. Thiel. Hamburg: Felix Meiner.

—— (1980b) [1884] *The Foundations of Arithmetic*. Evanston, IL: Northwestern University Press.

—— (1993) "On sense and meaning." In P. Geach and M. Black, *Translations from the Philosophical Writings of Gottlob Frege*, Oxford: Blackwell, pp. 56–78.

Gibbard, A. (1981) "Two recent theories of conditionals." In W. Harper, R. Stalnaker, and G. Pearce (eds.) *Ifs*, Dordrecht: Reidel, pp. 211–47.

Graff, D. (2001) "Descriptions as predicates." *Philosophical Studies* 102/1: 1–42.

Grice, Paul (1989a) "Further notes on logic and conversation." In *Studies in the Way of Words*, Cambridge, MA: Harvard University Press, pp. 41–57.

—— (1989b) "Indicative conditionals." In *Studies in the Way of Words*, Cambridge, MA: Harvard University Press, pp. 58-85.

—— (1989c) "Logic and conversation." In *Studies in the Way of Words*, Cambridge, MA: Harvard University Press, pp. 22–40.

Hazen, A. (1979) "Counterpart theoretic semantics for modal logic." *Journal of Philosophy* 76: 319–38.

Heck, R. (1993) "The development of arithmetic in Frege's *Grundgesetze der Arithmetik*." *Journal of Symbolic Logic* 58: 579–602.

—— (1998) "*Grundgesetze der Arithmetik* I §§29–32." *Notre Dame Journal of Formal Logic* 38: 437–74.

Heim, I. and A. Kratzer (1998) *Semantics in Generative Grammar*. Oxford: Blackwell.

Higginbotham, J. (1988) "Contexts, models, and meanings: a note on the data of semantics." In R. Kempson (ed.) *Mental Representations: The Interface between Language and Reality*, Cambridge: Cambridge University Press, pp. 29–48.

Hintikka, J. (1962) *Knowledge and Belief: An Introduction to the Logic of the Two Notions*. Ithaca, NY: Cornell University Press.

Jackson, F. (1987) *Conditionals*. Oxford: Blackwell.

Kaplan, D. (1968) "Quantifying in." *Synthèse* 19: 178–214.

—— (1986) "Opacity." In L. E. Hahn and P. A. Schilpp (eds.) *The Philosophy of W. V. Quine*, LaSalle, IL: Open Court, pp. 229–88.

—— (1989) "Demonstratives." In J. Almog, J. Perry, and H. Wettstein (eds.) *Themes from Kaplan*, Oxford: Oxford University Press, pp. 481–563.

Kamp, H. (1971) "Formal properties of 'now'." *Theoria* 37/3: 227–73.

King, J. (2003) "Tense, modality, and semantic value." In J. Hawthorne and D. Zimmerman (eds.) *Language and Philosophical Linguistics*, Philosophical Perspectives 17, Oxford: Blackwell.

Kripke, S. (1963) "Semantic considerations on modal logic." *Acta Philosophica Fennica* 16: 83–94.

—— (1980) [1972] *Naming and Necessity*. Cambridge, MA: Harvard University Press.

—— (2005) "Russell's notion of scope." *Mind* 114/456: 1005–37.

Larson, R., M. Den Dikken, and P. Ludlow (forthcoming) "Intensional transitive verbs and abstract clausal complementation." *Linguistic Inquiry*.

Lepore, E. (1982) "What model theoretic semantics cannot do." *Synthèse* 54: 167–87.

Lewis, D. (1968) "Counterpart theory and quantified modal logic." *Journal of Philosophy* 65: 113–26.

—— (1971) "Counterparts of persons and their bodies." *Journal of Philosophy* 68: 203–11.

—— (1973) *Counterfactuals*. Cambridge, MA: Harvard University Press.

—— (1976) "Probabilities of conditionals and conditional probabilities." *Philosophical Review* 85: 297–315.

—— (1979) "Scorekeeping in a language game." *Journal of Philosophical Logic* 8: 339–59.

—— (1981) "Index, context, and content." In S. Kanger and S. Ohman (eds.) *Philosophy and Grammar: Papers on the Occasion of the Quincentennial of Uppsala University*, Dordrecht: Reidel, pp. 79–100.

Meinong, A. (1910) *Ueber Annahmen*, rev. edn. Leipzig: Barth. Translated and edited by J. Heanue as *On Assumptions*, Berkeley, CA: University of California Press, 1983.

Montague, R. (1974a) "On the nature of certain philosophical entities." In *Formal Philosophy*, New Haven, CT: Yale University Press, pp. 148–87.

—— (1974b) "On the proper treatment of quantification in ordinary English." In *Formal Philosophy*, New Haven, CT: Yale University Press, pp. 247–70.

—— (1974c) "Pragmatics." In *Formal Philosophy*, New Haven, CT: Yale University Press, pp. 95–118.

Moore, G. E. (1899) "The nature of judgment." *Mind* 5/8: 176–93.

Neale, S. (1990) *Descriptions*. Cambridge, MA: MIT Press.

—— (2000) "On a milestone of empiricism." In A. Orenstein and P. Kotatko (eds.) *Knowledge, Language, and Logic*, London: Kluwer, pp. 237–346.

Parsons, T. (1969) "Essentialism and quantified modal logic." *Philosophical Review* 78/1: 35–42.

—— (1981) "Frege's hierarchies of indirect sense and the paradox of analysis." *Midwest Studies in Philosophy* 6: 37–57.

Partee, B. (1973) "Some structural analogies between tenses and pronouns in English." *Journal of Philosophy* 70: 601–9.

—— (1974) "Opacity and scope." In M. Munitz and P. Unger (eds.) *Semantics and Philosophy*, New York: New York University Press, pp. 81–101.

Perry, J. (1977) "Frege on demonstratives." *Philosophical Review* 86/4: 474–97.

Plantinga, A. (1974) *The Nature of Necessity*. Oxford: Clarendon Press.

Putnam, H. (1975) "Do true assertions correspond to reality?" In *Mind, Language, and Reality: Philosophical Papers*, vol. 2, Cambridge: Cambridge University Press, pp. 70–84.

Quine, W. V. O. (1943) "Notes on existence and necessity." *Journal of Philosophy* 40: 113–27.

—— (1947) "The problem of interpreting modal logic." *Journal of Symbolic Logic* 12: 43–8.

—— (1953) "Three grades of modal involvement." In *The Ways of Paradox and Other Essays*, Cambridge, MA: Harvard University Press, 1976, pp. 158–76.

—— (1955) "Quantifiers and propositional attitudes." In *The Ways of Paradox and Other Essays*, Cambridge, MA: Harvard University Press, 1976, pp. 185–96.

—— (1960) *Word and Object*. Cambridge, MA: MIT Press.

—— (1961) "Two dogmas of empiricism." In *From a Logical Point of View*, Cambridge, MA: Harvard University Press, pp. 20–46. (First published in *Philosophical Review*, 1951.)

—— (1976a) *The Ways of Paradox and Other Essays*. Cambridge, MA: Harvard University Press.

—— (1976b) "Worlds away." *Journal of Philosophy* 73/22: 859–63.

—— (1977) "Intensions revisited." *Midwest Studies in Philosophy* 2: 5–11.

Richard, M. (1987) "Quantification and Leibniz's Law." *Philosophical Review* 96: 555–78.

—— (1990) *Propositional Attitudes: An Essay on Thoughts and How We Ascribe Them*. Cambridge: Cambridge University Press.

—— (2001) "Seeking a centaur, adoring Adonis: intensional transitives and empty terms." In P. French and H. Wettstein (eds.) *Figurative Language*, Midwest Studies in Philosophy 25, Oxford: Blackwell, pp. 103–27.

Russell, B. (1905) "On denoting." *Mind* ns 14/56: 479–93.

—— (1919) *Introduction to Mathematical Philosophy*. New York: Simon & Schuster.

—— (1985) *The Philosophy of Logical Atomism*. La Salle, IL: Open Court.

—— (1988) *The Problems of Philosophy*. Buffalo, NY: Prometheus Books.

—— (1994) "On the nature of truth and falsehood." In *Philosophical Essays*, London: Routledge, pp. 147–59.

—— (1996) [1903] *The Principles of Mathematics*. New York: Norton.

Russell, B. and A. N. Whitehead (1910–13) *Principia Mathematica*. Cambridge: Cambridge University Press.

Salmon, N. (1981) *Reference and Essence*. Princeton, NJ: Princeton University Press.

Schiffer, S. (1987) *Remnants of Meaning*. Cambridge, MA: MIT Press.

Smullyan, A. F. (1947) "Review of W. V. Quine, The Problem of Interpreting Modal Logic," *Journal of Symbolic Logic* 12: 139–41.

—— (1948) "Modality and description." *Journal of Symbolic Logic* 13/1: 31–7.

Soames, S. (2002) *Beyond Rigidity: The Unfinished Semantic Agenda of Naming and Necessity*. New York: Oxford University Press.

Sosa, D. (2001) "Rigidity in the scope of Russell's theory." *Noûs* 35:1–38.

Stalnaker, R. (1968) "A theory of conditionals." In N. Rescher (ed.) *Studies in Logical Theory*, Oxford: Blackwell, pp. 98–112.

—— (1984) *Inquiry*. Cambridge. MA: MIT Press.

—— (1999a) "Indicative conditionals." In *Context and Content*, Oxford: Oxford University Press, pp. 63–77. (First published in *Philosophia*, 1975).

—— (1999b) "Pragmatics." In *Context and Content*, Oxford: Oxford University Press, pp. 31–46. (First published in *Synthèse*, 1970).

—— (2003a) "Anti-essentialism." In *Ways a World Might Be: Metaphysical and Anti-Metaphysical Essays*, Oxford: Oxford University Press, pp. 71–85.

—— (2003b) "The interaction of modality with quantification and identity." In *Ways a World Might Be: Metaphysical and Anti-Metaphysical Essays*, Oxford: Oxford University Press, pp. 144–59.

Stanley, J. (1996) "Truth and metatheory in Frege." *Pacific Philosophical Quarterly* 77: 45–70.

—— (1997a) "Names and rigid designation." In B. Hale and C. Wright (eds.) *A Companion to the Philosophy of Language*, Oxford: Blackwell, pp. 555–85.

—— (1997b) "Rigidity and content." In R. Heck (ed.) *Language, Thought, and Logic: Essays in Honor of Michael Dummett*, Oxford: Oxford University Press, pp. 131–56.

—— (1999) "Understanding, context-relativity, and the description theory." *Analysis* 59: 14–18.

—— (2002) "Modality and what is said." In J. Tomberlin (ed.) *Language and Mind*, Philosophical Perspectives 16, Oxford: Blackwell, pp. 321–44.

Stanley, J. and T. Williamson (1995) "Quantifiers and context-dependence." *Analysis* 55/4: 291–5.

Strawson, P. (1952) *Introduction to Logical Theory*. London: Methuen.

—— (1996) "On referring." In A. P. Martinich (ed.) *The Philosophy of Language*, 3rd edn., New York: Oxford University Press, pp. 208–30.

Szabo, Z. (2000) "Descriptions and uniqueness." *Philosophical Studies* 101: 29–57.

Tarski, A. (1983a) "On the concept of logical consequence." In *Logic, Semantics, Meta-Mathematics*, ed. J. Corcoran, trans. J. H. Woodger, Indianapolis: Hackett, pp. 409–20.

—— (1983b) "The concept of truth in formalized languages." In *Logic, Semantics, Meta-Mathematics*, ed. J. Corcoran, trans. J. H. Woodger, Indianapolis: Hackett, pp. 152–278.

—— (1983c) "The establishment of scientific semantics." In *Logic, Semantics, Meta-Mathematics*, ed. J. Corcoran, trans. J. H. Woodger, Indianapolis: Hackett, pp. 401–8.

Williamson, T. (2006) "Stalnaker on the interaction of modality with quantification and identity." In J. Thomason and A. Byrne (eds.) *Content and Modality: Themes from the Philosophy of Robert Stalnaker*, New York: Oxford University Press, pp. 123–47.

Zimmerman, T. E. (1993) "On the proper treatment of opacity in certain verbs." *Natural Language Semantics* 1: 149–79.

10

METAPHYSICS

E. J. Lowe

A synoptic overview of metaphysics in the twentieth century

Let me begin this chapter with a quick preview of the story that I am about to tell. And since it would defeat the purpose of such a sketch to expand it with elucidations of various semi-technical terms that will be fully explained in due course, I crave the reader's indulgence for including them at this stage of the proceedings. Unfortunately, academic philosophy is, for perfectly good reasons, replete with terms of this kind, which are mostly indispensable for a succinct and accurate characterization of its history.

The twentieth century saw the fortunes of metaphysics swing from high to low and back again. At the outset of the century, in the shadow of Kant and Hegel, idealism in the grand style still held sway, but was soon to be challenged by the method of logical analysis, in the hands of Gottlob Frege, Bertrand Russell, G. E. Moore and Ludwig Wittgenstein (see "The birth of analytic philosophy," Chapter 1). Then, for a short time, analytic ontology and metaphysical realism flourished in the form of the philosophy of logical atomism, rapidly to be overtaken by the rise of logical positivism with its scientistic bias and its hostility towards the traditional questions of metaphysics. This marked the beginning of the "linguistic turn," which placed the philosophy of language center-stage in analytic philosophy throughout the middle decades of the century (see "Philosophy of language," Chapter 9). Metaphysical questions became transmuted – some would say distorted – into semantic ones, inevitably encouraging anti-realist tendencies in some quarters. The immediate postwar period was characterized in the English-speaking world first by the prevalence of ordinary-language philosophy and then – through the influence of W. V. O. Quine – by the emergence of the naturalistic paradigm, the latter remaining a powerful force, especially in North America, for the remainder of the century (see "The development of analytic philosophy: Wittgenstein and after," Chapter 2, "American philosophy in the twentieth century," Chapter 5, and "Naturalism," Chapter 6). Meanwhile, in continental Europe, the demise of traditional metaphysics was repeatedly proclaimed in the wake of the phenomenological, existentialist, and structuralist movements (see "Phenomenolgy," Chapter 15 and "French philosophy in the twentieth century," Chapter 19). Thus, by the middle decades of the century, traditional metaphysics seemed to be dead everywhere and without hope of resurrection. And yet, by the 1970s its revival was already under way in Anglophone philosophy, stimulated at first by the work of Saul Kripke in modal logic and in due course epitomized by David Lewis's modal realism, with its vision of the plurality of possible worlds – a veritable metaphysician's paradise. Aristotelian essentialism, ridiculed by Quine as part of his onslaught on the analytic/synthetic distinction, was once more a subject of serious inquiry and a priori was no longer automatically a term of abuse. The Australian philosopher David Armstrong's work on universals undermined the prevailing nominalistic consensus, reopened debate on the nature of properties and, along with his promotion of the truth-maker principle, encouraged the burgeoning reaction against the linguistic turn and stimulated the resurgence of metaphysical realism. Serious ontology was back on the agenda of mainstream analytic philosophy, just as it had been in the heyday of logical atomism.

This, in barest outline, is the story of twentieth-century metaphysics as I shall be recounting it in this chapter. It is impossible to tell the story without being in any way partisan, because the most important issue for metaphysics in the twentieth century was the question of its very possibility, which was repeatedly denied by its most hostile critics. I tell the story from the point of view of one who does believe in the possibility of metaphysics and who believes this – I contend – with good reason. Indeed, I tell it from the point of view of one who maintains that the enemies of metaphysics attack it from positions that themselves are either incoherent or else involve covert metaphysical assumptions (see Lowe 1998: ch. 1). However, the question of whether, and if so how, metaphysics is possible – a question that Kant was famously the first to raise, in the *Critique of Pure Reason* (Kant 1929: B22) – cannot properly be posed without first asking what metaphysics is supposed to *be*. And here we immediately meet with a serious problem, because the answer to this very question is itself fraught with controversy. At this point, we need to cast our eyes briefly back to the history of metaphysics prior to 1900.

Metaphysics from Aristotle to Bradley: an opinionated thumbnail history

Kant himself held metaphysics to be possible – but only metaphysics conceived on his own terms. He rejected as incoherent or futile the conception of metaphysics that he attributed to the "rationalist" and "speculative" philosophers, such as Descartes, Spinoza, and Leibniz, who were amongst his prime objects of criticism. These philosophers, to whatever degree they may have proclaimed their distance from their Scholastic predecessors – and in this regard Leibniz was the least disrespectful of those roots – owed an inalienable debt to classical Greek metaphysics, especially to Aristotle and to a lesser extent to Plato. It is to the works of Aristotle that we owe the very term "metaphysics," his treatise on the subject taking its name from its position in the canonical ordering of his works *after* ("meta") the treatise on physics. Aristotle himself defined metaphysics as "the science of being qua being" (Aristotle 1928: Γ, 2–3), which we may loosely construe as being tantamount to *the systematic study of the most fundamental structure of reality as a whole*. The latter phrase certainly seems to capture the conception of metaphysics espoused by the great seventeenth-century metaphysicians who revitalized it in their own age, by incorporating into its pursuit a renewed concern with *natural* philosophy, that is, natural science, or the science of nature. This connection was intimately present in the thought of Aristotle himself, whence it was no accident that his *Metaphysics* was placed immediately after the *Physics* in the canonical ordering of his works. What distinguished Descartes, Spinoza, and Leibniz from their "empiricist" contemporaries, or near contemporaries – Locke, Berkeley, and Hume – was their confidence in the power of the human intellect to address and settle at least some of the central questions of metaphysics through the application of reason alone, that is, a priori, or without the benefit of or need for empirical evidence. It has scarcely ever been seriously questioned that the human intellect has access to some a priori knowledge, not least in the domain of mathematics. To suppose that such knowledge is to be had in the domain of metaphysics as well could not have seemed unreasonable to philosophers writing before David Hume (1711–76) – that same Hume who notoriously woke Kant from his "dogmatic slumbers" and prompted Kant's own "Copernican revolution." In this Kant transmuted metaphysics from Aristotle's study of being qua being into the study of *our thought* about being, seeking thereby to secure the apodictic certainty and a priori status of metaphysical knowledge at the expense of demoting the truth-evaluable content of metaphysical claims to something undeniably anti-realist in character. The succeeding nineteenth century was dominated by Kant-inspired idealist metaphysics, with Hegel constituting the pivotal figure of these developments – developments which, even in the natural home of empiricism, saw the domination of the British Idealists towards the end of the century, the pinnacle of whose achievements were the grandiose and – some would say – impenetrable systems of F. H. Bradley (1893) and J. M. E. McTaggart (1927).

So successful had Kant's redefinition of metaphysics been that, by the beginning of the twentieth century, metaphysics had more or less come to be identified with idealism and its realist orientation in the work of Aristotle had effectively been eradicated. Small wonder, then, that scientifically-minded philosophers for much of the twentieth century have proclaimed disgust for metaphysics. In Aristotle himself and the great metaphysicians of the seventeenth century no such antipathy between metaphysics and natural science was to be found. The antipathy between them that characterized so much of twentieth-century philosophy was the legacy of Kant's anti-realist redefinition of metaphysics as the study of the structure of *our thought* about reality rather than of the structure of reality itself. For the only empirical *science* that could have a central concern with the structure of our thought about reality is the science of *psychology*; this is a science which, however, can be pursued profitably only in conjunction with other empirical sciences, such as physics, chemistry, and biology, which are not concerned with the structure of our thought at all, but with quite other features of extra-mental reality. Indeed, it is not only the empirical sciences that sit uncomfortably with the Kantian conception of metaphysics; so too do logic and mathematics, for which Kant presents the specter of *psychologism*: the doctrine, in a nutshell, that the laws of logic are the laws of thought. Seen in this light, it is unsurprising that the revival of realist metaphysics in the twentieth century received its first major impetus from the work in formal logic and the foundations of mathematics of such scientifically-minded philosophers as Frege, Russell, and Whitehead. It will be with a consideration of the metaphysical implications of their work that I shall begin the story proper of metaphysics in the twentieth century, after a brief interlude discussing the idealist opposition against which they were reacting.

Monism, pluralism and the reality of relations

I shall concentrate on those features of idealism that provoked most hostility in the first generation of "analytic" philosophers. Psychologism was certainly a bugbear for Frege, who sought to rescue logic and mathematics from its grasp and therewith the objectivity and mind-independence of logical and mathematical truth (see Frege 1953: 1960) (see "The birth of analytic philosophy," Chapter 1 and "Kant in the twentieth century," Chapter 4). Undoubtedly, the single most important development in this connection was the discovery of first-order quantificational logic in its modern form, by Frege, Russell and Whitehead (see Russell and Whitehead 1910–13). Frege–Russell logic, as it may justly be called, has embedded within it certain important metaphysical assumptions of an ontological character, however metaphysically neutral its protagonists may sometimes claim it to be. At the core of this logic are the notion of an *atomic proposition* and the notion of *quantification*. An atomic proposition may either be monadic, in which case it is of the form "Fa," or it may be relational, in which case it is of the form "Rab" or "$Rabc$" and so on, depending on the "adicity" of the relation involved. Individual names or constants – "a," "b," "c" and so forth – are taken to denote particular objects, or individuals, whereas predicate letters – "F," "R" and so forth – are taken to express properties or relations that are predicable of such individuals. Quantification into a place in a sentence occupied by a name involves the replacement of that name by a variable which is then bound by a quantifier, as in "$\exists x Fx$" or "$\forall x \exists y Rxy$," these latter formulae affirming, respectively, that something has the property of being F and that everything stands in the relation R to something. The traditional logic that Frege–Russell logic replaced was not well equipped to express multiply-quantified propositions involving relations, such as "Every boy loves some girl," which is easily symbolized in Frege–Russell logic as "$\forall x(Bx \rightarrow \exists y(Gy \ \& \ Lxy))$." (With "$B$," "$G$," and "$L$" being taken to symbolize, respectively, the predicates "– is a boy," "– is a girl," and "– loves –," this formula may be read as follows: "For any x, if x is a boy, then, for some y, y is a girl and x loves y"; see further the Note on logical symbolism at the end of this chapter.) Traditional logic only accommodates sentences containing two "terms" linked by the copula, "is," as in "Every man is mortal" or "Some man is non-wise." This means, in effect, that such logic must "reduce" relations to properties of their relata, so that "Every boy loves some girl" is turned into "Every boy is a girl-lover," in which the property of being a girl-lover is predicated of every boy.

Now, as Fred Sommers has shown, it is in fact possible to formulate the traditional logic of terms in such a way as to render its expressive power equivalent to that of the first-order quantificational logic of Frege and Russell (see Sommers 1982). However, more important than such essentially verbal concerns are the underlying metaphysical assumptions of the two approaches. Frege–Russell logic is implicitly committed to a *two-category* ontology of *individuals* on the one hand and *properties and relations* on the other. It is, moreover, implicitly committed to a *pluralist* ontology, in the sense that it countenances the existence of *multiplicities* of individuals, properties, and relations. Idealists such as Francis Herbert Bradley (1846–1924), however, were deeply skeptical about the coherence of pluralism and the reality of relations. There can, of course, be relations in any serious sense only if there are distinct entities that can serve as their relata, so the two issues are intimately connected. For Bradley, reality is essentially *one* in a much more profound sense than is embodied in the mere idea that the world is *unified*: that there is one world, to which all of our truth-evaluable claims are responsible, with the implication that truth is not radically relative in character. A key consideration here is the regress that has come to be known as "Bradley's regress," which arises in connection with the problem of the so-called "unity of the proposition," but which might equally be characterized, in a less overtly linguistic guise, as the problem of the unity of facts, or of states of affairs.

In essence, the problem is this (see Bradley 1893: chs. 2, 3). If we suppose reality to be plural, in the sense of containing a multiplicity of distinct elements, various of which somehow combine together to constitute distinct facts, by corresponding to which our thoughts or assertions about reality acquire the status of truths, then we need to be able to comprehend how such "combination" is possible. Suppose, for instance, that we take a certain fact or state of affairs to contain, "combined together," certain individuals *a* and *b* and a certain relation *R* in which those individuals may truly be said to stand to one another. Then, it seems, the sole elements of reality that are involved in this state of affairs are the entities *a*, *b*, and *R*. But then we may ask in virtue of what it is that these entities may be said to be "combined" to form a distinct and unitary fact – the fact that *Rab* – as opposed to their forming the fact that *Rba* or indeed no fact at all. If we invoke some further *relation* between *a*, *b*, and *R* – saying, for instance, that the ordered pair, *a*, *b*> stands in the *exemplification* relation to R – then, it seems, we are saying that *a*, *b*, and *R* are *not*, after all, the only elements of reality involved in the putative fact that *Rab*, since the relation of exemplification is a further such element. But in that case it appears that we have got no further forward by invoking the supposed relation of exemplification in order to explain how the original elements *a*, *b*, and *R* are combined in the fact that *Rab*, because we are faced with exactly the same problem of explaining how the exemplification relation itself is combined together with the other three elements. If the exemplification relation is supposed to be some sort of metaphysical "glue" which binds *a*, *b*, and *R* together to make a unitary fact, then we need to be able to understand what it is that binds *this glue* – conceived as being just another element of reality – to each of the other three elements involved in the fact. And, clearly, invoking *yet another* element of reality to explain this in turn is just to embark on an infinite regress which has every appearance of being thoroughly vicious.

For Bradley, the lesson of this regress is that it was an error to suppose, in the first place, that reality is essentially plural, or composed of distinct elements, including "relations." On his sort of view, relations are spurious entities that metaphysical pluralists feel compelled to invoke in a necessarily vain attempt to unify reality: necessarily vain, because their pluralism fatally sunders reality into a multiplicity of distinct and disconnected fragments. Merely calling some of these fragments "relations" does not, on his sort of view, in any way serve to explain how they can bind together other fragments of reality so as to make reality as a whole unified. And along with his abandonment of pluralism and relations, the Bradleian idealist abandons the correspondence theory of truth, whereby true thoughts or assertions are those that "correspond" to distinct facts. In its place, we find a theory of truth that combines aspects of a *coherence* theory with aspects of a so-called *identity* theory, an identity theory of truth being one which refuses to distinguish between a true thought and what it is a thought *about*, that is, between "mind" and "world" (see Bradley 1893: ch. 24). For a philosopher like Bradley, nothing that finite minds like ours can say or think about reality can be *wholly* true, simply because reality does not admit of division into genuinely distinct parts such that one could, even in principle, say or think the *whole* truth about any one of those parts whilst remaining silent about the rest.

Logical analysis and logical atomism

Frege has an answer – of sorts – to the problem of the unity of the proposition, in terms of his notion of "saturation." For Frege, a proposition (or *Gedanke*, thought) is the *sense* of a meaningful sentence, its *reference* being a truth-value, that is, either *the True* or *the False* (see "On sense and reference," in Frege 1960). Each meaningful part of a sentence likewise has both sense and reference, the sense of the sentence being a function of the senses of its parts and its reference likewise being a function of the references of its parts. The meaningful parts of an atomic sentence are the proper names (*Eigennamen*) featuring in it and the predicate or predicates which remain when one or more such names are deleted from the sentence. Thus, in an atomic sentence such as "John loves Jill," three distinct predicates may be discerned, depending on how one analyses the sentence: "– loves Jill," "John loves –," and "– loves –." The proper names "John" and "Jill" refer to *objects* – the individual persons John and Jill respectively – and do so in virtue of the *senses* of those names. Each predicate has as its reference a *concept*, which, for Frege, is not to be thought of as something mental or psychological in character, but rather as being a mind-independent *function* (in the mathematician's sense), which takes one or more objects as its argument(s) and either the True or the False as its only possible values for those arguments. Thus, assuming that John *does* love Jill, the value of the function that is the reference of "John loves –" for Jill as its argument is *the True*. It is a consequence of Frege's approach to these matters that every true sentence or thought has the same reference – the True – rather than "corresponding" to a distinct "fact" or "state of affairs" which makes *it*, in particular, true. To this extent, Frege's ontology is not an ontology of states of affairs, but just an ontology of objects and concepts, with the True and the False residing amongst the objects. But – and this is the crucial point – the defining difference between objects and concepts is that the former, but not the latter, are "saturated," or complete in themselves, whereas concepts are essentially *un*saturated, demanding saturation or completion by objects (see "On concept and object," in Frege 1960). Because they are essentially unsaturated, concepts do not need to be "bound" to the objects that saturate them by further entities of any kind, that is, by any sort of metaphysical glue of the kind that Bradley's regress shows to be problematic. The obvious analogy is with a chemical compound, whose molecules are formed when electrons orbiting atoms of one kind fill up "gaps" in the outermost electron-shell of atoms of another kind, so as to make an electronically neutral and energetically stable unit.

Russellian propositions, unlike Fregean *Gedanken*, contain objects, properties, and relations as their constituents and are in this sense "world-involving" (see Frege 1980: 163, 169). That is to say, Russell's ontology – at the time of his allegiance to the philosophy of logical atomism – is indeed an ontology of facts or "states of affairs" and he is wedded to a correspondence theory of truth. For Russell, properties and relations – the counterparts of Fregean concepts – are *universals*, which differ from individual objects in being multiply exemplifiable and possessed of a fixed "adicity" (see "On the relations of universals and particulars," in Russell 1956). That is to say, each universal, in virtue of its adicity, is necessarily exemplifiable only by single individuals (if it is a monadic universal), or by pairs of individuals (if it is dyadic), or by triples of individuals (if it is triadic), and so on. At the same time, any given universal of a given adicity – say, a monadic universal – can be exemplified by more than one individual. Roundness, thus, may be exemplified by both of two distinct individual coins, which in that sense share this universal. Indeed, the sharing can even be construed quite literally if one favors, as Russell himself later did, the so-called "bundle theory," according to which individual objects just *are* "bundles" of co-present or co-exemplified universals (see Russell 1940: ch. 6). To the extent that this approach makes the adicity of a universal an essential feature of it, it resembles Frege's in its resources for answering the problem raised by Bradley's regress. For the thought, once again, is that universals do not need to be anyhow "glued" to individual objects in order for the latter to exemplify the former, since universals are, as it were, *ready-made* to "receive" individuals, rather as one piece of a jigsaw puzzle is ready-made to receive others. And to the extent that the approach involves allegiance to the bundle theory, Bradley's problem may appear to be still more easily solved, because it then turns out that a property "belongs" to an object simply in virtue of being a constituent part of it.

Russell arrived very early at his conviction that relations are real, through his examination of Leibniz's philosophy (which denied their reality) and his development, with Whitehead, of first-order quantificational logic, in which the addition of relational expressions brings with it a substantive and important augmentation of expressive power which is indispensable for mathematical purposes (see Russell 1900 and Russell and Whitehead 1910–13). He believed, indeed, that relations and other universals are possible objects of direct acquaintance (see Russell 1912: 51–2) and argued forcefully against nominalistic denials of their existence. Against those nominalists who seek to substitute resemblance-classes of individuals for universals, he famously argued that such an attempt to eliminate universals from our ontology founders on the role that it must acknowledge for the relation of *resemblance* itself, which cannot, on pain of a vicious infinite regress, be explained away in terms of further unanalyzed resemblances between individuals (see Russell 1912: ch. 9).

Russell's ontology can, in effect, be read off his *logical syntax*, as formulated in the rules for constructing well-formed formulae in first-order quantificational logic. The language of first-order logic is, in that sense, *ontologically perspicuous* as far as Russell is concerned. Atomic sentences of that language are true just in case they correspond to atomic facts, "*Fa*" being true, for example, just in case the individual *a* exemplifies the universal *F*. Not all compound sentences, however, need have distinctive atomic facts corresponding to them in order to be true. A disjunctive (that is, either/or) sentence, such as "*Fa* ∨ *Gb*," does not, since this will be true just in case there is *either* a fact corresponding to "*Fa*" or a fact corresponding to "*Gb*." There need be, then, no disjunctive *facts*. Russell does, however, think that there must be negative facts, and also general facts, such as the fact that all swans are white. This latter fact could not simply be a conjunctive fact, combining a finite number of facts about the whiteness of each individual swan. For even if *a* is white, and *b* is white, and *c* is white, and so on, for each individual swan, *a*, *b*, *c*, etc., it does not follow that *all* swans are white unless we are also given that *a*, *b*, *c*, etc. are all the swans there are; and this itself is a general fact (see "The philosophy of logical atomism," in Russell 1956: 183–4, 211). It is also a negative fact, because it is tantamount to the fact that there is no swan that is not identical with either *a*, or *b*, or *c*, etc.

Wittgenstein's version of logical atomism and of the correspondence theory of truth, embodied in his *Tractatus Logico-Philosophicus*, broadly resembles Russell's, while differing from it in some important respects, for example, in countenancing neither negative nor general facts as basic (see Wittgenstein 1922 and 1961: 2.04–2.06, 4.26, 4.51) (see "The birth of analytic philosophy," Chapter 1). Wittgenstein is also much less forthcoming than Russell about the nature of the "constituents" of atomic facts or states of affairs. These are said to be "objects," but it is unclear whether they are supposed to divide into two fundamental ontological categories: individuals on the one hand and universals on the other. Indeed, it is unclear whether it matters for Wittgenstein whether such a question is answerable by us or perhaps even at all. The *existence* of Wittgensteinian objects seems to be demanded by the intelligibility of our language and thought, on his account, but it doesn't seem to be required that *we* should be able to grasp their nature in order for them to serve this purpose. These, however, are deep exegetical waters, in which it is perhaps inadvisable to venture. Our main concern is with the general thrust of logical atomism and for that purpose a relatively broad-brush approach will suffice. The upshot is that it is a philosophy that is committed to metaphysical realism, ontological pluralism, and a correspondence theory of truth. The realism and pluralism it shares with Frege's philosophy, but not the account of truth. For Frege, truth – while indisputably objective and mind-independent – is indefinable and unanalyzable. On his view, it cannot at all illuminatingly be said to consist in "correspondence to fact," because no notion of "facts" as distinctly individuatable items is available that does not simply collapse them into true propositions. This is just the point, once again, that for Frege the only possible worldly "correlate" of a true thought or proposition is *the True* and is thus *the same* object for all such thoughts or propositions. If the worldly correlates of true thoughts or propositions were called "facts," then, there could be only *one* fact: the "Great Fact," as Donald Davidson calls it, with deliberate irony (see Davidson 1969). Thus the great dividing line, metaphysically speaking, between Frege's philosophy on the one hand and the philosophy of logical atomism on the other is that only the latter is committed to – in David Armstrong's phrase (see Armstrong 1997) – *a world of states of affairs*: to the view, as Wittgenstein expresses it at the outset of the *Tractatus*, that the world is the totality of *facts*, not of things (see Wittgenstein 1961: 1.1).

Logical positivism and the "linguistic turn"

The first seeds of doubt about the coherence of the philosophy of logical atomism were sown by Frank Plumpton Ramsey (1903–30). In the first place, he questioned the viability of the universal/particular distinction, which was central to Russell's version of logical atomism. According to F. P. Ramsey, this supposed distinction, far from being one of fundamental ontological significance, merely reflects a parochial grammatical distinction of natural language: the distinction between subject and predicate (see Ramsey 1925). To take his famous example: we suppose, he suggests, that "Socrates" is a quite different kind of entity from "wisdom" – the former being a particular, or individual object, whereas the latter is a universal or property – simply because it is customary to make the name "Socrates" the subject of any sentence concerning him, whereas any mention of wisdom is typically relegated to predicate position, as in "Socrates is wise." However, Ramsey points out, this same proposition could in fact be equally well expressed by the sentence "Wisdom is a characteristic of Socrates," in which the grammatical roles of the two expressions are reversed. Ramsey's challenge to the adherent of the universal/particular distinction is to say what *really* serves to distinguish so-called particulars from so-called universals, other than our predilection to make terms for the former the subjects of our sentences about them, a fact which provides no basis at all for an objective distinction between two supposedly quite different categories of entities. Russell does, in fact, have what seems to be the makings of an answer to this challenge, in his contention that universals have fixed "adicities," whereas particulars or individuals are free to combine with any number of other elements in atomic facts or propositions. So, for example, a dyadic relation, R, can only combine with *two* other elements, such as the individuals a and b, to form an atomic fact, in this case, the fact that Rab or the fact that Rba. By contrast, the individual a can combine with any number of other elements to form an atomic fact; for instance, it can combine with *one* other element, the monadic property F, to form the fact that Fa, or it can combine with *two* other elements, the dyadic relation R and the individual b, to form the fact that Rab, or it can combine with *three* other elements, the triadic relation S and the individuals b and c, to form the fact that Sabc; and so on. However, it would seem to be a contingent matter whether there really are universals of differing adicities, in that we can make sense of the thought that, for example, all universals might turn out to be dyadic relations. But in that case Russell's method of distinguishing between universals and particulars would not be applicable, since all atomic facts would then have to contain just three elements. Are we to say, then, that in such a world – which might conceivably turn out to be *our* world – the universal/particular distinction does not exist? If so, it hardly seems that it can be a deep and fundamental ontological distinction.

Ramsey also challenged the credentials of the correspondence theory of truth, by advancing in place of it his own *redundancy* theory, according to which the truth predicate, "– is true," serves only to effect expressive economy (see Ramsey 1927). The thought here is that any assertion of the form "p is true," where p is some proposition, amounts to nothing more than an assertion of p itself. And, indeed, it seems hard to say what more is being asserted when one asserts, for example, that it is true that Paris is the capital of France than when one simply asserts that Paris is the capital of France. In this case, of course, no economy at all is effected by the use of the truth predicate. But it *is* effected when, for instance, I assert that Paris is the capital of France and you respond by saying "That's true," for here your use of the truth predicate saves you the trouble of having to repeat my sentence. In other cases, however, it seems that the truth predicate is not so easily eliminable merely at the cost of greater longwind-edness, as, for example, when someone who does not know any geometry asserts that Pythagoras's Theorem is true; for such a person is not in any position simply to repeat the theorem in question. According to Ramsey, however, what such a person asserts has the logical form "$\forall p$(if Pythagoras's Theorem is p, then p is true)," which – given the equivalence between p and "p is true" – simply reduces to "$\forall p$(if Pythagoras's Theorem is p, then p)," from which the truth-predicate has duly been eliminated. (Notice that this latter sentence quantifies over *propositions*: it may be read as "For any (proposition) p, if Pythagoras's Theorem is p, then p" – although it is a matter of considerable debate whether using quantifiers and propositional variables in this way really makes sense.) If all of this is correct, it appears that the notion of truth has no deep metaphysical significance and that philosophers have once more been beguiled into thinking that it has by relatively superficial features of the natural languages that they speak.

In both of these attacks by Ramsey on metaphysical notions held dear by Russell, we see the effects of the "linguistic turn": the tendency, already present in Wittgenstein's work of the period, to focus on language and its logical structure as the starting point for philosophical discussion, rather than on extra-linguistic reality itself. On the one hand, there is here the thought that language, or at least *natural* language, can mislead us into positing illusory metaphysical distinctions and, on the other, the thought that the most that we can profitably study is language itself, rather than the extra-linguistic reality that it supposedly represents, because we have no guide to the structure of that reality other than is provided by the linguistic structures by means of which we seek to represent it. For already in Wittgenstein's *Tractatus* we find the idea that no sense can really be made of attempts to describe the putative relation *between* language and the world, since any such alleged description will just constitute another bit of *language*. We find there also the idea that all possibility and necessity is *logical* possi-bility and necessity, with logically necessary truths having that status in virtue of their logical form and lacking, as a consequence, any empirically significant content (see Wittgenstein 1961: 5.525, 6.375). This idea is inimical to realist metaphysics because any such metaphysics seems bound to posit *necessary connections between real entities* – such as between properties and the objects that possess them, or between states of affairs and their constituent elements – and purely logical relations, being relations between the sentences or propositions of a language, are connections of the wrong sort to serve the purposes of the metaphysical realist. For the philosopher who sees all modality as logical in character, Hume's conception of "objects" or "things," in the broadest sense of those terms – that is, entities of whatever kind – as all being "loose and separate" seems to be inevitable. On such a view, necessity resides only in our ways of *describing* the world, not in the world itself, and simply reflects the conceptual scheme that we happen to deploy.

From here it is but a short step to the *analytic/synthetic distinction* and a *verificationist theory of meaning* that were the central pillars of logical positivism and the chief basis of its adherents' hostility to traditional metaphysics. With the flourishing in the late 1920s of the Vienna Circle, the fountainhead of logical positivism whose leading lights included Moritz Schlick, Otto Neurath, and Rudoph Carnap – all strongly influenced by Wittgenstein, who had by now abandoned his allegiance to the philosophy of logical atomism – the linguistic turn was complete. In the English-speaking world, the clearest, if also the crudest, articulation of the doctrines of logical positivism was to be found in A. J. Ayer's overtly iconoclastic manifesto of 1936, *Language, Truth and Logic* (Ayer 1936; 1946). All meaningful statements were said to be divisible into two mutually exclusive classes, reminiscent of Hume's division between "relations of ideas" and "matters of fact": *analytic* statements, which are supposedly true solely in virtue of their logical or grammatical form and the meanings of the individual words contained in them, and *synthetic* statements which, if true, must be verifiable by means of experience or observation. And, just as Hume used his distinction to recommend that all works of "school" metaphysics should be "committed to the flames" (see Hume 1975: 165), so the logical positivists condemned as meaningless all "metaphysical" statements which failed to reduce either to logical tautologies or else to empirically verifiable claims of the sort that science supposedly deals with. Thus, Ayer had much irreverent fun at the expense of idealists like Bradley and some contemporary Continental philosophers by deriding the many seemingly obscure pronouncements to be found in their writings, such as Martin Heidegger's virtually untranslatable "Das Nichts selbst nichtet" (see Ayer 1946: 59, alluding to Heidegger 1929, usually translated as "The Nothing nothings"). One of many inescapable embarrassments for this doctrine, however, was its inability to accommodate its own central thesis, the *verification principle*, that is, the very claim that all meaningful synthetic statements must be empirically verifiable. For this claim itself appears not to be analytic, and yet to claim that it must itself be empirically verifiable would at best be question-begging as well as wholly implausible. Of course, one might simply *stipulate* that "meaningful," in this context, is to be understood as implying empirical verifiability, but that would deprive the principle of any interest. Furthermore, in any case, the logical positivists never satisfactorily explained what "empirical verifiability" is supposed to amount to, so that this key term constantly threatened to degenerate merely into a vacuous expression of vague approbation (see Berlin 1939; Popper 1934; 1968). But, quite apart from the technical difficulties that attended the formulation and justification of the verification principle, logical positivism was doomed to founder on its inadequate resources for accommodating the truths of mathematics, which are apparently indispensable for empirical scientific purposes and yet are seemingly at once a priori in character but not reducible to logical tautologies.

Untenable though the central doctrines of logical positivism undoubtedly were, its influence ran deep and succored the general hostility to realist metaphysics that was rampant amongst analytic philosophers of the period. The most sophisticated advocate of this approach was undoubtedly Rudolf Carnap, whose monumentally ambitious work *Der logische Aufbau der Welt* (Carnap 1928; 1967) sought to reconstruct all meaningful talk about physical reality on the basis of a single experiential datum: the relation of remembered similarity between experiences. Carnap's technical virtuosity in the field of formal semantics made him a formidable foe of traditional metaphysicians. Amongst other things, he sought to make the questions of traditional metaphysics literally unutterable – in a manner somewhat reminiscent of George Orwell's Ministry of Truth – by outlawing "external" questions and allowing only "internal" ones: internal, that is, to the linguistic practice of an appropriate scientific discipline (see Carnap 1950a). Thus, for example, it might be deemed intelligible and thus permissible for rival particle physicists to dispute whether *positrons* exist, but not permissible for philosophers to debate quite generally whether "material objects" do, as idealists and their materialist opponents have long attempted to. Hence, it is allegedly impossible to attach any sense to the question – raised in the context of a purely philosophical discussion – of whether positrons *really* exist or not, because in that context the sort of considerations that particle physicists would have in mind as bearing on the question of whether positrons exist simply would not be at issue.

Ordinary-language philosophy, descriptive metaphysics, and Quinean naturalism

Not many analytic philosophers had Carnap's taste for and facility with formal semantics and the construction of artificial logical languages – the only distinctive contributions, it would seem, that Carnap recognized philosophy as being able to bring to the scientific enterprise, enabling philosophers to "explicate" notions central to scientific method, such as the notion of the *degree of confirmation* conferred upon a scientific hypothesis by suitable empirical data (see Carnap 1950b). The idea of philosophy as a technical handmaiden to science was unattractively arid and uninspiring to those with residual hopes that "philosophy" might still be construed, however modestly, as meaning "the love of wisdom." But the linguistic turn had set in firmly and, if formal languages were not to be the focus of philosophical attention, this left only natural or "ordinary" language as the proper arena for philosophical inquiry. Encouragement for this came once again from the work of Wittgenstein, who had subtly shifted his ground once more and proclaimed ordinary language to be "in order as it is," requiring no revision or "improvement" at the hands of formal semanticists (see Wittgenstein 1953: 98). The shift in emphasis to ordinary language allowed traditional metaphysical questions to be raised once more, albeit only in the watered-down guise of questions about "our conceptual scheme," as articulated in the grammar and vocabulary of everyday talk. Thus was born *descriptive metaphysics*, as Peter F. Strawson (1919–2006) famously characterized it, in contradistinction to the suspect "revisionary" metaphysics of philosophy's supposedly disreputable past, as practiced by Spinoza, Leibniz, or Berkeley (see Strawson 1959: 9).

In effect, this was a linguistic version of Kant's conception of metaphysics, its modest aspiration being to render perspicuous certain very general features of the structure of our talk about the world, such as the commonplace distinction between persisting objects, which are said to undergo change, and passing events, which are not. Metaphysics was, in short, reconceived as a branch of the philosophy of language and thus also of the philosophy of *thought*, on the presumption – quite explicit, for example, in the work of Michael Dummett (1925–) – that the structure and content of thought can be effectively explored only through a study of the structure and meaning of the language in which thought is expressed (see Dummett 1991: Introduction; and 1993: ch. 13). Questions concerning identity and individuation came to the fore in this context; how, for example, do we identify *persons*, including ourselves, and re-identify them over time? Interest in these questions reached a peak in the wake of Derek Parfit's (1942–) controversial paper "Personal identity" (1971), maintaining that identity is not "what matters" where issues of personal survival, memory, and moral responsibility are concerned. Such questions were, however, typically given a semantic or epistemological gloss, rather than a genuinely ontological one. Instead of asking what persons *are*, if indeed they exist at all, and in what their identity over time consists, philosophers were supposed to inquire only into the meaning of the word "person" and the identity-criteria implicitly invoked in our practices of referring to persons at a time or over time (but see further Parfit 1984: x, where he makes it clear that he, at least – unlike many of his contemporaries – had more sympathy for revisionary than for descriptive metaphysics). The supposition was, of course, that questions of the former sort could be properly construed only as naive ways of addressing questions of the latter sort. When suitably reformulated, such questions could not seriously be taken to call into doubt the very *existence* of persons or – to use J. L. Austin's memorable phrase (see Austin 1962: 8) – "moderate-sized specimens of dry goods," such as tables and chairs, since everyday language is replete with words for such things. This, then, provided a comforting way of avoiding difficult issues about the degree of match or mismatch between the ontology of common sense, as embodied in everyday patterns of speech, and the real structure of the extra-linguistic world. Indeed, for a philosopher like Dummett, the traditional question of realism becomes transmuted into the seemingly much tamer question of whether sentences in this or that domain of discourse can be assigned "realist truth-conditions," the key consideration allegedly being whether or not the law of excluded middle (or, more cautiously, the principle of bivalence) can intelligibly be supposed to apply to sentences in a given domain – for example, to sentences about the past, or about other minds (see "Realism," in Dummett 1978).

But it was mainly British, or British-educated, philosophers who took wholeheartedly to ordinary-language philosophy with its attendant commonsense ontology and homely preference for descriptive rather than revisionary metaphysics. This reflected, perhaps, their tendency to have an educational background in the classics and the humanities rather than in the sciences. In the United States, the scientistic bias that had characterized logical positivism survived the demise of that school of philosophy, a demise finally secured by Quine's onslaught on the analytic/synthetic distinction in his "Two dogmas of empiricism" (see Quine 1953).(For further discussion of Quine, see "The development of analytic philosophy: Wittgenstein and after," Chapter 2; "American philosophy in the twentieth century," Chapter 5; and "Philosophy of language," Chapter 9.) It is significant that that onslaught was most firmly resisted in Britain, most notably in H. P. Grice and P. F. Strawson's rearguard defense of it, "In defense of a dogma" (see Grice and Strawson 1956). There it was defended precisely in the name of common sense and on the basis of everyday language, but without any of the positivist trappings that had been associated with it previously. In Quine's hands, however, the attack on the analytic/synthetic distinction marked the beginning of the ascendancy of *naturalism* amongst scientifically-minded philosophers (see "Epistemology naturalized," in Quine 1969). And here traditional metaphysics found itself faced not with a new ally but a new enemy even more formidable than logical positivism had been. For traditional metaphysics sees itself above all as *first philosophy*: an intellectual discipline whose task it is provide the general framework within which all more local pursuits of truth, as practiced by the special sciences, may be conducted. As such, it takes itself to be at heart an a priori discipline, attempting to determine to what fundamental ontological categories the elements of being must belong and how those elements are necessarily tied to one another in various relationships of ontological dependence. For the naturalistic philosopher, the idea of there being any such overarching or foundational intellectual discipline is thoroughly misbegotten, a product of our hubristic failure to acknowledge that we human beings and any knowledge of the world that we may attain to are merely outcomes of natural processes of biological evolution and adaptation. Accordingly, what we vaingloriously dignify as metaphysical knowledge, or the science of being qua being, is in reality nothing more than a set of cognitive structures that evolution has equipped us with to render us better adapted to our humble ecological niche here on the surface of an insignificant planet. The best we can do by way of exploring and explaining our metaphysical beliefs is, accordingly, to apply the thus-far successful methods of empirical science – and, more particularly, the methods of evolutionary psychology – *to ourselves*. Rather than metaphysics providing a foundation for empirical science, then, the tables are turned entirely and empirical science provides an explanation for our – no doubt parochial and in many ways highly idiosyncratic – metaphysical predilections. But in explaining our metaphysical beliefs it goes no way at all towards *justifying* them, in the sense of providing warrant for their truth. For deeply ingrained beliefs like these may certainly be "adaptive" – helping us to survive in a hostile environment – without needing to be *true*. So, at least, says the naturalistic philosopher.

And yet, it may be pointed out, Quine himself – the founding father of naturalized epistemology – is often associated with seemingly grandiose ontological pronouncements, epitomized by his two famous slogans, "To be is to be the value of a variable" and "No entity without identity" (see "Existence and quantification" and "Speaking of objects," in Quine 1969). Moreover, did not Quine favor an austere ontology of "desert landscapes," according to which the physical world consists entirely of spacetime occupied by material objects, where a "material object" is just any matter-filled region of spacetime, however "gerrymandered" its boundaries may be? Entities such as these – together with such sets or classes as are needed for the purposes of mathematics in its scientific applications – are all we need to "quantify over" for the purposes of physical theory, and they are all entities for which precise and determinate identity-conditions can be specified (see Quine 1995: 40–1). However, these Quinean doctrines must all be understood in the context of his thesis of *ontological relativity*, which implies that it is a mistake to suppose that the austere physicalist ontology just outlined really has any *philosophically* privileged status (see "Ontological relativity," in Quine 1969). Rather, it just turns out to be the implicit ontology of the language of physical science, whose methods have been pursued with great practical success for some three hundred years or so and thus have proved their worth in pragmatic terms. Hence, the strongest undercurrent in Quine's thought, driving his naturalism, seems to be in sympathy with the pragmatic philosophy of his illustrious compatriots of the preceding century, C. S. Peirce and William James (see "American philosophy in the twentieth century," Chapter 5). Metaphysics in the grand European style has always, one suspects, struck the American psyche as being somehow decadent and self-indulgent.

Kripkean essentialism and Lewisian modal realism

One of Quine's prime targets in attacking the analytic/synthetic distinction was the family of *modal* notions associated with it: the notions of necessity, possibility, and contingency. The logical positivists had held that all necessity is logical necessity, grounded in the a priori laws of logic and semantic connections between the meanings of words. But Quine was skeptical about the very idea that words have precisely identifiable individual "meanings" and thought that even logical laws are, in principle, revisable in the light of experience. Certainly, he had no sympathy for the idea of *modal logic*, conceived as an extension of first-order quantificational logic in which the standard truth-functional operators are supplemented by *modal operators* expressive of necessity and possibility. In particular, he considered the idea of so-called *de re* necessity or possibility to be incoherent, that is, the sort of necessity or possibility that is implicated when one "quantifies into" a context governed a modal operator, as in the formula '$\exists x \, \Im \, Fx$', asserting that there is something, x, such that, necessarily, x is F. To take one of his famous examples, Quine thinks that it is incoherent to assert that there is something, x, such that x is a number necessarily greater than 7 (see "Reference and modality," in Quine 1953). He allows that it may be acceptable to assert that, necessarily, 9 is a number greater than 7, but to infer "$\exists x \, \Im \, (x$ is a number $\& \, x > 7)$" from "($\Im \, 9$ is a number $\& \, 9 > 7$)" is illicitly to *quantify into* a context governed by the necessity operator, "$\Im$" ("it is necessarily the case that"). Why is this illicit? Because, in Quine's view, it is only as *described* or *referred to* in a certain way that anything can be said to be necessarily thus-and-so, since necessity at best resides only in our ways of talking about things, not in the things themselves. Thus, the number 9 may also be described as being "the number of the planets," but so-described it is *not* true that it is necessarily greater than 7, since it would plainly be false to assert that, necessarily, the number of the planets is greater than 7. Quine repudiates the notion of *de re* necessity as harking back to the obscurities of Aristotelian essentialism, with its distinction between the "essential" and the "accidental" properties of things. He dismisses this distinction in derisory fashion with his famous example of the mathematical cyclist. Should we say that Professor X, an illustrious mathematician with a predilection for cycling, is essentially a rational animal or that he is essentially a biped? Answer: to the extent that we describe him as being a mathematician, we should presumably also describe him as being rational; and, equally, to the extent that we describe him as being a cyclist we should presumably also describe him as being bipedal. But it is incoherent, Quine thinks, to suppose that Professor X is necessarily either rational or bipedal quite independently of how we choose to describe him, for this would be to suppose that necessity can reside *in things themselves* rather than merely in our descriptions of them (see Quine 1960: 199).

Highly influential though Quine's assault on the analytic/synthetic distinction was in its day, his dismissal of *de re* necessity, essentialism, and quantified modal logic proved far less successful. This was largely due to the impact of Saul Kripke's ground-breaking work in the formal semantics of modal logic and his famous lectures on naming and necessity (Kripke 1972; 1980). (For more on Kripke's approach, see "Philosophy of language," Chapter 9.) Using his model-theoretic framework of "possible worlds," Kripke showed how various systems of quantified modal logic could be consistently interpreted, thereby rebutting the Quinean charge that such logics harbor ineradicable incoherence in virtue of their allowing one to quantify into contexts governed by modal operators. For such formal model-theoretic purposes it mattered little what one took possible worlds *to be*, but this issue could not be ignored if the possible-worlds approach to modality was to be applied to the semantics of natural language – that is, if it was seriously to be suggested that what we ordinarily *mean* when we make modal claims in natural language is to say how matters stand in non-actual possible worlds. According to a possible-worlds semantics for modal statements, to say that it is *necessary* that *p* is to say that *p* is the case in *every* possible world (or, at least, in every possible world "accessible" to the actual world) and to say that it is *possible* that *p* is to say that *p* is the case in *some* possible world (or, at least, in some possible world "accessible" to the actual world). Of course, the notion of possible worlds was not a new one, although Kripke's formal use of it was. We owe it, ultimately, to that determinedly revisionist metaphysician, Leibniz. For Leibniz, however, possible worlds reside in the mind of God, apart from the one world that He chose to realize or make actual, and this theological conception of their ontological status is not readily adaptable to the purposes of a more secular generation of philosophers. Accepting Quine's criterion of ontological commitment, as encapsulated in his dictum "To be is to be the value of a variable," it is incumbent upon those who seriously purport to "quantify over" possible worlds to tell us what they take such entities *to be*. It was in recognition of this intellectual obligation that the metaphysics of possible worlds was born, a branch of metaphysics that has since burgeoned into a thriving industry.

Kripke himself, in *Naming and Necessity*, seemed to take a somewhat deflationary view of the ontological status of possible worlds, emphasizing that we are not to think of them as being, as it were, parallel universes existing alongside our own actual world. Other modal metaphysicians, while agreeing with Kripke on this negative point, were more explicit in their positive accounts of what possible worlds literally *are*. According to one very popular approach, possible worlds are taken to be *maximal consistent sets of propositions*: a set of propositions, S, being "maximal consistent" just in case S is a consistent set of propositions and, for any proposition, p, either S includes p or S includes the negation of p. The actual world, construed as one such world, thus turns out to be the set of all *true* propositions. Each non-actual possible world differs from the actual world, then, in including at least one proposition that is not (actually) true. Of course, it may sound bizarre to say that the actual world is a set of propositions, at least on the assumption that both sets and propositions are abstract rather than concrete entities. However, we can get around this seeming difficulty by distinguishing between "the actual world," construed as a set of true propositions, and the (at least partly concrete) reality of which those propositions are true. This latter might aptly be called "the universe," taken to include not only all actually existing concrete entities but also all actually existing abstract entities, such as the possible worlds themselves (conceived as maximal consistent sets of propositions). This sort of approach to the metaphysics of modality is rightly called *actualist*, since it acknowledges the existence of nothing that does not *actually* exist, including "possible worlds" themselves.

Theories of possible worlds like the foregoing are described by David Lewis as *ersatzist*, because, in his view, they offer pale substitutes for possible worlds in the form of actually existing abstract entities, when what are needed are *real* worlds, in a full-blooded sense (see Lewis 1986: ch. 3). Lewis was the inventor and foremost advocate of *modal realism*: the doctrine that, in addition to the concrete spatiotemporal universe which we inhabit, there are countless other such equally real and equally concrete universes – each spatiotemporally and causally isolated from one another – which collectively constitute the totality of all possible worlds. On Lewis's account, every world is "actual" to its own inhabitants, so that ours is not in any way special in that regard. This sort of approach to the metaphysics of modality is accordingly *possibilist* rather than actualist in character because, according to it, we can intelligibly and indeed truthfully say that some things exist that do not *actually* exist, to wit, all those things that exist in other possible worlds but not in our world. Against ersatzism, Lewis raises many complaints, one of which is that it cannot provide a reductive account of the *meaning* of modal expressions, since *ersatz* worlds are defined with the aid of modal notions, most obviously the notion of *consistency*. For to say that a set of propositions is consistent is just to say that it is *possible* for all of those propositions to be true together. Of course, the ersatzist may equally try to raise difficulties for Lewis's position, and Lewis frankly admits that this position is customarily met with "the incredulous stare" (see Lewis 1986: 133). In the end, though, he contends that modal realism is not really more ontologically extravagant than ersatzism and that its ontological commitments are well worth incurring in return for the explanatory power that they confer upon his theory of modality.

The debate between modal realism and ersatzism has still not been settled and it is not clear that it ever will be. Unsurprisingly, though, there are many philosophers for whom neither position is much to their taste, because they are skeptical about the pretensions of metaphysicians to make ontologically inflationary claims. One opposing deflationary approach to possible worlds is that of the *modal fictionalist*, whose position seems to have, in Russell's immortal phrase, all the benefits of theft over honest toil. The modal fictionalist seeks to retain all of the supposed explanatory benefits of Lewis's realism without incurring the ontological cost of having to acknowledge the existence of non-actual possible worlds (see Rosen 1990). Accordingly, "Necessarily p" is reconstrued as meaning not "In every possible world, p is the case" but, rather, "*According to the fiction of possible worlds, p is the case in every possible world.*" This, however, is just one example of a tendency, which emerged in the wake of the metaphysical revival engendered by Kripke and Lewis, to retreat from robustly realist positions in matters of ontology not so much to blatantly *anti*-realist positions as to deflationary or "minimalist" ones. We find it also, for instance, in the upsurge of minimalist or deflationary accounts of *truth* in the closing decades of the twentieth century (see Horwich 1990).

Kripke's revival of the Leibnizian notion of possible worlds gave birth to a new essentialism, no longer embarrassed by Quine's admonishments concerning its alleged incoherence. On Kripke's approach, we can say that a thing's essential properties are those that it possesses in every possible world in which it exists, while its accidental properties are those that it actually possesses but fails to possess in some possible worlds in which it exists. It turns out in the standard system of quantified modal logic that each thing's *identity* is provably essential to it, inasmuch as it is provable that true identity statements are *necessarily* true. This is intimately connected with Kripke's semantic doctrine concerning *proper names*: that these are *rigid designators*, denoting the same thing in every possible world in which they denote anything at all (see Kripke 1980: 4–15). Both Kripke himself and, at much the same time, Hilary Putnam (1926–) extended this doctrine to include *natural kind terms*, such as "water," "gold," and "tiger," the referents of which were likewise taken to possess "real essences," in the shape of their microstructural constitutions (see Kripke 1980: 116–55 and "The meaning of 'meaning'," in Putnam 1975). Most importantly, it was acknowledged and indeed emphasized that such essences could only be discovered a posteriori, by scientific investigation. It is chemistry, thus, that informs us that the real essence of water lies in its being H_2O, or that the real essence of gold lies in its having atomic number 79. And it is biochemistry that informs us that the real essence of tigers lies in their DNA. By breaking the traditionally assumed connection between necessity and the a priori, Kripke gave a new lease of life to both notions. At about the same time, David Wiggins (1933–) developed similar views about substance and essence, but drawing much more consciously on the Aristotelian roots of these notions than on the new technical apparatus of possible worlds, either Kripkean or Lewisian (see Wiggins 1980 and 2001).

According to Lewis's conception of possible worlds, of course, one cannot literally say that *the same thing* may exist in more than one possible world; at best one can say that something existing in one possible world may have a "counterpart" existing in another, its counterpart in any given world being the thing existing there, if any, that most closely resembles it in relevant respects (see Lewis 1986: ch. 4). Consequently, Lewis cannot usefully say that a thing's essential properties are those that *it* possesses in every possible world in which it exists, since it can exist in only one world. Instead, however, he can say that a thing's essential properties are those that are possessed by it and all of its counterparts. But since the counterpart relation may be differently determined when things in different worlds are compared in different respects, Lewisian essentialism turns out to be more fluid than the Kripkean variety. For some purposes, this may seem to be an advantage. Consider, for instance, the thorny question of whether or not we should identify a bronze statue with the lump of bronze of which it is made, on the assumption that both come into existence at the same time and go out of existence at the same time. According to Kripkean essentialism, we should not identify these objects, because the lump exists in worlds in which the statue does not, namely, in those worlds in which the lump was never fashioned into a statue. Lewis, however, can say that what we have in actuality is just *one* object – the lump/statue – which stands in two different counterpart relations to objects in other possible worlds, depending on whether it is compared to such objects in respect of its lumpish features or its statuesque features. There are worlds in which the lump/statue has a counterpart under the first of these relations but not under the second, that's all.

It should be remarked that Lewis originally presented his realist theory of possible worlds in the context of an account of the semantics of *counterfactual conditionals*: subjunctive conditional statements of the form "If it had been/were to be the case that *p*, then it would have been/would be the case that *q*," symbolized by Lewis as "$p \; \Box\!\!\rightarrow q$" (see Lewis 1973b). According to Lewis's account, a counterfactual of this form is true if and only if *q* is the case in the *closest* possible world(s) in which *p* is the case: where one world, w_1, is deemed to be *closer* to the actual world, w_a, than is another world, w_2, just in case w_1 is *more similar* to w_a than w_2 is. Robert Stalnaker advanced a very similar account at about the same time, although without advocating modal realism (see Stalnaker 1968). The Lewis–Stalnaker approach to the semantics of such conditionals has proved immensely influential and popular, opening the door to many attempts to analyze important metaphysical concepts in counterfactual terms, above all, the concept of *causation*, where again Lewis led the way. Lewis offered an analysis of event-causation according to which an event, *c*, is a cause of another event, *e*, just in case *c* and *e* are linked by a chain of events successive members of which stand in a relation of *counterfactual dependency* to their immediate predecessors in the chain; that is to say, where, if e_n is an event in the chain and e_{n+1} is its immediate successor, the following counterfactual conditional is true: 'If e_n had not occurred, then e_{n+1} would not have occurred' (see Lewis 1973a). This analysis had the advantage of being able to deal with certain problem cases involving causal *pre-emption*, that is, cases in which an event that did not actually cause a certain effect *would have* done so if another event had not. But other problem cases proved more difficult for Lewis's account, which he ultimately abandoned in favor of a different theory, albeit one still invoking counterfactuals (see Lewis 2000). The lasting legacy of Lewis's work in this area was, however, to make the counterfactual approach to causation the most popular in the closing decades of the twentieth century, even if the details of his own accounts were frequently challenged.

The metaphysics of time and persistence

It was perhaps inevitable that developments in modal logic and modal metaphysics would go hand in hand with developments in temporal logic and the metaphysics of time, for there are many interesting analogies between temporal and modal notions. Here once again the views of David Lewis came to dominate discussion in the closing decades of the twentieth century, perhaps unduly eclipsing the important earlier work of Arthur Norman Prior (1914–69). Two issues in particular came to the fore: the dispute between "tensed" and "tenseless" theories of time and the dispute between "endurantist" and "perdurantist" accounts of the persistence of objects through time. The two issues are connected, but not in a perfectly straightforward way. Prior was the pioneer of so-called *tense logic* and himself a firm advocate of the tensed view of time, according to which the notions of past, present and future are central to the metaphysics of time (see Prior 1968). Much earlier in the century, the British Idealist J. M. E. McTaggart (1866–1925) had famously pronounced time to be *unreal* because, he thought, these notions harbor an internal contradiction (see McTaggart 1927: ch. 33). The kernel of McTaggart's argument is that the predicates "past," "present," and "future" are mutually incompatible and yet we seem constrained to say that every event is past *and* present *and* future, in virtue of the passage of time. D. H. Mellor did much to revive interest in McTaggart's argument from the 1980s onwards, contending that its true lesson is not that *time* is unreal, but that *tense* is unreal (see Mellor 1981; 1998). Mellor acknowledged that irreducibly tensed *beliefs* are indispensable, because, for example, unless I believe, on December 5th, that *it is now December 5th*, knowing that December 5th is my uncle's birthday will not lead me to greet him appropriately on that day; but he held that such beliefs have *tenseless truth-conditions*. Thus, on this view, an utterance, *u*, of the sentence 'It is now December 5th, 2005' is true if and only if *u* is uttered on December 5th, 2005. That is to say, temporal expressions such as the word "now," which characteristically occur in tensed language, are so-called "token-reflexive" terms: "now" always refers to the time at which it is uttered, "tomorrow" to the day after it is uttered, and so on. The implication is supposed to be that it is an error – into which we fall by misunderstanding the semantics of token-reflexive expressions – to imagine that a word like "now" denotes an ontologically privileged moment of time which is somehow "more real" than other moments, past or future. All moments of time are equally real and words like "today," "yesterday," and "tomorrow" merely serve to locate one time relative to another, namely the time at which the words in question are uttered.

Naturally, supporters of tensed theories of time (also called "A-theorists," after McTaggart's *A-series* of past, present, and future events) rejected the arguments of tenseless theorists like Mellor (also called "B-theorists," after McTaggart's *B-series* of events standing in earlier/later relations to one another). Prior himself was a *presentist*, holding that only presently existing things are real, famously characterizing the present as the real considered in relation to two species of unreality, the past and the future (see Prior 1970). Though a fairly lone voice at the time, Prior was later joined by a growing band of presentists towards the end of the twentieth century. The catalyst for this development was work done by David Lewis on the metaphysics of persistence, which concerns the identity of objects over time. Of particular importance in this connection was a problem raised by Lewis that was called by him the *problem of temporary intrinsics* (see Lewis 1986: 202). This is the problem of explaining how one and the same persisting object can possess different intrinsic properties – properties such as shape or color – at different times. The same banana, for example, can be green at one time, t_1, and yellow at later time, t_2. But this seems to flout Leibniz's law, which affirms that objects are identical only if they have the same properties; for green and yellow are mutually incompatible properties. Lewis contends that there are only three possible solutions to this problem: either (1) we must say that the banana's properties are not green and yellow *simpliciter*, but greenness-at-t_1 and yellowness-at-t_2, which are indeed mutually compatible properties, but *relational* rather than intrinsic ones, or (2) we must deny, as the presentist does, that the same object may literally have different intrinsic properties at different times, on the grounds that only one time – the present – is real, or finally (3) we must attribute the intrinsic properties green and yellow to different things: not to the banana itself, but to two different temporal parts of it, one existing at t_1 and the other at t_2. Lewis himself favors the third solution and therewith the *perdurantist* account of persistence, which holds that objects persist through time by possessing different temporal parts at the different times at which they exist. Opposed to this is the *endurantist* account, according to which objects persist through time by being "wholly present" at each time at which they exist. Solutions (1) and (2) are consistent with endurantism, but are rejected by Lewis, the first because it seems to fly in the face of the obvious truth that properties like green and yellow are intrinsic properties of their bearers and the second because it is committed to a tensed theory of time and the unreality of the past and the future. At the time at which he was writing, Lewis evidently did not anticipate, however, just how many philosophers would be willing to embrace presentism as a solution to the problem of temporary intrinsics.

There is an obvious analogy between presentism in the philosophy of time and *actualism* in modal metaphysics. Similarly, if we call the position opposed to presentism *eternalism* – the view, that is, that all times are equally real – then there is a parallel analogy between eternalism and *possibilism*. For, just as the presentist holds that only the present time is real, so the actualist holds that only the actual world is real. And, just as the eternalist holds that all times are equally real, so the possibilist holds that all possible worlds are equally real. Of course, the actualist may *say* that possible worlds are "real," meaning thereby only that they are actually existing abstract entities, such as maximal consistent sets of propositions. To the modal realist, however, this is not taking possible worlds seriously; it is ersatzism. In like manner, the presentist may construe talk about past and future "times" as talk about abstract representations of unreal states of affairs – unreal because different from *present* states of affairs, which, according to the presentist, are the only states of affairs that are real. According to the presentist, to say that *p* was or will be the case at a past or future time, *t*, is just to say, in effect, that if *t* were *present*, then *p* would be the case; in other words, that if things were *really* as *t* represents them as being – remembering that *t*, a past or future "time," is here taken to be a mere abstract representation – then *p* would be the case. Analogously, according to the actualist, to say that *p* "is the case," or "is true" in a non-actual possible world, *w*, is just to say, in effect, that if the maximal consistent set of propositions *w* were *true*, then *p* would be true. Thus, "truth in a (non-actual) possible world" is not really *truth* for an actualist, any more than "existence at a past or future time" is really *existence* for a presentist.

Universals, tropes and the truth-maker principle

The 1980s saw, in the wake of David Armstrong's seminal work on universals, a revival of serious interest in *ontology*, that branch of metaphysics that seeks to identify the fundamental categories of being (see Armstrong 1978). Quine had virtually destroyed ontology in the minds of most analytic philosophers through his much-cited paper "On what there is" (Quine 1953), by persuading a whole generation of them to understand "ontology" in an altogether new way. In his characteristically laconic manner, Quine pronounced the fundamental question of ontology to be "What is there?" and its one-word answer to be "Everything": in other words, anything that should be taken to be amongst the values of the variables of our best-confirmed theories, when these are regimented in the style of first-order quantificational logic. Hence the famous slogan, "To be is to be the value of a variable." The reason why Quinean "ontology" is destructive of real ontology is that it allows of no fundamental distinctions between entities in respect of their ontological categories. In effect, Quine's ontology is a "no category" ontology. On Quine's view, the most we can say is just that there are *things* in the world – the values of our first-order variables – which can be variously described by means of different predicates, such as "– is red" or "– is a horse" or "– loves Jill." But predicates themselves do not denote or stand for anything, or, if they do, then at best they stand only for sets or classes of the things that they apply to: thus, *the set of red things* in the case of the predicate "is red." Quine is a thoroughgoing *nominalist*: he denies the existence of properties and relations, conceived as universals.

Armstrong gave us reasons to believe in the existence of universals, but not purely semantic reasons. He did not contend that we need to invoke universals as the *meanings* of predicates. Indeed, he thoroughly repudiated the view that every meaningful predicate must denote or stand for a corresponding property. More generally, he rejected the idea that language reflects ontology, or is our best and ultimately our only guide to ontology. One of his principal reasons for advocating an ontology including universals was that, he thought, *laws of nature* can properly be understood only as involving relations between universals (see Armstrong 1983). *Which* universals, precisely, we should include in our ontology is a question to be answered, ultimately, by empirical scientific inquiry, not by semantical considerations.

The laws acknowledged by our best-confirmed scientific theories will be our best guide to what universals there are. Here it is important to distinguish between laws themselves and *statements* of law. Many philosophers understand by a "law of nature" a true law-statement, but Armstrong takes a law to be, rather, the *truth-maker* of a true law-statement. Here we meet Armstrong's ultimate guiding principle in matters of ontology: the *truth-maker principle*, long championed by him and C. B. Martin (see Mulligan et al. 1984 and Armstrong 2004). This is the principle that all truths need to be *made true* by something existing in reality. Anything that makes a certain statement or proposition true is a truth-maker of that statement or proposition. But we should not assume that there is a one-to-one correspondence between truths and truth-makers. Rather, their relationship is many-to-many: the same truth may have more than one truth-maker, and the same truth-maker may make true more than one truth. This is one reason why we cannot read off ontology from language, why we cannot determine *what there is* simply on the basis of what we can truly say about the world.

In saying that laws of nature consist in relations between universals, Amstrong was rejecting a popular nominalist construal of laws as consisting in "constant conjunctions" amongst particulars, expressible by universally quantified conditionals – that is, in the simplest case, by statements of the logical form "$\forall x(Fx \rightarrow Gx)$" – a view traceable back to David Hume. Instead, he suggested, the logical form of a law is "$N(F, G)$," where "F" and "G" denote universals and "N" denotes the second-order relation of *necessitation* ("second-order" because it relates universals, not particulars (see Armstrong 1983: 85)). In other words, we should conceive of a law not as consisting in the fact that all Fs are Gs, but rather in the fact that F-ness necessitates G-ness; this is an idea that was also defended at about the same time by Fred Dretske and Michael Tooley, whence this view of laws is often referred to as the "Amstrong–Dretske–Tooley" account. According to Armstrong, "$N(F, G)$" *entails* but *is not entailed by* "$\forall x(Fx \rightarrow Gx)$," and this explains why law-statements support corresponding counterfactual conditionals, whereas statements of constant conjunction do not. That is to say, "$N(F, G)$" entails "If *a* were F, then *a* would be G," whereas the latter is *not* entailed by "All Fs are Gs." But Armstrong's account of these matters did not by any means go unchallenged by the nominalist opposition; in particular, Bas van Fraassen urged against it, amongst other things, that the supposed entailment of "$\forall x(Fx \rightarrow Gx)$" by "$N(F, G)$" is left unexplained and quite mysterious by Armstrong (see van Fraassen 1989: 96). However, Armstrong's advocacy of universals did not rest solely on the appeal that he made to them in his account of laws of nature; he had more general reasons for invoking their existence, based directly on the truth-maker principle (see Armstrong 1997: 115–16).

Consider any simple, contingent, predicative truth, of the form "*Fa*," such as "This ball is yellow." And let us ask what could be a *truth-maker* of this truth. Before we can attempt to answer that question, we need to say more specifically what the *truth-making relation* is supposed to be. At least to a first approximation, what we can say is this: an entity *e* is a truth-maker of a statement *S* just in case the existence of *e* entails the truth of *S*; or, in the language of possible worlds, just in case *S* is true in every possible world in which *e* exists. So, what sort of entity is it whose existence could entail the truth of "This ball is yellow"? Clearly, *this ball's* existence does not entail the truth in question: for, since it is merely *contingent* that this ball is yellow, there are many possible worlds in which this ball exists and yet "This ball is yellow" is not true. What seems to be required as a truth-maker in this case is not *an object*, such as this ball, nor even an object merely in conjunction with a property, such as this ball in conjunction with the property yellow: for, even granting that properties like this may exist, it seems clear that there are worlds in which *both* this ball *and* the property yellow exist, and yet in which it is not true that this ball *possesses* the property yellow – in other words, in which it is not true that *this ball is yellow*. It seems, rather, that what is required as a truth-maker for "This ball is yellow" is a *state of affairs*, containing this ball and the property yellow as its "constituents," with the former exemplifying the latter. We are thus led, by the truth-maker principle, to an ontology of states of affairs, whose ultimate constituents fall into two distinct ontological categories: individual objects or *particulars* on the one hand, and *universals* (properties and relations) on the other. But, of course, we have encountered this sort of position before, for it is essentially that of the philosophy of logical atomism as advocated by Russell. It is not, like Quine's ontology, a "no category" ontology but, as I have just said, a *two*-category ontology of particulars and universals. Here, however, it may be queried to what category, if any, *states of affairs* themselves are supposed to belong. Armstrong's own answer is clear enough: states of affairs that contain both particulars and universals as constituents are themselves *particulars*. He calls this "the victory of particularity" (see Armstrong 1997: 126–7).

Armstrong's two-category ontology soon acquired a formidable rival, in the shape of the one-category *trope* ontology advocated by, amongst others, Keith Campbell (see Campbell 1990). Although widely popular only in the closing two decades of the twentieth century, it already had by then a distinguished pedigree, having been defended early in the century by G. F. Stout and, in its middle years, by D. C. Williams, who coined the term "trope" (see Stout 1921 and Williams 1953). Armstrong is a realist about properties and relations, but takes them to be universals rather than particulars. Trope theorists, by contrast, take properties and relations to be particulars and deny the existence of universals. To understand this dispute, one has to have some sense of what is supposed to distinguish universals from particulars – which, it will be recalled, is precisely the question that F. P. Ramsey raised, claiming to find no satisfactory answer to it. And here a further distinction must be brought into play, this time between rival conceptions of universals: immanent or "Aristotelian" realism on the one hand, and transcendent or "Platonic" realism on the other. An immanent realist, such as Armstrong himself, maintains that there are no *unexemplified* or *uninstantiated* universals and that universals are "wholly present" wherever their particular instances are to be found. So, for example, the immanent realist who believes in the existence of color universals, such as the color red, will say that redness is *wholly present* wherever any individual red thing is to be found, *both* in the petals of this red flower *and* in the skin of that red tomato, and so forth. Thus, on this view, universals are *multiply located* entities, unlike particulars, whose existence is confined to a single place at any given time. By contrast, a transcendent realist will say, first, that not all universals need be exemplified or instantiated at all – they may altogether lack particular instances – and, second, that even when they are instantiated they are not literally *located* where their particular instances are, because universals, on this view, do not literally exist *in* space and time at all. Transcendent realism has its modern defenders, such as Michael Tooley (see Tooley 1987), but immanent realism is considerably more popular – largely, it would seem, because it is consistent with a broadly "naturalistic" metaphysics, that is, with a metaphysics that confines all real existence to the physical spacetime world. Certainly, Armstrong is motivated by this consideration in his advocacy of immanent realism. Setting aside, now, the dispute between immanent and transcendent realism, we are in a position to understand the dispute between immanent realists and trope theorists. The latter, as I have said, regard all properties and relations as being particulars rather than universals. This means, for example, that a trope theorist would hold that the redness of this red flower and the redness of that red tomato are not the *same* redness, wholly present in each of these individual objects and in that sense "shared" by them. Rather, they are two distinct *particular* rednesses, each present in one of the objects but not in the other. Not only that, however: the trope theorist goes further and contends that each of these objects – the red flower and the red tomato – is nothing but a "bundle" of coexisting or "co-present" tropes: a particular color, shape, mass, and so forth. This is why the trope ontology is a *one*-category ontology, for it contends that *everything* is ultimately composed of tropes, denying as it does that there is any fundamental distinction between objects, on the one hand, and properties and relations on the other.

The trope-ontologist, it seems clear, does not need to invoke states of affairs as the truth-makers of contingent, predicative truths such as "This ball is yellow." Such a theorist can maintain, for example, that *this ball's yellowness* – its yellow trope – is a truth-maker of the statement or proposition in question, at least on the plausible assumption that tropes are not "transferable" from one object to another and cannot exist save as part of a bundle of tropes that together compose an object. For, given this assumption, it follows that in any world in which this ball's yellow trope exists, it belongs to a bundle of tropes composing this ball, whence "This ball is yellow" is true in any such world. This may seem to give a clear advantage to trope theory over immanent realism, in point of its ontological economy. On the other hand, it may seem that immanent realism still has a distinct advantage over trope theory in respect of its account of laws of nature, for trope theory seems committed to the "constant conjunction" view of laws. However, matters may be more complicated than this, because in the closing decade of the twentieth century a *necessitarian* or *essentialist* view of laws began to be evolved by a number of analytic metaphysicians, notably Brian Ellis (see Ellis 2001). Although Ellis himself is a realist concerning universals, many philosophers sympathetic to trope theory are equally sympathetic to the necessitarian view of laws. According to this view, laws of nature are grounded in the *essences* of properties, so that it is a matter of *metaphysical necessity* what other properties any given property can combine with or interact with causally. C. B. Martin, for instance, holds this sort of view, even though he thinks that properties are particulars rather than universals (see Martin 1993). The implication of all this is that one can reject the idea that laws consist in mere "constant conjunctions" without adopting Armstrong's view that they consist in relations of necessitation between universals. For one can say, instead, that the laws that obtain in any possible world "supervene" upon the properties that exist there, with the implication that worlds in which the same properties exist are worlds in which the same laws necessarily obtain. Such a view of laws sits naturally alongside the idea that all properties are at least partly "dispositional" in nature, since they have built into their very essence their capacities for combination or causal interaction with other properties. This contrasts with Armstrong's long-held view, according to which all basic properties are "categorical" in nature and dispositions supervene upon these properties and the laws relating them to one another – laws which themselves are taken to be contingent in character (see Armstrong et al. 1996).

The problem of material composition and the ontology of ordinary objects

An issue that came to prominence in the 1990s was the problem of material composition, stimulated in large measure by Peter van Inwagen's book *Material Beings* (1990). In that book, van Inwagen raised what he called the *special composition question*: when is it that some objects, the xs, collectively compose another object, y? A noun-phrase of the form "the xs" is a plural referring-expression, examples in ordinary language being "the bricks in that wall" and "the sheep in that field." In these cases, of course, the xs are all (putative) objects of the same kind, bricks and sheep respectively. And in the first case there is an implicit assumption that the bricks in question *do* compose something, namely, a wall. It might also be supposed, very naturally, that in the second case, too, something is composed by the sheep, namely, a flock. Of course, bricks and sheep themselves are also taken to be composite objects, so that there is an implicit assumption that, if y is a brick or a sheep, then there are some xs such that the xs compose y. But it will seem extravagant to most philosophers – and even more so to most ordinary folk – to suppose that for any xs *whatever*, there is always some object y that they compose: for example, that there is an object composed by the following things: the Eiffel tower, my left foot, and the moon. However, some philosophers do indeed believe precisely this: they believe in *unrestricted mereological composition* (see, for example, Lewis 1991: 7). Mereology is the formal study of part–whole relations, which was axiomatized in the first half of the twentieth century by the Polish philosopher and logician Stanislaw Lesniewski and the American philosophers H. S. Leonard and Nelson Goodman (see Simons 1987: chs. 1–2). According to standard mereological principles, any plurality of objects, the xs, has a *sum*, y. If y is a sum of the xs, then the xs are *parts* of y and, since parthood is taken to be a *transitive* relation, it follows in standard mereology that y is also a sum of the *parts* of the xs. It is natural to assume that there are *some* objects that have *no* parts, these being described as *mereological atoms*. What *physicists* call "atoms" will not, of course, qualify as *mereological* atoms, because they *are* supposed to have parts, such as protons and neutrons. In standard mereology, any plurality of atoms has a *unique* sum and, consequently, any plurality of objects whatever – whether they are atoms or composite objects – has a unique sum, which is identical with the sum of the atoms composing all of those objects. From this point of view, then, every composite object whatever may simply be identified with a sum of atoms and every plurality of atoms composes an object. The implication is that the world contains vastly more composite objects than our ordinary commonsense ontology would suggest. On this view, "ordinary" objects, such as tables and chairs, bricks, walls, and sheep constitute just a tiny selection from all of the composite objects that the world really contains. The suggestion is, thus, that we focus on this tiny selection in our everyday ontology simply because these are the objects that are of interest to *us* and which consequently acquire names in human languages. Other creatures with different interests, it might well be supposed, populate "their" worlds with quite different selections of objects. This view is not exactly anti-realist, since it allows that "our" composite objects do indeed *exist*. But it does imply that our everyday ontology, even when supplemented by the ontology of our physical sciences, is partial and biased by our distinctively human interests.

Unsurprisingly, the doctrine of unrestricted mereological composition was challenged in many quarters. It seems bizarre to suppose that three apparently quite unrelated objects, such as the Eiffel tower, my left foot, and the moon should together compose a further object, distinct from each of these and containing them amongst its parts. The oddity of this suggestion is surely not solely due to the fact that we have in our language no familiar name for this object, or that it is not of any interest to us. The puzzle, rather, is how it could be so easy for composite objects to exist. Surely, a *real* composite object must have parts that are unified by some more substantive relation than mere coexistence. The problem, however, as van Inwagen makes clear, is that it is not at all easy to specify such a relation in a satisfactory way, so as to avoid various puzzles and paradoxes that are apt to arise. One such puzzle, concerning composite artifacts, is the famous problem of the ship of Theseus, whose original parts are successively replaced by new ones until the process of renovation is complete, whereupon the old parts are put together again to make a ship: we now have *two* ships, the renovated ship and the reconstructed ship, each of which seems to have a good claim to be identical with the original ship; but one ship cannot be identical with two distinct ships, on pain of contradiction. Van Inwagen's own position seems to some critics to be a rather extreme one: namely, that the *only* composite objects are living beings since, in his view, it is only when atoms are caught up together in the processes constituting a *life* that they collectively compose something. On his view, then, there are, strictly speaking, no such things as tables and chairs, bricks and walls, or indeed even the moon. The most we can strictly say is that there are atoms "arranged table-wise" or "arranged moon-wise" in various parts of the world. Fortunately, our own existence as composite beings is secured in virtue of the fact that we are living creatures.

Naturally, many philosophers are inclined to judge that van Inwagen's way of opposing the doctrine of unrestricted mereological composition is a case of "out of the frying pan and into the fire." Why make an exception of living things? Van Inwagen gives us his reasons, but they may not convince everyone. If we don't make such an exception, however, we shall end up having to say that *no composite things whatever exist*, which hardly seems credible. And what if it should turn out that there are no "atoms" – that nothing is "simple," in the sense of lacking all parts? That seems to be at least conceivable, but then it will follow that if there are no composite things there are *no things at all*. This is nihilism. However, whether or not one agrees with van Inwagen's solution, we have reason to be grateful to him for compelling us to confront some difficult questions about the ontology of everyday objects, questions that could not have been given a serious hearing in the heyday of ordinary-language philosophy. This, then, represents another victory for serious metaphysics in the closing years of the twentieth century.

How metaphysics stands at the end of the twentieth century

At the beginning of the twenty-first century, metaphysics in something like its traditional guise has come back from the dead and is in a healthier condition now than it was a hundred years earlier, even if its demise is still vigorously proclaimed in some quarters. It is healthier now partly because it has discovered a modus vivendi with empirical science, whereby each of these branches of intellectual inquiry can complement and learn from the other without either needing to secure its own credentials by trampling on the other's, even if this fact may as yet be apparent only to the metaphysicians and not, in general, to theoretical scientists. It is also healthier because it is far less under attack from within the ranks of philosophers themselves and is no longer under pressure to reinvent itself as something that it is not, for example, as an inquiry into the structure of "our conceptual scheme," or as a contribution to the semantics of everyday language. It can once again advertise itself in its true colors, as an inquiry into the fundamental structure of reality as a whole, without automatically meeting a hail of criticism that such an endeavor is by its very nature impossible or irredeemably misconceived. This is not at all to say that metaphysicians have reached broad agreement about fundamentals in ontology; as we can see from the preceding section, this is far from being the case. But at least it is now widely regarded as being perfectly respectable to engage in serious discussion about such matters as the existence of universals, the nature of persistence, and the reality of time.

Note on logical symbolism

The use of some logical symbolism has been unavoidable in this chapter, but for the benefit of those readers not conversant with it, here is a brief guide to current usage. Modern formal logic standardly deploys two *quantifiers*: the *universal* quantifier "$\forall$" and the *existential* quantifier "$\exists$," in conjunction with *variables*, "x," "y," "z" and so on. The expressions "$\forall x$" and "$\exists y$" are standardly read as "for all x" and "for some y" (or "there is some y") respectively. In addition, modern formal logic deploys the following *truth-functional operators*: "&" (conjunction), "$\vee$" (disjunction), "~" (negation) and "$\rightarrow$" (implication), which are read, respectively, as "and," "or," "not," and "if ... then." Thus, for example, the complex formula "$\exists x(Fx \vee \forall y(Rxy \rightarrow (\sim Gx \ \& \ Hy)))$" may be read as: "For some x, either x is F or for all y, if x is R to y, then x is not G and y is H." "F," "G," "H," and "R" here are *predicate letters*, symbolizing such predicates as "– is wise" or "– loves –" (the former being a *monadic* or *one-place* predicate and the latter a *dyadic* or *two-place* predicate). *Brackets* are used in complex logical formulae in much the same way that punctuation marks are used in written natural languages, in order to eliminate possible ambiguities. These basic logical symbols may be supplemented by, for example, the box "$\Box$" and the diamond "$\Diamond$," which are *modal operators* and can be read, respectively, as "necessarily" (or "it is necessary that") and "possibly" (or "it is possible that"). Another such additional symbol is David Lewis's symbol for the "if" of counterfactual conditionality, "$\Box\!\!\rightarrow$," discussed in the section "Kripkean essentialism and Lewisian modal realism."

References

Aristotle (1928) *The Works of Aristotle*, vol. VIII: *Metaphysica*, trans. D. Ross. Oxford: Clarendon Press.

Armstrong, D. M. (1978) *Universals and Scientific Realism*. Cambridge: Cambridge University Press.

—— (1983) *What is a Law of Nature?* Cambridge: Cambridge University Press.

—— (1997) *A World of States of Affairs*. Cambridge: Cambridge University Press.

—— (2004) *Truths and Truthmakers*. Cambridge: Cambridge University Press.

Armstrong, D. M., C. B. Martin, and U. T. Place (1996) *Dispositions: A Debate*, ed. T. Crane. London: Routledge.

Austin, J. L. (1962) *Sense and Sensibilia*, ed. G. J. Warnock. Oxford: Clarendon Press.

Ayer, A. J. (1936) *Language, Truth and Logic*. London: Victor Gollancz.

—— (1946) *Language, Truth and Logic*, 2nd edn. London: Victor Gollancz.

Berlin, I. (1939) "Verification," *Proceedings of the Aristotelian Society* 39: 225–48.

Bradley, F. H. (1893) *Appearance and Reality: A Metaphysical Essay*. London: Swan Sonnenschein.

Campbell, K. (1990) *Abstract Particulars*. Oxford: Blackwell.

Carnap, R. (1928) *Der logische Aufbau der Welt*. Berlin: Weltkreis Verlag.

—— (1950a) "Empiricism, semantics, and ontology." *Revue Internationale de Philosophie* 4: 20–40. Repr. in *Meaning and Necessity: A Study in Semantics and Modal Logic*, 2nd edn., Chicago: University of Chicago Press, 1956, pp. 205–221.

—— (1950b) *Logical Foundations of Probability*. Chicago: University of Chicago Press.

—— (1967) *The Logical Structure of the World and Pseudoproblems in Philosophy*, trans. R. A. George. London: Routledge & Kegan Paul.

Davidson, D. (1969) "True to the facts." *Journal of Philosophy* 66: 748–64.

Dummett, M. A. E. (1978) *Truth and Other Enigmas*. London: Duckworth.

—— (1991) *The Logical Basis of Metaphysics*. London: Duckworth.

—— (1993) *Origins of Analytical Philosophy*. London: Duckworth.

Ellis, B. (2001) *Scientific Essentialism*. Cambridge: Cambridge University Press.

Frege, G. (1953) *The Foundations of Arithmetic*, trans. J. L. Austin, 2nd edn. Oxford: Blackwell.

—— (1960) *Translations from the Philosophical Writings of Gottlob Frege*, trans. and ed. P. T. Geach and M. Black, 2nd edn. Oxford: Blackwell.

—— (1980) *Philosophical and Mathematical Correspondence*, ed. B. F. McGuinness, trans. H. Kaal. Oxford: Blackwell.

Grice, H. P. and P. F. Strawson (1956) "In defense of a dogma." *Philosophical Review* 65: 141–58.

Heidegger, M. (1929) *Was ist Metaphysik?* Bonn: Friedrich Cohen Verlag.

Horwich, P. (1990) *Truth*. Oxford: Blackwell.

Hume, D. (1975) *Enquiries Concerning Human Understanding and Concerning the Principles of Morals*, ed. L. A. Selby-Bigge and P. H. Nidditch. Oxford: Clarendon Press.

Kant, I. (1929) *Critique of Pure Reason*, trans. N. Kemp Smith. London: Macmillan.

Kripke, S. A. (1972) "Naming and necessity." In D. Davidson and G. Harman (eds.) *Semantics of Natural Language*, Dordrecht: Reidel, pp. 253–355.

—— (1980) *Naming and Necessity*. Oxford: Blackwell.

Lewis, D. K. (1973a) "Causation." *Journal of Philosophy* 70: 556–67. Repr. with postscripts in *Philosophical Papers*, vol. II, New York: Oxford University Press, 1986, pp. 159–213.

—— (1973b) *Counterfactuals*. Oxford: Blackwell.

—— (1986) *On the Plurality of Worlds*. Oxford: Blackwell.

—— (1991) *Parts of Classes*. Oxford: Blackwell.

—— (2000) "Causation as influence." *Journal of Philosophy* 97: 182–97.

Lowe, E. J. (1998) *The Possibility of Metaphysics: Substance, Identity, and Time*. Oxford: Clarendon Press.

McTaggart, J. M. E. (1927) *The Nature of Existence*. Cambridge: Cambridge University Press.

Martin, C. B. (1993) "Power for realists." In J. Bacon, K. Campbell, and L. Reinhardt (eds.) *Ontology, Causality and Mind: Essays in Honour of D. M. Armstrong*, Cambridge: Cambridge University Press.

Mellor, D. H. (1981) *Real Time*. Cambridge: Cambridge University Press.

—— (1998) *Real Time II*. London: Routledge.

Mulligan, K., P. Simons, and B. Smith (1984) "Truth-makers." *Philosophy and Phenomenological Research* 44: 287–321.

Parfit, D. (1971) "Personal identity." *Philosophical Review* 80: 3–27.

—— (1984) *Reasons and Persons*. Oxford: Clarendon Press.

Popper, K. R. (1934) *Logik der Forschung*. Vienna: Julius Springer.

—— (1968) *The Logic of Scientific Discovery*. London: Hutchinson.

Prior, A. N. (1968) *Papers on Time and Tense*. Oxford: Clarendon Press.

—— (1970) "The notion of the present." *Studium Generale* 23: 245–8.

Putnam, H. (1975) *Mind, Language and Reality: Philosophical Papers*, vol. 2. Cambridge: Cambridge University Press.

Quine, W. V. O. (1953) *From a Logical Point of View*. Cambridge, MA: Harvard University Press.

—— (1960) *Word and Object*. Cambridge, MA: MIT Press.

—— (1969) *Ontological Relativity and Other Essays*. New York: Columbia University Press.

—— (1995) *From Stimulus to Science*. Cambridge, MA: Harvard University Press.

Ramsey, F. P. (1925) "Universals." *Mind* 34: 401–17. Repr. in *The Foundations of Mathematics and Other Logical Essays*, London: Kegan Paul, 1931.

—— (1927) "Facts and propositions." Aristotelian Society Supplementary Volume VII: pp. 153–70. Repr. in *The Foundations of Mathematics and Other Logical Essays*, London: Kegan Paul, 1931.

Rosen, G. (1990) "Modal fictionalism." *Mind* 99: 327–54.

Russell, B. (1900) *A Critical Exposition of the Philosophy of Leibniz*. London: Allen & Unwin.

—— (1912) *The Problems of Philosophy*. London: Oxford University Press.

—— (1940) *An Inquiry into Meaning and Truth*. London: Allen & Unwin.

—— (1956) *Logic and Knowledge: Essays 1901–1950*, ed. R. C. Marsh. London: Allen & Unwin.

Russell, B. and A. N. Whitehead (1910–13) *Principia Mathematica*. Cambridge: Cambridge University Press.

Simons, P. (1987) *Parts: A Study in Ontology*. Oxford: Clarendon Press.

Sommers, F. (1982) *The Logic of Natural Language*. Oxford: Clarendon Press.

Stalnaker, R. C. (1968) "A theory of conditionals." In N. Rescher (ed.) *Studies in Logical Theory*, Oxford: Blackwell.

Stout, G. F. (1921) "The nature of universals and propositions." *Proceedings of the British Academy* 10: 157–72. Repr. in *Studies in Philosophy and Psychology*, London: Macmillan, 1930.

Strawson, P. F. (1959) *Individuals: An Essay in Descriptive Metaphysics*. London: Methuen.

Tooley, M. (1987) *Causation: A Realist Approach*. Oxford: Clarendon Press.

van Fraassen, B. C. (1989) *Laws and Symmetry*. Oxford: Clarendon Press.

van Inwagen, P. (1990) *Material Beings*. Ithaca, NY: Cornell University Press.

Wiggins, D. (1980) *Sameness and Substance*. Oxford: Blackwell.

—— (2001) *Sameness and Substance Renewed*. Cambridge: Cambridge University Press.

Williams, D. C. (1953) "On the elements of being." *Review of Metaphysics* 7: 3–18, 171–92.

Wittgenstein, L. (1922) *Tractatus Logico-Philosophicus*, trans. C. K. Ogden. London: Routledge & Kegan Paul.

—— (1953) *Philosophical Investigations*, trans. G. E. M. Anscombe. Oxford: Blackwell.

—— (1961) *Tractatus Logico-Philosophicus*, trans. D. F. Pears and B. F. McGuinness. London: Routledge & Kegan Paul.

Further reading

Jackson, F. (1998) *From Metaphysics to Ethics: A Defence of Conceptual Analysis*. Oxford: Clarendon Press. (A distinctive approach to the subject by a very distinguished philosopher).

Loux, M. J. and D. W. Zimmerman (eds.) *The Oxford Handbook of Metaphysics*. Oxford: Oxford University Press. (An authoritative multi-authored survey of contemporary analytic metaphysics).

Lowe, E. J. (1998) *The Possibility of Metaphysics: Substance, Identity, and Time*. Oxford: Clarendon Press. (A moderately advanced treatment of central issues in analytic metaphysics and ontology).

—— (2002) *A Survey of Metaphysics*. Oxford: Oxford University Press. (A fairly comprehensive survey of leading themes and issues in contemporary analytic metaphysics).

Strawson, P. F. (1959) *Individuals: An Essay in Descriptive Metaphysics*. London: Methuen. (A rather older but still very influential account of the nature of metaphysics and treatment of some of its key issues).

van Inwagen, P. (2002) *Metaphysics*, 2nd edn. Boulder, CO: Westview Press. (An outstanding account of the subject by one of the world's leading metaphysicians).

11

EPISTEMOLOGY IN THE TWENTIETH CENTURY

Matthias Steup

Synopsis

Epistemology, in the strict sense of the word, is concerned with the nature of knowledge and justified (or reasonable) belief. This twofold concern may be divided into five discernable questions:

1 What is knowledge?
2 What is justified belief?
3 How do we acquire knowledge?
4 What makes our beliefs justified?
5 Is the extent of justified belief and knowledge roughly what we take it to be, or are the skeptics right when they claim that it is much smaller than what we would like to think?

The first question differs from the third, and the second from the fourth, because we must distinguish between issues of definition and issues of substance.[1] Before we can address the substantive issues raised by questions 3 and 4, we must first settle what we *mean* when we talk of knowledge and justification. Thus, after a brief historical overview, this chapter focuses on the *conceptual* issues that arise when we try to answer questions 1 and 2. Here, we encounter issues such as: How can we distinguish between the kind of justification that is relevant to knowledge, and other kinds of justification? Is justification a deontological concept, to be understood in such terms as "ought," "permission," or "obligation"? How is justification related to knowledge? Can knowledge be understood as justified true belief? In the next section, turning to issues that arise when we attempt to answer questions 3 and 4, we shall examine two important debates – foundationalism vs. coherentism, and internalism vs. externalism – and review the most important theories on the nature of knowledge and justification, such as evidentialism, reliabilism, the conclusive reasons theory, and the tracking theory. After that, our topic will be a new approach – virtue epistemology – that received much attention during the last two decades of the twentieth century and that sheds new light on the problems that plague the theories previously examined. In the following section, we turn to the problem of how to respond to skeptical arguments. There, we will focus on the notorious brain-in-the-vat argument and discuss several responses to it: Moorean anti-skepticism, fallibilism, abandoning closure, the relevant alternatives theory, and contextualism. A brief overview of alternative approaches is then presented. The chapter will conclude with an outlook on the state of epistemology at the beginning of the twenty-first century.

Historical overview

Although epistemological and metaphysical issues are inextricably intertwined, it is important to bear in mind how they differ. While metaphysics is about the ultimate nature of reality, the subject matter of epistemology is knowledge of and reasonable belief about reality. Concern with epistemological questions can already be found in ancient philosophy. Plato (427–347 BC), for example, argued that sense perception cannot provide us with knowledge. And according to phyrrhonism, a school of skepticism founded by the Greek philosopher Pyrrho (260–227 BC), what skeptical puzzles teach us is that we ought not hold any beliefs but instead ought to suspend judgment. It was not until René Descartes (1596–1650), however, that epistemology was established as a philosophical discipline in its own right. In his *Meditations on First Philosophy* (1641), Descartes attempted to put knowledge on a firm foundation by finding a way to rebut the most powerful reason for doubt, which he found in the possibility of being deceived by an evil demon. Descartes attempted to dispel this doubt by proving the existence of God and his benevolent nature.

Descartes can be classified as a *rationalist*: a philosopher who relies on a priori insight – insight independent of any sense experience – afforded by the faculty of intuition. *Empiricists* are united in their opposition to viewing a priori insight as a genuine source of knowledge. Like Descartes, the British empiricists Bishop Berkeley (1685–1753), John Locke (1632–1704), and David Hume (1711–76) all addressed the question of how human knowledge is possible. Unlike Descartes, they downgraded the role of a priori knowledge and considered sense experience the only avenue to genuine knowledge of the world. What lies at the heart of the conflict between rationalists and empiricists is the *analytic/synthetic* distinction. Whereas analytic propositions express merely how ideas or concepts are related to each other, synthetic propositions state factual information about the world. Rationalists believe that a priori knowledge of the synthetic is possible. Rejecting this claim, empiricists lower the status of a priori knowledge by insisting that what's knowable a priori is restricted to the analytic.

There is, however, one thought with regard to which there was agreement among the rationalist and empiricist representatives of modern philosophy as it emerged during the sixteenth, seventeenth, and eighteenth centuries: knowledge of the external world – the world "outside" of our minds – is problematic, knowledge of the contents of our minds is not. Thus the emergence of epistemology as a philosophical discipline has been inextricably bound up with the problem of *skepticism*: How can we know that the world is really as our mind represents it to us? Berkeley's answer to this problem was idealism: reality consists of nothing but ideas. Locke's answer was that the existence of an external world is the best explanation of our experiences, and Hume's answer was that, since the logical gap between our experiences and our beliefs about external objects cannot be closed, such beliefs remain without rational justification. Immanuel Kant (1724–1804) devised his system of *transcendental idealism* as an attempt to forge a rationalist–empiricist compromise. We have, according to Kant, a priori knowledge of synthetic propositions because we can recognize our category-governed modes of synthesis in the sciences and the forms of our intuitions in mathematics and geometry. However, whereas the source of such a priori intuitions lies outside of our experiences, its legitimate subject matter is confined to what is possible for us to experience.

Epistemology in the twentieth century has to a large extent remained a response to the problems posed by the rationalist and empiricist thinkers of the modern period, especially with regard to the problems of explaining how we gain knowledge of the external world and defending such knowledge against skeptical arguments. In addition, however, we find a radicalization of the empiricist approach, and various ways in which philosophers have come to see traditional epistemology as an illegitimate enterprise. Let us briefly review the main movements and some of the central figures of twentieth-century epistemology.

There can be no doubt that Bertrand Russell (1872–1970) and G. E. Moore (1873–1958) must be counted among the most important contributors to twentieth-century epistemological thought. Russell conceived of epistemology broadly, as encompassing issues having to do with not only knowledge and rational belief, but also idealism vs. realism, truth, induction, causation, experience, and the mind. Knowledge of the external world, Russell held, is ultimately based on knowledge by *acquaintance*: knowledge of sense-data, to be understood as a kind of knowledge that is non-propositional or non-descriptive and constitutes the grounds on which descriptive knowledge of external reality is based.[2]

Moore's importance arises from his defense of approaching epistemological issues from the point of view of common sense, as defended in such seminal papers as "A defence of common sense" and "Proof of the external word."[3] (For further discussion of Moore, see "The birth of analytic philosophy," Chapter 1.) The second of these essays, in which he famously invoked the existence of his hands, can reasonably be interpreted as an intended refutation of idealism rather than a response to skepticism. Regarding the latter, Moore's chief point was that skeptical arguments fail because their premises are less certain than the rejection of their conclusions, a point to which we shall return later in this chapter.

In the first half of the twentieth century, empiricism evolved into *phenomenalism*, which can be seen as reviving Berkeley's approach without the theological framework. One of its chief advocates was A. J. Ayer (1910–89), who, like Russell, conceived of material objects as logical constructs of actual and possible sense-data. In his *The Foundations of Empirical Knowledge*,[4] he used the Argument from Illusion[5] to defend this claim, an argument that J. L. Austin (1911–60) famously criticized in *Sense and Sensibilia*.[6] Phenomenalism involves both a metaphysical and an epistemological aspect. Its metaphysical thesis is that the continued existence of physical objects is to be identified with stable and repeatable resemblance relations between sense-data. Its epistemological significance arises from the attempt to ground knowledge of physical objects in our knowledge of the immediate objects of our sense experiences.

While phenomenalism remains firmly within the confines of epistemology as a traditional philosophical discipline, *logical positivism* assumes the status of a movement advocating a new, science-oriented conception of philosophy. According to logical positivism, advocated prominently by Ayer and other members of the so-called Vienna Circle,[7] sentences that cannot (even in principle) be verified or falsified are literally meaningless. Consequently, the logical positivists viewed the questions of metaphysics, aesthetics, and ethics as illegitimate. Although logical positivism as a movement was short-lived, its science-oriented outlook retained lasting influence through the works of W. V. O. Quine (1908–2000), whose importance in epistemology is due to (1) rejecting reductionism (construing objects out of sense-data) and the analytic–synthetic distinction as two dogmas of empiricism; and (2) advocating the *naturalization of epistemology*, i.e., the project of transforming epistemology into a branch of the natural sciences, which would make empirical research, rather than a priori insight, the means to answer epistemological questions.[8] (For further discussion of Quine, see "The development of analytic philosophy: Wittgenstein and after," Chapter 2; "American philosophy in the twentieth century," Chapter 5; "Philosophy of language," Chapter 9; and "Metaphysics," Chapter 10.)

Ludwig Wittgenstein (1889–1951), another central figure of enormous influence among the great thinkers of the twentieth century, motivated, like Quine, a movement of devout followers. Whereas Wittgenstein's early opus, his *Tractatus Logico-Philosophicus*,[9] (see "The birth of analytic philosophy," Chapter 1) was a bold exercise in metaphysical speculation, his *Philosophical Investigations* and *On Certainty* express views more easily identifiable as being relevant to epistemology (see "The development of analytic philosophy: Wittgenstein and after," Chapter 2).[10] In this later period, Wittgenstein's basic idea was this: Paying close attention to the way we use ordinary language is the therapy needed to dissolve, rather than solve, the traditional philosophical problems. There is no point to accepting skepticism as a legitimate challenge and attempting to find an adequate response. Rather, the way to deal with traditional philosophical problems – such as skepticism, free will, and the relation between mind and body – is not to try to solve them but to understand how they arise from a misuse of words.[11]

In the context of viewing epistemology as an enterprise in need of therapy, Richard Rorty (1931–2007) deserves mention. Rorty argued, appealing to an assortment of thoughts by Quine, Sellars, Wittgenstein and Derrida, that epistemology was based on radically mistaken assumptions and thus was lingering towards its demise.[12] It would appear, however, that it was actually Rorty's diagnosis that was radically mistaken, as epistemology today is undoubtedly as healthy a philosophical discipline as there could be.

Philosophical movements come and go; the problems of epistemology remain. The last four decades of twentieth-century philosophy have seen a remarkable renaissance of traditional, a priori epistemology, a development that is in no small part due to the influence of Roderick M. Chisholm (1916–99). His works demonstrated that epistemology as an a priori discipline was not the hopeless endeavor that Quine and Wittgenstein claimed it was, but could bear a rich harvest of philosophical fruit.[13] Credit must be given as well to epistemologists such as William Alston (1921–), Laurence BonJour (1943–), Fred Dretske (1932–), Alvin Goldman (1938–), Gilbert Harman (1938–), Keith Lehrer (1936–), Robert Nozick (1938–2002), Alvin Plantinga (1932–), Wilfrid Sellars (1912–89), Ernest Sosa (1940–) and Barry Stroud (1935–) (among many others too numerous to mention here) for having contributed important works and advanced our understanding of the problems of epistemology and their possible solutions. In this chapter, I shall focus on the theories and issues of mainstream epistemology, narrowly defined, as they have emerged from the 1970s to the end of the century. The goal is to provide the reader with the background needed to understand cutting-edge epistemological literature at the outset of the twenty-first century.

The concepts of knowledge and justification

Knowledge as justified true belief

Let "S" stand for the subject who might have knowledge, and let the "p" in the schema "S knows that p" refer to the proposition S might know. An instance of "S knows that p" would be, for example, "Steup knows that he has hands," or "Steup knows that G. E. Moore was not a skeptic." To define what knowledge is, we must fill in the blank in "S knows that p iff ...," which requires of us to identify the conditions that are individually necessary and jointly sufficient for knowledge. Two of these conditions are fairly unproblematic. First, S knows that p only if p is true (the truth condition). The necessity of this condition can be recognized by considering cases of false belief. None of them intuitively qualify as cases of knowledge, whatever the details of the case may be. Second, S knows that p only if S believes that p (the belief condition). To suggest otherwise is to claim that a person can know that p without even believing that p. Even though this claim has received some support,[14] it may safely be said that the belief condition enjoys broad acceptance.[15]

The truth condition and the belief condition are not jointly sufficient for knowledge. Suppose Paul, who is away from home on a business trip, believes his house burned down. Suppose further Paul believes this solely because of a bout of paranoia. Finally, suppose Paul's belief happens to be true. Clearly, Paul does not know that his house burned down. He does not know this because his belief's being true is a matter of mere coincidence. Accidental truth like that, it is widely agreed, is incompatible with knowledge.

Thus, to ensure that S's true belief that p is not accidentally true, a third condition is needed. What, however, makes a belief's truth non-accidental?[16] This cannot be stated without immediately moving into controversial territory. According to what we might call the *traditional analysis of knowledge*, what makes S's belief non-accidentally true is S's being *justified* in believing that p, which requires S's having *good reasons* for p.[17] If we combine this condition (the justification condition) with the other two conditions, requiring truth and belief, we get the justified true belief (JTB) account of knowledge:

Knowledge as Justified True Belief (JTB)
S knows that *p* iff
(i) *p* is true;
(ii) S believes that *p*; and
(iii) S is justified in believing that *p*.

We will immediately see that conditions (i)–(iii) are not sufficient for knowledge. First, however, let us note that there is an alternative, *non-traditional* way of capturing the thought that knowledge of *p* is incompatible with *p*'s being accidentally true. The key idea motivating this alternative approach is that non-accidental truth requires *reliability*. If a true belief is to count as non-accidentally true, its origin must be reliable in the sense that beliefs having such an origin tend to be true. Think of your car. If your car tends to start each morning when you turn the ignition key, then it was not an accident that it started this morning. Likewise, if your belief that your car is in the garage is based on your memory of having it put there at an earlier time, and beliefs that you base on your memory tend to be true, then the truth of that belief is not accidental.

To sum up, a true belief qualifies as knowledge only if its truth is non-accidental. There are several ways in which epistemologists have tried to capture what it is for a belief to be non-accidentally true. We will discuss two of these. The first proceeds in terms of justification, the second in terms reliability. We will continue to focus on justification and return to the theme of reliability further below.

The Gettier problem

In his famous paper, "Is justified true belief knowledge?" Edmund Gettier (1927–) has persuasively argued that conditions (i)–(iii) in the JTB account of knowledge are not sufficient for knowledge.[18] Gettier describes two cases; in each, a subject forms a justified true belief that fails to be an instance of knowledge. Ever since, examples of that kind have been referred to as "Gettier cases." Let us briefly look at one such case. Suppose that during a road trip in the countryside you see what clearly appears to be a sheep in the field. Since you have no reason to suspect your sheep-like perceptual experience to be deceptive, you are justified in believing that there is a sheep in the field. Suppose further that the animal you take to be a sheep is in fact a poodle that its owner, who is a bit crazy, fixed up so it would look exactly like a sheep. Nevertheless, your belief is true since, lying in the deep grass and thus hidden from your view, there is an actual sheep. However, although your belief is justified and true, it can hardly be said to qualify as knowledge, as its truth is merely accidental.

What further condition do we need to ensure that the individual conditions of the analysis are jointly sufficient? Thus far, no widely agreed upon solution to this problem – known as the "Gettier problem" – has emerged.[19]

Justification

In response to the Gettier problem, advocates of the traditional analysis of knowledge retain the JTB core and try to find a suitable fourth condition that makes the intended account immune to Gettier cases. Within this approach, the concept of justification is of central importance. How is it to be understood? When we attempt to define what we mean when we use the term "justification," the problem is that there are different kinds of justification: moral, prudential, and epistemic. It's only the epistemic kind that is relevant in epistemology. Whether beliefs can be morally justified or unjustified is debatable. It seems clear, however, that they can be prudentially justified or unjustified. Positive beliefs about oneself can help one reach one's goals. Negative beliefs about oneself can stand in the way of accomplishing what one has set out to do. So positive beliefs about oneself can arguably be prudentially justified and negative beliefs about oneself prudentially unjustified. Epistemically, however, it might be otherwise. One's evidence might indicate that one is ill-equipped to reach the goal one has set for oneself. Prudential and epistemic justification can, therefore, diverge.

What distinguishes epistemic justification from other kinds of justification?[20] Above, we said that, from the traditional point of view, being justified in believing that p and having good reasons for p come to the same thing. For the moment, let's put the relevant point in terms of reasons. The standard move is to invoke the truth goal, that is, the goal of believing what is true and not believing what is false.[21] Reasons that help us attain this goal are of the epistemic kind, reasons that do not, of the non-epistemic kind. Instead of a person's epistemic reasons for p, we can also talk of a person's *evidence* for p. Evidence is what should guide us in the pursuit of truth. Employing the concept of evidence, we can characterize what epistemologists who favor the JTB approach have in mind when they talk of justification:

S is justified in believing that $p =_{df}$ S has adequate evidence for believing that p.

This is the core of what is called evidentialism.[22] A complete statement of evidentialism involves a definitional and a substantive component. The definitional component fixes the meaning of justification by linking evidence to the pursuit of truth. The substantive component would have to be an account of exactly what a person's evidence consists of. Candidates are beliefs, perceptual and introspective experiences, memories, and intuitions. We shall return to this issue further below.

Justification and deontology

According to some epistemologists, S's being justified in believing that p can be defined in deontological terms by saying that his believing that p is not *blameworthy* or *impermissible*, or that S is not *obliged* to refrain from believing that p, or that it's not the case that S *ought* to refrain from believing that p.[23] In each case, the deontological term used would have to be understood in a specifically epistemic sense. Blameworthiness, for example, would be of a kind solely having to do with matters related to the goal of believing what's true and not believing what's false.

There are two important objections to the deontological approach. It is argued that a deontological status such as epistemic permissibility or freedom from epistemic blame is more easily enjoyed than genuine epistemic justification. Consider, for example, members of a culturally isolated community who form beliefs on the basis of an obviously unreliable method such as reading the entrails of dead animals. Suppose S comes to believe that p on the basis of using that method. Since his community is culturally isolated, S does not have access to information that would allow him to view the method in question as epistemically defective. Therefore, basing his belief that p on reading the entrails of a dead animal does not deserve a negative deontological assessment. It is neither blameworthy nor impermissible for S to arrive at his belief in this way. However, S is not justified in believing that p, since obviously he could not come to know that p by using that method.[24] In response, advocates of the deontological conception could argue that epistemic defectiveness is transparent and thus recognizable even by subjects who are culturally isolated. If so, cultural isolation is no obstacle to judging that the belief in question does not conform to epistemic duty.

According to a second objection, the deontological conception of justification requires for our beliefs to be under our *voluntary control*. The prevailing view is that our beliefs don't meet that condition.[25] It is not clear, however, that the deontological approach really requires voluntary control over our beliefs.[26] Moreover, a case can be made for the conclusion that we can in fact exert about as much control over our beliefs as over our actions. If so, deontological evaluation of our beliefs should be no less problematic than deontological evaluation of our actions.[27]

It would seem, then, that the viability of the deontological approach remains an open question.

The nature of knowledge and justification

We have so far concerned ourselves with how to understand the concepts of knowledge and justification. Now we will turn our attention to more substantive issues. How do we acquire knowledge? According to the JTB approach, true beliefs qualify as knowledge if they are justified (and de-Gettiered, so to speak). But what makes our beliefs justified? According to *coherentists*, it is one and only one thing, namely the way they hang together, or cohere with each other. Coherence, though, is a complex affair. A belief system can be coherent because:

- it is logically consistent;
- some beliefs logically imply other beliefs;
- some beliefs make other beliefs probable by providing inductive support for them;
- some beliefs explain why other beliefs are true.

Coherentists claim that, in addition to such coherence relations among beliefs, there is nothing else that justifies our beliefs. *Foundationalists* deny this claim. They agree that coherence relations contribute to the justification of our beliefs, but insist that they are not by themselves sufficient for justifying a belief.[28]

Foundationalism

Foundationalists distinguish between the generation and the transfer of justification.[29] Inferential and explanatory support relations can transfer justification from one belief to another. Being part of a web of coherent beliefs can increase the justification individual beliefs enjoy. But for all of that to take place, foundationalists claim, justification must first be generated. Foundationalists hold that justification cannot be generated unless there are basic beliefs. A belief is *basic* if, and only if, it is justified without receiving any of its justification from other beliefs. Non-basic beliefs, in contrast, are justified by other beliefs. Ultimately, all non-basic beliefs owe their justification to basic beliefs. A person's belief system is, on this picture, divided into a superstructure of non-basic beliefs and a foundation of basic belief upon which the superstructure rests.

Why think that basic beliefs exist? The primary argument in support of their existence is called the *infinite regress argument*. It goes as follows: Suppose a first belief, B_1, is justified. If it is not basic, its justification must come from another belief, B_2. B_2 is either basic or not. If not, it must be justified by a further belief, B_3, and so forth. The point is that, unless this chain of justifying reasons eventually reaches a basic belief, the justification of B_1 will remain a mystery. In short, either there are basic beliefs or there are no justified beliefs at all. Note that this argument rests on two assumptions: first, a belief cannot be justified by an infinite chain of reasons; second, justification cannot be circular. Opponents of foundationalism have challenged both of these assumptions.[30]

How is it possible for a belief to be basic? Let us distinguish between *classical* and *moderate* foundationalism, each of which answers this question differently. According to classical foundationalism, there are various types of epistemic privilege. Two examples are infallibility and indubitability. An infallible belief is one that, by virtue of some special characteristic, C, cannot be false. An indubitable belief is one that, again by virtue of some special characteristic, C, cannot be doubted. Classical foundationalists would say that a belief is basic if it is infallible, or indubitable, or enjoys some other such privileged status.[31]

What kind of beliefs can be classified as infallible or indubitable? Obviously not beliefs about ordinary objects such as cats, cars, or trees. Such beliefs are sometimes false, and can sometimes be doubted. Thus classical foundationalists point to a different class of beliefs: those about our own mental states. Suppose, for example, you believe that the wall you are looking at is red. This belief might be mistaken, and thus can be doubted under certain circumstances. Perhaps the wall is really white, but looks red to you because it is illuminated by red light. Consider, in contrast, your belief that the wall *looks* red to you. It is not easy to see how that belief could be wrong, or how you could come to doubt that it is true. Classical foundationalists take their stand on beliefs like that. They claim that our beliefs about the world are ultimately justified by beliefs about the way the world appears to us in our perceptual experiences. These beliefs are justified not by other beliefs, but because they are infallible, indubitable, or enjoy some other kind of epistemically privileged status. In their totality, they constitute the foundation of our knowledge of the world.

Classical foundationalism is confronted with several serious problems. First, it seems clear that under ordinary circumstances, we don't form beliefs about the ways the world appears to us. We focus directly on the world, without bothering to dwell introspectively on the nature of our perceptual experiences. Hence it isn't clear how classical foundationalism can explain how our ordinary beliefs about external objects are justified. Second, it is unclear via what kind of inferences beliefs such as "This object *appears* F" to me can justify a belief such as "This object *is* F." Third, it is not easy to give a satisfactory account of exactly how a belief can be rendered basic by virtue of enjoying an epistemic privilege. Let us briefly dwell on this third problem, focusing on infallibility.

Suppose a classical foundationalist claims that beliefs are rendered basic by infallibility. We then need to know what it is that makes a belief infallible. Assume the classical foundationalist says: A belief is infallible if it's a belief about the way an object appears in one's experience. The belief "This tomato looks red to me" is a belief of that kind, and thus is infallible. This particular example seems unobjectionable. It is not easy to see how the belief in question could be mistaken. But there are more complex perceptual experiences. Suppose you believe that the object before you looks twelve-sided to you. Isn't that something you could be mistaken about? Perhaps the object really looks ten-sided to you.[32] It is doubtful, therefore, that the criterion we were given – a belief's being about the way the world appears to the subject – gives us the right results. In general terms, the difficulty for classical foundationalists is this: As soon as an account of infallibility is offered and a certain characteristic, C, is claimed to be sufficient for infallibility, there are likely to be examples involving instances of C that are not instances of infallibility. To avoid such counterexamples, C would have to be defined in a suitably narrow fashion. But then it is doubtful that enough beliefs have characteristic C for there to be a foundation rich enough to support the superstructure.

According to moderate foundationalism, we must understand a belief's being basic differently. What makes a belief basic is not an epistemic privilege of some sort, but rather this: its receiving its justification solely from an *experience*.[33] What makes foundationalism of this kind moderate is its deflationary conception of basic beliefs. Not enjoying an epistemic privilege, they are fallible, dubitable, and on occasion can be rendered unjustified by other things one believes.

To return to our example of the wall, moderate foundationalism says that your belief "The wall before me is red" is basic if and only if what justifies it is not another belief of yours, but solely the perceptual experience we describe when we say that the tomato looks red to you. Classical and moderate foundationalism, therefore, define basic beliefs rather differently. According to the former, beliefs about external objects are always non-basic. According to the latter, beliefs about external objects can be basic, just as beliefs about external objects appear in one's own experiences.

Moderate foundationalism has no problem explaining how ordinary perceptual beliefs are justified: they are justified by perceptual experiences. However, the claim that experiences can play a justificatory role is not unproblematic. Some would say they cannot because, unlike beliefs, they are lacking propositional content. According to that view, the relation between a belief and an experience can only be causal.[34] According to another kind of objection, perceptual experiences of kind K can be a source of justification for S, but only if S is justified in believing that perceptual experiences of kind K are reliable. If that's right, basic beliefs, as construed by minimal foundationalism, do not exist. For a belief such as "This tomato is red" would then be justified, not solely by a red-tomato-like visual experience, but rather by that experience *together* with beliefs about the reliability of such an experience.[35]

Coherentism

Coherentist theories tend to be complex. Avoiding complications that we do not have the space to discuss, let us focus on a simple model, the chief claim of which is that all beliefs are justified by other beliefs. Now, when we consider a simple perceptual belief, such as your belief that the wall you are looking at is red, how can we make sense of the claim that that belief is justified by other beliefs? Surely it must be admitted that, in typical cases, you do not infer the wall's color from any other beliefs. You simply see that it is red. According to our model of coherentism, your belief, even if it is a sponta-neous, non-inferential response to a perceptual experience, nevertheless receives its justification from other beliefs of yours. Let us say you believe, for example, that your perceptual experiences are reliable, and that the present conditions of observation allow for perceptual accuracy, and that you are not aware of anything that casts doubt on the accuracy of your present perceptions. According to our coherentist model, your belief that the wall is red is justified because it is embedded in the following coherent web of beliefs:

1 This wall is red.
2 I have, under favorable conditions of observation, a visual experience as though the wall before me is red.
3 Perceptual experiences of that kind are reliable.
4 I do not believe anything that would count as a reason for thinking that the wall before me is not red.

If we assume that, in addition to (1), you do in fact believe (2)–(4) as well, then it would indeed seem that there is an excellent case for claiming that you are justified in believing (1). Of course, (2) through (4) can justify (1) only if they are justified themselves. According to the coherentist model under consideration, (2) through (4) would be justified by yet further beliefs. None of them would be foundational.

The set of beliefs, (1)–(4), forms a coherent whole. Its coherence could be strengthened by adding further beliefs about the wall and its surroundings, corre-sponding features of current experiences, and by adding further beliefs about the physiology of perception. The latter would add to your belief system what is referred to as explanatory coherence. Here, the point would be that the best explanation of your present perceptual experience is that you are indeed perceiving a red wall, that is, a physical object that reflects light of a certain wave length, which in turn stimulates certain nerve endings in your eye. Such a causal account of what's going on would deepen your understanding of your cognitive situation, and would thus increase the justification you have for believing (1).

Our coherentist model liberally attributes to you quite a number of beliefs that are suitable as justifiers for your belief that the tomato is red. This is characteristic not just of the model considered here, but of coherentism in general. But such optimism about the richness of a person's belief system invites suspicion. Do people, under ordinary circumstances, really have the kind of beliefs that coherentists ascribe to them? It is doubtful that they do.

Another objection targets the coherentist claim that experiences themselves are epistemically inert, that is, neither justify nor take justification away.[36] Assume S and S* are two subjects who are observing a chameleon. Assume further that S and S* have belief systems that are nearly identical. Now let us consider two cases:

> Case 1: The chameleon changes its color from green to brown. S switches from believing that the chameleon is green to believing that it is brown. S* continues believing that it is green. Case 2: The chameleon remains green. S believes that the chameleon is green and continues believing this. S* first believes that the chameleon is green but then switches to believing that it is brown.[37]

Assume, in addition, that either belief about the chameleon's color coheres equally well with the rest of the belief system that S and S* share. Arguably, in each of the two cases, S's belief is justified, whereas S*'s belief is unjustified. The difference in justification is, in each case, solely due to a mismatch between belief and experience. The problem for coherentism is that it's difficult to see how this difference in justification can be explained solely in terms of coherence relations among S's and S*'s beliefs.[38]

Internalism and externalism

Even though foundationalists and coherentists disagree on how justification, and thus knowledge, comes about, they agree on this: justification depends on factors that are internal to the subject's mind. Those who favor the reliabilist approach mentioned on p. 474 disagree. They think that justification depends on factors that are external to the subject's mind. What exactly is it that they disagree about?[39]

As one might expect, how to define the terms "internalist" and "externalist" is not uncontroversial. According to one approach, the criterion to distinguish between internalist and externalist theories of justification is mentality.[40] Whereas internalist theories imply that mental states are the only things that can justify a belief, externalist theories imply that a belief can also be justified by things other than mental states. According to an alternative approach, the difference between internalism and externalism has to do with the accessibility of justification. Internalist theories assert a kind of accessibility to justification that externalist theories deny. For example, some internalists claim that, for any of S's beliefs, B, S can determine merely by reflection whether B is justified.[41] Externalist theories imply that a belief's justificational status is not always recognizable upon reflection.

For our purposes here, let us adopt a criterion that, while it allows us to identify various theories as either internalist or externalist, does not commit us to anything unduly controversial:

> Internal vs. external justification: If justification is internal, it is not possible to be massively deceived about the justificational status of one's beliefs. If justification is external, it is possible to be thus deceived.

The *massive deception* criterion allows us to classify a theory of justification as either internalist or externalist by applying what we might call the "evil demon test." The *evil demon*, a malevolent and omnipotent being, is a device of epistemological theorizing introduced by Descartes. If one imagines a subject to be deceived by the evil demon, one thinks of that subject's perceptual experiences as not portraying the world as it really is, but, owing to the evil demon's interference, as being completely misleading about what reality is really like.

To apply the evil demon test, we make the following assumptions: First, S and S* are mental duplicates; their beliefs and experiences are alike. Second, whereas S is a normal inhabitant of the actual world (such as yourself), S* is the victim of the evil demon. So S's beliefs about the world are pretty much correct, whereas S*'s beliefs about the world are mostly false. Now, what will S and S* say about the justificational status of their beliefs? S, whom we imagine to be a normal inhabitant of the actual world, will of course say that her beliefs about the world are by and large justified. Since S* is S's mental duplicate, S* will say the same. Bracketing skepticism about the justificational status of the beliefs of ordinary people, we will agree that S's judgment is correct. But what about S*'s judgment? When S* considers her beliefs about the world to be by and large justified, is she correct as well? If a theory is internalist, its answer is yes, if externalist, it is no.

Next, we will examine a number of theories that give us substantive conditions of either knowledge or justification. For each, we will determine whether it is internalist or externalist.

Evidentialism

Evidentialism was introduced earlier as an aid to understanding what epistemologists have in mind when they talk about justification. We stated the view thus:

> S is justified in believing that $p =_{df}$ S has adequate evidence for believing that p.

A person's evidence, we said, is constituted by the kind of reasons she should base her beliefs on if she aims at getting the truth and avoiding falsehood. Evidentialism turns into a substantive theory of justification once it offers us an account of what a person's evidence consists of. Unfortunately, there are various ways of construing what a person's evidence is. None of them are uncontroversial. Since we cannot dwell on this issue in any detail, we will consider what could reasonably be viewed as a typical construal of evidentialism. According to this construal, a person's evidence consists solely of her mental states. Things other than mental states do not count as evidence. For example, when I believe that there is a desk in room 115, my evidence for this belief would not be the desk itself, but might be a visual experience of the desk, or my memory of having seen the desk in that room, or my belief that the janitor told me that there was a desk in that room.[42]

A person's evidence includes, at a minimum, her justified beliefs. That much is uncontroversial. What is controversial is whether it also includes experiences and memories. As we saw earlier, some philosophers think that only beliefs can justify a belief. They would deny that memories and experiences are evidence. Rather, they would say that memories and experiences are relevant to justification only to the extent that we have beliefs about them. Other philosophers insist that experiences themselves do play a justificatory role.

Let us apply the evil demon test. Recall that, according to evidentialism, things other than mental states are not part of a person's evidence. Evidentialism implies, therefore, that subjects who are mental duplicates of each other have the same evidence. Hence evidentialism implies that, if S is correct in considering his beliefs about the world by and large justified, then S* is correct as well when he takes his beliefs to be by and large justified. So evidentialism implies that it's impossible to be massively misled about the justificational status of one's beliefs. It is, therefore, an internalist theory.

On what grounds would externalists object to evidentialism? The primary misgiving is that the connection between our evidence and the truth and our beliefs is not tight enough. Consequently, what determines whether or not a belief is justified is not solely a function of the subject's evidence. What matters as well is the question of whether the belief's origin is reliable.[43]

Goldman's process reliabilism

Earlier, we considered a reliabilist construal of the justification condition. In this section, we shall discuss a particular version of reliabilism, referred to as "process reliabilism" and due to Alvin Goldman, one of the most influential advocates of externalism.[44] The basic idea motivating process reliabilism is that our beliefs are justified if, and only if, they are produced by reliable cognitive processes. For example, cognitive processes rooted in perception, memory, or careful reasoning are typically reliable, and thus produce justified beliefs.

A rough and ready version of process reliabilism can be stated as follows:

> S is justified in believing that p iff S's belief that p is produced by a reliable cognitive process.

Goldman acknowledges that, as stated, the theory is vulnerable to counterexamples of the following kind: (1) S's belief that p is produced by a reliable process; (2) S has evidence for thinking that p is false. Thus Goldman says that the justificational status of a belief "is not only a function of the cognitive processes actually employed in producing it; it is also a function of processes that could and should be employed."[45] Consequently, the statement of the theory must be amended as follows:

> Process reliabilism: S is justified in believing that p iff (i) S's belief that *p* is produced by a reliable cognitive process; (ii) there is no alternative process available to S that, had it been used by S in addition to the process actually used, would have resulted in S's not believing that *p*.

Suppose, driving through town, you stop at an intersection because you see and thus believe that the traffic lights are red. If you have normal color vision, conditions (i) and (ii) are met, and we get the result we would expect: your belief is justified. Now suppose a hunch led you to believe that there is still enough gas in your car's tank. Since hunches are unreliable, your belief is unjustified. In this fashion, process reliabilism will yield correct results for a broad range of cases.

Applying the evil demon test, process reliabilism is easily identified as an externalist theory. The perceptual processes of S*, our evil demon victim, are extremely unreliable. So S*'s perceptual beliefs do not meet condition (i). Process reliabilism implies, therefore, that they are unjustified. However, the fact that his perceptual processes are unreliable is, so to speak, hidden from S*. Upon reflection, S* would therefore judge that his beliefs about the world are by and large justified. So process reliabilism implies that S* is massively deceived about the justificational status of his beliefs. Process reliabilism, then, is an externalist theory.

If process reliabilism is to succeed, its advocates must solve what has been labeled the *generality problem*. Considered broadly, perception is a reliable process. But some perceptual beliefs are unjustified because the specific perceptual processes employed are unreliable. For example, seeing someone from quite a distance, Jack believes it's his friend Jill. When we think of Jack's belief simply as a belief caused by vision, and assume that Jack's vision is reliable, process reliabilism says that Jack's belief is justified. But if we classify the belief as being caused by visually perceiving an object at a great distance, and assume that Jack's distance vision is not reliable, process reliabilism says that Jack's belief is not justified. If process reliabilism is to yield unequivocal judgments about particular cases, we need to be told how to select in a principled, non-arbitrary manner the actual process that is the one that caused the belief in question. It has turned out that this is no easy task.[46]

One objection to process reliabilism is that it cannot solve the generality problem. In addition, there are two further objections. The first of these turns the evil demon *test* into the evil demon *objection*. Internalists would argue that, since S and S* share their relevant beliefs and experiences, the outcome that S's and S*'s beliefs about the world differ in justificational status is highly implausible. Thus, if indeed we agree that S's beliefs are by and large justified, then we should say that S*'s beliefs are justified as well. But then we must conclude that reliability is not *necessary* for justification.[47]

According to the second objection, reliability is not *sufficient* for justification. Laurence BonJour[48] has argued that this can be seen by supposing that Norman is unknowingly equipped with a perfectly reliable faculty of clairvoyance, which causes him to believe that the president is in New York. Norman has no evidence for or against this belief, and no evidence for or against believing that reliable clairvoyance is possible. Given these assumptions, conditions (i) and (ii) of process reliabilism are met. So process reliabilism implies that Norman's belief is justified. According to BonJour, however, Norman's belief is unjustified, for Norman has no reason at all for judging, from his own point of view, that his belief is actually true. Hence BonJour concludes that a belief can be unjustified even though it was reliably produced.[49]

Dretske's conclusive reasons account

A true belief qualifies as knowledge only if its truth is non-accidental. Advocates of the JTB account of knowledge attempt to capture this non-accidentality requirement by saying that, if a true belief is to count as knowledge, it must be justified and de-Gettiered. Fred Dretske has proposed a different approach.[50] According to Dretske, knowledge requires the possession of a *conclusive reason*. He defines the concept of a conclusive reason by employing what's called a counterfactual.

> r is a conclusive reason for $p =_{df}$ If p were false, r would be false (or: if p were not the case, r would not be the case).

Counterfactuals are claims about what would (or would not) be the case if things were different from the way they in fact are. The standard method of evaluating the truth value of a counterfactual is to determine whether its consequent is true in the closest possible worlds in which its antecedent is true.[51] Let us apply Dretske's definition to two examples. First, suppose S believes

> (1) The house in front of me is blue.

S's sole reason for believing (1) is that the house looks blue to him. Suppose further that the house is in fact blue, but is also illuminated by a powerful blue light, and this is something that's hidden from S. Now let us consider the relevant counterfactual:

> C_1 If the house were not blue, it would not look blue to S.

C_1 is false. If the house were white, it would, since it is illuminated by blue light, still look blue to S. So S's reason for believing that the house is blue is not conclusive. Dretske's approach gives us the correct result: S does not know that the house is blue.

Now assume that the house is illuminated by bright sunlight. This time, C_1 is true because, if the house were not blue but (say) white instead, it would not look blue but white to S. S's reason for (1), therefore, is conclusive. Dretske's account gives us the desired result again: S knows that the house is blue.

To apply the evil demon test to Dretske's conclusive reasons account, we must slightly adjust our framework. Dretske doesn't think of conclusive reasons as giving subjects what internalists have in mind when they talk of justification. Rather, his is an account of knowledge. When S has a conclusive reason for p, and p is true, then S has knowledge of p. Accordingly, we must focus on the question of whether it is possible for a subject to be massively deceived about whether his reasons are conclusive. Let us tweak our evil demon test accordingly.

Upon reflection, S, the inhabitant of the actual world, would judge that her reasons in support of her ordinary beliefs about the world are by and large conclusive. S*, the evil demon victim, would judge analogously. Dretske's theory implies that, whereas S is right, S* is mistaken. The vast majority of S*'s reasons are reasons for propositions that are in fact false, and thus are not conclusive reasons. But, since S* is systematically deceived, this is something that's hidden from him. That's why he would judge, like S, that his reasons are by and large conclusive, when in fact they are not. Dretske's theory, therefore, must be classified as externalist.

Dretske's account will give us the intuitively right results for a wide range of cases. But there are cases where it just isn't clear what the theory implies about them. Consider the well-known case of barn facades.[52] Henry is on a road trip in the countryside and happens to be driving through an area where the locals, for the purpose of attracting tourists, have erected a vast number of barn facades (all of which, from the road, look like real barns). Among the many fake barns in this area, there is only one real barn. Suppose Henry believes

> B There is a barn over there

his reason being a barn-like visual experience. By sheer luck, Henry happens to be looking at the one real barn. Quite easily, Henry would have believed B while looking at a barn facade. So B's truth is merely accidental. Henry's belief should not, therefore, count as knowledge. What outcome do we get when we apply Dretske's theory to this case? To determine this, we must consider the following counterfactual:

> C_2 If B were false, Henry would not have a barn-like visual experience.

Let's say a world in which the antecedent of C_2 is true is a ~B world. The question to be answered is: In the ~B worlds that are closest to our hypothetical example (fixed by the assumption that there is an abundance of barn facades and only one real barn in the area), does Henry have a barn-like visual experience? Let's compare the following two ~B worlds:

> W_1 a ~B world in which Henry is looking at a barn facade; W_2 a ~B world in which Henry is looking at a tree.

Which world, W_1 or W_2, is closer to the world in our example? If we assume that the barn facades outnumber the trees, perhaps W_1 is closer. But the example is not typically described by saying that there are even more barn facades than trees in the area. If we assume that the trees outnumber the barn facades, then we might want to say that W_2 is closer. In that case, C_2 is true, and we get the intuitively wrong result: Henry knows B.[53] If W_1 is closer, then C_2 seems false, and Dretske's theory gives us the intuitively correct result: Henry does not know B.

So is Henry's reason for B conclusive? That's not easy to say, for, as John Hawthorne points out, counterfactuals are slippery, and our modes of evaluating them shifty. "Dangerous, then," Hawthorne observes, "to build an account of knowledge on them unless one is happy for the truth of knowledge claims to slip and slide with the varying similarity metrics that may guide verdicts about counterfactuals."[54]

The slippery nature of counterfactuals is one problem for Dretske's conclusive reasons account. Another arises because, to the extent we are confident in evaluating the truth values of counterfactuals, we can find counterexamples. Here is one devised by Hawthorne.[55] Suppose you suffer from the following affliction: when you consume ten or more glasses of beer, this causes you to have a false memory of having had exactly one glass of beer. Suppose you had a glass of beer and believe

G_1 I had less than two glasses of beer.

Your reason for G_1 is a memory of having had exactly one glass of beer. To assess whether this is a conclusive reason for G_1, we must consider:

C_3 If it's false that you had less than two glasses of beer, then you would not have a memory of having had exactly one glass of beer.

In the closest worlds in which G_1 is false, you had two or perhaps three glasses of beer. In those worlds, you don't have a memory of having had exactly one glass of beer. So C_3 is true, which is to say that your reason for G_1 is conclusive. Next, suppose you also believe

G_2 I had less than ten glasses of beer.

Your reason for this belief is, once again, your memory of having had exactly one glass of beer. To assess whether your memory of having had exactly one glass of beer is also a conclusive reason for G_2, a further counterfactual must be evaluated:

C_4 If it's false that you had less than ten glasses of beer, then you would not have a memory of having had exactly one glass of beer.

In the closest worlds in which G_2 is false, you had ten or perhaps eleven glasses of beer. In those worlds, because of your affliction, you would have a memory of having had exactly one glass of beer. So C_4 is false. Your memory of having had exactly one glass of beer, although it *is* a conclusive reason for G_1, is therefore *not* a conclusive reason for G_2. So it turns out that Dretske's theory implies you know you had less than two glasses of beer, but you do not know that you had less than ten glasses of beer. Not a happy outcome.

Nozick's tracking account

An account similar to Dretske's was suggested by Robert Nozick.[56] Its basic idea is that S knows that p iff (i) p is true, (ii) S believes that p, and (iii) in believing that p, S *tracks the truth* of p. Now, S's tracking the truth of p involves more than just p's being true. The two key conditions are these:

N₁ If p were true, S would believe that p.
N₂ If p were false, S would not believe that p.[57]

To see how truth tracking works, let us use the blue house example from the previous section. We distinguished between two scenarios. In the first, S looks at a blue house that is (unbeknownst to S) illuminated by a powerful blue light. In the second, the house is illuminated solely by bright sunlight. In both cases, S's belief about the house's color is based solely on how the house looks to him. Our intuitive assumption is that S knows that the house is blue in the second scenario, but not in the first. Assume again S believes

(1) The house in front of me is blue

solely on the basis of his perceptual experience of the house. The condition that allows us to discriminate between the two scenarios is N₂. In the first situation, since the house is illuminated by blue lights, S *would* believe that the house is blue if it wasn't blue but white instead. So condition N₂ is not met. We get the right result: S's belief does not track the truth; so S does not know (1). In the second situation, the light conditions are not misleading. If it were false that the house is blue, S *would not* believe it to be blue. So condition N₂ is met, and we get the right result again: S's belief tracks the truth. S knows that the house is blue.

Clearly, it is possible for a subject to be massively deceived about whether her beliefs track the truth. Consider again our mental twins, S and S*. Asked whether their beliefs about the world by and large track the truth, both would say yes. But whereas S would be right, S* would be wrong. Nozick's tracking account, therefore, must be classified as an externalist theory.

The tracking account has been at the receiving end of many objections.[58] Let us consider one of these, based on a modification of the barn facades case. Once again, although there is a vast number of barn facades in the area, Henry happens to be looking at the one real barn. Suppose, in addition, that the barn Henry is looking at is red, whereas none of the barn facades are red. Next, consider the following two propositions:

B I am looking at a barn.
Bᵣ I am looking at a red barn.

According to the objection, if B were false, that would be because Henry is looking at a barn facade, in which case he would believe himself to be looking at a barn.

Condition N_2 is not met; so Henry does not know B. Now, if B_r were false, that again would be because Henry is looking at a barn facade. But none of them are red. So Henry *would not* believe himself to be looking at a red barn. This time N_2 is met; so Henry knows B_r. Hence Nozick's theory appears to yield the result that Henry knows B_r but fails to know B. This looks like serious trouble.[59]

Is it so clear, however, that if B were false, that would be because Henry is looking at a fake barn? What if the closest ~B worlds are worlds in which Henry is looking at a tree? Looking at a tree, Henry would not believe himself to be looking at a barn. N_2 is met; so we get the outcome that Henry knows B. What, then, does Nozick's theory imply: that Henry knows B, or that he does not? Again, we should note that counterfactuals are slippery, and their truth values not easy to assess. As a result, Nozick's theory is confronted with problems analogous to those that plague Dretske's conclusive reasons account. To the extent we don't know how to assess the relevant counterfactuals, the theory remains vague and difficult to test. And to the extent we do feel confident about the truth-values of the relevant counterfactuals, it doesn't seem too difficult to devise painful counterexamples.

Internalism and externalism: reasons for and against

Having reviewed one internalist and three externalist theories, let us ask what kind of considerations motivate internalism and externalism. To begin with, internalism can be indirectly supported by pointing out the shortcomings of externalist theories, and vice versa. As for more direct ways of support, it is possible to argue for internalism using as a premise either a deontological or an evidentialist conception of justification. In the former case, the basic idea is that epistemic duty cannot be a function of external matters. In the latter case, the chief thought is that, since only mental states can play an evidential role, external factors are irrelevant to justification.[60] However, as mentioned on p. 476, the deontological conception of justification is highly problematic. Furthermore, many epistemologists will say that what determines the justificational status of a subject's beliefs goes beyond the subject's evidence. Hence neither argument is likely to settle the issue.

What arguments are there in support of externalism? One focuses on the connection between justification and truth. Justification, externalists claim, must be truth-conducive, that is, must generate objective probability.[61] As long as justification is solely a function of the subject's internal states, this desideratum is not met. The problem with this argument is that the demand for objective probability is difficult to reconcile with the thought that the beliefs of evil demon victims are justified. Another argument for externalism is based on the premise that animals have knowledge. Internalism makes justification too intellectual for animals to enjoy. Thus, if internalism were true, they couldn't have any knowledge. But that's not a plausible consequence. In response to this objection, internalists can argue either that evidence-based justification is available to animals as well, or that we should distinguish between two kinds of knowledge: animal knowledge that doesn't require justification and is available to both humans and animals, and reflective knowledge, which requires evidence and is available only to humans.

Virtue epistemology

Ernest Sosa's virtue epistemology

In ethics, the late twentieth century has seen the rise of a new approach: that of virtue ethics, inspired by an influential article by Elizabeth Anscombe (1919–2001).[62] A similar development has taken place in epistemology. However, how we are to conceive of virtue epistemology is not uncontroversial. Two of its main proponents, Ernest Sosa and Linda Zagzebski, disagree on what's distinctive of virtue epistemology. We shall begin with Sosa, whose turn toward virtue epistemology is articulated in his essay "The raft and the pyramid: coherence vs. foundations in the theory of knowledge."[63] There, Sosa asks us to consider the doctor who attended to Hitler's mother when she gave birth to her son, Adolf. A strict application of act utilitarianism gives us the result that the right course of action for the doctor would have been to kill the baby. Yet, since the doctor had no way of knowing what kind of a person the infant Hitler would develop into, we intuitively judge that infanticide would have been wrong. The problem is to explain why, when the doctor made sure the birth went well, he did the right thing. Sosa suggests the following:

> According to one promising idea, the key is to be found in the rules that [the doctor] embodies through stable dispositions. His action is the result of certain stable virtues, and there are no equally virtuous alternate dispositions that, given his cognitive limitations, he might have embodied with equal or better total consequences, and that would have led him to infanticide in the circumstances.[64]

The key idea is this: the doctor's action was the result of a moral virtue. Thus his action was right even though, on this occasion, infanticide would have led to better consequences. According to Sosa, when we conceive of moral rightness in this way, the concept of right action becomes *derivative*, and the distinction between right and wrong dispositions *primary*. Stable dispositions, if they are of the right kind, tend to produce desirable consequences. Actions are right when they originate in stable dispositions of the right kind. What is crucial here is the *order of analysis*. The rightness of stable disposition is not judged by recourse to right actions. Rather, we first identify which stable dispositions are virtues, and we do so by judging the desirability of their consequences. Subsequently, discriminating between actions that result from exercising moral virtues and those that do not allows us to discriminate between right and wrong actions.

According to Sosa, we can fruitfully employ the same strategy for the purpose of analyzing the notion of justified belief. Once we make the move to virtue epistemology, the concept of justified belief becomes derivative, resting on the primary distinction between epistemically virtuous and non-virtuous belief-forming, or intellectual, dispositions. Stable intellectual dispositions that contribute to getting us to the truth are epistemic virtues, those that do not are epistemic vices. Again, the order of analysis is crucial. Whether a belief-forming disposition is a virtue is judged by considering, not whether it produces justified beliefs, but instead whether it is instrumental in believing what's true and not believing what's false. Once we know which belief-forming dispositions are virtues, we can then proceed to discriminate between justified and unjustified belief by considering which beliefs are grounded in intellectual virtues and which are not. Thus goes the starting point of Sosa's epistemology, which he labels *virtue perspectivism*.

The two main concepts of virtue perspectivism are that of an intellectual virtue and an epistemic perspective.[65] An *intellectual virtue* is a subject's competence to distinguish between truth and falsehood in a field of propositions, F, under circumstances, C.[66] An example of an intellectual virtue is vision. Here, the relevant field of propositions would consist of propositions about visually detectable properties of suitably sized objects in the subject's environment, and the relevant circumstances would have to do with, for example, the lighting conditions and the distance between the subject and the objects about which she forms beliefs. Further examples of intellectual virtues are memory, introspection, and good reasoning.

An intellectual virtue, then, is a competence: a stable and reliable disposition to form true beliefs in a certain area under suitable conditions. A belief's having its origin in such a virtue makes it *apt*, which is Sosa's term for the kind of epistemic status that elevates true beliefs to the status of knowledge, or, more precisely, *animal knowledge*, as opposed to *reflective knowledge*. Animal knowledge is achieved when a belief is both true and apt. But how does one ascend from animal to reflective knowledge? It is here that the notion of an epistemic perspective comes into play.

For a belief to be an instance of reflective knowledge, it must be true and originate in an intellectual virtue. In addition to these two conditions, a third must be met: the subject's epistemic perspective must be such that she can coherently view her belief as having a virtuous origin. In other words, the subject must form *metabeliefs* that attribute reliability – not with precision and detail, but in a sketchy and generic way[67] – to the belief sources in question.

Sosa, then, distinguishes between external aptness and internal justification. Aptness is external because it is a function of reliability, about which a subject can be systematically misled. Justification, on the other hand, is a function of coherence, of how well a subject's beliefs and experiences hang together. Justification is internal because whether a belief of mine coheres with my other beliefs is internally accessible to me in a way the reliability of my belief's origin is not. The distinction between aptness and justification engenders Sosa's distinction between two kinds of knowledge: animal knowledge, resulting from the employment of apt faculties, and reflective knowledge, which we acquire when we achieve awareness of our faculties' aptness.

Sosa's virtue perspectivism may be viewed as a form of reliabilism. How does it differ from what we might call *simple reliabilism*, according to which a belief is justified if and only if it has its origin in a reliable process or method?[68] Let us examine three problems that bring the difference between simple reliabilism and virtue epistemology into clear focus.

The new evil demon problem

The old evil demon problem is the one posed by Descartes: How do I know I'm not deceived by an evil demon? The new evil demon problem is the one that we already encountered on p. 483. The belief systems of evil demon victims are marred by massive falsehood. The ways in which they form beliefs are, therefore, unreliable. Yet, the victims' beliefs intuitively strike us as justified, since there is no internally detectable difference between our own belief systems and those of the victims. Evil demon victims, then, pose a challenge to reliabilism because they seem to have beliefs that are justified, yet unreliably produced.

Sosa handles this problem by distinguishing between (1) same-world justification and (2) actual-world justification.[69] Consider a belief, B, produced by a faculty F, and held by a subject who is located in world W. B is *same-world justified* iff F is reliable in W itself. B is *actual-world justified* iff F is reliable in the actual world, that is, in our world. The beliefs of evil demon victims are not same-world justified, since, in their own world, the victims' faculties are unreliable. The victims' beliefs are, however, actual-world justified, since their faculties are reliable in our world. Hence, by employing the notion of actual-world justification, Sosa can account for the intuition that an evil demon victim's beliefs are justified.[70]

The problem of meta-incoherence

This problem is posed by BonJour's clairvoyance counterexamples to reliabilism.[71] Evil demon victims are a problem for simple reliabilism because, having unreliably produced beliefs that seem justified, they lend support to the claim that reliability is not *necessary* for justification. BonJour's clairvoyance counterexamples support the claim that reliability is not *sufficient* for justification. Recall Norman, whose perfectly reliable faculty of clairvoyance causes him to believe that the president is in New York, when Norman has no evidence for or against this belief, and no evidence for or against the possibility of reliable clairvoyance. Intuitively, Norman's belief seems unjustified even though it is reliably produced.

Sosa responds to this problem by employing the notion of an epistemic perspective.[72] Recall that Sosa distinguishes between external aptness, resulting from reliable faculties, and internal justification, resulting from the subject's coherent perspective on the reliability of her faculties. For a belief to enjoy the kind of justification that is required for reflective knowledge, the subject must be able to see – though merely in a generic and sketchy way – the belief as being grounded in an intellectual virtue. But Norman has no evidence at all in support of believing that his belief about the president's whereabouts has its origin in a virtuous faculty. The perspectival requirement, then, is clearly not met. Hence Sosa can agree with BonJour's intuition that Norman's belief is unjustified.[73]

The generality problem

For process reliabilism, this problem arises because, unless we are told exactly how to identify the cognitive processes that are relevant for the epistemic assessment of particular beliefs, there will be a wide range of assessments from which we can only arbitrarily choose (see the section "Goldman's process reliabilism," above). For Sosa's virtue perspectivism, the generality problem presents itself in a slightly different form. In Sosa's theory, the variables which we can describe in more or less general (or specific) terms are the field of propositions, F, and the circumstances, C. Characterizations that are too broad will lead to the ascription of knowledge in cases of ignorance. For example, a subject might lack competence within the narrow field F_1, where competence consists in the ability to discriminate reliably between makers of pick-up trucks, while being quite competent in field F_2, where competence consists in the ability to discriminate reliably between makers of automobiles in general. Now suppose S, who knows cars in general very well but is incompetent about brands of pick-up trucks, believes that the pick-up truck that just drove by was a Dodge. If S's belief is assessed relative to F_2, it would have to be classified as apt. If, on the other hand, S's belief is assessed relative to F_1, Sosa's theory would classify it, as it should be, as lacking aptness. Similar problems can be construed for more or less general descriptions of the circumstances, C. What recipe, then, does Sosa suggest for pinning down the right level of generality for describing F and C?

Sosa puts two constraints on the way we classify areas of competence and kinds of circumstances. First, they must be useful within the subject's epistemic community. For example, they must be useful for the purpose of recognizing dependable informants. Second, they must be useful for S herself when it comes to judging the reliability of her faculties, thus acquiring the perspectival meta-beliefs needed for the possession of reflective knowledge.[74] Let us apply the first of these conditions to the pick-up truck example. Since S's belief is about a pick-up truck, the relevant question is this: competence in which area, F_1 or F_2, makes S a dependable informant about pick-up trucks? Clearly, it would be competence in the more specific area F_1. Hence it is S's lack of competence about pick-up truck makers that is relevant for the assessment of the epistemic status of S's belief.

Problems for virtue perspectivism

Let us sum up the main points of the previous three sections. Sosa's brand of reliabilism differs from simple reliabilism because of three distinctive features. First, to solve the new evil demon problem, Sosa employs the distinction between same-world and actual-world justification. Second, to handle cases involving, so to speak, "blind" reliability (the problem of meta-incoherence), Sosa imposes the perspectival requirement that the subject must have meta-beliefs that attribute reliability to her belief sources. Third, as a solution to the generality problem, Sosa requires that the field and circumstances relative to which reliability is assessed must be useful for the recognition of dependable sources. In this section, we will briefly consider three further problems with which Sosa's virtue perspectivism is confronted. Here we will only briefly indicate how Sosa responds to these challenges.

To begin with, any form of reliabilism must deal with the problem of *accidental* reliability. When something functions reliably, it might just be a lucky accident. Consider Steup's 1988 Honda Accord, which has proved to be remarkably reliable for the sixteen years he had it in his possession. Suppose that, contrary to fact, when Steup went to the Honda dealer in 1988, he came home with an incredible lemon, a car that was going to break down on a daily basis. Alas, it so happened that, for sixteen years, Steup always had a friendly mechanic for a neighbor. Unbeknownst to Steup, this neighbor sneaked each night into Steup's garage and fixed his Honda, so it would hold up at least for the next day. Obviously, Steup would think that he had a most reliable car, when its seeming reliability was in fact nothing but a fantastic accident. Such luck can also occur in the workings of our cognitive faculties. Sosa considers as an example a deteriorated faculty that, owing to luckily compensating external circumstances, still continues to function reliably.[75] Such examples illustrate the need for giving an explanation of how we can distinguish between genuine and merely accidental reliability. Sosa proposes to articulate such an explanation in terms of the *epistemic access* the subject has to the workings of her faculties.[76]

Second, a problem that arises specifically because of the perspectival element of Sosa's reliabilism is this: Exactly what justifies the reliability attributing meta-beliefs that are needed for elevating mere animal knowledge to the status of reflective knowledge? According to BonJour, it is not entirely clear how Sosa's virtue perspectivism answers this problem. BonJour distinguishes between three ways in which perspectival metabeliefs might be justified:

> (A) entirely on the basis of internal coherence; (B) by virtue of being basic, in the way conceived of by internalist foundationalism; (C) entirely by virtue of being apt.[77]

None of these, BonJour argues, is satisfactory. (A) must be dismissed because there are good reasons for thinking that coherence by itself is not enough to generate justification. (B) is problematic because, if what justifies perspectival meta-beliefs is a foundational status of the internalist kind, we are left wondering why first-order beliefs can't be justified in the same way, and thus why the appeal to aptness should be necessary at all. Finally, (C) does not seem to be a good option because the purpose of perspectival meta-beliefs is to generate internal justification, which is necessary for reflective knowledge. Why, however, should we think that internal justification can result from external aptness, in the same way it can from internal coherence and internally accessible reasons? BonJour concludes, it is not easy to see how, on Sosa's theory, perspectival meta-beliefs are justified.[78]

In response, Sosa agrees that none of the options BonJour considers are satisfactory, but suggests that (A) through (C) do not exhaust the options. There is an additional option, namely to deny what is common to (A) through (C), which is the assumption that justification for believing *p* must necessarily involve a *reason* for thinking that *p* is true.[79] What, however, is Sosa's positive proposal about how perspectival meta-beliefs are justified? Since perspectival meta-beliefs are clearly not justified solely by virtue of coherence relations solely among our beliefs, Sosa proposes that what justifies them is a more *comprehensive* kind of coherence, a kind of coherence that includes coherence between beliefs and experiences, as well as a recognition of the reliability of one's belief sources.[80] Consider memory and perception. Meta-beliefs ascribing reliability to these faculties are justified by a coherent web that includes memorial and perceptual experiences and beliefs about the truthfulness of the beliefs formed on the basis of such experiences. Sosa is suggesting, then, that meta-beliefs about the reliability of memory and perception are justified in part by using memory and perception themselves.[81] This amounts to an endorsement of circularity, which brings us to the third and final problem for Sosa's virtue perspectivism.

Third, since perspectival beliefs about the reliability of our faculties cannot be formed without using those faculties, Sosa's brand of virtue epistemology is confronted with the problem of circularity. For example, you cannot find out whether your perceptual faculties are reliable without using perception, and you cannot find out whether memory is reliable without relying on memory. But is such circularity necessarily vicious? Alston, Fumerton, and Stroud think it is.[82] Fumerton, for example, writes:

> You cannot use perception to justify the reliability of perception! You cannot use memory to justify the reliability of memory! You cannot use induction to justify the reliability of induction. Such attempts to respond to the skeptic's concern involve blatant, indeed pathetic, circularity.[83]

Exactly what is objectionable about using a way of belief formation, W, to arrive at the belief that W is reliable? One chief worry is that, if establishing the reliability of W using W itself were legitimate, the reliability of *any* method, no matter how mad, can easily be accomplished. To establish the reliability of one's crystal ball, one may use the crystal ball itself. To show that astrology is reliable, one may use astrology itself. So if circularity is not an obstacle standing in the way of justification, what prevents someone certifiably mad from having a belief system that enjoys just as much justification as our belief systems?

If that is what is worrisome about circularity, Sosa argues, it's a discomfort we can live with. After all, we should remind ourselves that, before we attribute *knowledge* to subjects who are mad yet reason coherently, two further conditions must be met: their beliefs must be true, and moreover must have their origin in apt faculties. Presumably, in the case of coherent yet crazy beliefs, neither of these conditions is met. Hence, even though we are like the mad believers inasmuch as we, too, use circular reasoning, our beliefs, unlike theirs, are grounded in apt faculties and, if true, are instances of knowledge.[84]

Linda Zagzebski's virtue epistemology

Let us turn to Linda Zagzebski, who motivates virtue epistemology by diagnosing the concept of justification, considering how it is employed within traditional epistemology, as collapsing from internal pressures.[85] Even after decades of work on the Gettier problem it remains unclear how justification is related to knowledge. Moreover, the debate between internalists and externalists has resulted in an irresolvable deadlock. The remedy for the, in her judgment, hopeless state of traditional epistemology is to orient the discipline in a new direction: away from the focus on justification, towards a realignment with virtue ethics. Virtue *ethics* is an alternative recommended by the inherent and irresolvable difficulties involved in both deontological and consequentialist ethics. Analogously, virtue *epistemology* should be pursued as an alternative to epistemic deontology, as well as reliabilism, the latter being the epistemological analog to consequentialism in ethics.

Like Sosa's, Zagzebski's project is to account for the normative status of beliefs in terms of evaluative properties of the agent, which in turn are to be captured in terms of the distinction between virtuous and non-virtuous intellectual character traits. An intellectual virtue, according to Zagzebski, is a "deep and enduring acquired excellence of the human person that includes both a motivational component and a component of a reliable success in bringing about the end of the motivational component."[86] As examples of intellectual virtues, Zagzebski lists the following: open-mindedness, intellectual fairness, autonomy, trustworthiness, courage, perseverance, and attentiveness.[87] Such virtues do not differ importantly from moral virtues. In each case, they are "acquired by imitating virtuous persons and developing habits aimed at controlling emotions and developing the cognitive and perceptual abilities necessary to know how to apply the virtues in the appropriate circumstances."[88]

How, by appeal to virtues thus understood, does Zagzebski analyze the central notions of epistemic evaluation? She proposes the following:

1 A belief is *justified* iff it is a belief a virtuous agent would form in like circumstances.
2 A belief is *praiseworthy* iff it satisfies the criterion stated in (1), and moreover is virtuously motivated.
3 Believing that *p* is an *act of intellectual virtue* iff it satisfies the criteria stated in (1) and (2) and is successful in leading to truth and the end of the virtue in question.[89]

Zagzebski's virtue epistemology differs in two important aspects from Sosa's. First, Sosa and Zagzebski employ different notions of an intellectual virtue. Second, they differ on the relevance of reliability.

Zagzebski writes that "almost no effort has been made, either by Sosa or by others, to connect [the concept of an intellectual virtue] to the sense of virtue used in ethics, much less to integrate it into a general theory of virtue. In many cases, what an epistemologist calls a virtue is a virtue only by courtesy."[90]

What, specifically, is at issue here? According to Zagzebski, not just any reliable cognitive competence qualifies as an intellectual virtue. Rather, virtues, both moral and epistemic, must be *acquired*. If so, eyesight and memory would not be instances of intellectual virtues.[91] But according to Sosa, they are. He distinguishes between a narrow (Aristotelian) and a broad (non-Aristotelian) conception of virtues, and explicitly states that, according to the way he uses the notion of a virtue, anything can qualify as a virtue that has a natural or artificial function.[92] A related point is stressed by John Greco, who argues that, when we study historical sources (Plato and Aquinas, for example), the concept of a virtue is not as narrowly understood as Zagzebski construes it.[93]

Two kinds of virtue epistemology

The issue over the relevance of reliability arises when we examine how virtue epistemology differs from its traditional alternatives. There appear to be two different conceptions of what virtue epistemology is, even though, at first blush, Sosa and Zagzebski seem to be in agreement. In the passage cited at the beginning of the "Virtue epistemology" section, Sosa writes that what makes the virtue approach distinctive is this: it takes the evaluation of the subject's epistemic dispositions as primary, and the epistemic evaluation of beliefs as secondary. This fixes the order of analysis. We must first determine what it is that makes a person epistemically virtuous. Only then can we assess whether a person's beliefs are justified or not. Zagzebski defines the nature of virtue epistemology analogously. She writes:

> In a pure virtue theory the concept of a right act is derivative from the concept of a moral virtue. Similarly, I propose that in a pure virtue epistemology the concept of a justified belief is derivative from the concept of an intellectual virtue.[94]

Likewise, Greco says that the "defining characteristic of virtue epistemology … is that it makes the normative properties of persons conceptually prior to the normative properties of beliefs."[95] If that is how we are to conceive of virtue epistemology, Sosa is to count no less as a virtue epistemologist than Zagzebski, despite Zagzebski's suggestion that Sosa's isn't a virtue epistemology in the true sense. After all, Sosa first analyzes epistemic virtue in terms of reliable faculties, and then defines apt belief as belief originating in the exercise of such faculties.

Yet what Greco says about virtue ethics suggests that there is indeed a more narrow conception of virtue epistemology. Greco writes:

> In moral virtue theories, normative properties attaching to character are *basic*. The normative properties of actions are derivative, to be understood in terms of their relation to virtuous moral character. (Italics added.)[96]

What does it mean to say that the normative properties attaching to character are *basic*? If we take the term "basic" literally, it means that the concept of intellectual virtue is not in turn analyzed in terms of another notion. Compare how Richard Foley conceives of virtue ethics:

> In a genuine virtue-based ethics, virtue cannot be defined in terms of consequences, or for that matter in terms of rules ... For an approach to ethics to be virtue-based, it must treat virtue as the fundamental notion, not rules or consequences.[97]

If we conceive of virtue epistemology in strict analogy to virtue ethics thus understood, the notion of an intellectual virtuous character trait must be basic. It must be conceived of in a non-derivative way, that is, in such a way that

> the virtuousness of these traits isn't dependent upon their having a tendency to produce true beliefs and likewise isn't dependent upon their being in accordance with some independently defined notion of intellectual duty.[98]

Here, then, we see a significant difference between Sosa and Zagzebski. Let us distinguish between *reliabilist* and *pure* virtue epistemology. Sosa's is an example of the former, since he analyzes intellectual virtues in terms of their tendency to produce true beliefs. Zagzebski, on the other hand, objects to such epistemic consequentialism and conceives of intellectual virtue in a non-reliabilist way. Her approach, then, may be viewed as an instance of pure virtue epistemology.

However, is a pure virtue epistemology likely to meet with success? If the appeal to reliability is not permissible, is there a principled and informative way of distinguishing between virtuous and non-virtuous character traits? Can a non-reliabilist kind of virtue-epistemology give us results that stand up to vigorous testing against counterexamples? Greco says no. According to him, Zagzebski's virtue epistemology is deficient precisely because it does not make the appeal to reliability an essential ingredient. He argues that there are examples of knowledge, where knowledge results from the exercise of reliable faculties that are not examples of Zagzebski-style acts of virtue. Moreover, Greco claims, there are examples of belief that qualify as cases of knowledge on Zagzebski's account, but are in fact cases of ignorance because the beliefs in question are not really rooted in the exercise of reliable faculties.[99] On the basis of such considerations, a case could be made that a pure conception of virtue epistemology is indeed too narrow, and that a broader conception of it, allowing for a reliability-based conception of epistemic virtue, shows greater promise.[100]

Skepticism

The "brain in a vat" (BIV) argument

We shall turn our attention to various responses to skepticism. The kind of skeptical argument we shall consider invariably employs a skeptical hypothesis (or alternative) that is incompatible with the truth of most of our ordinary beliefs. Let an example of an ordinary belief be

H I have hands.

H is incompatible with, for instance, the alternative of being a brain in a vat (BIV). Suppose that your brain was removed from your body and is, with the aid of a powerful computer and sophisticated neuro-technology, stimulated in such a way that the perfect illusion of an ordinary life is created. Life continues just as you would expect it even though now you are a mere BIV. As a BIV, of course, you don't have hands. So if

B I am a BIV

is true, H is false. Employing the BIV alternative, a skeptic could argue as follows:

The BIV argument
(1) If you don't know that B is false, you don't know H. (2) You don't know that B is false. Therefore: (3) You don't know H.

This is the skeptical argument on which we shall focus. Its conclusion seems preposterous. Yet the argument is clearly valid. Moreover, neither of the two premises is in any *obvious* way lacking in plausibility. So the argument puts pressure on us to accept a conclusion that seems quite clearly false. It puts us in a rather uncomfortable intellectual position.

The first premise is plausible because it is supported by a principle that seems beyond reproach: the closure principle (*closure* for short). A simplified statement of it goes as follows:

Closure: If I know that *p*, and I know that *p* entails *q*, then I know *q*.[101]

Closure tells us that we can use entailments to expand our stock of knowledge. Its point can be put as follows. If you know an entailment, there are two possibilities: either you know both the entailing and the entailed proposition, or you know neither of them. That, certainly, seems plausible. Let's plug in "H" for "*p*" and "~B" for "*q*." Then we get: If you know that H, and you know that H entails ~B, then you know ~B. Now, that H entails ~B is an obvious entailment. So let's assume you know that this entailment holds. Given Closure, it now follows that, since you don't know ~B, you don't know H – which is the first premise of the BIV argument.

The second premise seems plausible because the BIV hypothesis is set up in such a way that it's hard to see on the basis of what evidence you could discriminate between being, and not being, a BIV. Suppose you say you know you're not a BIV because of evidence E. The problem is that, if you were a BIV, you would have exactly the same evidence E, and that in turn would lead you to think that you are not a BIV. So item E can't help you tell whether or not you are a BIV. And the same applies to *any* evidential item. So it looks as if it's impossible for you to know you are not a BIV.

The BIV argument, then, is valid and has plausible premises. Moreover, the argument can be generalized to any proposition about the external world that you take yourself to know. We must, therefore, either accept the conclusion that we have no knowledge of the external world, or we must find fault with the argument.

Moorean anti-skepticism

G. E. Moore deserves a special place in twentieth-century epistemology because of his advocacy of an uncompromisingly anti-skeptical position. According to Moore, when we are confronted with a skeptical argument, we should bear in mind the following two points. First, for a skeptical argument to succeed, it must not be the case that denying its conclusion is more plausible than accepting its premises.[102] Second, we can always turn a skeptical argument on its head, that is, reject one of its premises on the basis of denying its conclusion.[103]

Let us apply the first of these points to the BIV argument. According to the Moorean response, we must compare accepting the second premise with denying the conclusion. Moore would say that accepting the second premise (taking yourself not to know that B is false) is less reasonable than denying the conclusion (taking yourself to know that you have hands) – even if you cannot explain *how* you know that B is false.

Following Moore's recommendation, we might rebut the BIV argument with the following counterargument, thus turning the BIV argument on its head:

> *The reverse BIV argument*
> (1) If I don't know that B is false, I don't know H. (2) I know H. Therefore: (3) I know that B is false.

The limitation of Moore's response is obvious. Even though (bracketing the rejection of Closure) the reverse BIV argument seems *sound*, it is hard to convince oneself that rebutting skepticism takes no more than that. In the end, we do want to understand *how* we know that the skeptical alternative is false. Until such understanding is accomplished, the BIV argument is not effectively dealt with.

Let us distinguish between a *strict* and an *amended* construal of Moorean anti-skepticism. According to the strict construal, the reverse BIV argument is not only sound, but indeed cogent, in the sense that you can indeed come to know that you are not a BIV by deducing this from (1) and (2). According to the amended construal, a Moorean response to the BIV argument consists of rejecting its second premise, together with an explanation of how we know ~B *without* deriving ~B from our knowledge of H.

How, then, can you know that you are not a BIV? The first step towards explaining how such knowledge is possible is *fallibilism*: the rejection of Cartesian standards of knowledge such as certainty or infallibility. We could say that we must distinguish between a Cartesian concept of knowledge, according to which knowledge requires infallible evidence, and an ordinary concept of knowledge, according to which fallible evidence is enough to give us knowledge. The difference between fallible and infallible evidence is this: the former is compatible with error, the latter is not. For example, while I have infallible evidence for my own existence, and perhaps for some of my mental states, it is clear that my beliefs about the external world are *not* based on infallible evidence. With regard to those beliefs, error is always possible (although certainly not always likely).

Fallibilism says that fallible evidence, if good enough, gives us knowledge. But is your fallible evidence for thinking you're not a BIV good enough for knowledge? Arguably, you cannot come to know that you are not a BIV on the basis of your perceptual experiences. If you were a BIV, your perceptual experiences would be exactly the same as they are now. Therefore, they do not allow you to discriminate between being and not being a BIV. Let's consider an analogy. Suppose the wall before you looks red to you. Can you come to know that it is not white but illuminated by red light solely on the basis of its looking red to you? Surely not.[104] Its looking red does not enable you to discriminate between its being red and its being white while being illuminated by red light.

However, is coming to know that p on the basis of one's perceptual experiences really the *only* way of coming to know p, where p is some proposition about the external world? Consider:

W It's not the case that the wall before me is white and illuminated by red light.

You cannot come to know W on the basis of the wall's looking red to you. But that does not mean you can't come to know W at all. First of all, you know that objects are only infrequently illuminated by red light. Second, you might fail to notice any lighting equipment in the vicinity. Third, you might fail to find any explanation of why the wall should be illuminated by red light. This body of evidence arguably gives you knowledge of W.

Likewise, even though your perceptual experiences do not put you in a position to know that you are not a BIV, arguably you have background knowledge that does. For example, for there to be BIVs, there would have to exist the know-how and technology required for keeping brains alive and subjecting them to the kind of all-encompassing deception that the envatment scenario involves. But you know that the know-how and technology needed for envatment does not exist, just as you know that the know-how and technology does not exist for astronauts to travel to Mars and back to Earth within a couple of hours. Arguably, such background knowledge puts you in a position to know that you are not a BIV even though you can't come to know this on the basis of your perceptual experience alone.

The fallibilist response

Fallibilism, as we understand it here, is the view that your evidence for ~B is good enough for you to know ~B. Endorsing fallibilism, and drawing a conceptual distinction between ordinary knowledge (which can be had on the basis of fallible evidence) and Cartesian knowledge (which can only be had on the basis of infallible evidence), we can respond to the BIV argument by asserting that it is either unsound, invalid, or uninteresting. If the word "know" is to be understood as referring, each time it occurs in the argument, to ordinary knowledge, then the argument has a disturbing conclusion. But the second premise is false on that interpretation, and the argument may be rejected as unsound. If "know" refers to Cartesian knowledge in the second premise and to ordinary knowledge in the conclusion, then the argument has a disturbing conclusion and true premises. But in that case it may be rejected as invalid, because of equivocation between two different senses of "know." Finally, if the argument employs the Cartesian sense of "know" throughout, it is obviously sound. But then its conclusion is not disturbing. Who, after all, would have thought we have infallible evidence for thinking we are not BIVs? If that's all the skeptic means to tell us, then the argument's conclusion is utterly unsurprising.[105]

To sum up, according to the fallibilist response, there is just one interpretation on which the BIV argument is sound. On this interpretation, the argument's conclusion does not tell us anything new or disturbing. Hence there is no reason to worry about it.

The denial-of-closure response

Recall what Dretske means by a conclusive reason: r is a conclusive reason for you for believing if, and only if, if p were false, you would not have r. According to Dretske, knowledge requires conclusive reasons.[106] If so, closure fails. Let us see why. Suppose, visiting the zoo, you are in front of an enclosure with several zebras. Looking at them, you have a zebra-like perceptual experience. That's a conclusive reason for your belief that the animals in the pen are zebras. If there were polar bears or elephants in the enclosure instead, you wouldn't have zebra-like experiences. So you know

Z The animals in the pen are zebras.

But your zebra-like experience is not a conclusive reason for

~M The animals in the pen are not cleverly disguised mules.

Cleverly disguised mules look exactly like zebras. Just by looking at them, you cannot distinguish them from zebras. Therefore, if ~M were false (if the animals in the pen were cleverly disguised mules), you would still have those zebra-like experiences. Thus, on Dretske's theory, you do not know ~M. Of course you could come to know ~M by taking special steps, but we are assuming that you have not done that. Finally, let us suppose you notice, and thus come to know, that Z entails ~M. Putting all of this together, your situation is to be described thus: you know Z, you know that Z entails ~M, but you do not know ~M. It thus turns out that, if knowledge requires conclusive reasons, closure fails.

Since giving up closure is an effective way of rebutting skepticism, Dretske considers closure failure a virtue of his theory. Indeed, if we are prepared to deny closure, then we can reject the first premise of the BIV argument, and thus do not have to accept its conclusion. Let us look at the details of this move.

You believe you have hands because you have hand-like experiences. Are those experiences a conclusive reason for H? Indeed they are; if you didn't have hands, you wouldn't have hand-like experiences.[107] However, your hand-like experiences are not a conclusive reason for ~B, since if you were a BIV, you would still have hand-like experiences. So on Dretske's theory, even though you know that B entails ~H, the first premise of the BIV argument is false: you know H although you do not know ~B. Dretske's theory, then, blocks the skeptical conclusion by denying the closure.

Nozick's treatment of skepticism works analogously. In Nozick's account of knowledge, the condition that corresponds to Dretske's conclusive reason's requirement is the following:

> The sensitivity requirement: If S knows that p, then S would not believe that p if p were false.

Your belief that you have hands is sensitive. If you didn't have hands, you wouldn't believe you have hands. But your belief that you are not a BIV is not sensitive. If you were a BIV, you would still believe that you are not a BIV. Hence, on Nozick's account, you know H, but you do not know ~B, even though you know very well that H entails ~B. Once again, the skeptical conclusion ~H is blocked by denying closure.

There are two reasons why the closure-denial response to skepticism has not met with much enthusiasm among fellow epistemologists. First, the closure principle is highly plausible. If we deny it, we end up with rather unpalatable consequences. One is what Keith DeRose calls an *abominable conjunction*: You know that you have hands, but you do not know that you are not a handless BIV.[108] Another consequence of denying closure is that one can know a conjunction P & Q without knowing P.[109] Many epistemologists would say that such consequences are too high a price to pay for the denial of closure. Second, the Drestke–Nozick response to skepticism entails that we don't know we are not BIVs, and thus can be criticized for being too concessive.

Relevant alternatives theory

Dretske's response to skepticism is a version of what is referred to as the relevant alternatives theory (RAT).[110] An alternative to a proposition, p, is any proposition, q, that is incompatible with p.[111] While looking at the zebras in the pen, you don't have a conclusive reason for believing that they are not cleverly disguised mules. However, even though their being cleverly disguised mules is an alternative to their being zebras, to know Z you don't need to know ~M because M is not a *relevant* alternative. Likewise, you know H even though you don't know ~B, notwithstanding the fact that B is obviously incompatible with H. The trick is to say that, to know H, you don't *need* to know ~B because the alternative of your being a BIV is not relevant.

RAT, as advanced by Dretske, comes with the price of closure failure. Gail Stine argues that RAT should not be burdened with this consequence, and has proposed a way to make the theory work without abandoning closure.[112] Her version of RAT involves three essential ingredients:

1 A criterion of relevance: An alternative is relevant iff there is some reason to think that it is true.
2 A multiple-meaning semantics of "know": When we say "S knows that p" or "S does not know that p" what we *mean* is a function of our standards of knowledge, of which there are many.
3 Anti-evidentialism: Irrelevant alternatives are known to be false without any need for evidence. Knowledge does not always require evidence.

Here is how Stine's account avoids closure failure. Suppose again you are in the zoo, looking at several zebras in a pen. M (the cleverly disguised mule hypothesis) is an alternative incompatible with the truth of Z. But, as there is no reason to think M is true, M is not a relevant alternative. Hence you know M to be false without having evidence for ~M. Note the difference between Dretske and Stine. Although they agree that M is an irrelevant alternative, they differ with regard to what follows from that. For Dretske, it follows that, to know Z, you don't need to know ~M. For Stine, it follows that you know ~M even though you have no evidence for ~M. Consequently, unlike Dretske's conclusive reasons approach, Stine's theory preserves closure: you know Z, you know that Z entails ~M, and you know ~M.

Thus goes the story as long as we have our ordinary standards of knowledge in mind when we say "You know Z" and "You know ~M." What, however, if a skeptic somehow convinces us to endorse an extremely demanding standard of knowledge? Perhaps he convinces us that we know ~M only after applying a paint-removal test. Since you haven't done that, we must, having adopted the skeptic's high standard of knowledge, admit that the sentence "You know ~M" is false. And now it looks as if closure fails once again. Stine's response is that unless we wish to be guilty of the fallacy of equivocation, we must apply the same high-standard meaning of "know" when we assess whether you know Z. And given that the standards of knowledge are now extremely high, it turns out that "You know Z" is false, too. To sum up, on the ordinary understanding of "knowledge," we can correctly ascribe to you knowledge of both Z and ~M; on the high standard understanding of "knowledge" employed by the skeptic, which Stine considers perverse, we can correctly ascribe to you knowledge of neither Z nor ~M.

Let us compare Stine-type RAT with fallibilism and closure denial. Stinean RAT and fallibilism have this in common: Each of them concedes that we have Cartesian knowledge of neither H nor ~B. On the face of it, that looks like a compromise between skepticism and anti-skepticism. In fact, it is no such compromise, for according to each of these theories, the concession that we lack Cartesian knowledge bears no costs. According to Stine, it's no big deal because a concept of knowledge that, in Cartesian fashion, requires excessively high standards is perverse. And according to fallibilism, it's no big deal because the lack of Cartesian knowledge is nothing to worry about.[113] Both theories, therefore, may be classified as uncompromisingly anti-skeptical. In this regard, they differ from the closure-denial response, which safeguards knowledge of H by giving up knowledge of ~B. However, Stine's RAT differs from fallibilism with respect to whether we have evidence good enough to know ~B. Whereas fallibilism says we do, Stine-type RAT says we do not but know ~B nevertheless. This feature of Stine's view may be viewed as a liability. It's a bit thin to say we know ~M and ~B simply because M and B are irrelevant alternatives.[114] We want to know *how* we know that these alternatives are false. Unlike Stine's RAT, fallibilism offers us an account of that.

Contextualism

The contextualist response to skepticism is motivated by the following three desiderata:[115]

1 preserve closure;
2 preserve the truth of our ordinary knowledge claims;
3 explain why in our response to skepticism we vacillate between finding it compelling and finding it crazy.

Like Stine, contextualists hold that what the word "knowledge" means varies with the context within which we attribute knowledge or ignorance to others or ourselves. In fact, when contextualists speak of a subject's knowledge (or ignorance) of p, this is just a shorthand for saying, instead, that the sentence "S knows that p" is true (or that the sentence "S knows that p" is false).

Stine's RAT is an early prototype of the contextualist response. As developed by its three main advocates – Stewart Cohen, Keith DeRose, and David Lewis – contextualism goes beyond Stine's RAT in offering us a rather fine-tuned theory about how the meaning of the word "know" changes with context. The main thought is that, as soon as skeptical alternatives become salient, perhaps because someone mentioned them and we are now paying attention to them,[116] the standards of knowledge rise, and as a result we now mean something different when we use the word "know." Contextualists, then, distinguish between low-standards and high-standards contexts. As long as skeptical alternatives are ignored, the standards for our knowledge attributions remain low. In such low-standards contexts, a subject speaks truly when she says "I know I have hands." But when we do epistemology and consider skeptical alternatives, the standards of knowledge rise, and then we think we are unable to know that the skeptical alternatives are false, and thus, because of closure, unable to know what they are incompatible with.

Contextualism of this kind is called *attributor contextualism*, because what matters is not the context of the subject to whom knowledge is attributed, but instead the context of the attributor who utters a sentence of the form "S knows that p." Let us introduce two attributors: high-standards *Helga* and low-standards *Ludwig*. Helga, participating in an epistemological discussion of skepticism in a university classroom, is confronted with salient skeptical alternatives and thus is in a high-standards context. Ludwig is in a bar conversing about various things having nothing to do with epistemology. Skeptical alternatives are not salient to him. Thus, he is in a low-standards context. Suppose both of them have a friend in common, Fred. Helga and Ludwig (by sheer coincidence) happen both to be reflecting upon what Fred knows. Ludwig utters the sentence "Fred knows that he has hands," and Helga utters the sentence "Fred does not know that he has hands." In their respective conversations, both are right since, owing to the fact that they are in different contexts, each of them means something different when they use the word "know." Helga is right because relative to the high standards she has in mind when using the word "know," Fred does not know that he has hands. And Ludwig is right as well because, relative to the low standards Ludwig has in mind, Fred does have knowledge of his hands. Next, suppose Ludwig asserts "Fred knows that he is not a BIV," whereas Helga utters "Fred does not know that he is not a BIV."[117] Once again, Helga and Ludwig do not contradict each other but instead both speak truly. They both speak truly because, in their respective contexts, they employ different standards of knowledge.

According to Cohen, contextualism is a good news/bad news theory.[118] There is good news about closure: contextualism preserves it, since it implies that there are no situations in which one subject can truly say of another one that she knows she has hands, but she does not know that she is not a BIV. There is also good news about our ordinary knowledge attributions in contexts in which skeptical alternatives are not salient: in such contexts, our ordinary knowledge attributions are true. The bad news is that, when confronted with the BIV argument or some other such argument, we find ourselves in agreement with it.

It is precisely the good news/bad news aspect of contextualism that allows it to meet the desiderata identified at the beginning of this section. The good news of contextualism means that desiderata (1) and (2) are met. And the bad news affords contextualists with a way to meet desideratum (3), that is, with an explanation of why we find skepticism both crazy and compelling. The explanation goes like this: As long as we are in low-standards contexts we find skepticism crazy. In high-standards contexts, however, because of what we then mean by "knowledge," we cannot help but find skepticism compelling. Thus both sides of our vacillating response are explained in terms of the context sensitivity of the word "know."

Contextualism versus non-contextualism

If one rejects contextualism, to which view does one thereby commit oneself? According to DeRose, the plausibility of contextualism is to be judged against that of *invariantism*, which DeRose considers contextualism's big rival.[119] What, however, is invariantism? Let us consider two options.

> *Strict invariantism:* There is one and only one concept of knowledge; the word "know," therefore, is not context sensitive at all but always means the same.

> *Fallibilist invariantism:* There are two concepts of knowledge, the ordinary and the Cartesian one. The former is fallibilist, the latter infallibilist. Consequently, the meaning of "know" shows *some* variance, especially among epistemologists. But varying uses of "know" must be evaluated differently. There is one, and only

one, concept of knowledge that we should care about, which represents the meaning of "know" as it is typically used, and that is the fallibilist one. Hence utterances such as "S does not know that p," where "know" refers to infallibilist knowledge, can be classified as uninteresting or non-disturbing.

Contextualists tend to identify the negation of contextualism with strict invariantism which, on the face of it, does not look like a plausible option. However, fallibilist invariantism, even though it allows for *some* semantic variance, should also be considered a competitor for contextualism, for advocates of fallibilist invariantism reject pretty much everything that's distinctive about contextualism as advocated by Cohen, DeRose, and Lewis. Let us consider three of contextualism's distinctive and controversial features:

C_1 When we are confronted with skeptical arguments, we end up meaning by "know" what skeptics mean when they use that word, and thus, we cannot help accepting the conclusions the skeptics argue for.
C_2 The meaning of "know" varies (from context to context) to such an extent that focusing on knowledge itself, rather than focusing on knowledge attributions, is not the right way of doing epistemology.
C_3 There is only one way of giving a correct explanation of why our attitude towards skepticism vacillates, namely to appeal to the context-sensitivity of "know."

Advocates of fallibilist invariantism reject each of these claims. They would contend that C_1 is false because the word "know" can retain its low standards meaning even when used in situations in which skeptical alternatives are salient. Just think of anti-skeptics such as G. E. Moore and Roderick Chisholm. When they were thinking about and discussing skeptical arguments, they certainly did not switch from an ordinary to a Cartesian understanding of the word "know." Moreover, C_1 is not only false, it also makes contextualism too concessive in its treatment of skepticism, for it implies that, when confronted with a skeptical argument, we must agree with it. According to fallibilist invariantism, a more satisfying response to skepticism is one that allows us to avoid any kind of compromise with the skeptic. This is just what the fallibilist response allows us to do, which classifies skeptical arguments as either invalid, unsound, or if sound, uninteresting.[120]

Fallibilist invariantists would claim that C_2 is false since, even though the word "know" varies to some extent from speaker to speaker and situation to situation, this variance is much more limited than contextualists assert. Typically, when people use the word "know," what they have in mind is a non-Cartesian concept according to which knowledge that p requires only evidence for p that rules out reasonable doubt. Thus there is no need to replace talk of knowledge with talk of knowledge attributions. Rather, having made it explicit that we are concerned with not Cartesian but ordinary knowledge, we can do epistemology focusing on knowledge itself, without falling victim to any undue ambiguity.[121]

Finally, fallibilist invariantists would say that C_3 is false because we can explain the seeming cogency of skeptical arguments without appealing to the alleged context sensitivity of "know." Consider the distinction between the Cartesian and the ordinary concept of knowledge. Some people might find the BIV argument strangely compelling because they equivocate between these concepts. Alternatively, when confronted with a skeptical argument, one might mistakenly think that the Cartesian meaning is *the* real meaning of knowledge. If so, the skeptic managed to trick his victim into thinking that the *only* way to understand the concept of knowledge is in the Cartesian way. The fallibilist antidote for such trickery is to respond that there is low-standards and high-standards knowledge, and that there is nothing painful about the concession that we are rarely in possession of the latter.[122] In the next section, we will look at a further explanation of the vacillation phenomenon, an explanation that Sosa has suggested in response to DeRose's version of contextualism.

Sensitivity and safety

According to DeRose, when we pay attention to skeptical alternatives, we move into a high standards context, and therefore adopt the rule of sensitivity, according to which a belief qualifies as knowledge only if it is sensitive. Ernest Sosa has argued that skeptical arguments can seem sound when we confuse sensitivity with what Sosa calls safety.[123] Let us compare the two notions:

Sensitivity: S's belief that *p* is sensitive iff if *p* were false, S would not believe that *p*.

Safety: S's belief that *p* is safe iff if S were to believe that *p*, *p* would not be false.

It's tempting to think that sensitivity and safety amount to the same thing, just as "$p \supset q$" and "$\sim q \supset \sim p$," the latter being the contrapositive of the former, amount to the same thing. But whereas conditionals contrapose, counterfactuals do not. "If *p* were true *q* would be true" is not equivalent to "if *q* were false then *p* would be false." Sensitivity and safety are not, therefore, equivalent.[124] Hence there is the possibility that, whereas safety is a necessary condition of knowledge, sensitivity is not.

So what does knowledge require: sensitivity or safety? Sosa claims that it requires merely the latter, offering the following example in the way of support.

On my way to the elevator I release a trash bag down the chute from my high rise condo. Presumably I know my bag will soon be in the basement. But what if, having been released, it still (incredibly) were not to arrive there? That presumably would be because it had been snagged somehow in the chute on the way down (an incredibly rare occurrence), or some such happenstance. But none such could affect my predictive belief as I release it, so I would still predict that the bag would soon arrive in the basement. My belief seems not to be sensitive, therefore, but constitutes knowledge anyhow, and can correctly be said to do so.[125]

Sosa's example strongly suggests that the sensitivity requirement is false. At most, knowledge requires safety. Thus we have available to us an explanation of why the BIV argument can seem compelling. Sensitivity and safety, Sosa suggests, are easily confused. Thinking that knowledge requires sensitivity, and noting that your belief "I'm not a BIV" is not sensitive, you might think that the BIV argument's second premise is true. Sosa's advice is to recognize that sensitivity and safety are not equivalent, and that knowledge requires merely safety. Taking this advice, you might then note that your belief "I'm not a BIV" is indeed safe,[126] and then conclude that the second premise of the BIV argument is false.

Contextualists emphasize that in our response to skepticism, we vacillate between finding it crazy and compelling. They claim that there is only one way to explain this datum: to appeal to the context-sensitivity of the word "know." Sosa's distinction between sensitivity and safety affords us an alternative explanation. Hence the need to explain the vacillation datum would not appear to be a sufficient reason for endorsing contextualism.[127]

Alternative approaches

Naturalized epistemology

Epistemology, if naturalized, is an integral branch of the natural sciences. As mentioned in the historical overview, Quine (1969) recommended reorienting epistemology in this direction. To understand exactly what the naturalization project comes to, it is essential to distinguish between *epistemological naturalism* and *naturalizing epistemology*. The former is the view that that which makes beliefs justified, and if true might turn them into instances of knowledge, belongs to the natural world as revealed by science. Such naturalism does not yet add up to naturalization, for the armchair philosopher, engaging in conceptual analysis, might very well identify a natural property – reliability for example – as the ground from which reasonable belief and knowledge arises. If, however, epistemology is indeed naturalized, epistemologists may no longer enjoy the comforts of the armchair of a priori reflection. Instead, they must then determine the nature of knowledge and rational belief solely by employing the empirical methods used in the natural sciences.[128]

Why think that epistemology as an a priori discipline is doomed? Quine rejected traditional epistemology by identifying it with a narrowly-construed version of foundationalism that was indeed an easy target for effective criticism. There are two obvious objections to be made in response to Quine's reasoning. First, it is hard to see how the futility of traditional epistemology could be established without doing a good deal of traditional epistemology. If so, the naturalization project would remain incomplete, since a limited role would have to be assigned to a priori epistemology, namely that of securing the outcome that the pursuit of a priori epistemology is pointless. Second, at least thus far, arguments for the futility of a priori epistemology have not been blessed with success. There is, within traditional epistemology, a wide variety of theories that fall outside the scope of Quine's attack on foundationalism. Even if Quine's critique of his intended target was right, it would hardly follow that the alternative theories his argument missed are equally objectionable. In general terms, given the wide variety of approaches, maneuvers, and refinements that characterize a priori epistemology today, it seems rather unlikely that there could be an uncontroversial, general argument of the desired sort.

It would seem, then, that traditional epistemology is here to stay. This does not, however, mean that naturalistic epistemology must be rejected. There is no reason to think that it could not coexist and collaborate with a priori epistemology, for the mutual benefit of both approaches. Indeed, it seems obvious that what science tells us about the working of the mind and our perceptual faculties ought to be relevant to the a priori epistemologist. Furthermore, to the extent an epistemological theory proves inconsistent with well-established scientific results, there will be a prima facie reason for rejecting it.[129]

Evolutionary epistemology

Traditional epistemologists believe that empirical, merely descriptive methods simply cannot answer normative questions such as: Which of our beliefs are justified? How ought we arrive at our beliefs? Rejecting the traditional fact/value dichotomy, naturalistic epistemologists insist that they are indeed to be answered empirically. But how? According to evolutionary epistemology, which may be seen as a particular example of the naturalistic approach, natural selection has endowed us with a bias towards truth. Therefore, the belief-forming processes we in fact use must be good ones. Hence the questions we have just considered can be answered by appealing to the empirical theory of evolution and doing cognitive psychology.

It would appear, however, that evolution has not entirely succeeded in eliminating faulty reasoning from our cognitive practices. Even a cursory study of how people reason and form beliefs reveals abundant lapses of rationality. Such lapses, obviously, have thus far not stood in the way of reproductive success. Thus, at best, what evolutionary epistemology tells us is that our cognitive practices must, *by and large*, be good ones. But then we are left with the challenge of having to sort out which ones are good and which ones are bad. One wonders whether that in turn is a question that can be answered on the basis of evolutionary theory and cognitive psychology.[130]

Social epistemology

Narrowly defined, epistemology is concerned with the nature of knowledge and justified belief. There is, however, no point to being a stickler about exactly what the term "epistemology" denotes. Obviously, while the pursuit of epistemology narrowly understood is a worthy endeavor, questions of philosophical interest arise as well when we conceive of epistemology as a discipline that is also concerned with knowers and believers as subjects who are positioned within a particular social and historical context. Epistemology, pursued from this point of view, becomes social epistemology.

There is, however, no unanimity within this field on how to pursue it. Some view it as a novel extension of traditional epistemology, defined by the aim of correcting its overly individualist orientation. Others view it as a radical departure from traditional epistemology, which they, like naturalization advocates, see as a futile endeavor. Those who think of social epistemology as a discipline to be pursued in collaboration with traditional epistemology retain the thought that knowledge and justified belief are essentially linked to truth as the goal of our cognitive practices. According to this approach, there are objective norms of rationality that social epistemologists should aspire to articulate. Those who view social epistemology as a radical alternative reject the existence of objective norms of rationality, and reject truth as the goal of our intellectual and scientific activities. Within this approach, we find the claim that scientific facts are socially constructed. Such *constructivism*, if weak, asserts the epistemological thesis that scientific theories are laden with assumptions, presuppositions, and biases of a social, cultural, and historical nature; if strong, it asserts the metaphysical thesis that what is socially constructed is reality itself.[131]

Neo-Marxist and postmodernist epistemology

When studying a particular philosophical theory, how are we to assess it? This question can be seen as an epistemological one, since it can be understood equally well this way: When studying a particular philosophical theory, by which means can we arrive at a *justified* assessment of its plausibility? One way of doing this goes as follows: As a first step, we identify the various theses the theory asserts, and the arguments it offers in support of these theses. As a second step, we determine the validity of these arguments and the plausibility of their premises. Finally, we base our assessment of the theory on our findings in steps one and two.

According to Marxism, we should instead look at the historical, social, and economic background of the particular philosopher whose theory we study. Invariably, philosophical theories reveal the interests of the socio-economic class of their authors and are designed to further such interests. To the extent these interests are those of the bourgeoisie and its allies, the theory would have to be rejected as a mere ideology. Critics of Marxism would say that such reasoning is but an instance of the *ad hominem* fallacy. If, for example, we wish to assess the merits of John Locke's theory of private property, his socio-economic background is irrelevant. What matters is solely whether the arguments in favor of the theory are compelling.

According to Jürgen Habermas, a representative of the neo-Marxist Frankfurt School, the notion of interest is indeed of central importance to epistemology. (See "Critical Theory," Chapter 18.[132]) His employment of the notion, however, is nowhere near as crude as it is in classic Marxism. Habermas distinguishes between three areas of inquiry: natural sciences, historical-hermeneutic sciences, and critical social sciences. Unlike the former two, the latter aims at emancipation from oppression and exploitation. Each of these kinds of inquiry, Habermas holds, has its own set of quasi-transcendental preconditions for the acquisition of the kind of knowledge that is sought. Even though Habermas advocates a consensus theory of truth, his general outlook is opposed to *relativism*. When participating in intellectual discourse, he argues, we cannot help but adhere to objective, intersubjective standards of argumentation that make such discourse possible in the first place.

Whereas Habermas found merit in employing the notion of interest, Michel Foucault is known for introducing the notion of *power*. (For more on Foucault see "French philosophy in the twentieth century," Chapter 19.) Philosophical *archaeology*, according to Foucault, aims at revealing the total set of underlying, hidden yet constitutive elements of knowledge producing social processes, elements that determine both meaning and truth. Philosophical *genealogy* aims, in addition, at uncovering power relationships within the context of producing specific bodies of knowledge. A central ingredient of Foucault's thinking is the idea that criteria of truth are *contingent*: what counts as true is always a reflection of specific historical and social modes of inquiry.[133]

Foucault, together with figures such as Jacques Derrida, Jacques Lacan, and Emmanuel Levinas, may be seen as a contributor to what has become known as the *postmodernist* approach to philosophy in general and epistemology in particular. Metaphysical and epistemological relativism, it would seem, lies at the heart of this approach: objective truth, objective criteria of truth, objective principles of rationality, the objective meaning of a text, and objective standards for interpreting texts do not exist. Reality as well as meaning are nothing but social/historical constructs, and the criteria of truth and rationality we find employed in particular cognitive practices are mere reflections of social and historical contingency.

Critics would say that postmodernism is a necessarily incoherent and unstable view. Its adherents can hardly claim it to represent objective truth. What, then, is its status supposed to be? Moreover, critics would charge that, if the tenets of postmodernism were true, rational pursuit of truth would indeed be futile and theory choice would deteriorate into a cynical endorsement of whatever is viewed as serving best the quest for power.[134]

Feminist epistemology

Divided into a bewildering assortment of different approaches, feminist epistemology ranges from an uncontroversial expansion of scope to highly controversial versions of a postmodernist kind. Construed favorably, feminist epistemology may be viewed as a branch of social epistemology, studying issues having to do with fair and equal access of women to the institutions and processes through which knowledge is generated and transmitted. Conceived thus, it would of course be a worthwhile endeavor in its own right. Controversy ensues as soon as we move beyond this initial characterization. According to some, the task of feminist epistemology is to study and legitimize special ways in which women come to acquire knowledge. Even more controversial is the understanding of feminist epistemology as aiming at the political goal of opposing and rectifying oppression in general, and the oppression of women in particular. Although, obviously, oppression ought to be resisted and rectified wherever and whenever it in fact occurs, it remains unclear exactly *how* epistemology can be made subservient to the pursuit of that goal. When attempting to sort out the debates between foundationalists and coherentist, internalists and externalists, a priori epistemologists and advocates of naturalization, should we really favor one view over another because it appears to serve better the goal of opposing oppression? The alternative, of course, would be to endorse one view rather than another because it seems *true* to us, irrespective of perceived political consequences. Moreover, it is not easy to see what substantive connections there could possibly be between, for instance, the internalism–externalism debate and the political pursuits with which feminists identify.

At the extreme end, feminist epistemology is closely associated with postmodernism, and is then vulnerable to the battery of objections that can be and have been made in response to that approach. From a political point of view, the postmodernist, anti-objectivist turn of feminist epistemology remains baffling. Are the interests of women not better served if, say, violence against and exploitation of women is viewed as being *objectively* wrong? If postmodernism is right, there will be no objective standards of what constitutes oppression of women in the first place, and no objective criteria that favor the fight against over the defense and practice of oppression. On such grounds, among others, critics of the postmodernist kind of feminist epistemology would argue that such epistemology is neither a satisfying nor an effective platform from which the interests of women can be effectively pursued (see "Feminism in philosophy," Chapter 7).[135]

Outlook

Looking at the abundance of theories, issues, and arguments we have reviewed, certainly nothing definitive can be said about which developments we can expect to see in the future. Nevertheless, it might be safe to make the following points:

(1) When we consider debates such as that between foundationalists and coherentists, and that between internalists and externalists, it would seem each of the respective camps has in its arsenal serious objections to the theories advocated by the other camp. With the front lines clearly drawn, epistemologists in each camp know what to say in response to the main arguments coming from the opposite camp. If epistemology is to move beyond such deadlock, this will probably result from the pursuit of synthesis between the opposed theories. A respectable epistemology, it would seem, would have to weave an overall account of knowledge and justification by combining various foundationalist, coherentist, internalist, and externalist elements.

(2) In addition to all the rich and deep disagreements, there are also areas of overlap. There is almost unanimous agreement that knowledge requires belief and non-accidental truth. Although the question of what it is that makes a belief non-accidentally true generates controversy, even more common ground can be uncovered. Internalists agree that that which turns a true belief into knowledge would have to be a partly external type of thing. They diverge from the externalist point of view only inasmuch as they insist that knowledge involves, in addition to its external components, one internal factor: justification, understood as the possession of good reasons.

(3) As long as we assume that there is one single concept of knowledge that epistemology is about, the debate over whether knowledge involves an internal element or not becomes, it would seem, irresolvable, since intuitions favoring internalism as well

as externalism flow naturally from our ordinary cognitive practice. On the one hand, we tend to deny knowledge when we think that a subject is lacking a good, internally accessible reason. On the other hand, we freely attribute knowledge to animals, without thereby committing ourselves to the view that animals can have reasons in the way adult humans can. It would appear, therefore, that if we wish to reconcile our internalist and externalist leanings, we need to accept the thought that there are two grades of knowledge: one that does, and another one that does not, require the possession of internally accessible reasons.

(4) W. V. O. Quine recommended that epistemology be naturalized, that is, be turned into an branch of the natural sciences. It would however seem that the theories and arguments we have examined in this chapter have been, without exception, conceived in the philosopher's armchair. Hence it may safely be said that epistemology, notwithstanding efforts to naturalize it, has remained an armchair discipline, and as such has been flourishing indeed.

Notes

1 See Goldman 1979: 1 and Alston 1989: 81.
2 See, for example, Russell 1910–11; 1912; and 1914.
3 Both are reprinted in Moore 1959.
4 Ayer 1947.
5 Suppose you see a pencil in a glass of water. What you see is bent, but the pencil is not bent. Therefore, what you see is not the pencil. Similar reasoning can be found in the first chapter of Russell 1912.
6 Austin 1962.
7 Members of the Vienna Circle included Rudolf Carnap, Herbert Feigl, Kurt Gödel, Otto Neurath, Moritz Schlick, and Friedrich Waismann. Ayer and Quine also attended meetings of the circle.
8 See Quine 1953 and 1969. See also Kornblith 1987 and 1999.
9 Wittgenstein 1922.
10 See Wittgenstein 1953 and 1969.
11 Independently of Wittgenstein, J. L. Austin and Gilbert Ryle (1900–76) championed this approach as well. See Austin 1962 and Ryle 1949.
12 See Rorty 1979.
13 Roderick M. Chisholm is one of the main figures in twentieth-century philosophy, known for influential work in both metaphysics and epistemology. His main work in metaphysics is *Person and Object: A Philosophical Study* (Allen & Unwin, 1976); in epistemology, it is the textbook *Theory of Knowledge*. In metaphysics, Chisholm defended Platonism and an approach appealing to intentionality rather than causality. In epistemology, he advocated an internalist and foundationalist kind of epistemology in the tradition of Thomas Reid and G. E. Moore. Other major works are: *Perceiving: A Philosophical Study* (Cornell University Press, 1957); *The First Person: An Essay on Reference and Intentionality* (University of Minnesota Press, 1981); *The Foundations of Knowing* (University of Minnesota Press, 1982).
14 See Radford 1966.
15 Keith Lehrer (1990) argued that what knowledge requires is not belief but acceptance. This point should be seen, however, not as an outright rejection of the belief condition, but rather as a modification of it. On Lehrer's view, it is still true that knowledge of *p* requires a suitable attitude towards *p*, whereas an outright rejection of the belief condition amounts to the claim that knowledge that *p* requires no special attitude towards *p* at all.
16 For a systematic discussion of this issue, see Pritchard 2005.
17 Some philosophers would deny this. They would say that foundational beliefs are justified even without any reasons in support of them.

18 Gettier 1963.

19 For a book-length discussion of the analysis of knowledge and various responses to the Gettier problem, see Shope 1983.

20 From here on, unqualified use of the term "justified" should be understood as referring to epistemic justification.

21 See Alston 1989: 83f, and David 2001 and 2005.

22 See Conee and Feldman 1985.

23 For a defense of the deontological approach, see Ginet 1975; BonJour 1985; and Feldman 1988.

24 See Alston 1989: 95, and BonJour and Sosa 2003: 75ff.

25 See Alston 1989: 91ff. and 115–52.

26 See Feldman 1988 and 2001.

27 See Steup 2000. For further discussion, see also Ryan 2003.

28 See Lehrer 1974; 1990, and BonJour 1985 for important works defending coherentism. See Lewis 1929; 1946; Chisholm 1977; 1982; 1989; Fumerton 1995 and 2001; and BonJour 2001 for versions of foundationalism. For a foundationalism–coherentism compromise, see Haack 1993.

29 See Sosa 1991: 149–64 and Van Cleve 1985.

30 For a defense of the idea that justification via an infinite chain of reasons is possible, see Klein 1999 and 2005.

31 We can distinguish between different versions of foundationalism depending on how the connection between the foundation and the superstructure is construed. According to classical foundationalism as represented by Descartes, we must ascend from the foundation to the superstructure via deduction. Today's classical foundationalists are, in this regard, less ambitious. See BonJour 2001 and Fumerton 2001.

32 See Sosa 1991: 2 and BonJour and Sosa 2003: 119–40.

33 For the view that a belief can be justified solely by experience, see Pryor 2000; Huemer 2001; and Van Cleve 2005.

34 See Davidson 2001: 143.

35 Sellars 1963.

36 Recall that, according to coherentism, only beliefs can justify a belief.

37 If you wonder why S* forms beliefs in such an erratic fashion, simply assume that a momentary brain malfunction is responsible for that.

38 See Sosa 1991: 184. Sosa refers to the twin problems illustrated by Cases 1 and 2 as the problems of detachment from reality and alternative coherent systems. See also John Pollock's isolation argument against coherentism: Pollock 1986: 76f.

39 For literature on the internalism/externalism controversy, see Alston 1989: 185–226; Goldman 1999a; Kornblith 2001; BonJour and Sosa 2003; and Steup and Sosa 2005: ch. 9.

40 See Conee and Feldman 2004: 53–82.

41 See Chisholm 1977: 17.

42 Outside of philosophy, we would say that, at the scene of the crime, what the police gather are pieces of evidence: various items that will help to identify the perpetrator. One of these might be a bullet. This bullet might then be presented during the trial as a piece of evidence establishing the defendant's guilt. But from the evidentialist's point of view, what justifies the members of the jury in believing in the defendant's guilt is not the bullet itself, but suitable mental states, such as their beliefs about and perceptual experiences of the bullet.

43 For further discussion, see Greco 2005 and Feldman 2005.

44 See Goldman 1979; 1986; and 1991.

45 Goldman 1979: 20.

46 See Feldman 1985, and Conee and Feldman 2004: 135–59.

47 See Ginet 1985.

48 In his early work *The Structure of Empirical Knowledge*, BonJour defended coherentism, but later came to be an advocate of foundationalism. He is known as well for being a proponent of epistemic internalism and a rationalist account of a priori knowledge. Other major works are: *In Defense of Pure Reason* (Cambridge, 1998); *Epistemology: Classic Problems and Contemporary Responses* (Rowman & Littlefield, 2002): *Epistemic Justification: Internalism vs. Externalism, Foundations vs. Virtues* (co-authored with Ernest Sosa).

49 See BonJour 1985: ch. 1.
50 See Dretske 1971.
51 "Closest" is to be understood as "closest to the actual world." David Lewis puts the point thus: " 'If kangaroos had not tails, they would topple over' seems to me to mean something like this: in any possible state of affairs in which kangaroos have no tails, and which resembles our actual state of affairs as much as kangaroos having no tails permits it to, the kangaroos topple over" (1973: 1). When we assess the truth-value of a counterfactual about a hypothetical example, then "closest" is to be understood as meaning "closest to the world as described by the hypothetical example."
52 See Goldman 1976.
53 Dretske would not judge this outcome as intuitively wrong. He would say that, if C_2 is true, Henry knows B. See Dretske 2005: 24 n. 4.
54 Hawthorne 2005: 37. Compare Lewis, who writes: "Counterfactuals are notoriously vague. That does not mean that we cannot give a clear account of their truth conditions. It does mean that such an account must either be stated in vague terms … or be made relative to some parameter that is fixed only with rough limits of any given occasion of language use" (1973: 1).
55 Hawthorne 2005: 36f.
56 See Nozick 1981.
57 Nozick's complete account involves an appeal to the methods by which S's belief was formed.
58 See Luper-Foy 1987.
59 This counterexample is due to Saul Kripke, who presented it at the 1985 National Endowment for the Humanities Epistemology Institute in Boulder, CO.
60 For more details, see Steup 2001.
61 Alston 1989: 91 and 231f.
62 See Anscombe 1958.
63 Sosa 1980.
64 Sosa 1991: 189.
65 See Sosa 1994b: 29f.
66 See Sosa 1991: 284f.
67 See Sosa 1994b: 30.
68 See ibid.: 29–33.
69 See ibid.: 38f. and Sosa 2000: 108.
70 Alvin Goldman objects to Sosa's response to the new evil demon problem on the ground that the folk do not relativize justification to the subject's environment. See Goldman 1991: sect. II. In response to Goldman's objection, Sosa suggests that the "relativizing may be contextual and implicit." See BonJour and Sosa 2003: 156–8.
71 See BonJour 1985: ch. 1.
72 See Sosa 1991: 134.
73 This does not mean, however, that Sosa endorses BonJour's rejection of externalism. See BonJour and Sosa 2003: 204–6.
74 Sosa 1991: 281–4.
75 See Sosa 1991: 283.
76 For relevant literature on this issue, see Sosa 1991: 282f.; Foley 1994; and Sosa 1994b: 42–5.
77 See BonJour 2000: 93–6.
78 See ibid.
79 See Sosa 2000: 104.
80 See ibid.: 105.
81 For details, see Sosa 1997 and 2000: 106.
82 See Stroud 1989; Alston 1993: ch. 1; and Fumerton 1995: 177.
83 Fumerton 1995: 177.
84 For more on Sosa's views on circularity, see Sosa 1994a; 1997; and 1999: 106f.
85 See Zagzebski 2000: 169.
86 Ibid.: 172.
87 Ibid.
88 Ibid.: 173.

89 For the exact wording of Zagzebski's definitions, see Zagzebski 2000. For a full account of her version of virtue epistemology, see Zagzebski 1996.

90 Zagzebski 2000: 172.

91 See Zagzebski 1996: 9.

92 See Sosa 1991: 271.

93 See Greco 2000b: 180f.

94 Zagzebski 2000: 172.

95 Greco 2000b: 181. For Greco's own brand of virtue epistemology, which does not include the perspectival requirement Sosa imposes, see Greco 1999.

96 Greco 2000b: 181.

97 Foley 1994: 5.

98 Ibid.: 7.

99 See Greco 2000b.

100 For further literature on virtue epistemology, see Kvanvig 1992; Montmarquet 1993; Greco 1993 and 2000a; Axtell 1997 and 2000.

101 As stated, this formulation is open to objections. For example, even if I know p and know that p entails q, I might still not know q simply because I failed to form the belief that q. Thus, we would have to build into the antecedent that, in addition to recognizing the entailment, I form the belief that q. For discussion of the problems involved in finding a satisfactory articulation of the closure principle, see Hawthorne 2005. For our purposes in this part, the rough and ready version in the text will do, as long as we bear in mind that a satisfactory articulation of the principle requires fine-tuning.

102 See Moore 1922: 228; 1953: 120–6; and 1959: 226.

103 See Moore 1959: 247.

104 See Cohen 2002.

105 See Feldman 1986: 35ff.

106 See Dretske 1970.

107 Why say this? After all, if you were a BIV, you wouldn't have hands, but you would have hand-like experiences. Recall, however, that in assessing the truth value of the counterfactual "If I didn't have hands, I wouldn't have hand-like experiences," we need to consider the *closest* possible worlds in which you don't have hands. The BIV world is not a close world in which you don't have hands, and thus is to be ignored for the assessment of this counterfactual.

108 See DeRose 1995.

109 See Hawthorne 2005: 31f.

110 See Dretske 1970.

111 Saying that p and q are incompatible means that p and q cannot both be true.

112 See Stine 1976.

113 Perhaps these are just two different ways of articulating the same point.

114 A further problem for Stine's account arises from cases in which S has equally good evidence for and against a proposition. See Sosa 2003: sect. II.

115 See Cohen 1988; 1999; DeRose 1992; 1995; and 1999, and Lewis 1996.

116 See Lewis's "Rule of attention" in his 1996 article.

117 Our assumption raises a problem, though. Can Ludwig say "Fred knows he's not a BIV" without thereby making the BIV alternative salient, thus creating a high-standard context? It's not easy to see how he could, if merely paying attention to a skeptical alternative has the effect of having a person have high-standard knowledge in mind when he uses the word "know."

118 See Cohen 2005: 61f.

119 See DeRose 1999: 192.

120 For a defense of this approach, see Engel 2004 and Russell 2004.

121 A defense of this point would have to address various examples contextualists advance to show that there is contextual variance even in ordinary, non-philosophical situations, such as DeRose's bank case (DeRose 1992) and Cohen's airport case (Cohen 1999). It would also have to address the question of how, from the comfort of the a priori armchair, epistemologists can determine semantic facts about the word "know," which are, after all, empirical facts. Note, however, that contextualist face this problem as well.

122 How does this differ from contextualism? This way: A Moorean epistemologist's use of "know" retains its low-standard meaning even when confronted with a skeptical argument. She will respond to the argument by employing the tool of disambiguation. In contrast, contextualism is the view that, when confronted with a skeptical argument, what one means by "know" is fixed by the skeptic's high standards. The disambiguation tool is employed merely to distinguish between various contextually determined meanings of "know," but, according to contextualist semantics, is not available for the purpose of rebutting the skeptic.

123 See Sosa 1999 and 2003.

124 See Sosa 1999: 146 and Lewis 1973: 35. Here is Lewis's example: (1) If Boris had gone to the party, Olga would still have gone; (2) If Olga had not gone, Boris would still not have gone. Lewis assumes that "Boris wanted to go but stayed away solely in order to avoid Olga ... but Olga would have gone all the more willingly if Boris had been there." Given these two assumptions, (1) is true, but its contrapositive, (2), is false.

125 Sosa 1999: 145f.

126 The relevant counterfactual is "If I were to believe that I'm not a BIV, it would be true that I'm not a BIV." In the nearest possible worlds in which I believe I'm not a BIV, it is indeed true that I'm not a BIV. Hence my belief that I'm not a BIV is safe.

127 There is a further response to skepticism that has not been addressed in this chapter: semantic externalism. For relevant literature regarding this response, see DeRose and Warfield 1999. For a review of recent work on skepticism, see Pritchard 2002.

128 See Steup 1996: ch. 9.

129 For literature on the naturalization of epistemology, see Goldman 1986; Kornblith 1987 and 1999; Feldman 1999a and 1999b.

130 See Steup 1996: ch. 9; Kornblith 1997: introduction; and, for a general overview, Bradie and Harms 2004.

131 For some of the relevant literature, see Mannheim 1936; Fuller 1988, Longino 1990; Kitcher 1993; Schmitt 1994 and 1999; and Goldman 1999b and 2001.

132 See Habermas 1971. Other members of the Frankfurt School, all of whom advocated what is known as "Critical Theory," include Theodor Adorno, Max Horkheimer, and Herbert Marcuse.

133 See Foucault 1970; 1972; 1973; and 1980.

134 For a lucid and effective criticism of the rejection of objective truth, see Van Inwagen 2002: sect. 5. See also Searle 1995 and Haack 1998.

135 For useful overviews, see Longino 1999 and Anderson 2003. For a critical assessment of feminist epistemology, see Haack 1998: ch. 7.

References

Alston, W. (1989) *Epistemic Justification: Essays in the Theory of Knowledge*. Ithaca, NY: Cornell University Press.

—— (1993) *The Reliability of Sense Perception*. Ithaca, NY: Cornell University Press.

Anderson, E. (2003) "Feminist epistemology and philosophy of science." In E. N. Zalta (ed.) *The Stanford Encyclopedia of Philosophy*. http://plato.stanford.edu/entries/feminism-epistemology.

Anscombe, G. E. M. (1958) "Modern moral philosophy." *Philosophy* 33: 1–19.

Axtell, G. (1997) "Recent work on virtue epistemology." *American Philosophical Quarterly* 34: 1–26.

—— (ed.) (2000) *Knowledge, Belief, and Character: Readings in Virtue Epistemology*. Lanham, MD: Rowman & Littlefield.

Austin, J. L. (1962) *Sense and Sensibilia*. Oxford: Oxford University Press.

Ayer, A. J. (1947) *The Foundations of Empirical Knowledge*. London: Macmillan.

BonJour, L. (1985) *The Structure of Empirical Knowledge*. Cambridge, MA: Harvard University Press.

—— (2000) "Sosa on knowledge, justification, and 'aptness'." In G. Axtell (ed.) *Knowledge, Belief, and Character: Readings in Virtue Epistemology*, Lanham, MD: Rowman & Littlefield, pp. 87–97. First published in *Philosophical Studies* 78 (1995): 207–20.

—— (2001) "Towards a defense of empirical foundationalism." In M. De Paul (ed.) *Resurrecting Old-Fashioned Foundationalism*, New York: Rowman & Littlefield, pp. 21–38.

BonJour, L. and E. Sosa (2003) *Epistemic Justification: Internalism vs. Externalism, Foundations vs. Virtues.* Oxford: Blackwell.

Bradie, M. and W. Harms (2004) "Evolutionary epistemology." In E. N. Zalta (ed.) *The Stanford Encyclopedia of Philosophy*. http://plato.stanford.edu/entries/epistemology-evolutionary.

Chisholm, R. (1977) *Theory of Knowledge*, 2nd edn. Englewood Cliffs, NJ: Prentice-Hall.

—— (1982) *The Foundations of Knowing*. Minneapolis: University of Minnesota Press.

—— (1989) *Theory of Knowledge*, 3rd edn. Englewood Cliffs, NJ: Prentice-Hall.

Cohen, S. (1988) "How to be a fallibilist." *Philosophical Perspectives* 2: 91–123.

—— (1999) "Contextualism, skepticism, and the structure of reasons." *Philosophical Perspectives* 13: 57–89.

—— (2002) "Basic knowledge and the problem of easy knowledge." *Philosophy and Phenomenological Research* 65: 309–29.

—— (2005) "Contextualism defended." In M. Steup and E. Sosa (eds.) *Contemporary Debates in Epistemology*, Oxford: Blackwell, pp. 56–62.

Conee, E. and R. Feldman (1985) "Evidentialism." *Philosophical Studies* 48: 15–44.

—— and —— (2004) *Evidentialism: Essays in Epistemology*, Oxford and New York: Oxford University Press.

David, M. (2001) "Truth and the epistemic goal." In M. Steup (ed.) *Knowledge, Truth, and Duty: Essays on Epistemic Justification, Responsibility, and Virtue*. Oxford: Oxford University Press, pp. 151–69.

—— (2005) "Truth as the primary epistemic goal: a working hypothesis." In M. Steup and E. Sosa (eds.) *Contemporary Debates in Epistemology*, Oxford: Blackwell, pp. 296–312.

Davidson, D. (2001) "A coherence theory of truth and knowledge." In *Subjective, Objective, Intersubjective*, Oxford: Oxford University Press, pp. 137–53.

DeRose, K. (1992) "Contextualism and knowledge attributions." *Philosophy and Phenomenological Research* 52: 913–29.

—— (1995) "Solving the skeptical problem." *Philosophical Review* 104: 1–52.

—— (1999) "Contextualism: an explanation and defense." In J. Greco and E. Sosa (eds.) *The Blackwell Guide to Epistemology*, Oxford: Blackwell, pp. 187–205.

DeRose, K. and T. Warfield (eds.) (1999) *Skepticism: A Contemporary Reader*. Oxford: Oxford University Press.

Dretske, F. (1970) "Epistemic operators." *Journal of Philosophy* 67: 1007–23.

—— (1971) "Conclusive reasons." *Australasian Journal of Philosophy* 49: 1–22.

—— (2005) "The case against closure." In M. Steup and E. Sosa (eds.) *Contemporary Debates in Epistemology*, Oxford: Blackwell, pp. 13–26

Engel, M. (2004) "What's wrong with contextualism, and a noncontextualist resolution of the skeptical paradox." *Erkenntnis* 61: 203–31.

Feldman, F. (1986) *A Cartesian Introduction to Epistemology*. New York: McGraw-Hill.

Feldman, R. (1985) "Reliability and justification." *The Monist* 68: 159–74.

—— (1988) "Epistemic obligations." In J. E. Tomberlin (ed.) *Philosophical Perspectives* 2, Atascadero, CA: Ridgeview, pp. 235–56.

—— (1999a) "Methodological naturalism in epistemology." In J. Greco and E. Sosa (eds.) *The Blackwell Guide to Epistemology*, Oxford: Blackwell, pp. 170–86.

—— (1999b) "Naturalized epistemology." In E. N. Zalta (ed.) *The Stanford Encyclopedia of Philosophy*. http://plato.stanford.edu/entries/epistemology-naturalized/.

—— (2001) "Voluntary belief and epistemic evaluation." In M. Steup (ed.) *Knowledge, Truth, and Duty: Essays on Epistemic Justification, Responsibility, and Virtue*, Oxford: Oxford Univeristy Press, pp. 77–92.

—— (2005) "Justification is internal." In M. Steup and E. Sosa (eds.) *Contemporary Debates in Epistemology*, Oxford: Blackwell, pp. 270–84.

Foley, R. (1994) "The epistemology of Sosa." *Philosophical Issues* 5: 1–14.

Foucault, M. (1970) *The Order of Things*. New York: Random House.

—— (1972) *The Archaeology of Knowledge*. New York: Pantheon.

—— (1973) *The Birth of the Clinic: An Archaeology of Medical Perception*. New York: Vintage.

—— (1980) *Power/Knowledge: Selected Interviews and Other Writings*, ed. C. Gordon. New York: Pantheon.

Fuller, S. (1988) *Social Epistemology*. Bloomington: Indiana University Press.

Fumerton, R. (1995) *Metaepistemology and Skepticism*. Lanham, MD: Rowman & Littlefield.

—— (2001) "Classical foundationalism." In M. De Paul (ed.) *Resurrecting Old-Fashioned Foundationalism*, New York: Rowman & Littlefield, pp. 3–20.

Gettier, E. (1963) "Is justified true belief knowledge?" *Analysis* 23: 121–3.

Ginet, C. (1975) *Knowledge, Perception, and Memory*. Dordrecht: Reidel.

—— (1985) "Contra reliabilism." *The Monist* 68: 175–87.

Goldman, A. (1976) "Discrimination and perceptual knowledge." *Journal of Philosophy* 73: 771–91.

—— (1979) "What is justified belief?" In G. S. Pappas (ed.) *Justification and Knowledge*, Dordrecht: Reidel, pp. 1–23.

—— (1986) *Epistemology and Cognition*. Cambridge, MA: Harvard University Press.

—— (1991) "Epistemic folkways and scientific epistemology." In *Liaisons: Philosophy Meets the Cognitive and Social Sciences*. Cambridge, MA: MIT Press, pp. 155–77.

—— (1999a) "Internalism exposed." *Journal of Philosophy* 96: 271–93.

—— (1999b) *Knowledge in a Social World*. Oxford: Oxford University Press.

—— (2001) "Social epistemology." In E. N. Zalta (ed.) *The Stanford Encyclopedia of Philosophy*. http://plato.stanford.edu/entries/epistemology-social/.

Greco, J. (1993) "Virtues and vices of virtue epistemology." *Canadian Journal of Philosophy* 23: 413–32.

—— (1999) "Agent reliabilism." *Philosophical Perspectives* 13: 273–96.

—— (2000a) *Putting Skeptics in their Place: The Nature of Skeptical Arguments and their Role in Philosophical Inquiry*. Cambridge: Cambridge University Press.

—— (2000b) "Two kinds of intellectual virtue." *Philosophy and Phenomenological Research* 60: 179–84.

—— (2005) "Justification is not internal." In M. Steup and E. Sosa (eds.) *Contemporary Debates in Epistemology*, Oxford: Blackwell, pp. 257–70.

Haack, S. (1993) *Evidence and Inquiry: Towards Reconstruction in Epistemology*. Oxford: Blackwell.

—— (1998) *Manifesto of a Passionate Moderate: Unfashionable Essays*. Chicago: University of Chicago Press.

Habermas, J. (1971) *Knowledge and Human Interest*. London: Heinemann.

Hawthorne, J. (2005) "The case for closure." In M. Steup and E. Sosa (eds.) *Contemporary Debates in Epistemology*, Oxford: Blackwell, pp. 26–43.

Huemer, M. (2001) *Skepticism and the Veil of Perception*. New York: Rowman & Littlefield.

Kitcher, P. (1993) *The Advancement of Science*. New York: Oxford University Press.

Klein, P. (1999) "Human knowledge and the infinite regress of reasons." *Philosophical Perspectives* 13: 297–332.

—— (2005) "Infinitism is the solution to the regress problem." In M. Steup and E. Sosa (eds.) *Contemporary Debates in Epistemology*, Oxford: Blackwell, pp. 131–40.

Kornblith, H. (1987) *Naturalizing Epistemology*. Cambridge, MA: MIT Press.

—— (1999) "In defense of a naturalized epistemology." In J. Greco and E. Sosa (eds.) *The Blackwell Guide to Epistemology*, Oxford: Blackwell, pp. 158–69.

—— (2001) *Epistemology: Internalism and Externalism*. Oxford: Blackwell.

Kvanvig, J. (1992) *The Intellectual Virtues and the Life of the Mind*. Lanham, MD: Rowman & Littlefield.

Lehrer, K. (1974) *Knowledge*. Oxford: Oxford University Press.

—— (1990) *Theory of Knowledge*. Boulder, CO: Westview Press.

Lewis, C. I. (1929) *Mind and the World-Order*. New York: Charles Scribner's Sons.

—— (1946) *An Analysis of Knowledge and Valuation*. LaSalle, IL: Open Court.

Lewis, D. (1973) *Counterfactuals*. Cambridge, MA: Harvard University Press.

—— (1996) "Elusive knowledge." *Australasian Journal of Philosophy* 74: 549–67. Repr. in K. DeRose and T. Warfield (eds.) *Skepticism: A Contemporary Reader*, Oxford: Oxford University Press, 1999, pp. 220–39.

Longino, H. (1990) *Science as Social Knowledge*. Princeton, NJ: Princeton University Press.

—— (1999) "Feminist epistemology." In J. Greco and E. Sosa (eds.) *The Blackwell Guide to Epistemology*, Oxford: Blackwell, pp. 327–53.

Luper-Foy, S. (ed.) (1987) *The Possibility of Knowledge: Nozick and his Critics*. Totowa, NJ: Rowman & Littlefield.

Mannheim, K. (1936) *Ideology and Utopia*, trans. L. Wirth and E. Shils. New York: Hartcourt, Brace, & World.

Montmarquet, J. (1993) *Epistemic Virtue and Doxastic Responsibility*. Lanham, MD: Rowman & Littlefield.

Moore, G. E. (1922) *Philosophical Studies*. London: Routledge & Kegan Paul.

—— (1953) *Some Main Problems of Philosophy*. London: Allen & Unwin.

—— (1959) *Philosophical Papers*. London: Allen & Unwin.

Nozick, R. (1981) *Philosophical Explanations*. Cambridge, MA: Harvard University Press.

Pollock, J. (1986) *Contemporary Theories of Knowledge*. Totowa, NJ: Rowman & Littlefield.

Pritchard, D. (2002) "Recent work on radical skepticism." *American Philosophical Quarterly* 39: 215–57. Available online at www.philosophy.stir.ac.uk/staff/duncan-pritchard/publications.php.

—— (2004) "Some recent work in epistemology." *Philosophical Quarterly* 54: 604–13.

—— (2005) *Epistemic Luck*. Oxford: Oxford University Press.

Pryor, J. (2000) "The skeptic and the dogmatist." *Noûs* 34: 517–49. Available online at www.princeton.edu/~jimpryor/news/research/index.html.

Quine, W. V. O. (1953) *From A Logical Point of View*. Cambridge, MA: Harvard University Press.

—— (1969) "Epistemology naturalized." In *Ontological Relativity and Other Essays*. New York: Columbia University Press, pp. 69–90.

Radford, C. (1966) "Knowledge – by examples." *Analysis* 27: 1–11.

Rorty, R. (1979) *Philosophy and the Mirror of Nature*. Princeton, NJ: Princeton University Press.

Russell, Bertrand (1910–11) "Knowledge by acquaintance and knowledge by description." *Proceedings of the Aristotelian Society* 11: 108–28. Repr. in *Mysticism and Logic*, London: Allen & Unwin, 1963, ch. 10.

—— (1912) *The Problems of Philosophy*. Oxford: Oxford University Press.

—— (1914) "The relation of sense-data to physics." *Scientia* 16: 1–17. Repr. in *Mysticism and Logic*, London: Allen & Unwin, 1963, pp. 108–31.

Russell, Bruce (2004) "How to be an anti-skeptic and a noncontextualist." *Erkenntnis* 61: 245–55.

Ryan, S. (2003) "Doxastic compatibilism and the ethics of belief." *Philosophical Studies* 114: 47–79.

Ryle, G. (1949) *The Concept of Mind*. London: Hutchinson.

Schmitt, F. (ed.) (1994) *Socializing Epistemology*. Lanham, MD: Rowman & Littlefield.

—— (1999) "Social epistemology." In J. Greco and E. Sosa (eds.) *The Blackwell Guide to Epistemology*, Oxford: Blackwell, pp. 354–82.

Searle, J. (1995) *The Construction of Social Reality*. New York: Free Press.

Sellars, W. (1963) "Empiricism and the philosophy of mind." In *Science, Perception and Reality*, London: Routledge & Kegan Paul.

Shope, R. K. (1983) *The Analysis of Knowing: A Decade of Research*. Princeton, NJ: Princeton University Press.

Sosa, E. (1980) "The raft and the pyramid: coherence versus foundations in the theory of knowledge." *Midwest Studies in Philosophy* 5: 3–25. Repr. in *Knowledge in Perspective: Selected Essays in Epistemology*, Cambridge: Cambridge University Press, 1991, pp. 165–91.

—— (1991) *Knowledge in Perspective: Selected Essays in Epistemology*. Cambridge: Cambridge University Press.

——. (1994a) "Philosophical skepticism and epistemic circularity." *Aristotelian Society Supplementary Volume* 68: 263–90. Repr. in K. DeRose and T. Warfield (eds.) *Skepticism: A Contemporary Reader*, Oxford: Oxford University Press, 1999, pp. 93–114.

—— (1994b) "Virtue perspectivism: a response to Foley and Fumerton." *Philosophical Issues* 5: 29–50.

—— (1997) "Reflective knowledge in the best circles." *Journal of Philosophy* 96: 410–30. Available online at www.homepage.mac.com./ernestsosa/FileSharing3.html.

—— (1999) "How to defeat opposition to Moore." *Philosophical Perspectives*: 141–53. Available online at www.homepage.mac.com./ernestsosa/FileSharing3.html.

—— (2000) "Perspectives in virtue epistemology: a response to Dancy and BonJour." In G. Axtell (ed.) *Knowledge, Belief, and Character: Readings in Virtue Epistemology*, Lanham, MD: Rowman & Littlefield, pp. 99–110. First published in *Philosophical Studies* 78 (1995): 202–20.

—— (2003) "Relevant alternatives, contextualism included." *Philosophical Studies* 119: 35–65. Available online at www.homepage.mac.com./ernestsosa/FileSharing3.html.

Steup, M. (1996) *An Introduction to Contemporary Epistemology*. Upper Saddle River, NJ: Prentice-Hall.

—— (2000) "Doxastic voluntarism and epistemic deontology." *Acta Analytica* 15: 25–56. Available online at www.web.stcloudstate.edu/msteup/epis.html.

—— (ed.) (2001) *Knowledge, Truth, and Duty: Essays on Epistemic Justification, Responsibility, and Virtue*. Oxford: Oxford University Press.

Steup, M. and E. Sosa (eds.) (2005) *Contemporary Debates in Epistemology*. Oxford: Blackwell.

Stine, G. (1976) "Skepticism, relevant alternatives, and deductive closure." *Philosophical Studies* 29: 249–61.

Stroud, B. (1989) "Understanding human knowledge in general." In K. Lehrer and M. Clay (eds.) *Knowledge and Skepticism*, Boulder, CO: Westview Press, pp. 31–50.

Van Cleve, J. (1985) "Epistemic supervenience and the circle of beliefs." *The Monist* 6: 90–104.

—— (2005) "Why coherence is not enough: a defense of moderate foundationalism." In M. Steup and E. Sosa (eds.) *Contemporary Debates in Epistemology*, Oxford: Blackwell, pp. 168–80.

Van Inwagen, P (2002) *Metaphysics*. Boulder, CO: Westview Press.

Wittgenstein, L. (1922) *Tractatus Logico-Philosophicus*. London: Routledge & Kegan Paul.

—— (1953) *Philosophical Investigations*. Oxford: Blackwell.

—— (1969) *On Certainty*. Oxford: Blackwell.

Zagzebski, L. (1996) *Virtues of the Mind: An Inquiry into the Nature of Virtue and the Ethical Foundations of Knowledge*. Cambridge: Cambridge University Press.

—— (2000) "Précis of Virtues of the Mind." *Philosophy and Phenomenological Research* 60: 169–77.

Further reading

The following three introductory texts will be excellent first readings for the aspiring student of epistemology: Laurence BonJour, *Epistemology: Classic Problems and Contemporary Responses* (New York: Rowman & Littlefield, 2002); Richard Feldman, *Epistemology* (Upper Saddle River, NJ: Prentice-Hall, 2003): and Michael Williams, *Problems of Knowledge* (Oxford: Oxford University Press, 2001). For useful reviews of work in epistemology, see Pritchard 2002 and 2004. For further, more in-depth immersion into the epistemological literature, following collections cited in the bibliography will prove useful: DeRose and Warfield 1999; Greco and Sosa 1999; Axtell 2000; and Steup and Sosa 2005.

Part III

PHILOSOPHY OF MIND, PSYCHOLOGY, AND SCIENCE

12
PHILOSOPHY OF MIND
Sarah Patterson

Introduction

Philosophy of mind became one of the most active areas of philosophy in the latter part of the twentieth century. This chapter deals with developments in the so-called analytic or Anglo-American tradition; for an account of the Continental or phenomenological tradition, where philosophy of mind was a central topic, see Dan Zahavi's "Phenomenology," Chapter 15.

The place of the mind in a world increasingly regarded as fundamentally physical was a theme that ran through the century. Advances in scientific understanding of physical, chemical, and biological phenomena undermined the early emergentists' conviction that the mind was beyond the reach of reductive explanation. The "linguistic turn," applied in very different ways by Rudolf Carnap and by Gilbert Ryle, led to the view that the traditional conception of the mind as an immaterial private realm could be dissolved by a correct understanding of mental terms, contributing to the broadly materialist trend. The development of digital computing in mid-century and the advent of research into artificial intelligence provided a new way of understanding the mind which had a huge impact on philosophy as well as psychology. It held out the promise of an approach that was materialist but not reductionist, according to which the mind is to the brain as software is to hardware. It also held out the prospect of a mechanistic explanation of rational thought, leading to a focus on understanding intentionality and representation in physical systems. Consciousness and mental causation emerged as problems for the non-reductive physicalist consensus in the closing years of the century. Arguments were advanced to suggest that phenomenal consciousness could not be explained in physical terms. Some questioned whether physicalists could assure a causal role for mind while affirming the causal primacy of the physical. While physicalism came under increasing pressure, attention turned to the project of describing the mind itself, and of doing justice to the diversity of mental phenomena and the relationships among them.

The early years

The fission of psychology from philosophy and its emergence as an experimental discipline is often dated to 1879 and the founding of Wilhelm Wundt's laboratory at Leipzig (see Reed 1994 for an account of nineteenth-century developments leading to this point). The last major figure claimed both by philosophers and by psychologists was William James (1842–1910) (see "American philosophy in the twentieth century," Chapter 5). In 1875 James established a demonstration laboratory at Harvard, where he was the first professor of psychology. He moved to the Harvard philosophy department in 1879, and early in the new century published papers expounding his hypothesis of "a world of pure experience," according to which "there is only one primal stuff or material in the world, a stuff of which everything is composed" (1912: 4). Pure experience in James's sense is itself neither mental nor physical. An element of pure experience is called "mental" insofar as it is related to other elements making up what is called a stream of consciousness or personal biography, and called "physical" insofar as it is related to other elements making up what is called outer reality. Through the invocation of subjectless experience, James sought to erase the distinction between subject and object; one and the same element can be both *the real thing experienced* and *the experience of a real thing*, if it participates in two different series of relations, just as one and the same point can be on two intersecting lines:

> If … you follow it in the mental direction, taking it along with events of personal biography solely, all sorts of things are true of it which are false, and false of it which are true if you treat it as a real thing experienced, follow it in the physical direction, and relate it to associates in the outer world. (1912/1904: 14–15)

James's views exercised a strong influence on the neutral monism of Bertrand Russell (1872–1970), advanced in his book *The Analysis of Mind* (1921; see pp. 22–5). Russell was also influenced by the materialistic approach to mind adopted by contemporary behaviorist psychologists such as John Watson (1878–1958; see "Philosophy of psychology," Chapter 13). Russell was not a thoroughgoing behaviorist, holding that the existence of mental images should not be denied (as it was by Watson). But he was impressed by what he saw as the empirical success of behaviorist theorizing: "It is humiliating to find how terribly adequate this [behaviourist] hypothesis turns out to be" (1921: 27). Rejecting Franz Brentano's claim that relation to an object is an ultimate irreducible characteristic of mental phenomena (1921: 15), he concluded that "Mind is a matter of degree, chiefly exemplified in number and complexity of habits" (p. 308).

Russell saw a rapprochement between the materialistic tendencies of behaviorist psychology and what he regarded as the anti-materialistic tendencies of relativistic physics, a convergence leading naturally to a monist metaphysics in which "mind and matter alike are seen to be constructed out of a neutral stuff" (1921: 287). Matter is "a logical fiction, invented because it gives us a convenient way of stating causal laws" in physics, laws which are verified by appearances (p. 300). Psychology is concerned with the laws governing the appearances themselves. "When a sensation is used to verify physics, it is used merely as a sign of a certain material phenomenon ... But when it is studied by psychology, it is ... put into quite a different context, where it causes images or voluntary movements" (pp. 301–2). Russell concludes that "[p]hysics and psychology are not distinguished by their material" (p. 307).

Russell's is one of the metaphysical views discussed by Charles Dunbar Broad (1887–1971) in his master-work, *The Mind and its Place in Nature* (1925). Broad's book is a systematic survey of possible positions on the question of the metaphysical relationship between mind and matter, assessed in the light of empirical evidence. He classifies Russell's view as a form of mentalistic neutralism, according to which the fundamental stuff of which the world is made is neither mental nor material (1925: 632), and materiality is a delusive characteristic (pp. 610–11). As to the relationship between mentality and the neutral stuff, Broad argues that Russell's view is plausible only if mentality is an emergent rather than a reducible feature (p. 650).[1] To understand this distinction, we need to turn to one of the central divisions Broad discusses, that between mechanism and emergentism.

The distinction between mechanism and emergentism can be drawn in terms laid down by John Stuart Mill (1806–73) in the previous century (Mill 1843; see McLaughlin 1992 for discussion). Mill distinguishes between two ways in which causes may combine, the mechanical and the chemical. When causes *a* and *b* combine in the mechanical mode, the joint effect of their operation is the sum of the effects they would have if operating separately. When causes combine in the chemical mode, this is not the case; the combination produces an effect which is quite different from those found when *a* and *b* operate alone, or in combination with other causes. The laws governing such combinations can only be discovered inductively, as they are in chemistry (Mill 1843: 432). Lewes (1875) introduced the terms "emergent" and "resultant" to mark the distinction between the effects of the chemical and the mechanical modes of combination respectively (McLaughlin 1992: 65). Broad's distinction between mechanism and emergentism marks the same contrast: these views "differ according to the view that we take about the laws which connect the properties of the components with the characteristic behaviour of the complex wholes which they make up" (1925: 59). Both views can agree that the properties of wholes are *determined* by the components and their mode of combination (pp. 59, 64). But mechanism holds that the behavior of wholes can in principle be *deduced* from a knowledge of the way in which their components behave in isolation, while emergentism denies this. According to emergentism, wholes exhibit emergent behavior which can only be discovered inductively (p. 65).

Like Mill, Broad offers chemical examples to illustrate emergent characteristics: "most of the chemical and physical properties of water have no known connexion, either quantitative or qualitative, with those of Oxygen and Hydrogen" (1925: 63). The view of the mind which Broad himself finds most reasonable by the end of his survey is that mentality is "an emergent characteristic of certain kinds of material complex" (p. 647). He objects to a reductive materialist account of mentality, which he discusses under the heading of "Behaviourism," for a variety of reasons. "It has a mind" does not mean "It behaves thus and so" because the truth of the latter does not settle that of the former (pp. 614–15). Moreover, we do not ascribe experiences to ourselves on the basis of our behavior, but because we know we have them: "if we confine ourselves to bodily behaviour it is perfectly certain that we are leaving out something of whose existence we are immediately aware in favourable cases" (p. 614).

Broad's fundamental objection to materialism concerns this "sensational element" in perceptual experience (1925: 622). Materialists might mean one of two things in claiming, for example, that sensations can be reduced to molecular motions. They may mean that the characteristic of being a sensation of some kind and that of being a molecular motion of some kind are one and the same. Or they may mean that the two characteristics belong to the same event or substance. The second may be true, but it is a form of emergent, not reductive materialism (p. 623). The first cannot be true since it is "plainly nonsensical" (p. 622). This is shown by the following argument: "There is a something which has the characteristic of being my awareness of a red patch. There is a something which has the characteristic of being a molecular movement. It should surely be obvious … that whether these 'somethings' be the same or different, there are two different *characteristics*" (p. 622). Broad thinks it should be obvious because if the two phrases were "just two names for a single characteristic," they would be like "rich" and "wealthy" (p. 622); they would have the same meaning (though Broad does not put the point in these terms). This is a version of what came to be called the "Distinct Property" objection to materialism, which reappeared later in the century (see the sections "Materialism" and "Consciousness and qualia," below).

Broad observes that the choice between mechanism and emergentism has consequences for the unity of the sciences, even when we consider the sciences of the external world, leaving aside the study of consciousnesses. On the mechanist view, "the external world has the greatest amount of unity which is conceivable. There is really only one science, and the various 'special sciences' are just particular cases of it" (1925: 76). On the emergentist view, "we have to reconcile ourselves to much less unity in the external world and a much less intimate connexion between the various sciences. At best the external world and the various sciences that deal with it will form a kind of hierarchy" (p. 77). On this view, there might be one fundamental kind of stuff, but there would be fundamentally different types of law governing the properties of aggregates of that stuff.

Broad's book brings together several themes which were to reappear in philosophical discussions of mind in the twentieth century. One theme is that of explanation and reduction. Broad defines reducible properties epistemically, as those susceptible to a certain kind of explanation. Emergent properties are those which are not so susceptible (1925: 78). But the kind of reduction against which Broad deploys the Distinct Property objection is reduction in an ontological sense, where a is reduced to b iff $a = b$. How is explanatory reduction related to ontological reduction? This question is closely related to the second theme, that of the unity of science. Does one set of laws, one set of concepts, serve to explain and predict the behavior of all the things in the world? The final theme, not yet touched on, is that of the nature of the mental and of the material or physical. What are the distinctive features of mental and physical things? Broad's view is that both materiality and mentality are complex characteristics. The fundamental factor in materiality is extension (p. 633). Two of the central factors in mentality are what he calls sentience (which he glosses as "feeling somehow") and referential cognition (pp. 634–6). Such cognition may be intuitive (as in perceiving something) or discursive (as in thinking of something).[2] Broad's analysis thus manifests a distinction that was to become important in the ensuing decades: the distinction between mental states that feel a certain way (mental states with qualitative properties, as they came to be called) and mental states that are about or directed on something (mental states with intentional properties, as they came to be called).

Many of the further questions that became central to philosophy of mind in the twentieth century are connected to these themes. Scientific advances supplied physical explanations for chemical phenomena which Broad regarded as inexplicable, suggesting that there was more unity in the natural world than the emergentists imagined and fuelling the idea that reality, including mentality, is basically material or physical. But how should a plausible thesis of physicalism be formulated, and how can it be established? Is physicalism best construed as a thesis about things and properties, about concepts and terms, or about laws and explanations? And what exactly is it for something to be physical? Moreover, what is it for something to be mental? Is the concept of mentality an irreducibly disjunctive one – a state is mental if it feels some way to be in it, or it is directed on some object – or do such states have something in common? How are the qualitative and intentional properties of mental states to be explained? And how are such properties related to other distinctive features of minds such as subjectivity and consciousness?

As we have seen, Broad thought that reductive physicalism could be refuted by appealing to the fact that "being my awareness of a red patch" and "being a molecular movement" are not names for the same property. The physicalism espoused by the logical positivists of the Vienna Circle promised to sweep away such objections. The manifesto of this philosophical movement, published in 1929, advocated the unity of science in a strong and uncompromising form (Carnap et al. 1929) (see "Philosophy of science," Chapter 14).

Logical positivism

Two positivist theses of the unity of science should be distinguished. The first is what Herbert Feigl (1902–88) calls the thesis of the unity of the language of science. It asserts "a unity of the confirmation base of all factually cognitive (i.e., non-analytic) statements of the natural and of the social sciences" (Feigl 1963: 227). All factual scientific statements are confirmed in the same way, so fundamentally all the sciences employ the same method. The second thesis posits a unitary explanatory system, so Feigl calls it the thesis of "unitary science" (p. 227). It asserts that "the facts and laws of the natural and the social sciences can all be derived – at least in principle – from the theoretical assumptions of physics" (pp. 227–8). (This second thesis is evidently equivalent to what Broad calls "mechanism.") Feigl describes the first as a thesis about language, to be established via logical analysis, and the second as a thesis about laws, to be confirmed by the progress of science.

The physicalism characteristic of the Vienna Circle is a version of the thesis of the unity of the language of science. (For further discussion see "The birth of analytic philosophy," Chapter 1 and "Naturalism," Chapter 6.) Moritz Schlick (1882–1936) formulated the thesis thus in an early paper: "an absolutely complete description of the world is possible by the use of physical methods; … every event in the world can be described in the language of physics" (1935: 426). Rudolf Carnap (1891–1970) preferred to use the formal mode, regarding it as less misleading: "*physical language is a universal language*, that is, a language into which every sentence may be translated" (1932: 165). Ultimately this thesis was derived from the claim that statements in physical language are intersubjectively testable or confirmable. Schlick argues that intersubjective confirmability (objectivity) is essential to a language, "for without it the language could not serve as a means by which different subjects could arrive at an understanding" (1935: 426). As a matter of contingent empirical fact, Schlick argues, physical language provides such a means; statements in it are intersubjectively confirmable. Carnap calls it a "fortunate accident" that physical determinations are valid inter-sensorily and inter-subjectively (1934: 62, 65): "The determined value of a physical magnitude in any given case is independent not only of the particular sensory field used but also of the choice of the experimenter" (1934: 64). Different subjects agree in their reports of coincidences in the space-time order (Schlick 1935: 425). Of course this fortunate accident does not exclude the possibility that some other language enables intersubjective confirmability, but no such language is known (Carnap 1934: 96). Thus the claim that physical language *alone* permits intersubjective agreement is an empirical one (Schlick 1935: 427). That a meaningful statement must be intersubjectively confirmable is regarded as an analytic truth; that such statements can and must be couched in physical language is an empirical truth. On this view, the extent to which statements couched in psychological (or any other) language are intersubjectively confirmable is precisely the extent to which they are translatable into physical language, and precisely the extent to which they are meaningful. Of course the positivists had to account for the meaningfulness of mathematical statements, but these they regarded as true in virtue of meaning alone, as analytic and not empirical.

Carnap (1932) attempts to show that psychological statements can be translated into physical language by using an analogy between a sentence about the state of another's mind (e.g. "Mr A is now excited") and a sentence about a dispositional property of a physical object (e.g. "this wooden support is firm"). Both assert the existence of a physical structure characterized by the disposition to react in a specific manner to specific physical stimuli (1932: 172). This microstructural property of Mr A's body is specified in terms of the effects to which it gives rise, such as rapid pulse and "vehement and unsatisfactory answers to questions" (p. 172). Advances in science may be needed before we can describe this physical state in physiological terms, but the sentence about Mr A's excitement refers to a physical state nonetheless.

Carnap considers an "objection on the ground of analogy": that we experience a special feeling of anger when we are angry, as well as behaving in characteristic ways (recall Broad's objection that behaviorism leaves something out). We may conclude by analogy that others who behave in these characteristic ways probably have the same feeling. Carnap responds that analogy cannot be applied here. The objector seeks to argue from the premise "When I behave angrily, I feel anger" to the conclusion "When A behaves angrily, A feels anger." But, Carnap argues, the subject-predicate form of the premise is misleading. "I feel anger" does not assert that a property belongs to an entity; it simply records the existence of a feeling of anger ("anger now" or "anger occurs"). Correctly formulated, the premise reads "when I behave angrily, anger occurs." But now there is no argument from analogy. "When I behave angrily, anger occurs" and "A is now behaving angrily" cannot support the conclusion "A feels anger" (1932: 177).

However, people obviously do use sentences like "I feel anger." Carnap's analysis of sentences about the present state of one's own mind distinguishes *system* sentences such as "I am angry" from *protocol* sentences such as "(I am) angry now." Protocol sentences are the data; they need no justification and serve as foundation for all knowledge. In the misleading material mode, they refer to the given, to immediate experience (1934: 45). A system sentence such as "I am angry" may be *rationally* derived from protocol sentences recording the behavioral signs of anger (e.g. "My hands are now trembling") or *intuitively* derived from protocol sentences recording immediate perceptions such as "Anger now" (pp. 170–1, 193). But however it is justified, the sentence "I am angry" states that my body is in a certain physical state. My protocol sentence "Anger now" must be translatable into physical language if it is to be verifiable by another person; and it can be intelligible to another only if it is verifiable by another. When the speaker is competent and sincere, his avowal of his own mental state serves as a sign of the very state which it describes (p. 196). That which is private and subjective cannot be spoken of, if language is (as Schlick argued) essentially public and objective. A sentence which referred to a non-physical experience could not be understood by anyone other than the subject of the experience; it would be a sentence of a solipsistic language (pp. 78–80). As Carnap notes, establishing that physical language is a universal language would not show that "the present system of physical laws is sufficient to explain all phenomena" (p. 98). But it would show that any meaningful statement is about a physical phenomenon, and thereby dispose of Broad's Distinct Property argument.

The account of mental states given by Carnap (1934) is similar to one later advanced by David Armstrong (see the subsection "Armstrong and Lewis," below). Both regard mental states as physical states of the body underlying a disposition to react in certain ways to certain stimuli. Carl Hempel's "The logical analysis of psychology" (1949) presents a view closer to textbook logical or analytical behaviorism. According to the textbook version, statements about minds are translatable without loss of meaning into statements about behavior alone. Hempel's argument starts from the claim that knowing the meaning of a statement is knowing the conditions under which it would be verified; so, he concludes, the meaning of a statement is established by the conditions of its verification. Two statements have the same meaning just in case they are true or false in the same conditions. Now, a psychological statement such as "Paul has a toothache" is verified in circumstances in which Paul utters certain words and makes certain gestures, and Paul's body exhibits certain physiological conditions. Hence this psychological statement has the same meaning as the conjunction of the "test sentences" describing its verification conditions. It is "simply an abbreviated expression of … all its test sentences" (1949: 17). But even this is not textbook analytical behaviorism, since the translation includes non-behavioral test sentences referring to processes in Paul's central nervous system. It is scarcely credible that knowledge of such verification conditions is required for understanding the everyday meaning of "Paul has a toothache." The inclusion of such verification conditions in the meaning of the original statement also has the consequence that the development of a new way of verifying the statement makes for a change in its meaning. Consequences such as these were exploited by Hilary Putnam (1968) in his influential attack on logical behaviorism, discussed below in the section "Problems with behaviorism".

Ordinary-language philosophy

The logical positivists pursued a program of reform: traditional philosophical problems were to be dissolved by the adoption of a physical language suitable for science. By contrast, ordinary-language philosophers sought to dissolve such traditional problems through an analysis of everyday usage. One of the most influential examples of this approach is Gilbert Ryle's *The Concept of Mind* (1949) (see also "The development of analytic philosophy: Wittgenstein and after," Chapter 2). This work has been described as "a remarkable literary object and perhaps the best book to read to get an idea of the linguistic philosophy of the period 1945–60" (Quinton, recorded in Magee 1971: 10). Quinton credits it with making philosophy of mind a central field of interest in that period.

Ryle's book begins with an attack on what he takes as the received philosophical view of the mind, "Descartes's Myth" of the ghost in the machine: the para-mechanical hypothesis of an immaterial consciousness interacting with a material body. He claims that the myth originates in a category mistake, a mistake about the logical type to which mental concepts belong. According to the myth, minds are things which are the subjects of mental states, in which mental processes, changes, causes, and effects take place. They differ from bodies, which are the subjects of physical states, and in which physical processes, changes, causes, and effects take place, in being non-physical. Intelligent human behavior has non-mechanical (mental) causes, while unintelligent behavior has mechanical (physical) causes. Since these non-mechanical causes cannot be observed – they are private, accessible only to the mind in which they occur – onlookers cannot tell whether some behavior is genuinely intelligent or not. But this, Ryle argues, shows the absurdity of the myth. Descartes sought to explain how minded beings differ from mere machines. But the explanation he gave made it impossible in practice to tell the difference between them, since we have no access to the "postulated immaterial causes" of the behavior of other minded beings (1949: 21). For Ryle, the fact that we apply mental-conduct concepts "regularly and effectively" to others without such access shows that Descartes's causal hypothesis must be false (p. 21).

Most of Ryle's book is devoted to the positive task of "rectify[ing] the logic of mental-conduct concepts" (1949: 16) through an examination of their use. One of the central category mistakes he diagnoses is that of treating *hypothetical* statements about how someone is disposed to behave as *categorical* statements about hidden episodes and processes occurring in that person's immaterial mind. The clown and the clumsy person may trip and fall in just the same way; but the clown's fall is intelligent and deliberate, while the clumsy person's fall is neither. According to the Cartesian myth, the clown's fall is intelligent and deliberate because it has a certain immaterial mental cause, witnessable only by the clown; that is why what makes the difference cannot be seen in the fall itself, which is simply a bodily movement. But according to Ryle, what makes the difference must be something we spectators can witness; otherwise we could never know that the clown's fall is deliberate, while the clumsy person's is not. We come to know this by observing other aspects of the clown's behavior: "he trips and tumbles on purpose and after much rehearsal and at the golden moment and where the children can see him and so as not to hurt himself" (p. 33). The clown's fall is the exercise of a skill, while the clumsy person's is not. But to say this is to say something general and hypothetical, something about how the clown is disposed to act on other occasions. It is not to say something categorical about this particular occasion: that his fall is the effect of an unseen inner act. A disposition is "of the wrong logical type to be seen or unseen" (p. 33). The traditional myth has misconstrued the contrast between an unwitnessable disposition and its witnessable exercise as the contrast between unwitnessable mental causes and their witnessable physical effects (p. 33).

Ryle's treatment of motives provides an important example of the central role he assigns to dispositions. Actions are frequently explained in terms of motives. Suppose we say that a skater is keeping to the edge of the pond because he fears the ice is thin. According to the Cartesian myth as Ryle construes it, this means that the skater's behavior is *caused* by a *feeling* of fear. This account makes two assumptions about the motive for the skater's action: that it is a feeling, and that it is the cause of the action. Ryle rejects both assumptions. He argues that motives are not feelings, but dispositions; and that to explain an action in terms of a motive is not to give its cause, but to reveal it as the manifestation of a disposition. "The imputation of a motive for a particular action is not a causal inference to an unwitnessed event but the subsumption of an episode proposition under a law-like proposition. It is therefore analogous to … the explanation of the fracture of the glass by reference to its brittleness" (1949: 90). To ascribe the dispositional property of brittleness to the glass is to assert a law-like general hypothetical proposition: "that the glass, *if* sharply struck or twisted, etc. *would* not dissolve or stretch or evaporate but fly into fragments" (p. 89). To say that the glass fractured when struck *because* it was brittle is to say that it fractured when it was struck, and that is the sort of thing it would do. To say that the skater kept to the edge *because* he feared that the ice was thin is to say that he kept to the edge, and that is the sort of thing he would do. "It is to say 'he *would* do that'" (p. 93).

Obviously this non-causal account of motive explanations is grounded in Ryle's analysis of motives as dispositions. If having some motive just is behaving in a certain way, the motive is not sufficiently distinct from the behavior to be its cause. Moreover, Ryle assumes with his Cartesian opponent that causes are events or happenings (1949: 88); since dispositions are neither, they are not even the right kinds of thing to be causes (though feelings are). But Ryle sees no alternative to his dispositional account. If motives were feelings privy only to their possessors, as the Cartesian has it, others' motives could never be discovered; but we do discover others' motives, by observing regularities in their behavior which justify us in asserting law-like propositions about them (p. 90). We discover our own motives in the same way. In general, Ryle holds that "the sorts of things that I can find out about myself are the same as the sorts of things I can find out about other people, and the methods of finding them out are much the same" (p. 155). This view reflects his rejection of the notion of "Privileged Access" (p. 154) and his non-causal account of mental dispositions. If to attribute a belief to me is to assert a hypothetical proposition about how I am disposed to behave in certain circumstances, and the disposition itself is not a causal factor in the production of that behavior, I can presumably only come to know that I have it by observing regularities in my behavior.

Many of the themes of *The Concept of Mind* are also themes in the work of the later Wittgenstein. The Blue and Brown books, precursors of Wittgenstein's *Philosophical Investigations* (1953), circulated in Oxford and Cambridge before the Second World War, and exerted an important influence in postwar Oxford philosophy (Magee 1971: 10). Methodologically, Wittgenstein and Ryle both think that philosophical mistakes can be dissolved by a proper attention to linguistic usage; and both regard the view of the mind which Ryle calls Cartesian as a philosophical mistake. (For discussion of Ryle's notion of a category mistake, see "The development of analytic philosophy: Wittgenstein and after," Chapter 2.) Both stress the irrelevance of inner feelings or experiences to questions of meaning and understanding; both deny that meaning and understanding are inner processes (Ryle 1949: 295; Wittgenstein 1953: §154). For Wittgenstein, the meaning of a word is its use in a language-game, not an inner process accompanying it use. Both stress the importance of behavioral criteria for the application of mental terms. However, there are also important differences between their views. Unlike Ryle, Wittgenstein holds that avowals such as "I am in pain" do not express knowledge; they are expressions of pain, rather than reports of it (1953: §244). And he offers an influential argument against the possibility of a private language, a language which is unintelligible to others because its terms refer to the private experiences of its user (§§243, 256). The terms of the private language would have to be associated with the sensations they name by private ostensive definition. Wittgenstein imagines concentrating one's attention on a sensation when it occurs, thinking "*This* is called S." But this does not serve to define the correct use of "S," since it does not specify the criteria a thing must satisfy to be relevantly similar to the paradigm. Wittgenstein concludes, "in the present case I have no criterion of correctness. One would like to say: Whatever is going to seem right to me is right. And that only means that here we can't talk about 'right'" (§258). When can we talk about "right"? Wittgenstein states that there are "criteria in a man's behaviour ... for his understanding [a] word right" (§269); it is precisely because such criteria are public that they can fix correct usage. The sensation as private object "drops out of consideration as irrelevant" to the question of meaning (§293). Famously, Wittgenstein concludes that "An 'inner process' stands in need of outward criteria" (§580). The view that claims about the mind must be criterially or logically connected to outward behavior links Wittgenstein with Ryle.

Problems with behaviorism

Jerry Fodor (1935–) once said that the original sin of the behaviorist tradition is the confusion of mentalism with dualism. (For further discussion of behaviorism and its critique, see "Philosophy of psychology," Chapter 13.) Fodor's point is that the behaviorists did not envisage the possibility of a materialistic mentalism: a view according to which there are states and processes which are mental, but also physical. There is certainly some truth in this as applied to Ryle, who tends to argue as though dualism and behaviorism exhaust the alternatives. But Fodor's dictum is misleading if it suggests that the behaviorist opposition to mentalism was primarily metaphysical, an opposition to *immaterial* entities. Behaviorist opposition to mentalism was primarily epistemological, an opposition to *private* entities. In the case of the logical positivists, the dualism they reject is a methodological one: the view that the mind cannot be studied by the methods of the natural sciences. They have no objection to entities which are mental *and* physical, since, being physical, they are intersubjectively available. In the case of Wittgenstein, the opposition to private entities is clear. In the case of Ryle, if there is a confusion, it is a confusion of private entities with immaterial entities. He complains that the mental states of the dualist myth are ghostly, when his true complaint is that they are occult, or hidden. His presentation of "the official doctrine" concentrates on its epistemological elements:

> When someone is described as knowing, believing or guessing something, as hoping, dreading, intending or shirking something, as designing this or being amused at that, these verbs are supposed to denote the occurrence of specific modifications in his (to us) occult stream of consciousness. Only his own privileged access to this stream in direct awareness and introspection could provide authentic testimony that these mental-conduct verbs were correctly or incorrectly applied. (Ryle 1949: 15)

What Ryle really objects to in this doctrine is the conjunction of two claims:

1 that mental phenomena are private episodes, and
2 that these episodes are the causes of public behavior.

So Ryle rejects a materialist account of mental phenomena for the same reason that he rejects a dualist account: he regards it as committed to claims (1) and (2).

Of course the physical occurrences with which the materialist mentalist identifies mental phenomena are not private *in principle*, as the dualist's episodes in a stream of consciousness are; but they are certainly not open to observation in the ordinary course of things. Mental-conduct verbs are applied to others on the basis of observation of their public behavior, not on the basis of observation of their brains. Motives construed as neural events would still be imputed on the basis of "a causal inference to an unwitnessed event" (1949: 90); and this, fundamentally, is what Ryle rejects.

If we are looking for the original sin of the behaviorist tradition, verificationism has a better claim to be the culprit. A crude form of behaviorism, which claims that statements containing mental terms can be translated into statements about behavior, is refuted by showing that no such translations can be given. "Paul has a toothache" is not even equivalent in truth-value to a conjunction of statements about behavior couched in purely physical terms. Even if he has a toothache, Paul will only say "Yes" when asked "Do you have a toothache?" if he understands English and wants to answer truthfully. But more sophisticated forms of behaviorism, such as Ryle's, do not make such claims of translatability. Ryle does not assume a verificationist theory of meaning; his behaviorism is motivated by a conception of justification rather than a conception of meaning.

Ryle argues that attributions of mental states and processes cannot be claims about private episodes in consciousness, because such claims could not be justified by observations of behavior alone. In effect, he reasons as follows:

1 At least some attributions of mental states to others are justified.
2 Such attributions are made on the basis of observations of behavior alone.
3 All that such observations can justify are claims about behavioral dispositions.
4 Therefore, attributions of mental states must be claims about behavioral dispositions.

Claims about private episodes in consciousness "would lack any possibility of observational corroboration" (1949: 14–15). They are "untestable" (p. 46). One might observe a correlation between episodes in one's own consciousness and movements of one's own body, and hypothesize that similar movements of others' bodies are correlated with similar episodes in their consciousnesses; but the hypothesis could never be corroborated by observation of the hypothesized episodes. "It would be like water-divining in places where well-sinking was forbidden" (p. 90). We cannot directly observe others' behavioral dispositions, but via "an inductive process" we can justify claims about them through observation of their previous behavior (p. 90). Given premise (3), which expresses the crucial assumption about justification, attributions of mental states must be claims about behavioral dispositions.

For Ryle and the Wittgensteinian tradition, the relationship between mental states and behavior is logical or criterial and not causal. This claim came under increasing pressure in the 1960s. The behaviorist presupposes that unless there are behavioral criteria for the application of mental predicates – that is, behavioral conditions in which the application of the mental predicate is guaranteed to be correct, as a matter of conceptual necessity – then no applications of mental predicates could be justified. Since there are such criteria, the application of mental predicates can be justified. But since these criteria are fixed by the meaning of the predicates in question (the concepts they express), any change in criteria is a change in meaning (a change in concept expressed). Opponents such as Putnam (1968) and Chihara and Fodor (1965) argued that the conception of justification which motivates the behaviorist analysis is flawed; they claimed that mental states are causally related to behavior, and attributions of mental states are justified by inference to the best explanation.

Putnam exploits an analogy with disease concepts such as that of polio. Before the viral origin for polio was discovered, the disease was diagnosed by the presence of certain symptoms; once the virus was discovered, infection with the virus became diagnostic. It then became plain that there were asymptomatic cases of polio, and cases where the symptoms but not the virus were present. If the symptoms were taken to be criteria, one would have to say that the meaning of "polio" changed after the discovery. So a prescient doctor who said of an asymptomatic case, "this is polio" before the discovery of the virus must have been speaking falsely. But this claim is hardly plausible. The discovery of the virus made for a new way of testing for the presence of the same disease, not a change of subject. Statements about polio are not translatable into statements about symptoms, because causes are not logical constructions out of their effects (Putnam 1968: 7). If the relationship between pains and behavior is similarly causal, the attribution of pains to others can be justified on the basis of the fact that this (along with the attribution of other mental states) provides the best explanation of their behavior. "Such justifications depend … on appeals to the simplicity, plausibility, and predictive adequacy of an explanatory system as a whole" (Chihara and Fodor 1965: 292).

Brentano's thesis and the flight from intension

In a paper published in 1956 entitled "Sentences about believing," Roderick M. Chisholm (1916–99) argued that the use of "intentional language" was essential in describing mental phenomena, and that the behaviorist attempt to translate psychological statements into purely physical language must therefore fail (1956; see also Chisholm 1957: ch. 11). Chisholm's criticisms of behaviorism were important, but his work was especially influential for its exposition and defense of what he called Brentano's thesis: the thesis that intentionality is the mark of the mental.

Chisholm (1957) quotes Brentano's claim that all mental phenomena are

> characterised by what the scholastics of the Middle Ages referred to as the intentional (or mental) inexistence of an object, and what we might call, though not wholly unambiguously, reference to a content, direction toward an object (which is not to be understood here as meaning a thing), or immanent objectivity. (Brentano 1874: 88).

As Chisholm notes, Brentano claims that this intentional inexistence differentiates the mental from the physical: "No physical phenomenon exhibits anything like it' (Brentano 1874: 89).

Brentano was the founder of the phenomenological tradition (see "Phenomenology," Chapter 15) and centrally concerned with the phenomenological analysis of the way in which objects are presented to consciousness. Chisholm did not share these interests; his version of Brentano's thesis is a thesis about language.[3] His linguistic version states that intentional language is essential for the description of mental phenomena, but not essential for the description of physical phenomena. Moreover, intentional sentences cannot be translated into non-intentional sentences. Contrary to the claims of the logical positivists, "the language of physical things" is not adequate for the description of psychological phenomena. (Arguments from Ayer and Carnap are criticized in Chisholm 1957.)

What does Chisholm mean by "intentional language"? A non-compound intentional sentence as he defines it is a sentence satisfying at least one of three criteria:

1 Neither it nor its negation implies the existence or nonexistence of any thing referred to by the purportedly referring terms which it contains.
2 If it contains a propositional clause, neither it nor its negation implies that the propositional clause is true or that it is false.
3 Its truth-value can be altered by substituting a co-referring singular term for a singular term which it contains.

Chisholm's first and third criteria for the intentionality of sentences are essentially the same as the two criteria for what came to be known as the intensionality of contexts: failure of existential generalization and failure of substitutivity. Consider Chisholm's example of a sentence satisfying his first criterion of intentionality:

(a) Diogenes looked for an honest man.

(a) does not imply that there are any honest men to be found. So we cannot represent it thus:

(b) There is an x such that x is an honest man and Diogenes looked for x,

since (b) does imply that there is at least one honest man. There is a singular term in (a) to which existential generalization cannot be applied; so (a) contains an intensional context. Consider an example of a sentence satisfying Chisholm's third criterion of intentionality:

(c) Ada believes that the Evening Star is bright.

From (c) and

(d) The Evening Star = the Morning Star

we cannot infer

(e) Ada believes that the Morning Star is bright.

Suppose that (c) is true, but Ada is ignorant of (d) and even denies that the Morning Star is bright. It seems that (e) is false. Substituting the occurrence of "the Evening Star" in (c) with a co-referring term has changed the sentence's truth-value; so (c) contains an intensional context. In terminology popularized by Quine (1960: §30), (a) and (c) contain terms in positions which are opaque (to substitution and quantification).

Quine notes that "believes" and other mental verbs may be transparent or opaque (1960: 145). We may say, despite Ada's denials, that since the Evening Star is the Morning Star, and she believes that the Evening Star is bright, she believes that the Morning Star is bright. (e) is true on the transparent reading of "belief" but not on the opaque reading, while (c) is true on both. This distinction between what Quine calls the transparent and opaque senses of belief is now more commonly made in different terminology, which he also popularized: the terminology of *de re* (transparent) and *de dicto* (opaque) attitude ascriptions. (c) interpreted as an ascription of belief in the transparent sense may be represented thus, quantifying into the referentially transparent position within the scope of the verb:

(e′) There is an *x* such that *x* is the Evening Star and Ada believes that *x* is bright.

This is the *de re* reading, since Ada's belief is said to relate her to an object (*res*). If (c) is interpreted in the opaque sense, the quantifier stays within the scope of the verb:

(e″) Ada believes that *there is an x such that x* is the Evening Star and *x* is bright.

This is the *de dicto* reading, which relates Ada to a proposition or dictum.

Willard Van Orman Quine (1908–2000) took up Chisholm's linguistic version of Brentano's thesis in his highly influential book *Word and Object* (1960). He agreed with Chisholm's view that "there is no breaking out of the intentional vocabulary by explaining its members in other terms" (Quine 1960: 220), but drew a very different conclusion:

> Brentano's thesis of the irreducibility of intentional idioms is of a piece with the thesis of the indeterminacy of translation. One may accept the Brentano thesis either as showing the indispensability of intentional idioms and the importance of an autonomous science of intention, or as showing the baselessness of intentional idioms and the emptiness of a science of intention. My attitude, unlike Brentano's, is the second. (1960: 221)

To understand the first claim Quine makes here, we must turn to his thesis of the indeterminacy of translation. Quine considers the situation of the radical translator, who has to construct a translation manual for an unknown and unfamiliar language simply by observing the verbal behavior of its native speakers. His conclusion is that this project could be completed in different ways: "manuals for translating one language into another can be set up in divergent ways, all compatible with the totality of speech dispositions, yet incompatible with one another" (1960: 27). Suppose the translator is in the jungle with a native informant; a rabbit hops by, and the informant says "gavagai." Quine argues that "gavagai" can be translated as *rabbit* or as *rabbit-stage*, modulo compensating adjustments:

> if ... we take "are the same" as translation of some construction in the jungle language, we may proceed on that basis to question our informant about sameness of gavagais from occasion to occasion and so conclude that gavagais are rabbits and not stages. But if instead we take "are stages of the same animal" as translation of that jungle construction, we will conclude from the same subsequent questioning of our informant that gavagais are rabbit stages. (1960: 72)

Quine concludes that linguistic meaning is indeterminate, since it is not fully determined by the totality of speech dispositions. But, he argues, the intentional vocabulary delineated by Chisholm represents the meaning of terms as determinate; "gavagai" means "rabbit" just in case the speaker is disposed to apply it to what he believes to be rabbits. Only if the speaker is disposed to apply it to what he believes to be rabbit-stages does it mean "rabbit-stage" (1960: 220). But no distinction in behavioral dispositions corresponds to this putative distinction in meaning and belief. Hence intentional idioms cannot be translated into behavioral ones (Chisholm's irreducibility thesis); but hence too Quine's conclusion that a science of intention is empty. The determinacy of intentional objects that such a science assumes is an illusion fostered by an "uncritical mentalistic theory of ideas" (p. 4): the myth of the mental museum of meanings (Quine 1969). The intentional idioms, talk of what people want and believe, are indispensable in daily life, but the scientist must forswear them:

> if we are limning the true and ultimate structure of reality, the canonical scheme for us is the austere scheme that knows no quotation but direct quotation and no propositional attitudes but only the physical constitution and behavior of organisms. (1960: 221)

The reference to direct quotation here reflects Quine's account of propositional attitude ascriptions. We can quote or report others' words directly "in the strictest scientific spirit," "almost as we might a bird call," and do so accurately or inaccurately (1960: 218–19). When we come to indirect quotation, saying what others mean or what they think, we leave the realm of objective reporting for that of imaginative projection: "we project ourselves into what, from his remarks and other indications, we imagine the speaker's state of mind to have been, and then we say what, in our language, is natural and relevant to us in the state thus feigned" (p. 219). There are no clear standards for the accuracy of what is "an essentially dramatic act" (p. 219).

Quine's indeterminacy thesis and his attack on the myth of the mental museum converged with Wittgenstein's attack on private language to fuel suspicion about the idea of determinate mental meanings. His remarks about the prospects for a science of intention presented defenders of intentional psychology with a dilemma: either such a psychology will be autonomous and vacuous, or it will be reducible and dispensable. Some philosophers who reject Quine's behaviorist approach to language, such as Fodor, have accepted the challenge of *naturalizing* intentionality, or explaining it without the help of semantic or intentional notions (Quine 1960: 220; Fodor 1987: ch. 4).

Brentano's thesis that intentionality is the mark of the mental attracted renewed interest later in the century. When Richard Rorty (1980) raised again Brentano's question of what differentiates mental phenomena from others, he remarked that "the attempt to hitch pains and beliefs together seems ad hoc – they don't seem to have anything in common except our refusal to call them 'physical'" (1980: 22). He rejected Brentano's answer on the grounds that pains are not intentional: "they do not represent, they are not *about* anything" (ibid.). But later philosophers defended Brentano's thesis, arguing for example that pains are sensory representations of damage to the body (e.g. Tye 1990; see Crane 1998 for a different account of the intentionality of pains).

Chisholm's linguistic reinterpretation of Brentano's thesis should be distinguished from the original. Chisholm makes three claims: that intensionality is the criterion of the intentional, that intentionality so defined is the mark of the mental, and that intentionality so defined is irreducible. The first claim is implausible; modal state-ments are intensional in that they can be opaque to substitution, and admit of *de re* and *de dicto* readings. But the idea that the nature of propositional attitudes can be illuminated by studying the semantics of attitude ascriptions – a descendant of the "linguistic turn" applied by Chisholm and Quine – was very influential. There was a period of intense debate about the interpretation of *de re* ascriptions, with some claiming that *de re* beliefs involve a special direct relation to their objects (Burge 1977). This fed into the debate about externalism and object-dependent thought (see the section "Mental content," below) in ways which were not always helpful. Obviously a theory of belief must be informed by what we say about beliefs, but caution is needed in moving from claims about the logical form of belief ascriptions to claims about the nature of beliefs. The existence of two kinds of belief reports, *de re* and *de dicto*, does not by itself establish the existence of two kinds of belief involving different objects; further argument is needed to support the inference.

Materialism

Quine (1960) took the view that "the true and ultimate structure of reality" is physical, but stopped short of identifying mental states with physical states (although he later expressed sympathy with the view; see Quine 1990). However, versions of mind/brain identity theory were advanced by U. T. Place (1924–2000) in 1956, by Herbert Feigl in 1958 and by J. J. C. Smart (1920–) in 1959. Place's influential paper emerged from discussions with C. B. Martin and J. J. C. Smart at the University of Adelaide, during which Smart was converted from behaviorism to materialism (Presley 1967). The view was for a time known as "Australian materialism," although Smart was influenced by Feigl's work (Heil 1989).

It is notable that all three of these advocates restricted their original claim of identity to phenomenal states, thereby endorsing the idea that intentional and phenomenal states should be given separate treatment. The reason for the restriction to phenomenal states in the work of Place and Smart was the belief that a behaviorist approach to intentional states such as believing and wanting was basically sound (Place 1956: 44). Only in the case of phenomenal states was an analysis in terms of behavioral dispositions inadequate: "there would seem to be an intractable residue of concepts clustering around the notions of consciousness, experience, sensation, and mental imagery, where some sort of inner process story is unavoidable" (Place 1956: 44; see also Smart 1959: 144). Feigl's reason for restricting the identity claim to phenomenal states is different. He certainly agrees that a behaviorist analysis of such states is inadequate, but holds that the same is true of a behaviorist analysis of intentional states (Feigl 1958: 394–5). His reason for not proposing that intentional states are neural states is the problem of naturalizing intentionality. Intentionality is a logical notion, not a purely psychological one (1958: 417–18), and it would be "a category mistake of the most glaring sort" (p. 445) to identify intentionality with a physical phenomenon; designation is not an empirical relation (p. 418).

These early pioneers of materialism saw their main task as defending the cogency of mind/brain identity claims against charges of conceptual confusion. The first goal was to argue that the identity thesis *could* be true; arguing that it *was* true took second place. As Place put it in the abstract of his paper, "The thesis that consciousness is a process in the brain is put forward as a reasonable scientific hypothesis, not to be dismissed on logical [sc. conceptual] grounds alone" (1956: 44). He pointed out that "table" and "old packing-case" do not mean the same thing, and nor do "lightning" and "motion of electric charges"; but for all that, it may be true that

(1) His table is an old packing-case,

and it is true that

(2) Lightning is a motion of electric charges.

These statements are not true by definition; they are not necessary truths, as can be seen by the fact that their denial is not self-contradictory. (1) and (2) are contingent truths which can only be verified empirically (1956: 45). The truth of (2) is established because a well-confirmed scientific theory enables us to explain observations of lightning as the effect of motions of electric charges through the atmosphere. When we observe flashes of lightning, we are observing motions of electrical charges. Similarly, Place argues, if it could be shown that "the introspective observations reported by the subject can be accounted for in terms of processes which are known to have occurred in his brain," this would establish that consciousness is a process in the brain (p. 48).

What would it be for such introspective observations to be explained by brain processes? Place cautions against what he calls the "phenomenological fallacy" (1956: 49). This leads to the mistaken belief that the subject's report that she sees a green afterimage, for example, can only be explained by positing a green object on which she is reporting. Since no brain process is green, this belief excludes any explanation in terms of brain processes. The phenomenological fallacy derives from the assumption that ascriptions of real properties (properties of objects) are parasitic on ascriptions of phenomenal properties (properties of experiences). In fact, Place argues, the reverse is true; descriptions of experiences are parasitic on descriptions of objects. The subject uses "green" to describe her afterimage because her experience is similar to the experience she has when she sees a green object. Suppose the physiologist discovers that the brain process which is causing the subject to describe her experience in this way is the sort which normally occurs when she is seeing something green (Place 1956: 50). Then the subject's introspective observation of her experience will be explained by the brain process.

This approach to introspective reports of experience is a precursor of the "topic-neutral" analysis advanced by Smart (1959). Smart offers his analysis in response to Objection 3, a version of Broad's Distinct Property argument advanced by Max Black (1909–88). Like Broad's, the argument concludes that "the qualities of sensations are something over and above the qualities of brain-processes" (Smart 1959: 148). So it threatens the materialist with a residue of "irreducibly psychic" properties. How does Smart respond to this objection? Like Place, Smart insists the identity thesis is a contingent thesis, to be established empirically and a posteriori. This claim is central to their defense of the cogency of the thesis: if it is contingent, if it makes a claim of fact, not meaning, it cannot be confirmed *or refuted* a priori by linguistic considerations. In this respect, it resembles this identity statement:

(3) The evening star is the morning star.

This statement is contingent because the property of being the star that appears in the evening is distinct from the property of being the star that appears in the morning. As it happens, the same thing has both properties; so two expressions which pick it out via its possession of different properties pick out the same thing. Now consider:

(4) The experience of a green afterimage is a brain process of kind X.

Again, Smart claims that two expressions with different meanings may refer to the same thing. But they must pick out the thing via different properties it possesses, otherwise the statement would be a necessary one, known to be true a priori. But this seems to imply that the property of being an experience of a green afterimage is a non-physical or irreducibly psychic property, leaving us with the Distinct Property objection. Smart's solution is to analyze the property in question in topic-neutral terms, as a relational property. He proposes that "I see a yellowish-orange afterimage" means "There is something going on which is like what is going on when I see an orange" (1959: 149). This relational property of the experience is distinct from the property of being a brain process of kind X, so the identity claim is contingent; but it is not an irreducibly psychic property.

Feigl, like Smart, formulates the identity theory in semantic terms: the referents of phenomenal terms of the language of introspection, raw feels, may as a matter of empirical fact be identical to the referents of terms of neurophysiological language, neural events (1958: 447). The object of knowledge by acquaintance is identical with the object of knowledge by (neurophysiological) description (pp. 446, 448). Place, Smart, and Feigl assume that the truth of the identity thesis would be empirically established only if correlations between kinds of experience and kinds of brain process were observed. Smart emphasizes the view that the adoption of a claim of identity rather than simple correlation would be justified on methodological grounds of parsimony and simplicity (1959: 156). To rest with mere correlation would be to leave a comprehensive, unified physical theory disfigured by what Feigl called nomological danglers, irreducible laws correlating hugely complex physical states with sensations.

Smart's topic-neutral analyses of the meaning of reports of experience have generally been regarded as unsatisfactory (e.g. Shaffer 1963). But the relational aspect of topic-neutral analysis made it an important precursor of the functionalist approach to the mind (see the section "Functionalism," below). Smart's insistence on the contingency of the identity thesis made him vulnerable to Kripke's attack on the notion of contingent identity. Kripke's work was instrumental in revising the semantic and epistemological framework within which Smart had formulated and defended the identity theory (see Boyd 1980 for discussion).

Kripke's conceivability argument

Smart responded to the objections that one could talk and think about sensations without knowing about brains, and that we can imagine having sensations but not having a body, by stressing the fact that the identity thesis is, if true, contingently true. It is an empirical claim, to be established a posteriori via investigation, not a priori via conceptual analysis. Similarly, we can imagine that lightning is not electrical discharge, but it is; this just shows that the identity is contingent, not necessary. However, Kripke argued that theoretical identities such as "Lightning is a motion of electric charges" and "Heat is molecular motion" are, if true, necessarily true, although they are neither analytic nor knowable a priori. According to his analysis, these statements involve natural kind terms which are *rigid designators*: they refer to the same thing in every possible world. This being so, if these natural kind terms co-refer in the actual world, they co-refer in every possible world. Smart and Feigl formulate the identity theory in terms of co-reference: to say that pain is C-fiber firing is to say that the terms "pain" and "C-fiber firing" refer to the same thing, as a matter of empirical fact. But if "pain" and "C-fiber firing" are natural kind terms, they co-refer in every possible world if they co-refer in the actual world. So if the identity statement is true, it is necessarily true. Of course it is not *analytically* true, since it is true not in virtue of the meanings of words, but in virtue of facts about what they refer to; so its truth is not knowable a priori. The identity theorists are right about that. But they are wrong if they think they can accommodate the intuition that there could be pain in the absence of brain processes – what Kripke calls the "Cartesian intuition" – by saying that the identity thesis is only contingently true (Kripke 1972: 148).

However, there may be a way out for the identity theorist, if the Cartesian intuition can be shown to be misleading. Consider Smart's response to the intuition: "I can imagine that the electrical theory of lightning is false, that lightning is merely some sort of optical phenomenon" (1959: 152). Yet according to Kripke's analysis (2), if true, is necessarily true; so the appearance of contingency must be misleading. Kripke's analysis of the lightning case is this: what we imagine is a situation in which flashes of light in the sky turn out to be an optical, not an electrical phenomenon. But that is a situation in which something that looks like lightning, something qualitatively indistinguishable from lightning to observers, is not an electrical phenomenon. Contra Smart's description, it is not a situation in which *lightning* is not an electrical but an optical phenomenon. Given that lightning *is* an electrical phenomenon, such a situation is impossible. Thus Kripke accounts for the illusion that (2) is contingent. However, he argues, the identity theorist cannot apply this way out to

(5) Pain is C-fiber firing.

A situation in which there is something that feels like pain, something qualitatively indistinguishable from pain, without C-fiber firing just *is* a situation in which there is pain without C-fiber firing. This is because something qualitatively indistinguishable from pain just *is* pain (Kripke 1972: 152). There is no room for illusion here, and so no room for an illusion of contingency. The intuition of contingency is an intuition of the real possibility of pain existing without C-fiber firing, Kripke claims, and this implies the falsity of (5).

Most responses to Kripke's objection in the literature of the time challenged his Cartesian assumption that the essence of pain is manifest in how it feels. The most direct response rejected his assumption that something qualitatively indistinguishable from pain is pain. Advocates of this move took a robustly materialist line, holding that pain could turn out to be a type of sensation with a physical essence (e.g. Lycan 1987). The more popular response was to argue that Kripke's argument was irrelevant, since the most plausible account of mental states was not committed to the type of identities, exemplified by (5), which were its target. One such response exploits a distinction between particular or token pains, felt by a specific individual at a specific time, and pain as a type of experience. It was argued that a token identity thesis, identifying particular pains with particular physical occurrences, was not vulnerable to Kripke's objection. A pain which feels just like the pain I felt in my toe last Thursday is not ipso facto the same thing as that pain; so token identity claims allow for an illusion of contingency (McGinn 1977). Another response was to advocate a functionalist account which allowed for the possibility of non-physical realizations of mental states. Kripke's challenge received renewed attention with the resurgence of interest in phenomenal consciousness in the final decades of the century (see the section "Consciousness and qualia," below).

Functionalism

Functionalism is the view that what makes for mentality is the right kind of functional organization. Mental states are characterized in terms of their causal role within this organization, particularly their relationships to sensory inputs, behavioral outputs, and other mental states. Functionalism first emerged in the late 1960s (Lewis 1966; Putnam 1967) and was much discussed in the 1970s. Its dominance in the ensuing decades of the century owed as much to the defects of its competitors as to its own merits.

Functionalism originally emerged in two distinct forms, differing in their attitude towards the type identity theory and typified by Lewis (1966) and Putnam (1967). The Australian functionalists (Armstrong, Lewis, Smart) used functionalist analyses of mental states to argue *for* the type identity theory. They regarded mental states as *functionally specified* physical states (see functional specification theory, Block 1978). American functionalists (Putnam, Fodor) motivated their functionalist accounts by arguing *against* the type identity theory. They regarded mental states as functional states, not physical states (functional state identity theory, see Block 1978). These differences were due largely to the differing theoretical interests of the two camps. The functional specifications offered by the Australian functionalists were descendants of Smart's topic-neutral analyses. They reflected the view that mental concepts could be analyzed as concepts of states with a range of typical causes and effects; if the states in question proved to be physical, this would yield an argument for type identity (Lewis 1966; 1972). Putnam and Fodor were concerned with developments in artificial intelligence and cognitive psychology, not with the analysis of mental concepts. They took an explicitly anti-reductionist line, arguing that systems sharing the same mental or psychological properties need not share precisely the same physical properties (Putnam 1967; Fodor 1968).

Putnam and Fodor

Putnam's original functionalist proposal was inspired by similarities between mental states and Turing machine table states. The Turing machine states in question are defined entirely in terms of their relations between inputs, outputs, and one another. They can be realized in any system which possesses inputs, outputs, and states which stand in the appropriate relations, whatever its physical constitution. If mental states are Turing machine states then they can be relationally defined, but not solely in terms of their relationship to the system's output or behavior. And if mental states are Turing machine states then they can occur in systems which are physically diverse. This means, Putnam argues, that the functional state hypothesis is more plausible than the hypothesis that mental states are behavioral dispositions or the hypothesis that they are types of brain state. The behaviorist hypothesis fails because it specifies mental states solely in terms of their relations to behavior, omitting their relations to one another. The type identity hypothesis is empirically implausible, since it requires that the same type of physico-chemical state is invariably correlated with the same type of mental state. It is far more plausible that mental properties can be shared by systems which are physically diverse; that they are multiply realized (though Putnam does not use this terminology).

Fodor rejects the identification of mental states with machine table states, since a system can only be in one machine table state at a time, but can be in more than one mental state at a time (Block and Fodor 1972). But he holds that mental properties are computational properties which are multiply realizable: "there are possible – and, for all we know, real – information processing systems which share our psychology (instantiate its generalizations) but do not share our physical organization ... it looks as though type physicalism does carve things up in the wrong ways, assuming that the sort of psychological theories that are now being developed are even close to being true' (Fodor 1983: 9).[4] The conception of mental properties psychology requires is a relational or functional one, and the conception of materialism it requires is token physicalism, the view that mental particulars are physical (1983: 9–10). Moreover, Fodor argues that the view that all particulars are physical serves as a defensible form of the unity of science thesis (1974). Fodor thus advances a form of non-reductive physicalism, a view which holds that mental particulars are identical to physical particulars, but denies that mental properties are identical to physical properties. This type of view was to become standard (see the sections "Anomalous monism" and "Mental causation," below).

Armstrong and Lewis

Armstrong (1968) sets out to give a materialist account of mind, one compatible with the view that a human being is "nothing but a physico-chemical mechanism." Reflection on two inadequacies of Ryle's behaviorism points the way. The first is the now familiar point that such behaviorism fails to recognize that the mind is not behavior, but what brings about behavior. The second is less familiar: it is that dispositions to behave in certain ways should be construed realistically, as states that bring about the behavior in question. Consider fragility, one of Ryle's favorite examples of a disposition. We certainly think that objects that are fragile behave in characteristic ways; they tend to break when struck, for example. But we also think that there is an underlying basis for this behavior in the inner structure of the fragile thing. The fragility of the thing consists in its having a structure that causes it to break when struck. This line of thought leads to the idea of psychological dispositions as structural features of persons, ones that cause them to behave in characteristic ways. Putting these two points together yields a causal conception of a mental state as a state of a person apt for producing certain ranges of behavior. Such a state may in fact be a physical state of the brain. This conception guides Armstrong's analysis of specific concepts such as those of sensation, emotion, belief, purpose, and desire.

Armstrong's analyses of mental concepts, like Smart's topic-neutral analyses of sensations, are supposed by their authors to be compatible with type physicalism, but not to entail it. Both Armstrong and Smart suppose that the claim of identity will be defended on grounds of parsimony and simplicity. But Lewis offers an argument designed to force the identification of mental types with physical types. Its form is as follows (Lewis 1972, summarizing Lewis 1966):

Mental state M = the occupant of causal role R (by definition of M)

Neural state N = the occupant of causal role R (by physiological theory)

Therefore, mental state M = neural state N (by transitivity of identity)

In his later paper (1972), Lewis develops a causal analysis of mental states via the device which became known as Ramseyfication. We are invited to think of folk or commonsense psychology as a term-introducing theory. The theory can be constructed by conjoining commonsense platitudes about mental states, in particular those which concern their causal relations to behavioral outputs, sensory inputs, and one another. This theory can then be Ramseyfied by replacing the names of types of mental states with (indexed) variables, and binding these variables with existential quantifiers. The resulting Ramsey sentence says that the commonsense theory has at least one realization; that is, there is at least one set of states which occupy the causal roles implicitly defined by the theory. Lewis takes it that if the theory is (largely) true, it has a unique realization; there is a unique set of states which occupy the causal roles it defines. Once physiologists discover which neural states these are, psychophysical identity claims will follow as a matter of logic.

The argument of Lewis's earlier paper (1966) is more programmatic. Citing Smart's topic-neutral analysis, he proposes that types of experiences are defined by their causal roles, their typical causes and effects. His second premise is that the causes of physical phenomena are exclusively physical. Lewis takes this to follow from the plausible hypothesis that all physical phenomena are explicable in terms of physical phenomena (the explanatory adequacy of physics, Lewis 1966: 23). From the fact that the behavioral effects of experiences are physical phenomena, he concludes that the experiences must themselves be physical; if they were not, they could not be the causes of these physical effects.

Both these papers advance ideas with appeal and significance beyond the ranks of functionalists. Lewis (1966) anticipates a causal argument for physicalism which later became the focus of much debate (see the section "Mental causation," below). Lewis (1972) makes use of the idea of folk psychology as a theory of the causes of behavior. This idea had been introduced by Sellars (1956) to explain how names for experiences could be theoretical, yet also play a reporting role. The idea of folk psychology as a theory took on a life of its own, becoming particularly influential in the debate over the nature of propositional attitudes (see the section "Folk psychology and a science of intention," below).

Problems for functionalism

Functionalism attempts to give an account of what mental states are. The basic idea is that mental states are states that have certain relations to sensory inputs, behavioral outputs, and one another. Different versions of functionalism give different accounts of the functional organization characteristic of mentality. But any such functionalist account attempts to specify necessary and sufficient conditions for the possession of mental states. An account that fails to specify the right sufficient conditions is too *liberal*; it attributes mentality to systems that lack it. An account that fails to specify the right necessary conditions is *chauvinistic*; it denies mentality to systems that have it. This terminology comes from Block (1978), who raised a number of influential objections to functionalism. Functionalism is supposed to avoid the liberalism of logical behaviorism and the chauvinism of the type identity theory, but Block doubts that any functional account of mentality will avoid both these failings.

One argument that functionalism is too liberal is this: we can imagine systems that have the right functional organization, but, intuitively, lack any mental states. Block asks us to imagine a system made up of the inhabitants of China and a robot body which instantiates his functional organization. It is particularly implausible, Block argues, that there is anything it is like to be such a system; it seems to lack any qualitative mental states. Another thought-experiment used to argue that functionalism cannot account for qualitative states is the Inverted Spectrum argument: suppose that what it is like for you to see ripe tomatoes is what it is like for me to see unripe ones (and vice versa). It seems (though this has been challenged) that this inversion need not be reflected in any functional difference (Block and Fodor 1972). If so, we will be in the same functional state but in different qualitative states when we both look at a ripe tomato. Both these "Absent Qualia" and "Inverted Qualia" arguments trade on the thought that some mental states have an intrinsic qualitative character which is not determined by their causal role.

John Searle (1932–) presented a thought-experiment specifically intended to show that a functionalist approach cannot account for intentional mental states such as understanding (Searle 1980). Suppose that Searle, who understands no Chinese, is shut in a room with a collection of slips of paper bearing Chinese characters and an enormous book of rules, written in English. Slips of paper bearing strings of Chinese characters come into the room, and Searle matches the slips to rules in the book which tell him how to put other characters together to make a string which he passes out of the room. Unbeknownst to him, he is producing cogent answers, written in Chinese, to incoming questions which are also written in Chinese. By following the rules in the book, Searle executes a program for answering questions in Chinese. Yet Searle himself understands no Chinese as a result; so, he argues, executing a program is not sufficient for understanding.

Searle originally used this "Chinese Room" thought-experiment to attack what he called "strong artificial intelligence (AI)," the view that the mind is to the brain as computer software is to computer hardware. What this means is that the nature of the hardware is unimportant; all that matters is the program. An attack on this view is also an attack on functionalism, since functionalism holds that the right kind of functional organization makes for mentality; the nature of the physical realization is unimportant. If this view were right, Searle argues, then executing the right kind of program for manipulating symbols should make him understand Chinese. But no amount of symbol manipulation in the Chinese Room can do that; for the occupant of the room, the Chinese symbols remain mere shapes, devoid of meaning.

Searle's argument provoked heated debate, in psychology and Artificial Intelligence as well as in philosophy (see Preston and Bishop 2002 for a collection of responses). One obvious response for a functionalist to make is that since it is the system as a whole which instantiates the right functional organization, functionalism does not imply that the occupant of the Chinese Room understands Chinese; it implies that the system does. Searle responds by supposing that he memorizes the rules and symbols, so that he internalizes the system; still he will not understand Chinese. Some critics argued that he would nonetheless harbor a system that does understand Chinese. A further functionalist response is that the Room cannot have the same functional organization as a genuine Chinese speaker; for that we need a system with a body which can interact with its environment. Searle responds that even if we envisage him as controlling a robot body, receiving symbol strings which encode perceptual inputs and issuing symbol strings which encode motor commands, he is still shuffling symbols without understanding them. Critics argued that once the system is enriched in this way, it is plausible to say that it does understand Chinese. Searle's insistence that this is absurd owes much to his conviction that intentionality requires consciousness, and that there is no consciousness of meaning in such a system.

Functionalist accounts also face the problem of specifying the functional roles of mental states. Since a functional state is individuated by its role in a system, any difference in functional organization makes for a difference in functional states. To steer a course between liberalism and chauvinism, the account must specify the functional organization common to all and only the systems with minds. But how could the sensory inputs and behavioral outputs of such a system be specified, to say nothing of the interrelations of its internal states? If we specify them with reference to our bodies or nervous systems, the account will be chauvinistic, but if we specify them in the abstract, liberalism threatens; the economy of a country might have the right inputs, outputs, and internal states (Block 1978).

Contemporary responses to these problems tended to accept the price of chauvinism; some advocated a hybrid of functionalism and type identity, tying qualitative states to particular physical realizations. The Absent and Inverted Qualia arguments were later recognized as versions of the problem of the explanatory gap (see the section "Consciousness and qualia," below). Perhaps the most influential legacy of functionalism was a negative one: the rejection of type physicalism. Even those who were not convinced that the essence of mental states is functional were persuaded that it is not physical by the argument from multiple realizability. Meanwhile, Donald Davidson (1917–2003) had developed another influential argument against type physicalism.

Anomalous monism

Donald Davidson's papers "Actions, reasons and causes" (1963) and "Mental events" (1970) exerted immense influence on the development of philosophy of mind in the latter part of the twentieth century, even among philosophers who did not share Davidson's interpretationist view of the mind. "Actions, reasons and causes" was instrumental in rehabilitating the view that explanations of actions in terms of reasons are causal explanations. This view had been attacked by Ryle and by followers of Wittgenstein, including G. E. M. Anscombe (1919–2001), whose influential study *Intention* (1957) was much admired by Davidson. Anscombe argued that an action could be intentional under one description (when described as the flipping of a light switch, for example) but not under another (as the alerting of a prowler, for example). Davidson endorses this idea, but disputes Anscombe's non-causalist view of action explanations. He sets out to defend what he calls the "ancient – and common-sense" position that explanations of actions in terms of reasons relate reason and action as cause and effect. He does so largely by pointing out defects in the arguments offered against the view. One such is the argument (advanced by Ryle; see the section "Ordinary-language philosophy," above) that motives or beliefs cannot be the causes of actions because they are not events. Davidson points out that standing conditions are often cited as causes; for example, the bridge collapsed because it had a structural defect. He agrees that in such cases there must be a precipitating event. But the acquisition of a belief or a motive can be such an event; those who dispute the existence of mental events precipitating actions "have often missed the obvious" because they have assumed (as Ryle does) that such an event would have to be a feeling or a twinge, something of which the agent is aware (Davidson 1963: 12).

Another argument offered by Ryle is that motives are not sufficiently distinct from actions to be their causes; when we give the motive, we re-describe the action itself. But, Davidson points out, we often describe effects in terms of what we know to be their causes. If I describe the red patch on my skin as sunburn, I imply that it was caused by the sun. Nonetheless, the action of the sun and the condition of my skin are distinct, and the first may have caused the second (and must have, if my description is true).

What positive reason does Davidson give for believing that reasons are causes? He points out that someone may have a reason R to perform an action A, and perform A, yet not do it for R. In such a case, it would be wrong to explain A in terms of R. "Central to the relation between a reason and an action it explains is the idea that the agent performed the action *because* he had the reason" (1963: 9). The best argument for the view that reasons are the causes of the actions they explain is that we have no other satisfactory account of the relation between them (p. 11).

The later paper, "Mental events," argued for a metaphysical position labeled "anomalous monism" (1970: 214). According to this view, mental events are (identical to) physical events (hence "monism"), but there are no laws correlating mental kinds of events with physical kinds of events (hence "anomalous"). In other words (which Davidson does not use), the position offers token physicalism (token identity) without type physicalism (type identity). Although Davidson denies that there are psychophysical laws, he does maintain that "mental characteristics are in some sense dependent, or supervenient, on physical characteristics"; for example, "there cannot be two events alike in all physical respects but differing in some mental respect" (1970: 214).

This marks a first way in which the paper is important; anomalous monism provides a paradigm of the *non-reductive physicalism* which became orthodoxy in the latter part of the century.[5] Davidson himself took pains to stress the non-reductive character of his view: "such a bland monism, unbuttressed by correlating laws or conceptual economies, does not seem to merit the term 'reductionism'" (1970: 214). Anomalous monism maintains that all events are physical, but denies that mental properties can be reduced to (or even lawfully correlated with) physical properties, even if they supervene on them. As Davidson points out (pp. 212–13), early advocates of the identity theory assumed that the identities in question would be identities between kinds of events, such as "pains are C-fiber firings." Smart, for example, assumes that empirical evidence for the identity theory would take the form of psychophysical laws (1959: 142). The distinction between type and token identity claims had been remarked before, notably by Feigl: "Psychophysiological identity may be identity of particulars (*this* twinge of pain with a specific cerebral event at a certain time), or of universals (pain of a certain *kind*, and a *type* of cerebral process)" (1958: 463). But Davidson was the first to argue for token identity via the rejection of a type identity. He was also the first to suggest that mental properties might be supervenient on physical properties. Supervenience theses became the focus of an enormous literature, and were regarded by some as defining a minimal physicalism; others came to regard them as too minimal (see the section "Conclusion," below).

Davidson's defense of physicalism was novel not only in grounding token identity in the rejection of psychophysical correlations, but also in its focus on intentional mental events rather than sensations. This brings us to a second way in which the paper is important: it advances Davidson's distinctive interpretationist approach to the mind. For Davidson, "the distinguishing feature of the mental is not that it is private, subjective, or immaterial, but that it exhibits what Brentano called intentionality" (1970: 211). An event is mental if and only if it can be picked out by a mental description, and a mental description is one that contains a verb of propositional attitude which is referentially opaque (p. 210). Davidson thus adopts the Chisholm–Quine linguistic criterion of intentionality. Mental events are attitudes such as believings, desirings, intendings, identified by their content: what is believed, desired, intended.

For Davidson, the key to the nature of these attitudes is the fact that they are ascribed via interpretation; and the key to understanding interpretation is the notion of radical interpretation. Davidson's radical interpretation is a descendant of Quine's radical translation. But while the goal of radical translation is to assign meanings to the alien's language, the goal of radical interpretation is to assign meanings to the alien's language *and* contents to the alien's attitudes. Davidson's point is that the radical translator must solve for attitude and meaning together:

we could not begin to decode a man's sayings if we could not make out his attitudes towards his sentences, such as holding, wishing, or wanting them to be true. Beginning from these attitudes, we must work out a theory of what he means, thus simultaneously giving content to his attitudes and to his words. (1970: 222)

Attributions of propositional attitudes need not be mere dramatic projections, as Quine (1960) had claimed; they emerge as a product of radical translation broadly construed. The theory of content the interpreter arrives at is constrained by the aim of making sense of the alien's behavior, including verbal behavior; she wants to reveal the system of beliefs and motives which provide his reasons for acting, the rational causes of his behavior. "But in inferring this system from the evidence we necessarily impose conditions of coherence, rationality and consistency" (1974: 231). We succeed in attributing attitudes only to the extent that we succeed in imposing a pattern of coherence, rationality and consistency on the agent's behavior and its causes. This may be done in more than one way; interpretation, like translation, is indeterminate.

Davidson makes his case for anomalous monism by arguing that it follows from the reconciliation of three premises which might appear to be inconsistent. The first is the Principle of Causal Interaction (PCI), which states that some mental events interact causally with physical events. To use Davidson's example, if someone sank the *Bismarck*, then various perceivings and judgments caused bodily movements which led to the sinking of a ship. The second is the Principle of the Nomological Character of Causality (PNCC): events related as cause and effect fall under strict laws. The third is the Principle of the Anomalism of the Mental (PAM): there are no strict laws containing mental descriptions. These principles appear to conflict because causally related mental and physical events must, by PNCC, fall under a strict law; but, by PAM, there are no strict laws which events described as mental can instantiate. Davidson reconciles the three principles and establishes token identity as follows:

1 m, a mental event, is causally related to p, a physical event. (instance of PCI)
2 m and p are subsumed by a strict law. (by PNCC)
3 The strict law which subsumes m and p does not contain any mental description. (by PAM)
4 The strict law which subsumes m and p contains only physical descriptions.
5 So m has a physical description, i.e. it is physical event.

Obviously this form of argument, if sound, can be used to show that any mental event forming part of a causal chain which includes a physical event is itself a physical event.

This argument yields the monist element of anomalous monism; PAM provides the anomalism. Davidson's argument for the anomalism of the mental is based on his interpretationist view of the mind. In essence, the argument is that rationality plays a constitutive role in the application of mental descriptions, but plays no role in the application of physical descriptions. Because of these "disparate commitments" of the mental and physical schemes, there can be no strict psychophysical laws; "there cannot be tight connections between the [mental and physical] realms if each is to retain allegiance to its proper source of evidence" (1970: 222). This line of reasoning, with its relatively a priori character, is most naturally read as ruling out psychophysical bridge laws: if mental and physical predicates are applied on the basis of quite different considerations, we cannot expect any two such predicates to be co-extensive ("no purely physical predicate ... has, as a matter of law, the same extension as a mental predicate"; 1970: 215). But what premise 3 of the argument for token identity requires is that there be no strict psychophysical causal law subsuming m and p under their mental and physical descriptions; so the argument against psychophysical laws must be more complex (see McLaughlin 1985; Patterson 1995 for further discussion).

Two points about Davidson's argument for token identity are worth noting. One is that it assumes that the everyday events mentioned in premise 1, such as intendings and ship sinkings, can be picked out by predicates occurring in the strict laws of a precise and comprehensive physical theory. It is not obvious that descriptions of such complex events would figure in the strict laws of a completed (micro?) physics (see Sturgeon 1998 for discussion). Some argument is needed to make this assumption plausible. The second point (which is not unrelated) concerns the gap between premise 3 and premise 4 of the argument for token identity. Premise 3 says that no strict psychological or psychophysical law subsumes m and p. But what guarantees that there is a strict *physical* law that subsumes them? Davidson (1970: 223–4) comes close to saying that physical theory provides a comprehensive closed system describing all events in a vocabulary amenable to strict law. Such a claim would close the gap between the premises, but make the anomalism of the mental irrelevant to the argument for monism. If all causes and effects can be subsumed by strict physical laws, monism will follow from PCI and PNCC alone.

This brings us to a third way in which Davidson's paper has been important: in offering a novel kind of causal argument for the identity theory. Lewis had offered a causal argument for type identity earlier (Lewis 1966), but he assumed that mental state types could be defined in causal terms. Davidson's argument relies on the weaker and far more plausible assumption that some mental events interact causally with physical events. Versions of causal arguments for token identity continued to be important (e.g. Peacocke 1979; see the section "Mental causation," below). But the versions subsequently advanced generally eschewed Davidson's commitment to the Nomological Character of Causality and his argument for the Anomalism of the Mental, relying instead on the principle that all physical events have physical causes (as did Lewis). This principle of the causal closure of the physical is close to a claim that Davidson's own argument tacitly assumes, as noted in the previous paragraph (see Crane 1995 for discussion).

Although Davidson's anomalous monism provided a paradigm for non-reductive physicalism and his argument for token identity provided a model for the argument from causal closure, his interpretationist approach to the mental proved less popular. Non-reductive physicalists preferred to defend the irreducibility of mental properties by appeal to their multiple realizability in a functionalist style, rather than by arguing from the constitutive role of rationality and the disparate commitments of the mental and physical schemes. Davidson's claim that there is no more to the mind than radical interpretation can reveal, and his concomitant remarks about the impossibility of a science of psychology (e.g. Davidson 1974), placed him too close to Quine for those who sought to defend the possibility of a science of intention. Although Davidson was no eliminativist, his conception of the mind was not realist enough for most tastes. This reaction was reflected in the criticism that anomalous monism is epiphenomenalist, that it deprives mental properties of any causal efficacy. Eventually the threat of epiphenomenalism came to be seen as a wider problem for non-reductive physicalism in general.

Folk psychology and a science of intention

The views of the early type physicalists and functionalists, like Davidson's anomalous monism, entailed or at least allowed for a causal role for mental states and events in the production of behavior. They also entailed or at least allowed for token physicalism, the identity of particular mental states or events with physical states or events. Of course, this was no accident. The rehabilitation of mentalism, the conception of mental phenomena as inner causes, involved its detachment from the "Cartesian" conception of mental phenomena as immaterial causes which were "inner" in the sense of being private, of being subjective phenomena uniquely accessible to a single consciousness. When mental causes were conceived of as neural events or processes, they could be conceived of as "inner" simply in the sense of being internal, of occurring within a person's body. Of course this means that everyday ascriptions of mental states to others cannot be based on direct observations of the states themselves, since others' brains are not open to view. But mental states conceived of as causes of behavior can be regarded as inferred or theoretical entities; ascriptions of such states are warranted by their utility in explaining and predicting behavior. This view comports naturally with the idea of commonsense or "folk" psychology as a theory, an idea already encountered in the context of Lewis's argument for psychophysical identity (Lewis 1972).

The idea of folk psychology as a theory was combined with a variety of differing views about the nature and status of that theory. For eliminative materialists such as Feyerabend (1963), Rorty (1965), and especially Churchland (1981), our commonsense conception of mental phenomena embodies a bad theory of the causes of behavior, one which will be displaced by a neurophysiological account devoid of mental terminology. For a realist such as Fodor, folk psychology is a well-confirmed theory of the causes of behavior which will be vindicated by developments in cognitive psychology (see especially Fodor 1987). For an instrumentalist such as Dennett (1987), folk psychology is an indispensable tool in our dealings with one another, but it works because it enables us to latch on to patterns in human behavior, not because it latches on to the inner causes of behavior.

Quine (1960) had described the ascription of beliefs to another as "an essentially dramatic act"; he depicted it as involving imaginative projection into the other's situation. The idea that we predict what others will do through what came to be called simulation – by imagining that we are in their situation, and deciding what to do – was developed in the 1980s as an alternative to the view of folk psychology as a theory. Gordon (1986) defended the simulation approach by appealing to empirical evidence that the ability to pretend and the ability to predict others' behavior develop in tandem in young children. Goldman (1989) developed the idea of off-line simulation, the idea that we use ourselves as a model for another by feeding pretend beliefs and desires into our own practical reasoning mechanisms, and taking the resulting pretend decision as a prediction of what the other will do. Jane Heal (1986) argues for the simulation hypothesis on grounds of its greater parsimony. On the simulation view, to predict your response to the question, "What is 26×7?" I do not need to have a theory about how people reason arithmetically; I just need to be able to reason arithmetically myself. This enables me to replicate the thinking you would do to answer the question, and thereby predict your answer. Heal and Gordon developed and defended simulation as a theory of what goes on at the personal level when we predict or explain others' thoughts and actions, while Goldman developed it as an account of what goes on at the subpersonal level.

The debate between proponents of simulation theory and defenders of the rival "theory theory" (the view that we explain and predict others' thoughts and actions by deploying a tacit psychological theory) became genuinely interdisciplinary, involving psychologists as well as philosophers (see Davies and Stone 1995 for a useful overview). The simulation approach seemed to some philosophers to offer an effective rebuttal of eliminativism. If folk psychology is not a theory, it cannot be a false theory, so the practice of ascribing beliefs and desires is insulated from the threat of elimination (Stich and Nichols 1992). Others argued that this response is too hasty. Suppose that our ability to predict and explain others' actions does not rest on any internally represented psychological theory, but involves simulation alone. It might still prove possible to reconstruct a folk psychological theory by systematizing platitudes, in the manner originally proposed by Lewis (1972), or by reconstructing the psychological theory reflected by the explanations and predictions themselves. So it is not obvious that the truth of the simulation theory would deprive eliminativism of a target (Stich and Ravenscroft 1994).

Eliminative materialism

Early advocates of eliminative materialism such as Feyerabend (1963), Rorty (1965), and Churchland (1981) were concerned chiefly to argue for the elimination of terms putatively referring to sensations, "raw feels" and other qualitative mental phenomena. The reason for opting for elimination rather than reduction was succinctly put by Feyerabend; if sensations are identified with brain processes, the indiscernibility of identicals dictates that brain processes have all the problematic properties that sensations seem to have, such as private phenomenal qualities. (This is the problem encapsulated in Smart's Objection 3, discussed above.) The materialist ought rather to say that there are no sensations as traditionally conceived, and to support this claim by arguing that the elimination of sensation terminology, with the false conceptions it brings with it, "would leave our ability to describe and predict undiminished" (Rorty 1965: 181). Reference to sensations would go the way of reference to demons and phlogiston; we would speak instead of C-fiber firings and the like.

With Churchland's "Eliminative materialism and the propositional attitudes" (1981), the focus shifted from phenomenal states such as sensations to intentional states such as beliefs and desires. This paper is the most influential expression of eliminativism about propositional attitudes and one of the clearest statements of the thesis that folk psychology is a theory. Churchland describes the laws of the theory as generalizations quantifying over agents and propositions, such as:

> For any agent x, and any proposition p, if x fears that p, then x desires that not-p.

Obviously only propositional attitudes can be subsumed by laws quantifying over propositions; but Churchland assumes that such attitudes "form the systematic core of folk psychology" (1981: 70). The intentionality of these central theoretical posits constitutes one of the reasons for Churchland's pessimism about the folk theory. Churchland argues that folk psychology is a bad theory because it is incomplete, stagnant, and shows little sign of being integrated with established science (especially neuroscience). "Its intentional categories stand magnificently alone, without visible prospect of reduction to that larger corpus" (p. 75). The standard functionalist response to a demand for reduction to neuroscience is that mental states are irreducible to physical ones because they are functionally specified, and can be realized in physically different systems. Churchland replies that this stratagem of pleading functional individuation could be used to save any bad theory, such as alchemy, which failed to integrate with lower-level sciences.

Defenders of folk psychology responded that even if it can be regarded as a theory, it is not a developed science, and should not be judged as such (see Horgan and Woodward 1985; Jackson and Pettit 1990). Research in cognitive psychology, based on concepts derived from folk psychology, is not stagnant and promises to explain many phenomena on which the folk theory is silent. Reduction is not the only way in which intentional psychology might be integrated with lower-level theories; integration could be secured by providing lower-level mechanisms which explain how we conform to intentional laws.

Churchland raises and responds to the objection that it is self-defeating to advocate the elimination of belief because advocacy itself implies belief. This question of the coherence of eliminativism about propositional attitudes also prompted discussion (see the forum discussion in the summer 1993 issue of *Mind & Language*).

Fodorian intentional realism

Jerry Fodor is one of the most active defenders of folk psychology and one of the most influential figures in philosophy of mind in the latter part of the century. It would be more accurate to describe him as a defender of propositional attitude psychology, since he, like Churchland, regards such attitudes as the systematic core of folk psychology; but unlike Churchland, he regards folk psychology as a largely true theory of the causes of behavior. He stresses three points about folk psychology: that it works; that it is theoretical; and that it is indispensable (Fodor 1987: 2). Attributing propositional attitudes to others enables us to predict their behavior with a considerable degree of success (it works); we know of no other conceptual framework which enables us to do this (it is indispensable); and the generalizations of folk psychology quantify over interacting causes of behavior which are not directly observable (it is theoretical). Given that folk psychology is such a successful theory, we have good reason to believe that it is largely true, and to believe that the states and processes it posits exist. Hence we should expect that folk psychology will be vindicated by scientific theory, not displaced by it; and this expectation is borne out by theories in cognitive psychology, which posit states essentially similar to the attitudes. Fodor's view is that although work in cognitive science will of course extend, elaborate, and in some ways revise folk wisdom, it will do so within an explanatory framework which is essentially that of propositional attitude psychology.

To understand and assess this claim, we need to know what Fodor regards as the essence of propositional attitudes. The attitudes of folk psychology are, he claims, states which are causally efficacious, have intentional properties, and conform to generalizations which are both causal and intentional. The last point is especially significant because it means that the causal powers of the attitudes are correlated with their intentional properties. The chief importance of the computational approach in cognitive psychology, for Fodor, is that the idea of computation enables us to understand how there can be states which are such that their causal powers are correlated with their semantic properties. Computers are precisely devices in which the causal roles of symbols are determined by their syntactic properties, and the semantic properties of symbols are correlated with their syntactic properties. If propositional attitudes are computational states, we can see how they can be states of a physical system which have interlinked causal and semantic properties. Computation supplies a mechanism for intentional causation (Fodor 1987).

The theory of mind Fodor advocates, then, is both representational and computational. It is representational insofar as it takes propositional attitudes to be relations to mental representations, and it is computational insofar as it takes those relations to be computational and those mental representations to be the objects of computational processes. According to the Representational Theory of Mind (RTM), to believe that cats like fish is to stand in a certain functional relation to a mental representation with the content *cats like fish*. To use Fodor's image, it is to have a sentence of the Language of Thought, or Mentalese, which means *cats like fish* in one's belief-box. According to the Computational Theory of Mind (CTM), mental processes are computational processes; they operate on mental representations in virtue of their formal or syntactic properties. Different sentences of the Language of Thought have different formal properties, to which computational processes are sensitive: "computers ... just are environments in which the causal role of a symbol token is made to parallel the inferential role of the proposition that it expresses" (Fodor 1990: 22).

Fodor has vigorously defended this representational, computational theory of mind from the 1970s onwards, though the emphasis has altered over time as the battle lines have shifted. In his earlier work, the stress was on the view of propositional attitudes as relations to sentence-like mental representations. *The Language of Thought* (1975) argued that empirically adequate theorizing in cognitive psychology required such a construal of the attitudes. "Propositional attitudes" (1978) advanced more a priori reasons for the construal, arguing, for example, that it provides an explanation of the opacity of attitude ascriptions. If beliefs are relations to sentence-like mental representations, we can see how Ada can believe that the morning star is bright without thereby believing that the evening star is bright. All that is required is that the two beliefs be constituted by relations to distinct sentences of Mentalese (1978: 188, 194). (This style of argument came perilously close to reading an empirical claim about the nature of beliefs from the logical features of attitude ascriptions; see the section "Brentano's thesis and the flight from intention," above.)

In the 1980s, the computational theory of mental processes came to assume as much importance as the representational theory of propositional attitudes. "Methodological solipsism ..." (Fodor 1980) argued that a propositional attitude psychology supplies just what a computational psychology demands: an intentional taxonomy of the attitudes which matches a formal taxonomy of their representational objects. This happy conclusion was soon challenged; the idea that *de dicto* or opaque attitude ascriptions attribute narrow content, content that supervenes on the intrinsic properties of thinkers, fell prey to the externalist arguments of Burge and Putnam (see the section "Mental content," below). Over the next ten years, Fodor grappled with the problem of constructing a naturalistic theory of mental content suited to the demands of a representational computational psychology, first defending and then abandoning narrow content. The resulting asymmetric dependence theory of content is a variation on the causal theory, according to which a mental symbol represents its normal environmental cause (Fodor 1990).

Fodor continued to defend his Language of Thought hypothesis, deploying a new argument in response to a new threat from connectionism. The argument, first advanced in his 1987 article and developed in the 1988 article co-authored with Pylyshyn, is based on the systematicity of thought: the fact that the ability to entertain some thoughts brings with it the ability to entertain semantically related thoughts. A person who can think that John loves Mary can think that Mary loves John. If these thoughts are construed as relations to language-like mental representations – representations which are language-like in having a compositional syntax and semantics – there is a ready explanation for this fact, Fodor claims. If the person's language of thought contains symbols which can combine to form a complex representation with the content *John loves Mary*, it contains symbols which can combine to form a complex representation with the content *Mary loves John*. Although Fodor has expressed pessimism about the explanatory power of the computational theory of mental processes, his enthusiasm for mental representation and the language of thought remains vigorous. He describes it as "something like an unmitigated success" (2000: 4).

Fodor's work set the agenda for many debates in the final decades of the century, in particular those concerning narrow content (see "Mental content," below), the Language of Thought, and the naturalization of intentionality (see "Philosophy of psychology," Chapter 13). He has been an influential advocate of the "divide and conquer" approach to the mind, dividing the "great metaphysical puzzles about the mind" into three: "How could anything material have conscious states? How could anything material have semantical properties? How could anything material be rational?" (1991: 285). The Fodorian project of vindicating folk psychology via a theory of mind that is both representational and computational is addressed to the latter two questions. The project has been challenged for a variety of reasons. The proposed vindication of folk psychology is highly schematic; it largely consists in showing that there could be a naturalistic reduction of intentionality and a mechanism for intentional causation. This is no mean achievement, but it is not obvious that it provides an account of the propositional attitudes attributed in folk psychological explanations. Yoking folk psychology to classical computationalism may be dangerous to both; a research program in cognitive science is freighted with metaphysical baggage, while the fate of folk psychology becomes hostage to empirical fortune (see Matthews 1991 for discussion).

Dennett's instrumentalism

Daniel Dennett (1942–), like Fodor, sought to construct a theory of mind informed by work in cognitive psychology, especially computational psychology. But Dennett's approach to folk psychology was very different. Whereas for Fodor the notion of intentional causation provides the key to understanding propositional attitudes, for Dennett the key notion is that of an intentional system (Dennett 1971). An intentional system is one whose behavior can be predicted by assuming that it is *rational*, and ascribing beliefs, desires, and other intentional states accordingly. To adopt this strategy for predicting the system's behavior is to adopt the intentional stance towards it. To have intentional states such as beliefs and desires is simply to be an intentional system, one whose behavior is predictable via the intentional stance.

So far, Dennett's approach might seem similar to that of Davidson, who also assigns a central role to rationality and takes an interpretationist view of mental states. Both were influenced by Quine's strictures against determinate mental meanings, but Dennett's view differs from Davidson's in a number of important ways. While Davidson argues that only language-using creatures are fit subjects for radical interpretation, Dennett points out that we adopt the intentional stance towards a wide variety of systems; we can use it to predict the behavior of growing plants (which want to reach the light), thermostats (which want to keep the temperature constant) and chess-playing computers (which want to get the Queen out early), as well as animals. The attribution of belief is made solely on pragmatic grounds, to enable prediction of behavior; it is not made in order to enable the interpretation of language. The diversity of the systems which can be approached via the intentional stance provides Dennett with one of his motivations for rejecting intentional realism of a Fodorian variety. Surely there are no inner structures which all such systems share; what they have in common in simply the fact that their behavior can be predicted via the intentional stance (see Dennett 1981b).

Another way in which Dennett's account differs from Davidson's is that while the latter stresses the fact that intentional interpretation yields causal explanations of behavior, the former stresses its utility for prediction. This is obviously connected to the fact that Davidson identifies a mental event, such as the acquisition of a belief, with a physical event in the believer's nervous system, while Dennett avoids such "misplaced concreteness" (1981a: p. 55). Dennett regards the belief and desires of folk psychology as abstracta, logical constructs akin to centers of gravity (1987: 72). The use of these constructs enables us to reveal and exploit genuine patterns in human behavior, but we should not conclude from the success of this enterprise that belief-like and desire-like objects exist in human heads (1987: 81). Though few wanted to join Dennett on his knife-edge between realism and relativism (1987; 37), his methodological critique of Fodorian realism was influential.

Mental content

Propositional attitudes are identified in part by their contents, which are traditionally taken to be given by the that-clauses of attitude ascriptions. The appearance of Putnam's Twin Earth thought-experiment (1975), and his conclusion that "meanings ain't in the head," began a debate about the determinants of mental content which continued until the end of the century. Putnam asks us to imagine a planet, Twin Earth, which is just like Earth except for the fact that the colorless, odorless liquid which runs in the rivers, flows from the taps, and so on has a different chemical composition from its analogue on Earth. The Twin Earth liquid is not H_2O but a complicated compound which Putnam refers to as XYZ. Now, consider Oscar, a chemically unsophisticated Earthling, and Twin Oscar (or Toscar), his doppelganger on Twin Earth. Oscar and Twin Oscar are physical duplicates (modulo the fact that Oscar's body contains H_2O and Toscar's XYZ). But, Putnam argues, Oscar's word "water" means H_2O, i.e. water, whereas Toscar's word "water" means not H_2O but XYZ – what we might call twin water, or twater for short. Putnam concludes that the meaning of natural kind terms like "water" depends on the speaker's physical and social environment; "meanings ain't in the head" because they are not determined only by what's in the speaker's mind.

Although Putnam introduced terminology that became standard in the ensuing debate, he did not in his original paper conclude that what's in the mind – the content of mental states – is not in the head, in the sense of not being determined just by what's in the head. Putnam drew a distinction between mental states in the *narrow* sense – states which do not presuppose the existence of any individual apart from the subject to whom the state is ascribed – and mental states in the *wide* sense, states which do presuppose the existence of other individuals (1975: 220). (He gives jealousy as an example of a wide mental state; x is jealous of y implies that y exists.[6]) The target of Putnam's paper is a traditional view about meaning which he ascribes to

Frege and Carnap (pp. 218–19). On this view the meaning or intension of a word (1) is determined by narrow mental state and (2) determines its extension (pp. 219–22). Twin Earth provides a counterexample, he argues, because the twins are in the same narrow mental state, yet their words mean different things. In fact, Putnam calls it "absurd" to suppose that my twin's mental state is "one bit different" from mine (p. 227). However, Twin Earth was soon used to support this very conclusion. Burge (1979 n. 2; 1982) argued that the twins differ not only in the meanings of their words but also in the contents of their beliefs. Suppose Oscar sincerely asserts, "water is wet"; we would naturally ascribe him the belief that water is wet. But when Toscar sincerely asserts "water is wet," we cannot report his belief in the same way. To do so would be to ascribe him a belief about water (that is, H_2O), a stuff he has never seen or even heard of. To capture the content of his belief, we must say "Toscar believes that twater is wet." So the contents of the twins' beliefs about natural kinds partly depend on their physical and social environments, just as the meanings of their natural kind terms do.

Burge (1979) provided central impetus to the debate by using another thought-experiment to argue that the content of a thinker's beliefs and other propositional attitudes depends on the thinker's social environment. Burge presented this conclusion as a challenge to received views of the mind which he described as "individualistic." Such approaches

> seek to see a person's intentional mental phenomena ultimately and purely in terms of what happens to the person, what occurs within him, and how he responds to his physical environment, without any essential reference to the social context in which he or the interpreter of his mental phenomena are situated. (1979: 103)

The thought-experiment which Burge takes to undermine such views runs as follows. Suppose a patient (call him Alfred) has "a large number of attitudes commonly attributed with content clauses containing 'arthritis' in oblique occurrence"; for example, he believes that he has had arthritis for years, that he has arthritis in his ankles, and so on (p. 77). After feeling aches and pains in his thigh, he comes to believe that he has developed arthritis in his thigh, and voices this fear to his doctor. The doctor tells him that this cannot be the case, since arthritis is an inflammation of the joints. Alfred is surprised, but relinquishes his view and asks what might be wrong with his thigh. Now consider a counterfactual situation which differs from the actual one only in that the word 'arthritis' is used differently: it is standardly used to refer to inflammations of the bones and joints. This difference between the actual and counterfactual situations affects only Alfred's social environment; he has the same physiological history, he makes the same physical movements and sounds, he is the subject of the same mental phenomena, non-intentionally described. But when he goes to the doctor and says "I fear I have arthritis in my thigh," the doctor's reaction is different. Instead of saying "That can't be so," she says "Let's see if you're right." Burge argues that it would be incorrect to describe Alfred as believing that he has arthritis in his thigh in the counterfactual situation. This is a belief which cannot be true, yet (as the doctor's reaction shows) the belief Alfred has in the counterfactual situation is a belief that may be true. In fact, it would be incorrect to describe him as believing that he has had arthritis for years, that he has arthritis in his ankles, and so on. His word "arthritis" does not mean *arthritis* – it does not refer to rheumatoid inflammations of the joints – and it is hard to see how he could have picked up the notion of arthritis. To capture the content of the belief he has in the counterfactual situation, we would have to coin a term for inflammations of the bones and joints, such as tharthritis; then we could say that in the counterfactual situation, he believes that he has tharthritis in his thigh. So the contents of Alfred's attitudes differ between the actual and counter-factual situations: "the patient's mental contents differ while his entire physical and non-intentional mental histories, considered in isolation from their social context, remain the same … The difference in his mental contents is attributable to differences in his social environment" (Burge 1979: 79).

These thought-experiments generated considerable debate. On the one hand, there were the arguments of Burge and Putnam, which seemed to demonstrate the existence of a type of mental content which depended on physical and social environment. This type of content came to be known as wide or broad. On the other, there was the intuitive pull of the idea of a type of mental content that was shared by twins, despite the difference in their environments; after all, Putnam originally took it as obvious that the twins' mental states are the same. This type of content came to be known as narrow. So a debate developed between those who held that all content was wide (who came to be known as externalists) and those who held that some content was narrow (the internalists). The notion of narrow content was defended in different ways. Some appealed to causal or explanatory considerations, arguing that the twins, being physical duplicates, will behave in the same way; the difference in the (wide) contents of their attitudes makes no difference to their behavior. Since we attribute intentional states to others to explain their behavior, the argument concluded, we should attribute states with the same content to the twins. A related way of motivating shared content appealed to the idea that the world seems the same to the twins; the difference between their environments is not one that affects their perspective on those environments. If they were to be switched overnight from one environment to the other, they would never notice the difference. Since in attributing attitudes with content to others we attempt to capture their perspective on the world – how the world seems to them, how they would like it to be, how they fear it might be – we should attribute the same contents to the twins, to capture their shared perspective.

Opponents of narrow content regarded these arguments as begging the question against broad content attributions. The causal or explanatory argument assumes that the twins behave in the same way. This is true, if behavior is individuated in physical terms. But we generally attribute intentional states to explain *actions*, behavior under an intentional description. And we have as much reason to say that the twins' actions are different as we have to say that their attitudes are different. Oscar goes to his kitchen tap to get a drink of water. Toscar goes to *his* kitchen tap to get a drink of twater. Oscar wants water, Toscar wants twater, and each acts to get what he wants.

Ordinary broad content ascriptions provide perfectly good explanations of their respective behaviors. The appeal to perspectives, or how the world seems to the twins, was also regarded as begging the question, and castigated as a relic of a discredited Cartesianism. To speak of how the world seems to the twins is just to speak of how each thinks the world is; and broad content attributions do a perfectly good job of portraying this. Oscar thinks that there is water in his glass; Toscar thinks that there is twater in his glass.

It might seem that this debate would end in a stalemate, but opponents of narrow content had a trump card. How was the supposed narrow content of the twins' beliefs to be expressed? Ascribing both twins beliefs about water, or beliefs about twater, would land one twin with false beliefs about a stuff unknown to him; this move is a non-starter. Ascribing both twins beliefs about the local colorless, odorless liquid that runs in the rivers ... etc. – that is, using a description which picks out water on Earth and twater on Twin Earth – appears to be a more promising way of expressing the narrow content of their shared beliefs. But this proposal does not supply belief ascriptions which are true on an opaque construal. In "Methodological solipsism ..." Fodor had proposed that the type of content picked out by opaque attitude ascriptions was just the type of content required by a computational psychology. His thought was that terms in the content-clause of an attitude ascription are opaque to substitution precisely because they pick out the object of the attitude in the way that the thinker conceives of it (cf. Fodor 1978; see the section "Fodorian intentional realism," above). But Oscar may simply conceive of water as water; he may not conceive of it as the local colorless, odorless liquid that runs in the rivers, and so on. He need not even have the concept of a colorless, odorless liquid in order to have beliefs about water, i.e. beliefs attributed using the word "water" in the content-clause of an opaque ascription. But if narrow content is not what is picked out by ordinary opaque attitude attributions, its defenders must give some account of what it is and how it is individuated. In particular, they must explain why it deserves to be regarded as content. Just saying that narrow content is attitude content shared by physical and functional duplicates is not only inadequate to define the notion but also question-begging. Obviously such duplicates share many properties, but what is the argument for assuming that a notion of *content* is determined by them?

A natural proposal, advanced in slightly different forms by White (1982), Fodor (1987), and Loar (1987), is to model narrow content on the content of indexicals. In fact, Putnam had originally interpreted his thought-experiment as showing that "natural-kind words like 'water' are indexical" (1975: 234). The indexical word "I" has different extensions when used in different contexts; "I" used by me refers to me, while "I" used by you refers to you. But, as Putnam points out, this variation in the extension of the term is not matched by a difference in intension; it is precisely because "I" means what it does that it refers to different individuals in different contexts. Kaplan describes the character of indexicals as a function from contexts to meanings; Fodor and White propose that narrow content is a function from contexts to truth-conditions, or wide contents. Narrow content determines wide content relative to a context. Fodor (1987) accepts that narrow contents are inexpressible, but maintains that they are more fundamental than wide contents, since they determine them. Loar (1988) describes the narrow content of beliefs as determining context-indeterminate realization conditions, and argues that we can in fact pick out such contents using ordinary opaque ascriptions, although such ascriptions do not express narrow contents.

Loar and Fodor motivate talk of narrow content in very different ways. Loar (1988) uses thought-experiments to argue that our everyday practice of attitude ascription recognizes a notion of explanatorily relevant psychological content which cannot always be captured by opaque ascriptions. He tackles Burge on his own ground, arguing that ordinary ascriptive practice is not as externalist as Burge claims. Fodor assumes (with Stich 1978) that any scientifically respectable notion of psychological content must yield content that is shared by physical and functional duplicates. This is the formality condition that Fodor (1980) motivated by appeal to the computational theory of mind: "two thoughts can be distinct in content only if they can be identified with relations to formally distinct representations" (1980: 227). Physical and functional twins will have symbols of the same form in their heads; so a theory of mind which is representational and computational cannot allow their thoughts to be distinct in content. The Burge and Putnam thought-experiments threatened to split apart the computational and representational elements of Fodor's theory of mind; narrow content was needed to hold them together. He finally abandoned narrow content in his 1994 book, arguing that a nomological rather than a metaphysical link would suffice to hold content and computational form together. This change in view was due in large measure to Fodor's espousal of an informational account of content which was strongly externalist.

By the end of the century, the debate over narrow content was generally regarded as having been won by the externalists. The view that mental content is wide, dependent on a thinker's environment, became the standard view. Sometimes it is regarded as obvious, once we reflect on what it is for mental states to have content. The idea of content goes with the idea of intentionality or aboutness; mental states which have content are about something beyond themselves. If you believe that water is wet, you have a belief about something external to you; your state of mind relates you to that stuff. To say what you believe is (in part) to say what it is your belief is about, to relate your state of mind to that thing. The idea that there could be a kind of content which didn't involve any relation to anything outside your head looks absurd. So does the idea of a kind of content which could be specified without referring to anything external to the thinker. Such "content" would be content without the content – which is just how narrow content was described by its detractors.

But this rapid response to the debate about the determinants of content trades on a confusion. Your belief relates you to water in that it is about water; but this fact does not settle the question of what relations (if any) must obtain between you and your environment for you to have a belief that is about water. Subject S's possession of a belief about x does not directly entail the existence of an x in S's environment (or indeed anywhere) to which S is related, as beliefs about Santa Claus and phlogiston show (see Crane 2001). This point can be obscured by the conflation of two different conceptions of narrow content (distinguished by Burge 1986: 4). On the first, mental states with narrow content are states that can be explicated solely in terms of a subject's intrinsic physical and functional states, non-intentionally described. On the second, mental states with narrow content are states that supervene on a subject's intrinsic physical and functional states, non-intentionally described. States which cannot be explicated solely by reference to intrinsic states may nonetheless supervene on intrinsic states. Consider solubility in water: this is a disposition which cannot be explicated without reference to something extrinsic to water-soluble things (i.e. water), but it nonetheless supervenes on their intrinsic physical structure. Of course these are not the only possible conceptions of narrow content; the notion need not be tied to physical and functional constitution (see Crane 2001). And of course showing that the notion is not incoherent is not showing that a defensible account of it can or needs to be given (see Segal 2000 for an attempt to do this).

Self-knowledge and externalism

One challenge put to externalists early in the debate about content was this: if the content of our thoughts is wide, if it depends in part on the nature of our environment, how can we know the contents of our own thoughts without investigating the nature of our environment? Neither Oscar nor Toscar knows anything about the chemical differences between water and twater; they cannot tell them apart. But according to the externalist, their thought contents differ in ways which depend on those chemical differences. So the content of the twins' thoughts depends on features of their environment (the chemical composition of the stuffs they call "water") of which they are ignorant. How then can they know what they are thinking?

Tyler Burge (1946–) argues in response that the twins do not need to be able to discriminate water from twater, or water-thoughts from twater-thoughts, in order to know what they are thinking. They simply need to be able to think the thoughts in question and think that they are thinking them. The content of the second-order, self-ascriptive thought is inherited from the content of the first-order thought, which in turn is determined by the environment. "One knows one's thought to be what it is simply by thinking it while exercising second-order, self-ascriptive powers" (Burge 1988: 72). But if knowledge of one's thoughts can be shown not to require knowledge of one's environment, a second challenge awaits. The second problem is that knowledge of our thoughts seems to enable us to know about our environment without investigating it, if externalism is true. Suppose I know that I am thinking that water is wet. Suppose further that externalism is true, and I know it is; and that if externalism is true, my having thoughts about water entails that water exists in my environment, and that I know this. Then it seems that I can deduce that my environment contains water simply from the fact that I have thoughts about water, without needing to engage in any empirical investigation of my environment (see McKinsey 1991). Discussion of this problem in the last decade of the century centered on the question of whether any substantive empirical presuppositions of my having the thoughts I have could be established without empirical investigation (see Ludlow and Martin 1998).

These debates about the compatibility between externalism and self-knowledge helped to motivate a renewal of interest in the topic of self-knowledge itself. How can such knowledge be substantive, yet not based on evidence? (For discussion, see Wright et al. 1998; Moran 2001.)

Consciousness and qualia

In 1974 Thomas Nagel (1937–) published a paper ("What is it like to be a bat?") in which he argued that it is consciousness that poses the deep challenge for physicalism, that "makes the mind–body problem really intractable" (1974: 435). The basic argument of the paper is this: "If physicalism is to be defended, the phenomenological features [of experience] must themselves be given a physical account. But when we examine their subjective character it seems that such a result is impossible" (p. 437). Nagel's paper exerted an enormous influence on subsequent discussions of the phenomenal or qualitative features of conscious experience.[7] It popularized the phrase "what it is like" as a formula for referring to the qualitative character of experience. Frank Jackson cites it as an influence on his Knowledge Argument against physicalism (Jackson 1982: 131 n. 10), an argument which in turn sparked extensive debate. And it helped to inspire a paper by Levine (1983: n. 3), which employs the notion of an *explanatory gap* to illuminate a number of qualia-based objections to physicalism.

Nagel uses the "what it is like" locution to pick out what he calls the subjective character of experience: "fundamentally an organism has conscious mental states if and only if there is something that it is like to be that organism – something it is like for that organism. We may call this the subjective character of experience" (1974: 436). He claims that this subjective character is not captured by any available reductive analysis of the mental in physical or functional terms, "for all of them are logically compatible with its absence" (p. 436). And he offers an argument designed to show that a physical account of the subjective character of experience appears impossible. In essence, the argument turns on two claims. The first is that facts about the subjective character of a given type of experience are understandable only by adopting the point of view of the experiencer. The second is that understanding facts about the physical and functional structure of the experiencer does not enable others to adopt that point of view. These latter are objective facts, accessible and understandable from many points of view; but precisely for that reason, knowledge of them does not take us closer to the subject's point of view (pp. 444–5). Nagel uses the example of the bat to illustrate this claim. Unlike humans, bats rely on echolocation to find their way around their environment. Presumably there is something it is like for a bat to perceive the world through this sense modality, some subjective character to the bat's perceptual experience. But, Nagel argues, we cannot understand this subjective character. The bat's perceptual experience is just too different from our own for us to be able to imagine what it is like, and gathering information about bat anatomy and physiology does not enable us to adopt the bat's point of view.

Nagel does not conclude from this that physicalism is false; he concludes that we do not yet understand how it might be true. The cases usually cited by the physicalist, such as the identity of lightning with electrical discharge, are cases in which two objective phenomena are identified, and so do not help us to understand how psycho-physical identity claims could be true. "The idea of how a mental and a physical term might refer to the same thing is lacking, and the usual analogies with theoretical identification in other fields fail to supply it" (1974: 447).

Nagel's remark that functionalist accounts are compatible with the absence of experience with subjective character echoes the "absent qualia" objection to functionalism (Block and Fodor 1972; Block 1978; see the section "Problems for functionalism," above). His claim that psychophysical identities are disanalogous to other theoretical identities recalls Kripke's insistence that "Heat is molecular motion" is metaphysically necessary, while "Pain is C-fiber firing" is not (see the section "Kripke's conceivability argument," above). Nagel discusses Kripke's Conceivability Argument in a footnote; "like Kripke," he comments, "I find the hypothesis that a certain brain state should necessarily have a certain subjective character incomprehensible without further explanation" (1974: 445 n. 11). But unlike Kripke, he does not conclude that such psychophysical identities are contingent and therefore false; in fact, he suggests a way of explaining how they could appear contingent even if they were understood to be necessary. (Hill 1997 develops this suggestion into a reply to Kripke's argument.)

Levine's "Materialism and qualia: the explanatory gap" (1983) draws these threads together. Levine argues that Kripke's Cartesian objection to psychophysical identities and the absent qualia objection to psychofunctional identities are fueled by the same underlying intuition about the qualitative properties of mental states. Furthermore, he argues that the intuition in question supports an epistemological thesis rather than a metaphysical one: the thesis that the identities in question leave an explanatory gap. Kripke points out that both

(5) Pain is C-fiber firing

and

(6) Heat is molecular motion

appear to be contingent; it seems conceivable that they be false (Levine 1983: 355). As we have seen, Kripke argues that the apparent contingency of (6) is only apparent; it can be explained away. The explanation appeals to the conflation of (6) with the genuinely contingent identity statement (7):

(7) The phenomenon we experience through feelings of warmth, which is caused by friction, which causes metals to expand and ice to melt, etc., is molecular motion.

Thus the explanation appeals to a distinction between heat as it appears or feels to us, and heat as it is in itself. But we cannot make this distinction in the case of (5), since pain as it feels to us is pain as it is in itself. Similarly, Block (1978) argues that we can conceive that the psychofunctional identity

(8) Being in pain is being in functional state F

is false. He does this by describing a situation in which a system (the China-body simulation; see the section "Problems for functionalism," above) is in state F, but has no feeling of pain.

Levine proposes a diagnosis of the intuition that (5) and (8) are contingent: they express identities that are not fully explanatory. By contrast, he claims, (6) expresses an identity that is fully explanatory. The content of the explanation is given by an expanded version of (7). Once we understand how molecular motion can be caused by friction and can bring about the expansion of metals, the melting of ice, and the other effects of heat – once we understand how molecular motion can fill the causal role of heat – we understand the nature of heat. Before we know the essential nature of heat, we conceive of heat simply as something that plays a certain causal role; and once we see how molecular motion can play that role, "there is nothing more we need to understand" (Levine 1983: 356). In the case of pain, the situation is different. We conceive of pain not only as something that plays a certain causal role, but also as something that feels a certain way, that has a distinctive qualitative or subjective character. Even if we understand that the causal role of functional state F is that of pain, and even if we understand that C-fiber firing occupies that role in humans, this does not provide an explanation of why pain feels as it does: "there seems to be nothing about C-fibre firing which makes it naturally 'fit' the phenomenal properties of pain, any more than it would fit some other set of phenomenal properties" (1983: 356).

Levine's point is not that this is reason to think that pain cannot be C-fiber firing, but that it explains why we can conceive of one occurring without the other. The truth of (5) does not explain why having one's C-fibers fire feels as pain does. Compare (6) and (7); before we learn the physical nature of heat, the fact that it causes metals to expand is just a brute fact. Once we learn about molecular motion, we understand why (or how) it does this; it is no longer a brute fact. Not so, Levine claims, with (5); the connection between the physical and qualitative nature of pain remains simply a brute fact. (See Sturgeon 1994 for a similar argument.) Inability to close this explanatory gap does not make identity claims like (5) false; but it does mean, Levine argues, that we cannot know that they are true (1983: 360). So advocates of physicalism must try to find a way of bridging the explanatory gap.

Nagel argued that extant physical and functional accounts of conscious states leave something out; they ignore the subjective character of experience. But, like Levine, he did not take this to show that physicalism is false. Frank Jackson's Knowledge Argument does draw this conclusion; it states that because a complete physical account of the world leaves out the qualitative properties of mental states, physicalism is false. The argument proceeds via a thought-experiment. Jackson (1982) asks us to imagine a brilliant scientist, Mary, who is locked in a black and white room and receives all her information about the world via a black and white monitor and black and white books. By these means she acquires all the physical information there is to obtain about what goes on when human beings see colors. Despite this, Jackson argues, when Mary is released from her room and sees a red thing for the first time, she learns something new: she learns *what it is like* to see red. Mary acquires information about the qualitative character of a certain type of experience which she did not have before. This means that even when Mary knew everything physical there is to know, there was something she did not know; so not everything there is to know is physical. Since Mary's exhaustive knowledge of "matters physical" did not include knowledge of the qualitative features of experience, these features are not physical and physicalism is false (Jackson 1982; 1986).

The story of Mary is anticipated by Broad (1925: 71) and by Feigl, who asks what it is that a blind scientist cannot know about color qualities (1958: 431, 435). Jackson's presentation of the Knowledge Argument provoked much discussion, and helped to stimulate the renewal of philosophical interest in conscious experience. The anti-physicalist conclusion Jackson (1943–) seeks will follow only if the story of Mary shows that on her release she gains information or knowledge about a *new subject-matter*. Since she already knows all there is to know about matters physical, the new knowledge must be knowledge of something non-physical. This conclusion has been challenged in a variety of ways, but two popular lines of resistance can be distinguished. The first denies that Mary acquires any new propositional knowledge on her release; what she acquires is knowledge how, not knowledge that. She acquires the ability to recognize, imagine, and remember experiences of seeing red. Knowing how to do these things is knowing what it's like to see red. This so-called Ability Response is associated particularly with Nemirow (1990) and Lewis (1988).[8] Jackson (1986) responds that although Mary does acquire such abilities on her release, it remains plausible that she also acquires new propositional knowledge. The second line of resistance agrees that Mary acquires such knowledge, but denies that it is knowledge about a new subject matter. This type of response is elaborated in various ways in the literature (see Van Gulick 1993 for a more fine-grained taxonomy). But the basic idea is that the Knowledge Argument exploits two different senses of "knowledge" or "information." The premises of the argument are that Mary *first* knows "everything physical there is to know" and *then* comes to know something more (Jackson 1986). This could mean that she first knows all the truths about physical things, and then comes to know about things that are not physical (reading "knowledge" transparently). Or it could mean that she first knows all the truths that can be expressed in physical terms, and then comes to know truths that are expressed in non-physical terms (reading "knowledge" opaquely). The reading Jackson needs to secure his anti-physicalist conclusion is the first, but the physicalist will grant the premises only on the second reading (see Horgan 1984; Loar 1990).

Another qualia-based argument which provoked much debate in the closing years of the century was David Chalmers' Zombie Argument (Chalmers 1996), essentially a type of absent qualia argument against physicalism and functionalism. The zombies in question are not the lumbering monsters depicted in B-movies, but physical and functional duplicates of us whose experiences lack any qualitative character. Chalmers (1966–) argues that we can not only conceive of such creatures, but also conceive of a zombie world, a physical duplicate of our world in which there is no phenomenal consciousness. From the conceivability of zombies and a zombie world, Chalmers infers that they are metaphysically possible; and if they are metaphysically possible, physicalism is false. This argumentative strategy is obviously analogous to that of Kripke, and exploits the explanatory gap in a similar way. Chalmers also introduces a distinction between the easy and the hard problems of consciousness, which is closely related to the notion of the explanatory gap. The easy problems of consciousness are the problems of explaining how the brain performs various cognitive functions such as processing environmental stimuli and integrating and accessing information (1996: xi–xii). The hard problem is the problem of experience itself: the problem of explaining why and how the performance of these functions is accompanied by "an experienced inner life" (p. xii). Chalmers's distinction is similar to the distinction drawn by Ned Block (1995) between access consciousness and phenomenal consciousness. A state is access-conscious (A-conscious) if it is poised for direct control of thought and action. A-conscious states are always states of consciousness of something; propositional attitudes are the paradigm examples of A-conscious states. A state is phenomenally conscious (P-conscious) if there is something it is like to be in it; these are experiential states with distinctive qualitative character. P-conscious states may or may not be states of consciousness of something. Sensations are the paradigm examples of P-conscious states, though occurrent thoughts can be P-conscious too. As Block notes, the conscious states for which an explanatory gap is believed to arise are P-conscious states. How and why does a certain kind of neural activity give rise to a certain kind of experience? What Chalmers refers to as the hard problem of consciousness is the problem of experience, the problem of explaining P-consciousness. Relative to this, explaining A-consciousness is one of the easy problems. This is not because it is easy to solve in practice, but because A-consciousness is a functional notion, and so there seems to be no obstacle to explaining it computationally or neurophysiologically. Levine's diagnosis of the explanatory gap suggests why phenomenal consciousness would be hard to explain; if phenomenal properties are not individuated by their causal role, it is difficult to see how they could be explained functionally.

Kripke's Conceivability Argument, Jackson's Knowledge Argument, and Chalmers's Zombie Argument all infer an ontological gap from the explanatory gap; they draw a metaphysical conclusion about what there is from epistemological premises about what is conceivable or explicable. These arguments have elicited a variety of physicalist responses. All such responses, being physicalist, deny that there is any ontological gap; but they differ in their attitudes to the explanatory gap. At one pole is the view that there is no such gap. One way of eliminating the gap is to eliminate phenomenal properties. Dennett (1988), for example, argues that qualia are simply a philosophical fiction, so there is no need to explain them; the so-called mysteries of consciousness are artifacts of a misguided Cartesian picture (see his *Consciousness Explained*, 1991). A completely different way is to argue that the appearance of a gap is simply an artifact of neurobiological ignorance and philosophical prejudice. Searle

(1992), for example, argues that consciousness is simply an evolved biological feature of certain brains, caused by brain processes, for which we should eventually find a neurobiological explanation. Consciousness seems mysterious only because we make the mistake of thinking that because it is irreducibly subjective, it cannot be a physical phenomenon (Searle 1992: 95, 102). At the opposite pole is the view that the explanatory gap is so deep that we can never cross it. McGinn (1989a) is the paradigmatic exponent of this view. He argues that we cannot explain consciousness because we are constitutionally incapable of forming a concept of the property of the brain that accounts for it. Nonetheless, there is such a property, so there is no ontological gulf to match the epistemological one. Between these two extremes lie a range of views offering proposals for crossing or narrowing the epistemic gap. Loar (1990) offers an interesting defense of one such view. He sets out to provide the kind of account that Nagel (1974) said was needed: an account of how phenomenal and physical concepts could apply to the same properties despite being conceptually independent. Loar argues that phenomenal concepts are recognitional properties which pick out their referents directly (compare Feigl 1958: 448). The aim of such accounts is to show that there is no need for a priori conceptual linkages (modern-day synonymies) to establish psychophysical identities, and thus to show that distinct concepts – even concepts divided by an explanatory gap – can apply to the same properties.

Mental causation

As we have seen, both Lewis (1966) and Davidson (1970) presented causal arguments for physicalism. Both arguments made use of disputed assumptions: Lewis assumed that mental properties are defined by their causal role, while Davidson assumed that causation requires strict deterministic laws. Christopher Peacocke (1950–) advanced a causal argument for physicalism which employed a less controversial assumption, the assumption that the effects of mental events are not regularly overdetermined (Peacocke 1979). This style of Overdetermination Argument for physicalism attracted much interest. The basic strategy of all three arguments is the same: to argue that mental phenomena must be physical if they are to have physical effects. All three arguments rely on a claim that is sometimes called the Completeness of Physics, or the Causal Closure of the Physical. This is made precise in various ways, but the basic idea is this:

(a) All physical effects have physical causes. (Physical Completeness)

This is conjoined with a second premise:

(b) Mental causes have physical effects. (Mental Causation)

Claims (a) and (b) together entail that the effects of mental causes also have physical causes, but leave open the possibility that their mental and physical causes are distinct; a further step is needed to force the identification of the two. The three arguments take this step in different ways. Lewis takes it that mental states are by definition the causes of certain physical effects; so by definition, they are identical to the (physical) causes of those effects. Davidson assumes that causation requires strict deterministic laws, and claims that such laws employ only physical predicates; this yields both (a) and the identification of mental with physical causes. The Overdetermination Argument claims that the effects of mental events are not overdetermined; but if they had distinct mental and physical causes, they would be. So their mental and physical causes are not distinct. The net effect of all these moves is to exclude the possibility that physical effects have mental and physical causes which are distinct:

(c) No physical effect has a mental cause distinct from its physical cause. (Causal Exclusion)

Claims (a), (b), and (c) combined yield the conclusion that mental causes are physical causes:

(d) The mental causes of physical effects are not distinct from their physical causes. (Identity)

This argument exemplifies what I shall call the exclusion strategy for arguing for physicalism. The causes and effects of which the argument speaks may be types or tokens, properties or particular events. Lewis applies the exclusion strategy to mental properties (types of experience), yielding type physicalism, while Davidson applies it to individual mental events, yielding token physicalism. Since type physicalism is generally rejected on grounds of the multiple realizability of mental properties, the favored overdetermination style of causal argument for non-reductive physicalism applies the exclusion strategy to token events.

Familiarly, non-reductive physicalism combines token physicalism with property dualism. To many this seemed the ideal combination, providing a robust causal role for mental particulars while acknowledging that mental kinds can cross-cut physical kinds.[9] However, worries about whether this view provides a causal role for mental properties began to surface in the 1980s. Concern about the causal efficacy of mental properties had three main sources. First, the debate between externalists and internalists focused attention on the causal role of mental content, particularly wide content properties. Fodor argued that mental causation demands content which is locally (i.e. narrowly) supervenient on physical properties: "causal powers supervene on local microstructure ... mind/brain supervenience ... is our only plausible account of how mental states could have the causal powers that they do have" (1987: 44). The idea that causally efficacious properties are local and intrinsic while wide content is environmental and extrinsic prompted questions about its causal efficacy:

what happens at the causal nexus is local, proximate and intrinsic: the features of the cause that lead to the effect must be right there where the causal interaction takes place … The causal powers of a state or property must be intrinsically grounded; they cannot depend essentially upon relations to what lies entirely elsewhere. (McGinn 1989b: 133)

Defenders of wide content accused their opponents of begging the question; since wide content has causal powers, such powers are not local and intrinsic (Burge 1993). Skeptics asked *how* wide content properties made a causal difference. Where do different wide contents get a causal foothold in physically and computationally identical brains? From here it was a short step to the question: How do content properties get a causal foothold in *any* brain where physical and computational mechanisms do the causal work?

Second, Davidson's anomalous monism, with its commitment to the nomological character of causality and the anomalousness of the mental, was charged with rendering mental properties causally inert or epiphenomenal. If causal relations require strict causal laws, and only physical properties figure in strict laws, then it seems that a mental event's causal relations are determined by its physical properties alone. Variations in its mental properties would make no causal difference (Honderich 1982; Sosa 1984; Kim 1989). Davidson defends himself against the charge by appealing to the supervenience of mental properties on physical properties; an event's mental properties cannot change unless its physical properties change, so a change in an event's mental properties does make for a change in its causal relations. Faced with the complaint that it is still the event's physical properties that are causally efficacious, he repudiates the idea that properties can be causes at all (Davidson 1993; see McLaughlin 1993 for discussion). Properties can be relevant to causal explanation, but here mental properties come off well, since we know many reliable causal generalizations subsuming events described in mental terms (Davidson 1963; see Crane 1995). Though consistently Davidsonian, this response has the disadvantage of depriving *all* properties of causal efficacy. But it also suggests a way of securing causal efficacy for mental properties: simply appeal to the fact that they figure in (non-strict) reliable laws (Fodor 1990), or in counterfactual dependencies (LePore and Loewer 1987). But epiphenomenal properties can figure in such laws too; so epiphenomenalist worries were not fully assuaged.

The rediscovery of emergent materialism provided a third source of concern about mental causation and non-reductive physicalism (see McLaughlin 1993 for an account of emergentism). The emergentists held that mental properties emerge only when suitable physical conditions are instantiated; they are dependent on physical properties, but distinct from them. Moreover, mental properties have genuine causal powers, not reducible to the causal powers of their physical bases. Kim (1993) argued that contemporary non-reductive physicalism is a form of emergentism, and that it cannot reconcile the causal closure of the physical with the causal powers of mental properties. The sufficiency of physical causes guaranteed by causal closure leaves no place for the distinctive causal powers putatively possessed by mental properties.

This line of argument points the way to the basic Exclusion Argument for epiphe-nomenalism about mental properties (Yablo 1992; Kim 1998). Consider the exclusion strategy for arguing for physicalism, applied to properties. This yields:

(a') The physical effects of physical events are caused by the physical properties of those events. (Physical Completeness for properties)

(b') The physical effects of mental events are caused by the mental properties of those events. (Mental Causation for properties)

(c') No physical effect has a mental cause distinct from its physical cause. (Causal Exclusion)

(d') The mental and physical properties of mental events causing the events' physical effects are not distinct. (Identity for properties)

Non-reductive physicalism rejects the conclusion, since it rejects the identification of mental properties with physical properties; so it must reject one of the premises. The Exclusion Argument for epiphenomenalism says that the non-reductive physicalist must reject (b') Mental Causation for properties. It deduces the negation of (b') from the negation of (d') conjoined with (a') and (c'). The non-reductive physicalist who wants to affirm Mental Causation for properties must deny another premise, and the Causal Exclusion premise (c') is an obvious choice. Yablo (1992) targets this premise in an elegant way, arguing that mental and physical properties do not compete for causal influence over physical effects because they are too closely linked; physical properties are determinates of mental determinables. However, mental and physical properties do compete for the title of "cause," and here mental properties have an advantage; they are proportional to the physical effects in question in a way that more specific physical properties are not. This part of Yablo's argument casts doubt on premise (a').

The Exclusion Argument not only threatens epiphenomenalism, but also throws the exclusion strategy of argument for physicalism into sharp relief. Of course non-reductive physicalists use that strategy to argue for token identity, not property identity. But an attack on the Causal Exclusion premise threatens the crucial step in the exclusion argument for token identity. And if, as Yablo suggests, mental events may have a better claim to be the causes of actions than microphysical events, premise (a) of that argument is called in question (see Sturgeon 1998 for a different argument to the same conclusion). Perhaps the moral is that physicalism is better motivated by empirical and methodological considerations than by armchair metaphysics.

Conclusion

The story of philosophy of mind in the twentieth century is in part the story of the fortunes of physicalism. C. D. Broad in 1925 rejected the mechanist claim that all phenomena can be explained in physical terms, because he found it empirically implausible. He rejected reductive materialism because he thought it obvious that phenomenal concepts and physical concepts pick out different properties. He thus rejected the explanatory and ontological reduction of mental properties to physical properties. The logical positivists defined ontological physicalism semantically, arguing that all the facts about the mind are statable in physical terms, since all facts are physically verifiable. This thesis does not entail that psychological laws are deducible from physical laws, but it does entail that there are no conceptual barriers to such a reduction. With the recognition of the inadequacies of verificationism, physicalism was defended in a weaker form. Smart, Place, and Feigl defended the ontological reduction of sensations to brain processes on grounds of empirical plausibility and methodological simplicity. Most philosophers came to reject the identification of mental properties with physical properties on grounds of empirical implausibility, finding it more likely that mental properties are multiply realizable. Non-reductive physicalism became the orthodox view.

Non-reductive physicalism has been formulated in different ways. Davidson's anomalous monism is simply the view that all mental events are physical events (token physicalism). This form of physicalism is weak in saying nothing about mental properties; it is compatible with the view that their distribution is entirely indifferent to the distribution of physical properties. Token physicalism plus the supervenience of mental properties on physical properties is a stronger view. And since supervenience provides a way of tying mental properties to physical properties without identifying the two, it seems well suited for formulating non-reductive physicalism. The debate about wide and narrow content indicates that it would be too restrictive to say that mental properties supervene on physical properties at the level of the individual; but a claim of global supervenience seems tailor-made to capture the claim that the world is fundamentally physical. Suppose that duplicating our world physically suffices for duplicating our world simpliciter. This looks like physicalism without reduction (see Haugeland 1982; Horgan 1982; Jackson 1998).

As the end of the century approached, this physicalist supervenience thesis came under attack for two very different reasons. On the one hand, it was argued that the supervenience thesis is too strong to be plausible, since the conceivability of a zombie world – a physical duplicate of our world where there is no phenomenal consciousness – shows that it is false (Chalmers 1996). On the other, it was argued that the super-venience thesis is too weak to capture physicalism (Horgan 1995). It simply states that mental properties must co-vary with physical properties without explaining why this is so. But this means that it leaves open the possibility that there is no explanation, or that the explanation is non-physical. A satisfying form of physicalism must explain why physical properties determine mental properties.

Much discussion of the first argument focused on the move from the conceivability of zombies to their possibility as an instance of the move from an explanatory gap to an ontological gap. Critics point out that conceivability and intelligibility are epistemic notions, not metaphysical ones; a gap between concepts need not imply a gap between the properties to which they apply. But by the same token, closing an ontological gap by asserting a metaphysical relation of supervenience or identity between mental and physical properties brings little explanatory gain. That is the lesson of the second argument, and it raises the question of why one should accept a physicalist account of the mental in the first place. Physicalism itself has now come under scrutiny. What is the reason for affirming that everything is physical, and what does "physical" mean in this context? (Crane and Mellor 1990; Stoljar 2001).

But the story of philosophy of mind in the twentieth century is much more than just the story of physicalism. Particular mental phenomena such as emotion, sensation, memory, and perception have been the focus of philosophical investigation. With the recent revival of interest in Brentano's thesis that intentionality is the mark of the mental, the question of the relationship between the intentional and qualitative aspects of mind has been reopened. This is a particular focus of work on perception (see, e.g., Crane 1992). Moves to integrate the intentional and phenomenal aspects of mind run counter to the "divide and conquer" strategy which has been dominant for many years. Understanding the mind will ultimately require that accounts of different areas of mental life be brought together; and understanding the mind itself is a prerequisite for understanding the place of the mind in a physical world.

Notes

1 Broad claims that higher forms of mentality, such as referential cognition, cannot be reduced to lower forms, such as sentience (feelings and sensations). He argues that even if we suppose that an event which is the perception of a pink rat consists entirely of feelings and sensations, it would still be impossible to deduce that the event would be the perception of a pink rat simply from laws about feelings and sensations (1925: 638).

2 Broad's analysis of mentality is more complex than this. He includes two other factors, acquaintance and affective attitudes. The first is awareness of feeling somehow (which, he acknowledges, some will identify with feeling somehow, or sentience; see 1925: 635). The second involves "feeling some*how towards* something" (p. 636; italics in original). Broad claims that while sentience/acquaintance can exist without referential cognition, the converse is not true; and that while affective attitudes require sentience/acquaintance and referential cognition, the converse is not true (p. 637).

3 Moran (1996) argues persuasively that Chisholm's interpretation obscures both Brentano's conception of intentionality and his phenomenological conception of the contrast between mental and physical.

4 It should be noted that although Fodor holds that mental attitudes such as believing and desiring are functionally distinguished, he rejects a functionalist account of the content of such attitudes.

5 It provides a paradigm, not the paradigm; Davidson employs an ontology of events, while non-reductive physicalism is more often formulated in terms of states and events.

6 Putnam also uses the phrase "methodological solipsism" to denote what he regards as a traditional philosophical assumption: the assumption that psychological states properly so-called are states in the narrow sense (1975: 220). Fodor (1980) defends the assumption.

7 It should be noted that B. A. Farrell's paper "Experience" (1950) anticipates many of Nagel's points, even using the example of a bat's experiences.

8 Compare Feigl's remark that if we were blind we would not know color experiences "by *acquaintance*; i.e., (1) we would not *have* them; (2) we could not *imagine* them; (3) we could not *recognize* (or *label*) them as 'red', 'green', etc." (1958: 415; italics in original). However, unlike Nemirow and Lewis, Feigl regards knowledge by acquaintance as propositional (p. 435). Nemirow 1990 discusses Feigl's view.

9 See Fodor 1974 for a defense of this view that does not employ the exclusion strategy.

References

Anscombe, G. E. M. (1957) *Intention*. Oxford: Blackwell.

Armstrong, D. (1968) *A Materialist Theory of the Mind*. London: Routledge & Kegan Paul.

Block, N. (1978) "Troubles with functionalism." In N. Block (ed.) *Readings in Philosophy of Psychology*, vol. 1. Cambridge, MA: Harvard University Press, 1980, pp. 268–305.

—— (1995) "On a confusion about a function of consciousness." *Behavioral and Brain Sciences* 18: 227–47.

Block, N. and J. A. Fodor (1972) "What psychological states are not." *Philosophical Review* 81: 158–81.

Boyd, R. (1980) "Materialism without reductionism: what physicalism does not entail." In N. Block (ed.) *Readings in Philosophy of Psychology*, vol. 1. Cambridge, MA: Harvard University Press, pp. 67–106.

Brentano, F. (1874) *Psychologie vom empirischen Standpunkt*. Repr. as *Psychology from an Empirical Standpoint*, trans. L. L. McAlister, London: Routledge, 1973, to which page references are made.

Broad, C. D. (1925) *The Mind and its Place in Nature*. London: Routledge & Kegan Paul.

Burge, T. (1977) "Belief de re." *Journal of Philosophy* 74: 338–62.

—— (1979) "Individualism and the mental." In P. A. French, T. E. Uehling, and H. K. Wettstein (eds.) *Midwest Studies in Philosophy* 4, Minneapolis: University of Minnesota Press, pp. 73–122.

—— (1982) "Other bodies." In A. Woodfield (ed.) *Thought and Object*, Oxford: Clarendon Press, pp. 97–120.

—— (1986) "Individualism and psychology." *Philosophical Review* 95: 3–45.

—— (1988) "Individualism and self-knowledge." *Journal of Philosophy* 85: 649–63.

—— (1993) "Mind–body causation and explanatory practice." In J. Heil and A. Mele (eds.) *Mental Causation*, Oxford: Oxford University Press, pp. 97–120.

Carnap, R. (1932) "Psychologie in physikalischer Sprache." *Erkenntnis* 3: 107–42. Repr. as "Psychology in physical language," in A. J. Ayer (ed.) *Logical Positivism*, New York: Free Press, 1959, pp. 165-98, to which page references are made.

Carnap, R. (1934) *The Unity of Science*, trans. Max Black. London: Kegan Paul. Originally published in *Erkenntnis* 2 (1931): 432–65.

Carnap, R., H. Hahn, and O. Neurath (1929) *Wissenschaftliche Weltauffassung – Der Wiener Kreis*. Vienna: Wolf.

Chalmers, D. (1996) *The Conscious Mind*. Oxford: Oxford University Press.

Chihara, C. S. and J. A. Fodor (1965) "Operationalism and ordinary language: a critique of Wittgenstein." *American Philosophical Quarterly* 2: 281–95.

Chisholm, R. (1956) "Sentences about believing." *Proceedings of the Aristotelian Society* 56: 125–48.

—— (1957) *Perceiving: A Philosophical Study*. Ithaca, NY: Cornell University Press.

Churchland, P. M. (1981) "Eliminative materialism and propositional attitudes." *Journal of Philosophy* 78: 67–90.

Crane, T. (ed.) (1992) *The Contents of Experience: Essays on Perception*. Cambridge: Cambridge University Press.

—— (1995) "The mental causation debate." *Proceedings of the Aristotelian Society, Supplementary Volume* 69: 211–36.

—— (1998) "Intentionality as the mark of the mental." In A. O'Hear (ed.) *Current Issues in the Philosophy of Mind*. Cambridge: Cambridge University Press, pp. 229–51.

—— (2001) *Elements of Mind*. Oxford: Oxford University Press.

Crane, T. and H. Mellor (1990) "There is no question of physicalism." *Mind* 99: 185–206.

Davidson, D. (1963) "Actions, reasons and causes." *Journal of Philosophy* 60: 685–700. Repr. in *Essays on Actions and Events*, Oxford: Oxford University Press, 1980, pp. 3–20, to which page references are made.

—— (1970) "Mental events." In L. Foster and J. W. Swanson (eds.) *Experience and Theory*, London: Duckworth. Repr. in *Essays on Actions and Events*, Oxford: Oxford University Press, 1980, pp. 207–25, to which page references are made.

—— (1974) "Psychology as philosophy." In S. C. Brown (ed.) *Philosophy of Psychology*, London: Macmillan. Repr. in *Essays on Actions and Events*, Oxford: Oxford University Press, 1980, pp. 229–39, to which page references are made.

—— (1987) "Knowing one's own mind." *Proceedings and Addresses of the American Philosophical Association* 60: 441–58.

—— (1993) "Thinking causes." In J. Heil and A. Mele (eds.) *Mental Causation*, Oxford: Oxford University Press, pp. 3–17.

Davies, M. and T. Stone (eds.) (1995) *Folk Psychology: The Theory of Mind Debate*. Oxford: Blackwell.

Dennett, D. (1971) "Intentional systems." *Journal of Philosophy* 68: 87–106.

—— (1981a) "Three kinds of intentional psychology." In R. F. Healy (ed.) *Reduction, Time and Reality*, Cambridge: Cambridge University Press. Repr. in *The Intentional Stance*, Cambridge, MA: MIT Press, 1987, pp. 43–68, to which page references are made.

—— (1981b) "True believers: the intentional strategy and why it works." In A. F. Heath (ed.) *Scientific Explanations*, Oxford: Oxford University Press, pp. 53–75. Reprinted in *The Intentional Stance*, Cambridge, MA: MIT Press, 1987, pp. 13–35.

—— (1987) *The Intentional Stance*. Cambridge, MA: MIT Press.

—— (1988) "Quining qualia." In A. Marcel and E. Bisiach (eds.) *Consciousness in Contemporary Science*, Oxford: Oxford University Press, pp. 42–77.

—— (1991) *Consciousness Explained*. London: Little, Brown.

Farrell, B. A. (1950) "Experience." *Mind* 59: 170–98.

Feigl, H. (1963) "Physicalism, unity of science and the foundations of psychology." In P. A. Schilpp (ed.) *The Philosophy of Rudolf Carnap*, La Salle, IL: Open Court, pp. 227–67.

—— (1958) "The 'Mental' and the 'Physical'." In H. Feigl, M. Scriven, and G. Maxwell (eds.) *Minnesota Studies in the Philosophy of Science 2*, Minneapolis: University of Minnesota Press, pp. 370–497.

Feigl, H. and W. Sellars (eds.) (1949) *Readings in Philosophical Analysis*. New York: Appleton-Century-Crofts.

Feyerabend, P. (1963) "Mental events and the brain." *Journal of Philosophy* 60: 295–6.

Fodor, J. A. (1968) *Psychological Explanation*. New York: Random House.

—— (1974) "Special sciences." *Synthèse* 28: 77–115. Repr. in *Representations: Philosophical Essays on the Foundations of Cognitive Science*, Cambridge, MA: MIT Press, 1983, pp. 127–45.

—— (1975) *The Language of Thought*. Cambridge, MA: Harvard University Press.

—— (1978) "Propositional attitudes." *The Monist* 6: 501–23. Repr. in *Representations: Philosophical Essays on the Foundations of Cognitive Science*, Cambridge, MA: MIT Press, 1983, pp. 177–203, to which page references are made.

—— (1980) "Methodological solipsism considered as a research strategy in cognitive psychology." *Behavioral and Brain Sciences* 3: 63–73. Repr. in *Representations: Philosophical Essays on the Foundations of Cognitive Science*, Cambridge, MA: MIT Press, 1983, pp. 225–53, to which page references are made.

—— (1983) *Representations: Philosophical Essays on the Foundations of Cognitive Science*. Cambridge, MA: MIT Press.

—— (1987) *Psychosemantics: The Problem of Meaning in the Philosophy of Mind*. Cambridge, MA: MIT Press.

—— (1990) "Making mind matter more." In *A Theory of Content and Other Essays*, Cambridge, MA: MIT Press, pp. 137–59.

—— (1991) "Replies." In B. Loewer and G. Rey (eds.) *Meaning in Mind: Fodor and his Critics*, Oxford: Blackwell, pp. 255–319.

—— (1994) *The Elm and the Expert: Mentalese and its Semantics*. Cambridge, MA: MIT Press.

—— (2000) *The Mind Doesn't Work That Way*. Cambridge, MA: MIT Press.

Fodor, J. A. and Z. Pylyshyn (1988) "Connectionism and cognitive architecture." *Cognition* 28: 3–71.

Goldberg, S. and A. Pessin (eds.) (1996) *The Twin-Earth Chronicles*. New York and London: M. E. Sharpe.

Goldman, A. (1989) "Interpretation psychologized." *Mind & Language* 4: 161–85.

Gordon, R. (1986) "Folk psychology as simulation." *Mind & Language* 1: 158–71.

Haugeland, J. (1982) "Weak supervenience." *American Philosophical Quarterly* 19: 93–103.

Heal, J. (1986) "Replication and functionalism," In J. Butterfield (ed.) *Language, Mind and Logic*, Cambridge: Cambridge University Press, pp. 135–50.

Heil, J. (ed.) (1989) *Cause, Mind and Reality: Essays Honouring C. B. Martin*. London: Kluwer.

Hempel, C. (1949) "The logical analysis of psychology." In H. Feigl and W. Sellars (eds.) *Readings in Philosophical Analysis*, New York: Appleton-Century-Crofts. Repr. in N. Block (ed.) *Readings in Philosophy of Psychology*, vol. 1, Cambridge, MA: Harvard University Press, 1980, pp. 14–23, to which page references are made.

Hill, C. (1997) "Imaginability, conceivability, possibility, and the mind–body problem." *Philosophical Studies* 87: 61–85.

Honderich, T. (1982) "The argument for anomalous monism." *Analysis* 42: 59–64.

Horgan, T. (1982) "Supervenience and microphysics." *Pacific Philosophical Quarterly* 63: 29–43.

—— (1984) "Functionalism, qualia, and the inverted spectrum." *Philosophical and Phenomenological Research* 44: 453–69.

—— (1995) "From supervenience to superdupervenience: meeting the demands of a material world." *Mind* 102: 555–86.

Horgan, T. and J. Woodward (1985) "Folk psychology is here to stay." *Philosophical Review* 94: 197–226.

Jackson, F. (1982) "Epiphenomenal qualia." *Philosophical Quarterly* 32: 127–36.

—— (1986) "What Mary didn't know." *Journal of Philosophy* 83: 291–5.

—— (1998) *From Metaphysics to Ethics: A Defense of Conceptual Analysis.* Oxford: Clarendon Press.

Jackson, F. and P. Pettit (1990) "In defence of folk psychology." *Philosophical Studies* 57: 7–30.

James, W. (1912) "Does consciousness exist?" In *Essays in Radical Empiricism*, New York: Longman Green, pp. 1–38. Originally published in *Journal of Philosophy, Psychology, and Scientific Methods* 1 (1904): 477–91.

Kim, J. (1989) "The myth of non-reductive materialism." *Proceedings and Addresses of the American Philosophical Association* 63: 31–47.

—— (1993) "The non-reductivist's troubles with mental causation." In J. Heil and A. Mele (eds.) *Mental Causation*, Oxford: Oxford University Press, pp. 189–210.

—— (1998) *Mind in a Physical World.* Cambridge, MA: MIT Press.

Kripke, S. (1972) *Naming and Necessity.* Cambridge, MA: Harvard University Press.

LePore, E. and B. Loewer (1987) "Mind matters." *Journal of Philosophy* 84: 630–42.

Levine, J. (1983) "Materialism and qualia: the explanatory gap." *Pacific Philosophical Quarterly* 64: 354–61.

Lewes, G. H. (1875) *Problems of Life and Mind*, vol. 2. London: Kegan Paul, Trench, Trubner.

Lewis, D. (1966) "An argument for the identity theory." *Journal of Philosophy* 63: 17–25.

—— (1972) "Psychophysical and theoretical identifications." *Australian Journal of Philosophy* 50: 249–58.

—— (1988) "What experience teaches." In *Proceedings of the Russellian Society* (University of Sydney). Repr. in W. G. Lycan (ed.) *Mind and Cognition: A Reader*, Oxford: Blackwell, 1990, pp. 499–519.

Loar, B. (1988) "Social content and psychological content." In R. Grimm and D. Merrill (eds.) *Contents of Thought*, Tucson: University of Arizona Press, pp. 180–91.

—— (1990) "Phenomenal states." In J. Tomberlin (ed.) *Philosophical Perspectives*, vol. 4, Atascadero, CA: Ridgeview, pp. 81–108. Rev. version in N. Block, O. Flanagan, and G. Guzeldere (eds.) *The Nature of Consciousness*, Cambridge, MA: MIT Press, 1997, pp. 597–616.

Ludlow, P. and Martin, N. (eds.) (1998) *Externalism and Self-Knowledge.* Stanford, CA: CSLI Press.

Lycan, W. G. (1987) *Consciousness.* Cambridge, MA: MIT Press.

McGinn, C. (1977) "Anomalous monism and Kripke's Cartesian intuitions." *Analysis* 37: 78–80.

—— (1989a) "Can we solve the mind–body problem?" *Mind* 98: 349–66.

—— (1989b) *Mental Content.* Oxford: Blackwell.

McKinsey, M. (1991) "Anti-individualism and privileged access." *Analysis* 51: 9–16.

McLaughlin, B. (1985) "Anomalous monism and the irreducibility of the mental." In E. LePore and B. McLaughlin (eds.) *Actions and Events: Perspectives on the Philosophy of Donald Davidson*, Oxford: Blackwell, pp. 331–68.

—— (1992) "The rise and fall of British emergentism." In A. Beckermann, H. Flohr, and J. Kim (eds.) *Emergence or Reduction? Prospects for Nonreductive Physicalism.* Berlin: de Gruyter, pp. 49–93.

—— (1993) "On Davidson's response to the charge of epiphenomenalism ." In J. Heil and A. Mele (eds.) *Mental Causation*, Oxford: Oxford University Press, pp. 27–40.

Magee, B. (1971) *Modern British Philosophy.* London: Secker & Warburg.

Matthews, R. (1991) "Is there vindication through representationalism?" In B. Loewer and G. Rey (eds.) *Meaning in Mind: Fodor and his Critics*, Oxford: Blackwell, pp. 137–49.

Mill, J. S. (1843) *A System of Logic.* London: Longmans, Green, Reader & Dyer.

Moran, D. (1996) "Brentano's thesis." *Proceedings of the Aristotelian Society, Supplementary Volume* 70: 1–27.

Moran, R. (2001) *Authority and Estrangement: An Essay on Self-Knowledge.* Princeton, NJ: Princeton University Press.

Nagel, T. (1974) "What is it like to be a bat?" *Philosophical Review* 83: 435–50.

Nemirow, L. (1990) "Physicalism and the cognitive role of acquaintance." In W. Lycan (ed.) *Mind and Cognition*. Oxford: Blackwell, pp. 490–9.

Patterson, S. (1995) "The anomalism of psychology." *Proceedings of the Aristotelian Society* 96: 37–52.

Peacocke, C. (1979) *Holistic Explanation*. Oxford: Clarendon Press.

Place, U. T. (1956) "Is consciousness a brain process?" *British Journal of Psychology* 47: 44–50.

Presley, C. F. (1967) *The Identity Theory of Mind*. St Lucia: University of Queensland Press.

Preston, J. and M. Bishop (eds.) (2002) *Views into the Chinese Room: New Essays on Searle and Artificial Intelligence*. New York: Oxford University Press.

Putnam, H. (1967) "Psychological predicates." In W. H. Capitan and D. D. Merrill (eds.) *Art, Mind and Religion*, Pittsburgh: University of Pittsburgh Press, pp. 37–48. Repr. as "The nature of mental states," in N. Block (ed.) *Readings in Philosophy of Psychology*, vol. 1, Cambridge, MA: Harvard University Press, 1980, pp. 223–31.

Putnam, H. (1968) "Brains and behavior." In R. J. Butler (ed.) *Analytical Philosophy II*, Oxford: Blackwell, pp. 1–19. Repr. in N. Block (ed.) *Readings in Philosophy of Psychology*, vol. 1, Cambridge, MA: Harvard University Press, 1980.

—— (1975) "The meaning of 'meaning'." In *Mind, Language and Reality: Philosophical Papers*, vol. 2, Cambridge: Cambridge University Press, pp. 215–71. Originally in K. Gunderson (ed.) *Language, Mind and Knowledge*, *Minnesota Studies in the Philosophy of Science* 7, Minneapolis: University of Minnesota Press, 1975, pp. 131–93.

Quine, W.V. O. (1960) *Word and Object*. Cambridge, MA: MIT Press.

—— (1969) *Ontological Relativity and Other Essays*. New York: Columbia University Press.

—— (1990) *Pursuit of Truth*. Cambridge, MA: Harvard University Press.

Reed, E. S. (1994) "The separation of psychology from philosophy." In C. L. Ten (ed.) *Routledge History of Philosophy*, vol. 8: *The Nineteenth Century*, London: Routledge, pp. 297–356.

Rorty, R. (1965) "Mind–body identity, privacy and categories." *Review of Metaphysics* 19: 24–54.

—— (1980) *Philosophy and the Mirror of Nature*. Oxford: Blackwell.

Russell, B. (1921) *The Analysis of Mind*. London: Allen & Unwin.

Ryle, G. (1949) *The Concept of Mind*. New York: Barnes & Noble.

Schlick, M. (1935) "De la relation entre les notions psychologiques et les notions physiques." *Revue de Synthèse* 10: 5–16. Repr. as "On the relation between psychological and physical concepts," trans W. Sellars, in M. Schlick, *Philosphical Papers*, vol. 2, London: Reidel, 1979, pp. 420–36, to which page references are made.

Searle, J. (1980) "Minds, brains and programs." *Behavioral and Brain Sciences* 1: 417–24.

—— (1992) *The Rediscovery of Mind*. Cambridge, MA: MIT Press.

Segal, G. (2000) *A Slim Book about Narrow Content*. Cambridge, MA: MIT Press.

Sellars, W. (1956) "Empiricism and philosophy of mind." In H. Feigl and M. Scriven (eds.) *Minnesota Studies in the Philosophy of Science* 1, Minneapolis: University of Minnesota Press, pp. 253–329.

Shaffer, J. (1963) "Mental events and the brain." *Journal of Philosophy* 60: 160–6.

Smart, J .J. C. (1959) "Sensations and brain processes." *Philosophical Review* 68: 141–56.

Sosa, E. (1984) "Mind–body interaction and supervenient causation." *Midwest Studies in Philosophy* 9, Minneapolis: University of Minnesota Press, pp. 271–81.

Stich, S. (1978) "Autonomous psychology and the belief–desire thesis." *The Monist* 61: 573–91.

Stich, S. and S. Nichols (1992) "Folk psychology: simulation vs. tacit theory." *Mind & Language* 7: 29–65.

Stich, S. and I. Ravenscroft (1994) "What is folk psychology?" *Cognition* 50: 447–68.

Stoljar, D. (2001) "Two conceptions of the physical." *Philosophy and Phenomenological Research* 62: 253–81.

Sturgeon, S. (1994) "The epistemic view of subjectivity." *Journal of Philosophy* 91: 221–35.

—— (1998) "Physicalism and overdetermination." *Mind* 107: 411–32.

Tye, M. (1990) "A representational theory of pains and their phenomenal character." In J. Tomberlin (ed.) *Philosophical Perspectives*, vol. 9, Atascadero, CA: Ridgeview, pp. 223–39.

Van Gulick, R. (1993) "Understanding the phenomenal mind: are we all just armadillos?" In M. Davies and G. Humphreys (eds.) *Consciousness: Philosophical and Psychological Aspects*. Oxford: Blackwell, pp. 137–54.

White, S. (1982) "Partial character and the language of thought." *Pacific Philosophical Quarterly* 63: 347–65.

Wittgenstein, L. (1953) *Philosophical Investigations*, trans. G. E. M. Anscombe. Oxford: Blackwell.

Wright, C., B. C. Smith, and C. Macdonald (eds.) (1998) *Knowing Our Own Minds*. Oxford: Clarendon Press.

Yablo, S. (1992) "Mental causation." *Philosophical Review* 101: 245–80.

Further reading

Braddon-Mitchell, D. and F. Jackson (2007) *Philosophy of Mind and Cognition*. Oxford: Blackwell. (Clear introduction to recent philosophy of mind, with particular emphasis on debates about mental content).

Chalmers, D. J. (ed.) (2002) *Philosophy of Mind: Classical and Contemporary Readings*. New York: Oxford University Press. (Readings drawn mostly from the twentieth century, grouped thematically; particularly wide coverage of topics relating to consciousness).

Kim, J. (1996) *Philosophy of Mind*. Boulder, CO: Westview Press. Rev. edn., 2005. (Clear survey of major twentieth-century metaphysical views of mind, with particular emphasis on problems of mental causation).

Rosenthal, D. M. (ed.) (1991) *The Nature of Mind*. New York: Oxford University Press. (A useful collection of key readings in philosophy of mind drawn largely from the latter half of the twentieth century, grouped thematically).

13
PHILOSOPHY OF PSYCHOLOGY

Kelby Mason, Chandra Sekhar Sripada, and Stephen Stich

Introduction

The twentieth century has been a tumultuous time in psychology, a century in which the discipline struggled with basic questions about its intellectual identity, but nonetheless managed to achieve spectacular growth and maturation. It is not surprising, then, that psychology has attracted sustained philosophical attention and stimulated rich philosophical debate. Some of this debate was aimed at understanding, and sometimes criticizing, the assumptions, concepts, and explanatory strategies prevailing in the psychology of the time. But much philosophical work has also been devoted to exploring the implications of psychological findings and theories for broader philosophical questions such as: Are humans really rational animals? How malleable is human nature? and Do we have any innate knowledge or innate ideas?

One particularly noteworthy fact about philosophy of psychology in the twentieth century is that, in the last quarter of the century, the distinction between psychology and the philosophy of psychology began to dissolve as philosophers played an increasingly active role in articulating and testing empirical theories about the mind and psychologists became increasingly interested in the philosophical underpinnings and implications of their work. It isn't possible to distinguish sharply between philosophy of psychology and philosophy of mind but, roughly speaking, philosophy of psychology at the end of the twentieth century and start of the twenty-first has two distinctive features: (a) as just mentioned, it is naturalistic, presenting itself as continuous with natural science; and therefore (b) it typically starts from psychological research, and attends to it closely, where philosophy of mind often starts from folk psychological observation or more general theoretical considerations.[1] We present here a survey of five important themes in twentieth-century psychology which have been the focus of philosophical attention and have benefited from philosophical scrutiny.

Perhaps the two most important events in the history of psychology in the twentieth century were the emergence of the *behaviorist* approach, which dominated psychology for the first half of the century (see "Philosophy of mind," Chapter 12), and its displacement by *cognitivism* as the century drew to a close. Philosophers played an important role in both of these events, developing a philosophical companion to psychological behaviorism, and clarifying the nature and assumptions of the cognitivist approach to psychological theorizing. Our first section will be devoted to the transition from behaviorism to cognitivism.

The linguist Noam Chomsky (1928–) is widely considered one of the founders of the cognitivist approach in psychology; he was also the central figure in a second major movement in contemporary psychology, *nativism*, which is the topic of our second section. Nativism and empiricism have traditionally been philosophical doctrines regarding the structure of the mind and the sources of the justification of belief. Contemporary cognitive psychology complements and extends traditional philosophical inquiry by providing a sophisticated methodology for investigating nativist structures in the mind. But nativism is a problematic notion, and in this section we discuss philosophical attempts to clarify both what nativism claims and what it entails about human nature.

Nativism is closely related to, but importantly distinct from, another topic which has been center-stage in both psychology and the philosophy of psychology for the last two decades: *modularity*. Jerry Fodor's seminal *Modularity of the Mind* (1983) suggested that an important structural principle in the organization of the mind is that at least some cognitive capacities are subserved by specialized, largely independent subsystems. Recent work in psychology has sought to delineate the modular structure of a number of important cognitive capacities, including language and mathematical cognition. Philosophy of psychology has contributed to this endeavor by helping to clarify the notion of a module. Philosophers have also debated whether modularity, if it is true, forces us to abandon traditional views about the transparency of the mental and to reconsider prevailing accounts of epistemic justification. These are some of the issues we'll consider in the third section "Modularity," below.

A fourth theme which attracted a great deal of attention during the twentieth century, both in philosophy and in psychology, is *rationality*. Philosophers have traditionally debated the nature and the extent of both theoretical rationality, or the rationality of belief, and practical rationality, or the rationality of action. During the last three decades of the twentieth century psychologists became increasingly interested in these topics as well, and a large experimental literature emerged exploring the ways in which people actually reason and make decisions. Much of what they found was both surprising and troubling. In the fourth section, we recount some of the more disquieting empirical findings in this tradition and consider how both philosophers and psychologists have attempted to come to grips with them.

The final topic we consider is *intentionality*. Cognitive psychology, as it is currently practiced, appears to be committed to the existence of intentional states, like beliefs, desires, plans, goals, and fears, which are conceived of as being *representational* – they are *about* states of affairs in the world. Thus it would seem that cognitive psychology must grapple with "Brentano's problem," the problem of how to accommodate intentional notions within a naturalistic view of the world (see the discussion in "Philosophy of mind," Chapter 12). In our final section we discuss debates surrounding attempts by philosophers to "naturalize" the intentional. It may well be the case that more philosophical ink has been spilled on the topic of naturalizing the intentional than on the preceding four topics combined. Despite this, we suspect that the question of how to naturalize the intentional is not well posed, and the importance of the answer is far from obvious. Perhaps a new century of philosophy of psychology will decide that the question, once made more precise, was not worth all the fuss.

From behaviorism to cognitivism

A great deal of contemporary psychological research and theorizing is unabashedly *mentalistic*. Psychological theories explain outward behavior by positing internal psychological states and structures such as beliefs, desires, perceptions, memories, and various and sundry other kinds of mental states. In the first half of the twentieth century, however, a very different ethos prevailed. Psychological theorizing was dominated by *behaviorist* thinking in which the positing of unobservable mental entities was explicitly shunned. Perhaps the most important event in the history of psychology in the twentieth century was the demise of behaviorism and the rise of *cognitivism*, a thoroughly mentalistic approach to mind. We'll begin our survey of key issues in twentieth-century philosophy of psychology by discussing this transition.

Logical behaviorism

There are actually two quite distinct versions of behaviorism that flourished in the first half of the twentieth century, one primarily in philosophy and the other primarily in psychology. *Logical behaviorism*, which prevailed primarily in philosophical circles, is a thesis about the meaning of mental state concepts (see also "The development of analytic philosophy: Wittgenstein and after," Chapter 2). According to logical behaviorists, mental state concepts such as belief or desire don't refer to hidden, and potentially mysterious, internal states of a person. Rather, talk of mental states is actually talk about dispositions to behave in certain ways under certain circumstances. For example, consider the claim that Paul has a headache. Superficially, this claim appears to refer to some inner state of Paul, perhaps some "achy" subjective sensation. But according to logical behaviorists, this appearance is mistaken. Talk of Paul's headache actually refers to a complex set of dispositions, for example the disposition to groan, wince, avoid bright lights, reach for the aspirin, say "Ouch" when he moves his head too quickly, and so on. (See Ryle 1949 for the classic exposition of logical behaviorism.)

One of the main attractions of logical behaviorism is that it provides an account of the reference of mental state concepts without positing anything metaphysically spooky or mysterious, such as a Cartesian *res cogitans*. If mental state concepts are about behavior, then their materialistic bona fides cannot be denied. A second attraction of logical behaviorism is epistemological. People routinely attribute states such as beliefs and desires to others. If beliefs and desires are understood as hidden inner states of a person, then it is hard to see how we might come to have knowledge of these states in others, and the potential for skepticism regarding other minds looms large. On the other hand, if mental states are understood as dispositions to behave in certain ways, as logical behaviorists contend, then our knowledge of these states is readily explained and skepticism about other minds is dispelled.

Despite its attractions, logical behaviorism ultimately foundered. A key stumbling block for the program is that there appears to be no *straightforward* connection between mental states and dispositions to engage in certain behaviors in the way that logical behaviorism appears to require. Rather, connections between mental states and behavior invariably appear to be mediated by a number of factors, most notably by other mental states. Let us return to the example of Paul who has a headache. The logical behaviorist says that Paul's having a headache means that Paul is disposed to engage in a host of behaviors, including, among others, reaching for the aspirin. But it seems that whether Paul does in fact reach for the aspirin depends critically on Paul's other mental states, including his other beliefs, desires, preferences, etc. For example, suppose that Paul believes that aspirin will upset his stomach, or that Paul dislikes medicines and prefers natural remedies, such as a massage. In each of these cases, Paul will not reach for an aspirin.

The lesson for logical behaviorism, as philosophers such as Donald Davidson and Jerry Fodor emphasized, is that beliefs, desires, and other mental states are embedded in a dense network of other mental states, and these states invariably act only in *concert* in the production of behavior (Davidson 1963; Fodor 1968). The systematic causal interdependency of mental states in the production of behavior makes it impossible to assign to each mental state its own unique set of behavioral ramifications in the way that logical behaviorists envisioned.

Psychological behaviorism

Even if one rejects logical behaviorism's claims about the centrality of behavior in the meaning of mental state concepts, one might still insist on the centrality of behavior in the formulation of psychological *explanations*. This latter view is at the core of the position often called *psychological behaviorism* or *methodological behaviorism*. According to psychological behaviorism, psychologists should restrict themselves to describing relationships between observable external features of the organism, for example relationships between histories of stimuli impinging on the organism and behavioral responses, without invoking hidden internal states of the organism. Psychological behaviorism is independent of logical behaviorism, since one can be a psychological behaviorist and still maintain that mental states such as beliefs and desires exist and that our concepts of belief and desire and other mental states do in fact refer to these hidden causes of behavior. But one might also be a psychological behaviorist and deny these claims, that is, one might be a psychological behaviorist *and* a logical behaviorist, and in fact many theorists were.

There are two important reasons why psychological behaviorists wanted to dispense with talk of mental states. The first reason is broadly epistemological. Many psychological behaviorists were attracted to the positivist doctrine that scientific theories should only invoke explanatory entities that are publicly observable. Since mental states are "inner" events that are not publicly observable, and there is no observational test to determine when such states occur, mental states are not the sorts of things that should be invoked by scientific psychological theories.

The second motivation for psychological behaviorism is in many ways more interesting and more deeply revealing about why psychological behaviorism ultimately failed as a research program. Many psychological behaviorists saw the task of psychology as formulating law-like generalizations about behavior. In pursuing this endeavor, they viewed the positing of mental states that mediate between environmental inputs and behavioral outputs as *explanatorily superfluous*. The basic idea is that if we assume that there are lawful connections between environmental stimuli (or histories of exposure to environmental stimuli) and inner mental states, and lawful connections between inner mental states and the production of behavior, then there will be lawful connections between environmental stimuli and behavior that can be stated without adverting to inner mental states as mediators. The positing of inner mental states does no additional explanatory work, and given that these inner states are epistemically inaccessible, psychology is better off without them. B. F. Skinner (1904–90) puts the point succinctly:

> If all linkages are lawful, nothing is lost by neglecting a supposed nonphysical (mental) link. Thus, if we know that a child has not eaten for a long time, and if we know that he therefore feels hungry and that because he feels hungry he then eats, then we know that if he has not eaten for a long time, he will eat. (Skinner 1953: 59)

Psychological behaviorism rose to prominence with John Watson's (1878–1958) influential 1913 manifesto "Psychology as the behaviorist views it" (Watson 1913), and the movement held sway, especially in North America, for about five decades. Among the most significant of the behaviorists' accomplishments was the formulation of a number of important learning rules. An example of such a rule is Thorndike's Law of Effect, named after the behaviorist psychologist Edward Thorndike (1874–1949), which says very roughly that if an organism performs some behavior X and X is followed by reinforcement, then the probability of the organism performing X again in the future increases (Thorndike 1911: 244). Behaviorists formalized many such learning rules and generated a substantial body of empirical results demonstrating how these rules successfully predict animal behavior, at least in certain experimental contexts. But despite their successes, there were two fundamental problems with psychological behaviorism that eventually led to the movement's mid-century demise.

One problem with psychological behaviorism was that it dogmatically insisted that the purpose or goal of psychological explanation is, and rightfully should be, the prediction of behavior. But this claim is actually quite puzzling. Even if we grant, for argument's sake, that positing internal mental states and processes is not *necessary* for the prediction of behavior, it does not follow that the elucidation of these states and processes is thereby rendered uninteresting and unworthy of study. The question of what is, or what is not, interesting or worthy of scientific study simply cannot be legislated in this way. Ironically, in the last several decades, psychologists and neuroscientists have had enormous success in identifying the neural and synaptic mechanisms that underlie several of the learning rules that behaviorist psychologists such as Pavlov, Thorndike, and Skinner originally formulated. (For example, see Rescorla and Wagner 1972 and Kandel et al. 2000.) It seems, then, that psychological behaviorism was needlessly restrictive. The identification of behavioral regularities and the elucidation of internal states that mediate these regularities are *both* worthy projects, and there is simply no reason to privilege one at the expense of the other.

A second problem with psychological behaviorism is the fact that behaviorist explanations appear most plausible when applied to relatively simple animals confronted with certain highly restricted, and indeed somewhat contrived, experimental tasks (for example, pigeons that learn to peck at a lever to obtain food pellets). But when we consider more sophisticated kinds of behavior displayed in more realistic ecological contexts, the idea that this behavior might be explained by simple learning rules such as the Law of Effect begins to look much less plausible. For example, the human capacity to produce and comprehend language is extraordinarily complex, and, as we shall see in the following section, behaviorist accounts of language are particularly implausible.

Noam Chomsky and the rise of cognitivism

Perhaps no figure is more closely associated with the downfall of psychological behaviorism than Noam Chomsky. In a series of influential works, including his 1965 classic *Aspects of the Theory of Syntax*, Chomsky initiated an alternative approach to the study of language that deviated from the explanatory strategy of psychological behaviorism in two crucial respects. (For further discussion of Chomsky, see "American philosophy in the twentieth century," Chapter 5 and "Philosophy of language," Chapter 9.)

First, while behaviorists sought to explain the acquisition of all patterns of behavior by means of just a few domain-general learning mechanisms, Chomsky argued that many kinds of behaviors, or behavioral capacities, are importantly *innate*. Chomsky pressed this claim even in the behaviorists' favored turf of the explanation of relatively simple behaviors in lower animals. For example, in his seminal critique of Skinner's (1957) *Verbal Behavior*, Chomsky noted that many animal behaviors, such as the gaping response of the nestling thrush (a species of bird), appear to be innate in the sense that these behaviors emerge early, reliably, and without the need for learning (Chomsky 1959). In later works, Chomsky assembled a series of arguments that suggested, quite persuasively, that human language too is importantly innate. For example, according to Chomsky's celebrated *poverty of the stimulus argument*, human languages are too complex and the inputs available for the child to learn these languages are too meager for language acquisition to be explicable on the behaviorist model of learning. We'll discuss the poverty of the stimulus argument, and the broader issue of innateness claims in psychology, in more detail in the section entitled "Nativism," below.

The second respect in which Chomsky deviated from psychological behaviorism is that, while behaviorists eschewed positing internal mental states, he argued that in the explanation of complex behavior, the postulation of such states is *unavoidable*. A striking fact, largely ignored by behaviorists, but emphasized by Chomsky, is that language is *productive*; a competent speaker can produce, comprehend, and make judgments about an infinite (or at least unbounded) number of sentences (Chomsky 1965). For example, a competent speaker can judge any of a potentially infinite number of sentences to be grammatical or ungrammatical. Behaviorists are hard pressed to explain the productivity of language, since they would seemingly need to appeal to an infinite number of stimulus-response links. Even worse, speakers can readily produce and comprehend sentences *that they've never heard before*, suggesting that the behaviorist's explanation of these abilities in terms of previously learned stimulus-response links is singularly implausible.

Chomsky argued that the explanation of a productive capacity like language demands that we acknowledge the existence of a sophisticated set of formal processes inside the head of the person. In particular, he postulated the existence of a mentally represented set of rules called a *generative grammar* that underlies speakers' grammaticality judgments. A key feature of a generative grammar is that it specifies *recursive* rules for how words and phrases can be assembled into sentences, thus explaining how speakers with finite minds are able to form judgments of the grammaticality of any of an infinite number of sentences.

Chomsky's work in language was part of a broader effort already under way by other theorists including George Miller in psychology and John McCarthy (1927–), Allan Newell (1927–92), and Herbert Simon (1916–2001) in artificial intelligence (see Gardner 1985). These theorists were heavily influenced by new developments in mathematical logic and computer science, and together, they laid the foundations for an alternative to behaviorism in the study of the mind called *cognitivism*.

The central hypothesis of cognitivism is that the mind can be understood as a kind of computer. Computers process information by executing step-by-step operations, called *algorithms*, on internally encoded bodies of information, called data structures or *representations*. Very roughly, representations are elements within the computer that *stand for* objects and properties in the world. For example, consider a computer that plays checkers. One way such a computer might work is that it might possess internal elements that stand for the various pieces on a checkerboard. By manipulating these internal representations in the appropriate ways, the computer can identify moves that are more likely to lead to unsuccessful outcomes and avoid moves that lead to unsuccessful outcomes.

Cognitivists claim that minds process information in much the same way as computers. Chomsky's explanation of language, which appeals to recursive algorithmic processes that operate over internal representational structures, is a classic example of a cognitivist theory. Cognitivist explanations of other capacities, including perception, categorization, reasoning, and many others, take a similar form (see the chapters in Posner 1989). Cognitivism has flourished since the 1960s and has been an enormously fruitful research program. A central achievement of cognitivism is that it has thrown off the behaviorists' strictures against talking of the mental and made it possible to develop a rigorous theory of the mind, and not just of behavior. However, in opening up the realm of the mental to theoretical exploration, cognitivism also raises a number of fundamental questions that are of great interest to the philosophy of psychology. In the next four sections of this chapter, we'll explore four important issues in the philosophy of psychology that are, in one way or another, deeply influenced by the cognitivist turn in psychology.

Nativism

The nature of nativism

In the previous section, we noted that Noam Chomsky was a central figure in the development of cognitivism. He also played a pivotal role in the emergence of a second theoretical perspective that has loomed large in contemporary cognitive psychology: *nativism*. Nativists believe that the mind comes equipped with a great deal of innate structure and this innate structure plays an important role in explaining our mature cognitive capacities and abilities. It is useful to distinguish three types of cognitive structure that nativists might endorse as being innate: *concepts* (e.g. "triangle," "God," or "cow"), *beliefs* or *bodies of information* (e.g. mathematical beliefs, geometric beliefs, or beliefs about physical objects) and *mechanisms* (e.g. mechanisms for language acquisition, mechanisms for reasoning). Nativists might endorse the innateness of any the preceding types of cognitive structure, and historically, nativists of various stripes have endorsed the innateness of various combinations of these three (see Cowie's (1999) lucid discussion).

Nativists are opposed by empiricists, who argue that the mind comes equipped with relatively little innate structure, and this structure is relatively unimportant in explaining our mature cognitive capacities and abilities. For example, one particularly extreme version of empiricism, sometimes attributed to the British empiricists of the eighteenth century such as Locke and Hume, claims that the newborn infant's mind is a tabula rasa, or blank slate. According to these theorists, experience is the source of almost all of our mature concepts and beliefs as well as our mature cognitive abilities and capacities. It's important to recognize that even extreme empiricists don't claim that the mind possesses *no* innate structure whatsoever. Rather, empiricists attempt to explain the development of our mature cognitive repertoire by adverting to a minimum of innate structure. Thus, they typically assert that the mind comes equipped with just a few learning mechanisms and these mechanisms are *domain-general*; that is, they operate over a wide variety of cognitive domains. Paradigm examples of empiricist learning mechanisms include associative learning mechanisms (e.g. Pavlovian conditioning) and general-purpose inductive learning mechanisms (e.g. Bayesian approaches to learning).

During the first half of the twentieth century, empiricist ideas dominated psychology and other sciences of human behavior. As we saw in the previous section, behaviorist psychologists such as Watson and Skinner emphasized the role of learning, and in particular, histories of conditioning or reinforcement, in the explanation of behavior.

A similar picture prevailed in the social sciences. Anthropologists such as Franz Boas (1858–1942) and sociologists such as Émile Durkheim (1858–1917) denied that there were rich innate features of the mind shared by all humans. Like behaviorist psychologists, these theorists viewed the human mind as a tabula rasa, although they emphasized the role of social learning and cultural conformity, rather than histories of conditioning or reinforcement, as the primary shapers of human behavior (see Laland and Brown 2002: 53–4).

By the mid-1960s however, the tide had turned. Empiricism no longer enjoyed a position of unquestioned dominance as psychologists increasingly began to emphasize the innate basis for a number of cognitive capacities. Chomsky was a key figure in the resuscitation of nativism. He pointed out that there are a number of features of language that suggest that important aspects of language are in fact innate. For example, Chomsky noted that language is universal in all human groups, and within each human group, it is reliably the case that virtually all normal individuals achieve competence in the native language. These features are predicted on the hypothesis that important aspects of language are innate, and less readily explained on the hypothesis that language is acquired by general-purpose learning.

Perhaps Chomsky's most influential argument for the innateness of language is the *poverty of the stimulus argument*. According to Chomsky, children learn their native language with remarkable ease and rapidity, despite the fact that children are seldom explicitly instructed in their language, and their linguistic experience consists of little more than a fairly limited set of examples of often degraded adult speech. Thus, Chomsky claimed, there is a gap between the learning target achieved by the child, i.e. the child's mature linguistic competence, and the meager inputs available to the child. He argued that the only way to bridge this gap is to postulate that the child antecedently possesses extensive *innate* knowledge of language and brings this knowledge to the language learning task.

Since Chomsky's seminal early investigations of language, nativism has flourished as a theoretical perspective in cognitive psychology. For example, in addition to language, theorists have proposed that there are innate mechanisms or innate bodies of information that subserve our capacities to attribute intentional states to others (Leslie 1994), explain and predict the motion of middle-sized physical objects (Spelke 1988), classify animals and plants (Atran 1998), and many other abilities as well (see the essays in Hirschfeld and Gelman 1994). It's worth emphasizing, however, that although nativist hypotheses were certainly important and influential at the end of the twentieth century, they were by no means uncontested, and vigorous debate between nativists and empiricists raged on (see Elman et al. 1996 for an important defense of broadly empiricist approaches to cognitive development).

Problems with the notion of innateness

As we've seen, the crux of the argument between nativists and empiricists concerns the quantity of innate structure in the mind and the importance of this innate structure in explaining our mature cognitive capacities. Notice, however, that in formulating the preceding core disagreement between nativists and empiricists, we helped ourselves to the term "innate." What exactly does this term mean? As it turns out, there is no consensus on what it means to say that some element of mental structure is innate, and different theorists often appear to mean quite different things by the term. Given the plethora of meanings, debates between nativists and empiricists are often fraught with confusion, with theorists talking past one another.

An important ongoing project for philosophers of psychology is to clarify the meaning of "innate" and thus help to reduce some of the controversy that surrounds the use of the term in psychological theorizing. This is no easy task since theorists often emphasize different threads of meaning in different contexts. Let us examine a few ways in which the concept of innateness is used in the contemporary literature.

One quite popular way of characterizing innateness is in terms of *developmental invariance* (the phrase is from Samuels 2002). According to these invariance accounts, a trait is innate if it reliably develops over a wide range of normal environments. Put another way, an innate trait is one that is not dependent on any *specific* developmental environment; it is not the case that the trait develops in one way in one environment and another quite distinct way in another environment. Descartes appears to have had developmental invariance in mind when he suggested that certain diseases which recur in families, such as gout, serve as a model for understanding innateness. In *Comments on a Certain Broadsheet*, he notes that diseases such as gout are not literally inborn in the sense that "babies of such families suffer from these diseases in their mother's womb" (Descartes 1985: 304) Rather, he argues, they are innate in the sense they reliably emerge during the course of development, and their emergence does not depend on any specific environment (see also Stich 1975).

Notice, however, that even if a trait reliably develops over a large range of environments, there will inevitably be certain environments in which the trait does not emerge. For example, if we deprive an immature organism of important nutrients or expose it to drugs like thalidomide, its development will be severely stunted and certain traits of the organism that would otherwise reliably develop might not develop at all. Should we, on this basis, discount these traits from being considered innate? A more reasonable alternative is to relativize our account of innateness to some range of "normal" environments. But which range of environments should we count as normal? One proposal might be to count an environment as normal if it is sufficiently similar to the environment in which the organism evolved. Another proposal counts an environment as normal if it is one that is compatible with the organism's "surviving and thriving" (Kitcher 1996: 243). Neither of these proposals is terribly precise and they both leave a good deal of room for disagreement about what counts as a normal environment.

Invariance accounts capture one conception of innateness that is particularly widely used in the biological sciences, although it is found in psychology as well. There is another important meaning of "innate," however, that is much more specific to psychology. Recall that certain leading empiricists argued that the mind is a tabula rasa at birth and that most of a person's stock of concepts, beliefs, abilities, and capacities are acquired through experience, that is, they are *learned*. Implicit in this doctrine is the idea that elements of mental structure are of one of two types: they are either innate or learned. This provides us with another characterization of the notion of innateness: an element of mental structure is innate if it is not learned.[2]

A problem with the preceding account, however, is that learning is itself a contested notion, and there are a number of problematic cases in which it is difficult to know whether to classify a particular kind of acquisition process as an instance of learning. For example, consider Chomsky's highly influential model of language acquisition, which he calls the "Principles and Parameters Model" (Chomsky 1988). According to this model, the language faculty is associated with a set of parameters which can be set in various permissible ways (in most cases just two). For example, one putative parameter governs the ordering of phrases in a sentence. English is subject-verb-object, Hindi is subject-object-verb, while virtually no languages are object-subject-verb. According to Chomsky, the linguistic experience that the child confronts sets the parameters associated with the language faculty, thus accounting for the child's mature language competence (1988: 133–4). If language acquisition does in fact consist of parameter-setting, as Chomsky proposes, it is hard to know whether we should count this acquisition process as an instance of learning. Chomsky himself has argued that language is not in fact learned. Rather, he claims, the language organ simply "grows" in much the way the heart or any other somatic organ grows (1988; see Cowie 1999 for a critique).

In addition to the two accounts of innateness discussed above, there are a number of others. The biologist Patrick Bateson (1938–) has identified at least seven important usages of the notion of innateness in the literature. According to him, theorists at different times use "innate" to mean:

- caused by genetic factors
- caused or driven by internal factors
- shared by all members of the species
- adapted by natural selection over the course of evolution (Bateson 1991)

Given that there are a large number of quite distinct accounts of innateness in the literature, it is tempting to ask which of them is correct. In our view, this temptation should be resisted, since it is unlikely that there is a unique right answer. Rather, we think, "innate" has several legitimate meanings, and each meaning has its uses in the context of distinct scientific and explanatory projects. The philosopher Paul Griffiths suggests that in order to avoid confusion, scientists should simply specify which among the many meaning of innateness they intend to signify by their use of the term (Griffiths 2002). For example, a scientist who intends "innate" to connote *not learned* should simply specify this so as to not confuse her meaning of the term with other meanings. We think this is an eminently reasonable proposal.

The malleability of human nature

While we are ecumenical in endorsing a number of different legitimate uses of "innate," there is one use of the term that is worth flagging because it is particularly problematic. It is sometimes assumed that if some element of mental structure is innate, then it is more or less fixed, implastic, and resistant to change or environ-mental manipulation. This usage of the term suggests that an innate trait is one that is more or less *immalleable*.

However, it's important to realize that while there may be a connection between a trait's being innate and its being immalleable, this connection must be explicitly defended on a case by case basis, and it is certainly not inevitable. To take a stock example from the literature, phenylketonuria is a genetic disorder in which an affected individual is unable to break down the amino acid phenylalanine from the diet, and the disorder was once routinely life-threatening. However, advances in medical science have made low phenylalanine diets and phenylalanine-free formulas widely available, thus mitigating much of the illness associated with the disorder. The cluster of life-threatening symptoms associated with phenylketonuria is an example of a trait that is innate according to several of the accounts listed above, but it is nonetheless susceptible to substantial environmental manipulation.

Too often, theorists assume that if a trait is innate it is immalleable. This is unfortunate because the question of the malleability of human nature is an emotionally-charged issue with important social, political, and normative implica-tions. The debate between nativism and empiricism is quite distinct from the debate over the malleability of human nature, and keeping these two debates separate will eliminate much unnecessary controversy.

Modularity

In 1983, Jerry Fodor revived a tradition of faculty psychology which he traced back, tongue only partly in cheek, to Franz Joseph Gall (1758–1828), the founder of phrenology (Fodor 1983). On Fodor's view, then-contemporary cognitive science had produced evidence that the human mind contained a number of distinct cognitive mechanisms, which were dedicated to specific tasks; Chomsky (1980) called such mechanisms "mental organs," but Fodor called them "modules." This view, that the mind is at least partly modular, can be contrasted with the view that it is composed only of mechanisms and processes which are entirely domain-general – that is, which can operate indifferently on all tasks and topics. Attention, memory, and reasoning are putative examples of domain-general processes.

Fodorian modules

Fodor did not seek to define the term "module" with necessary and sufficient condi-tions. Rather, he offered a characterization of the sorts of mechanisms that seemed to be invoked by cognitive science, in particular vision science and linguistics. Fodorian modules are characterized by having a cluster of the following features, each of which is itself a matter of degree:

1 Their operation is mandatory (i.e. they respond automatically to input).
2 Their operation is fast.

3 They are domain-specific (i.e. they operate on a limited range of inputs, defined by some task such as domain like vision or language processing).
4 They are neurally localized.
5 They are informationally encapsulated (i.e. they have limited access to information in other systems).
6 Other mental systems have only limited access to their computations.
7 Their outputs are shallow (i.e. not very conceptually elaborated).
8 They show characteristic and specific breakdowns.
9 Their development shows a characteristic pace and sequence.

The most important of these features, for Fodor, was informational encapsulation. A clear example of encapsulation is the persistence of perceptual illusions like the Müller–Lyer illusion in Figure 1. Even when we know that the two lines are the same length – by measuring them, say, or having drawn them ourselves – they continue to appear of different lengths. The information that they are the same length can't "get into" the visual system.

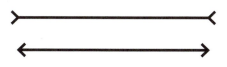

Figure 1: Müller–Lyer illusion

Because of their informational encapsulation, Fodor argued that modules would only be found at the input and output sides of the mind. To function properly, central processes such as reasoning, decision-making, and belief-fixation must be able to access and integrate information from many different domains and different sources. Moreover, it seems that central systems do in fact have such general access to information; therefore, Fodor maintained, they can't be modular.

Evolutionary psychology and massive modularity

Since the publication of *The Modularity of Mind*, the notion of modularity has been highly influential in cognitive science. And, *pace* Fodor, some psychologists and philosophers have posited the existence of modules in more central domains of cognition. For instance, Scott Atran has argued that there is a module for folk biology—people's intuitive understanding of the living world (Atran 1998); Alan Leslie has argued that there is a module for folk psychology—people's understanding of other people's mental states (Scholl and Leslie 1999); while Simon Baron-Cohen has argued that folk psychology is subserved by several distinct modules (Baron-Cohen 1995).

The most extreme statement of this trend can be found in evolutionary psychology, and in particular the work of Leda Cosmides and John Tooby. Not only have Cosmides and Tooby posited the existence of modules for central processes such as cheater-detection (e.g. Cosmides and Tooby 1992), but they have also offered a general evolutionary argument that we should expect the mind to be, in Samuels' (1998) phrase, "massively modular" (Cosmides and Tooby 1994). That is, there are supposedly general evolutionary reasons to expect that the mind (including central cognition) will be largely or even entirely composed of modules rather than domain-general processes.

Cosmides and Tooby offer two main reasons: first, our ancestors would have faced different adaptive problems – e.g. foraging, navigation, mate selection – which required different sorts of solutions. An organism with domain-specific ways to solve these problems would have been faster, more efficient, and more reliable than a "jack of all trades" organism which could only solve them in some domain-general way; therefore modular organisms would have been selected over "jack of all trades" organisms in our ancestral lineage. Thus our own evolved cognitive architecture is likely to be massively modular.

The second putative reason to expect massive modularity is that only massively modular minds could have produced "minimally adaptive behavior in ancestral environments" (Cosmides and Tooby 1994: 91). "Jack of all trades" organisms could not have learned by themselves and in their own lifetimes the benefits of avoiding incest or helping kin, especially since what counts as error and success differs from one domain to another. Creatures with domain-specific knowledge of what to do and when to do it would have selective advantage over "jack of all trades" creatures who had to figure it all out themselves.

Even if we grant the general soundness of these just-so stories, they fall far short of establishing that the mind is massively modular in the Fodorian sense of "module," which is that of a *computational* module. Computational modules are distinct computers which only interact with the rest of the mind at the input and output ends, and which contain their own proprietary mental operations.[3] By contrast, there is another, non-computational notion of modularity which Samuels et al. (1999) call a *Chomskian* module. Chomskian modules are mentally represented bodies of domain-specific knowledge which are supposed to underlie our cognitive abilities in various domains. They get their name from Chomskian linguistics, which posits the existence of such a module for grammar: an internally represented body of knowledge of the grammar of our language which explains our ability to comprehend, produce, and make judgments about sentences (Chomsky 1980). As noted in the previous section, developmental psychologists have posited the existence of such domain-specific knowledge for other domains such as intuitive physics (Carey and Spelke 1994) and number (Gelman and Brenneman 1994). Whereas computational modules are distinct little computers, Chomskian modules, by contrast, are merely distinct databases of information about specific domains; these databases may be looked up and used, not by specialized computers, but by general cognitive processes.

If the arguments from evolutionary psychology show anything at all, it is the need for some domain-specific knowledge of the sort contained in Chomskian modules. Perhaps successful organisms do need substantial amounts of knowledge about the adaptive problems their ancestors would have faced. But, as Samuels (1998) has argued, this does not support the existence of separate computational modules. For it is entirely possible that all this domain-specific knowledge is operated on by the same domain-general cognitive processes. It is one thing to argue that the mind must have a vast library of domain-specific information; it is another thing to show that it must also have a vast network of different computers dedicated to using that information.

Philosophical implications of modularity

Why should philosophers care whether the mind is composed of modules, of either the computational or Chomskian sort? Apart from the inherent empirical interest in uncovering the structure of the mind – and there is a long history of philosophers speculating about this structure – there are more directly philosophical reasons why it matters. For one thing, the issue of modularity is relevant to the nativist–empiricist debate discussed in the previous section. Granted, the mere existence of a module does not itself show that the module is innate, since some features of modules (like informational encapsulation and neural localization) might come about through individual development (Karmiloff-Smith 1992). Even so, if the mind did turn out to be considerably modular, it would be implausible that *none* of that structure was innate. For that would mean that the exact same cognitive architecture and domain-specific information had been constructed in a billion different heads, with a billion different learning histories, by the undirected operation of purely domain-general processes, which is singularly unlikely. Substantial modularity, then, would be supportive of at least some nativist cognitive structure.

Substantial modularity might also seem to undermine the possibility of epistemic justification. Consider, for instance, a coherentist theory of justification, according to which a belief is justified if and only if it belongs to a coherent set of beliefs. This naturally implies that organisms that want to have justified beliefs ought to try to get their beliefs to mutually cohere. But if the organism has a cluster of modules, and if some of the information in those modules counts as *beliefs*, then it may find this task impossible. Whether it has fully computational or merely Chomskian modules, some of its beliefs may well be out of its control, immune to revision or rational consideration. In such a case, Quinean assertions to the contrary notwithstanding (e.g. Quine 1951), not every strand in the web of belief would be revisable, not even in principle.

More generally, modularity raises the prospect of epistemic boundedness, since our cognitive architecture might place regrettable limits on the possibility of our epistemic progress towards the truth. To illustrate this possibility, we adapt an example from Fodor (1983), who likened his input/output modules to a reflex such as protective blinking. Suppose your helpful neighbor sees a mote in your eye and, deciding to remove it, quickly moves her finger to your eye. No matter how much you trust your neighbor, your blink reflex will kick in and you will flinch from her approaching digit. The belief that your neighbor is unlikely to harm you etc., has no effect on your reflexive behavior. To move to a more cognitive case, while staying at the level of input processes, recall the Müller–Lyer diagram in Figure 1. Here your belief that the lines are of the same length has no effect on your perception; they still look unequal.

So far this is epistemically harmless; indeed, as Fodor points out, it's positively beneficial that creatures' wishful thinking can't impair the accuracy of their perception. But now suppose that certain more central parts of cognition were modular. This could either mean, as in the case of computational modules, that certain processes of belief-fixation are informationally encapsulated and therefore cannot be affected by all the available information in the mind; or, as in the case of Chomskian modules, it could mean that certain beliefs are relatively fixed. Either way, some of your beliefs would not be sensitive to everything you know; and while your modules might be good at dealing with certain problems in their domain, they might be very bad at dealing with other problems they are required to handle. In other words, you would be epistemically bounded.

A modular agent might actually be epistemically bounded in two different ways. First, the agent might be bounded with respect to the thoughts it can entertain. If it has different computational modules for working on different domains, then it might not be able to entertain thoughts with contents which cross those domains. Second, a modular agent might be epistemically bounded with respect to the information it can access in assessing a certain thought. Indeed, this type of boundedness is the very essence of informational encapsulation.

Human beings certainly don't appear to be epistemically bounded in the first way. Not only can we entertain thoughts about minds, bodies, numbers, animals, and so on, we can entertain thoughts that are about any combination of these things. The flexibility of our thought has thus been offered as an argument that our cognition couldn't possibly be *massively* modular and that there must be some sort of domain-general, "central workspace" (this argument is developed in Fodor 2000; see Carruthers 2003 for a response).

By contrast, the extent to which humans are epistemically bounded in the second way is still an open question. On the one hand, our abductive reasoning processes generally seem to be able to use many sorts of information. In trying to predict what Jean Valjean will do next, Inspector Javert might consider facts about Valjean's character, the weather, contemporary social conditions in France, Valjean's basic biological needs, and so on. On the other hand, it is not at all clear that humans always do, or can, take into account all the available and relevant information in forming certain judgments, and this might well be explained by our modular cognitive architecture.

Rationality

Once it became acceptable again in psychology to talk about thoughts, it was also acceptable to study how people string thoughts together, that is, how they reason. Newell and Simon, for instance, ran studies in which subjects worked through logic problems while thinking aloud, in order to investigate the reasoning they went through (Newell and Simon 1963). Unfortunately, just as the headline results of social psychology often showed people behaving badly – e.g. Milgram's (1963) work on compliance or that of Latane and Darley (1970) on the bystander effect – so too, the study of reasoning soon seemed to show people reasoning badly.

These and other results, two of which we present shortly, widely prompted the question, To what extent are humans rational? Aristotle, of course, defined man as the rational animal, but throughout the centuries cynics and nay-sayers like Hume, Hobbes, and Freud have held a dissenting opinion. It would be good if actual psychological data could help answer this question, but first two complications must be noted.

The first is that the rules of logic and probability are not themselves normative principles. They describe the relations between propositions and probabilities but do not give advice on how to reason or what to believe (Goldman 1986: ch. 5; Harman 1986). There is, however, a natural way to derive normative principles of reason from logic and probability via what Stein (1996) calls the "standard picture of rationality." According to this picture, principles of rationality can be derived, fairly straightforwardly, from logic and probability theory. For instance, the conjunction rule is a basic rule of probability:

CR: The probability of (A & B) cannot be greater than the probability of either A or B on its own.

From this rule we can plausibly derive a normative conjunction principle:

CP: Don't assign a greater probability to the conjunction of A and B than to either event alone.

The standard picture also makes the deontological claim that rationality, or good reasoning, is reasoning in accord with these derived principles. If we adopt the standard picture, then the measure of how well (or poorly) people reason is the extent to which they follow principles of reason derived from logic and probability theory.

The second complication is that people's mistakes sometimes fail to show anything about their underlying abilities. Suppose that in the last sentence we had mistakenly written "they're" for "their." We might have done this because we were tired, or distracted, or drunk while writing this chapter, in which case the error wouldn't show that we didn't know the correct spelling. When mistakes are due to such extraneous factors, they are merely performance errors and show nothing about the underlying competence. In our example, our competence with English spelling would be impugned only if we routinely used "they're" for "their," even when fully awake, attentive, sober, etc.

Like our English spelling ability, our reasoning competence can be affected by such relatively extraneous factors as fatigue, level of attention, and intoxication. Our rationality can only be impugned if our mistakes are not mere performance errors but indicative of our competence. Hence the question "to what extent are people rational?" is concerned not with our reasoning performance but with our underlying reasoning competence. There are difficulties involved with spelling out the notion of human reasoning competence (discussed in Stein 1996: ch. 2), but here we will assume that some such notion is to be had. We now present two of the most famous cases of apparent irrationality, the conjunction fallacy and failure on the selection task, to give a flavor of the psychological data.

Human irrationality?

The conjunction fallacy:

Consider the following character sketch (from Tversky and Kahneman 1982):

Linda is 31 years old, single, outspoken, and very bright. She majored in philosophy. As a student, she was deeply concerned with issues of discrimination and social justice, and also participated in anti-nuclear demonstrations.

Now rank the following statements from least to most probable:

1 Linda is a teacher in elementary school.
2 Linda works in a bookstore and takes Yoga classes.
3 Linda is active in the feminist movement.
4 Linda is a psychiatric social worker.
5 Linda is a member of the League of Women Voters.
6 Linda is a bank teller.
7 Linda is an insurance salesperson.
8 Linda is a bank teller and is active in the feminist movement.

Most people rank (8) as being more probable than (6). Alas, this falls afoul of the conjunction principle described above. The probability that Linda is a bank teller *and* that she is a feminist – $p(A \& B)$ – simply cannot be greater than the probability that she is a bank teller – $p(A)$ – and so we shouldn't judge it as greater.

The selection task:

Now consider the following task (from Wason 1966): There is a set of cards, each of which has a letter on one side and a number on the other. You are shown four cards which show "A," "K," "4," and "7" (see Figure 2). Which cards do you need to turn over to test the truth of the following rule?

If a card has a vowel on one side, then it has an even number on the other side.

Figure 2

The correct answer is "A" and "7." If the "A" card has an odd number on the back, then the rule is false; if the "7" card has a vowel on the back, then the rule is false. Hence these two cards must be turned over. As for the "4" card, it is irrelevant to the rule; regardless of whether there is a vowel or consonant on the other side, the rule could be true or false, and similarly for the "K" card. Hence these cards do not need to be turned over. Most people, however, choose both "A" and "4" but don't choose "7."

There's plenty more bad news where that came from, with experiments showing overconfidence in the accuracy of one's judgments (Lichtenstein and Fischhoff 1977), hindsight bias (Fischhoff 1975), the gambler's fallacy (Tversky and Kahneman 1971), the perception of illusory correlations (Chapman and Chapman 1967), and neglect of base rate information (Kahneman and Tversky 1973), to mention just a few.[4] Kahneman and Tversky published a series of articles in the early 1970s, many of them collected in Kahneman et al. (1982), which presented some of these apparent failures of rationality and suggested some possible cognitive explanations. This inspired an ongoing research program to do, essentially, more of the same: the *heuristics and biases* program. (See Nisbett and Ross 1980 for a good review of early work, and Gilovich et al. 2002 for a collection of later papers.)

These errors in reasoning were originally studied to cast light on the cognitive mechanisms at work (just as visual illusions can tell us much about the visual system) but, as Kahneman and Tversky (1982) themselves noted, the method quickly became part of the message. Some psychologists, especially in the heuristics and biases tradition, interpreted these and similar results as having "bleak implications" for human rationality (Nisbett and Borgida 1975). Our susceptibility to such errors was taken to show that we are much less rational than we would like to be. The idea here is not, of course, that we are incapable of ever conforming to the principles of reason – we can apply the conjunction principle when it is made explicit and salient. Rather the "bleak implications view" is that much of the time we don't conform to the principles, and not just because of performance errors. Ergo, humans are substantially irrational.

Arguments against irrationality

Although the bleak implications view might seem vague enough to be immune to challenge – how much is much of the time? –there are actually several ways it might be challenged. First, one could try to explain away the data by invoking the influence of pragmatic and other confounding factors in subjects' understanding of the questions they are asked. Perhaps, for instance, subjects in the Linda experiment interpret (6) as meaning "Linda is a bank teller and not a feminist," in which case it could be perfectly rational to assign it a lower probability than (8). This approach can certainly explain away some of the experiments, but it won't work for them all. There are simply too many experiments, many of them designed to control for such confounds, and too many phenomena are robust under variations in experimental design.

Alternatively, one might claim that systematic human irrationality is not something that could ever be demonstrated empirically, because of the very nature of rationality.

One way this argument could go is by invoking ideas about the constraints on inter-pretation from Quine (1960), Davidson (1984), or Dennett (1987), who provides the clearest expression of the argument. According to Dennett, we attribute to people the intentional states that it would be rational for them to have. (For further discussion of Dennett see "Philosophy of mind," Chapter 12.) Hence, if we could discover that people were massively irrational, then we could no longer attribute beliefs and desires to them; but since we *do* attribute beliefs and desires, we must assume that they are rational. Unfortunately for this argument, in the considerable literature on "mind-reading" or "folk psychology" there is little evidence that considerations of rationality play a role in attribution of mental states; and in our everyday practice we have no trouble attributing inconsistent beliefs to someone, or less than fully rational reasoning.[5] So Dennett's argument will not rule out the bleak implications view.

In a much discussed article, Cohen (1981) offered an even stronger epistemological argument that human reasoning competence must be, not just mostly rational, but fully rational. Stripped to its essentials, Cohen's argument was that the principles of reason are derived from people's intuitions by a process of reflective equilibrium – which is, near enough, the same way we discover people's reasoning competence. Any deviations from the principles of reason must therefore be classed as performance errors. Where this argument founders is its tendency to relativism about rationality. Consider Poor Jim, who bets his entire life savings that the next toss of a fair coin will be heads, because the last ten times the coin landed tails. No matter how much reflective equilibrium we try to induce in Jim, no matter how much statistical training he gets, he persists in committing this gambler's fallacy. Nonetheless, according to Cohen, Poor Jim is not being irrational – at least, not for him. His own principles of reason, derived via reflective equilibrium on things like his intuitions about the next coin toss, countenance the gambler's fallacy. Since Poor Jim is clearly not rational, what this example shows is that Cohen is simply wrong about how the principles of reason are derived.[6]

The third main response to the bleak implications view has come from evolutionary psychology. Its basic thrust is to challenge the ecological validity of most experiments on human reasoning, and to claim they have not been properly designed to elicit responses that reflect the subject's reasoning competence. If instead we considered problems similar to those which our ancestors would have faced in the environment of evolutionary adaptation (EEA) and which human cognition evolved to handle, then we would find much more evidence of human rationality than is allowed by the bleak implications view.

One specific instance of this response concerns the Wason selection task. This task has been extensively studied with a variety of rules, some of which do elicit the correct response. For instance, when the subjects are asked to test the rule "If someone is drinking alcohol, they must be over 21" (see Figure 3), they readily choose the correct responses, "beer" and "18" (Griggs and Cox 1982). To account for the differ-ences between cases that elicit the correct response and cases that don't, Cosmides and Tooby (1992) proposed the cheater-detection hypothesis. According to this hypothesis, one problem our ancestors would have faced was detecting people who would try to cheat them in social exchanges, and so humans probably have a module devoted to solving this problem. Selection tasks which have the form of a "social contract," as in Figure 3, will trigger this module, which produces the right response. Selection tasks which don't have this form, as in Figure 2, won't trigger the module.[7]

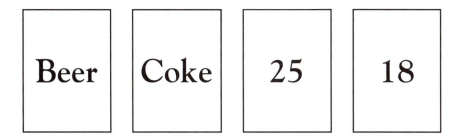

Figure 3

Another application of the challenge from evolutionary psychology concerns the format in which information is presented. Cosmides and Tooby (1996) and Gigerenzer (1994) have argued that, in the EEA, statistical information would have been presented as frequencies rather than probabilities of particular events: "two out of every ten times you go hunting you meet a tiger" rather than "the probability of meeting a tiger on today's hunt is 0.2." It is thus no surprise that people reason poorly about single-event probabilities, but they should be able to reason quite well about frequencies. And, indeed, several studies have shown that subjects can choose normatively correct responses when the information is given as frequencies. For instance, in one study subjects were told that 200 women met the "Linda" description, and were then asked to estimate how many of those women were feminists, bank tellers, and feminist bank tellers (Gigerenzer 1994). Only 13 percent of subjects committed the conjunction fallacy (by estimating that there were more feminist bank tellers than bank tellers), far fewer than the 85 percent who committed the fallacy in the analogous probabilistic version of Tversky and Kahneman (1982).

Evolutionary psychology and the heuristics and biases program have been depicted as necessarily opposed, but this is mistaken (Samuels et al. 2002). There is indeed a difference in emphasis, with evolutionary psychology focusing on reasoning successes and the heuristics and biases program focusing on failures, but this is only a difference in emphasis. Evolutionary psychology is not committed to the Panglossian view that humans are perfect reasoners, especially not in a modern environment so different from the EEA; nor is the heuristics and biases program committed to the bleak implications view.

At a more fundamental level, the challenges from evolutionary psychology haven't yet managed to disprove the bleak implications view. Granted, on the right sorts of EEA-friendly problems, people answer correctly, but this leaves untouched our failures on all the other problems. Hence it is still an open possibility that, in many of the cases where information is not presented in the appropriate format or where the problem does not resemble a problem from the EEA, humans are indeed as irrational as they have been in the classic studies.

An alternative view of rationality

There is, however, a second, more interesting component to Gigerenzer's program which leads to a deeper issue in evaluating human rationality. The bleak implications view, and the entire enterprise of assessing rationality by seeing whether people follow the principles of reason, relies on the standard picture and its deontological account of rationality. According to the alternative consequentialist account that Gigerenzer advocates, good reasoning is reasoning which (reliably) produces the best outcome. If we adopt this consequentialist approach, then the truth or falsity of the bleak implications view, and thus the extent of human rationality, become contingent on the sort of world we live in and not on our following the principles of reason. Even if people violate principles of reason, and fall short of being perfect Bayesians, our reasoning mechanisms might still manage to produce the best outcomes overall.

For instance, a plausible principle of reason might be "consider all the available evidence when making a decision" but Gerd Gigerenzer (1947–) and colleagues have shown that *not* considering all the evidence can be a better strategy in the right sort of environment (Gigerenzer et al. 1999: Parts II and III). The work of Robyn Dawes (e.g. Dawes 1979) has similarly shown that prediction rules which are prima facie normatively deficient (e.g. rules which weight all predictive factors equally, regardless of their predictive validity) can outperform more complicated rules.

There are good reasons for favoring a consequentialist view of rationality which we won't go into here.[8] To assess the extent of human rationality, on a consequentialist account, we will have to learn much more not only about human psychology, but also about the task environments we actually face (see Martignon 2001). In any event, whether we accept the standard deontological picture of rationality or opt for an alternative consequentialist picture, we are still a long way from being able to say just how rational humans are.

Naturalization of intentionality

We have now considered four central questions in the philosophy of psychology: Do we need to invoke inner representational states to explain behavior? How much innate information and structure does the mind have? How modular is the mind? How rational are we? While all four involve some conceptual and philosophical heavy lifting, they are largely empirical questions. To answer them, at the very least we need to know a lot of facts about human psychology.

Our final topic, the naturalization of intentionality, is quite different. The enterprise here looks considerably more like traditional philosophy: X proposes a theory,

Y comes up with a counterexample, X adds a complication or two to keep her theory going; repeat as necessary. To naturalize intentionality, it seems, we don't need to know a lot of facts about human psychology. The question is not *whether* the human mind has intentionality,[9] or *how much* intentionality it has, but *how* it has it.

Nonetheless, even this philosophical enterprise has been strongly influenced by developments in psychology, at least indirectly. As we have seen, during the 1960s, the ruling orthodoxy of behaviorism was overthrown by cognitivism, and one of the distinctive features of cognitivism was its positing of representational states: mental states which are *about* things. As cognitivism became more widespread, the question thus arose: how to develop a scientifically respectable account of representation? Or, in other words, how to naturalize intentionality?

Intentionality and naturalization

But first the basics: What is intentionality, and what would it take to naturalize it? In our everyday folk psychological reasoning, we attribute thoughts to one another, and these thoughts are *about* things: suppose you want a beer, believe there's a beer in the fridge, wonder whether Guinness is better than Foster's, and so on. Your thoughts are *about* beer, the fridge, Guinness and Foster's, etc. Similarly, cognitivist psychology also posits mental states which are about things. Intentionality is this property of *aboutness*: the property that mental states (as well as things like words and maps) can have of being about one thing or another, of having a particular *content*. The notion of intentionality was reintroduced to philosophy and psychology in 1874 by Franz Brentano, who adopted it from medieval Scholastic philosophy. Brentano claimed that what distinguished mental states from (merely) physical states was that mental states were intentional; hence what came to be known as *Brentano's thesis* that the intentional is the mark of the mental.

Taking up these ideas, Chisholm (1957) argued that mental states were ineliminably intentional, that they could not be described or explained except in intentional terms. As Quine (1960) put it, Brentano's thesis shows either "the indispensability of intentional idioms and the importance of an autonomous science of intention" or "the baselessness of intentional idioms and the emptiness of a science of intention." Quine, the arch-behaviorist, was happy to take the second option, but almost everyone else has preferred the first.

Hence the attempts from the 1970s onwards to naturalize intentionality, that is, to come up with a theory of intentionality which is scientifically respectable. If intentionality is a real feature of mental states as posited by cognitivism, then we want to know how it fits into the rest of our scientific (and physicalist) picture of the world. Intentionality doesn't look to be part of the basic stuff in the world like atoms and quarks, and so we want to know how you get intentionality out of the basic stuff (Fodor 1987). Attempts to naturalize intentionality are attempts to show how you can do this, to explain intentionality in a naturalistic vocabulary which does not itself invoke intentionality (see also "Philosophy of mind," Chapter 12).

In addition to showing how intentionality arises from non-intentional stuff, there are two thorny problems an adequate naturalistic theory must solve: first, the *problem of misrepresentation*. You can believe your chocolate is in the cupboard, even though someone has secretly moved it elsewhere. You can mistake fool's gold for gold. You can believe that unicorns exist. In each of these cases, your mental states do not match up with the way the world really is. A naturalistic theory of intentionality must explain how this mismatch is possible. Second, the problem of *grain*. You can think about Hesperus, or you can think about Phosphorus. These are different thoughts, and have different content, but of course Hesperus just is Phosphorus. A naturalistic theory of intentionality must be able to draw such fine-grained distinctions between related but distinct contents.

Finally, before discussing the theories themselves, a word about narrow versus wide content. Since Putnam (1975), philosophers have debated whether the contents of mental states are to be individuated widely (by including factors which "ain't in the head") or narrowly (by not including such factors).[10] Most of the naturalistic accounts of intentionality are externalist, favoring wide individuation conditions. But even internalists, who favor narrow content, have to explain how mental states can be about things. Hence they too need to provide an account of intentionality (see Botterill and Carruthers 1999).

Three accounts of intentionality

Three main approaches have been taken to naturalizing intentionality: informational theories, teleosemantic theories, and conceptual role semantics. As they have developed in response to various problems and objections, these theories have accrued epicycles like barnacles on a shipwreck. To discuss the finer points of these theories would be well beyond the scope of this chapter (and beside the point, as we argue below). It is enough for our purposes to present them in somewhat simplified form.[11]

The informational approach is most closely associated with Fred Dretske (1981; 1988). This approach analyzes the content of a mental state in terms of the information it carries; your beer-thoughts are about beer because they carry information about beer. Information here is understood as causal co-variance. If there is a reliable law (typically, a causal law) that "whenever X obtains, so does Y," then Xs carry information about Ys. Spots carry information about measles, smoke carries information about fire, and beer-thoughts carry information about beer.

A pure informational approach has trouble both with misrepresentation and with grain. Suppose that Brenda reliably mistakes toads for frogs. Then her frog-thoughts would carry information about toads as much as about frogs, so how can we say that her frog-thoughts are mistaken when they occur in the presence of toads? Aren't they instead perfectly accurate frog-or-toad-thoughts? The informational approach cannot deal easily with misrepresentation. Similarly, Hesperus-thoughts may carry information about Hesperus, but they also carry information about Phosphorus. So why aren't our Hesperus-thoughts equally well Phosphorus-thoughts; that is to say, how can an informational approach solve the problem of grain? Another problem concerns causal chains. Smoke-thoughts carry information about smoke, but they also carry information about fire (since, generally, where there's smoke, there's fire). So why aren't our smoke-thoughts equally well fire-thoughts?

Informational theorists have developed two main ways of dealing with these problems. The first is Fodor's, which is to introduce a requirement of *asymmetric causal dependence* (Fodor 1990). Suppose that there were two laws in Brenda's psychology:

(1) frogs → frog-thoughts

(2) toads → frog-thoughts

Brenda's frog-thoughts are about frogs and not toads if (2) asymmetrically depends on (1). This means that if (1) did not hold, then (2) would not hold either but even if (2) did not hold, (1) still would. If frogs were no longer reliably linked to frog-thoughts, then toads wouldn't be linked to frog-thoughts either, but the converse is not true. The notion of asymmetric dependence, however, has serious problems of its own, which have been well rehearsed elsewhere (Adams and Aizawa 1994; Adams 2003). The main problem is spelling it out in a way which is properly naturalistic and not ad hoc, and this looks to be difficult, if not impossible.

The second way of dealing with these problems for the informational approach, and the way Dretske has taken, is to incorporate teleological elements into the theory. But the teleosemantic approach has also been pursued in its own right, primarily by Ruth Millikan (1984; 1989) and David Papineau (1987; 1993). The basic idea of teleosemantics is that the content of a particular mental state is given by its biological function: frog-thoughts are about frogs just in case their biological function is to carry information about frogs. A thing's biological function is then defined, following Wright's (1973) analysis, as the job that natural selection designed that thing to do. The function of hearts is to pump blood and, similarly, the function of frog-thoughts is to carry information about frogs.

Such a teleological approach deals well enough with the problem of misrepresentation. We could generally be mistaken about toads – indeed, our ancestors could have been as well – and our frog-thoughts would still be about frogs. All that matters is that frog-thoughts were selected to carry information about frogs, not toads. Where the teleosemantic approach runs into trouble is dealing with the problem of grain. For instance, suppose that in our evolutionary history we had only ever come into contact with one particular species of frog. Then what (if anything) makes it the case that our frog-thoughts are about frogs in general rather than that one particular species? Teleosemantic approaches must assume that evolutionary theory will pick out one content rather than the other as the appropriate biological function, but this assumption may not be well founded. Even if an appeal to evolution can solve this problem, it is not clear how it could also solve the Hesperus/Phosphorus problem.

The final approach we shall consider has been variously called conceptual, functional, inferential, or causal role semantics (Block 1986; Field 2001). The idea here is that thoughts are individuated in terms of their inferential or functional role in a person's overall cognitive economy, and so such an approach has typically been restricted to theories of narrow content (e.g. Field 1978; Loar 1981). But to explain intentionality – the relation between thoughts and the world – and to specify contents, functional role semantics must construe functional role broadly, so as to include relations between mental states and the world. The reason beer-thoughts are about beer as opposed to scotch (or, for that matter, the reason they are about anything at all) surely has something to do with how the world is and how we are hooked up to it. A broad functional role semantics would explain this by including various thought–world interactions as part of the thought's functional role; for instance, part of the functional role of beer-thoughts is that they are produced in the presence of beer, and that they lead to consumption of beer when one so desires.

It is difficult to assess the merits of functional role semantics as a naturalistic account of intentionality. While various philosophers have gestured at the approach as a way to naturalize intentionality, no one has actually offered a detailed account that would assign specific content to mental states. For instance, what is the functional role of the belief that the beer is in the fridge, as opposed to the belief that the scotch is in the fridge, or that the beer is in the cupboard? Moreover, all beer-thoughts are about beer, but what is common to the functional role of beer-thoughts? It is one thing to say that functional roles can answer these questions, but it is another thing to show how and, as yet, no one has come even close to doing this.

Doubts about naturalization

So much for the main approaches to naturalizing intentionality. Each of these approaches has its own problems, which we have only sketched here; they are well summarized in Adams (2003) and Loewer (1997). There are also more general doubts about the overall project of naturalizing intentionality. First, a suggestion made by Horgan (1994) and Loewer (1997). Perhaps intentionality is indeed naturalistically respectable – that is, intentionality is built out of basic physical features of the world – but there is no way for us to understand how this happens. The problem of explaining intentionality may be simply intractable, or beyond our limited cognitive capacities.[12]

This sort of cognitive closure with respect to intentionality is certainly a possibility, but its significance ought not be overstated. Maybe we *can't* provide a fully naturalistic account of intentionality but that's no argument against trying. You've got to be in it to win it. To be fair to Horgan and Loewer, they were not arguing that we should give up on naturalizing intentionality. Rather, the possibility of cognitive closure was offered as a potential explanation of why we haven't succeeded so far, and why we might never succeed. Even so, there is no reason why, having recognized this possibility, we shouldn't keep trying.

There is another general doubt about the project, however, which we think is more serious and which lies in the fuzziness of the demand for naturalization (Stich 1992; Tye 1992; Stich and Laurence 1994; Botterill and Carruthers 1999). What, exactly, would *count* as having naturalized intentionality? As we noted at the start of this section, the debates over intentionality resemble good old-fashioned conceptual analysis (well, old-fashioned conceptual analysis, anyway). X offers a theory of intentionality, Y brings up a counterexample (often outlandish), and X goes back to the drawing board. So the call for naturalization looks like a call to provide necessary and sufficient conditions for something's being intentional, and for something's having the particular content that it does. That is, it looks like a call for a definition of the term or concept "intentionality."

But if that's what naturalization amounts to, then why suppose that we can naturalize intentionality – or anything else? Fodor himself has argued in a different context that necessary and sufficient conditions won't be forthcoming for even the most innocuous concept like "paint" (Fodor 1981), so it would be surprising if we *could* produce a definition for "intentionality." Indeed, if certain views about conceptual structure are right, it's not just that definitions for concepts are hard to come by, it's that there *aren't* any. If concepts have exemplar or prototype structure, for instance, then they don't have definitions and so cannot be analyzed in terms of necessary and sufficient conditions.[13]

What unites these two general doubts (about cognitive closure and about the very project of naturalization) is their skepticism about the urgent need to naturalize. Fodor predicts, quite literally, apocalypse if the intentional can't be naturalized: it would be "the end of the world" (1990: 156) and "the greatest intellectual catastrophe in the history of our species" (1987: xii). This is because he thinks that intentional irrealism would follow; other putative consequences include the causal/explanatory impotence of intentionality and the impossibility of an intentional psychology.

The prospect of "failure" to naturalize, then, has been seen by some as tantamount to opening the seventh seal. Against this alarmism, we caution: don't believe the hype. Regardless of the actual structure of our concepts, there are plenty of other features of the world for which we lack definitions despite a lot of sophisticated effort aimed at producing them. Necessary and sufficient conditions have not been found for something's being a phoneme, or a gene, or a species, or just about anything except being a bachelor or a triangle. You don't find biologists gnashing their teeth because they can't give necessary and sufficient conditions for "gene" or "species," and this "failure" seems hardly to impugn the realism, efficacy, or scientific respectability of genes or species.

More generally, however the demand to naturalize intentionality is meant, the apocalypse will not ensue if we fail (see Stich and Laurence 1994). This is not to say that there are no interesting questions about intentionality and mental content. It is not yet settled, for instance, what sort of mental states a mature psychology will be committed to, what sorts of intentional properties, if any, those states will have, and how this is related to the intentional properties invoked by everyday folk psychology (Stich 1992). But answering these questions is a long way from "naturalizing intentionality."

Conclusion

Of necessity, this survey of important developments in twentieth-century philosophy of psychology has been selective. There are many issues we have not discussed, or only touched on, including the following.[14]

The nature of concepts

What is the structure of mental representation, or concepts? Philosophers since Plato have typically assumed that our concepts are defined by a set of necessary and sufficient conditions. Since the pioneering work of Eleanor Rosch (1938–) in the 1970s (Rosch and Mervis 1975), psychologists have developed at least two other, competing accounts of our conceptual structure. Philosophers have participated actively in the (still unresolved) empirical debate which has ensued, as well as teasing out the philosophical implications of these alternatives. Margolis and Laurence 1999 offers an excellent overview of this work.

Connectionism

According to the "classical" or symbol-manipulation view in cognitive psychology, thinking is computation, i.e. the manipulation of symbolic representations. By contrast, according to connectionism there is no separation between representations and processes operating over those representations. Rather, cognition is modeled as a network of interconnecting nodes, loosely inspired by neural networks, and information is distributed over the entire network. Since the re-emergence of connectionism in 1986 (Rumelhart et al. 1986), some have argued that connectionist models were more plausible descriptions of human psychology; philosophers have debated whether connectionism and classical models are genuine alternatives, and the potential consequences if the human mind were indeed connectionist (see Bechtel and Abrahamsen 2002).

Extended cognition

Psychologists and philosophers have generally conceived of thinking as something that goes on purely "in the head"; both connectionist and classical models of cognition make this assumption. The idea of extended cognition challenges this by recasting cognition as reaching out "into the world": for example, the mobile phone you store important phone numbers in is not just a tool for your thinking, it is a part of your thinking. Andy Clark has advocated this idea in his 2003 book and elsewhere.

The emotions

What are the emotions, and how do they relate to the rest of our thinking? In the late twentieth century, there was extensive work in both philosophy and psychology trying to address this question. Unfortunately, most of the philosophy simply ignored the psychology, although this situation has been partly remedied in later years (e.g. Griffiths 1997; Prinz 2004).

Theory of mind and simulation in folk psychological reasoning

How do we detect and think about other people's mental states? For instance, how do we predict your behavior given what we know about your beliefs and desires? According to the theory theory, we use a mentally represented theory of mind which includes general psychological laws. By contrast, according to simulation theory, proposed independently by philosophers Robert Gordon and Jane Heal (Gordon 1986;

Heal 1986), we must simulate being you; that is to say, we imagine having your mental states, and see what we would do. Much research on the psychological mechanisms for mentalizing was done during the last three decades of the twentieth century, and philosophers actively contributed to this research and the broader debates (Nichols and Stich 2003; Goldman 2006).

Consciousness

Philosophers at least since Dennett (1969) have tried to develop accounts of consciousness informed by psychology; this trend increased in the 1990s with the revival in psychology itself of research into consciousness (see the papers in Baars et al. 2003). Much of the philosophy of consciousness, however, is still only tangentially connected, if that, with the psychology of consciousness.

Eliminativism and the role of the propositional attitudes in psychology

In our everyday folk psychology we naturally ascribe mental states like beliefs and desires to one another, and to ourselves. Will such propositional attitudes appear in our finished scientific psychology and, if not, does that not mean we should reject them as empirically inadequate concepts (like "witch" or "phlogiston")? It has seemed to some philosophers that cognitive psychology or connectionist models leave no room for propositional attitudes, but this has been hotly contested (see Horgan and Tienson 1991).

The rise of evolutionary psychology

One of the most striking facts about psychology since the 1990s has been the increasing influence (not least in the arena of public debate) of evolutionary psychology. Broadly speaking, evolutionary psychology is any psychology influenced by evolutionary theory; more commonly, however, it refers to a specific research paradigm closely associated with Cosmides and Tooby (Barkow et al. 1992). This paradigm has found both philosophical advocates (e.g. Samuels et al. 1999) and opponents (e.g. Buller 2005).

The growing importance of neuroscience

During the closing decades of the twentieth century, technological improvements have made possible increasingly detailed investigation into the actual neurological circuitry of human and animal cognition. Inevitably, this work has received increasing philosophical attention (Bechtel et al. 2001), which is only likely to increase further as more and more is discovered in neuroscience.

This represents just a sample of philosophically relevant research in psychology at the start of the twenty-first century. More so than in the twentieth century even, psychology today moves fast, in hundreds of different directions. Scarcely a week goes by without some new research plowing up fertile ground for philosophical work. What we hope to have shown in this overview is that philosophers of psychology have proved themselves up to the task. Philosophy of psychology is not the handmaiden of psychology. In the last century at least, philosophy and psychology worked hand-in-hand to uncover truths about the human mind. May they stay partners in the next.

Notes

1 We stress that this is only a rough characterization; it is both too broad and too narrow. Ultimately, nothing really hangs on whether a specific issue is considered part of philosophy of psychology or philosophy of mind.

2 Richard Samuels offers an account of innateness that is related to the present account, but is quite a bit more sophisticated. See Samuels 2002 for a lucid discussion.

3 In fact, evolutionary psychologists are generally committed to a specific type of computational module, namely one which was produced by natural selection and is universal across all (normal) humans. Since these further features aren't relevant here, we will pass over them.

4 *Overconfidence*: people's confidence in their own judgments can far outstrip their actual accuracy. *Hindsight bias*: once they know an event has occurred, people typically overestimate how likely they would have thought that event in advance. *Gambler's fallacy*: e.g. after seeing a long run of heads in a series of coin tosses, many people think that tails must be "due" and therefore more likely to occur. *Illusory correlations*: people will often see correlations (in a set of data) that aren't there. *Base-rate neglect*: given information about the base-rate frequency of a particular outcome in a population (e.g. frequency of colon cancer), and diagnostic evidence about a specific case (e.g. Smith's bioscopy), most people ignore the base-rate information when predicting the likelihood that the outcome has occurred in this case (i.e. that Smith has colon cancer).

5 The psychologists Csibra and Gergely have interpreted their results in a Dennettian framework (e.g. Gergely et al. 1995; Csibra et al. 1999) but this seems an over-interpretation. For more on the relation of rationality theories to human rationality and to folk psychology, see Stich 1985 and Nichols and Stich 2003: sect. 3.4.4.

6 Admittedly, the argument here is hardly conclusive. For more extended criticism of Cohen, see Stich 1985; 1990; and Stein 1996.

7 There are other hypotheses to explain the pattern of results, from outside evolutionary psychology (e.g. Cheng and Holyoak 1989; Oaksford and Chater 1994; Cummins 1996). Which of these hypotheses is correct is still a hotly debated issue.

8 They are persuasively put by Bishop (2000) and Bishop and Trout (2004).

9 Certainly, irrealism about intentionality is a possible view, but few contemporary philosophers have adopted it with any gusto (but see the discussion of Quine, below). Dennett's instrumentalism might seem close (e.g. Dennett 1987), but he denies that his position is irrealist (Dennett 1991).

10 Pessin and Goldberg 1996 contains many papers on this externalism/internalism debate.

11 For more detail, see the selections in Stich and Warfield 1994.

12 This suggestion is analogous with what McGinn (1993) has claimed about consciousness.

13 See Margolis and Laurence 1999 and Murphy 2002 for discussion of psychological theories of concepts and categorization.

14 This list is *far* from exhaustive.

References

Adams, F. (2003) "Thoughts and their contents: the structure of cognitive representations." In S. Stich and T. A. Warfield (eds.) *The Blackwell Guide to Philosophy of Mind*, Oxford: Blackwell, pp. 143–71.

Adams, F. and K. Aizawa (1994) "Fodorian semantics." In S. Stich and T. A. Warfield (eds.) *Mental Representation*, Oxford: Blackwell, pp. 223–42.

Atran, S. (1998) "Folk biology and the anthropology of science: cognitive universals and cultural particulars." *Behavioral and Brain Sciences* 21: 547–609.

Baars, B. J., W. P. Banks, and J. B. Newman (2003) *Essential Sources in the Scientific Study of Consciousness*. Cambridge, MA: MIT Press.

Barkow, J., L. Cosmides, and J. Tooby (eds.) (1992) *The Adapted Mind: Evolutionary Psychology and the Generation of Culture*. Oxford: Oxford University Press.

Baron-Cohen, S. (1995) *Mindblindness: An Essay on Autism and Theory of Mind*. Cambridge, MA: MIT Press.

Bateson, P. (1991) "Are there principles of behavioural development?" In P. Bateson (ed.) *The Development and Integration of Behaviour*, Cambridge: Cambridge University Press, pp. 19–39.

Bechtel, W. and A. Abrahamsen (2002) *Connectionism and the Mind: Parallel Processing, Dynamics, and Evolution in Networks*, 2nd edn. Oxford: Blackwell.

Bechtel, W., R. Stufflebeam, J. Mundale, and P. Mandik (2001) *Philosophy and the Neurosciences: A Reader*. Oxford: Blackwell.

Bishop, M. (2000) "In praise of epistemic irresponsibility: How lazy and ignorant can you be?" *Synthèse* 122: 179–208.

Bishop, M. and J. D. Trout (2004) *Epistemology and the Psychology of Human Judgment*. Oxford: Oxford University Press.

Block, N. (1986) "Advertisement for a semantics for psychology." *Midwest Studies in Philosophy* 10: 615–78.

Botterill, G. and P. Carruthers (1999) *The Philosophy of Psychology*. Cambridge: Cambridge University Press.

Brentano, F. (1973) [1874] *Philosophy from an Empirical Standpoint*. London: Routledge & Kegan Paul.

Buller, D. J. (2005) *Adapting Minds: Evolutionary Psychology and the Persistent Quest for Human Nature*. Cambridge, MA: MIT Press.

Carey, S. and E. Spelke (1994) "Domain-specific knowledge and conceptual change." In L. Hirschfeld and S. Gelman (eds.) *Mapping the Mind*, Cambridge: Cambridge University Press, pp. 169–200.

Carruthers, P. (2003) "On Fodor's problem." *Mind and Language* 18: 502–23.

Chapman, L. J. and J. P. Chapman (1967) "Genesis of popular but erroneous psychodiagnostic observations." *Journal of Abnormal Psychology* 73: 193–204.

Cheng, P. and K. Holyoak (1989) "On the natural selection of reasoning theories." *Cognition* 33: 285–313.

Chisholm, R. (1957) *Perceiving: A Philosophy Study*. Ithaca, NY: Cornell University Press.

Chomsky, N. (1959) "A review of Skinner's *Verbal Behavior*." Repr. in N. Block (ed.) *Readings in Philosophy of Psychology*, Cambridge, MA: Harvard University Press, 1980, pp. 48–63.

—— (1965) *Aspects of the Theory of Syntax*. Cambridge, MA: MIT Press.

—— (1988) *Language and Problems of Knowledge*. Cambridge, MA: MIT Press.

—— (1980) *Rules and Representation*. New York: Columbia University Press.

Clark, A. (2003) *Natural-Born Cyborgs: Minds, Technologies, and the Future of Human Intelligence*. Oxford: Oxford University Press.

Cohen, L. (1981) "Can human irrationality be experimentally demonstrated?" *Behavioral and Brain Sciences* 4: 317–70.

Cosmides, L. and J. Tooby (1992) "Cognitive adaptations for social exchange." In J. Barkow, L. Cosmides, and J. Tooby (eds.) *The Adapted Mind: Evolutionary Psychology and the Generation of Culture*, Oxford: Oxford University Press, pp. 163–228.

—— and —— (1994) "Origins of domain specificity: the evolution of functional organization." In L. Hirschfeld and S. Gelman (eds.) *Mapping the Mind*, Cambridge: Cambridge University Press, pp. 85–116.

—— and —— (1996) "Are humans good intuitive statisticians after all? Rethinking some conclusions from the literature on judgment under uncertainty." *Cognition* 58: 1–73.

Cowie, F. (1999) *What's Within? Nativism Reconsidered*. New York: Oxford University Press.

Csibra, G., G. Gergely, S. Biro, O. Koos, and M. Brockbank (1999) "Goal attribution without agency cues: the perception of 'pure reason' in infancy." *Cognition* 72: 237–67.

Cummins, D. (1996) "Evidence for the innateness of deontic reasoning." *Mind and Language* 11: 160–90.

Davidson, D. (1963) "Actions, reasons and causes." *Journal of Philosophy* 60/23: 685–700.

—— (1984) *Inquiries into Truth and Interpretation*. Oxford: Oxford University Press.

Dawes, R. M. (1979) "The robust beauty of improper linear models in decision making." *American Psychologist* 34: 571–82.

Dennett, D. (1969) *Content and Consciousness*. London: Routledge & Kegan Paul.

—— (1987) *The Intentional Stance*. Cambridge, MA: MIT Press.

—— (1991) "Real patterns." *Journal of Philosophy* 88: 27–51.

Descartes, R. (1985) *The Philosophical Writings of Descartes*, vol. 1, trans. J. Cottingham, R. Stoothoff, and D. Murdoch. Cambridge: Cambridge University Press.

Dretske, F. (1981) *Knowledge and the Flow of Information*. Cambridge, MA: MIT Press.

—— (1988) *Explaining Behavior*. Cambridge, MA: MIT Press.

Elman, J., E. Bates, M. H. Johnson, A. Karmiloff-Smith, D. Parisi, and K. Plunkett (1996) *Rethinking Innateness: A Connectionist Perspective on Development*. Cambridge: Cambridge University Press.

Field, H. (1978) "Mental representation." *Erkenntnis* 13: 9–61.

—— (2001) *Truth and the Absence of Fact*. Oxford: Oxford University Press.

Fischhoff, B. (1975) "Hindsight is not equal to foresight: the effect of outcome knowledge on judgment under uncertainty." *Journal of Experimental Psychology: Human Perception and Performance* 1: 288–99.

Fodor, J. (1968) *Psychological Explanation*. New York: Random House.

—— (1981) *Representations*. Cambridge, MA: MIT Press.

—— (1983) *The Modularity of Mind*. Cambridge, MA: MIT Press.

—— (1987) *Psychosemantics*. Cambridge, MA: MIT Press.

—— (1990) *A Theory of Content and Other Essays*. Cambridge, MA: MIT Press.

—— (2000) *The Mind Doesn't Work That Way*. Cambridge, MA: MIT Press.

Gardner, H. (1985) *The Mind's New Science: A History of the Cognitive Revolution*. New York: Basic Books.

Gelman, R. and K. Brenneman (1994) "First principles can support both universal and culture-specific learning about number and music." In L. Hirschfeld and S. Gelman (eds.) *Mapping the Mind*, Cambridge: Cambridge University Press, pp. 369–90.

Gergely, G., Z. Nadasy, G. Csibra, and S. Biro (1995) "Taking the intentional stance at 12 months of age." *Cognition* 56: 165–93.

Gigerenzer, G. (1994) "Why the distinction between single-event probabilities and frequencies is important for psychology (and vice versa)." In G. Wright and P. Ayton (eds.) *Subjective Probability*, New York: John Wiley, pp. 129–61.

Gigerenzer, G., P. Todd, and the ABC Research Group (1999) *Simple Heuristics that Make Us Smart*. New York: Oxford University Press.

Gilovich, T., D. Griffin, and D. Kahneman (2002) *Heuristics and Biases: The Psychology of Intuitive Judgment*. Cambridge: Cambridge University Press.

Goldman, A. (1986) *Epistemology and Cognition*. Cambridge, MA: Harvard University Press.

—— A. (2006) *Simulating Minds: The Philosophy, Psychology and Neuroscience of Mindreading*. Oxford: Oxford University Press.

Gordon, R. (1986) "Folk psychology as simulation." *Mind and Language* 1: 158–71.

Griffiths, P. (1997) *What Emotions Really Are*. Chicago: University of Chicago Press.

—— (2002) "What is innateness?" *The Monist* 85/1: 70–85.

Griggs, R. and J. Cox (1982) "The elusive thematic-materials effect in Wason's selection task." *British Journal of Psychology* 73: 407–20.

Harman, G. (1986) *Change of View*. Cambridge, MA: MIT Press.

Heal, J. (1986) "Replication and functionalism." In J. Butterfield (ed.) *Language, Mind, and Logic*, Cambridge: Cambridge University Press, pp. 135–50.

Hirschfeld, L. and S. Gelman (eds.) (1994) *Mapping the Mind: Domain Specificity in Cognition and Culture*. Cambridge: Cambridge University Press.

Horgan, T. (1994) "Computation and mental representation." In S. Stich and T. A. Warfield (eds.) *Mental Representation*, Oxford: Blackwell, pp. 302–11.

Horgan, T. and J. Tienson (eds.) (1991) *Connectionism and the Philosophy of Mind*. Dordrecht: Kluwer.

Kahneman, D. and A. Tversky (1973) "On the psychology of prediction." *Psychological Review* 80: 237–51.

—— and —— (1982) "On the study of statistical intuitions." In D. Kahneman, P. Slovic, and A. Tversky (eds.) *Judgment under Uncertainty: Heuristics and Biases*, Cambridge: Cambridge University Press, pp. 493–508.

Kahneman, D., P. Slovic, and A. Tversky (eds.) (1982) *Judgment under Uncertainty: Heuristics and Biases*. Cambridge: Cambridge University Press.

Kandel, E., J. H. Schwartz, and T. M. Jessell (2000) *Principles of Neural Science*. New York: McGraw-Hill.

Karmiloff-Smith, A. (1992) *Beyond Modularity*. Cambridge, MA: MIT Press.

Kitcher, P. (1996) *The Lives to Come*. New York: Simon & Schuster.

Laland, K. N. and G. R. Brown (2002) *Sense and Nonsense: Evolutionary Perspectives on Human Behavior*. New York: Oxford University Press.

Latane, B. and J. M. Darley (1970) *The Unresponsive Bystander: Why Doesn't He Help?* New York: Appleton-Century-Crofts.

Leslie, A. (1994) "ToMM, ToBY, and agency: core architecture and domain specificity." In L. Hirchfeld and S. Gelman (eds.) *Mapping the Mind*, Cambridge: Cambridge University Press, pp. 119–48.

Lichtenstein, S. and B. Fischhoff (1977) "Do those who know more also know more about how much they know?" *Organizational Behavior and Human Performance* 20: 159–83.

Loar, B. (1981) *Mind and Meaning*. Cambridge: Cambridge University Press.

Loewer, B. (1997) "A guide to naturalizing semantics." In B. Hale and C. Wright (eds.) *A Companion to the Philosophy of Language*, Oxford: Blackwell, pp. 108–26.

Margolis, E. and S. Laurence (eds.) (1999) *Concepts: Core Readings*. Cambridge, MA: MIT Press.

Martignon, L. (2001) "Comparing fast and frugal heuristics and optimal models." In G. Gigerenzer and R. Selten (eds.) *Bounded Rationality: The Adaptive Toolbox*, Cambridge, MA: MIT Press, pp. 147–71.

McGinn, C. (1993) *Problems in Philosophy: The Limits of Inquiry*. Oxford: Blackwell.

Milgram, S. (1963) "Behavioral study of obedience." *Journal of Abnormal and Social Psychology* 67: 371–78.

Millikan, R. (1984) *Language, Thought, and Other Biological Categories*. Cambridge, MA: MIT Press.

—— (1989) "Biosemantics." *Journal of Philosophy* 86: 281–97.

Murphy, G. (2002) *The Big Book of Concepts*. Cambridge, MA: MIT Press.

Newell, A. and H. Simon (1963) "GPS, a program that simulates human thought." In E. Feigenbaum and J. Feldman (eds.) *Computers and Thought*, New York: McGraw-Hill, pp. 279–93.

Nichols, S. and S. Stich (2003) *Mindreading: An Integrated Account of Pretence, Self-Awareness, and Understanding of Other Minds*. Oxford: Oxford University Press.

Nisbett, R. E. and E. Borgida (1975) "Attribution and the psychology of prediction." *Journal of Personality and Social Psychology* 32: 932–43.

Nisbett, R. E. and L. Ross (1980) *Human Inference: Strategies and Shortcomings of Social Judgment*. Englewood Cliffs, NJ: Prentice-Hall.

Oaksford, M. and N. Chater (1994) "A rational analysis of the selection task as optimal data selection." *Psychological Review* 101: 608–31.

Papineau, D. (1987) *Reality and Representation*. Oxford: Blackwell.

—— (1993) *Philosophical Naturalism*. Oxford: Blackwell.

Pessin, A. and S. Goldberg (eds.) (1996) *The Twin Earth Chronicles: Twenty Years of Reflection on Hilary Putnam's "The Meaning of 'Meaning'."* Armonk, NY: M. E. Sharpe.

Posner, M. I. (1989) *Foundations of Cognitive Science*. Cambridge, MA: MIT Press.

Prinz, J. (2004) *Gut Reactions: A Perceptual Theory of Emotion*. Oxford: Oxford University Press.

Putnam, H. (1975) "The meaning of 'meaning'." In K. Gunderson (ed.) *Language, Mind and Knowledge*, Minneapolis, MN: University of Minnesota Press, pp. 131–93.

Quine, W. V. O. (1951) "Two dogmas of empiricism." *Philosophical Review* 60: 20–43.

—— (1960) *Word and Object*. Cambridge, MA: MIT Press.

Rescorla, R. A. and A. R. Wagner (1972) "A theory of Pavlovian conditioning: variations in the effectiveness of reinforcement and nonreinforcement." In A. H. Black and W. F. Prokasy (eds.) *Classical Conditioning II: Current Research and Theory*, New York: Appleton-Century-Crofts, pp. 64–99.

Rosch, E. and C. Mervis (1975) "Family resemblances: studies in the internal structure of categories." *Cognitive Psychology* 8: 382–439.

Rumelhart, D. E., J. L. McClelland, and the PDP Research Group (1986) *Parallel Distributed Processing Explorations in the Microstructure of Cognition*. Cambridge, MA: MIT Press.

Ryle, G. (1949) *The Concept of Mind*. London: Hutchinson.

Samuels, R. (1998) "Evolutionary psychology and the massive modularity hypothesis." *British Journal for the Philosophy of Science* 49: 575–602.

—— (2002) "Nativism in cognitive science." *Mind and Language* 17: 233–65.

Samuels, R., S. Stich, and P. D. Tremoulet (1999) "Rethinking rationality: from bleak implications to Darwinian modules." In E. LePore and Z. Pylyshyn (eds.) *What Is Cognitive Science?*, Oxford: Blackwell, pp. 74–120.

Samuels, R., S. Stich, and M. Bishop (2002) "Ending the rationality wars: how to make disputes about human rationality disappear." In R. Elio (ed.) *Common Sense, Reasoning, and Rationality*, Oxford: Oxford University Press, pp. 236–68.

Scholl, B. and A. Leslie (1999) "Modularity, development and 'theory of mind'." *Mind and Language* 14: 131–53.

Skinner, B. F. (1953) *Science and Human Behavior*. New York: Macmillan.

—— (1957) *Verbal Behavior*. New York: Appleton-Century-Crofts.

Spelke, E. S. (1988) "The origins of physical knowledge." In L. Weiskrantz (ed.) *Thought Without Language*, Oxford: Clarendon Press, pp. 168–84.

Stein, E. (1996) *Without Good Reason*. Oxford: Clarendon Press.

Stich, S. (1975) "The idea of innateness." In S. Stich (ed.) *Innate Ideas*, Los Angeles: University of California Press, pp. 1–22.

—— (1985) "Could man be an irrational animal?" *Synthèse* 64: 115–35.

—— (1990) *The Fragmentation of Reason*. Cambridge, MA: MIT Press.

—— (1992) "What is a theory of mental representation?" *Mind* 101: 243–61.

Stich, S. and S. Laurence (1994) "Intentionality and naturalism." *Midwest Studies in Philosophy* 19: 159–82.

Stich, S. and T. A. Warfield (eds.) (1994) *Mental Representation*. Oxford: Blackwell.

Thorndike, E. L. (1911) *Animal Intelligence*. New York: Macmillan.

Tversky, A. and D. Kahneman (1971) "Belief in the law of small numbers." *Psychological Bulletin* 76: 105–10.

—— and —— (1982) "Judgments of and by representativeness." In D. Kahneman, P. Slovic, and A. Tversky (eds.) *Judgment under Uncertainty: Heuristics and Biases*, Cambridge: Cambridge University Press, pp. 84–98.

Tye, M. (1992) "Naturalism and the mental." *Mind* 101: 421–41.

Warfield, T. A. and S. Stich (1994) Introduction. In S. Stich and T. A. Warfield (eds.) *Mental Representation*, Oxford: Blackwell.

Wason, P. C. (1966) "Reasoning." In B. Foss (ed.) *New Horizons in Psychology*, Harmondsworth: Penguin, pp. 135–51.

Watson, J. B. (1913) "Psychology as the behaviorist views it." *Psychological Review* 20: 158–77.

Wright, L. (1973) "Functions." *Philosophical Review* 82: 139–68.

Further reading

General philosophy of psychology

G. Botterill and P. Carruthers, *The Philosophy of Psychology* (Cambridge: Cambridge University Press, 1999) provides a more in-depth treatment of most topics covered here, as well as others. R. Cummins and D. Cummins, *Minds, Brains and Computers: The Foundations of Cognitive Science* (Oxford: Blackwell, 2000) reprints many seminal papers in cognitive science. Most general anthologies of philosophy of mind also contain selections relevant to topics discussed here (e.g. W. Lycan (ed.) *Mind and Cognition*, 2nd edn., Oxford: Blackwell, 1999).

Cognitivism

H. Gardner, *The Mind's New Science: A History of the Cognitive Revolution* (New York: Basic Books, 1985) remains an accessible history of the development of cognitive science. The first part of N. Block (ed.) *Readings in Philosophy of Psychology* (Cambridge, MA: Harvard University Press, 1980) reprints some of the historically important texts. For a valuable collection of philosophical reactions to Chomsky's work, see L. Antony and N. Hornstein, *Chomsky and His Critics* (Oxford: Blackwell, 2003).

Nativism

L. Hirschfeld and S. Gelman (eds.) *Mapping the Mind: Domain Specificity in Cognition and Culture* (Cambridge: Cambridge University Press, 1994) is an influential collection of nativist papers. F. Cowie,

What's Within? Nativism Reconsidered (New York: Oxford University Press, 1999) and J. Elman et al., *Rethinking Innateness: A Connectionist Perspective on Development* (Cambridge: Cambridge University Press, 1996) are important critiques.

Modularity
J. Fodor, *The Modularity of Mind* (Cambridge, MA: MIT Press, 1983) is the locus classicus of modularity. Fodor, *The Mind Doesn't Work That Way* (Cambridge, MA: MIT Press, 2000) presents his later view, and R. Samuels, "Evolutionary psychology and the massive modularity hypothesis" (*British Journal for the Philosophy of Science* 49, 1998) is critical in various ways of modularity.

Rationality
The anthologies D. Kahneman et al. (eds.) *Judgment under Uncertainty: Heuristics and Biases* (Cambridge: Cambridge University Press, 1982) and T. Gilovich et al. (eds.) *Heuristics and Biases: The Psychology of Intuitive Judgment* (Cambridge: Cambridge University Press, 2002) provide copious empirical evidence. The alternative approach advocated by Gigerenzer and colleagues is presented in a series of books, including their *Simple Heuristics that Make Us Smart* (New York: Oxford University Press, 1999). E. Stein, *Without Good Reason* (Oxford: Clarendon Press, 1996) is a good overview of the debate.

Intentionality
S. Stich and T. A. Warfield (eds.) *Mental Representation* (Oxford: Blackwell, 1994) collects many of the important papers.

14

PHILOSOPHY OF SCIENCE

Stathis Psillos

Synoptic overview

Philosophy of science emerged as a distinctive part of philosophy in the twentieth century. It set its own agenda, the systematic study of the metaphysical and epistemological foundations of science, and acquired its own professional structure, departments and journals. Its defining moment was the meeting (and the clash) of two courses of events: the breakdown of the Kantian philosophical tradition and the crisis in the sciences and mathematics at the beginning of the century. The emergence of the new Frege–Russell logic (see "The birth of analytic philosophy," Chapter 1), the arithmeticization of geometry and the collapse of classical mechanics called into question the neat Kantian scheme of synthetic a priori principles (see "Kant in the twentieth century," Chapter 4). But the thought that *some* a priori (framework) principles should be in place in order for science to be possible had still had a strong grip on the thinkers of the European continent. A heated intellectual debate started concerning the status of these a priori principles. The view that dominated the scene after the dust had settled was that the required framework principles were conventions. The seed of this thought was found in Poincaré's writings, but in the hands of the logical positivists, it was fertilized with Frege's conception of analyticity and Hilbert's conception of implicit definitions. The consolidation of modern physics lent credence to the view that a priori principles can be revised; hence, a new conception of *relativized* a priori emerged. The linguistic turn in philosophy reoriented the subject matter of philosophical thinking about science to the *language* of science (see "The development of analytic philosophy: Wittgenstein and after," Chapter 2). Formal-logical methods and conceptual analysis were taken to be the privileged philosophical tools. Not only, it was thought, do they clarify and perhaps solve (or dissolve) traditional philosophical problems; they also make philosophy rigorous and set it apart from empirical science. In the 1930s, philosophy of science became the logic of science; it became synonymous with anti-psychologism, anti-historicism, and anti-naturalism. At the same time, philosophy of science, in Vienna and elsewhere, was completing the project of the Enlightenment: the safeguarding of the objectivity and epistemic authority of science.

The havoc brought about by the Nazis liquidated most philosophical thinking on the Continent and many continental philosophers of science took refuge in the US. There, their thought came under the pressure of American pragmatism. Pragmatism's disdain for drawing sharp distinctions where perfect continua exist shook up the rationale for doing philosophy of science in the way the logical positivists practised it. Quine challenged the fact/framework distinction and argued that no a priori principles were necessary for science. Sellars refuted a foundationalist strand that was present in the thought of some logical positivists. And Kuhn restored the place of history in philosophical thinking about science. By the 1960s, philosophy of science had seen the advent of psychologism, naturalism, and history. The historical turn showed that attempted rational reconstructions of science were paper tigers. Yet the historicists' grand models of science were no less of paper tigers, if only because the individual sciences are not uniform enough to be lumped under grand macro-models. The 1980s saw the mushrooming of interest in the individual sciences. The renaissance of scientific realism in the 1960s resulted in an epistemic optimism with regard to science's claim to truth, though new forms of empiricism emerged in the 1980s. At the same time causation came out of the empiricist closet. In the last two decades of the century, philosophers of science had started taking seriously a number of traditional metaphysical issues that were considered meaningless in the 1930s.[1]

Pressures on Kantianism

Much of the philosophical thinking before the beginning of the twentieth century had been shaped by Kant's philosophy. Immanuel Kant (1724–1804) had rejected empiricism (which denied the active role of the mind in understanding and representing the world of experience) and uncritical rationalism (which did acknowledge the active role of the mind but gave it an almost unlimited power to arrive at substantive knowledge of the world on the basis only of the lights of Reason). He famously claimed that although all knowledge starts with experience it does not arise from it: it is actively shaped by the categories of the understanding and the forms of pure intuition (space and time). The mind, as it were, imposes some conceptual structure onto the world, without which no experience could be possible. There was a notorious drawback, however. Kant thought there could be no knowledge of things as they were in themselves (the *noumena*) and only knowledge of things as they appeared to us (*phenomena*). This odd combination, Kant thought, might well be an inevitable price one has to pay in order to defeat skepticism and forgo traditional idealism. Be that as it may, his master thought was that some synthetic a priori principles should be in place for experience to be possible. These synthetic a priori principles (e.g. that space is Euclidean, that every event has a cause, that nature is law-governed, that substance is conserved, the laws of arithmetic) were necessary for the very possibility of science and of Newtonian mechanics in particular. If we were to sum up Kant's conception of a priori knowledge, this would be helpful: it is knowledge

1 universal, necessary and certain;
2 whose content is formal: it establishes conceptual connections (if analytic); it captures the form of pure intuition and formal features that phenomena have

because they are partly constituted by the pure concepts of the understanding (if synthetic);

3 constitutive of the form of experience;

4 disconnected from the content of experience; hence, unrevisable.

The new physics

A century after Kant's death, a major crisis swept across the reigning Newtonian physics. Classical mechanics crumbled. Two kinds of pressure were exerted on it.

The first came from Einstein's Special Theory of Relativity in 1905. Drawing on important considerations of symmetry, Albert Einstein (1879–1955) suggested that understanding the electrodynamics of moving bodies required a radical departure from classical mechanics. Where classical mechanics, and its extension to the electrodynamics of moving bodies by Hendrik Antoon Lorentz (1853–1928), had relied on the existence of absolute space and time, Einstein showed that no such commitment was necessary. Indeed, by taking the concept of simultaneity to be relative to a frame of reference, on the basis of the postulate that the speed of light is constant and identical in all reference frames, he showed that there was no such thing as *the* time in which an event happened. And, by postulating that laws of nature must remain invariant in all inertial frames, he showed that there was no need to posit an absolute frame of reference, typically associated with the absolute space (and the aether). In the able hands of the mathematician Hermann Minkowski (1864–1909), space and time were united in a four-dimensional spacetime framework. In 1915 Einstein advanced his General Theory of Relativity, according to which the laws of nature are the same in *all* frames of reference.

The second kind of pressure came from Max Planck's quantum of action in 1900. He showed that the explanation of a number of phenomena which were within the purview of classical mechanics required admitting a radical discontinuity: energy comes in fundamental quanta. In 1905, Einstein used Planck's idea to explain the photoelectric effect, suggesting that light radiation comes in quantized photons, while many other physicists employed it to develop an alternative to classical mechanics, known as (old) quantum theory. Its culmination came in 1913, where Neils Bohr (1865–1962) explained the structure and the stability of atoms, positing that electrons orbit the nucleus in discrete orbits. By the 1920s, Newtonian mechanics had given its place to Quantum Theory and the General Theory of Relativity.

Geometry and arithmetic

It had been already known, from the work of Nikolai Ivanovich Lobachevsky (1792–1856), János Bolyai (1802–60), and Bernhard Riemann (1826–66), that there could be consistent *geometrical* systems which represented non-Euclidean geometries. Euclid's fifth postulate, that from a point outside a line exactly one line parallel to this can be drawn, can be denied in two ways. Lobachevsky and Bolyai developed a consistent (hyperbolic) geometry which assumed that an infinite number of parallel lines could be drawn. Riemann developed a consistent (spherical) geometry which assumed that no parallel lines could be drawn. These non-Euclidean geometries were originally admitted as interesting mathematical systems. The Kantian thought that the geometry of physical space had to be Euclidean was taken as unassailable. Yet Einstein's General Theory suggested that this Kantian thought was an illusion. Far from being flat, as Euclidean geometry required, space – that is, *physical* space – is curved. Actually, it's a space with variable curvature, the latter depending on the distribution of mass in the universe. This was a far-reaching result. All three geometries (Euclidean, Lobachevkyan, and Riemannian) posited spaces of constant curvature: zero, negative, and positive respectively. They all presupposed the Helmholtz–Lie axiom of free mobility, which, in effect, assumes that space is homogeneous. Einstein's General Theory called this axiom into question: objects in spacetime move along geodesics whose curvature is variable.

Another Kantian thought that came under fire was that space and time were the a priori forms of pure intuition. In *The Foundations of Arithmetic* (1884), Gottlob Frege (1848–1925) challenged the thought that *arithmetic* was synthetic a priori knowledge. He suggested that arithmetical truths are analytic: they are provable on the basis of general logical laws plus definitions. No intuition was necessary for establishing, and getting to know, arithmetical truths: rigorous deductive proof was enough. Arithmetic, to be sure, was still taken to embody a corpus of a priori truths. But being, in effect, logical truths, they make no empirical claims whatsoever. Frege, however, agreed with Kant that geometrical truths were synthetic a priori.

It was David Hilbert (1862–1943) in *The Foundations of Geometry* (1899) who excised all intuition from geometry. He advanced an axiomatization of geometry and showed that the proof of geometrical theorems could be achieved by strictly logical-deductive means, without *any* appeal to intuition. Hilbert's result was far-reaching because, among other things, it made available the idea of an *implicit definition*. A set of axioms implicitly defines its basic concepts in the sense that it specifies their interpretation collectively: any system of entities that satisfies the axioms is characterized by these axioms. There is no need to have an "independent" or intuitive grasp of the meanings of terms such as "point," "line," or "plane": their meaning is fully specified collectively by the relevant axioms.

These developments in physics and mathematics, mixed up with the dominant Kantian tradition, created an explosive philosophical brew. The instability of the Kantian synthetic a priori principles became evident. Principles that were neatly classified in light of the three Kantian categories (analytic a priori; synthetic a priori; synthetic a posteriori) started to move about. In particular, the category of synthetic a priori truths was being drained away. The crisis in the sciences made possible the claim that the basic principles of classical mechanics and of Euclidean geometry were not a priori since they were revis*able* (they were revis*ed*). The crisis in arithmetic suggested that arithmetical truths, alongside the logical ones, were analytic. It wouldn't be an exaggeration to claim that much of philosophy of science in the first half of the twentieth century was an attempt to come to terms with the apparent collapse of the Kantian synthetic a priori.

Convention and the relativized a priori

The Kantian conception did find some support in the work of the neo-Kantian school of Marburg. In *Substance and Function* (1910) Ernst Cassirer (1874–1945) argued that, although mathematical structures were necessary for experience, in that the phenomena could be identified, organized, and structured *only* if they were embedded in such structures, these structures need not be fixed for all time and immutable. He thought that mathematical structures, though a priori (since they are required for objective experience), are revisable yet convergent: newer structures accommodate within themselves old ones. But it was Hans Reichenbach (1891–1953) in *The Theory of Relativity and A Priori Knowledge* (1921) who set the agenda for what was to come by unpacking two elements in the Kantian conception of the a priori: on the one hand, a priori truths are meant to be necessary; on the other hand, they are meant to be constitutive of the object of knowledge. Reichenbach rejected the first element of a priori knowledge, but insisted that the second was inescapable. Knowledge of the physical world, he thought, requires principles of coordination, namely, principles that connect the basic concepts of the theory with reality. These principles were taken to be constitutive of experience. Mathematics, Reichenbach thought, was indispensable precisely because it provided a framework of general rules according to which the coordination between scientific concepts and reality takes place. Once this framework is in place, a theory is presented as an axiomatic system, whose basic axioms – the "axioms of connection" – are broadly empirical in that they specify the relationships among certain physical-state variables. The axioms of coordination, Reichenbach thought, logically precede the most general axioms of connection: they are a priori, and yet revisable. Against Kant, Reichenbach argued that a priori principles, though constitutive of the object of knowledge, could be rationally revised in response to experience.

How is this possible? In *Science and Hypothesis* (1902), Henri Poincaré (1854–1912) had shown that a theoretical system T that comprised Euclidean geometry plus some strange physics (which allowed the length of all bodies to be distorted when they were in motion) was empirically indistinguishable from another theoretical system T′ which comprised non-Euclidean geometry plus normal physics (which admitted rigid motion). Poincaré's own suggestion was that the choice between such systems (and hence the adoption of a certain geometry as *the* physical geometry) was, by and large, a matter of convention. Indeed, Poincaré extended his geometrical conventionalism further by arguing that the principles of mechanics too were conventions (or definitions in disguise). His starting point was that the principles of mechanics were not a priori truths, since they could not be known independently of experience. Nor were they generalizations of experimental facts. The idealized systems to which these principles apply are not to be found in nature. Besides, no experience can conclusively confirm, or falsify, a principle of mechanics.

Poincaréan conventions are general principles which are held true, but whose truth can neither be the product of a priori reasoning nor be established by a posteriori investigation. But calling them "conventions" did not imply, for Poincaré, that their adoption (or choice) was arbitrary. He repeatedly stressed that some principles were more convenient than others. He thought that considerations of simplicity and unity could and should "guide" the relevant choice. Indeed, he envisaged a certain hierarchy of the sciences, according to which the very possibility of empirical and testable physical science requires that there are in place (as, in the end, freely chosen conventions) the axioms of Euclidean geometry and the principles of Newtonian mechanics.

Reichenbach was influenced by this Poincaréan view, but gave it a double twist. On the one hand, he took it to imply that seemingly unrevisable principles could be revised. On the other hand, he thought that Poincaré's own particular suggestion regarding Euclidean geometry was wrong. For whereas going for T (thereby admitting the existence of universal forces that affect indiscriminately and uniformly all moving bodies) does not allow for a unique coordination between theory and reality, the alternative framework T' (which revises the geometry of physical space) does allow for unique coordination. Einstein's General Theory of Relativity, Reichenbach thought, falsified the claim that the geometry of physical space was Euclidean (thereby leading to a deep revision of a seemingly unassailable a priori principle). His prime thought was that *within* Einstein's General Theory, geometry and physics become one. Hence, there is no space to play with the one at the expense of the other, as Poincaré thought.

Drawing on the thought of Poincaré and Pierre Duhem (1861–1916), Moritz Schlick (1918) argued that no theory could be tested in isolation from others. Accordingly, when geometry and physics are tested together, if there is a conflict with experience, there is space for choice about which component is to be revised, the choice being guided, by and large, by considerations of simplicity. On Schlick's early view, there is no principled difference between constitutive principles (e.g. the principles of geometry) and other principles (e.g. the laws of physics). Reichenbach's thought, however, was importantly different. Although he too accepted that both kinds of principle were revisable, he argued that there was a *logical* difference between them. The constitutive principles marked off the a priori, whereas the axioms of connection marked off the empirical. Reichenbach was naturally led to the conclusion that the only workable notion of a priori should be relativized: each and every theoretical framework needs some constitutive (and hence, a priori) principles, but these principles are revisable, and revised when the framework fails to come to terms with experience. Unfortunately, Reichenbach abandoned this distinction. Following Schlick in the way his thought developed, Reichenbach (1928) was led to adopt a more full-blown conventionalism, according to which even in light of Einstein's theory, the choice of the geometry of physical space was conventional.

Logical positivism

Armed with the notion of convention, Schlick (1882–1936) and his Vienna Circle tried to show that there could be no synthetic a priori at all. They extended conventionalism to logic and mathematics, arguing that the only distinction there is is between empirical (synthetic a posteriori) principles and conventional (analytic a priori) ones. The logical positivists thought they were completing Frege's agenda. Like him, they took logic and arithmetic to embody analytic truths. Unlike him, and informed by Hilbert's arithmetization of geometry, they took (pure) geometry too to embody analytic truths. So they fully rejected synthetic a priori knowledge. All a priori knowledge was analytic and, thanks to their conventionalist account of analyticity, grasping a priori (= analytic) truths required no special faculty of intuition.

The logical positivists took analytic truths to be constitutive of a language. They are true by virtue of definitions or stipulations that determine the meanings of the terms involved in them. Hence, they issue in linguistic prescriptions about how to speak about things. Attendant on this doctrine was the so-called linguistic doctrine of necessity: all and only analytic truths are necessary. This doctrine, which, following Hume, excised all necessity from nature, had already played a key role in Wittgenstein's *Tractatus Logico-Philosophicus*.

If analytic statements acquire their meaning by linguistic stipulation, how do empirical (synthetic) statements acquire theirs? Being empiricists, the logical positivists took to heart Russell's *Principle of Acquaintance*: that all meaning (of descriptive concepts) should originate in experience. They elevated this principle into a criterion of meaningfulness, known as the verifiability criterion. Non-analytic statements are meaningful (cognitively significant) if and only if their truth can be verified in experience. In slogan form: meaning is the method of verification. The logical positivists utilized this criterion to show that statements of traditional metaphysics were meaningless, since their truth (or falsity) made no difference in experience. This consequentialist criterion was akin to that employed by the American pragmatists. But unlike the pragmatists, the logical positivists did not adopt a pragmatist theory of truth. (For a discussion of pragmatism, see "American philosophy in the twentieth century," Chapter 5.)

In the course of the 1930s, the concept of verifiability moved from a strict sense of provability on the basis of experience to the much more liberal sense of confirmability. The chief problem was that the strong criterion of cognitive significance failed to deliver the goods. Apart from metaphysical statements, many ordinary scientific assertions, those that express universal laws of nature, would be meaningless, precisely because they are not, strictly speaking, verifiable. In response to this, diehard advocates of verificationism, following Schlick, took the view that law-statements were inference-tickets: their only role was to serve as major premises in valid deductive arguments, whose minor premise and conclusion were singular observational statements. The immediate challenge to this view was that it was hard to see how a statement of the form "All *F*s are *G*s" could serve as a premise in a valid deductive argument without having a truth-value.

According to the logical positivists, if put together, the Hilbert approach to geometry and the Duhem–Poincaré hypothetico-deductive account of scientific theories, give a powerful and systematic way to represent scientific theories. The basic principles of the theory are taken to be the axioms. But the terms and predicates of the theory are stripped of their interpretation/meaning. Hence, the axiomatic system itself is entirely formal. The advantage of the axiomatic approach is that it lays bare the logical structure of the theory. What is more, the axiomatic approach unambiguously identifies the content of the theory: it is the set of logical consequences of the axioms. However, treated as a formal system, the theory lacks any empirical content. In order for the theory to get some such content, its terms and predicates should be suitably interpreted. It was a central thought of the logical positivists that a scientific theory need not be completely interpreted to be meaningful and applicable. They claimed that it is enough that only *some*, the so-called "observational," terms and predicates be interpreted. The rest of the terms and predicates of the theory, in particular those which, taken at face value, purport to refer to unobservable entities, were deemed "theoretical," and were taken to be only partially interpreted by means of correspondence rules, that is *mixed* sentences that linked theoretical terms with observational ones. However, it was soon realized that the correspondence rules muddle the distinction between the analytic (meaning-related) and synthetic (fact-stating) part of a scientific theory, which was central in the thought of logical positivists. For, on the one hand, they specify (even partly) the meaning of theoretical terms and, on the other, they contribute to the factual content of the theory.

Hence, it became pressing for the logical positivists to restore a way in which a theory is divided into two distinct parts, one that fixes the meaning of its theoretical terms (and which cannot be falsified if the theory is in conflict with experience) and another part of the theory which specifies its empirical content (and which can be rejected in case of conflict with experience).

Objectivity and structure

It's been a popular thought, stressed by Quine (1969), that the logical positivists, and Rudolf Carnap (1891–1970) in particular, were epistemological foundationalists. The *locus classicus* of this view is supposed to be found in Carnap's (1928) *The Logical Structure of the World*. (For further discussion of Carnap see "The birth of analytic philosophy," Chapter 1 and "The development of analytic philosophy: Wittgenstein and after," Chapter 2.) The received view, in outline, comes to this. Being an empiricist and, in particular a foundationalist, Carnap aimed to materialize Russell's "supreme maxim of philosophizing," that is, the claim that "Whenever possible logical constructions are to be substituted for inferred entities." By showing how all concepts that can be meaningfully spoken of can be constructed out of logicomathematical concepts and concepts which refer to immediate experiences, Carnap's *Structure* would (a) secure a certain foundation for knowledge; (b) secure empiricism about meaning and concept formation; and (c) show how the content of talk about the world could be fully captured by an unproblematic-for-empiricists talk about the "given." Although there is something in the received view, it seems that Carnap, far from being an unqualified foundationalist empiricist, had a broadly neo-Kantian axe to grind. Carnap's main aim was to show how the epistemological enterprise should be conducted for an empiricist if the objectivity of the world of science is to be secured. That is, it was *objectivity* and not foundations that Carnap was after.

Carnap's two kinds of objectivity

There are two ways to think of objectivity. The first is akin to inter-subjectivity, understood as the "common factor" point of view: the point of view common to all subjects (see Carnap 1928: §66). Looked at in that way, Carnap's *Structure* aimed to show how the physical world could emerge from within his constructional system as the "common factor" of the individual subjective points of view (see §§148–9). Given the gap between the world of experience and the world of science, Carnap's attempt was to specify the assumptions that should be in place (or the structure that needs to be added to the world of experience) in order to make possible the connection between the world of experience and the world of science (see §§125–9). The Kantian connection should be obvious here. Carnap stressed that, because his construction was based on the new Frege–Russell logic, he had no place for the Kantian synthetic a priori. Carnap's first way to explicate objectivity came to grief: there is no way to draw the distinction between subjective and objective *within* Carnap's constructional system, since the subjective is simply equated with whatever is *outside* the system of unified science.

But objectivity may well be conceived in more radical terms: as being totally subject-independent. This is what Carnap called "desubjectivized" science (see §16). Looked at in this light, Carnap's *Structure* amounts to an endorsement of structuralism, where structure is understood as logical structure in the sense of Russell and Whitehead's *Principia Mathematica*. Carnap tied content (the material) to subjective experience and made formal structure the locus of objectivity. His task then was to characterize all concepts that may legitimately figure in his system of unified science by means of "purely structural definite descriptions" (see §§11–15).

Russell's structuralism

Structuralist approaches to objectivity and knowledge had been advanced before Carnap. But it was Bertrand Russell (1872–1970) who made structuralism popular by claiming, in his *The Analysis of Matter* (1927), that the abstract character of modern physics, and of the knowledge of the world that this offers, could be reconciled with the fact that all evidence for its truth came from experience. To this end, he advanced a *structuralist* account of our knowledge of the world. According to this, only the structure, i.e. the totality of formal, logico-mathematical properties, of the external world can be known, while all of its intrinsic (qualitative) properties are inherently unknown. This logico-mathematical structure, he argued, can be legitimately *inferred* from the structure of the perceived phenomena. Russell explicitly noted that this view was an attempt to show how *some* knowledge of the Kantian *noumena* (namely, their structure) can be had. Relying on the causal theory of perception (which gave him the assumption that there are external physical objects which cause perceptions), and on other substantive principles (which connect differences in the percepts with differences in their causes, and conversely), he argued that there is an isomorphism between the structure of the percepts and the structure of their causes (stimuli). But Russell's structuralism was met with a fatal objection, due to the Cambridge mathematician M. H. A. Newman (1928); this was that the structuralist claim is *trivial* in the sense that it merely recapitulates Russell's assumption that there is a set of physical objects which cause perceptions. Given that this set of objects has the right cardinality, Newman showed that Russell's supposed further substantive conclusion, namely that of *this* set it is also known that it has certain structure W, is wholly insubstantial. Russell conceded defeat to Newman, but it might be ironic that the very same objection applies to Carnap's structuralism. Carnap insisted on building his account of structural objectivity out of a single relation of "recollection of similarity" among elementary experiences, which (relation) he aimed to characterize in purely structural terms. But there is no guarantee that such a purely structural description can characterize the relevant relation uniquely. Besides, that *there is* a relation with the required structure is a trivial claim, as Newman pointed out.

Structural convergence

Writing at the beginning of the twentieth century, Poincaré and Duhem too favored a structuralist account of scientific knowledge. Although Poincaré took the basic axioms of geometry and mechanics to be conventions, he thought that scientific hypotheses proper, even high-level ones such as Maxwell's laws, were empirical. Faced with the problem of discontinuity in theory-change (the fact that some basic scientific hypotheses and law-statements have been abandoned in the transition from one theory to another), he argued that there is, nonetheless, some substantial continuity at the level of the mathematical equations that represent empirical as well as theoretical relations. From this, he concluded that these retained mathematical equations – together with the retained empirical content – fully capture the objective content of scientific theories. By and large, he thought, the theoretical content of scientific theories is structural: if successful, a theory represents correctly the *structure* of the world.

As in many other cases, Poincaré's structuralism had a Kantian origin. He took it that science could never offer knowledge of things as they were in themselves. But he did add to this that their relations could nonetheless be revealed by structurally-convergent scientific theories. Duhem advanced this thought further by arguing that science aims at a natural classification of the phenomena, where a classification (that is, the organization of the phenomena within a mathematical system) is *natural* if the relations it establishes among the experimental phenomena "correspond to real relations among things" (1906: 26–7). He went on to draw a principled distinction between, as he put it, the explanatory and the representative part of a scientific theory. The former advances hypotheses about the underlying causes of the phenomena, whereas the latter comprises the empirical laws as well as the mathematical equations that are used to systematize and organize these laws. His novel thought was that in theory-change, the explanatory part of the theory gets abandoned while its representative (structural) part gets retained in the successor theory. Perhaps for the first time in the history of the philosophy of science, someone was trying to substantiate his claim by looking in detail into the history of science, and especially the history of optical theories and of mechanics. One may wonder, however, whether the explanatory/representative distinction on which Duhem's argument rests is sound. One might say that explanatory hypotheses are representative in that they too are cast in mathematical form and, normally, entail predictions which can be tested. And conversely, mathematical equations that represent laws of nature are explanatory in that they can be used as premises for the derivation of other low-level laws.

Structural realism

Poincaré and Duhem found in structuralism an account of the objectivity (and the limits) of scientific knowledge. But they worked with a notion of *mathematical* structure as this is exemplified in the mathematical equations of theories. In this sense, their structuralism was different from Russell's and Carnap's, who worked with a sharper notion of *logical* structure (see Carnap's relevant remarks in 1928: §16). But their account of objectivity as structure-invariance reappeared in the 1960s under the guise of structural realism, in the writings of Grover Maxwell (1918–81) and, in the 1980s, of John Worrall and Elie Zahar. The twist they gave to structuralism was based on the idea of Ramsey-sentences.

This idea goes back to *Theories* (1929), by Frank Ramsey (1903–30) (see also "Philosophical logic," Chapter 8). Ramsey noted that the excess content that a theory has over and above its observational consequences is best seen when the theory is formulated as expressing an *existential judgment*: there are entities which satisfy the theory. This is captured by the Ramsey-sentence of the theory, which replaces the theoretical terms with variables and binds them with existential quantifiers. Ramsey thought that reference to theoretical entities does not require names; the existentially bound variables are enough. The Ramsey-sentence of a theory, which has exactly the same observational consequences as the original theory and the very same deductive structure, is truth-evaluable and committed, if true, to the existence of entities over and above observable ones.

Structural realists offered a structuralist reading of Ramsey-sentences: the empirical content of a theory is captured by its Ramsey-sentence and the excess content that the Ramsey-sentence has over its empirical consequences is purely *structural*. Given that the Ramsey-sentence captures the logico-mathematical form of the original theory, the structuralist thought is that, if true, the Ramsey-sentence also captures the structure of reality: the logico-mathematical form of an empirically adequate Ramsey-sentence mirrors the structure of reality.

It is a historical irony that the Newman-problem which plagued the Russell–Carnap structuralism is equally devastating against the Maxwell–Worrall–Zahar structuralism. For unless some non-structural restrictions are imposed on the kinds of things the existence of which the Ramsey-sentence asserts, that is, unless structuralism gives up on the claim that *only* structure can be known, it turns out that an empirically adequate Ramsey-sentence is bound to be true: truth collapses to empirical adequacy.

The analytic/synthetic distinction

In the 1930s, Carnap had to re-shape his agenda. Epistemology gave way to the "logic of science," where the latter was taken to be a purely formal study of the language of science.

Logic of science

The thought, developed in Carnap's *The Logical Syntax of Language* (1934), was that the development of a general theory of the logical syntax of the logico-mathematical language of science would provide a neutral framework in which: (a) scientific theories are cast and studied; (b) scientific concepts (e.g. explanation, confirmation, laws, etc.) are explicated; and (c) traditional metaphysical disputes are overcome. The whole project required a sharp analytic/synthetic distinction: philosophical statements would be analytic (about the language of science) whereas scientific ones would be synthetic (about the world). Carnap conceived of (artificially constructed) languages as systems of two kinds of rule: (a) formation rules, which specify how the sentences of the language are constructed and (b) transformation rules, which express inference rules. He distinguished between two kinds of transformation rule, namely (b₁) L-rules (the logical rules of syntax) and (b₂) P-rules (physical rules, such as the empirical laws of science). A logical language, then, consists of only L-rules, whereas a physical language (the language of a scientific theory) comprises P-rules too. The object of the general theory of logical syntax was such logical and physical languages. Carnap then equated analyticity with (suitably understood) provability *within* a language system: those sentences are analytic that are provable by means of the L-rules of the language. Hence, analyticity requires a sharp distinction between L-rules and P-rules and an equally sharp distinction between logical and descriptive symbols. But Carnap's project came to grief. This was the result of many factors, but prominent among them were Tarski's work on truth (which suggested that truth was an irreducibly semantic notion) and Kurt Gödel's incompleteness theorem. Although Carnap was fully aware of Gödel's limitative results, his own attempt to provide a neutral and minimal meta-theoretical framework (the framework of General Syntax) in which the concept of analyticity was defined fell prey to Gödel's proof that there are mathematical (i.e. analytic) truths which are not provable within such a system.

The web of belief

Carnap's enduring thought was that the analytic/synthetic distinction was necessary for any attempt to have a scientific understanding of the world, since the latter requires the presence of a linguistic and conceptual framework within which empirical facts are grafted. This view might plausibly be thought of as the last remnant of Kantianism in Carnap's philosophy. This last remnant (that is, some notion of analytic a priori truths) came under heavy attack by W. V.

O. Quine (1908–2000). In "Truth by convention" (1936), Quine issued a deep challenge to the view that logic was a matter of convention. Logical truths, he argued, cannot be true by convention simply because if logic were to be derived from conventions, logic would be needed to *infer* logic from conventions. In "Two dogmas of empiricism" (1951), he went on to argue that the notion of analyticity is deeply problematic, since it requires a notion of cognitive synonymy and there is no independent criterion of cognitive synonymy. Quine's master argument against the analytic/synthetic distinction rested on the view that "analytic" was taken to mean "unrevisable." If analytic statements have no empirical content, experience cannot possibly have any bearing on their truth-value. So analytic statements can suffer no truth-value revision. But, Quine argued, nothing (not even logical truths) is unrevisable. Hence, there cannot be any analytic truths. Here Quine took a leaf from Duhem's (and indeed Carnap's) book. Confirmation and refutation are holistic: they accrue to systems (theories) as a whole and not to their constituent statements, taken individually. If a theory is confirmed, then everything it asserts is confirmed; and conversely, if a theory is refuted, then any part of it can be revised (abandoned) in order for harmony with experience to be restored. Accordingly, anything (i.e. any statement, be it logical or mathematical or empirical) can be confirmed (hence, everything has empirical content). And anything (i.e. any statement, be it logical or mathematical or empirical) can be refuted (hence, everything can be such that experience can refute it). *Ergo*, there are no analytic (= unrevisable) statements.

The image of science that emerges has no place for truths of a special status: all truths are on a par. This leads to a blurring of the distinction between the factual and the conventional. What matters, for Quine, is that a theory acquires its empirical content as a whole, by issuing in observational statements and by being confronted with experience. The whole idea, however, rests on the claim that observational statements are privileged. They are not, to be sure, privileged in the way foundationalists thought they were: they are not the certain and incorrigible foundations of all knowledge. But they are privileged in the sense that all evidence for or against a theory comes from them and also in the sense that they can command intersubjective agreement. Quine did not deny that some principles (those of logic, or mathematics, or some basic physical principles) do *seem* to have some special status. He argued, however, that this is not enough to confer on them the status of a priori truths. Rather, they are very central to our web of belief. When our theory of the world clashes with experience, they are the last to be abandoned. But they *can* be abandoned if their rejection results in a simpler web of belief. In contemplating what kind of changes we should make, Quine argued, we should be guided by principles such as simplicity, or the principle of minimal mutilation. Yet the status of these methodological principles remained unclear. Why for instance couldn't *they* be seen as a priori principles that govern belief-revision? And if they are not, what is the argument which shows that they are also empirical principles? Surely, one cannot read them off experience in any straightforward way.

Carnap meets Quine

The cogency of Quine's attack on the a priori rests on the cogency of the following equation: a priori = unrevisable. We have already seen a whole strand in post-Kantian thinking that denied this equation, while holding on to the view that some principles are constitutive of experience. It might not be surprising then that Carnap was not particularly moved by Quine's criticism. For he *too* denied the foregoing equation (see Carnap 1934: 318). He took the analytic/synthetic distinction to be *internal* to a language and claimed that analyticity (a priority) is not invariant under language-change. In radical theory-change, the analytic/synthetic distinction has to be re-drawn within the successor theory. "Being held true, come what may" holds for both the analytic and the synthetic statements, when minor changes are required. Similarly, both analytic statements and basic synthetic postulates may be revised, when radical changes are in order.

Quine did have a point. For Carnap, analytic statements are such that (a) it is rational to accept them within a linguistic framework; (b) it is rational to reject them, when the framework changes; and (c) there is some extra characteristic which all and only analytic statements share, in distinction to synthetic ones. Even if Quine's criticisms are impotent *vis-à-vis* (a) and (b), they are quite powerful against (c). The point was simply that the dual role of correspondence rules (and the concomitant Hilbert-style implicit definition of theoretical terms) made the drawing of this distinction impossible, even *within* a theory. It took a great deal of Carnap's time and energy to find a cogent explication of (c). In the end, he had to re-invent the Ramsey-sentences to find a plausible way to draw the line between the analytic and the synthetic (see Psillos 2000).

Confirmation and induction

The logical empiricists thought that, by devising a formal and algorithmic account of confirmation, they could kill two birds with one stone. They could bypass the problem of induction and solve the problem of the objectivity of scientific method. The former, it was thought, could be bypassed by transforming it into a logico-syntactic theory of confirmation, according to which, as it rolls in, the evidence increases the probability of a hypothesis. The latter, it was thought, could be solved by showing how the scientific method (and induction, in particular) was based on purely logical rules.

Confirmation: syntax and semantics

Hempel's (1945) logico-syntactic theory of confirmation was based on the idea that given any hypothesis of the form "All As are Bs," and given any positive instance of this hypothesis (that is an object *a* which is both A and B), this positive instance confirms the hypothesis that "All As are Bs." This view came under attack when Hempel himself noted that it leads to paradox, known as the Ravens paradox.

However, it was Nelson Goodman (1906–98) who dealt a fatal blow to Hempel's logico-syntactic approach by introducing a new predicate, "grue," which is defined as follows: observed before 2010 and found green, or not observed before 2010 and be blue. (For further discussion of Goodman, see "American philosophy in the twentieth century," Chapter 5.) Clearly, all *observed* emeralds are green. But they are also "grue." Why then should we claim that the observation of a green emerald confirms the hypothesis that *All emeralds are green* instead of *All emeralds are grue*? These two generalizations are consistent with all current evidence, but they disagree on their predictions about emeralds that are observed after 2010. Hempel's logico-syntactic theory is blind to this difference: the two competing hypotheses have exactly the same syntactic form. Goodman (1954) argued that only the first statement ("All emeralds are green") is capable of expressing a law of nature because only this is confirmed by the observation of green emeralds. He disqualified the generalization "All emeralds are grue" on the grounds that the predicate "is grue," unlike the predicate "is green," does not pick out a natural kind. But the very idea of having suitable (natural-kind) predicates featuring in confirmable generalizations speaks against a purely syntactic account of confirmation.

Inductive logic

Carnap, following John Maynard Keynes (1883–1946), took pains to advance an inductive *logic* (which, in certain respects, would mimic the content-insensitive structure of deductive logic). In his *Logical Foundations of Probability* (1950) he devised a quantitative confirmation function that expressed the *degree of partial entailment* of a hypothesis by the observational evidence. The evidence (cast in observational statements) is supposed to confirm a hypothesis to the extent in which it partially entails this hypothesis, where partial entailment was a formal relation between the range of the evidence and the range of the hypothesis.

In his system of inductive logic, Carnap claimed, true sentences expressing relations of partial entailment are analytic. And if inductive logic is analytic, it is also a priori. He went as far as to claim that the contentious principle of uniformity of nature, a principle that Hume criticized not as false but as of illegitimate use in any attempt to justify induction, was also analytic within his system of inductive logic: it is statement of logical probability asserting that "on the basis of the available evidence it is very *probable* that the degree of uniformity of the world is high" (Carnap 1950: 180–1). Carnap was certainly right in noting that, expressed as above, the principle of uniformity of nature could neither be proved nor refuted by experience. But for this principle to be acceptable, we need to assume another principle, namely what Keynes called "the Principle of Limited Variety" (1921: 287). Suppose that although C has been invariably associated with E in the past, there is an unlimited variety of properties $E_1, \ldots, E_n$ such that it is possible that future occurrences of C will be accompanied by any of the E_i's, instead of E. Then, and if we let n (the variety index) tend to infinity, we cannot even start to say how likely it is that E will occur, given C and the past association of Cs with Es. The Principle of Limited Variety excludes the possibility just envisaged. It is necessary for making inductive inferences of any sort. This, no doubt, is a substantive, synthetic, principle *about* the world. Carnap cannot simply relegate it to yet another analytically true principle. Indeed, as was pointed out by Keynes long before Carnap, the very possibility of inductive inference requires that some hypotheses are given non-zero prior probability, for otherwise fresh evidence cannot raise their probability.

If "inductive logic" had to rely on substantive synthetic principles, it was no longer *logic*. Carnap's attempt to use the quasi-logical Principle of Indifference, which dictated that all equally possible outcomes should be given equal prior probabilities of happening, led to inconsistent results. In the end, when Carnap devised the continuum of inductive methods, he drew the conclusion that there can be a variety of actual inductive methods whose results and effectiveness vary in accordance to how one picks out the value of a certain parameter, where this parameter depends on formal features of the language used. But obviously, there is no a priori reason to select a particular value of the relevant parameter; hence there is no explication of inductive inference in a unique way. Carnap suggested that it is left to the scientists to choose among different inductive methods, in view of their specific purposes. Where an a priori justification of induction was sought, the end product was based on a pragmatic decision.

Naturalism: the break with neo-Kantianism

The emergence of naturalism was a real turning point in the philosophy of science. It amounted to an ultimate break with neo-Kantianism in all of its forms (see also "Naturalism," Chapter 6).

Against a priorism

The challenge to the very possibility of a priori knowledge was a central input in the *naturalist turn* in the philosophy of science in the 1960s. The old a prioristic way of doing philosophy of science was nicely summarized by Reichenbach: "We see such a way in the application of the *method of logical analysis* to epistemology. The results discovered by the positive sciences in continuous contact with experience presuppose principles the detection of which by means of logical analysis is the task of philosophy" (1921: 74).

Quine's "Epistemology naturalized" (1969) claimed that, once the search for secure foundations of knowledge is shown futile, philosophy loses its presumed status as the privileged framework (equipped with a privileged source of knowledge: a priori reflection and logical analysis) aiming to validate science. Philosophy becomes continuous with the sciences in that there is no privileged philosophical method, distinct from the scientific method, and that the findings of empirical sciences are central to understanding philosophical issues and disputes. Quine went as far as to suggest a replacement thesis: epistemology, as traditionally understood, should give way to psychology. The aim of this psychologized epistemology should be the understanding of the link between observations (the meager input of scientific method) and theory (its torrential output), an issue that, strictly speaking, belongs to psychology.

Why, then, call it epistemology? Because, Quine says, we are still concerned with a central question of traditional epistemology: how do theories relate to *evidence*? Quine made capital on the vivid metaphor of Neurath's boat: "Neurath has linked science to a boat which, if we are to rebuild it, we must rebuild plank by plank while staying afloat in it" (1960: 3). Accordingly, philosophy has no special status; nor are there parts of our conceptual scheme (the findings of science in particular) that cannot be relied upon when revision elsewhere in it are necessary.

Against anti-psychologism

Naturalism's other input was the rejection of anti-psychologism that had dominated philosophy of science in the first half of the twentieth century. Broadly speaking, anti-psychologism is the view that the content of the key concepts of epistemology and philosophy of science (knowledge, evidence, justification, method, etc.) should be analyzed independently of the psychological processes that implement them to cognitive subjects. More specifically, anti-psychologism holds that logical questions should be sharply distinguished from psychological questions. This distinction led to a sharp separation between the *context of discovery* and the *context of justification* (which was introduced by Reichenbach). In *The Logic of Scientific Discovery* (1959), Karl Popper (1902–94) argued that, being psychological, the process of coming up with theories is not subject to rigorous logical analysis, nor is it interesting philosophically (on Popper, see also "The development of analytic philosophy: Wittgenstein and after," Chapter 2). He lumped it under the rubric of devising conjectures and argued that the important philosophical issue was how hypotheses are tested after they have been suggested. He took it that the process of testing is a formal process of trying to find an *inconsistency* between the predictions of a theory and the relevant observations.

Popper's anti-psychologism was based on his stance on Hume's problem of induction. But whereas Hume, who was a proto-naturalist, thought that induction was an inevitable natural-psychological process of forming beliefs, Popper went as far as to argue that induction was a myth: real science (as well as ordinary thinking) doesn't (and shouldn't) employ induction. In its place he tried to put the idea that scientific method needs no more than deduction: even if scientific theories cannot be proved (or confirmed) on the basis of experience, they can still be falsified by the evidence. This thought, however, is simplistic. For one thing, as Duhem and Quine have pointed out, no theory is, strictly speaking, refutable. Typically, in mature sciences, the theory being tested cannot generate empirical predictions without the use of several auxiliary assumptions. Hence, if the prediction is not fulfilled, the only thing we can *logically* infer is that either the auxiliaries are, or the theory is, false. That is, logic alone cannot distribute blame to the premises of an argument with a false conclusion. For another, the key Popperian thought, namely that deductive logic is the only logic that we have or need and that the only valid arguments are deductively valid arguments, is deeply problematic. This last view, known as deductivism, is flawed both as a descriptive and as a normative thesis.

The historical turn

Although the logical positivists favored inductivism and Popper deductivism, an assumption shared by both was that scientific method should be justified a priori. Popper, to be sure, was more inclined to the view that scientific methods are conventions, but he did subscribe to the positivist idea that a theory of scientific method is a *rational reconstruction* of the scientific game: a reconstruction that presents science as a rule-governed activity. These rules are meant to constitute the very essence of the scientific game very much like the rules of chess are constitutive of a game of chess. This idea gives rise to an important question: if there are many competing rational reconstructions of the scientific game, which one is to be preferred? As was fully acknowledged by the history-oriented methodologies of science that succeeded Popper and the positivists, this question could be answered only if the very game of rational reconstruction gave way to accounts informed by the actual history and practice of science.

The historical turn of the 1960s was a central component of the naturalist turn. Thomas S. Kuhn's (1922–96) theory of science should be seen as the outcome of two inputs: (a) a reflection on the actual scientific practice as well as the actual historical development and succession of scientific theories, and (b) a reaction to what was perceived to be the dominant logical empiricist and Popperian images of scientific growth: a progressive and cumulative process governed by specific rules on how evidence relates to theory. A coarse-grained explication of Kuhn's *The Structure of Scientific Revolutions* (1962) goes as follows. The emergence of a scientific discipline is characterized by the adoption by a community of a paradigm, that is, as of a shared body of theories, models, exemplars, values, and methods. A long period of "normal science" emerges, in which scientists attempt to apply, develop, and explore the consequences of the paradigm. This activity is akin to puzzle-solving, in that scientists follow the rules (or, the concrete exemplars) laid out by the paradigm in order (a) to determine which problems are solvable and (b) to solve them. This rule-bound (or, better, exemplar-bound) activity that characterizes normal science goes on until an anomaly appears. An anomaly is a problem that falls under the scope of the paradigm, is supposed to be solvable, but persistently resists solution. The emergence of anomalies signifies a serious decline in the puzzle-solving efficacy of the paradigm. The community enters a stage of crisis that is ultimately resolved by a revolutionary transition (paradigm shift) from the old paradigm to a new one. The new paradigm employs a different conceptual framework, and sets new problems as well as rules (exemplars) for their solutions. A new period of normal science emerges. Crucially, for Kuhn the change of paradigm is not rule-governed. It's nothing to do with degrees of confirmation or conclusive refutations. Nor does it amount to a slow transition from one paradigm to the other. Rather, it's an abrupt change in which the new paradigm completely replaces the old one. The new paradigm gets accepted not because of superior arguments or massive evidence in its favor, but rather because of its proponents' powers of rhetoric and persuasion.

The Kuhnian approach had a mixed reception. Many philosophers of science thought that it opened up the way to relativist and irrationalist views of science.

Imre Lakatos's (1922–74) lasting contribution to this debate was his attempt to combine Popper's and Kuhn's images of science in one model of theory-change that preserves progress and rationality while avoiding Popper's naive falsificationism *and* doing justice to the actual history of radical theory-change in science. To this end, Lakatos (1970) developed the "Methodology of Scientific Research Programmes." A research program is a sequence of theories and consists of a hard core, the negative heuristic, and the positive heuristic. The *hard core* comprises all those theoretical hypotheses that any theory which belongs to the research program must share. The advocates of the research program hold these hypotheses immune to revision. This methodological decision to protect the hard core constitutes the negative heuristic. The process of articulating directives about how the research program will be developed, either in the face of anomalies or in an attempt to cover new phenomena, constitutes the positive heuristic. It creates a *protective belt* around the hard core, which absorbs all potential blows from anomalies. A research program is progressive as long as it issues in novel predictions, some of which are corroborated. It is degenerating when it offers only *post hoc* accommodations of facts, either discovered by chance or predicted by a rival research program. Progress in science occurs when a progressive research program supersedes a degenerating one. But although this Lakatosian program is highly plausible and suggestive, it suffers from a severe drawback: as an account of scientific methodology, it is retroactive. It provides no way to tell which of two *currently* competing research programs is and will continue to be progressive. For even if one of them seems stagnated, it may stage an impressive comeback in the future.

Methodological naturalism

The real bite of the naturalist turn is that it made available a totally different view of how scientific methods are justified. The core of methodological naturalism is the view that methodology is an empirical discipline and that, as such, it is part and parcel of natural science. This approach suggests the following. (1) Normative claims are *instrumental*: methodological rules link up aims with methods which will bring them about, and recommend what action is more likely to achieve one's favored aim. (2) The soundness of methodological rules depends on whether they lead to successful action, and their justification is a function of their effectiveness in bringing about their aims. Where traditional approaches to method were seen as issuing in *categorical imperatives*, the naturalist suggestion was that methodological claims should be seen as issuing in *hypothetical imperatives*. These imperatives were seen as resting on (supervening upon) factual claims which capture correlations, causal links or statistical laws between "doing X" and "achieving Y." Hence, these (hypothetical) imperatives depend on contingent features of the world. This view implied a big break with the traditional a prioristic conception of method. After all, we want our methods to be effective in this world, i.e. to guide scientists to correct decisions and correct strategies for extracting information from nature. In this sense, the methods scientists adopt must be amenable to substantive information about the actual world.

Methodological naturalism carried a number of problems in its train. The first is the problem of circularity: were methods to be justified empirically, wouldn't some methods (the very same ones?) be presupposed in coming to legitimately accept the empirical findings that are relevant to their vindication? There are many things one could say in reply to this charge. But the short answer is that we are all passengers on HMS Neurath. There is no dry-dock in which we can place our conceptual scheme as a whole and examine it bit by bit. Rather, we are engaged in a process of mutual adjustment of its pieces while keeping it afloat: we fix our methods in light of empirical facts and ascertain facts while keeping our methods fixed. If the aim of philosophy of science is no longer to validate science and its method, the ensuing threat of circularity is moot.

The second problem with methodological naturalism is that it seems to lead to epistemic relativism. This concern forces naturalism to adopt an axiology, that is, a general theory of the constraints that govern rational choice of aims and goals. More specifically, naturalism has to accept truth as the *basic cognitive virtue*. This move blunts the threat of relativism. In fact, naturalism should take a leaf from the book of reliabilism in epistemology. Its central point is that justification is issued by reliable processes and methods, where a process or method is reliable if it tends to generate true beliefs. Accordingly, methodological and reasoning strategies should be evaluated by their success in producing and maintaining true beliefs, or tending to do so, where judging this success, or establishing the tendency, is open to empirical findings and investigation. Methodological naturalism should appeal to reliabilism in order to meet the third challenge it faces, namely that it leaves no room for normative judgment. Reliabilism supplements methodological naturalism with a normative meta-perspective of truth-linked judgments.

Semantic holism and the theory/observation distinction

A new approach to meaning – semantic holism – started to become popular in the 1960s. Instead of trying to specify the meaning of each and every term in isolation from the others, semantic holism claimed that terms (and, in particular, so-called "theoretical terms") get their meaning from the theories and network of nomological statements in which they are embedded. Although the logical empiricists subscribed to semantic atomism, they advocated confirmational holism, that is, the view that theories are confirmed as wholes. Already in Syntax, Carnap stressed: "Thus *the test applies, at bottom, not to a single hypothesis but to the whole system of physics as a system of hypotheses*" (Duhem, Poincaré) (1934: 318). But confirmational holism, conjoined with the denial of the analytic/synthetic distinction and the thought that confirmable theories are meaningful, leads to semantic holism. Later empiricists, notably Carl Hempel (1907–97), accepted semantic holism. But Carnap (1956) resisted this conclusion to very end.

Theory-ladenness and incommensurability

An increasingly popular view in the 1960s was that there was no way to draw a sharp line between theoretical statements and observational ones. In its *strong* version, it claimed that, strictly speaking, there can be *no* observational terms at all. This claim, inspired by the view that all observation is theory-laden, led to the thought that there cannot *possibly* be a theory-neutral observation language. This view was supported by Norwood Russell Hanson (1924–67), Kuhn, and Paul Feyerabend (1924–94). But it was advanced at the beginning of the century by Duhem (1906). In the 1960s, when this thesis resurfaced, it drew on a mass of empirical evidence coming from psychology to the effect that perceptual experience is theoretically interpreted. Hanson, Kuhn, and Feyerabend pushed the theory-ladenness-of-observation thesis to its extremes, by arguing that each theory (or paradigm) determines the meaning of *all* terms that occur in it and that there is *no* neutral language which can be used to assess different theories (or paradigms). If the meanings of terms are determined by the theory as a whole, it could be claimed that every time the theory changes, the meanings of *all* terms change, too. We have then a thesis of radical meaning variance. If, on top of that, it is accepted that meaning determines reference (as the traditional descriptive theories of meaning have it), an even more radical thesis follows, namely, reference variance.

Kuhn argued that a paradigm defines a world. Accordingly, there is a sense in which when a new paradigm is adopted, the world changes: Priestley, with his phlogiston-based paradigm lived in a different world from Lavoisier, with his oxygen-based theory. Remarks such as this have led to a lot of interpretative claims. But, I think, the best way to understand Kuhn's general philosophical perspective is to say that Kuhn's underlying philosophy is relativized neo-Kantianism. It's neo-Kantianism because it implies a distinction between the world-in-itself, which is epistemically inaccessible to cognizers, and the phenomenal world, which is constituted by the cognizers' concepts and categories. But Kuhn's neo-Kantianism is *relativized* because he thought there was a plurality of phenomenal worlds, each being dependent on, or constituted by, some community's paradigm. The paradigm imposes, so to speak, a structure on the world of appearances: it carves up this world into "natural kinds." This is how a phenomenal world is "created." But different paradigms carve up the world of appearances in different networks of natural kinds. Incommensurability then follows (even if it is local rather than global) since it is claimed that there are no ways to match up the natural-kind structure of one paradigm with that of another.

Social constructivism

Kuhn's views inspired social constructivists. Social constructivism is an agglomeration of views with varying degrees of radicalness and plausibility. Here is a sketchy list of them. The truth of a belief has nothing to do with its acceptability; beliefs are determined by social, political, and ideological forces, which constitute their causes. Scientific facts are constructed out of social interactions and negotiations. Scientific objects are created in the laboratory. The acceptability of scientific theories is largely, if not solely, a matter of social negotiation and a function of the prevailing social and political values. Science is only one of any number of possible "discourses," no one of which is fundamentally truer than any other. What unites this cluster of views are (vague) slogans such as "scientific truth is a matter of social authority" or "nature plays (little or) no role" in how science works. It might be useful to draw a distinction between a weak form of social constructivism and a strong one. The weak view has it that some categories (or entities) are socially constructed: they exist because we brought them into existence and persist as long as we make them do so. Money, the Red Cross, and football games are cases in point. But this view, though not problem-free, is almost harmless. On the strong view, all reality (including the physical world) is socially constructed: it is a mere projection of our socially inculcated conceptualizations. I am not sure anyone can really *believe* this. But there is a rather strong argument against the (more sensible) Kuhnian relativized neo-Kantianism. Roughly put, the argument is that the world enters the picture as that which offers *resistance* to our attempts to conceptualize it. Unless we think there is a world with an objective natural-kind structure, we cannot explain the appearance, persistence, and stubbornness of anomalies in our theories.

Causal theories of reference

The advent of the causal theories of reference in the 1970s challenged the alleged inevitability of incommensurability. Hilary Putnam (1973) extended Saul Kripke's (1972) causal theory of proper names to the reference of natural-kind terms and to physical-magnitude terms. (For further discussion of Kripke, see "American philosophy in the twentieth century," Chapter 5 and "Philosophy of language," Chapter 9.) The thrust of the causal theory is that the relation between a word and an object is *direct* – a direct causal link – unmediated by a concept. Generally, when confronted with some observable phenomena, it is reasonable to assume that there is a physical magnitude, or entity, which causes them. Then we dub this magnitude with a term and associate this magnitude with the production of these phenomena. The descriptions that will, typically, surround the introduction of the term might be incomplete, misguided, or even mistaken. Yet, on the causal theory of reference, one has nonetheless introduced *existentially* a referent: an entity causally responsible for certain effects to which the introduced term refers.

It is easily seen that the causal theory disposes of semantic incommensurability. Besides, it lends credence to the claim that even though past scientists had partially or fully incorrect beliefs about the properties of a causal agent, their investigations were continuous with the investigations of subsequent scientists, since they were aiming to identify the nature of the same causal agent. Yet there is a sense in which the causal theory of reference makes reference-continuity in theory-change all too easy. If the reference of theoretical terms is fixed purely existentially, then insofar as *there is* a causal agent behind the relevant phenomena, the term is bound to end up referring to it. Hence, there can be no referential failure, even in cases where it is counterintuitive to expect successful reference. This, and other problems, have led many theorists to combine elements of both the causal and the descriptive theories of reference into a causal-descriptivist account. On this mixed account, the burden of reference of theoretical terms lies with *some* descriptions which specify the kind-constitutive properties in virtue of which the referent, if it exists, plays its causal role.

The role and structure of scientific theories

In spite of the empiricists' best efforts, the meaning of a theoretical term cannot be exhausted by a set of empirical applications. It should also include the *entity* to which this term putatively refers. Consequently, terms such as "electron" or "magnetic flux" are no less meaningful than terms such as "table" or "is red." The latter refer to observable entities, whereas the former can be seen as putatively referring to unobservable entities.

Semantic realism and instrumentalism

This breath of fresh air came to be known as "semantic realism." It was championed in the 1950s by Herbert Feigl (1902–88). He claimed that the empiricist program had been a hostage to verificationism for too long. Verificationism runs together two separate issues: the evidential basis for the truth of the assertion and the semantic relation of designation (i.e. reference). It thereby conflates the issue of what constitutes evidence for the truth of an assertion with the issue of what make this assertion true. If evidence-conditions and truth-conditions are separated, verificationism loses its bite. An observational statement as well as a theoretical statement are true if and only if their truth-conditions obtain. Accordingly, theoretical terms as well as (and no less than) observational terms have putative factual reference. If theoretical statements cannot be given truth-conditions in an ontology that dispenses with theoretical entities, then a full and just explication of scientific theories simply requires commitment to irreducible unobservable entities, no less than it requires commitment to observable entities.

A strong pressure on semantic realism came from the application to philosophy of science of Craig's theorem: for any scientific theory T, T is replaceable by another (axiomatizable) theory Craig(T), consisting of all and only the theorems of T which are formulated in terms of the observational vocabulary (Craig 1956). The gist of Craig's theorem is that a theory is a conservative extension of the deductive systematization of its observational consequences. This point was readily seized upon by instrumentalists. Instrumentalism claims that theories should be seen as (useful) instruments for the organization, classification, and prediction of observable phenomena. So, the "cash value" of scientific theories is fully captured by what theories say about the observable world. Instrumentalists made use of Craig's theorem in order to argue that theoretical commitments in science were dispensable: theoretical terms could be eliminated *en bloc*, without loss in the deductive connections between the observable consequences of the theory.

This debate led Hempel (1958) to formulate what he called "the theoretician's dilemma." If the theoretical terms and the theoretical principles of a theory do not serve their purpose of a deductive systematization of the empirical consequences of a theory, they are dispensable. But, even if they do serve their purpose, given Craig's theorem, they can be dispensed with. Theoretical terms and principles of a theory either serve their purpose or they do not. Hence, the theoretical terms and principles of any theory are dispensable. But is this dilemma compelling? As Hempel himself stressed, it is implausible to think of theories as establishing solely a deductive system-atization of observable phenomena. Theories also offer inductive systematizations in the sense that they are used to establish inductive connections among them: they function as premises in *inductive* arguments whose other premises concern observable phenomena and whose conclusions refer to observable phenomena. But then, the Craig-theorem-based instrumentalist argument is blocked: theories, seen as aiming to establish inductive connections among observables, are *indispensable*.

The semantic view of theories

In the 1970s, the dominant formal-syntactic view of theories came under heavy attack by a number of philosophers of science. What emerged was a cluster of views known as the *semantic view of theories*. The core of this view was that theories represent via models and hence that the characterization of theories, as well as the understanding of how they represent the world, should rely on the notion of model. Where the logical empiricists favored a formal axiomatization of theories in terms of first-order logic, thinking that models can play only an illustrative role, the advocates of the semantic view opted for a looser account of theories, based on mathematics rather than meta-mathematics. As an answer to the question "What is a scientific theory?," the semantic view claims that a scientific theory should be thought of as something *extra-linguistic*: a certain structure (or class of structures) that admits of different linguistic garbs. This thought goes back to Patrick Suppes and was further pursued by Fred Suppe and Bas van Fraassen. Accordingly, to present a theory amounts to presenting a family of models. A key argument for the semantic view was that its own characterization of theories tallies better with the actual scientific conception of theories.

An immediate challenge to this view was that it was unclear how theories can represent anything empirical and hence how they can have empirical content. This challenge has been met in several ways, but two ways became prominent. The first way was that the representational relation was, ultimately, some mathematical *morphism*. The theory represents the world by having one of its models *isomorphic* to the world or by having the empirical phenomena *embedded* in a model of the theory. However, mathematical morphisms preserve only structure and hence it is not clear how a theory acquires any specific empirical content, and in particular how it can be judged as true. The second way, which was advanced to meet this last challenge, was that theories are mixed entities: they consist of mathematical models plus theoretical hypotheses. The latter are linguistic constructions which claim that a certain model of the theory represents (say by being similar to) a certain worldly system. On this view, advanced by Ronald Giere (1988), theoretical hypotheses provide the *link* between the model and the world. But in light of this mixed account of theories, it may well be that a proper understanding of theories requires the applications of both linguistic and extra-linguistic resources and that, in the end, there is not a single medium (the mathematical model) via which theories represent the world: theories may well be complexes of representational media.

Empiricism versus realism

Empiricists thought that a theory-free observational language was necessary for the existence of a neutral ground on which competing theories could be confirmed and compared. However, at least some them also thought that such a language could capture "the given" in experience, which acted as the certain foundation of all knowledge. Yet these two functions do not come to the same thing. Even if observation is theory-laden, it can be laden by theories (or beliefs) that are accepted by all sides of a theoretical dispute. Observations can be fallible and corrigible and yet they can confirm theories. That observations can be the epistemic foundation of all knowledge, in the sense of being an autonomous stratum of knowledge, is a dogma of empiricism that was refuted by Wilfrid Sellars (1912–89) in his famous attack on the "myth of the given" (1956). (For further discussion of Sellars, see "American philosophy in the twentieth century," Chapter 5.)

Realism and explanation

Sellars took a further step. He claimed that there was another popular myth that empiricism capitalized on: *the myth of the levels* (1963). This myth rested on the following image. There is the bottom level of observable entities. Then there is the intermediate level of the observational framework, which consists of empirical generalizations about observable entities. And finally, there is yet another (higher) level: the theoretical framework of scientific theories which posits unobservable entities and laws about them. It is part of this image that while the observational framework is explanatory of observable entities, the theoretical framework explains the inductively established generalizations of the observational framework. But then, Sellars says, the empiricist will rightly protest that the higher level is dispensable. For all the explanatory work vis-à-vis the bottom level is done by the observational framework and its inductive generalizations. Why then posit a higher level in the first place? Sellars's reply was that the unobservables posited by a theory explain *directly* why (the individual) observable entities behave the way they do and obey the empirical laws they do (to the extent that they do obey such laws). He, therefore, offered an indispensability argument for the existence of unobservable entities: they are indispensable elements of scientific explanation.

By the 1960s, the tide had started to move the scientific realists' way. Jack (J. J. C.) Smart (1963) put the scientific realism issue in proper perspective by arguing that it rests on an abductive argument, *aka inference to the best explanation*. Smart attacked the instrumentalists' position by saying that they must believe in cosmic coincidence. On the instrumentalist view of theories, a vast number of ontologically disconnected observable phenomena are "connected" only by virtue of a purely instrumental theory: they just *happen* to be, and just *happen* to be related to one another in the way suggested by the theory. Scientific realism, on the other hand, leaves no space for a cosmic-scale coincidence: it is *because* theories are true and *because* the unobservable entities they posit exist that the phenomena are, and are related to one another, the way they are.

Smart's point was that scientific realism (and its concomitant view of science) should be accepted because it offers the best explanation of why the observable phenomena are as they are predicted by scientific theories. Hilary Putnam (1975) and Richard Boyd (1973) argued that inference to the best explanation is the very method scientists use to form and justify their beliefs in unobservable entities and that realism should be seen as an overarching empirical hypothesis which gets support from the fact that it offers the best explanation of the success of science. The Putnam–Boyd argument came to be known as "the no-miracles argument" since, in Putnam's words, "The positive argument for realism is that it is the only philosophy that does not make the success of science a miracle" (1975: 73).

Explanation and metaphysics

Oddly enough, a similar debate had been conducted at the beginning of the twentieth century. But then it was mostly shaped by an emergent scientific theory, atomism, and some philosophical reactions to it. Atomism posited the existence of unobservable entities – the atoms – to account for a host of observable phenomena (from chemical bonding to Brownian motion). Although many scientists adopted atomism right away, there was some strong resistance to it by some eminent scientists. Ernst Mach resisted atomism on the basis of the concept-empiricist claim that the very concept of "atom" was problematic because it was radically different from ordinary empirical concepts. Poincaré was initially very skeptical of the atomic hypothesis, but near the end of his life he came to accept it as a result of the extremely accurate calculation of Avogadro's number by the French physicist Jean Perrin (1870–1942), who employed thirteen distinct ways to specify the precise value of this number. This spectacular development suggested to Poincaré an irresistible argument in favor of the reality of atoms: we can calculate how many they are, therefore they exist. Yet resistance still persisted and was best exemplified in the writings of Duhem. He built his resistance to atoms on a sharp distinction between science and metaphysics. He claimed that explanation by postulation – that is, explanation in terms of unobservable entities and mechanisms – belonged to metaphysics and not to science.

Duhem's theory of science rested on a very restricted understanding of scientific method, which can be captured by the slogan: *scientific method = experience + logic*. On this view, whatever cannot be proved from experience with the help of logic is irredeemably suspect. The irony is that Duhem himself offered some of the best arguments against an instrumentalist conception of theories. The central one comes from the possibility of novel predictions: if a theory were just a "rack filled with tools," it would be hard to understand how it can be "a prophet for us" (1906: 27). Duhem's point was that the fact that some theories generate *novel* predictions could not be accounted for on a purely instrumentalist understanding of scientific theories. However, he thought that explanatory arguments were outside the scope of scientific method. Yet this thought is deeply problematic. Scientists employ explanatory arguments in order to accept theories. So, contrary to Duhem, it is *part and parcel* of science and its method to rely on explanatory considerations in order to form and defend rational belief. In fact, this point was forcefully made by the American pragmatist Charles Saunders Peirce (1839–1914) in his spirited defense of abduction.

Duhem's understanding of metaphysics as bound up with any attempt to offer explanation by postulation became part of the empiricist dogma for many decades. It led many empiricists to reject scientific realism. However, the key question is what kinds of methods are compatible with empiricism. Even if we grant, as we should, that all knowledge starts with experience, its boundaries depend on the credentials of the methods employed. It is perfectly compatible with empiricism, as Reichenbach and others noted, to accept ampliative (inductive) methods and to accept the existence of unobservable entities on their basis. So there is no incompatibility between being an empiricist (which, after all, is an epistemological stance) and being a scientific realist (which, after all, is a metaphysical stance).

Constructive empiricism

The rivalry of realism and empiricism was fostered by van Fraassen's influential doctrine of constructive empiricism in the 1980s. This is a view about science according to which science aims at empirically adequate theories, and acceptance of scientific theories involves belief only in their empirical adequacy (though acceptance involves *more* than belief, namely commitment to a theory). Van Fraassen (1941–) took realism to be, by and large, an *axiological* thesis: the aim of science is true theories. He supplemented it with a *doxastic* thesis: acceptance of theories implies belief in their truth. Seen that way, realism and constructive empiricism are rivals. But of course, a lot depends on whether an empiricist ought to be a *constructive* empiricist. There is no logical obstacle for an empiricist (who, ultimately, thinks that all knowledge stems from experience) to fostering methods that warrant belief in the truth of theories in a way that goes beyond belief in their empirical adequacy, and hence, to be scientific realist. Similarly, there is no logical obstacle for an empiricist to being stricter than constructive empiricism. Constructive empiricism does set the boundaries of experience a little further than strict empiricism, and since what empiricism is is *not* carved in stone, there is no logical obstacle to setting the boundaries of experience (that is, the reach of legitimate applications of scientific method) even further, as realists demand.

Van Fraassen tied empiricism to a sharp distinction between observable and unobservable *entities*. This is a step forward *vis-à-vis* the more traditional empiricist distinction in terms of observational and theoretical terms and predicates. Drawing the distinction in terms of entities allows for the description of observable entities to be fully theory-laden. Yet, van Fraassen insisted, even theoretically described, an entity does not cease to be observable if a suitably placed observer *could* perceive it with the naked eye. Long before van Fraassen, Grover Maxwell (1962) had denied this entity-based distinction, arguing that observability is a vague notion and that, in essence, *all* entities are observable under suitable circumstances. He rested on the view that "observability" should be best understood as detectability through or by means of something. If observability is understood thus, there are continuous degrees of observability, and hence there is no natural and non-arbitrary way to draw a line between observable and unobservable entities. The rebuttal of Maxwell's argument requires that naked-eye observations (which are required to tell us what entities are *strictly* observable) form a special kind of detection that is set apart from any other way of detecting the presence of an entity (e.g. by the microscope). Be that as it may, the issue is not whether the entity-based distinction can be drawn but its epistemic relevance: why should the observable/unobservable distinction define the border between what is epistemically accessible and what is not?

What is scientific realism?

I take scientific realism to consist in three theses (or stances) (see Psillos 1999).
The metaphysical thesis: The world has a definite and mind-independent structure.
The semantic thesis: Scientific theories should be taken at face-value.
The epistemic thesis: Mature and predictively successful scientific theories are (approximately) true of the world.

In the last quarter of the twentieth century it was the third thesis of scientific realism that was primarily the focus. Briefly put, this is an epistemically optimistic thesis: science can and does deliver theoretical truth no less than it can and does deliver observational truth. The centrality of this thesis for realism was dictated by the perception of what the opposing view was: *agnostic* or *skeptical* versions of empiricism. A strong critique of realism was that the abductive-ampliative methodology of science fails to connect empirical success and truth robustly. Hence, it was argued, the claim that scientific theories are true is never warranted. Two arguments were put forward in favor of this view. The first relies on the so-called underdetermination of theories by evidence: two or more mutually incompatible theories can nonetheless be empirically congruent and hence equally empirically warranted. Given that at most one of them can be true, the semantic thesis can still stand but accompanied by a skeptical attitude towards the truth of scientific theories. The second argument was so-called pessimistic induction. As Larry Laudan (1984) pointed out, the history of science is replete with theories which were once considered to be empirically successful and fruitful, but which turned out to be false and were abandoned. If the history of science is the wasteland of aborted "best theoretical explanations" of the evidence, it might well be that current best explanatory theories will take the route to this wasteland in due course.

The argument from underdetermination rests on two questionable premises. (1): for any theory T there is at least another one incompatible theory T′ which is empirically congruent with T. (2): if two theories are empirically equivalent, then they are epistemically equivalent too. Both premises have been forcefully challenged by realists. Some have challenged (1) on the grounds that the thesis it encapsulates is not proven. Others have objected to (2). There are, on the face of it, two strategies available. One (2a) is to argue that even if we take only empirical evidence to bear on the epistemic support of the theory, it does not follow that the class of the observational consequences of the theory is coextensional with the class of empirical facts that support to the theory. An obvious counterexample to the claim of coextensionality is that a theory can get *indirect* support from evidence it does not directly entail. The other strategy (2b) is to note that theoretical virtues (and explanatory power, in particular) are epistemic in character and hence they can bear on the support of the theory. Here again, there are two options available to realists: (2b.i) to argue (rather implausibly) that some theoretical virtues are constitutive marks of truth; or (2b.ii) to argue for a broad conception of evidence which takes the theoretical virtues to be broadly empirical and contingent marks of truth. Option (2b.ii) is an attractive strategy because it challenges the strictly empiricist conception of evidence and its relation to rational belief.

When it comes to the pessimistic induction, the best defense of realism has been to try to reconcile the historical record with some form of realism. In order to do this, realists should be more selective in what they are realists about. A claim that has emerged with some force is that theory-change is not as radical and discontinuous as the opponents of realism have suggested. Realists have aimed to show that there are ways to identify the theoretical constituents of abandoned scientific theories which essentially contributed to their successes, separate them from others that were "idle" and demonstrate that those components which made essential contributions to the theory's empirical success were retained in subsequent theories of the same domain (see Kitcher 1993; Psillos 1999). Then, the fact that our current best theories may be replaced by others does not, necessarily, undermine scientific realism. All it shows is that (a) we cannot get at the truth all at once; and (b) our judgments from empirical support to approximate truth should be more refined and cautious, in that they should only commit us to the theoretical constituents that do enjoy evidential support and contribute to the empirical successes of the theory. Realists ground their epistemic optimism on the fact that newer theories incorporate many theoretical constituents of their superseded predecessors, especially those constituents that have led to empirical successes. The substantive continuity in theory-change suggests that a rather stable network of theoretical principles and explanatory hypotheses has emerged, which has survived revolutionary changes, and has become part and parcel of our evolving scientific image of the world.

Causation and explanation

The collapse of the synthetic a priori took with it the Kantian idea that the principle of causation ("everything that happens, that is, begins to be, presupposes something upon which it follows by rule"), was synthetic a priori. The logical positivists took to heart Hume's critique of the supposed necessary connection between cause and effect. The twist they gave to this critique was based on their verificationist criterion of meaning: positing a necessary link between two events would be tantamount to committing a kind of nonsense since all attempts to verify it would be futile.

Causal explanation

A central element of the empiricist project was to legitimize – and demystify – the concept of causation by subsuming it under the concept of lawful explanation, which in turn, was modeled on deductive arguments. This project culminated in Hempel and Oppenheim's (1948) Deductive-Nomological (DN) model of explanation. According to this, to offer an explanation of an event *e* is to construct a valid deductive argument of the following form:

Antecedent/initial conditions

Statements of laws

Therefore, *e* (event/fact to be explained)

So, when the claim is made that event *c* causes event *e*, it should be understood as follows: there are relevant laws in virtue of which the occurrence of the antecedent condition *c* is nomologically sufficient for the occurrence of the event *e*. It has been a standard criticism of the DN-model that, insofar as it aims to offer sufficient and necessary conditions for an argument to count as a bona fide explanation, it fails. A view that became dominant in the 1960s was that the DN-model fails precisely because it ignores the role of *causation* in explanation. In other words, there is more to the concept of causation than what can be captured by DN-explanations.

The Humean view may be entitled the "regularity view of causation." But an opposite view that became prominent in the twentieth century, owing mostly to the work of Curt John Ducasse (1881–1969), is that what makes a sequence of events causal is a local tie between the cause and the effect, or an intrinsic feature of the particular sequence. Causation, non-Humeans argue, is essentially singular: a matter of *this* causing *that*. Concomitant to this view is the thought that causal explanation is also singular. It is not a matter of subsuming the explanandum under a law but rather a matter of offering causally relevant information about why an event occurred.

The platitudes of causation

No matter how one thinks about causation, there are certain platitudes that this concept should satisfy. One of them may be called the "difference platitude": causes are difference-makers, that is, things would be different if the causes of some effects were absent. This platitude is normally cast in two ways. The first is the *counterfactual* way: if the cause hadn't been, the effect wouldn't have been either. David Lewis (1941–2001) defined causation in terms of the *counterfactual dependence* of the effect on the cause: the cause is rendered counterfactually necessary for the effect (1986). The other is the *probabilistic* way: causes raise the *chances* of their effects, namely, the probability that a certain event happens is higher if we take into account its cause than if we don't. This thought has led to the development of theories of *probabilistic causation*. Some philosophers, most notably Patrick Suppes (1984) and Nancy Cartwright (1983), claimed that the existence of probabilistic causation is already a good argument against the view that causation is connected with invariable sequences or regularities.

The origin of the probabilistic understanding of causation is found in Hempel's (1965) attempts to offer a general model of statistical explanation. Hempel argued that singular events whose probability of happening is less than unity can be explained by being subsumed under a statistical (or probabilistic) law. He advanced an *inductive-statistical* model of explanation according to which to explain an event is to construct an inductive argument one premise of which states a statistical generalization. But it became immediately obvious that this model suffered from problems. For instance, it can only explain events that are likely to happen, although unlikely events do happen and they too require explanation. Besides, statistical laws require fixing reference classes and it is not obvious what principles should govern this fixing. Wesley Salmon (1925–2001) advanced an alternative model of statistical explanation (1971), known as the *statistical-relevance* model, according to which in judging whether a factor C is relevant to the explanation of an event that falls under type E, we look at how taking C into account affects the probability of E. In particular, a factor C explains the occurrence of an event E, if $\text{prob}(E/C) > \text{prob}(E)$. Note that it is *not* required that the probability $\text{prob}(E/C)$ be high. All that is required is that there is a difference, no matter how small, between the two probabilities. Although it was initially thought that this model could offer an account of causal relevance, Salmon soon accepted the view that there is more to probabilistic causation than relations of statistical dependence. Mere correlations can conform to the statistical relevance model, but they are not causal. The theories of probabilistic causation that emerged in the 1980s attempted to figure out what more should be added to relations of statistical relevance to get causation.

Another central platitude of the concept of causation may be called the "recipe platitude": causes are recipes for producing or preventing their effects. This platitude is normally cast in terms of manipulability: causes can be manipulated to bring about certain effects. G. H. von Wright (1906–2003) developed this thought into a full-blown theory of causation. Since manipulation is a distinctively human action, he thought that the causal relation is dependent upon the concept of human action. But his views were taken to be too anthropomorphic. Yet in the last quarter of the century there were important attempts to give a more objective gloss to the idea of manipulation (mostly developed by James Woodward).

In the same period, several philosophers tried to show that there is more to causation than regular succession by positing a *physical mechanism* that links cause and effect. Salmon advanced a mechanistic approach (1984), saying roughly that an event *c* causes an event *e* if and only if there is a causal process that connects *c* and *e*. He characterized as "causal" those processes that are capable of transmitting a mark, where a mark is a modification of the structure of a process. Later on, Salmon and Phil Dowe took causation to consist in the exchange or transfer of some conserved quantity, such as energy-momentum or charge. Such accounts may be called "transference models" because they claim that causation consists in the transfer of something (some physical quantity) between the cause and its effect. But there is a drawback. Even if it is granted that these models offer neat accounts of causation at the level of physical processes, they can be generalized as accounts of causation *simpliciter* only if they are married to strong reductionist views that all worldly phenomena (be they social or psychological or biological) are, ultimately, reducible to physical phenomena.

Despite the centrality of the concept of causation in the ways we conceptualize the world and in the analysis of a number of other concepts, there is hardly any agreement about what causation is. It might not be implausible to think that, although traditionally causation has been taken to be a single, unitary, concept, there may well be two (or more) concepts of causation.

What is a law of nature?

The Deductive-Nomological model of explanation, as well as any attempt to tie causation to laws, faced a significant conceptual difficulty: the problem of how to determine what the laws of nature were. Most Humeans adopted the "regularity view of laws": laws of nature are regularities. Yet they had a hurdle to jump: not all regularities are causal. Nor can all regularities be deemed laws of nature. So they were forced to draw a distinction between the good regularities (those that constitute the laws of nature) and the bad ones, i.e. those that are, as John Stuart Mill put it, "conjunctions in some sense accidental." Only the former can underpin causation and play a role in explanation. The predicament that Humeans were caught in is this. Something (let's call it the property of lawlikeness) must be added to a regularity to make it a law of nature. But what can this be?

Humean conceptions of laws

The first systematic attempt to pin down this elusive property of lawlikeness was broadly epistemic. The thought, advanced by A. J. Ayer (1901–89), Richard Braithwaite (1900–90), and Nelson Goodman among others, was that inquirers have different epistemic attitudes towards laws and accidents. Lawlikeness was taken to be the property of those generalizations that play a certain epistemic role: they are believed to be true, and they are so believed because they are confirmed by their instances and are used in proper inductive reasoning. But this purely epistemic account of lawlikeness fails to draw a robust line between laws and accidents.

A much more promising attempt to draw the line between laws and accidents is what may be called the "web of laws" view. According to this, the regularities that constitute the laws of nature are those that are expressed by the axioms and theorems of an ideal deductive system of our knowledge of the world, a system that strikes the best balance between simplicity and strength. Whatever regularity is not part of this best system is merely accidental: it fails to be a genuine law of nature. The gist of this approach, which was advocated by Mill, and in the twentieth century by Ramsey and Lewis, is that no regularity, taken in isolation, can be deemed a law of nature. The regularities that constitute laws of nature are determined in a kind of holistic fashion by being parts of a structure. Despite its many attractions, this view faces the charge that it cannot offer a fully objective account of laws of nature. For instance, it is commonly argued that how our knowledge of the world is organized into a simple and strong deductive system is, by and large, a subjective matter. But this kind of criticism is overstated. There is nothing in the web of laws approach that makes laws mind-dependent. The regularities that are laws are fully objective, and they govern the world irrespective of our knowledge of them, and of our being able to identify them. In any case, as Ramsey pointed out, it is a fact about the world that some regularities form, objectively, a system; this is that *the world has an objective nomological structure*, in which regularities stand in certain relations to each other; these relations can be captured (or expressed) by relations of deductive entailment in an ideal deductive system of our knowledge of the world. Ramsey's suggestion grounds an objective distinction between laws and accidents in a *worldly* feature: that the world has a certain nomological structure (see Psillos 2002).

Non-Humean conceptions of laws

In the 1970s, David Armstrong (1983), Fred Dretske (1977), and Michael Tooley (1977) put forward the view that lawhood cannot be reduced to regularity. Lawhood, they claimed, is a certain necessitating relation among properties (i.e. universals). An attraction of this view is that it makes clear how laws can cause anything to happen: they do so because they embody causal relations among properties. But the central concept of nomic necessitation is still not sufficiently clear. In particular, it is not clear how the necessitating relation between the property of F-ness and the property of G-ness makes it the case that All Fs are Gs.

Both the Humeans and the advocates of the Armstrong–Dretske–Tooley view agreed that laws of nature are *contingent*. But a growing rival thought was that if laws did not hold with some kind of objective necessity, they could not be robust enough to support either causation or explanation. Up until the early 1970s, this talk of objective necessity in nature was considered almost unintelligible. It was Kripke's (1972) liberating views that changed the scene radically. He broke with the Kantian tradition which equated the necessary and the a priori as well as with the empiricist tradition which equated the necessary with the analytic. He argued that there are necessarily true statements which can be known a posteriori.

As a result of this, there has been a growing tendency among non-Humeans to take laws of nature to be metaphysically necessary. This amounts to a radical denial of the contingency of laws. Along with it came a resurgence of Aristotelianism in the philosophy of science. The advocates of the view that the laws are *contingent* necessitating relations among properties thought that, although an appeal to (natural) properties is indispensable for the explication of lawhood, the properties themselves are passive and freely recombinable. Accordingly, there can be possible worlds in which some properties are not related in the way they are related in the actual world. But the advocates of metaphysical necessity took the stronger line that laws of nature flow from the essences of properties. Insofar as properties have essences, and insofar as it is part of their essence to endow their bearers with a certain behavior, it follows that the bearers of properties *must* obey certain laws, those that are issued by their properties. Essentialism was treated with suspicion in most of the twentieth century, partly because essences were taken to be discredited by the advent of modern science and partly because the admission of essences (and the concomitant distinction between essential and accidental properties) created logical difficulties. Essentialism required the existence of *de re* necessity, that is, natural necessity, since if it is of the essence of an entity to be thus-and-so, it is *necessarily* thus-and-so. But before Kripke's work, the dominant view was that all necessity was *de dicto*, that is, it applies, if at all, to propositions and not to things in the world.

The thought that laws are metaphysically necessary gained support from the (neo-Aristotelian) claim that properties are active powers. Many philosophers argue that properties are best understood as powers since the only way to identify them is via their causal role. Accordingly, two seemingly distinct properties that have exactly the same powers are, in fact, one and the same property. And similarly, one cannot ascribe different powers to a property without changing this property. It's a short step from these thoughts to the idea that properties are not freely recombinable: there cannot be worlds in which two properties are combined by a different law from the one that unites them in the actual world. Actually, on this view, it does not even make sense to say that properties are united by laws. Rather, properties – qua powers – *ground* the laws.

The emergence of a new dogma?

From the 1970s on, a new over-arching approach to many problems in the philosophy of science has emerged: Bayesianism. This is a mathematical theory based on the probability calculus that aims to provide a general framework in which key concepts such as rationality, scientific method, confirmation, evidential support, and sound inductive inference are cast and analyzed. It borrows its name from a theorem of probability calculus: Bayes's Theorem. Let H be a hypothesis and e the evidence. Bayes's theorem says:

prob(H/e) = prob(e/H)prob(H)/prob(e), where prob(e) = prob(e/H)prob(H) + prob(e/-H)prob(-H).

The unconditional prob(H) is called the prior probability of the hypothesis, the conditional prob(H/e) is called the posterior probability of the hypothesis *given* the evidence, and the prob(e/H) is called the likelihood of the evidence given the hypothesis. (The theorem can be easily reformulated so that background knowledge is taken into account.) In its dominant version, Bayesianism is subjective or personalist because it claims that probabilities express subjective degrees of belief. It is based on the significant mathematical result – proved by Ramsey and Bruno de Finnetti (1906–85) – that subjective degrees of beliefs (expressed as fair betting quotients) satisfy Kolmogorov's axioms for probability functions. The central idea, known as the Dutch-book theorem, is that unless the degrees of beliefs that an agent possesses, *at any given time*, satisfy the axioms of the probability calculus, she is subject to a Dutch-book, that is, to a set of synchronic bets such that they are all fair by her own lights, and yet, taken together, make her suffer a net loss come what may. The thrust of the Dutch-book theorem is that there is a *structural incoherence* in a system of degrees of belief that violate the axioms of the probability calculus.

There have been attempts to extend Bayesianism to belief-revision by the technique of conditionalization. It is supposed to be a canon of rationality that agents should *update* their degrees of belief by conditionalizing on the evidence: $\text{Prob}_{\text{new}}(-) = \text{Prob}_{\text{old}}(-/e)$, where e is the total evidence. (Conditionalization can be either strict, where the probability of the learned evidence is unity, or Jeffrey (due to Richard Jeffrey, 1926–2002) where the evidence one updates on can have probability less than 1.) The penalty for not conditionalizing on the evidence is liability to a Dutch-book strategy: the agent can be offered a set of bets over time such that (a) each of them taken individually will seem fair to her at the time when it is offered; but (b) taken collectively, they lead her to suffer a net loss, come what may. But critics point out that there is no general proof of the conditionalization rule (see Earman 1992: 46–51).

The Bayesians' reliance on subjective prior probabilities has been a constant source of dissatisfaction among their critics. It is claimed that purely subjective prior probabilities fail to capture the all-important notion of rational or reasonable degrees of belief. But, in all fairness, it's been extremely difficult to articulate the notion of a *rational* degree of belief. Attempts to advance a more objectivist Bayesian theory (based on the principle of indifference, or, worse, based on Keynes's thought that "logical intuition" enables agents to "see" the logical relation between the evidence and the hypothesis) have failed. This has led Bayesians to insist on the indispensability of subjective priors in inductive reasoning. It has been argued that, in the long run, the prior probabilities wash out: even widely different prior probabilities will converge, in the limit, to the same posterior probability, if agents conditionalize on the same evidence. But this is little consolation because, apart from the fact that in the long run we are all dead, the convergence theorem holds only under limited and very well-defined circumstances that can hardly be met in ordinary scientific cases. Since the 1980s, subjective Bayesianism has become the orthodoxy in confirmation theory. The truth is that this theory of confirmation has had many successes. Old tangles, like the Ravens paradox or the grue problem, have been resolved. New tangles, like the problem of old evidence (how can a piece of evidence that is already known and entailed by the theory raise the posterior probability of the theory above its prior?), have been, to some extent, resolved. But to many, this success is not very surprising since the subjective nature of prior probabilities makes, in effect, prior probabilities free parameters that Bayesians can play with.

Can there be non-probabilistic accounts of confirmation? Clark Glymour (1980) developed his own "bootstrapping" account of confirmation that was meant to be an improvement over Hempel's theory. Glymour's key idea was that confirmation is three-place relation: the evidence confirms a hypothesis *relative* to a theory (which may be the very theory in which the hypothesis under test belongs). This account gave prominent role to explanatory considerations, but failed to show how confirmation of the hypothesis can give us reasons to believe in the hypothesis. The thought here is that unless probabilities are introduced into a theory of confirmation, there is no connection between confirmation and reasons for belief.

Among the alternatives to Bayesian confirmation that were developed over the last two decades of the century and that relied on probabilities, two stand out. The first is Deborah Mayo's (1996) error-statistical approach, which rests on the standard Neyman–Pearson statistics and utilizes error-probabilities understood as objective frequencies. They refer to the experimental process itself and specify how reliably it can discriminate between alternative hypotheses. Mayo focuses on learning from experiments and argues that experimental learning has a life and a model of its own. Experimental learning may be messy and piecemeal, it may require a tool-kit of techniques that ensure low error probabilities, but it can be embedded in a rather neat statistical framework that makes a virtue out of our errors. Yet, in Mayo's account, it is not clear how theories are confirmed by the evidence.

The other alternative to Bayesian confirmation is by Peter Achinstein (2001). He has advanced an absolute notion of confirmation, according to which e is evidence for H only if e is not evidence for the denial of H. This is meant to capture the view that evidence should provide a good reason to believe. But Achinstein's real novelty consists in his claim that this absolute conception of evidence is not sufficient for reasonable belief. What must be added is that there is an *explanatory connection* between H and e in order for e to be evidence for H.

Indeed, to many philosophers, explanatory considerations should be a rational constraint on inference and should inform any account of scientific method which tallies with scientific practice. But it is hard to see how explanatory considerations can be accommodated within the Bayesian account of scientific method, which, in effect, accepts the following equation: *scientific method = experience + probability calculus (including logic)*. This is certainly an improvement over Duhem's equation: *scientific method = experience + logic*. The need to import explanatory considerations into the scientific method (almost) swayed Duhem away from his strict equation (though Duhem rightly noted that explanatory considerations do not admit of an algorithmic account since they are values, broadly understood). Bayesians may not be easily swayed out of their own equation, since they may argue that explanatory considerations can be reflected in a suitable distribution of subjective prior probabilities among competing theories. But this kind of answer is inadequate if only because explanatory considerations are supposed to be objective, or in any case, not merely subjective. In fact, Bayesian accounts of confirmation fail to account for the methodological truism that goodness of explanation goes hand in hand with warrant for belief. It's not hard to see that on a Bayesian account of confirmation, and given that the theory T entails the set of its observational consequences T_O, no theory T can ever be more credible than a "theory" T_O. Yet T may well explain T_O, whereas T_O does not explain itself. As Glymour (1980: 83) put it, Bayesians render theories a "gratuitous risk."

Bayesianism is an admirable theory but, to my mind, there is more to scientific method than subjective prior probability and Bayes's Theorem. Of course, the tough issue is to offer a systematic and well-worked-out alternative to Bayesianism. Perhaps this alternative should be based on the broad idea that the kernel of scientific method is eliminative induction, where elimination is informed by explanatory considerations. But any account of scientific method should make room for epistemic values. Philosophy of science in the twentieth century has been animated by a legend: that theory-testing and theory-evaluation in science is based on a fully objective and general, value-free, presuppositions-free, evidence-driven, and domain-neutral scientific method. The naturalist turn did a lot to rebut the a prioristic version of the legend but it seems it's not gone all the way!

Outlook

Kant raised the question "How is metaphysics possible at all?" and went on to answer it by defending the synthetic a priori character of metaphysical propositions, which he thought would make science possible too. In the twentieth century, some of the philosophers who were deeply influenced by Kant's thought ended up considering metaphysics meaningless because it transgresses the bounds of meaningful discourse captured by mathematics and science. But as the century was drawing to a close, the genie came out of the bottle again: philosophers of science had to swim in deep metaphysical waters in order to address a number of key issues. Far from being a philosophical dirty word, "metaphysics" captures a legitimate and indispensable area of philosophical engagement with science. Understanding the basic structure of the world requires doing serious metaphysics, although now we know full well that no metaphysics can be seriously engaged with in abstention from what science tells us about the world. The big movement of the twentieth century was from issues related to language and meaning to issues related directly to the furniture of the world. It was also a movement from rational reconstructions and macro-models of science to the details of the individual sciences (especially, sciences other than physics).

Much to my disappointment, the present survey has not touched upon a number of issues. My greatest regret is that there is no discussion of feminist philosophies of science, a distinctive product of the twentieth century that has brought to light a key aspect of the issue of scientific objectivity. As the twentieth century recedes into history, what kinds of issue are dead and what are still alive?

Although in philosophy no issue really dies, it's safe to say that some positions are no longer viable (e.g. reductive understandings of the meaning of theoretical terms, strong instrumentalist accounts of scientific theories, naive regularity views of laws, algorithmic approaches to scientific method, global type-reductive accounts of inter-theoretic relations). Perhaps the whole philosophical issue of conceptual change is pretty much exhausted (with the exception of empirical studies of cognitive models of science), as is the issue of devising grand theories of science. Perhaps one should also be skeptical about the insights that can be gained by formal approaches to the nature and structure of scientific theories.

Surprisingly, the realism debate keeps coming back. The nature of rational judgment and the role of values in it are certainly fertile areas. And so are the nature of causation and the structure of causal inference. Adequate descriptions of ampliative reasoning are still in demand. And the prospects of structuralism occupy the thought of many philosophers of science. Most importantly, more work should be done on the relations between central issues in the philosophy of science and topics and debates in other areas of philosophy (most notably, metaphysics and epistemology).

A breath of fresh air has come from the conscious effort of Michael Friedman (1999) and many others to re-evaluate and reappraise the major philosophical schools and the major philosophers of science of the twentieth century. The philosophical battlegrounds of the twentieth century saw many attacks on strawmen and a number of pyrrhic victories. The time is now ripe to start repainting the complex landscape of twentieth-century philosophy of science.

Note

1 This survey reflects my own prides and prejudices; my own intellectual influences and debts. Others would have done things differently. I hope that I have not been unfair to the broad tradition I have been brought up in. Many thanks to Marc Lange and to three anonymous readers for their encouragement and insightful comments.

References

Achinstein, P. (2001) *The Book of Evidence*. New York: Oxford University Press.

Armstrong, D. M. (1983) *What Is a Law of Nature?* Cambridge: Cambridge University Press.

Boyd, R. (1973) "Realism, underdetermination and the causal theory of evidence." *Noûs* 7: 1–12.

Carnap, R. (1928) *The Logical Structure of the World*. English translation by R. A. George, Berkeley: University of California Press, 1961.

—— (1934) *The Logical Syntax of Language*. English translation by A. Smeaton, London: Kegan Paul, 1937.

—— (1950) *Logical Foundations of Probability*. Chicago: University of Chicago Press.

—— (1956) "The methodological character of theoretical concepts." In *Minnesota Studies in the Philosophy of Science* 1, Minneapolis: University of Minnesota Press, pp. 38–76.

Cartwright, N. (1983) *How the Laws of Physics Lie*. Oxford: Clarendon Press.

Cassirer, E. (1910) *Substance and Function*. English translation by W. C. and M. C. Swabey, Chicago: Open Court, 1923.

Craig, W. (1956) "Replacements of auxiliary assumptions." *Philosophical Review* 65: 38–55.

Dretske, F. I. (1977) "Laws of nature." *Philosophy of Science* 44: 248–68.

Duhem, P. (1906) *The Aim and Structure of Physical Theory*. English translation by P. Wiener, Princeton, NJ: Princeton University Press, 1954.

Earman, J. (1992) *Bayes or Bust? A Critical Examination of Bayesian Confirmation Theory*, Cambridge MA: MIT Press.

Frege, G. (1884) *The Foundations of Arithmetic*. English translation by J. L. Austin, Evanston, IL: Northwestern University Press, 1980.

Friedman, M. (1999) *Reconsidering Logical Positivism*. Cambridge: Cambridge University Press.

Giere, R. (1988) *Explaining Science: A Cognitive Approach*. Chicago: University of Chicago Press.

Glymour, C. (1980) *Theory and Evidence*. Princeton, NJ: Princeton University Press.

Goodman, N. (1954) *Fact, Fiction and Forecast*. Cambridge, MA: Harvard University Press.

Hempel, C. (1945) "Studies in the logic of confirmation." *Mind* 54: 1–26.

—— (1958) "The theoretician's dilemma: a study in the logic of theory construction." In *Minnesota Studies in the Philosophy of Science* 2, Minneapolis: University of Minnesota Press, pp. 37–98.

—— (1965) *Aspects of Scientific Explanation*. New York: Free Press.

Hempel, C. and P. Oppenheim (1948) "Studies in the logic of explanation." *Philosophy of Science* 15: 135–75.

Hilbert, D. (1899) *The Foundations of Geometry*. English translation by L. Unger, La Salle, IL: Open Court, 1971.

Keynes, J. M. (1921) *A Treatise on Probability: The Collected Works of J. M. Keynes*, vol. 7. London and Cambridge: MacMillan and Cambridge University Press.

Kitcher, P. (1993) *The Advancement of Science*. Oxford: Oxford University Press.

Kripke, S. (1972) "Naming and necessity." In D. Davidson and G. Harman (eds.) *Semantics of Natural Language*, Dordrecht: Reidel, pp. 253–355, 763–9.

Kuhn, T. S. (1962) *The Structure of Scientific Revolutions*. 2nd, enlarged edn., 1970. Chicago: University of Chicago Press.

Lakatos, I. (1970) "Falsification and the methodology of scientific research programmes." In I. Lakatos and A. Musgrave (eds.) *Criticism and the Growth of Knowledge*, Cambridge: Cambridge University Press, pp. 91–196.

Laudan, L. (1984) *Science and Values*. Berkeley: University of California Press.

Lewis, D. (1986) "Causation." In *Philosophical Papers*, vol. 2, Oxford: Oxford University Press, pp. 159–213.

Maxwell, G. (1962) "The ontological status of theoretical entities." In *Minnesota Studies in the Philosophy of Science* 3, Minneapolis: University of Minnesota Press, pp. 3–27.

Mayo, D. G. (1996) *Error and the Growth of Experimental Knowledge*. Chicago: University of Chicago Press.

Newman, M. H. A. (1928) "Mr. Russell's 'Causal theory of perception'." *Mind* 37: 137–48.

Poincaré, H. (1902) *Science and Hypothesis*. English translation, New York: Dover, 1905.

Popper, K. (1959) *The Logic of Scientific Discovery*. London: Hutchinson.

Psillos, S. (1999) *Scientific Realism: How Science Tracks Truth*. London and New York: Routledge.

—— (2000) "An introduction to Carnap's 'Theoretical concepts in science'" (with Carnap's: "Theoretical concepts in science"). *Studies in History and Philosophy of Science* 31: 151–72.

—— (2002) *Causation and Explanation*. Montreal: McGill-Queens University Press.

Putnam, H. (1973) "Explanation and reference." In G. Pearce and P. Maynard (eds.) *Conceptual Change*, Dordrecht: Reidel, pp. 199–221.

—— (1975) *Mathematics, Matter and Method: Philosophical Papers*, vol.1. Cambridge: Cambridge University Press.

Quine, W. V. O. (1936) "Truth by convention." In O. H. Lee (ed.) *Philosophical Essays for A. N. Whitehead*, New York: Longmans, pp. 90–124. Repr. in Quine's *The Ways of Paradox and Other Essays*, Cambridge, MA: Harvard University Press, 1976, pp. 77–106.

—— (1951) "Two dogmas of empiricism." *Philosophical Review* 60: 20–43.

—— (1960) *Word and Object*. Cambridge, MA: MIT Press.

—— (1969) "Epistemology naturalized." In *Ontological Relativity and Other Essays*, Cambridge, MA: Harvard University Press, pp. 69–90.

Ramsey, F. (1929) "Theories." In *The Foundations of Mathematics and Other Essays*, ed. R. B. Braithwaite, London: Routledge & Kegan Paul, 1931, pp. 212–36.

Reichenbach, H. (1921) *The Theory of Relativity and A Priori Knowledge*. English translation by M. Reichenbach, Berkeley: University of California Press, 1965.

—— (1928) *Philosophy of Space and Time*. English translation by M. Reichenbach and J. Freund, New York: Dover, 1958.

Russell, B. (1927) *The Analysis of Matter*. London: Routledge & Kegan Paul.

Salmon, W., R. C. Jeffrey, and J. G. Greeno (eds.) (1971) *Statistical Explanation and Statistical Relevance*. Pittsburgh: University of Pittsburgh Press.

—— (1984) *Scientific Explanation and the Causal Structure of the World*. Princeton, NJ: Princeton University Press.

Schlick, M. (1918) *General Theory of Knowledge*. 2nd German edn., 1925. English translation by A. E. Blumberg, Vienna and New York: Springer-Verlag, 1974.

Sellars, W. (1956) "Empiricism and the philosophy of mind." In *Minnesota Studies in the Philosophy of Science* 1, Minneapolis: University of Minnesota Press, pp. 253–329.

—— (1963) *Science, Perception and Reality*. Atascadero, CA: Ridgeview, 1991.

Smart J. J. C. (1963) *Philosophy and Scientific Realism*. London: Routledge & Kegan Paul.

Suppe, Frederick. (1980). *The Semantic Conception of Theories and Scientific Realism*. Urbana: Univerity of Illinois Press

Suppes, P. (1984) *Probabilistic Metaphysics*. Oxford: Blackwell.

Tooley, M. (1977) "The nature of laws." *Canadian Journal of Philosophy* 7: 667–98.

van Fraassen, Bas C. (1980) *The Scientific Image*. Oxford: Clarendon Press.

Further reading

Bird, A. (1998) *Philosophy of Science*. Montreal: McGill-Queens University Press. (A thorough critical introduction to most central areas and debates in the philosophy of science, written with elegance and insight).

Hempel, C. (1966) *Philosophy of Natural Science*. Englewood Cliffs, NJ: Prentice-Hall. (An all-time classic introduction to the philosophy of science, tantalizingly modern).

Hitchcock, C. (ed.) (2004) *Contemporary Debates in Philosophy of Science*. Oxford: Blackwell. (Well-known contemporary thinkers present opposing arguments on eight hotly debated issues in the philosophy of science).

Ladyman, J. (2002) *Understanding Philosophy of Science*. London and New York: Routledge.

Lange, M. (ed.) (2006) *Philosophy of Science: An Anthology*. Oxford: Blackwell. (A comprehensive collection of influential papers on a number of central topics in the philosophy of science arranged thematically and accompanied by thoughtful introductions by the editor).

Papineau, D. (ed.) (1996) *The Philosophy of Science*, Oxford: Oxford University Press. (A short collection of the most influential papers on general methodological issues in the philosophy of science, with an excellent introduction by the editor).

Psillos, S. (2007) *Philosophy of Science A–Z*. Edinburgh: Edinburgh University Press. (A dictionary of most central concepts, schools of thought, arguments, and thinkers; especially suitable for beginners).

Psillos, S. and M. Curd (eds.) (2008) *The Routledge Companion to the Philosophy of Science*. London and New York: Routledge. (Fifty-five specially commissioned chapters on all major issues in the philosophy of science, written by distinguished authors and offering a balanced critical assessment of the discipline and issues of current debate).

Salmon, M. et al. (eds.) (1992) *Introduction to the Philosophy of Science*. Englewood Cliffs, NJ: Prentice-Hall. (Written by members of the History and Philosophy of Science Department of the University of Pittsburgh, it contains thought-provoking advanced introductions to major debates about general issues (such as confirmation and explanation) as well as more special issues in the foundations of the sciences)

Part IV

PHENOMENOLOGY, HERMENEUTICS, EXISTENTIALISM, AND CRITICAL THEORY

15
PHENOMENOLOGY

Dan Zahavi

Is there something like a phenomenological tradition? Opinions are divided. According to one view, phenomenology counts as one of the dominant traditions in twentieth-century philosophy. Edmund Husserl (1859–1938)[1] was its founder, but other prominent exponents include Adolf Reinach (1883–1917), Max Scheler (1874–1928), Edith Stein (1891–1942), Martin Heidegger (1889–1976),[2] Aaron Gurwitsch (1901–73), Roman Ingarden (1893–1970), Alfred Schütz (1899–1959), Eugen Fink (1905–1975), Jean-Paul Sartre (1905–80), Maurice Merleau-Ponty (1908–61),[3] Simone de Beauvoir (1908–86), Emmanuel Lévinas (1906–95), Hans-Georg Gadamer (1900–2002), Paul Ricoeur (1913–2005), Jacques Derrida (1930–2004), Michel Henry (1922-2002), and Jean-Luc Marion (1946–) (see also "Twentieth-century hermeneutics," Chapter 16; "German philosophy (Heidegger, Gadamer, Apel)," Chapter 17; "French philosophy in the twentieth century," Chapter 18). Given that phenomenology has been a decisive precondition and persisting interlocutor for a whole range of later theory formations, including hermeneutics, deconstruction, and post-structuralism, it rightly deserves to be considered as the cornerstone of what is frequently and somewhat misleadingly called Continental philosophy.

Husserl is the founding father of phenomenology but it has often been claimed that virtually all post-Husserlian phenomenologists ended up distancing themselves from most aspects of his original program. Thus, according to a second competing view, phenomenology is a tradition by name only. It has no common method and research program. It has even been suggested that Husserl was not only the founder of phenomenology, but also its sole true practitioner.

The thesis to be defended in this chapter is that the latter view, which for opposing reasons has been advocated by ardent Husserlians and anti-Husserlians alike, is wrong. It presents us with a distorted view of the influence of phenomenology in twentieth-century philosophy, and it conceals to what extent post-Husserlian phenomenologists continued the work of the founder. Although phenomenology has in many ways developed as a heterogeneous movement with many branches; although, as Ricoeur famously put it, the history of phenomenology is the history of Husserlian heresies (Ricoeur 1987: 9); and although it would be an exaggeration to claim that phenomenology is a philosophical system with a clearly delineated body of doctrines, one should not overlook the overarching concerns and common themes that have united and continue to unite its proponents.

Many still tend to think of Husserl's transcendental phenomenology and Heidegger's and Merleau-Ponty's hermeneutical and existential phenomenology as excluding alternatives. The argument given is frequently that only the latter introduced the topics of intersubjectivity, sociality, embodiment, historicity, language, and interpretation into phenomenology and that this led to a decisive transformation of the Husserlian framework. For some, this conviction has been so strong that they have even questioned the sincerity and validity of Merleau-Ponty's own rather positive appraisal of Husserl. Thus it has been argued that Merleau-Ponty's writings on Husserl are not so much about what Husserl did say, as they are about what Merleau-Ponty thought he should have said, and that they must consequently be read as an exposition of Merleau-Ponty's own thoughts rather than as a genuine Husserl interpretation (Madison 1981: 170, 213, 330; Dreyfus and Rabinow 1983: 36; Dillon 1997: 27).

Given Merleau-Ponty's persistent and rather enthusiastic (though by no means uncritical) interest in Husserl – an occupation that lasted throughout his life, and which actually increased rather than diminished in the course of time – why this unwillingness to take his Husserl interpretation seriously? Why this certainty that the philosophies of the two are antithetical and that Merleau-Ponty must have misrepresented Husserl's position more or less knowingly in order to make it less offensive? The reason seems to be that many scholars are convinced that Husserl remained an intellectualist, an idealist, and a solipsist to the very end, regardless of what Merleau-Ponty might have said to the contrary. Thus, according to the received view, Husserl's commitment to a Cartesian foundationalism made him conceive of phenomenology as an investigation of a detached transcendental ego for whom its own body, worldly things, and other subjects were but constituted objects spread out before its gaze.

If this standard interpretation had been correct, it would indeed have been difficult to maintain that Husserl's phenomenology had much in common with Merleau-Ponty's or Heidegger's phenomenology. But we are dealing with a pejorative caricature that recent Husserl research has done much to dismantle. The continuing publication of *Husserliana* has made an increasing number of Husserl's research manuscripts available, and a study of these has made it clear that Husserl is a far more complex thinker than the standard reading is suggesting. He frequently anticipated and formulated many of the critical moves made by subsequent phenomenologists.[4]

During the twentieth century, phenomenology made major contributions in most areas of philosophy, including philosophy of mind, social philosophy, philosophical anthropology, aesthetics, ethics, philosophy of science, epistemology, theory of meaning, and formal ontology. It has provided ground-breaking analyses of such topics as intentionality, embodiment, self-awareness, intersubjectivity, temporality, historicity, truth, evidence, perception, and interpretation. It has delivered a targeted criticism of reductionism, objectivism, and scientism, and argued at length for a rehabilitation of the life-world. By presenting a detailed account of human existence, where the subject is understood as an embodied and socially and culturally embedded being-in-the-world, phenomenology has also provided crucial inputs to a whole range of empirical disciplines, including psychiatry, sociology, literary studies, architecture, ethnology, and developmental psychology.

Since it will be impossible to treat all of these topics in a single chapter, I will in the following address a rather meta-philosophical issue. I will focus on the very conception of philosophy found in phenomenology. I will discuss the question of method, the rejection of objectivism, scientism, metaphysical realism, and the focus on the first-person perspective. I will argue that phenomenology is a type of transcendental philosophy, but also that it differs rather markedly from other more traditional (Kantian) types of transcendental philosophy, for instance by emphasizing the embodied and intersubjectively embedded nature of subjectivity. I will conclude the chapter with a discussion of some of the challenges facing phenomenology in the twenty-first century.

Given that it will also be impossible to do justice to all the phenomenologists, my main focus will be on Husserl, (the early) Heidegger, and Merleau-Ponty, three thinkers whose decisive influence on the development of twentieth-century philosophy is undeniable.[5] Rather than articulating their differences, differences that in my view have frequently been overstated, my emphasis will be on their commonalities, and will be guided by what I consider to be some of Husserl's most promising attempts at articulating and capturing the basic thrust of phenomenology. A close reading of Merleau-Ponty's preface to his *Phénoménologie de la perception* of 1945 will serve as my point of departure.

Merleau-Ponty's Phenomenology of Perception

In his famous preface to *Phénoménologie de la perception* (*Phenomenology of Perception*), Merleau-Ponty seeks to provide a short answer to the question "What is phenomenology?" Merleau-Ponty starts out by noting that even half a century after Husserl's first writings a univocal definition of phenomenology is still missing. In fact, many of the proposals given seem to point in different directions:

1 On the one hand, phenomenology is characterized by a form of essentialism. It is not interested in a merely empirical or factual account of different phenomena, but seeks on the contrary to disclose the invariant structures of, for example, the stream of consciousness, embodiment, perception, etc. On the other hand, however, the point of departure for its investigation of the world and human existence remains factual existence. Phenomenology is not simply a form of essentialism, it is also a philosophy of facticity.
2 Phenomenology is a form of transcendental philosophy (see "Kant in the twentieth century," Chapter 4 and "German philosophy (Heidegger, Gadamer, Apel)," Chapter 17). It seeks to reflect on the conditions of possibility of experience and cognition, and it suspends our natural and everyday metaphysical assumptions (in particular, our assumption about the existence of a mind-independent world) in order to investigate them critically. At the same time, however, it admits that reflection must start from an already existing relation to the world, and that the main task of philosophy consists in reaching a full comprehension of this immediate and direct contact with the world.

3 Phenomenology seeks to establish a strictly scientific philosophy, but it also has the task of accounting for our life-world and of doing justice to our pre-scientific experience of space, time, and world.
4 Phenomenology is frequently described as a purely descriptive discipline. It describes our experiences just as they are given. It is interested neither in the psychological nor biological origin of the experiences, nor does it seek to provide a causal account. But at the same time, Husserl himself has emphasized the importance of developing a genetic phenomenology, i.e. a phenomenology that analyzes the origin, development, and historicity of the intentional structures.

As Merleau-Ponty remarks, it might be tempting to seek to overcome these apparent discrepancies by simply differentiating between Husserl's (transcendental) phenomenology, which has often been seen as an attempt to thematize the pure and invariant conditions of cognition, and Heidegger's (hermeneutical and existential) phenomenology, which has frequently been interpreted as an attempt to disclose the historical and practical contextuality of cognition. But Merleau-Ponty rejects this suggestion as being far too naive. As he points out, all the contrasts can be found internally in Husserl's thinking. Moreover, and more important, we are not dealing with true contrasts or alternatives, but rather with complementary aspects that phenomenology must include and consider (Merleau-Ponty 1945: i–ii; for Merleau-Ponty on Husserl, see Zahavi 2002b).

Husserl's dictum "to the things themselves" should be interpreted as a criticism of scientism, and as a call for a disclosure of a more original relation to the world than the one manifested in scientific rationality. It is a call for a return to the perceptual world that is prior to and a precondition for any scientific conceptualization and articulation. Scientism seeks to reduce us to objects in the world, objects that can be exhaustively explained by objectifying theories like those of physics, biology, or psychology. But as Merleau-Ponty points out, we should never forget that our knowledge of the world, including our scientific knowledge, arises from a first-person perspective, and that science would be meaningless without this experiential dimension. The scientific discourse is rooted in the world of experience, in the experiential world, and if we wish to comprehend the performance and limits of science, we have to investigate the original experience of the world of which science is a higher-order articulation. The one-sided focus of science on what is available from a third-person perspective is for Merleau-Ponty both naive and dishonest, since the scientific practice constantly presupposes the scientist's first-personal and pre-scientific experience of the world (Merleau-Ponty 1945: ii–iii).

Phenomenology's emphasis on the importance of the first-person perspective should not be confused with the classical (transcendental) idealistic attempt to detach the mind from the world in order to let a pure and worldless subject constitute the richness and concreteness of the world. This attempt was also naive. The subject has no priority over the world, and truth is not to be found in the interiority of man. There is no interiority, since man is in the world, and only knows him- or herself by means of inhabiting a world. To put it differently, the subjectivity disclosed by the phenomenological reflection is not a concealed interiority, but an open world relation. To use Heidegger's phrase, we are dealing with a "being-in-the-world," a world that moreover shouldn't be understood as the mere totality of positioned objects, or as the sum total of causal relations, but rather as the context of meaning that we are constantly situated within (ibid.: iii–v).

Had idealism been true, had the world been a mere product of our constitution and construction, the world would have appeared in full transparency. It would only possess the meaning that we ascribe to it, and it would consequently contain no hidden aspects, no sense of mystery. Idealism and constructionism deprive the world of its transcendence. For such positions, knowledge of self, world, and other are no longer a problem. But things are more complicated. Phenomenological analyses reveal that I do not simply exist for myself, but also for an other, and that the other does not simply exist for him- or herself, but also for me. The subject does not have a monopoly, either on its self-understanding or on its understanding of the world. On the contrary, there are aspects of myself and aspects of the world that only become available and accessible through the other. In short, my existence is not simply a question of how I apprehend myself, it is also a question of how others apprehend me. Subjectivity is necessarily embedded and embodied in a social, historical, and natural context. The world is inseparable from subjectivity and intersubjectivity, and the task of phenomenology is to think world, subjectivity, and intersubjectivity in their proper connection (ibid.: vi–viii, xv).

Our relation to the world is so fundamental, so obvious and natural, that we normally do not reflect upon it. It is this domain of ignored obviousness that phenomenology seeks to investigate. The task of phenomenology is not to obtain new empirical knowledge about different areas in the world, but rather to comprehend the basic relation to the world that is presupposed in any such empirical investigation. When phenomenology emphasizes the methodological necessity of a type of reflective reserve – what Husserl has called the *epoché* or the reduction (see below) – this is not because phenomenology intends to desert the world in favor of pure consciousness, but because we can only make those intentional threads that attach us to the world visible by slacking them slightly. The world is, as Merleau-Ponty writes, wonderful. It is a gift and a riddle. But in order to realize this, it is necessary to suspend our ordinary blind and thoughtless taking the world for granted. Normally, I live in a natural and engaged world-relation. But as a philosopher, I cannot make do with such a naïve being-in-the-world. I have to distance myself from it, if ever so slightly, in order to be able to describe it. This is why Merleau-Ponty argues that an analysis of our being-in-the-world presupposes the phenomenological reduction (ibid.: viii–ix).

The analysis of intentionality, the analysis of the directedness or aboutness of consciousness, is often presented as one of the central accomplishments of phenomenology (on intentionality, see also "Philosophy of mind," Chapter 12 and "Philosophy of psychology," Chapter 13). One does not merely love, fear, see, or judge, one loves a beloved, fears something fearful, sees an object, and judges a state of affairs. Regardless of whether we are talking about a perception, thought, judgment, fantasy, doubt, expectation, or recollection, all of these diverse forms of consciousness are characterized by intending objects, and cannot be analyzed properly without a look at their objective correlate, i.e., the perceived, doubted, expected object. It is consequently not a problem for the subject to reach the object, since its being is intentional. That is, the subject is per se self-transcending, per se directed towards something different from itself. But apart from having analyzed our theoretical object-directedness in great detail, phenomenology has also made it clear that the world is given prior to any analysis, identification, and objectification. There is, in short, a pre- and a-theoretical relation to the world. As Merleau-Ponty points out, this is why Husserl distinguished two types of intentionality. There is what Husserl in the Fifth Logical Investigation called *act-intentionality*, which is an objectifying form of intentionality. But there is also a more fundamental passive or *operative* form of non-objectifying intentionality, which Husserl analyzed in detail in later works such as *Analysen zur passiven Synthesis*.[6] According to Merleau-Ponty, this original and basic world-relation cannot be explained or analyzed further. All phenomenology can do is to call attention to it, and make us respect its irreducibility (1945: xiii, xv).

Phenomenology is a perpetual critical (self-)reflection. It should not take anything for granted, least of all itself. It is, to put it differently, a constant meditation. As Merleau-Ponty points out in closing, however, the fact that phenomenology remains unfinished, the fact that it is always under way, is not a defect or flaw that should be mended, but rather one of its essential features. As a wonder over the world, phenomenology is not a solid and inflexible system, but rather in constant movement (ibid.: xvi).

The question of method

Husserl's *Logische Untersuchungen* (*Logical Investigations*, 2001) in 1900/1 heralded the birth of a new method for studying consciousness, a method called *phenomenology* (Husserl 1962: 28, 302). The aim was to explore the intentional structures involved in our perception, thinking, judging, etc. This might seem like a simple continuation of the project commenced by Brentano in his *Psychologie vom empirischen Standpunkt* of 1874 (*Psychology from an Empirical Standpoint*). But although Brentano should be praised for his rediscovery of the concept of intentionality, his analysis of intentionality remained – as Husserl points out – naturalistic and psychological, whereas Husserl's own analysis was neither (Husserl 1962: 37, 310). Thus it is important to realize that the stated purpose of *Logische Untersuchungen* was not to establish a new foundation for psychology, but rather to provide a new foundation for epistemology. According to Husserl, this task would call for an "unnatural" change of interest. Although it had turned out to be impossible to reconcile scientific objectivity with a psychological foundation of logic (cf. Husserl's devastating criticism of psychologism) one was still confronted with the apparent paradox that objective truths are known in subjective acts of knowing. And, as Husserl points out, this relation between the object of knowledge and the subjective act of knowing must be investigated and clarified if we wish to attain a more substantial understanding of the possibility of knowledge. Thus, instead of merely paying attention to the objects, we need to reflect on, describe, and analyze the intentional experiences (Husserl 1984b: 14). Although this was not yet fully realized in *Logische Untersuchungen*, such a task would ultimately necessitate a clear distinction between two quite different takes on consciousness, a psychological and a transcendental (Husserl 1962: 42).

But why introduce a new science entitled phenomenology when there is already a well-established explanatory science dealing with the psychic life of humans and animals, namely psychology? More specifically, psychology is a science of naturalized consciousness. And could it not be argued that a mere description of experience – which is supposedly all that phenomenology can offer – does not constitute a viable scientific alternative to psychology, but merely a – perhaps indispensable – descriptive preliminary to a truly scientific study of the mind (Husserl 1987: 102)? As Husserl remarks, this line of thought has been so convincing that the term "phenomenological" is being used in all kinds of philosophical and psychological writings to describe a direct description of consciousness based on introspection (1987: 103).

In many of his writings, Husserl contrasts his own phenomenological investigation of consciousness with a natural scientific account of consciousness, and argues that the attempt to naturalize consciousness has not only failed, but that it is fundamentally flawed (1987: 17, 41). Husserl's criticism of naturalism can provide us with a clue to the difference between phenomenology and psychology, for according to Husserl, one of the main problems with naturalism is that it is blind to the constituting, transcendental, dimension of subjectivity. To refer to this dimension, to speak of transcendental subjectivity is not to introduce a new and additional subject next to the empirical subject. The empirical subject and the transcendental subject are not two different subjects, but rather two different takes on one and the same subject (1962: 294): It is a difference between conceiving of the subject as an object in the world, and conceiving of the subject as a subject for the world, i.e. as a meaning-bestowing and world-disclosing subject of intentionality. The whole thrust of the phenomenological analysis is to unearth the latter, thereby disclosing what phenomenology takes to be a *non-psychological* dimension of consciousness. This is also why phenomenologists have repeatedly denied that they should be engaged in some form of introspective psychology (see Merleau-Ponty 1945: 69–70; Gurwitsch 1966: 89–106; Husserl 1984a: 201–16; Heidegger 1993: 11–17). The argument is simple. Phenomenology must be appreciated as a form of transcendental philosophy; it is not a kind of empirical psychology. Phenomenology is not concerned with the psychological question of how a pre-existing reality (objectivity) is subjectively apprehended by psychical beings; rather it is concerned with the question of what it means for something to be real and objective in the first place and in particular with the transcendental questions concerning the very condition of possibility for manifestation. Its investigation of the essence of phenomenality is prior to any divide between psychical interiority and physical exteriority, since it is an investigation of the dimension in which any object – be it external or internal – manifests itself. Thus, phenomenologists would typically argue that it would be a metaphysical fallacy to locate the phenomenal realm within the mind, and to suggest that the way to access and describe it is by turning the gaze inwards (*introspicio*). As Husserl had already pointed out in the *Logische*

Untersuchungen, the entire facile divide between inside and outside has its origin in a naive commonsensical metaphysics and is phenomenologically suspect (Husserl 1984b: 673, 708),[7] but this divide is precisely something that the term "introspection" buys into and accepts.[8] To speak of introspection is (tacitly) to endorse the idea that consciousness is inside the head and the world outside. But as Merleau-Ponty put it, "Inside and outside are inseparable. The world is wholly inside and I am wholly outside myself" (1945: 467; 1962: 407), and as Heidegger wrote in *Being and Time* (*Sein und Zeit*, 1927):

> In directing itself toward … and in grasping something, Dasein does not first go outside of the inner sphere in which it is initially encapsulated, but, rather, in its primary kind of being, it is always already "'outside" together with some being encountered in the world already discovered. Nor is any inner sphere abandoned when Dasein dwells together with a being to be known and determines its character. Rather, even in this "being outside" together with its object, Dasein is "inside" correctly understood; that is, it itself exists as the being-in-the-world which knows. (1986: 62)

Husserl's rejection of any straightforward identification of phenomenology with psychology was fully shared by Heidegger. Not only does Heidegger categorically reject that his own analysis of the existential structures of Dasein is a psychological analysis (Heidegger 1986: 45–50), but he also writes that the attempt to interpret Husserl's investigations as a kind of descriptive psychology completely fails to do justice to their transcendental character. In fact, as Heidegger adds, phenomenology will remain a book sealed with seven or more seals to any such psychological approach (1993: 15–16). For both Husserl and Heidegger, phenomenology differs from psychology by not simply accepting the ontological (or metaphysical) presuppositions of the natural attitude.

Naturalism has denied the existence of a particular philosophical method, and has claimed that philosophy should employ the same method that all strict sciences are using, the natural scientific method (see "Naturalism," Chapter 6). But for Husserl this line of reasoning merely displays that one has failed to understand the true nature of philosophy. Philosophy has its own aims and methodological requirements; requirements that for Husserl are epitomized in his notion of *phenomenological reduction* (Husserl 1984a: 238–9). For Husserl, the reduction is meant to make us maintain the radical difference between philosophical reflection and all other modes of thinking. As he had already written in 1907: "*Thus, the 'phenomenological reduction' is simply the requirement always to abide by the sense of the proper investigation, and not to confuse epistemology with a natural scientific (objectivistic) investigation*" (1984a: 410, my translation). Every positive science rests upon a field of givenness or evidence that is presupposed but not investigated by the sciences themselves. In order to make this dimension accessible, a new type of inquiry is called for, a type of inquiry that "*lies before all ordinary knowledge and science, and lies in a quite different direction than ordinary science*" (1984a: 176; my translation).

According to Husserl, the positive sciences are so absorbed in their investigation of the natural (or social/cultural) world that they do not pause to reflect upon their own presuppositions and conditions of possibility. The positive sciences operate on the basis of a natural (and necessary) naivety. They operate on the basis of a tacit belief in the existence of a mind-, experience-, and theory-independent reality. This realistic assumption is so fundamental and deeply rooted that it is not only accepted by the positive sciences, it even permeates our daily pre-theoretical life, for which reason Husserl calls it the *natural attitude*. But this attitude must be philosophically investigated. That such an investigation is required should not, however, be taken as an endorsement of skepticism. That the world exists is, as Husserl writes, beyond any doubt. But the great task is to truly understand this indubitability (which sustains life and positive science) and to clarify its legitimacy (Husserl 1971: 152–3; 1954: 190–1).

How is this investigation to proceed if it is to avoid prejudicing the results beforehand? Husserl's answer is deceptively simple: our investigation should turn its attention towards the *givenness* or *appearance* of reality, i.e. it should focus on the way in which reality is given to us in experience. However, to turn towards the given is far easier said than done. It calls for a number of methodological preparations. In order to avoid presupposing commonsensical naivety (as well as a number of different speculative hypotheses concerning the metaphysical status of reality), it is necessary to suspend our acceptance of the natural attitude. We keep the attitude (in order to be able to investigate it), but we bracket its validity. This procedure, which entails a suspension of our natural realistic inclination, is known by the name of *epoché*. Strictly speaking, the *epoché* must be distinguished from what Husserl terms the *transcendental reduction*, which is his name for the analysis of the correlation between subjectivity and world. Both the *epoché* and the reduction can, however, be seen as closely linked elements of a transcendental reflection, the purpose of which – as Merleau-Ponty also pointed out in his preface – is to liberate us from a natural(istic) dogmatism and to make us aware of our own constitutive (i.e. cognitive, meaning-disclosing) contribution.

Are the *epoché* and the reduction something that phenomenology cannot do without, are they methodological tools that make phenomenology be what it is, or do they simply reveal Husserl's commitment to some form of methodological solipsism or Cartesian foundationalism?

Some have argued that Husserl takes a solipsistic, disembodied Cartesian ego as his starting point, and that he advocates a transcendental idealism which brackets all questions concerning external reality (e.g. Blackburn 1994: 181). But to claim that Husserl brackets all concern with the external world in order to focus on the internal structures of experience (Smith and McIntyre 1982: xiv, 87–8); to argue that the phenomenological reduction involves an exclusion of the world and that the world is henceforth ignored in favor of the mental representations that make intentionality possible (Dreyfus 1991: 50); to claim that questions concerning the being of reality are suspended, that existing reality is lost sight of, and that no attention is paid to the question of whether that which we are intentionally directed at does at all exist, are, in my view, all misunderstandings. Generally speaking, they succumb to what might be called a mentalistic misinterpretation of the phenomenological dimension. Rather than seeing the field of givenness, the phenomena, as something that questions the very subject/object split, as something that stresses the co-emergence of self and world, the phenomena are interpreted phenomenalistically, as part of the mental inventory. Moreover, these criticisms slight all the places where Husserl explicitly denies that the true purpose of the *epoché* and the reduction is to doubt, neglect, abandon, or exclude reality from our research, but rather emphasizes that their aim is to suspend or neutralize a certain dogmatic *attitude* towards reality, thereby allowing us to focus more narrowly and directly on reality just as it is given. In short, the *epoché* entails a change of attitude towards reality, and not an exclusion of reality. As Husserl makes clear, the only thing that is excluded as a result of the *epoché* is a certain naivety, the naivety of simply taking the world for granted, thereby ignoring the contribution of consciousness (Husserl 1989: 173). To put it differently, the *epoché* and the reduction do not involve an exclusive turn towards inwardness. On the contrary, they permit us to investigate reality in a new way, namely in its significance and manifestation for consciousness. And as Husserl repeatedly insists, the turn from a naive exploration of the world to a reflective exploration of the field of consciousness does not entail a turning away from the world; rather, it is a turn that for the first time allows for a truly radical investigation and comprehension of the world (1989: 178). Although this reflective investigation differs from a straightforward exploration of the world, it remains an investigation of reality; it is not an investigation of some otherworldly, mental, realm. Only a mistaken view of the nature of meaning and appearance would lead to such a misunderstanding. To put it differently, to perform the *epoché* and the reduction makes a decisive discovery possible and should consequently be understood as an *expansion* of our field of research (Husserl 1950a: 66; 1954: 154). This is why Husserl in *Krisis* (*The Crisis of European Sciences and Transcendental Phenomenology*) can compare the performance of the *epoché* with the transition from a two-dimensional to a three-dimensional life (1954: 120). In fact, as he points out in *Erste Philosophie II*, it is actually better to avoid using the term *Ausschaltung* ("exclusion," "disconnection," see *Ideas* I §31) altogether, since the use of this term might easily lead to the mistaken view that the being of the world is no longer a phenomenological theme, whereas the truth is that transcendental research includes "the world itself, with all its true being" (1959: 432).

Husserl has repeatedly insisted that one will have no chance of comprehending what phenomenology is all about, if one considers the *epoché* and the transcendental reduction as irrelevant peculiarities (1971: 155: 1976: 200); but what about later phenomenologists? It is indisputable that neither Heidegger nor Merleau-Ponty made many references to the *epoché* and the reduction. But is this because they rejected Husserl's methodology, or is it because they simply took it for granted? In §§ 27–33 of *Ideen I* (*Ideas I*), Husserl describes the natural attitude in detail and argues that the fundamental structures of our relation to the world, as well as the special character of our own subjectivity will remain concealed as long as we simply continue to live naively in the natural pre-philosophical attitude. It is by suspending our natural attitude that we discover that there is more to our subjectivity than merely being yet another object in the world. If we move from *Ideen I* to *Sein und Zeit*, we will find Heidegger arguing in a very similar manner. For Heidegger, human existence is characterized by a tendency to self-forgetfulness and self-objectification. It has a tendency to let its own self-understanding be guided by and therefore covered over by its habitual and commonsense understanding of worldly matters (Heidegger 1986: 21). Phenomenology can be described as a struggle against this leveling self-understanding. This is why Heidegger in *Sein und Zeit* writes that the phenomenological analysis is characterized by a certain violence, since its disclosure of the being of Dasein is only to be won in direct confrontation with Dasein's own tendency to cover things up. In fact, it must be wrested and captured from Dasein (1986: 311). As for Merleau-Ponty, we will find him arguing that we need to break with our familiar acceptance of the world if we are to understand the latter properly. In the preface to *Phénoménologie de la perception*, for instance, he explicitly writes that the phenomenological reduction, far from being a procedure of idealistic philosophy, belongs to existential philosophy, and that Heidegger's analysis of our being-in-the-world presupposes the work of the phenomenological reduction (Merleau-Ponty 1945: ix).

Furthermore, and this is even more important, all of the phenomenologists deny that the task of phenomenology is to describe objects or experiences as precisely and meticulously as possible, and they do not take it to be concerned with an investigation of the phenomena in all their factual diversity. No, for them its true task is to examine the very dimension of appearance or givenness, and to disclose its structure and condition of possibility. But this move from a straightforward metaphysical or empirical investigation of objects to an investigation of the very dimension of manifestation, i.e. to an exploration of the very framework of meaning and intelligibility that makes any such straightforward investigation possible in the first place, calls for a transcendental stance quite unlike the one needed in the positive sciences. The *epoché* and the reduction are precisely Husserl's terms for the reflective move that is needed in order to attain the stance of transcendental philosophy. Despite the disagreements they might have with the details of Husserl's program, both Heidegger and Merleau-Ponty are fully committed to this reflective move. As Heidegger writes in 1927 in the lecture course *Grundprobleme der Phänomenologie* (*Basic Problems of Phenomenology*): "We call this basic component of phenomenological method – the leading back or re-duction of investigative vision from a naively apprehended being to being – *phenomenological reduction*" (1989: 29).[9] A few years earlier, in the lecture course *Prolegomena zur Geschichte des Zeitbegriffs* (*History of the Concept of Time: Prolegomena*), Heidegger spends time accounting for Husserl's phenomenological methodology, and at one point, he delivers the following quite acute characterization:

> This bracketing of the entity takes nothing away from the entity itself, nor does it purport to assume that the entity is not. This reversal of perspective has rather the sense of making the being of the entity present. This phenomenological suspension of the transcendent thesis has but the sole function of making the entity present in regard to its being. The term "suspension" is

thus always misunderstood when it is thought that in suspending the thesis of existence and by doing so, phenomenological reflection simply has nothing more to do with the entity. Quite the contrary: in an extreme and unique way, what really is at issue now is the determination of the being of the very entity. (1979: 136)

When Heidegger speaks of being, he is not referring to any commonsense metaphysics; he is referring to the transcendental conditions of possibility for manifestation and intelligibility. Thus it is no coincidence that Heidegger calls the science of being a transcendental science (1989: 23), and that he argues that the mode of being of Dasein is such that it permits transcendental constitution (cf. Husserl 1962: 601–2).

I am obviously not arguing that there is complete agreement between Husserl, Heidegger, and Merleau-Ponty. There are many differences, and some of these are quite crucial. One should never forget that we are dealing with three independent thinkers who were also influenced by quite different figures in the philosophical tradition.[10] However, the disagreement and the later phenomenologists' criticism of Husserl take place within a horizon of shared assumptions. It is an immanent criticism, a criticism internal to phenomenology, and not a break with or general rejection of it.[11] To put it differently, a comprehension of the Husserlian framework is indispensable if one is to understand and appreciate the *phenomenological* aspect of Heidegger's and Merleau-Ponty's thinking.

Heidegger famously accuses Husserl for remaining too focused on logical and epistemological issues, and thereby for operating with a too narrow concept of being. Givenness is reduced to object-givenness, and according to Heidegger, Husserl thereby fails to disclose not only the unique mode of being peculiar to intentional subjectivity as such, he also fails to address the truly transcendental question adequately, namely the question concerning the condition of possibility for givenness as such (Heidegger 1979: §§ 10–13). Whether this criticism is justified or not is not the main issue.[12] The main issue is that the character of the criticism makes it clear that Heidegger's own project remains within the framework of transcendental phenomenology. This is also acknowledged by Tugendhat, who observes that it is

> through the *epoché* that Husserl enters the dimension of Heidegger's being-in-the-world. Heidegger does not need the *epoché* any more in order to gain entrance to the dimension of the modes of givenness, since he, after it was opened by Husserl, from the very start stands in it, and from now on can articulate it according to its own conditions – and not simply in exclusive orientation towards a world of objects. (Tugendhat 1970: 263; my translation)

And as the French philosopher Jean-Luc Marion has more recently put it, "Heidegger does not abandon Husserlian phenomenology any more than he refutes it – he revives its temporarily slackened impetus" (1998: 76).

To sum up, properly understood the *epoché* and the reduction are essential for phenomenology. They are elements in the transcendental reflection that makes

phenomenology a philosophical enterprise. Any attempt to downplay the significance of the phenomenological method runs the risk of confusing phenomenological
analyses with psychological or anthropological descriptions.

Husserl has frequently been accused of being a foundationalist. To some extent this
is correct. Husserl is a transcendental philosopher, and he would insist that transcendental phenomenology investigates the condition of the possibility for experience,
meaning, and manifestation, and thereby also the very framework of intelligibility that
conditions every scientific inquiry. However, Husserl also quite explicitly denies that
transcendental subjectivity could ever serve as the starting point for a transcendental
deduction (Husserl 1954: 193; 1950a: 63). Phenomenology is not a *deductive* discipline, but a *descriptive* discipline (Husserl 1976: 158). To put it differently, the truths
that transcendental phenomenology might uncover do not make up a foundation
which the contents of the positive sciences could be deduced from. Moreover, Husserl
did not conceive of his own transcendental analysis as a conclusive, final analysis. It is
an exploration of a field, which in an absolute sense, is unavoidable (*unhintergehbar*). It
is an analysis of the processes by and in which everything is constituted. It is an investigation into the conditions in virtue of which anything is given to us. But the analysis
of this domain can always be refined, deepened, and improved. Thus, for Husserl the
full and conclusive truth about the transcendental dimension remains a regulative
ideal. Philosophy as a science based on ultimate justification is an idea which can only
be realized in an infinite historical process (Husserl 1959: 186; 1954: 439).

One way to understand Husserl's foundationalism might consequently be to see it
as a way of emphasizing and maintaining the difference between the empirical and
the philosophical stance, between the mundane and the transcendental attitude. It
is by insisting upon this difference that Husserl can maintain that philosophy has
something cognitively distinctive to offer the scientific enterprise. This is a vision not
unlike the one to be found (with different emphasis to be sure) in Merleau-Ponty and
(the early) Heidegger as well.

Subjectivity and metaphysics

All the phenomenologists have emphasized the importance of analyzing the first-
person perspective. All of them have been occupied with the problem of subjectivity.
This is also true of Heidegger. Although he has occasionally been interpreted as a
radical critic of the philosophy of subjectivity, it is undeniable that he in *Sein und Zeit*
attributes a decisive role to Dasein. Not only architectonically, insofar as the analysis
of Dasein constitutes the larger part of the book, but also systematically, which is
evident from passages where Heidegger writes that without Dasein there would be
neither being, truth nor world (Heidegger 1986: 212, 226, 365). As he declares, a
clarification of the fundamental ontological questions must proceed via an investigation of Dasein's understanding of being, since this is what defines the horizon within
which worldly beings can be. Being is investigated "in so far as it stands within the
intelligibility of Dasein" (1986: 152, cf. 207). It could of course be objected that this
is quite irrelevant, since Heidegger's concept of Dasein should not be confused with

the traditional concept of subjectivity. To some extent this is true, namely if one has an isolated, self-contained, worldless substance in mind. Heidegger rejects this notion of subjectivity, and that is why he argues that one would misunderstand Dasein if one interpreted it as an ego or a subject (1986: 46, 322–3). However, the pertinent question is whether Dasein has something to do with a phenomenologically clarified concept of subjectivity. Heidegger provides the answer himself, when in works such as *Sein und Zeit, Die Grundprobleme der Phänomenologie, Einleitung in die Philosophie* (*Introduction to Philosophy*), and *Kant und das Problem der Metaphysik* (1929) (*Kant and the Problem of Metaphysics*) he argues that it is necessary to commence a phenomenological investigation of the subjectivity of the finite subject. He also writes that his own thematization of the ontology of Dasein equals an analysis of the subjectivity of the subject, and that an ontological comprehension of the subject will lead us to the existing Dasein (1986: 24, 366, 382; 1991: 87, 219; 1989: 207, 220; 1996: 72, 115; cf. Marion 1998; Overgaard 2004).

But why have phenomenologists been so preoccupied with this examination of subjectivity and selfhood? Had it been a goal in itself, phenomenology would have remained a form of philosophical psychology or anthropology. But the phenomenological interest in subjectivity is not motivated by the relatively trivial insight that we need to include the first-person perspective if we wish to understand mental phenomena. Rather the analysis is transcendental philosophical in nature. We cannot look at our experiences from sideways on to see whether they match with reality, nor can we consider our experiences and structures of understanding as mere elements within the world that we experience and understand. The relation between mind and world is an internal one, a relation constitutive of its relata, and not an external one of causality. The reason why the phenomenologists have been so preoccupied with describing and analyzing the fundamental features of subjectivity, whether its structures of intentionality, of embodiment, of temporality, of historicity, of intersubjective embeddedness, is that they have been convinced that a thorough philosophical understanding of the structures of knowledge, truth, meaning, reference must include an investigation of the first-person perspective. If we wish to understand how physical objects, mathematical models, chemical processes, social relations, cultural products, can appear as they do and with the meaning they have, then we will also have to examine the subject to whom they appear. If we wish to understand the world that we experience and live in, we also have to investigate subjectivity. Truth, meaning, reality are always a truth, meaning, and reality *for* somebody. As Heidegger writes in the lecture course *Grundprobleme der Phänomenologie* from 1927:

> World exists – that is, it is – only if Dasein exists, only if there is Dasein. Only if world is there, if Dasein exists as being-in-the-world, is there understanding of being, and only if this understanding exists are intraworldly beings unveiled as extant and handy. World-understanding as Dasein-understanding is self-understanding. Self and world belong together in the single entity, the Dasein. Self and world are not two beings, like subject and object, or like I and thou, but self and world are the basic determination of the Dasein itself in the unity of the structure of being-in-the-world. (Heidegger 1989: 422)

One can find similar statements in both Husserl and Merleau-Ponty. As the latter writes, the world is inseparable from the subject, and the subject inseparable from the world (Merleau-Ponty 1945: 491–2). Thus phenomenologists would not only deny that the mind is self-contained, they would say the same *vis-à-vis* the world. The mind is tied to the world, but the world is also tied to the mind.

By adopting the phenomenological attitude we become aware of the givenness of objects. But we do not simply focus on the objects precisely as they are given; we also focus on the subjective side of consciousness, thereby becoming aware of our subjective accomplishments and of the intentionality that is at play in order for the objects to appear as they do. When we investigate appearing objects, we also disclose ourselves as datives of manifestation, as those to whom objects appear. The topic of the phenomenological analyses is consequently not a worldless subject, and phenomenology does not ignore the world in favor of consciousness. On the contrary, phenomenology is interested in consciousness because it is world-disclosing.

Phenomenology is supposed to be concerned with phenomena and appearances and their conditions of possibility, but what precisely is a phenomenon? For many philosophers, the phenomenon is understood as the immediate givenness of the object, it is how it appears to us, it is how *apparently* is. If one wishes to discover what the object is really like, however, one has to transcend the merely phenomenal. Had it been this concept of phenomenon that phenomenology was employing, phenomenology would have been nothing but a science of the merely subjective, apparent, or superficial. But this is obviously not the case. As Heidegger argues in §7 of *Sein und Zeit*, the phenomenon is to be understood as that which shows itself, as beings' own manifestation. Phenomenology should therefore be understood as a philosophical analysis of the different modes of givenness, and in connection with this as a reflective investigation of those structures of understanding that permits different types of beings to show themselves as what they are. In contrast to the objective or positive sciences, phenomenology is not particularly interested in the substantial nature of the objects, such as their weight, rarity, or chemical composition, but in the way in which they show themselves, i.e. in their modes of givenness. There are essential differences between the ways in which a physical thing, a utensil, a work of art, a melody, a state of affairs, a number, an animal, a social relation, etc., manifests itself. Moreover, it is also possible for one and the same object to appear in a variety of different ways: from this or that perspective, in strong or faint illumination, as perceived, imagined, wished for, feared, anticipated, or recollected. Rather than regarding questions concerning the manifestation or givenness of objects as something insignificant or merely subjective, phenomenologists insist that such an investigation is of crucial philosophical importance.

Although the distinction between appearance and reality must be maintained (some appearances are misleading), it is according to transcendental phenomenology not a distinction between two separate realms (falling in the province of phenomenology and metaphysics, respectively), but a distinction internal to the world we are living in. It is a distinction between how the objects might appear at a superficial glance, and how they might appear in the best of circumstances, be it in practical use or in the light of extensive scientific investigations. Thus, the reality of the object is not to be located behind its appearance, as if the appearance in some way or another hid the real object. As Heidegger points out, it is phenomenologically absurd to argue that the phenomenon hides something more fundamental which it merely represents (1979: 118). Whereas metaphysical realists might claim that the phenomena are something merely subjective, a veil or smoke screen that conceals the objectively existing reality, phenomenologists insist that one is in contact with the thing in itself when and insofar as it is a phenomenon. This is not to say that phenomena cannot be deceptive, but even when deceived we remain in contact with the world. It is after all the world that we are deceived about. Moreover, one cannot expose such deceptive phenomena by appealing to some mysterious view from nowhere, rather the only justification obtainable and the only justification required is one that is internal to the world of experience and to its intersubjective practices. In this sense, Davidson is entirely right when he writes: "A community of minds is the basis of knowledge; it provides the measure of all things. It makes no sense to question the adequacy of this measure, or to seek a more ultimate standard" (2001: 218).

In order not to misunderstand this position, it is, however, as already mentioned, vital not to commit the mistake of interpreting the phenomena mentalistically. For the phenomenologists, the phenomenon is not a psychological item. On the contrary, one of the decisive merits of phenomenology has been its introduction of a new non-mentalistic notion of phenomenon (Benoist 1997: 228). As Husserl himself writes in *Einleitung in die Logik und Erkenntnistheorie* (*Introduction to Logic and Epistemology*) from 1906–7,

> If consciousness ceases to be a human or some other empirical consciousness, then the word loses all psychological meaning, and ultimately one is *led back to something absolute that is neither physical nor psychical being in a natural scientific sense*. However, in the phenomenological perspective this is the case throughout the field of givenness. It is precisely the apparently so obvious thought, that everything given is either physical or psychical that must be abandoned. (1984a: 242; my translation)

It cannot be emphasized too much how important it is to keep this admonition in mind.

Given the strong emphasis on the interdependency of subjectivity and world and given the phenomenological definition of phenomena, what are the metaphysical implications? Is transcendental phenomenology a kind of idealism?

Some have argued that transcendental phenomenology must be viewed as a meta-philosophical or methodological endeavor rather than as a straightforwardly metaphysical doctrine about the nature and status of worldly objects (see Crowell 2001). As already mentioned, Husserl's *epoché* and reduction are methodological tools permitting us to overcome the naivety of the naturalistic attitude, which simply presupposes the world as a pre-given source of validities. One encounters objects as given, but does not reflect upon what givenness means, nor how it is possible. Transcendental phenomenology, however, thematizes objects in terms of their givenness, validity, and intelligibility, and such an investigation calls for a reflective stance unlike the one needed in the positive sciences. From this point of view, a metaphysical interpretation of transcendental phenomenology would entail a dramatic misunderstanding of what phenomenology is all about. It would misunderstand the notion of reduction, and it would overlook the decisive difference between the natural attitude and the phenomenological attitude. From the perspective of phenomenology, metaphysics remains a pre-critical or naive enterprise. In its attempt to map out the building blocks of reality, it never leaves the natural attitude. It doesn't partake in the reflective move that is the defining moment of transcendental thought.

It is true that transcendental phenomenology is not engaged in straightforward metaphysics, and it is important to emphasize the difference between the object-oriented nature of metaphysics and the reflective orientation of transcendental phenomenology. But to interpret phenomenology as non-metaphysical,[13] to argue that it has no metaphysical implications or impact, and that it therefore remains compatible with a variety of different metaphysical views, including metaphysical or scientific realism is to make it sound as if phenomenology operates with a two-world theory. On the one hand, we would have the world as it is for us, the world of significance and appearance, the world phenomenology is supposed to investigate. On the other hand, we would have the world as it is in itself, the real world, the world metaphysics and positive science are supposed to investigate. But this way of cutting the cake would be unacceptable to phenomenologists. Transcendental phenomenology is not merely a theory about the structure of subjectivity, nor is it merely a theory about how we understand and perceive the world. It is not even a theory about how the world appears to us, *if*, that is, such a theory is supposed to be complemented by a further investigation (left to metaphysics) of what the world itself is like. To construe phenomenology in such a way would make it vulnerable to the objection that it engages in an unphenomenological abstraction: Something crucial would be missing from its repertoire; being and reality would be topics left for other disciplines. But this interpretation does not respect nor reflect Husserl's, Heidegger's, or Merleau-Ponty's own assertions on the matter. As Eugen Fink (1905–75), Husserl's last assistant, for instance pointed out back in 1939, only a fundamental misunderstanding of the aim of phenomenology would lead to the mistaken but often repeated claim that Husserl's phenomenology is not interested in reality or the question of being, but only in subjective meaning-formations in intentional consciousness (Fink 1939: 257).

Phenomenology investigates the intelligibility, significance, and appearance of the world. To engage in a reflective exploration of the structures and conditions of worldly significance and appearance differs from any direct metaphysical investigation of the real word. But what needs to be stressed is that the significance and appearance being investigated is the significance and appearance of the real world, not of some other-worldly realm. Phenomenology has insisted upon this, and rightly so, but by doing that, it can no longer claim metaphysical neutrality. Transcendental phenomenology cannot permit itself to remain neutral or indifferent to the question concerning the relationship between the phenomena and reality. But by having to take a stand on this relationship, by having to elucidate what it means for a given object to exist and be real, phenomenology by necessity has metaphysical implications.

Of course, metaphysics can mean a lot of different things, and given certain understandings of the term phenomenology is indeed non-metaphysical, or even better anti-metaphysical. Thus if metaphysics is, for instance, seen as being wedded inseparably to an objectivistic framework, phenomenology is not metaphysical and has no dealing with it, except of course in so far as it criticizes it, and does not simply leave it untouched and unquestioned. To argue that transcendental phenomenology is metaphysically neutral, to argue that it is concerned with meaning rather than being, and that it lacks the resources to tackle metaphysical issues, is not only to make transcendental phenomenology tamer and lamer than it really is. The true paradox is that such a view is exactly giving in to a certain kind of traditional metaphysics, accepting as it does the classical distinction between meaning and being, and between appearance and reality.

Continuing this line of thought some might want to argue that the term "metaphysics" is so loaded that it might be prudent to simply avoid using it. If one really wants to insist that phenomenology has metaphysical implications, it might be better to specify that the kind of metaphysics at play is a *post-critical* metaphysics. I have no quarrel with this suggestion. In fact, there is no reason to quarrel over terminology. All that is important is to recognize the scope of transcendental phenomenology (transcendental phenomenology does have something to say about existing reality, about being and objectivity) and not to misconstrue it in such a way that it becomes indistinguishable from some kind of descriptive psychology.[14] Such a misconstrual would be particularly harmful these days, given the widespread but misleading use of the term "phenomenology" in analytical philosophy. Phenomenology is not another name for a kind of psychological self-observation, nor is it simply to be identified with a first-person description of what the "what it is like" of experience is really like.

For phenomenology the world that appears to us, be it in perception, in our daily concerns, or in our scientific analyses, is the only real world. To claim that in addition to this world there exists a hidden world, which transcends every appearance, and every experiential and theoretical evidence, and to identify this world with true reality is according to the phenomenologists an empty and countersensical proposition. But to repeat the question, does this mean that phenomenology is committed to idealism? It all depends on what we mean by "idealism." Since the term is notoriously ambiguous, it might be more informative to say that phenomenology is committed to a criticism of metaphysical realism. Phenomenologists share this criticism with leading figures in analytical philosophy, e.g. Wittgenstein, Davidson, Dummett, Putnam, and Rorty.

According to metaphysical realism, there is a clear distinction to be drawn between the properties things have "in themselves" and the properties which are "projected by us." Whereas the world of appearance, the world as it is for us in daily life, combines subjective and objective features, the world that science describes is the world as it is in itself, and science gains access to this world by transcending all subjective perspectives, structures, and categories. Knowledge is consequently taken to consist in a faithful mirroring of a mind-independent reality; a reality independent of subjectivity, interpretation, and historical community. But to think that science has access to a non-perspectival reality, and that science can provide us with an *absolute* description of reality, that is, a description from a view from nowhere; to think that science is the only road to metaphysical truth, and that science simply mirrors the way in which Nature classifies itself, is illusory. In truth, one of the things that pre-scientific experience and scientific exploration have in common is that both are concerned with the world of appearance. The latter simply enlarges it.

For phenomenology, science is not simply a collection of systematic interrelated justified propositions. Science is performed by somebody; it is a specific theoretical stance towards the world. This stance did not fall down from the sky; it has its own presuppositions and origin. Science is, as Merleau-Ponty remarks in the Preface to *Phénoménologie de la perception*, rooted in the life-world, it draws on insights from the pre-scientific sphere, and it is performed by embodied and embedded subjects. In its urge towards idealization, in its search for exact and objective knowledge, science has made a virtue out of its decisive showdown with subject-relative evidence, but it has thereby had a tendency to overlook that its own more refined measurements inevitably continue to draw on the contribution of intuition, as when one looks in the microscope, reads the measuring instruments, or interprets, compares, and discusses the results with other scientists.

The contribution of phenomenology does not consist in providing a scientific explanation of human existence. Rather it is an attempt to make science, i.e. scientific rationality and practice, comprehensible through a detailed analysis of the forms of intentionality that are employed by the cognizing subject. One of the central tasks is to account for the way in which the theoretical attitude which we employ when doing science originates from, influences, and transforms our basic being-in-the-world.

The phenomenological criticism of metaphysical realism is fully compatible with an endorsement of what has occasionally been called empirical realism. Whether something is real or not does not depend upon whether it can be fitted into the procrustean bed of reductionism. Our common world of experience, our life-world, has its own (pragmatic) criteria for truth and validity, and does not have to await the warrant of science. In contrast, metaphysical realists have frequently made the idealist move of making a certain restricted theoretical outlook the measure of what counts as real. As a result, the existence of everyday objects such as tables, chairs, nations, economic crises, and wars has been denied with the argument that none of these entities figures in the account of reality provided by natural science (Putnam 1987:2). Although metaphysical realism was once heralded as a strong antidote against idealism and skepticism, we are consequently confronted with one of those cases where the medicine has turned out to be part of the sickness it was supposed to cure and in the end just as deadly.

Intersubjectivity and embodiment

As Husserl admits in *Erste Philosophie I* (*First Philosophy*, vol. 1), when he decided to designate his own phenomenology as transcendental, he was employing a Kantian concept (1956: 230). But although a reference to Kant is appropriate, and although such a reference can certainly be helpful in the attempt to explain why phenomenology is not simply a form of introspective psychology, one should also be careful in not overlooking some rather decisive differences between Kantianism and phenomenology. To put it differently, it would be a mistake to think that transcendental philosophy is all one thing, and to ignore the difference between a Kantian transcendental philosophy and the form of transcendental philosophy we find in phenomenology.

If we look closer at some of Husserl's scattered remarks about Kant, we will find Husserl faulting Kant for not having had a proper concept of the a priori, for operating with a too strong distinction between sensation and understanding, for remaining too metaphysical, for having overlooked a number of foundational issues in his critique of knowledge, for being too oriented towards the natural sciences, for confusing noetic and noematic analyses, and for lacking methodological rigor (Husserl 1956: 198–9, 235, 282; 1954: 420–1; 1984a: 729, 732; 1976: 246;1950b: 48). In one of his longest texts on Kant, a talk written and presented in commemoration of Kant's bicentennial in 1924, entitled *Kant und die Idee der Transzendentalphilosophie* ("Kant and the idea of transcendental philosophy," 1974), reprinted in *Husserliana* VII, Husserl writes that transcendental philosophy should be based upon a systematic description and analysis of consciousness in all of its modalities (1956: 234–5). And he then criticizes Kant's method for being regressive-constructive. It lacks an intuitive basis and is unable to provide us with a proper account of consciousness. In fact, as Husserl points out in the conclusion, phenomenology insists upon an in-depth investigation of consciousness, and this demand necessitates an *extension* of Kant's concept of the transcendental. It proves necessary to include the humanities and the manifold of human sociality and culture in the transcendental analysis (1956: 282). This remark is amplified a few years later when Husserl writes that the possibility of a transcendental elucidation of subjectivity and world is lost if one follows the Kantian tradition in interpreting transcendental subjectivity as an isolated ego and thereby ignores the problem of transcendental intersubjectivity (1993: 120). Thus it is no coincidence that Husserl at times describes his own project as a *sociological* transcendental philosophy (1962: 539) and even writes that the development of phenomenology necessarily implies the step from an " 'egological' ... phenomenology into a transcendental sociological phenomenology having reference to a manifest multiplicity of conscious subjects communicating with one another" (1981: 68). Ultimately, and this is something that only recently has been properly appreciated, Husserl's phenomenology must be seen as entailing an intersubjective transformation of transcendental philosophy (see Zahavi 2001 and 2005).

Already in *Ideen II* (*Ideas* II, posthumously published in 1952 as *Husserliana* IV) Husserl argued that I, we, and world belong together (1952: 288). From the start, Husserl stressed the constitutive relationship between subjectivity and world. But he eventually came to the realization that (1) the subject does not remain untouched by its constitutive performance, but is, on the contrary, drawn into it, just as (2) constitution is not simply a relation between a single subject and the world, but an intersubjective process. The problem he then faced was to clarify the precise relation between subjectivity, world, and other. This is most explicit in his last writings, where the three are seen as being increasingly intertwined. It does not matter which of the three one takes as a starting point, for one will still inevitably be led to the other two: the subjectivity that is related to the world only gains its full relation to itself, and to the world, in relation to the other, i.e. in intersubjectivity; intersubjectivity only exists and develops in the mutual relationship between subjects that are related to the world; and the world is only brought to articulation in the relation between subjects (see Husserl 1959: 505; 1973a: 480; 1973b: 373). This core insight is shared by later phenomenologists. Merleau-Ponty insists that a phenomenological description, rather than disclosing subjectivities that are inaccessible and self-sufficient, reveals continuity between intersubjective life and the world. The subject realizes itself in its presence to the world and to others – not in spite of, but precisely *by way of* its corporeality and historicity (Merleau-Ponty 1945: 515). The subject must be seen as a worldly incarnate existence, and the world as a common field of experience, if intersubjectivity is at all to be possible (Merleau-Ponty 1964: 322). As for Heidegger, he describes the life-world as an interpenetration of the three domains: "surrounding world" (*Umwelt*), "with-world" (*Mitwelt*), and "self-world" (*Selbstwelt*) (1993: 33, 39, 62), and argues that Dasein as world-experiencing is always already being-with. As he writes in the lecture course *Grundprobleme der Phänomenologie* from 1927,

> just as the Dasein is originally being with others, so it is originally being with the handy and the extant. Similarly, the Dasein is just as little at first merely a dwelling among things so as then occasionally to discover among these things beings with its own kind of being; instead, as the being which is occupied with itself, the Dasein is with equal originality being-with others *and* being-among intraworldly beings. (1989: 421)

Self, world, and others belong together; they reciprocally illuminate one another, and can only be understood in their interconnection. This idea is not unique to phenomenology. As Davidson wrote in his *Subjective, Intersubjective, Objective*:

> There are three basic problems: how a mind can know the world of nature, how it is possible for one mind to know another, and how it is possible to know the contents of our own minds without resort to observation or evidence. It is a mistake, I shall urge, to suppose that these questions can be collapsed into two, or taken in isolation. (2001: 208)

It is important to recognize that a transcendental philosophy that takes intersubjectivity seriously must also take embodiment and thereby facticity seriously. Intersubjectivity is a relation between embodied creatures. And our bodies are present in every project and in every perception. They are our *point de vue* and *point de départ* (Sartre 1976: 373–4; 1956: 326). There is no pure point of view and there is no view from nowhere, there is only an embodied (and contextually embedded) point of view.

As Sartre points out, an object cannot appear perspectival unless the perceiver is situated in the perceptual field as well:

> [T]he perceptive field refers to a center objectively defined by that reference and located *in the very field* which is oriented around it. Only we do not see this center as the structure of the perceptive field considered; *we are the center*.... Thus my being-in-the-world, by the sole fact that it *realizes* a world, causes itself to be indicated to itself as a being-in-the-midst-of-the-world by the world which it realizes. The case could not be otherwise, for my being has no other way of entering into contact with the world except to *be in the world*. It would be impossible for me to realize a world in which I was not and which would be for me a pure object of a surveying contemplation. But on the contrary it is necessary that I lose myself in the world in order for the world to exist and for me to be able to transcend it. Thus to say that I have entered into the world, "come to the world," or that there is a world, or that I have a body is one and the same thing. (1943: 365–6; 1956: 317–18)[15]

The phenomenological emphasis on the body obviously entails a rejection of Cartesian mind/body dualism. The notion of embodiment, the notion of an embodied mind or a minded body, is supposed to replace the ordinary notions of mind and body, both of which are considered to be derivations and abstractions. But it also entails a rejection of the Cartesian mind/world dualism. The body is not to be understood as a medium between me and the world. Rather, our primary being-in-the-world has the form of an embodied existence. Thus, we cannot first study the body, and next investigate it in its relation to the world. The world is given to us as bodily explored, and the body is revealed to us in its exploration of the world (Husserl 1971: 128; 1973b: 287). This is also why both Husserl and Merleau-Ponty emphasize the constitutive importance of sensuous affectivity and passivity. For both of them, a theory of intentionality must necessarily include a discussion of pre-predicative bodily and sensuous experience (thereby countering a certain type of linguistic constructivism). As Merleau-Ponty would say, language presupposes our pre-linguistic, perceptual contact with the world, and language retains a reference to pre-linguistic reality (1945: ix–x).

Husserl's and Merleau-Ponty's focus on embodiment eventually made them enter fields that had traditionally been reserved to psychopathology, sociology, anthropology, and ethnology; it made them consider the philosophical relevance of such issues as generativity, historicity, and normality. Whereas a traditional Kantian type of transcendental philosophy would have considered such empirical and mundane domains as without any transcendental relevance, owing to their interest in both intersubjectivity and embodiment, Husserl and Merleau-Ponty were forced to reconsider the traditional divide between the empirical and the transcendental (Zahavi 2001). Thus, already in his first major work, *La Structure de Comportement* (*The Structure of Behavior*) Merleau-Ponty discusses such diverse authors as Pavlov, Freud, Koffka, Piaget, Watson, and Wallon. The last sub-chapter of the book carries the heading "Is there not a truth in naturalism?"; it contains a criticism of Kantian transcendental philosophy, and on the very final page of the book, Merleau-Ponty calls for a redefinition of transcendental philosophy that makes it pay heed to the real world (1942: 241). Rather than making us choose between either an external scientific explanation or an internal phenomenological reflection, a choice which would rip asunder the living relation between consciousness and nature, Merleau-Ponty consequently asks us to reconsider the very opposition, and to search for a dimension that is beyond both objectivism and subjectivism. What is particularly significant, however, is that he didn't conceive of the relation between transcendental phenomenology and positive science as a question of how to apply already established phenomenological insights on empirical issues. It wasn't simply a question of how phenomenology might constrain positive science. On the contrary, Merleau-Ponty's idea is that phenomenology itself can be changed and modified through its dialogue with the empirical disciplines. In fact, it needs this confrontation if it is to develop in the right way. And Merleau-Ponty holds this view without thereby reducing phenomenology merely to yet another positive science, without thereby dismissing its transcendental philosophical nature.

In *Les Mots et les choses* (translated into English as *The Order of Things: An Archaeology of the Human Sciences*) Foucault argues that phenomenology exemplifies a type of modern discourse that in its investigation of experience seeks to separate as well as integrate the empirical and the transcendental. It is an investigation of experience that in the face of positivism has tried to restore the lost dimension of the transcendental, but which at the same time has made experience concrete enough to include both body and culture. To Foucault it is quite clear that this modern type of transcendental reflection differs from the Kantian type by taking its point of departure in the paradox of human existence rather than in the existence of natural science. Although Husserl had apparently succeeded in unifying the Cartesian theme of the *cogito* with the transcendental motif of Kant, the truth is that Husserl was only able to accomplish this union insofar as he changed the very nature of transcendental analysis. It is this transformation that in Foucault's view has resulted in phenomenology's simultaneously promising and threatening proximity to empirical analyses of man (Foucault 1966: 331–6).

I think Foucault's diagnosis is basically correct,[16] and I think it holds true not only in the case of Husserl, but also for many of the post-Husserlian phenomenologists. As Merleau-Ponty would write in *Signes* (*Signs*):

> Now if the transcendental is intersubjectivity, how can the borders of the transcendental and the empirical help becoming indistinct? For along with the other person, all the other person sees of me – all my facticity – is reintegrated into subjectivity, or at least posited as an indispensable element of its definition. Thus the transcendental descends into history. (1960: 134; 1964: 107)

The fact that transcendental phenomenology operates with an enlarged notion of the transcendental gives it an advantage in comparison with a more traditional Kantian type of transcendental philosophy. But of course it would also be fair to say that this enlargement and transformation generate new problems and challenges as well.

Phenomenology in the twenty-first century

Obviously, phenomenology did not come to an end with the passing of Merleau-Ponty and Heidegger. Much has happened since then, particularly in French phenomenology. Thinkers such as Paul Ricoeur, Michel Henry, Jacques Derrida, Emmanuel Lévinas, and Jean-Luc Marion have all questioned the adequacy of the classical phenomenological investigations of intentionality, time-consciousness, intersubjectivity, language, etc. In their attempt to radicalize phenomenology they have disclosed new types and structures of manifestation, and thereby made decisive contributions to the development of phenomenology.

Steven Crowell has argued that the future prospects of phenomenology will depend on the talent of those who take it up (2002: 442). However, it will also depend upon their ability to articulate and strengthen what is common to the phenomenological enterprise instead of getting involved in the sectarian trench warfare that has regrettably plagued the history of phenomenology.

In my view, phenomenology should adopt a two-pronged strategy. On the one hand, it needs to "look inward," and to continue developing the kind of philosophical analyses that are unique to this tradition. On the other hand, it also needs to "look outward"; it should not fail to realize that it shares topics and interests with other philosophical traditions.[17] Let me by way of conclusion say a few words about this second task.

Many scientists have until recently considered consciousness to be unsuitable for scientific research. As Damasio remarks, "studying consciousness was simply not the thing to do before you made tenure, and even after you did it was looked upon with suspicion" (1999: 7). Prompted by technological developments as well as conceptual changes, this attitude has changed since the early 1990s, and an explanation of consciousness is currently seen by many as one of the few remaining major unsolved problems of modern science. It has become customary to describe this change in terms of an ongoing "consciousness boom."[18]

Much empirical research aims at locating and identifying particular neural correlates of consciousness. But one should not forget that we will not get very far in giving an account of the relationship between consciousness and the brain if we do not have a clear conception of what it is that we are trying to relate. Any assessment of the possibility of reducing consciousness to more fundamental neuronal structures, any appraisal of whether a naturalization of consciousness is possible, will not only involve metaphysical and epistemological clarifications, it will also call for a detailed analysis and description of consciousness. To put it differently, although much current research focuses on questions concerned with the precise relation between brain and consciousness, questions of this kind by no means exhaust the challenges currently facing the study of consciousness. To mention just a few quite different urgent questions: What is the relation between intentionality and self-consciousness?; What is the temporal structure of the stream of consciousness?; What is it like to think abstract thoughts?; How does social interaction influence the structures of experience?; Is it possible to conceptualize experiential life?; What is the cognitive function of affective experiences?; Is self-experience always embedded and embodied?; What does it at all mean to be a subject, to be a self? But questions like these are not new. They have been analyzed extensively by phenomenologists.

To put it bluntly, given some of the developments in cognitive science and analytical philosophy of mind taking place at the turn of the twenty-first century, given the upsurge of theoretical and empirical interest in the subjective or phenomenal dimension of consciousness, given that an increasing number of analytical philosophers argue that an important and non-negligible feature of consciousness is the way in which it is experienced by the subject, it would simply be counterproductive to continue to ignore the analyses of consciousness that phenomenology can provide. The fact that subjectivity has always been of central concern for phenomenologists, and that they have devoted much time to a scrutiny of the first-person perspective, the structures of experience, time-consciousness, body-awareness, self-awareness, intentionality, and so forth, makes them into obvious interlocutors. Phenomenology addresses issues and provides analyses that are crucial for an understanding of the true complexity of consciousness – but which are nevertheless frequently absent from the current debate. It offers a conceptual framework for understanding subjectivity that might be of considerably more value than some of the models currently in vogue in cognitive science. By ignoring the tradition and the resources it contains, analytical philosophy of mind might miss out on important insights that in the best of circumstances end up being rediscovered decades or centuries later (see Zahavi 2002a). Conversely, were phenomenology to engage in discussions with cognitive science and analytical philosophy, it could make a major contribution to the burgeoning field of consciousness research. It would be a pity to miss such a unique opportunity. In fact, phenomenology needs to engage more in critical dialogue with other philosophical and empirical positions than is currently the case. It is precisely by confronting, discussing, and criticizing alternative approaches that phenomenology can demonstrate its vitality and contemporary relevance. Of course this is not to deny that phenomenology has its own quite legitimate agenda, but the very attempt to engage in such a dialogue with analytical philosophy of mind, developmental psychology, or psychopathology (to mention just a few possible partners) might force phenomenology to become more problem-oriented and thereby counteract what is currently one of its greatest weaknesses: its preoccupation with exegesis.

Although it is important to encourage the exchange between phenomenology and empirical science, the possibility of a fruitful cooperation between the two should not make us overlook their difference. To paraphrase Putnam, it is entirely possible to insist that philosophy needs to be informed by the best available scientific knowledge, while at the same time insisting that philosophical and scientific questions differ fundamentally (see Putnam 1992: 34). Husserl for his part would insist that although there might be a considerable overlap when it comes to the content of transcendental and empirical science – he even speaks of a parallelism between the two – their difference is precisely not a difference in content, but in attitude. Phenomenology and, say, psychology might both investigate consciousness, but they do so with quite different agendas in mind, and it would make just as little sense to identify the phenomenologists' transcendental analysis of consciousness with a psychological investigation as it would be to identify, say, the discussions of linguistic frameworks or conceptual schemes found in analytical philosophy with phonetic or syntaxical analyses. It is this fact that makes the recent interest in the study of consciousness a mixed blessing. With few exceptions this interest has gone hand in hand with a strong commitment to naturalism. Whereas classical analytical philosophy (of language) might have been less interested in consciousness, its basic conception of language as a framework of intelligibility could easily be given a transcendental philosophical twist. Rather than engaging in first-order claims about the nature of things (which it left to various scientific disciplines) it concerned itself with the conceptual preconditions for any such empirical inquiries. The situation is now more or less reversed by philosophers who subscribe to the slogan "reduce or eliminate," and who consider their own work to be directly continuous with the natural sciences. For phenomenology, however, it is important to retain both aspects: the interest in subjectivity and the transcendental perspective.

Let me anticipate a critical objection: Couldn't (and shouldn't) one simply discard the (outdated) transcendental philosophical aspect of phenomenological philosophy and simply preserve what is of lasting value, namely those concrete phenomenological analyses that remain pertinent for, e.g., social philosophy, philosophical anthropology, and philosophy of mind? The reply should at this stage be obvious. Were one to do so, one would also abandon the properly philosophical aspect of phenomenology. One might retain a form of psychological or sociological phenomenology, but one would no longer be dealing with phenomenology in the sense of a philosophical discipline, tradition, and method.[19]

Notes

1 Edmund Husserl studied physics, mathematics, astronomy, and philosophy in Leipzig, Berlin, and Vienna. He obtained his doctoral dissertation in mathematics in 1882, and in the following years he attended lectures by the psychologist and philosopher Franz Brentano in Vienna. His first major work, *Logische Untersuchungen* was published in 1900–1, and it was on the basis of this work, that Husserl received a call to Göttingen, where he taught from 1901 to 1916. His next major work, *Ideen zu einer reinen Phänomenologie und phänomenologischen Philosophie I* was published in 1913. In 1916, Husserl moved to Freiburg, where he took over the chair in philosophy from the neo-Kantian Heinrich Rickert. In the following years, both Edith Stein and Martin Heidegger worked as his assistants. When Husserl retired in 1928, he was succeeded by Heidegger. Shortly after his retirement, Husserl published *Formale und Transzendentale Logik* (1929) and *Méditations cartésiennes* (1931). After the Nazi assumption of power, Husserl became increasingly isolated from German academic life, but in 1935, he was invited to give lectures in Vienna and Prague, and these lectures constituted the foundation for his last work, *Die Krisis der europäischen Wissenschaften und die transzendentale Phänomenologie* (1936). Shortly after Husserl's death on April 27, 1938, the young Franciscan Van Breda succeeded in smuggling Husserl's many research manuscripts out of Germany and into safety in a monastery in Belgium. Before the start of the Second World War, the Husserl archives were already established in Leuven, where the original manuscripts are still to be found.

2 Heidegger started out studying Catholic theology and medieval philosophy in Freiburg, but decided to concentrate on philosophy in 1911. In 1913 he defended his dissertation *Die Lehre vom Urteil im Psychologismus*, and two years later his habilitation *Die Kategorien- und Bedeutungslehre des Duns Scotus*. The later work was submitted to Rickert, the philosopher whose successor was Husserl. Heidegger

worked as Husserl's assistant from 1918 until 1923, when he became extraordinary professor at the university in Marburg. In 1927 Heidegger's main opus *Sein and Zeit* was published, and in 1928 he took over Husserl's chair in Freiburg. In 1929, Heidegger gave his famous inaugural lecture *Was ist Metaphysik?* After the Nazi assumption of power, he was elected rector of Freiburg University, and became a member of the Nazi Party. Less than a year later, however, he stepped down from his rectorship and slowly withdrew from university politics. Until 1944 Heidegger gave regular lectures, but after the end of the war he was prohibited from teaching because of his Nazi sympathies, and in 1946 he was deprived of his professorship. Heidegger was reinstated as professor emeritus in 1949, and from then until shortly before his death he lectured extensively, and it was in this context that central pieces such as *Die Kehre* (1949), *Die Frage nach der Technik* (1953), and *Die onto-theo-logische Verfassung der Metaphysik* (1957) were written.

3 Merleau-Ponty studied philosophy at the prestigious École Normale Supérieure. He published his first book, *La Structure du comportement* in 1942, and what is arguably his main work *Phénoménologie de la perception* in 1945. In 1949 he obtained the chair of child psychology at the Sorbonne, and in 1952 he was elected to the chair of philosophy at the Collège de France, the youngest ever appointed to the position, which he held until his death in May 1961. After the Second World War, Merleau-Ponty became increasingly engaged in politics, and he published a number of books with political essays, including *Humanisme et terreur* (1947), *Sens et non-sens* (1948), and *Les Aventures de la dialectique* (1955). In parallel with his political interest, Merleau-Ponty continued teaching, and many of his lectures from Sorbonne and Collège de France bear witness to his extensive interest in empirical work, including in child psychology, structural linguistics, ethnology, and psychoanalysis. In 1960 *Signes*, another volume consisting of essays, was published, and in 1964 the fragmentary *Le Visible et l'invisible*, which many consider to be Merleau-Ponty's second main work, was published posthumously.

4 The complexity in question also makes it close to impossible to reconcile all of his claims into one coherent theory; for one thing, although it would be an exaggeration to speak of veritable ruptures between his early and later works, there are certainly developments and differences to be reckoned with. For a concise introduction to Husserl's phenomenology that takes recent research results into consideration, see Zahavi 2003b.

5 My reason for including only some passing references to an otherwise central figure like Sartre in the following is due to the fact that I don't think Sartre's most important and influential phenomenological contributions are to be found in his more overarching meta-philosophical and methodological reflections on the status of phenomenology. Rather, Sartre's decisive contributions are to be found in his many concrete analyses, be it of imagination, embodiment, selfhood, self-awareness, intersubjectivity, intentionality, etc.

6 See E. Husserl, *Analyses Concerning Passive and Active Synthesis: Lectures on Transcendental Logic*, trans. A. J. Steinbock, Husserl Collected Works vol. IX (Dordrecht: Kluwer, 2001). For an in-depth discussion of this aspect of Husserl's philosophy, see for instance Montavont 1999.

7 This is one of the many reasons why it is problematic simply to classify Husserl as a traditional internalist (see Zahavi 2004).

8 Let me anticipate a critical objection. Doesn't Husserl make frequent use of the terms "immanence" and "transcendence," terms used to designate consciousness and worldly objects respectively? Doesn't the repeated use of these concepts show the unmistakably Cartesian tenor of Husserl's thinking? Doesn't it reveal to what extent Husserl's theory of intentionality, his conception of the mind/world relation, remains committed to a form of representationalism, where any experience and cognition of the external world requires the presence of some inner representation in the mind? Doesn't the use of the terms unequivocally demonstrate how far removed Husserl ultimately is from Merleau-Ponty and Heidegger's understanding of our being-in-the-world? In fact, the answer to all of these questions is no. Throughout his philosophical career Husserl is unequivocal in his rejection of representationalism. He considers the suggestion that my access to external objects is mediated by representations internal to my mind to be not only false, but completely nonsensical (see Husserl 1950a: 118; 1976: 207–8; 1979: 305; 1984b: 436–7; 2003: 106). Moreover, Husserl's use of the concepts of immanence and transcendence (unfortunate as it might be, given the kind of misunderstandings it has occasioned) is meant to capture a certain phenomenological difference in the mode of givenness pertaining to consciousness and worldly entities respectively (Husserl 1976: 88). To put it even more simply,

according to Husserl, experiences are not given in the same manner as chairs and symphonies, nor are we aware of our own experiences in the same way we are aware of worldly objects. Thus the distinction between immanence and transcendence is one internal to the phenomenological realm and is not meant to demarcate what belongs to phenomenology from what does not. For a classical exposé of Husserl's use of the concepts transcendence and immanence, see Boehm 1968: 141–85. For a discussion of similarities between the Husserlian overcoming of the inner/outer dichotomy and central ideas in Buddhist philosophy, see Fasching 2003.

9 In the lecture course "Prolegomena zur Geschichte des Zeitbegriffs" Heidegger explicitly rejects Husserl's phenomenological reduction (Heidegger 1979: 150), but the interpretation he there offers of it is quite problematic. For more extensive reflections on Heidegger's use of *epoché* and reduction, see Tugendhat 1970: 262–80; Courtine 1990: 207–47; Caputo 1992; Marion 1998; Crowell 2001: 182–202; Overgaard 2004.

10 Whereas Husserl at different stages of his thinking was influenced in turn by Brentano, Lotze, Bolzano, Hume, Locke, Descartes, Kant, Leibniz, and Fichte, Heidegger's sources of inspiration include, for instance, Aristotle, Luther, Kierkegaard, Nietzsche, and the pre-Socratics.

11 This is not to deny that Heidegger occasionally presented his own work as constituting a radical break with Husserl's phenomenology, but then again, Heidegger was always anxious to emphasize his own originality *vis-à-vis* the old teacher (see Zahavi 2003a). To put it differently, if one wishes to understand the relation between Heidegger and Husserl, Heidegger's own account might not be the most reliable source. At the same time, however, it should certainly also be conceded that Husserl failed to understand the basic thrust of Heidegger's (early) work, failed to realize to what extent this work remained committed to a form of transcendental phenomenology. Husserl's characterization of *Sein und Zeit* as a piece of anthropology is a case in point (cf. Breeur 1994).

12 I have elsewhere questioned the adequacy of the criticism; see Zahavi 1999: 2003c.

13 It should be emphasized that to be non-metaphysical is not the same as to be anti-metaphysical.

14 For more on the relationship between phenomenology and metaphysics, cf. Zahavi 2002c; 2003d.

15 For an illuminating discussion of Sartre's analysis of the body see Cabestan 1996.

16 However, I would not concur with Foucault's subsequent criticism of phenomenology.

17 Recently, the habitual stance of analytical philosophy towards phenomenology, which has ranged from complete disregard to outright hostility, also seems to be slowly changing. This may be because prominent philosophers from the analytical tradition have started to rediscover the common roots of both traditions (see Dummett 1996) – Husserl and Frege were both anti-psychologists – or because analytical philosophy since the mid-1990s has regained an interest in some of the topics that for many years have remained on the phenomenological agenda.

18 For further discussion of the concept of consciousness, see "Philosophy of mind," Chapter 12.

19 This study has been funded by the Danish National Research Foundation.

References

Benoist, J. (1997) *Phénoménologie, sémantique, ontologie*. Paris: PUF.

Blackburn, S. (1994) *The Oxford Dictionary of Philosophy*. Oxford: Oxford University Press.

Boehm, R. (1968) *Vom Gesichtspunkt der Phänomenologie*. The Hague: Nijhoff.

Breeur, R. (1994) "Randbemerkungen Husserls zu Heideggers *Sein und Zeit* und *Kant und das Problem der Metaphysik*." *Husserl Studies* 11/1–2: 3–63.

Brentano, F. (1995) *Psychology from an Empirical Standpoint*, trans. A. C. Rancurello, D. B. Terrell, and L. L. McAlister, 2nd edn. with new introduction by P. Simons. London: Routledge.

Cabestan, P. (1996) "La constitution du corps selon l'ordre de ses apparitions." *EPOKHE* 6: 279–98.

Caputo, J. D. (1992) "The question of being and transcendental phenomenology: reflections on Heidegger's relationship to Husserl." In C. Macann (ed.) *Martin Heidegger: Critical Assessments I*, London: Routledge, pp. 326–44.

Courtine, J.-F. (1990) *Heidegger et la phénoménologie*. Paris: Vrin.

Crowell, S. G. (2001) *Husserl, Heidegger, and the Space of Meaning*. Evanston, IL: Northwestern University Press.

_____ (2002) "Is there a phenomenological research program?" *Synthèse* 131/3: 419–44.

Damasio, A. (1999) *The Feeling of What Happens*. San Diego, CA: Harcourt.

Davidson, D. (2001) *Subjective, Intersubjective, Objective*. Oxford: Oxford University Press.

Dillon, M. C. (1997) *Merleau-Ponty's Ontology*. Evanston, IL: Northwestern University Press.

Dreyfus, H. L. (1991) *Being-in-the-World*. Cambridge, MA: MIT Press.

Dreyfus, H. L. and P. Rabinow (1983) *Michel Foucault: Beyond Structuralism and Hermeneutics*. Chicago: Chicago University Press.

Dummett, M. (1996) *Origins of Analytical Philosophy*. Cambridge, MA: Harvard University Press.

Fasching, W. (2003) *Phänomenologische Reduktion und Mushin: Edmund Husserls Bewusstseinstheorie und der Zen-Buddhismus*. Munich: Karl Alber.

Fink, E. (1939) "Das Problem der Phänomenologie Edmund Husserls." *Revue Internationale de Philosophie* 1: 226–70.

Foucault, M. (1966) *Les Mots et les choses*. Paris: Gallimard. Translated as *The Order of Things*, New York: Vintage, 1973.

Gurwitsch, A. (1966) *Studies in Phenomenology and Psychology*. Evanston, IL: Northwestern University Press.

Heidegger, M. (1979) *Prolegomena zur Geschichte des Zeitbegriffs*. Gesamtausgabe Band 20. Frankfurt am Main: Vittorio Klostermann.

_____ (1986) *Sein und Zeit*. Tübingen: Max Niemeyer.

_____ (1989) *Grundprobleme der Phänomenologie*. Gesamtausgabe Band 24. Frankfurt am Main: Vittorio Klostermann. First published 1982.

_____ (1991) *Kant und das Problem der Metaphysik*. Frankfurt am Main: Vittorio Klostermann.

_____ (1993) *Grundprobleme der Phänomenologie (1919/1920)*. Gesamtausgabe Band 58. Frankfurt am Main: Vittorio Klostermann.

_____ (1996) *Einleitung in die Philosophie*. Gesamtausgabe Band 27. Frankfurt am Main: Vittorio Klostermann.

Husserl, E. (1950a) *Cartesianische Meditationen und Pariser Vorträge*. Husserliana I. The Hague: Nijhoff.

_____ (1950b) *Die Idee der Phänomenologie. Fünf Vorlesungen*. Husserliana II. The Hague: Nijhoff.

_____ (1952) *Ideen zu einer reinen Phänomenologie und phänomenologischen Philosophie II*. Husserliana IV. The Hague: Nijhoff.

_____ (1954) *Die Krisis der europäischen Wissenschaften und die transzendentale Phänomenologie. Eine Einleitung in die phänomenologische Philosophie*. Husserliana VI. The Hague: Nijhoff.

_____ (1956) *Erste Philosophie (1923/24). Erster Teil. Kritische Ideengeschichte*. Husserliana VII. The Hague: Nijhoff.

_____ (1959) *Erste Philosophie (1923/24). Zweiter Teil. Theorie der phänomenologischen Reduktion*. Husserliana VIII. The Hague: Nijhoff.

_____ (1962) *Phänomenologische Psychologie*. Husserliana IX. The Hague: Nijhoff.

_____ (1966) *Analysen zur passiven Synthesis. Aus Vorlesungs- und Forschungsmanuskripten 1918–1926*. Husserliana XI. The Hague: Nijhoff.

_____ (1971) *Ideen zu einer reinen Phänomenologie und phänomenologischen Philosophie. Drittes Buch: Die Phänomenologie und die Fundamente der Wissenschaften*. Husserliana V. The Hague: Nijhoff.

_____ (1973a) *Zur Phänomenologie der Intersubjektivität I*. Husserliana XIII. The Hague: Nijhoff.

_____ (1973b) *Zur Phänomenologie der Intersubjektivität III*. Husserliana XV. The Hague: Nijhoff.

_____ (1976) *Ideen zu einer reinen Phänomenologie und phänomenologischen Philosophie I*. Husserliana III/1–2. The Hague: Nijhoff.

_____ (1979) *Aufsätze und Rezensionen (1890–1910)*. Husserliana XXII. The Hague: Nijhoff.

_____ (1981) *Shorter Works*, ed. P. McCormick and F. A. Elliston. Notre Dame, IN: University of Notre Dame Press.

_____ (1984a) *Einleitung in die Logik und Erkenntnistheorie*. Husserliana XXIV. The Hague: Nijhoff.

_____ (1984b) *Logische Untersuchungen II*. Husserliana XIX/1–2. The Hague: Nijhoff.

_____ (1987) *Aufsätze und Vorträge (1911–1921)*. Husserliana XXV. Dordrecht: Nijhoff.

_____ (1989) *Aufsätze und Vorträge (1922–1937)*. Husserliana XXVII. Dordrecht: Kluwer.

_____ (1993) *Die Krisis der europäischen Wissenschaften und die transzendentale Phänomenologie. Ergänzungsband. Texte aus dem Nachlass 1934–1937*. Husserliana XXIX. Dordrecht: Kluwer.

_____ (2003) *Transzendentaler Idealismus. Texte aus dem Nachlass (1908–1921)*. Dordrecht: Kluwer.

Madison, G. B. (1981) *The Phenomenology of Merleau-Ponty*. Athens: Ohio University Press.

Marion, J.-L. (1998) *Reduction and Givenness*. Evanston, IL: Northwestern University Press.

Merleau-Ponty, M. (1942) *La Structure du comportement*. Paris: PUF.

_____ (1945) *Phénoménologie de la perception*. Paris: Gallimard.

_____ (1960) *Signes*. Paris: Éditions Gallimard.

_____ (1964) *Le Visible et l'invisible*. Paris: Tel Gallimard.

Montavont, A. (1999) *De la passivité dans la phénoménologie de Husserl*. Paris: PUF.

Overgaard, S. (2004) *Husserl and Heidegger on Being in the World*. Dordrecht: Kluwer.

Putnam, H. (1987) *The Many Faces of Realism*. LaSalle, IL: Open Court.

_____ (1992) *Renewing Philosophy*. Cambridge, MA: Harvard University Press.

Ricoeur, P. (1987) *A l'école de la phénoménologie*. Paris: Vrin.

Sartre, J.-P. (1943) *L'Être et le néant*. Paris: Tel Gallimard. Repr. 1976.

_____ (1956) *Being and Nothingness*, trans. H. E. Barnes. New York: Philosophical Library.

Smith, D. W. and R. McIntyre (1982) *Husserl and Intentionality*. Dordrecht: Reidel.

Tugendhat, E. (1970) *Der Wahrheitsbegriff bei Husserl und Heidegger*. Berlin: de Gruyter.

Zahavi, D. (1999) *Self-awareness and Alterity: A Phenomenological Investigation*. Evanston, IL: Northwestern University Press.

_____ (2001) *Husserl and Transcendental Intersubjectivity*. Athens: Ohio University Press.

_____ (2002a) "First-person thoughts and embodied self-awareness: some reflections on the relation between recent analytical philosophy and phenomenology." *Phenomenology and the Cognitive Sciences* 1: 7–26.

_____ (2002b) "Merleau-Ponty on Husserl: a reappraisal." In T. Toadvine and L. Embree (eds.) *Merleau-Ponty's Reading of Husserl*, Dordrecht: Kluwer, pp. 3–29.

_____ (2002c) "Metaphysical neutrality in logical investigations." In D. Zahavi and F. Stjernfelt (eds.) *One Hundred Years of Phenomenology: Husserl's Logical Investigations Revisited*. Dordrecht: Kluwer, pp. 93–108.

_____ (2003a) "How to investigate subjectivity: Natorp and Heidegger on reflection." *Continental Philosophy Review* 36/2: 155–76.

_____ (2003b) *Husserl's Phenomenology*. Stanford, CA: Stanford University Press.

_____ (2003c) "Inner time-consciousness and pre-reflective self-awareness." In D. Welton (ed.) *The New Husserl: A Critical Reader*, Bloomington: Indiana University Press, pp. 157–80.

_____ (2003d) "Phenomenology and metaphysics." In D. Zahavi, S. Heinämaa, and H. Ruin (eds.) *Metaphysics, Facticity, Interpretation*, Dordrecht: Kluwer, pp. 3–22.

_____ (2004) "Husserl's noema and the internalism–externalism debate." *Inquiry* 47/1: 42–66.

_____ (2005) "Husserl's intersubjective transformation of transcendental philosophy." In R. Bernet, D. Welton, and G. Zavota (eds.) *Edmund Husserl: Critical Assessments of Leading Philosophers IV*. London: Routledge, pp. 359–380.

Further reading and translations of cited works

General introductions to phenomenology

Hammond, M., J. Howarth, and R. Keat, *Understanding Phenomenology*. Oxford: Blackwell, 1991. (A good introduction that is especially helpful for those coming from an analytic perspective).

Moran, D., *Introduction to Phenomenology*. London: Routledge, 2000. (A comprehensive introduction to the different figures in the phenomenological tradition).

Sokolowski, R., *Introduction to Phenomenology*. Cambridge: Cambridge University Press, 2000. (A thematic introduction to a number of phenomenological (mainly Husserlian) concepts).

Works by Husserl

Analyses Concerning Passive and Active Synthesis: Lectures on Transcendental Logic, trans. A. J. Steinbock. Husserl Collected Works, vol. IX. Dordrecht: Kluwer, 2001.

Cartesian Meditations, trans. D. Cairns. The Hague: Nijhoff, 1967.

Experience and Judgement: Investigations in a Genealogy of Logic, rev. and ed. L. Landgrebe, trans. J. S. Churchill and K. Ameriks. Evanston, IL: Northwestern University Press, 1973.

Formal and Transcendental Logic, trans. D. Cairns. The Hague: Nijhoff, 1969.

Ideas Pertaining to a Pure Phenomenology and to a Phenomenological Philosophy I, trans. F. Kersten. Dordrecht: Kluwer, 1983.

Ideas pertaining to a Pure Phenomenology and to a Phenomenological Philosophy II, trans. R. Rojcewicz and A. Schuwer. Dordrecht: Kluwer, 1989.

"Kant and the idea of transcendental philosophy," trans. T. E. Klein and W. E. Pohl. *Southwestern Journal of Philosophy* 5 (fall 1974): 9–56.

Logical Investigations, 2 vols., trans. J. N. Findlay, ed. with a new introduction by D. Moran and new preface by M. Dummett. London and New York: Routledge, 2001.

Phenomenological Psychology: Lectures, Summer Semester, 1925, trans. J. Scanlon. The Hague: Nijhoff, 1977.

The Crisis of European Sciences and Transcendental Phenomenology, trans. D. Carr. Evanston, IL: Northwestern University Press, 1970.

The Idea of Phenomenology, trans. L. Hardy. Dordrecht: Kluwer, 1999.

Works on Husserl

Bernet, R., I. Kern, and E. Marbach, *An Introduction to Husserlian Phenomenology*. Evanston, IL: Northwestern University Press, 1993. (A comprehensive and technical introduction by three leading experts).

Moran, D., *Edmund Husserl: Founder of Phenomenology*. Cambridge: Polity, 2005. (Readable introduction to Husserl that discusses his early descriptive phenomenology as well as his later commitment to transcendental idealism).

Sokolowski, R., *Husserlian Meditations*. Evanston, IL: Northwestern University Press, 1974. (A classical analysis of a number of central themes in Husserl's phenomenology).

Welton, D. (ed.) *The New Husserl: A Critical Reader*. Bloomington: Indiana University Press, 2003. (An excellent collection of articles by major interpreters of Husserl).

Zahavi, D., *Husserl's Phenomenology*. Stanford, CA: Stanford University Press, 2003. (A very accessible and up-to-date introduction).

Works by Heidegger

Being and Time, trans. J. Macquarrie and J. Robinson. Oxford: Blackwell, 1978.

Being and Time, trans. J. Stambaugh. Albany: State University of New York Press, 1996 (includes the pagination of the 1986 German edn.).

History of the Concept of Time: Prolegomena, trans. T. Kisiel. Bloomington: Indiana University Press, 1985 (includes the pagination of the 1979 German edn.).

Kant and the Problem of Metaphysics, trans. J. S. Churchill. Bloomington: Indiana University Press, 1962.

The Basic Problems of Phenomenology, trans. A. Hofstadter. Bloomington: Indiana University Press, 1982 (includes the pagination of the 1989 German edn.).

Works on Heidegger

Crowell, S. G., *Husserl, Heidegger, and the Space of Meaning*. Evanston, IL: Northwestern University Press, 2001. (A good discussion of the relation between Husserl and Heidegger).

Dreyfus, H., *Being in the World: Commentary on Heidegger's "Being and Time": Division 1*. Cambridge, MA: MIT Press, 1991. (A clear and helpful commentary).

Kisiel, T., *The Genesis of Heidegger's "Being and Time."* Berkeley: University of California Press, 1993. (A scholarly masterpiece).

Steiner, G., *Martin Heidegger*. Chicago: University of Chicago Press, 1991. (A very readable introduction).

Works by Merleau-Ponty

Phenomenology of Perception, trans. C. Smith. London: Routledge, 1962.

Signs, trans. R. McCleary. Evanston, IL: Northwestern University Press, 1964.

The Structure of Behavior, trans. A. L. Fisher. Boston: Beacon Press, 1963.

The Visible and the Invisible, trans. A. Lingis. Evanston, IL: Northwestern University Press, 1968.

Works on Merleau-Ponty

Madison, G. B., *Merleau-Ponty's Phenomenology*. Athens: Ohio University Press, 1981. (A well-organized and clearly written general introduction).

Dillon, M. C., *Merleau-Ponty's Ontology*. Evanston, IL: Northwestern University Press, 1997. (A thorough and perceptive examination of Merleau-Ponty's philosophy).

16
TWENTIETH-CENTURY HERMENEUTICS

Nicholas Davey

Nothing is perfectly clear, everything demands the work of interpretation.

Frank (1974: 141)

The twentieth-century transformation of hermeneutics

Contemporary hermeneutics has been characterized as "a preparing for the other" (Caputo 2000: 8). Given the mercurial aspirations of hermeneutics as the messenger of understanding and the catastrophic political understandings of the last century, such a description of hermeneutics offers some pause for thought. The often deliberate "misunderstandings" between ideologies might speak in favor of Nietzsche's will to power and question the adequacy of the hermeneutic endeavor. However, it might be just as forcefully argued that the political disasters of the twentieth century only serve to show how great the need is for understanding. Achieving "understanding" between human communities remains as pressing a task as it ever was. Hermeneutic philosophy is accordingly not a mere academic exercise. Its dialogical *modus operandi* and its philosophical disposition towards openness enable hermeneutic practice not merely to prepare for the other but to allow the other to be other. The hermeneutic pursuit of "understanding" has a practical urgency about it which is often absent from other areas of philosophical operation. This chapter will emphasize the "practical" nature of hermeneutics and, furthermore, since it will be impossible to discuss and do justice to all aspects of recent hermeneutics, we shall offer an in-depth discussion of the German roots and development of this key philosophical discipline.

Hermeneutics underwent a fundamental transformation during the nineteenth century. Prior to the 1800s, the discipline was broadly speaking accorded the philological task of clarifying and authenticating obscure texts as a prelude to any philosophical analysis of their content. Hermeneutics tended to be regarded either as a philological *aide de philosophie* or as a prelude to theology. Friedrich Schleiermacher (1768–1834) was amongst the first to question this.

> Treatments [of hermeneutics] generally, originate with people who had an ulterior purpose. Theologians and Jurists. For the latter the main thing is the logical interpretation which goes beyond the real content of the utterance. (Schleiermacher 1998: 229)

Schleiermacher further grasped that the object of understanding was neither independent of nor unaffected by our means of understanding it. To grasp the content of an expression, it was necessary to understand its grammatical form, but an appreciation of its grammatical form would in its turn change one's grasp of the individual content. Understanding was thus in constant movement. Schleiermacher was amongst the first to recognize that understanding could never be complete. His was a hermeneutics of participatory engagement and not methodological exegesis.

Because of the further interventions of Friedrich Nietzsche (1844–1900) and Wilhelm Dilthey (1833–1911) initially and, then, of Martin Heidegger (1889–1976) and Hans-Georg Gadamer (1900–2002), hermeneutics has continued to lose its reputation as a mere midwife to philosophy and has become an autonomous mode of philosophical reflection itself. The difficulties, challenges, and limitations of interpretation have become emblematic of how philosophy conceives of itself. The turn to language in twentieth-century thought has meant that philosophy has become increasingly hermeneutic. Inquiry into how philosophy undertakes the interpretation of moral and aesthetic issues is, after all, an attempt on philosophy's part to understand itself and its place in the world. We offer the following provisional description of hermeneutics as a mode of philosophical reflection.

Hermeneutics as a mode of philosophical reflection accepts that misunderstanding, that cultural and historical difference, is the starting point of hermeneutic engagement. The task of hermeneutics is not to remove such differences but to articulate them and to uncover what is at stake in another's perspective. Only on the basis of discovering the differences at issue between the outlooks which govern a text or an artwork and those which govern our attitudes to such works can the labor of dialogical negotiation begin. Gadamer and Ricoeur regard difference and historical distance as the drivers of understanding more of a text and of the presuppositions which can aid or distort our grasp of it rather than as obstacles to such engagement. Hermeneutic philosophy is deeply historicist in nature. It nurtures a healthy skepticism towards any "definitive" reading of a text. All texts and all readings of them are historically circumstantial by nature. Not only is a text a product of its own historical world but how that world appears to us will alter according to the historical circumstances from which we approach it. All understanding is thus provisional and incomplete. Despite such skepticism, hermeneutic philosophy betrays an optimistic intellectual disposition. The fact that no definitive readings are possible opens the reader to the possibility of ever new readings and learning. Hermeneutic philosophy is marked by the mercurial character and nature of its divine agent Hermes. Like him, it is always on the move, sliding deftly between the twilight gloom of ignorance and the ever-approaching dawn of better insight.

The variety of twentieth-century hermeneutics is extensive (see Ormiston and Schrift 1990a; 1990b and Mueller-Vollmer 1986). As Heidegger appreciated, hermeneutics faced two challenges at the beginning of the century. First: Nietzsche's philosophy of flux deconstructed epistemology as interpretation. Its culminating claim "Alles ist Interpretation" ("Everything is interpretation") suggested that no definitive reading of a text could be arrived at and that which was eventually preferred, was so only because it energized and enhanced the reader's sense of being alive (will to power). Dilthey clearly recognized the threat his own methodological aspirations were under from Nietzsche's perspectivism. In his essay "Present-day culture and philosophy," Nietzsche's subjectivism is charged with robbing what is valid and lasting in philosophy. Perspectivism amounts to the inescapable prison of the "I" (Dilthey 1976: 116–18). Second: Dilthey's expansive hermeneutics celebrated the diversity of mankind and the variety of its historical experience. The self-understanding of the human community was to be enriched by internalizing the diverse life of each individual. Yet because Dilthey articulated the knowing subject in a neo-Kantian fashion, the insurmountable problem arose of whether the interpreting subject confronted a genuine other or merely its own representation of the other. This chapter will focus for the most part on Heidegger's and Gadamer's response to the challenges posed by Nietzsche and Dilthey (see Davey 2002). It will do so for two reasons. First, the responses of Heidegger and Gadamer to the challenges set by Nietzsche and Dilthey alter how hermeneutics is conceived (see Hahn 1993: 5–7). Second, their reworking of the ontological basis of hermeneutics re-positions our understanding of philosophy. The detractors of ontological hermeneutics, Foucault and Derrida, do not achieve a fundamental re-working of either philosophy or hermeneutics. (For further discussion of Foucault and Derrida, see "French philosophy in the twentieth century," Chapter 19.) Their particular genius is to reveal and to extend the challenging critical implications of Nietzsche's *Interpretationsphilosophie* (philosophy of interpretation) (see Derrida 1979 and Foucault 1985). Nevertheless, as will become apparent, recent studies of interpretation place considerable pressure on the status of the *concept* of understanding within hermeneutics.

Focusing on Heidegger's and Gadamer's response to both Dilthey and Nietzsche is not merely to be persuaded by a dialogical account of philosophy's history but it is also to be convinced of how exchanges between particular thinkers afford intense glimpses into the operation of ideas beyond individuals. The life of ideas resides, according to an Italian proverb, in "tradition, translation and treason." However, it would be churlish not to acknowledge the virtues of other historical approaches to twentieth-century hermeneutics.

In his *The Conflict of Interpretations*, Paul Ricoeur (1913–2005) utilizes the notion of a "hermeneutics of suspicion" in order to distinguish those schools of interpretation which seek meaning in intentional consciousness, i.e. Dilthey and Husserl, from those who view the representations of consciousness as the epiphenomenal product of subconscious forces such as Marx, Nietzsche, and Freud (Ricoeur 1974). As a methodological operation, the hermeneutics of suspicion has expanded. It now includes Foucault's post-structuralist analysis of cultural meaning as a site in which competing fields of power configure and confront one another and Derrida's linguistic deconstruction, which radicalizes Saussure's structuralist account of meaning in order to dissolve the latter of any canonical or authorial status (Derrida 1978 and 1997). The inclusion of Foucault and Derrida within the hermeneutics of suspicion undoes what earlier "hermeneuticians" within Ricoeur's category were attempting. Nietzsche indeed proclaimed "Alles ist Interpretation." Late twentieth-century hermeneutics of suspicion indeed affirms interpretation as the only "fact," i.e. the irreducible manifestation of a "meaningless" play of signifiers. However, the consequence of this is that the idea of a "deep" or "hidden truth" to be discovered by interpretation (as, for example, defended by Habermas), must be dismissed as "myth" (see Norris 1985 and Teichman and White 1995).

The inclusion of post-structuralist thinkers within the hermeneutics of suspicion opens a rift in the grouping. The works of Jürgen Habermas (1929–) are, for example, consistent with Ricoeur's use of "suspicion" but radically opposed to the arguments of Derrida and Foucault (Habermas 1978; 1987). Like Nietzsche and Marx, Habermas questions the veracity of consciousness's presentation of its subject matter on the grounds that subconscious neurosis can always distort whatever an artist claims the meaning of her work to be. Habermas's thinking is clearly influenced by Critical Theory (see "Critical Theory," Chapter 18). A projected "emancipatory truth" serves as a critical device to expose the narrowness and limitations of a particular idiom of thought. For Habermas all readings of a text strive towards an ideal consensus over how its truth content can be best articulated. The anticipation of an ideal truth-content becomes the gauge against which to measure the limitations and distortions of more ideological readings of such a text. Habermas says that if "the understanding of meaning [in tradition] is not to remain ... indifferent towards the idea of truth then we have to anticipate ... the concept of a kind of truth which measures itself on an idealised consensus achieved in unlimited communication free from force" (1980: 206). Wolfhart Pannenberg (1928–), a theological hermeneutician of the same generation as Habermas, suggests a similar argument. All traditions of understanding are temporally conditioned. It is only when the question of the "truth" of the tradition arises that a critique of its temporally conditioned elements becomes possible. He argues,

> the hermeneutical process as process of productive appropriation is possible only because the elements of tradition, both in their content and in the process of their transmission, stand in relation to a truth which lies ahead of them and which in its own shape is still open, and which because of this can be made to refute its own "temporally conditioned" shape by the freedom of the interpreter. (Pannenberg 1976: 198)

The hermeneutics of suspicion remained for Habermas the basis of a more therapeutic "depth hermeneutics" in which an individual subject renegotiated the influences which distorted his or her understanding of a given theme on the basis of an appeal to an anticipated truth. However, it is precisely the ability of depth hermeneutics either to drill to a core meaning or to anticipate a more complete meaning where interpretation is fulfilled, that the post-structuralist hermeneuticians of suspicion deny. As Foucault reputedly remarked, "we are interpretation all the way down."

The institutionalization of the hermeneutics of suspicion as a distinct school prompted defenders of Dilthey, Heidegger, and Gadamer to appeal to a "hermeneutics of tradition," a diverse grouping which includes Hans Kimmerle (1978), Peter Szondi (1995), Manfred Franck (1977; 1979), Karl-Otto Apel (1967; 1980) and Wolfgang Iser (1978; 2000). This is in certain ways a regrettable schematization which obscures the individuating detail of each position. The hermeneutics of tradition has little to do with an apologetics for conservatism as is so often assumed. For the most part, these authors insist that the canon is constantly shifting: tradition is inseparable from transmission. Tradition does not constitute the stability and identity of the subject matters transmitted but is the ongoing process of cultural transmission itself. Critique, questioning the scope of an interpretation, exposing its assumptions, challenging its universality, drives transmission. Gadamer insists that it is not a body of texts which constitute an intellectual tradition, but a central core of *questions*.

Although broadly useful, set historical schemas of interpretation can be rather shortsighted and simplistic. The device of dividing thinkers who fall within the hermeneutics of suspicion from those who support the hermeneutics of tradition (Ormiston and Schrift 1990a; 1990b) tends to overlook the hermeneutic significance of the works of Ludwig Wittgenstein (1958; 1967), Peter Winch (1958), Mikhail Bakhtin (1990), Michael Oakeshott (1987; 1991), Alasdair MacIntyre (1988; 1993), and Donald Davidson (1984). On one level, such insensitivity is inexcusable. Wittgenstein's conception of "understanding," not as a mental act but as a knowing-how-to-behave within the circumstances of a given *Lebensform*, both anticipates the participatory epistemology central to Iser's notion of interpretation and forms the basis of the social hermeneutics of Peter Winch and Hans Peter Duerr (Duerr 1985). Wittgenstein's participatory notion of understanding offers an obvious solution to the subjectivism which compromised Dilthey's hermeneutic. Charles Taylor's concern with understanding the other takes the problems of mutual participation as its starting point (see Malpas 2002: 279). Wittgenstein's notion also stimulated the development of accounts of language as a social practice which in their turn influenced the growth of philosophies of practice in the works of Oakeshott and MacIntyre (see "Twentieth-century political philosophy," Chapter 21). The parallels between these two thinkers and Hans-Georg Gadamer are easy to see. All three are rooted in the classics, especially in the works of Aristotle. The substantive link shared with Wittgenstein is a conviction characteristic of much twentieth-century philosophy that the days of "grand theory"are past. Whatever understanding is, we can only grasp it as an activity rooted in local communicative practices and their assumptions. Twentieth-century hermeneutics embodies the language-turn in philosophy. It bears witness to a consequence of that shift, namely, the turn in philosophy and hermeneutics from theory to practice (see Schatzki et al. 2001). Whereas Dilthey's hermeneutics sought an appropriate method to understand individuality, more recent aesthetic turns in hermeneutics demand that the singularity of a work take precedence over any theoretical analysis of it (see Clark 2005).

If the history of twentieth-century hermeneutics were written in terms of structural shifts instead of the customary groupings of "Continental" (Franco-German) and "analytic" philosophers, the works of Mikhail Bakhtin (1895–1975) would have to be given a place. Bakhtin's arguments that utterance is never originary, that within language there is a simultaneity of the said and the unsaid, and that self-understanding is a matter of ongoing dialogical exchange, all bear comparison with positions in Gadamer and Iser. Ignorance of Russia's formidable philological tradition has been lamentable. However, questions of method must not needlessly detain us.

Twentieth-century Continental hermeneutics is the tradition we are primarily concerned with. This tradition concerns itself less with questions of method and more with the transformation of the aims and ambitions of philosophy. As Heidegger and Gadamer have contributed most to this transformation, this chapter will primarily examine their central arguments and consider some of their consequences. A brief outline of the primary *Leitmotifen* of hermeneutics will place their subsequent arguments in context. However, our purpose is not merely historical. It is also partici-patory. Our thesis is, then, that twentieth-century hermeneutics does indeed transform an understanding of the endeavours of philosophy but in so doing it initiates, perhaps, an eclipse of understanding itself.

Hermeneutics: what lies in a word?

It is not possible to use the word "hermeneutics" without invoking a deep archae-ology of meaning. This is, perhaps, a key problem for twentieth-century hermeneutics itself: can it escape some of the awkward philosophical associations attached to one of its pivotal concepts, understanding (*verstehen*)? Placing this question aside for the moment, "we should never underestimate what a word can tell us" for, as Gadamer observes, a word gives us our first orientation to "the accomplishment of thought" (the received traditions of meaning) within it (1986: 12). The word "hermeneutics" invokes Hermes, the messenger of the Greek gods and his Roman counterpart Mercury. His allotted task was to interpret what the gods wished to communicate to mortals and to translate it into terms humans might understand. Hermes' predicament addresses all who work with expression, for what is given to us through insight or revelation has to be understood and *translated* into forms permitting others to grasp what we have understood. Hermes presides over the in-between, caught between the gods and mortals, translating the language of each into that of the other. He is in an awkward situation that neither gods nor mortals can properly appreciate. Hermes commands the precarious space between apprehending a truth and communicating it. He was revered by robbers and by those who traveled dark and difficult roads. In the classical world he lent his name to the wayside marker (*herm*) which frequently portrayed him in the company of Aphrodite who evidently "aroused" his interest. Hermes was renowned for his nocturnal disclosures, indeed, night is the realm of his proper governance: darkness reveals our need for guidance and allows things to be seen in a new light (How 1995: 7–8).

To speak of Hermes is to speak not just of the classical world but of the mythopoeic inversion by means of which that world externalized its grasp of common phenomeno-logical predicaments: the perpetual need for understanding and guidance, the sense of being robbed of peace of mind when a dark thought strikes, the struggle to find, to follow and to keep to a path, the experience of being excited by and drawn on by an insight, the mercurial nature of others, the anticipation and the fear of where a dedicated route or journey might lead, and, perhaps, the realization that we too are not unlike Hermes who is always on the way somewhere but with no place of his own finally to dwell in. Indeed, the hermeneutic experience of being caught between an irrecoverable past and an uncertain future speaks just as much of modernity as it does of the classical world (see Giddens 1995: ch. 6). Twentieth-century hermeneutics does not talk in mythopoeic terms, but like those terms, it addresses the phenomenology of loss and discovery which animate the dialectic of so much human experience and "understanding." Heidegger's *Destruktion* of metaphysical language is a hermeneutical attempt to strip philosophical discourse of its historical encrustations so as to regain a sense of the primal power of words to summon the mystery and wonder of existence. (For further discussion of Heidegger, see "German philosophy," Chapter 17.) Gadamer's thought pursues a similar path. The philosophical task of hermeneutics is to awaken "in our thought, what in truth *already* lies in our life-world experience and its sedimentation in language" (1992: 216; 1986: 12). As we shall see, late-twentieth-century hermeneutics holds to its word.

Hermeneutics: the recuperative gesture

If the word "hermeneutic" stands on "an accomplishment of thought," what figure of thought accomplishes itself in the word? Hermeneutics is a recuperative gesture concerned in part with the recovery of the indistinct in meaning and experience. Heidegger's and Gadamer's opposition to the hegemony of the propositional form in philosophical argument suggests that hermeneutics is involved with the linguistically indistinct and the vaguely expressible. However, as early as 1934, Julius Stenzel (1883–1935) argued that the meaning of words is set within unexpressed semantic horizons that shade from relatively clear cores of definition into indefiniteness. Yet it is precisely because words are incompletely defined that a proposition can be formulated with precision. Definition is not opposed to the indefinite but depends on surrounding horizons of indistinct meanings (Pannenberg 1976: 217). Meaning is, in Baumgarten's phrase, a *campos confusionis*, a point of confluence between the distinct and the indistinct. The classic hermeneutic maneuver strives to discern what underlies a communicative practice, to see how the distinct in expression is configured by the indistinct. Charles Taylor (1931–) speaks of the hermeneutic as an attempt to reveal what must underlie an established practice (2004: 7). This repeats a formulation of 1971: a hermeneutic aims to bring to light an *underlying* coherence or sense (1985: 15).

Taylor's remark touches on what is a principal figure of hermeneutic thought, namely, a *recuperative* gesture which takes several forms. For Schleiermacher, to overcome ambiguities of individual expression it is necessary to recover its underlying grammar which, in turn, cannot be understood other than through the particularities of individual usage (1998: 11–12). In Dilthey's mind, to understand an expression is to discern what it is an expression *of*. This requires a *re-construction* of the *Weltanschauung* that *in*-forms (underlies) agency, enabling an interpreter empathetically to (re) *in*-habit (*nacherleben*) the intentionality of an agent's perspective. For Heidegger, hermeneutical awareness is not a reconstruction but a reawakening of a common *restiveness* (*Unrühe*) which animates the *situatedness* characteristic of human existence (*Dasein*). Rejecting the neo-Kantian notion that understanding is a subject's act, he attempts a more radical recuperation. Subjective acts (interpretation) are both dependent upon and give expression to a more fundamental set of relations indicative of a mode of being which is shared. Heidegger suggests that Dilthey's understanding never grasps itself: it always over-flies its ontological ground. An interpreting subject cannot hypostasize its acts and subject them to hermeneutic inquiry since interpreting *is* its being. If interpreting is this subject's mode of being, an interpretative disposition towards *being* must *already* be presupposed. Heidegger's "hermeneutics of facticity" strives to articulate and to reactivate both what underlies the act of interpretation and what is entailed within the (often overlooked) interpretative disposition towards *being* which pre-reflectively shapes our interpretative modes. Gadamer's recuperative gesture is one of ontological re-engagement. Whereas Heidegger pursues a formal hermeneutic analytic of the phenomenological forms of situatedness per se, Gadamer propounds a dialogical (or applied) hermeneutics of content the orientation of which is practical rather than concerned with metaphysical or theoretical questions relating to the question of being. It seeks to reawaken cultural practices (conversations) not so much to "the fundamental question of being" but to those fundamental, controversial, and ongoing questions of subject matter (*Sachen*) from which interpretative practices derive their initial orientation and being (tradition).

Taylor's concern with what underlies a practice is vulnerable to Foucault's criticism that exposing the underlying norms of a practice neither broadens nor challenges a subject's understanding (Kögler 1996). To the contrary, it uncritically consolidates that understanding by encouraging a subject to bring the indeterminate elements of its practice under greater methodological control. Of Dilthey, the criticism is fair. Dilthey's recuperative gesture tends towards cognitive reappropriation. He requires that interpretation rest on systematic and valid knowledge (Dilthey 1976: 62). Understanding is conceived as the act of an epistemological subject. Consequently, that which cannot be brought under a subject's methodological scrutiny cannot become a proper object of its understanding. The circularity is evident. Interpretation retrieves from the outward (and seemingly irrational aspects) of human expression, its underlying rationality and by reconstructing it within a systematic framework of supposedly shared experience, translates it into a form which conforms to and can be assimilated by a subject's understanding (Duerr 1985: 129). Yet because they locate understanding ontologically, the criticism cannot be made of Heidegger and Gadamer. The ontological preconditions of any interpretative practice are placed beyond a subject's (reductive) capture. The recuperative gesture of Heidegger and Gadamer does not involve reappropriation – a taking back into the subject – but a reorientation, a returning of the hermeneutic subject to the underlying ontological circumstances of its interpretative practices. Human existence is always situated (*Dasein*) and, thus, always in an indissoluble relation to the world (*Sein*). What Heidegger intends by the word *Sein* is notoriously difficult to grasp but he clearly associates it with the power to appear and to hide simultaneously, to disclose and to remain undisclosed. *Sein* is aligned with the still power of the possible, with the letting be of what can be (1962: 405). In Heidegger's eyes, human beings notoriously shun possibility, especially that of their death. Fearing death and an uncertain future, humans allow their anxieties to close themselves to the openness of being. Heidegger's *Destruktion* (destruction) strives to break the fearful intellectual (en)closures humans place around themselves and to reawaken a reverence for *Sein* and the gift of its hidden possibilities. The maneuver is a literal re-minding (bringing back to mind) that what we readily refer to as *the* world is not a body of substantive fact but a corpus of responsive interpretations which, as Nietzsche would argue, have acquired the status of fact because their nature as interpretation has been forgotten. Uncovering their status as interpretation reveals what underlies them. They are disclosed as one amongst many other possible ways of negotiating our situatedness, a disclosure which, in its turn, reveals other possible ways of being in the world. The recuperative gesture in Heidegger's hermeneutics is implicit within his "destructive" maneuver. His argument links with Gadamer's in an unexpected fashion.

Tradition has to be deconstructed (Heidegger says "destroyed," *destruiert*) since received interpretations of the world interpolate themselves between the hermeneutic subject and its ability to treat of being-in-the-world more directly (1962: 405). Heidegger's recuperative gesture is a reverse *pentimento*: it removes tradition's surface layers in order to re-engage with the underlying possibilities that being-in the-world opens us towards. Gadamer's interests are more prosaic. His concern is not with "the forgotten question of being" which philosophical tradition has allegedly obscured but with recovering from tradition the open (and sometimes alternative) horizons of questions which institutional prejudice and dogma can conceal. Gadamer's *Destruktion* dispossesses intellectual tradition of its *monopolizing* claim to universal truth by exposing it as a particular and far from conclusive dialogical response to a set of canonical questions. This permits the contemporary interlocutor critically to re-engage with the questions driving the tradition that finds its confluence in his being. Taylor's description of hermeneutics as discerning what underlies a given practice has clear merit. Heidegger's and Gadamer's recuperative gestures restore a horizon of questioning to our understanding of both being-in-the-world and being-in-a-tradition, not replacing something lost but restoring to existence a vital sense of engagement and openness.

Hermeneutics and biblical interpretation

The twentieth century has borne witness to a fundamental reversal in the relationship between theology and hermeneutics. Whereas, traditionally speaking, the religious reader deployed methods of hermeneutic decipherment to discern in religious texts the signs of divine intentionality, the reader's own understanding has now become the mystery. Understanding has truly come to earth: understanding itself is now in question. How does participation in a process of understanding affect the subject matter understood? How does participation in understanding alter the *being* (the self-understanding) of he or she who understands? As the works of Heidegger, Gadamer, and Ricoeur attest, hermeneutics no longer refers exclusively to those instrumental procedures which a subject might use to clarify an obscure text but to those processes of engagement with a text which challenge the very self-understanding of the interpreter. As we shall see when we discuss the consequences of Gadamer's hermeneutics, in becoming reflexive, understanding becomes difficult to itself, aware of its limits and finitude. The mystery to be discerned no longer lies in the external text but in the being of the hermeneutic subject itself. If understanding is dialogical, what we understand of ourselves is dependent upon what the other reveals to us (Williams 2000: 239–41). If the perspective of the other is necessarily particular and culturally specific, self-understanding is never complete: it remains an open task and can never achieve full transparency. The self-understanding of the hermeneutic subject reveals itself as mystery (Louth 1989: 144) which engagement with the other can only partially unravel (Davies 2001: 288–9 Hampson 2002: ch. 7). The inheritance of biblical hermeneutics can be discerned in how twentieth-century hermeneutics has evolved into a form of philosophical humanism (Said 2003: xix).

Protestant hermeneutics in particular has shaped the way contemporary hermeneutics shuns semiotic methods of deciphering the text of a transmitted message in favor of determining how the practice of *reading* folds the received meaning into the horizon of the reader. A text does not itself speak. A reader must determine its import. For Gadamer, wherever meaningfulness is present, so too are hermeneutic subjects. Subjects are always in dialogue with themselves and with the voices of the received: they exist in proximity to each other *within* dialogical relations. Each is the co-being of the other within language. Reading (interpreting) is one such relation, a practice of exchange between what addresses a subject and how that subject answers.

It is ironic that contemporary dialogical hermeneutics and traditional Protestant hermeneutics should share a concern over the vulnerability of the hermeneutic subject to another's claim. Gadamer retrieves tradition from its denigration by Enlightenment rationalism whilst in its attack upon the arbitrary (biblically unsustainable) authority of Catholic tradition, Protestant Reformation theology established the precedent for such defamation. Reformation theology nurtured what for Gadamer is the quite unhermeneutical myth of the natural reader who reads a text *de novo*, who reads alone and who reads the "Word" alone (*sola scriptura*) (Cunningham 2002: 7). Nevertheless, what betrays Gadamer's philosophical hermeneutics as a Protestant hermeneutic par excellence is its humanist emphasis upon reading practice.

Reformation hermeneutics framed its privileging of solitary biblical reading with questionable suppositions about the "purity" of transmission between an undeceiving God who "says it as it is" and a reader innocent of tradition's distortions. Gadamer and Bakhtin insist that the power of the word to disrupt the assumptions of the reader lies not in its *divine* provenance but in its *dialogical* status as the word of an *other*. The meanings of a word are never owned by a speaker. Thus the "other" in a speaker's words can undo what the speaker intends (Iser 2000: 46). As a language speaker the hermeneutic subject neither belongs to nor coincides with itself. Its self-understanding depends upon inexhaustible sets of "I–Thou" relationships. Such understanding is unknowing: what "will come to pass" is already held within (written into) possible but yet to be realized I–Thou relationships which, like language itself, are "always-already-there," preceding what is presently understood. The self-understanding of a hermeneutic subject can never be solitary. It is accompanied by an enabling otherness which is just beyond being articulated (Holquist 1990: 39). The being of the herme-neutic subject is inseparable from its dialogical relationships with "significant others" (Eagleton 2003: 139). This renders the hermeneutic subject vulnerable to the other. In the other's text, the relationships that make the subject presently intelligible to itself can be dramatically reconfigured. Reading may occasion the emergence of the other's meaning but for the reader such emergence is potentially always an emergency, a disarraying of the dialogical configurations of established understandings. Reformation hermeneutics attributed the emergencies of revelation to divine agency. Contemporary hermeneutics sees no agency, only the dialogical play of language. The life of the "Word" is no longer God's but *Sprache*'s. *Sprachlichkeit* (linguisticality) as the always-already-there of social and cultural meaning. *Sprache* (speech, language) displaces God as the *fons et origo* of *human* existence. Heidegger's *Sprachsphilosophie* (philosophy of language) entails a *Destruktion* of theological hermeneutics, stripping phenomenological experiences of wonder and ecstasy of the heavy veneer of doctrinal prejudice imposed on them by institutionalized religion (Mueller-Vollmer 1986: 252–3). The practice of reading exposes the hermeneutic subject not to the word of God but to the speculative murmurings of language (*Sprache*) itself. The practice remains an act of discipleship, an act of faith in the fact that as dialogical creatures we are embedded in a language-world capable of transforming our understanding of the other and ourselves. Reading practices transcendence. It is noteworthy that in the hermeneutics of Heidegger and Gadamer, the psychologistic categories of *feel as one* (*einfüllen*) and *re-experience* (*nacherleben*) are replaced with the terms *listen* (*zuhören*) and *attentiveness* (*Aufmerksamkeit*) (Fiumara 1990 and Lafont 1999).

Hermeneutics: language and the ontological turn

The linguistic turn of twentieth-century philosophy attains a central prominence in the hermeneutics of Heidegger and Gadamer. (For further discussion of the linguistic turn, see "The development of analytic philosophy: Wittgenstein and after," Chapter 2.) They share with Wittgenstein the conviction that with the word one is never alone. Language is always located and circumstantial. In our innermost thoughts we are *already* involved with dialogue, with the semantic traces of the other and with the residues of past meanings. Nor can we, hermeneutically speaking, be "alone with our thoughts." What we grasp as our "own" is not our own at all but an idiom of thought already inflected with the nuanced voices of historical others. Contemporary hermeneutics presents linguistic consciousness as a historically formed *fluidium* which, though it mediates individual consciousness, also transcends it. For Gadamer linguistic consciousness (*Bewußtsein*) is more "being" (*Sein*) than "knowing" (*bewußt*) or, to put it differently, linguistic being is more "deeply knowing" than any individual consciousness can grasp. Hermeneutics as dialogical involvement embraces an episte-mology of participation. It is not a "theory" of understanding that stands apart from what it describes. Given its grasp of linguistic consciousness, it is impossible for it not to become involved (not to be already involved) with what it strives to under-stand. Heidegger articulates hermeneutics accordingly as a mode of being, a mode of being-in-language, whilst Gadamer presents it not as a philosophical method but as a philosophical disposition which strives both to discern and to engage the historical other within one's position. This is no antiquarianism but dialogism with a dialectical purpose. The task of understanding is not to assimilate the other's position (bring the conversation to an end) but to strengthen it so that it stands out against one's own more poignantly. Heightening the contrast between positions generates opportunities for inducing the hidden assumptions within one's position to come to light. Gadamer's hermeneutic is a midwife to otherness. Enhancing the voice of the other occasions the possibility of becoming other to our own previously held assumptions (Ricoeur 1974: 17). We learn through difference and, through such learning, become different to ourselves: if we understand at all we understand differently (1989: 398). In other words, twentieth-century hermeneutics becomes *philosophical*.

As an interpretative practice, hermeneutics has always been concerned with questions of how to understand a text, an art work, or a musical composition. Not unnaturally for a discipline bearing Hermes' name, it asks how his work is best done? Questions regarding what constitutes *best practice* in interpretation and translation and about how the "message" of a text is best conveyed, concern the appropriate *method* of hermeneutic practice. The task of establishing a universal method for hermeneutics inspired Dilthey, whose works or, more specifically, whose limited methodological assumptions, set the agenda for the emergence of twentieth-century hermeneutics. Disconcerted by the "scandal of subjectivity" which he believed to afflict the status of the humanities, Dilthey sought to articulate a neo-Kantian framework of inter-subjective experience (*Erlebnis*) from which claims about what lay within a historical expression could be made with epistemological confidence (Mueller-Vollmer 1986: 152). The methodological orientation of Dilthey's hermeneutics poses obvious questions.

Gadamer is emphatic in his charge that Dilthey's hermeneutics rests on a Cartesian dualism which supposes that it is methodologically necessary for a knowing subject to be distanced from the historical texts to which an interpretative method is to be applied (see 1989: 238–9). This methodological orientation effectively separates the interpreting subject from the historical horizons which shape both it and the objects of its interpretation. Dilthey unwittingly turned hermeneutics into a process of decipherment rather than engagement (dialogue) with the past (see 1989: 240). He was led by the overtly rationalist assumption questionably derived from Schleiermacher that texts can be fully understood as a "Thou" in an I–Thou relationship: an author's meaning can be discerned *directly* from her text. The lodgment of meaning in the intentionality of an author is defended by thinkers such as E. D. Hirsch (1928–) and the Italian Emilio Betti (1890–1968) but for Heidegger and Gadamer, Dilthey's assumption involves an unwarranted restriction of meaning to subjectivity (Hirsch 1967). Contemporary worries about whether we "intend" what we say or over whether words are fully under an author's control, make Dilthey's commitments appear naive.

Dilthey presumes texts to have stable meanings. Texts recorded and fixed their authors' intentions. Although such philological positivism is ardently defended in the study of classics and musical texts (Martindale 1993: ch. 1) for twentieth-century hermeneutics any reading of a text or score becomes a part of its reception process and, in so doing, an element in the transmission and reception of its meaning (Jauss 1982). Understanding is not based on methods of decipherment but upon dialogical processes of engagement (Murray 1978: 141–60). Thus, largely in response to Dilthey, twentieth-century hermeneutics has moved away from an epistemology of practice which assumes understanding to be the exclusive act of subjective consciousness and towards an ontology of practice which treats understanding as an event in a language world. Heidegger's notion of "language as the house of being" and Gadamer's related concept of *Sprachlichkeit* (linguisticality) not only committed twentieth-century hermeneutics to a language ontology but demonstrated that hermeneutics was not alone in taking the "language-turn" of much twentieth-century philosophy. As a consequence, the notion of understanding became embedded in a language ontology in which the object of understanding was no longer primarily the text but the way in which a dialogical encounter with a text changed the self-understanding and hence the being of those who engaged with it. Grounding understanding upon its linguistic foundations turned twentieth-century hermeneutics into a fundamentally *dialogical* practice.

Heidegger and the interpretation of understanding

If Dilthey's hermeneutics was concerned with reconstructing a narrative (under-standing a subject's own account of its actions), Heidegger's hermeneutic focuses on what must come *before*, i.e. a narrativity or narrative sense that guides and disposes the subject towards re-presenting its existence to itself in narrative form. Heidegger's hermeneutic re-awakens a pre-literary notion of reading such as in the "reading of dreams" (*onirocritica*) or "the reading of stars" (*astrologia*) (Baumgarten 1983: 74, 97–8). In Dilthey's hermeneutic, the part–whole structures and the anticipation of completeness are deployed methodologically by a hermeneutic subject so as to arrive at an understanding of a text. He assumes that the interpreting subject and the subject interpreted share the same a priori structures of mental life. For Heidegger, however, this neo-Kantian doctrine of intersubjective understanding achieves nothing. To impose interpretative categories upon a text is to presuppose that we are already acquainted with what it is for something to reveal itself in time. An exegesis of texts is possible because of a *prior* acquaintance with an "exegesis of things" (Ricoeur 1981: 57). It is the structure of this prior acquaintance with exegesis (*fore-understanding*) that inclines us towards narrative readings of ourselves and others. We are inclined towards narrativity because its structures indicate the existential structures which characterize our mode of being-in-the-world (*Dasein*).

Without attempting to negotiate the question of its nature, Heidegger conceives of Being (*Sein*) as that which shows or presents (*darstellen*) itself in time. Being's eschatological characteristics are far from clear since temporality hides them, but what temporality discloses – patterns in how *Sein* shows itself – suggest a continuous but always inconclusive sense of the presence of *Sein's* unfolding eschatology (Moran 2000: 225). *Sein* is not a meta- or a master narrative. Rather, the character of its disclosures hints at possible continuities. The narrativity of the parts insinuates a whole to which they belong. Such a narrativity of the parts provokes and renews the *question* of what the whole or the narrative and, by implication, what *Sein* might be. The key point is that were we not already in the world and oriented towards it in fundamental ways, the question of what Being (*Sein*) is would not arise for us. Without a prior prereflective acquaintance with existence, we could not be reawakened to or *re-cognize* what the question was asking. Heidegger's argument suggests, therefore, that narrativity precedes narrative. To ask for a definition of what a text or narrative is, is, within the framework of his thought, a necessarily superficial exercise. Instrumental reflection discounts or blocks off precisely what the question assumes, namely, that prior understanding of what it is for something to be readable in the first place. The prominence of the figure of the question in Heidegger's hermeneutic does not emphasize the pursuit of lucid (reflective) definitions. It is a declaration of meditative intent. Questioning what a text is, or what Being is, strives to elucidate (to literally, re-mind us of) the as yet undisclosed but ever present region wherein, whereof, and wherefrom the question itself speaks. The task of hermeneutical questioning is in Heidegger's mind to return us to that understanding of the world that is prior to any questioning but which guides it nevertheless.

The priority of that more fundamental (though inchoate) understanding of what it is to be in the world over our more theoretical interpretations of what we take the world to be, is demonstrated by Heidegger's example of equipment breaking down. A writer reaching for a pen does so in the full expectancy that he can, *without thinking about it*, sit in front of a piece of paper, collect his thoughts, and write them down. Thus, the writer is already oriented towards and taken up by his task: the moment he reaches for his pen, it is "available" to him (*Zuhandensein*, "readiness to hand," "avail-ability"). That we are already unthinkingly given over to the structure of such projects normally remains hidden, yet the moment the pen fails and the writing project is jeopardized, the extent of our prior embedment in the pre-reflective assumptions of a practice and how they shape our anticipation, becomes manifest. The practice of *reading* illustrates the seminal point as effectively as the example of malfunctioning tools. When a "reading" breaks down and a text becomes unintelligible, we sense that a meaning eludes or is withheld from us. Yet the failure of such "reading" reveals not so much what is absent (an anticipated meaning) but "lights up" the effective presence of what indeed *is* normally hidden, namely, those working assumptions concerning not *the* meaning of what is read but about what would count as a plausible or possible meaning (reading) in the first place. We must, therefore, be in some fundamental way already acquainted with, understand, and have some sense of what a plausible reading might be in order to recognize – whenever a reading fails – the presence of its absence. To accept a given interpretation as a legitimate reading presupposes a prior understanding of what it would be for something to be a credible reading in the first place. Anticipating Gadamer's reworking of *mimesis*, Heidegger's argument suggests that we recognize an interpretation as such because we recognize it as filling out one of several possibilities within what we already understand. In a fundamental sense, we already know what it is for something to be acceptable as a plausible reading. Heidegger writes,

> Interpretation is grounded existentially in understanding; the latter does not arise from the former. Nor is interpretation the acquiring of information about what is understood; it is rather the working out of the possibilities in understanding. (1962: 188)

> Whenever something is interpreted as something, the interpretation will be founded essentially upon a fore-having, fore-sight and fore conception. An interpretation is never a presuppositionless apprehending of something presented to us. (1962: 191)

> In interpreting, we do not, so to speak, throw a signification over some naked thing which is present at hand, we do not stick a value on it; but when something within the world is encountered as such, the thing in question has an involvement which is disclosed in our understanding of the world, and this involvement is one which gets laid out by the interpretation. (1962: 190)

Heidegger's distance from Dilthey's hermeneutic is plain. For Dilthey, understanding is the methodological consequence of interpretation: it remains an act of the subject. For Heidegger, interpretation is made possible by the fact that the hermeneutic subject has already acquired a knowing orientation towards existence by virtue of its being in the world. It is precisely what is entailed within this Dasein that Heidegger's "hermeneutics of facticity" strives to elucidate. Before we turn to this position, several comments are called for.

First: it is striking how many discussions of Heidegger's hermeneutics have missed the poignancy of reading and its breakdown as a way of illustrating the ontological priority of our existential orientations. Second: if narrativity precedes narrative, reading cannot return to an underlying text. Dasein offers the necessary analogy. The common predicament of Dasein involves a "thrownness" (*Geworfenheit*) into the world. According to Richardson we are always "in the throw" of being in the world and cannot get behind that fact (Richardson 1986: 34). Dasein does not veil or cover up *Sein* and narrativity does not obscure an underlying narrative or forgotten text. Caputo is, therefore, not unjustified in recruiting Heidegger to the cause of the hermeneutics of suspicion: "the saving message is that there is no saving message": there are no special instructions coming from Milesia (Caputo 1987: 185–6). There is no text before (prior) to Dasein. Third: what Caputo misses, however, is another connotation of "before," namely, that which is ahead of us. The notion of projection claims

Heidegger as belonging to the hermeneutics of anticipation, a hermeneutics which is more fully developed in the thought of Habermas. It places the text before the reader, the narrative ahead of narrativity, and the question of *Sein* before Dasein. Hermes may never arrive and, worse, we may be mistaken about his arrival. Yet lost or irretrievable mail is not the point. Heidegger's genius is to suggest a hermeneutics of what it is to come. Our different senses of what a plausible reading might be are not reflections of a lost text but of a possible text to come. Dasein does not hide *Sein*; rather, it opens us towards what *Sein* might yet be thought of as being (Pannenberg 1976: 198). In other words, Heidegger's argument points towards a hermeneutic of futurity: it upholds what might be possible against what is actual. "In every case ... interpretation is grounded in something we have in advance – in a fore-having (*Vorhabe*)" (BT 32). It is what we have *in advance* that draws us out within a practice and allows us to advance. Gadamer judged Heidegger perfectly: "working out appropriate projections, anticipatory in nature" (1989: 252 and 267) is the task of hermeneutics. This theme is readily explained.

Interpretation is the filling out of possibilities already held within understanding. Interpretation is enabled by understanding. Insofar as an interpretation realizes one set of determinate possibilities within understanding, interpretation reveals that which was already on the way to us. In Heidegger's words, "origin" (the undisclosed possibilities within understanding) will "always comes to meet us from the future" (be disclosed by future interpretations).

Michel Foucault (1926–84), however, contends that the projective character of modern hermeneutics is its very weakness. "It dooms us to an endless task ... an exegesis, which listens ... to the Word of God, ever secret, ever beyond itself ... (but) for centuries we have waited in vain for the decision of the Word" (Foucault 1975: xvi–xvii). Yet this criticism misconceives Heidegger's grasp of understanding as a modality of existence both incomplete and open-ended. Instead of revealing the true meaning of history, the end of history would spell the end of understanding: understanding is possible *only* as an unfinished, future-oriented *activity* (Bauman 1978: 170).

The theme of remembering the future reveals the ethical component within Heidegger's hermeneutics of facticity. The ontology of understanding sustaining Heidegger's hermeneutics of *facticity* points to the argument that because *we are what we do*, we can become, i.e. *act on*, who we are (Nietzsche). We are a mode of being (Dasein) whose *being* is expressed in interpretative *action*. Interpretation discloses (fills out) *possibilities* within understanding. Interpretation does not recover the past for its own sake but for the sake of discerning in it possibilities for future action. In antici-pation of Gadamer's hermeneutics of application, Heidegger orients hermeneutics towards the practical: the hermeneutician strives to discern unrealized possibilities in a text to escape the burden of canonic reception. The anticipation of alternative ways of completing a text opens different outcomes for that text and exposes, thereby, further *pre*-conceptions about textuality that we might have entertained within our understanding. This explains Heidegger's allusions to the "restiveness" (*Unruhe*) of hermeneutic activity. A projective interpretation anticipates how a text might be completed and, as a consequence, uncovers previously undisclosed possibilities within our understanding which, when revealed, alter the direction of future interpretations which in their turn ... etc., etc. The figure/ground relationship of interpretation and understanding constitutes a *perpetuum mobile* whose ceaselessness is not to be mocked (Foucault) but to be valued because it brings and continually keeps to the *fore* an awareness of being grounded in something larger than our immediate subjectivity. Reading is once again tied to the theme of transcendence. The ineliminable *Unrühe* between interpretation and understanding in Heidegger's hermeneutic articulates the temporal boundaries of *human* existence. Our being is hermeneutical because like Hermes we are always *between* something understood and something to be understood.

The hermeneutics of facticity: a reading of "the fall"

The hermeneutics of "facticity" (*Faktizität*) is an unfortunate rendering of the German term and has little to do with the English words "fact" or "factive." *Faktizität* concerns that which is actual and actualizable. In contrast to the "closed" world of fact, human existence is *faktisch*, that is, despite its particularity and contingency, it remains open to a range of concrete possibilities. It does so because an incontrovertible feature of *Dasein* (being-in-the world) is its "thrownness.". Being-in-the-world does not denote a neutral mode of existence but a mode of being with precise concerns about its well-being. *Dasein* is always situated and located. Only because *Dasein* has already orientated itself towards existence can the question of what *Sein* is emerge for it. Heidegger therefore distinguishes between existence (*being*-in-the-world) and (an) *existentiell* (a mode of being-in-the world). An *existentiell* is one interpretation of, one response to being-in-the-world. That we so readily confuse religious or political interpretations of our existential condition for our actual condition provides Heidegger with a "deconstructive" account of the "fall" of humanity.

The confusion of existence with *existentiell* is indicative of a "fall," of a deliberate avoidance of the unpredictable and open nature of the existential in preference for hiding ourselves from the latter within a seemingly reliable and stable *existentiell*. By choosing to "fall," we delude ourselves that we *are* the roles we project. In an argument which mirrors Nietzsche's thesis that the Apollonian quest for aesthetic self-forgetfulness is driven by a desire to suppress a Dionysian awareness of the horrors of existence, Heidegger contends that the ontological insecurity of having to face the openness of Being is suppressed by adopting those readily available interpretations and dispositions which religion and ideology provide. The basic situation of having "been thrown" into a groundless *choice* of such roles is ignored if not denied (Richardson 1986: 140). Heidegger's reading of the fall involves not merely avoiding an explicit and proper understanding of our being-in-the-world but because of an incorrect grasp of our *existential* possibilities, a purposeful misunderstanding of it (ibid.). This deconstruction of "the fall" suggests that because of a fearfulness of the open, we avoid the precariousness of actuality in favor of the constructed closures of the factual. There is then, in Heidegger's mind, an all too human tendency to flee the risky and return to familiar horizons in which we feel at home. Yet to flee the risky is nevertheless to admit to recognizing it. The hermeneutics of facticity, therefore, offers a reading of both the inauthentic existence that avoids the existential implications of being–in–the-world and outlines the character of an authentic existence which remains "resolutely" open to the uncertainties and enigmas of human existence.

The burden of the traditional and the gift of tradition

That all hermeneutical reading is contextualized does not represent a problem for Heidegger. The historical contingency in which we find ourselves is not an immutable given. Its *facticity* lies in it being not just the residue of the realized but also the promise of the yet-to-be realized. An authentic acceptance of Dasein embraces the openness of existence as opposed to the closedness of an *existentiell*. Our present being-in-the world is portrayed not as a fixed determination of the past but as an openness to a future yet to be determined, as a conscious pursuit of the past's unrealized possibilities. Embracing the past does not involve a passive acceptance of the historical as monumental, immutable, and irrevocably "given." To the contrary, authentic existence is a "handing to oneself" (*ein Sichüberliefern*) and a "taking over" of the possibilities in the circumstances of one's thrownness as one's own. Heidegger's conceives of history as "no brutal factuality but (as) a constellation of possibilities ... delivered over to us" (Caputo 1987: 88). As the handing over of "possibilities habored within one's heritage," tradition transforms *Geworfenheit* from a condition of random chance into a gift of possible futures. Heidegger's hermeneutics is, indeed, recuperative: it strives to overcome the burden of historicism with an engaged sense of historicity and allows the interpreter to recover the past as a restorative for future action. The hermeneutic disposition here is not to return to the past per se, but to view the past as a particular and instructive response to the question of being. Reading the past as offering particular responses to the existential predicament aims at a re-sourcing of future interpretative possibilities.

Heidegger's notion of historicity is not a philosophy of history. It offers the reader access to the historical *within* hermeneutic practice not to the end of venerating the past but as the occasion for reappropriating the potential for action within it. Heidegger's hermeneutic positions the reader between the achieved and the yet-to-be-achieved within a textual tradition. Such a positioning permits the reader to become "more fully present" to herself – more "authentic" (*eigentlich*) by opening herself towards a future of those unrealized potentials held within her past (Niethammer 1994: 149). Heidegger's hermeneutics does not "read" history in the manner of Dilthey. It does not read history as an expression of human choice and action but reappropriates the historical as the basis for *recovering* authentic choice and action.

The recuperative elements within Heidegger's hermeneutics of facticity respond to both the burden of the traditional and the disruptive elements of European modernism. Heidegger's argument with tradition is an argument with the traditional rather than with tradition per se. His critique of the western metaphysical tradition claims that what is transmitted as the traditional and, hence, supposedly proper way of articulating being and truth, blocks access to the "primordial sources" – the open question of Being – from which our thinking has traditionally been drawn (1962: ?43). What is ossified as the traditional becomes increasingly immune to critique whereas tradition proper returns to and repeats the questions that animate it in the first place (Kisiel and van Buren1994: 128). Once recovered, such questions open the reader towards her own response to what they ask of what it is to be in the world.

European modernism also entertained a suspicion of the traditional but, unlike Heidegger, rejected tradition as well. The illusion that one can step away from the past and adopt a mode of being-in-the-world as easily as making a lifestyle decision was, for Heidegger, nihilistic. Against the modern illusion of being able to become what we like, an illusion which suggests that how we are in the world is the consequence of an unsituated *subjective* act, Heidegger advocates the deliberate choosing of what we already are. The historicity of human existence means that we cannot but be situated. The point is, however, what being situated opens us towards. To choose one's past as one's own is not to adopt the life of a reactionary cliché but to seize those opportunities for future action which are grounded in one's past. A writer does not find her voice *ex nihilo* but develops it in *response* to those questions which her literary tradition has left often or not answered adequately. It is, in other words, being grounded in a tradition of responses that enables the writer to find her voice. Such a writer would no longer be adrift in a given life-world. Her creativity would be shaped not by a groundless act of subjective will but by its seizing the potentialities within its received world *as its own*. The undecided and unresolved within tradition (that which, ontologically speaking, keeps the writer afloat) has to be taken in hand and made her own.

> Our situation is not that of the rescuing coast; it is a leap into a drifting boat. Everything now depends on our taking the sails' tack into our hands and looking to the wind. It is precisely the difficulties that we must see ... Only by appropriating to myself the structure of my having to decide; only be realising that it is within and upon such having that I shall come to see; only in this way can illumination sustain the fundamental motivation for the temporal unfolding of philosophizing. (Kisiel and van Buren 1994: 365)

The resolute reappropriation of tradition is not the conservative act of one who in the face of uncertainty grasps for an established role or *traditional* identity. Such an act seeks the self-forgetfulness of a return to the known and trusted. Heidegger's reappropriation of tradition calls us away from the complacency and oblivion of the traditional towards confronting for ourselves the unsettling question of Being that philosophical tradition proper transmits to us. The hermeneutical retrieval of a tradition's *unrealized* potentials frees the subject from the fixity of the habitual and the traditional by recovering for it a horizon of admittedly determinate possible actions from within which, nevertheless, it can choose a grounded and actualizable future.

Being, disclosure and linguistic mysticism

Being and Time's comprehensive attempt at a hermeneutic analytic of human facticity is renowned. The range and novelty of its categories –"thrownness," "situatedness," and "the projective" – serve to radicalize hermeneutics' conception of the ontological underlay of being-in-the-world. Yet Heidegger's later *Sprachsphilosophie* despairs of youthful philosophical ambition and turns instead to a poetically orientated account of "language as the house of Being." Even so, Heidegger's early and late thought do take common cause: the hermeneutical task of reading and listening is to achieve both an openness towards and a communion with what presents (*darstellen*) itself from within a text or art work. The hermeneutics of facticity stresses commitment to the horizons of a life-world *not* out of conservative loyalty to one such world but because being committed to a life-world is the only way general questions about our being-in-the-world can be drawn into the open. There is no unmediated access to *being*, no innocent reading of Being. Were we not already in the world and able to "read" patterns of events and their possible portents, the question of what Being (*Sein*) is would not arise for us. Being is not a text to be read off *de novo*. The question of *being* only makes sense in relation to (but is never reducible to) what we already have, namely, a prereflective sense of what it is to be in the world (Dasein). Heidegger's early hermeneutic inverts the palimpsest image which dominates Nietzsche's and Foucault's hermeneutics of suspicion. Interpretation is certainly dependent upon the understanding that precedes it but interpretation does not itself overwrite, distort, or obscure that understanding. John D. Caputo is right to suggest that for Heidegger there is no hidden meaning, no original text for interpretation to uncover. To the contrary, the understanding which sustains interpretation only makes itself apparent *in* the disclosures of interpretation. In other words, Heidegger's hermeneutic calls for a type of unforced reading, a meditative thinking (*besinnliches Denken*), with an ear for how words orientate themselves towards what has been and what has yet to be understood. The task of interpretation is thus to set free and thereby "let be" (*Gelassenheit*, "letting be") what is already at play within understanding (Blond 1988: 188–9).

What understanding encompasses will never be grasped in its entirety. Its full import is withheld and yet it still upholds human existence. The ontological dimension of Heidegger's hermeneutic is in effect a metaphysical meditation upon the insight that "what it is to be human ... (is) ultimately the gift of something non-human" (Taylor 1995: 124–6) that our thinking is indeed rooted in a being-in-the-world which takes us beyond ourselves (Kerr 1997: 156–8). The key point is not that Dasein is located and circumstantial but rather that the understanding which is beyond its grasp not only upholds Dasein but keeps it in (its) place in relation to what transcends it. Heidegger's hermeneutic does not appeal to any *Geistes/Naturwissenschaft* distinction; rather, the human world is disclosed to itself as a "world" in relation to that which surpasses it. But herein lies the weakness of this hermeneutic. It is a hermeneutic which sets itself the task of holding the boundary between Dasein and the understanding which sustains it. The boundary simultaneously differentiates the two realms and binds them together. It is only in relation to understanding that Dasein can show itself as a world and it is also only in relation to Dasein that the presence of understanding can disclose itself. Heidegger's anti-subjectivist hermeneutic has a religious inflection: it patrols the boundary between understanding and Dasein so as to remind us reverentially of the non-human (transcendental) ground of human existence. This is why Heidegger's hermeneutic is disquieting. It does not address the conflicts of *this* world but meditates long on the conflict between the non-human realm and the human, between "earth" and "world." Heidegger's later philosophy venerates language not as a means to dialogical exchange but as an expressive medium capable of disclosing a (mystical) sense of that which underlies words. Language calls us to be attentive to that generative silence which calls forth words. Taylor remarks, "the silence is where there are not yet the right words, but where we are interpellated by entities to disclose them as things ... we are pushed to find unprecedented words, which we draw out of silence." The majesty and the poverty of Heidegger's hermeneutic is obvious. It is an incontestably forceful reminder that human existence rests on that which transcends it but it is also breathtaking in its forgetfulness of how humans must not just assume each other (*mitsein*) but also *need each other* in order understand their predicament. Gadamer explicitly returns to the *negotiated* elements of understanding. His is a hermeneutics at once both more classical and Protestant in orientation: it is the fact that we are capable of and culpable for unintended errors of judgment, rather than being mindful of the ontological difference between understanding and Dasein, that marks us out as being human. The pain of misunderstanding marks the path towards a more human and humane form of understanding.

Hermeneutics and Anglo-American philosophy

Before we pass to Hans-Georg Gadamer's formulation of hermeneutics it is appropriate to consider briefly some of the Anglo-American philosophical responses to hermeneutics. Heidegger's ontological turn within hermeneutics constituted his response to the epistemological impasse posed by Wilhelm Dilthey's hermeneutics: if empathetic understanding involves the reconstruction within myself of the same mental contents of the other I seek to understand, how can I distinguish between my mental states and those I have reconstructed? R. J. Collingwood (1889–1943) was the first to respond by suggesting that the aim of historical understanding is not to *re-experience* (*nacherleben*) the other but to imaginatively re-think the thoughts which led the other to act in the way that he did (Collingwood 1946:138). W. A. Hodges and P. Rickman continued the dissemination of Dilthey's work in Britain, influencing such historians as Gordon Leff. However, it was not until the late 1950s and 1960s that idioms of Dilthey's thought had an impact upon liberal social theory in its fight against the reductionism of behaviorism. Dilthey's notion of a *Weltanschauung* – an individual's grasp of the value-horizons within which he or she lived – was frequently cited as a necessary reflexive component in understanding a subject's account of his or her agency. Dilthey's influence can be detected in Anthony Giddens' *New Rules of Sociological Method*, in which he argued, "the (communicative) production and reproduction of society ... has to be treated as a skilled performance on the part of its members, not as a merely mechanical series of processes ... Structures must not be conceptualised as simply placing constraints upon human agency, but as enabling" (1976: 160–1). Dilthey's notion of *Weltanschauung* also shaped Winch's reception of Wittgenstein's notion of a "form of life" (*Lebensform*). Understanding an act was not a matter of identifying the causal laws that prompted it nor a matter of grasping the psychology behind it but a question of acquiring a grasp of the *Lebensform* within which the act took place. Winch's notion of understanding was, like the later Wittgenstein's, far from relativistic; it was robustly participatory. Wittgenstein's notion of "having a feel for a word," of having a sense for what wheels it could and could not turn, promised an empathetic account of understanding which was reducible to participatory competencies (how to go on with an argument or improvisation), and not to the sharing of psychological states. These and other themes were ably explored in such works as *Hermeneutics and Social Science* (1978) by the Polish-born sociologist Zygmunt Bauman (1925–). However, along with Alasdair MacIntyre (1929–), Charles Taylor (1931–) has emerged as the most influential of the English-speaking philosophers to handle hermeneutical themes in the late twentieth century.

Alasdair MacIntyre holds to Gadamer's stance that moral concepts are not timeless but embodied within and constitutive of forms of social life. Values are not theoretical entities but expressions of participation in practices, their traditions, and their pursuit of excellence. Though multiple and various, they are all indicative of a cooperative pursuit of "goods." MacIntyre shares with Gadamer a clear respect for the enabling horizons of intellectual and practical traditions, but unlike Gadamer who tends like Pannenberg to look within the projections of tradition for its critical norms, he has surprisingly more in common with Habermas. In his book *Whose Justice? Which Rationality?* (1988), although he concedes that no rational inquiry escapes the standpoint of a particular historical tradition, he defends the view that it is the "force of reason" which after due debate and anguish recommends one line of thought against another. MacIntyre's hermeneutics is one of ardent adversarial debate, a place of constrained disagreement, of imposed initiation into and participation in hermeneutical conflicts (1990). Charles Taylor's hermeneutics has a less troubled tenor.

If Dilthey's quest for methodological autonomy within the *Geisteswissenschaften* was to make them more science-like, a constant *Leitmotif* in Taylor's work has been the philosophical resistance to modeling the study of human kind on the natural sciences (Taylor 1985: 1). The natural sciences fail to recognize that a sense of self is a crucial feature of our understanding of human agency (ibid.). In the second volume of his influential *Philosophical Papers*, Taylor contends that,

> A fully competent human agent not only has some understanding (which may be also more or less misunderstanding) of himself, but is partly constituted by this understanding ... Our self-understanding essentially incorporates our seeing ourselves against a background ... of distinctions between things that are recognised as of categoric or unconditioned or higher importance ... To be a full human agent, to be a person or self ... is to exist in a space defined by distinctions of worth. (1985: 3)

In the essay "Interpretation and the sciences of man," first published in 1971, Taylor insists that "man is a self-defining animal," that is, our understanding of what it is to be human is reflexive. It is defined against collectively posited notions of worth. Notions of worth are subject-referring in that they only have relevance in a world in which there are, phenomenologically speaking, real subjects of experience. The elimination of self-referring notions of worth by behaviorist and indeed structuralist accounts of the human world render it unintelligible as a *human* world. Taylor is accordingly very resistant to Foucault's analysis of power stratagems instituting themselves in the body social. Tellingly, Taylor remarks that Dostoyevsky's analysis of modern political terrorism in terms of projected self-hatred and as a response to a sense of emptiness could not and would not be acknowledged by Foucault's mode of analysis (Taylor 1985: 170). Taylor is an eloquent advocate of the thesis that our sense of self is necessarily situated in the history of social practices and political institutions. His *magnum opus*, *Sources of the Self* (1989) echoes his earlier study of Hegel and argues that a sense of self is inescapably situated historically and depends upon the conceptual and linguistic inheritance which articulate our intellectual and practical horizons. However, in his more recent work Taylor reaches beyond his Diltheyean inheritance. He is not just interested in elaborating a common *Weltanschauung* of practices or evaluative outlooks. His book *Modern Social Imaginaries* speaks of a social imaginary which is that common understanding *that makes possible* common practices (2004: 23). The social imaginary extends beyond the background that makes sense of our particular practices (p. 25).

> It is in fact that largely unstructured and inarticulate understanding of our whole situation, within which particular features of our world show up for us in the sense they have. It can never be adequately expressed in the form of explicit doctrines because of its unlimited and indefinite nature. That is another reason for speaking of an imaginary rather a not a theory. (2004: 25)

Taylor contends that the relation between practices and the social imaginary is not one-sided. If the understanding makes the practice possible, the practice also carries the understanding. The question which Taylor's work points to an indeed awaits an answer: "what is exactly involved when a theory penetrates and transforms the social imaginary?" (2004: 25). It is possible to discern some aspects of Gadamer's approach to tradition in Taylor's notion of the social imaginary and it is to Gadamer that we shall now turn.

Hans-Georg Gadamer and philosophical hermeneutics

> And I – it is the shudder of meaning I interrogate, listening to the rustle of language, that language which for me ... is my Nature.
>
> Barthes (1989: 79)

Gadamer's *Truth and Method* (first published in 1960) fulfils its own definition of art: the transformation of the familiar into the unfamiliar. It is one of the great crossroads of European philosophy. Plato's metaphysics of forms is reshaped into a phenomenology of historically evolved subject matters (*Sachen*), Hegel's dialectic of experience is developed into an account of how such subject matters appear to consciousness and, furthermore, the historically revealed nature of subject matters are deployed to give structure to Heidegger's argument that "language is the house of being." (For further discussion of Hegel, see "Hegelianism in the twentieth century," Chapter 3.) Combining Hegel's claim that historical substantialities (*Sachen*) underpin subjective experience with Heidegger's view of time as the medium of experience, Gadamer propounds a philosophy of meaningful experience that strikes simultaneously at Nietzsche's nihilism and the privileging of impersonal method as the high road to understanding. Philosophical hermeneutics is not a traditional theory of interpretation. It does not seek to establish a generally acceptable method for the reading of obscure and difficult texts. Philosophical hermeneutics is, much rather, an interpretation of interpretation, a prolonged meditation upon what "happens" to us within "hermeneutic experience" when we are challenged by texts and art works. Although it eschews formal methodologies of reading, it does not privilege subjective responses to a text. Philosophical hermeneutics is *philosophical* in that it strives to discern objectivities within the subjective voice. It reflects on the historical and cultural preconditions of individual hermeneutic experience and seeks to discern in it something of the predicament, character, and mode of being of those who "undergo" such experience. Yet the philosophical within philosophical hermeneutics remains *hermeneutical* for it is not concerned with the abstract nature of such objectivities but with how they manifest themselves and are encountered within the particularities of experience and its ramifications.

Gadamer's hermeneutic shares with Heidegger's a certain transcendental trajectory. Both resist Dilthey's reduction of understanding to a reconstruction of a subject's conscious experiences (*Erlebnisse*). Gadamer strongly objects in Dilthey to the neo-Kantian reduction of knowledge to an act of the subject. He does so not just because he finds a subject's naivety concerning its use of "objective" method as an instrument of individual power offensive, but because to start with subjectivity is to miss the point. Understanding is less a subjective act and more participation in that which both underlies and reaches beyond individual consciousness. "All self-knowledge," Gadamer argues, "arises from what is historically pre-given, with what with Hegel we call substance because it underlies all subjective intentions." Philosophical hermeneutics sets itself the task of discovering in the subjective, the substantiality that determines it (1989: 302). The argument parallels Heidegger's thesis that we need to surpass the "ready-at-hand" in order to glimpse how subjective consciousness is grounded in a mode of being-in-the-world that exceeds it. Gadamer's case against the neo-Kantian reduction of "knowledge" to subjectivity claims that such subjectivity is always more than it knows itself to be. Gadamer's hermeneutic surpasses Heidegger's in a number of ways. Heidegger's hermeneutic entails an "ontology of location" (locating the "human world" in relation to that which transcends it) whilst

Gadamer's involves an ontology of participation: how does the subject participate in and alter the understanding that guides its existence? In short, extending Heidegger's notion of understanding as an *event* into one of play, Gadamer's hermeneutic focuses on the question, How does a hermeneutic subject read, participate in and alter the direction of that play? (1989: 101–29).

Gadamer's hermeneutic is a prolonged reflection on the consequential nature of hermeneutic practice: "What happens to us when we interpret a text or art work?" Heidegger's answer had a binary form: interpretation reveals and fills out aspects of its grounding understanding. Gadamer's triadic response has a Hegelian inflection. A subject's interpretation indeed fills out aspects of the historically received *understandings* which underwrite it but in so doing the nature of the subject's own understanding changes.

The problematic inheritance of tradition

Hermeneutics for Gadamer engages with what shows itself as meaningful. Although the meaningful is not reducible to an interpreting subject's opinions, it discloses itself to subjects in experience (*Erfahrungen*). What discloses itself to the subject as meaningful may seem to the interpreter to be a psychological event *ex nihilo* but, ontologically speaking, the disclosure is *always* located and circumstantial. The practice of reading may occasion the disclosure of unexpected revelations of meaning but there are clear preconditions governing the possibility of such events. Interpretative practice invariably takes for granted what history and traditions *grant* it. Whereas Heidegger talks in terms of thrownness, Gadamer speaks of traditions and their horizons. These silently shape our expectancies of texts and their subject matters (*Sachen*). Such foreknowledge is indicative of our historical placement and provides the acquired know-how in orientating ourselves towards texts and their subject-matters. It is prejudicial in that it guides us towards the possibility of articulate judgment and learning: nothing can be learned or unlearned if prereflective assumptions are not challenged. Tradition is not disabling, rather, it is a precondition of being open to other modes of outlook. For the most part, Gadamer holds, we are unaware of the "hidden persuader" of tradition for, when properly effective, it hides itself. However, when profound experience confounds expectancy, the assumptions of our foreknowledge are forced to the surface. Such experience manifests the hidden or assumed horizons of reader and text.

In Gadamer's hermeneutic, interpretation is in part ritualistic. The reading of text or the viewing of picture requires that we forget our everyday purposes and give ourselves to the work at hand. In other words, the practice of reading occasions an event: it clears a space within the everyday whereby the hidden assumptions within the interpreter's and the work's horizon can be put in play and, indeed, be played out. The ritual of reading solicits an occurrence, the bringing of something to light. What emerges does so not as a consequence of a reader's volition: what happens, discloses itself, "happens to us over and above our wanting and our doing" (1989: xviii). "Understanding begins when something addresses us" (1989: 299). Hermeneutical reading does not impose itself on a text, it requires that its own (pre)understanding be probed and be questioned by what emerges in the process of interpretation. The fission between interpretive horizons is much closer to what Gadamer means by a "fusion" of horizons. The later does not imply a meeting of minds, a blending of opinions or the attainment of consensus. Much rather, the fusion of horizons suggests a moment of differentiation when the assumptions of a work stand out against those of our own about that work. Understanding is not to do with recovering the meaning of a text, as many of Gadamer's post-structural critics suggest, but with recognizing what exactly is *at issue* between that text and ourselves. Understanding for Gadamer does not mark a point of arrival as its does for Dilthey but rather a point of departure: dialogue and exchange is possible only on the basis of recognizing difference.

"Just the thing!" Understanding the subject at issue

The dialogical issue between text and interpreter concerns the different assumptions about the nature of a given subject matter. What interpretive engagement with a text gives us a sense of is the *Sache*, or the significant-content-in-dispute. Interpretation solicits such subject matters but, in effect, they show themselves. Gadamer cites how in a conversation unexpected insights come to mind of their own accord. He speaks of "the coming into language of the thing itself" (1989: 378). The *Sache* ("matter" or "thing" itself) is a highly a nuanced notion in Gadamer. Four aspects of his argument are important for our discussion:

(1) *A Sache is an intentional object.* It is that which a work refers to or intends. It can denote the subject matter of an expression or the substance of what it is being addressed. A *Sache* is not a physical object. That the subject matter "landscape" can be rendered in many ways by artists neither relativizes the motif, nor suggests that it exists apart from the ways it is interpreted. For Gadamer, a *Sache* is equivalent to what Husserl presents as the "thing-itself" (as opposed to the Kantian noumenal thing-in-itself). Husserl contends that over a period of time a *Sache* shows itself as that continuity of perceptions in which various perspectives on similar objects shade into one another. For instance, although Altdorfer's and Turner's approaches to landscape are different, each perspective helps co-constitute (with other related perspectives) the *Sache* which then becomes historically effective as the *genre* "landscape."

(2) *A Sache is a transcendent object.* A *Sache* is always larger than its portrayal in a work. Although a subject matter has a historical genesis, how it is grasped across history surpasses how any one epoch interprets it. A *Sache* has an inherent scope of cultural and historical reference beyond the grasp of any one individual. A work can never exhaust what lies within a *Sache*, nor monopolize its content. Because a *Sache* is always more than the work in and through which it presents itself, a work of art can never be fully complete. There is always more to be said. A work that brings its subject matter to mind points beyond itself to what has yet to be shown.

(3) *A Sache is historically mutable.* Though a *Sache* is an *objective* entity that transcends the horizon of an individual's understanding and has a denotation and connotation of meaning beyond the orbit of a single language user, *Sachen* are not

fully independent of individuals and their understanding. Subject matters would lie forever dormant if they were not made to function. Their cultural effectiveness rests upon their being addressed (Iser 2000: 154). The acquisition of any expressive or interpretive practice entails engaging with the cultural forms (*Sachen*) that enable that practice. The *Sachen* which underwrite pre-understanding operate as the precondition of individual interpretive practices but only the effective operation of the latter allow the *Sachen* underwriting them to function and be renewed.

(4) Gadamer's notion of *Sachen* constitutes a brilliant reworking of Plato's doctrine of the forms (universals). Both *Sachen* and forms serve as the intentional points of reference of texts and arguments. As the subject matters addressed, both transcend their instances. How they reveal themselves in appearance is never exhaustive: there is always more to be understood. Yet whereas for Plato the literary or artistic interpretations of a form distance us from and corrupt our understanding of the metaphysical original, for Gadamer, they enhance the historical being of a *Sache*, substantiating its presence and effectiveness. Although both transcend their particular instances, *Sachen*, unlike forms, have their genesis and their being in historical practices. Theirs is the realm of becoming. Not only do they underwrite interpretive practices but insofar as such practices unfold their inner possibilities, *Sachen* develop in history.

Gadamer's articulation of the ontological underlay of what texts and works address has clear practical consequences for hermeneutics.

Gadamer and the practical consequences of hermeneutics

Although he does not directly use Heidegger's language, Gadamer's position echoes the ontological primacy given by Heidegger to understanding and the derivative status accorded to interpretation. First: *the Husserlian perspective that Gadamer adopts is future oriented*. Each perspective of a given object adds to the "ideality" of that object. There is no object-in-itself behind interpretation. Nor can we approach a *Sache* other than through the point of view we adopt towards it. This does not relativize interpretation for there is no object-in-itself apart from interpretation. Each interpretation of a *Sache* leads to an extended view of the subject matter, each suggesting an infinitely perfectible notion of what that *Sache* can be. Interpretation is therefore anticipatory in nature, pointing towards and contributing towards what is to come. Second: *it is not surprising, therefore, that Gadamer's notion of interpretation should share with Heidegger's hermeneutic an exegetical role rather than that of commentary.* If there is no text – no original – to be read off or commented on the task of interpretation cannot be that of re-presentation (commentary or elucidation) but that of presentation (exegesis – bringing forth). Gadamer always insists that a *Sache* is not really the object of statements but comes to language in statements (1989: 446). Thus, interpretation brings forth that which is already at play in language and allows it to show itself in a new, more fulsome way: "understanding and interpretation are not constructions based on principles, but the *furthering* of an event that goes *further* back" (1989: xxiv). Interpretation fills out what is already (in part) understood and allows what has been understood, to be understood differently. Three: *interpretation for Gadamer is essentially participatory*. Although *Sachen* are not reducible to our point of view, they nevertheless ground that point of view. To interpret a *Sache* is not only to engage with what shapes our horizon but to alter its effective future by expanding the possibilities for meaning within it.

Gadamer's hermeneutic is not, however, merely derivative of Heidegger's. It significantly extends Heidegger's key hermeneutic proclamation that "language is the house of Being" and demonstrates that a dialogical conception of hermeneutics reveals what Heidegger means when he speaks of being *disclosing* itself. It also offers a precise explanation of why *Sachen* are never revealed in isolation.

The limit of my (subjective) world may indeed be language but language is not reducible to what I grasp of it in my world. The linguistic horizons that shape my world, extend beyond my immediate grasp. Thus the language that grounds me in my present horizon also enables me to transcend it. The transcendence of linguisticality *per se*, however, is not possible. A *Sache* cannot be experienced other than against a backdrop of received expectations. Past as well as unrealized future potentialities of meaning are held within a *Sache*. Following Heidegger, Gadamer describes these aspects of meaning as "the withheld." These lend to a *Sache* a sense of weight and depth. Furthermore, it is because we experience the nature of a *Sache* against the backdrop of previous experience that we are able to "recognize its independent otherness" (1989: 445). The magnitude of a *Sache* arises from a consciousness of its negative dimension: we find ourselves in the presence of dimensions of meaning that are partially withheld from us. This explains why philosophical hermeneutics holds that *Sachen* and our understanding of them can never be fully objectified in statements but only made manifest by the speculative dynamics of language. Thus Gadamer's hermeneutic offers an open explication of Heidegger's claim noted above that "language is the house of Being."

Everything that shows itself as being part of our world, shows itself through language. Gadamer uses the activities of language to explicate Heidegger's conception of "being as disclosure." Just as Being reveals itself, it also hides itself. Gadamer does not take up the metaphysical dimensions of these assertions but chooses to reside in what he has realized, namely, that what being is cannot be stated but shows itself though what the word manifests. What the word "being" *shows* is that, like other words, its meaning is a simultaneous coming forth and a falling away. In revealing part of its meaning it also reveals that another aspect of its meaning remains withheld. There always remains more to be said. In this sense, the word "being" reveals what *being* is.

For Gadamer interpretation is a *practical device* for drawing the withheld aspect of *Sache* to mind. The untheorized aspects of *Sachen* are apprehendable through language's *speculative* capacity. This has nothing to do with the use of propositions to reduce a *Sache* to a series of assertions but with that careful and sensitive use of words which aims not to state what a subject matter is, but to bring us to an awareness of its full depth and resonance.

> Every word breaks forth as if from a centre and is related to a *whole*, through which alone it is a word. Every word causes the whole of the language to

which it belongs to resonate and the whole world view that underlies it to appear. Thus, *every word*, as the event of a moment, *carries with it the unsaid*, to which it is related by responding and summoning. The occasionality of human speech is not a causal imperfection of its expressive power; it is, rather the logical expression of the living virtuality of speech that brings a totality of meaning into play without being able to express it totally. All human speaking is finite in such a way that there is laid up within it an infinity of meaning to be explicated and laid out. That is why the hermeneutical phenomenon also can be illuminated only in light of the fundamental finitude of being, which is wholly verbal in character. (1989: 458, emphases added)

The passage makes several things clear. The nexus of meaning which constitutes a *Sache* serves as the historically received enabling condition of statements about such a thematic: "*every word breaks forth from a centre and is related to whole*" and "*carries with it the unsaid.*" The being of such a nexus of meaning is in part "withheld." As a semantic field, although a *Sache* may sustain the practice of everyday judgments, the full extent of its nature remains hidden from us: it is that "infinity" of the unsaid, that "totality of meaning" which cannot be expressed. However, insofar as the resonance of a statement about a *Sache* depends upon being "backed up by the ground" of the withheld, the withheld is as such brought to light. It is not objectified in language per se but brought to mind by language as an intentional object of our understanding: "*every word causes* the world view underlying it to appear." The nexus of meaning which constitutes the *withheld* dimension of *Sache* is essentially a linguistic phenomenon. It is not, in principle, an entity alien to language. What makes it inexpressible is the finitude of linguistic understanding. It is the finitude of language rather than any incommensurability between the nature of the object and language which prevents a nexus of meaning from being presented as a whole. Though *withheld* from us, the *withheld* is not as such incommensurable with our mode of understanding. It is, ontologically speaking, the other of us. Held within it are possibilities for understanding which have not yet been grasped, possibilities which would enable us to become other to our present selves. It is the withheld within the *Sachen* that uphold the possibilities for hermeneutical transcendence.

Question and answer

The unpredictable dynamics of dialogue demonstrates that for philosophical hermeneutics understanding is not arrived at by "method." Insights emerge in conversational exchanges that interlocutors neither expect nor necessarily want. Although Gadamer defends the "art" of conversation, it would be disingenuous of him to deny the effective employment of methodical (rhetorical) devices within dialogue. Collingwood's notion of a dialectic of question and answer plays a central role in his hermeneutic (1989: 370–5, 513–16). The Socratic dimension of this appeal to dialogue can be misleading. In Plato, dialogical exchange is presented as the gateway to dialectic (reason). Dialogue is the prelude to an inward dialectic focused on what lies behind the vagaries of linguistic meaning, namely, its underlying ideas. Gadamer suggests that this misrepresents Socrates, who also claimed "not to know" (Silverman 1991: 23–41). This claim implies that dialogue is not merely a path to the dialectical recovery of established but forgotten concepts but a device that utilizes the speculative capacity of language to explore the undisclosed aspects of our thinking. The virtue of dialogue – the conversational dialectic of question and answer – is that it can catch our hermeneutic expectations off-guard. Questions are directed at a text not because certain answers are expected but because questioning a text demands the reader's engagement and it is precisely the unpredictable consequences of that engagement that can prompt the unexpected transformative insight. The question serves to draw out a hitherto withheld aspect of a subject matter. Philosophical hermeneutics may not deploy a method but it does employ a range of dialogical devices. It is not "the forgotten question of being" that drives Gadamer's hermeneutic but the question of what we have overlooked, become blind to, or indeed may have forgotten in our own practices.

Gadamer and Heidegger articulate their hermeneutics in outright opposition to the Cartesian "philosophy of consciousness." Both contend that neither the question of being nor that of meaning can be reducible to subjective consciousness. Gadamer is acutely aware of the problem posed by both the Nietzschean and Derridean school of thought: how does interpretation avoid being the projection of subjectivity, of a subject's will to power? Philosophical hermeneutics deploys several tactical devices to expose a reader's unreflective assumptions. Gadamer is well aware that what we regard and present as a canonical text is, more often than not, a consequence of our particular view of a canon rather than of our evaluations of the text per se. His appeal to the text itself is, then, not an unwitting lapse into philological positivism but an effort to read the text as a dialogical response to a question, i.e. the question of what it addresses, of what its subject matter is. The hermeneutical ambition of the question is to force the reader to separate her (contemporary) understanding of a subject matter from how an author of the past would have grasped it. This is the first part of Gadamer's attempt to separate the reader's initial assumptions about a received text from the text itself. The task is then to read the text against its own understanding of its subject matter in order to assess the adequacy of its response. Now, if this were the sole ambition of Gadamer's hermeneutic it could rightly be dismissed as academic. However, its real ambition is to bring the reader into dialogue with the text and this is achieved, paradoxically, by radicalizing the difference between reader and text.

Not only does Gadamer advocate interpreting the text in the light of how it grasps and responds to its subject matter but he also adopts Aristotle's argument that a reader should attempt to *strengthen* the argument of the author she is studying. This is not hermeneutic altruism but a deliberate tactic aimed at soliciting a hermeneutic epiphany. Its aim is to facilitate the emergence of that *unexpected* insight into our *own* way of thinking about a subject matter. As conversation demonstrates, such insights are fickle. They emerge spontaneously from within dialogue and are for the most part contrary to a subject's willing and doing. They are not the result of subjective (methodological) projection. The dialectic of question and answer aims to enhance what is already at play in the relationship between reader and text and to occasion the arrival in the reader's mind of those insights that are in a certain sense already under way to her. The dialectic of question and answer supposes that a subject matter transcends its particular renditions. The historical character of a subject matter is such that it is always capable of being more. Like a symbol, its capacity for meaningfulness is inexhaustible. Uncovering how past authors dealt with a subject matter has immediate implications for how we might deal with it. The dialectic of question and answer initially demands that a reader separate a text from its subject matter in order to access the adequacy of its response. This not only allows the reader to consider other possibilities available to an author regarding the treatment of the subject matter but it also exposes the reader to questions about her own grasp of it. In effect, Gadamer's Aristotelean tactic of strengthening an author's argument is intended to put the hidden assumptions of our own view of a subject matter under such pressure that they are forced into the open. Whilst the dialectic of question and answer may be directed at a text, its primary aim is to bring to light the implicit assumptions about a subject matter at play within a reader. Gadamer's dialogical hermeneutics does not resolve the differences between past and present approaches. To the contrary, it aims at strengthening the differences between them. Strengthening that which is different from our own position places our implicit assumptions about a subject-matter in question. Gadamer's hermeneutic does not resolve difference. It seeks to understand what is at issue within differences, to grasp what they bring to and place in question.

Ways of understanding

Compared to Heidegger's account of interpretation as the elucidation of what already lies in understanding, Gadamer's approach to the two terms is less dichotomous but more ambiguous. What does Gadamer's hermeneutic call us to be attentive to? If Heidegger's hermeneutic constitutes a metaphysical meditation upon the insight that our thinking is rooted in a being-in-the world which takes us beyond ourselves, what is Gadamer's hermeneutic appealing to? Gadamer's hermeneutic invokes at least four modes of (interrelated) understanding: the academic and aesthetic, the religious and the ethical.

Gadamer's classicist foundations insure that part of his hermeneutic practice is to contribute to the academic understanding of received texts. Correcting the philological provenance of ancient manuscripts and clarifying the ways ancient authors received, digested, and communicated their subject matters is an attempt to get to the text itself. This is no positivistic *faux pas* which supposes that a text can be read independently of the broad tradition in which it is received. Gadamer's purpose is in fact "aesthetic." By concentrating upon what the text seeks to address, he seeks to strengthen the a text's approach to a subject matter, to make it stand out against our own assumptions about its content, to let us glimpse it without our more contemporary prejudices. However, as we have seen, the pursuit of such academic understanding is not an end in itself. Dialogue cannot commence with the text alone. The pursuit of the text-in-itself is a necessary hermeneutic *praeludium* to exposing our more immediate historical assumptions about the text and its subject matter, in other words, it is a prelude to establishing the difference that will then drive dialogue and the conflict of interpretation.

The practice of hermeneutic engagement aims at what Gadamer grants is a form of religious insight. Hermeneutic practice aims at transcendence, at being receptive to disclosures that expose the limits of present understanding. Heidegger's initial Catholic orientation perhaps shows itself in the fact that his hermeneutic celebrates the *event* of disclosure as a revelation of a power larger than and beyond ourselves. Gadamer's orientation is at once more Protestant and more classical. It is the power of negation within disclosures that are important. The revelation of a subject matter as enigmatic, the uncovering of a point of interpretation that we had not anticipated, and the disclosure of our hidden assumptions about a text, are always double edged. On the one hand, they widen the horizons of our understanding and allow us to transcend the limits of our present point of view, but on the other hand, they reveal the limits, oversights, and inadequacies of our understanding. The shock of hermeneutic disclosure is not just that it brings us to see familiar subject matters in unfamiliar ways but that it reveals the extent of our blindness to what was actually before us but which we failed to see. In short, the hermeneutic revelation is valued because of its regulative nature. First, it reminds humans that we are not gods: the time and place of insight is beyond our control. Second, the disclosure of the enigmatic nature of a text or art work reveals that the object of our understanding is always in excess of our understanding. The disclosure thereby marks a limit to what can be grasped by reason and method. Third, the disclosure reminds us of the incompleteness of understanding. Although a disclosure may uncover a hitherto unseen aspect of a subject matter, the inevitably partial and perspectival nature of the disclosure also suggests that which has yet to be disclosed. Gadamer's hermeneutic forces the reader to confront the frailty of her understanding and to moderate any claim to completeness. Philosophical hermeneutics exposes us to the recognition that there is no final word in understanding, only a careful appeal to more words and to a more careful understanding.

Finally, Gadamer's hermeneutic exposes the ethical dimension of understanding. If there is no last word in hermeneutics, neither is there a first word. Heidegger's invocation of "thrownness" and Gadamer's appeal to the enabling powers of tradition serve to remind us that we are part of a "conversation" that is already under way. This implies that the hermeneutic subject is a being whose being always remains a being-in-question precisely because how it grasps itself is always a consequence of being party to unending dialogical exchanges. The subject is not a transcendental condition of hermeneutic exchange but an integrity that comes into existence within dialogical exchange. As Bakhtin might have argued, as far as self-understanding is concerned, the exchanges of conversation and negotiation *are* the essence of what is going on. This suggests an ethical dependence upon the *otherness* of the other. It is only in relation to the difference of the other that the hermeneutic subject gains a consciousness of its own difference. Indeed, it is only because the other sees me differently that I can begin to see myself differently (see Davey 2006). Self-understanding is thus ethically dependent upon the other and upon tradition, for only by reaching out to what is not self does the subject achieve a proximate understanding of itself.

Before we consider some of the philosophical problems posed by the difficulties within the hermeneutic endeavor, some of the key aspects of Paul Ricoeur's
(1913–2005) hermeneutics should be discussed. Although Ricoeur shares the phenomenological tutelage of Heidegger and Gadamer (he worked with Mikel Dufrenne
(1910–95) on translations of Husserl during their shared internment as German
prisoners of war), he does not share their background of ancient philosophy. Rather
Ricoeur brings to hermeneutics an attentiveness to the text, an availablity to others
(*disponibilité*) which owes much to his Protestant commitments and to his early mentor
Gabriel Marcel (1889–1973). Unlike Gadamer's thought, Ricoeur's hermeneutics
is not a hermeneutics of experience but a one of action, for it is in action that the
phenomenological truths of individual consciousness are tried and tested against the
hermeneutical claims of tradition, texts and "others." It is only in the commitment to
action – specifically the reflective actions of reading and writing – that the individual
is able to explore the Being he or she is rooted in. Ricoeur upholds Marcel's claim
that the individual is *au fond*, that is, inextricably bound up with and a participant
in, Being and the life of the other. Two points are worth noting. The first concerns
the quasi Neoplatonic character to Ricoeur's thought and the second involves the
direction of his account of understanding per se.

Gadamer's hermeneutics of language has a Neoplatonic character inasmuch as
the universal aspects of language do not exist apart from particular utterances but
are inherent within them. His account of *Sachen* is similarly structured in that the
element of meaning which transcends an individual instantiation of a *Sache* does not
exist apart from that instantiation but is implicated in and by the latter. Ricoeur's
hermeneutic is not concerned to retrieve "the things themselves" but to demonstrate
that they constitute the mythic meaning-sediments which ground the plurality of
philosophy's traditions. Ricoeur's adopted task is not so much to "graft" hermeneutics
on to phenomenology but to reveal the dependence of the first-person world of the
phenomenological upon the third-person world of hermeneutical meaning structures.
Ricoeur argues accordingly that,

> Consciousness is not transparent to itself ... but a relation of conceal/reveal
> which calls for a specific reading, a hermeneutics. The task of hermeneutics
> has always been to read a text and to distinguish the true sense from the
> apparent sense, to search for the sense under the sense ... There is them, a
> proper manner of uncovering what was covered, of unveiling what was veiled,
> of removing the mask. (Kearney 1987: 105)

It is vital to Ricoeur's position that the otherness revealed in the meaning-sediments
of myth and tradition is not an alterity absolutely alien to the individual subject.
This risks positing the other as an other whose voice will not be heard and whose self
will be unaffected "in the mode of being-enjoined" (Smith 1997: 56). Ricoeur insists
that the other must be sufficiently in the self for it to matter to that self (ibid.). The
hidden meaning-sediments of myth and tradition thus constitute the "hermeneutic
community" in relation to which the subject becomes a self and to which that self

is answerable. "Action" is the ontological axis along which self and community both meet and moderate each other. This gives a specific inflection to Ricoeur's notion of understanding.

In the essay "On interpretation" (1983), Ricoeur states that "to understand oneself is to understand oneself as one confronts the text and to receive from it the conditions for a self other than that which first undertakes the reading" (1983: 193). The interpreting subject is not the precondition of understanding, rather the hermeneutic process subjectivizes its participants.

> The act of subjectivity is not so much what initiates understanding as what terminates it. This terminal act can be characterised as appropriation. [But] it does not purport ... to rejoin the original subjectivity which would support the meaning of the text. Rather it responds to the matter of the text, and hence to the proposals of meaning which the text unfolds. It is thus the counterpart of the distanciation which establishes the autonomy of the text with respect to its author, its situation and its original addressee. Thus appropriation can be integrated into the theory of interpretation without surreptitiously re-introducing the primacy of subjectivity. (Kearney 1987: 111)

The distance of history or the autonomy of the art work initially resists the unreflective orientations of their recipients. In order to engage with such works, the reader must lose herself to the text, become exposed to it and enter its world. It is not a question of projecting our understanding upon a work but of allowing the text to increase our understanding of life. A greater sense of one's own subjectivity is the result of engagement with a text, not a precondition of one's involvement: "as a reader, I find myself only by losing myself" (Simms 2003: 42). To read and to write is to engage with and mediate the sedimented layers of collective meaning in one's being. There is no end to such activity for it is only in and through such activity that, first, the subject comes to grasp more of itself and, second, that the collective ground of the subject sustains its being. Hermeneutic action for Ricoeur is an expression of faith not in the sense of a formal *credo* but in the sense that the act of understanding always points to a future "more-to-be understood." Such futural openness means that Ricoeur is never guilty of the discourtesies of the pious. His work grants equal rights to opposed interpretations in that they open the reader to conflicting but plausible worlds. Philosophy for Ricoeur demands neither speedy resolution nor aggressive defensiveness. The conflict of interpretations demands sincere, anguished contemplation. Understanding, like eternity, lives in the momentary act: there in is its agony and its hope.

Interpretation as *perpetuum mobile*

Gadamer attributes the incompleteness of understanding to the finitude of human experience and its ontological predicament: there always remains in the said something "unsaid" and what is unsaid can always undo the said. The capacity of the "other" to confront us with a perspective we have overlooked invariably exceeds what we imagine.

What Gadamer overlooks, or at least underplays, is that it is the process of interpretation itself which induces an inherent negativity within the experience of understanding. Wolfgang Iser insists that it is not the ontological circumstances of understanding which limit its completeness. It is the process of interpretation itself which renders understanding impossible in the sense that it can never achieve complete closure. To return to the beginning of this essay, it was noted that Hermes is associated with nocturnal thieving. The question which twentieth-century hermeneutics poses for the twenty-first century is whether Hermes has stolen the possibility of understanding itself. In Werner Hamacher's words, is not understanding always in want of understanding? (Hamacher 1996: 1). To pose the question another way, what is actually lost if the concept of understanding is removed from hermeneutics? After all, Wolfgang Iser's *The Range of Interpretation* (2000) and Umberto Eco's *The Limits of Interpretation* (1994) hardly mention the concept. Iser's argument is of particular interest as it suggests that it is not the ontological circumstances of understanding which render understanding incomplete but the interpretative process itself.

Wolfgang Iser's (1926–2007) early work concentrates for the most part on the reader's role in literary reception, but in *The Range of Interpretation* the process of interpretation becomes the central subject matter (2000). He strips interpretation (hermeneutics) of the post-metaphysical language of Heidegger and Gadamer and treats it pragmatically as a translation process. This does not separate hermeneutics from its ethical import, as we shall see. Iser follows Husserl and Gadamer in claiming that interpretation concerns the assimilation of subject matters. However, interpretative assimilation is marked by an ineluctable duality. Philosophical or literary subject matters cannot simply be transposed from their original horizons. In order to function within a contemporary horizon, they have to be translated into the latter's terms. Understanding is essentially interpretative: it translates a subject matter from one historical idiom into another in order to secure its functionality (2000: 154). Yet this very process generates an ineliminable difference. To translate a subject matter from one idiom into another presupposes that interpretation recognizes that something of the transposed subject matter is left behind (i.e. cannot be translated into a contemporary idiom). When the transposed subject matter is made functional, it is different from the form it took before translation (p. 60). Thus interpretation opens a space between "the from" and "the to," a space which serves only to drive further interpretation. Interpretation generates a hermeneutic differential. Iser argues that the subject matter to be interpreted is invariably shaped by the approach brought to bear, and yet "the approach is not just a superimposition but a register into which the slanted subject matter is translated." "Fashioning the subject matter points to a difference between what is to be interpreted and the register into which it is transposed" (ibid.). Interpretation is performative: it gives rise to the emergence of a liminal space which cannot be eliminated in its entirety. This residual untranslatability drives the need for further interpretation and so the process of understanding rather than being "completed" is once more driven forward or, in Derrida's terms, "postponed." The residual untranslatability produced by the effort to make a subject matter functional, drives the need for further interpretation *ad infinitum*.

Iser's succinct hermeneutical pragmatics have several consequences. First: they demonstrate why understanding is, in Werner Hamacher's phrase, always in want of understanding (i.e. cannot be theoretically grounded). It is not because the practice of interpretation can never grasp the full extent of the foreknowledge that grounds it but because the practice of interpretation generates its own incompleteness. Second: if interpretation produces an ineliminable space, why do human beings continue to interpret? Iser suggests that the ground from which human beings spring is unfathomable and "appears to be withheld from them" (2000: 155). In a manner that is reminiscent of Dilthey's dictum that "only what we do will tell us what we are," Iser argues that human beings are unavailable to themselves: we *are* (exist) but do not know what it is to be. Being human is therefore defined by two constitutive blanks. It is precisely because the "fundamentals are unplumbable" that the unending process of interpretation is driven along. Interpretation reveals what we are capable of. In a way that echoes a central theme in the thinking of Nietzsche, Marx, and Gianni Vattimo (1936–), interpretation discloses that human beings live by what they produce and that interpretation is not only "world-making" but shows what human beings are capable of making of themselves. Iser is adamant that the liminal space of interpretation must not be closed either by ideology, by rigid concepts, or by attempts to colonize the content of a subject matter. Such "colonisation converts interpretation into an act that determines the intended meaning of a subject-matter" and "when this happens interpretation ceases" (2000: 151). The cessation of interpretation and the lapse into another master narrative of the human condition threatens the possibilities for further modes of understanding and, hence, of human *being*: "life cannot be frozen into a hypostatization of any of its aspects, for it is basically unrepresentable and can therefore be conceived only in terms of the transient figurations of interpretation" (ibid.). Interpretation, in effect, renders understanding in the objectivist or cognitivist sense impossible.

Iser's analysis does not displace the ontological notion of understanding that underwrites interpretation. Heidegger and Gadamer never thought that an understanding of "understanding" (i.e. its reduction to a concept) was possible. The actuality of the ontological dimensions of understanding is always in excess of conceptualization. *What Iser's argument strikes out at is the Diltheyean notion that interpretation has its culmination in understanding.* The dynamics of difference and duality within interpretation are such that there can be no end, no terminus, to interpretation. If there is no end to interpretation and understanding never arrives, can "anything be said and in consequence, written about *anything*"? (Steiner 1990: 53). Is this the "open secret which hermeneutics ... (has) laboured to exorcize or to conceal" (ibid.)? Derrida's negative hermeneutics is in large part consistent with key aspects of Iser's argument: the constant play of linguistic signifiers suggests that we never arrive at *the* meaning of a text or assertion, for whatever meaning an interpretation suggests always defers to other combinations of meaning. A not unrelated argument is put by Wittgenstein in *Zettel*: there is no logical terminus to interpretation, no *final* interpretation, only a psychological (i.e. logically arbitrary) terminus to interpretation.

(It) is not that this symbol cannot be further interpreted, but: I do no more interpreting. I do not interpret, because I feel at home in the present picture … What we have reached is a psychological, not a logical terminus. (1967: sect. 234 and 231)

To return to our earlier discussion of biblical hermeneutics, the word of hermeneutics would appear to suggest a world without end and be "beyond *all* understanding." Foucault's observation that hermeneutics waits endlessly for the revelation of "the Word" is not unfounded. Yet the argument is *far* from what it seems.

Wittgenstein's comment serves as a "hermeneutic reminder" of something obvious but easily overlooked: namely, that underlying much twentieth-century hermeneutics is the much older conflict between language and reason in philosophy. Wittgenstein's later philosophy bids us recall that understanding is not a specifiable concept: it is more a mode of life, a knowing "how to go on." Ways of life like understanding itself have key elements of vagueness within them. Understanding how to use a word does not presuppose that I have a clear concept of all that the word stands for. All that is supposed is that I have sufficient grasp of some of its associations in order to play the particular language-game that the word is a part of. In other words, dialogical exchange continues irrespective of understanding not being reducible to a concept and may, indeed, depend upon a certain looseness of definition. In other words, Derrida's negative hermeneutics and Iser's analysis of interpretation only render understanding impossible, if and only if it is supposed that understanding and its objects are reducible to the fixity of concepts, that understanding something is the same thing as knowing something. However, *Sachen* (the objects of understanding) are not reducible to determinate concepts; rather, they are constellations or fields of meaningfulness capable of sustaining multiple interpretations. The issue is not whether an interpretation arrives at *the* meaning of a text but whether the interpretation arrived at illuminates, expands, or offers a new vector across the accumulated meanings which constitute the hermeneutic field of that text. This is reminiscent of Gadamer's reworking of *mimesis*. That we cannot say definitely what a work is, is not a cause for despair, since what we are able so say of a work allows it to become more what it is. The perspective which we might offer adds to and changes the historically accretion of perspectives which *is* the work.

Interpretation will never arrive at the definitive meaning of a work. A profound text such as Kant's *Critique of Pure Reason* is, with regard to interpretation, inexhaustible. Trouble starts, as Iser observes, whenever sectional interests strive to colonize a text and claim their view of it to be *the* meaning. Language and its infinite potential for new meaning cannot offer the same certainties as reason. The perspectival meanings that our interpretations arrive at are inherently unstable, always referring and deferring to other potential combinations of meaning. In this respect, Iser's analysis successfully illuminates Heidegger's reference to the *Unruhe* of interpretation: if interpretation both produces and is driven by the ineliminable gaps that hermeneutic translation (application) produces, interpretation actually depends upon the irresolvable difference between the text as received and the text as applied. Interpretation, in other words, becomes a matter of dialogical relations and, insofar as it does so, it honors Hermes: it stands in the irresolvable tensions *between* the horizon of the received and the applied. Yet arguably, that interpretation never affords a definitive understanding of text is no cause for despair.

That a definitive understanding is never arrived at is not necessarily a negative outcome. The subject matters of hermeneutic inquiry are *not* concepts to be seized on: they are shifting fields or constellations of interests which appear differently depending on how and where one is placed within them. Extending hermeneutic inquiry is a matter of striving to see around one's own corner, to adopt another perspective with regard to where one once stood. Hermeneutic inquiry may lead to the adoption of a new perspective but it does not arrive at the underlying meaning of a *Sache*, merely another perspective. In other words, hermeneutic inquiry is a matter of *dialogical* relations. As Ricoeur appreciates, when one's grasp of a text changes, the nature of the conversation with that text changes: one's dialogical relation to it is altered. One *proceeds* with it differently. In other words, with regard to the concept of understanding, nothing is lost by abandoning the last vestiges of the Neoplatonic inheritance within hermeneutics. If that which is to be understood is not an underlying idea or concept but a constellation of shifting meanings and associations, and if understanding is not a matter of grasping the alleged concept lying beneath the surface of a text but a matter of taking up a dialogical relation to a cluster of different interpretations, the ethical dimension of hermeneutics remains unaffected. The emergence of a new interpretation of a *Sache* can still catch us out, expose the bias of our preconceptions, as well as open us towards new horizons of meaning. According to this argument, hermeneutics is not a matter of laying siege to *the* meaning of a text or reducing it to a body of concepts, but a matter of engaging with and participating in the fields of meaning which surround the text as a dialogical object. That linguistic meaning is a matter of usage, application, and participation, that linguistic meaning is always open and never reducible to fixed concepts is thus positively advantageous to this view of hermeneutic practice. It is precisely because the realms of linguistic meaning are never fixed and closed that our interpretations of a subject matter are subject to challenge. Negative hermeneutics does indeed render objective understanding in the pejorative sense of the word "impossible" but then, the constant slippage of linguistic meaning and the unavoidable historicity of our interpretations which render objective understanding impossible guarantee that our interpretations are indeed subject to change and development.

What Iser's view of interpretation and Derrida's negative account of hermeneutics suggest is the need to differentiate between "understanding" as that which one does (understanding as a dialogical-relation) and "understanding" as that which is sought (*the* meaning of text or the underlying *concept* that a text supposedly expresses). Iser's and Derrida's position intimate that hermeneutics might do well to abandon the objectivist notion of understanding altogether. This is not just because hermeneutic practice grasped as dialogical exchange can function perfectly well without appealing to the objectivist notion of understanding but also because of the difficult and misleading associations attached to the objectivist notion. Heidegger and Gadamer strove to separate hermeneutics from the "philosophy of consciousness" and the "philosophy of identity" which underwrote Dilthey's hermeneutics. By grounding interpretation in a language-ontology they resisted the argument that understanding is a faculty of the knowing subject, rooted in the forms of the knowing subject's consciousness. Understanding is not a mode of a subject's consciousness, they argued, but a mode of its being. Fore-understanding and the expectancies of tradition are forms of Dasein. In this sense of the term, understanding is clearly possible. Understanding entails participation in the enabling prejudices (Giddens) that facilitate a certain way of life. Yet whenever Gadamer spoke of profound understanding as the negativity of *experience*, he unwittingly reinvoked the neo-Kantian view of understanding as that which relates to a conscious subject. This is indeed unfortunate, for as soon as the neo-Kantian position is reinvoked, it becomes difficult to escape Nietzsche's charge that all understanding is subjectivist, that is, tainted by a subject's will to power. There is, then, much to recommend the suggestion that hermeneutics should be thought of as a philosophy of interpretation rather than a philosophy of understanding. Yet an important twist in the argument remains. If the concept of understanding and its subjectivist associations were parted from hermeneutics, how could one make sense of "the conflict of interpretations" (Ricoeur)?

The advantages of separating hermeneutics from the philosophy of consciousness and its attendant notions of the epistemological subject are plain. Nevertheless, can hermeneutics with its notions of interpretation and perspective be separated entirely from notions of subjectivity? "Interpretation" and "perspective" cannot be separated from a point of view. However, a point of view need not summons the notion of a subject-identity in the classic epistemological sense of the term. It can belong to a "subjectivity" understood in a pluralistic sense, as when one speaks of a government or military perspective. The constellation or grouping of interests that cluster within such a subjectivity are not and do not have to be reduced to one, but can, in Nietzsche's words, act as one (*Will to Power*, sect. 490). They can engage with, become involved with, or resist other interpretations that express interests and concerns different from its own. Furthermore, it is difficult to understand how Gadamer's notion of the play of interpretations might be grasped unless *participation* is supposed. Participation presupposes involvement and involvement speaks of concerns and interests. Gadamer's appeal to the educative capacity of the negativity of experience would not make sense unless the interests (prejudices) of a "subjectivity" are challenged. The ability to learn and become different to oneself demands participation in dialogical exchange. When presented as an interpretative practice, hermeneutics *can* be thought of as a process of translation and transposition that invokes understanding neither as the definitive goal of interpretation nor as a faculty of an epistemological subject. However, although the practice of hermeneutics as dialogical exchange is perfectly plausible without an appeal to the classical concept of understanding, the notion of dialogical exchange without an appeal to subjectivity in the restricted sense of a constellation of interests is not. Without such a conception of subjectivity, there would be no points of view to exchange, to challenge, or to be challenged. Thus, without the *concept* of understanding, hermeneutics as dialogical exchange would lose none of its capacity for insight and revelation. The conflict of interpretations could still release presuppositions within a subjectivity which the latter was blind to and, in consequence, alter that subjectivity's sense of itself. Is there any loss if it is argued that such a subjectivity does not achieve self-understanding in any definitive sense but does perhaps reach other more intensive and suggestive interpretations of itself?

The question which Iser's analysis of interpretation poses is a question which the twenty-first century will have to find an answer to. "Is hermeneutics better grasped without appealing to the notion of 'understanding' and its subjectivist associations? Are not our relations to texts and to others better thought of as the continuous, difficult, and tireless practice of dialogical exchange and interpretative negotiation? This points to a conception of hermeneutics with genuine ethical promise. The weakness of Heidegger's hermeneutics is that it is more concerned with patrolling the boundary between human understanding and its non-human foundation than with resolving the conflicts which confront human beings in this world. The ethical emphasis in Gadamer's hermeneutics remains inward, concerned about its good conscience. It dwells on the pathos of individual hubris and what hermeneutic arrogance is blind to. In conclusion, separating hermeneutics from the concept of understanding with its traditional and somewhat misleading associations has the advantage of emphasizing the hard and demanding business of converse, exchange, and negotiation. Such a separation would strengthen the *exchange* character of hermeneutics and prioritize the mutuality of ethical involvement. If the process of interpretation creates liminal spaces that can never be closed, understanding can never be arrived at. But, then, if no final understanding is possible, then everything that we have and have yet to become aware of will depend upon upholding continuing hermeneutical exchanges with the other. The consequence of Iser's argument is plain. If interpretation renders understanding impossible in the sense that it is the process of interpretation which prevents understanding from ever becoming closed, then, the traditional "objectivist" concept of understanding is rendered irrelevant. What remains relevant is that the processes of interpretation and dialogical exchange are kept in motion, for it is precisely that motion which generates new and transformative insights. The questions which Iser's notion of interpretation pose for the coming century are whether a hermeneutics freed from a cognitivist concept of understanding and whether a practical hermeneutics willing to undertake the modest but strenuous tasks of conversing and of negotiation are not, after all, better prepared to meet the other? If they are, there are reasons to doubt whether hermeneutics will escape the notion of understanding and its subjectivist associations. Instead of escaping the notion, Iser's arguments suggest that the processes of interpretation will reproduce it. Is it not the case that the dynamics of dialogue "subjectivize" its participants in relation to each other? If so, will not a subject's 'understanding' remain perspectival not in Nietzsche's cognivist sense of the term but because an understanding will express a mode of relation within a process of converse. This suggests something on which all twentieth-century hermeneuticians will agree, namely, that when all is said and done (which in hermeneutics it never will be), understanding will always reach beyond itself.

References

Apel, K.-O. (1967) *Analytic Philosophy of Language and the Geisteswissenschaften*. Dordrecht: Reidel.

—— (1980) *Towards a Transformation of Philosophy*. London: Routledge & Kegan Paul.

Bakhtin, M. (1990) *Art and Answerability: Early Philosophical Works of* M. M. *Bakhtin*. Austin: University of Texas Press.

Barthes, R. (1989) *The Rustle of Language*. Berkeley: University of California Press.

Bauman, Z. (1978) *Hermeneutics and Social Science*. London: Hutchinson.

Baumgarten, A. G. (1983) *Texte zur Grundlegung der Ästhetik* [c.1748]. Hamburg: Felix Meiner.

Blond, P. (1988) *Post-Secular Philosophy*. London: Routledge.

Caputo, J. D. (1987) *Radical Hermeneutics, Repetition, Deconstruction and the Hermeneutic Project*. Bloomington: Indiana University Press.

—— (2000) *More Radical Hermeneutics*. Bloomington: Indiana University Press.

Clark, T. C. (2005) *The Poetics of Singularity: The Counter-Culturalist Turn in Heidegger, Derrida, Blanchot and the later Gadamer*. Edinburgh: Edinburgh University Press.

Collingwood, R. J. (1946) *The Idea of History*. Oxford: Clarendon Press.

Cunningham, V. (2002) *Reading After Theory*. Oxford: Blackwell.

Davey, N. (2002) "Between the human and the divine: on the question of the inbetween." In *Between the Human and the Divine: Philosophical and Theological Hermeneutics*, ed. A. Wiercinski, Toronto: Hermeneutic Press, pp. 88–97.

—— (2006) *The Unquiet Understanding: Gadamer and Philosophical Hermeneutics*. Albany: State University of New York Press.

Davidson, D. (1984) "Truth and meaning." In *Inquiries into Truth and Meaning*, Oxford: Clarendon Press.

Davies, O. (2001) *A Theology of Compassion*. London: SCM Press.

Derrida, J. (1979) *Spurs: Nietzsche's Styles*. Chicago: University of Chicago Press.

—— (1997) *Limited Inc*. Evanston, IL: Northwestern University Press.

Dilthey, W. (1976) *Selected Writings*, ed. P. Rickman. Cambridge: Cambridge University Press.

Duerr, H. P. (1985) *Dreamtime: Concerning the Boundary between Wilderness and Civilization*, trans. F. D. Goodman. Oxford: Blackwell.

Eagleton, T. (2003) *After Theory*: Harmondsworth: Penguin.

Eco, U. (1994) *The Limits of Interpretation*. Bloomington: Indiana University Press.

Fiurmara, G. C. (1990) *The Other Side of Language*: London: Routledge.

Foucault, M. (1975) *The Birth of the Clinic: An Archaeology of Medical Perception*, trans. A. M. Sheridan. New York: Vintage.

—— (1985) *The Order of Things*. London: Tavistock.

Frank, M. (1977) *Das individuelle Allgemeine. Textstrukturierung und -interpretation nach Schleiermacher*. Frankfurt: Suhrkamp.

—— (1979) *"Was heisst einen Text verstehen."* In *Texthermeneutik, Aktualität, Geschichte, Kritik*, ed. U. Nassen. Paderborn: Schoningh.

—— (1982) "Textauslegung." In *Erkenntnis und Literatur, Theorien, Konzepte, Methode der Literaturwissenschaft*, ed. D. Harth and P. Gebhardt, Stuttgart: J. B. Metzler, p. 58–77.

Gadamer, H.-G. (1976) *Philosophical Hermeneutics*. Berkeley: University of California Press.

—— (1986) *The Relevance of the Beautiful*. London: Cambridge University Press.

——(1989) *Truth and Method*. London: Sheed & Ward.

—— (1992) *On Education, Poetry and History: Applied Hermeneutics*, ed. D. Misgeld and G. Nicholson. Albany: State University of New York Press.

Giddens, A. (1976) *New Rules of Sociological Method*. London: Hutchinson.

—— (1995) *Modernity and Self Identity*. London: Polity.

Habermas, J. (1978) *Knowledge and Human Interests*. London: Heinemann.

—— (1980) "The hermeneutic claim to universality." In J. Bleicher (ed.) *Contemporary Hermeneutics: Hermeneutics as Method, Philosophy and Critique*, London: Routledge.

—— (1987) *The Philosophical Discourse of Modernity*. Oxford: Polity.

Hahn, L. E. (1993) *The Philosophy of Hans-Georg Gadamer*. Chicago: Open Court.

Hamacher, W. (1996) *Premises: Essays on Philosophy and Literature from Kant to Celan*. Cambridge, MA: Harvard University Press.

Hampson, D. (2002) *After Christianity*. London: SCM Press.

Heidegger, M. (1962) *Being and Time*, trans. J. Macquarrie and E. Robinson. New York: Harper & Row.

Hirsch, E. D. (1967) *Validity in Interpretation*. New Haven, CT and London: Yale University Press.

Holquist, M. (1990) *Dialogism*. London: Routledge.

How, A. (1995) *The Habermas–Gadamer Debate and the Nature of the Social*. Aldershot: Avebury.

Iser, W. (1978) *The Act of Reading: A Theory of Aesthetic Response*. Baltimore: Johns Hopkins University Press.

—— (2000) *The Range of Interpretation*. New York: Columbia University Press.

Jauss, H. R. (1982) *Towards an Aesthetic of Reception*. Minneapolis: University of Minnesota Press.

Kearney, R. (1987) *Modern Movements in European Philosophy*. Manchester: Manchester University Press.

Kerr, F. (1997) *Immortal Longings: Versions of Transcending Humanity*. London: SPCK.

Kimmerle, H. (1978) *Philosophie der Geisteswissenschaften als Kritik ihrer Methoden*. The Hague: Nijhoff.

Kisiel, T. and J. van Buren (eds.) (1994) *Reading Heidegger from the Start: Essays in His Earliest Thought*. Albany: State University of New York Press.

Kögler, H. H. (1996) *The Power of Dialogue: Critical Hermeneutics after Gadamer and Foucault*. Cambridge, MA: MIT Press.

Lafont, C. (1999) *The Linguistic Turn in Hermeneutic Philosophy*. Cambridge, MA: MIT Press.

Louth, A. (1989) *Discerning the Mystery: An Essay on the Nature of Theology*. Oxford: Clarendon Press.

MacIntyre, A. (1988) *Whose Justice? Which Rationality?* London: Duckworth. For a recent discussion of Gadamer by MacIntyre, see *Gadamer's Century: Essays in Honor of Hans-Georg Gadamer*, ed. J. Malpas, U. Arnswald, and J. Kertscher, Cambridge, MA: MIT Press, 2002, pp. 157–72.

—— (1990) *Three Rival Versions of Moral Inquiry*. Notre Dame, IN: Notre Dame University Press.

—— (1993) *After Virtue*. London: Duckworth, chs. 15, 16.

Malpas, J., U. Arnswald, and J. Kertscher (eds.) (2002) *Gadamer's Century: Essays in Honor of Hans-Georg Gadamer*. Cambridge, MA: MIT Press.

Martindale, C. (1993) *Redeeming the Text: Latin Poetry and the Hermeneutics of Reception*. Cambridge: Cambridge University Press.

Moran, D. (2000) *Introduction to Phenomenology*. London: Routledge.

Mueller-Vollmer, K. (ed.) (1985) *The Hermeneutics Reader*. Oxford: Blackwell.

Murray, M. (ed.) (1978) *Heidegger and Modern Philosophy*. New Haven, CT: Yale University Press.

Niethammer, L. (1994) *Posthistoire: Has History Come to an End?* London: Verso.

Nietzsche, F. (1968) *The Will to Power*, trans. W. Kaufman and R. J. Hollingdale. London: Weidenfeld & Nicolson.

Norris, C. (1985) *Contest of Faculties*. London: Methuen.

Okeshott, M. (1987) *Rationalism in Politics*. London: Methuen.

—— (1991) *On Human Conduct*. Oxford: Clarendon Press.

Ormiston, G. L. and A. D. Schrift (eds.) (1990a) *The Hermeneutic Tradition*. Albany: State University of New York Press.

—— and —— (eds.) (1990b) *Transforming the Hermeneutic Context*. Albany: State University of New York Press.

Pannenberg, W. (1976) *Theology and the Philosophy of Science*. London: Darton, Longman & Todd.

Richardson, J. (1986) *Existential Epistemology*. Oxford: Clarendon Press.

Ricoeur, P. (1974) *The Conflict of Interpretations*. Evanston, IL: Northwestern University Press.

—— (1981) *Hermeneutics and the Human Sciences*, ed. J. B. Thompson. Cambridge: Cambridge University Press.

—— (1983) "On interpretation." In A. Montefiore (ed.) *Philosophy in France Today*, Cambridge: Cambridge University Press, pp. 175–97.

Said, E. (2003) *Orientalism*. Harmondsworth: Penguin.

Schatzki, T. R., K. K. Cetina, and E. von Savigny (eds.) (2001) *The Practice Turn in Contemporary Theory*. London: Routledge.

Schleiermacher, F. (1998) *Hermeneutics and Criticism and Other Writings*, trans. A. Bowie. Cambridge: Cambridge University Press.

Silverman, H. (ed.) (1991) *Gadamer and Hermeneutics*. London: Routledge.

Simms, K. (2003) *Paul Ricoeur*. London: Routledge.

Smith, N. (1997) *Strong Hermeneutics*. London: Routledge.

Steiner, G. (1990) *Real Presences*. London: Faber and Faber.

Stenzel, J. (1934) *Philosophie der Sprache*. Munich and Berlin: R. Oldenbourg.

Szondi, P. (1995) *Introduction to Literary Hermeneutics*. Cambridge: Cambridge University Press.

Taylor, C. (1975) *Hegel*. Cambridge: Cambridge University Press.

—— (1985) "Interpretation and the sciences of man." In *Philosophical Papers*, vol. 2, Cambridge: Cambridge University Press, pp. 15–57.

—— (1995) *Philosophical Arguments*. Cambridge, MA: Harvard University Press.

—— (2004) *Modern Social Imaginaries*. London: Duke University Press.

Teichman, J. and G. White (1995) *An Introduction to Modern European Philosophy*. Basingstoke: Macmillan.

Vattimo, G. (1997) *Beyond Interpretation*. London: Polity.

Wiercinski, A. (ed.) (2003) *Between the Human and the Divine: Philosophical and Theological Hermeneutics*. Toronto: The Hermeneutic Press.

Williams, R. (2000) *On Christian Theology*. Oxford: Blackwell.

Winch, P. (1958) *The Idea of a Social Science and its Relation to Philosophy*. London: Routledge & Kegan Paul. Repr. 1988.

Wittgenstein, L. (1953) *Philosophical Investigations*. Oxford: Blackwell.

—— (1958) *The Blue and Brown Books*. Oxford: Blackwell.

—— (1967) *Zettel*. Oxford: Blackwell.

Further reading

The following volumes offer broad discussions of the primary philosophical characteristics of twentieth-century hermeneutics.

Coltman, R. (1998) *The Language of Hermeneutics: Gadamer and Heidegger in Dialogue*. Albany: State University of New York Press.

Dostal, R. (ed.) (2001) *The Cambridge Companion to Gadamer*. Cambridge: Cambridge University Press.

Gallagher, S. (1992) *Hermeneutics and Education*. Albany: State University of New York Press.

Grondin, J. (1995) *Introduction to Philosophical Hermeneutics*. New Haven, CT: Yale University Press.

—— (1996) *Sources of Hermeneutics*. Albany: State University of New York Press.

Howard, R. (1978) *Three Faces of Hermeneutics: An Introduction to Current Theories of Understanding*. Berkeley: University of California Press.

Kögler, H. H. (1996) *The Power of Dialogue: Critical Hermeneutics after Gadamer and Foucault*. Cambridge, MA: MIT Press.

Madison, G. (1988) *The Hermeneutics of Post-Modernity: Figures and Themes*. Bloomington: Indiana University Press.

Smith, P. C. (1990) *The Hermeneutics of Original Argument, Demonstration, Dialectic, Rhetoric*. Evanston, IL: Northwestern University Press.

Wachterhauser, B. (1999) *Beyond Being: Gadamer's Post-Platonic Hermeneutic Ontology*. Evanston, IL: Northwestern University Press.

Weinsheimer, J. (1991) *Philosophical Hermeneutics and Literary Theory*. New Haven, CT: Yale University Press.

17
GERMAN PHILOSOPHY

The hermeneutics of Being (Heidegger, Gadamer) versus transcendental hermeneutics or transcendental pragmatics (Apel)

Karl-Otto Apel

translated by Brian Elliott

Introduction

This review of twentieth-century German philosophy is necessarily selective and
perspectival. Nevertheless, allowing for certain preconditions, it may also have a valid
claim to be representative. Admittedly, it excludes important elements of German (or,
more accurately, German-speaking) philosophy of the twentieth century; however,
those elements could also be incorporated under other philosophical categories not
restricted specifically to Germany. Thus Wittgenstein and the Vienna Circle may
be considered as the German-language point of departure for (*linguistic*) *analytic*
philosophy, whose center of gravity later shifted to the Anglo-American world (see
"The development of analytic philosophy: Wittgenstein and after," Chapter 2). This is
similarly the case with Karl R. Popper's *critical rationalism* (see "Philosophy of science,"
Chapter 14). It is certainly true, also, that Edmund Husserl's classical *phenomenology*
originally developed in Germany and exerted great influence there on significant
philosophers, such as Max Scheler (1874–1928), Nicolai Hartmann (1882–1950)
and, indeed, Martin Heidegger (1889–1976) (see "Phenomenology," Chapter 15).
However, phenomenology should more properly be regarded as an international
movement, whose continuation took place primarily in France. This is also the case
with *Existenzphilosophie* or *existentialism*, whose true founder was the Danish thinker
Søren Kierkegaard (1813–55), and whose German representatives (Karl Jaspers and
again Heidegger) were soon replaced by French philosophers, such as Gabriel Marcel
(1889–1973), and Jean-Paul Sartre (1905–80). Western *neo-Marxism* should also be
considered as an international movement, although admittedly it did have a particular
focus in Germany with *Critical Theory*, a school of thought still represented today in
the philosophy and sociology of Jürgen Habermas (1929–). However, this aspect of
German philosophy should properly be treated as a separate subject (see "Critical
Theory," Chapter 18). In my opinion, separate treatment should similarly be accorded
also to *philosophical anthropology*, which was represented in Germany by a group of
very original – and currently somewhat neglected – thinkers, such as Max Scheler

(1874–1928), Helmuth Plessner (1892–1985), Arnold Gehlen (1904–76), and Erich Rothacker (1888–1965).

Compared with these well-known thematic divisions the three philosophical positions specifically treated in this chapter – those of Martin Heidegger, Hans-Georg Gadamer, and Karl-Otto Apel (1922–) – relate to just one aspect of twentieth-century German philosophy, an aspect which in my view brings to light a certain dialectical interconnection between the three positions. According to this interconnected treatment, Heidegger will be treated not primarily as an existential philosopher, but rather as the founder of the *hermeneutics of human existence*, of the *understanding of Being* and, finally, of the *history of Being*. As such, he inspired the *philosophical hermeneutics* of Hans-Georg Gadamer (1900–2002) and also – admittedly only with critical limitations – my own transcendental hermeneutics or "transcendental pragmatics."

In order to discuss the dialectical interconnection between the three positions treated here I shall present them in a rough, preliminary sketch in terms of a possible confrontation between the first two basic conceptions and the third. From the perspective of *transcendental pragmatics* (which in my view co-founds a *transcendental hermeneutics*) this possible confrontation can be highlighted with the following question: can or must the *logos* of the argumentative discourse of philosophy – as a philosophical hermeneutics – ultimately find its foundation of validity in temporal being or in the history of Being? Or must every specifically *philosophical* proposition – as a possible proposition also about temporal being or about the history of Being – be able ultimately to justify its claim to universal validity before the *logos* of discourse understood as raised above time and history?

The answer to this question today cannot anymore be given in a metaphysically fundamental manner, but must, in my view, be given in a strictly transcendental-reflective way, in the sense of a linguistic- or meaning-critical (*sprach- und sinnkritische*) transformation of Kant.

Heidegger's new philosophical approach: What is the bearing of the attempted answer on the question concerning the "meaning of Being"?

Heidegger's philosophical approach in his (albeit incomplete and subsequently never completed) *magnum opus, Being and Time* (1927),[1] was immediately recognized by contemporaries to be something wholly new, that is, in comparison with the tendencies that were representative of German philosophy at the beginning of the twentieth-century; these tendencies were: *neo-Kantianism* which predominated from the end of the nineteenth-century (see "Kant in the twentieth century," Chapter 4), *phenomenology* founded by Edmund Husserl at the beginning of the twentieth century (see "Phenomenology," Chapter 15), and also the new approaches to ontology and ethics developed by Max Scheler (1874–1928) and Nicolai Hartmann (1882–1950), which related critically to neo-Kantianism and phenomenology. Only the affinity between the Heideggerian approach and the *Existenzphilosophie* founded by Karl Jaspers and inspired by Kierkegaard appeared initially to be illuminating.

Only gradually did readers come to understand the approach of *Being and Time* – and even later, perhaps also the historical reasons for its non-completion – on the basis of Heidegger's own programmatic indications, above all according to his conception of the *ontological difference* and the corresponding question concerning the *meaning of Being*. This question was in fact – in contradistinction to the classical question of being in the ontological tradition – not to be understood and answered as such according to the abstract-logical structure of the "beingness" of beings (*Seiendheit des Seienden*), but rather by recourse to the "operative" (*vollzugshaft*) (and thus temporal and existential) understanding-of-Being (*Zu-sein-verstehen*) of human existence. Heidegger's basic question thus referred to the internal relationship between the conception of a fundamental ontology and a quasi self-reflective existential ontology directed toward the human understanding of Being.

Amidst all entities, only the human being *exists* in the manner of both an operative and reflexive relationship with its own Being – in the manner of a "having-to-be" (*Zu-sein-haben*) and a "care" (*Sorge*) of self. Heidegger's approach may therefore be understood to imply that one can expect an internally intelligible answer to the question of the meaning of Being based on one's self-reflection on existence.

On the one hand, this latter consideration opened up the theoretical field for an existential ontology (thus of an *Existenzphilosophie* or philosophy of existence); on the other hand, however, an indication was given of this philosophy's epistemological method of "inner understanding." Wilhelm Dilthey (1833–1911) had previously characterized this method as that of the cultural-scientific cognition of human life (*geisteswissenschaftliche Erkenntnis des menschlichen Lebens*), in contradistinction to the external, nomological "explanation" (*Erklären*) of the natural sciences. (For more on Dilthey, see "Twentieth-century hermeneutics," Chapter 16.) Heidegger laid claim to the internal understanding of one's own being as *the* mode of being of human existence and therefore was able to understand the method of philosophical existential analysis as that of a "hermeneutics" of existence.

By so doing, the cognitive side of fundamental ontology was characterized and at the same time the task was set of deepening Kant's transcendental question as that about the conditions of the possibility of ontological understanding. For the existentially grounded ontological understanding of Dasein was meant to function both as the fundamental ontological and as the transcendental foundation for the very varied forms of constitution pertaining to the different ontological modes of those entities that can be humanly experienced in any way whatsoever. Although the internally intelligible being of Dasein – as "that with which *Dasein* is always concerned" – is essentially distinct in its constitution from the objective being of the objects of experience in Kant's sense, Heidegger was able to show, from the standpoint of fundamental ontology, that Dasein (both as understanding Being-in-the-world and as care of self) has always already been made manifest in its experiencability and thus at the same time has always already constituted the ontological modes of the entities of its environment. This does not relate primarily to the "presence-at-handness" (*Vorhandensein*) of the objects of theoretical science, but in the first instance rather to the "readiness-to-hand" (*Zuhandenheit*) of the "equipment" (*Zeug*) with a practical "end" or "appliance" (*Bewandtnis*) within the horizon of "concernful having-to-do-with" (*besorgenden Zutunhabens*). It is the case, however, that Dasein's constitution does nevertheless relate to the mere "presence-at-hand" of objects in those cases where an instrument does not function as it should and thereby becomes conspicuous in its mere presence-at-hand. The difference between these distinct modes of ontological understanding is also characterized by Heidegger as the difference between the "pre-predicative synthesis" of the "hermeneutic" disclosure of "something as something" in its "significance" (*Bedeutsamkeit*) and the "predicative synthesis" of the traditional epistemological determination of objects present-at-hand in cognitive judgment.

In *Being and Time* Heidegger had also already indicated a radically deepened constitutional problematic with respect to the Being of other subjects of existence. Rather than the "transcendental solipsism" (Husserl) of the "I think" – which dominated the subject–object problematic of critical epistemology from Descartes on – Heidegger maintained that what he termed "being-with" ("*Mitsein*") others should be the existential and transcendental presupposition of the relevant constitutional problematic, and in such a way that solitary being (*Alleinsein*) is to be understood from the outset as a deficient mode of social being or "being with one another" (*Miteinandersein*).

However, according to Heidegger, the difference between Being or its modes of Being (as manifested in the ontological understanding of *Dasein*) and entities (*das Seiende*) or "beingness" or "essence" (*Seiendheit*) only becomes intelligible when time as the horizon of ontological understanding is taken into consideration. Then the "ecstatic" temporality – that is, at once related to presence, having-been (*Gewesenheit*) and future – pertaining to the "existential" (later "ec-sistential") ontological constitution of Dasein shows itself to be the condition of the possibility of the constitution of all ontological modes. The mode in question is, first, the existential one of finite Dasein itself, that is, of "being-towards-death" (*Sein zum Tode*); second, the relational structures of the environment of concerned having-to-do-with; and finally, the deficient mode of the mere "presence-at-hand" of objects and their properties. According to Heidegger this last mode, presence-at-hand, as the only ontological mode traditionally thematized in ontology and epistemology, shows itself to be the correlative (*Reflex*) of the continuously posited "presence" (*Anwesenheit*) of entities merely contemplated in the present. Over and against this presence, the common understanding of time takes the "having-been" of Dasein and its world as "having-passed" (*Vergangenheit*) – that is, as *no longer being* – and the future is recognized as not yet being (*noch nicht seiend*). The structure of time itself is recognized solely as a succession of now-moments in time, whereas the "ecstatic" temporality of Dasein itself remains wholly unthematized.

According to Heidegger, along with the reduction of ontological understanding in the "common understanding of time" (with its fixation on constant presence) there goes a suppression of the existentially constitutive structures relating to the finitude of human being-in-the-world; specifically, a suppression of the "facticity" of "thrownness" into the *there* (*Da*) and of the limitation of Dasein's "projective" possibilities by death. Similarly, if knowledge is understood solely as the analysis of present evidences of sense (*gegenwärtige Sinnes-Evidenzen*) by means of timeless ideational concepts, then the "destinal historicity" (*Geschichtlichkeit*) of human existence founded in the existential temporality of the "thrown project" – which is connected in the "herme-neutics" of Dasein with a cultural and above all linguistic pre-understanding of the world – cannot be recognized as the transcendental condition of the possibility of the understanding of world.

In short, the phenomenological exposition of the "originary temporality" of human Being-in-the-world and of the ontological understanding founded therein clarifies why Heidegger accuses the whole philosophical tradition of the "forgetfulness" of Being. Initially, the existential hermeneutics of human Dasein (as carried out in the published sections of *Being and Time*) is meant to set out phenomenologically the presuppositions of an ontological understanding affected by the "forgetfulness of Being." The prospective "destruction" (*Destruktion*) of traditional ontological metaphysics (announced but not carried out in *Being and Time* §6) – above all of its Greek foundation and modern reformulation from Descartes on – was to follow.

The envisaged completion of *Being and Time* gave way, however, to what Heidegger himself called, in his 1947 *Letter on Humanism*, the "turning" (*die Kehre*) of the philosophy of *Being and Time*. This philosophical turning coincided, at least chrono-logically, with the politically determined new orientation of Heidegger's thinking from 1933. What is the significance of this turning, and its continuation in Heidegger's later philosophy, for the approach of *Being and Time* as we have explicated it thus far?

There are unmistakable characteristics of an altered overall position and conception of Heideggerian thought in connection with the turning, as well as indications of a deep-rooted continuity that stretches from *Being and Time* to the later period. Let us consider initially those characteristics of the turning which Heidegger himself signaled and commented on and which are certainly unmistakable to his readers.

Heidegger says, in his *Letter on Humanism*, concerning the fact that the third division of the first part of *Being and Time* was "withheld": "Here the whole matter is turned around" (*Hier kehrt sich das Ganze um*). Nevertheless he emphasizes the fact that the turning of his thought that begins here is not an "alteration of the standpoint" (*Änderung des Standpunktes*) of *Being and Time*. Rather, here his thought is said for the first time to turn "into the locale of the dimension from out of which *Being and Time* is experienced, that is, from out of the basic experience of forgetfulness of Being" (*in die Ortschaft der Dimension, aus der "Sein und Zeit" erfahren ist, und zwar erfahren aus der Grunderfahrung der Seinsvergessenheit*) (GA 9, 328; P, 250). Yet he also accounts for the turning with reference to the fact that his thought "did not succeed" with the help of the language of metaphysics. Does this mean that Heidegger's late work – already beginning, as we know, with his *Beiträge zur Philosophie: Vom Ereignis* (English translation: *Contributions to Philosophy (From Enowning)*), written between 1936 and 1938 though not published until 1989 – no longer belongs to metaphysics in the trans-formed sense earlier proclaimed as "existential ontology" or "fundamental ontology"? Is the turning not limited to the fact that, having revealed the "originary temporality" of existence in the hermeneutics of Dasein, Heidegger now takes up the already postu-lated "destruction" of traditional ontology from out of this temporal horizon?

Indeed, just about every phase of the history of European metaphysics, whose "destruction" was envisaged in *Being and Time*, receives treatment in Heidegger's late work. For instance, among the texts published during Heidegger's lifetime, the beginning of metaphysics is considered in "Plato's doctrine of truth" (1942), the post-Cartesian metaphysics of subjectivity in the essay "The age of the world picture" (1938), and Kant's *Critique of Pure Reason* is discussed in two comprehensive though divergent interpretations (1929 and 1935/6). Among the lectures and treatises (already published or still to be published in the "last hand edition" of the *Gesamtausgabe*) we find studies of German Idealism (Fichte, Hegel and especially Schelling's text on freedom), Aristotle, Leibniz on the foundation of logic, and above all comprehensive interpretations of Nietzsche's philosophy (the doctrines of the will to power and "eternal recurrence of the same") with which, according to Heidegger, European metaphysics ends in nihilism.

Yet in each of these later texts – with the exception of the first Kant book (*Kant and the Problem of Metaphysics*, 1929), which was written before the turning – time in the sense of the existential ("ecstatic") and the transcendental temporality of Dasein – is no longer the foundation for the destruction of traditional ontology, but rather temporal being itself. Admittedly, this latter concept had already found a "revelatory" (*erschlossen*) locale of intelligible sense in the ecstatic temporality of Dasein. Now, however, it is factically distinguished as the "truth of Being itself" from the "revealedness" (*Erschlossenheit*) of Dasein. (At times it is even designated by the archaic German word for being, *Seyn*; although, according to Heidegger, this suggestion must yield to the insight that Being (*Sein*) cannot be thought without entities (*Seiendes*) and thus not without the ontological understanding of the entity Dasein.) Only then Being itself might still be thematically understood within the horizon of the temporality of Dasein when one connects these insights with Heidegger's hermeneutics of anxiety (*Angst*) in his 1929 text "What is metaphysics?" which characterizes Dasein as "Being held in nothingness" and "nothingness" as the "veil of Being." "Nothingness" would then belong to the finitude of Dasein's ecstatic temporality and at the same time – as the "nothingness of all entities" – be testimony to the manifestness (*Offenbarkeit*) of Being itself.

It is certainly true that, with the turning, the language and – one could also say – the momentum and pathos of Heidegger's philosophy alter in an astonishing manner. In short: fundamental ontology no longer appears as existential ontology. Dasein's "forgetfulness of Being" is no longer explicated by means of the (also designated "existentiell") differentiation of the "they" (*das Man*) and the "authenticity" of existence in "angst-prepared anticipation of death" (*Vorlaufen zum Tode*) as the "most authentic possibility" of Dasein. The "resoluteness" (*Entschlossenheit*) of authentic existence which Dasein must prove in the "project" of its ontological possibilities, appears to be replaced by the "revealedness" (*Erschlossenheit*) of "ec-sistence" as the "going-beyond" (transcendence) or "standing out" of "Da-sein" into the "open" of the "clearing of Being" (*Lichtung des Seins*). Accordingly, Heidegger, in his *Letter on Humanism* of 1947, rejects Sartre's talk of existentialism as humanism because in "ec-sistence" (no longer "existence") the essential matter is not the human but rather *Being*. Admittedly the highest "worth" of human beings – and thus of the human – resides precisely in the fact that they do not exist for their own sake but rather, as the "shepherd of Being" (*Hirte des Seins*), undertake the "warding" (*Hut*) of Being at Being's behest and so to speak in obedience (*Hörigkeit*) to the command (*Zuspruch*) of Being.

In my opinion, both the rupture and, at the same time, the continuity in Heidegger's thought, both before and after the turning, can be discussed with utmost philosophical rigor with respect to the problematic of *time* or *history* and *truth*. I shall now attempt to do this in more detail.

Initially, it is striking that, in the texts after the turning, the distinction developed by Heidegger between the "originary," threefold "ecstatic" temporality of Dasein and the "vulgar" time or "inner temporality" (*Innerzeitigkeit*) of now-moments – this latter understood on the basis of "fallenness" (*Verfallen*) onto the "presence" (*Anwesenheit*) of "present-at-hand" entities encountered in the present (*Gegenwart*) – no longer plays any role. Instead, Heidegger now speaks of *the* (temporal) "Being" and *the* "history of Being" whose "epochs" correspond respectively to the "event" of "the clearing and at once renewed covering over" of Being. Here is to be found, in my opinion, an incontestable privileging of the "inner temporality" of now-moments (corresponding to the primacy of the present), even though Heidegger does not want to use the word *Ereignis* (event) in the plural and prefers to understand the history of Being as the "production or temporalization" (*Zeitigung*) of Being rather than as a succession of occurrences in time. In short: in the onto-historical thinking of the late Heidegger a very radical version of historicism becomes apparent, although Heidegger would reject this characterization as a regression to the subjective metaphysics of the nineteenth century (as later does Gadamer, as will be shown). However, the specific historicism of the later Heidegger resides in the fact that the *logos* of truth understood as universal validity – implicitly adopted by Heidegger himself in his philosophical propositions – is rendered completely ineffective by the conception of the "history of Being" in favor of the putatively sole authority of the "destiny of Being" (*Seins-Geschick*).

This is most clearly shown by Heidegger's constant reassurance that his destruction – or what he later calls the "overcoming" (*Verwindung*) – of European metaphysics does not represent a critique of the canonical thinkers. All attempted refutation in the domain of "essential thinking" is putatively unwise, because in the unfolding of metaphysics from Plato to Nietzsche the destiny (*Schickung*) of Being itself is at work. An alternative to this destiny – leading from Plato's subjugation of temporal Being to the eternally present Ideas, through the modern assertion of the "enframing" (*Gestell*) in the subject–object relation in science and technology, up to the inversion of Platonism in Nietzsche's philosophy of the will to power and to the nihilism of the present – is at best to be hoped for in an "originary" (*anfänglich*) thought and poetry, such as is found, for example, prior to Plato in Parmenides and Heraclitus (and in the poet Sophocles and much later still in Hölderlin).

In his first book on Kant after *Being and Time* – the 1929 *Kant and the Problem of Metaphysics*, which still preceded the *Kehre* – Heidegger once again, in my view, argued most carefully. Here he attempted, in an almost desperate manner, to show that in the problematic of the schematism and the imagination, found in the First Edition of the *Critique of Pure Reason*, Kant is in accord with the conception of "ec-static" temporality and that in the recognition of the identity of the future projections of ontological understanding Kant provides a de facto confirmation of the temporal basis of finite reason or even of reason's identity with "originary time." Admittedly, so Heidegger's argument continues, Kant drew back from the "abyss" of this insight in the Second Edition of the *Critique* in favor of an allegedly "time free" synthesis of understanding.

This obviously must be understood as criticism. Against this it can be objected that Kant, in contradistinction to Heidegger, was not primarily interested in the meaning-projection (*Sinn-Entwurf*) of ontological understanding but rather in the constitution of objectivity and so also in the "intersubjective validity" of thought and knowledge. For this reason he wished to keep temporality and historicity (as also the concrete reality of language) at a distance from transcendental logic. Admittedly, Kant does not thereby engage directly with Heidegger on this issue, and no decision concerning the charge made by Heidegger can so far be arrived at. However, this issue points back to Heidegger's central interpretation of truth as "manifestness" (*Offenbarkeit*) or "unconcealedness" (*Unverborgenheit*) (*Aletheia*). In light of this conception of truth, the idea of the intersubjective validity of scientific thought and knowledge, which stands in the foreground in Kant in the guise of transcendental truth, suffers a radical devaluation.

Thus Heidegger says in the 1934 lecture *On Logic as the Question Concerning Language*:

> Is there then no absolute truth? Indeed not. And it is about time that we rid ourselves of the estrangement about it, i.e. become clear about being above all humans and not gods. That does not mean, however, that there is no truth whatever. Truth is the manifestness of entities. What is true in this sense of truth suffices completely for a human life. A truth does not become a lesser truth when it is not valid for everyone. (1934: 36) (trans. Brian Elliott)

And in the *Contributions to Philosophy* (*From Enowning*) from 1936–8 Heidegger remarks:

> Where truth conceals itself in the form of "reason" and the "reasonable" its non-being [*Unwesen*] is at work, that destructive power of the universally valid by means of which everyone is arbitrarily put in the right and that pleasure arises in the fact that of course no one has a genuine advantage over the others. It is this "magic" of universal validity that has consolidated the dominant interpretation of truth as correctness and made it virtually unshakeable. (GA 65, 343; C, 240) (trans. Brian Elliott)

Leaving aside the fact that these pronouncements by Heidegger are logically confused – for in no way does the "universal validity" of truth "put everyone arbitrarily in the right" – their polemic against the validity of truth for all rational beings is truly terrifying. For these pronouncements must be considered together with numerous other utterances of the same period which validate the relationship to a people and its destiny as the sole normative imperative (*normative Verbindlichkeit*) of truth.[2] (In actual fact the intersubjectivity of "Being-with" in Heidegger nowhere went beyond this horizon.)

However, the fact remains that, although this has scarcely been noticed, in the 1964 essay "The end of philosophy and the task of thinking" (clearly under the influence of Ernst Tugendhat's critique[3]) Heidegger revoked the identification of truth with "unconcealedness" along with the thesis of the "essential transformation of truth" in the sense of correctness in Plato that he had maintained for decades. There he writes: "*Aletheia*, unconcealedness conceived as the clearing of presence, is not yet truth"; and again: "The natural concept of truth does not mean unconcealedness, nor is this so in the philosophy of the Greeks ... But then neither is the assertion of the essential transformation of truth ... defensible" (SD, 78; BW, 447).

Nevertheless, Heidegger drew the consequences of this revocation only in a very one-sided manner, that is, he remained insistent on the primacy of the *historical* "clearing of meaning" (*Sinn-Lichtung*) over universally valid truth (which might be understood counterfactually as a "regulative idea" in Kant's sense). In his final position Heidegger holds that the correctness or falsity of a proposition is only possible "in the element of the clearing of presence." The possible truth or falsity of empirical propositions in science would thereby be rendered dependent in a one-sided manner on the historical clearing of meaning (similar to the manner in which the results of "normal science" are dependent on incommensurable paradigms in Thomas Kuhn). However, might it not be the case that clearings of sense are not simply destinally (*geschickhaft*) (thus a-rationally) determined, but also for their own part dependent on true and false propositions (for example, on verifications and falsifications of scientific hypotheses) which would have to be grasped as points of departure for historical, indeed transculturally valid, processes of learning? Proponents of semantic reference realism such as Hilary Putnam appear to speak in favor of this view, according to which cognitive priority is granted to the extension as opposed to the intension of concepts, thereby providing a counterbalance to Heidegger's hypostasizing of language as the "house of Being."[4]

In any event, concerning the question of truth the following opposition remains: the "unconcealing" (*Entbergung*) or "clearing" (*Lichtung*) of the meaning of Being is in actual fact historical and it always includes as the unconcealing of linguistically determinable being the concealing (*Verbergung*) of another possible being. This insight, which was already connected in *Being and Time* with the discussion of existential meaning-projections that are at the same time failed apprehensions of possible sense, is one of Heidegger's great, though ambivalent, discoveries, one which dominates his entire work.

In my view the most compelling illustration of the unconcealment conception is to be found in the later Heidegger's treatise "The origin of the work of art" (1935). (For further discussion of this treatise see "Twentieth-century aesthetics," Chapter 22.) Here it becomes clear – in the "strife" of "earth" and "world" – that the "clearing of Being" in art (and also in language) not only concerns, in a quasi-idealist way, pure "meaning" constitution, but also the formation of "the other" of meaning-clearing, which is indeed the "earth" as that which tends to conceal itself in all meaning-clearing but as such can still be formed.

Linguistically constituted meaning-clearing is prior to propositional truth insofar as it opens and limits the domain of possible questions which true and false propositions attempt to answer. On the other hand, it remains the case that true (and false) propositions are valid independently of time, that is, for every rational being (*zon logon echon*, animal possessing reason). And this truth-correctness-validity is not only canonical for "normal science" (which according to Heidegger "does not think") but also for philosophy that attempts "to think Being."[5]

That this is so can be shown easily with respect to the truth claim of Heidegger's own propositions. Undoubtedly, these propositions – as propositions of temporally present thinking – are dependent on the "fore-structure" of understanding Being-in-the-world as explicated by Heidegger. That is, they are dependent on the structure of an onto-historically "thrown projection," which is to be understood solely as an answer to a situation. However, as Heidegger's self-correction on the question of the definition of truth showed in veritably propositional explicitness, it is not possible for the philosopher to evade discussion (and to this extent also possible refutation) on the level of his necessarily universal and therefore non-historically relative claim to truth. This is also the case – and in my view in our time with particular urgency – for the non-propositional, non-explicitly but rather performatively and implicitly acknowledged claims to truth connected with every philosophical proposition. It is the case, for example, for Nietzsche's performative truth claim in the (in)famous proposition: "Truth is a kind of error without which a certain kind of living being could not live." (Heidegger, who places this proposition at the end of metaphysics, does not take seriously the performative element and accepts as meaningful only Nietzsche's propositionally explicit claim; he comments: "If truth according to Nietzsche is a kind of error, then the essence of this truth resides in a manner of thinking which falsifies the real always and necessarily" ("Plato's doctrine of truth"). In my opinion his commentary should have read: "then Nietzsche annuls his own performatively necessary truth claim and thereby the philosophical proposition becomes meaningless."

Gadamer's conception of a "philosophical hermeneutics" and of a "hermeneutical philosophy"

Hans-Georg Gadamer lived from 1900 to 2002, but he did not publish his magnum opus, *Truth and Method*, until 1960. In contrast to the way in which his teacher, Heidegger, responded to the historical situation with his major work *Being and Time* (and then later, after the turning, with his philosophy of the "history of Being"), these dates indicate something about how Gadamer's philosophy was conditioned by the historical situation in a manner fundamentally different from Heidegger. Starting in the 1920s and persisting even after the turning (which, for Heidegger himself, was a response to what he regarded as the failure of the philosophical language of *Being and Time*), Heidegger's philosophy displayed a revolutionary character in that it insisted on the necessity for a totally new beginning in relation to the tradition and the social context which he called the "with-world" (*Mitwelt*). This radicalism of "destruction" became even more pronounced as the later Heidegger finally condemned all concepts of academic philosophy (including those he had himself introduced) in favor of a poeticized language of thinking after the "end of philosophy." Such an attitude, which puts the whole philosophical tradition into question, is completely absent in Gadamer.

Instead, Gadamer endeavors, in his founding of a hermeneutical philosophy (which appeared in a time of reconstruction after the German catastrophe), to utilize the structures of Heidegger's thought, presupposed in his approach, for what is on the whole a culturally conservative task of reintegrating contemporary philosophy into the European tradition. The classical Greek thinkers (Socrates, Plato, and Aristotle), who already were, for Heidegger, the founders of metaphysics, thereby play a thoroughly positive role that Gadamer explicitly defends *against* Heidegger's "destruction."

What Gadamer terms the "effective history" (*Wirkungsgeschichte*) of Heidegger's "enframing" (*Gestell*), that is, of the technological scientism that renders the world serviceable (which Heidegger had already seen as founded in Plato's doctrine of the Ideas) begins, according to Gadamer, with the post-Cartesian establishment of the epistemological subject–object relation, in other words, with the modern absolutizing of method and the autonomy of the subject. (Kant's "Copernican turn" and the conception of a constitutive transcendental philosophy following this turn must be understood as absolutely in contrast to the "happening of truth" (*Wahrheitsgeschehen*) of hermeneutical understanding, which Gadamer opposes to the absolutizing of what he terms "method." This is also the case, on the level of practical philosophy, in relation to the Categorical Imperative, as abstract principle of universalization, and, on the level of the philosophy of art, in relation to the aesthetic consciousness of the "critique of the power of judgment," which according to Kant requires the abstraction of the judgment of taste from all relations to truth as revelation of mundane meaning (*Weltsinnerschließung*) and to the human moral-practical life orientation.)

Regarding the basic positive orientation of Gadamer's *hermeneutical* philosophy, in my opinion two points of departure must be noted corresponding to what has already been said, while still bearing in mind Gadamer's academic background.[6] These are, on the one hand, Heidegger's approach and, on the other, the dialogical model traceable back to Plato or, more accurately, to the Platonic Socrates.

What is new and quasi-revolutionary in Gadamer's approach – an approach which above all lies in his critical and still often disputed connection with the hermeneutics concerned with the founding of the human or cultural sciences (*Geisteswissenschaften*) in the nineteenth century (Schleiermacher, Droysen, Boeckh, and above all Dilthey) – evidently stems from his identification of understanding (*Verstehen*) with the temporal mode of being of human existence. (For further discussion of Gadamer's hermeneutics, see "Twentieth-century hermeneutics," Chapter 16.) In this way Gadamer has recourse both to the existential-ontological approach of the early Heidegger and also to Heidegger's late philosophy, grasped by Gadamer as the *hermeneutics of the history of Being*. Admittedly, Gadamer saw this existential-ontological approach not primarily as a matter of the understanding realization (*Nachvollzug*) of the projected possibility of Dasein that relates to the future (that is, of Dasein's "most authentic being-able" or, in late Heidegger, of the hope for a "new beginning" on the basis of the "destining" of Being), but rather as concerning the "hermeneutics of facticity" of Dasein. This hermeneutics of facticity already relates, in Heidegger, to the historically conditioned "thrownness" (*Geworfenheit*) which also affects the projections of our being-able. Thus it relates to the whole "pre-understanding" of our Being-in-the-world, insofar as it is conditioned by the fact of the cultural tradition, a fact which is above all linguistically determined. This pre-understanding, which constitutes the "fore-structure" of our understanding of Being-in-the-world, precedes, for Gadamer as also for Heidegger, all intentional-cognitive "achievements" of consciousness (in Husserl's sense). As such, according to Gadamer, it must function in "philosophical hermeneutics" as a more basic presupposition and so be foundational for all methodological achievements of a hermeneutics considered as an art of interpretation.

According to Gadamer, as a result of this presupposition it is impossible to separate a purely objective method of understanding and meaning-interpretation from the subjective practice whereby understanding is *applied* to the life-world (*Lebenswelt*). Consequently, it is also impossible to secure, in a manner analogous to, but different from, the methodology of the natural sciences, the scientific dignity of hermeneutics as an autonomous methodology. This was precisely what Dilthey wanted to do in the nineteenth century and, according to Gadamer, it was the unfeasibility of this project that led to Dilthey's entanglement in historicism.

For, on the one hand, Dilthey had already also recognized the historicity of the subjective conditions of the possibility of understanding in his philosophy of life (*Lebensphilosophie*). However, in his effort to found an objective methodology of the human sciences, Dilthey did not follow the insight of his philosophy of life into the ontological unity of understanding, interpretation and historical life-practice, but rather attempted, following Schleiermacher, methodologically to separate the episte-mological problem of the objectively identical retrospective understanding of psychic acts from the understanding's conditions of application. Against this, Gadamer wanted – following Heidegger's existential ontology – to recognize unconditionally the *historicity* of understanding as Dasein's practice and precisely in this way solve the problem of historicism. (We shall return to this approach, which, in the case of representatives of hermeneutics derived from Dilthey such as Emilio Betti and E. D. Hirsch, met with heavy resistance.)

Gadamer summarizes the existential-ontological approach of his philosophical hermeneutics as follows:

> Through Heidegger's ... interpretation of understanding the problem of hermeneutics gains a universal compass, indeed it gains a new dimension. The connection of the interpreter to his object, which in the reflection of the historical school was not able to find any proper legitimation, now receives a concretely demonstrable meaning, and it is the task of hermeneutics to provide the demonstration of this meaning. That *Dasein's* structure is thrown

projection, that *Dasein* is understanding according to its proper act of Being [*Seinsvollzug*] – that must also be the case for the act of understanding which occurs in the human sciences. The universal structure of understanding attains its concretion in historical understanding, whereby concrete attachments to morals and tradition and their corresponding possibilities of one's own future become effective in understanding itself. (WM, 249; TM, 264)

However, before we explicate the positive consequences for his own philosophical hermeneutics that Gadamer derives from the Heideggerian approach, we must introduce the second point of departure that Gadamer refers to: the approach of a "dialectic of the dialogue," which Gadamer himself traces back to his studies of Platonic philosophy that preceded the completion of *Truth and Method*. This approach, which Gadamer introduces in his magnum opus wrapped up, so to speak, in his *language* ontology, contains references to structural elements that are absent from Heidegger's existential ontology but are prerequisites for a "concretion" of existential understanding in the sense of the "historical understanding" of the human sciences (for example, in the understanding of texts). The approach is in fact a question of replacing in some manner the Cartesian subject–object relation, which was a fundamental posit of modern methodology up to and including Dilthey, with a hermeneutically more appropriate relationship between the interpreter and interpretandum (what is to be interpreted). Gadamer has recourse here to the I–thou relationship of the communicative understanding on "the matter" (*die Sache*), which is itself in the light of language in each case already discovered *as something*. Although he admits in advance that the hermeneutical situation in relation to texts is not fully equivalent to that between two conversation partners, he believes he is entitled to speak of a "hermeneutical conversation" (WM, 365; TM, 386–7).

From this perspective, derived from Gadamer's two points of departure, there arises at this point the basic problem of Gadamer's hermeneutics: how is the position (inspired by Heidegger) of the radical *historicity* of understanding as a *temporal happening of truth* consistent with the point of departure of an *understanding through dialogue*? Indeed, in my opinion, all the characteristic theses and key concepts of Gadamer's hermeneutics can be understood as an answer to this question. However, thereby an ontologically conditioned asymmetry is immediately apparent, which is difficult to reconcile with the relationship of partners, especially their validity claims, within an argumentative dialogue or discourse.

The text represents, according to Gadamer, the claim of tradition to be revalidated by the interpreter with the aim of advancing the tradition. The condition of the possibility of such advancement through interpretation resides ultimately in the fact that the interpreter is, in his pre-understanding of the life-world, ontologically conditioned by the same historical process of tradition that he must hermeneutically develop. (This ontological relation of the transmission of tradition cannot, according to Gadamer, be genuinely rendered ineffective by modern processes of what is often called the "disempowerment of tradition" (*Traditionsentmachtung*) – for example, by secularization, "decay of values" (*Werteverfall*), or by the museum enculturation of art's effectiveness.[7])

Gadamer also proceeds from the assumption, however, that between the "horizon" of mundane pre-understanding on which the interpreter is dependent and the corresponding horizon of the interpretandum there exists a historically conditioned difference that has to be bridged hermeneutically. This bridging occurs, according to Gadamer, by means of what he terms the "fusion of horizons" (*Horizontverschmelzung*), and thereby the fundamental answer of his hermeneutics to the question of the reconcilability of the dialogue-model with the onto-historical model is indicated.

However, this talk of a fusion of horizons is very vague and immediately raises further questions, for example, the question of the normatively appropriate fusion of horizons. Gadamer constantly offers reassurance that he does not wish to issue any methodological instructions but merely to give an answer to the philosophical question "how understanding is at all possible." In this sense he refers to the fact that the transmission of tradition by *understanding, interpretation and their application to the practice of life* always proceeds by means of fusion of horizons. However, even if one posits this as an existential-ontological precondition of all hermeneutics, one can still ask in the present – after the development of philosophy and the "disciplines of *logos*" (*technai logikai*), such as grammar, logic, rhetoric, and hermeneutics) – whether the constant precondition of fusion of horizons also in itself provides the sufficient condition for *valid* or correct understanding, interpreting and applying, that is, for an understanding that can also supply the preconditions of a critical judgment and a development of cultural transmission based on them.

Moreover, this question is unavoidable especially when Gadamer is understood in such a way that hermeneutical understanding cannot be restricted methodologically, through a "hermeneutical abstraction," to a retrospective understanding of meaning intentions that is free of evaluation, but rather originarily and thus in the final analysis as striving for a (dialogical) understanding (*Sich-Verständigen*) on matters with the goal of a justified consensus. In my view, the question (itself also methodologically relevant) of how – in the sense of a normatively appropriate fusion of horizons – the controlled procedure of understanding or interpretation is to be realized is unavoidable. Indeed, even some of the most well-known conceptions of Gadamer's hermeneutics can only be understood as methodologically relevant answers in the manner indicated. These conceptions include above all the "preconception of perfection," the "hermeneutical circle," the "logic of question and answer" (following Collingwood), and always at least in part Gadamer's attempts to rehabilitate normatively relevant concepts discredited by Descartes and the Enlightenment, such as *sensus communis* ("the common sense"), "prejudices," "authority," and "classical" in the sense of "exemplary." Let us consider these conceptions more closely.

The "preconception of perfection" must be understood as unambiguous and unquestionable in the minimal sense of a methodological-heuristic priority of the interpretandum before possible opposed prejudices of the interpreter. It relates, in my view, both to the concern and truth-claim of the interpretandum and also to its consistency of meaning and coherence. Its (at least initial) priority corresponds absolutely to the authentic knowledge interest of the interpreter who would naturally like to learn as much as possible from the interpretandum representing the tradition.

To this extent the preconception of perfection also corresponds to the traditional (e.g. humanistic) idea of the "authority" of the "classic" texts. However, in my opinion this foregoing (methodological-heuristic) attitude must not be equated with a dogmatic immunization of the interpretandum against all possible critique or even the rejection of its truth claims. Instead it can be justified as a necessary precondition of every critique that is not founded on a misleading prejudice or misunderstanding. (Such a methodological-heuristic interpretation of Gadamer's principle also in my view makes evident its difference from Donald Davidson's "principle of charity," which really represents a "metaphysical" precondition of every possible interpretation, i.e. before all possible critique or application.)

A methodologically relevant relation can also be established between the preconception of perfection and the hermeneutical circle. The hermeneutic circle, which Gadamer borrows directly from Heidegger, is not solely related to the reciprocal relationship of correction between the understanding of the text as a whole and the understanding of its parts – as is the case in the long prehistory of hermeneutics that stretches back to Melanchthon's pupil, Matthias Flacius Illyricus (1520–75) – but rather related from the outset to the act of fusion of horizons of mundane pre-understanding in relation to interpretandum and interpreter. For the methodologically controlled realization of this procedure by the interpreter the preconception of perfection in relation to the interpretandum must clearly be decisive at least as an initial, transitory precondition.

It appears to me to be methodologically even more precise to position the logic of question and answer here, although Gadamer only explicated this in the form of indications (see WM, 376ff.; TM, 398ff.; GW 2, 226). According to Gadamer, the meaning of this logic of question and answer, in the context of a dialogical dialectic of Socratic-Platonic provenance, is meant to reside evidently in the fact that all propositions with which philosophy is concerned are already answers to historically determined questions (and not, for example, problems raised above history in some "third world," as the neo-Kantians held, along with Nicolai Hartmann and, finally Karl Popper). Therefore, the questions, and the interests, which constitute their background and belong to the life-world, are also hermeneutically more important than the propositions (these arise in Heidegger's sense out of the clearings or concealments of the history of Being).

In the sense of the methodologically relevant explication of the logic of question and answer it is the relationship between the questions for which traditional texts provide answers and the questions which arise out of the pre-understanding of the interpreter and thus of the present that call for critical inquiry. The hermeneutical domain of tasks would thereby be designated within whose bounds the prejudices of the interpreter, which are necessary as a condition of the possibility of understanding, can according to Gadamer, "be put in play," so that they may either validate themselves or not. But we must ask further: must not also the prejudices (i.e. the questions and the interests which lie behind them) of the texts representing the tradition validate themselves in the dialogical/dialectical confrontation between the interpreter and interpretandum; and, if so, what would constitute the normative standards of such a discursive-dialogical validation?

We have now arrived at the point at which the heuristically justified prioritizing of the interpretandum reaches its limit, if the hermeneutical process is not only to be understood as a historical-temporal occurrence that transmits tradition, but also – from the perspective of the *dialogue*-model – as an argumentative and discursive confrontation. The principal difficulty in answering our question on the normative standards of communicative understanding as confrontation resides in the fact that Gadamer can clearly only locate the resources of socially binding norms themselves in tradition, indeed in the "effective history" emitted by an interpretandum and received into the hermeneutical consciousness of the interpreter. In this way Gadamer's talk of the hermeneutical "productivity of temporal distance" in relation to possible expectations of the reader contains no reference to the essential possibility of a reflectively conditioned advance in the hermeneutical understanding and judgment of the tradition.

This crucial aspect of the problem within Gadamerian hermeneutics can be best elucidated, in my opinion, by means of the famous idea (often discussed in *Truth and Method*) that one can or should understand an author better than he understands or understood himself. Gadamer distinguishes two versions of the idea: (1) the reference found in Fichte, and already in Kant, to the possible advance in factual or conceptual clarity in the thoughts of an author by the subsequent interpreters; and (2) Schleiermacher's version, which draws attention to rendering reproductively conscious a productive process in an author – especially an artistic genius. According to Gadamer, for the psychologically orientated hermeneutics of the nineteenth century only the second version became decisive, and it is only against this version (so it at first appears) that Gadamer's critique is aimed. In contrast, the first version, which goes back to the Enlightenment, appears to be justified owing to the situation, repeatedly emphasized by Gadamer, that the semantic content (*Sinngehalt*) of a text with which hermeneutics is concerned can under no circumstances be identified with the subjective opinion of the author, but rather arises out of the totality of factual and contextual conditions.

However, Gadamer surprisingly condemns both versions of the idea in his concluding evaluation and maintains:

> Understanding is in truth not understanding-better [*Besserverstehen*]: neither in the sense of factually knowing-better by means of clearer concepts nor in the sense of the fundamental superiority that conscious production possesses over unconscious. It is enough to say that one understands *differently*, if one understands at all. (WM, 280; TM, 296–7)

How is this verdict, which appears to relate not only to the idea dealt with but also to the possible advance of textual interpretations in relation to one another, to be understood? At this point Gadamer has recourse to Heidegger's philosophy and declares:

> it is only on the basis of the ontological transition which Heidegger brings about in understanding as an "existential" and of the temporal interpretation

which he bestows on *Dasein*'s mode of being that temporal distance could be conceived in its hermeneutical productivity. Time is no longer primarily an abyss that is to be bridged because it separates and keeps at a distance, rather it is in truth the ground that bears the event [*tragender Grund des Geschehens*] in which what is present is rooted. This temporal distance is not something to be overcome. That was rather the naïve presupposition of historicism: that one should place oneself in the spirit of the times, think in its concepts and ideas and not in one's own, and in this way be able to attain historical objectivity. In truth it is a question of recognising temporal distance as a positive and productive possibility of understanding. (WM, 281; TM, 297)

However, at this point one might again assume that the "positive possibility of understanding" opened by temporal distance could also consist precisely of improved understanding of factual and conceptual presuppositions of the interpretandum, subject in general to the conditions of experience. This possibility of improved understanding in relation to the presuppositions contained within the interpretandum could evidently also be related to the process of rendering conscious the mental presuppositions which are expressed in the interpretandum – for there is also precisely such a thing as a *semiologically* conditioned experience of textual meaning. (Such a possibility is in my opinion suggested by Gadamer himself when he remarks in another place that Hegel's conception of "the spirit's self-interpenetration" (*Selbstdurchdringung des Geistes*) is in principle superior to the historical hermeneutical conception of identical retrospective understanding.)

However, Gadamer fails to mention this just-indicated possibility of a temporally conditioned and improved understanding. For him there exists, "an ineradicable difference between the interpreter and the creator that is produced by historical distance. Every age has to understand the transmitted text in its own way" (WM, 280; TM, 296). Although temporal distance is "to be recognised as a positive and productive possibility of understanding," the intended productivity consists for Gadamer evidently solely in the fact that the distance can be filled "by the continuity of provenance and of the tradition in whose light all legacy [*Überlieferung*] appears to us" (WM, 281; TM, 297).

Evidently, the "principle of effective history" is also to be grasped in the sense of the evaluation of the positive possibilities of temporal distance just indicated (something that is also characterized by Gadamer, in my view quite correctly, as "a new *demand*, not on research but rather on its methodological consciousness") (WM, 284; TM, 300). Gadamer is correct to state that effective history is never "known completely." He says this against Hegel's claim to absolute knowledge in the course of which history attains to complete self-transparency and is thus raised to the perspective of the Concept (see WM, 285; TM, 301). Nevertheless, it is simplistic of Gadamer to suggest at this point that the task of historical hermeneutics be determined as a reversal of the direction of the Hegel's historical reflection: "[hermeneutics] must retreat along the path of the Hegelian phenomenology of spirit to the extent that one reveals the substantiality that determines all subjectivity" (WM, 286; TM, 302). On the basis of such recourse to the pre-given of effective history the "explication of the hermeneutical situation" should, according to Gadamer, result in "attaining the right horizon of questioning for those questions that occur to us in relation to the tradition" (ibid.).

Even for attaining the right hermeneutical horizon of questioning for the present, therefore, the normative orientation is, according to Gadamer, only to be sought and found in the "pre-given" of that history to which we have always belonged. However, if hermeneutical textual interpretation is to be understood also as dialogical confrontation – indeed, as argumentative discourse – of the present with the truth claims of the tradition, must not then a normative directive for the "right" questions in relation to traditional texts also be attainable on the basis of the present discursive situation, indeed on the basis of any discursive situation whatsoever? Is consensus (*Einverständnis*) with a "thou" about something, with which the understanding of texts is, also for Gadamer, ultimately concerned, merely the occasion for validation (or at least "continued development" (*Fortbildung*)) of social consensus that in fact must from the first carry the normative prescriptiveness of the cultural tradition? Or can it also be a matter of a new consensus that is only gained through a critical-hermeneutical confrontation with the tradition and its "effective history"? And is a (transcendental-hermeneutical) criterion (*Maßstab*) of a consensus, which is always to be attained anew, not ultimately (certainly since Socrates) to be found in the very idea of dialogue as argumentative discourse – that is, as the regulative idea recognized from the outset in argumentation, according to which philosophically acceptable consensus is not valid for a particular traditional community but rather for an unlimited communicative community (*Kommunikationsgemeinschaft*)?

However, in Gadamer, such an ideal criterion (*Richtmaß*) (Kant) of possible dialogical confrontation is utterly absent, although his description of the "productivity of temporal distance" often appears to evoke just that. This is the case when he writes: "Temporal distance ... allows the true meaning that lies in the thing itself to emerge fully for the first time" (WM, 282; TM, 298), or: "It is not only the case that new sources of error are eliminated time and again so that the true meaning is filtered out through all kinds of obscurity, but new sources of understanding also repeatedly emerge, which make manifest unanticipated semantic connections" (ibid.). And finally and decisively:

> [Temporal distance] does not merely allow prejudices of a particular nature to die away, but also those which provide genuine understanding to emerge as such. Nothing other than this temporal distance is capable of making the genuinely critical question of hermeneutics resolvable, namely, to separate the *true* prejudices by which we *understand* from the *false* ones by which we *misunderstand*. (WM, 282; TM, 298–9)

One can only agree! Yet nowhere did Gadamer transcend the limits of a temporal-historical conception to a normatively reasoned progressive conception in his evaluation of temporal discourse. As a consequence, he failed to validate the second model of his philosophical hermeneutics – that of dialogue or argumentative discourse.

As far as I can see, Gadamer is prevented from replacing the conception of "objective" (i.e. evaluation-free) retrospective understanding, which he rightly criticizes as a scientistic illusion, with a conception of improved understanding related to historical progress, by three interconnected "prejudices":

(1) Fundamental is the idea, taken over from Heidegger, of the temporality (*Temporalität*) of Being or of the history of Being, that, through its linguistically constituted "clearings" and "coverings" of meaning, determines in the manner of a destiny the presupposition of possible – true and false – judgments (and also precisely the "prejudices") from the outset. (According to this conception, Gadamer manifestly failed to anticipate, as did Heidegger, that the historical, linguistically articulated clearings and coverings of meaning might, conversely, also be normatively influenced by empirical processes of learning and rational arguments.[8] In my opinion, this reciprocally determining relation could even be understood as an expression of the structure of the hermeneutical circle as explicated by Heidegger in *Being and Time*.

(2) On the basis of the Heideggerian temporality of Being-in-the-world in the sense of "facticity" and "thrownness" there emerges Gadamer's specific conviction that understanding is a further development of a tradition and that *all* prejudices which make understanding possible themselves belong to the tradition to be further developed, to its facticity, because prejudices are also constitutive of the historical being of humanity. Thus there are no such prejudices which, as a rational a priori, make possible the hermeneutical dialogue with the tradition as argumentative discourse. That is, there are no rational, historically independent presuppositions of hermeneutics.

(3) Consequently, there is for Gadamer (as also for Heidegger) no normative dimension to hermeneutics that could be legitimized through something like a transcendental principle of hermeneutical discourse. Thus, Gadamer does not consider a transcendental-hermeneutical extension and transformation of the Cartesian-Kantian presuppositions of modern philosophy to be possible. (This transcendental philosophical way of thought, according to Gadamer, was still being pursued by Heidegger in *Being and Time* but then was, rightly, left behind in the turning to the history of Being.)

On the basis of these observations, I think it is already possible to make intelligible the dialectical transition within twentieth-century German philosophy from Gadamer's position to Apel's. However, before doing this, I want at least to indicate two further aspects of Gadamer's philosophical hermeneutics that make manifest the effectively *relativist* consequences of his approach for contemporary philosophy.

First, there is the seldom noticed consequence for the history of science, a consequence that Gadamer refers to as the "retrieval of the fundamental hermeneutical problem" (WM, 291–5; TM, 307–11). Gadamer wishes to some extent to reverse the uncoupling – effected by the Enlightenment and in particular by Schleiermacher and Dilthey – of the epistemological function of hermeneutical understanding (specifically in relation to the human sciences) from its centuries-long utilization by theological and juridical dogmatics. (In a broader sense, he also wants to restore the connection to classical humanism as the informal dogmatics of philology or classical studies.) He would like, contrary to the constitution of the human sciences in Germany in the nineteenth century, to clarify the unity of the possible legitimation of hermeneutics' pre-understanding precisely by appealing to the dogmatic paradigm of juridical and theological hermeneutics. For here the normative application of understanding and interpretation in fact constitutes along with the cognitive function an obligatory unity, which in the nineteenth century was reduced to a value-free, scientistically understood conception of "understanding."

However, it is significant that Gadamer fails to consider that the decoupling of hermeneutics from its (existentially proper) dimension of application must in no way lead to the possible alternative of a dogmatic integration of the application of understanding to the practice of life. In a post-Enlightenment hermeneutics also such a thing as a comparative history of law and religion could and would have to be considered within the proper dimension of application. Admittedly, a normatively engaged hermeneutics would then have to achieve a realization of understanding and interpretation, which ideally would have to be transmitted through a critical judgment of all the formal and informal dogmas of various cultural traditions. In order to make this possible it would be necessary to have recourse not only to the actual basis of consensus of one's own cultural tradition, but minimally also to a basis of consensus that (as in the case, for example, for human rights) could be decisive for all human cultural traditions, without appeal to metaphysical, religious, or simply traditionally conditioned dogmas.

This postulate, which is rather irritating for today's historicist-leaning tradition of thought in the broadest sense, can and must, in my opinion, be realized in principle by a transcendental-hermeneutical reflection. Such reflective thought (reflexive Besinnung) would relate not only to the fore-structure (Gadamer along with Heidegger) of "my or our respective" pre-understanding of the life-world, but also to the fore-structure of philosophical propositions about the respective facticity of world-understanding fundamental for reflection. The truth-claim of these propositions is manifestly dependent on presuppositions that can no longer be relativized historically in intercultural dialogue, but rather must be constantly recognized as universally valid. To these presuppositions there also belongs the equal justification of the different partners of an intellectual dialogue and so also of the interpreter and interpretandum according to the hermeneutical dialogue model.

However, from the outset Gadamer cuts himself off from transcendental-reflective thought of this kind through his critique of "reflective philosophy" (WM, 294ff.; TM, 311ff.). Gadamer (with appeal to Heidegger) condemns reflective philosophy's argument that the propositions of a relativist involve self-refutation as an "attempted ambush" (Überrumpelungsversuch), i.e. as an argument that, while formally correct, is of no relevance for determining the contingent dependency of all the normative presuppositions of our mundane understanding on history (see WM, 327; TM, 344). Further, the usual method in the human sciences of inter- and intracultural comparison stems, according to Gadamer, from the fact that thereby one separates in advance the interpretation of the interpretanda to be compared from the cultural dimension of application to which they belong and renders the interpretanda, as natural formations

(*Gestalten*), to some extent synchronous and objective (see WM, 220; TM, 234). The comparison is thus not made possible by anything like a realization of reflection that relates in advance to the dimension of application of understanding in such a way as to be able to emancipate this dimension, so to speak, for a responsible, post-dogmatic option.

As indicated thus far, the basic features of the partially post-Heideggerian histor-icism of Gadamer's hermeneutics are in no way untypical of the philosophy of the twentieth century. They do not refute but rather outdo Dilthey's historicism (and this indeed without any appreciation or even mention of the refutation of the scientism orientated towards the natural sciences – introduced by Dilthey and others time and again – by means of the differentiation of nomological "explanation" and the "under-standing" of the human sciences[9]). In the meantime the specifically Gadamerian historicism-hermeneutics has even undergone extensive confirmation in the "post-empirical" theory of science (above all in Thomas Kuhn) and also particularly in the practical philosophy of Anglo-American "communitarianism." (For further discussion of communitarianism, see "Twentieth-century political philosophy," Chapter 21.)

This last circumstance refers to the second aspect, emphasized by Gadamer himself, of the implications of his hermeneutics: its affinity with Aristotle's practical philosophy (just as late twentieth-century neo-Aristotelianism has absolved itself from any metaphysical grounding of "natural law") (see WM, 295–307; TM, 312–24). The applied function of understanding is, for Gadamer, given here as a prototype in the concept of *phronesis* (practical wisdom). For, according to Gadamer, in this fundamental concept of practical philosophy (distinguished by Aristotle himself from *episteme* (theoretical knowledge) as the fundamental concept of theoretical philosophy) a mediation between the normative generality of an *ethos* and the particularity of a situation is conceived for the first time, not in the manner of a logical subsumption, but quasi "dialectically." This mediation can then also be grasped in the present as a structural prototype for the continued development of a historical tradition in herme-neutics. Just as normative knowledge is both applied to the situation by *phronesis* and also constituted by this concretization time and again, so the hermeneutical inter-preter must "not ignore himself and the concrete hermeneutical situation in which he finds himself," if he wishes to understand at all (see WM, 307; TM, 324).

Although this analogy of the application-problematic is perspicuous one must note once again in this case the partiality, indeed the implicitly dogmatic presupposition of Gadamer's orientation in relation to a given tradition of normative knowledge. The given tradition of normative knowledge is as little problematized in Gadamer as the traditional *ethos* of the good polis is by Aristotle in the *Nicomachean Ethics*. In both cases the problem of a critical understanding of the *ethos*-tradition is not so much as even raised. Albeit, there was already in Aristotle's lifetime a controversial discussion of whether, as assumed by Aristotle, slaves, barbarians, and women really had a lesser share in the universal *logos* than the free, male Hellenes. In the sixteenth century there was a discussion between the Scholastic theologian Juan Ginés de Sepulveda (1494–1573) and the Spanish Dominican priest and advocate for the indigenous people of the Americas, Bartolomé de Las Casas (1484–1566) over whether Aristotle's doctrine that there are born slaves could be applied to the Indians recently subjugated by the Spanish. In the present there exists the universal hermeneutical, ethical, and ethno-juridical problem over which traditionally determined norms can be universally binding or at least tolerably accepted in a multicultural global society.

What is inadequate about the model of the respective continued transmission of tradition for a post-dogmatic hermeneutics and also for a post-conventional ethics is in my opinion explicated in its paradigmatic significance by Gadamer in the essay, "On the possibility of a philosophical ethics" (1963). His concise answer to the question reads: *hos dei* plus *phronesis* (I would translate: *What is seemly for a good society* plus *prudent application to the concrete situation*). That is in actual fact the neo-Aristotelian reduction of the problem of ethics and of hermeneutics. However, in view of the challenge of a globalized and continual development of human cultural traditions the question arises: can the claim to universality for hermeneutics made by Gadamer be cashed out in this way?

Karl-Otto Apel's conception of transcendental hermeneutics or transcendental pragmatics. The a priori of discourse as the reflective basis of philosophy's claim to universality

The claim to universality made by Gadamer in *Wahrheit und Methode* (1960) regarding philosophical hermeneutics or hermeneutical philosophy became the point of departure for a philosophical debate in the 1960s in which, among others, Jürgen Habermas and Karl-Otto Apel participated. For these thinkers the answer to the question raised by Gadamer became, in the course of the subsequent clarification of meaning, the point of crystallization for their basic philosophical position. This basic position appeared in part to be identical in Habermas and Apel. Thus, for example, in the volume *Hermeneutik und Ideologiekritik* (see Apel 1971), both proceeded, as critics of Gadamer, from the epistemological (or epistemological-anthropological) architectonic of three "quasi-transcendental," "knowledge directing" (*erkenntnisleitend*) interests: the techno-logical, hermeneutical, and emancipatory knowledge interests. Even with the basic approach of universal pragmatics that came later – which proceeded from linguistic communication or, more precisely, from discourse understood as the quasi-transcendental condition of the possibility for cashing in argumentative validity-claims – there still appeared to be extensive agreement between Habermas and Apel.

However, later still it became apparent that Habermas's sociologically broad program, whereby transcendental philosophy (together with metaphysics if not with autonomous philosophy as such) appears rather as something historically obsolete and thus to be methodologically overcome (*Aufzuhebendes*), had instead to be understood from the perspective of the Frankfurt School's Critical Theory (see "Critical Theory," Chapter 18). By contrast, Apel understood "universal pragmatics" as in actual fact transcendental pragmatics, i.e. in its discourse-theoretical core as a transformation of classical transcendental philosophy. On the one hand this makes necessary, owing to the overcoming of the metaphysics of subjectivity, a significant restriction of the Kantian a priori, but, on the other hand, it reveals the possibility of – with reflective recourse to the incontestable presuppositions of argumentative discourse – a new non-deductive form of ultimate transcendental philosophical legitimation. In what follows, on the basis of an autobiographical retrospection, I shall attempt to reconstruct the approach and explication of Apel's conception of transcendental pragmatics.

If one compares Habermas's and Apel's conception of the three "knowledge leading interests" and their function within the architectonic of the anthropologically and quasi-transcendentally extended epistemology and theory of science, then it is noticeable that the relationship of this architectonic to philosophy is in each case different.

In Habermas the technological knowledge interest of the natural sciences and the practical knowledge interest of the hermeneutical human sciences both differ from that of philosophy, which reflects on the distinction between the former two interests. Only the emancipatory knowledge interest of ideology critique – which reflects on the self-alienation of the subject by means of a connection of deep hermeneutical and causally explanatory methods of psychoanalysis and the social sciences – is, however, ultimately identical with the knowledge interest of philosophy (in the sense of practical reason in Fichte). The emancipatory knowledge interest thus far represents a synthesis of the other two and to this extent corresponds to rational interest as such.[10] The emancipatory knowledge interest of the critical social sciences, and not pure hermeneutics – so it appears – represents philosophy's claim to universality. The conception of pure hermeneutics, one might conclude, corresponds to an idealist illusion of the human sciences, which overlooks for example the fact that traditional texts are not the expression of discursive relations free from violence but are also in each case symptoms of ideologically distorted communication and so open to criticism in the sense of the emancipatory knowledge interest.

It appears to me, as it already did then, that the main critical argument advanced by Habermas is incontestable to the extent that it relates to the interpretation of tradition in the context of a reconstructed universal history.[11] In this way the hermeneutical methods of the human sciences always require, in my opinion, supplementation by the critical social sciences – not only in the Marxist but also in the Freudian sense and indeed in the sense of the Foucauldian critique of power as well. One could integrate these approaches into a correspondingly extended "hermeneutics of suspicion" as understood by Paul Ricoeur.[12] However, such an extension in the function of hermeneutics would fail to acknowledge adequately the difference between such interpretative methods – which are grounded in the methodical (kunstmäßig) extension of communicative understanding – and those methods grounded in the suspension of communicative understanding and its temporary replacement by causal explanation of pathological symptoms, in other words, grounded in the mediation of two distinct knowledge interests.

However, precisely this mediation of two distinct knowledge interests (which according to Habermas has its paradigmatic model in psychoanalytic method) shows that the hermeneutical deepening of communication (Verständigung) must not only constitute the goal of the critical mediation of communicative understanding by means of the explanation of pathological symptoms, but also and above all represent the permanent philosophical presupposition of all methods of this kind. Neither psychoanalysis nor the socially orientated critique of ideology can realize the suspension of communicative reasoning and the unmasking of motives on the level of inter-subjective communication of the research subjects themselves. This means that within the critical connection of the social sciences to the cultural tradition the continued development of hermeneutical communication must have priority. Thus, in my opinion, this aspect of Gadamer's argumentation in *Hermeneutik und Ideologiekritik* must be accepted, insofar as it does not signify abrogation of the supplementation of the hermeneutical methods of the empirical human sciences by those of the critical social sciences, but denotes rather a reflective recognition of the philosophical presupposition of all sciences in the sense of a transcendental hermeneutics.

As I had already – even prior to reading *Truth and Method* – selected this term "transcendental hermeneutics" for my relationship with Heidegger, signaling thereby a transformation of transcendental philosophy,[13] I returned to it in my confrontation with Gadamer.[14] Later, however, I began primarily to use the term "transcendental (speech-) pragmatics" for my own position, in order to mark the reflectively valid basis for the unavoidable argumentative discourse over and against any historical dependency of philosophy.

In contrast to Habermas I emphasized that the difference between two functions of reflection should be recognized for an architectonic of knowledge interests in the theory of science.[15] On the one hand, there is the empirically relevant function of (deep psychological or ideology-critical) human self-reflection directed by emancipatory knowledge interests; on the other hand, there is the transcendental reflection of philosophy (on the level of argumentative discourse) upon knowledge-directing interests as quasi-transcendental conditions of the possibility for the constitution of meaning in experience (in contrast to the transcendental conditions of the possibility for the inter-subjective validity of epistemological truth-claims which are discursively cashed in. More on this later). In this sense of a subordination of the problematics of the social and human sciences to the transcendental reflection of philosophy, I also later made use of the conception of three fundamental knowledge interests, in particular in my attempt at a monographical reconstruction of the "explanation-understanding controversy,"[16] which, at least in Germany, accompanied the differentiation of empirical natural and human or social sciences from Hegel onwards. Habermas by contrast, after the publication of his resoundingly pioneering book *Erkenntnis und Interesse* (1968; English translation: *Knowledge and Human Interests*), surprisingly did not pursue the triadic concept of knowledge interests further, but rather resolved it into the conception of a "universal pragmatics" or "reconstructive sciences."

In relation to the conception of a universal pragmatics or, from my perspective, a transcendental pragmatics, the issue became for me in the following decades a matter of realizing the program of a transformation of transcendental philosophy (which I continue to carry on, always in constant confrontation with the realization of Habermas's program). Besides the critical connection to my beginnings in the name of a transcendental hermeneutics, which went back to my Habilitation thesis on the idea of language in the humanistic tradition,[17] it was above all my confrontation, stretching over many years, with analytic and in particular Anglo-American philosophy (which first became known in Germany in around 1950) that helped me during the 1960s to arrive at the basic position that I have represented since then.

More precisely, this confrontation began with the study of the beginnings of analytic language philosophy in the Vienna Circle (Rudolf Carnap, Moritz Schlick) and above all with Ludwig Wittgenstein (see "The development of analytic philosophy: Wittgenstein and after," Chapter 2). I interpreted the *Tractatus Logico-Philosophicus* of the young Wittgenstein in a similar manner to Erik Stenius,[18] above all from a Kantian perspective as a critique of pure language, and attempted to grasp the conception of language-games of the later Wittgenstein to some extent as the pragmatic-pluralistic differentiation of this transcendental language critique.[19] It was important for me to avoid interpreting the pragmatic dimension of language use or language-games behavioristically, in the way this was usually done in the "pragmatic turn" related to the conception of unified science in neo-positivism (along the lines of Carnap and Charles W. Morris). On the contrary, I strove to understand the comportment (*Verhalten*) of language use and the form of life belonging to it on the (quasi-transcendental) presupposition of the possibility in principle of communicative participation in a language-game. Peter Winch's quasi-hermeneutical Wittgenstein interpretation afforded me significant help in this regard.[20]

Admittedly, I was at the same time confronted by Winch with the specific relativism of Wittgenstein's theory of language-games and social forms of life.[21] In order to respond argumentatively to this (and to the numerous relativisms of contemporary philosophy which have recourse to the later Wittgenstein) one must in my view engage in radical (semantic-critical (*sinnkritisch*) and therapeutic) questioning of the function of philosophical language-games. On the one hand, I earnestly attempted this and came to the conclusion that the primacy of the critique of knowledge (*Erkenntniskritik*) in modern philosophy in actual fact is to be resolved into the primacy of semantic criticism (*Sinnkritik*) with respect to language-games in contemporary philosophy after Wittgenstein. Furthermore, I concluded that this semantic criticism is in a position to unmask a good part of the conclusions and before this even the problems of modern epistemology as meaningless language use (for example, Descartes's dream argument or Kant's distinction between the unknowable "thing in itself" and the mere "appearance" which supposedly is knowable).

On the other hand, I could not fail to notice that Wittgenstein never poses the reflective question, which the (necessarily "healthy") language-game of philosophy itself enables him (if only from time to time) to make evident the linguistic sickness of philosophy as such and, by recourse to the essential "interconnectedness" (*Verwobenheit*) of language-games, activities, and forms of life, to show "the fly the way out of the bottle." Wittgenstein cannot conceal the fact that, despite all the use of examples and paucity of theory in his investigations, here a claim is made to universally valid philosophical insight. Rather it is apparent that – as in Heidegger[22] and Gadamer – there exists an essential difference between the respective exemplifying fore-structure of linguistic and mundane understanding relative to forms of life and the employed fore-structure of *philosophical* language analysis. With respect to its truth claim the latter cannot be relativized either in relation to the plurality of distinct language-games and forms of life or in relation to "clearings of the history of Being"; rather its universal truth claim must be admitted in order to save the meaning of self-critical philosophy.

With this insight I have of course employed a reflective, transcendental-pragmatic argument. In analytical philosophy proper such an argument is shot through with a suspicion of meaninglessness which goes back to the proscription of self-referential language use in Bertrand Russell's theory of types (or Alfred Tarski's theory of an infinite hierarchy of meta-languages).[23] However, around that time, I became convinced that the pragmatic turn in linguistic philosophy could only avoid the reduction of the pragmatic dimension in language use to an object of empirical science (and thus of semantics) and thus understand actual interpreters of signs semiotically (along with Peirce) as a third instance of sign relation,[24] if self-reflection upon present language use were to be recognized as an intrinsic feature of the language-game itself (although admittedly not self-reflection as understood by introspective psychology, but rather self-reflection understood as the "self-hierarchizing" (Selbstaufstufung) of argumentation in the sense of reflectively ascertaining the philosophical validity claims of argumentation).[25]

On this presupposition it is not the self-referentiality of language use in philosophy as such that is semantic-critically proscribed (as is the case in the logical semantics of formalizable languages since Russell and Tarski), but rather the lack of reflection of the arguer upon the validity claims he presently makes, and which is expressed, for example, in the performative self-contradiction. Such a self-contradiction is present in numerous examples: thus, when Russell has to formulate his theory of types, which forbids self-referential language use, with the help of a philosophical para-language meant to relate to *all* languages and hence also to itself; further, when the numerous representatives of historical relativism (skeptics, reductionist naturalists, and holists in Quine's sense) set out their own position by means of a priori universal truth claims; again, returning to semiotics, when Jacques Derrida attempts to *communicate* and *make clear* to his readers that the *presentation* in communication of a signified (*signifié*) is impossible because of continuous dissemination (*dissémination*) due to the *différance* in the play of signs in linguistic usage. (According to Derrida, moreover, Heidegger was prohibited from posing his basic question concerning the "meaning of Being" owing to his own presuppositions relating to the dependence of the clearing (*Lichtung*) of meaning upon the difference-constituting "event" (*Ereignis*) of the history of Being.)

In short, it emerges that the semantic validity (*Sinngeltung*) of argumentation and the "self-concordance [*Selbsteinstimmigkeit*] of reason" (Kant) in philosophy is above all a matter of the reflectively tested consistency of the semantics of propositions with the corresponding pragmatics of performative speech acts in which the argumentative validity claims are set out. Precisely this insight, which for me constitutes the point of the pragmatic turn in analytic philosophy of language, appeared to me at this time to be systematically explicated by Habermas in his theory of universal pragmatics in connection with the speech act theory of Austin and Searle.[26] The principal achievement of this theory consists in my view, first, in the synthesizing presentation of four discursive validity claims, that is, of the claim to meaning and intelligibility and of the three claims relating to the world: the objective truth claim (*Wahrheitsanspruch*) in relation to the external world, the subjective claim to truthfulness (*Wahrhaftigkeitsanspruch*) in relation to the internal world, and the intersubjective moral-normative correctness claim (*Richtigkeitsanspruch*) in relation to the social world. Second, the other achievement of Habermas's theory consists in the recognition of the performative-propositional twofold structure of facts of human discourse. This latter insight, which characterizes the *pragmatic* basis of speech act reflection, implies in my view a considerable deepening in understanding of the *logos*-structure of human language whose concept had been determined since Aristotle by a limitation to the structure of the propositional sentence.[27] (Heidegger's polemic against the *logos* of "enframing" in metaphysics and Derrida's corresponding polemic against the "logocentrism" of western philosophy were evidently directed against the narrow *logos* of the propositional sentence and apodictic logic and can thus be corrected in different ways by means of a transcendental pragmatic recognition of the dialogical and self-reflective deep structure of the human *logos* of language.)

From the perspective of this transcendental pragmatic interpretation, I connected several strong interpretations with the conception of "universal language pragmatics" from the outset.

Thus for me the meaning or intelligibility claim cannot be the condition of the possibility of all other discursive validity claims merely on the basis of being linguistically (syntactically and semantically) well formed, but rather only on the basis of a genuine claim to semantic validity (*Sinngeltungs-Anspruch*) that can be defended against arguments of meaninglessness, especially those pertaining to philosophy. (Thus, for example, the assertion "the present King of France is bald," can be neither true nor false as the sentence asserted lacks meaning on account of non-fulfillment of the existential presupposition relating to the King of France. However, a much more relevant verdict of meaninglessness is directed towards the supposition that *everything* which seems real is in fact only a dream (or my dream); or that there is no external world whatsoever, but rather everything is merely in consciousness; or I am always deceived, for example by a "deceiving spirit" or "'deceiving god" (Descartes's *dieu trompeur*). Or, along with Kant: all our scientifically testable and to that extent empirically valid knowledge of experience is in fact only knowledge of knowable "appearances" of unknowable things in themselves.

In all these examples from modern epistemological critique (and in many others), while the intelligibility claim in the sense of being linguistically well formed is satisfied, the pragmatic consistency of the language-game is nevertheless destroyed. This is because a paradigmatic presupposition of the language-game in relation to doubt (for example, the usual contrast between dream and reality or between the external world and my consciousness, or between knowable reality and mere appearance) was suspended by means of a putatively radical universalizing of doubt.

Wittgenstein indicated in his last work, *On Certainty*,[28] that one cannot doubt all things because every concrete doubt presupposes such a thing as a paradigmatic certainty. I applied this argument to the absolutized thesis of "fallibilism" of the late

Popperians (Hans Albert, William W. Bartley III, Gerard Radnitzsky) and inquired after the *paradigmatic certainties* that make the application of the concept "fallible" within a language-game of philosophy intelligible in the first place.[29] It emerged that to such application (along with reflection on Descartes's *cogito, ergo sum*) there belongs the whole language-game of argumentative discourse (I shall return to this in connection with the argument for the transcendental-pragmatic ultimate grounding of philosophy).

A further transcendental-pragmatic strengthening in the interpretation of Habermas's conception of universal pragmatics relates to the a priori status of the "unavoidable" presuppositions of argumentation. According to Habermas these also belong to the conditions of the possibility of all scientific testing of hypotheses. However, their investigation should on the other hand fall within the domain of the tasks belonging to the so-called competence-reconstructive sciences, among which should be numbered linguistics, the structural genesis of Piaget and Kohlberg, and finally also philosophical logic.[30] Accordingly, Habermas compares, for example, Chomsky's strong but empirical hypotheses about the ultimately congenital precondi- tions of linguistic competence with the precondition of "communicative competence" analyzed by universal pragmatics and comes to the conclusion that all "presuppositions of argumentation" must also be in principle empirically tested in relation to the widest possible extension of examples. In my opinion, however, this demand cannot be meaningful, because otherwise the transcendental-pragmatic preconditions of every test could be thereby possibly falsified.

One could however perhaps object that testing might show that the tested presuppo- sitions are not yet in fact the necessary presuppositions of every argument. However, in my opinion, at this point there comes into play the transcendental-pragmatic argument, which I introduced as *the ultimate grounding criterion (Letztbegründungskriterium)*.[31] It is a question of whether or not, by means of rigorous reflection upon one's own non-circumventible argumentation, the presuppositions under discussion can be contested without performative self-contradiction. If it is not possible then it has been proved that the presuppositions are transcendentally necessary and thus ultimately valid.

It is of decisive importance that this transcendental-pragmatic test is carried out in rigorous reflection, for otherwise the suspicion will be raised that one is presenting in a formal logical manner a presupposition of argumentation whose incontestability rests on the foregoing definition of "argumentation," for example, the incontestability of the equality of rights in principle of all participants in discourse on the basis of a corre- sponding definition of "discourse." (This accusation of circularity is doubtless at once the most common counterargument and the most characteristic misunderstanding of the transcendental-pragmatic ultimate validation.)

However, the necessity of the argumentative presuppositions does not rest upon a logical operation of this kind, but rather first *appears* as necessary with the reflective attempt of contestation, along with performative self-contradiction. Accordingly, I have proposed the following formulation for ultimate validation: "Those presupposi- tions of argumentation are ultimately validated, which cannot be contested without performative self-contradiction and (precisely because of this) cannot be logically validated without *petitio principii*"[32] (i.e. the logical fallacy of "begging the question").

With respect to the relationship between transcendental pragmatics with its reflection upon the argumentative presuppositions and competence reconstructing science I, like Habermas, consider close coherence and cooperation between the two sides to be necessary. This is so because thereby even a mutual correction of the results of philosophy and the competence reconstructing (social and human) sciences can be effected. However, I consider this to be possible only on the precondition that both sides presuppose their own respective criteria for testing: on the one hand, the empirical criteria (also including those of hermeneutical understanding) of the reconstructive social sciences and, on the other hand, philosophy's criteria of a priori testing with the help of the criterion that the performative self-contradiction of argumentation is to be avoided. In the case of Kohlberg's theory of ontogenetic levels of morality I attempted to apply these presuppositions to the relationship between philosophical justification and psychological theory concerning the development of moral judgment.[33] Ultimately Kohlberg recognized the absolute necessity of a normative justificatory function of moral philosophy to complement psychology.[34]

With these remarks I have indicated the structure of a program for applying transcendental pragmatics, understood as a justification of theoretical and practical philosophy (or of the corresponding sciences), measured in terms of the complementarity and difference between transcendental and empirical presuppositions. In the last three decades of the twentieth century I attempted to work out this program, on the one hand, in terms of the epistemic truth-claim present in argumentative discourse and, on the other, in terms of the claim to a discourse ethics residing therein at the same time.

Before I go into this in more detail I would like to introduce briefly my confrontation with American pragmatism (beginning in 1965), in particular in relation to Charles Sanders Peirce, in my view that movement's most important and significant representative. Peirce's work – to which I dedicated a German edition of selected writings (1967/70), a monograph (1975), and also a series of investigations from 1973 to 2007[35] – was for me the most important contribution of Anglo-American philosophy to my conception of transcendental pragmatics. That may be in part determined by my German interpretative perspective, for example, my insistence on the Kantian question concerning conditions of the possibility of the objective (= inter-subjective) validity of scientific knowledge. However, it was Peirce's own critical confrontation with Kant that helped me arrive at a very radical (semantic-critical, semiotic and epistemological) transformation of Kant's classical transcendental philosophy.[36] On the one hand, this transformation allowed for confirmation and supplementation of Wittgenstein's motif of meaning critique (*Sinnkritik*) in the sense of Peirce's "pragmatic maxim" of meaning clarification. On the other hand, however, Peirce's prescriptive and future-relating orientation of the "pragmatic motif" and its explication in a normative logic of investigation could also serve as a corrective for the relativistic reductionism of the use-theory of meaning at least hinted at by Wittgenstein.[37] Wittgenstein's reference to normal language use can certainly serve a critical and therapeutic function in relation to the linguistically conditioned pseudo-problems of metaphysics, but he offers no help to the creative scientist in the clarification of more obscure concepts.

If such a scientist were to ask, for example, what the relationship of space and time *means* for experiential practice (e.g. for the possible measurement of the simultaneity of two events), then the answer cannot be directed towards normal language use (which understands temporal relations as independent of spatial relations owing to the practically infinite velocity of light in everyday life). Rather, he or she must carry out thought-experiments relating to the future (Peirce's "mellonization") in order to arrive at possible new determinations of the relevant concepts: space, time, simultaneity. Such a thing was undertaken by Einstein in the Special Theory of Relativity. But the American political philosopher John Rawls also set up a similar experiment when he attempted to present to himself the limiting conditions under which an "original position" could be conceived, in which human beings could reach a consensus about the meaning of a just ordering of society.

I was able to derive a different but complementary correction from the philosophy of Wittgenstein and Peirce with regard to the question of overcoming the "methodological" or "transcendental solipsism" (Husserl) characteristic of modern philosophy. According to Husserl, the position of the *ego cogito cogitatum* going back to Descartes is the transcendental residual position of a radical thinker who must first bracket belief in the existence of the real world. He is thus faced with the task of first "constituting" the existence of the real world including that of all other thinking subjects on the basis of the intentional achievements of just his consciousness.

Against this basic situation of the modern philosophy of the subject, conceived by Husserl – in a form that is already presupposed through the formulation of the *cogito* – without any transcendental philosophical consideration of public language, Wittgenstein proved that "one cannot follow a rule alone and only once" and that "a private language" is inconceivable. I adopted this famous argument absolutely, though I cannot further elucidate it here. I constantly asked myself, however, how one could explain, following Wittgenstein, rules relating to linguistic or social innovations that cannot yet be actually followed by a given community of rule-followers. Must such following be merely *possible*, subject to possible ethical abrogation or is it not meaningful at all to conceive of the existence and function of a rule in the absence of *actual* rule-following in a community, since a rule-Platonism not permitted by Wittgenstein? In a discussion of the collection *Die pragmatische Wende* [*The Pragmatic Turn*] (1986)[38] ethically disastrous consequences were drawn from the answer to the latter question.[39]

In my opinion the normative or transcendental-pragmatic supplement of the supposition of the practice of a rule community for overcoming "methodological solipsism" is to be found in Peirce. Peirce asks about the "grounds of the validity of the laws of logic" of research. However, this question (which in Peirce replaces Kant's transcendental question) cannot be answered for him by recourse to the rule presuppositions (categories, first principles) of the "synthesis of apperception" possible for a finite consciousness. According to Peirce, the presupposed rules can only be those pertaining to processes of semantic interpretation and "synthetic" conclusion (induction and abduction), which deliver in the long run acceptable results for an "indefinite community of investigators." All principles or judgments (Kant's a priori valid "first principles" of science as well as perceptual judgments) are, according to Peirce, only more or less certain, though in principle *fallible* sedimentations of potentially infinite processes of semantic interpretation and conclusion. The truth in relation to the real, however, would (we must counterfactually anticipate it) be represented in the final (i.e. not to be further questioned by arguments) opinion of the research community. According to Peirce, by this is to be understood not a condition one can expect to attain with time but rather a "regulative hope" (Kant spoke of a "criterion (*Richtmaß*) of "regulative ideas of reason"). Peirce also demands moral commitment to such a community of rule-following from everyone who desires to think rationally: a moral commitment that presupposes a "self-surrender" with respect to all private interests (even those of spiritual well-being).

I attempted to make Peirce's philosophy of the indefinite community and regulative hopes productive by connecting it with the incontestable presuppositions of argumentation (in the sense of reflective ultimate grounding). It was easiest to do this in the case of the truth theory of natural science, insofar as it is related to a reality whose structure can be conceived of as being independent of actual but not of possible knowledge. Here there emerges from Peirce's perspective, as also from that of the transcendental-pragmatic presuppositions relating to the incontestable truth claim of argumentation, the conception of a consensus theory of truth manifestly superior to traditional conceptions. Such conceptions include the correspondence theory (externalist-realist) of classical metaphysics, the methodologically solipsistic evidence theory, the coherence theory excluding empirical evidence and naturally also the common pragmatic utility theory as related to individual or particular collective usefulness. Peirce's consensus theory is in my view capable of "sublating" (*aufheben*) the (weak) truth criteria recognized by the truth theories just enumerated into the argumentative context of the consensus or discourse theory.[40] I have defended this truth theory on many occasions, including against philosophers who for a time adopted it along with me, such as Habermas and Putnam.[41]

It proved more difficult to justify a consensus or discourse theory of truth for the hermeneutical human and cultural sciences. It is simply assumed by Peirce and all other participants known to me in the contemporary discussion of truth that the reality with which knowledge is concerned is not dependent on what we actually think about it. But it is precisely this assumption that is not valid for the historical reality of human culture. Rather, along with human action human knowledge (including even its errors and shortcomings) enters persistently into this reality. (Giambattista Vico, the founder of the human sciences and of the modern philosophy of history, at least touched upon this problem.) I myself looked for the solution in light of the supposition that the problem of true knowledge in relation to history cannot be solved independently of the problem of the ethically correct interpretation of history directed towards continuation.[42] (We have already touched upon this problem aporetically as that of an application of philosophical hermeneutics in Gadamer.) I see a formal precondition for solving this problem in the fact that here, on the one hand, the cultural sciences presuppose an ethics of responsibility relating to history, although this ethics, on the other hand, always presupposes for its part the empirical reconstruction of the historical situation by the cultural and social sciences.

That brings me to the problem of the legitimation of ethics that I first approached in the late 1960s. The connection with Peirce's ethics of the community of scientists was relevant here in two respects. Naturally one could not fail to notice that Peirce's ethics of "self-surrender" was at best an ethics for scientists and not at all acceptable as an ethics for everyone. To a certain extent William James's essay *The Will to Believe* (1887), which James himself originally wanted to entitle "The right to believe," can be understood as a counterargument to Peirce's. Nevertheless, in 1967, it was Peirce's position that was inspirational for me.

On the one hand this was because Peirce had at least shown that science, as a paradigm of rationality, does not show that something like a rational legitimation of ethics is impossible (as was generally assumed at that time, following Max Weber and according to the convictions of logical positivism), but rather precisely presupposes this grounding. For although it is correct that science must proceed in a value-free manner in Max Weber's sense with respect to its *object* insofar as it consists only of facts and laws, value-free natural science must presuppose (in a manner that complements its object relation) a discourse ethics in the intersubjective dimension of the communicative community (*Kommunikations-gemeinschaft*) of scientists. Such ethics is, however, as an ethics of science in Peirce's sense, not *universally* valid. That is, it cannot demand from all human beings in all situations a "self-surrender" in relation to extra-scientific interests. On the contrary, as universally valid discourse ethics it must in actual fact demand the balanced investigation and consideration of all mutually consistent human interests. However, the ethics of an ideal argumentative community, which is presupposed from the outset in the community of scientists, must also demand a self-surrender, that is, a restriction to consideration of such methods of representation of interest as are permissible in an ideal argumentative community.

It is precisely this demand that clearly corresponds to the moral claim to correctness (*Richtigkeitsanspruch*) belonging to the incontestable presuppositions of argumentation as such. This fore-structure of argumentation can be explicated in the following manner: we presuppose in the case of every genuine argument a transcendental structure (which is also fundamental for empirically isolated thought), namely a twofold communicative a priori:

1 connectedness to a *real* (i.e. representative of our actual, traditionally determined pre-understanding of the world) communicative community, and
2 thereby at once the (counterfactually anticipated) connectedness to an ideal communicative community in which consensus would be attained concerning our justified moral claims to correctness as universal validity claims.

In view of this twofold a priori condition and in view of knowledge concerning the difference between actual reality and the necessarily anticipated ideal (even the skeptic who genuinely argues must share these argumentative presuppositions), we also presuppose the obligation to reduce the difference in the long term. (Without the constantly repeated attempt at such a reduction the responsible application of discourse ethics would not be in the least conceivable.)

With this explication of the argumentative a priori (first presented in a lecture in Göteborg in 1967 and published as an essay, "The *a priori* of the communicative community and the foundations of ethics" in my book of 1973)[43] a transcendental pragmatic grounding of discourse ethics was in my view outlined. In the decades that followed, in numerous books and articles, I was engaged in the development of this ethics.[44] This involved, in rough terms, the following problematics:

1 defense of the transcendental-pragmatic ultimate grounding of discourse ethics;
2 responsible application of discourse ethics under conditions sympathetic and inimical to dialogue;
3 discourse ethical grounding of moral and juridical norms in relation to the values of the "good life";
4 relation of discourse ethics to the functional "objective compulsions" (*Sachzwängen*) of social institutions.

The program of mutually interrelated tasks indicated in this way is far from complete and can be only very selectively presented in what follows.

Concerning (1): The difference between the transcendental-pragmatic, reflective ultimate grounding and the usual paradigm of logical-semantic (in the strict case deductive) ultimate grounding (which leads to a trilemma, as Hans Albert was the last to demonstrate[45]) was already emphasized above. To this point of difference there could be added reference to the debate concerning the possibility of "transcendental arguments," initiated by Peter Strawson and continuing over many years. The transcendental-pragmatic ultimate grounding is indeed also a "transcendental argument." However, in this case the concern is not, as it is for Strawson and his followers, with objectively (logically and semantically) demonstrable preconditions of a "descriptive metaphysics" in relation to "categorial schemes" of objective knowledge, but rather with presuppositions of every argument which can be demonstrated in a strictly reflective manner. The latter are also a priori valid under the conditions of a post-Quinean and post-Davidsonian holism that questions the transcendental status of categorial schemes.

A putatively more radical argument is specifically directed against the ultimate grounding of ethics; such justification is said to be impossible because skeptics can refuse argumentation.[46] But this is clearly an argument in philosophical discourse and this discourse is not circumventible (*nicht hintergehbar*). (This is in actual fact the most important characterizing term for the strictly reflective, transcendental-pragmatic ultimate grounding.) Thus someone must present the refusing argument in discourse and so the proponent cannot apply it to himself. Therefore such an argument is self-defeating (*selbstaufhebend*).

Concerning (2): Admittedly, a quite serious argument with respect to the *application* of discourse ethics might be concealed behind the pseudo-argument just presented, an argument which I have dealt with in the past and continue to deal with in great detail in the present under the heading of a "Part B" of discourse ethics.[47] One novelty of discourse ethics over and against every rational ethics grounded in a methodologically solipsistic manner is the fact that the grounding of the material (ultimately situational) norms of action is essentially referred to real discourse with the persons affected, in order that the interests of all affected parties can be considered in the construction of the consensus aimed at. (In political practice this happens mostly by means of the representation of interest, although this is also essentially – even in the case of empirically isolated deliberation – always referred back to supposed real discourses.) How should we behave when our genuinely necessary partners refuse moral discourse (or do not even possess the competence for such discourse), when they prefer to behave *strategically*, whether this means amoral actions, bargaining, or even open violence?

With respect to these not uncommon cases I have not resorted to the usual solutions that merely obscure the problems (e.g. the separation of private morality, judicial process and amoral politics),[48] but rather tentatively introduced a Part B of applied discourse ethics in which moral and strategic orientations of action can no longer – as in ideal discourse – be separated.[49] In contradistinction to the ideal Part A of discourse ethics, which can be understood as purely deontological in the sense of abstracting from history, in Part B the historically situated condition of discourse ethics as applicable ethics of responsibility is also considered. Discourse ethics must take into consideration from the first the fact that the conditions of ideal discourse, counterfactually anticipated in the discourse of ultimate grounding, are nowhere already historically realized, but rather are still to be realized. Thus a teleological dimension enters into discourse ethics as an ethics of responsibility. However, this also makes it possible to make binding a long-term moral strategy for the strategy-counter strategy licenses, which must be admitted in Part B of discourse ethics (such as, for example, necessary lying and violence to oppose violence). Such a moral strategy is able to mark the difference between an ethics of responsibility related to history and a purely strategic *Realpolitik*.

The difference just indicated also makes clear that discourse ethics in the sense of its Part A is also absolutely applicable as an ethics of responsibility with respect to reality. Under discourse ethics in the sense of its Part B, the ideal principle of Part A – the criterion of the acceptability of all solutions of moral problems according to the measure of interests of all affected parties – is to be constantly presupposed as a necessary limit condition of moral action, including cases of strategic solutions of problems.[50] (The principle of the capacity for consensus of all affected parties is thereby a regulative ideal principle that may be distinct from any currently politically realizable principle of an "overlapping consensus" in Rawls's sense[51]).

The applicability of discourse ethics as an ethics of grounding norms is currently primarily manifest on the level of the "reasoning world public" (*räsonierende Weltöffentlichkeit*) (Kant) and of the quasi-institution of thousands of discussions and conferences about problems of humanity rhetorically related to this reasoning world public.[52] Despite all the predominance of strategic rationality in the negotiations that go on here, scarcely any party dares to contradict publicly in discussion with the media the principles of discourse ethics which I have sketched out. There is also a "material compulsion" (*Sachzwang*) of the meta-institution of discourse that is also vitally important in this regard (see below) about the property of institutions.

Concerning (3): If we understand the application of discourse ethics as that of grounding norms, then the following distinctions formally arise: (1) fundamental norms, (2) material moral norms, (3) legal norms, (4) values of an "ethics of the good life."

Fundamental norms are normative conditions of the possibility of the discursive grounding of norms. They are implied in the incontestable presuppositions of argumentation and are therefore a priori valid. The most important fundamental norms of discourse ethics relate to the equal legitimacy of all discourse partners and the shared co-responsibility (*Mit-Verantwortung*) of all discourse partners for the solution of moral problems by means of the discursive grounding of material norms that are always situation dependent and therefore both fallible and temporary. *Material moral norms* are to be distinguished from *legal norms*, i.e. the *norms of positive law* (*positives Recht*). These latter are, with respect to their grounding, not only dependent on dominance free discourse (*herrschaftsfreier Diskurs*) of an ideal communication community, but still draw their normative authority from the sovereignty of the state of law (*Rechts-Staat*) that is able to assert its authority by virtue of a monopoly on violence. Thereby positive law exonerates the subordinated national citizens from the burden of the rational ultimate grounding of moral norms (above all from the problematic of Part B of an ethics of responsibility).[53] Nevertheless, a democratic state of law presupposes the grounding of norms of a discourse ethics as a model to the extent that it presupposes the identity of citizens as sovereign founders and addressees of the legislature who must follow a corresponding regulative principle of consensus formation.[54]

The problematic of human rights, of the rights of peoples and of the international organizations that represent them (above all of the United Nations) raises at present the question whether the representation and enforcement of a "cosmopolitan" system of law and order (*weltbürgerliche Rechts-und-Friedensordnung*) (as already found in Kant's demand for eternal "peace" in his *Zum ewigen Frieden* (*Eternal Peace*) of 1795) can be established, whether it be on the basis of a world state or of a "confederation of peoples."[55]

The problematic of the *values* in the sense of the good life to be chosen (in Aristotle's sense or also in the sense of existential philosophy) can be distinguished from the problematic of the grounding of norms just sketched out.[56] The former problematic can be relativized with respect to individual or collective life-projects to the extent that these projects need not be limited by universally valid moral norms of justice. (So, for example, the age-old project of the prince's life for martial honor can no longer be accepted.) On the other hand, in my view a universally valid norm (e.g. the duty to commit oneself to progress in the sense of the realization of a cosmopolitan system of law and order as already proclaimed by Kant) can also be understood as a "value" in the sense of a good life to be chosen by all persons.

Concerning (4): With the discussion of the problem of grounding legal norms we have touched on the relationship of discourse ethics to social institutions or functional systems. Since the 1990s I have turned to this problem from the perspective of the problem of applying responsibility relating to history.[57] Here the problematic of the relation of discourse ethics to social institutions can be connected in my view to that of Part B of discourse ethics, if one also takes into consideration two conditions of human action – conditions to be anthropologically and socio-philosophically thematized:

(1) In concrete social situations, human beings cannot act solely by means of their rationality in an unmediated and exclusive manner – neither solely by means of abstract, strategic rationality (as they are analyzed in decision and game theories), nor solely by means of reciprocal, ideal communicative rationality (as, for example, Kant assumes in the conception of an intelligible "kingdom of ends," which in actual fact must count as a metaphysical prototype of the ideal communicative community that we must assume both counterfactually and as a regulative ideal in argumentation). In concrete social situations (also in situations of social emergency relief on the basis of ethical responsibility evoked by the singular claim of the other in Levinas's sense[58]) human beings must always act on the basis of the relevant presuppositions of institutions which relate to the situation (e.g. in the sense of professional duties, competences and appertaining conventions). Therein resides not only an exoneration from rational ultimate grounding (which is a matter of reflection), but also alienation of autonomic reason and a greater or lesser admission of institutional material compulsions which are often morally restrictive.

(2) The significance of the latter can be clarified in my opinion with reference to the difference between the rationality of action (the strategic as well as the communicative-moral rationality of persons and the functional rationality of social systems. The relevant difference of rationality types[59] may be clarified by means of an old commonplace of social and historical philosophy. The difference between human *intentions* of action and the *effects* of actions on the level of society and of history is evident both in the frustration of good intentions and also conversely in the collective achievements of purely egoistic and strategic action. (An example of the latter is the case of the "invisible hand" of the market economy assumed by Adam Smith and in the "cunning" [*List*] of nature or providence or the idea, or the world spirit, in essence supposed first by Kant and then explicitly by Hegel).

In connection with Part B of discourse ethics this problematic can be explained in the following manner:

The unavoidable concessions to the (often morally restrictive) material compulsions of institutions (those of politics, the economy, and also positive law) correspond in the first instance to the necessity of acting also in a strategically correct manner, i.e. with the responsibility of being successful. In some situations strategically correct practical rationality and functional rationality as it relates to a social system can even coincide (as may be the case for example in wartime, in a politically or economically relevant negotiation, or in an action which enforces the law by means of the police). The difference between action in the sense of a systemic material compulsion and an action in the sense of the practical rationality of Part B of discourse ethics nevertheless resides in the fact that in the first case an institutional exoneration from thinking through the grounding of practical rationality to its end is in each case effected. Not uncommonly this exoneration extends so far that the part of the strategic rationality of action meant to serve Part B of ethics is practically annulled. Human action is thereby not only institutionally exonerated in the indicated ethical sense, but rather totally determined in its motivation by the material compulsions of institutions (We recognize this state of affairs from the special domain of politics that pertains to the military, but also from the broader domain of the political subjection of thinking to the *raison d'état*. Correspondingly, in recent times the total reduction of "economic ethics" to "institutional ethics" in the sense of the functional rationality of the economic system is demanded.[60])

In the face of this situation I have attempted, by means of a differentiating reconstruction of the concept of responsibility, both to recognize the necessity of material compulsions and to subordinate them to the transcendental-pragmatically grounded ethics of responsibility.[61] One has to admit that individually attributable responsibility for certain duties and tasks is extensively dependent on institutions and their material compulsions. In this conventional sense it is always already *assigned* responsibility. Besides this, the only other possibility (in a post-conventional sense) appears to be the self-apportioning of specific responsibility on the basis of particular insights, capacities, and positions of power, for example, initiatives of responsibility on the part of scientists, technicians, economists, and politicians, who have discovered a new problem, in particular a risk of the existing institutions for the general public. However, on the basis of these preconditions alone collective responsibility for the testing and possible amendment of existing institutions in the face of the globalization of almost all human cultural problems cannot be ethically grounded. Why should every individual feel responsible for the contemporary problems of humanity, such as, for example, those of the ecological crisis, of multiculturalism, of the global economic system, and of the cosmopolitan system of law and order?

However, here the reflective ultimate grounding of ethics can contemplate the circumstance that, in earnest discussion of this problem in primordial discourse, we have at once already assumed a co-responsibility beyond all institutions. It is not a question here of an individually attributable responsibility for particular duties and tasks, but rather of the equally apportioned shared responsibility for the identification and solution of all discursively resolvable problems that accompanies the equal authority of all discourse partners. There also belongs to these problems, as is evident today, the apportioning of individually attributable responsibility on the basis of arguments amenable to consensus. This shared responsibility of human beings as discourse partners beyond all institutions has today already found a counterpart at the level of political institutions (albeit only approximately and partially): the relationship of the voters to those voted for, within a democracy – a relation that, so to speak, has taken the place of the legitimation of princes' power by appeal to God's mercy. This seems to be the place where discourse ethics – along with the grounding of the norms of positive law and of the legal system of the economy – also has to introduce the accommodation (*Vermittlung*) of its responsible application with the particular reality of social institutions in the present.

Notes

Quotations from the German texts have been translated by Brian Elliott.

1 Originally *Being and Time* was meant to have two parts: "First Part: the interpretation of *Dasein* with respect to temporality and the explication of time as the transcendental horizon of the question of Being. Second Part: basic features of a phenomenological destruction of the history of ontology orientated towards the problematic of temporality" (*Being and Time*, Introduction §8). The whole of the second half and the third division of the first half, which was to be entitled "Time and Being," did not, however, appear. See what is said below about the "turning" in Heidegger's philosophy.

2 Accordingly Heidegger remarks, for example in the lecture series from 1934–5: "The truth of the people is the respective manifestness of Being as a whole according to which the powers which bear and dispose and direct receive their ranks and effect their concordance. The truth of a people is that manifestness of Being in virtue of which a people knows what it wants historically and through *willing itself* wills its self."

3 Ernst Tugendhat's critique is elaborated in the book *Der Wahrheitsbegriff bei Husserl und Heidegger* [*The Concept of Truth in Husserl and Heidegger*] (1967), but it had already been presented for the first time in February 1964 in his Heidelberg lecture "Heidegger's idea of truth" (see Pöggeler 1969). In April 1964 Heidegger, whether he knew of the critique or not, substantially confirmed it.

4 See Lafont 1994.

5 See Apel 1998a: 505–68.

6 After an initial phase of philosophical research with Heidegger at Freiburg and Marburg (1923–5), Gadamer completed studies in classical philology. Subsequently he was able, in his Habilitation under Heidegger on Plato's *Philebus* (published under the title *Plato's Dialectical Ethics*), both to present to and to oppose to his teacher an independent interpretation of Plato.

7 Here Gadamer distinguishes himself fundamentally from authors such as Joachim Ritter (1961), who assumed that the break of modern culture with the quasi-natural function of tradition (*Überlieferung*) is precisely a presupposition of the human sciences. However, this raises the question whether, even under the precondition of an existential ontological concept of the historicity of understanding, one does not still need to distinguish a pre-reflective and a reflectively determined post-Enlightenment situation of the transmission of tradition. On this see the contributions of Karl-Otto Apel and Jürgen Habermas in *Hermeneutik und Ideologiekritik* (Apel 1971).

8 The debates between Thomas Kuhn and Imre Lakatos on the structure of the history of science offer illuminating counterexamples here. (For further discussion of Kuhn and Lakatos, see "Philosophy of science," Chapter 14.) Although "normal science" (which in Heidegger's view "does not think") is dependent, according to Kuhn, on "incommensurable paradigms" (corresponding to Heideggerian "clearings/coverings"), nevertheless the historian of science must, according to Lakatos, distinguish between the "internal" (i.e. rationally reconstructible) and "external" (i.e. merely psychologically or sociologically explicable) history of science, in order to be able to identify minimally the object of investigation. See Kuhn 1962 and Lakatos 1974.

9 See Apel 1979.

10 See Habermas 1968; see also Habermas 1970, "Der Universalitätsanspruch der Hermeneutik" ("The hermeneutic claim to universality").

11 See Apel 1971.

12 See Ricoeur 1970.

13 See Apel 1963: Introduction.

14 See Apel 1970.

15 See Apel 1973b, 2: 128–54.

16 See Apel 1979.

17 See Apel 1963.

18 See Stenius 1960.

19 See in particular Apel 1965; 1973b, 2: 28–95.

20 See Winch 1958.

21 See Apel 1973b, 2: 28–95, 220–63 (*Towards a Transformation of Philosophy*, pp. 136–79); 1998a: 609–48.

22 See my comparison of Wittgenstein and Heidegger in Apel 1973b, 2: 223–334 (*Towards a Transformation of Philosophy*, pp. 1–45); 1998a: 459–504.

23 See Apel 1995a.

24 See my confrontation with Charles W. Morris in Apel 1973a.

25 See Apel 2001c.

26 See Habermas 1976.

27 See Apel 1986.

28 See Wittgenstein 1979.

29 See Apel 1998a: 9f., 33–194.

30 See Habermas 1976: 183–204.

31 See Apel 1976a; 1998a: 69. See also Kuhlmann 1985.

32 See Apel 1976a.

33 See Apel 1988: 306–69.

34 See Kohlberg 1984.

35 Apel 1973a; 1973b; 1993; 1995b; 1995c; 2001e; 2002; 2007.

36 See most recently Apel 2007.

37 See Apel 1998a: 9–42; 1998b: 459–505, in particular 494ff.

38 See Böhler et al. 1986.

39 See Rossvaer 1986. It is stated there, for example, in relation to the behavior of the SS: "The decisive point is … that the categorical imperative as a *universal* rule was adhered to and yet on the basis of a practice that was distinct from ours … The rule always becomes binding through some practice, be it ours or theirs. There is no rationality and no moral rationality that could be binding for us independently of practice" (p. 199). There is, however, for rational (philosophical) ethics, a *post-conventional* problem of the situationally correct application of moral rules. Yet precisely for this problem of practical reason Wittgenstein appears to offer merely reference to (arbitrary) empirically constant "habits," that is, conventions. In my opinion that would be in fact the capitulation of practical reason.

40 See Apel 1998a: 81–194; 1998b: 64–102.

41 See Apel 2002.

42 See Apel 2004.

43 See Apel 1973b.

44 See Apel 1984a; 1984b; 1988; 1990; 1992b; 1993; 1994a; 1996a; 1997a; 1997b; 1998a (especially pp. 221–412 and 609–838); 1999b; 2000; 2001b; 2001d; 2002.

45 Albert 1968: 13.

46 See Habermas 1983: 108ff.; also Reese-Schäfer 1990: 125ff. On this, see Apel 2001e: 81ff.

47 See Apel 1988 and 2001e.

48 See, e.g., my case study on the Kosovo conflict in Apel 2001a.

49 See Apel 1988: 143ff.

50 In this way the moral strategy of action of Part B of discourse ethics does not annul the ideal principle of discourse ethics, but rather complements it, but only with respect to Part A, which presupposes ideal conditions of application. (In the primordial, fundamental discourse of grounding pertaining to philosophy the ideal conditions of discourse are of course always presupposed. However, in relation to the application of discourse ethics, the primordial discourse must presuppose, along with the precondition for appropriate application, the distinction between A and B.)

51 See Apel 2001d.

52 See Apel 2000.

53 See Apel 1990 and 1992.

54 Cf. Habermas 1992. On this see Apel 1998a: 727–838 and 1999b.

55 See Apel 2000 and 2005.

56 See Habermas 1991: 100–18. On this see Apel 1998a: 772ff.

57 See Apel 1992a and 1992b; 1996a: 13–14; 1997b; 2001b.

58 See Mosès 1993.

59 See Apel 1995a and 1995b.

60 See Homann and Blome-Drees 1992. On this see Apel 1997b.

61 See Apel 2000 and 2001b.

References

Albert, H. (1968) *Traktat über kritische Vernunft*. Tübingen: Mohr. Translated as *Treatise on Critical Reason*, Princeton, NJ: Princeton University Press, 1985.

Apel, K.-O. (1955) "Das *Verstehen*: eine Problemgeschichte als Begriffsgeschichte." In *Archiv für Begriffsgeschichte*, vol. 1, Bonn: Bouvier, pp. 142–99.

—— (1963) *Die Idee der Sprache in der Tradition des Humanismus von Dante bis Vico*. Bonn: Bouvier. 3rd edn. 1980.

—— (1965) "Die Entfaltung der sprachanalytischen Philosophie und das Problem der Geisteswissenschaften." *Philosophie Jahrbuch* 72, pp. 239–89. Repr. in Apel 1973b, vol. 2, pp. 28–95. Translated as "Analytic philosophy of language and the 'Geisteswissenschaften'," in *Foundations of Language*, vol. 5, Dordrecht: Reidel, 1967. Repr. in Apel 1994b: 1–50.

—— (ed.) (1967, 1970) C. S. Peirce, *Schriften* I und II, Frankfurt am Main: Suhrkamp.

—— (1970) "Szientismus oder transzendentale Hermeneutik." In R. Bubner et al. (eds.) *Hermeneutik und Dialektik. H.-G. Gadamer zum 70 Geburtstag*, 2 vols., Tübingen: Mohr/ Siebeck, vol. 1, pp. 105–44.

—— (1971) "Szientistik, Hermeneutik, Ideologiekritik: Entwurf einer Wissenschaftslehre in erkenntnis anthropologischer Sicht." In K.-O. Apel et al. (eds.) *Hermeneutik und Ideologiekritik*, Frankfurt am Main: Suhrkamp, pp. 7–44. Repr. in Apel 1973b, 2: 96–127. Translated in K. Mueller-Vollmer (ed.) *The Hermeneutics Reader*, New York: Continuum, 1985, pp. 320–45.

—— (1972) "The apriori of communication and the foundations of the humanities." *Man and World* 5/1: 3–37.

—— (1973a) "Charles W. Morris und das Programm einer pragmatisch interpretierten Semiotik." In Ch. W. Morris, *Zeichen, Sprache und Verhalten*, Düsseldorf: Schwan, pp. 9–66. Repr. in A. Eschbach (ed.) *Zeichen über Zeichen über Zeichen*, Tübingen: G. Narr, 1981, pp. 25–82.

—— (1973b) *Transformation der Philosophie*, 2 vols., vol. 1 *Sprachanalytik, Semiotik, Hermeneutik*; vol. 2: *Das Apriori der Kommunikationsgemeinschaft*. Frankfurt am Main: Suhrkamp. Partial English translation: *Towards a Transformation of Philosophy*, London: Routledge & Kegan Paul, 1980. Repr. Milwaukee, WI: Marguette University Press, 1998.

—— (1974) "Zur Idee einer transzendentalen Sprachpragmatik." In J. Simon (ed.) *Aspekte und Probleme der Sprachphilosophie*, Freiburg: Alber, pp. 283–326.

—— (1975) *Der Denkweg von Charles S. Peirce*. Frankfurt am Main: Suhrkamp. Translated as *Charles S. Peirce: From Pragmatism to Pragmaticism*, Amherst, MA: University of Massachusetts Press, 1981. Repr. Atlantic Highlands, NJ: Humanities Press, 1995.

—— (1976a) "Das Problem der philosophischen Letztbegründung im Lichte einer transzendentalen Sprachpragmatik." In B. Kanitscheider (ed.) *Sprache und Erkenntnis, Festschrift für Gerhard Frey*, Innsbruck, 1976, pp. 55–82. Repr. in Apel 1998a, pp. 33–80. Translated as "The problem of philo-sophical fundamental grounding in light of a transcendental pragmatics of language," *Man and World* 8/3 (1975): 239–75. Repr. in Apel 1996b; and in K. Baynes et al. (eds.) *After Philosophy: End or Transformation?*, Cambridge, MA: MIT Press, 1987, pp. 250–90.

—— (ed.) (1976b) *Sprachpragmatik und Philosophie*. Frankfurt am Main: Suhrkamp. Includes "Sprechakttheorie und transzendentale Sprachpragmatik zur Frage ethischer Normen," pp. 10–173.

—— (1979) *Die "Erklären-Verstehen"- Kontroverse in transzendentalpragmatischer Sicht*. Frankfurt am Main: Suhrkamp. Translated as *Understanding and Explanation: A Transcendental-Pragmatic Perspective*, Cambridge, MA: MIT Press, 1984.

—— (1986) "Die Logos-Auszeichnung der menschlichen Sprache. Die philosophische Relevanz der Sprechakttheorie." In G. Bosshardt (ed.) *Perspektiven auf Sprache*, Berlin: de Gruyter, pp. 45–87.

—— (1988) *Diskurs und Verantwortung. Das Problem des Übergangs zur postkonventionellen Moral*. Frankfurt am Main: Suhrkamp.

—— (1990) "Diskursethik als Verantwortungsethik. Eine postmetaphysische Transformation der Ethik Kants," In R. Fornet-Betancourt (ed.) *Ethik und Befreiung*, in *Concordia, Monographien*, Aachen: Augustinus-Buchhandlung, pp. 10–40. Repr. in G. Schönrich, and Y. Kato (eds.) *Kant in der Diskussion der Moderne*, Frankfurt am Main: Suhrkamp, 1996, pp. 326–59.

—— (1992) "Diskursethik vor der Problematik von Recht und Politik." In K.-O. Apel and M. Kettner (eds.) *Zur Anwendung der Diskursethik in Politik, Recht und Wissenschaft*, Frankfurt am Main: Suhrkamp, pp. 29–61.

—— (1993) "How to ground a universalistic ethics of co-responsibility for the effects of collective actions and activities." In M. Batens et al. (eds.) Problèmes moraux: vie privée, vie publique, *Philosophica* 52/2: 9–29.

—— (1994a) "Die Diskursethik vor der Herausforderung der latein-amerikanischen Philosophie der Befreiung." In R. Fornet-Betancourt (ed.) *Konvergenz oder Divergenz? Eine Bilanz des Gesprächs zwischen Diskursethik und Befreiungsethik*, Aachen: Augustinus-Buchhandlung, pp. 17–38, and Porto Alegre: Editora Voces.

—— (1994b) *Towards a Transcendental Semiotics: Selected Essays*, vol. 1. Atlantic Highlands, NJ: Humanities Press.

—— (1995a) "Rationalitätskriterien und Rationalitätstypen. Versuch einer transzendentalpragmatischen Rekonstruktion des Unterschiedes zwischen Verstand und Vernunft." In A. Wüstehube (ed.) *Pragmatische Rationalitätstheorien*, Würzburg: Königshausen & Neumann, pp. 29–64.

—— (1995b) "The rationality of human communication: on the relationship between consensual, strategical, and systems rationality." In *Graduate Faculty Philosophy Journal* 18/1: 1–25. German version in K.-O. Apel and M. Kettner (1996) *Die eine Vernunft und die vielen Rationalitäten*, Frankfurt am Main: Suhrkamp, pp. 17–41.

—— (1995c) "Transcendental semiotics and hypothetical metaphysics of evolution: a Peircean or quasi-Peircean answer to a current problem of post-Kantian philosophy. " In K. L. Ketner (ed.) *Peirce and Contemporary Thought*, New York: Fordham University Press, pp. 366–97.

—— (1996a) "Das Anliegen der Befreiungsethik als Anliegen des Teils B der Diskursethik (Zur Implementation moralischer Normen unter den Bedingungen sozialer Institutionen bzw. Systeme)." In R. Fornet-Betancourt (ed.) *Armut-Ethik-Befreiung*, Aachen: Augustinus-Buchhandlung, pp. 13–44.

—— (1996b) *Ethics and the Theory of Rationality: Selected Essays*, vol. 2. Atlantic Highlands, NJ: Humanities Press.

—— (1997a) "Das Problem der Gerechtigkeit in einer mulitkulturellen Gesellschaft." In R. Fornet-Betancourt (ed.) *Armut im Spannungsfeld zwischen Globalisierung und dem Recht auf eine eigene Kultur*, Aachen: Augustinus-Buchhandlung, 106–30. Translated as "The problem of justice in a multicultural society," in R. Kearney and M. Dooley (eds.) *Ethics in Question*, London and New York: Routledge, 1998, pp. 145–63.

—— (1997b) "Institutionenethik oder Diskursethik als Verantwortungsethik? Das Problem der institutionellen Implementation moralischer Normen im Falle des Systems der Marktwirtschaft." In J. P. Harpes and W. Kuhlmann (eds.) *25 Jahre Diskursethik. Ein Symposion*, Münster: LIT-Verlag, pp. 167–209.

—— (1998a) *Auseinandersetzungen – in Erprobung des transzendentalpragmatischen Ansatzes*. Frankfurt am Main: Suhrkamp.

—— (1998b) *From a Transcendental-Semiotic Point of View*. Manchester: Manchester University Press.

—— (1999a) "Husserl, Tarski oder Peirce? Für eine transzendentalsemiotische Konsenstheorie der Wahrheit." In S. Bøe et al. (eds.) *I første, andre og tredje person*, Trondheim: NTNU Filosofisk instituts publikasjonsserie, pp. 3–14.

—— (1999b) "Zum Verhältnis von Moral, Recht und Demokratie. Eine Stellungnahme zu Habermas' Rechtsphilosophie aus transzendentalpragmatischer Sichte." In P. Siller and B. Keller (eds.) *Rechtsphilosophische Kontroversen der Gegenwart*, Baden-Baden: Nomos, pp. 27–40. Translated as: "Regarding the relationship of morality, law and democracy: on Habermas' Philosophy of Law from a transcendental-pragmatic point of view." In M. Aboulafia (ed.) *Habermas and Pragmatism*, London: Routledge, 2001, pp. 17–30.

—— (2000) "First things first: Der primordiale Begriff der Mitverantwortung." In M. Kettner (ed.) *Angewandte Ethik als Politikum*, Frankfurt am Main: Suhrkamp, pp. 21–50.

—— (2001a) "Das Spannungsfeld zwischen Ethik, Völkerrecht und politisch-militärischer Strategie in der Gegenwart. Philosophische Retrospektive auf den Kosovo-Konflikt." In M. Niquet (ed.) *Diskursethik: Grundlegungen und Anwendungen*, Würzburg: Königshausen & Neumann, pp. 205–18. Translated as "On the relationship between ethics, international law and politico–military strategy in our time: a philosophical retrospective on the Kosovo conflict," *European Journal of Social Theory* 4/1 (2001): 29–40.

—— (2001b) "Diskursethik als Ethik der Mit-Verantwortung vor den Sachzwängen der Politik, des Rechts und der Marktwirtschaft." In K.-O. Apel and H. Burkhart (eds.) *Prinzip Mitverantwortung. Grundlage von Ethik und Pädagogik*, Würzburg: Königshausen & Neumann, pp. 69–96.

—— (2001c) "Intersubjektivität, Sprache und Selbstreflexion – ein neues Paradigma der Transzendentalphilosophie?" In W. Kuhlmann (ed.) *Anknüpfen an Kant. Konzeptionen der Transzendentalphilosophie*, Würzburg: Königshausen & Neumann, pp. 63–78.

—— (2001d) "May a political conception of 'Overlapping Consensus' be an adequate basis of political justice?" In D. M. Rasmussen (ed.) *Proceedings of the 20th World Congress of Philosophy*, Boston, 1998, vol. 11, Philosophy Documentation Center, pp. 1–15. Repr. in *Concordia* 46 (2004): 29–44.

—— (2001e) *The Response of Discourse Ethics*. Leuven: Peeters.

—— (2002) "Pragmatismus als sinnkritischer Realismus auf der Basis regulativer Ideen. In Verteididung einer Peirceschen Theorie der Realität und der Wahrheit." In M. L. Raters and M. Willaschek (eds.) *Hilary Putnam und die Tradition des Pragmatismus*, Frankfurt am Main: Suhrkamp, pp. 117–50. Published in English as "Pragmatism as sense-critical realism based on a regulative idea of truth: in defense of a Peircean theory of reality and truth," in *Transactions of the C. S. Peirce Society* XXXVII/4 (2001): 445–74.

—— (2004) "Il concetto di verità e la realtà della culture humana." *La Cultura* XLII/2: 283–96.

—— (2005) "Internationale Beziehungen. Was ist wünschenswert: das Imperium als Weltstaat oder die Völkergemeinschaft?" In R. Fornet-Betancourt (ed.) *Neue Kolonialismen in den Nord-Süd Beziehungen*, Frankfurt am Main and London: Iko-Verlag, pp. 29–44.

—— (2007) "La réflexion pragmatique transcendentale comme perspective principale d'une transformation actuelle de la philosophie kantienne." In C. Berner and F. Capeilleres (eds.) *Kant et les kantismes dans la philosophie contemporaine 1804–2004*, Villeneuve d'Ascq: Presses Universitaires du Septentrion, pp. 193–215.

—— (2008) "Discourse ethics, democracy, and international law: toward a globalization of practical reason." In S. Hicks and D. E. Shannon (eds.) *The Challenges of Globalization*, Oxford: Blackwell, pp. 49–70. Also in *The American Journal of Economics and Sociology* 66/1 (2007): 49–70.

Apel, K.-O. et al. (eds.) (1984a) *Funkkolleg Praktische Philosophie. Ethik: Dialoge*, 2 vols., Frankfurt am Main: Fischer.

Apel, K.-O., D. Böhler, and K. Rebel (eds.) (1984b) *Funkkolleg Praktische. Ethik: Studientexte*, 3 vols., Weinheim and Basle: Beltz.

Betti, E. (1962) *Die Hermeneutik als allgemeine Methodik der Geisteswissenschaften*. Tübingen: Mohr/Siebeck.

Böhler, D. et al. (eds.) (1986) *Die pragmatische Wende. Sprachspielpragmatik oder Transzendentalpragmatik?* Frankfurt am Main: Suhrkamp.

Böhler, D. et al. (eds.) (2003) *Reflexion und Verantwortung. Auseinandersetzugen mit Karl-Otto Apel*. Frankfurt am Main: Suhrkamp.

Gadamer, H.-G. (1931) *Platons dialektische Ethik. Phänomenologische Untersuchungen zum "Philebos."* Leipzig: Felix Meiner.

—— (1960) *Wahrheit und Methode. Grundzüge einer philosophischen Hermeneutik*. Tübingen: Mohr/Siebeck; 3rd expanded edn., 1972 (Referred to as WM in citations, with page nos. of the 3rd edn.). Also in *Gesammelte Werke*, vol. 2: *Hermeneutic II: Ergänzungen, Register*, Tübingen: Mohr/Siebeck, 1993. English translation of 2nd edn. by J. Weinsheimer and D. G. Marshall: *Truth and Method*, New York: Crossroad, 1989. (Referred to as TM in citations).

—— (1963) "Uber die Möglichkeit einer philosophischen Ethik." In *Sein und Ethos. Untersuchungen zur Grundlegung der Ethik*, ed. P. M. Engelhart, Walberberger Studien der Albertus-Magnus-Akademie, Philosophische Reihe 1, Mainz: Matthias-Grünewald, pp. 11–24. Also in *Gesammelte Werke*, vol. 4, pp. 175–88. Translated by M. Kelly as "On the possibility of a philosophical ethics" in R. Beiner and W. J. Booth (eds.) *Kant and Political Philosophy: The Contemporary Legacy*, New Haven, CT and London: Yale University Press, 1993, pp. 361–73.

—— (1967) *Kleine Schriften*, I und II. Tübingen: Mohr/Siebeck.

—— (1985–95) *Gesammelte Werke*, 10 vols. Tübingen: Mohr/Siebeck. (Referred to as GW in citations).

Grondin, J. (1999) *Hans-Georg Gadamer. Eine Biographie*. Tübingen: Mohr/Siebeck. Translated by J. Weinsheimer as: *Hans-Georg Gadamer: A Biography*, New Haven, CT and London: Yale University Press, 2003.

—— (2001) *Von Heidegger zu Gadamer. Unterwegs zur Hermeneutik*. Darmstadt: WBG.

Habermas, J. (1968) *Erkenntnis und Interesse*. Frankfurt am Main: Suhrkamp. Repr. with Postscript, 1973.

—— (1970) "Der Universalitätsanspruch der Hermeneutik." In K. Cramer and R. Wiehl (eds.) *Hermeneutik und Dialektik*, 2 vols., Tubingen: Mohr. Repr. in K.-O. Apel (ed.) *Hermeneutik und Ideologiekritik*, Frankfurt am Main: Suhrkamp, 1971, and in R. Bubner et al. (eds.) *Hermeneutik und Dialektik. H.-G. Gadamer zum 70 Geburtstag*, 2 vols., Tübingen: Mohr/Siebeck, 1970, vol. 1, pp. 73–104. Translated by J. Bleicher as "The hermeneutic claim to universality," in *Contemporary Hermeneutics*, London: Routledge & Kegan Paul, 1980, pp. 181–211.

—— (1971) "Zu Gadamers 'Wahrheit und Methode'." In K.-O. Apel et al. (eds.) *Hermeneutik und Ideologiekritik*, Frankfurt am Main: Suhrkamp, pp. 45–56.

—— (1976) "Was heißt Universalpragmatik?" In K.-O. Apel (ed.) *Sprachpragmatik und Philosophie*, Frankfurt am Main: Suhrkamp, pp. 174–272.

—— (1983) *Moralbewußtsein und kommunikatives Handeln*. Frankfurt am Main: Suhrkamp. Including "Diskursethik – Notizen zu einem Begründungsprogramm," pp. 53–126.

—— (1991) *Erläuterungen zur Diskursethik*. Frankfurt am Main: Suhrkamp. Including "Vom pragmatischen, ethischen und moralischen Vernunftgebrauch," pp. 100–19.

—— (1992) *Faktizität und Geltung*. Frankfurt am Main: Suhrkamp.

Heidegger, M. (1927) *Sein und Zeit*. Halle: Niemeyer.

—— (1929a) *Kant und das Problem der Metaphysik*. Frankfurt am Main: Klostermann.

—— (1929b) *Was ist Metapyhsik?* Bonn: Friedrich Cohen.

——(1934) *Logik als Frage nach der Sprache*. Lecture course from Sommersemester 1934, in *Gesamtausgabe* (1910–76), II. Abteilung.

—— (1935/6): *Die Frage nach dem Ding. Zu Kants Lehre von den transzendentalen Grundsätzen*. Tübingen: Niemeyer, 1962. (Publication of lecture course from winter semester 1935/6).

—— (1947a) *Brief über den Humanismus*. Berne: Franke.

—— (1947b) *Platons Lehre von der Wahrheit*. Berne: Franke.

—— (1950a) "Der Ursprung des Kunstwerkes," In *Holzwege*, Frankfurt am Main: Klostermann, pp. 7–68. Also in *Gesamtausgabe*, vol. 5, ed. F.-W. von Hermann, Frankfurt am Main: Klostermann, 1977; repr. 2003.,

—— (1950b) "Die Zeit des Weltbildes." In *Holzwege*, Frankfurt am Main: Klostermann, pp. 69–104. Also in *Gesamtausgabe*, vol. 5, ed. F.-W. von Hermann, Frankfurt am Main: Klostermann, 1977; repr. 2003.

—— (1962–4) *Zur Sache des Denkens*. In *Gesamtausgabe*, I. Abteilung. Frankfurt am Main: Klostermann. This Gesamtausgabe edn. is now vol. 14: *Zur Sache des Denken (1962–1964)*, 2007. (Referred to as SD in citations).

—— (1975–) *Gesamtausgabe*, 102 vols. projected. Ausgabe letzter Hand. I Abteilung: Veröffentlichte Schriften 1910–76, 16 vols. II Abteilung: Vorlesungen 1923–44. III Abteilung: Unveröffentlichte Abhandlungen. Vorträge-Gedachtes. IV Abteilung: Aufzeichnungen und Hinweise. Frankfurt am Main: Klostermann.

—— (1989) *Beiträge zur Philosophie (Vom Ereignis)*. Frankfurt am Main: Klostermann.

—— (1993) *Basic Writings*, 2nd edn. San Francisco: Harper. (Referred to as BW in citations).

—— (2000) *Contributions to Philosophy (From Enowning)*, trans. P. Emad and K. Maly (Studies in Continental Thought). Bloomington: Indiana University Press. (Referred to as C in citations).

Hirsch, E. D. (1967) *Validity of Interpretation*, New Haven, CT: Yale University Press.

Hohmann, K. and F. Blome-Drees (1992) *Wirtschafts- und Unternehmensethik*, Göttingen: Vandenhoeck.

Husserl, E. (1963) *Cartesianische Meditationen*, 2nd edn. The Hague: Nijhoff.

James, W. (1997) *The Will to Believe*. New York: Dover.

Kettner, M. (ed.) (2000) *Angewandte Ethik als Politikum*. Frankfurt am Main: Suhrkamp.

Kohlberg, L. (1984) *The Philosophy of Moral Development*. San Francisco: Harper & Row.

Kuhlmann, W. (1985) *Reflexive Letztbegründung*. Freiburg and Munich: Alber.

—— (ed.) (2001) *Anknüpfen an Kant. Konzeptionen der Transzendentalphilosophie*. Würzburg: Königshausen & Neumann.

Kuhn, Thomas S. (1962) *The Structure of Scientific Revolutions*. Chicago: University of Chicago Press. 2nd edn., with Postscript, 1970.

Lafont, C. (1994) *Sprache und Welterschließung. Zur linguistischen Wende der Hermeneutik Heideggers*. Frankfurt am Main: Suhrkamp.

Lakatos, I. (1974) "Die Geschichte der Wissenschaft und ihre rationalen Rekonstruktionen." In W. Diederich (ed.) *Beiträge zur Wissenschaftstheorie*, Frankfurt am Main: Suhrkamp, pp. 55–119.

Morris, C. W. (1938) *Foundations of the Theory of Signs: International Encyclopedia of Unified Science.* Chicago: University of Chicago Press.

—— (1946) *Signs, Language, and Behavior.* New York: Braziller.

Mosès, S. (1993) "Gerechtigkeit und Gemeinschaft bei Emanuel Lévinas." In M. Brumlik and H. Brunkhorst (eds.) *Gemeinschaft und Gerechtigkeit,* Frankfurt am Main: Fischer, pp. 364–84.

Niquet, M. (1991) *Transzendentale Argumente. Kant, Strawson und die Aporetik der Detranszendentalisierung.* Frankfurt am Main: Suhrkamp.

—— (1999) *Nichthintergehbarkeit und Diskurs. Prolegomena zu einer Diskurstheorie des Transzendentalen,* Berlin: Duncker & Humblot.

—— (2001) *Diskursethik. Grundlegung und Anwendungen.* Würzburg: Königshausen & Neumann.

Pöggeler, O. (1963) *Der Denkweg Martin Heideggers.* Freiburg: Alber.

—— (1969) *Heidegger. Perspektiven zur Deutung seines Werkes.* Cologne: Kiepenheuer & Witsch.

—— (ed.) (1972) *Hermeneutische Philosophie.* Munich: Nymphenburger Verlagshandlung.

Reese-Schafer, W. (1990) *Karl-Otto Apel. Zur Einfuhrung* (with a Postscript by J. Habermas). Hamburg: Junis.

Ricoeur, P. (1970) *Freud and Philosophy: An Essay on Interpretation,* trans. D. Savage. New Haven, CT: Yale University Press. First published as *Die Interpretation. Ein Versuch über Freud,* Frankfurt am Main: Suhrkamp, 1969.

Ritter, J. (1961) *Die Aufgabe der Geisteswissenschaften in der modernen Gesellschaft.* Münster: Gesellschaft zur Förderung der Westfälischen Wilhelms-Universität.

Rossvaer, V. (1986) "Transzendentalpragmatik, transzendentale Hermeneutik und die Möglichkeit, Auschwitz zu verstehen." In D. Böhler et al. (eds.) *Die pragmatische Wende. Sprachspielpragmatik oder Transzendentalpragmatik?,* Frankfurt am Main: Suhrkamp, pp. 187–202.

Stenius, E. (1960) *Wittgenstein's Tractatus.* Oxford: Blackwell.

Tugendhat, E. (1967) *Der Wahrheitsbegriff bei Husserl und Heidegger.* Berlin: de Gruyter.

Winch, P. (1958) *The Idea of a Social Science.* London: Routledge & Kegan Paul.

—— (1964) "Understanding a primitive society." *American Philosophical Quarterly* 1: 317–24.

Wittgenstein, L. (1922) *Tractatus Logico-Philosophicus.* London: Routledge & Kegan Paul.

—— (1960) *Philosophische Untersuchungen.* In *Schriften* 1. Frankfurt am Main: Suhrkamp, pp. 280–544.

—— (1979) *Über Gewißheit.* Frankfurt am Main: Suhrkamp.

Further reading

German philosophy

Bowie, A. (2003) *Introduction to German Philosophy: From Kant to Habermas.* Cambridge: Polity.

Bubner, R. (1981) *Modern German Philosophy,* trans. E. Mathews. Cambridge: Cambridge University Press.

Gorner, P. (2000) *Twentieth-Century German Philosophy.* Oxford: Oxford University Press.

O'Hear, A. (ed.) (1999) *German Philosophy since Kant.* Cambridge: Cambridge University Press.

Rintelen, F.-J. von, H. W. Schneider, and G. Funke (1970) *Contemporary German Philosophy and its Background.* Bonn: Bouvier.

Roberts, J. (1992) *The Logic of Reflection: German Philosophy in the 20th Century.* New Haven, CT: Yale University Press.

Schnädelbach, H. (1983) *Philosophy in Germany 1831–1933,* trans. E. Mathews. Cambridge: Cambridge University Press.

Stegmueller, W. (1970) *Main Currents in Contemporary German, British and American Philosophy.* Bloomington: Indiana University Press.

Works by Heidegger

Heidegger, M. (1956) *What Is Philosophy?* New Haven, CT: College & University Press.

—— (1962) *Being and Time,* trans. J. Macquarrie and J. Robinson. Oxford: Blackwell.

—— (1976) *What Is Called Thinking?* New York: Harper & Row.

—— (1982a) *On the Way to Language*. New York: Harper & Row.

—— (1982b) *The Question Concerning Technology, and Other Essays*. New York: HarperCollins.

—— (1988) *The Basic Problems of Phenomenology*. Bloomington: Indiana University Press.

—— (1992a) *History of the Concept of Time* (Studies in Phenomenology and Existential Philosophy). Bloomington: Indiana University Press.

—— (1992b) *The Metaphysical Foundations of Logic* (Studies in Phenomenology and Existential Philosophy). Bloomington: Indiana University Press.

—— (1993) *Basic Writings*, 2nd edn. San Francisco: Harper.

—— *The Principle of Reason* (Studies in Continental Thought). Bloomington: Indiana University Press.

—— (1997) *Kant and the Problem of Metaphysics* (Studies in Continental Thought). Bloomington: Indiana University Press.

—— (1998a) *Basic Concepts*. Bloomington: Indiana University Press.

—— (1998b) *Pathmarks*. Cambridge: Cambridge University Press.

—— (1999a) *Contributions to Philosophy: (From Enowning)* (Studies in Continental Thought). Bloomington: Indiana University Press.

—— (1999b) *Ontology: The Hermeneutics of Facticity* (Studies in Continental Thought). Bloomington: Indiana University Press,

—— (2000) *Introduction to Metaphysics*. New Haven, CT: Yale University Press.

—— (2001a) *Poetry, Language, Thought*.

—— (2001b) *The Fundamental Concepts of Metaphysics: World, Finitude, Solitude*. Bloomington: Indiana University Press.

—— (2002a) *Heidegger: Off the Beaten Track*. Cambridge: Cambridge University Press.

—— (2002b) *Identity and Difference*. Chicago: University of Chicago Press.

—— (2002c) *On Time and Being*. Chicago: University of Chicago Press.

—— (2002d) *The Essence of Truth: On Plato's Cave Allegory and Theaetetus*. London: Athlone Press.

Works on Heidegger

Allemann, B. (1954) *Hölderlin und Heidegger*. Zurich: Atlantis.

Ballard, E. G. and C. F. Scott (eds.) (1973) *Martin Heidegger: In Europe and America*. The Hague: Nijhoff.

Beaufret, J. (1947) "Heidegger et le problème de la verité." *Fontaine* 63: 758–85.

—— (1973–4) *Dialogue avec Heidegger*, 3 vols. Paris : Minuit.

Biemel, W. (1976) *Heidegger: An Illustrated Study*. New York: Harcourt, Brace, Jovanovich.

Birault, H. (1978) *Heidegger et l'experience de la pensée*. Paris: Gallimard.

Bretschneider, W. (1965) *Sein und Wahrheit. Über die Zusammengehörigkeit von Sein und Wahrheit im Denken Heideggers*. Meisenheim: Hain.

Gadamer, H.-G. (1959) "Vom Zirkel des Verstehens." In *Martin Heidegger zum siebzigsten Geburtstag*, Pfullingen: Neske, pp. 24–34; repr. in H.-G. Gadamer, *Gesammelte Werke*, vol. 2, pp. 57–65.

—— (1970) "Zur Einführung in Martin Heideggers 'Der Ursprung des Kunstwerks'," In M. Heidegger, *Der Ursprung des Kunstwerks*, Stuttgart: Reclam, pp. 102–25.

Gethmann-Siefert, A. and O. Pöggeler (eds.) (1998) *Heidegger und die praktische Philosophie*. Frankfurt am Main: Suhrkamp.

Herrmann, F.-W. (1980) *Heideggers Philosophie der Kunst*. Frankfurt am Main: Klostermann.

Kockelmans, J. J. (ed.) (1972) *On Heidegger and Language*. Evanston, IL: Northwestern University Press.

—— (1984) *On the Truth of Being: Reflections on Heidegger's Later Philosophy*. Bloomington: Indiana University Press.

—— (1985) *Heidegger on Art and Art Works*. Dordrecht: Nijhoff.

Marx, W. (1971) *Heidegger und die Tradition*. Evanston, IL: Northwestern University Press.

Pöggeler, O. (1972) *Philosophie und Politik bei Heidegger*. Freiburg and Munich: Alber.

—— (1983) *Heidegger und die hermeneutische Philosophie*. Freiburg and Munich: Alber.

Richardson, W. J. (1963) *Heidegger: Through Phenomenology to Thought*. The Hague: Nijhoff.

Schwan, A. (1965) *Politische Philosophie im Denken Heideggers*. Cologne: Westdeutscher Verlag.

Sallis, J. (ed.) (1970) *Heidegger and the Path of Thinking*. Pittsburgh: Duquesne University Press.

Sheehan, T. (ed.) (1981) *Heidegger: The Man and the Thinker*. Chicago: Precedent Publishing.

Durchblicke (1970) *Martin Heidegger zum 80 Geburtstag*. Frankfurt am Main: Klostermann.

Works by Gadamer

Gadamer, H.-G. (1985–95) *Gesammelte Werke*, 10 vols. Tübingen: Mohr/Siebeck.

—— (1976a) *Hegel's Dialectic: Five Hermeneutical Studies*, trans. P. C. Smith. New Haven, CT: Yale University Press.

—— (1976b) *Philosophical Hermeneutics*, ed. and trans. D. E. Linge. Berkeley: University of California Press.

—— (1980) *Dialogue and Dialectic: Eight Hermeneutical Studies on Plato*, ed. and trans. P. C. Smith. New Haven, CT: Yale University Press.

—— (1982) *Reason in the Age of Science*. Cambridge, MA: MIT Press.

—— (1985) *Philosophical Apprenticeships*. Cambridge, MA: MIT Press.

—— (1986a) *The Idea of the Good in Platonic-Aristotelian Philosophy*, trans. P. C. Smith. New Haven, CT: Yale University Press.

—— (1986b) *The Relevance of the Beautiful and Other Essays*, trans. N. Walker, ed. R. Bernasconi. Cambridge: Cambridge University Press.

—— (1989) *Truth and Method*, 2nd rev. edn., trans. J. Weinsheimer and D. G. Marshall. New York: Crossroad.

—— (1993) *Literature and Philosophy in Dialogue: Essays in German Literary Theory*, trans. R. H. Paslick. Albany, NY: State University of New York Press.

—— (1994) *Heidegger's Ways*, trans. J. W. Stanley. Albany, NY: State University of New York Press.

—— (1997) *Gadamer on Celan: 'Who Am I and Who Are You?' and Other Essays*, trans. and ed. R. Heinemann and B. Krajewski. Albany, NY: State University of New York Press.

—— (1998) *Praise of Theory*, trans. C. Dawson. New Haven, CT: Yale University Press.

Gadamer, H.-G. and G. Boehm (eds.) (1976) *Seminar philosophische Hermeneutik* (Texte von M. Flacius Illyricus, Spinoza, J. J. Rambach, J. M. Chlademius, K. Ph. Moritz, J. G. Herder, A. F. J. Thibaut, Fr. Ast, Fr. Schleiermacher, H. Steinthal, J. G. Droysen, W. Dilthey, E. Rothacker, R. Bultmann, M. Heidegger, H. Lipps, H.-G. Gadamer). Frankfurt am Main: Suhrkamp.

Works on Gadamer

Code, L. (ed.) (2003) *Feminist Interpretations of Hans-Georg Gadamer*. University Park: Pennsylvania State University Press.

Coltman, R. (1998) *The Language of Hermeneutics: Gadamer and Heidegger in Dialogue*. Albany, NY: State University of New York Press.

Dostal, R. L. (ed.) (2002) *The Cambridge Companion to Gadamer*. Cambridge: Cambridge University Press.

Grondin, J. (1982) *Hermeneutische Wahrheit. Zum Wahrheitsbegriff Hans-Georg Gadamers*. Königstein: Hain.

—— (2002) *The Philosophy of Gadamer*, trans. K. Plant. New York: McGill-Queens University Press.

—— (2004) *Hans-Georg Gadamer: A Biography*, trans J. Weinsheimer. New Haven, CT: Yale University Press.

Hahn, L. E. (ed.) (1997) *The Philosophy of Hans-Georg Gadamer*, Library of Living Philosophers 24. Chicago: Open Court.

Malpas, J., U. Arnswald, and J. Kertscher (eds.) (2002) *Gadamer's Century: Essays in Honor of Hans-Georg Gadamer*. Cambridge, MA: MIT Press.

Pöggeler, O. (ed.) (1972) *Hermeneutische Philosophie* (Texte von Dilthey, Heidegger, Gadamer, Ritter, Apel, Habermas, Ricoeur, O. Becker, Bollnow). Munich: Nymphenburger Verlagshandlung.

Scheibler, I. (2000) *Gadamer: Between Heidegger and Hermeneutics*. Lanham, MD: Rowman & Littlefield.

Wachterhauser, B. (1999) *Beyond Being: Gadamer's Post-Platonic Hermeneutic Ontology*. Evanston, IL: Northwestern University Press.

Warnke, G. (1987) *Gadamer: Hermeneutics, Tradition and Reason*. Stanford, CA: Stanford University Press

Weinsheimer, J. (1985) *Gadamer's Hermeneutics: A Reading of "Truth and Method"*. New Haven, CT: Yale University Press.

Wright, K. (ed.) (1990) *Festivals of Interpretation: Essays on Hans-Georg Gadamer's Work*. Albany, NY: State University of New York Press.

Works by Habermas

Habermas, J. (1979) *Communication and the Evolution of Society*, trans. and intro. T. McCarthy. Boston: Beacon Press.

—— (1991) *The New Conservatism: Cultural Criticism and the Historians' Debate*. Cambridge, MA: MIT Press.

—— (1992) *Moral Consciousness and Communicative Action*. Cambridge, MA: MIT Press.

—— (1994) *Postmetaphysical Thinking*. Cambridge, MA: MIT Press.

—— (1996) *Between Facts and Norms: Contributions to a Discourse Theory of Law and Democracy*. Cambridge, MA: MIT Press.

—— (2000a) *On the Pragmatics of Communication*. Cambridge, MA: MIT Press.

—— (2000b) *The Inclusion of the Other: Studies in Political Theory*. Cambridge, MA: MIT Press.

—— (2001a) *The Liberating Power of Symbols: Philosophical Essays*. Cambridge, MA: MIT Press.

—— (2001b) *The Postnational Constellation: Political Essays*. Cambridge, MA: MIT Press.

—— (2002a) *On the Pragmatics of Social Interaction: Preliminary Studies in the Theory of Communicative Action*. Cambridge, MA: MIT Press.

—— (2002b) *Religion and Rationality: Essays on Reason, God and Modernity*. Cambridge, MA: MIT Press.

—— (2003a) *Philosophy in a Time of Terror: Dialogues with Jürgen Habermas and Jacques Derrida*. Chicago: University of Chicago Press.

—— (2003b) *Truth and Justification*. Cambridge, MA: MIT Press.

Works on Habermas

Cooke, M. (1994) *Language and Reason: A Study of Habermas's Pragmatics*. Cambridge, MA: MIT Press,

Kearney, R. (ed.) (1994) *The Routledge History of Philosophy*. London: Routledge, vol. 8, pp. 254–89.

McCarthy, T. (1978) *The Critical Theory of Jürgen Habermas*. London: Hutchinson.

Outhwaite, W. (ed.) (1996) *The Habermas Reader*. Cambridge: Polity.

Rasmussen, D. (2002) *Reading Habermas*. Oxford: Blackwell.

Thompson, J. B. (2003) *Critical Hermeneutics: A Study in the Thought of Paul Ricoeur and Jürgen Habermas*. Cambridge: Cambridge University Press.

White, S. K. (ed.) (1995) *The Cambridge Companion to Habermas*. Cambridge: Cambridge University Press.

Works on Apel

Böhler, D. (1985) *Rekonstruktive Pragmatik. Von der Bewußtseinsphilosophie zur Kommunikationsreflexion*. Frankfurt am Main: Suhrkamp.

Fornet-Betancourt, R. (1992) *Diskursethik oder Befreiungsethik*. Aachen: Augustinus-Buchhandlung.

—— (ed.) (1994) *Konvergenz oder Divergenz? Eine Bilanz des Gesprächs zwischen Diskursethik und Befreiungsethik*. Aachen: Augustinus-Buchhandlung.

—— (ed.) (1996) *Diskurs und Leidenschaft. Festschrift für K.-O. Apel zum 75. Geburtstag*. Aachen: Augustinus-Buchhandlung.

—— (ed.) (2002) *Karl-Otto Apel und die lateinamerikanische Philosophie*. In *Concordia 2002*. Aachen: Wissenschaftsverlag Mainz.

—— (2003) "Transzendentalpragmatik und Diskursethik. Elemente und Perspektiven der Apelschen Diskursphilosophie." *Journal for General Philosophy of Science* 34: 221–49.

Gottschalk-Mazouz, N. (2000) *Diskursethik. Theorien, Entwicklungen, Perspektiven*. Berlin: Akademie-Verlag.

Harpes, J.-P. and W. Kuhlmann (eds.) (1997) *Zur Relevanz der Diskursethik. Anwendungsprobleme der Diskursethik in Wirtschaft und Politik*. Münster: LIT-Verlag.

Kuhlmann, W. (1992a) *Kant und die Transzendentalpragmatik*. Würzburg: Königshausen & Neumann.

—— (1992b) *Sprachphilosophie, Hermeneutik, Ethik. Studien zur Transzendentalpragmatik*. Würzburg: Königshausen & Neumann.

Kuhlmann, W. and D. Böhler (1982) *Kommunikation und Reflexion. Zur Diskussion der Transzendentalpragmatik*. Frankfurt am Main: Suhrkamp.

Mendieta, E. (2002) *The Adventures of Transcendental Philosophy: Karl-Otto Apel´s Semiotics and Discourse Ethics*. Lanham, MD, Boulder, CO, and New York: Rowman & Littlefield.

Niquet, M. (2002) *Moralität und Befolgungsgültigkeit. Prolegomena zu einer realistischen Diskurstheorie der Moral.* Würzburg: Königshausen & Neumann.

Reese-Schäfer, W. (1990) *Karl-Otto Apel zur Einführung* (with a Postscript by J. Habermas). Hamburg: Junius.

—— (1997) *Grenzgötter der Moral: der neuere europäisch-amerikanische Diskurs zur politischen Ethik.* Frankfurt am Main: Suhrkamp.

Tschentscher, A. (2000) *Prozedurale Theorien der Gerechtigkeit. Rationales Entscheiden, Diskursethik und prozedurales Recht.* Baden-Baden: Nomos.

18

CRITICAL THEORY

Axel Honneth

translated by Brian Elliott

With the transition to the twenty-first century Critical Theory appears now to be a form of thought belonging to the past. It is as though the merely chronological break between centuries has considerably widened the distance that separates us from the theoretical beginnings of that school. The names of those authors, which were still vital for the founders of the school, suddenly sound very remote to us and the theoretical challenges from which they drew their insights threaten to lapse into oblivion. Today, a younger generation carries on the task of social criticism with little more than a nostalgic memory of the heroic years of western Marxism.

Accordingly, it can hardly be overlooked that the political changes of the last decade of the twentieth century have not been without influence on the status of social criticism. With growing consciousness of the plurality of cultures and of the manifest differences between the various social movements of emancipation, expectations of what criticism should be, and might do, have had to be considerably scaled down. In general, a liberal concept of justice now prevails, whose criteria for the normative identification of social injustices are invoked without any particular desire to explain their institutional foundedness in a particular type of society. Even where such a procedure is regarded as unsatisfactory, social-critical models are invoked that emulate rather the spirit of Michel Foucault's genealogical method or the style of Michael Walzer's critical hermeneutics.[1] In these cases, however, criticism is grasped as nothing more than the reflexive form of a rationality that is itself anchored in the historical process. In contradistinction, Critical Theory insists, in what might be a unique manner, on the *mediation* between theory and history through the concept of a socially efficacious reason. According to this concept, the historical past has to be understood precisely as a *process of development* (*Bildungsprozess*), whose pathological distortion, brought about by capitalism, can be overcome only by initiating a process of enlightenment among those affected. This conceptual model (*Denkmodel*) concerning an intertwining of theory and history underpins the unity of Critical Theory in its multiplicity of voices. Whether it is in the positive manner of the young Max Horkheimer (1895–1973), Herbert Marcuse (1898–1979), or Jürgen Habermas (1929–), or in the negative manner of Theodor Adorno (1903–69) or Walter Benjamin (1892–1940), the context of their different projects is always constituted by the thought that a particular historical process of development is distorted by social relations, and that this distortion can only be remedied through a kind of praxis. Identifying the legacy of Critical Theory for the new century must therefore mean: preserving the explosive force latent in the thought of this social pathology of reason and thereby maintaining its vitality for current thinking. In opposition to the tendency to reduce social critique to a project of normative, situational, or local position-taking, the relationship of Critical Theory to the requirements of a historically developed reason has to be made clear.

In what follows I shall endeavor to take a first step in this direction: first, I shall explicate the ethical core contained within Critical Theory's idea of a deficient social rationality; second, I shall delineate the extent to which capitalism can be grasped as the cause of this distortion of social rationality; third, and finally, I shall set out the connection with praxis that has to be acknowledged in the envisaged overcoming (*Aufhebung*) of the social suffering produced by this deficient rationality. At each step, it will be a question of finding the right language to make manifest the contemporary significance of what is meant. Here I have to restrict myself mostly to mere indications of the direction which the realization of these arguments would have to take for the contemporary period.

The initial idea: social pathologies as a shortcoming of reason

Although it may be difficult to discover an underlying systematic unity across the multifarious forms of Critical Theory, nevertheless what may count as an initial point of shared agreement is the recognition that the proper point of departure is from a socio-theoretical negativism (*Negativismus*).[2] Not only the members of the inner circle but also those on the periphery of the Institute for Social Research[3] regard the social situation which they seek to influence as a condition of *social negativity*. Extensive agreement exists, moreover, that this negativity should not be measured in the narrow sense in terms of infringements against principles of social justice, but rather in the broad sense of violations of the conditions for good or successful living.[4] All the various expressions employed by members of the circle to characterize the given condition of society issue from a socio-theoretical vocabulary grounded in a fundamental distinction between "pathological" and "intact" or non-pathological relations. Max Horkheimer speaks early on of the "irrational orientation" of society; Adorno later of the "administered world"; Marcuse uses concepts such as "one-dimensional society" or "repressive tolerance"; and, finally, Jürgen Habermas uses the formula: the "colonization of the social life-world."[5] In all these formulations there is the constant normative presupposition of a constitution of social relations which ought to be "intact," in the sense of affording all members the chance of successful self-realization. What is specific about this terminology is not sufficiently clarified, however, by merely pointing to how it differs from the more usual discourse about social injustice within moral philosophy. Rather, the particularity of these expressions only becomes apparent when the initially opaque relationship thought to exist between the social pathology and a deficient reason is brought to light.

All the aforementioned authors take their point of departure from the notion that the cause of the negative condition of society must be recognized as residing in a *deficit of social reason*. They posit an internal relationship holding between the pathological relations and the constitution of social rationality, a relationship that explains their interest in the historical process according to which reason is realized. Every attempt to render the tradition of Critical Theory fruitful once more for the present day must therefore start with the attempt to realize this coupling, which is grounded in an ethical idea whose roots are to be found in G. W. F. Hegel (1770–1831).

The thesis that social pathologies are to be understood as a result of deficient rationality is derived ultimately from Hegel's political philosophy. In his *Philosophy of Right* (1821) Hegel worked with the basic presumption that the manifold tendencies toward the loss of meaning (*Sinnverlust*) apparent in his day could be accounted for only on the basis of an inadequate appropriation of an "objectively" already possible rationality.[6] The presupposition for this diagnosis of his time resided in a comprehensive conception of reason, according to which Hegel established a connection between historical progress and ethics. Accordingly, reason unfolds in the historical process in such a way that, at every stage, it creates anew general "moral" (*sittliche*) institutions, whose consideration permits individuals to plan their life according to socially recognized goals and so experience their life as meaningful. By contrast, anyone who does not allow his or her life to be determined by such objective, rational ends will suffer from the consequences of this "indeterminacy" (*Unbestimmtheit*) and will develop symptoms attendant upon such loss of orientation. If this ethical insight is carried over into the context of social processes as a whole, then the outlines emerge of the diagnosis of his time which Hegel held as basic in his *Philosophy of Right*. In the society of his day Hegel saw systems of thought predominate and ideologies installed that hindered subjects from apprehending the already established morality (*Sittlichkeit*), so that symptoms of loss of meaning were seen to emerge on a very broad basis. To this extent Hegel was convinced that social pathologies had to be understood as resulting from an incapacity of societies to express fully a rational potential that they already possessed within themselves, in their institutions, practices, and everyday routines.

If this conception is extracted from the particular context in which Hegel had embedded it then it leads to the general thesis that a successful form of society is only possible by maintaining at the highest level the appropriate standard of rationality. Accordingly, this connection is justified by Hegel by means of the ethical premise that only what is of *rational generality* (*vernünftiges Allgemeine*) can provide members of the society with the points of orientation needed to direct their lives in a meaningful way. A residue of this substantive conviction must still be in play among the representatives of Critical Theory when, according to their own distinct approaches, they assert that a lack of social rationality causes the pathologies of capitalist society. Without this ethical presupposition (already implicit in Hegel), there can be no grounds for asserting such a connection. It must be possible to say of the members of a society that they are able to lead successful, non-distorted lives only when they all orientate themselves by means of principles or institutions which they can recognize as rational goals for their own self-realization. Every deviation from this ideal as outlined must lead to a social pathology insofar as the subjects recognizably suffer from the loss of general, communal ends.

In the various programs of Critical Theory, however, the genuinely ethical core of this initial hypothesis remained mostly hidden behind anthropological presuppositions. The rational generality which is meant to guarantee an intact form of sociality is grasped as the potential for an invariant manner of human activity. In Horkheimer, such an element is contained within his version of the concept of labor, according to which human dominance over nature is "immanently" directed toward the goal of a social constitution in which individual contributions mutually complement each other in a transparent manner. Here, it may be said, the emergence of the social pathology is made to depend, as in the thought of Karl Marx (1818–83), upon the circumstance of the actual organization of society remaining behind the standards of the rationality that was already embodied in the forces of production. This thought, which presents the ethical core of his considerations in the form of a materialist theory of history, is justified by Horkheimer in his seminal article "Traditional and Critical Theory."[7] Epistemologically, this key article aims at a systematic critique of positivism; methodologically, its goal is the development of a Critical Theory founded on the assumption of a historically developed rational potential.[8]

The key to Horkheimer's critique of positivism lies in the *materialist epistemology* of the early Marx. Following Marx's somewhat fragmentary considerations, as found in his early writings, Horkheimer works on the basic presupposition that the empirical sciences, right down to their methodology, are determined by the exigencies of social labor. The attainment of theoretical propositions is here subject to the same interest in dominating physical nature, the same dominance as that which already directs labor on a pre-scientific level. As soon as this "transcendental" constitutional complex (*Konstitutionszusammenhang*) of the sciences is described epistemologically, the misunderstanding to which positivism inevitably leads necessarily becomes apparent: by justifying the sciences in a merely methodological manner positivism cuts them off both from their social roots and from the knowledge of their practical goals. In this denial of the realm of life-practice pertaining to scientific theories Horkheimer discerns, to be sure, not only the error of contemporary positivism but also the shortcomings of the modern understanding of theory in general. He traces right back to Descartes the roots of the positivist consciousness according to which the sciences appear as a pure endeavor completely absolved from practical interests. He named this tradition of scientism that spans the whole of modernity "traditional theory." To this traditional theory, he opposes "critical theory" as a form of science that constantly remains conscious both of its social context of development and its practical context of application.

To be sure, Horkheimer is convinced that Critical Theory can only tackle its assumed task once it has a theory of history at its disposal, a theory that is in fact capable of explicating its own position and role in the historical process. Accordingly, the foundation of a critical theory of society demands, already on epistemological grounds, a historical-philosophical reflection on the form for which the contemporary division of labor between philosophy and the sciences envisages no legitimate place. Implicitly, the approach to such a theory of history is already contained within the materialist epistemology on which Horkheimer was able to base his critique of positivism. This approach, then, by extending it through a fundamental supposition of historical materialism, becomes a complete field of interpretation.

In Horkheimer's article two quite distinct tendencies stand out that make the Marxian assumptions about the course of history fruitful for the foundation of Critical Theory. On the one hand, Horkheimer appears to want to anchor the entire endeavor of such a theory "transcendentally" in the process that Marx conceived of as "augmentation of productive forces" (*Steigerung der Produktivkräfte*). According to this interpretation, Critical Theory would be a reflective form, not of instrumental action, but rather of the rational potential which time and again drives all manipulation of nature beyond the boundaries set by the particular social relations of production operative at the time. Here the "rational generality" is in a certain manner anchored in the cooperative relationships by means of which members of the human race secure their material reproduction communally in a progressive sequence. On the other hand however, Horkheimer also appears, in some places in his text, to be putting forward the idea that Critical Theory is constitutionally anchored in that sphere of historical development that Marx described by means of the concept of "critical activity." Accordingly, the task set up by Horkheimer would be that of a critical form of reflection, not on social labor in the widest sense, but rather on those social struggles and conflicts in which the up-to-now suppressed collective rises up against injustice and disadvantage. Admittedly, this attractive alternative model, which would have tied Critical Theory, both epistemologically and normatively, back into a constitutionally conceived sphere of social struggles,[9] does not receive adequate articulation in Horkheimer's article. Instead, over long stretches of it, the former conception dominates, according to which Critical Theory must understand itself as serving, in the form of its instrument of reflection, the rational potential immanent in the development of productive forces.

For the other members of the Frankfurt School's inner circle, it is also the case that the ethical idea of a rational generality is present within the layout of their philosophy of history only in a relatively obscure manner. Methodologically speaking, the most interesting case here is certainly presented by Theodor W. Adorno's early theory. His theory is grounded in a "materialistically" understood hermeneutics which has the task of deciphering the traces of a rational generality indirectly from what is attested to by a history that has become naturalistic and meaningless. Adorno arrived at the idea of a *materialist hermeneutics* of natural history – an idea he never relinquished throughout his life – through his intellectual exchanges with Walter Benjamin.[10] In contrast to Benjamin, however, from early on Adorno gave this idea a rational-theoretical form, crucially regulated by German Idealism's concept of reason.[11] For both authors, as for many of their contemporaries, the thought became decisive that the social extension of commodity exchange would necessarily lead to the deformation of human praxis, and it was further understood in a more extended sense as forcing subjects into objectifying relations not only with nature but also with themselves and their fellow interaction partners. Benjamin and Adorno therefore saw the historical-social world of modernity as a paralyzed space that had become "second nature," in which human relations had lost their transparency for practical reasons, having been transformed into mere "natural occurrences."[12] They also agreed about the methodological consequences for philosophy that had to be drawn from this historical point of departure. If the extension of commodity exchange consigned the modern world to a process of reification (*Verdinglichung*) then the "crisis of idealism"[13] could be overcome neither through Simmel's philosophy of life nor through Husserl's phenomenology; neither through Heidegger's analysis of Dasein nor through Scheler's material analysis of value. All those movements lacked in their very fundamental concepts *the fact of historicity* – if such a shorthand may be permitted to express the idea that the actual state of the human mind has to be seen as a result of a social change – by means of which the loss of meaning resulting from a basic transformation of social structure could be accounted for. To be equal to this regression of the social to nature a philosophical method was instead required that intended from the outset to recognize the social dynamic for what it was, namely a directionless concatenation of events that has been rendered unintelligible. Benjamin and Adorno both agreed that this "nature" of capitalism, distorted in meaning from the outset, could only be deciphered by a specific form of hermeneutics that subjected the empirically given material to variation with respect to possible constellations, up to the point where a cipher possessing objective meaning-content (*Bedeutungsgehalt*) became apparent in one of the figures thus produced.

Admittedly, just what the particular meaning of this hermeneutical idea might be was a matter of dispute between the Adorno and Benjamin from the beginning. As is well known, Benjamin tended toward the view that the production of such meaningful figures had to be yielded by the collective unconscious itself, in which archaic potentialities of a figurative imagination were present. Thus, for Benjamin, the methodologically skilful reproduction of such dream-like images alone was required in order to trace the obscure secret that had been produced by the fetishism of commodities in the social life of capitalism.[14] For Adorno, in contrast, the philosophical task of interpretation is quite different and in this respect he stands at once closer to and further from the hermeneutical method. Adorno remains closer to hermeneutics because he insists, in opposition to Benjamin, that the interpretation of a reality, distorted in meaning and rendered enigmatic, is solely the theoretical concern of the interpreter. As though in anticipation of his later critique, in his inaugural lecture Adorno already remarks:

> the historical images ... are not simply self-given [*Selbstgegebenheiten*]. They are not to be found organically in history. No sight [*Schau*] and no intuition [*Intuition*] is required to become cognisant of them; they are not magical divinities of history. Rather, they must be produced by human beings and can only be legitimated insofar as reality forms together around them with compelling evidence.[15]

The concept of "production" (*Herstellung*) to be found in this last sentence certainly brings into relief the full distance that separates Adorno from the contemporary hermeneutics which at that time was generally associated with Wilhelm Dilthey (see also "Twentieth-century hermeneutics," Chapter 16). Owing to the fact that social reality has to a large extent become a complex of events rendered meaningless (*intentionslos*) under the pressure of generalized commodity exchange, there can no longer be any historically mediated meaning into which the researcher might be able to enter mimetically (*nachahmend*). Rather, what is initially called for is constructive "composition of the analytically isolated elements," so that ultimately, within the "complete, contradictory and fragmentary" text of the social, figures are produced which might act as indicators of the objective meaning of the historical condition. However, many of the methodological formulations used by Adorno more closely to characterize this idea of an "interpretative grouping" remain vague and are therefore of negligible help. Nevertheless, the fact that he speaks in the same context time and again of explosive (*aufsprengend*) "key categories" may indicate that Weber's category of the "ideal type" stands in the background of his considerations.

A brief glance at a parallel text by Max Weber (1864–1920) in fact already makes it clear that there is scarcely a methodological thought in Adorno's inaugural lecture that could not already have been formulated by the author of *Economy and Society* (1914). In almost literal accord with Adorno, Weber states in his "'Objectivity" article that the ideal type must be understood as the "composition of a plenitude of distinct and discrete, to a greater or lesser degree existent or even in places non-existent particular phenomena … into a unitary structure of thought."[16] This conceptual construction, Weber continues, possesses a merely instrumental function, insofar as it serves the objective possibilities in making evident the "cultural significance" of a process by means of "cognitive intensification (*gedankliche Steigerung*) of certain elements of reality."[17] With the exception of the concept of "cultural significance," which I shall discuss below, Weber's methodological proposal is in complete accord with Adorno's considerations. Furthermore, the "figures," represented by the latter as a goal of the work of philosophical interpretation, are the result of a hyperbolic "construction" of reality on the basis of empirical material. The "elements of social analysis," Adorno holds, must be "grouped" in such a way that their connection constitutes a figure in which every single component is annulled (*aufgehoben*).[18] For the conceptual construction of these figures or "ideal types" (*Idealtypen*), Adorno says – using the same word as Weber – an "exact fantasy" (*Phantasie*) is necessary that stretches out beyond the given empirical material insofar as it brings into focus or neglects the "features" (*Züge*) residing therein and orders them as a whole in a new way.[19] In Weber the corresponding thought is expressed with the remark that the construction productive of ideal types requires a "fantasy"[20] which renders the composed elements sufficiently constitutive of reality so as to make them appear "objectively possible." Finally, the two authors also agree about the determination of the goals of research practice which are connected with the construction of such ideal types or figures. Just as one can read in Weber that the ideal types are not "hypotheses" but rather should merely "indicate the direction"[21] for "hypothesis construction," so too Adorno holds of the constructively formed figures that they represent "models," "with which *ratio* tentatively and experimentally approaches a reality which is inaccessible to the rule."[22] Later there can be found in Adorno, in connection with discussions of scientific theory, many formulations that point even more strongly in the direction of Weber's idea that the construction of reality according to ideal types constitutes a kind of basic principle to which the projection of empirical hypotheses is meant to conform.

However, can anything be found in Adorno's methodological reflections that is equivalent to the concept of "cultural significance" that plays such a central role in Weber's account of the "ideal type"? This question leads us to the center of the program which Adorno explicated in his inaugural lecture in order to delineate the idea of a materialist hermeneutics of the capitalist form of life. As is well known, Weber has recourse to neo-Kantianism when he asserts that the concepts involving ideal types serve to render evident the cultural significance of certain processes or phenomena. "Cultural significance" signifies in this connection the extra-personal, historically given value-perspective in virtue of which the chaotic mass of particular data can be organized at all, so that therein groupings of events and acts relevant to research can be distinguished.[23] The example used by Weber for illustrative purposes appears to be chosen as if it were related directly to the later example given by Adorno.

> One can, [says Weber] ... attempt to sketch the utopia of a "capitalist" culture, that is, one solely dominated by the exploitative interest of private capital. It would have to combine single, diffused features of modern and material cultural life, intensified in their singularity into a contradiction-free ideal image for our observation. That would then be an attempt to sketch an "idea of capitalist culture.[24]

Admittedly, if, in 1931, it was already Adorno's intention to sketch out such a comprehensive ideal type, then he would certainly not have posited the merely cultural significance of capitalist exploitation as its foundation of validity (Geltungsgrundlage). Rather, in those years he was already far too convinced of the truth of the Marxist analysis of society to have had recourse to the cultural perspectivism of Weber's theory of science. In fact the justification Adorno gives for his program of a constructive, ideal-type interpretation of the "second nature" of capitalism is quite different from that of Weber and rests on Hegelian premises. Adorno is convinced that the rational process of development of the human race is so profoundly disturbed by the universalization of commodity exchange that the conditions of life under capitalism as a whole have been reduced at every level to reified relations. The assertion of such a regression of the social to natural conditions is not the result of the adoption of a particular evaluative perspective, but rather follows from the fact of the failure of all other traditional theoretical approaches. For Adorno, as for Horkheimer, the theme of the crisis of contemporary philosophy and sociology plays the role of a justifying authority. Owing to the fact that all historically given projections of thought have systematically failed to grasp the specific essence of the modern manner of existence (Daseinsweise), the hermeneutical approach alone must emerge, through a process of elimination, as theoretically adequate to the phenomenon of reification. The necessary failure of every post-idealist theory in the face of the phenomenon that equally affects all those present, provides Adorno with sufficient grounds for assuming the superiority of his own position.

What is most significant about the Hegelian premises of Adorno's hermeneutical approach, however, is the fact that they force him into drawing a direct parallel between the social condition and the constitution of reason. This equation is not a trivial affair precisely because it has to be shown that the social pathology of reification has an intrinsic connection with a deformation of the capacity of human reason. Among the many places in his work where Adorno suggests approaches to account for why the generalization of commodity exchange should at the same time signify a deformation of human reason, those which utilize the concept of "imitation" (*Nachahmung*) have always appeared to me to be the most fruitful. In the long Aphorism 99 ("Gold assay") of *Minima Moralia* one finds a terse sentence that could function as the key to a corresponding theory: "What is human adheres to imitation: a human being only becomes human by imitating other humans."[25] From this position (which also accords with the observations of more recent social anthropology, in which imitation is similarly granted central significance for the development of the human spirit),[26] one can reconstruct why Adorno saw the reification of commodity exchange as being directly responsible for the deformation of reason. Only by means of imitative behavior, behavior that for Adorno derives originally from a feeling of loving care,[27] do we humans attain to our rational capacity, owing to the fact that we learn to relate to the world from the perspective of others by means of the gradually apparent intentionality of our interactive partners. Reality no longer represents for us merely a domain provoking adaptive relations, but rather becomes laden with a growing mass of intentions, wishes, and positions, which we learn to appreciate in our action. This capacity to perceive the world from the "inside," so to speak, is something which Adorno does not wish to restrict to the domain of behavior between humans. On the contrary, he sees our specific, imitatively grounded capacity of reason as residing in the ability to experience also the adaptive goals of beings lacking language, indeed even of objects, as intentions that call for rational appreciation. He was convinced, therefore, that all genuine knowledge must preserve within itself in a sublimated form the original impulse of loving imitation, in order to be able to do justice to the rational structure of the world from our perspective.[28]

Adorno sees the extension of a schema of praxis as connected with the institutionalization of commodity exchange in such a way that the schema disposes us humans to lose once more the capacity for rational respect for other intensions. Reification signifies for him a process of the "recentering" of human beings because they forget, following the rule of exchange, how to perceive the world from the perspective of those intentions and wishes whose significance they originally realized in imitation. To this extent Adorno is right in a certain sense to assert that the extension of commodity exchange at the same time represents a process of the deformation of reason. The compulsion to act solely according to the exchange schema of praxis in ever more practical spheres demands from human beings that they concentrate their rational capacity on the egocentric calculation of utilizable conditions. It is this idea of a social pathology of reason that accounts for the methodological operational position that is meant to be taken up by Adorno's hermeneutical procedure in the context of his analysis of capitalism. The renaturalization of social relations – that reification which is meant to consist in the extinguishing of our talents for imitation – precludes internal access to the phenomenal sphere of the social from the perspective of participants. Instead, the scientific researcher must be satisfied with the perspective of an observer to whom the social world is given as a context of occurrences emptied of meaning and populated by use-calculating individual subjects. Admittedly, the researcher also knows which historical or indeed objective significance pertains to the alien occurrence, as he possesses insight into the social causes of the process whereby the social is diminished. He will therefore strive to attain a method suited to rendering evident in a pointed manner this objective meaning of the social processes of praxis. This is the task Adorno allots to ideal-type constructions. They are meant to produce, by means of the conceptual accentuation of certain elements of social reality, figures in which the pathology of reason arising from generalized commodity exchange is mirrored in an exemplary manner. The heading under which Adorno carries out this program in his writings is that of a *physiognomy of the capitalist form of life*.

Herbert Marcuse, having freed himself from the Heideggerian roots of his original conception, also followed in Hegel's footsteps in order to outline an ethical concept of rational generality. In his later writings, however, this decisive concern is increasingly repositioned within the sphere of an aesthetic praxis which appears as the medium of a social integration in which subjects can satisfy their social needs in unforced co-operation.[29] According to this version, the social pathology starts at the moment in which the institution of society begins to suppress that rational potential that resides within the power of imagination anchored in the life-world. Finally, in Jürgen Habermas, the Hegelian idea of a rational generality is preserved in the concept of a communicative understanding whose idealizing presuppositions are meant to guarantee that the potential of discursive reason is revalidated at every new level of social development. We can therefore speak of a social pathology as soon as the symbolic reproduction of society is no longer subordinated to those standards of rationality which reside in the highest developed form of discursive understanding.[30] In all these approaches found in Critical Theory, the Hegelian idea that there is constant need of a rational generality to make possible for subjects a fulfilled manner of self-realization within society is reprised in merely different determinations of originary human praxis. Just as in Horkheimer's concept of "human work," Adorno's idea of "imitation," or Marcuse's thought of an "aesthetic life," so Habermas's concept of communicative understanding serves, in the first instance, the purpose of establishing the form of reason, in whose developed figure the medium of a satisfactory, and not merely rational, interpretation of society is provided. It is this reference to such an authoritative measure of rational praxis that permits the authors to set out their analysis of society as a rational and theoretical diagnosis of social pathologies. Deviations from the ideal that would be attained with the social realization of rational generality can be described as social pathologies because they are accompanied by a painful loss of chances with respect to intersubjective self-realization.

Of course, in the course of the intellectual development from Horkheimer to Habermas, this idea of a rational generality has changed both with respect to its content and its methodological form. While Horkheimer still links his concept of work with a rational potential which is meant to serve subjects directly as a goal of cooperative self-realization in a "society of free human beings,"[31] Habermas no longer grasps the idea of a communicative understanding as a rational goal but rather merely as the rational form of a successful mode of socialization. For Habermas, the idea that a felicitous common life of societal members is granted only with a perfected rationality is rendered radically procedural insofar as the rationality of praxis oriented toward understanding ensures only the *conditions for* and no longer the *fulfillment of* an autonomous self-realization.[32] However, this formulation still cannot conceal the fact that behind this anthropological mode of discourse about an originary mode of human praxis there lies hidden an ethical idea. The concept of a communicative praxis whose rationality imposes on human beings an unvarying compulsion still contains, albeit in an indirect manner, the idea of a successful sociality, which the concepts of work or aesthetic praxis in Horkheimer and Marcuse directly involve. The representatives of Critical Theory share Hegel's conviction that the self-realization of the individual can only be successful when his or her goals are intertwined with the self-realization of all other members of society by means of generally accepted principles or ends. Indeed, one may go beyond this and claim that, in the idea of a rational generality, the concept of a common good is contained about which the members of a society must have rationally agreed in order to be able to relate their individual freedoms cooperatively to each other. The differing modes of praxis, offered by Horkheimer, Adorno, Marcuse, and Habermas, are therefore as a whole proxies of this one thought, according to which the socialization of human beings can only be successful under the conditions of cooperative freedom. In whatever particular manner the anthropological notions may be constituted, in the final analysis they stand for the ethical idea of distinguishing a form of communal praxis in which subjects can attain self-realization cooperatively with one another.[33]

This conception of a rational generality of cooperative self-realization, which all the adherents of Critical Theory fundamentally share, is related to liberalism in just as critical a manner as it is related to that tradition of thought which is today called "communitarianism." More recently, a certain rapprochement with liberal doctrines has become apparent among Critical Theorists, including Habermas, owing to the fact that the legal autonomy of the individual has been granted greater scope in their theories, but this nevertheless has not led to the point where the differences between Critical Theory and liberalism regarding the socio-ontological premises of their doctrines have been eliminated. Rather Habermas is still convinced – no less than Marcuse, Horkheimer, or Adorno – that the realization of individual freedom is connected with the precondition of a common praxis which is more than the result of a coordination of individual interests. All concepts of a rational praxis arrived at in Critical Theory are in their fine detail tailored to actions whose execution demands a higher level of intersubjective consensus than is allowed for in liberalism. To be able to cooperate with equal legitimacy, aesthetically collaborate, or agree without compulsion, requires a shared conviction that a value pertains to the respective activity that justifies in certain cases the subordination of individual interests. To this extent Critical Theory presupposes a normative ideal of society which is irreconcilable with the individualistic premises of the liberal tradition. In contrast, the orientation toward the notion of cooperative self-realization entails that subjects are unable to arrive at a successful life within society for as long as they have not recognized a core of common evaluative convictions behind their respective individual interests. The idea of a "community of free human beings," which Horkheimer had already formulated in his article "Traditional and Critical Theory," constitutes the leitmotif of Critical Theory even where the concept of "community" is most strictly avoided because of its ideological misuse.

When this line of thought is followed further the impression can easily be given that the normative concern of Critical Theory coincides with that of "communitarianism."[34] However, just as Critical Theory is distinguished from liberalism because of its orientation toward a "generality" of self-realization, so also it is distinguished from communitarianism through its attachment to the link between that generality and reason. None of the authors who belong to Critical Theory has ever given up the Hegelian notion that cooperative praxis and thereby shared values must possess a rational character. Indeed, it is precisely the central purpose of their approach to see individual self-realization as bound to the precondition of a communal praxis that can only be the result of a realization of reason. Far from understanding the connection to overarching values as a purpose in itself, the establishment of a cooperative context fulfills for the representatives of Critical Theory the function of an augmentation of societal rationality. Otherwise it could not be comprehended why the forms of praxis respectively aimed at should always be the result of societal rationalization, or why the negative situation of the present must always be indicative of a lack of reason. In contrast to communitarianism, Critical Theory subordinates the generality, which must be embodied and realized through social cooperation, to the criterion of rational justification. However much the concepts of reason (from Horkheimer to Habermas) may differ, they all lead back to the notion that the inclination toward the emancipating praxis of cooperation must not result from affective connection, feelings of belonging, or feelings of unanimity, but rather must result from rational insight.

Accordingly, the tradition of Critical Theory differs from liberalism and communitarianism, through an ethical perfectionism of a quite distinct kind. In a different manner from the liberal tradition, the normative goal of societies should consist in the reciprocal enabling of self-realization, although what favors this goal is grasped as the grounded result of a certain analysis of the process of human development. Just as is already the case in Hegel, so also here the boundaries between description and prescription, between mere description and normative justification, appear to be blurred. The explanation of the conditions which have blocked or unbalanced the process of rational realization is meant to possess in itself the rational power to convince subjects to create a social praxis of cooperation. The perfection of society that is envisaged by all adherents of Critical Theory must, according to their shared conception, be the result of an enlightenment through analysis. The explicative interpretation which they offer to this end is admittedly no longer expressed in the language of Hegel's philosophy of spirit (*Geistphilosophie*). Rather, there is agreement that a decisive sociologizing of the categorial frame of reference (*kategorialer Bezugsrahmen*) is necessary in order to be able to carry out this analysis. This attempt to explicate the process of a pathological deformation of reason in sociological terms constitutes the second specific characteristic of Critical Theory. It also deserves a legacy today, as does the idea of a cooperative self-realization.

The sociological foundation: the shortcomings of reason as a result of capitalism

There exists today a growing tendency to carry out social criticism in such a way that it manages to get by without any component of sociological explanation. This development arises because it is for the most part seen as sufficient to uncover certain evils in society on the basis of well-grounded values or norms. By contrast, the question why those affected do not problematize or attack such moral evil no longer falls within the area of competence of social criticism as such. The separation thereby established is, however, shaken as soon as a causal connection is produced between the existence of the identified social evils and the absence of public reaction. Social iniquity would then possess, among other properties, the property of itself causing precisely that silence or apathy which the lack of public reaction expresses.

Such a supposition is fundamental to most of Critical Theory's approaches. However strongly they may be influenced by Marx in particular, on this point their approaches almost all share a central premise drawn from Marx's analysis of capitalism: the social conditions that constitute the pathology of capitalist societies evince the structural peculiarity precisely of veiling those states of affairs that would provoke particularly strong public criticism. This supposition sketched in Marx in his theory of "fetishism" or "reification"[35] is correspondingly to be found in the authors of Critical Theory in conceptions such as the "context of obfuscation" (*Verblendungszusammenhang*), "one-dimensionality," or "positivism."[36] With such concepts a system of convictions and practices is constantly characterized which possesses the paradoxical property of removing from recognition those social conditions through which this system is at the same time structurally produced. Accordingly, for the type of social criticism practiced by Critical Theory, an extension of the tasks to be carried out arises through this realization. In contradistinction to those approaches that have come to predominate today, Critical Theory has to connect the critique of social evils with an explanation of the processes that have contributed to their general obfuscation. For only when those addressed can be convinced by such an explanatory analysis that they are deceiving themselves about the actual character of social conditions can their injustice be demonstrated publicly with the prospect of agreement. To this extent, owing to a relation of cause and effect being posited between the social evil and the lack of negative reaction to it, in Critical Theory normative critique has to be extended by means of an element of historical explanation. The lack of a rational generality which constitutes the social pathology of the present must be explained by a historical process of rational deformation, which at the same time renders comprehensible the public dethematizing of social evils.

Right from the beginning there is agreement within Critical Theory concerning the fact that these historical processes of rational deformation can only be explained within a sociological frame of reference. Although, in the final analysis, the ethical intuition of the entire enterprise is nourished by the Hegelian idea of a rational generality, its protagonists are nevertheless inheritors of the sociological classics to such a degree that they are no longer able to rest their explanation of the divergence from that generality upon the idealist conception of reason. The processes of deformation which have contributed to a lack of social rationality and to the formation of a "particular rationality,"[37] are rather analyzed within a categorial framework, which, from Horkheimer to Habermas, arises out of a theoretical synthesis of Marx with Weber. Marx had already turned Hegel's concept of reason from its "head" onto its "feet," when he tied the extension of justificatory knowledge to the extension of a social praxis in virtue of which subjects gradually improve the conditions of their material reproduction. It is no longer the internal compulsions of spirit but rather the external challenges of nature that, according to Marx, within empirical science lead to the processes of learning that allow talk of a realization of reason to be justified. However, the epistemological-anthropological ideas of Marx were not sufficient for the adherents of Critical Theory to provide actual sociological interpretation of the historical process that had been described by Hegel in his philosophy as a process of spiritual self-unfolding. It was the reception of Max Weber's conceptuality – at first repeatedly fragmented by Lukács's idiosyncratic reading[38] – that first completed the notion so that, with the passing of time, the connection between processes of learning bound to praxis and social institutionalization became much clearer. In the fusion of Weber and Marx the members of the Frankfurt School arrived at the common conviction that the human potential of reason unfolds in historical processes of learning in which the rational solutions of problems are inextricably bound up with conflicts about the monopolization of knowledge. Although subjects react to the objective challenges that are posed on every level by nature and social organization with a constant improvement of their practical knowledge, this involves social confrontations about power and rule to such an extent that quite often lasting institutional form is only attained with the exclusion of certain groups. For Critical Theory it is therefore beyond doubt that the Hegelian realization of reason must be understood as a conflictual, many-layered process of learning in which knowledge capable of generalization only gradually forges ahead in the course of improved solutions of problems and against the resistance of dominant groups.

Of course, this fundamental thought has been subject to constant change in the history of Critical Theory. At the beginning, in Horkheimer, the process of learning in all its socially conflictual character was related only to the dimension of the handling of nature, so that it could not be comprehended how rational improvements were meant to have also been played out in the organization of social life.[39] Adorno had already broadened the spectrum in that, following Weber's sociology of music, he took account of a rationalization in the handling of artistic material, this rationalization serving the purpose of extending calculable sovereignty within aesthetic praxis.[40] This imitative rationality, whose unfolding in human history is inhibited by the extension of commodity exchange, gets the chance, at least in works of art, of a methodological refinement and growing precision. There are also some indications in Marcuse's theory that appear to justify the supposition of a collective process of learning together with corresponding setbacks due to power formation in the area of the appropriation of inner nature.[41] However, Habermas is the first to arrive at a systematic organization of different processes of learning which he grounds in the fact of distinct world-relations in linguistic praxis. According to his outlook, we can expect human rational potential to develop along at least two paths: in one case in the direction of a growth in knowledge about the objective world, and in another in the direction of a more just solution of international conflicts.[42] The gain in differentiation here is admittedly at the cost of no longer being able to conceive the historical growth in rationality in conjunction with those social conflicts which, in connection with Weber's sociology of domination (*Herrschaftssoziologie*), appeared to the older representative of Critical Theory more clearly. Between the dimension that Bourdieu, for instance, has investigated in processes of cultural monopoly construction[43] and the rational processes of learning there exists within Habermas's work a divide which is in principle irreconcilable with the original concern of the tradition.

All the same, Critical Theory cannot manage without the supposition of degrees of differentiation possessed by Habermas's concept of rationality, because it requires a post-Idealist rendering of the thesis Hegel outlines in his conception of rational realization. To grasp the respects in which socially institutionalized knowledge has become rationalized, in the sense of evincing a growing degree of reflexivity in the overcoming of social problems, it is necessary to differentiate as many aspects of rationality as there are socially perceivable challenges in the consensus-dependent reproduction of societies. In contrast to Habermas's approach, which carries out such a differentiation on the basis of the structural peculiarities of human language, a concept which binds the aspects of social rationalization, in the sense of an internal realism, more strongly to the problem-solving power of socially established values, would perhaps emerge as superior. Rather than the invariant validation aspects of linguistic understanding it would then be the historically produced validity-aspects of social spheres of value that would prescribe the direction in which the rationalization of social knowledge is realized. Also, the concept of reason, with which Critical Theory attempts to understand increases in rationality in human history, is subjected to the pressure of incorporating alien and novel, indeed non-European, perspectives. It is therefore not surprising that the concept of social rationality must be constantly extended and differentiated in order to account for the manifold nature of social processes of learning. In any case, it is a post-Idealist version of Hegel's thought of rational realization that provides the necessary background for the idea that may be supposed to constitute the innermost core of the whole tradition from Horkheimer to Habermas. According to this idea, the process of social realization is interrupted or rendered one-sided by the social structural peculiarities pertaining to capitalism, in such a way that the social pathologies are unavoidable insofar as they result from the loss of a rational generality.

The key for the thesis in which all the elements thus far treated separately are combined constitutes a concept of capitalism carrying a rational-theoretical charge. It is not difficult to see that Critical Theory arrived at such a conception less through a reception of Marx's work than through the impulse of Lukács's early theory. In *History and Class Consciousness*, Lukács could first suggest the thought that, in the institutional reality of modern capitalism, an organizational form of society can be made out which is structurally connected with a limited constitution of rationality. For Lukács, who for his part was essentially influenced by Max Weber and Georg Simmel (1858–1918), the peculiarity of this form of rationality consists in the fact that subjects are forced into a type of praxis that renders them "spectators without influence" of a course of events removed from their needs and intentions. Mechanized practical work and commodity exchange demand a form of perception in which all other humans appear as thing-like beings lacking sensation, so that social interaction is robbed of any attention to properties valuable in themselves. In terminology that stands closer to our present notions, the result of Lukács's analysis can be represented in such a way that with capitalism a form of praxis attains predominance that compels indifference with respect to the aspects of value of other human beings. Instead of relating to each other in recognition, subjects perceive themselves as objects to be grasped according to the measure of their own interest.[44] Certainly, it is this diagnosis of Lukács which provides Critical Theory with the categorial framework according to which one can speak of an interruption, or rendering one-sided, of the process of rational realization. On the basis of a historical process of learning, the social structural exigencies which Lukács accentuated within modern capitalism represent blockages of a rational potential already socially stored up until the threshold of modernity. The organizational form of social relations in capitalism prevents the application of those rational principles already available in terms of cognitive possibility within the praxis of life.

Conversely, by way of limitation, it must also be said that this explanatory schema in Critical Theory varies in each case with the assumptions presupposed in relation to the manner and course of the historical process of reason. Thus, one finds in Horkheimer, on the basis of his premises, the thesis that the capitalist organization of production brings about an opposition of individual interests which "prevents ... application of the entire mental and physical means of the mastery of nature."[45] Later, together with Adorno, he broadened his deliberations through the rather implausible assumption that in the form of interaction that took place within the nineteenth-century bourgeois family there resided an emotional rationality whose potential could not develop, owing to increasing monopolization, under which competition decreased.[46] In Adorno's work there can be found numerous places in which his materialist hermeneutics achieves application in virtue of the fact that a diagnosis of the growing impossibility of imitative reason is provided in the form of a conceptual ideal-type constitution. Certain traits of a given reality are stylistically brought together by a new grouping in such a way that the social pathology of reason is prominently represented. The idea that such conceptual constructions concern "interpretations" and thus a specific form of understanding also receives a precise meaning in this connection. As soon as one succeeds in producing a certain "figure" with a corresponding intuitive function, at the same time an interpretation is realized, because an entire ensemble of practices, perspectives, or regulations has been rendered comprehensible as a symptom of a missing process of development. None of the concepts that act as leitmotifs in Adorno's analysis of capitalism lacks an interpretative character of this sort. A multitude of social phenomena is always combined into a closed unity or "figure" which, in virtue of the new grouping, can show that in those phenomena it is always at the same time a matter of the mode of appearance of a deformation of our original rational capacity. Adorno's analysis of capitalism is in principle and execution the deep hermeneutics of a social pathology of human reason. The behavioral paradigms – purified and intensified according to ideal types representing a praxis purely oriented toward exchange value – are meant to make comprehensible the extent to which the capitalist form of life forces our rational capacities into a merely instrumental, egocentric use. In this closest of affinities between societal analysis and rational diagnosis Adorno's theory of capitalism may well count as unique.

The manner in which Adorno succeeds in each case in extending his sociological key categories to the point of the diagnosis of reason may be explicated, by way of example, in relation to the concepts of "organization" and "collective narcissism." In the construction of the concept of "organization," which occupies a key place within the categorial network of Adorno's analysis of capitalism, one trait is conspicuous which until now had not been sufficiently noticed. The partial phenomena brought together in the ideal-typical "figure" are introduced through reference to an experience that has an inherent irreducible historical character insofar as it possesses significance only for the present or modernity. The analyst of society who is thus mindful of the natural relations of capitalism is therefore not so alienated from his or her society to be ignorant of historically particular states and expectations. Rather, the analyst's findings that need to be assembled in order to render evident the social pathology, at the same time always include a resultant experience that can only be explained historically. In the case of "organization" Adorno begins his conceptual construction with the observation that today the "organizational overshadowing of ever more spheres of life"[47] provokes above all else a feeling of powerlessness, because it collides with the historically developed expectation of individual freedom. Only in a social epoch in which – as it is described in almost literal agreement with Hegel – the "potential" of individual autonomy has become generally "visible,"[48] can the extension of bureaucratic organizations be accompanied by the feeling of growing powerlessness. In any event, contributory to this diffuse state, which must enter into the construction of the ideal type as an essential phenomenon, are two developmental tendencies of modern organizations that can already only be explicated in terms of rational-theoretical concepts. On the one hand, the rational purpose which the arrangement of an organization as a "consciously created," technical "purposive association"[49] is meant to serve in the first place, has become in the course of mere "functioning" increasingly non-transparent, so that finally it has begun severing itself from its original "validating principle" (Rechtsgrund).[50]

Within his conceptual construction Adorno holds to the phenomenon according to which today a "self-purpose" has emerged out of the instrumental "implement" (Werkzeug) of the organization, without subjects possessing any longer the chance of influencing or indeed directing.[51] It is only with the obverse of this process of becoming autonomous, however, that Adorno arrives at the result which he places at the center of his construction of categories in order to complete, with its help, the bridge to the diagnosis of reason. The more the purpose has been rendered autonomous within organizations, so that they carry on routinely for the sake of mere functioning, the more clearly the tendency to exclude arbitrarily the members of certain groups grows. "Precisely the organisations which cover everything," so Adorno remarks, "possess paradoxically the quality of being exclusive and particular … That one can be excluded from an organisation belongs just as much to the concept of the organisation as the process of exclusion contains traces of the dominance exercised by group opinion."[52] It is this last partial sentence which explains why the administrative "arbitrariness within what is lawful" (*Willkür im Gesetzmäßigen*) is meant to represent as such the symptom of a deformed reason. For, according to Adorno, exclusion rests on the principle of being in each case insulated against that "which does not equate with the dominant group opinion."[53] The tendency to exclude what does not so equate is the vanishing point which allows Adorno to bring his construction of the category "organization" to a point with a diagnosis of reason. The incapacity to imitate what is immediately alien, and thereby to give up one's own particular standpoint, precisely indicates the separation of dominant, instrumental reason from its original potential. In Adorno's concept of "organization" the three phenomena of omnipresent power-lessness, the reversal of means into ends, and the growing tendency toward arbitrary exclusion of "what is dissimilar" find themselves grouped into a single figure which is meant, by means of over-stylization, to make evident the extent to which our present form of life is due to a pathological deformation of human reason.

Adorno's intention to carry out the analysis of capitalism as a diagnosis of reason by means of an ideal-type intensification becomes ever more evident in the categories of his social psychology. Here all the central concepts (based on the psychoanalysis of Sigmund Freud) are so arranged that they assemble several modes of behavior and character traits within a single type in order to demonstrate the regression of the capacity for taking a perspective determined by the requirements of exploitation. This may be briefly explicated by means of the concept of "collective narcissism," which plays a significant role in Adorno's late social psychology.[54] As with the concept of "organization" so in this case Adorno begins with the phenomenon of a mere state of being (*Befindlichkeit*) for which he once again uses expressions such as "powerlessness" or "impotence."[55] In connection with "collective narcissism," however, it becomes clearer than in other places of his work that this diffuse situational state arises out of the collective experience of a real loss of autonomy. The traceable crisis of "techno-logical unemployment" – as he puts it in the "Remarks on politics and neurosis" – "the economic impossibility of mastering life through one's own power,"[56] thus in sum the growing feeling "of being redundant in the dominant social mechanism,"[57] lead in their combined effect to the mass feeling of individual powerlessness. If this collective state is the first phenomenon which enters into the construction of the concept of "collective narcissism," then the second phenomenon derives from the social psychological finding that today the formation of a constant object-connection in the socialization process of early childhood increasingly fails. Instead of flowing into the "love of other human beings," libidinal energy is directed to "one's own ego."[58] Whatever is the case in relation to the empirical utilizability of these conceptual components – and here certainly considerable doubts are in order – for Adorno they constitute the necessary, indeed causal, connection between the initial phenomenon and the third element of his social psychological category. Owing to the fact that one's own ego is experienced as too weak, too powerless, one seeks narcissistic "compensation in an omnipotent, bloated collective construction that nevertheless profoundly resembles one's own weak ego."[59] With this latter phenomenon Adorno does not, admittedly, merely mean subordination to the authoritarian leader of a totalitarian movement, but in more general terms the mechanism of an "obstinate identification" with an "in-group."[60] Conversely, the partial phenomena are brought together within the concept of "collective narcissism" in such a way that they render recognizable as a complete figure the intrinsic connection between modes of behavior and a deformation of our reason. The tendency to remain locked into the conviction of one's own group in a state of "insensibility" (*Affektlosigkeit*) towards others, in the form of collective narcissism, also expresses the regression of imitative reason. It would now probably be easy to show, for the other key concepts of the analysis of capitalism, to what extent they represent ideal-typical constructions insofar as they render evident a social pathology of our reason. Both the concept of the "culture industry"[61] and that of "semi-development" (*Halbbildung*)[62] are so constituted that the phenomena collectively falling under them emerge in the final point of construction as phenomenal ways in which imitative behavior is rendered impossible. In each case the ideal-typical figures are conceived of in such a way that they can be used to orient the empirical construction of hypotheses. Instead of dealing with further examples, however, as a final step, I wish to discuss briefly the question of how Adorno connected his ideal-typical method with the proof of an irrevocable potential for resistance.

Marcuse orients himself, roughly speaking, towards Schiller's letter on "aesthetic education," when he sees the end of the process of intensified aesthetic sensibility in modern capitalism, which he describes, like Lukács, but with recourse to Heidegger, as a condition of generalized utility knowledge (*Verfügungs-wissen*).[63] Finally, in Habermas's theory one finds the idea that, under the conditions of capitalism, the potential for communicative rationality cannot be released because the imperative of economic exploitation itself penetrates through to the spheres of the social life-world. Although the family and the political public have long since emancipated themselves from their traditional basis of legitimation, the principles of a rational understanding cannot attain validity because they are more strongly infiltrated by mechanisms of system control.[64] As different as these explanatory approaches may be, however, the basic schema of the critique of capitalism which in each case underlies them is nevertheless just as unitary. In a rather similar manner to that found in Lukács, although with greater differentiation and without the historical-philosophical exaggeration of the proletariat, the authors of Critical Theory perceive capitalism as a social form of organization in which practices and modes of thought predominate that prevent the social utilizability of a rationality already rendered historically possible. This historical blockage represents at once a moral and ethical challenge because it renders impossible orientation toward a rational generality whose impulses could only derive from a completed rationality. It is certainly an open question whether the rational-theoretical concept of capitalism that underlies this interpretation of history can be reproduced again today. The possibilities of the organization of the capitalist economic action appear too multifarious – too much shot through with other, non-rationally purposive modes of social commerce – to permit the reduction of the perspectives of the agents involved in only the one model of instrumental rationality. At the same time, more recent investigations suggest that, in capitalist societies, those attitudes or orientations are first and foremost awarded social success whose fixation on individual advantage compels merely strategic dealings with oneself and others.[65] It cannot therefore be excluded that capitalism can still be interpreted as the institutional result of a cultural style of life or of a social imaginary[66] in which a certain type of limited, "reifying" rationality possesses practical predominance.

What is common within Critical Theory, however, goes beyond this point. Its central representatives share not only the formal schema of a diagnosis of capitalism as a social condition of blocked or one-sided rationality, but also the idea about the appropriate therapeutic means to overcome this onesidedness. The forces that can contribute to overcoming the social pathology must derive from just that rationality whose realization is precisely prevented by the capitalist social form of organization. As in the other element of the theory so here again a classical figure of modern thought plays a prominent role. The same significance accorded to Hegel, Marx, Weber, and Lukács for the core content of Critical Theory is also possessed by Freud's psychoanalysis. From psychoanalysis, the authors take over the thought that social pathologies precipitate the suffering that keeps alive interest in the emancipatory power of reason.

The emancipatory perspective: social suffering as openness to reasoning

The question of how the conditions of injustice can be practically overcome generally no longer falls within the set of tasks pertaining to social criticism. With the exception of those approaches which are oriented toward Foucault and grasp a transformation of the individual self-relation as a precondition of criticism,[67] the question concerning the relationship of theory and praxis remains excluded from contemporary considerations. The perspectival determinations of the conversion of knowledge into praxis belong just as little to the business of criticism as the explanation of the causes which may be responsible for silence concerning social evils. Such a perspective demands a social psychology or theory of the subject that explains why the individuals themselves should still be amenable to the rational content of theory while still under the conditions of dominance by certain modes of thought and praxis. It must be explained whence the subjective powers can be derived which offer the guaranteed chance of a conversion of knowledge into praxis despite all obfuscation, one-dimensionality, and fragmentation. As heterogeneously constituted as the field of social criticism may be today, it is characteristic that scarcely any approach grasps such a determination as part of its proper task. The question concerning the motivational constitution of subjects which must be central here is instead to a great extent left out of account, because reflection on the conditions of conversion into praxis is no longer expected of criticism itself.

By contrast, Critical Theory is, from the outset, so strongly indebted to the tradition of left-Hegelianism[68] that it regards as an essential part of its task the initiation of a critical praxis that can contribute to the overcoming of this social pathology. Even where skepticism about the possibility of practical enlightenment is predominant among its authors,[69] the drama of the question arises solely from the presupposed necessity of an *inner relation between theory and praxis*. Admittedly, Critical Theory no longer sees the determination of this mediation between theory and praxis as a task that can be addressed by means of philosophical reflection alone. In contrast to historical-philosophical speculation, still unquestionable for Marx or Lukács, Critical Theory relies rather on the new instrument of empirical social research in order to be informed about the critical preparedness of the public.[70] The consequence of this methodological reorientation, which constitutes a further peculiarity of Critical Theory, is a more modest estimation of the conscious condition of the proletariat. Contrary to the assumption of the Marxist wing of left-Hegelianism, the working class does not automatically develop, in the execution of mechanical partial work, revolutionary preparedness to convert the critical content of theory into socially transformative practice.[71] Hence, it is now impossible for Critical Theory to establish the connection between theory and praxis merely by appealing to the predetermined addressees. Instead, all considerations consequently come down to the idea of expecting the conversion into praxis of precisely that rationality which is merely deformed by the social pathology but not eliminated. In place of the proletariat, whose social situation counted previously as the guarantee of applicability for the critical content of theory, a *submerged rational capacity* (*verschüttete Vernunftfähigkeit*) must now arise for which all subjects in principle possess the same motivational aptitude.

Admittedly, such a change of perspective demands an additional train of thought, because at first sight it is far from clear why the motivation of critical praxis is expected from such a rationality, which is, according to the theory, highly deformed. How can the authors be sure that they will encounter sufficient rational preparedness for the conversion into praxis when socially practiced reason is meant to be either rendered pathologically one-sided or debilitated? The answer to this question is contained within a theoretical domain of Critical Theory that may be located somewhere within a continuum between psychoanalysis and moral psychology. Accordingly, it is always a matter of revealing the motivational roots which keep alive preparedness for moral knowledge in the individual subject, despite all rational diminution. It is sensible to separate out two steps in the argument, even though the authors of Critical Theory have not always drawn a clear line between them:

(1) Lack of social rationality leads to symptoms of a social pathology, the subject's suffering from the condition of society is initially concluded. As a consequence of the deformation of reason no individual can escape either being diminished or being described as such, because the chances of successful self-realization stemming from reciprocal cooperation have been submerged along with this loss of a rational

generality. In other words, this loss must affect individuals in their well-being, such that they too suffer from the more general situation of diminished rationality. Freud's psychoanalysis certainly served as a methodological paradigm in Critical Theory for the manner in which, in this first step, a connection is made between deficient rationality and individual suffering. Indeed, a similar connection can be found in Hegel's critique of Romanticism, which cannot have been without influence upon the representatives of the Frankfurt School. However, the motivation to connect the category of suffering with pathologies of social rationality is certainly in the first instance derived from the Freudian idea that every neurotic illness arises out of a diminution of the rational ego and must cause suffering to the individual. Habermas was not the first Critical Theorist to transpose this fundamental psychoanalytic thought into the domain of social analysis.[72] In his early articles Horkheimer described social irrationality in concepts that were in accord with Freud's doctrine to the extent that they measured the degree of the social pathology by the effect of drives alien to the ego.[73] Furthermore, everywhere that Adorno speaks of individual or social suffering some trace remains of the Freudian supposition according to which subjects must suffer from the neurotic limitation of their truly rational capacities.

The concept of suffering used by Adorno is not meant to connote an explicit, linguistically articulated experience. Rather, it is "transcendentally" posited whenever human beings have been assumed to have experienced a diminution of full self-realization and happiness by being restricted in their rational capacities. The thesis that every limitation on reason, every loss of our rational potential, objectively entails psychical suffering, Adorno owes to the implicit anthropology of Freud's doctrine. He shares with Freud the conviction that we human beings are disposed to react to a curbing of our rationality with a somatic sensation of suffering. As is the case for neurotic symptoms,[74] according to Freud, such suffering must include some pre-reflective consciousness or trace of the fact that the exercise of rationality is curbed or blocked. Adorno expresses this first step in the formulation that every somatic impulse possesses an "inward" (*inwendig*) form of reflection: "The somatic aspect [of suffering] declares the knowledge that suffering should not exist, that it should be otherwise."[75]

The use of this concept of suffering, which arises here as proof of the experience of the interplay between mental and physical forces, has unfortunately remained largely unexamined in the reception of Critical Theory.[76] A more precise analysis would likely show that in the case of suffering, as Freud maintains, the felt experience of being unable to bear the "loss of ego (capacities)"[77] needs to be expressed. From Horkheimer to Habermas, therefore, Critical Theory is directed by the idea that the pathological distortion of social rationality leads to diminutions which insignificantly increase the painful experience of the loss of rational capacities. Finally, this idea leads to a strong, almost anthropological, thesis that human subjects cannot be indifferent to the limiting of their rational capacities. Because their self-realization presupposes a cooperative utilization of their reason, they cannot escape the mental suffering due to its deformation. This insight that there is an internal connection between mental wholeness and undamaged rationality is perhaps the strongest impetus Critical Theory received from Freud. All current investigations, albeit conducted with superior methodologies, still accommodate this basic concern of Critical Theory.

(2) It is only with the second step, however, which is carried out within Critical Theory in a similarly implicit manner, that a means is derived from this thesis to enable the interrupted relation to praxis to be restored. Once again it is Freud who provides the decisive impetus when, with the continuation of the first step, it is now asserted that the pressure of suffering impels a cure that draws on the very rationality whose function was damaged by the pathology. What is presupposed is that the obvious condition in which to begin psychoanalytic treatment exists here: the sufferer of a neurotic illness wishes to be free of his or her suffering. In Critical Theory it is not always clear whether this motivation that distress provides to find a cure may only be spoken of as a subjective experience or also as an objective occurrence. Whereas Adorno, who speaks of suffering as a "subjective impulse," appears to have the former in mind, Horkheimer often uses formulations in which social suffering is treated as an objectively ascribable quantity of sensation. Conversely, in Habermas's *Theory of Communicative Action* there are many indications of the use of the subjective mode of discourse,[78] whereas Marcuse, finally, oscillates between both alternatives.

In any case, in Critical Theory it is presupposed that this subjectively experienced or objectively ascribable suffering leads members of society to the same wish for a cure, for emancipation from social evil, that the analyst must ascribe to his or her patients. And in both cases the interest in one's own healing is meant to be documented by the preparedness to reactivate against opposition those rational powers which were precisely deformed by the individual or social pathology. All the inner circle of Critical Theory believers assumed, on the part of those they addressed, a latent interest in rational explanations or interpretations, because the wish to be liberated from suffering can only be fulfilled by regaining an undamaged rationality. It is this risky presupposition which permits the construction of a connection of theory to praxis in a manner other than that found in the Marxian tradition. The advocates of Critical Theory share with those they address not a space of shared goals or political projects, but rather a space of potentially common reasons (*Gründe*) which keeps the pathological present open to the possibility of a transformation through rational insight. Of course, here as before, the differences between the individual members of the Frankfurt School must be acknowledged. These differences are for the most part colored by the kind of social psychological or anthropological assumptions used to ground the thesis that, despite all deformation of social life, an individual receptivity for rational arguments remains. In Horkheimer one finds at this point the idea that the memory of emotional security in early childhood keeps alive the interest in overcoming that form of rationality which is fixed to a merely instrumental order. Admittedly, it remains unclear whether he considered to what extent such a mental impulse can also be directed toward an unimpaired, full rational capacity.

For Adorno, the sensation of suffering not only reveals in a rudimentary way the knowledge that one's rational potential can only develop in a restricted manner, but also entails the wish to be liberated from the deformation thus sensed. Here Adorno once again implicitly connects with Freud in taking over his idea that neurotic suffering motivates a "need for healing."[79] Adorno transposes the discussion into the critique of capitalism but continues to follow this line of thought in maintaining, in relation to the "suffering" of subjects, that the negative experiences of the deformation of rationality are constantly accompanied by the wish for liberation from the social pathologies. To this extent the impulses of suffering guarantee, to speak pointedly, the subjects' ability to resist the instrumental expectations of the capitalist form of life.

It may however be the case that at this point in his interpretation of capitalism Adorno brings another thought to bear, one that comes to light whenever he speaks emphatically about childhood. Adorno supposes, as we have seen, that human reason develops when the child imitates beloved persons. It is only with the mimetic comprehension of the other's perspective that the infant has the chance to decenter his or her own perspective to such a degree that he or she can progress to a considered and thereby rational evaluation of states of affairs. On the basis of these infantile experiences in which our thinking develops through love Adorno appears to assume that these situations also continue to exist, as traces of memories, in the process of the socially compelled instrumentalization of our mind. Even the adult who behaves in complete conformity to the instrumental compulsions of the capitalist form of life preserves a weak recollection of the origin of his or her thinking from the early moments of empathy and care. It is upon such a residue of early experiences that, in various places, Adorno rests his confidence that despite all obfuscation subjects still possess an interest in the liberation of their reason. Memory of childhood brings, time and again, in the midst of instrumental realizations of life, the wish to be liberated from the social limitations which are imposed upon the activity of our mind. If this is the determining thought which lies concealed behind Adorno's stubborn confidence, then his physiognomy of the capitalist form of life would have to be anchored in a normative conception.[80]

In Marcuse such determinations of the subject's resistance can be found in a theory of drives wherein it is supposed that the erotic impulses of a life instinct long for an aesthetic realization which also needs a "conscious enactment of free reason."[81] For sure, this project has often been questioned about whether it in actual fact offers sufficient guarantee of an extended concept of social rationality.[82] Habermas, finally, within a kind of epistemological anthropology, has ascribed to the human race an "emancipatory interest" embedded within the experience of discursive praxis, which is structurally concerned with non-compulsion and equal rights.[83] Although this concept has given way in the meantime to a discourse theory that no longer makes any anthropological claims, the supposition has remained that the praxis of argumentative discourse can be ascribed to individuals for better reasons.[84] All these considerations represent answers to the question: what are the experiences, practices, or needs that permit the continued existence of an interest in the completion of reason within human beings, despite all deformation and one-sidedness of social rationality? For, argued in this way, it is only insofar as one can reckon with such a rational impulse that theory is capable of being related reflectively to a potential praxis in which its explicative offerings can be converted for the purpose of liberation from suffering. Thus Critical Theory (in the form in which it has been developed from Horkheimer to Habermas) can continue to exist in the future only if it not does not renounce the proof of such an interest. Without a realistic concept of the "interest in emancipation," which supposes an incorruptible core of rational susceptibility on the part of the subjects for the purpose of criticism, this theoretical project has no future.

With this final thought the development of the themes that constitute the core content of Critical Theory as it may be inherited is brought to a substantial conclusion. The sequence of systematic ideas developed above makes up a unity of thought from which a constituent part cannot be removed without consequences. As long as the intent to understand Critical Theory as the reflective form of a historically efficacious rationality is not abandoned, neither will the normative motive of a rational generality, the idea of a social pathology of reason, and the concept of an emancipatory interest be simply given up. In any event, it has been shown at the same time that scarcely a single one of these three conceptual components can still be retained in the theoretical form in which it was originally developed by the members of the Frankfurt School. These ideas all require new conceptual formation and communication with the present condition of our knowledge, if they are still to fulfill the function for which they were initially intended. Thereby, a set of tasks is outlined which may be handed over to the inheritors of Critical Theory in the twenty-first century.

Notes

1 For social criticism in Michel Foucault's sense see, for example, J. Tully, "Political philosophy as critical activity," in *Political Theory* 30/4 (2002): 533–55. On Michael Walzer, see *Kritik und Gemeinsinn*, Berlin: Rotbuch, 1990. I have attempted to develop a critique of this model of social criticism in Axel Honneth, "Idiosynkrasie als Erkenntnismittel. Gesellschaftskritik im Zeitalter des normalisierten Intellektuellen,", in U. J. Wenzel (ed.) *Der kritische Blick*, Frankfurt am Main: Suhrkamp, 2002, pp. 61–79.

2 On the concept of "negativism," above all on the distinction between negativism of content and of method, see the work of Michael Theunissen: *Das Selbst auf dem Grund der Verzweiflung. Kierkegaards negativistische Methode*, Frankfurt am Main: Suhrkamp, 1991; and "Negativität bei Adorno," in L. von Friedeburg and J. Habermas (eds.) *Adorno-Konferenz 1983*, Frankfurt am Main: Suhrkamp, 1983, pp. 41–65.

3 On the distinction between the center and periphery of Critical Theory see "Kritische Theorie. Vom Zentrum zur Peripherie einer Denktradition," in A. Honneth, *Die zerrissene Welt des Sozialen. Sozialphilosophische Aufsätze*, expanded edn., Frankfurt am Main: Suhrkamp, 1999, pp. 25–72; 1st edn. 1990. English translation: "Critical Theory," in *The Fragmented World of the Social: Essays in Social and Political Philosophy*, ed. C. W. Wright, New York: State University of New York Press, 1995.

4 See on this distinction "Pathologien des Sozialen. Tradition und Aktualität der Sozialphilosophie," in A. Honneth, *Das Andere der Gerechtigkeit*, Frankfurt am Main: Suhrkamp, 2000, pp. 11–87.

5 See M. Horkheimer, "Traditional and Critical Theory," in *Critical Theory: Selected Essays*, New York: Continuum, 1982, pp. 188–243; T. W. Adorno, "Cultural criticism and society," in B. O'Connor (ed.) *The Adorno Reader*, Oxford: Blackwell, 2000, pp. 195–210; H. Marcuse, *One-Dimensional Man*, London and New York: Routledge, 2006; H. Marcuse "Repressive tolerance," in *A Critique of Pure Tolerance*, Boston: Beacon Press, 1965; J. Habermas, *Theory of Communicative Action*, Cambridge: Polity Press, 1987, vol. 2, ch. VIII.

6 See A. Honneth, *Suffering from Indeterminacy: An Attempt at a Reacturalization of Hegel's Philosophy of Right*, Assen: Van Gorchum, 2000 (*Leiden an Unbestimmtheit. Eine Reaktualisierung der Hegelschen Rechtsphilosophie*, Stuttgart, 2001); M. Theunissen, *Selbstverwirklichung und Allgemeinheit. Zur Kritik des gegenwärtigen Bewusstseins*, Berlin and New York: de Gruyter, 1982.

7 Horkheimer, "Traditional and Critical Theory."

8 Ibid.

9 A. Honneth, *The Critique of Power: Reflective Stages in a Critical Social Theory*, trans. K. Baynes, Cambridge, MA: MIT Press, 1991, ch. 1.

10 See, for example, W. Benjamin, "On the program of the coming philosophy," in *Selected Writings*, 4 vols. (1996–2003), Cambridge, MA: Harvard University Press, 1996, vol. 1, pp. 100–110.

11 On the differences see, for example, J. Habermas, "Walter Benjamin: consciousness-raising or rescuing critique," in *Philosophical-Political Profiles*, Cambridge, MA: MIT Press, 1985, pp. 129ff. ("Walter Benjamin. Bewußtmachende oder rettende Kritik," in *Philosophisch-politische Profile*, 3rd expanded edn., Frankfurt am Main, 1981, pp. 336–76).

12 T. W. Adorno, "The actuality of philosophy," trans. B. Snow, in B. O'Connor (ed.) *The Adorno Reader*, Oxford: Blackwell, 2000, pp. 23–39 ("Die Aktualität der Philosophie," in *Gesammelte Schriften*, vol. 1, Frankfurt am Main: Suhrkamp, 1973, pp. 325–44).

13 Adorno, "Actuality," p. 25.

14 See, for example, W. Benjamin, *Charles Baudelaire: A Lyric Poet in the Age of High Capitalism*, New York and London: Verso, 1997; see. in general, A. Honneth, *The Fragmented World of the Social* ("Kommunikative Erschließung der Vergangenheit. Zum Zusammenhang von Anthropologie und Geschichtsphilosophie bei Walter Benjamin" in: *Die zerrissene Welt des Sozialen*, Frankfurt am Main: Suhrkamp, 1999, pp. 93–113).

15 Adorno, "Actuality," p. 36 (translation revised by B. Elliott).

16 M. Weber, "The 'objectivity' of social scientific and socio-political knowledge," in S. Whimster (ed.) *The Essential Weber*, London: Routledge, 2004, pp. 359–404, p. 388. ("Die 'Objektivität' sozialwissenschaftlicher und sozialpolitischer Erkenntnis," in *Gesammelte Aufsätze zur Wissenschaftslehre*, ed. J. Winckelmann, 3rd edn., Tübingen: Mohr, 1968, pp. 146–214).

17 Weber, "Objectivity," p. 387.

18 Adorno, "Actuality," p. 33.

19 Ibid., p. 37.

20 Weber, "Objectivity'," p. 390.

21 Ibid., p. 387.

22 Adorno, "Actuality," p. 36.

23 See D. Henrich, *Die Einheit der Wissenschaftslehre Max Webers*, Tübingen: Mohr/Siebeck, 1952; M. Schmid, "Idealisierung und Idealtypus. Zur Logik der Typenbildung bei Max Weber," in G. Wagner, H. Zipprian (eds.) *Max Webers Wissenschaftslehre*, Frankfurt am Main, 1994, pp. 415–44.

24 Weber, "Objectivity'," p. 388.

25 T. W. Adorno, "Gold assay," in *Minima Moralia*, London and New York: Verso, 1984, pp. 152–5.

26 See, for example, M. Tomasello, *The Cultural Origins of Human Cognition*, Cambridge, MA: Harvard University Press, 1999, especially chs. 2 and 3; P. Hobson, *The Cradle of Thought*, Oxford: Oxford University Press, 2002, especially chs. 3 and 4. See,. on these "mimetic" or emotive-intersubjective preconditions of human thought in general, M. Dornes, "Die intersubjektiven Ursprünge des Denkens," in *West End. Neue Zeitschrift für Sozialforschung*, vol. 2 no. 1 (April 2005).

27 Adorno, "Gold assay."

28 Ibid.

29 See H. Marcuse, "Treatise on emancipation," in *Philosophy, Psychoanalysis and Emancipation: Collected Papers of Herbert Marcuse*, London and New York: Routledge, 2007 ("Versuch über die Befreiung," in *Schriften*, vol. 8, Frankfurt am Main: Suhrkamp, 1984, pp. 237–319); and H. Marcuse, *Eros and Civilization*, Boston: Beacon Press, 1955, especially Part 2 (*Triebstruktur und Gesellschaft*, in *Schriften*, vol. 5, Frankfurt am Main: Suhrkamp, 1979).

30 J. Habermas, *Theory of Communicative Action*, vol. 2, especially ch. VI/1; see on this M. Cooke, *Language and Reason: A Study of Habermas's Pragmatics*, Cambridge, MA: MIT Press, 1994, especially ch. 5.

31 Horkheimer, "Traditional and Critical Theory."

32 This intention of rendering procedural the Hegelian idea of rational generality becomes particularly clear in J. Habermas, "Können komplexe Gesellschaften eine vernünftige Identität ausbilden?," in J. Habermas and D. Henrich, *Zwei Reden aus Anlass der Verleihung des Hegel-Preises 1973 der Stadt Stuttgart an Jürgen Habermas am 19 Januar 1974*, Frankfurt am Main: Suhrkamp, 1974, pp. 23–84.

33 It is this ethical perspective that I am convinced represents a certain point of contact between Critical Theory and American pragmatism. It is all the more astonishing that a productive reception of pragmatism begins first with Habermas, whereas the reaction of the first generation of Critical Theory ranged from essentially skeptical to dismissive. On the history of this reception, see H. Joas, "The underestimated alternative: America and the limits of Critical Theory," in *Pragmatism and Social Theory*, Chicago: University of Chicago Press, 1993, pp. 79–93.

34 On communitarianism, see A. Honneth, *Kommunitarismus. Eine Debatte über die moralischen Grundlagen moderner Gesellschaften*, Frankfurt am Main: Suhrkamp, 1993.

35 K. Marx, "The fetishism of the commodity and its secret," in *Capital: A Critique of Political Economy*, vol. 1, pp. 163ff.; an excellent analysis is provided by G. Lohmann, *Indifferenz und Gesellschaft. Eine kritische Auseinandersetzung mit Marx*, Frankfurt am Main: Suhrkamp, 1991, especially ch. 5.

36 See, in this order, M. Horkheimer and T. W. Adorno, *Dialectic of Enlightenment*, Stanford, CA: Stanford University Press, 2002; Marcuse, *One-Dimensional Man*; T. W. Adorno, "Introduction," in *The Positivism Dispute in German Sociology*, London: Heinemann, 1976, pp. 1–67; J. Habermas, *Technik und Wissenschaft als "Ideologie"*, Frankfurt am Main: Suhrkamp, 1968.

37 Adorno, "Cultural criticism and society," p. 201.

38 G. Lukács, "Reification and the consciousness of the proletariat," in *History and Class Consciousness*, London: Merlin, 1968, pp. 83–222; on the significance of Lukács's analysis of reification for Critical Theory, see Habermas, *Theory of Communicative Action*, vol. 1, ch. VI.

39 Horkheimer, "Traditional and Critical Theory"; on the problematic see Honneth, *The Critique of Power*.

40 T. W. Adorno, *Introduction to the Sociology of Music*, New York: Seabury Press, 1976.

41 H. Marcuse, *Eros and Civilization*, Boston: Beacon Press, 1955, especially ch. 6.

42 Habermas, *Technik und Wissenschaft als 'Ideologie'*; *Theory of Communicative Action*, vol. 2, ch. VI, pp. 113–98.

43 See on this P. Bourdieu and J.-C. Passeron, *Reproduction in Education, Society and Culture*, London: Sage, 1977.

44 In the meantime I have attempted to reactivate this concept of reification myself: Axel Honneth, *Verdinglichung. Eine anerkennungstheoretische Studie*, Frankfurt am Main: Suhrkamp, 2005.

45 Horkheimer, "Traditional and Critical Theory."

46 M. Horkheimer, "Authority and the family in the present," in *Critique of Instrumental Reason*, New York: Continuum, 1983; Horkheimer develops the same motif with unmistakably religious undertones in "Die verwaltete Welt kennt keine Liebe" ("The governed world knows no love"), *Gesammelte Schriften*, Frankfurt am Main: Suhrkamp, 1985, pp. 358–67.

47 T. W. Adorno, "Individuum und Organisation," in *Gesammelte Schriften*, vol. 8, Frankfurt am Main: Suhrkamp, 1977, pp. 440–56.

48 Ibid., p. 443.

49 Ibid., p. 441.

50 Ibid., p. 442.

51 Ibid.

52 Ibid.

53 Ibid.

54 In what follows my remarks rest upon Adorno's 1954 "Bemerkungen über Politik und Neurose" ("Remarks on politics and neurosis"), in *Gesammelte Schriften*, vol. 8, pp. 434–9.

55 Ibid., p. 438.

56 Ibid.

57 Adorno, "Individuum und Organisation," p. 446.

58 Adorno, "Bemerkungen," p. 437.

59 Ibid.

60 Ibid., p. 436.

61 Adorno, "Culture industry reconsidered," in *The Adorno Reader*, pp. 230–8.

62 Adorno, "Theorie der Halbbildung," in *Gesammelte Schriften*, vol. 8, pp. 93–121.

63 Marcuse, *Eros and Civilization*, ch. IV; see on this J. P. Arnason, *Von Marcuse zu Marx*, Neuwied and Berlin: Luchterhand, 1971, especially ch. V.

64 Habermas, *Theory of Communicative Action*, vol. 2, ch. VIII.

65 See,. for example, A. Giddens, *Modernity and Self-Identity: Self and Society in the Late Modern Age*, Cambridge: Cambridge University Press, 1991, especially pp. 196ff.

66 Of significance in this connection are studies by Max Weber's successors (W. Hennis, *Max Webers Fragestellung: Prolegomena zu einer dialektischen Anthroplogie*, Tübingen: Mohr, 1987) or the writings of Cornelius Castoriadis (*The Imaginary Institution of Society*, Cambridge, MA: MIT Press, 1998). Also worth mentioning is: L. Boltanski and E. Chiapello, *Le Nouvel Esprit du capitalisme*, Paris: Gallimard, 1999.

67 See, for example, J. Butler, *The Psychic Life of Power: Theories in Subjection*, Stanford, CA: Stanford University Press, 1997; chs. 2, 3, and 4.

68 See K. Löwith, *From Hegel to Nietzsche: The Revolution in Nineteenth Century Thought*, New York: Columbia University Press, 1991, Part I, sect. II, pp. 65–120; Habermas, *The Philosophical Discourse of Modernity*, Cambridge, MA: MIT Press, 1987, ch. III.

69 See, for example, T. W. Adorno, "Resignation," in *Critical Models*, New York: Columbia University Press, 1998, pp. 289–93.

70 See E. Fromm, *Arbeiter und Ungestellte am Vorabend des Dritten Reiches. Eine sozialpsychologische Untersuchung*, Stuttgart: DVA, 1980.

71 See H. Dubiel, *Wissenschaftsorganisation und politische Erfahrung. Studien zur frühen kritischen Theorie*, Suhrkamp: Frankfurt am Main, 1978, Part A, ch. 5.

72 J. Habermas, *Knowledge and Human Interests*, Cambridge: Polity Press, 1987, ch. 12.

73 M. Horkheimer, "Geschichte und Psychologie," in *Kritsiche Theorie*, ed. A. Schmidt, Frankfurt am Main: Suhrkamp, 1968, pp. 9–30.

74 See, for example, S. Freud, "Further recommendations in the technique of psychoanalysis," in *Collected Papers*, vol. 2, ed. J. Rivière, London: Hogarth Press, 1957, pp. 342–65.

75 T. W. Adorno, *Negative Dialektik*, in *Gesammelte Schriften*, vol. 6, Frankfurt am Main: Suhrkamp, 2003, pp. 7–410, p. 203.

76 An exception to this is represented by J. Früchtl, *Mimesis: Konstellation eines Zentral-begriffes bei Adorno*, Würzburg: Königshausen & Neumann, 1986, ch. III, 2

77 Adorno, "Bemerkungen," p. 437.

78 See, for example, the considerations concerning Marx in Habermas, *Theory of Communicative Action*, vol. 2, ch. VIII. All the same, Habermas oscillates here between an experiential (*lebensweltlich*) and a merely functional use of the idea of a social pathology.

79 S. Freud, *Outline of Psychoanalysis*, Penguin Freud Library, vol. 15, Harmondsworth: Penguin, 1986, pp. 375–443, p. 415.

80 On this, see aphorisms 2, 72, 79 and 146 from *Minima Moralia*.

81 Herbert Marcuse, *Triebstruktur und Gesellschaft (Eros and Civilization)*, in *Schriften*, vol. 5, Frankfurt am Main: Suhrkamp, 1979, p. 191.

82 See Jürgen Habermas, Silvia Bovenschen, et al., *Gespräche mit Herbert Marcuse*, Frankfurt am Main: Suhrkamp, 1978.

83 Habermas, *Knowledge and Human Interests*, ch. III.

84 J. Habermas, "Noch einmal: Zum Verhältnis von Theorie und Praxis," in *Wahrheit und Rechtfertigung*, Frankfurt am Main: Suhrkamp, 1999, pp. 319–33; e.g. p. 332.

Further reading

Monographs

Agger, B., *The Discourse of Domination: From the Frankfurt School to Postmodernism*. Evanston, IL: Northwestern University Press, 1992.

Arato, A. and E. Gebhardt (eds.) *The Essential Frankfurt School Reader*. Oxford: Blackwell, 1978.

Benhabib, S., *Critique, Norm and Utopia: A Study of the Foundations of Critical Theory*. New York: Columbia University Press, 1986.

Berman, R., *Modern Culture and Critical Theory: Art, Politics, and the Legacy of the Frankfurt School*. Madison: University of Wisconsin Press, 1988.

Bottomore, T., *The Frankfurt School*. London: Tavistock, 1984.

Bronner, S. E., *Of Critical Theory and its Theorists*. New York: Routledge, 2002.

Connerton, P., *The Tragedy of Enlightenment: An Essay on the Frankfurt School*. Cambridge: Cambridge University Press, 1980.

Cooke, M., *Language and Reason: A Study of Habermas's Pragmatics*. Cambridge, MA: MIT Press, 1994.

Dubiel, H., *Theory and Politics: Studies in the Development of Critical Theory*. Cambridge, MA: MIT Press, 1985.

Feenberg, A., *Lukács, Marx, and the Sources of Critical Theory*. Totowa, NJ: Rowman & Littlefield, 1981; New York: Oxford University Press, 1986.

Friedman, G., *The Political Philosophy of the Frankfurt School*. Ithaca, NY and London: Cornell University Press, 1981.

Geuss, R., *The Idea of a Critical Theory: Habermas and the Frankfurt School*. Cambridge: Cambridge University Press, 1981.

Habermas, J., *The Philosophical Discourse of Modernity*. Cambridge, MA: MIT Press, 1987.

——, *The Theory of Communicative Action*, vol. 2: *Lifeworld and System: A Critique of Functionalist Reason*. Cambridge: Polity Press, 1987.

Hanssen, B., *Critique of Violence: Between Poststructuralism and Critical Theory*. London: Routledge, 2000.

Held, D., *An Introduction to Critical Theory*. London: Hutchinson, 1980.

Honneth, A., *The Critique of Power: Reflective Stages in a Critical Social Theory*, trans. K. Baynes. Cambridge, MA: MIT Press, 1991.

——, *The Struggle for Recognition: The Moral Grammar of Social Conflicts*, trans. J. Anderson. Cambridge, MA: MIT Press, 1996.

——, *Pathologien der Vernunft. Geschichte und Gegenwart der Kritischen Theorie*. Frankfurt am Main: Suhrkamp, 2007.

Hoy, D. C. and T. McCarthy, *Critical Theory*. Cambridge, MA: Blackwell, 1994.

Ingram, D., *Critical Theory and Philosophy*. New York: Paragon House, 1990.

Jay, M., *The Dialectical Imagination: A History of the Frankfurt School and the Institute for Social Research 1923–1950*. Berkeley: University of California Press, 1973; rev. edn. 1996.

——, *Marxism and Totality: The Adventures of a Concept from Lukács to Habermas*. Berkeley: University of California Press, 1984.

Kellner, D., *Critical Theory, Marxism, and Modernity*. Baltimore: Johns Hopkins University Press, 1989

McCarthy, T., *The Critical Theory of Jürgen Habermas*. Cambridge, MA: MIT Press, 1978; rev. edn. 1982.

——, *Ideals and Illusions: On Deconstruction and Reconstruction in Contemporary Critical Theory*. Cambridge, MA: MIT Press, 1993.

Morrow, R. A. and D. D. Brown, *Critical Theory and Methodology*. London and Thousand Oaks, CA: Sage Publications, 1994.

Outwaite, W., *New Philosophies of Social Science: Realism, Hermeneutics, and Critical Theory*. New York: St Martin's Press, 1987.

Wellmer, A., *Critical Theory of Society*, trans. J. Cumming. New York: Herder & Herder, 1971.

——, *The Persistence of Modernity: Essays on Aesthetics, Ethics and Postmodernism*. Cambridge, MA: MIT Press, 1991.

——, *Endgames: The Irreconcilable Nature of Modernity: Essays and Lectures*. Cambridge, MA: MIT Press, 1998.

Whitebook, J., *Perversion and Utopia: A Study in Psychoanalysis and Critical Theory*. Cambridge, MA: MIT Press, 1994.

Wiggershaus, R., *The Frankfurt School: Its History, Theories and Political Significance*, trans. M. Robertson. Cambridge, MA: MIT Press, 1994.

Wolin, R., *The Terms of Cultural Criticism: The Frankfurt School, Existentialism, Poststructuralism*. New York: Columbia University Press, 1992.

Collections

The following edited collections offer useful critical discussions of Critical Theory:

Bronner, S. E. and D. M. Kellner (eds.) *Critical Theory and Society: A Reader*. New York: Routledge, 1989.

Brosio, R. A. (ed.) *The Frankfurt School: An Analysis of the Contradictions and Crises of Liberal Capitalist Societies*. Muncie, IN: Ball State University Press, 1980.

Hohendahl, P.-U. and J. Fisher (eds.) *Critical Theory: Current State and Future Prospects*. New York: Berghahn Books, 2001.

Honneth, A. and H. Joas (eds.) *Communicative Action: Essays on Jürgen Habermas's* The Theory of Communicative Action, trans. J. Gaines and D. L. Jones. Cambridge, MA: MIT Press, 1991.

Honneth, A., T. McCarthy, C. Offe, and A. Wellmer (eds.) *Cultural-Political Interventions in the Unfinished Project of Enlightenment*. Cambridge, MA: MIT Press, 1992.

Kelly, M. (ed.) *Hermeneutics and Critical Theory in Ethics and Politics*. Cambridge, MA: MIT Press, 1990.

O'Neill, J. (ed.) *On Critical Theory*. New York: Seabury Press, 1976.

Rasmussen, D. M. (ed.) *Handbook of Critical Theory*. Oxford and Cambridge, MA: Blackwell, 1996.

Roblin, R. (ed.) *The Aesthetics of the Critical Theorists: Studies on Benjamin, Adorno, Marcuse, and Habermas*. Lewiston, NY: E. Mellen Press, 1990.

Rush, F. (ed.) *The Cambridge Companion to Critical Theory*. Cambridge: Cambridge University Press, 2004.

19

FRENCH PHILOSOPHY IN THE TWENTIETH CENTURY

Gary Gutting

Introduction: science and philosophy

French philosophy from (roughly) 1890 to 1990 is open to a number of philosophically illuminating perspectives. An instructive story can be told, for example, in terms of the problems of freedom and of consciousness.[1] Here, however, I will take the relation of philosophy to science as my leitmotif, showing how French thought from Poincaré and Bergson to Foucault and Derrida can be understood in terms of opposing views of the cognitive authority of science in relation to philosophical inquiry.

At the beginning of the twentieth century, French philosophers were fundamentally concerned with the question of how to reconcile the authority of a scientific worldview with the centrality of the free individual subject. Reflection on this issue operated between two poles: positivism, originating with Auguste Comte (1798–1857) in the nineteenth century, saw science as the sole legitimate cognitive authority and reduced all reality to the material world of science; spiritualism, traceable back to Maine de Biran (1766–1824) in the eighteenth century and in a sense to René Descartes (1596–1650) himself, insisted that our autonomy as free subjects in a world created by God showed the need to complement science with distinctively philosophical knowledge of the world. It is plausible to read the subsequent development of French philosophy in terms of the conflict of positivist and spiritualist positions. This may seem an odd claim, since both the radical empiricism of positivism and the religious metaphysics of spiritualism quickly became distinctly marginal in twentieth-century French thought. We shall see, however, that thinkers who reject the specific doctrines of classical positivism and spiritualism nonetheless are generally oriented to a worldview centered either on the objective concepts of science or on our experience of ourselves as free existents. In Michel Foucault's terminology, French thought has been divided into the philosophy of the concept and the philosophy of experience. In the same vein I will speak of a positivist orientation and a spiritualist orientation, and will trace the development of the positivist orientation from Poincaré and Duhem, through Brunschvicg, Bachelard, and Canguilhem, to Michel Foucault. Correspondingly, I will follow the spiritualist orientation from Bergson, through Blondel, Marcel, Sartre, and Merleau-Ponty, to Derrida and Levinas. These two interweaving threads will guide us through the history of twentieth-century French philosophy, leading to some conclusions about the value of the French experience for Anglophone philosophers.

In the early years of the twentieth century, even French philosophers who most firmly rejected positivism recognized the centrality of science for philosophical reflection. Jules Lachelier (1832–1918) and Émile Boutroux (1845–1921), for example, offered unified accounts of nature that tried to synthesize the truths of science and of human freedom into a coherent whole. Their accounts presented science as limited by, for example, its indeterminism and failure to take account of finality, limitations that make it fall short of full concreteness and require supplementation by philosophy. The philosophy (or metaphysics) of nature they sought could not, however, be developed in a scientific vacuum. It required reflection on actual scientific achievements and, therefore, familiarity with the methods and results of contemporary science. This philosophical approach to science also incorporated Comte's conviction that science had to be studied through its history. The convergence of these desiderata led to the rapid development in France of what came to be known as the "epistemology of science," a philosophico-historical effort to understand the cognitive structure of science. As the effort developed, however, it moved away from Lachelier's and Boutroux's subordination of science to philosophy and towards an autonomous study of science in its own terms. The new "philosophers of science," as they came to be known, no longer tried to incorporate scientific truth into a synthetic metaphysical view of nature as a concrete whole.

Founders of the philosophy of science: Poincaré and Duhem

Henri Poincaré (1854–1912) is the best example of this new orientation. Himself an eminent mathematician and scientist, Poincaré had little training in philosophy and no tendency toward spiritualism. He focused on the methodology of science considered in its own right as the paradigm of knowledge and provided a model for what became analytic philosophy of science: the careful study of the content of specific scientific theories as a basis for sophisticated analyses of the key notions of observation, law, theory, and explanation.

Poincaré, however, like French philosophers in general, avoided the empiricist foundationalism characteristic of the logical positivism that followed him. He recognized the theory-laden character of scientific observation and formulated a sophisticated conventionalism that gives the mind an active role in constituting empirical objects. Poincaré's work remains, however, more positivist than Kantian, more a codification of what he saw as current scientific practice than deduction from a priori philosophical principles; and his a priori categories, such as simplicity, are pragmatic conditions of scientific progress rather than transcendental conditions of experience.

Pierre Duhem (1861–1916), a scientist of some importance but much more prominent as a historian of science, did not share Poincaré's positivist dismissal of traditional metaphysics. However, he sharply distinguished the world known by science from the world of metaphysical truth. Science deals with only sensory appearances; the real world beneath these appearances – according to Duhem, a domain of Aristotelian substances – is unknowable to science, although open to non-empirical philosophical reasoning.

Despite Duhem's metaphysical proclivities, his account of science is, as he himself emphasized, strictly positivist in the sense of rejecting any underlying ontology for scientific theories. Science has no metaphysical content beyond the commonsense world given in the "practical facts" of ordinary experience. Theories are mere means of calculation that tell us nothing about the reality beneath the appearances of ordinary experience. Scientific results are, therefore, strictly independent of any metaphysical claims about the real natures of things.

Poincaré and Duhem developed a new and distinctive approach to philosophical reflection on science, positivist in its aversion to metaphysical assumptions and empiricist in its emphasis on observation and experiment. But their positivism does not dogmatically eliminate all metaphysical inquiry and their empiricism is a sophisticated sort that leaves room for the mind's active role in both theory and experience. Not only their spirit but also many of their specific formulations of problems and solutions are directly relevant to later analytic discussions, and their thought has maintained a significance outside of France unusual in French thinkers of their period.

Correspondingly, their positivism and empiricism separated the new philosophy of science from the spiritualist orientation that continued to define mainline French philosophy in the Third Republic. The separation was deepened by the specialized training in science and its history that the new discipline required. Some, such as Bergson and Brunschvicg, combined traditional interests with specialized work in philosophy of science. Eventually, however, French philosophy of science became an essentially autonomous domain, respected and influential in the French university, but, especially after the rise of existential philosophy, mostly left to a small circle of specialists. Gaston Bachelard (1884–1962) and Georges Canguilhem (1904–95) were, as we shall see, important figures in the general education of successive generations of students at the Sorbonne. But, apart from the exceptional case of Michel Foucault (1926–84), they had relatively little influence on existentialist and post-structuralist philosophers dominant from the 1940s on.

Outside of France, after the rise of logical positivism, philosophy of science took a formal, non-historical turn for which the French tradition was uncongenial. (For further discussion of logical positivism, see "The development of analytic philosophy: Wittgenstein and after," Chapter 2 and "Philosophy of science," Chapter 14.) The French, in turn, dismissed what they saw as the naive epistemological foundationalism of logical positivism and its insensitivity to the actual practice of science. Later, when the historicist reaction against positivism took hold, English-speaking philosophers of science rediscovered major themes of the French tradition, such as the theory-ladenness of observation and the irreducibility of scientific rationality to logic. But by then the two approaches were too far apart for fruitful interaction. The French were cool to what they rightly saw as old news, and the British and Americans had scant interest in discussions that, if they read them at all, lacked the analytic clarity and rigor to which they were accustomed and that ignored logical-positivist philosophy of science as hardly worth refuting.

As a result, the rest of the story of French philosophy of science in the twentieth century is one quite separate from the parallel story outside France (see "Philosophy of science," Chapter 14). This history is of great philosophical interest in its own right and, moreover, a fertile basis for comparative assessments of the strengths and weaknesses of standard analytic work on science. But there is no sense in denying the essential historical isolation, after the seminal work of Poincaré and Duhem, of French philosophy of science.

Science and idealism: Léon Brunschvicg

Léon Brunschvicg (1869–1944) continues the line of French philosophy of science, but also integrates it with significant elements of spiritualism. He is, indeed, an idealist in the sense that he thinks that the very notion of a thing-in-itself, material or spiritual, is unintelligible. Any being exists only as the object or act of thinking, which thinking itself must not be reified as, for example, a substantial mind. But the ultimate dependence of reality on thought does not mean that the truth about the world can be read off of or deduced from any abstract reflection of thought on itself. Truth must arise from reflection on the mind, but this is mind as a positive reality in human history, not an ahistorical object of philosophical intuition. Further, the history through which truth is revealed is precisely the history of *science*. Brunschvicg characterizes his position as a "philosophy of thought," in contrast to absolute idealist "philosophies of nature" and rationalist "philosophies of science." A philosophy of nature (e.g. Hegel's) offers a view of the natural world, derived entirely from philosophical insight and reasoning, that claims to be independent of and superior to the empirical constructions of natural scientists. Brunschvicg rejects such philosophies as chimeras, refuted by their obvious inconsistency with scientific facts. By contrast, philosophies of science (e.g. Descartes's and Kant's) effectively oppose these systems of dogmatic metaphysics by refusing to go beyond the results of science. But they go wrong in thinking that they can discover in the science of their time final truths that define the framework of all subsequent science. Brunschvicg's own "philosophy of thought" purports to balance the claim that only science can provide the definitive account of reality with a realization that the content of this account cannot be extracted from the science of any given time. What is required instead is historical reflection on the full sweep of science as it has developed over the centuries. Through such reflection we simultaneously recognize the ultimate authority of science as arbiter of the real and the ultimate dependence of this authority on human thought.

The details of Brunschvicg's philosophy of science are developed in the three massive historical studies that constitute the bulk of his life's work. The first was *Les Étapes de la pensée mathématique*, 1912 (*The Stages of Mathematical Thinking*), which follows the entire history of mathematics and of mathematically inspired philosophy from the ancient Greeks through twentieth-century logicism and intuitionism. Brunschvicg rejects the idea that mathematics is a pure study of merely ideal relations and instead views it as essentially tied to our efforts to understand the world. His history shows how novel mathematical ideas emerge from the mind's creative efforts to make sense of our experience of the world. At the same time, Brunschvicg follows the work of philosophers – particularly, Plato, Descartes, Leibniz, and Kant – who were inspired by the mathematical achievements of their times. He acknowledges the resulting advances in philosophical understanding but denounces the philosophical systems that present those results as the final word on the nature of reality, arguing that the subsequent history of mathematics always creates new ideas that undermine the old systems. The only philosophical conclusion supported by the history of mathematics is Brunschvicg's own anti-systematic view of the mind responding to ever new and unpredictable "shocks" of nature with its own new and unpredictable interpretations. A second volume, *L'Expérience humaine et la causalité physique*, 1922 (*Human Experience and Physical Causation*), develops the same general viewpoint, this time through a study of scientific and philosophical conceptions of causality.

Brunschvicg speaks of his philosophy of thought as being "progressive" and in tune with the "rhythm of progress" (1922: 552). Given his strong claims about the unpredictability of the future direction of science, it is hard to see how even the most well-informed history could give us a real sense of where science is going in the long run. But Brunschvicg thinks there is something substantial that can be said about the moral and religious progress of humankind, a progress that he sees as intimately connected with the development of science and which he treats in his third volume, *Le Progrès de la conscience dans la philosophie occidentale*, 1927 (*The Development of Consciousness in Western Philosophy*).

A philosophy of scientific change: Gaston Bachelard

Brunschvicg's approach was continued, although in a much less idealistic manner, by Gaston Bachelard (1884–1962). Much more than Brunschvicg, Bachelard insists on radical discontinuities in the history of science. Over thirty years before Thomas Kuhn's *The Structure of Scientific Revolutions*, Bachelard read the history of physics as a series of epistemic "breaks" (*coupures épistémologiques*) whereby one conception of a natural domain is replaced by a radically different conception. (For further discussion of Thomas Kuhn, see "Philosophy of science," Chapter 14.) Philosophy, which, as Bachelard put it, always has to "go to the school of the sciences," must develop new conceptions corresponding to each new historical stage of science. The philosophy of an age of relativity and quantum physics has to be essentially different from a philosophy of the Newtonian era, since Newtonian concepts are now "epistemological obstacles" to an adequate understanding of nature. Bachelard accordingly worked to develop a philosophical standpoint that would mirror the radically new conceptions of physics. He proposes, for example, a "non-Cartesian epistemology" (a notion meant to parallel "non-Euclidean geometry"), based on a rejection of Descartes's (and many subsequent philosophers') foundationalist privileging of the "givens" of immediate experience. This epistemology will, of course, also be "non-Kantian" in its denial of the eternal validity of categories that in fact are contingent expressions of Newtonian science. Bachelard further suggests the need for a "psychoanalysis of knowledge" that will expose the unconscious role outdated common sense and scientific concepts play in our thinking. In another vein, he pursued the positive role of such images in the non-scientific contexts of poetry and art and developed what he called a "psychoanalysis" of the attraction of primordial images such as earth, fire, air, and water (see, for example, *La Psychoanalyse de feu*, 1938, published in English as *The Psychoanalysis of Fire*). But he denied any fundamental ontological significance to these non-scientific images.

Bachelard's insistence on breaks and discontinuity might seem to reject Brunschvicg's view of science as an essentially progressive enterprise. Bachelard, however, maintains that progress does not require continuity. Even though there are sharp conceptual and methodological breaks from one scientific worldview to another, we are still justified in speaking of progress because some specific achievements of past science are preserved as special cases within later theories. Non-Euclidean geometry, for example, denies the Euclidean claim that all triangles have 180 degrees as the sum of their interior angles, while admitting a special class of triangles ("Euclidean triangles") for which this is true. In the same way, concepts such as specific heat (developed by Black in terms of the now superseded caloric theory) and mass (as understood by Newton) have been reformulated in the context of later theories.

There is deeper tension between Bachelard and Brunschvicg on the issue of idealism. Bachelard does criticize a position he calls "realism," characterized as believing "in the prolix richness of the individual sensation and in the systematic impoverishment of abstractive thought" (1929: 206). Realism in this sense asserts the epistemic and metaphysical primacy of ordinary sense objects over what it regards as abstract accounts in terms of the theoretical entities of science. Bachelard's critique of realism is in effect an assertion of the ontological primacy of theoretical entities as concrete realities. To this extent, it amounts to a defense of what analytic philosophers of science nowadays call "scientific realism."

Whatever its relation to realism, Bachelard's applied rationalism also introduces the crucial idea that scientific instrumentation has a central role in the constitution of the physical world. Instruments are, he says, "theories materialized," and a concept is truly scientific only to the extent that it receives concrete reality through a "technique of realization" (1934: 13, 16). Husserl's phenomenology describes how the mind constitutes the objects of everyday experience (see also "Phenomenology," Chapter 15), but, according to Bachelard, we also require a "phenomeno-technics" that will describe the constitution of scientific objects by instrumental technology.

Living time: the metaphysics of Bergson

Henri Bergson (1859–1941), the most important French philosopher prior to the Second World War, returns to a strongly spiritualist orientation. In contrast to both

Brunschvicg and Bachelard, he rejects the ultimate cognitive authority of both science and the thought that it expresses. According to him, the products of thought (particularly science) are abstractions from the concrete intuition through which we experience "lived time" (duration, *la durée*). Bergson's philosophical project is the articulation of our experience of duration, the contrast of this experience with our standard ("spatialized") modes of experience and thought, and the reassessment of fundamental philosophical questions in the light of this articulation and contrast. In his first book (*Essai sur les données immédiates de la conscience*, 1889, translated as *Time and Free Will*, 1910), for example, he argues that traditional aporiae over freedom can be resolved by attending to the continuous temporal nature of our psychological states. Similarly, his second book *Matière et mémoire*, 1896 (*Matter and Memory*) deals with the mind/body problem by attacking materialism along with dualism as inadequate to our concrete experience, which shows that both the mental and the physical are abstractions from the unified flow of lived time.

Creative Evolution (*L'Evolution créatrice*, 1907) offers a general metaphysical account of the duration that the earlier two books encountered only in specific contexts. Here Bergson presents science as essentially tied to the "cinematographical method," which views reality not as a continuous flux (the duration that it in fact is) but as a series of instantaneous "snapshots" extracted from this flux. Bergson ties this method to science's ultimate goal of controlling nature for the sake of effective action. Effective action requires nothing more than moving from a given starting point to a given end point with no concern for whatever might exist between the two. This leads science to reduce its objects to static frames, abstracted from the concrete temporal flux in which we experience them. Admittedly, modern science, in apparent contrast to ancient thought, conceptualizes the world as a continuous manifold, open to the technique of the differential calculus, with time itself as the fundamental independent variable. But Bergson maintains that the time of modern science is not the continuous flux of duration but a spatialized, immobile surrogate. Science "always considers moments, always virtual stopping-places, always, in short, immobilities. Which amounts to saying that real time, regarded as flux, or, in other words, the very mobility of being, escapes the hold of scientific knowledge" (1907: 366). Modern philosophy from Descartes through Kant has failed to recognize this essential incompleteness of the scientific worldview and the corresponding need for a philosophical account of what science leaves out: the fullness of lived time (duration).

In *Creative Evolution* Bergson says that life in general shares the active, creative character of the duration of consciousness. In particular, the entire bio-historical process of evolution is driven by a dynamic impulse, the *élan vital*, that is the principle of all life. This impulse, now presented as the highest metaphysical principle, is also the creative force within conscious duration.

Creative Evolution also tries to show just why and how the intellect, although it is biologically the distinctive human trait, is a limited instrument of knowledge, formed to deal only with inert matter. Bergson further argues that the antidote to intellect lies on the side of instinct, which is directed to the singular, concrete object, that is, to time as duration. Ordinarily, instinct lacks the distance from objects needed for theoretical knowledge of them; its access to duration remains an unreflective sympathy that goes no further than an implicit know-how. But, according to Bergson, it is possible for instinct to become disengaged, to "become disinterested, self-conscious, capable of reflecting on its object" (1907: 194). Instinct then becomes *intuition*, the privileged vehicle of philosophical knowledge. But this does not mean that philosophy is a simple rejection of intellect. Rather, philosophy is born from a fundamental cooperation between two complementary powers: "There are things that intelligence alone is able to seek, but which, by itself, it will never find. These things instinct alone could find; but it will never seek them" (p. 167, emphasis omitted). Intuition is precisely instinct directed toward the intellect's goal of general, theoretical knowledge.

Bergson's affinity with spiritualism is particularly apparent in his positive stance toward religion. The philosophy of the Third Republic, like the Republic itself, was an essentially secular enterprise. Its neo-Kantian standpoint insisted on no particular religious commitment, but it did present a world of finality and freedom in which faith could find a comfortable enough intellectual niche. Jules Lachelier's spiritualist idealism, for example, by asserting the metaphysical and moral autonomy of individuals and avoiding materialist reductions, kept open the way for his Catholic commitment to personal salvation and immortality. But Lachelier (1832–1918) was quite clear that the move to religious commitment could not be motivated by philosophical reflection. Nor did he see his faith as in any way guiding or grounding his philosophical reflection. He – like Boutroux and Duhem – was Catholic and a philosopher but not, in any strong sense, a Catholic philosopher.

Henri Bergson, however, found his philosophical thought, particularly in his last book, *Les Deux Sources de la morale et de la religion*, 1932 (*The Two Sources of Morality and Religion*), moving him closer and closer to religious conviction. Bergson makes a key distinction between static and dynamic religion. In its static form, religion functions to preserve the stability of society against challenges from intelligence. Although human society is analogous to the entirely instinctual societies of ants and bees, it differs in that its individuals are capable of understanding and questioning their situation, a fact that raises the real possibility of refusing social obligations. Static religion responds with myths about the universe and our place in it that counter such questioning by, for example, promising rewards and punishments in an afterlife and offering magical instruments for the control of nature.

The God of static religion is a tribal god, insisting on our loyalty to a particular social group. By contrast, dynamic religion moves from the guardian gods of one tribe to a divinity whose love embraces everyone. On Bergson's view, dynamic religion flows from the experiences of a select group of religious "geniuses," the mystics, with, however, the understanding that the most perfect form of mysticism involves not only detached contemplation but also practical action in the world. The greatest mystics are those who, like Christ himself, also profoundly transformed human affairs.

Bergson defines mysticism quite explicitly:

> In our eyes, the ultimate end of mysticism is the establishment of a contact, consequently of a partial coincidence, with the creative effort which life itself

manifests. This effort is of God, if it is not God himself. The great mystic is to be conceived as an individual being, capable of transcending the limitations imposed on the species by its material nature, thus continuing and extending the divine action. (1932: 220–1)

In the highest forms of mysticism (which Bergson thinks occur primarily in Christianity), "visions are left far behind" and all that remains is a total and final union with God, "who is acting through the soul ... with an irresistible impulse that hurls it into great enterprises" (1932: 232). The mystic's love has the same direction as the vital impulse, indeed, "it *is* this impetus itself, communicated in its entirety to exceptional men who in their turn would fain impart it to all humanity" (p. 235). The goal is the paradox of turning a biological species, which is precisely a stable product of the vital impulse, into the creative movement of that impulse.

But mysticism faces the same obstacle that always obstructs the vital impetus: the inertness of matter, in this case, the human need for physical sustenance, which takes up almost all our energies and turns us away from higher things. Hinting at an ultimately political direction of his thought, Bergson suggests that the total fulfillment of mysticism's spiritual goal requires "a profound change in the material conditions imposed on humanity by nature" (p. 236), a change that in the end might be best effected by "a vast system of machinery such as might set human activity at liberty, this liberation being, moreover, stabilized by a political and social organization which would ensure the application of the mechanism to its true object" (p. 235). Such radical transformations are not immediately possible, and mystics have instead limited themselves to the more feasible tasks of planting and sustaining the mystical flame in established social institutions, particularly those of static religion, mainly by founding religious communities. At the end of his life, Bergson himself became strongly drawn to one such community, the Catholic Church. He stopped short of the public commitment of baptism only because, in the midst of the German occupation, he did not want to seem to renounce his Jewish origin.

The first existentialists: Blondel and Marcel

The disastrous absurdities of the First World War produced a new generation of philosophers cynical about what they saw as the comfortable truths of their teachers and eager for a philosophy based in the immediacy of experience. Their motto, "to the concrete," was taken from the title of Jean Wahl's (1888–1974) influential book, *Vers le concret* (*To the Concrete*). (For further discussion of Wahl, see "Hegelianism in the twentieth century," Chapter 3.) To this extent, they might have looked to Bergson, as opposed to Brunschvicg and the other neo-Kantians, for inspiration. But, as Jean Hyppolite (1907–1968) has pointed out, the young Turks saw Bergson (like Brunschvicg and the rest) as offering philosophies of "final serenity" that ignored the tragic drama of human existence, made so apparent by recent history (Hyppolite 1971: 453). Bergson's turn to religion – even Catholicism – toward the end of his life also had an alienating effect.

Existential philosophy, as it was called by the 1930s, was, however, by no means a repudiation of the spiritualist orientation. The existentialists retain the central commitments to the priority of the free individual, in opposition to positivist reduction and absolute–idealist assimilation. Even the explicitly religious commitments of spiritualism are paramount in the two thinkers who developed existentialist themes well before Sartre and Merleau-Ponty: Maurice Blondel and Gabriel Marcel.

In his famous thesis, Action (L'Action), defended in 1893, Maurice Blondel (1861–1949) did not go so far as to employ his Catholic beliefs as premises of his philosophical arguments or to try to derive these beliefs from naturally known philosophical premises. But he did maintain that a proper philosophical understanding of the human condition would show that our deepest aspirations could not be satisfied in the natural realm, that the intelligibility and fulfillment we desire are possible only if the Christian doctrine of salvation through supernatural grace is true.

Action begins with the urgent question: "Yes or no, does human life make sense, and does man have a destiny?" (1963: 1), and this dramatic, proto-existentialist tone is interwoven throughout its complex and sometimes tediously extended philosophical discussions. This tone corresponds, moreover, to Blondel's insistence that human life is a matter of concrete engagement in the world through action, where "action" means the totality of our thought, feeling, and willing in direct relation with their objects. The question is what sort of overall meaning, if any, we must ascribe to our life of action.

It might seem possible to reject Blondel's question, to refuse even to consider whether life has any meaning. Such a rejection, he maintains, entails a "dilettantism" that would endlessly explore a random variety of human experiences and activities with no concern for finding a unified or even consistent pattern in the variety. Blondel (like Kierkegaard) has enough empathy with dilettantism to provide a vivid and nuanced evocation of its attitude. But he concludes that the standpoint is ultimately incoherent. Dilettantes claim to have no interest in overall meaning but are in fact committed to understanding everything in terms of their own selfish project of an endless succession of enjoyments. The pessimist (Schopenhauer is an explicit example) accepts the validity of Blondel's question but gives it an entirely negative answer: life has no meaning, and our attitude toward it should be one of pessimistic denial. Blondel argues, however, that pessimism is, like dilettantism, incoherent, since its project of willing nothing must be parasitic on the willing of some positive reality. Negation is always a relative matter of replacing one positive reality with another.

The largest part of Action offers a systematic survey of possible positive views of the meaning of life, with an ultimate goal of showing that only the existence of the Christian God provides what we require. Blondel's discussion places him firmly within the French spiritualist tradition. Although his final goal is to support the Catholic faith, his philosophical precursors are not Augustine or Aquinas but Maine de Biran, Félix Ravaisson (1813–1900), Lachelier, and Léon Ollé-Laprune (1839–98), his teacher at the École Normale.

Blondel begins with the possibility that scientific materialism answers his question of the meaning of life but rejects this possibility on the standard spiritualist grounds that consciousness is not reducible to matter. Similarly, he rejects an answer in terms of psychological determinism, arguing that freedom, concretely expressed in action, is an essential feature of consciousness. Here Blondel even anticipates Sartre's existentialist language: "The substance of man is action; he is what he makes himself" (see Lacroix 1963: 33). But Blondel insists that the life of the individual alone cannot sustain the meaning we require. Our action inevitably extends to the social world, seeking meaning first in the family, then in the nation, then in the community of all humankind, and even in projections of humanity into idols of superstitious worship.

At every stage, action is driven to seek further levels of meaning because of the gap between what our willing has achieved so far (what Blondel calls the "willed will," *volonté voulue*) and what we most profoundly will (the "willing will," *volonté voulante*). No matter how successful our willing, no matter how extensive the realm of objects it attains, the will (*volonté voulue*) is never entirely satisfied. This is because, at the very least, our willing itself, the very root of our action, is not something we have willed.

The will is not content that its action be finally derived from outside. Our ultimate desire is to be entirely self-sufficient; to be, in a word, God: "Man aspires to be a god." Once again, Blondel anticipates Sartre. But, unlike Sartre, he does not conclude that the our desire to be God is a "useless passion," collapsing under the impossibility of a being that would be both in-itself and for-itself. According to Blondel, the impossibility follows only if we choose "to be god without God and against God." But there is another alternative: "to be God through God and with God" (1963: 328). To take this route is to open myself to the will of another being, but one that is the source of my being and hence of my very will. In union with this being (God), I can achieve the self-sufficiency that is my ultimate volition. It is this alternative that opens the way to our rebirth in a supernatural order of grace.

Philosophy, according to Blondel, can take us as far as the possibility of this supernatural order. But it cannot tell us whether the order is actual or whether we ought to choose the alternative it would present. Blondel sees the whole of *Action* as operating within this limited domain of the philosophical and so respecting the boundary between what is knowable to natural reason and what is grasped only by supernatural faith.

Despite his insistence on the strictly philosophical grounding of *Action*, Blondel's secular colleagues were not convinced that his project stood independent of his Catholicism. Accordingly, his influence was mostly restricted to Catholic circles and was further limited by his failure to follow *Action* with any other books for over forty years. It was only in 1934 that he began to publish an immense trilogy, with a revised version of *Action* preceded by treatises on thought (*La Penseé*) and ontology (*L'Être et les êtres*). But the trilogy came too late to have much impact on the general direction of French philosophy.

There was, however, a Catholic philosopher whose views were much closer to what was becoming the mainstream and who can even be plausibly put forward as the first French existentialist. This is Gabriel Marcel (1889–1973), who, while Sartre and the other fledging existentialists were still in school, was publishing, in his *Metaphysical Journal* (1927), careful descriptions of how embodied subjectivity experiences concrete existence, the human situation, the other, and being itself. There is, in fact, no major theme of existentialism that is not treated, thoroughly and perceptively, in his work.

In *The Mystery of Being* (1951), Marcel presents his philosophy as a matter of what he calls "secondary reflection" rather than "primary reflection." Primary reflection is primary only in that it corresponds to the descriptions of our experience that are nearest to the surface and that we are, therefore, most likely to put forward first when we begin thinking about the human situation. It expresses the standpoint of common sense and of science. Primary reflection makes a sharp distinction between the objects of the world and the mind that experiences and knows them. Likewise, it sharply distinguishes the body from the mind, regarding the body as just another object in the world, knowable in the same objective way as other objects. The knowledge attained by primary reflection is not only objective but also general, formulated in terms of abstract concepts applicable to entire ranges of similar objects. This generality is expressed by universal laws such as those of natural science.

Marcel has no quarrel with the validity or importance of primary reflection. Its truths – especially the truths of science – are undeniable and essential for our pragmatic dealings with the world. But he vigorously opposes the idea that primary reflection provides the only or the most important truth about our world and our lives. There is also what he calls "secondary reflection": secondary not in the sense of subordinate or marginal but in the sense of operating at a further, deeper level. Secondary reflection is the inverse at every point of primary reflection. Its knowledge is concrete rather than abstract, personal rather than objective, and based on our involvement with the world rather than our separation from it.

Correlated with the distinction between primary and secondary reflection is Marcel's distinction between problems and mysteries. Primary reflection deals with problems, that is, with precisely formulable questions with answers that can be judged in a public way by clear criteria. A crossword puzzle is a problem, but so are extremely complex scientific questions (e.g. What are the ultimate constituents of matter?) that may take centuries to answer. I may or may not be interested in a given problem, and once it is solved I can turn my attention to something else. Even if I am desperately interested in solving a problem, the solution has nothing to do with who I fundamentally am. By contrast, a mystery is a question that implicates me in my deepest reality. There are no objective criteria for answering it, and no answer can have universal validity. Indeed, it is wrong to think that there is any pre-established answer that I could ever discover. Responding to a mystery is as much a matter of creatively transforming as of discovering some truth about myself. Examples of questions that lead to mysteries rather than problems are: "Am I free?," "Have I been created by God?," "Should I despair in the face of death?," "Do I love this person?" Such questions are not unanswerable, but they cannot be answered in the manner of a solution to a problem. This is because, in contrast to a problem, a mystery is not something from which I can withdraw to attain an objective perspective. In response to a mystery, I can only try to journey further into a reality that is an essential part of me. Such a journey will simultaneously reveal and create this reality.

According to Marcel, the mistake of much philosophical thought is to treat the self, other people, and God as objects about which we pose and solve problems. The true task of philosophy is to abandon this quest for objective knowledge, modeled on science, in favor of creative intuitions of these realities as mysteries of existence (where "existence" means the fullness of concrete reality). Through such intuitions I not only encounter my self in its full existential concreteness, I also encounter other people, not as alien beings but as members with me of a community essential to us all. For Marcel, the fundamental experience of philosophy is not "I am" but "we are." Further, this "we" eventually is seen to involve not just finite creatures but even God. Of course, for Marcel, there is no question of proving the existence of God by logical or scientific argument. That is impossible because it would require that God be just another thing in an objective multiplicity of things. The reality of God must be that of a person (a "thou," as Marcel, like Martin Buber, puts it) with whom I have direct communication; and this communication is not an exchange between separated subjects but a shared life whereby I participate in the divine reality.

The experience of secondary reflection is thoroughly personal in two senses: it is undergone by a person and it is directed toward persons. As such, the experience is fraught with the emotional and moral substance of personal life. Accordingly, Marcel maintains that this experience must take the form of the most fundamental and intense modes of human feeling and values: fidelity (or faith), hope, and love. I become fully aware of myself, of how I am one with others, and how we are all one with God only by opening myself to the world through a faithful, hopeful, and loving life. Some of Marcel's most impressive work consists of his close descriptions of just what is involved in such a life. Faith, he says, is that whereby the self is created, hope is ultimately for salvation, and love involves the affirmation that the beloved shall not die.

Despite the priority of his work, Marcel had limited influence on the younger existentialists. They engaged much more with twentieth-century Germans such as Husserl and Heidegger, philosophers to whom Marcel's thought owed little or nothing. Moreover, Marcel was a theist (and, from 1929 on, a Catholic) who thought that faith, hope, and love could overcome the absurdity, despair, and conflict of the atheistic existentialists. (Also, his political positions alone, such as support for Franco's Spain, alienated him from these philosophers.) As a result, Marcel remained the odd man out among French existentialists.

The apex of existentialism: Jean-Paul Sartre (1905–80)

The work of the major existentialists, especially Sartre, is (often explicitly) anti-religious. To this extent, of course, this means that, as philosophers, they take religion much more seriously than do philosophers who are indifferent to belief or who see philosophy as having nothing to do with whatever religious beliefs they might have. In Sartre's case, his metaphysical system is based on a conception of human freedom that seems to exclude a priori the possibility of its being created by God. In general, the "humanism" of the French existentialists rejected religion on the broadly Nietzschean grounds that it was incompatible with a thoroughgoing commitment to our temporal world. But in another sense the existentialists did not take religion seriously: they did not see it as anything approaching a real option and so spent little time understanding it, even for purposes of refutation.

The canonical exposition of Sartre's existentialism is his philosophical masterpiece, *L'Être et le néant*, 1943 (*Being and Nothingness*) Here he begins from two fundamental claims about consciousness: it is always *of something*, but is itself *not something*. To be conscious implies that there is some object that I am conscious of. Consciousness is, as Husserl said, essentially *intentional*: directed toward something else. (For further discussion of Sartre, see "Phenomenology," Chapter 15.) But objects are not physically or substantially in consciousness, the way a fish is in a river or even a pain is in a leg. Consciousness is not a thing, not a material thing but also not an immaterial thing such as a soul or a spiritual substance. It has no content or structure of its own; rather, its entire existence consists in its relation to its objects. Consciousness is a totally "transparent" intending of its objects and nothing more. In view of this, Sartre is prepared to say that consciousness is *nothing*. Consciousness is also transparent in the sense of being always aware, directly and immediately, of itself as consciousness. Because consciousness is always self-aware, Sartre says that it has *being-for-itself*: its very existence involves an internal relation to itself. The objects of consciousness, which, as such, are not self-aware have, by contrast, the solid positivity of intrinsic content, which Sartre calls *being-in-itself*. In a very characteristic displacement, Sartre puts the psychological self – the subject of our habits, character, etc. – on the side of being-in-itself. The self, in this sense, is not consciousness (or even part of it); it exists only as an object of consciousness, one of the many things that make up my world.

Being-in-itself has no intrinsic intelligibility; it is a brute, unstructured given, merely existing with no meaning. Being-in-itself becomes meaningful only to the extent that it is an object of consciousness, which is the ultimate source not of the reality of being-in-itself but of its meaning. Sartre holds not a metaphysical idealism of being but an idealism of meaning.

Sartre understands the relation of being-for-itself (consciousness) to being-in-itself in terms of negativity (nothingness). Consider a paradigm phenomenological analysis he presents *in Being and Nothingness*: as I enter a café, late for an appointment with Pierre, I at first seem to encounter a fullness of being; everywhere I look there are objects or activities. But, since I am looking for Pierre and worried that he may have already left, every element of this scene falls back, as soon as it begins to present itself, because I see it as merely not-Pierre. This negative experience is an example of "nihilation" (*néantisation*), Sartre's neologism for the process whereby negation is introduced on the concrete level of immediate perception (as opposed to the reflective level of intellectual judgment). Correspondingly, *nothingness* denotes the reality of negation that is introduced by nihilation. The upshot of Sartre's account is that nothingness is required as a distinct ontological category, existing in the midst of being-in-itself and being-for-itself like "a worm in the heart of being." But nothingness is also derived from consciousness, "secreted," Sartre says, by consciousness's determination of being-in-itself as meaning this and *not* that.

Consciousness negates being-in-itself not by annihilating it but by *withdrawing* from it. Sartre identifies this withdrawal as *freedom*. Freedom exists as consciousness's ability to withdraw from (revise or even reject) the self. Because I am free, I can deny what I am (that is, what I have been up to now) and constitute at any moment a new meaning for my existence as a self. Negation enters the world in virtue of consciousness's choice to make its self mean *this* and not *that* in relation to the rest of the world. Freedom is not a matter of determining what happens but of determining the meaning of what happens. Within the human domain of meaning, we are absolutely sovereign.

With this sovereignty comes anguish, the awareness of our total responsibility for the meaning of our existence, as well as the effort to flee the burden of freedom through what Sartre calls *bad faith* (*mauvaise foi*, sometimes translated as "self-deception"). Bad faith is essentially a lie to oneself, in particular, the lie that my character and life have been determined by outside forces. Sartre seizes on the intrinsic paradox of *self-deception* (the liar knows the truth and the one lied to does not) as an indication of the distinctive ontological status of human reality. Since I am both a psychological self (being-in-itself) and a consciousness (being-for-itself) other than and aware of this self, I (as consciousness) am not what I am (as self). This ontological complexity is the root and explanation of the possibility of bad faith.

Sartre's distinctively existentialist understanding of freedom both continues and radically transforms the French spiritualist exaltation of the free individual. He accepts the traditional view that freedom is the irreducible prerogative of the human individual as well as the standard ethical claim that true freedom requires freedom *from* a standard set of evils: the lies and values of popular materialistic culture (in Sartre's terms bad faith and bourgeois morality). But he rejects the traditional view that freedom must also be regarded as freedom *for* some objective *summum bonum* (truth, happiness, virtue), itself grounded in an objective, pre-given order (Platonic Forms, human nature, scientific laws, divine providence). For Sartre, there is nothing outside human freedom that is normative for it. Accordingly, the central positive features of traditional ideas of freedom (freedom for) become negative features (freedom from) for Sartre. Specifically, Sartrean freedom requires freedom from God (anti-theism) and freedom from objective ethical values (anti-moralism).

For Sartre humans actions are entirely free in the sense that there are no external conditions, moral or causal, that constrain them. Freedom has limits, but only those that it implicitly imposes on itself. Any obstacle or constraint is entirely the result of my decision to act. For example, a mountain is an obstacle only once I have decided to climb it; it is no obstacle to the tourist who is merely interested in admiring its grandeur. The same is true of so-called psychological causes of behavior. It may seem that I really want to keep climbing the mountain but my feeling of fatigue is so great that I simply cannot go on. According to Sartre, however, whether or not the feeling is "great enough" as to stop me depends on whether or not I really want to go on no matter what. In fact, I could keep pushing myself to the point of collapse or even death. The fatigue is an obstacle only to the extent that I allow it to be.

It is often argued that, by deriving values themselves from our choices, Sartre has destroyed the possibility of meaningful ethical standards. Although he never completed his long-awaited treatise on morality, the main thrust of his response is clear: he excludes all external goals for freedom but takes freedom itself as its own goal. Freedom ceases to be a means to something else (freedom for) and becomes an absolute end in itself. As a result, Sartre's fundamental ethical category becomes authenticity, in the sense of accepting one's status as a radically free agent. Authenticity rejects the temptation of bad faith to flee from our freedom.

Sartre's account of freedom exemplifies a tension that is found throughout *Being and Nothingness*. On the one hand, he develops a systematic structure in terms of his fundamental ontological categories (being-in-itself, being-for-itself, nothingness, etc.); this is his ontology. At the same time, he shows how concrete phenomenological descriptions (e.g. of negativities, bad faith, situated freedom) complement and deepen this structure; this is his phenomenology. The result is, overall, a very effective dual approach, but it involves two limitations. First, the abstract ontological categories, dialectically deployed simply in their own terms, are not always adequate to the richness of the phenomenological descriptions. This is particularly apparent in the case of freedom, where the sharp conceptual separation of being-for-itself from being-in-itself makes it difficult to appreciate the phenomenology of situated freedom. The problem is that any ontological categories – and especially Sartre's – abstract from the concrete situation of man-in-the-world. The obvious solution is to give priority to the phenomenological descriptions and modify the apparent import of the categories accordingly.

Further, even the descriptive enterprise of *Being and Nothingness* is limited, at least in the earlier parts of the book, by an implicit restriction to a hyper-individualistic viewpoint that ignores the social embeddedness of consciousness. It is no accident that so many examples are taken from the often disengaged life of the Parisian café. As the discussion develops, Sartre's descriptive examples expand to include the commitment of situated agents struggling with the natural and historical worlds. But the early examples join the abstract ontology in supporting a radically disengaged conception of freedom inconsistent with the later examples. In Sartre's second systematic philosophical treatise, *The Critique of Dialectical Reason* (*Critique de la raison dialectique*, 1960), he develops a social ontology, inspired by Marx, that tries to provide a more nuanced account of freedom, without, however, backing away from the core existentialist theses about the priority and irreducibility of individual freedom.

From existential phenomenology to structuralism: Merleau-Ponty

The other major proponent of existential phenomenology was Maurice Merleau-Ponty (1908–61), Sartre's friend and collaborator on their influential journal, *Les Temps Modernes*. In his major work, *The Phenomenology of Perception* (*Phénoménologie de la perception*, 1945), Merleau-Ponty, in contrast to Sartre, mostly eschews systematic ontology for more accurate and nuanced phenomenological description (see also "Phenomenology," Chapter 15). Regarding freedom, for example, Merleau-Ponty maintains that Sartre ignores the fact that freedom can exist only in a field of possibilities that specify the probabilities, given my situation, that I will act in one way rather than another (1945: 442). Sartre is right that nothing appears as an obstacle except as a result of a project that I have chosen. But, Merleau-Ponty notes, freedom constitutes obstacles only in a general way, by constituting a context in which certain things will appear as obstacles, others as aids, etc. But what the *particular* obstacles are depends on the situation, not on freedom. The cliff is an obstacle only because I choose to climb it, but the particular physical structures of the cliff and of my body determine just what these obstacles will be. Similarly, regarding internal factors such as fatigue, Sartre ignores the crucial fact that, although I always *can* alter my deep-rooted attitudes or patterns of reaction, it is improbable that I *will*. Probability is a genuine phenomenon of "weight" (or "tendency") that is given in immediate experience.

More generally, Sartre poses a false dichotomy between being-in-itself and being-for-itself, ignoring the fact that these categories are only abstractions from the concrete reality of consciousness-in-the-world. To avoid this ontological dualism, Merleau-Ponty centers his phenomenological analyses on the body. The body is not an object on a par with other objects. As *my* body it is the ineradicable locus of experience, the standpoint from which I must perceive the world. Merleau-Ponty agrees with Sartre (following Husserl) that to be conscious is to be conscious of an object or – taking account of the entire context in which an object appears – a world. But having a world as an object is not a matter of having disengaged, objective consciousness of a world. Consciousness is not just of-the-world but in-the-world, incarnated in a body that is itself part of that world. Accordingly, there is no sharp separation between me as subjective perceiver and the objects that I perceive. There is, rather, a structure (meaning) of my situation that defines the limits within which my engagement with the world must occur. But this defining structure is not wholly determinate; it is partially ambiguous and thus consistent with a certain range of attitudes and actions. By recognizing the priority of the body as the locus of consciousness, Merleau-Ponty replaces the sharp abstract dichotomies of Sartre's ontology with the ambiguities of our incarnation in the world.

The strength of Merleau-Ponty's philosophy is, then, the extent to which, unlike Sartre, he refuses to simplify the complexity of our experience via ontological abstractions. Nonetheless, he realized that eventually ontological questions must be raised, since (contrary to Husserl) even the most rigorous phenomenological descriptions will be based on assumptions about what sorts of things consciousness and its objects are. Because of phenomenology's insistence on what Merleau-Ponty himself called the "primacy of perception,", its own ontological inclination is toward some form of idealism. We have already seen how the central place of being-for-itself in Sartre's scheme led him to an idealism of meaning. In *The Phenomenology of Perception*, Merleau-Ponty moved toward a similar position in his notion of a "tacit cogito," a "self-awareness" that lies "behind all our particular thoughts" (1945: 400), through which he recognized "an element of final truth in the Cartesian return of things or ideas to the self" (p. 369).

In writings after *Being and Nothingness* and *The Phenomenology of Perception*, both Sartre and Merleau-Ponty were at pains to see that these idealistic tendencies did not take the form of any relapse into neo-Kantian or even Hegelian absolute idealism. To this end, they both connected phenomenological meaning to the social meanings of material culture. Sartre did this in his effort to synthesize existentialism and Marxism. Merleau-Ponty tried to effect a rapprochement of phenomenology and structural social science (particularly the anthropology of his good friend, Claude Lévi-Strauss). Sartre's effort was lost in the self-indulgent obscurity of *The Critique of Dialectical Reason* and the increasing turn of French intellectuals from Marxism. But Merleau-Ponty's enterprise – abandoned by his later turn to something like a Heideggerian ontology in the unfinished *The Visible and the Invisible* (*Le Visible et l'invisible*, 1964) – laid the basis for what soon became, in Derrida's phrase, the "structuralist invasion" of French philosophy.

The connection of phenomenology to structuralism is apparent in a crucial sentence of Merleau-Ponty's essay on the anthropologist Claude Lévi-Strauss (1908–): "For the philosopher, the presence of structure outside of us in natural and social systems and within us as symbolic function points to a way beyond the subject–object correlation which has dominated philosophy from Descartes to Hegel" (1960: 123). While positivism tried to replace social meanings with causal relations among objects, Kantian versions of spiritualism thought of them as constituted by the intellectual activity of the mind. Neither approach was satisfactory.

Lévi-Strauss's cultural anthropology provided, Merleau-Ponty thought, a viable alternative by giving an account of social realities (e.g. language, kinship relations) in terms of structures. These structures are meanings and therefore not reducible to causal relations among objects. At the same time, they are not the idealist's "crystal-lized ideas," since the subjects who live in accord with meanings typically have no conscious grasp of them.

Because structures are both objective realities, independent of any mind, and meanings informing the lives of individuals, they can be the vehicle of the concrete unity of man-in-the-world. We cannot limit ourselves to the study of structures alone. We also need to understand how structures enter into the lives of individuals, an understanding available in our direct experience of meanings in our ordinary life, reflectively accessible through phenomenological description. But there is also a need for what Merleau-Ponty calls "ethnological experience," which results from inserting ourselves into another culture through anthropological fieldwork.

By understanding structure and its relation to lived experience, we overcome tradi-tional philosophical mistakes of privileging the subject over the object or the object over the subject. Structuralism thus appears as the essential complement to phenomenological philosophy. What often appears as an overthrow of existentialism from the outside by struc-turalism in fact originated from the internal logic of existential phenomenology. Why then did structuralism come to be instead regarded as a stark alternative to existential phenom-enology? A first level of explanation lies in the rivalry between Lévi-Strauss and Sartre for the position of reigning French master-thinker. Lévi-Strauss's explicit, sometimes virulent, challenge to Sartre's dominant position (as in the concluding chapter of *The Savage Mind*) left no room for cooperative inquiry. If Merleau-Ponty, with his close ties to Lévi-Strauss, had lived long enough and succeeded Sartre (whose interests were becoming much less narrowly philosophical) as the leading existential phenomenologist, the relations between structuralism and phenomenology might well have been very different.

The philosophy of the concept: Georges Canguilhem

In any case, there had long been a much deeper philosophical challenge to the spiritualist orientation of existential phenomenology. We mentioned earlier Foucault's distinction of "philosophy of the concept" from "philosophy of experience." In Foucault's student days, the "philosophy of experience" was, of course, existential phenomenology (but Foucault located earlier instantiations of it in various versions of spiritualism from Lachelier to Bergson). The "philosophy of the concept" was historically tied to the French tradition, ultimately traceable to Comte, of the history and philosophy of science.

But for the contingencies of the war, there might well have been a "conceptual" appropriation of Husserl to rival Sartre's and Merleau-Ponty's "experiential" readings. Jean Cavaillès (1903–44), writing in the 1940s, had offered a brilliant formal reading of Husserl that moved his thought away from its Heideggerian future and back toward its origins in logic and the philosophy of mathematics. Unfortunately, Cavaillès, who was one of the founders of the French Resistance to the Nazi occupation of France, was captured by the Germans and executed. His "rationalist" development of phenomenology was continued by, for example, Suzanne Bachelard (the daughter of Gaston Bachelard) and by the Belgian Jean Ladrière (1921–). But the existentialized Husserl remained dominant in France.

As it turned out, however, the philosophy of the concept was primarily the work of Georges Canguilhem, Bachelard's successor as director of the Sorbonne's Institut d'Histoire des Sciences et des Techniques. Canguilhem trained a large number of historians and philosophers of science, and even non-specialists frequently followed his courses. Although Canguilhem starts from an essentially Bachelardian view of science, the foci of his work are different from Bachelard's: philosophical history rather than historical philosophizing, the biological and medical sciences rather than physics and chemistry. Further, his results suggest a number of important modifications in Bachelard's position.

Canguilhem's most important methodological contribution was his distinction between concepts and theories. In much twentieth-century philosophy of science, concepts are functions of theories, deriving their meaning from the roles they play in theoretical accounts of phenomena. Newtonian and Einsteinian mass, for example, are regarded as fundamentally different concepts because they are embedded in fundamentally different physical theories. This subordination of concept to theory derives from the view that the interpretation of phenomena (that is, their subsumption under a given set of concepts) is a matter of explaining them on the basis of a particular theoretical framework. For Canguilhem, by contrast, there is a crucial distinction between the interpretation of phenomena (via concepts) and their theoretical explanation. According to him, a given set of concepts provides the preliminary descriptions of a phenomenon that allow the formulation of questions about how to explain it. Different theories (all, however, formulated in terms of the same set of basic concepts) will provide competing answers to these questions. Galileo, for example, introduced a new conception of the motion of falling bodies to replace the Aristotelian conception.

Galileo, Descartes, and Newton all employed this new conception in their description of the motion of falling bodies and in the theories they developed to explain this motion. Although the basic concept of motion was the same, the explanatory theories were very different. This shows, according to Canguilhem, the "theoretical polyvalence" of concepts: their ability to function in the context of widely differing theories. His own historical studies (for example, of reflex movement) are typically histories of concepts that persist through a series of theoretical formulations.

The philosophy of the concept, in Canguilhem and others, is a much more important and enduring aspect of twentieth-century French philosophy than the structuralism that proposed subordinating subjectivity to unconscious social and linguistic structures that could be analyzed in a rigorous, even quasi-mathematical scientific manner. Thus understood, structuralism had a relatively short strut upon the French intellectual stage. It was most important in psychoanalysis (Jacques Lacan, 1901–81) and literary theory (Roland Barthes, 1915–80), at one stage. Its philosophical influence was most apparent in Louis Althusser's anti-humanist reading of Marx and in several books from Michel Foucault's "archaeological period" in the 1960s. But, especially in philosophy, structuralism quickly yielded to post-stucturalism. Structuralism purported to provide rigorously objective scientific accounts of the human domain. But it was readily apparent that this claim was based on a confusion of genuine science, grounded in exacting empirical tests, and the esoteric technical vocabulary and complex logical systems that, by themselves, are mere trappings of science. Post-structuralism produced a discourse in the style of structuralism – preserving its veneer of scientific rigor – but rejected the key structuralist claim that there is a deep objective truth about human nature that can be expressed by such discourse. This rejection, moreover, was not aimed only or even primarily at the passing phenomenon of structuralism. It was especially directed to the entire mainline tradition of philosophical thought, from Plato through Husserl, defined by the goal of knowing the fundamental nature and meaning of human reality.

This goal had, in particular, defined French philosophy since Descartes and had, during the twentieth century, been pursued through various forms of the spiritualist orientation, from critical idealism, through Bergson, to phenomenology. Positivism, which maintained that final truth was scientific truth, challenged not the ideal of ultimate truth but the claim that philosophy rather than science was the means to the ideal. Perennially, the only other alternative seemed to be a skeptical denial of all serious truth claims.

As the 1960s began in France, the traditional claims of philosophy were represented by phenomenology and the perennial positivist challenge by structuralism. As we have seen, after Merleau-Ponty, the major issue seemed to be that of complementing the subject-centered standpoint of phenomenology with the objectivist stance of scientific structuralism and somehow basing the synthesis on an ontology more adequate than Sartre's. But the new generation of thinkers, led by Foucault and Derrida, had a far more radical project. They questioned the ideal of ultimate knowledge that defined not only phenomenology and structuralism but the very enterprise of philosophy. This questioning, however, was not based on the poverty of a skeptical denial of knowledge as such. The idea was not merely to undermine the old ideal but to replace it with a new mode of philosophizing, one that did not seek ultimate truth but could claim to be the legitimate successor to the tradition that had.

It was not, accordingly, structuralism that undermined existential phenomenology. The claim that it did was an illusion due to an indefensible reading of structuralism as the final scientific truth that would replace subjectivist phenomenology. Once this pretension collapsed, it would have been entirely feasible to return to Merleau-Ponty's project of synthesizing phenomenological description with structuralist interpretation. That this never happened was due to the post-structuralist questioning of the assumption, shared by phenomenology and structuralism alike, that we could attain deep truths about the human situation. Phenomenology fell not to an external scientific critique but to an internal meta-philosophical revolution, led in quite different ways by Michel Foucault and Jacques Derrida. As we shall see, the differences between Foucault and Derrida mirror the pervasive French division of the positivist and the spiritualist orientations.

Positivist post-structuralism: Michel Foucault

Foucault (1926–84) rejects the standard philosophical project of discovering necessary or essential truths about ourselves and our world in favor of the inverse project of discovering cases in which what are presented as necessary truths about our condition are in fact only contingent products of our historical situation. His writings, therefore, offer not a coherent vision of what we must be but rather a series of histories designed to show how we might be different.

Canguilhem supervised Michel Foucault's doctoral thesis (on the history of madness), and his history of concepts was a model for what Foucault called his "archaeological" histories of knowledge. Foucault's primary focus was the social sciences, and *The Birth of the Clinic* (1963) and much of *The Order of Things* (*Les Mots et les choses*, 1966) can be read as history of concepts, à la Canguilhem.

A good case can be made for thinking of Foucault's attitude toward science as broadly positivist, in the sense defined above of recognizing no cognitive authority beyond that of science. Here a first point to note is that, although both critics and supporters often classify Foucault as an epistemological skeptic or relativist, he never questions the objective validity of mathematics and the natural sciences. He does show how the social sciences (and the medicalized biological sciences) are essentially implicated in social power structures but does not see such implication as automatically destroying the objective validity of a discipline's claims. Sometimes a discipline's role in a power regime is in part due precisely to its objective validity (if, for example, objectivity is a social value). Further, Foucault does not, like the neo-Kantians and even Bachelard, recognize any body of truth achieved by philosophical theorizing. He spins out the occasional philosophical theory (e.g. of language or of power), most often of Nietzschean or Heideggerian inspiration. But this is for the ad hoc purpose of understanding a particular historical phenomenon and has no pretensions to universal validity. The only general epistemic standard to which Foucault holds his own work is that of historical accuracy. If we count history as a broadly scientific enterprise, then Foucault recognizes no knowledge outside the scientific domain and so counts as a positivist.

Unlike mainstream positivists, however, Foucault has little interest in questions about the methodology or ontology of science. This is no doubt because his focus was almost entirely on "dubious" scientific disciplines, such as psychiatry and criminology, or, at best, on the dubious aspects of more respectable disciplines, such as economics and anthropology. Here a discipline is "dubious" to the extent that what it presents as unquestionable objective truths about a certain domain (say, the mad, criminals, or homosexuals) are rather (or also) part of an eminently questionable system of social power. So, for example, Foucault argues in his *Madness and Civilization* (*Folie et déraison*) that the modern conception of madness as "mental illness" is grounded much more in the effort of bourgeois morality to control the mad than in any scientific truth about the nature of madness. Foucault's concern with the cognitive limitations of disciplines implicated in the power network left little room for standard discussions of the positive (methodological and ontological) achievements of science.

On the other hand, Foucault's critical historiography was very fertile in developing new ways of viewing science, ways that would reveal aspects not available to the self-understanding of a discipline. Here his two great innovations were the archaeology and the genealogy of thought. Archaeology is a synchronic technique of unearthing and comparing the deep structures (the epistemic "unconscious") of historical bodies of thought. Foucault's assumption was that there are rules of "discursive formations" (the bodies of discourse that express the scientific and would-be-scientific disciplines), beyond those of grammar and logic. These rules materially constrain the possibilities of what can be said and define a limited conceptual domain in which the thought of a certain period about a given subject matter must operate. Genealogy is a complementary diachronic technique for understanding the emergence of new disciplines and the discursive formations that structure them. Its two main postulates are that systems of knowledge develop in symbiotic relations with systems of social power and that social power consists of a diffuse network of many micro-centers of power, with no centralized, hierarchical structure. As a result, a genealogical history of knowledge avoids unitary teleological narratives of domination (such as Marxism) while still allowing us to question alleged cognitive necessities that mask techniques of disciplinary control.

We can get a more detailed sense of Foucault's approach by looking at his "archaeological" history of the origins of the social sciences in *The Order of Things* and his "genealogical" study of the origins of the modern prison in *Discipline and Punish* (*Surveiller et punir*, 1975).

The Order of Things operates, as Foucault typically does, with a standard chronological division of the Renaissance, the classical age (combining the seventeenth-century "age of reason" and the eighteenth-century Enlightenment) and the modern age, following the French Revolution. Each period, Foucault maintains, has general epistemic structure (its *episteme*) in terms of which the disciplines that are the counterparts of today's human sciences can be understood. He argues that these earlier disciplines (e.g. classical analysis of wealth) are not halting anticipations of the modern human sciences (e.g. economics) but autonomous alternatives for construing human reality.

The Order of Things is the fruit of the archaeological method toward which Foucault was groping in his earlier work on the history of madness and of clinical medicine. Archaeology reveals the conceptual structures that underlie and make possible the entire range of diverse (and often conflicting) concepts, methods, and theories characterizing the thought of a given period. The level of concepts, methods, and theories corresponds to the conscious life of individual subjects. By reading texts to discover not the intentions of their authors but the deep structure of the language itself, Foucault's archaeology goes beneath conscious life to reveal the epistemic "unconscious" that defines and makes possible the knowledge of individuals.

Foucault's archaeologies explore the structural features of knowledge at given times, with no pretension to causal accounts of radical changes in thinking from age to age. With *Discipline and Punish*, he deploys what he calls, with a deliberate allusion to Nietzsche, a "genealogical" method designed to provide such accounts. Genealogy deals with the connection between non-discursive practices and systems of discourse (bodies of knowledge). Foucault argues for an inextricable interrelation of knowledge (discourse) and power (expressed in non-discursive practices, in particular, the control of bodies). He does not have in mind the standard Baconian idea, which sees knowledge as first existing as an autonomous achievement, which is then used as an instrument of action (e.g. pure science vs. technology). Rather, according to Foucault, knowledge simply does not exist in complete independence of power; the deployment of knowledge and the deployment of power are simultaneous from the beginning.

On the other hand, knowledge and power are not simply identical; for example, knowledge is not simply an expression of social or political control. Rather, Foucault maintains that systems of knowledge express objective (and perhaps even universally valid) truth in their own right, but are nonetheless always more or less closely tied to the regimes of power that exist within a given society. Conversely, regimes of power necessarily give rise to bodies of knowledge about the objects they control, and this knowledge may – in its objectivity – go beyond and even ultimately threaten the project of domination that generated the knowledge.

Discipline and Punish analyzes the connections between modern (post-French-Revolution) disciplinary practices and modern social-scientific disciplines. Foucault begins with imprisonment as a way of punishing criminals in relation to criminology and related social scientific disciplines. But he goes on to argue that this case is a paradigm for modern disciplinary practices in general. Schools, factories, the military, etc. are all modeled on the prison, so that we live in what Foucault calls a "carceral archipelago."

Modern disciplinary practices were self-consciously introduced as human transformation of earlier brutality. Foucault agrees that there is a striking difference between the violent and flamboyantly public nature of the pre-modern punishment (drawing and quartering, etc.) and the milder, "low profile" modern punishment of imprisonment. But Foucault's power/knowledge hypothesis suggests that there was more going on than mere humanitarianism, and he makes a strong case that punishment becomes milder not for the sake of mildness but to implement new, more effective, and more extensive forms of control. The point, he says, was not so much to punish less as to punish (and control) better. The elimination of the spectacle of violent punishment was paralleled by the emergence of a society of surreptitious surveillance and control.

Spiritualist post-structuralism: Jacques Derrida

Foucault's post-structuralist critique of philosophy is almost always covert, a subtext implicit in his reconception of the philosophical project. But the thought of Derrida (1930–2004) typically involves an explicit attack on the limitations of traditional philosophy, carried out through his remarkably perceptive and inventive readings of philosophical texts. Derrida's focus is always on the tensions, the ambivalences, the contradictions of writing since, on his view, these are not ultimately just contingent failings of a particular text but revelations of the essential limitations of thought. A written text will always escape total clarification. There will always be textual difficulties that remain unresolvable and prevent us from understanding fully "what the author really means." Nor is this due to limitations merely in the medium of writing as opposed to speech, which, given unbridgeable gaps between interlocutors, likewise excludes perfect understanding. Even when I eliminate the other person and attempt a linguistic formulation of my own thoughts or feelings, the gap between my own experience and language prevents adequate expression. We are forced back to the limit of the pure immediacy of experience's pre-linguistic presence to itself, but, Derrida argues, this is a phantom, since all thought is mediated through language.

The above line of thought is typical of Derrida's repeated demonstrations, in different contexts and terms, that the apparently contingent and remediable defects of writing are in fact inevitable features of all thought, all expression, all reality. Derrida's philosophical project is an unending extrapolation of our inability to master a text. However, although we can never achieve perfect understanding or expression, all thought and language aims at these ideals, which evoke our constant, unavoidable effort to think through hierarchically ordered pairs of opposing concepts. These are the sharp dichotomies, from, for example, hot/cold, through dark/light and male/female, to true/false and being/non-being that characterize what Derrida calls *logocentric* thought – from which, indeed, there is never an escape.

Derrida's readings reveal the dichotomies (binary oppositions) of a text and at the same time show how these divisions collapse as the alleged relations of logical exclusion and hierarchical priority are implicitly undermined by the words deployed to express them. He characterizes such readings, in a term borrowed from Heidegger, as *deconstructions*, not in the sense of destruction through external assault but of careful teasing out of radical instabilities. According to Derrida, the dominant term of a basic dichotomy always expresses a reality that is positive, complete, simple, independent, and fundamental – in short, some form of presence (God, truth, reality, etc.), as opposed to an absence (creatures, falsity, appearance), which is negative, incomplete, complex, dependent, and derivative.

Deconstruction does not exclude positive philosophical efforts, merely the pretension that they will eliminate the root instabilities of thought and language. Such efforts are part of thinking itself, and Derrida himself introduces philosophical vocabularies designed to adumbrate an ontology of dissolving dichotomies and perpetually reversing oppositions. His vocabularies are systematic both in their comprehensive applicability and in their complex interconnections. One of the earliest, most developed, and most important of these vocabularies is that of *différance*.

Différance, a neologism derived from the French verb *différer*, means both *to differ* and *to defer*. *Différance*, accordingly, expresses both the fact that there are irreducible differences between the structure of any phenomenon (a historical event, a text, a personality) and the dichotomies required to think or talk about it; and the consequent fact that efforts to impose the sharp distinction required by binary oppositions must always be "put off" (deferred) in the face of the recalcitrance of the phenomenon. Further, in forming a noun from *différer*, Derrida has introduced a "misspelling": *différance* instead of the standard *différence*. The deviant *a* follows the French pattern for forming verbal nouns (gerunds). As a result, *différance* maintains a pointed ambivalence between an action (a making different) and the state resulting from this action (a difference), suggesting a reality not caught by such standard metaphysical dichotomies as active/passive, event/state, action/passion. Also, the fact that in French there is a written but no spoken difference between *différance* and *différence* evokes Derrida's famous attack on the privileging of speech over writing (with writing considered as a derivative and less reliable expression). In this case, the standard hierarchy is undermined, since writing alone can express the distinction between "*différance*" and "*différence*."

Derrida's use of "*différance*" mimics the technical vocabularies of traditional metaphysics; he speaks, for example, of *différance* underlying the movement of thought and reality, producing differences and then undermining them. But he at the same time insists that *différance* itself is subject to the play of differences; there is no standpoint outside of this play from which we can overlook and master them. We can use "*différance*" to indicate the limitations of our concepts and language. But this new way of speaking neither overcomes these limitations nor eliminates our need to employ the concepts that are subject to them.

The fact that *différance* must always play among the concepts of traditional philosophy – and the freedom involved in this play – suggests the fundamentally spiritualist orientation of Derrida's philosophy. "Spirit," we might say, retains its place through the constant action of deconstructing differences. Despite Derrida's explicit animus toward Sartre, there are deep parallels between *différance* and Sartre's nothingness. Derrida's spiritualist orientation is further apparent in his turn to ethical and religious thought.

Derrida's interest in religion came rather late and is closely tied to his ethical sensibilities. For example, in strong contrast to Kierkegaard, he reads Abraham's sacrifice of Isaac as a case of ethical responsibility, not of the distinction between ethics and religion. According to Kierkegaard, in *Fear and Trembling*, God is the other to whom Abraham has an absolute responsibility, overriding all others. But, for Derrida, this is precisely the situation of any of us when we find ourselves ethically responsible to another person. To accept fully any one responsibility – say to my children – is to be prepared, in principle, to renounce any competing responsibility (say to my job). Derrida seems, therefore, to reject a distinctly religious attitude toward God by refusing to distinguish it from ordinary ethical obligation.

But Derrida's view is more complex, as becomes apparent in his distinction between faith and religion (see Derrida et al. 1997: 15). Faith, as he uses the term, is simply acceptance of the ethical "call" of the other as an absolute responsibility. The object of this acceptance is "merely human" in that it does not posit any entities beyond the human. But, at the same time, this Derridean faith is not directed toward human ethical values as we encounter them in our actual lives. His faith is, rather, directed toward the ethical conceived as the inaccessible limit of any possible human thought or experience. In this sense, Derrida's "ethical" faith is directed toward the divine. This faith contrasts with the "religion" of many believers and institutions, for whom God who is not the non-deconstructible limit of all thought and experience but a being of whom we can know the actions, desires, and commands.

On Derrida's view, religion absolutizes all-too-human categories by *identifying* the other with one particular conceptual formulation, positing a God who is categorical rather than transcendent, a reflection rather than a limit of thought and experience. For Derrida religion in this sense is the ultimate form of idolatry.

The metaphysics of post-structuralism: Deleuze

According to Derrida, difference represents the unsurpassable boundary of thought and, therefore, the inadequacy of traditional philosophizing. Philosophy may still survive as an essential critical or disruptive dimension of our thought, but the grand pretensions of, say, systematic metaphysics must be pronounced dead. Gilles Deleuze (1925–95), however, is deaf to proclamations of the death of philosophy and is even prepared to endorse a sort of systematic metaphysics. He is still a post-structuralist, rejecting the unifying devices of traditional philosophy (subject, object, representation, cause, etc.), and construing philosophical systems not as representations of truth but as creations of new concepts. But, with these post-structuralist modifications, Deleuze continues the tradition of spiritualist metaphysics, particularly, as we shall see, that of Bergson.

Deleuze's thought develops from two fundamental "intuitions," one of being, the other of the thinking that grasps being. The first intuition is that being is radically diverse, the second that, correspondingly, thought is a recognition of ontological diversity, not a reduction to unity. He develops these two intuitions in terms of his notion of *difference*.

The significance of Deleuze's difference is apparent in his radical reformulation of the classical problem of the one and the many, carried out particularly in *Difference and Repetition* (*Différence et répétition*, 1968). This problem arises out of our experience of *different* individuals that are nonetheless examples of the same kind of thing: there are many trees in the forest, many human beings on the earth. How, we naively but also profoundly ask, can many things all be what would seem to be just one thing? Traditionally, metaphysicians have responded by distinguishing between the general structure (form), defined by the essential characteristics of a kind to which individuals belong, and the unstructured stuff (matter) that, when appropriately related to the general structure, becomes a concrete individual of the given kind. Classic metaphysical debates concern the precise ontological status of this form and matter and the precise nature of the relation between the two.

Deleuze rejects the assumption, shared by the participants in these debates, that there must be principles of unity (forms, whatever their ontological status) that constitute the essential nature of concrete realities. According to traditional metaphysics, unifying form is the basis and explanation of all differences. There are differences between kinds because one kind includes forms that another lacks. Within a given kind, differences between individuals arise because the individuals belong to different sub-kinds. In both cases, differentiation (of kinds or of individuals) is entirely due to the unifying forms that determine reality.

Traditional metaphysics, therefore, denies Deleuze's intuition that the fundamental principle of reality (being) is not unity but difference, that to be is not to be one but to be diverse. This denial is not always as straightforward as the (roughly, Leibnizian) metaphysics of forms sketched above. Traditional metaphysics does often recognize the irreducibility of the many (difference) to the one (form) by introducing a special principle corresponding to the many, such as the non-being of Plato's *Sophist* or Aristotle's prime matter. But in traditional metaphysical systems, such principles are always subordinated to the principles of unity, serving merely as unintelligible surds on which forms are somehow impressed.

Deleuze, on the other hand, sets out to develop concepts and language that express his view that "the thing differs with itself," that to be is to be different. Consider, for example, the distinction between difference and repetition. On the standard view, for which the being of concrete realities is understood in terms of forms, two concrete things differ by expressing different forms or they repeat one another by expressing the same form. Difference and repetition are, therefore, exclusive alternatives. Deleuze, however, asks us to think that to repeat is to differ, and not just in the trivial standard sense that every instance (repetition) of a form differs non-essentially from other repetitions of the form (having, for example, a different spatial or temporal location). For Deleuze a repetition is essentially different from what it repeats. This is absurd in terms of our standard understanding, for which to be is to be the same (that is, to be this sort of thing rather than any other). But, given the Deleuzian intuition that to be is to be different, repetition can be only an expression of a being's difference with itself.

Identifying being with difference does not, according to Deleuze, simply reverse the traditional view by giving ontological priority to negation. Deleuzian difference is affirmation not denial, which presupposes something *else* that is negated and so would lead to what Deleuze is trying to avoid: defining difference by its relation to sameness. For Deleuze, difference is what a being is in itself, not how it is related to other things. A being, simply as a being, is a locus of heterogeneity (novelty, creativity). The repetition of a being – for example, its continued existence through time or a new instantiation of it – can only be an expression of this heterogeneity, of this difference.

Deleuze's ontology also requires radical revision of our epistemological conception of what it is to think about beings. The epistemic counterpart of traditional metaphysics is representationalism, which regards knowledge as the accurate reproduction in the mind of the forms defining an entity. Such knowledge is formulated in concepts that express the unity (form) common to many instances. We attain truth by finding concepts that accurately represent the individuals falling under them. Deleuze rejects this representationalist view of concepts because he rejects its assumption that being is defined by structural identities (forms). For Deleuze, a concept is not a meaning (comprehension) under which instances (extension) fall, but a continuum of variations in several dimensions, embracing numerous relations among the varying elements but providing them no overall sense or order.

Deleuze's metaphysics of difference can be read (as he encourages us to do, e.g. in *Bergsonisme*, 1965) as a post-structuralist version of Bergsonian metaphysics, his rejection of representationalism corresponding to Bergson's critique of abstraction and spatialization and his concept of difference a parallel to Bergson's duration. In both cases, Deleuze continues, admittedly by very different means, the spiritualist rejection of science's epistemic hegemony. Similarly, his ethical and political thought (developed in joint works with Félix Guattari, such as *Anti-Oedipus* (*L'Anti-oedipe*, 1972)) develops a radical version of the spiritualist assertion of individual freedom, through a complex psycho-social account of desire understood as individuals' drives to become other than (different from) what they have been.

Phenomenology and ethics: Emmanuel Levinas

One of the many ironies of post-structuralism was that, for all its subordination of subjectivity to unconscious linguistic structures, its own development depended on the force of strong intellectual personalities such as Foucault and Derrida. The death of the author was itself proclaimed by major authors. Correspondingly, post-structuralism declined for lack of new champions as compelling as its originators. From Sartre through Derrida, French philosophy had been driven by major intellectual figures who, although trained in French universities, had thrived primarily outside this system, in the general intellectual culture. After Foucault and Derrida, there was a return to philosophy centered in the universities, just as in the earlier years of the twentieth century. There has been a long vigil for the new master-thinker, with many premature announcements of arrival (Lyotard, Nancy, Badiou ...), but no one attained a cultural status transcending success as a university professor. French philosophy since the 1980s has, as a result, become less creative but more solid, exchanging, we might say, the virtues of the avant-garde for those of the bourgeoisie.

One particularly important development has been a return of French philosophy to themes – and figures – of its phenomenological past. Here the case of Emmanuel Levinas (1906–95) is particularly striking. As early as the 1930s Levinas had an important impact by introducing Husserl (and Heidegger, through whose lens he read Husserl) to France. Through the 1950s, his publications were primarily critical commentaries on Husserl and Heidegger, with his own distinctive philosophy only gradually and partially emerging. In 1961 he published *Totalité et infini* (*Totality and Infinity*) which immediately established him as an important independent thinker, although one scarcely in tune with the developing turn to structuralism. The book is grounded in careful phenomenological descriptions, although it soon becomes apparent that Levinas has come to see Husserl and even Heidegger as implicated in a fundamental mistake that tainted all of western philosophy: the subordination of the Other to the Same.

The "Same" corresponds to the "totality" of Levinas's title: an encompassing whole to which each part entirely owes its intelligibility. In Levinas's jargon, to belong to a totality and thus to be understood solely as part of a whole is to be "reduced to the Same." Reduction to the Same has been the relentless project of western philosophy, which has sought understanding entirely in terms of self-intelligible wholes, such as Platonic Forms, Aristotelian substances, the divine Pure Act of Aquinas, or Hegel's Absolute. Levinas rejects this project with his fundamental claim that no totality truly encompasses all reality, that there is always an Other irreducible to any totality.

The full force of Levinas's position does not, however, emerge until we realize that on the most concrete level the Other is the *other person* as an absolute ethical demand, requiring my unconditional respect and responsibility. The ontological ideal of a totality is overturned by the ethical imperative of the Other. Contrary to the western tradition, ethics not metaphysics is "first philosophy."

Levinas formulates the ethical demand of the Other in the simplest terms: "Do not kill me." This demand is neither a utilitarian threat (e.g. "If you kill me, society will punish you") nor an appeal to a deontological general principle ("Killing is wrong, so don't do it to me"). It is simply an assertion of the inviolability of this person before me, of my absolute responsibility to respect this person's presence. The demand imposes a responsibility that is both infinite and asymmetrical: infinite in that there are no considerations, not even that of my own death, able to limit it; asymmetrical because, unlike Kant's categorical imperative, it does not of itself involve a recip-rocal obligation to me on the part of the Other. Any such obligation must arise from another's own experience of an Other.

Levinas's depiction of the Other in terms of its radical alterity and absolute demands often evokes the language of religion, particularly as it has been deployed by Kierkegaard and others set on opposing the subordination of religious experience to totalizing philosophical conceptions. This is no accident, and in his later writings, especially *De Dieu que vient à l'idée*, 1982 (*Of God Who Comes to Mind*), Levinas is not reluctant to develop the experience of the Other in a religious direction. He does not, however, identify the Other with God since, in his view, this would destroy the utter alterity of the divine. At the same time, our only access to God is through the Other.

Levinas is nearly obsessive in his caution regarding any efforts to speak of God. He is even hesitant to adopt the standard move of negative theology, concerned, presumably, that even to deny an attribute A of God is to suggest that he at least falls within the conceptual domain defined by A and its negation (as, for example, saying God is not blue suggests that he is some other color). In response to this difficulty, Levinas introduces a number of linguistic maneuvers, of which the most effective is his substitution of *à-Dieu* for *Dieu*, with the striking double meaning of "towards (*à*) God" (suggesting that we can never actually reach the divine) and "farewell" (*adieu*) (suggesting both that we are going beyond standard categories and that we encounter God only as he is leaving).

Levinas's philosophical discussions of God are meant to be independent of any particular religious community, despite his own deep commitment to Judaism, expressed in his "confessional texts," which he sharply distinguishes from his philosophical writings. Nonetheless, there is considerable overlap in terminology and ideas between Levinas's philosophical texts and his explicitly Jewish texts, and the two shed considerable light on one another.

Like Levinas, Paul Ricoeur (1913–2005) began as a commentator on German phenomenology and moved beyond that starting point with important works that received their full due only after the turn away from post-structuralism. A devout Protestant who wrote on theological topics such as biblical exegesis, he nonetheless, again like Levinas, has insisted on a strict separation between philosophy and faith, although even strictly as a philosopher, he has taken religious themes and commitments very seriously indeed. His religious orientation was a major reason for the long neglect of his work in France.

Ricoeur's first major enterprise was the application of phenomenology to describe the affective dimension of human existence, particularly volition. *Le Voluntaire et l'involuntaire*, 1960 (*The Voluntary and the Involuntary*) aimed to do for will and feeling what Merleau-Ponty had done for perception. Ricoeur also tried to show how involuntary factors, from the body and its environment through emotion and character, are necessary correlates of voluntary action, thereby effecting an implicit critique of Sartre's radical existentialist view of freedom.

Ricoeur emphasized that a phenomenology, which could present only the essential structure of volition, could not explain the contingent but – especially for a Christian – crucial phenomenon of the evil will. Rather, according to Ricoeur, evil must be understood in hermeneutic terms specifically, through the interpretation of religious and cultural symbols and myths of evil. The hermeneutic turn is required because, given our tendency to hide or deny our evil, efforts directly to confront the phenomenon of evil will always fail. Rather, we must extract from artistic and religious traditions their implicit understanding of evil. More generally, Ricoeur thinks that there is an opaqueness in consciousness that limits all phenomenological projects of self-knowledge and requires the "detour" of hermeneutic interpretation of cultural symbols and myths. Without denying the validity of phenomenology in its limited domain or rejecting the central role of subjectivity in human existence, Ricoeur insists that the philosophical study of human reality needs both phenomenological description and hermeneutic interpretation.

The need to develop a hermeneutics led Ricoeur through many years of second-order discussions of the languages by which we must understand ourselves. (For further discussion of hermeneutics, see "Twentieth-century hermeneutics," Chapter 16.) One such language is that of narrative, of which Ricoeur developed, in *Time and Narrative* (*Temps et récit*, 1983–5), a powerful account that led him, in accord with Aristotle's principle that narrative is an imitation (*mimesis*) of action, back to his original project of explicating the volitional and affective roots of action. In particular, he developed Aristotle's insight by showing how actions can, for analytic purposes, be treated as texts, since agents are distanced from what they do in the same way that authors are distanced from what they write. This tie between action and language also allowed him to integrate his hermeneutic approach with approaches of analytic philosophy such as Searle's speech-act theory and Davidson's action theory. (For more on analytic philosophy of language, see "Philosophy of language," Chapter 9.) Particularly important here is Ricoeur's effort to dissolve the purported dichotomy, often central in analytic discussions, between the causal explanation of actions and the hermeneutic understanding of their meaning. His work on action also naturally led him into the areas of ethics and political theory.

This later work of Ricoeur's eventually brought him back to his phenomenological roots. He stands by his earlier criticisms of phenomenology but contends that they apply only to the foundationalist version of the method that Husserl puts forward, for example, in his *Cartesian Meditations*. It is only the demand that phenomenology provide rigorous foundations for all knowledge, which in turn leads to demands for total self-reflective transparency and apodictic certainty, that is undermined by structuralism and hermeneutics. Hermeneutics, like phenomenology, seeks the meanings implicit in human existence and must acknowledge the phenomenological claim that these meanings are ultimately rooted in subjective consciousness. We need, therefore, only separate the phenomenological search for subject-centered meaning from the Cartesian demand for foundational certainty to realize that "phenomenology remains the unsurpassable presupposition of hermeneutics" (Ricoeur 1995: 34).

Conclusion

Our survey of twentieth-century French philosophy has emphasized the persistence of both the positivist and the spiritualist orientations throughout the century. On the one hand, this history belies the common impression that, from the 1930s on, French thought is dominated by anti-scientific versions of existential phenomenology and of post-structuralism. To the contrary, we have seen the enduring role of concept-based philosophy of science, first in Bachelard and Canguilhem and then continuing, with significant twists, in Foucault. On the other hand, our story also undermines the easy conclusion that, after the 1930s, spiritualism is at best an object of conservative nostalgia. Rather, existentialism and much of post-structuralism should be read as a new (secular and radicalized) variant of the spiritualist defense of individual autonomy.

This dual persistence is a signal feature of French philosophy in contrast to Anglophone philosophy of the twentieth century. Although twentieth-century Anglophone thought begins with similar tensions between acceptance and critique of the cognitive authority of science, the triumph, from the 1950s on, of analytic philosophy effectively ended discussion about the relation of science and philosophy. Mainstream Anglophone philosophers either accepted science as the only knowledge of the world or, if they thought philosophy had independent standing, nevertheless saw its standards of justification as modeled on those of science. Moreover, even within the positivist orientation, Anglophone philosophers of science have been far less reflective than their French counterparts about the relation of philosophy and science. The cognitive dominance of science is simply taken as an unthematized given. Particularly now that Anglophone philosophers of science have abandoned naive positivist views and reached the epistemological sophistication of Bachelard and Canguilhem, they would do well to follow the French philosophers in developing an explicit case for the unique cognitive authority of science.

Apart from highly marginalized enterprises such as neo-Thomism and process philosophy, there has been no Anglophone counterpart to the spiritualist orientation. Late twentieth-century developments in analytic philosophy of mind, ethics, and philosophy of religion suggest, however, that there may be a place in future Anglophone thought for forthright claims of philosophical knowledge inaccessible to science. (Here I am thinking, for example, of moves toward dualism, anti-naturalist ethics, and theism.) I myself have strong reservations about the viability of any such move toward a spiritualist orientation, and I am even more certain that there is no possibility of providing "Continental" solutions to analytic problems. But analytic philosophers seeking inspiration for their own efforts to move beyond the positivist orientation of analytic philosophy would do well to consult the path followed by French philosophers in the twentieth century.

For its own part, French philosophy seems on a path to move beyond the high degree of isolation that characterized its twentieth-century history. The return of French thought to phenomenology as well as a parallel return to neo-Kantian themes in ethics and political philosophy show the continuing strength of the spiritualist orientation into the twenty-first century. The positivist orientation has also renewed itself through late twentieth-century openings to analytic philosophy, particularly philosophy of mind and cognitive science. But both these movements, to the extent that they represent the future of French philosophy, suggest an assimilation to general international trends and may well signal the end of a century of creative philosophical individuality in France. There is and will be much highly competent and interesting work, but French philosophy may be losing its distinctive twentieth-century flamboyance.

Note

1 I have developed the theme of freedom in the concluding chapter of my *French Philosophy in the Twentieth Century*. Much of this chapter consists of condensations and revisions of material in that book.

References

Bachelard, G. (1929) *La Valeur inductive de la relativité*. Paris: Vrin.

_____ (1934) *Le Nouvel Esprit scientifique*. Paris: Alcan. Translated by A. Goldhammer as *The New Scientific Spirit*, Boston: Beacon, 1984. Page references are to this translation.

_____ (1938) *La Psychoanalyse de feu*. Paris: Gallimard. Translated by G. C. Waterston as *The Psychoanalysis of Fire*, New York: Orion, 1969.

Bergson, H. (1889) *Essai sur les données immédiates de la conscience*. In Henri Bergson, *Oeuvres*, Paris: Presses Universitaires de France, 1959. Translated by F. L. Pogson as *Time and Free Will*, London: Sonnenschein, 1910.

_____ (1907) *L'Evolution créatrice*. Repr. in Henri Bergson, *Oeuvres*, Paris: Presses Universitaires de France, 1959. Translated by A. Mitchell as *Creative Evolution*, New York: Modern Library, 1944. Page references are to this translation.

Bergson, H. (1932) *Les Deux Sources de la morale et de la religion*. Repr. in Henri Bergson, *Oeuvres*, Paris: Presses Universitaires de France, 1959. Translated by R. Audra and C. Brereton as *The Two Sources of Morality and Religion*, Notre Dame, IN: University of Notre Dame Press, 1977. Page references are to this translation.

_____ (1896) *Matière et mémoire*. Repr. in Henri Bergson, *Oeuvres*, Paris: Presses Universitaires de France, 1959. Translated by N. M. Paul and W. S. Winter as *Matter and Memory*, New York: Zone Books, 1988.

Blondel, M. (1963) *L'Action*. Paris: Presses Universitaires de France. Translated by O. Blanchette as *Action*, Notre Dame, IN: University of Notre Dame Press, 1984. Page references are to this translation.

Brunschvicg, L. (1912) *Les Étapes de la philosophie mathématique*. Paris: Alcan.

_____ (1922) *L'Experience humaine et la causalité physique*. Paris: Alcan.

_____ (1927) *La Progrès de la conscience dans le philosophie occidentale*. Paris: Presses Universitaires de France.

Deleuze, G. (1965) *Bergsonisme*. Paris: Presses Universitaires de France. Translated by H. Tomlinson and B. Habberjam as *Bergsonism*, New York: Zone Books, 1988.

_____ (1968) *Différence et répétition*. Paris: Presses Universitaires de France. Translated by P. Patton as *Difference and Repetition*, New York: Columbia University Press, 1994.

Deleuze, G. and F. Guattari (1972) *L'Anti-oedipe*. Paris: Minuit. Translated by R. Hurley, M. Seem, and H. Lane as *Anti-Oedipus*, Minneapolis: University of Minnesota Press, 1983.

Derrida, J. (1999) *Donner la mort*. Paris: Galilée. Translated by D. Wills as *The Gift of Death*, Chicago: University of Chicago Press, 1995.

Derrida, J. et al. (1997) "Villanova Roundtable." In J. Caputo (ed.) *Deconstruction in a Nutshell*, New York: Fordham University Press.

Foucault, M. (1966a) *Folie et déraison*. Paris: Gallimard. Translated by R. Howard as *Madness and Civilization: A History of Insanity in the Age of Reason*, New York: Pantheon, 1965.

_____ (1966b) *Les Mots et les choses*. Paris: Gallimard. Translated by A. Sheridan as *The Order of Things: An Archeology of the Human Sciences*, New York: Vintage, 1973.

_____ (1975) *Surveiller et punir*. Paris: Gallimard. Translated by A. Sheridan as *Discipline and Punish*, New York: Pantheon, 1977.

_____ (1997–9) *Essential Works of Foucault, 1954–1984*, 3 vols., ed. P. Rabinow. New York: New Press.

Hyppolite, J. (1971) *Figures de la pensée philosophique*. Paris: Presses Universitaires de France.

Lacroix, J. (1963) *Maurice Blondel*. Paris: Presses Universitaires de France.

Lévinas, E. (1961) *Totalité et infini*. The Hague: Nijhoff. Translated by A. Lingis as *Totality and Infinity*, Pittsburgh, PA: Duquesne University Press, 1969.

_____ (1982) *De Dieu que vient à l'idée*. Paris: Vrin. Translated by B. Bergo as *Of God Who Comes to Mind*, Stanford, CA: Stanford University Press, 1998.

Lévi-Strauss, C. (1962) *La Pensée sauvage*. Paris: Plon. Translated by D. Weightman as *The Savage Mind*, Chicago: University of Chicago Press, 1966.

Marcel, G. (1927) *Journal métaphysique*. Paris: Gallimard. Translated by B. Wall as *Metaphysical Journal*, Chicago: Regnery, 1952.

_____ (1951) *Mystère de l'être*. Paris: Aubier. Translated by R. Hague as *The Mystery of Being*, Chicago: Regnery, 1951.

Merleau-Ponty, M. (1945) *Phénoménologie de la perception*. Paris: Gallimard. Translated by C. Smith as *Phenomenology of Perception*, London: Routledge, 1962. Page references are to this translation.

_____ (1960) *Signes*. Paris: Gallimard. Translated by R. McCleary as *Signs*, Evanston, IL: Northwestern University Press, 1964. Page references are to this translation.

_____ (1964) *Le Visible et l'invisible*, ed. C. Lefort. Paris: Gallimard. Translated by A. Lingis as *The Visible and the Invisible*, Evanston, IL: Northwestern University Press, 1964.

Ricoeur, P. (1960–3) *Philosophie de la volonté*, 3 vols.: *Le Volontaire et l'involuntaire*, *L'Homme fallible*, and *La Symbolique du mal*. Paris: Aubier. Translated by E. V. Kohák as *Freedom and Nature: The Voluntary and the Involuntary*, Evanston, IL: Northwestern University Press, 1966; by C. A. Kelbley as *Fallible Man*, Chicago: Regnery, 1965; by E. Buchanan as *The Symbolism of Evil*, New York: Harper & Row, 1967.

_____ (1983–5) *Temps et récit*, 3 vols. Paris: Éditions du Seuil. Translated by K. McLaughlin and D. Pellauer as *Time and Narrative*, 3 vols., Chicago: University of Chicago Press, 1984–8.

_____ (1995) "Intellectual biography." In L. Hahn (ed.) *The Philosophy of Paul Ricoeur*, La Salle, IL: Open Court.

Sartre, J.-P. (1943) *L'Être et le néant*. Paris: Gallimard. Translated by H. Barnes as *Being and Nothingness*, New York: Washington Square Press, 1956.

_____ (1960) *Critique de la raison dialectique*, vol. I. Paris: Gallimard. Translated by A. Sheridan-Smith as *Critique of Dialectical Reason*, vol. I, London: New Left Books, 1976.

Wahl, J. (1932) *Vers le concret*. Paris: Vrin.

Further reading

General histories

Gutting, G. (2001) *French Philosophy in the Twentieth Century*. Cambridge: Cambridge University Press. (A comprehensive and detailed history in English).

Matthews, E. (1996) *Twentieth-Century French Philosophy*. Oxford: Oxford University Press. (A lucid and judicious discussion of major figures).

Bachelard

Tiles, M. (1984) *Bachelard: Science and Objectivity*. Cambridge: Cambridge University Press. (A helpful analysis of some of Bachelard's main ideas on science and mathematics).

Bergson

Lacey, A. R. (1989) *Bergson*. London: Routledge. (A close analysis of some of Bergson's major lines of argument, especially helpful for those coming from an analytic perspective).

Kolakowski, L. (1985) *Bergson*. Oxford: Oxford University Press. (An excellent brief and lucid introduction).

Deleuze

Hardt, M. (1993) *Gilles Deleuze: An Apprenticeship in Philosophy*. Minneapolis: University of Minnesota Press. (A helpful discussion of Deleuze's writings on major modern philosophers).

May, T. (2005) *Gilles Deleuze: A General Introduction*. Cambridge: Cambridge University Press. (A very lucid and perceptive introduction to Deleuze).

Derrida

Caputo, J. (ed.) (1997) *Deconstruction in a Nutshell*. New York: Fordham University Press. (Extremely helpful commentary combined with accessible discussions with Derrida).

Howells, C. (1999) *Derrida: Deconstruction from Phenomenology to Ethics*. Cambridge: Polity Press. (A clear and comprehensive introduction).

Norris, C. (1988) *Derrida*. Cambridge, MA: Harvard University Press. (A good discussion of Derrida's earlier writings).

Foucault

Gutting, G. (1989) *Michel Foucault's Archaeology of Scientific Reason*. Cambridge: Cambridge University Press. (Close explications of Foucault's major books of the 1960s, with particular attention to his relation to Bachelard and Canguilhem).

_____ (2005) *Foucault: A Very Short Introduction*. Oxford: Oxford University Press. (An essay for the general reader that approaches Foucault's thought from a variety of disciplinary perspectives).

McNay, L. (1994) *Foucault: A Critical Introduction*. New York: Continuum. (A clear and helpful general introduction).

Levinas

Bernasconi, R. and S. Critchley (eds.) (2002) *The Cambridge Companion to Levinas*. New York: Cambridge University Press. (An excellent collection of articles by major interpreters of Levinas).

Davis, C. (1991) *Levinas: An Introduction*. Notre Dame, IN: University of Notre Dame Press. (A well-organized and clearly written general introduction).

Peperzak, A. (1993) *To the Other*. West Lafayette, IN: Purdue University Press. (A thorough and perceptive scholarly examination of Levinas's thought).

Marcel

Schilpp, P. and L. Hahn (eds.) *The Philosophy of Gabriel Marcel*. Library of Living Philosophers, La Salle, IL: Open Court. (A large collection of articles about Marcel, along with his autobiographical essay and responses to the articles).

Merleau-Ponty

Carman, T. and M. B. N. Hanson (eds.) (2004) *The Cambridge Companion to Merleau-Ponty*. New York: Cambridge University Press. (A comprehensive set of essays by leading authorities on Merleau-Ponty).

Poincaré

Zahar, E. (2001) *Poincaré's Philosophy: From Conventionalism to Phenomenology*. La Salle, IL: Open Court. (Discusses Poincaré's philosophy of science both in its historical development and in its systematic structure).

Ricoeur

Kearney, R. (2004) *Paul Ricoeur: The Owl of Minerva*. London: Ashgate. (An authoritative exposition by one of the most knowledgeable commentators on Ricoeur).

Regan, C. (1996) *Paul Ricoeur: His Life and Work*. Chicago: University of Chicago Press. (A survey of both Ricoeur's life and his writings).

Part V

POLITICS, ETHICS, AND AESTHETICS

20

TWENTIETH-CENTURY MORAL PHILOSOPHY

Rowland Stout

Introduction

Despite being somewhat long in the tooth at the time, the giants of twentieth-century moral philosophy were Aristotle (384–322 BC), Hume (1711–76), and Kant (1724–1804). Much of the progress made in that century comes down to a detailed working through of each of their approaches by the expanding and increasingly professionalized corps of academic philosophers. And this progress can be measured not just by the quality and sophistication of moral philosophy at the end of that century, but also by the narrowing of some of the gaps between Aristotelian, Humean, and Kantian philosophers.

The more significant legacies from the nineteenth century were utilitarianism represented by Bentham (1748–1832) and Mill (1806–73), and by contrast the nihilism of Nietzsche (1844–1900). The hold that utilitarianism had over the discourse remained practically undiminished across the twentieth century despite the numerous attempted refutations. And coming from a completely different philosophical perspective Nietzsche had generated an intoxicating mixture of skepticism, mysticism, and the promise of freedom from conventional morality.

All this was worked through the great twentieth-century philosophical movements such as positivism, linguistic philosophy, and existentialism (see "The development of analytic philosophy: Wittgenstein and after," Chapter 2 and "French philosophy in the twentieth century," Chapter 19). And in subtler ways the great cultural shifts of the twentieth century left their mark. What became described as agent-centered morality reflected the reaction to the various threats of industrial mechanization, self-righteous genocide, totalitarian politics, and paternalism. And in addition to the abiding interest in the role of ethics in politics and law, moral philosophy developed a concern with the role of ethics in medicine, business, and our relationship with the environment.

The big questions that concerned twentieth-century moral philosophers were largely inherited from previous ages. Very roughly they fell into five categories: (1) the conceptual: how we should understand ethical language; (2) the metaphysical:

whether ethical value is real; (3) the epistemological: how moral judgments are grounded or justified; (4) the moral psychological: how morality is related to the will; and (5) the normative: what, if any, are the proper structuring principles of an ethical system. I will deal with these roughly in turn, but I will not try too hard to squeeze every aspect of twentieth-century moral philosophy into a particular category. Most work in ethics has addressed several of these questions simultaneously.

That there was any answer to the conceptual question of what "good" *means* was challenged early on by G. E. Moore's attack on the naturalistic fallacy. This was supposed to be the fallacy of providing a definition of the evaluative word, "good," in non-evaluative terms. This did not stop a series of "naturalistic" attempts to answer the question (though not always in terms of a definition), from John Dewey (1859–1952) and Ralph Barton Perry (1876–1957) in the early part of the century through to the Cornell Realists and Frank Jackson (1943–) right at the end of it.

More significant perhaps was the discovery by so-called "non-cognitivist" philosophers such as Charles Stevenson (1908–79) and Richard Hare (1919–2002) that an account of the expressive significance of moral language might be attempted while denying that moral terms had any descriptive meaning as such. The non-cognitivists were following up David Hume's famous dictum that morality was not derived from reason alone, arguing instead that it was merely an expression of individual or social attitudes. Expressing these attitudes was seen to be distinct from describing them. Just as, for example, frowning may be an expression of disapproval but not a description of disapproval, so it was claimed moral utterances were merely expressions and not descriptions.

The metaphysical questions about the reality of moral values and the factuality of moral claims rumbled on throughout the century. Non-cognitivists generally argued that there were no moral facts corresponding to ethical judgments. But then so did some cognitivists such as Gilbert Harman (1938–), who thought that moral judgments were derived from reason but just never objectively true. With advances in the philosophy of language the issue became subtler. Moral realists did not after all have to be committed to some Platonic realm in which moral values dwelled or to the existence of natural or unnatural properties in virtue of which moral claims had objective truth. They just needed to argue that the norms for the correctness of moral judgments were in some cases not dependent on the attitudes of the individual or of their cultural community.

Intuitionism was one way to answer the epistemological question for realist philosophers who had rejected a naturalistic answer to the conceptual question. They claimed that we know the answers to moral questions directly and not through a process of inference. This view, which may have started off looking horribly like hand-waving, has turned out to have a real force as it developed through the work of G. E. Moore (1873–1958), H. A. Prichard (1871–1947), W. D. Ross (1877–1971), and later philosophers such as Jonathan Dancy (1946–) and Robert Audi (1941–).

This kind of intuitionism was often associated with an Aristotelian approach to moral psychology in which moral judgments, rationality, *emotions* and action are related to one another. The Oxford philosophers Iris Murdoch (1919–99) and John

McDowell (1942–) were particularly influential in developing this *sensibility* approach to ethics, although the role of emotions in ethical thinking had been examined much earlier in the century by Continental philosophers, Max Scheler (1874–1928) among them.

The alternative, developed by Kantian philosophers such as Stephen Toulmin (1922–) and Alan Gewirth (1912–2004) was to say that we know the answers to moral questions through a process of reasoning. The central issue in moral psychology for such Kantians is the relationship between moral judgment, rationality, and action, with emotional attitudes having less significance.

With the fifth of these big questions – normative ethics – there was no agreement about whether the abstract discipline of philosophy could really say anything useful. The rather tired distinction between consequentialist and deontological approaches remained stubbornly in play throughout the century. Consequentialism was the view that the rightness or wrongness of an action should be determined by the goodness or badness of its consequences or expected consequences. Utilitarianism was the classic example of a consequentialist approach. Deontology, represented paradigmatically by Kantian ethics, was the view that the rightness or wrongness of an action should be determined by whether or not the action conformed to proper principles of morality – principles which made explicit the duties of the agent.

In some taxonomies virtue theory was added to this pair. According to virtue theory, represented by Philippa Foot (1978) and Michael Slote (1992) among other philosophers, it was important to consider the qualities of the agent in assessing the rightness or wrongness of their actions. This Aristotelian approach to ethics was usually associated with the so-called "particularist" view that there were no true universal principles that could determine the rightness or wrongness of an action. Having a properly virtuous character, and thus having a properly attuned moral sensibility, meant that one was sensitive to the moral considerations that applied in a situation in its infinite particularity. Any general principle would be bound to ignore important moral distinctions. In continental Europe this particularist approach was developed by philosophers in the phenomenological tradition, including Martin Buber (1878–1965) and Emmanuel Levinas (1906–95) (for more on Levinas, see "French philosophy in the twentieth century," Chapter 19).

Moore's challenge

The century began more or less with G. E. Moore's (1903) broadside on Mill and others whom Moore accused of trying to derive an understanding of what was good from a basic definition of "good" in morally neutral terms. In other words Moore was rejecting a reductionist analysis of "good."

Moore distinguished what we would now call extensional and intensional definitions of "good." He took it to be a useful task of philosophical ethics to spell out the extension of the predicate – to determine the set of all things that are good. And it was also a useful task to *characterize* this extension in various illuminating ways – to provide a sort of taxonomy of goodness. But he took it to be an error to try to *define* the predicate intensionally – i.e. to try to capture its *meaning* – in terms of other predicates. In particular it would be a mistake – and this is what he called the "naturalistic fallacy" – to do an extensional analysis and then think that one had captured the meaning or intension of the predicate. This would be like observing that all yellow things reflected light of a certain frequency range and then to conclude that the meaning of the word "yellow" was "reflects light in such and such a frequency range."

If the meaning of the term "yellow" were given by this sort of characterization of its extension then the claim that yellow things reflect light in such and such a frequency range would be empty and pointless, since it would just mean that things that reflect light in such and such a frequency range reflect light in such and such a frequency range. And the same goes for an attempt to define "good" as "desired" or as "involving pleasure" for instance. To say that things that are desired are good would be to say nothing significant if it were just a statement of a definition of the term "good."

Moore proposed a test – the open question argument – for whether a statement might count as providing the meaning (intension) of a predicate. If some statement just tells us what we mean by the term then that statement is not open to further questioning. Suppose I ask whether vixens are foxes, and I am told that it is part of what we mean by the word "vixen" that it is a female fox. If that is the right answer then this closes off the question; no further discussion is needed. But if I ask whether good things are things that give people pleasure, the question remains open however much I know the meaning of the word "good." So it cannot be part of the meaning of the word "good" that good things give people pleasure.

This test has to be applied with great care, however, since meaning itself is not always completely transparent. It may seem to be an open question just what some word means even when one can use the word reasonably well in most contexts.

An extension of Moore's open question argument that was applied by various philosophers through the course of the century depended on accepting David Hume's internalism: his claim that motivation is internal to moral judgment. You cannot truly judge something to be right or good without thereby having some motivation to act or feel accordingly. If that is right there should be no room for the following version of an open question: "I can see that this is good, but why should I care?" And likewise, for any attempted analysis, A, of "good," there should be no room for the question: "I can see that this is A; but why should I care?" For example, in response to an analysis of good in terms of conventional acceptance I might say: "I can see that obeying the law is conventionally accepted, but why should I care about that?" To the extent that the question makes sense the putative analysis fails.

The diagnosis of the naturalistic fallacy has been ridiculed in approximate proportion to how enormously influential it has been.[1] It is common to say that the naturalistic fallacy is neither naturalistic nor a fallacy. To say it is not a fallacy is to say there is no mistake made in confusing extensional and intensional definitions. And saying this might be justified by accepting Quine's (1951) attempted demolition of the analytic/synthetic distinction. But I think that would be an anachronism. Moore was writing at the heyday of the analytic/synthetic distinction, and he was criticizing attempts to provide *analyses* of our moral concepts, although the extent to which such criticism hit the mark with Mill is questionable. And Moore's claim that although such accounts have said useful things about the extension of the predicate "good," they failed to provide analyses of meaning, fits happily with Quine's rejection of the notion of analytic truth. Quine was rejecting the idea of providing analyses generally; Moore was rejecting the idea of providing an analysis of "good."

Naturalistic ethics

Certainly, however, it may seem odd to call the fallacy "naturalistic." But Moore recognized that the fallacy could also apply to non-naturalistic definitions. The fallacy was not just to posit a definition of "good." It was to treat an extensional account as if it were an intensional account. And Moore just took it for granted that extensional accounts would usually be in naturalistic terms, though he did also think that a non-naturalistic Kantian account might involve the same fallacy. The reason for calling the fallacy naturalistic was that, according to Moore, any naturalistic account of "good" must be extensional rather than intensional; and so a naturalistic intensional analysis would automatically be fallacious. This was because "good" was a non-natural term and so any intensional analysis of "good" must also be non-naturalistic.[2]

Roughly speaking, a natural quality was taken to be a quality that is either present in ordinary experience or is the sort of quality that science deals with. It would have been common ground that goodness was neither of these. With the sustained attack on the fact/value distinction, made especially by the sensibility theorists of the second half of the century, the natural/non-natural distinction would seem less clear. It was no longer so clear that goodness could not figure in ordinary experience. But as with the rejection of the analytic/synthetic distinction, this would do no harm to Moore's argument. For Moore was aiming his argument at those who took goodness to be definable in what they took to be naturalistic terms – thus naturalizing the non-natural.

The sorts of things that might count as naturalistic sources for our moral concepts are individual preferences, individual feelings of desire, enjoyment, pleasure, etc., individual emotions, individual judgments of approbation, individual acts or dispositions of will, social agreements and rules, and cultures of praise and blame. But many naturalistic accounts of ethics did not attempt to *define* moral terms in such naturalistic terms. Generally, in the spirit of Aristotle, they sought to *ground* our use of moral language in naturalistic terms, not by reducing the moral to the natural but by anchoring the moral to the natural. So Aristotle himself, who took a virtuous character to be one that fulfilled human nature, certainly did not take virtue to be reducible to human nature.

And one of the twentieth century's most influential naturalists, John Dewey, argued that value is connected with experiences of enjoyment, but only in the sense that these experiences provide the material that is elaborated in the process of rational discourse to construct value (on Dewey, see "American philosophy in the twentieth century," Chapter 5).[3] He argued that morality should not float free of human experience as it did in what he took to be the empty rationalism of Kant. But he was just as concerned to avoid the sensationalist approach which identified morality with human experience and so left it useless as a means for providing direction to conduct.

Very much in the spirit of both Aristotle and Hume he claimed that the formation of taste is the chief matter wherever values enter in. "The formation of a cultivated and effectively operative good judgement or taste with respect to what is aesthetically admired, intellectually acceptable and morally approvable is the supreme task set to humans by the incidents of experience" (1929: 209).

Dewey took the experimental method that is acknowledged as the way to arrive at scientific truth to be the way to arrive at moral truth. Moral rules and principles were hypotheses to be tested in the imagination and in practice. Only by trying out particular moral stances and adapting and refining them in response to their success or failure at guiding in a clear and settled way could these stances be validated. This was an early example of what became known in moral philosophy following John Rawls (1951 and 1971) as the method of reflective equilibrium.

Indeed the practice of interacting with situations in order to test moral hypotheses for stability and clarity not only determines the correctness of these hypotheses; it also *constructs* the correctness of these hypotheses, according to Dewey. A situation does not come to us with a solution that we are initially too puzzled to find. By interacting with the situation we make it morally determinate. We invest it with rightness and wrongness.

This might be taken in a weaker or stronger way. The weaker way to understand it would be to observe that a moral situation is not just a blankly external state of affairs. It is a set of questions and problems, which depend essentially on how the state of affairs is conceptualized and interacted with. By engaging imaginatively with a moral situation we can describe it in terms of alternative possible courses of action. There is no canonical description of a state of affairs that fixes the moral issues and dilemmas. So in this sense we might be said to construct the goodness in a situation.

The stronger sense would take the moral truth of a situation to be a function of what we do with it in our process of rational interaction with it. Something has value if it is associated with the feeling of enjoyment at the end of the rational process of experimentation guided by the goal of "cultivated and effectively operative good judgement and taste." When you have interacted with a situation in the designated way and as a result object X is judged to have value, then that is what it is for object X to have value.

This stronger – anti-realist – sense of the idea of the *construction* of good might be vulnerable to Moore's naturalistic fallacy argument. Moore would pose the open question: is the thing that emerges with a judgment of value from such a process really good? And if this is genuinely an open question, then the notion of goodness is not captured by this definition. But it is by no means clear that this anti-realism is the right claim to pin on Dewey. He was usually very cautious about making such a strong claim. And if he was not making any attempt to define "good" in his notion of the construction of good, then he was not vulnerable to Moore's naturalistic fallacy argument.

Perhaps the very fact that there are so few twentieth-century approaches to moral philosophy that can be properly criticized as committing the naturalistic fallacy should be taken to be a testament to the influence of Moore's argument rather than, as it is often taken, an indication of its irrelevance. The naturalistic definition of color that Moore took to reveal more clearly the absurdity of naturalistic definitions of non-natural terms has turned out to have many more adherents than naturalistic definitions of goodness. And this is presumably because philosophers of color did not feel they had Moore breathing down their necks.

One approach which was often taken to be subject to Moore's attack at the time was that of the Finnish social anthropologist, Edvard Alexander Westermarck (1862–1939) in his *The Origin and Development of Moral Ideas* (1906–8). This was a sociological, psychological, and evolutionary approach, and Westermarck was not really a philosopher; so he was an easy target. Westermarck defined the wrongness of an action in terms of an individual's inclination to disapprove of it and sometimes too of a tendency across society to disapprove of it. Moore's argument presents this account with the question of whether it is wrong to do something that you (or society) are inclined to disapprove of. If this question is genuinely an open question – one whose answer does not just fall out of the meanings of the terms – then it cannot be the meaning of something's being wrong that you or society are inclined to disapprove of it.

Another naturalistic approach to ethics that might fall under the terms of Moore's naturalistic fallacy was that of R. B. Perry (1926). Like Dewey, he was influenced by pragmatism, in particular by William James, but, also by behaviorism. And in the iconoclastic spirit of early behaviorism he was much less cautious about making reductionist claims. He defined value as follows: "Any object, whatever it be, acquires value when any interest whatever it be, is taken in it; just as anything whatsoever becomes a target when anyone whatsoever aims at it" (section 49).

In a manner reminiscent of Mill's apparent confusion of desired and desirable, Perry identified having value with being valued rather than with being valuable, and then assimilated being valuable to that. It is precisely this sort of account that Moore was targeting. It is an open question whether there is any value in some thing or activity that a particular person is interested in. It is not an open question whether such a thing is valued.

But perhaps Perry could have conceded that at this stage of the story he was talking about something having value only in the sense of its being valued. The notion of right behavior comes later when considering "overall value." Overall value is determined by a harmony of interests. Like Dewey he considered the process of reflective agreement to determine ultimate value. And like Dewey, if this is taken to be the idea that ultimate value is a function of the process of reflective agreement, then he was vulnerable after all to Moore's naturalistic fallacy argument.

Certainly the development of this kind of approach into what became known as Ideal Observer theory seems to be so vulnerable. Roderick Firth (1917–87) defended this sort of analysis, which construes "statements of the form '*x* is P,' in which P is some particular ethical predicate, to be identical in meaning with statements of the form: 'Any ideal observer would react to *x* in such and such a way under such and such conditions' " (Firth 1952). An ideal observer is omniscient, dispassionate, disinterested, and consistent (though in other ways perfectly normal!).

If the ideal observer and the appropriate conditions for the ideal observer can be characterized in naturalistic terms, then we have here a straightforwardly naturalistic definition of ethical terms. And Moore's open question argument can be applied here. "An omniscient, dispassionate … observer would react positively to this; but is it good?"

The reason that question seems open is that it seems to be possible to make the judgment about the reactions of an ideal observer without being thereby committed to have the same reactions oneself. "Why should I care how an ideal observer would react when determining how I should react? If an angel would judge that this is what should be done in this situation, I might still demur and say that I don't care what an angel would judge; it is not how I judge I should behave."

A similar account to Firth's was defended by Richard Brandt (1910–97) in *Ethical Theory* (1959). He thought that ethical terms usually corresponded to some particular sort of attitude. "Desirable" corresponds to desire, "blameworthy" corresponds to blame, "hateful" corresponds to hate, "right" corresponds to approval of the action, etc. So generally an ethical predicate means something like "worthy of such and such an attitude." As a definition this is naturalistic only in the innocuous sense that Dewey and Aristotle were naturalists: namely that ethical terms are anchored in natural aspects of our condition. But it does not represent any sort of reductive definition, since the word "worthy" is thoroughly ethical. So the open question argument cannot apply yet, as it makes no sense to ask why you should admire something that is worthy of admiration.

But then Brandt developed this in terms of a definition that has just enough substantial content to be subject to Moore's argument. It is as follows:

> The quasi-naturalist definition proposes that "x is E" (where E is some ethical term) means the same as "The E-corresponding attitude … to x satisfies all the conditions that would be set, as a general policy, for the endorsement of attitudes governing or appraising choices or actions, by anyone who was intelligent and factually informed and had thought through the problems of the possible different general policies for the endorsement of such attitudes." (1959: 265–6)

Brandt had a view about what sort of method such an intelligent and factually informed person would adopt. He called it the Qualified Attitude method and it amounts to something quite similar to what Firth required of the Ideal Observer. But mindful of Moore's challenge, Brandt did not include it in his definition of ethical predicates. Still, what he did include is far from trivial. And it is certainly open to someone who is not particularly intelligent (whatever that is) or well informed to ask why they should approve of something just because it meets some condition laid down by someone who is.

Gilbert Harman's picture of ethics, developed for example in his 1977 textbook, *Morality*, is subject to the same sort of worry. The picture is explicitly relativistic.

> For the purposes of assigning truth conditions, a judgement of the form, it would be morally wrong of P to D, has to be understood as elliptical for a judgement of the form, in relation to moral framework M, it would be morally wrong of P to D. Similarly for other moral judgements. (1977: 17)

This certainly does not look like a naturalistic definition of "morally wrong," not least because the phrase "morally wrong" figures on both sides of the explanation. But the problem arises when what it would be for something to be wrong in a moral framework is understood, as Harman does understand it, as a claim about the attitudes and conventions of that moral framework. Something is taken to be wrong in a moral framework if an ideal reasoner adopting the conventions and basic attitudes of the moral framework would judge it to be wrong. Yet it seems a perfectly good open question to say: "I know that an ideal reasoner adopting my moral framework would judge this to be wrong, but is it really wrong?" To put it even more bluntly, a relativistic account like Harman's may be criticized because there is always an open question about whether one's own moral framework is the right moral framework. And this question should be closed off according to his relativism.

In response to Harman among others there sprang up in the last couple of decades of the century a group of moral realist philosophers often called Cornell Realists. These included Richard Boyd and Nicholas Sturgeon.[4] Their view was that moral properties were natural kinds. Saying that something is good is like describing an animal as healthy. They claimed that although it is not possible to provide an intensional definition, we can point to paradigms of good things or healthy things and conceive of the whole extension of the term as a natural extension of these cases. A similar suggestion was made later by Frank Jackson (1998) who argued that something is right if and only if it has whatever property plays the rightness role in mature folk psychology, and that this property will turn out to be expressed by an infinite disjunction of descriptive predicates.

For Boyd, a moral term is associated with a cluster of mutually supporting natural properties: a "homeostatic" cluster. Because the extension of the term is partly determined by this natural and causal idea of mutually supporting properties there is no objection in principle to moral properties being causally significant, and therefore real. According to Sturgeon the best explanation for someone's judging that something is bad is that that thing is bad. Alternatively, the best explanation for someone acting in a certain way might be that he or she is a good person. And this is what is required for realism.

The open question argument does challenge this approach in proportion to the degree to which the approach spells out what makes it the case that some natural cluster of properties is associated with a moral term. The open question here is: "Why should I care about whether some action, situation, or person belongs to such a cluster when deciding how to act? I can see that this thing belongs to such a cluster but is it really good?"

One response on behalf of the Cornell Realists is to appeal to the idea that the cluster of natural properties associated with a moral term is determined partly by a process of critical reflection – a process that precisely matches the process an individual must go through to work out what to do, how to be, or what state to value. Like Dewey, these realists believe that there is continuity between scientific method and ethical method. In both cases we look for explanations of our experiences in hypotheses about how things are. And in both cases we test these hypotheses by considering new and untried situations. The real challenge then is to explain how what makes a set of natural properties cluster together in a self-supporting way coincides with the results of rational ethical reflection.

Non-cognitivism

Those philosophers inclined towards a strongly naturalistic approach but finding it unsustainable, perhaps because they accepted Hume's internalism, found what they were looking for when in 1923 C. K. Ogden (1889–1957) and I. A. Richards (1893–1979) introduced the idea of emotivism. Ogden and Richards were linguistic philosophers concerned with how language works, how it sometimes symbolizes things and sometimes merely appears to symbolize things. In their book on language called *The Meaning of Meaning*, there is one paragraph on ethical language (1923: 125):

> The peculiar ethical use of "good" is, we suggest, a purely emotive one. When so used the word stands for nothing whatever, and has no symbolic function. Thus, when we use it in the sentence, "*This* is good," we merely refer to *this*, and the addition of "is good" makes no difference whatever to our reference. When on the other hand, we say, "*This* is red," the addition of "is red" to "this" does symbolize an extension of our reference, namely, to some other red thing. But "is good" has no *comparable* symbolic function; it serves only as an emotive sign expressing our attitude to *this*, and perhaps similar attitudes in other persons, or inciting them to action of one kind or another.

This idea chimed with the American pragmatists' principle that the meaning of words was a function of how they were used and their rejection of the realist principle that this must always be understood in terms of how this use of words was related to some independently existing reality. The idea also coincided with the development and influence of logical positivism. Assuming that ethical language could not meet the conditions of properly scientific discourse, the hard-line positivist conclusion was that it was meaningless. But the positivists, especially the so-called Left Vienna School, were ethical thinkers like everyone else, and some significance had to be found for such thinking. The linguistic analysis of Ogden and Richards suggested what this significance might be. The function of ethical language was to express attitudes and persuade or incite people to act, but not to describe anything.

In other words the significance of moral judgments was *non-cognitive*. A moral judgment was not taken to be the application of a shared concept to a situation by the application of perception and reason. So the normal categories of truth and falsity were taken not to apply to moral judgments. Instead a moral judgment was taken to be the *expression* of a personal or interpersonal attitude, emotion, instruction, or norm. As such it might be described as authentic or inauthentic, but not as true or false.

A. J. Ayer (1910–89) developed this idea in *Language, Truth and Logic* (1936), and Charles Stevenson did so the following year. Stevenson wrote: "Doubtless there is always some element of description in ethical judgements, but this is by no means all. Their major use is not to indicate facts, but to *create an influence*" (1937: 18). C. D. Broad (1934) described it as the "interjectional" theory. To say, "That act of self-sacrifice is good," is to say something that functions precisely like "That is an act of self-sacrifice. Hurrah!" To say, "That deliberately misleading statement is bad," is to say something that functions precisely like "That is a deliberately misleading statement. Blast!"

Non-cognitivism is a way of responding to Moore's open question argument. In fact Darwall et al. (1992: 118) have described it as "the real historical beneficiary" of that argument. There are two possible reasons for this. On the one hand, there is no possibility of accusing non-cognitivists of making the naturalistic fallacy, since they are denying that moral terms have intensions in the normal sense. Moral terms do not correspond with concepts that may be applied correctly or incorrectly to situations. So non-cognitivists are certainly not illegitimately defining moral concepts in terms of their extensions. Also the more general internalist worry with naturalistic accounts does not apply to non-cognitivists. There is no room for someone to say: "This is an action of giving money to charity – Hurrah! But so what?" Expressing the positive attitude to that action commits the speaker to accepting that the action is right – that they should do it.

However there is room for some sort of open question argument at an *interpersonal* level for a non-cognitivist. Suppose person A says to person B, "You should not smoke in this compartment." Person B may reply: "I understand what you are saying – and see that you are expressing your disapproval of my smoking in this compartment, but why has that got any relevance to me? It is still an open question for me whether or not I should smoke."

The problem for non-cognitivism is that when someone tells me what I should not do and I think I should do it I am disagreeing with her. But according to non-cognitivism I am merely not complying with her instruction or attitude. The basis of someone's instruction to me or attitude about what I am to do is not automatically a basis for me to give myself the instruction or have the attitude, and so act in that way. And yet if I accept someone's reasons for judging that I should not smoke in this compartment, it seems that I can't deny that I have a reason for not smoking.

This is just to say that non-cognitivism, by eschewing objectivity, gives an account of moral judgments that falls short of what we might have thought was required by our actual practice of moral discourse. During the second half of the century non-cognitivism developed by putting back as much objectivity into the story as was possible while denying that moral judgments were simply descriptions of how things were. But however close to objectivity non-cognitivism came it never dealt with the problem of the interpersonal open question argument. For a non-cognitivist one person's moral judgment being correct and appropriate provides no reason for another person to accept it; and this consequence just has to be swallowed.

So Richard Hare, in his *Language of Morals* (1952), argued for something he called "universal prescriptivism." One minor departure from his emotivist predecessors was his insistence that the core function of moral judgments was to command or prescribe. He was less interested in the larger range of attitudes and feelings that they had taken to be expressed in moral discourse.

More significant was his introduction of universalizability to provide something like a descriptive element to his non-cognitivism. The idea was that the function of the moral assertion "You should not smoke in this compartment," was the same as that of the instruction "Do not smoke in this compartment!" But there was one extra aspect to the moral prescription, namely its universalizability. The latter does not commit you to the claim, "Do not smoke in any compartment exactly like this one in all morally relevant respects!" whereas the former does. Unlike mere instructions, the prescriptions expressed by moral assertions must be universalizable in that they commit one to the equivalent prescription in morally similar situations.

Hare's theory generated a huge amount of argument. One problem was with the status of the universalizability requirement. It appears in the theory as a merely logical condition of a prescription *counting* as a moral prescription. But universalizability appears to be a substantive moral requirement of our moral discourse not a merely logical condition of that discourse counting as moral. A related problem was with the correct characterization of universalizability and in particular with the notion of morally relevant properties. It seems to be a notion that can only be charac-terized through moral reflection, which would threaten Hare's account with a sort of circularity.

A further difficulty raised by Peter Geach (1958) is that the expressivist approach seems to break down when the moral part of a judgment is logically embedded in a larger judgment. We might accept that "Stealing is wrong," is functionally equivalent to "Stealing – Blast!" But what about saying, "If stealing is wrong then taxation is immoral." It seems to make no sense to identify this with, "If stealing – blast, then taxation – blast." The "if then" structure does not operate on expressions of attitudes but only on descriptive components that have truth values.

One way to respond to the Geach problem would be to say that in this sort of context, the use of "if … then" is itself expressive. It expresses a commitment or an attitude of approval towards a certain transition of attitudes – the transition from disapproving of stealing to disapproving of taxation. Simon Blackburn (1984) explored this idea in his non-cognitivist account of quasi-realism. And Alan Gibbard (1990) did something similar by applying non-cognitivism to rationality itself.

Moral realism

These developments of non-cognitivism in which our use of logical forms like "if … then" and our talk of normativity in general are taken to be expressive have taken non-cognitivism quite close to allowing talk of truth in moral judgments. An expressivist approach to truth itself, like that of Robert Brandom (1994) would in theory allow moral expressivism to be compatible with moral judgments being genuinely true and false.

The twentieth-century debate about the nature of truth between correspondence theorists, deflationists, anti-realist assertibility theorists, etc. has made the related issues of moral truth, moral realism, and moral objectivism very complex. Anti-realists about truth would be anti-realists about morality but still accept that moral judgments were true or false if they satisfied the pragmatic constraints of a certain kind of discourse. One such constraint might be that moral attitudes must converge in response to their being open to higher-order attitudes about these very attitudes, i.e. something like critical reflection.

David Wiggins (1991) took the issue of whether moral judgments might be true to depend on an evaluation of whether moral discourse met such constraints – what he called "marks of truth." And he argued that only some sorts of moral judgments met such constraints and only in a qualified way. In the process he made what he took to be a moral subjectivist position, inspired in particular by David Hume, as close to objectivism as he could.

A more extreme subjectivism was defended by John Mackie (1977), who argued that moral truth would require moral truth-makers: real values somehow out there in the world. And he argued that both metaphysically and epistemologically these real external values would have to be very queer things indeed, so queer that it would be reasonable to assume that no such things existed. They were not discernible by normal perceptual means; so they would have to be discernible by some very queer extra faculty. They would have to be both out there and in here simultaneously, since moral values were action-guiding, and that would make them pretty queer too.

Mackie was not content with the non-cognitivist response that our moral talk was not committed to the existence of such external standards but merely expressed our own internal standards and attitudes. He thought our moral talk was committed to the existence of these queer real external values and consequently just about every straightforward first-order moral judgment we make is strictly false. This was his *error theory* of ethics.

Some moral realists, like the Cornell Realists mentioned earlier, tried to meet this challenge head on and argued that moral properties were real external causally active and explanatory features of the world. Others, like John McDowell (1985), take a deflationary stance to truth. He denies that ethical standards are or need to be *blankly* external, but neither are they mere expressions of actual attitudes. Helping himself to the analogy with secondary qualities often employed by anti-realists, he argues that things were colored red independently of any actual experience of this, but that to be red is to be such as (in certain cases) to look, precisely, red. So secondary quality judgments are grounded in the notion of human experience, but are still correct or incorrect independently of any particular experience or set of experiences – and so *objective*. Similarly, moral judgments are grounded in the attitudes generated by human sensibility, but are still objective.

Thomas Nagel (1937–), in a series of articles and books from "Subjective and objective" (1979) onwards, developed the idea of a certain kind of progression in ethics from subjective viewpoints to more objective detached ones in which one's own interests and attitudes were removed from the viewpoint and treated as parts of the objective world, along with everyone else's interests and attitudes. For Nagel, our task in ethics is not to eliminate the subjective perspective, but to integrate it with more objective perspectives. Given this model, his way of understanding the question of moral realism then is whether from an objective viewpoint there would be any reasons to act.

His first book, *The Possibility of Altruism* (1970), employing a strongly Kantian approach, answered yes to this question. Altruism was taken to be a rational requirement for action and from this requirement moral principles could be derived. He began by pointing out that even self-interest theories of rationality take rationality itself to involve a substantial requirement, namely prudence. The very structure of means–ends rationality requires that the interests of oneself *in the future* are to be of concern.

In the case of altruism the argument is that if you have a reason to further your own interests or meet you own needs you are committed to thinking of such needs and interests as providing reasons objectively, and thus as providing reasons for other people too. This then commits you to thinking of other people's needs and interests as providing you with reason to act. In this way Nagel mirrored Moore's (1903) argument against ethical egoism.

Christine Korsgaard has developed this Kantian project, and at the same time attempted to make a synthesis between it and Aristotle's approach to ethical behavior. She claims that by reflecting on our nature as agents (on our "practical identity") we find that consciousness of our own humanity gives us a kind of authority for action; and "it is this authority that gives normativity to moral claims" (1996: 20).

Intuitionism

Mackie's attack on external ethical values as having to be queer both metaphysically and epistemologically was in part an attack on G. E. Moore's conception of the good as a simple non-natural property knowable through intuition. Moore's own approach had a huge influence in the first half of the twentieth century, although it was itself strongly influenced by a work of the nineteenth century, Henry Sidgwick's *The Methods of Ethics* (1874), whose seventh edition was published in 1907.

Both Sidgwick (1838–1900) and Moore articulated a conception of ethics one step on in the Aristotelian direction from Mill. While seeing no alternative to utilitarianism as an account of what actions are right, they were fiercely critical of Mill's half-hearted attempt to ground the principle of utilitarianism in definitions and proofs. Instead they talked of intuitive knowledge. As I will try to show here, this intuitionistic approach developed almost seamlessly into the much more Aristotelian approaches of late twentieth-century sensibility theories of ethics.

But Sidgwick explicitly rejected the Aristotelian idea that decisions about how to act in particular situations were to be arrived at through some kind of intuitive conception of the merits of the case. He described this as the phase of perceptional intuitionism, and thought of it as a primitive stage in the process of moral development. The next stage is to ground these judgments in general principles and rules.

But when you have no argument for these principles and rules of conduct, but merely intuit them as correct, you are at what he calls the phase of dogmatic intuitionism. You can do better than this by grounding your choice of principles and rules in some fundamental philosophical principles about the nature of ethics. But these philosophical principles cannot be grounded in anything more fundamental. The process of providing ever deeper justifications must stop, not as Mill suggested in some definition of "desirable," but in fundamental unargued intuitions. This is the phase of philosophical intuitionism, and we must rest there.

However, Sidgwick's construction of the progress of phases in the rational development of ethics positively invites a further extension of his sequence. Why should the correct choice of fundamental philosophical principles when we are faced with a decision between incompatible ways of grounding our rules of conduct not be determined by some further justification rather than by intuition? This question seems particularly pressing since what he takes to be the basic philosophical principle underlying ethics now seems so arbitrary – namely that the right action is the one that will maximize the good.

Moore criticized Sidgwick's claim that human happiness is the only thing good in itself, arguing, perhaps rather strangely, that faced with an alternative between two worlds, one beautiful and one ugly, neither of which contained any people or other creatures capable of judgment, it would by rational to try to bring about the beautiful one (1993: 83). But Moore accepted Sidgwick's claim that we can know through intuition the general truth that the right action is the one that will produce the greatest possible amount of good. And in this respect his theory of what actions are right (as opposed to what things are good) was criticized by W. D. Ross (1930). Applying our moral intuition sensibly, we can still say, "I can see that doing this would maximize the amount of good, but is it right for me to do it?" For example, if our intuition is that in some situation where utilitarianism is in conflict with a conception of justice based on rights and obligation justice should prevail, then this seems incompatible with utilitarianism itself being an intuitive truth.

Ross, an Oxford moral philosopher influenced in about equal parts by Aristotle and Kant, argued that we do not always look to the future, but often to the past, when determining how to behave (1930: 17). So Ross, following H. A. Prichard (1912) and in parallel with C. D. Broad (1930), rejected Sidgwick's and Moore's idea that the issue of how to act – what is right – depended on some grand intuitively knowable principle linking right and good. Just as Moore rejected any grand a priori principle concerning what is good, Ross rejected any such overarching principles concerning what is right, and argued that knowledge of what is right is based on more piecemeal and particular considerations.

Ross claimed that there is a set of morally relevant considerations that give us reason to act – what he called prima facie duties – some of which are consequential and others of which are not. Broadly they come under the following headings: fidelity, reparation, gratitude, justice, beneficence, self-improvement, and non-malificence. As with Sidgwick's and Moore's grand consequentialist principle, our knowledge of these prima facie duties is intuitive. Broad said similar things, talking about considerations that made actions *fitting* or *unfitting*.

Since there is a plurality of prima facie duties they will often conflict. Whereas we can know intuitively what are the prima facie duties, we do not always know how to weigh them, whether we have missed any in the particular situation and, with respect to the consequentialist ones, what the consequences are. So we can only come up with judgments that are more or less probably correct about the rightness or wrongness of particular actions.

Ross's approach to ethics generally was echoed much later, when medical ethics started to develop. An influential book by Beauchamp and Childress (1979) argued that there were four basic principles of medical ethics: autonomy, non-maleficence, beneficence, and justice. Although looking like a sort of ragbag approach to ethics, this has proved to be a remarkably robust tool in this branch of practical ethics.

The faculty of intuition sounds like a fig leaf for mere opinion or prejudice. And it has been a common criticism of intuitionism that talk of intuition just waves a hand at the epistemological problem rather than providing an answer. The criticism was particularly acute when targeting Moore's idea that we could be intuitively aware of simple non-natural properties. But with Ross's idea that good and right are complex things, it is not so clear that we have to posit some mysterious faculty to explain our intuitive knowledge of them.

The key thing about intuitive knowledge is that it is non-inferential. The intuitionists were keen to deny that our knowledge of what is good (and of what is right for the ones who did not follow Moore on the definability of "right" as opposed to "good") is derived through inference from some more basic principle or definition. But it does not follow that perception and reason do not go to make up intuition. If a tree surgeon looks at a tree and judges that it is unhealthy he may not be inferring this from some principle that says that whenever a tree has a certain property it is unhealthy. Tree surgeons are able to recognize that a tree is unhealthy because they have refined their capacity to apply this concept. There is no need to posit a special faculty, just a special conceptual or recognitional skill.

Aristotle's ethical insights were employed to develop this idea in intuitionism in several ways simultaneously, very often by Oxford philosophers. One Aristotelian development of intuitionism was particularism: the idea that moral judgments did not need to be grounded by general principles. Ross made some use of general principles with his list of *prima facie* duties, but these were not supposed to determine moral judgments even though they provided some grounds for them. Later particularists, such as John McDowell (1979) and Jonathan Dancy (1983), rejected even this role for principles, arguing that sensitivity to morally relevant properties need not be mediated by recognition of the application of any universal principles.

Such sensitivity must of course be learnt and developed. Moral sensibility must be refined. This is another feature of Aristotle's approach that fed into later twentieth-century successors to intuitionism. The approach, sometimes called sensibility theory, accepted Aristotle's principle that moral judgment depended on the exercise of a sensibility constituted from properly refined and rationally moderated *emotions*. It was still a conceptual exercise since these emotions were subject to justification, but one grounded in human nature.

G. H. von Wright (1963: 171) developed a conception of practical reasoning rooted in the knitting together of "wanting an end, understanding a necessity, and setting oneself to act." Martha Nussbaum (1978: 178) describes the appeal of explanations of action in terms of such a notion of sensibility as lying "in their ability to link an agent's desires and his perceptions of how things are in the world around him, his subjective motivation and the objective limitations of his situation (as he sees them)." David Wiggins (1987: essays 5 and 6) finds this idea in Hume and in his non-cognitivist successors, as well as in Aristotle's notion of aesthesis, which Wiggins translates as situational appreciation.

In this tradition the notion of intuition amounts to something like seeing things properly. It is bound up with having the capacity to *feel* things properly. Emotions are rationally assessable. And, as John McDowell (1979) has argued, the ethical concepts that one applies on the basis of this knitting together of reason, perception, and emotion are irreducible to concepts that one can grasp fully from a non-emotional perspective. Nevertheless, moral judgment is taken to be an exercise in concept application, just like any other form of judgment that aims to be true. It is just that the ability to apply these concepts properly depends on having the sensibility that goes with properly realized and moderated emotions; i.e. it depends on being virtuous.

This is why Moore's open question argument has no force against a thoroughgoing Aristotelian sensibility theory. The initial worry might be that it makes sense for a non-virtuous person to say: "I can see that that is what a virtuous person would do; but not being perfectly virtuous myself, why should I care?" Identifying the right act with the act of a good person appears to risk alienating normal people from morality. But McDowell's point is that being virtuous enables you to tell what is the right act. He is not simply recommending the following decision procedure for the less than fully virtuous person: work out what the virtuous person would do and act accordingly. For this decision procedure is not fully available to the non-virtuous person. There may be good reasons to emulate people who seem virtuous to you in order to acquire virtue, but this is a much weaker claim than the putative decision procedure. McDowell's point, echoing Moore (but more obviously Aristotle) is that knowledge of what is good or right is not available from outside the practice of moral thinking, and such a moral practice requires the properly moderated and modulated emotional sensibility that goes with being virtuous.

This idea served feminist approaches to ethical knowledge (see also "Feminism in philosophy," Chapter 7). The feminist psychologist Carol Gilligan (1936–) developed a distinction between two ways of approaching a moral problem (Gilligan 1982). One way, which might be associated with a man's approach, was to look for a solution to the problem *as stated*. Principles are brought to bear and argued about, and eventually one side or other of the argument is assumed to win. The language is adversarial.

The other way, which might be associated with women, is to work around the problem; not to accept the problem as stated but to redefine it if possible. No situation comes fully conceptualized. Any description of a moral problem can be improved upon until it looks much less like a moral *problem* as such. By talking through the situation with lateral thinking, it might be possible to avoid a clash of principles, but to reach an acceptable course of action through consensus. On the one hand is defined the ethics of justice and duty. On the other hand is the ethics of care. Aristotelian sensibility theory provided an intellectual arena for the ethics of care.[5]

According to Bernard Williams (1929–2003), the various ethical concepts are more or less "thick," ranging from concepts like "gratitude," "brutality," and "bravery," which are ineliminably ethical but have a lot of descriptive content, to thin concepts like "good" and "right" (Williams 1985). No attempt to give an account of the application of thin concepts can work without recourse to thick ones, but the application of thick ones is itself a messy business. In the same way Philippa Foot (1958) had argued that evaluative concepts like "rude" have clear conventionally accepted criteria for application and still express the attitude of disapproval. The only way to avoid being committed to such an attitude when faced with these clear criteria is to refuse to use the concept of rudeness.

As Iris Murdoch (1970: 34) wrote, "Moral language which relates to a reality infinitely more complex and various than that of science is often unavoidably idiosyncratic and inaccessible." Murdoch's work in the 1960s culminating in her 1970 book, *The Sovereignty of Good*, was highly influential in the development of sensibility theory in Oxford. More influenced by Plato than by Aristotle and more concerned to respond to French existentialist philosophy than most of her colleagues were, she brought to bear Simone Weil's (1959) notion of "attention" to capture the idea of a loving and humble gaze directed upon particular individuals and situations. The central idea was that there is no way to fix a description of a particular person and their situation or even fix the concepts that apply to them, but that the process of trying to perfect our ways of seeing things is essentially the moral project – a project in which art and literature are more useful than more theoretical pursuits.

One of the important contributions of Murdoch's work was to make a bridge between the work on ethics in the analytical Anglo-American tradition and the work being done in an existentialist or phenomenologist mode on the continent of Europe. For example, Anglo-American sensibility theory bears a striking but unacknowledged resemblance to the idea of Martin Buber (1937) that ethical understanding requires adopting a non-objective perspective towards others – what he called an "I–thou" relationship.

In one respect this was to treat people in a Kantian way as always ends in themselves rather than as merely means to achieving ends. But Buber rejected Kant's conception of the moral law, arguing, in the spirit of existentialism (and indeed Aristotelian particularism), for what became known as "situation ethics." A concrete situation of infinite particularity is presented to us, and what constitutes our responsibility is to answer to this situation in the fullness of our being. Somehow this also constitutes our relationship with God. This idea was developed by Emmanuel Levinas in his *Totality and Infinity* (1961). There he argued that ethics involves an encounter with the unknowable Other.

The role of emotions in our moral sensibility was more explicitly brought out in the work of Max Scheler (1954), which defined what became known as "axiology" or the philosophy of values. Values, for Scheler, were phenomenologically disclosed in emotional experience. His conception of an emotion was of an experience with both a subjective and an objective aspect, the objective aspect revealing real values. To this extent our conception of the evaluative world was partly constituted by our nature as feeling creatures, while our nature as feeling creatures was partly constituted by our capacity to perceive values. This virtuous Aristotelian circle of values and emotions was precisely what McDowell and other sensibility theorists were so keen to defend.

In a 1958 article Elizabeth Anscombe mounted an attack on all moral systems based on general principles, whether consequentialist or Kantian. In the same way as Nietzsche had attacked morality generally, Anscombe argued that there was no place in current ethical thinking for an *authority* backing up these moral obligations. The only role left for sensible moral discourse was in understanding human virtue; and this would need to wait until moral psychology was more developed.

This paper is often taken to herald what is known as Virtue Theory, the idea that actions are right or wrong in virtue of whether or not they issue naturally from good or virtuous character dispositions. Virtue Theory is an aspect of Aristotelian sensibility theory, since according to sensibility theory, having good character dispositions is part of having a properly moral sensibility, which is what enables one to tell what is the right thing to do in any particular situation. And knowing what is right will naturally lead to acting well.

So sensibility theory leads to the slogan that the right act is the one that the good person will perform, which is Virtue Theory. But it reaches this slogan via the Socratic claim that virtue enables you to *know* what is right. And this claim about knowledge is not always taken to be part of Virtue Theory. For example, Alasdair MacIntyre (1981) does not identify virtue and knowledge, but argues that we can gain insight into a culture's moral practice by investigating its conception of moral virtues. His approach, in the spirit of Virtue Theory is to reject the search for a grounding of our concept of virtues in anything else. But, in the spirit of the postmodernism of the 1960s and 1970s he goes on to make the further move that there was no room for rational argument in favor of one or other conception of virtue. This move is certainly not warranted by Aristotelian sensibility theory.

Bernard Williams (1973), while not endorsing anything like a systematic virtue theory, was in the forefront of the argument for so-called agent-centered ethics. He argued against utilitarian and Kantian approaches by claiming that they failed to acknowledge the particular moral viewpoint of the individual agent. Moral thinking must be relevant to the moral agent; it must be action-guiding. And as such it must reflect the agent's interests and concerns. It must respect their integrity as a moral agent.[6]

For Williams, this position was associated with a view about moral reasons and indeed about practical reasons generally. In his paper, "Internal and external reasons" (1981: ch. 8) he argued that anything that counts as a reason for someone to do something must be grounded in that person's motivational set of desires and other attitudes. Something simply does not count as a reason for someone to act if it cannot be derived from this motivational set.

The significance of this idea depends to a large extent on what resources can be appealed to in the process of deriving reasons from a motivational set. Although

Williams would have rejected the possibility, it is compatible with his view of internal reasons that some moral reasons may apply to everyone and still count as internal reasons inasmuch as they could be derived from any motivational starting point whatsoever once it was properly worked out. In any case the paper represented the start of a resurgence of interest in the nature of practical reasons. For example, Michael Smith (1994) defends a Humean conception of what he called "motivational reasons" in which such reasons are determined by the agent's beliefs and desires while he rejects Williams's claim that all reasons for action (including what Smith called "normative reasons") are rooted in the agent's beliefs and desires. On the other hand Jonathan Dancy (2000) argues against a psychological conception of motivating reasons as well; only in odd cases do one's beliefs and desires count as reasons for one to act. The issue is complicated, however, with various important distinctions – e.g. between reasons for acting and reasons why one acts – still not having been properly worked out by the end of the century.

Agency, free will, and responsibility

Underlying the central issue of how morality is related to the will is the question of what agency is. Hume identified agency with the causal role of a subject's psychological states – their beliefs and desires – while Kant identified agency with the role of practical reason. These two approaches continued to characterize work on the philosophy of agency through the century. The high point was perhaps Donald Davidson's (1963) article bringing Hume and Kant together by characterizing the primary reason in the light of which an action is intelligible as being constituted by a belief/desire pair, and then insisting that explaining an action in terms of reasons is simultaneously to make it rationally intelligible and to cite causes that explain why it happened. In claiming that reasons were simultaneously causes he was replying to the influential non-causal approaches then prevalent deriving from Gilbert Ryle (1949), Elizabeth Anscombe (1957), and Alfred Melden (1961).

There was still an issue about whether agency in this sense was sufficient for moral responsibility. Many philosophers thought that it made sense to say that someone might act but not of their own free will and so not be morally responsible for doing so. Two principles in particular were often suggested as providing further requirements of free and therefore responsible agency. The first was the causal origination principle: that to be responsible for one thing you must also be responsible for what caused it. Philosophers from Paul Edwards (1958) to Galen Strawson (1986) have defended this principle and at the same time argued that we are not responsible for the ultimate causes of our achievements and so not responsible for these achievements either.

The other principle, often called the principle of alternative possibilities, is that to be acting freely and responsibly it must be possible that one acted otherwise. This is an attempt to capture the general ethical principle that "ought" implies "can." If there is no alternative possibility then it can never be right to say that you ought to have done otherwise and so it is never right to blame you for doing what you did do. This principle was used by, for example, van Inwagen (1975) to argue for the incompatibility of free will and determinism.

What bothered these twentieth-century philosophers as much as it had bothered earlier philosophers was whether there was space for the idea of moral responsibility in the naturalistic scientific world picture, where every event was either determined by previous events according to the laws of physics or was the realization of some quantum probability function. The "hard" determinists thought this was a real problem. The "soft" determinists or "compatibilists" thought that free will and responsibility were not threatened by any of this. And the libertarians rejected that particular aspect of the scientific worldview that seemed to threaten free will, namely determinism.

One important version of this rejection of determinism was the idea of agent causation, developed in different ways by Richard Taylor (1966) and Roderick Chisholm (1966). Taylor was concerned that an account of agency that worked with the idea of mental events causing behavior missed out the central role of the agent herself in agency – a role that could only be accommodated by assuming that the idea of an agent making something happen was irreducible to that of states of the agent making things happen. Chisholm's concern was with free will; he argued that the possibility of free will required that some events were not caused by other events but only by the agent. While this came at too high a metaphysical price for most philosophers since 1966, there were some notable exceptions later in the century, for example Tim O'Connor (1995).

Many compatibilists – e.g. Daniel Dennett (1984: ch. 6) – have remarked that the question of whether you could or could not have done otherwise in some situation depends entirely on how the notion of possibility here is being understood. There is no single answer to the question of whether you could have jumped four foot in the air. It depends on what is taken as given and what is allowed to vary when considering the possibility. So it is argued that a fallacy of equivocation is made in concluding from the deterministic (or fatalistic for that matter) claim that things could not have been otherwise to the incompatibilist conclusion that I could not have done otherwise.

That conclusion was dealt a further body blow by Harry Frankfurt (1929–), who argued that it is in any case not relevant to a consideration of free will or responsibility whether or not you could have done otherwise (1969). Suppose you are contemplating some vile act, which you eventually decide to do of your own free will and for which you are fully responsible. But suppose also that unknown to you there had been someone standing behind you ready to intervene and make you decide to do it (perhaps by manipulating your brain) if it had looked as though you were not going to go through with it. In the event that person did not need to intervene, but the very presence of that person meant that there was no possible world in which you did not decide to do that vile act. You were responsible for the vile act even though you could not have done otherwise.

Peter Strawson's article, "Freedom and resentment" (1962), presented a more radical rejection of the free will/determinism dialectic. He maintained that whatever we think of grand metaphysical arguments against a certain sort of liberty this has no relevance to our attributions of moral responsibility. These grand arguments depend on adopting an "objective" point of view when considering someone's agency, i.e. treating them as an object rather than as one of us. The perspective from which moral responsibility is attributed is one in which our conception of someone's agency is partly constituted by our own reactive attitudes to them – or the reactive attitudes that would be appropriate towards them. These are attitudes of resentment, gratitude, etc. The grand metaphysical arguments have no role in this perspective, nor do they undermine it.

In the spirit of the Aristotle renaissance in Oxford at the time, Strawson developed an account of how we attribute responsibility to an agent in terms of a properly tuned reactive sensibility towards her: we build up our ability to attribute responsibility from a starting point of being able to feel resentment and gratitude to others for the respect or otherwise that they show to us. We then develop the ability to feel vicarious resentment and gratitude on behalf of others, and then to say when such resentment and gratitude would be appropriate. In some circumstances it might not be appropriate to resent someone who acted freely and wrongly if he was in a very difficult situation, and in some circumstances it might be appropriate to resent someone for the lack of respect she showed in her behavior and general attitudes, whatever her status as a "free" agent. At this point when our reactive attitudes are rationally moderated we have developed a concept of objective responsibility.

In a more Kantian vein, Charles Taylor (1976) developed the view that determination of the will by reason constitutes free agency, but added the Hegelian twist that rationality was essentially dynamic. So freedom consisted in the capacity, when faced with incompatible courses of action recommended by different evaluations, to reconceptualize one's situation and develop a further evaluation that incorporates the earlier ones and avoids the contradiction. This act of reconceptualization is an act of self-definition very much in the spirit of the existentialist identification of freedom and self-definition.

Taylor disagreed with Sartre (1948), however, by claiming that an act of self-definition, although it is not itself derived from any deeper more basic rational evaluation, is not somehow outside of rationality. The new conception of oneself and one's place in the world is straightaway subject to rational assessment and the possibility of revision, even though there may be no competing evaluation that requires such an assessment straightaway. And in this sense such self-definition is sensitive to rationality.

For the existentialists, self-definition was a radical choice, one that was neither guided by any basic conception of oneself, nor sensitive to rationality as a whole. It was a blind leap. In virtue of being unconstrained even by rationality as a whole this possibility was supposed to capture freedom in the very strongest sense. Value was there to be created by such a leap; in this respect twentieth-century existentialists set themselves apart from Nietzschean skepticism. But value was not external to such self-definition and could not guide it.

Starting from this idea of radical choice and of authentic moral thinking emerging from such unconstrained choice, it is not surprising that the existentialists had relatively little systematic to say about ethics. Perhaps in tension with the apparently unguided nature of free self-definition Simone de Beauvoir (1948) claimed that freedom was an end in itself and that dishonesty, inauthenticity, and tyranny were all failures in this regard. But no definitive answers were provided by these generalities. Every instance of something having significance had to be created freely, and was always open to being recreated differently. And every realization of freedom in some act of self-definition, by fixing meaning, at the same time constrains freedom. This is the tension that she called ambiguity.

Utilitarianism

The general principle that one should promote the good by one's actions guided much ethical thinking in the twentieth century. This principle by itself might be innocuous, but when combined with the assumption that the good to be promoted can be understood independently of the particular agent's concerns, obligations, and entitlements, we get the theory known as consequentialism. If the good is treated as happiness in some sense, then we have utilitarianism; and if the good is taken to consist of other things too, like beauty, knowledge, etc., then we have what Hastings Rashdall (1907) dubbed "ideal utilitarianism." Sidgwick was a utilitarian, indeed a "hedonistic" utilitarian, since his conception of happiness was a hedonistic one in which happiness was understood in terms of pleasure and enjoyment. Moore was an ideal utilitarian, since he included other things than just happiness in his conception of a good state – for example beauty. More recently, James Griffin (1986: 67) presented a kind of ideal utilitarianism in which the central prudential values were accomplishment, fulfilling requirements of human existence, and flourishing, understanding, enjoyment, and personal relations.

Utilitarianism based on a hedonistic conception of happiness as pleasure or enjoyment and indeed any conception of happiness as an internal mental state is often thought to have fallen foul of Robert Nozick's (1974) example of the experience machine. Nozick (1938–2002) asks you to think of the things that you would most value achieving and experiencing in life and offers you the imagined chance to go into a machine that would simulate in complete detail the experience of achieving such things. If you valued writing a great book, you could go into the machine and become convinced that you really did write such a book and feel all the satisfaction that would come from that. Would you choose to go into the machine? If not, then what you take to matter is not an internal mental state of happiness but actual achievements.

The most influential departure from a hedonistic conception of happiness was a preference satisfaction conception. There were hints of this sort of approach even in Mill's *Utilitarianism*, but it only really took off when Frank Ramsey (1931) developed a behaviorist calculus of preferences. He showed that it was possible to construct a measure of utility associated with different possible outcomes just by determining how subjects would choose between different outcomes. He also showed that it was possible to construct a measure of their degree of belief in certain possible outcomes by determining how they would bet on these outcomes.

Ramsey's aim was to develop a subjective approach to probability. But his calculus quickly became the basis of a self-interest conception of rationality: rational choice theory. This was developed into game theory in a book by von Neumann and

Morgenstern (1944). The idea was that the rational thing to do is to satisfy your preferences optimally; and Ramsey had provided the basis of an axiomatization of what this involved. John Harsanyi (1982) worked this up into what he called "preference utilitarianism."

It is often thought that this approach as an account of rationality is based on a fairly simple fallacy. It is trivially true that you only ever do what you want. So it is supposed to follow that you only ever *aim* for what you want. You only do what you prefer to do; so you *should* do what you prefer to do. The desired becomes the desirable, as in Mill. The valued becomes the valuable as in Perry. If satisfaction of your preferences is taken to be the fundamental axiomatic principle of practical rationality, then these preferences are themselves taken to be determined outside of practical rationality. They are not the results of moral evaluation and consideration of others, but are given psychologically. We seem to have moved from the truism that you only do what you want to do or prefer to do to the extraordinary claim that rationality consists entirely in responding effectively to your preferences.

But as a way to approximate a measure of happiness, preference theory was a shot in the arm for utilitarianism. It turned out that utility can be measured after all. In social policy cost–benefit analysis and welfare economics were born. Civil servants applied utility calculations based on experimental research into people's preferences to establish the degree to which large-scale projects would lead to the outcome most desired by the population. The practical significance of this branch of ethics was immense.

A central issue for utilitarianism, though one that at the same time spread into other areas of moral philosophy in the twentieth century – especially theories of rights – was the question of which beings were to be included in calculations of overall happiness. Whether one is a utilitarian or not, morality is concerned with respecting the interests of others; but which others should one be concerned with? Peter Singer's *Animal Liberation* (1975) made the case on behalf of utilitarianism that all (and only) sentient beings counted in any estimate of overall happiness. This has led Singer (1946–) to bite the bullet in many controversial ethical debates concerning animal rights, abortion, and euthanasia. Abstracting from other factors that Singer concedes are bound to muddy the question in practice, he argued that if a newborn child has less capacity for feeling pain than a cow we should be more concerned with the well-being of the cow.

Derek Parfit (1942–) has raised the same question about future generations. In his *Reasons and Persons* (1984) he maintains that as yet unborn people count alongside existing beings in one's moral concern for the interests of others. Given his rejection of a strict conception of personal identity, even one's concern with one's own interests in the future is a concern with a distinct though psychologically connected being – one that does not yet exist. Along with the problems that the interests of future generation raise for utilitarianism, issues are raised in practical ethics concerning how we should treat the environment and whether we should apply genetic filtering to human embryos to ensure that children are born with the best possible set of genetic resources (see, e.g., Steiner 1994).

Rule-based systems

The law was another area of public morality to which utilitarianism had been fruit-fully applied since the time of the nineteenth-century philosopher of law, John Austin (1790–1859). The structure and details of the judicial system could be put into a utility calculation and the system of laws that maximized overall happiness would be recommended. Indeed, having any such system at all could be justified in this way. But what could not be justified in this way was an *individual's* decision to be bound by the law – or indeed any self-constructed law either.

If a judge knows that as a good utilitarian he or she should abandon proper procedure and summarily dismiss the case of someone known to be a murderer in order to avoid riots and massive loss of life, then even if the law itself is justified on utilitarian grounds, utilitarianism dictates that the judge should ignore the law and release the murderer. Anti-utilitarians have argued all through the century that this sort of case shows that as a basis for individual decision utilitarianism leads to patently unethical results and fails to make proper space for the ideas of rights and justice.

The problem is that the utilitarian justification of following a rule is contingent on expected consequences, whereas our intuitions about rights and justice suggest that rules are obligatory in a way that is at least partially independent of the consequences of particular instances of following or not following them. This raises the question of whether it might be possible to provide a utilitarian justification of the claim that one's action should be in accordance with the best set of universal rules or principles.

The idea would be that although following a particular rule on a particular occasion might not be justified on utilitarian grounds, being a rule-follower might be justified on such grounds, and the decision on a particular occasion might then be fixed by this prior decision. So before the judge calculates whether letting the murderer go free has better consequences than convicting him according to the principles of justice, she should decide the prior issue of whether or not to be principled.

The criticism of this sort of utilitarianism was that only the weakest conception of being principled could possibly be justified on utilitarian grounds. It is useful to have rules of thumb to apply to situations in which the expected reduction in happiness from making a time-consuming utilitarian calculation outweighs the expected gain from getting the calculation right. But this will not help the judge in the example just given. We can assume that he or she knows straightaway that releasing the murderer will result in more happiness than following through with justice. So whatever rule of thumb is employed, he or she should still in this situation do the unprincipled thing.

Another way to justify being principled is to justify having a principled character. One of the things good utilitarians should do is act to develop in themselves the character that will lead to the best consequences. It may be that having a horror of injustice is a good thing to have in one's character from a utilitarian point of view (though this would need quite a good argument). So the utilitarian judge would in this case feel a horror in letting the murderer go. Robert Adams (1976) developed something like this view in defending "motive-utilitarianism."

But the utilitarian judge should still let the murderer go despite feeling horror. Richard Hare (1981) developed the distinction between intuitive level thinking and critical level thinking to make just this point. Rules of thumb, deeply felt principles, and character dispositions might be developed according to utilitarian principles, and these might lead one to be more principled than utilitarianism on an act by act basis (act-utilitarianism) would do. Acting according to such rules or character dispositions is working at the intuitive level. But the good utilitarian should have the capacity to go against these intuitive level recommendations and when the need arises apply a critical utilitarian approach to whether or not to follow such rules or character dispositions in a particular situation. The judge faced with the possibility of riots if he or she does not release the murderer would have to apply critical level thinking to the case, and would have to choose the unfair course of action as a result.

The difficulty for this sort of utilitarian justification of rules can be put in a different way. If the principles or rules are supposed to apply across the board and not be trumped and undermined by further critical thinking, then the rules would have to be highly qualified. For example, the judge would have to construct a rule that went something like this: "Follow the rules of the system with complete impartiality unless not doing so would have a clear benefit for overall happiness." Principles play no significant part in this system.

Faced with the impossibility of constructing a utilitarian justification of following rules in morality, R. F. Harrod (1936) employed something more like a Kantian justification of following rules, when he introduced the idea of rule-utilitarianism. His idea was to combine utilitarianism with the so-called generalization principle that in itself has nothing to do with utilitarianism.

According to the generalization principle a rule is good if it would be good if everyone followed it. If we can appeal to a Kantian justification of basing moral action on principles and also appeal to something like Kant's first formulation of the categorical imperative – act only on that maxim that you would at the same time wish to be universal moral law – then utilitarianism might still have a role in determining which would be the best set of universal moral laws. In other words, utilitarianism was taken to plug what was perceived to be a serious gap in the Kantian system – the transition from the formulation of the categorical imperative to substantial moral principles.[7]

As David Lyons (1965: 136) formulated it in an influential criticism of the different possible forms of rule-utilitarianism: "An act is right if, and only if, it conforms to a set of rules general acceptance of which would maximise utility."

Many utilitarians have taken this proposal to be flawed as it simply rejects the basic utilitarian claim that when deciding how to act you should aim at achieving the best consequences. For example J. J. C. Smart (1956) maintained a sustained defense of act-utilitarianism in the face of this hybrid theory. One of his arguments was that even this more Kantian rule-utilitarianism must collapse into act-utilitarianism. Wouldn't the world be as good as it could be if everyone simply followed the act-utilitarian principle that they should do their best to maximize overall happiness? Against the response that no one would trust anyone in such a world one might reply that in a world where you could rely on everyone being a good act-utilitarian there would be no need for institutions of trust. As Lyons (1965) argued, there are ways of formulating rule-utilitarianism that do not collapse into act-utilitarianism, but these are not always the most plausible theories in themselves.

A parallel debate was carried on by those moral philosophers who, in the spirit of Thomas Hobbes, were trying to base an adherence to moral principles on self-interest instead of overall happiness. Many philosophers in this tradition were persuaded by the argument that it is in all of our interests to have a system of rules that everyone sticks to. One's world is safer; interpersonal relationships are stronger; generally one will be happier and more able to achieve one's goals in a world where everyone is principled. So morality seems to be justified on the grounds of self-interest.

Kurt Baier (1917–) was a key figure in the development of this sort of approach. He argued that morality involved a special sort of reason, one that took account of the interests of others (1958). In this he was following Stephen Toulmin (1950). But Toulmin did not attempt to ground moral practices in self-interest but in their conduciveness to an overall harmony of interests. For Baier, moral reasons overrode those of simple self-interest, but the fact that they had this priority was itself supposed to be grounded in considerations of self-interest.

The challenge for this sort of approach was the Prisoners' Dilemma. While it may be the case that we would all be better off if we all followed rules rather than all seeking our own self-interest in an unprincipled way, it would still be in any particular individual's interest to cheat when presented with a case where being principled would go against his own interest. So every individual would cheat when it was in his own interest, and as a result everyone would be worse off than they would have been if everyone had been principled.

If the only principle determining rational action is self-interest, it looks as if people will not work within a system of moral principles at all, but will be bound to collapse into unprincipled behavior which paradoxically leaves them worse off than in the moral system. So some further Kantian constraint on rationality has to be found if anything recognizable as a moral perspective can be grounded.

In this spirit David Gauthier (1967; 1986) claimed that rationality essentially involved commitment. Commitment was part of the very idea of having intentions. Out of this he tries to show that the self-interested decision would be to commit oneself to morality, where such a commitment would carry one through prisoners' dilemmas. Alan Gewirth (1978) introduced the idea that it was in one's interests to have generic rights respected, and argued that it would be irrational to insist on one's own rights without respecting the rights of others.

The idea that rights were fundamental to ethical thinking was one that characterized much moral philosophy of the twentieth century. For example Judith Thomson (1976), developing Philippa Foot's (1967) discussion, used the idea of rights to explain why it is morally permissible to turn a trolley from a track where it was going to kill five people onto a track where it will kill just one, whereas it is not morally permissible for a surgeon to kill one person in order to harvest his or her organs to save five others. She also worked out an influential argument in the abortion debate (1971), which appealed to the mother's right to have a say in who was allowed to feed off her body.

Joseph Raz (1984: 195) developed a powerful theoretical proposal for linking rights with duties and duties with interests: "*x* has a right if and only if *x* can have rights, and other things being equal, an aspect of *x*'s well-being (his interest) is a sufficient reason for holding some other person(s) to be under a duty." Raz's proposal, in opposition to rights-based theorists such as Dworkin (1977) and Mackie (1978), did not take rights to be morally basic. The proposal can be applied if we can presume that we have some independent grasp on the idea of the *interests* of members of a certain group, whether this is a preference-based conception of utility or a more Aristotelian conception of what the members of a group need in order to fulfill their nature as members of that group, i.e. to flourish. Then the rules that should govern the members of a group can be determined according to the principle that these should be the rules that enable the members of the group to flourish as such. These rules determine duties for the members of the group, and these duties determine specific rights for the members of the group.

This sort of discussion of rights, although it belongs squarely in moral philosophy, was brought into the remit of political philosophy as it developed in the second half of the century. Political philosophy's concern with the ethical foundation of institutional systems, tax systems, judicial systems and so on, saw the role of rights – whether property rights (Nozick 1974; Steiner 1994), or rights based on freedom – to be central in this discussion.

Even more central was "contractualism," the idea that actual or hypothetical social contracts should determine the right political systems and ground the individual's moral commitment to such systems. Thomas Scanlon applied a "contractualist" approach to *individual* morality by arguing that an act "is wrong if its performance under the circumstances would be disallowed by any system of rules for the general regulation of behaviour which no one could reasonably reject as a basis for informed, unforced general agreement" (1982: 110). And this kind of approach, often developed in a Kantian spirit as an exploration of the constraints that a certain conception of rationality imposed on moral systems, was a major force in political philosophy in the twentieth century.

Two of the most influential figures in political philosophy, John Rawls (1958) and Jürgen Habermas (1984), were neo-Kantians in this sense and tried to establish foundations for determining just institutional systems by describing what would count as a rational or reasonable way to *agree on* such things (on Rawls, see "Twentieth-century political philosophy," Chapter 21). Rawls argued that it would be reasonable to accept a system that we would all agree on were we deciding the matter from behind a veil of ignorance, where we had no idea where we ourselves would figure in the system. And Habermas argued that it would be reasonable to accept a system that was agreed upon in a properly inclusive debate, where everyone had to respect everyone else's perspective. But at this point the narrative moves into the field of political philosophy.

Notes

1 An important early attack came from William Frankena (1939).
2 See especially Moore's preface to the second edition of *Principia Ethics*, where he tries to sort this out.
3 Some of Dewey's most significant work on ethics was done in the 1920s, in his *Human Nature and Conduct* (1922) and "The construction of good," which formed chapter 10 of his *The Quest for Certainty* (1929).
4 Boyd's "How to be a moral realist" and Sturgeon's "Moral explanations" are both in Sayre-McCord 1988.
5 To be stuck with the ethics of care has not suited all feminist thinkers. Sandra Bartky (1990) has warned of the consequences for disempowerment.
6 This sort of criticism of utilitarianism has itself been criticized by Shelley Kagan (1991), who has maintained that moral requirements may diverge from intuitively acceptable requirements, in which case, as moral agents, we should aim to change ourselves so that what seems acceptable lines up better with what is morally required.
7 As Urmson (1953) argued, there are signs of this sort of approach in Mill's own utilitarianism. Other significant rule-utilitarians include Mabbot (1953) and Brandt (1963).

References

Adams, R. (1976) "Motive Utilitarianism." *Journal of Philosophy* 73: 467–81.
Anscombe, G. E. M. (1957) *Intention*. Oxford: Blackwell.
_____ (1958) "Modern moral philosophy." *Philosophy* 33: 1–19.
Ayer, A. J. (1936) *Language, Truth and Logic*. London: Gollancz.
Baier, K. (1958) *The Moral Point of View*. Ithaca, NY: Cornell Univerisity Press.
Bartky, S. (1990) *Femininity and Domination*. London: Routledge.
Beauchamp, T. and J. Childress (1979) *Principles of Biomedical Ethics*. Oxford: Oxford University Press.
Beauvoir, S. de (1948) *The Ethics of Ambiguity*, trans. B. Frechtman. New York: Philosophical Library.
Blackburn, S. (1984) *Spreading the Word*. Oxford: Oxford University Press.
Brandom, R. (1994) *Making it Explicit*. Cambridge MA: Harvard University Press.
Brandt, R. B. (1959) *Ethical Theory*. New York: Prentice-Hall.
_____ 1963, "Toward a credible form of utilitarianism." In H.-N. Castañeda and G. Nakhnikian (eds.) *Morality and the Language of Conduct*, Detroit: Wayne State University Press, pp. 107–43.
Broad, C. D. (1930) *Five Types of Ethical Theory*. London: Routledge & Kegan Paul.
_____ (1934) "Is 'goodness' a name of a simple non-natural property?" *Proceedings of the Aristotelian Society* 34: 249–68.
Buber, M. (1937) *I and Thou*, trans. R. G. Smith. Edinburgh: T. & T. Clark.
Chisholm, R. (1966) "Freedom and action." In K. Lehrer (ed.) *Freedom and Determinism*, New York: Random House, pp. 11–44.
Dancy, J. (1983) "Ethical particularism and morally relevant properties." *Mind* 92: 530–47.
_____ (2000) *Practical Reality*. Oxford: Oxford University Press.
Darwall, S., A. Gibbard, and P. Railton (1992) "Towards fin de siècle ethics: some trends." *Philosophical Review* 101: 115–89.
Davidson, D. (1963) "Actions, reasons and causes." *Journal of Philosophy* 60: 685–700.
Dennett, D. (1984) *Elbow Room*. Cambridge, MA: MIT Press.
Dewey, J. (1922) *Human Nature and Conduct*. New York: The Modern Library.
_____ (1929) *The Quest for Certainty*. New York: Putnam.
Dworkin, R. (1977) *Taking Rights Seriously*. Cambridge, MA: Harvard University Press.
Edwards, P. (1958) "Hard and soft determinism." In S. Hook (ed.) *Determinism and Freedom*, New York: Collier, pp. 117–25.
Firth, R. (1952) "Ethical absolutism and the Ideal Observer." *Philosophy and Phenomenological Review* 12: 317–45.
Foot, P. (1958) "Moral arguments." *Mind* 67: 502–13.

_____ (1967) "The problem of abortion and the doctrine of double effect." *Oxford Review* 5: 5–15.

_____ (1978) *Virtues and Vices*. Oxford: Blackwell.

Frankena, W. (1939) "The naturalistic fallacy." *Mind* 48: 464–77.

Frankfurt, H. (1969) "Alternate possibilities and moral responsibility." *Journal of Philosophy* 66: 829–39.

Gauthier, D. (1967) "Morality and advantage." *Philosophical Review* 76: 460–75.

_____ (1986) *Morals by Agreement*. Oxford: Oxford University Press.

Geach, P. (1958) "Imperative and deontic logic." *Analysis* 18: 49–56.

Gewirth, A. (1978) *Reason and Morality*. Chicago: University of Chicago Press.

Gibbard, A. (1990) *Wise Choices, Apt Feelings*. Cambridge, MA: Harvard University Press.

Gilligan, C. (1982) *In a Different Voice*. Cambridge, MA: Harvard University Press.

Griffin, J. (1986) *Well-Being*. Oxford: Oxford University Press.

Habermas, J. (1984) *The Theory of Communicative Action*. Boston: Beacon Press.

Hare, R. (1952) *The Language of Morals*. Oxford: Oxford University Press.

_____ (1981) *Moral Thinking*. Oxford: Oxford University Press.

Harman, G. (1977) *Morality*. Oxford: Oxford University Press.

Harrod, R. F. (1936) "Utilitarianism revisited." *Mind* 44: 137–56.

Harsanyi, J. (1982) "Morality and the theory of rational behaviour." In A. Sen and B. Williams (eds.) *Utilitarianism and Beyond*, Cambridge: Cambridge University Press, pp. 39–62.

Jackson, F. (1998) *From Metaphysics to Ethics*. Oxford: Oxford University Press.

Kagan, S. (1991) *The Limits of Morality*. Oxford: Oxford University Press.

Korsgaard, C. (1996) *The Sources of Normativity*. Cambridge: Cambridge University Press.

Levinas, E. (1961) *Totality and Infinity*, trans. A. Lingis. Pittsburgh: Duquesne University Press.

Lyons, D. (1965) *Forms and Limits of Utilitarianism*. Oxford: Oxford University Press.

Mabbott, J. D. (1953) "Moral Rules." *Proceedings of the British Academy* 37: 97–117.

McDowell, J. (1979) "Virtue and reason." *The Monist* 62: 331–50.

_____ (1985) "Values and secondary qualities." In T. Honderich (ed.) *Morality and Ojectivity*, London: Routledge & Kegan Paul, pp. 110–29.

MacIntyre, A. (1981) *After Virtue*. London: Duckworth.

Mackie, J. (1977) *Ethics: Inventing Right and Wrong*. Harmondsworth: Penguin.

_____ (1978) "Can there be a rights-based moral theory?" *Midwest Studies in Philosophy* 3: 350–9.

Melden, A. (1961) *Free Action*. London: Routledge.

Moore, G. E. (1993) [1903] *Principia Ethica*, rev. edn., ed. T. Baldwin. Cambridge: Cambridge University Press.

Murdoch, I. (1970) *The Sovereignty of Good*. London: Routledge & Kegan Paul.

Nagel, T. (1970) *The Possibility of Altruism*. Princeton, NJ: Princeton University Press.

_____ (1979) "Subjective and objective." In *Mortal Questions*, Cambridge: Cambridge University Press, pp. 196–214.

Nozick, R. (1974) *Anarchy, State and Utopia*. New York: Basic Books.

Nussbaum, M. (1978) *Aristotle's de motu animalium*, Princeton, NJ: Princeton University Press.

O'Connor, T. (1995) "Agent causation." In T. O'Connor (ed.) *Agents, Causes, and Events*, Oxford: Oxford University Press, pp. 173–200.

Ogden. C. K. and I. A. Richards (1923) *The Meaning of Meaning*. New York: Harcourt, Brace & World.

Parfit, D. (1977) *Reasons and Persons*. Oxford: Clarendon Press.

Perry, R. B.(1926) *General Theory of Value*. New York: Longmans, Green & Co.

Prichard, H. A. (1912) "Does moral philosophy rest on a mistake?" *Mind* 21: 21–37.

Quine, W. V. O. (1951) "Two dogmas of empiricism." *Philosophical Review* 60: 20–43.

Ramsey, F. P. (1931) "Truth and probability." In R. B. Braithwaite (ed.) *Foundations of Mathematics and other Essays*, London: Routledge & Kegan Paul, pp. 156–198.

Rashdall, H. (1907) *The Theory of Good and Evil*. Oxford: Oxford Univeristy Press.

Rawls, J. (1951) "Outline for a decision procedure for ethics." *Philosophical Review* 60: 177–97.

_____ (1958) "Justice as fairness." *Philosophical Review* 67: 154–94.

_____ (1971) *A Theory of Justice*. Cambridge, MA: Harvard University Press.

Raz, J. (1984) "The nature of rights." *Mind* 93: 194–214.

Ross, W. D. (1930) *The Right and the Good*. Oxford: Oxford University Press.

Ryle, G. (1949) *The Concept of Mind*. London: Hutchinson.

Sartre, J-P. (1948) *Existentialism and Humanism*, trans. P. Mairet. London: Methuen.

Sayre-McCord, G. (ed.) (1988) *Essays on Moral Realism*, Ithaca, NY: Cornell University Press.

Scanlon, T. (1982) "Contractualism and utilitarianism." In A. Sen and B. Williams (eds.) *Utilitarianism and Beyond*, Cambridge: Cambridge University Press, pp. 103–28.

Scheler, M. (1954) *The Nature of Sympathy*, trans. P. Heath. London: Routledge & Kegan Paul.

Sidgwick, H. (1874) *The Methods of Ethics*. London: Macmillan.

Singer, P. (1975) *Animal Liberation*. New York: Random House.

Slote, M. (1992) *From Morality to Virtue*. Oxford: Oxford University Press.

Smart, J. J. C. (1956) "Extreme and restricted utilitarianism." *Philosophical Quarterly* 6: 344–54.

Smith, M. (1994) *The Moral Problem*. Oxford: Blackwell.

Steiner, H. (1994) *An Essay on Rights*. Oxford: Blackwell.

Stevenson, C. (1937) "The emotive meaning of ethical terms." *Mind* 46: 14–31.

Strawson, G. (1986) *Freedom and Belief*. Oxford: Oxford University Press.

Strawson, P. (1962) "Freedom and resentment." *Proceedings of the British Academy* 48: 1–25.

Taylor, C. (1976) "Responsibility for self." In A. Rorty (ed.) *The Identities of Persons*, Berkeley: University of California Press, pp. 81–99.

Taylor, R. (1966) *Action and Purpose*. Englewood Cliffs, NJ : Prentice-Hall.

Thomson, J. (1971) "A defense of abortion." *Philosophy and Public Affairs* 1: 47–66.

_____ (1976) "Killing, letting die and the trolley problem." *The Monist* 59: 204–17.

Toulmin, S. (1950) *An Examination of the Place of Reason in Ethics*. Cambridge: Cambridge University Press.

Urmson, J. O. (1953) "The interpretation of the moral philosophy of J. S. Mill." *Philosophical Quarterly* 3: 33–9.

Weil, S. (1959) *Lectures on Philosophy*. Cambridge: Cambridge University Press.

Westermarck, E. (1906–8) *Origin and Development of Moral Ideas*, vols. 1 and 2. London: Macmillan.

Wiggins, D. (1980) "Deliberation and practical reasoning." In A. Rorty (ed.) *Essays on Aristotle's Ethics*, Berkeley: University of California Press, pp. 221–40.

_____ (1987) *Needs, Values, Truth*. Oxford: Blackwell.

_____ (1991) "Moral cognitivism, moral relativism and motivating moral beliefs." *Proceedings of the Aristotelian Society* 91: 61–86.

Williams, B. (1972) *Morality*. Cambridge: Cambridge University Press.

_____ (1973) "Integrity." In J. J. C. Smart and B. Williams, *Utilitarianism: For and Against*, Cambridge: Cambridge University Press, pp. 108–17.

_____ (1981) *Moral Luck*. Cambridge: Cambridge University Press.

_____ (1985) *Ethics and the Limits of Philosophy*. Cambridge, MA: Harvard University Press.

van Inwagen, P. (1975) "The incompatibility of free will and determinism." *Philosophical Studies* 27: 185–99.

von Neumann, J. and O. Morgenstern (1944) *Theory of Games and Economic Behavior*. Princeton, NJ: Princeton University Press.

von Wright, G. F. (1963) *Varieties of Goodness*. London: Routledge & Kegan Paul.

Further reading

Crisp, R. and M. Slote (eds.) (1997) *Virtue Ethics*. Oxford: Oxford University Press. (A collection of significant essays on this developing area in ethics).

Darwall, S. (1998) *Philosophical Ethics*. Boulder, CO: Westview Press. (Accessible introduction to philosophical ethics including the work of key historical figures along the way).

Mackie, J. (1977) *Ethics: Inventing Right and Wrong*. Harmondsworth: Penguin. (Accessible introduction to a subjectivist approach to ethics).

Singer, P. (1979) *Practical Ethics*. Cambridge: Cambridge University Press. (Singer presents an uncompromising utilitarian approach to practical ethics).

Smart, J. J. C. and B. Williams (eds.) (1973) *Utilitarianism: For and Against*. Cambridge: Cambridge University Press. (Influential debate about utilitarianism).

Williams, B. (1985) *Ethics and the Limits of Philosophy*. Cambridge, MA: Harvard University Press. (Laid out as a sustained critique of classic approaches to ethics from Aristotle to Kant, the book at the same time develops Williams's own individualistic approach to ethics).

21
TWENTIETH-CENTURY POLITICAL PHILOSOPHY

Matt Matravers

Introduction

There is a commonly told story about political philosophy in the twentieth century that begins with Peter Laslett's famous statement of 1956 that "for the moment, anyway, political philosophy is dead" (Laslett 1956: vii). The tale continues with Isaiah Berlin's 1962 claim that "no commanding work of political philosophy" had been written in the twentieth century (Berlin 1962: 1) before ending with the publication of Rawls's *A Theory of Justice* – a "commanding work" by any measure – which is credited with breathing life back into the moribund body of political philosophy.

The punch line of the story depends on the truth of the claim that political philosophy was dead, or at least pretty lifeless, before John Rawls (1921–2002). If so, that is a remarkable fact that calls for explanation. The century had witnessed two world wars, the Holocaust, the murderous regimes of Stalin and Mao, the development and use of the atomic bomb, decolonization and nationalism, the extension of the suffrage in many places, the rise of the Welfare State, and so on. Political philosophers, it might be thought, must have had something to say about all that?

In what follows, I shall first try to explain why it was plausible – if not entirely accurate – to write political philosophy's obituary in 1956. Second, I will offer an alternative reading of the history of the discipline to the 1960s. Third, I will describe the impact of Rawls before, in the remaining sections, saying something of political philosophy after Rawls and into the twenty-first century. However, before embarking on that, it is necessary to say something about what I take political philosophy to be.[1]

Undertaking a survey of a discipline as "mongrel" (Dryzeck et al. 2006: 5) as political philosophy is a risky business. For example, whereas in the philosophy of mind one might be accused of giving too much, or too little, space to "eliminativists," in political philosophy oversights are more likely to be taken as indications of personal moral failure; omitting some or other figure being evidence of (sub)conscious "ethnocentrisms," "racism," or "sexism." At the same time, political philosophy is not merely a "topic" within philosophy, but is itself a discipline and this means that in surveying developments within it one inevitably marginalizes those who already feel that their input is underappreciated by "professional" political philosophers.

In what follows, my focus is mainly, but not exclusively, on the discipline of political philosophy within the (broadly) analytic tradition. Although political philosophy is located between, and borrows from, the social sciences, history, and philosophy, I shall – again mainly – be interested in the application of philosophy to politics and not with the broader category of all normative thinking about political questions. I shall take the central issue of politics to be the question: what political practices and institutions are justified and ought to be established?

Finally, the focus will be on the application of philosophy to political questions within a broadly liberal tradition. That is, the main concern of the writers discussed is to find secular, normative principles to regulate societies of free and equal citizens. That said, these restrictions only regulate the broad flow of what follows, and I deviate from them whenever it seems that definitional *fiat* would get in the way of accurately capturing the flavor of political philosophy in the twentieth century.[2]

The strange death of political philosophy

Laslett is not alone in his analysis of the condition of political philosophy in the first half to two-thirds of the twentieth century. Philip Pettit (1945–) writes of a "long silence" from "late in the [nineteenth] century to about the 1950s" (Pettit 1993: 8) and Alan Haworth remarks that "with the onset of the twentieth century ... English-speaking philosophy entered a period during which it was to be dominated by a succession of movements of ideas which ... could be of no help whatsoever when it came to politics" (Haworth 2006: 2542). The story goes as follows: at the turn of the century, English-speaking political philosophy was dominated by an idealist intellectual tradition that was fast running out of steam. The great works of this tradition – for example, Bernard Bosanquet's (1848–1923) *The Philosophical Theory of the State* and F. H. Bradley's (1846–1924) *Ethical Studies* – had been published at the end of the nineteenth century and, although idealists remained in place in British universities, in particular in Oxford, the tradition was about to be fatally wounded by the rise of logical positivism and ordinary-language philosophy under the influence of the Vienna Circle and Wittgenstein (see "The development of analytic philosophy: Wittgenstein and after," Chapter 2). These positions, though, were not simply hostile to idealism, but to political philosophy as a whole. Thus, Laslett had no hesitation in declaring that "the Logical Positivists" (Laslett 1956: ix) were responsible for the death of political philosophy.

Laslett's analysis might best be taken as shorthand for a number of interconnected phenomena. On the one hand, within analytic philosophy Bertrand Russell and others pursued the goal of developing a language that accurately reflected the world, the propositions of which were either empirically verifiable or analytically true. Since value judgments are not analytically true, they were quickly relegated to being either meaningless or merely expressions of approval or disapproval (Ayer 1936). On the other, the later Wittgenstein and those influenced by him confidently expected seemingly deep and intractable problems to disappear once one did away with too much theorizing and concentrated on the use to which language was put. As Brian Barry (1936–) remarks, this means that political ideas and concepts only happen to be the subject of study if one happens to find them interesting (Barry 1990: xxxiv–xxxv). Moreover, Barry adds, nobody had much reason to think the application of philosophy to politics would be interesting because of "the prevalence of utilitarianism among philosophers in the 1950s and early 1960s." As Barry remarks, "adherence to utilitarianism makes for very boring political philosophy, because once the goal has been postulated ... everything else is a matter of arguing about the most efficacious means to that end" (p. xxxv).

The precise diagnosis of the illness, then, is different, but Pettit, Barry, Laslett, and Haworth all agree that, if not dead, political philosophy was, at best, ailing and infirm in the first half of the century. The one book they all cite, T. D. Weldon's *The Vocabulary of Politics*, published in 1953, appears to confirm the situation: political philosophers, Weldon wrote, "have formulated questions to which no empirically testable answers could be given, and such questions are nonsensical" (Weldon 1953: 74).

Signs of life

The above analysis depends, to an extent, on the restrictive definition of political philosophy given at the beginning. Were one to be more inclusive, one could, for example, point to many volumes produced by Harold Laski (1893–1950) between 1917 and 1945. Even keeping within the narrow definition, however, it is possible to discern signs of life within political philosophy in the period under discussion (which we might take to be that between the 1903 publication of G. E. Moore's *Principia Ethica* and Brian Barry's 1965 *Political Argument*). On the one hand, there are individual authors who, it might be thought, are simply exceptions to the rule. On the other hand, there are continuing traditions of thought, most notably Marxism and utilitarianism.

Amongst the notable individual authors, a number were clearly influenced by the rise and effects of totalitarianism. Although different in numerous important ways, Karl Popper (1902–1994) (*The Open Society and Its Enemies*, 1945; *The Poverty of Historicism*, 1957); Isaiah Berlin (1909–97) ("Two concepts of liberty," 1958); Friedrich von Hayek (1899–1992) (*The Constitution of Liberty*, 1960); and Michael Oakeshott (1901–90) (*Rationalism in Politics*, 1962) all offered a vision of a recognizably liberal society against background warnings of the dangers of totalitarianism. (For further discussion of Karl Popper, see "Philosophy of science," Chapter 14.) Popper and Hayek were both émigrés from the Nazis (Popper from Germany and Hayek from German-occupied Austria) and Berlin clearly had both Soviet Russia and Nazi Germany in mind when connecting positive liberty with the rise of totalitarianism. Hannah Arendt's *The Origins of Totalitarianism* (1951) of course specifically focuses on the Soviet and Nazi regimes as new, modern forms of government and to some extent her *The Human Condition* (1958) celebrates the freedom individuals can find in political action. Finally, Leo Strauss (1899–1973) – like Arendt (1906–75) a refugee from Germany – published *Natural Right and History* in 1953.

Although these writers are important and all continue to be influential, their publications in the period do not blunt the general thrust of Laslett's analysis. Political philosophy – including some profound and long-lasting political philosophy – was being done here and there, but it was neither mainstream in departments of philosophy or political science nor publicly influential. Indeed, of the authors mentioned, Popper was primarily and professionally a philosopher of science, Hayek an economist, Berlin and Strauss historians of political thought. Of the remaining two, Oakeshott thought "political philosophy" an oxymoron, which leaves Arendt who is, by any reckoning, an unusual case.

Turning to the continuing traditions of thought, although (as Barry noted) utilitarianism continued to be the prevalent political philosophy in the postwar period, it remained the case that if one wanted to refer to the most recent "commanding" defense of utilitarianism one would have to go back to Henry Sidgwick's (1838–1900) *The Methods of Ethics*, the first edition of which came out in 1874. Nevertheless, utilitarianism dominated the emerging science of economics and found sophisticated supporters in the moral philosophy of Richard Hare in the UK and that of Richard Brandt in the USA. (For further discussion of these issues, see "Twentieth-century moral philosophy," Chapter 20.) Although, ironically, the essay from the period in defense of a utilitarian position that remains a standard reference is John Rawls's "Two concepts of rules" (1955).

In the case of Marxism, no account of twentieth-century political philosophy could be complete without some reference to the development of Marx's thought. In part, Marxism compels attention because of politics. The 1917 revolution in Russia caused reverberations through much of the world; the Cold War defined the period after the Second World War; and for most of the century, a significant proportion of the globe was governed by regimes that defined themselves as Marxist. The main currents of Marxist philosophy were found away from the Anglophone world. Putting aside Mao's idiosyncratic development of the tradition, it is in Germany, France, and Italy that Marxism flourished as a distinctive political philosophy. That said, Marxist thought and categories have seeped into a number of theoretical developments in the century and Marxism itself has become so fragmented that some, like contemporary analytical Marxists, bear little resemblance to, say, the Leninist orthodoxy that prevailed at the beginning of the century.

From the perspective of the development of political philosophy to the mid-1960s, arguably the two earliest, most significant Marxist theorists were Georg Lukács (1971) and Antonio Gramsci (1971). Lukács's significance lies in his focus on the Hegelian roots of Marxist thought, which in turn meant the giving of a more significant place to consciousness and agency, and in his attack on the interpretation of Marxism as a positivistic science. Rather than the triumph of Communism being the inevitable result of the unstable economics of capitalism, Lukács argued that revolution would be the outcome of free action by a self-conscious proletarian class. In achieving this, humankind would realize its own imminent nature and (in an Hegelian spirit) history would be completed. Those Marxists who had attempted to present Marxism as a science, and reduce the revolution to the inevitable outcome of economic laws, were not only wrong, according to Lukács, but positively damaging. For, in reducing the role of agency, Marxists contributed to the process of "reification" that sustained capitalism. For Lukács, reification – a development of Marx's "commodity fetishism" – was the process by which relations between agents and between agents and the world become relations between "things" or "objects" governed by impersonal laws. Capitalist modes of production, and in particular the division of labor, encapsulated reification and atomized individuals. (For discussion of reification, see "Critical Theory," Chapter 18.) Thus, according to Lukács, it was only once the proletariat, through their agents the Communist Party, came to self-consciousness that the meaning of history could be revealed and achieved. Lukács's work, particularly his focus on Hegel, laid the foundations subsequently built upon by the Frankfurt School, surely the most significant development of Marxist thought within the western tradition (see "Critical Theory," Chapter 18).

Antonio Gramsci's claim to inclusion in any serious study of political philosophy lies primarily in his development of the idea of hegemony, which he bequeathed not just to Marxist thought, but to political philosophy generally. Like Lukács, Gramsci (1891–1937) built upon Hegel and was severely critical of the positivistic interpretation of Marx. Again like Lukács, he argued for Marxism to move its focus from the economic to the cultural, social, and political. For Gramsci, this was necessary because the ruling classes occupied a hegemonic position; that is, through their control of social, cultural, and political forces, the ruling classes were able to attain the consent of the working classes to capitalism and thus to their own domination. In developed societies, Gramsci argued, Marxist leaders and other "organic" intellectuals ought to concentrate on civil society with the aim of undermining the hegemonic position of the ruling classes.

In their focus on an "Hegelian Marx" and on subjects beyond economics, Gramsci and Lukács anticipate much of what would make the Frankfurt School distinctive and, to an extent, what would make it "Critical" rather than "Marxist." This focus also serves to differentiate them from the most significant French Marxist thinker of the century, Louis Althusser (1918–90), (see Althusser 1971; 1977).

Far from recovering Marx through his early work and connections with Hegel, Althusser claimed that Marx's work was marked by a radical "epistemological break" which occurred with the "Theses on Feuerbach" of 1845. Marxism proper, Althusser claimed, begins with Marx's rejection of Hegelian idealism and of philosophy and their replacement with a scientific theory of history. One target of Althusser's work was undoubtedly Jean-Paul Sartre, whose aspiration was to build a grand theory encompassing existentialism, humanism, and Marxism. Another was Hegel, who had, through Alexandre Kojève, become a critical figure in French thought. In this, he joined forces with French philosophers of science and with structuralist and ultimately post-structuralist thinkers such as Claude Lévi-Strauss and Michel Foucault (see also "French philosophy in the twentieth century," Chapter 19). Indeed, it is perhaps as a leading and influential French intellectual, rather than as a Marxist thinker, that Althusser has had his most lasting effect on political philosophy.

The coming of Rawls

If political philosophy was largely marginalized and moribund in the first half of the century, what happened to revive it? As already noted, the standard answer to this question is that John Rawls's *A Theory of Justice* was published. Yet the prevailing mood amongst political scientists in the United States whilst Rawls was writing his book was not propitious (which may account for political philosophy being transformed by a *moral* philosopher). The 1950s and 1960s witnessed the rise of political *science*, with the emphasis firmly on the word "science." First, "the new science of politics" and then "behaviorism" put the emphasis on value-neutrality, scientific procedures, and the objective analysis of predictive laws of politics. Commenting on Madison's *Federalist Paper No. 10*, Robert Dahl (1915–) wrote that "the theory of populist democracy is not an empirical system. It consists only of logical relations among ethical postulates. It tells us nothing about the real world. From it we can predict no behavior whatsoever" (1956: 51). Instead, Dahl and others pushed for greater respect for the fact/value distinction and for the usefulness of empirical political science.

The advent of the new political science did not go unchallenged. Leo Strauss famously attacked it in 1962, but it is noticeable that the only American book one might add to the list of individual exceptions to the "death of political philosophy" is Sheldon Wolin's *Politics and Vision*, which came out in 1960; it is primarily a work in the history of political thought, a subfield the new political scientists were happy to cede to the historians and other non-scientists.

It would be wrong to say that *A Theory of Justice* burst into the field, transforming the subject, in 1971. For a start, a draft of at least the first two parts of *A Theory of Justice* were circulating as early as 1961. However, this is only one reason why it would be wrong to focus on the publication of the book, and a relatively trivial one at that. More important in understanding the context in which *A Theory of Justice* had the impact it had were first, other events in the academy, and second, events outside in the "real world" so prized by the new political scientists. Within the academy, there were exciting developments in the social sciences. Von Neumann's and Morgenstern's *Theory of Games and Economic Behavior* had been published in 1944 (and applied to the arms race by the RAND Corporation and in Schelling's *The Strategy of Conflict* in 1960); Arrow's *Social Choice and Individual Values* had been published in 1951, Buchanan's and Tullock's *The Calculus of Consent* in 1962; Brian Barry's *Political Argument* in 1965; and the first volume of the journal *Philosophy and Public Affairs* in 1971. In addition, H. L. A. Hart (1907–92) had single-handedly reinvented analytical jurisprudence in *The Concept of Law*, published in 1961. Not only were many of these works referred to in *A Theory of Justice*, but as Philip Pettit remarks, one of the things that marks out the "end" of the long silence in political philosophy was Barry's and Rawls's willingness to "contaminate ... pure philosophical analysis with materials from the empirical disciplines in developing a picture of how to institutionalize [their] preferred package of values and in considering whether the institutions recommended are likely to be stable" (1993: 12).

The impact of *A Theory of Justice*, though, perhaps has as much to do with events outside the academy as within it. In the United States and beyond, the era in which the book was written witnessed the civil rights movements, "women's liberation," the Vietnam War, and the conflict over the draft. As Arlene Saxonhouse (1944–) makes clear in a review of political philosophy "then and now," whatever political scientists said about the non-normative purity of the discipline, these real world events forced values firmly back into the center of politics: "What were the grounds of civil disobedience or resistance? What was the source of obligation – and to whom and what was one obliged? And what was justice anyway?" (Saxonhouse 2006: 851). If these, and many others, were the questions buzzing around the common rooms, in contrast to those being asked in the adjoining seminar rooms, then it is little surprise that Rawls's book was not just an important contribution to political philosophy, but was timely.

Of course, being timely is not quite the same as rescuing from the dead, and perhaps the two have become too tightly connected in the retelling of the fall and rise of political philosophy, but that is not to deny the importance or long-term significance of what Rawls achieved. In one sense, that achievement was simply a general one. As Barry puts it:

> The difference that Rawls made in A *Theory of Justice* was that he raised the stakes in political philosophy to a quite new level. Although the structure of the book works to conceal this, A *Theory of Justice* represents a return to the grand manner of political philosophizing, complete with a theory of the human good, a moral psychology, a theory of the subject-matter (the "basic structure of society") and the objects (the "primary goods") of justice, and, of course, an immensely elaborate structure of argument in favour of specific principles of justice.

Barry concludes, "Rawls has made writing general treatments of political philosophy hard in much the same way as Beethoven made writing symphonies hard: much more is involved than before" (Barry 1990: lxx).

A Theory of Justice

As Barry says, Rawls's A *Theory of Justice* is a grand work in the tradition of the classics of political philosophy from Plato to Sidgwick. Rawls's purpose is to give an account of what is politically right – of the principles of justice for what he calls "the basic structure of society" – and to show that these principles can be shown to be reasonable to every citizen reflecting on the question of how her society ought to be governed. The first question, then, is one of method: *how* can we identify the appropriate principles of justice given the secular, "non-metaphysical" constraints described above?

Rawls's answer is to "present a conception of justice which generalizes and carries to a higher level of abstraction the familiar theory of the social contract as found, say, in Locke, Rousseau, and Kant" (1971: 11). In an early presentation of this, "Justice as fairness" (1958), Rawls considered the choice of principles that would be made by actual people from a range of alternatives. However, A *Theory of Justice* introduces one of the ideas for which Rawls has become famous: the "veil of ignorance" (1971:

§24). As its name suggests, the function of the veil of ignorance is to deny certain information to the choosers in Rawls's hypothetical state of nature, which he calls the "original position." What is denied to the people in the original position is any knowledge of their particular situations: "no one knows his place in society, his class position or social status; nor does he know his fortune in the distribution of natural assets and abilities, his intelligence and strength, and the like." Moreover, the person in the original position deliberates without knowledge of his own aims and values – "his conception of the good, the particulars of his rational plan of life" – and of the generation to which he belongs, and the particular details of his society ("its economic or political situation [and] the level of civilization and culture it has been able to achieve") (all in Rawls 1971: 137).

What the parties do know is that the "circumstances of justice" apply (that is, they know that there are conditions of moderate scarcity and that people's demands over the distribution of resources reflect their beliefs about political and moral value), and they know "whatever general facts [about human society] affect the choice of the principles of justice" (1971: 137). However, depriving the parties of all particular knowledge, including knowledge of their conceptions of the good, would render them unable to choose principles of any kind. They would not know, for example, what kind of "stuff" principles of justice should distribute. Thus, Rawls allows the parties knowledge of a "thin theory of the good" (1971: §60), which includes an assumption that "they would prefer more primary social goods rather than less" (p. 142). Primary social goods are the distribuand of Rawls's theory of justice and are "things which it is supposed a rational man wants whatever else he wants ... rights and liberties, opportunities and powers, income and wealth [and] a sense of one's own worth" (p. 92).

Controversially, Rawls argues that in these circumstances the parties would adopt a maximin rule of choice. That is, they would "rank the alternatives by their worst possible outcomes" and then adopt that alternative "the worst outcome of which is superior to the worst outcomes of the others" (1971: 152–3). Using this rule of choice, they would choose two principles of justice as follows:

> *First Principle* Each person is to have an equal right to the most extensive total system of equal basic liberties compatible with a similar system of liberty for all.
> *Second Principle* Social and economic inequalities are to be arranged so that they are both: (a) to the greatest benefit of the least advantaged, consistent with the just savings principle, and (b) attached to offices and positions open to all under conditions of fair equality of opportunity. (1971: 302)

Furthermore, the people in the original position would choose a lexical ordering of these principles such that the first principle, often called the "equal liberty" principle, has strict priority over the second, and within the second, part (b), often called the "fair equality of opportunity principle," has priority over part (a), Rawls's famous "difference principle."

The point of the original position, and the veil of ignorance, is to ensure that the choice of principles is uncorrupted by bias or self-interest; in short, to ensure that the principles are *fair*. In this sense, Rawls's theory is, as he says, procedural: the mechanism for discovering principles of justice is to ask what people would agree to in a suitably constructed choosing situation (1971: §14).

Rawls's contractualist method, and in particular the hypothetical nature of the original position, have attracted considerable criticism. The obvious question is one Rawls puts to himself on the final page of A *Theory of Justice*: given the hypothetical nature of the original position, "why should we take any interest in it, moral or otherwise?" (p. 587). To understand Rawls's answer, it is necessary to understand the original position not just as a heuristic device that allows us to identify the principles of justice, but as part of the method by which Rawls argues that the principles are *justified*.

Rawls's method of justification is "reflective equilibrium" (1971: 48–51) (see also the discussion in "Twentieth-century moral philosophy," Chapter 20). The idea is to use the original position to capture generally shared conditions that are appropriate when reasoning about justice. From these, we can develop principles of justice and then these principles are to be tested against our considered convictions about what justice requires. If the principles fail this test, then we can return to the original position and re-examine the conditions imposed (the veil of ignorance, and so on), or we can revise our considered convictions. Once we have developed principles from the original position that match our considered convictions, we are in reflective equilibrium and the principles are justified. As Rawls puts it (1971: 579), "justification is a matter of the mutual support of many considerations, of everything fitting together in one coherent view." Thus the answer to Rawls's rhetorical question – why should we be interested in the choice made in the initial situation? – is "that the conditions embodied in this situation are ones that we do in fact accept," or can be persuaded to accept given the arguments of A *Theory of Justice* (p. 587).

On the face of it, this may seem an unpromising method of *justifying* principles of justice. Rather, reflective equilibrium seems little more than a way of systematizing our moral opinions and prejudices and then identifying principles that will support them. However, this is to misunderstand both Rawls's method and the promise of moral and political philosophy. It is to misunderstand the method because reflective equilibrium does not start from just any old beliefs about what is appropriate when thinking about justice, and the principles are not tested against just any old convictions about what justice requires. Rather, the original position captures restrictions that are both reasonable and widely accepted (for example, it is both reasonable and widely accepted that one's gender or race should not matter when thinking appropriately about justice and thus knowledge of both is excluded from the persons in the original position by being included in the veil of ignorance). Similarly, the convictions against which the principles of justice are tested are *considered*; that is, they are the moral judgments in which we have the greatest confidence, "which we feel sure must be answered in a certain way ... for example ... that religious intolerance and racial discrimination are unjust" (1971: 19; see also p. 47).

The criticism is mistaken about the promise of political philosophy, Rawls argues, because reflective equilibrium is as good as it gets. Whilst we might like to think that we can deduce the theory of justice from self-evident first principles, or reduce moral categories to non-moral ones that can then be subject to "scientific" inquiry, neither is plausible (1971: §87). Thus we are left with reflective equilibrium, but this should not be thought of as a poor second-best. As the Canadian political philosopher Will Kymlicka puts it in an introduction to political philosophy:

> if on reflection we share the intuition that slavery is unjust, then it is a powerful objection to a proposed theory of justice that it supports slavery. Conversely, if a theory of justice matches our considered intuitions, and structures them so as to bring out their internal logic, then we have a powerful argument in favour of that theory. (Kymlicka 2002: 6)

Nevertheless, it might be thought that *if* this is the best we can do – and many people would deny that – it is still a method by which we can merely get agreement on what we and other like-minded people think. After all, ancient Greeks may have been able to come to agreement on principles of justice that matched their considered convictions, but which would – for example with respect to slavery – look very different from ours.

Rawls, of course, accepts that his theory is not the final word in political philosophy and that future generations will revise and reformulate the principles; the book after all is called "A" not "*The*" *Theory of Justice*. Nonetheless, at the very end of the book he offers an impassioned plea for the relevance of the perspective of the original position – of looking at justice from an impartial point of view – in seeing the human situation *sub specie aeternitatis*. As Rawls says, this "perspective from eternity is not a perspective from a certain place beyond the world, nor the point of view of a transcendent being." Rather, he explains, "it is a certain form of thought and feeling that rational persons can adopt within the world" (1971: 587).

By the time of his second book, *Political Liberalism* (1993), Rawls had changed his view on the scope of the theory, but before dealing with that shift, and the reasons for it, it is worth considering some of the reactions to A *Theory of Justice*. Although these were legion – and the discipline continues to be dominated by Rawls such that it is possible to say of almost any political philosophy published after 1971 that it is, in some sense, a reaction to his work – they can be usefully subdivided into those whose criticisms were "internal," that is, concerned with whether the arguments worked and that have led to developments of a broadly "Rawlsian" theory, and those that attacked Rawls's whole approach and argued for some different approach to political philosophy.

Internal criticisms of and developments from A Theory of Justice

The choice of the two principles

Amongst the first responses to A *Theory of Justice* were a number of books and papers that queried whether the people in the original position would choose the two principles, and the associated priority rules, identified by Rawls. Some rejected the use of the maximin decision rule and argued that when choosing in conditions of uncertainty it would be rational for the parties to adopt a form of utilitarianism (Arrow 1973; Harsanyi 1982). A related challenge questioned whether those in the original position would give priority to the worst-off group, as required by the difference principle (Barry 1973). Finally, in an influential paper, H. L. A. Hart (1975) criticized Rawls's understanding of the value of liberty and the argument for the lexical priority of the first principle. In short, a number of critics were broadly sympathetic to Rawls's approach and to the general liberal, egalitarian, thrust of the two principles, but were not convinced that his derivation of the two principles from the original position as described was valid. Although Rawls revised his account of the basic liberties in response to Hart (see Rawls 1982; 1993: lecture viii), he resisted the pressure to revise the maximin method of choice (see 1974a; 1974b) not least because what was being pressed upon him was to adopt a form of utilitarianism. Although a significant part of the initial reception of A Theory of Justice, these debates have fallen somewhat into the background as Rawls's work developed in a way that made the derivation of the two principles from the original position less central.

Rawls's treatment of differences in natural talents and the problem of desert

A particularly controversial aspect of Rawls's theory was his inclusion of "natural assets and abilities" in the veil of ignorance, that is, as amongst the factors to be put to one side when thinking appropriately about justice. Rawls's argument appears largely in chapter II of A Theory of Justice, and is taken by some to constitute a separate, and more compelling, case for the principles of justice than the argument from the original position (see, e.g., Barry 1989: ch. 6; 1995b: §§9–10; Kymlicka 2002: ch. 3). Rawls begins with the idea of equality of opportunity and asks what is required to satisfy that value. A society that merely abolished formal inequalities would, Rawls claims, fail to instantiate equality of opportunity in part because outcomes would still be influenced by irrelevant differences in people's social background. A liberal advance on this position would try to mitigate the effect of social class and similar factors so that "there should be roughly equal prospects of achievement for everyone similarly motivated and endowed" (Rawls 1971: 73). This is a familiar position, but Rawls insists that it is still inadequate. "For one thing," he writes, "it still permits the distribution of wealth and income to be determined by the natural distributions of abilities and talents." This is problematic in the same way as it would be problematic to allow distribution to track social class for "there is no more reason to permit the distribution of income and wealth to be settled by the distribution of natural assets than by historical or social fortune" (1971: 73–4).

This argument seems to end in equality of outcome, since ruling out inequalities that arise from both environmental and genetic factors (from the social and natural lotteries) leaves no features by which to distinguish between people, but Rawls insists that rather than eliminating differences in outcome we should endorse the difference principle. "No one deserves his greater natural capacity nor merits a more favorable starting place in society," as Rawls puts it, "but it does not follow that one should eliminate these distinctions." Rather, he argues,

> the basic structure can be arranged so that these contingencies work for the good of the least fortunate. Thus we are led to the difference principle if we wish to set up the social system so that no-one gains or loses from his arbitrary place in the distribution of natural assets or his initial position in society without giving or receiving compensating advantages in return. (1971: 102)

Rawls's argument for the moral arbitrariness of natural talents and abilities has proved enormously controversial. Some critics allege that, in assigning all differences between people to the natural and social "*lotteries*," Rawls leaves no room for responsibility and the significance of choice. Thus, Robert Nozick, for example, interprets Rawls as claiming that all inequalities are undeserved because the sources of those inequalities are not themselves within the control of the agent, and are thus morally arbitrary. Reading Rawls in this determinist fashion opens him up to two criticisms that Nozick presses. First, that embracing a wholly deterministic account "is a risky line to take for a theory that otherwise wishes to buttress the dignity and self-respect of autonomous beings" (Nozick 1974: 214). Second, that the incompatibilist denial that people could be responsible for things that emerge from processes over which they had no control is not convincing because "it needn't be that the foundations underlying desert are themselves deserved, *all the way down*" (1974: 225).

Nozick's account has itself been severely criticized as based on a misreading of *A Theory of Justice* (see, for example, Cohen 1989: 914–15). Although some of what Rawls writes appears to leave insufficient room for the significance of choice, nowhere does he endorse the kind of deterministic thesis that Nozick foists upon him.

A more important line of criticism is neatly captured by a discussion of Will Kymlicka's that also foreshadows the development of the most significant movement in post-Rawlsian liberal egalitarian thought: responsibility-sensitive egalitarianism (see below). According to Kymlicka, Rawls endorses equality of opportunity because it ensures that "people's fate is determined by their choices, rather than their circumstances" (Kymlicka 2002: 58). He goes on to impute to Rawls the desire to develop a theory that is (in terms owed to Ronald Dworkin (1931–) upon whose work Kymlicka builds) "ambition-sensitive" and "endowment-insensitive" (R. Dworkin 1981: 311; Kymlicka 2002: 74). Given this, Kymlicka argues that Rawls's theory fails on both counts. The difference principle, which allows inequalities only if they are to the benefit of the least advantaged, does not distinguish between those whose choices have resulted in them being least advantaged and those in that group because of circumstances. It is, therefore, not properly ambition-sensitive. Moreover, in governing only the distribution of primary *social* goods – such as income and wealth – the difference principle ignores the impact of differences in primary *natural* goods – such as health – and is, therefore, not properly endowment-insensitive (Kymlicka 2002: 70–4. Here Kymlicka echoes a criticism of Rawls first developed by Amartya Sen 1980; see also Rawls 1988).

The interpretation of Rawls as instigating the development of responsibility-sensitive egalitarianism by provoking the criticisms of Dworkin and Sen, whilst himself offering an inadequate account of the same is popular, but deeply problematic. The difficulty lies in attributing to Rawls the motivation of developing a theory based on the significance of the distinction between chance and choice. Like Nozick, Kymlicka takes Rawls to be concerned with the problem of luck – and like Nozick, Kymlicka thinks Rawls ascribes too much to luck and ignores choice (although, unlike Nozick, Kymlicka also thinks that Rawls is insensitive to luck in his dealing with natural goods) – and there is indeed much in what Rawls writes that supports this interpretation. However, it is difficult to sustain this reading across the whole of A *Theory of Justice*. In particular, Rawls himself states that "the difference principle is not of course the principle of redress. It does not require society to try to even out handicaps as if all were expected to compete on a fair basis in the same race." The principle of redress being "that undeserved inequalities call for redress; and since inequalities of birth and natural endowment are undeserved, those inequalities are somehow to be compensated for" (1971: 100–1). Moreover, Rawls is not hesitant in ascribing responsibility for actions in retributive justice, describing the propensity to commit criminal acts as a "mark of bad character" and as rightly attracting "legal punishments ... in a just society" (p. 315).

Given that reading Rawls as trying to develop an ambition-sensitive, endowment-insensitive account of justice both stretches interpretive credibility and leaves his account open to obvious challenges, it is worth considering whether there is an alternative reading available.

Read in context, Rawls's remarks about the contingency of our natural talents and abilities has less to do with the distinction between choice and chance, and more with an attack on the idea that justice requires that "income and wealth, and the good things in life generally, should be distributed according to moral desert" (Rawls 1971: 310). As Rawls recognizes, the idea of justice as giving people what they deserve has both a long history and an intuitive appeal. Nevertheless, Rawls is explicit: "justice as fairness rejects this conception" (p. 310). The reason for that is not that Rawls is committed to determinism, or to negating the effects of luck, but is that the distribution of natural talents and abilities has no authority in distributive justice and neither can nor should translate into distributive shares.[3] Thus Rawls propounds a system of "legitimate expectations." It is reasonable to reward those who do what the system of justice declares will be rewarded, but this is a sense of desert that is "post-justicial"; what one deserves depends on the system of justice (see Rawls 1971: §48; Scheffler 2001: ch. 10; 2003; Matravers 2007: ch. 3, §6.2).

Criticisms of the original position

Other responses to A *Theory of Justice* were more critical of the argument from the original position as a whole. Rather than attack Rawls's claim that the two principles would be chosen by the parties, they found fault with the construction itself or with its role in the argument. One of the most important criticisms honed in on Rawls's inclusion of conceptions of the good in the veil of ignorance (Nagel 1975). The purpose of the veil of ignorance being to put appropriate constraints on the reasoning of the parties, critics argued that whilst it was clear that, for example, reference to race or gender would not be appropriate, reference to what people believed to be of moral value would be. The easiest way to see this is to consider an example: a religious believer in a modified original position (modified because knowledge of beliefs about the good was allowed) – who knew of his beliefs about the good, but was otherwise ignorant of particular facts as dictated by Rawls's veil of ignorance – would choose principles to advance the good (in this case, the religious good) of everyone in the society (Nagel 1975: 8). This is clearly not the same as allowing knowledge of, say, race and the parties then choosing to advance the good of only, say, white-skinned people. The former case is impartial; in the eyes of the religious believer he is advancing everyone's good equally.

Rawls's inclusion of knowledge of value and conceptions of the good in the veil of ignorance is, of course, essential to his theory since without it he could not posit unanimous choice in the original position. That is to say, given that there are a number of diverse accounts of the good (religious and otherwise), the parties could never come to agreement on justice. Christians would advance Christian principles for the good of all; Muslims, Muslim principles; hedonists, hedonistic principles, and so on. It is for this reason, as noted above, that Rawls uses a *thin* theory of the good, which is meant to be such that it can appeal to all as advancing their goods no matter what the content of those goods. However, as Nagel points out (1975: 7–10), the thin theory of the good is unlikely to appeal to all equally. Thus, the original position loses its main appeal, which is to represent a situation that is *fair* to all.

Nagel's criticism was the forerunner of a line of attack that has accompanied Rawls's work from beginning to end and that re-emerges in discussions of Rawls's later work. This is that, whilst Rawls claims that his theory is neutral and fair with respect to differing theories of the good, it is in fact little more than a restatement of a dominant individualistic liberal position; it does not so much deny knowledge of conceptions of the good from those choosing in the original position as ensure that they choose principles that advance the liberal conception. To decide what one thinks about this, one needs to decide whether one believes that there is qualitative difference between a society in which a dominant substantive conception of the good is imposed on everyone (say, a society that is Catholic and whose public rules are derived from Catholic teaching), and one in which what is imposed is the rule that no group is allowed to impose its beliefs on any other. Both involve the imposition of a rule that will not suit many – in the first case, all non-Catholics and, in the second, all non-liberals (although it is important to note that a liberal society is likely to be the second-best option for all since if one is a Catholic, for example, it is surely better to live in a liberal society than an Islamic one) – but the two positions might nevertheless strike one as importantly different.

Another line of argument that has remained significant in the reaction to Rawls's work concerns neither the content of, nor the choice made in, the original position, but its *role* in the overall argument. The first, and still one of the most influential versions of this argument was given by Ronald Dworkin in 1975. Dworkin argued that the whole idea of justifying principles by reference to what people *would* have chosen in some hypothetical situation was mistaken. As he puts it in a much quoted sentence, "a hypothetical contract is not simply a pale form of an actual contract; it is no contract at all" (1975: 18). However, Dworkin argued, this was not as serious a problem as might be imagined, since the original position and contract argument are not the things really doing the work in A *Theory of Justice*. Rather, they presuppose "a deep theory that assumes natural rights" (1975: 46) and it is this deep theory that underpins Rawls's argument.

This criticism has been repeated in a variety of forms. The "contract," it is said, cannot be a contract at all since the veil of ignorance means that the parties in the original position are effectively identical, and, since they have no knowledge of their own positions, cannot bargain with one another. As Brian Barry puts it, "faced with identical information and reasoning in an identical fashion, they [the parties in the original position] arrive at identical conclusions. We might as well talk of computers having the same program and fed the same input reaching an agreement" (1995a: 58).[4] Similarly, Will Kymlicka concludes that "all the major issues of justice" have to be settled before constructing the original position or any alternative choosing situation, thus rendering the contract "redundant," but not "entirely useless." It is not useless, according to Kymlicka, because it has a role in rendering our intuitions about justice both "vivid" and "more precise," and it can be a useful means by which to test the consequences of different intuitions (2002: 68).

In the face of this barrage of criticism (in addition to Barry and Kymlicka, see Gauthier 1977 and Hampton 1980) and the undeniable fact – which Rawls himself acknowledged in A *Theory of Justice* – that the original position does not contain bargaining and is not, in this sense, a contract, it might be expected that Rawls would have jettisoned the contract argument in his later work. However, this is not the case. To understand why, it is necessary to re-examine the idea of the contract as it appears in A *Theory of Justice*.

Rawls's contractualism: towards Barry, Scanlon, and Habermas

As Samuel Freeman notes, the objection that Rawls's theory is not contractual because the original position does not feature bargaining between persons with distinctive interests "assumes that all contracts are like economic contracts." Rawls's contract, Freeman argues – like Locke's, Rousseau's, and Kant's – is not of this form. Rather, the idea is "that every member of society should be able to accept the same terms of cooperation because they achieve certain interests everyone has." The "contract" in Rawls is, according to Freeman, really a combination of the "*mutual acknowledgement*" of the appropriate principles of justice for what Rawls calls "a well-ordered society" and the "*mutual precommitment*" of each of the parties (each of us) to agree only on condition that others do, too, such that 'all tie themselves into social and political relations permanently to achieve certain common purposes as well as their individual interests' (all quotations from Freeman 2003: 19).

Freeman's argument locates Rawls's contractualism in the overall approach Rawls takes to the idea of a well-ordered society, rather than merely within the argument from the original position. A well-ordered society is one in which "all reasonable persons accept the same public principles of justice, their agreement on these principles is public knowledge, and these principles are realized in society's laws and basic institutions" (Freeman 2007: 4). In performing the thought-experiment required to put oneself in the original position, then, one commits oneself (on condition that others do, too) to the necessity of justifying the social, economic, and political institutions under which one lives to other citizens on terms that they can accept given their status as free, equal co-citizens (and so, in that sense, co-contractors).

Freeman's account of Rawls's contractualism may not rescue it from Barry's complaint that the original position as constructed by Rawls does not adequately capture the commitment to the idea of principles of justice that can be justified to each reasonable citizen, but it does connect Rawls's project to Barry's own *Justice as Impartiality* in the way in which Barry himself suggests (Barry 1995b: ch. 3). Barry builds on T. M. Scanlon's "contractualist account of the nature of moral wrongness," which holds that "an act is wrong if its performance under the circumstances would be disallowed by any system of rules for the general regulation of behaviour which no one could reasonably reject as the basis for informed, unforced general agreement" (Scanlon 1982: 110; an idea developed further in Scanlon 1998). Barry's claim is that "the Scanlonian approach … achieves Rawls's objectives better than does the construction proposed by Rawls himself' (Barry 1995b: 70) and his *Justice as Impartiality* remains the most important contractualist development of this idea.

Finally, understanding Rawls's work as centered on the idea of a well-ordered society also explains the apparent "collision" in the trajectories of Rawls and Habermas that saw them engage with one another's work late in their careers. It is when the idea of the well-ordered society is stressed that the similarities between it and Habermas's conception of a legitimate society as one that can command the support of citizens involved in collective debate under ideal speech conditions become most clear (although there are also important differences. See Habermas 1995, and also "Critical Theory," Chapter 18).

The problem of stability and the second coming of Rawls

Emphasizing Rawls's ideal of a well-ordered society also helps to explain his concern for *stability*. As Freeman puts it, Rawls was primarily occupied by two questions, "what does justice require of us?" and "given what justice requires, are humans capable of it?" (2007: 323). The two principles tell us what justice requires. Whether we are capable of it is a matter of whether a society regulated by justice as fairness will be stable, and whether people will embrace and be motivated by the principles and the institutions that follow from these first principles. Stability, for Rawls, is a moralized concept. Mere Hobbesian *modus vivendi* agreements are not acceptable, although they may be a stepping-stone to stability properly understood.

Rawls's concern for stability is often associated with his second book, *Political Liberalism*, which he describes as addressing the question, "how is it possible that there may exist over time a stable and just society of free and equal citizens profoundly divided by reasonable though incompatible religious, philosophical, and moral doctrines?" (1993: xviii). However, the problem is integral to A *Theory of Justice*, and the answer given there is essential in understanding Rawls's later work.

In Part III of A *Theory of Justice*, Rawls approaches the problem of stability in two ways. First, in chapter VIII, he explains how people can come to have an effective sense of justice (the disposition to act in accordance with, *and out of respect for*, justice). Chapter IX asks the far more difficult and profound question of whether it can be shown that acting in accordance with one's sense of justice is congruent with one's good.[5] To answer this question, Rawls called upon the Kantian interpretation of his theory (1971: 256; 1980; for discussion see Barry 1995a; Mendus 1999). The idea being to show that we achieve moral autonomy and fully realize our natures in acting in accordance with our sense of justice.

In retrospect, Rawls identified this Kantian argument for stability as "a serious problem" and as "not consistent with the view as a whole" (1993: xv–xvi). This change of position is sometimes attributed to the communitarian challenge to liberalism (see below). For example, William Connolly claims that the communitarian writer Michael Sandel (1953–) "almost singlehandedly motivated Rawls to redefine his theory in an attempt to remove metaphysical elements from it" (Connolly 2006: 831), but there is no evidence for this (indeed, the evidence is quite the opposite, see Rawls 1993: xix n.; Freeman 2007: 6). Rather, Rawls realized that invoking a comprehensive account of Kantian autonomy was incompatible with the requirement that free and equal citizens, who differ profoundly in their views about the good, ought to be able to give public endorsement to the justification of the two principles as regulative of their way of life together.

Thus *Political Liberalism* reworks the argument for stability and in doing so narrows the scope of the theory as a whole. Justice as fairness is presented as a "freestanding," "political" conception of justice. That is, it is neutral with respect to moral, epistemological, and metaphysical questions. Similarly, the idea of free and equal persons in A *Theory of Justice* is transformed in the later work into a description of citizens and the way in which they view one another when engaged in public matters. Thus, whilst a committed Christian may regard herself and others as fundamentally made in the image of God, as a citizen she respects other citizens, who have different views, as "free and equal." When reasoning together about the demands of justice, then, she will understand the need to present her arguments in terms all can accept, which Rawls calls terms of "public reason."

Rawls's idea is to put to one side questions of the deep justification of the principles of justice since on this it would unreasonable to expect agreement in circumstances of profound pluralism. Nevertheless, using resources "implicit in the public political culture" (1993: 13) of democratic societies, Rawls argues that agreement is still possible on the principles of justice. The issue, though, is how such principles can be the basis of a stable society (in Rawls's sense) if questions of their deep justification are removed from the public domain. His answer is that the principles can be the subject of an "overlapping consensus" (1993: Lecture IV). The idea is that reasonable citizens will be able to endorse the freestanding conception of justice each in accordance with her own beliefs about the good. So, a Kantian, a utilitarian, and a Catholic, for example, will endorse the demands of justice on the basis of autonomy, the promotion of utility, and accordance with God's will, respectively. Of course, when engaging with one another, each must "translate" their beliefs into reasons that are publicly acceptable – into public reason – for not to do so would be to fail to respect the political status of the other as a free and equal citizen.

Political Liberalism has attracted admiration and criticism, but has not had the kind of profound effect on political philosophy that is associated with A *Theory of Justice*. In reworking his theory as appropriate for, and applicable only to, modern democratic societies, Rawls restricted its ambition. That said, in emphasizing the importance and apparent permanence of pluralism, and in promoting the idea of public reason as an appropriate response to that, the later Rawls has had a significant influence on the debate over "multiculturalism" (see below).

Other contracts

Robert Nozick

Rawls's main target in A *Theory of Justice* was utilitarianism, which he criticized for being insensitive to "the distinction between persons" (1971: 27). Right at the start of the book, Rawls declares that "each person possesses an inviolability founded on justice that even the welfare of society as a whole cannot override" (p. 3). Perhaps the most significant challenge to Rawlsian theory to emerge soon after A *Theory of Justice* begins in a seemingly similar vein: "individuals have rights," according to Robert Nozick, "and there are things no person or group may do to them (without violating their rights)" (Nozick 1974: ix).

Nozick's *Anarchy, State, and Utopia* builds from this starting point in addressing what he takes to be "the fundamental question of political philosophy … whether there should be any state at all" (1974: 4). The rights that individuals have, according to Nozick, extend to the use and control over their own bodies and to ownership of such external resources as they have justly acquired. In this, he explicitly follows John Locke, from whom he also borrows his account of just acquisition (1974: 175–82).

Nozick adopts the traditional contract device and follows how individuals would reason from a state of nature, that is, from a condition of having no political authority at all. He argues that persons in these circumstances would entrust their security to "protective associations." The role of these associations would be to defend their customers from rights violations, or, where these occur, to extract compensation and deliver punishments to offenders on behalf of their clients (1974: 12–15). He goes on to argue for the emergence of a "dominant protective association," which – despite initial appearances (see p. 25) – is of the form of a "minimal state." Thus, although an agent may use her freedoms and rights together with others in pursuit of some good, the state is restricted to the role of "rights protector" and can raise funds through taxation *only* to serve this purpose.

Nozick's attitude to the state, and the seriousness with which he treats the possibility of anarchism, is representative of a small, but significant movement within the literature on political obligation. Although it was in some sense the dominant question of the early modern social contract theorists – and, in the form of the justification of civil disobedience, an important issue during the civil rights and nuclear disarmament movements – the question of political obligation was overshadowed by that of justice in the second half of the twentieth century. That said, a number of philosophers have continued to engage with it and, amongst those, a number have sustained the anarchist tradition (see, for example, Wolff 1970; Simmons 1979). However, it is Nozick's entitlement theory of justice, and assault on Rawlsian "pattern" theories, rather than his account of the state that continues to attract the most attention.

An "entitlement" theory of justice flows naturally from Nozick's starting point that people have rights over their justly acquired holdings. Once we have organized things such that each person is entitled to her holdings, then a just distribution will simply be whatever results from free exchange between her and others. Of course, tracing whether current actual holdings were justly acquired (in accordance with Nozick's account of just acquisition) will be difficult and may be impossible. If so, we may need to engage in some kind of "one off" redistribution, but after that we should respect the fact that justice is whatever results from people's free choices: "from each as they choose, to each as they are chosen" (Nozick 1974: 160).

Nozick's argument has a certain intuitive appeal. In a famous example, he asks the reader to imagine a starting point in which all people have exactly that to which they are justly entitled under whatever scheme of justice (Rawlsian, utilitarian, egalitarian, etc.) the reader prefers. Many of these people – a million of them in a season – freely choose to go to see a famous basketball player, Wilt Chamberlain, play. Chamberlain has negotiated a contract with his team such that 25 cents from the ticket price goes to him. The spectators know this and when they go to see the game they drop a quarter into buckets labeled "Chamberlain." At the end of the season, Chamberlain is $250,000 richer. The starting point was just – indeed, it was the reader's preferred starting point; each transfer was free and voluntarily engaged in, so, Nozick claims, the outcome must be just (1974: 161). Moreover, any attempt to alter it – for example, to tax Chamberlain in order to re-establish the initial (say, Rawlsian) pattern of distribution – must be unjust. Thus, justice is "historical" in that whether a state of affairs is just depends on how it came about (p. 153), and "liberty upsets patterns" because once people use their holdings any pattern theory of justice will break down (pp.160–4).

The intuitive appeal of the Wilt Chamberlain example, though, is deceptive. Nozick draws the reader in by inviting her to choose her preferred account of justice to fix the initial holdings, but once that is done he treats those holdings in his own preferred way, as *absolute*. But, liberal egalitarians need not endorse any such account. They can claim that Chamberlain's income is held as part of a general scheme that includes taxation. In short, Nozick's conclusions follow from the very first sentence, quoted above, which grants absolute rights over person and property to rights holders. Once this is granted, his argument for the entitlement theory follows, but critics allege that the first claim is unsupported and so Nozick's theory is simply "libertarianism without foundations" (Nagel 1981; see also Barry 1975).

David Gauthier

Both Rawls and Nozick use the contract to tease out the implications of certain moral commitments. Rawls begins with people as free and equal, Nozick with people as rights holders. Both are instances of what Brian Barry calls "justice as impartiality" because they ask "what can freely be agreed on by equally well placed parties" (Barry 1995b: 51), although Barry would take issue with Nozick's account of what it is to be "equally well placed." Such an approach is liable (as we have seen) to two critical questions: first, if people's prior moral commitments differ, then won't it be the case that different theories will simply replicate this disagreement in different "contracts"? Second, even if some contractualist theory can demonstrate what is demanded by some moral concern, what reason do agents have to respect those demands in the real world?

So-called Hobbesian or contractarian (as against "contractualist") theorists take both these challenges seriously. They argue that the contract must not simply reflect prior moral convictions, but must explain morality, and our commitment to it, in terms of non-moral reasons. An early example of such an approach was Buchanan's *The Limits of Liberty* (1975), but its canonical modern statement appears in David Gauthier's *Morals by Agreement* (1986).

Gauthier (1932–) embraces Rawls's claim that society is a "co-operative venture for mutual advantage" (Rawls 1971: 4; Gauthier 1986: 10), but interprets that as requiring that each person must benefit from cooperation. Starting from a completely free market in which people act as they wish entirely unconstrained by moral rules, why, asks Gauthier, would people agree to cooperate with others under rules? The answer is that cooperation must give rise to mutually advantageous gains for all parties. If one party would not gain because she is all-powerful and so does not need the cooperation of others, then she has no reason to engage with others under rules. Similarly, if a different party is so weak that his participation brings nothing to the bargain then others have no reason to cooperate with him. For the great majority of people, though, cooperation is mutually beneficial.

However, cooperation brings with it risks. In particular, it would seem that each person's ideal would be for others to cooperate whilst he free-rides, picking up the benefits of cooperation whilst not paying the costs. Moreover, even if this problem could be overcome (say, because people were involved in multiple enterprises and so did not want to jeopardize future cooperation), Gauthier would not have a theory of *morality*, but merely one of rational cooperation. To justify calling his account "morals," and not simply "rules," by agreement, Gauthier must show that agents have reason to constrain the pursuit of their self-interest by rules even when defection from the agreement promises greater benefit. He does this by arguing that we have reason to become "constrained" rather than "straightforward" maximizers; where the latter simply do that which will maximize their self-interest, but the former "reason in a different way" (1986: 170). The difference is that the constrained maximizer is disposed not to consider the benefits of defecting, but only whether the offer is worked out properly and whether the benefit to him is greater than it would be if there was universal non-cooperation.

Gauthier's argument that we have reason to become constrained maximizers has been subject to persistent criticism (see Copp 1991; Matravers 2000: 168–75). However, that criticism is muted when compared to the reaction to his overall project. The problem, the critics allege, is that whilst the principles that would emerge as mutually advantageous would coincide with some of our existing moral beliefs, the overlap would only be partial. In particular, justice as mutual advantage leaves out those who have nothing to bring to the bargain. As Gauthier puts it, "animals, the unborn, the congenitally handicapped and defective, fall beyond the pale of a morality tied to mutuality" (1986: 268). It is this, more than anything, that has attracted the hostility of critics (see Barry 1995b: 39–46; Hampton 1991: 48–9) and led some to suggest that justice as mutual advantage is not so much an alternative theory of morality as a theory of an alternative morality (Kymlicka 1991: 190–1).

It is possible that Gauthier, and other mutual advantage theorists, would accept Kymlicka's claim. It is interesting to note that, for Rawls and Gauthier, the basic problem is fundamentally different. For Rawls, the world is, in a sense, filled with too much morality. People believe different things about the good and the right and what is needed, given that pluralism, is agreement about how to live together. Gauthier, of course, would not deny that pluralism is a fact, but his starting point is that moral rules need rational justification or must (rationally) be abandoned. In this sense, we live in a world without morality (unless it can be rationally defended). Thus, for Rawls and others, insofar as justice as mutual advantage cannot generate principles that match our moral intuitions, it is to be condemned. For Gauthier, insofar as it generates any moral principles at all it is a triumph, for the test is not how far short it falls from our existing practices, but how far it can get from nothing given that we live in a "post-anthropomorphic, post-theocentric, post-technocratic world" (Gauthier 1988: 385).[6]

Post-Rawlsian theorizing

Communitarianism

For some time in the 1980s, Anglo-American political philosophy was dominated by the so-called "liberal/communitarian" debate (for a comprehensive analysis, see Mulhall and Swift 1996). The "communitarian" critique was contained in a flurry of books that came out between 1981 and 1985: Alasdair MacIntyre's *After Virtue* (1981, rev. edn. 1984), Michael Sandel's *Liberalism and the Limits of Justice* (1982), Michael Walzer's *Spheres of Justice* (1983), and Charles Taylor's *Philosophical Papers* (1985). At one time or another, all these writers have disowned the label "communitarian," but nevertheless they were (and are) grouped together as offering an interconnected set of criticisms of the orthodox liberal individualist position. In particular: first, they alleged that liberalism was universalistic and abstract, whereas moral reasoning should proceed from local shared practices and traditions (see Walzer 1983: xiv; MacIntyre 1984: chs. 4–5). Second, that the liberal emphasis on individual rights left too little room for the communitarian "politics of the common good" (Sandel 1984: 7). Third, that liberalism mistakenly thought of agents as "unencumbered," as "never defined by [their] aims and attachments" (Sandel 1984: 5). In contrast, communitarians insisted that some of the roles are partly constitutive of the self. In short, the prevailing communitarian thought was that moral and political theorizing had gone horribly wrong and in this it reflected modern, atomistic, liberal societies. For Alasdair MacIntyre, we are in a new "dark age" in which "the barbarians are not waiting beyond the frontiers; they have already been governing us for some time." The only sensible response to which is to retreat to build small communities in which the virtues could flourish whilst waiting for "another – doubtless very different – St Benedict [the patron saint of small communities]" (MacIntyre 1984: 263).

The liberal/communitarian debate largely fizzled out because it was rightly perceived that in their starkest form, the communitarian criticisms were of positions that liberals neither needed to, nor in fact did, hold (for a detailed analysis, see Caney 1992). Liberals did not hold to a metaphysical conception of the self as prior to its ends, but to the view that thinking of people in this way was necessary in determining principles of justice for pluralistic societies. Similarly, the liberal commitment to abstracting from local understandings and practices was not an attempt to occupy some strange "view from nowhere," but a necessary step back to gain some critical distance from what might be nothing but local prejudice.

In addition, the debate lost some of its edge as the two sides crept closer together. Liberals recognized the need to think more about the place of identity and community in their theories, and communitarians recognized that not all communities were admirable places which respected basic moral norms. The exception to this remains Alasdair MacIntyre, who has sustained his sophisticated Aristotle and Aquinas inspired critique of both liberalism and modernity (MacIntyre 1988; 1990).[7]

Multiculturalism

Although superficially similar to the debate between liberals and communitarians, the growing concern in political philosophy with multiculturalism and identity politics in fact represents an independent movement. What is captured by these labels is a sense that the dominant liberal model of society, and the dominant concern within political philosophy over questions of the distribution of income and wealth, fail to engage with the problems of those who are socially and culturally marginalized. In Nancy Fraser's terminology, we are too fixated by the "politics of redistribution." This approach focuses on socio-economic injustices that it aims to reduce by redistribution, thus bringing classes closer together. What we ignore is the "politics of recognition," which focuses on status inequalities that it aims to reduce by re-affirming "difference" (Fraser 1998; 2000).

Using these terms to provide the framework, it is possible to see why multiculturalism and identity politics embrace issues of importance to groups as diverse as homosexuals and the Amish, indigenous peoples and those – like the Québécois, Flemish, and Catalans – who wish to secede and establish their own liberal democratic states. In all these cases, what is alleged is that liberal individualism cannot accommodate *group* concerns, and is blind to the oppression from which some people suffer as members of groups (Young 1990; Kymlicka 1995a; Tully 1995; Ivison et al. 2000).

Debates over multiculturalism have given rise to philosophically interesting work on the idea of "groups" and "group" rights, as well as to intriguing practical political questions about how to deal with minorities living in liberal states (Goldberg 1995; Kymlicka 1995b; and Willet 1998 provide excellent guides to the field). They have also attracted some trenchant liberal criticisms (see Barry 2001).

Responsibility-sensitive egalitarianism

As was indicated in the discussion of Kymlicka's reading of Rawls, a plausible (if not Rawlsian) account of egalitarianism would have it that inequalities are permissible when they are the result of people's choices, but not when they are the result of chance or circumstance. Much of the initial motivation for the development of this account was owed to the search for a "currency of egalitarian justice" (Cohen 1989) or, to put it another way, an answer to Amartya Sen's question "equality of what?" (Sen 1980). So, for example, it might be wondered whether two people are treated equally if they are given the same resources or if they are given the resources each needs to ensure equality of outcome in terms of welfare (R. Dworkin 1981; Matravers 2007).

Although seemingly simple, this question has given rise to ever more complicated answers. There are now "resourcists," "welfarists," advocates of "equal access to advantage," "prioritarians," and "sufficientarians," all offering competing answers (for a good summary and collection, see Clayton and Williams 2000). The basic underlying issue, however, remains how far a liberal society is required to intervene in the lives of its citizens if it is to realize the ideal of equality of opportunity. The egalitarian push in answering this question has given rise to some of the most interesting work at the boundary of political philosophy and policy analysis. For example, John Roemer (1998) has developed a mechanism for measuring the impacts of advantage and disadvantage, which shows how radical the redistributive implications would be of taking seriously what he argues to be a standard liberal interpretation of equality of opportunity. And Philippe van Parijs (1951–) makes an argument that a liberal society should try to achieve a condition in which each person has an equal opportunity to fulfill his life plan, even if that life plan precludes paid employment (for example, life plans dedicated to caring for others, artistic endeavor, or voluntary work). To do this, van Parijs argues (1995), the liberal state should provide all its citizens with an unconditional basic income sufficient to live on. This proposal has given rise to an entire "basic income" literature – including the specialist journal *Basic Income Studies* – that is both philosophical and aimed at public policy.[8]

Feminism

It is customary to divide feminism into first, second, and third waves: the first predating the beginning of the century and lasting until the 1930s, the second occurring in the 1970s, and the third breaking in the late 1980s. Of course, all such divisions (in any area of philosophy) need to be treated with caution (and this one more than most since it tracks periods of political activism rather than intellectual inquiry). And, of course, the relative absence of campaigning feminist movements in the 1940s and 1950s needs to be put alongside the publication of Simone de Beauvoir's *The Second Sex* in 1949 (see also "Feminism in philosophy," Chapter 7).

The description "the first wave of feminism" is broadly meant to capture the political movements in support of the suffrage, education, and legal personhood that occurred throughout much of the world between (roughly) the middle of the nineteenth century and the 1930s. As indicated above, the gap between the end of this wave and the next set of feminist struggles incorporates the publication of de Beauvoir's book (de Beauvoir 1997). Drawing on Hegel's master–slave dialectic, de Beauvoir sought to explain the dominance of men over women and women's complicity in that relationship of domination. The critical issue for de Beauvoir was men's success at asserting their subjective consciousness through the recognition they receive from submissive women.

De Beauvoir's analysis, which involved looking at the myriad ways in which masculinity and femininity were depicted, and through which men and women understood themselves, as well as juxtaposing women and men as "other" and "subject," paved the way for a great deal of later theorizing. An example is the later focus on the many and various ways in which women are oppressed as well as, as Susan James puts it, the use of "pairs such as mind and body, public and private, and reason and emotion" in that oppression (James 2003: 504). Finally, for de Beauvoir the very category "woman" is a social construction, forged in childhood and through social practices; as she famously puts it "one is not born, but rather becomes, a woman" (de Beauvoir 1997: book II), which is an anti-essentialism that echoes through much – but importantly not all – feminist writing.

Within the second wave of feminism, spurred on by the emerging radical politics of the 1970s, the most significant shift was from a broadly Marxist analysis of the structural and economic oppression of women to an analysis in terms of men's sexual domination of women. This involved, in part, a focus on marriage, domestic violence, rape, and pornography (A. Dworkin 1981; MacKinnon 1989). Combining this approach with existing analyses of women's oppression gave a broad account of the various ways in which patriarchy was sustained. In particular, it was argued, many of these ways fell beyond the normal boundaries of both political inquiry and political practice. For example, women's domestic work was not thought to be part of "the economy" and the domestic abuse of women by their partners not thought to be a legitimate interest of the state in its role as upholder of the criminal law. Breaking this mold required recognizing that, as the famous slogan has it, "the personal is political."

The assault on political philosophy as incorporating a fundamentally gendered idea of the subject has taken a number of forms. First, feminist critics have alleged that the mere existence of equal political rights does not ensure equality if those rights are understood in the same way as when they were reserved strictly for men (Elshtain 1981; Pateman 1989). Second, they believed that the liberal state, and liberal theorizing about the state, extended a notion of a private sphere that contributed to the marginalization of women (Young 1990). Third, and explicitly directed at Rawls, their objection was that the liberal focus on impartial justice as "the first virtue of social institutions" (Rawls 1971; 3) failed both to deal with inequalities in the family (Okin 1989) and to accommodate women's different approach to moral theorizing (Gilligan 1982).

Feminism's third wave shares a great deal with the rise of multicultural and identity politics discussed above. That is, whereas the first and second waves were largely concerned with "women," the third is more sensitive to differences between, say, black and white, western and non-western, women (see, for example, Ong 1988; Spelman 1988; Ang 1995). To an extent, this is a sign of the success of feminist philosophy in moving from being a discrete area of inquiry to being an important part of the mainstream of political philosophy.

Concluding remarks: the contribution of the twentieth century and looking to the future

If it were true that political philosophy is nothing other than a series of "footnotes to Plato," then it is unlikely that one could say much about the contribution made to the discipline by those working in the twentieth century. Fortunately, it is not true, or not wholly true. Nevertheless, it is difficult to know by what criterion one should judge "contribution" because to make a contribution one must normally take something forward or improve it, and it is hard to say what it is to take political philosophy forward, or to make it better.

What one can say, I think, is that the interdisciplinarity re-established in the twentieth century – which involves, for example, the incorporation of rational choice and game theory into political philosophy – has done much to improve the discipline. Moreover, political philosophy has contributed to the defeat (at least for the moment) of the kinds of theories that provided intellectual support to the murderous regimes (in Nazi Germany, China, the former USSR, Cambodia, and so on) that blighted the twentieth century. That is a significant achievement, and whether it can be sustained depends in part on the imagination of liberal political philosophers faced with the next set of outrages, whether perpetrated by terrorists flying into buildings in New York or (although I do not think them equivalent) by our own governments ignoring, in Guantanamo Bay, the hard-won gains of the twentieth century.

Where the discipline will go in the future is, of course, more difficult to say. Perhaps there will be a continuation of the kind of grand theorizing epitomized by *A Theory of Justice*, except applied to the kinds of global issues such as the distribution of resources internationally, and global warming, that appeared only towards the end of last century. An example of such theorizing is Martha Nussbaum's development of Sen's "capabilities" approach applied to the problems that she identifies as being at the frontiers of justice: disability, nationality, and inter-species justice (Nussbaum 2006). Certainly, if Bernard Williams (1929–2003) is right that "living political philosophy arises only in a context of political urgency" (2006: 155), then the future states of humanity and the planet should (depressingly enough) give it more than enough to feed on (see for a start, Caney 2005; Barry 2005: Part VI).

Perhaps as likely is that political philosophy will turn away from theorizing about the precise nature of justice, and with it away from the close relationship it established with moral philosophy during the second half of the twentieth century. If so, its guiding lights from that period may well not be any of the thinkers discussed above, but the likes of Bernard Williams, Michael Oakeshott, and Michel Foucault, for all of whom – despite their many differences – the application of philosophical ideas to political practice is a matter of the particular, local, and historically informed (see Oakeshott 1962; 1975; Foucault 1977; 1980; Williams 2005; 2006).

Notes

1 Earlier versions of this chapter were papers given at Durham and York Universities. The discussion at Durham was extremely helpful at a very early stage and I would like to thank the audience and the organizers, Stamatoula Panagakou and Maria Dimova-Cookson. My colleagues at York were (as ever) stimulating, critical, and helpful. I am very grateful to them for that and for their continuing intellectual companionship.

2 I should add that I have not dealt with the philosophy of law. Thus, there is no discussion of the legal theory of, for example, Kelsen, Hart, Dworkin, and Raz. But for a review of philosophy of law and punishment covering the latter half of the twentieth century, see Calvin G. Normore, "Philosophy of Law," in John V. Canfield (ed.) *Routledge History of Philosophy*, vol. X: *Philosophy of Meaning, Knowledge and Value in the Twentieth Century* (London and New York: Routledge, 1997), pp. 342–63.

  I have also not dealt with changes and advances in the history of political thought.

3 Not least because, as Rawls points out, in a market society it is true that what one "deserves" – is entitled to – depends on the contribution one makes. The extent of one's contribution, however, varies in accordance with supply and demand. Were one committed to a *pre*-justicial notion of desert one would have to hold that "when someone's abilities are less in demand or have deteriorated (as in the case of singers) his moral deservingness undergoes a similar shift" (Rawls 1971: 311).

4 Rawls himself writes of the people in the original position that "it is clear that since the differences among the parties are unknown to them, and everyone is equally rational and similarly situated, each is convinced by the same arguments. Therefore, we can view the choice in the original position from the standpoint of one person selected at random" (1971: 139).

5 Thus, to return to Brian Barry's comment on Rawls, chapter VIII in A *Theory of Justice* contains an account of moral psychology and chapter IX a theory of the human good. Rawls's congruence question is, of course, the first question of political philosophy (in the sense that it is Socrates' question in *Republic*: is justice valuable both for its own sake and for its consequences?).

6 In a memorable phrase, Gauthier insists that *Morals by Agreement*, in eschewing reference to natural rights, and in refusing to assume that human beings have equal moral value, is "an attempt to write moral theory for adults" (Gauthier 1988: 385).

7 It is worth adding a political note. Despite its relatively brief philosophical life, communitarianism became, and remains, a remarkably active political movement, which, in the form of "The Communitarian Network," has been politically influential in both the UK and USA.

8 A good example of the collaboration is the Basic Income Earth Network (http://www.etes.ucl.ac.be/bien/Index.html) formed by philosophers, political scientists, and policy wonks.

References

Althusser, L. (1971) *Lenin and Philosophy, and Other Essays*. New York: Monthly Review Press.

_____ (1977) *For Marx*. London: New Left Books.

Ang, I. (1995) "I'm a feminist but . . . 'other' women and postnational feminism." In B. Caine and R. Pringle (eds.) *Transitions: New Australian Feminisms*, New York: Palgrave Macmillan, pp. 57–73.

Arendt, H. (1951) *The Origins of Totalitarianism*. New York: Harcourt Brace & Co.

_____ (1958) *The Human Condition*. Chicago: University of Chicago Press.

Arrow, K. J. (1951) *Social Choice and Individual Values*. New York: Wiley.

_____ (1973) "Some ordinalist-utilitarian notes on Rawls's sense of justice." *Journal of Philosophy* 70: 245–63.

Ayer, A. J. (1936) *Language, Truth and Logic*. London: Victor Gollancz.

Barry, B. M. (1973) *The Liberal Theory of Justice: A Critical Examination of the Principal Doctrines in A Theory of Justice by John Rawls*. Oxford: Clarendon Press.

_____ (1975) Review of Nozick, Anarchy, State and Utopia. *Political Theory* 3: 331–6.

_____ (1989) *Theories of Justice*: vol. 1 of *A Treatise on Social Justice*. Hemel Hempstead, Herts.: Harvester-Wheatsheaf.

_____ (1990) *Political Argument: A Reissue with a New Introduction*. Berkeley and Los Angeles: University of California Press.

_____ (1995a) "John Rawls and the search for stability." *Ethics* 105: 874–915.

_____ (1995b) *Justice as Impartiality*: vol. 2 of *A Treatise on Social Justice*. Oxford: Clarendon Press.

_____ (2001) *Culture and Equality: An Egalitarian Critique of Multiculturalism*. Cambridge: Polity Press.

_____ (2005) *Why Social Justice Matters*. Cambridge: Polity Press.

Beauvoir, S. de. (1997) *The Second Sex*. London: Vintage.

Berlin, I. (1962) "Does political theory still exist?" In P. Laslett and W. G. Runciman (eds.) *Philosophy, Politics and Society*, 2nd series. Oxford: Blackwell, pp. 1–33.

_____ (1969) "Two concepts of liberty" [1958]. In *Four Essays on Liberty*, Oxford: Oxford University Press.

Buchanan, J. M. (1975) *The Limits of Liberty: Between Anarchy and Leviathan*. Chicago: University of Chicago Press.

Buchanan, J. M. and G. Tullock (1962) *The Calculus of Consent: Logical Foundations of Constitutional Democracy*. Ann Arbor: University of Michigan Press.

Caney, S. (1992) "Liberalism and communitarianism: a misconceived debate." *Political Studies* 40: 273–89.

_____ (2005) *Justice Beyond Borders: A Global Political Theory*. Oxford: Oxford University Press.

Clayton, M. and A. Williams (eds.) (2000) *The Ideal of Equality*. London: Palgrave.

Cohen, G. (1989) "On the currency of egalitarian justice." *Ethics* 99/4: 906–44.

Connolly, W. (2006) "Then and now: participant observation in political theory." In J. Dryzeck, B. Honig, and A. Phillips (eds.) *The Oxford Handbook of Political Theory*, Oxford: Oxford University Press, pp. 827–43.

Copp, D. (1991) "Contractarianism and moral skepticism." In P. Vallentyne (ed.) *Contractarianism and Rational Choice: Essays on David Gauthier's Morals By Agreement*. New York: Cambridge University Press, pp. 196–228.

Dahl, R. (1956) *A Preface to Democratic Theory*. Chicago: University of Chicago Press.

Dryzeck, J., B. Honig, and A. Phillips (2006) Introduction. In *The Oxford Handbook of Political Theory*, Oxford: Oxford University Press, pp. 3–41.

Dworkin, A. (1981) *Pornography: Men Possessing Women*. London: Women's Press.

Dworkin, R. (1975) "The original position." In N. Daniels (ed.) *Reading Rawls: Critical Studies on Rawls' A Theory of Justice*, New York: Basic Books, pp. 16–52.

_____ (1981) "What is equality? Part I: Equality of welfare; Part II: Equality of resources." *Philosophy and Public Affairs* 10/3: 185–246, 10/4: 283–345.

Elshtain, J. (1981) *Public Man, Private Woman: Women in Social and Political Thought*. Princeton, NJ: Princeton University Press.

Foucault, M. (1977) *Discipline and Punish: The Birth of the Prison*. London: Allen Lane.

_____ (1980) *Power/Knowledge: Selected Interviews and Other Writings, 1972–1977*. New York: Pantheon Books.

Fraser, N. (1998) "Social justice in the age of identity politics: redistribution, recognition, and participation." *The Tanner Lectures on Human Values*, XIX, ed. G. Peterson, Salt Lake City: University of Utah Press.

_____ (2000) "Rethinking recognition." *New Left Review* 3: 107–20.

Freeman, S. R. (2003) "Introduction: John Rawls – an overview." In S. R. Freeman (ed.) *The Cambridge Companion to Rawls*, Cambridge: Cambridge University Press.

_____ (2007) *Justice and the Social Contract: Essays on Rawlsian Political Philosophy*. Oxford: Oxford University Press.

Gauthier, D. (1977) "The social contract as ideology." *Philosophy and Public Affairs* 6: 130–64.

_____ (1986) *Morals by Agreement*. Oxford: Oxford University Press.

_____ (1988) "Moral artifice." *Canadian Journal of Philosophy* 18: 385–418.

Gilligan, C. (1982) *In a Different Voice: Psychological Theory and Women's Development*. Cambridge, MA: Harvard University Press.

Goldberg, D. (ed.) (1995) *Multiculturalism: A Critical Reader*. Oxford: Blackwell.

Gramsci, A. (1971) *Selections from the Prison Notebooks*. London: Lawrence & Wishart.

Habermas, J. (1995) "Reconciliation through the public use of reason: remarks on John Rawls's political liberalism." *Journal of Philosophy* 92: 109–31.

Hampton, J. (1980) "Contracts and choices: does Rawls have a social contract theory?" *Journal of Philosophy* 77/6: 315–38.

_____ (1991) "Two faces of contractarian thought." In P. Vallentyne (ed.) *Contractarianism and Rational Choice: Essays on David Gauthier's Morals by Agreement*, New York: Cambridge University Press, pp. 31–55.

Harsanyi, J. C. (1982) "Morality and the theory of rational behaviour." In A. Sen and B. A. O. Williams (eds.) *Utilitarianism and Beyond*, Cambridge: Cambridge University Press, pp. 39–62.

Hart, H. L. A. (1961) *The Concept of Law*. Oxford: Clarendon Press.

_____ (1975) "Rawls on liberty and its priority." In N. Daniels (ed.) *Reading Rawls*, New York: Basic Books, pp. 230–52.

Haworth, A. (2006) "Political philosophy." In A. Grayling, A. Pyle and N. Goulder (eds.) *Encyclopedia of British Philosophy*, Bristol: Thoemmes Continuum, pp. 2537–43.

Hayek, F. A. von (1960) *The Constitution of Liberty*. Chicago: University of Chicago Press.

Ivison, D., P. Patton, and W. Sanders (eds.) (2000) *Political Theory and the Rights of Indigenous Peoples*. Cambridge: Cambridge University Press.

James, S. (2003) "Feminisms." In T. Ball and R. Bellamy (eds.) *The Cambridge History of Twentieth-Century Political Thought*, Cambridge: Cambridge University Press, pp. 493–516.

Kymlicka, W. (1991) "The social contract tradition." In P. Singer (ed.) *A Companion to Ethics*, Oxford: Blackwell, pp. 186–96.

_____ (1995a) *Multicultural Citizenship: A Liberal Theory of Minority Rights*. Oxford: Oxford University Press.

_____ (ed.) (1995b) *The Rights of Minority Cultures*. Oxford: Oxford University Press.

_____ (2002) *Contemporary Political Philosophy: An Introduction*, 2nd edn. Oxford: Oxford University Press.

Laslett, P. (1956) Introduction. In *Philosophy, Politics and Society*, 1st series, Oxford: Blackwell, pp. vii–xv.

Lukács, G. (1971) *History and Class Consciousness*. London: Merlin Press.

MacIntyre, A. (1984) [1981] *After Virtue: A Study in Moral Theory*. Notre Dame, IN: University of Notre Dame Press.

_____ (1988) *Whose Justice? Which Rationality?* Notre Dame, IN: University of Notre Dame Press.

_____ (1990) *Three Rival Versions of Moral Enquiry*. Notre Dame, IN: University of Notre Dame Press.

MacKinnon, C. A. (1989) *Toward a Feminist Theory of the State*. Cambridge, MA: Harvard University Press.

Matravers, M. (2000) *Justice and Punishment: The Rationale of Coercion*. Oxford: Oxford University Press.

_____ (2007) *Responsibility and Justice*. Cambridge: Polity Press.

Mendus, S. (1999) "The importance of love in Rawls's theory of justice." *British Journal of Political Science* 29: 57–75.

Mulhall, S. and A. Swift (1996) *Liberals and Communitarians*. Oxford: Blackwell.

Nagel, T. (1975) "Rawls on justice." In N. Daniels (ed.) *Reading Rawls: Critical Studies on Rawls' A Theory of Justice*, New York: Basic Books, pp. 1–15.

_____ (1981) "Libertarianism without foundations." In J. Paul (ed.) *Reading Nozick*, Totowa, NJ: Rowman & Littlefield.

Nozick, R. (1974) *Anarchy, State and Utopia*. New York: Basic Books.

Nussbaum, M. (2006) *Frontiers of Justice: Disability, Nationality, Species Membership*. Cambridge, MA: Harvard University Press.

Oakeshott, M. J. (1962) *Rationalism in Politics and Other Essays*. London: Methuen.

_____ (1975) *On Human Conduct*. Oxford: Clarendon Press.

Okin, S. (1989) *Justice, Gender, and the Family*. New York: Basic Books.

Ong, A. (1988) "Colonialism and modernity: feminist re-presentations of women in non-western societies." *Inscriptions* 3/4: 79–93.

Pateman, C. (1989) *The Disorder of Women*. Cambridge: Cambridge University Press.

Pettit, P. (1993) "Analytical philosophy." In R. Goodin and P. Pettit (eds.) *A Companion to Contemporary Political Philosophy*, Oxford: Blackwell, pp. 7–38.

Popper, K. R. (1945) *The Open Society and its Enemies*. London: Routledge.

_____ (1957) *The Poverty of Historicism*. London: Routledge & Kegan Paul.

Rawls, J. B. (1955) "Two concepts of rules." In J. Rawls and S. R. Freeman (eds.) *Collected Papers*, Cambridge, MA: Harvard University Press, 1999, pp. 20–46.

_____ (1958) "Justice as fairness." In J. Rawls and S. R. Freeman (eds.) *Collected Papers*, Cambridge, MA: Harvard University Press, 1999, pp. 47–72.

_____ (1971) *A Theory of Justice*. Cambridge, MA: Harvard University Press.

_____ (1974a) "Reply to Alexander and Musgrave." In J. Rawls and S. R. Freeman (eds.) *Collected Papers*, Cambridge, MA: Harvard University Press, 1999, pp. 232–53.

_____ (1974b) "Some reasons for the maximin criterion." In J. Rawls and S. R. Freeman (eds.) *Collected Papers*, Cambridge, MA: Harvard University Press, 1999, pp. 225–31.

_____ (1980) "Kantian constructivism in moral theory." In J. Rawls and S. R. Freeman (eds.) *Collected Papers*, Cambridge, MA: Harvard University Press, 1999, pp. 303–58.

_____ (1982) "The basic liberties and their priority." *The Tanner Lectures on Human Values, III*, ed. S. M. McMurrin, Salt Lake City: University of Utah Press, pp. 1–87.

_____ (1988) "The priority of right and ideas of the good." In J. Rawls and S. R. Freeman (eds.) *Collected Papers*, Cambridge, MA: Harvard University Press, 1999, pp. 449–72.

_____ (1993) *Political Liberalism*. New York: Columbia University Press.

Roemer, J. (1998) *Equality of Opportunity*. Cambridge, MA: Harvard University Press.

Sandel, M. (1982) *Liberalism and the Limits of Justice*. Cambridge: Cambridge University Press.

_____ (1984) Introduction. In *Liberalism and its Critics*, Oxford: Blackwell, pp. 1–11.

Saxonhouse, A. (2006) "Exile and re-entry: political theory yesterday and tomorrow." In J. Dryzeck, B. Honig, and A. Phillips (eds.) *The Oxford Handbook of Political Theory*, Oxford: Oxford University Press, pp. 844–58.

Scanlon, T. M. (1982) "Contractualism and utilitarianism." In A. Sen and B. A. O. Williams (eds.) *Utilitarianism and Beyond*, Cambridge: Cambridge University Press, pp. 103–28.

_____ (1998) *What We Owe to Each Other*. Cambridge, MA: Harvard University Press.

Scheffler, S. (2001) *Boundaries and Allegiances: Problems of Justice and Responsibility in Liberal Thought*. Oxford: Oxford University Press.

_____ (2003) "What is egalitarianism?" *Philosophy and Public Affairs* 31/1: 5–39.

Schelling, T. C. (1960) *The Strategy of Conflict*. Cambridge, MA: Harvard University Press.

Sen, A. (1980) "Equality of what?" *The Tanner Lectures on Human Values, I*, ed. S. M. McMurrin, Salt Lake City: University of Utah Press, pp. 353–69.

Simmons, A. J. (1979) *Moral Principles and Political Obligations*. Princeton, NJ: Princeton University Press.

Spelman, E. (1988) *Inessential Women: Problems of Exclusion in Feminist Thought*. Boston: Beacon Press.

Strauss, L. (1953) *Natural Right and History*. Chicago: University of Chicago Press.

_____ (1962) "An epilogue." In H. Storing (ed.) *Essays on the Scientific Study of Politics*, New York: Holt, Rinehart and Winston, pp. 305–27.

Taylor, C. (1985) *Human Agency and Language: Philosophical Papers I; Philosophy and the Human Sciences: Philosophical Papers II*. Cambridge: Cambridge University Press.

Tully, J. (1995) *Strange Multiplicity: Constitutionalism in an Age of Diversity*. Cambridge: Cambridge University Press.

van Parijs, P. (1995) *Real Freedom For All*. Oxford: Oxford University Press.

von Neumann, J. and O. Morgenstern (1944) *Theory of Games and Economic Behavior*. Princeton, NJ: Princeton University Press.

Walzer, M. (1983) *Spheres of Justice: A Defence of Pluralism and Equality*. Oxford: Blackwell.

Weldon, T. D. (1953) *The Vocabulary of Politics*. Harmondsworth: Penguin.

Willet, C. (ed.) (1998) *Theorizing Multiculturalism: A Guide to the Current Debate*. Oxford: Blackwell.

Williams, B. A. O. (2005) *In the Beginning Was the Deed: Realism and Moralism in Poltical Argument*. Princeton, NJ: Princeton University Press.

_____ (2006) *Philosophy as a Humanistic Discipline*. Princeton, NJ: Princeton University Press.

Wolff, R. (1970) *In Defense of Anarchism*. New York: Harper.

Wolin, S. (1960) *Politics and Vision: Continuity and Innovation in Western Political Thought*. Boston: Little, Brown.

Young, I. M. (1990) *Justice and the Politics of Difference*. Princeton, NJ: Princeton University Press.

Further reading

Two excellent introductions to contemporary political philosophy (largely dealing with Rawls and after) are:

Kymlicka, W. (2002) *Contemporary Political Philosophy: An Introduction*, 2nd edn. Oxford: Oxford University Press. (Includes chapters on Marxism, multiculturalism, and feminism, in addition to covering liberalism and utilitarianism).

Swift, A. (2006) *Political Philosophy: A Beginner's Guide for Students and Politicians*, 2nd edn. Cambridge: Polity Press. (Shorter, and more narrowly focused, than Kymlicka, but provides a useful, intelligent, discussion of the main issues).

There are several useful compendia for information about all aspects of contemporary political philosophy:

Ball, T. and R. Bellamy (eds.) (2003) *The Cambridge History of Twentieth Century Political Thought*. Cambridge: Cambridge University Press.

Dryzeck, J., B. Honig, and A. Phillips (eds.) (2006) *The Oxford Handbook of Political Theory*. Oxford: Oxford University Press.

Goodin, R. and P. Pettit (eds.) (1993) *A Companion to Contemporary Political Philosophy*. Oxford: Blackwell.

The sister volume to this on ethics is also useful:

Singer, P. (ed.) (1991) *A Companion to Ethics*. Oxford: Blackwell.

Barry, B. M. (1990) *Political Argument*. Berkeley: University of California Press. (Contains a new Introduction that sets the scene for the original publication of the book in 1965 and for the emergence of Rawls's work).

_____ (1989) *Theories of Justice*, vol. 1 of *A Treatise on Social Justice*. Hemel Hempstead, Herts.: Harvester-Wheatsheaf. (A magisterial work that has been influential in setting the terms of debate in contemporary political philosophy, in particular in contrasting justice as impartiality and justice as mutual advantage. Includes discussions of the historical antecedents of contemporary debates in Hume and Hobbes).

22
TWENTIETH-CENTURY AESTHETICS

Paul Guyer

Introduction

Western aesthetics began on a negative note with Plato's attempt to restrict the role of music, poetry, and drama in the education of the guardians of his ideal republic. Plato attacked the prestige of these arts in Greek culture on two fronts: he held mimetic works of art to be of little cognitive value, since they merely imitate concrete objects and events that are themselves merely imitations of the true objects of knowledge, the Forms, and thus artists, poets in particular, do not possess the expertise about real life they claim; and many of the kinds of art that were most popular among the Greeks, such as tragedy, are morally deleterious, since the reception and especially the performance[1] of works of such arts encourage indulgence in emotions that are inconsistent with virtuous self-control. Plato would allow only truthful hymns to the gods and properly refined forms of music and dance into the educational system of his well-ordered republic.[2] Most subsequent philosophers have loved the arts too much to accept Plato's epistemological and moral critique. So throughout history (even though the name for the discipline was coined by Alexander Baumgarten (1714–62) only in 1735),[3] the central task of philosophical aesthetics has been to respond to Plato, either by defending the value of a form of human experience that is essentially independent from the ordinary concerns of both cognition and action, or by arguing for fruitful relations between aesthetic experience on the one hand and our fundamental cognitive or moral objectives on the other without surrendering what seems to be distinctive in aesthetic experience and its objects.

In the eighteenth century, when aesthetic theorizing was well launched in Britain and France before Baumgarten baptized it in Germany, these options were all explored. Francis Hutcheson (1694–1746), for example, argued that our sense of beauty is completely independent of conceptual judgments in general and therefore judgments of practical value – interest – in particular, and that although our possession of the sense of beauty is a sign of God's benevolence toward us it has no direct influence on our conduct.[4] By contrast, Anthony Ashley Cooper (1671–1713), the third Earl of Shaftesbury, was a Neoplatonist who asserted the underlying identity of the beautiful with the true and the good, arguing that the ultimate goal of knowledge is the recognition of cosmic order, that the ultimate goal of action is augmenting that order, and that our experience of order in the form of beauty – primarily natural rather than artistic – can support us in both of these endeavors.[5] Immanuel Kant (1724–1804) then tried to bridge the gulf between these two approaches. He argued that disinterested pleasure in the beautiful, although, as Hutcheson argued, it is not a form of cognition, is nevertheless rooted in a distinctive yet universally valid condition of the cognitive powers, the state that he characterized as a free play between imagination and understanding with the representation of an object. It is precisely because our response to a beautiful object is free from constraint by cognition or morality that beauty can nevertheless serve as a palpable symbol of the autonomy, or positively law-governed freedom of the will, that is the foundation of morality. On this basis Kant held that the experience of beauty, whether natural or artistic, can prepare us to love disinterestedly, that is, apparently, can cooperate at the phenomenal level with our noumenal commitment to do what morality requires. Thus the beautiful is connected to the good, as Shaftesbury argued, although only indirectly. Kant also added an interpretation of the sublime, the other great subject of eighteenth-century aesthetics, according to which our feeling of the sublimity of nature (Kant did not think that art could be truly sublime) is a distinctive play between imagination and reason which yet can make palpable to us the power of our reason over our mere inclinations and thus prepare us to love even against our self-interest, as morality often requires.[6]

In the twentieth century, the arts underwent numerous convulsions of innovation in both form and content that seemed to break fundamental ties with artistic traditions and conventions going back to the Renaissance or even antiquity. The twentieth-century revolution in the arts certainly stimulated an enormous amount of aesthetic theorizing, and it can seem as if redefining the concept of art so that it could comprehend works that look or sound nothing like traditional art must have been the fundamental issue for twentieth-century aesthetics, replacing the traditional concern to define aesthetic experience by means of its differences from but connections to cognition and action.[7] But this appearance is misleading. On the one hand, finding a definition for art that will suffice to distinguish it from things with which it might be confused has often been a goal of traditional aesthetics as well; thus Kant's lectures on topics in aesthetics always defined the difference between poetry and rhetoric,[8] and Hegel began his lectures on fine art by discussing the differences between art, religion, and philosophy.[9] On the other hand, the basic task of understanding our experience of art and of the beauty and sublimity of nature in such a way that it is either independent of our cognitive and practical concerns or else distinctive but nevertheless valuably supportive of them has remained the basic project of most twentieth-century aesthetics. The present chapter will narrate the history of twentieth-century aesthetics on the basis of this assumption.

Aesthetics at the turn of the twentieth century

For some historiographical purposes, the "long" nineteenth century ended only in August 1914. For our purposes, however, although of course the cataclysm of World War I was a central event in the history of all aspects of western culture and therefore aesthetics as well, the history of twentieth-century aesthetics begins in the ten years from 1892 to 1902, the period that saw the publication of Bernard Bosanquet's *A History of Æsthetic* (1892), George Santayana's *The Sense of Beauty* (1896), Leo Tolstoy's *What is Art?* (published in English in 1898 before any Russian edition), and Benedetto Croce's *Aesthetics as the Science of Expression and General Linguistics* (1902). I will argue here that Tolstoy (1828–1910) and Santayana (1863–1952) can be taken as defining two extremes between which much of twentieth-century aesthetics was to seek a middle way along lines first laid down by Bosanquet (1848–1923) and Croce (1866–1952).

Emotional infection

Tolstoy's tract is a violent response to the ideology of "art for art's sake" or "aestheticism" that was celebrated in various artistic and intellectual circles through much of the nineteenth century. (The phrase "art for art's sake" first gained popularity from Théophile Gauthier's 1834 novel *Mademoiselle de Maupin*, and was later identified with writers such as Gustave Flaubert, Walter Pater, and Oscar Wilde.[10] The attitude it represents was often traced back to Kant,[11] but should really be traced back to a 1785 essay by Karl Philipp Moritz (1756–1793).[12]) Tolstoy rebelled at the thought that any form of pleasure, a fortiori pleasure in art for its own sake, could be intrinsically valuable (Tolstoy 1898: 35), and also argued that the mere pleasure that its consumption could deliver to a wealthy elite could not justify the human and economic costs of the production of expensive works of fine art such as grand opera (pp. 4–8). Instead, he insisted, the costs of the production and consumption of art could be justified only when art is the vehicle for the communication of socially valuable feelings other than pleasure itself, so that art is a means of communication among people" (p. 37). Tolstoy in fact transformed this normative claim about the value of art into a definition of art:

> To call up in oneself a feeling once experienced and, having called it up, to convey it by means of movements, lines, colours, sounds, images expressed in words, so that others experience the same feeling – in this consists the activity of art. Art is that human activity which consists in one man's consciously conveying to others, by certain external signs, the feelings he has experienced, and in others being infected by those feelings and also experiencing them. (1898: 39–40)

Tolstoy's model of communication requires that the artist actually experience the feeling his work is supposed to communicate – thus making the artist's sincerity a necessary condition of genuine art (in popular art criticism this allegedly necessary condition often seems to become a sufficient condition for artistic success) – and the audience in turn is supposed to experience the very same feeling. It is also striking that Tolstoy characterizes the relation between artist's feeling and audience's feeling in the strictly causal terminology of "infection"; there is no great emphasis on the freedom of the artist's imagination in artistic production, which had been an essential component of Kant's conception of genius, and even less emphasis on any freedom of imagination on the part of the audience – the freedom that was the central idea in Kant's explanation of the response to beauty as a free play of imagination and understanding and would be re-emphasized by many subsequent writers.[13] Finally, Tolstoy places a decisive restriction on what sorts of feelings are supposed to be infectiously communicated by genuine art: "The appreciation of the merits of art – that is, of the feelings it conveys – depends on people's understanding of the meaning of life, on what they see as good and evil," where "Good and evil in life are determined by what are called religions" (p. 42). All human individuals and societies, he holds, have "this religious consciousness ... of what is good and what is bad, and it is this religious consciousness that determines the worth of the feelings conveyed by art" (p. 43).[14]

Tolstoy thus rejects not only the aestheticism of the late nineteenth century, but central assumptions of aesthetic theory going back to the beginning of the eighteenth century: that pleasure in response to nature and art is intrinsically (even if not unconditionally) valuable, and that the freedom of the imagination that is central to such pleasure means that the aesthetic cannot simply be reduced to either the cognitive or the moral, even if it can stand in indirect but valuable relations to one or both of these. Tolstoy's inflamed moralism thus represents a return to Plato's attempt to exclude amoral and immoral arts from his ideal republic. The religious inflection of Tolstoy's moralism would not enjoy widespread acceptance among twentieth-century intellectuals, although his (and Plato's) insistence that art is valuable only insofar as it advances preferred moral or more specifically political ends would certainly be accepted by some, especially by some Marxist aestheticians.

Emotional isolation

The aestheticism of late nineteenth-century artists and intellectuals found many more defenders among turn of the century aestheticians. In the United States, Santayana's *The Sense of Beauty* rejected nineteenth-century metaphysical theories of art such as those of Schelling, Schopenhauer, and Hegel with the trenchant comment that "Such value as belongs to metaphysical derivations of the nature of the beautiful, comes to them not because they explain our primary feelings, which they cannot do, but because they express, and in fact, constitute some of our later appreciations" (Santayana 1896: 7) – later appreciations that are possible if we have accepted "metaphysical derivations" on independent grounds. Santayana (1863–1952) held that no metaphysical derivation or justification of the value of aesthetic experience is necessary or even possible because the "reduction of all values to immediate appreciations, to sensuous or vital activities, is so inevitable that it has struck even the minds most courageously rationalistic" (p. 20). He clearly returned to a Kantian foundation for aesthetic theory when he held that "it is in the spontaneous play of his faculties that man finds himself and his happiness," and identified the pleasures of aesthetic experience with those arising from the spontaneous play and freedom of the imagination. Like Kant and indeed other eighteenth-century philosophers such as Hutcheson and Hume, Santayana also interpreted beauty as the objective correlative of our subjective response, or as the reflection of the capacity of an object to stimulate us to aesthetic response. On his account, beauty is "value positive, intrinsic, and objectified ... pleasure regarded as the quality of a thing" (p. 31). By calling beauty a value, he meant that "it is not a perception of a matter of fact or a relation," but is "an emotion, an affection of our volitional and appreciative nature," thus not any emotion but pleasure itself. By calling it positive, he meant that "beauty is a pure gain which brings no evil with it" (p. 31). And by calling it objectified, he meant that it presents itself to us as if it were a quality "rather of things than of consciousness" (p. 32), although this is a claim about the phenomenology rather than the etiology of beauty. But Santayana then departed from Kant, or at least from the restrictive formalism of Kant's initial analysis of the proper object of judgments of taste,[15] by arguing that we can find beauty in the *materials* of works of both nature and art (Part II), in their *forms* (Part III), and in *expression*; this he defined quite abstractly as the affinities of experienced objects "to what is not at the time perceived ... a meaning and tone which upon investigation we shall see to have been the proper characteristics of other objects and feelings, associated with them once in our experience ... [t]he quality ... acquired by objects through association" (Part IV, p. 119). Here Santayana combined with Kant's formalism one of its main historical rivals, the British associationism that reached its zenith in a work exactly contemporaneous with Kant's third *Critique*, Archibald Alison's *Essays on the Nature and Principles of Taste*.[16]

Santayana's conceptions of material, form, and expression are broad, and his examples of them are varied, so the generosity of his conception of the sources of aesthetic value is a striking contrast to Tolstoy's puritanism. What is even more striking is his reversal of Tolstoy's form of moralism. As already noted, Santayana holds pleasure in beauty to be intrinsically valuable. By contrast, he holds morality to be concerned with the remediation of the ills of human life, and thus of great but strictly speaking only negative value, conditional upon the presence of ills and unfulfilled needs. If morality's "attempt to remove from life all its evils" were ever to be completely successful, then "we shall have little but æsthetic pleasures remaining to constitute unalloyed happiness" (pp. 19–20). In fact, Santayana holds, "Obedience to God or reason can originally recommend itself to a man only as the surest and ultimately least painful way of balancing his aims and synthesizing his desires" (p. 22), thereby maximizing scope for free play and aesthetic appreciation. To be sure, Santayana knows full well that morality's project of removing the ills of life never is complete, and thus that "The appreciation of beauty and its embodiment in the arts are activities which belong to our holiday life, when we are redeemed for the moment from the shadow of evil and the slavery to fear" (p. 17). In the actual conditions of human life, pursuit of the intrinsic value of aesthetic experience must often be foregone because of the urgent demands of morality. But this does not undermine the claim that the value of morality is ultimately instrumental and only that of aesthetic experience truly intrinsic.

A very similar view was advocated seven years later by a British philosopher whose immediate as well as subsequent influence was certainly greater than Santayana's, namely G. E. Moore (1873–1958). (For further discussion of Moore, see "The birth of analytic philosophy," Chapter 1 and "Twentieth-century moral philosophy," Chapter 20.) In his *Principia Ethica* of 1903, which would become the bible for many British intellectuals until the Great War and remain important for philosophers long after, Moore also maintained that beauty is an ultimate intrinsic value: "By far the most valuable things, which we know or can imagine, are certain states of consciousness, which may be roughly described as the pleasures of human intercourse and the enjoyment of beautiful objects" (Moore 1903: 237). Indeed, Moore's two intrinsic goods can be thought of as giving philosophical expression to the creed of the "Bloomsbury" group of artists, writers, and intellectuals (the most enduringly famous of whom are the novelist Virginia Woolf and the economist John Maynard Keynes (1883–1946)): the ultimate value is the creation and enjoyment of beautiful things within a community of friends.[17]

Moore's statement is the conclusion of a long argument in ethics that cannot be recounted here, but is the starting point for a brief yet trenchant discussion of aesthetics. His first claim is that "aesthetic appreciation" is an "organic whole" consisting of consciousness of both the beautiful qualities of an object and of a feeling of its beauty, "an appropriate emotion towards the beautiful qualities" that are cognized, as contrasted to the mere recognition that the object *has* those qualities (1903: 238). By calling different emotions appropriate to different kinds of beauty, he continues, he means "that the [organic] whole which is formed by the consciousness of that kind of beauty *together with* the emotion appropriate to it, is better than if any other emotion had been felt in contemplating that particular object" (p. 239). It should be noted here, however, that Moore restricts his conception of aesthetic qualities to kinds of *beauty*, and thus presumably restricts the range of appropriate emotions to kinds of *pleasure*, the general class of emotion that beauty would be thought to produce; this would be consistent with his general thesis that what is intrinsically good is not pleasure alone but organic unities that include pleasure. He then adds, in what can only be seen as a conscious reversal of the Kantian thesis that aesthetic value lies entirely in what we can make of the representation of an object and not in the existence of the object itself,[18] that the actual existence of something good *adds* to the goodness of an organic whole of which it is a part, so that

> the emotional contemplation of a natural scene, supposing its qualities equally beautiful, is in some way a better state of things than that of a beautiful landscape: we think that the world would be improved if we could substitute for the best works of representative art *real* objects equally beautiful. (1903: 243)

By means of this remarkable argument, Moore may have given a status to natural beauty that it had not enjoyed since Hegel had largely eliminated it from aesthetics,[19] and in so doing Moore may have guaranteed a certain degree of schizophrenia for his art-worshipping followers. But he may also have prepared the way for the acceptance of twentieth-century artistic movements that attempted to efface the traditional boundary between actual things and mere representations of them.[20] Next, however, in what sounds like a return to Kant as well as agreement with Santayana, Moore defines beauty "as that of which the admiring contemplation is good in itself" (p. 249). Like Kant, he is also at pains to distinguish between merely subjectively valid "admiring contemplation" by someone and the objective fact that some objects *ought* to be admiringly contemplated by anyone. Finally, although nothing more than that can be said by way of a definition of the beautiful, Moore is willing to say more about the objects that can prompt such contemplation, namely that

> beautiful objects are themselves, for the most part, organic unities, in this sense, that the contemplation of any part, by itself, may have no value, and yet that, unless the contemplation of the whole includes the contemplation of that part, it will lose in value.

Here Moore is applying his concept of "organic unity" a second time: in addition to the experience of beauty being an organic whole consisting of cognition of a quality plus an appropriate emotional response to that quality, the quality to which we so respond can itself be understood only as an organic unity. And from this, Moore claims, "it follows that there can be no single criterion of beauty" (p. 250). That is, there may be certain characteristics that "are more or less universally present in beautiful objects," but they can never amount to necessary and sufficient conditions for beauty. This was a thesis that had already been stated by Hume and Kant, and that would frequently be restated in twentieth-century aesthetics.[21]

Moore thus makes the appreciation of beauty the end to which ethical conduct is a mere means, like Santayana, thereby also making it the obvious goal of all art. Unlike Santayana, he thinks that not much can be said about what makes objects beautiful except that it is organic unity, indeed it is precisely because beauty is organic unity that not much more can be said about what sorts of properties of objects characteristically produce it. Apart from the apotheosis of the enjoyment of beauty that Moore shares with Santayana, what would particularly influence the leading writers in the decade remaining before the Great War is the thought that there is a distinct emotion or set of emotions appropriate to beauty, and that aesthetic pleasure is inextricably linked to the occurrence of this emotion. Thus, in contrast to Tolstoy, who taught that art serves to communicate morally ("religiously") valuable emotions, Moore taught that morality exists only as a means to a distinctive aesthetic emotion or set of emotions.

The names of Clive Bell (1881–1964) and Roger Fry (1866–1934) are invariably linked as the leading aestheticians of the Bloomsbury group, and in 1910 and 1912 they did collaborate on two important exhibitions of "post-impressionists," especially Cézanne.[22] But there are important differences in their views. Bell was a strict adherent of Moore.[23] He defended an "aesthetic hypothesis" comprising the claims that aesthetic experience is based on a distinct kind of emotion "provoked by every kind of visual art" and by no other objects; that to arouse this distinct emotion is "the essential quality in a work of art"; and that the property in a work of art that arouses this emotion is its "significant form" (Bell 1914: 17). He also blocked the objection that by distinguishing the emotional core of the experience of art from all other emotions he must deprive art of all moral significance with an appeal to Moore's thesis that aesthetic experience is an intrinsic good to which morality is a mere means. Thus he stated that "Art is not only a means to good states of mind, but, perhaps, the most direct and potent that we possess" (p. 83). By contrast, Fry, at least in a "Retrospect" to a 1920 collection of some of his earlier essays, argued that Bell had gone too far in postulating a special aesthetic emotion, and instead defended the view that a work of art uses its special formal means to communicate "some emotion of actual life" in a way made possible by the distinctive "detachment" of the artist. He also altered the Moorean subordination of morality to aesthetic experience, maintaining instead that while "Morality … appreciates emotion by the standard of resultant action[, a]rt appreciates emotion in and for itself" (Fry 1920: 19). On this account, the aesthetic experience of emotion remains intrinsically rather than instrumentally valuable while in moral contexts emotions are only instrumentally valuable, but there is no suggestion that the actions to which the latter are the means must themselves derive their value from anything connected with aesthetic experience.

Among the post-Mooreans, the writer who was most influential on but perhaps also most misunderstood in the subsequent history of aesthetics was Edward Bullough (1880–1934). Like Bell and Fry, he was not a trained philosopher, but he was an academic – ultimately Professor of Italian Literature at Cambridge – and in 1907 he offered the first course on aesthetics at Cambridge. In a famous essay of 1912 he argued for "psychical distance" as a "factor in art and an aesthetic principle."[24] If while sailing through a fog at sea one can abstract from worries about delays and danger and focus on the fog itself, then one can find the fog a "source of intense relish and enjoyment" arising from "attention to the features 'objectively' constituting the phenomenon," such as "the veil surrounding you with an opaqueness as of transparent milk," "the curious creamy smoothness of the water, hypocritically denying as it were any suggestion of danger; and, above all, the strange solitude and remoteness of the world" (Bullough 1957: 93–4). Bullough has often been read to argue here, like Moore or Bell, that by setting aside all of one's ordinary responses one opens oneself up to a unique aesthetic emotion, but a close reading of his words suggests instead that by setting aside purely *self-regarding* emotions such as worries about danger or delay one opens oneself up to a wide range of other thoughts, such as the thoughts of solitude and remoteness, and the variety of quite intense emotions that can accompany such thoughts. Thus aesthetic experience can actually enrich our range of emotional experiences. And in his 1907 lectures, Bullough maintained that the aesthetic experience of an object depends upon "the recognition of its uniqueness, of those distinctive qualities, which are its exclusive property, and make it different from, and incommensurable with, any other work," by means of which we become "imbued with its spirit and enveloped by its peculiar atmosphere," thereby all the more strongly realizing "its uniqueness and its solitary perfection" (p. 46). This suggests that each work of art can convey a distinct emotional atmosphere, not that all works of art convey the same special aesthetic emotion.

Between Tolstoy on the one hand and Santayana and Moore on the other there was a clear opposition between the view that artistic beauty exists only to convey morally valuable feelings and the view that morality exists only to facilitate the experience of a unique and intrinsically valuable feeling of beauty. Bell followed Moore closely, but Fry and Bullough complicated the picture by suggesting that aesthetic experience in general and art in particular allow us to experience a wide range of emotions. This brought them closer to what would become the central theme of much twentieth-century aesthetics, namely that the essential function of art is to find form for the expression of emotion. The figures who most clearly occupied this ground in pre-World War I aesthetics, however, were the neo-Hegelian philosophers Bernard Bosanquet (1848–1923) in Britain and Benedetto Croce (1866–1952) in Italy, whose work was also quickly and widely received in Britain and the US (see also "Hegelianism in the twentieth century," Chapter 3). The neo-Kantian Hermann Cohen (1842–1918) might also be mentioned as a representative of this tendency in Germany, although if his work had any influence on later developments it would only be through his student Ernst Cassirer (1874–1945).

The expression of emotion

Bosanquet wrote widely on metaphysics and moral and political philosophy. His *History of Æsthetic*, originally published in 1892, was one of his earlier works, and presents his own view of the aesthetic only through the vehicle of a long history of the subject from the ancients to the nineteenth century.[25] One central theme of this work is that the traditional conception of beauty in general and beauty in art as merely the "regular and harmonious, or as the simple expression of unity in variety," has had to give way, particularly through a history centrally involving the eighteenth century's addition of the sublime to the beautiful, to a conception of beauty, but especially artistic beauty, as "demanding ... characteristic expression for sense" (Bosanquet 1892: 5–6). In other words, the concept of beauty as triggering a distinctive emotion of its own is ultimately transformed into the concept of the expression of a wide range of thoughts and emotions. The concept of beauty is transformed, not replaced, because in expression there is still harmony, but harmony between form and content rather than within form alone. As Bosanquet writes,

> The content gets into the product through being in the man, and through being in the man in such a way that in as far as he is free in his producing activity, the content will, by means of his disciplined habit together with his overmastering impulse, modify his production with satisfaction to himself.... The content which appears in art seems then to operate through that expansion of self which comes in utterance, and which from the nature of the content claims to be a harmonious expansion. (1892: 453)

Or as Croce would put it ten years later, "It seems appropriate to us to define the beautiful as successful expression, or better, as expression *simpliciter*, since expression, when it is not successful, is not expression" (Croce 1902: 87). In his later lectures on aesthetics, Bosanquet himself would also make his original abstraction more concrete. Here he says plainly that art is that in which human "feeling becomes 'organized,' 'plastic' or 'incarnate'." Art has "the power to draw out or give imaginative shape to the object and material of experience," to submit feeling "to the laws of an object" through which it "must take on permanence, order, harmony, meaning, in short value" and thereby cease to be "mere self-absorption" (Bosanquet 1915: 7–8).

Hermann Cohen began his career with commentaries on each of Kant's three critiques, treating his aesthetics in *Kant's Establishment of Aesthetics* (Cohen 1889). He then presented his own neo-Kantianism in three treatises, concluding with an *Aesthetics of Pure Feeling* (Cohen 1912). Cohen's task was to find a form of lawfulness in aesthetic experience, an imperative because Kant had insisted upon such a possibility, but a challenge because the laws of nature and the laws of morality had already been explained as laws of human consciousness, with which the aesthetic might otherwise be identified. Cohen's solution was to argue that while the laws of the other domains stem from the pure forms of human consciousness, those laws do not present themselves to us phenomenologically *as* forms of consciousness, while the aesthetic concerns the conscious feelings that accompany the constitutive functioning of human consciousness, and those feelings themselves have their own forms, which are revealed in their purest form by aesthetic experience, particularly by the experience of art. Cohen characterized this distinctively aesthetic aspect of consciousness as the "concept of pure feeling" (Cohen 1912, I: 98), and presented a lengthy description of the different dimensions of pure feeling and different forms of the "lawfulness" of pure feeling brought out in the different arts. But what places his theory in the camp of Bosanquet and Croce rather than that of Moore and Bell is his view that "pure feeling" is not a unique and isolated form of experience but rather the affective dimension of all the other forms of human consciousness.

In contrast to Tolstoy, then, writers such as Bosanquet, Croce, and Cohen denied that art exists merely to infect an audience with a morally valuable emotion, pretty much regardless of the active cognitive participation of that audience. In contrast to Moore and Bell, they did not hold that the experience of beauty simply produces a distinctively aesthetic feeling of emotion, and in contrast to Santayana they did not hold that beauty is simply pleasure objectified, that is, projected by us upon the object that engenders it. Instead, they held that genuine beauty, thus the goal of art, consists in objectifying or expressing through clearly apprehensible form the full gamut of human emotions, for both the cognitive satisfaction and the liberation from domination by inadequately understood emotions that can arise from such apprehension allow us to reach a state of "active" – rather than merely passive – "and productive feeling" (Bosanquet 1892: 453). This is the idea that would be further developed by the giants of interwar aesthetics, John Dewey and R. G. Collingwood, and by many, although of course not all, of the other leading aestheticians of the next period.

Aesthetics between the wars

While some disciplines and schools of philosophy came back to life almost immediately after the end of World War I – such as the areas of philosophy of language, logic, and science in Vienna and elsewhere that received such a boost from the publication of Ludwig Wittgenstein's *Tractatus Logico-Philosophicus* in 1921 – the most important interwar work on aesthetics was done in the 1930s. Indeed, this part of our narrative can almost be confined to the few years from 1934 to 1938; it saw in 1934 the publication of John Dewey's *Art as Experience* and the delivery of Martin Heidegger's lectures "On the origin of the work of art"; in 1936 Walter Benjamin's essay "The work of art in the age of its technical reproducibility" and A. J. Ayer's *Language, Truth, and Logic*; and in 1938 both the publication of R. G. Collingwood's *The Principles of Art* in Oxford and Ludwig Wittgenstein's lectures on aesthetics in Cambridge (although these were not published until 1967 and were not the vehicle for Wittgenstein's main influence on aesthetics). After the outbreak of World War II in September 1939, of course, philosophical activity in Europe and shortly afterwards in the US was largely suspended, and the renewal of activity in aesthetics beginning in the 1950s would take place in an intellectual landscape that was in some ways very new and in other ways continuous with that of the 1930s.

Some interwar work in aesthetics, such as the aesthetics of orthodox Marxism, carried on the Tolstoyan tradition of finding the value of art solely in the communication of morally – now of course understood politically rather religiously – valuable emotions. Other approaches, such as the logical positivism epitomized by Ayer and the "emotivism" subsequently developed by Charles L. Stevenson, can be seen as continuing the tradition of isolating aesthetic phenomena from other experiences in the fashion of Moore and Bullough. (For further discussion of emotivism, see "Twentieth-century moral philosophy," Chapter 20.) But the mainstream of the period, represented by Dewey and Collingwood, can be seen as developing Bosanquet's claim that the purpose of art is to give "imaginative shape" to experience, particularly the experience of emotion. I will first discuss this central project, and then turn to some of the alternatives to it.

Consummatory experience

John Dewey (1859–1952) came to aesthetics only late in his long career (perhaps as the result of his friendship with the famous collector Albert Barnes), devoting one chapter to the subject in his 1925 book *Experience and Nature* and then treating it at length in his 1930–1 William James lectures at Harvard, published in 1934 as *Art as Experience* and perhaps still the most widely read of Dewey's numerous works.[26] (For further discussion of James and Dewey, see "American philosophy in the twentieth century," Chapter 5.) The central idea of the latter work is already present in the chapter "Experience, nature and art" in the former. In Dewey's synthesis of Hegel, Darwin, and earlier American pragmatism, existence is depicted as a constant interaction between an organism and its environment, in which the organism seeks equilibrium in the exchange of energy with its environment.[27] Sentient human beings can become aware of and enjoy the moments in which such equilibrium is reached in "consummatory" experiences. Such moments are experienced as moments of meaning: "Thus to be conscious of meanings or to have an idea marks a fruition, an enjoyed or suffered arrest of the flux of events" (Dewey 1925: 301). And the experience of art – whether the experience that leads to the creation of art or the experience that results from the reception of art – is the paradigmatic form of consummatory experience: "art is the solvent union of the generic, recurrent, ordered, established phase of nature with its phase that is incomplete, going on, and hence still uncertain, contingent, novel, particular"; thus in art "the contingent and ongoing no longer work at cross purposes with the formal and recurrent but conmingle in harmony ... in it the instrumental and the final, meanings that are signs and clews and meanings that are immediately possessed, suffered and enjoyed, come together in one" (p. 291). In the experience of art in particular the usual distinction between means and end is dissolved, so that art is simultaneously "means and consequence, process and product, the instrumental and [the] consummatory" (p. 292).

Dewey continues this line of thought in *Art as Experience*, asserting that "Art is the living and concrete proof that man is capable of restoring consciously, and thus on the plane of meaning, the union of sense, need, impulse and action characteristic of the live creature" (1934: 25). But in this work he also makes his approach more precise and connects it more explicitly to the mainstream of the discipline by identifying "the esthetic quality that rounds out an experience into completeness and unity as emotional" (p. 41) and then arguing that art has a special role in the expression of emotion. The attempt to express the emotional quality of their own experience to others is a normal part of their ongoing interaction with their environment for human beings, and thus creating and enjoying art is also a central part of human life. But a work of art is not simply a refined sigh or cry; art works by objectifying emotion, that is, it does not simply project it onto an object as we are supposed to do with our sensations of color or smell, but presents the content of our emotion through a representation of the context of the object that engenders it. Dewey clearly distinguishes his view from that of predecessors such as Santayana and Bell when he writes that "emotion as thus 'objectified' is esthetic," but then adds that "Esthetic emotion is thus something distinctive and not yet cut off by a chasm from other and natural emotional experiences, as some theorists in contending for its existence have made it to be" (p. 78).

Dewey holds that the aesthetic "is the clarified and intensified development of traits that belong to every normally complete experience" (p. 46). His theory that experience is an ongoing process of interaction with the environment including emotionally charged moments of heightened awareness of that interaction and of equilibria in it allows him to give some substance to this statement, which could easily have been written by Bosanquet or Croce. Because the ongoing flow of experience is experience of relations among things, its moments of equilibrium and their emotional tone can be captured, represented, and re-experienced through the sensible relations among things at some level of abstraction. Thus, for example, while "the ultimate subject matter of still life painting is highly 'realistic' – napery, pans, apples, bowls ... a still life by Chardin or Cezanne presents these materials in terms of relations of lines, planes and colors inherently enjoyed in perception" (p. 94). Art in any medium necessarily involves "selection" and "abstraction" precisely because it must get past the surface of experience to the relations that create its ebb and flow. Of course, Dewey adds, "There is no *a priori* rule to decide how far abstraction may be carried" (p. 94).

A central theme of *Art as Experience* is that both the creation and the reception of art involve interaction between subject and object, so there are deep affinities between the experience of the producer of art and that of the consumer of art, indeed there are elements of each in the other. Dewey notes that the term "art" "denotes a process of doing and making ... molding of clay, chipping of marble, laying on of pigments, construction of buildings, singing of songs," and so on, while "The word 'esthetic' refers ... to experience as appreciative, perceiving, and enjoying," denoting "the consumer's rather than the producer's standpoint." But, he continues, "the distinction between esthetic and artistic cannot be pressed so far as to become a separation" (1934: p. 47). Rather, the artist must also play the role of the consumer at those moments in his creation of a work when he steps back to gauge his progress by seeing how it will look to another, and the experience of the consumer involves activity as well as receptivity: the experience of taking in a work of art is also a flow in which an appreciator, just like an artist, takes in external stimuli, forms conjectures about their meaning and about experiences to come, refines those expectations in light of further observation of the object, and so on. Since the "real work of art is the building up of an integral experience out of the interaction or organic and environmental conditions and energies" (p. 64), the audience of a work of art is engaged in productive activity as well as the artist who in the conventional sense produces an object for an audience. Breaking down a rigid distinction between artist and audience is as central to Dewey's project as breaking down a rigid distinction between aesthetic emotion and the rest of our emotions.

The clarification of emotion

In *The Principles of Art*, R. G. Collingwood (1889–1943) notoriously asserted that "a work of art may be completely created when it has been created as a thing whose only place is in the artist's mind" (1938: 130), and thereby seemed to deny any importance to an audience for art. But in fact a central theme of his work is also to emphasize the need for real interaction between the standpoint of the artist and the standpoint of the audience. Like Dewey, he combines this theme with the argument that art is not in the business of capturing a special aesthetic emotion but of clarifying all the emotions of human life.[28]

Collingwood grew up around art – his father was an archaeologist as well as a biographer of John Ruskin – and addressed issues of aesthetics several times in his career. He began his early work *Speculum Mentis, or the Map of Knowledge*, with a chapter on art, and began that chapter with the assertion that art is "pure imagination," indifferent to the reality or unreality of a represented object (Collingwood

1924: 61) and aims instead at the creation of an independent world structured by the demands of beauty rather than by anything else (pp. 65–7). However, the artist, in this regard like any normal human being, inevitably seeks to put his imaginative vision before "real minds other than his own – including among these his own future and past mind – with which he desires to communicate, teaching them and learning from them" (p. 99). This leads to the creation of physical works of art, but also to criticism, and thus to "discord in the life of the artist." The artistic frame of mind is thus not in enduring equilibrium, to borrow Dewey's term, but is instead engaged in a dialectic; and in Hegelian fashion, Collingwood goes on to describe how art must be supplemented by religion, science, history, and ultimately philosophy. In the *Outlines of a Philosophy of Art* of one year later, Collingwood largely drops the Hegelian subordination of art to other forms of thought and increasingly emphasizes that the artist must stand back from his own imagining – adopting, as it were, the position of a possible audience for his work – as part of the process of creation:

> The artist, then, is always doing two things: imagining and knowing that he is imagining. His mind is as it were a twofold mind and has before it a twofold object: as imagining, he has before him the imagined object; as thinking, he has before him his own act of imagining that object.

But there is still a lingering Hegelianism in Collingwood's assertion that the artist "is not a philosopher," and that while "he knows that something is controlling his imaginative activity … [he] does not know that this something is his own thought" (1925: 47–8). That the artist's stance toward his own activity remains intuitive rather than clearly conceptual is an important part of what distinguishes art from other human activities. Nevertheless, this distinction between the intuitive and the conceptual should not be confused with a distinction between the private and the public; a central theme of the *Outlines* is that the imaginative activity of the artist breaks down any rigid barrier between the personal and the interpersonal:

> The life of imagination is a life in which all human beings participate. Hence the work which the artist creates in order to advance his own aesthetic life is in principle capable of the same function in any one else's aesthetic life. In the act itself, this truth is not explicitly present. The artist does not paint for an audience, but for himself; and it is only by truly satisfying himself that he can truly satisfy others. But what he is trying to satisfy in himself is, whether he knows it or not, that imaginative activity which is the same in himself and others; and it is not more possible that a work of art should be truly and ultimately beautiful to one person and not to others than that a scientific demonstration should be truly and ultimately cogent to one person and not to others. (1925: 81–2)

Here Collingwood reaches back beyond Hegel to touch a central chord of the eighteenth-century conception of taste.

Collingwood's mature work of 1938 begins with the insistence of his earlier works that the primary goal of art is the imaginative activity of the artist and that its expression through the creation of a physical object is only secondary, but in the end undermines any such separation between what is expressed and its external vehicle of expression. It also definitively leaves behind any lingering Hegelianism by arguing that what art expresses is the emotion that accompanies all human perception, thought, and action, and that there is nothing that replaces or supersedes art in doing this. The supposed idealist Collingwood thus ultimately reaches a position much closer to that of the naturalist and pragmatist Dewey than initially appears.

In Part I of *The Principles of Art*, Collingwood argues that we all know that "art proper" is different from "craft." Craft always involves a clear-cut distinction between means and end, planning and execution, raw material and finished artifact, and form and matter (1938: 15–16). In the case of art proper, none of these distinctions is clear-cut: a poem, for example, is not a means to an end (p. 20), nor are the words of its language mere raw materials for a finished artifact (pp. 22–3). Of course, a literary work such as a poem is the best example for Collingwood's case, and other media of art, for example sculpture, do seem to transform raw material into a finished artifact in an ordinary sense. But the heart of Collingwood's thesis is the claim that art proper is not a mere means to an end outside of it, and this leads to – or, perhaps better, rests upon – Collingwood's argument that the goal of art cannot be amusement, the arousal of emotion simply to enjoy it, nor magic, the arousal of emotion for the sake of its practical value, nor stimulation of the intellectual faculties either for the mere sake of their exercise or for instruction, nor or advertisement, propaganda, or exhortation (p. 32). Further, Collingwood's rejection of the equation of art with craft leads to – or again rests upon – his view that the work of art is not a physical object per se, which is the goal of craft, but an act of imagination. Thus Collingwood claims that the artist produces two different things:

> Primarily ... an "internal" or "mental" thing, something (as we commonly say) "existing in his head" and there only: something of the kind we commonly call an experience. Secondarily ... a bodily or perceptible thing (a picture, statue, &c.) ... Of these two things, the first is obviously not anything that can be called a work of art, if work means something made in the sense in which a weaver makes cloth. But since it is the thing which the artist as such primarily produces ... we are entitled to call it "the work of art" proper. The second thing, the bodily and perceptible thing ... [is] only incidental to the first. (1938: 36–7)

A key inference that Collingwood draws from his distinction between art proper and craft is that the mere creation of a representation cannot be the goal of art, because the creation of representations is a craft with definite goals and techniques (1938: ch. III).

This hardly means that art proper does not in fact sometimes create representations. Likewise, Collingwood's insistence that art proper does not aim at the arousal of emotion for its own sake by means of amusement, magic, and propaganda hardly means that art has nothing to do with emotion. Collingwood emphatically rejects Tolstoy's theory that art is a means for infecting others with emotion, using Tolstoy's language although not mentioning his name: "young men who, learning in the torment of their own bodies and minds what war is like, have stammered their indignation in verses, and published them in the hope of infecting others and causing them to abolish it … have nothing to do with poetry." But it is the essential goal of art – Collingwood cannot, after all, avoid talking of means and ends for art – to clarify our emotions: thus "it is not her ability to weep real tears that would mark out a good actress; it is her ability to make it clear to herself and her audience what the tears are about" (1938: 122–3). "The artist proper is a person who, grappling with the problem of a certain emotion, says, 'I want to get this clear'" (p. 114) and thereby solve a certain problem, indeed remove a certain burden (p. 117). What does remain from Collingwood's distinction between art and craft, however, is the thesis that while such clarification of emotion is indeed the goal of a "directed process" of the "exploration" of the artist's emotion, there is no "technique" for such exploration, and the end of such a process "is not something foreseen and preconceived" (p. 111).

Collingwood sets this conclusion of Part I of the *Principles* within a framework in Part II that both supports and refines it. While his conclusion that art aims at the clarification of emotion might seem too narrow for many kinds of art, Collingwood makes it maximally extensive by arguing that all perception, thought, and activity are accompanied with some feeling. He also argues that we ordinarily fail to distinguish between the underlying perception or thought and its attendant feeling, but that we have the freedom to make the latter rather than the former the focus of our attention, thereby holding a feeling "before the mind; rescuing it from the flux of mere sensation, and conserving it for so long as may be necessary in order that we should take note of it … perpetuating the act by which we feel it" (1938: 209). This is the primary work of the imagination because imagination in its original sense is the capacity to entertain a thought in the absence of its object and thus in the absence of the immediate sensation if it. The essence of imagination is that "instead of having our field of view wholly occupied by the sensations and emotions of the moment, we also become aware of ourselves, as the activity of feeling these things." And this leads to the possibility of control over our emotions: "Their brute power over us is thus replaced by our power over them: we become able on the one hand to stand up to them so that they no longer unconditionally determine our conduct, and, on the other, to prolong and evoke them at will. From being impressions of sense, they thus become ideas of imagination" (p. 222).

The second key claim of Part II is, then, an argument that the clarification as well as communication of emotion is effected through language, broadly understood. Collingwood begins his analysis of language with the claim that the original use of language is not to denote objects but to express emotions: when the baby whose mother typically says "Hatty off" when she takes its hat off "says in tones of great satisfaction, 'Hattiaw!' … when it takes its own bonnet off and throws it out of the perambulator," it is not trying to denote the hat or the act of removing it, but is instead expressing "the peculiar satisfaction which for some reason the child takes in removing it. That is to say, it expresses the feeling which the child has in doing that act" (1938; 228). Collingwood then concludes that language consists in "Bodily actions expressing certain emotions, in so far as they come under our control and are conceived by us, in our awareness of controlling them, as our way of expressing these emotions." Collingwood does not mean by language here simply speech, but "any activity of any organ which is expressive in the same way in which speech is expressive" (p. 238). Language in this broad sense transforms primitive noises and gestures like the baby's "Hattiaw!" into an infinite range of signs and gestures for the expression of clarified emotions: "Thus the imaginative experience creates for itself, by an infinite work of refraction and reflection and condensation and dispersal, an infinity of emotions demanding for their expression an infinite subtlety in the articulations of the language it creates in expressing them" (p. 238). This is the work – that is, the labor rather than the product – of art.

This view of "Art as language" (chapter XII) leads in Part III to a radical revision of Collingwood's apparently idealist model of the work – now both labor and product – of art from Part I. Even if "the artist is a person who comes to know himself, to know his own emotion" (1938: 291), insofar as coming to know one's emotion requires finding a language in which to express it and a language is a system of physical noises and gestures that is publicly accessible, coming to know one's own emotions requires articulating them in a publicly accessible fashion, in a medium, whether it be words, paint, stone, or movement, to which others can respond. The artist is not "a missionary or a salesman of the aesthetic experience" (p. 301) who uses a public means of expression *in order to* infect others with his feelings, but he has to use a publicly accessible medium in order to clarify his own feelings. Thus the production of a physical object such as a painting is not "identical" to the "artist's aesthetic activity," but its "production is somehow necessarily connected with the aesthetic activity" (p. 305). In order to clarify his emotion, the artist must use a publicly accessible medium as a language, must in the course of clarifying his emotion stand back from it and look at it from the point of view of such a language, and in so doing thereby makes his own emotion and its clarification accessible to others who can understand that language as well.

That the imaginative work of art requires a language and therefore is open to a public does not of course guarantee that the artist will not exploit language for the sake of mere amusement or propaganda. The artist must choose to take "it as his business not to express his own private emotions, irrespectively of whether any one else feels them or not, but the emotions he shares with his audience," and instead of being a "mystagogue," to "be a humbler person, imposing upon himself the task of understanding his world, and thus enabling it to understand itself" (1938: 312). Collingwood's work may not at first seem political, but his hostility to the use of art as propaganda was part of his deeply felt anti-fascism (see Collingwood 1989), and what really drives his philosophy of art is the recognition that "bad art" is "corruption of consciousness" (1938: 285), while the clarity about our emotions that art and only art can – although does not automatically – provide is an antidote to the use of bad art to poison the wells of truth. But the freedom of imagination that is the origin of art must be freedom in a full sense if this is to be achieved.

Art as symbolic form

Although he came out of the German neo-Kantian tradition rather than the British neo-Hegelian tradition like Collingwood or for that matter the American neo-Hegelian tradition like Dewey, Ernst Cassirer (1874–1945) thought about art in terms fundamentally similar to theirs. Surprisingly, there is no discussion of art in Cassirer's *magnum opus*, *The Philosophy of Symbolic Forms* (1923–9), but he had written extensively about "the discovery of the world of aesthetic forms" from Leibniz to Winckelmann in his 1916 *Freedom and Form* (1916), made aesthetics central to his *Philosophy of the Enlightenment* (1932), and finally stated his own position, worked out during the 1920s and 1930s, in his 1944 English-language summary of his philosophy, *An Essay on Man* (1944). As a follower of the Marburg version of neo-Kantianism, Cassirer held that human beings organize their experience by means of various systems of symbols, such as those of discursive language, mathematics, and the visual arts, and for various purposes, such as those of natural science, government, and art. A symbolic form can be considered as the use of a particular kind of symbol system, such as mathematics, for a particular purpose, such as that of astronomy or mechanics. Unlike neo-Hegelians, such as the Collingwood of *Speculum Mentis*, Cassirer did not arrange the different symbolic forms in a hierarchy. But he did hold that there is a fundamental difference between such symbolic forms as the use of language and mathematics in natural science on the one hand and the artistic use of language or other media: science depends upon abstraction to identify and organize what is universal and repeatable in the flux of experience, whereas art is aimed at capturing the form of particular experiences in their individuality.[29] A landscape painter, for example, "does not portray or copy a certain empirical object – a landscape with its hills and mountains" – as he might if he were illustrating a concept or classification in a treatise on geology, but instead aims to use the same medium that could be used for the former purpose for the different goal of revealing "the individual and momentary physiognomy of the landscape" (Cassirer 1944: 144). But even more characteristically, art has the special task of clearly fixing the form and physiognomy of human passion and emotion: in a sentence that could have been written by Collingwood, he states that in art "Our passions are no longer dark and impenetrable powers; they become, as it were, transparent" (p. 147). Like Bosanquet, Croce, Dewey, and Collingwood, Cassirer also holds that the special function of art, regardless of medium and style, is to capture and clarify the subjective aspects of the whole variety of human experience in a way that no other symbolic form can.

The American Suzanne K. Langer (1895–1985) was influenced by Cassirer as well as by mainstream philosophers of language such as Russell, Wittgenstein, and Carnap. Although her main work on aesthetics, *Feeling and Form* (dedicated to "the happy memory of Ernst Cassirer"), appeared in 1953, thus after World War II, the germ of her thought about the arts was worked out earlier and was already present in her 1942 book *Philosophy in a New Key*. Langer held that human thought is essentially symbolic rather than representational, that is, that it uses a variety of media to structure our experience rather than simply copying structures it finds in experience. Like Cassirer, she resisted the assimilation of all forms of symbolism to the models and artificial languages of mathematics and natural science. Specifically, she argued that the arts do not employ "discursive" symbol-systems to analyze experience; rather, they use non-discursive symbols to capture the felt quality of experience itself. Using music as an example, she argued that "music has not the characteristic properties of language – separable terms with fixed connotations, and syntactical rules for deriving complex connections ... Yet it may be a presentational symbol, and present emotive experience through global forms that are as indivisible as the elements of chiaroscuro" (1942: 232). Thus Langer also argued that the arts have the special function of capturing and clarifying the nature of human emotion.

Emotivism

This widespread approach to art as the vehicle for the expression of emotion must be distinguished from the narrower form of "emotivism" associated with Alfred Jules Ayer (1910–89) and Charles L. Stevenson (1908–79). Shortly after graduating from Oxford in 1932, Ayer spent several months in Vienna, and on his return wrote *Language, Truth and Logic*, which successfully introduced logical positivism to the British and American public. Ayer argued that the criterion for "the genuineness of apparent statements of fact is the criterion of verifiability," namely, "that a sentence is factually significant to any given person, if, and only, if, he knows how to verify the proposition which it purports to express – that is, if he knows what observations would lead him, under certain conditions, to accept the propositions as being true, or reject it as being false" (1936: 35), although he also argued that no factual statement is ever *conclusively* verified or falsified (p. 38). He then argued that apparent "judgments of value" are either "ordinary 'scientific' statements," statements about the effects of actions that would be either verifiably true or verifiably false, or else not genuine statements at all, but only "expressions of emotion which can be neither true nor false" (p. 103) – although of course it can be a verifiable matter of fact that a person actually has or had the feeling expressed. More precisely, the contents of ethical philosophy can be divided into four types: "propositions which express definitions of ethical terms"; "propositions describing the phenomena of moral experience, and their causes"; "exhortations to moral virtue"; and the "actual ethical judgments" which are mere expressions of emotion (p. 103). Only the first class of ethical propositions belong to philosophy proper, which is supposed to analyze concepts; the second class belong to empirical psychology or sociology; and both the third and fourth are actually non-propositional properties of ethical utterances, the expression of felt emotion at an actual or proposed course of action on the one hand and on the other hand the command or commendation of such an action or response to others. Finally, Ayer argued that "Æsthetic terms are used in exactly the same way as ethical terms": "Such æsthetic words as 'beautiful' and 'hideous' are employed, as ethical words are employed, not to make statements of fact, but simply to express certain feelings and evoke a certain response." From this Ayer inferred that "there is no sense in attributing objective validity to æsthetic judgments, and no possibility of arguing about questions of value in æsthetics, but only about questions of fact" (p. 113). That is, such disciplines as psychology, sociology, and art history can investigate the causes of feelings, tastes, and the production of various works of art, but there is no possibility for a philosophical justification of aesthetic norms or for a philosophical foundation of critical discourse. "There is nothing in æsthetics, any more than there is in ethics, to justify the view that it embodies a unique type of knowledge" (p. 114). Stevenson extended Ayer's view with an elaborate theory of definition, arguing that many definitions are actually "persuasive" rather than factual in character (Stevenson 1944: 206–26). He also supported emotivism by arguing that the fact that our expression of moral judgments is accompanied with dispositions to act in accordance with them is evidence that those judgments are expressions of those dispositions. But he did not substantially change the view. The "emotivists" thus saw aesthetic language as the expression of emotion in one sense of expression, a purely causal sense in which an utterance is the effect of an emotion in the one who makes the utterance and possibly a cause of a response in another, but did not allow that the aesthetic and thus art significantly shapes or clarifies emotion, or acquires either cognitive or moral value by so doing. The emotivist view is thus more of a reversion to Tolstoy's view of the communication of emotion through art than part of the mainstream view that art is the means to clarifying and understanding emotions.

Wittgenstein I

Two years after Ayer's book was published in London and in the same year that Collingwood published *The Principles of Art* in Oxford, Ludwig Wittgenstein (1889–1951) lectured on aesthetics to a small group in Cambridge. It would be almost thirty years before some student notes from these lectures were published (Wittgenstein 1967), and indeed Wittgenstein's main influence on aesthetics would come from the *Philosophical Investigations*, posthumously published in 1953, and will thus be considered later. (For further discussion of the later Wittgenstein, see "The development of analytic philosophy: Wittgenstein and after," Chapter 2.) But the earlier lectures are interesting both for what they share with emotivism and for how they differ. Wittgenstein began by arguing that there can be no "science" of aesthetics. For that idea he had nothing but scorn: "You might think Aesthetics is a science telling us what's beautiful – almost too ridiculous for words. I suppose it ought to include also what sort of coffee tastes well" (1967: 11). This might have been meant to share Ayer's view that apparent aesthetic value judgments are not factual and verifiable, but perhaps it was instead meant to reject even Ayer's allowance that such sciences as psychology and sociology can properly study the causes and effects of tastes – a proposal that Wittgenstein was familiar with from the nineteenth-century work of Hermann von Helmholtz (1821–94) and Gustav Theodor Fechner (1801–87). Wittgenstein then spent much of his time arguing that general terms like "beautiful" and "lovely," while they certainly do not express objective values, are also not the typical terms of aesthetic appraisals. Instead, he argued that "in real life, when aesthetic judgments are made," we typically say things like "'Look at this transition', or 'The passage here is incoherent' ... [or] 'His use of images is precise'" (1967: 3). Such utterances do not merely express our own feelings nor command or exhort others to have certain responses, but are instead used to direct the attention of others to specific features of objects that we take to be the source of our satisfaction with them, but which we could not link up with that satisfaction by means of any general laws.[30] Finally, Wittgenstein maintains that particular aesthetic terms are used within particular "ways of living" – what would later become a central concept in his philosophy under the name of "forms of life." "In order to get clear about aesthetic words you have to describe ways of living," for such words are "used something like a gesture, accompanying a complicated activity" (p. 11). For example, we use certain words in discussing with our tailor how our suit should be cut or altered, with our landlady whether a certain picture should be hung in our apartment and if so just where, and so on. In all of this, Wittgenstein seems to be describing ways in which various feelings may enter into "ways of living" and thus into our interactions with others, but he gives no indication that any of the aesthetic terms he discusses play any special role in clarifying our feelings. A fortiori, there is no suggestion that the creation or reception of art plays any such role.

Art and being

While Ayer was writing *Language, Truth, and Logic* and thus a few years before Wittgenstein's lectures, another set of lectures were being given that would become influential only after their delayed publication: Martin Heidegger's (1889–1976) lectures "On the origin of the work of art," first given in 1931 and 1934, written up in 1935–6, but not published until 1950. The argument of this work is complicated and obscure,[31] and while in some ways Heidegger's idea that a work of art expresses a "world" might seem analogous to Wittgenstein's notion that aesthetic terms play roles within a "way of living," other aspects of Heidegger's thought seem opposed to any idea that works of art are expressions of a distinctively human standpoint, whether that is embodied in any special aesthetic emotion, in the whole range of ordinary human emotions, or in ordinary human activities. For Heidegger seems to oppose to all of these archetypically subjective concerns an objective world, what he calls "Being," and to argue that the primary function of art is to allow Being to be revealed. Heidegger thus sets his face against the aestheticism of the turn of the century but also against the mainstream view that art is specially concerned with the clarification of human emotions; for him, art seems rather to be about the transcendence of the specifically human.

The Origin of the Work of Art was composed after Heidegger's famous "turn" (*Wende*) from the "analytic of *Dasein*" or phenomenology of human experience that is the heart of his 1927 masterpiece *Being and Time* to the "question of Being." (For further discussion of Heidegger's turn, see "German philosophy," Chapter 17.) In the most general terms, this is a turn toward realism, a turn from the idea that the human mind imposes the structure of truth on the world to the idea that the world imposes the structure of truth on the human mind. Perhaps Heidegger took up the problem of art so early in his *Wende* precisely because art was so universally regarded as the expression of human subjectivity that if he could show that even in art some sort of objective truth reveals itself to human beings rather than being created by them, the way would be smoothed for the rest of his new philosophy. In any case, the "turn" happens quite early in Heidegger's essay, where he argues that works of art reveal the "thingliness" of things better than ordinary artifacts, where "thingliness" is suppressed in behalf of instrumentality or "to-handedness" (*Zuhandenheit*, "readiness to hand"), a concept that had figured centrally in the phenomenology of *Being and Time*. To be sure, works of art also convey "workliness," that is, we are more immediately conscious that a work of art is a product of human hands than we are conscious that a tool is, and this would seem to create a special consciousness of the productive activity of the artist. But perhaps the most fundamental move of Heidegger's argument is to reinterpret the labor of producing art as the struggle it takes for the artist (let alone the rest of us) to let Being reveal itself. On Heidegger's account, in a genuine work of art the artist does not merely become "something inconsequential in comparison with the work – almost like a passageway which, in the creative process, destroys itself for the sake of the coming forth of the work" (1950: 19); rather, the work itself tends to disappear in behalf of truth or Being: "The work's becoming a work is a mode of the becoming and happening of truth" (p. 36), where truth is essentially "the unconcealment of beings" (p. 28). Heidegger's central idea is thus that the artist does not express something subjective or create something but simply reveals something fundamental about reality.

This is revealed only somewhat gradually in Heidegger's exposition, for at first he emphasizes that a work of art reveals a "world" where that might be understood as a way of life and its accompanying emotions. This is in his famous (or infamous)[32] discussion of van Gogh's painting of some battered peasant shoes: "From out of the dark opening of the well-worn insides of the shoes the toil of the worker's tread stares forth. In the crudely solid heaviness of the shoes accumulates the tenacity of the slow trudge through the … field swept by a raw wind… This equipment is pervaded by uncomplaining worry as to the certainty of bread, wordless joy at having once more withstood want, trembling before the impending birth, and shivering at the surrounding menace of death" (1950: 14). If all of this could really be read off of the painting, it would be a paradigmatic example for the mainstream theory that art is the vehicle for the expression of ordinary human emotions. However, Heidegger next turns to the example of a Greek temple (apparently at Paestum), and interprets that as a work that "opens up a world" yet at the same time sets "this world back onto the earth which itself first comes forth as the ground of the dwelling" (p. 25).[33] By "world" here Heidegger does seem to mean something close to a human way of life. But in characterizing "earth" as the ground for a work of art he wants to get past the traditional distinction between form and matter, in which the material for a work of art (for example, stone) is submerged into the form imposed upon it (p. 24), and instead to suggest that the subjective, human element remains rooted in something chthonic, something that transcends mere human being. He will then argue that the real task of art is precisely to let "earth" reveal itself as the ground of mere "world."

Heidegger's peculiarly passive conception of the work of artistic production is part of his general opposition to "modern subjectivism," which "of course[!] misinterprets creation as the product of the genius of the self-sovereign subject" (Heidegger 1950: 48). Opposition to the "subjectivism" of modern aesthetics would be a central theme in *Truth and Method*, the main work of Hans-Georg Gadamer (1900–2002), the student of Heidegger who would become most influential in later literary theory (see Gadamer 1960, Part I, and Gadamer 1977). Heidegger also had considerable influence on the theory and perhaps even the practice of architecture, through his characterization of materials as if they had a will of their own – "Color shines and wants only to shine" (p. 25) – and especially his emphasis that space is not so much to be enclosed as to be revealed by a building – "A work, by being a work, allows a space for that spaciousness" (p. 23) – has found resonance (see Heidegger 1950).[34] But Heidegger's drastic reinterpretation of the nature of artistic creativity has not found much resonance within the mainstream of twentieth century-aesthetics.

Marxist aesthetics I

Before we return to the post-World War II development of the mainstream of aesthetic theory, we need to consider one element of interwar aesthetics that has thus far gone unmentioned, Marxist aesthetics.[35] What we have been examining thus far might well be considered to consist largely in analyses and justifications for the aesthetic tastes and practices of the bourgeoisie or even wealthier elites, so Marxist aesthetics might be expected to have very different concerns. But it may be illuminating to consider one tendency within Marxist aesthetics to be in the Tolstoyan vein, arguing simply that the arts should be used to arouse revolutionary fervor, while other tendencies recommend the use of the arts, if not simply for the clarifying expression of human emotion, then to reveal the contradictions of capitalist society within which current emotions, especially feelings of repression and alienation, arise, and further to reveal at least the possibility of change.

The most orthodox form of Marxist aesthetics was represented by the first leader of the Soviet Union himself, Vladimir Ili'ich Ulyanov or "Lenin" (1870–1924).[36] Lenin did not recognize art as a distinctive sphere of human activity expressing a distinct type of emotion, but treated it as a category of "intellectual work" which, like any other form of labor, could be used against or for the revolution. He expected art to serve the political education of the proletariat and to remain accessible by the use of conventional forms. Lev Bronstein, alias "Trotsky" (1879–1940), also thought that art should serve as a "hammer" for building the new society, but recognized that it must also be a "mirror" of existing society so that revolutionaries could see where their work needed to be done. Unlike Lenin, however, he kept in mind that the ultimate point of revolution was supposed to be the extension of the benefits of freedom to all, and kept in mind that art should not be merely instrumental but should also enjoy some form of freedom.[37]

Trotsky's recognition that traditional forms of art could be used as a mirror for the flaws of existing society was developed by the Hungarian György Lukács (1885–1971).[38] Lukács's first work, *The Soul and the Forms* (1910), was in a neo-Kantian vein; his next book, *The Theory of the Novel* (1916), was a mixture of Hegelian language and *fin de siècle* pessimism, arguing that a novel presents a whole world or way of life, but always as something "fragile" to which "Art always says 'And yet' ... The creation of forms is the most profound confirmation of a dissonance" (Lukács 1916: 72). That art serves to reveal the dissonances within existing society would remain Lukács's view even after he became an active Communist in the aftermath of World War I, when he served in the government of the short-lived Hungarian Soviet Republic (after its fall, he lived for years in Moscow). While the role of art did not figure centrally in his first Marxist work, *History and Class Consciousness* (1923), it would be the central theme in the flood of writing he produced from the 1930s into the 1960s, culminating in his massive (and untranslated) *Eigenart des Ästhetischen* ("Uniqueness of the aesthetic," 1963). His central argument would always be that every society is a complex but integrated whole in which all aspects of life reflect its underlying economic and political realities; that individual psychologies form types that reflect the possibilities of the society as a whole; and that art, but especially the novel, represents the complex reality of a society and its psychological types. Lukács became deeply hostile to "modernist" literature such as that of Kafka and Joyce, which he saw as an expression merely of the individual psychology of its authors, and espoused the value of "realism," that is, art that self-consciously represents its society and the contradictions therein. Lukács admitted that all art involves some element of abstraction, but disavowed abstraction as itself an aim for art. Instead, he maintained, in a 1938 polemic with Ernst Bloch, the goal of art as realism "is to penetrate the laws governing objective reality and to uncover the deeper, hidden, mediated not immediately perceptible network of relationships that go to make up society ... not just a subjectively perceived moment isolated from the totality in an abstract and over-intense manner" ("Realism in the balance," in Taylor 1977: 38–9). From a very different political position, Lukács shared Heidegger's hostility to "subjectivism."

The playwright Bertolt Brecht (1898–1956) would in turn reply to Lukács that realism is not a matter of how a society is represented but rather requires opening the mind of the audience for art to the reality outside of art. To this end, abstract and unconventional means of presentation might work more effectively than traditional forms of mimesis. In his own dramaturgy, Brecht strove to break the conventions of naturalistic illusion through what he called *Verfremdungseffekten* ("alienating effects"), which began with the removal of the proscenium arch between actors and audience and went on to include all sorts of interruptions to the traditional flow of action in the play: – placards, background projections, bursts of song, direct addresses to the audience, and the like. Brecht agreed that art is aimed at "discovering the causal complexes of society/unmasking the prevailing view of those who are in power/writing from the standpoint of the class which offers the broadest solution for the pressing difficulties in which human society is caught up," but argued that precisely in order to do this "we shall allow the artist to employ his fantasy, his originality, his humour, his invention.... We shall not stick to too detailed literary models; we shall not bind the artist to too rigidly defined modes of narrative" ("Against Georg Lukács," from "Popularity and realism," written in 1938; from Taylor 1977: 62).

Less influential than Brecht while he was alive but far more widely read now is the literary critic Walter Benjamin (1892–1940).[39] Benjamin made his name with studies of the "play of mourning" in the German baroque (Benjamin 1928) and of German romanticism (see Benjamin 1996–2003, vol. 1), but much of his work studied modernist writers beginning with Baudelaire, and he spent much of the last part of his life working on the so-called *Passagenwerk* or "Arcades Project," an attempt to study the conditions of modern life through the lens of the nineteenth-century shopping mall, leading to a vast accumulation of materials of all sorts, from high art to advertising, that is an inspiration for contemporary cultural studies (see Benjamin 1999). Among academic aestheticians, his most widely read work is the 1936 essay "The work of art in the age of its technical reproducibility," first published in the organ of the Frankfurt School, the *Zeitschrift für Sozialforschung*, and included in the first and highly influential collection of Benjamin's writings published in English as *Illuminations* in 1968. (For further discussion of the Frankfurt School, see "Critical Theory," Chapter 18.) In this essay, Benjamin argued that works of art traditionally had an "aura" due not merely to their uniqueness but also to their function in ritual or "cult," which readily allowed for the manipulation and domination of their audience. In an age of mechanical reproducibility and therefore widespread accessibility – although in taking the cinema as his model, Benjamin actually elides the difference between works that are produced as unique instances but then widely reproduced in another medium (such as oil paintings reproduced by photolithography) and works that exist only in multiple instances to begin with (such as music, much photography, and cinema) – works of art would necessarily lose this aura, allowing for "a tremendous shattering of tradition which is the obverse of the contemporary crisis and renewal of mankind" (1968: 223). "For the first time in world history," Benjamin continues, "mechanical reproduction emancipates the work of art from its parasitical dependence on ritual" (p. 226). However, it is not clear what may follow from this: while the end of aura may allow for a "progressive reaction ... characterized by the direct, intimate fusion of visual and emotional enjoyment," it may also lead to the predetermination of "individual reactions ... by the mass audience response" (p. 236), and "So long as the movie-makers' capital sets the fashion," the "film-industry" may simply exploit the ready access to the cinema "to spur the interest of the masses through illusion-promoting spectacles and dubious speculations" (pp. 233–4). In the end, perhaps Benjamin splits the difference between Lukács and Brecht by recognizing that characteristically modern forms and media of art can be used for either progressive or retrogressive purposes – which is no doubt true.

After the German conquest of France made his refuge in Paris worthless, Benjamin committed suicide at the Spanish border in 1940. His Frankfurt colleagues Max Horkheimer, Theodor W. Adorno, and Herbert Marcuse had better luck, escaping to the US and surviving to become the leading Marxist aestheticians after the war. We will return to them later.

Postwar aesthetics

Any "return to normalcy" that might have been taking place in philosophy after World War II was quickly shattered, at least in Britain and America,[40] by the publication of Gilbert Ryle's *The Concept of Mind* in 1949, of Ludwig Wittgenstein's *Philosophical Investigations* in 1953, and by such works of John Langshaw Austin as his William James lectures *How to Do Things with Words* of 1955 (though not published until 1962) and "A plea for excuses" of 1956. Although their approaches are ultimately quite distinct, at the time they were seen as collectively initiating "ordinary language" philosophy (see also "The development of analytic philosophy: Wittgenstein and after," Chapter 2). This movement had a tremendous effect on aesthetics.[41]

Wittgenstein II

Here we may focus on several themes from Wittgenstein that would prove most influential.[42] First, Wittgenstein held that "For a *large* class of cases ... in which we employ the word 'meaning' it can be defined thus: the meaning of a word is its use in the language" (Wittgenstein 1953: §43). By this Wittgenstein meant that the meaning of a word is not fixed by some mental event with which it is always correlated, but by a variety of features of the context in which the word is used and the purposes for which it is used – "Just as a move in chess doesn't consist simply in moving a piece in such-and-such a way on the board – nor yet in one's thoughts and feelings as one makes the move: but in the circumstances that we call 'playing a game of chess', 'solving a chess problem', and so on" (§33). This was the aspect of Wittgenstein's thought that was closest to Ryle (and for that matter to pragmatism, an affinity which may have explained the ready acceptance of Wittgenstein in the US and, ironically, the eclipse of pragmatism for several decades). Second, Wittgenstein's theory that meaning is use precluded essentialism, or any thought that the meaning of concepts could be exhaustively analyzed into a determinate set of necessary and sufficient conditions, because common terms typically have a variety of uses that are only loosely connected by "a complicated network of similarities overlapping and criss-crossing," like "family resemblances." In a crucial example, Wittgenstein argued that this was true of the concept of games (§§66–7), and he called different uses of language "language-games" precisely to emphasize that they cannot be reduced to a single model, say of picturing, as he himself had argued in his earlier work (see §23). In this context, Wittgenstein also argued that language-games are ways of acting, like other games are: "the term 'language-*game*' is meant to bring into prominence the fact that the *speaking* of language is part of an activity, or a form of life" (§23). Finally, in the second part of the *Investigations*, in which he investigated the use of a variety of psychological terms, Wittgenstein offered a famous explication of "Two uses of the word 'see'," one, what we might call an objective or extensional use, in which a person is simply said to see an object without any specification of how it presents itself to him, and the other, which we might call a subjective or intensional use, in which a person sees an object in a certain way or under a certain aspect. Wittgenstein called the latter form of seeing

"seeing as," and his introduction of it was clearly meant to break down any rigid barrier between perception and conceptualization (see Wittgenstein 1953: Part II, section xi, especially pp. 193e–197e, 204e, 211e).

Analytical aesthetics

At least four different tendencies in subsequent Anglo-American aesthetics can be seen as arising from these ideas. Wittgenstein's "family resemblance" conception of concepts lay behind a widespread argument that the search for a determinate concept of art, thought to be the fundamental aim of traditional aesthetics, is hopeless, for while there are certainly "overlapping and criss-crossing" similarities between different media of art and works within those different media, there are also too many differences to allow for an informative definition of art. One of the earliest versions of this argument was offered by Morris Weitz in a 1956 article on "The role of theory in aesthetics," which he summed up twenty years later by saying

> art is an open concept ... it performs its main jobs of describing and evaluating certain objects under conditions less than definitive and, in particular, under sets of conditions, none of which is necessary or sufficient, but ... which must accommodate the unforeseeably new works of art that are demanded by the development of art. (1977: 155)

To some considerable degree, the argument of Weitz and others like William Kennick (Kennick 1958) was based on the fact that works of art in different media and, especially in the twentieth century, even in the same medium, just *look* (or sound, or read) so different from one another that it is obvious that they cannot be instances of a single concept specifying necessary and sufficient conditions for its application. However, a decisive response to the position that art is necessarily an "open" or "family-resemblance" concept was soon offered by Maurice Mandelbaum, who argued that even radical changes in art do not by themselves "prove that new sorts of instantiation of a previously defined concept will necessarily involve us in changing the definition of that concept" (1965: 149).

At the same time, Arthur C. Danto (1924–) first argued that not only do works of art, especially avant-garde works of visual art in the twentieth century, often look very unlike previous art, but also sometimes look remarkably *like* things that are clearly not works of art at all. His favorite example was Andy Warhol's *Brillo Boxes*, plywood boxes silk-screened to look very much like the shipping cartons for an ordinary household product and stacked in the art gallery much as the real boxes might have been stacked in a supermarket display. So Danto argued that what makes Warhol's boxes art – which he assumes they are – cannot be anything *perceptible*, for they are perceptibly indistinguishable from ordinary objects that are not art. (Warhol's *Brillo Boxes* are not actually perceptually indistinguishable from ordinary Brillo boxes, as Danto would sometimes later acknowledge, but the perceptible differences between them, he was surely right to argue, are of no obvious *aesthetic* significance – Warhol's boxes are if anything slightly cruder, not more beautiful, than the ordinary ones.) But from this Danto did not infer that there is nothing uniquely necessary to make something art, only that what makes something art is not anything perceptible. Instead, he argued, "To see something as art requires something the eye cannot decry – an atmosphere of artistic theory, a knowledge of the history of art: an artworld" (1964: 177). "What in the end makes the difference between a Brillo box and a work of art consisting of a Brillo box is a certain theory of art. It is the theory that takes it up into the world of art, and keeps it from collapsing into the real object" (p. 180). Kendall Walton's influential 1970 article, "Categories of art," also stressed that works of art are created and responded to within a particular framework of conceptions and expectations, so that they cannot be treated as if they were immediate objects of unmediated perception (Walton 1970).

In his early article, which thus far did not make a point to which Dewey or Collingwood would have objected, Danto did not say what makes a theory an *artistic* theory, thus what kind of theory is necessary to take an object up into the world of art. This allowed his position to be confused at first with one that was actually quite different, and that should be associated with Wittgenstein's idea that a language is a form of life rather than with his family-resemblance theory of concepts. This other theory was George Dickie's "institutional analysis of art." Dickie began his work by rejecting the idea that there is a psychologically distinctive aesthetic attitude such as Bullough's "psychical distance," and thus the idea that art could be defined as that which aims to produce such an attitude. And like all writers of the period, he recognized that there is nothing common to the appearance of all works of art, thus no prospect for defining art on the basis of a common objective rather than subjective feature. Instead, he thought he could build upon Danto's introduction of the idea of an "artworld" by using it "to refer to the broad social institution in which works of art have their place" (Dickie 1974: 29). That is, he thought that we could all readily recognize the form of life in which works of art are produced and received – art schools, museums, art galleries, art journals, theaters, concert halls, and so on – and that he could then define a work of art simply as "(1) an artifact (2) a set of the aspects of which has had conferred upon it the status of a candidate for appreciation by some person or persons acting on behalf of a certain social institution (the artworld)" (p. 34). This would suffice for a definition of art, he held, even though there could be no definition of a special aesthetic form of appreciation and no set of necessary and sufficient conditions for membership in the artworld and thus no statable criteria for acting on its behalf. Our recognition of the artworld as a form of life would do all the work.[43]

Although widely discussed for a time,[44] this theory eventually fell before the weight of the objections that without either a definition of aesthetic appreciation or non-circular criteria for membership in the artworld, there would be no way to tell whether someone offering us an object for some sort of appreciation was actually acting on behalf of the artworld and offering us a work of art.[45] But it also became clear that this sociological conception of the artworld was not at all what Danto had in mind;[46] by an artworld he meant an "atmosphere" of *theory*, thus that what makes something a work of art is that it is made and offered under the license of a theory of what art is in general and what makes that work a work of art in particular. That made it incumbent upon him to offer an informative general theory of art, a challenge he took up in his 1981 book *The Transfiguration of the Commonplace*.[47] This work begins with Danto's original point that a particular work of art differs from either another work of art or a non-artwork that is perceptibly indistinguishable from it in virtue of the meaning it is intended to have or the interpretation it is intended to bear. But since all sorts of things have meanings that are intended to be interpreted, Danto now raises the question of what makes a sign that bears interpretation "an *artistic* representation" (Danto 1981: 135). The answer to this question is that "works of art, in categorical contrast with mere representations, use the means of representation in a way that is not exhaustively specified when one has exhaustively specified what is being represented" (pp. 147–8), and that what remains beyond the latter, denotative content is precisely the *expression* of a point of view – the artist's point of view – about the denoted content, through rhetorical means such as metaphor (pp. 164–8) and through the artist's distinctive style (pp. 197–201). In his subsequent writing, Danto characterizes his view by saying that art is "embodied meaning" (2003: 24, 139). Danto thus aligns himself with the mainstream modern view that "art *is* expression" (1981: 165), although he does not equate the "point of view" that a work of art expresses with emotion. Yet he takes it that the point of art is to *engage* the emotional response of its audience, to *arouse* emotions (2003: 120), "to *cause* the viewer to feel an appropriate emotion," or even "to *seduce* the feelings of viewers and auditors" (p. 122, emphases added; see also Danto 1981: 167). So while Danto's definition of art as embodied meaning distinguishes works of art from mere real things, which even when they have meaning do not embody it, it is not clear whether on his view there is any essential difference between art and other forms of rhetoric – although this is something that many theorists going back to Kant had been at pains to establish (see Kant 1790: §§51, 53). At the end of *The Abuse of Beauty* Danto does appeal to Kant to support the suggestion that through the experience of art "we learn something fundamental about ourselves ... We learn that we are not 'pure intelligences' but creatures of feelings, and not simply of feelings, but of powerful feelings, such as astonishment and awe" (Danto 2003: 156). But this appeal to a cognitive rather than merely causal connection between art and emotion may come too late to save his theory from the objection that it conflates art with mere rhetoric, if that is an objection.

Let us now return to the more immediate influence of Wittgenstein. Wittgenstein's insistence that general terms like "game" or even "language" itself really connote a variety of much more specific uses and practices can be seen, along with the work of Austin, as lying behind the position of Frank Sibley (1923–96), himself a student of Ryle. Sibley argued, first, that aesthetic theory should focus on specific terms such as "unified, balanced, integrated, lifeless, serene ... tragic" and the like (Sibley 1959: 1) rather than on vague and general terms like "beautiful," and, second, that when we do so focus on specific terms of aesthetic appraisal and description we will see that although such terms "always ultimately depend upon the presence of features which ... are visible, audible, or otherwise discernible without any exercise of taste or sensibility" (p. 3), such "non-aesthetic features" never "serve in *any* circumstances as logically *sufficient conditions* for applying aesthetic terms" (p. 4). Sibley thus held that disputes over the application of aesthetic terms could never be settled by demon-strative arguments, although at the same time aesthetic judgments can be objective, their rightness or wrongness determined not by logically necessary and sufficient conditions but by appropriate or optimal conditions for judgment, like judgments about color (Sibley 1968: 71–3) – an argument that goes back to Hume (Hume 1757) and would later be picked up by John McDowell (McDowell 1983). A similar line of thought was developed by the American philosopher Arnold Isenberg in a famous paper, "Critical communication" (Isenberg 1949). Although Sibley's work continues to draw interest – his collected papers and an accompanying volume of commentary were published as recently as 2001 (Brady and Levinson 2001) – it is striking that what he presents as if it were the result of a new method in philosophy of language is of course the same result that Kant had derived from his theory that aesthetic response results from a free play between the imagination and understanding induced by the representation of an object but not reducible to any perceptual laws (Kant 1790: §§9, 17, 22). In the wake of Wittgenstein and Ryle, Sibley refuses to offer a psychological explanation for linguistic phenomena that traditional aesthetic theory thought it necessary to explain. Isenberg, writing just before the influence of those figures became full-blown, does not preclude the possibility of a psychological explanation of the non-condition-governed character of critical communication, but does think that close analysis of the actual practice of critics provides more conclusive evidence for it than does psychological theory.

Finally, Wittgenstein's discussion of "seeing as" was also influential. In *Art and its Objects* (1968), Richard Wollheim (1923–2003) explicitly applied Wittgenstein's concept of a "form of life" to the case of art, arguing that art is a form of life constituted by characteristic practices and expectations on the basis of both artist and audience. But his specific concept of "life" clearly connected his view to the mainstream view that art exists to give shape to the expression of emotion, for the "life" to which "form" must in fact be given by art is nothing other than the life of human emotions: "Art rests on the fact that deep feelings pattern themselves in a coherent way all over our life and behaviour" (Wollheim 1960: 112). Wollheim was willing to entertain the idea that artist and audience come to share a language for the expression of emotions, but only as long as the concept of a language is not reduced to that of a code (pp. 132–6). He also emphasized that the spectator of art "should be able to structure or interpret the work of art in more ways than one," but "not at the expense of the artist," who in turn "is characteristically operating at the intersection of more than one intention" (p. 139). Wollheim rejected what he conceived of as the idealism of Collingwood because it did not do justice to art as a form of life, but his view that art develops forms of expression for feeling connects him to Collingwood's deeper message, and his emphasis on the freedom of interpretative imagination for both artist and spectator connects his view not only to Collingwood but also to Kant. The Wittgensteinian theme of "seeing as," however, is the focus of Wollheim's second main work in aesthetics, *Painting as an Art* (1987). Here Wollheim offers a psychological account of pictorial meaning. He says that the psychological theorizing that "has quite rightly been chased out of the field of language, most notably through the influence of Wittgenstein, is at home in painting" (1987: 22), but the kind of account of painting that he goes on to give is itself Wittgensteinian. The basic idea is that a painter engages in the activity of "seeing in," seeing an image or a meaning in an object, and actively places that seen meaning in his work through his own distinctive choice of theme and style. The role of the spectator – which of course can be and is often occupied by the artist as well, in the course of creation (another Collingwoodian theme) – is then to "see-in" the work what the artist has seen-in it – although presumably with the degree of freedom insisted upon in Wollheim's earlier work. All of this is enabled by the fact that "seeing-in" is a fundamental human capacity, "logically and historically" prior to artistic representation: we can see images in clouds, Wollheim argues, before or without any specific practice of making images (pp. 47–8). The practice of painting, and presumably of other arts as well, is a later development, but one rooted in one of the deepest features of human psychology.

Another author who erected a theory of aesthetic appreciation on an account of imagination based on the notion of "seeing as" is Roger Scruton (Scruton 1974). Starting under the influence of Wittgenstein, both Wollheim and Scruton ended up returning to fundamental insights of pre-Wittgensteinian aesthetics. For others, the route was less tortuous.

The return of beauty

Several of the most important figures who self-consciously continued to work in the mainstream of twentieth-century aesthetics even through the upheaval of ordinary-language philosophy are Monroe Beardsley (1915–85), Mary Mothersill, and Anthony Savile. Influenced by both Dewey and Kant, Beardsley[48] steadfastly defended the informativeness of the concept of aesthetic experience throughout the heyday of linguistic philosophy (his chief work was first published in 1958), and defined art as work intentionally aimed to produce experience with a marked "aesthetic character" (Beardsley 1981: 59). Experience has such a character, he summarizes, "when it has some of the following features, including the first one: attention firmly fixed on a perceptual or intentional object; a feeling of freedom from concerns about matters outside that object; notable affect that is detached from practical ends; the sense of exercising powers of discovery; and the integration of the self and of its experiences" (p. lxii). A central part of his detailed argument is that in a "unified experience the percepts are integrated with affects of various kind" (p. lxi) but separated from the need or urge for immediate action. In developing the idea that an aesthetic experience is perceptually unified, Beardsley is clearly extending the Kantian idea that there is a free but harmonious play between the imagination and the demands of the under-standing in aesthetic experience. Beardsley devotes much space to this theme, arguing that we experience aesthetic objects as part–whole complexes (pp. 82–3) and showing in detail how this is the case in our experience of music and literature as well as of the visual arts. But in arguing that there is also a unity between percept and affect in aesthetic experience, Beardsley is equally clearly developing the thought of both

Dewey and Collingwood that aesthetic experience requires the shaping and clarifying of emotion rather than its mere communication. In a concluding defense of the value of art, after accepting the view of Santayana and Moore that the pleasure afforded by art is itself intrinsically valuable (p. 572), Beardsley lists a number of further benefits of aesthetic experience. It "develops the imagination, and along with it the ability to put oneself in the place of others," and it "fosters mutual sympathy and understanding"; but perhaps above all it "resolves lesser conflicts within the self, and helps to create an integration, or harmony," specifically "a remarkable kind of *clarification*, as though the jumble in our minds were being sorted out" (pp. 574–5). But art rarely sorts out purely cognitive confusions; what Beardsley must have in mind is primarily the clarification of emotions.

Two books published during the 1980s also defended traditional aesthetic theorizing, in particular defending the concept of beauty from the ravages it had suffered at the hands of both twentieth-century art and the Wittgenstein-inspired de-emphasis on the importance of the term "beautiful" in ordinary aesthetic discourse. Both of these works drew inspiration directly from Hume and Kant. In *Beauty Restored*, the American Mary Mothersill, influenced by Arnold Isenberg as well, drew on both eighteenth-century authors in defending two theses as the parameters for any plausible aesthetic theory: that there are no laws of taste (Mothersill 1984: 115), and yet that some judgments of taste are genuine judgments, with a sustainable claim to intersubjective acceptability (p. 164). On Mothersill's account, these two theses are not self-evident or a priori truths, as Kant might have thought (p. 168), nor yet need we give them up at the first whiff of skepticism; they are the product of serious reflection on our actual practices, but they do need an explanation by a theory of beauty. Mothersill then goes back to Plato and Aquinas to begin developing a theory of beauty. From Plato she accepts the premises that beauty is "(i) a kind of good (ii) which can be possessed by items of any kind and (iii) which is linked with pleasure and inspires love" (p. 262). Contrary to recent fashion, she argues that pleasure can be considered a genuine inner state that can stand in a causal relation to external objects; but she accepts the recent consensus that there is no phenomenologically specific aesthetic pleasure, thus that beauty cannot be defined and identified by a special type of pleasure that it causes. Instead, she turns to the object of pleasure to find beauty. Here her argument takes what might seem a paradoxical turn. She argues that an object is beautiful when it causes pleasure by means of its aesthetic properties (pp. 342–7), where aesthetic properties are simply properties that objects share only to the extent that they are perceptually indistinguishable from one another (p. 344). In other words, aesthetic properties are what make an object perceptually unique. This explains why there can be no laws linking beauty to determinate classes of objects or properties, for classes always allow for some recognizable differences among their members as well. But why should such properties please? Here is where Mothersill turns to Aquinas, arguing that "beauty is a disposition ... actualized on each occasion when someone is pleased by the *apprehensio ipsa* of the beautiful object," where "what is grasped in an *apprehensio ipsa* (and not otherwise) is the aesthetic properties of individuals" (p. 347). In other words, pleasure in beauty is pleasure in contemplation of what is unique in objects. This seems open to the objection, however, that objects can also be uniquely ugly, so uniqueness alone is no explanation of pleasure in contemplation. At this point it seems that something like Beardsley's Kantian–Deweyian, positive account of the integrated character of the experience of contemplation of the unique complex of parts offered by some perceptual or intentional object is needed to complete the account of beauty.

Two years earlier, the British philosopher Anthony Savile had resurrected aspects of traditional aesthetics by asking what could allow works of art to withstand the "test of time" in spite of the historicist contention that art is inextricably linked to its time and place, which was such a prominent feature of much nineteenth- and twentieth-century art criticism and historiography. Savile argued that successful art withstands the test of time for three main reasons. First, precisely because it is representative of one place and time, great art can enlarge the "sense of possibility" of an audience receiving it at another time. Here he appeals to Friedrich Schiller's *Letters on the Aesthetic Education of Mankind* (1795) for the insight that because we are so "inclined to understand the world from the point of view of the assumptions that we bring to it," great artworks from other times and places can offer us "alternatives to the ways in which we are accustomed to believe events are guided" and thereby enable "us to detach ourselves from our assumptions" (Savile 1982: 96–7). Second, here appealing to the nineteenth-century critic William Hazlitt, Savile argued that great art reveals constancies in human nature underlying the superficial differences that are so often emphasized by historicism, and appeals to our "*general* preference for the deep over the shallow" (p. 146). Finally, appealing both to Kant, but more to Kant's analysis of the spirit of works of artistic genius (p. 167; Kant 1790; §§46–9) than to his initial analysis of "free beauty," and also to Wittgenstein's suggestion that we find an object beautiful when it "clicks" (p. 169), Savile argues that we find an object beautiful when we recognize it as a satisfying solution to its underlying problem or problems – problems that may be set by its genre as well as by more specific objectives, e.g. by the genre of portraiture as well as by the task of capturing a particular personality – within its own style (pp. 168–9, 177–80). Here the underlying thought is that the human satisfaction in the original and successful solution of a problem can transcend the limits of the original spatio-temporal context of the problem itself.

Savile admits that his account is extremely abstract: while there is nothing in it "to preclude assessment of fit in the representational field from involving a judgment about the broadly human or anthropocentric character of the represented world – of its emotional, intellectual, and even its moral nature," he also concedes that he has "said next to nothing by way of description of this beauty-constituting fit at all" (1982: 184–5). Even more recent attempts to restore the concept of beauty to its traditional place in aesthetic theory do say more about this. In *The Abuse of Beauty* Danto, who had previously focused his aesthetic theorizing on those paradigms of twentieth-century art that had seemed to make beauty irrelevant to the aims of art, for example, in addition to the pop art of Andy Warhol, the ready-mades of Marcel Duchamp and "disturbational" art (Danto 1986: ch. VI), acknowledges that the creation of beauty may indeed sometimes be "internal" to the intentions of a work of art even if it is not always so (2003: 86–93), and that when it is, the intended role of the beauty of the work will typically be to engage or transform our emotions, as when Robert Motherwell's *Elegies for the Spanish Republic* or Maya Lin's Vietnam Memorial transform "pain from grief into sorrow, and with that into a form of release" (p. 111). In his 2002 Tanner Lectures, Alexander Nehamas has also stressed the connection between beauty and our deepest emotions, although his conception of the emotional impact of art is more active than Danto's peculiarly passive, rhetorical model. On Nehamas's account, "A work we admire, a work we love, a work we find, in a word, beautiful, sparks within us the same sense that it has more to offer, the same willingness to submit to it, the same desire to make it part of our life" (2002: 205). A beautiful work draws us down a path of further engagement with it and other objects to which it leads, as loving Proust could lead one to go back to Ruskin, whom Proust admired, to travel to Normandy, where much of Proust's novel is set, and more. Further, Nehamas argues, beauty is a medium for our emotional connection with others: "to find something beautiful is to want to make it part of your life and of the life of others whose taste you already admire" (p. 215). The idea here is not Tolstoy's idea that a work of art passively infects its audience with feelings deemed to be valuable from some objective "religious" standpoint, but rather that we at least in part actively shape our lives, individually and in communities of taste, around what we find beautiful. Successful art does not merely shape and clarify our emotions considered as it were individually, but can shape and clarify our whole lives, or their emotional dimensions.

Languages of art

With these recent works on beauty and its significance in art, Anglo-American aesthetics has returned to issues that centrally concerned it before the episode of ordinary-language philosophy. Before leaving Anglo-American aesthetics for a while, one other alternative to the ordinary-language approach to aesthetics needs to be considered. This is the approach of Nelson Goodman in his 1968 book *Languages of Art* (see also Goodman 1972, Part III, and Goodman 1984, Part IV). (For further discussion of Goodman, see "American philosophy in the twentieth century," Chapter 5.) Goodman was concerned with the traditional problems of representation and the expression of emotion in art, but approached them from a conception of language that was informed by both the theory of symbol-systems developed by Suzanne Langer and the nominalism that Goodman had earlier developed with W. V. O. Quine. Goodman treated natural language as one instance of a wide range of symbolic systems with certain commonalities as well as key differences, and interpreted various media of art as exploiting the possibilities of symbolic systems in a variety of ways. He may also be seen as carrying on the pragmatic tradition of Dewey, although in a very different way from Monroe Beardsley, in his insistence that our response to art is cognitive and thus problem-solving – but also in his refusal to draw a rigid distinction between the cognitive and emotional dimensions of aesthetic experience, his aim being instead to show that emotions are part of the way in which we come to know works of art. Further, although he shies away from the term, Goodman shows that all use of symbols and language is an exercise in imagination, creating ways for thinking about the world that are not automatically given to us (what he would ultimately call "ways of world-making"; see Goodman 1978). Goodman's exploration of aesthetic symbol-systems is thus an examination of the nature and scope of the aesthetic imagination as well.

One key feature of languages in Goodman's view is that they allow for both denotation and exemplification, denotation when a sign is taken to refer to an object or property and exemplification when an object is used as a sign (like a tailor's fabric swatches) that is, denotes one or more features (color or texture, for example) that it possesses itself; thus, "exemplification is reference plus possession" (Goodman 1968: 53–4). Further, language can be used both literally and metaphorically, although the difference between these two modes of use is only a matter of habit and familiarity, because no uses of language are mechanically determined by their objects. Literal usage is just that way of representing the world with which we are more familiar, and metaphorical usage is that which is more unfamiliar and non-habitual (although of course metaphors can become habitual, and then they tend toward the literal). Artistic representation is then interpreted as a form of denotation rather than, as traditionally thought, resemblance:[49] a picture of Winston Churchill represents him just insofar as it is taken to denote him within some symbol system that artist and audience know how to use. The representation of fictional objects is interpreted as the use of predicates to denote certain sorts of signs themselves – e.g. unicorn-pictures – when those predicates cannot be used to denote actual objects – e.g. unicorns (p. 21). Most importantly, artistic expression is metaphorical exemplification: a sad piece of music is of course not a person who is actually sad, but nevertheless "comes under a transferred application of some label coextensive with 'sad'," (p. 85) where we may have various reasons for seeing it as and calling it "sad" other than that it is literally sad or that it makes us literally sad. Because of Goodman's nominalism,[50] there is no need for an essentialist explanation of why we classify both persons and music or pictures as sad, although we do the former habitually, thus literally, and the latter less literally, thus metaphorically. The importance of his analysis of exemplification for Goodman's aesthetics becomes clear when he subsequently argues that art is not meant to arouse emotions but emotions are a chief way in which we come to know works of art: how such works feel to us will be a key factor in what we take them to exemplify.

The influence of Langer – Goodman explicitly acknowledges that many of his results "may well have been anticipated" by Charles Sanders Peirce, Cassirer, Charles W. Morris, and Langer (Goodman 1968: xii–xiii) – becomes evident in Goodman's detailed exploration of the syntactical and semantic differences between artistic languages or symbol-systems and various ordinary and scientific ones. Scientific languages tend to employ discrete symbols, with clear boundaries between one another and between significant and insignificant variations among the symbols themselves, whereas the symbol-systems of the arts tend to be dense and rich, and any difference between one symbol or region of a work and another can be aesthetically significant. Symbols tend to be aesthetic when the following characteristics are present: syntactic density; semantic density, such as ambiguity; repleteness, that is, having a multiplicity of dimensions of meaning; the use of metaphorical as well as literal exemplification; and finally the existence of multiple reference relations for a single symbol,[51] although

Goodman emphasizes that all these are "symptoms" rather than necessary and sufficient conditions of the aesthetic.

Goodman abjures virtually all discussion of beauty, maintaining instead that "beauty" is only "an alternative and misleading word for aesthetic merit" (1968: 255). He is also critical of any attempt to make the occurrence of pleasure definitive of aesthetic experience. Instead, he emphasizes the cognitive dimension of aesthetic experience:

> Aesthetic experience is dynamic rather than static. It involves making delicate discriminations and discerning subtle relationships, identifying symbol systems and characters within these systems and what these characters denote and exemplify, interpreting works and reorganizing the world in terms of works and works in terms of the world.... . The aesthetic "attitude" is restless, searching, testing – is less attitude than action: creation and re-creation. (1968: 241–2)

But Goodman hardly means to deny that the kinds of cognitive activities with which we respond to works of art are among our deepest sources of pleasure. In fact, the cognitive activities with art that Goodman describes seem to be good examples of what Kant had in mind in his idea of the free play between imagination and understanding, and which have been central to so many subsequent accounts, such as those of Collingwood, Beardsley, and more recently Nehamas. Goodman's thought is not as far from the mainstream as his iconoclastic tone may initially suggest.

Further, while Goodman's account of expression seems to downplay any thought that we call a picture sad because it either has the same emotion that a sad person has or evokes the same emotion in another that a sad person does, in the end he by no means excludes emotions from our response to art. On the contrary, he emphasizes –and this is perhaps the chief point of his work – "that in aesthetic experience the *emotions function cognitively*. The work of art is apprehended through the feelings as well as through the senses." "Emotions must be felt –that is, must occur, as sensations must – if they are to be used cognitively" (1968: 248). To be sure, our response to art is not *simply* emotional: "emotions function cognitively not as separate items but in combination with one another and with other means of knowing. Perception, conception, and feeling intermingle and interact" (p. 249). Goodman certainly rejects Tolstoy's view that art simply communicates emotion and Danto's suggestions that art simply engages or seduces our emotion. But he does not so much reject the mainstream view of Bosanquet, Collingwood, and Dewey that art shapes and clarifies our emotions as he supplements it with the recognition that our emotions also shape and clarify our understanding of art and indeed of the world in general. In his distinctive way, Goodman is therefore also part of the mainstream of twentieth-century aesthetics.

Marxist aesthetics II

The most important Marxist aestheticians of the postwar period also moved toward rapprochement with the mainstream of twentieth-century aesthetics. Although Walter Benjamin has had his greatest influence after the 1960s, he had died in 1940, and while György Lukács published his system of aesthetics only in the 1960s, the main lines of his position had already been established in the 1930s. So those figures will not be further discussed here. The present section will focus on Theodor Wiesengrund Adorno (1903–69) and Herbert Marcuse (1899–1979).

Adorno began the serious study of philosophy as a teenager, reading the *Critique of Pure Reason* with Siegfried Kracauer, later famous as a film theorist. But he also came from a musical family, and spent the first years after earning his first degree studying composition in Vienna with Alban Berg. His vast output includes many writings on music, including a *Philosophy of Modern Music* (1949), and multiple volumes of *Notes to Literature* (1958–65). But here we will focus on the theoretical background and content of his work in philosophical aesthetics.

Adorno taught at the university in Frankfurt and was associated with the Institut für Sozialforschung, what would later become known as the "Frankfurt School," prior to the Nazi takeover. (For further discussion of Adorno, see "Critical Theory," Chapter 18.) He escaped first to Oxford, where he worked upon but did not complete a doctorate, and then rejoined Max Horkheimer, the leader of the Frankfurt institute, in Los Angeles. During this period he contributed to a famous volume, *The Authoritarian Personality* (Adorno et al. 1950), and co-authored *The Dialectic of Enlightenment* with Horkheimer (Adorno and Horkheimer 1947).[52] This work made the rather fantastical argument that the European Enlightenment actually continued the repressive tendencies of the religious worldview that it purported to replace by seeking the same totalizing control over individual lives; but it also included a more perspicuous analysis of the "culture industry" that revealed the repressive tendencies inherent in the commercialization of art. This was of course a theme that Benjamin had already touched upon in 1936.

Adorno's two major theoretical works were completed (or nearly so) only in the final decade of his life, after he had returned to Frankfurt. Adorno's general philosophical position was laid out in a complicated work, *Negative Dialectics* (1966), in which he criticized the non-dialectical philosophy of Edmund Husserl. He also bit the Hegelian hand that had fed him by arguing that intellectual and social contradictions reveal themselves dialectically, but in a dialectic that does not by itself cause, let alone guarantee their resolution – hence his term *negative* dialectics.[53] In the posthumously published *Aesthetic Theory* (1970), he argued that art goes beyond other forms of social and intellectual production by revealing not only the existence of contradictions in the structure of society but also at least the *possibility* of resolving them. This work is long, involuted, and eschews any linear pattern of argumentation, trying to replicate at the level of theory the irreducibility of art itself to conceptual rules.[54] But the basic idea of the work emerges early on. Adorno maintains that "The concept of art is located in an historically changing constellation of elements," and "refuses definition" precisely because it "can be understood only by its laws of movement" – "art's substance could be its transitoriness" (1970: 2–3). Nevertheless, Adorno is willing to generalize that art has always "turned against the status quo and what merely exists just as much as it has come to its aid by giving form to its elements" (p. 2): art can be used to beautify existing society with all of its contradiction and repression, but can also be used to make us aware of the possibility of something better as well. The latter possibility is clearly essential if not definitional in Adorno's conception of art.

> Only by separation from empirical reality, which sanctions art to model the relation of the whole and the part according to the work's own need, does the artwork achieve a heightened order of existence. Artworks are afterimages of empirical life insofar as they help the latter to what is denied [it] outside [its] own sphere and thereby free it from that to which [it is] condemned by reified external experience.... Art negates the categorial determinations stamped on the empirical world and yet harbors what is empirically existing in its own substance. (1970: 4-5)

Adorno interprets the traditional concept of the autonomy of art with its potential for negating the limitations of current society as pointing to the real possibility of a life beyond those limits: "The moment a limit is posited, it is overstepped and that against which the limit was established is absorbed. Only this, not moralizing, is the critique of the principle of *l'art pour l'art*" (p. 6). Adorno also appeals to the traditional conception of art as integrative, as in Moore, Dewey, and Beardsley, but with a twist: art shows both the "fissures" that exist in the kinds of integration currently imposed by society, but also the possibility of a non-coercive integration beyond those fissures (p. 9).

One of the distinctive features of Adorno's *Aesthetic Theory* is its treatment of natural beauty. As is only to be expected, Adorno's attitude toward natural beauty is complex and ambivalent. On the one hand, "the identity of nature with itself" of which we are aware in the appreciation of natural beauty offers a model of integration or reconciliation – indeed, not just a model but a real possibility and necessity, since ultimately human beings must recognize that they are part of nature and must live within nature if they are to continue living at all – which art strives to copy. For this reason, "Authentic artworks, which hold fast to the idea of reconciliation with nature by making themselves completely a second nature, have consistently felt the urge, as if in need of a breath of fresh air, to step outside of themselves … they have sought consolation in nature. Thus the last act of *Figaro* is played out of doors …" (1970: 63). On the other hand, it is all too easy to let the existence of natural beauty seduce us into thinking that reconciliation will come automatically instead of by our own intentional action. Thus Adorno writes:

> That the experience of natural beauty … is entirely distinct from the domination of nature, as if the experience were at one with the primordial origin, marks out both the strength and the weakness of the experience: its

strength, because it recollects a world without domination, one that probably never existed; its weakness, because through this recollection it dissolves back into that amorphousness out of which genius once arose and for the first time becomes conscious of the idea of freedom that could be realized in a world free from domination. The amamnesis of freedom in natural beauty deceives because it seeks freedom in the old unfreedom. Natural beauty is myth transposed into the imagination and thus, perhaps, requited. (1970: 66)

The involutions and ultimately ambivalence of this passage are typical of Adorno's prose throughout the book. And ultimately Adorno's message is perhaps less optimistic than it initially appears. Thus much later in the work he writes "Art desires what has not yet been, though everything that art is has already been. It cannot escape the shadow of the past" (p. 134). Thus, "aesthetic experience is that of something that spirit may find neither in the world nor in itself; it is possibility promised by its impossibility. Art is the ever broken promise of happiness" (pp. 135–6).

A more optimistic as well as more accessible assessment of the value of art was offered by Herbert Marcuse, another émigré from the Frankfurt School who, however, remained in the US after the war. Marcuse was obviously impressed with the Frankfurt critique of the "culture industry," and in one of his best-known works, *One-Dimensional Man* (1964), warned of the power of society to defang criticism by co-opting it, thus transforming serious resistance into mere entertainment. In his unique synthesis of Freud with the young Marx, however, Marcuse had argued that human beings can use the productive power of modern society to create room for the expression of human freedom, typified for him by "Eros" or libidinal energy. In his last work, *The Aesthetic Dimension*, he argued for an unequivocally positive role for art in the fulfillment of the human wish for life rather than death. Marcuse cast this short work as a critique of orthodox Marxist aesthetics. In spite of the traditional Marxist interpretation of art as merely part of the superstructure of society that is entirely determined by the economic substructure, Marcuse argued that "by virtue of its aesthetic form, art is largely autonomous vis à vis the given social relations." Like Adorno, he held that art "protests these relations," but unlike Adorno he unequivocally held that art "at the same time transcends them" (Marcuse 1978: ix) in virtue of essential characteristics that realize value beyond the limits of specific places, times, and social circumstances. "Aesthetic form, autonomy, and truth" are each "a socio-historical phenomenon," yet "each *transcends* the socio-historical arena." And they do this for the sake of "an emancipation of sensibility, imagination, and reason in all spheres of subjectivity and objectivity" (p. 9). This possibility is grounded "in the commitment of art to Eros, the deep affirmation of the Life Instincts in their fight against instinctual and social oppression" (pp. 10–11). Specifically, Marcuse maintains that art "challenges the monopoly of the established reality to determine what is 'real,' and it does so by creating a fictitious world which is nevertheless 'more real than reality itself'" (p. 22) (he acknowledges at the outset that his account will be based primarily on literature), thus appropriating Schiller's idea that art can show us the possibility of a better reality that was also invoked by Savile. Further, Marcuse interprets aesthetic form as consisting precisely in its ability to provide an image of unity better than "a society in which subjects and objects are shattered, atomized, robbed of their words and images," turned "into bits and pieces" (p. 49), although to be sure he recognizes the catastrophic risk that aesthetic form can also be used to create an illusion of integration in a society that is still atomizing its subjects and robbing them of their words and images (p. 50). Nevertheless, Marcuse maintains that art is capable of genuine beauty, an

> erotic quality ... which persists through all changes in the "judgment of taste." As pertaining to the domain of Eros, the Beautiful represents the pleasure principle. Thus, it rebels against the prevailing reality principle of domination. The work of art speaks the liberating language, invokes the liber-ating images of the subordination of death and destruction to the will to live. This is the emancipatory element in aesthetic affirmation. (1978: 62–3)

Above all by representing a particular domain of emotions, namely "the brief moments of fulfillment, tranquility ... the 'beautiful moment' which arrests the incessant dynamic and disorder.... . The Beautiful belongs to the imagery of liberation" (pp. 64–5). Finally, Marcuse concludes that "Against all fetishism of the productive forces, against the continued enslavement of individuals by the objective conditions (which remain those of domination), art represents the ultimate goal of all revolutions: the freedom and the happiness of the individual" (p. 69).

In that conclusion, Marcuse follows Trotsky, who had reminded Lenin that the point of revolution was not simply to remodel society in the abstract but to allow and promote the freedom of individuals in the concrete. But he argues that art will do this, once of course it has revealed to us the contradictions of existing society, primarily by capturing the feeling of moments of repose and tranquility, thus holding out to us the promise of happiness in a society committed to life rather than death. Here he exploits the conception of art as the vehicle for the clear and shapely expression of emotion that has been at the heart of twentieth-century aesthetic theory.

Subsequent developments

There are numerous fields in contemporary aesthetics that have produced large bodies of literature worthy of comment: the ontology of artworks and fictional characters; the philosophy of particular arts such as literature, cinema, music, and architecture; feminist aesthetics; comparative studies in western and non-western aesthetics; and many more. I will conclude, however, by touching upon two debates in contemporary aesthetics that resume discussions that have been central throughout the history of modern aesthetics. We have already observed the defense of the concept of beauty, after its attack in both avant-garde art and aesthetic theory, beginning in the 1980s with the work of Mothersill and Savile and continuing more recently with the work of Nehamas and even Danto. Several works from outside of the precincts of profes-sional philosophy that have also received wide attention are books and catalogues by the art critic Dave Hickey (e.g. Hickey 1993) and the Tanner Lectures of Elaine

Scarry (Scarry 1999).[55] What I will mention now is discussion of the "aesthetics of the natural environment," as one recent collection calls it (Carlson and Berleant 2004), and the extensive debate over the relation between art and morality that has been going on since the mid-1990s.

Discussion of natural beauty within analytical aesthetics was spurred by R. W. Hepburn's paper "Contemporary aesthetics and the neglect of natural beauty" (1966). Hepburn raised the problem that natural beauty is "frameless": unlike a painting, for example, where our gaze may be directed to the relevant object by a frame, which itself embodies all the conventions that we have for looking at and comprehending paintings, we have no authorial or conventional guidance for looking at nature. Hepburn doubted that there is any single way in which to appreciate nature aesthetically. Since then, two main alternatives have dominated discussion. On the one hand, authors including Allen Carlson (1979; 2000) and Malcolm Budd (1996; 2002) have argued that aesthetic appreciation of nature must be based on a conception of what is being appreciated *as* nature and a scientifically appropriate classification of the kind of natural object being appreciated. Carlson has argued specifically that nature must be appreciated as our own environment, that is, the ecological system of which we are a part. On the other hand, Arnold Berleant (1992) and Emily Brady (1998; 2003) have argued, with appeal to Kant, that objects and vistas in nature offer suitable objects for the free play of imagination independent of an ecological perspective and scientific classification. Hepburn has restated the position that there is a "duality within our [aesthetic] commerce with nature – a respect for its own structures and the celebrating of those, and the annexation of natural forms" (Hepburn 2001: 7), his term for imaginative play with natural forms independent of any thought about their scientific significance. It is indeed hard to see why both of these should not provide aesthetically satisfactory engagements with nature, or how one could be ranked as more important than the other – absent, of course, moral arguments for the importance of recognizing our position within and dependence upon the ecology of nature, which, however, would clearly be extra-aesthetic.[56]

Debate about the moral significance of the aesthetic diminished during the early phase of analytical aesthetics, perhaps as a lingering effect of the misinterpretation of Bullough's conception of "psychical distance." But it has become very lively again since the 1980s and 1990s, yielding a literature far larger than can be surveyed here.[57] There have been two separate questions in this debate: one about the ethical import of the aesthetic, the other about the aesthetic import of the ethical. That is, one question concerns the moral value of the aesthetic experience of works of art, and the other concerns the impact on the aesthetic experience, again of works of art, of moral views that may be expressed in or advocated by those works. The first of these questions concerns whether we can learn anything of moral value from works of art, primarily narrative works of art such as novels and films. One view denies that we can, holding that any moral principles that might be expressed in works will be so obvious and banal that we can hardly be said to learn from them. The opposing view admits that this may be true about moral principles, but argues that we can learn a great deal from narrative art about the emotions of both agents and patients in morally fraught and demanding situations, indeed that narrative art may well be the primary means by which that level of our moral education proceeds. The latter view has been defended by Martha Nussbaum in many of her works (see for example Nussbaum 1986; 1990; 1995; and 2001) and by Noël Carroll in several discussions of narrative art (1997; 1998).

The second debate concerns what has come to be called "ethical criticism" (Gaut 1998). Here the question is whether what are perceived as ethical "defects" in the morality expressed by a work of art are necessarily also aesthetic defects in the work, or whether our appreciation of the purely aesthetic properties of the work – form, inventiveness, and so on – is entirely independent of any moral stance or attitudes in the work. The latter position, which has been dubbed "autonomism," has been provocatively defended by Daniel Jacobson (see Jacobson 1997), while Carroll and Gaut have defended the position that Carroll calls "moderate moralism" (Carroll 1996). Moderate moralism is the view that moral defects are prima facie or *pro tanto* aesthetic defects, because they may interfere with our "aesthetic uptake" of the work, that is, in Carroll's version, our appreciation of the artistic project of the work, but these defects may or may not be outweighed by the aesthetic merits of the work. In the former case we are left with an overall favorable aesthetic appreciation and evaluation of the work in spite of its moral defects. However, in the absence of a fuller account of aesthetic appreciation than some of the participants of this debate have thus far been willing to give, it is sometimes difficult to appraise the strength of the arguments on each side.

A quite distinctive approach to the relation between aesthetics and morality has long been the foundation of the philosophical criticism of again mostly narrative art that has been a central part of the work of Stanley Cavell (1926–). Although Cavell was deeply influenced by the work of Wittgenstein and Austin at the time of its original appearance, and although he was concerned with the possibility of ordinary-language philosophy at the outset of his career (see the earlier essays in Cavell 1969), he could not be associated with any of the obvious influences of Wittgenstein earlier discussed, and his continuing interest in the problem of the ordinary owes as much to his interest in Heidegger and Emerson as to the influence of Wittgenstein and Austin. In the domain of aesthetics (in which he has written philosophical criticism rather than a systematic treatise), Cavell's concern with the ordinary can be at least partially parsed as a concern for what we can learn about the conditions of our ordinary life from a works of narrative art ranging from Shakespeare's tragedies (Cavell 1987) to Hollywood screwball comedies of remarriage and melodramas of unknown women (Cavell 1981; 1996). Thus Cavell's general concern falls more into the first debate here mentioned, about the role of art in moral education, than into the second, about the role of moral considerations in art criticism. But instead of arguing simply that we learn about the nature of our own emotions and their proper place in moral deliberation and action from works of narrative art, Cavell has argued that we learn about the *condition* within which we can understand and act upon our emotions, namely, the condition in which complete certainty about our own feelings and intentions as well as those of those with whom we interact, whether child, spouse, or ex-spouse, is, literally, humanly impossible, and in which we must therefore learn to acknowledge our own vulnerability and the imperfection of others – the human condition. Cavell notably illustrated this thesis with interpretations of *King Lear* (Cavell 1969; 1987), in which the tragedy is caused by Lear's insistence on avowals of unconditional love from his daughters in order to mask his own human vulnerability, and *Othello* (Cavell 1979), in which the tragedy is caused by Othello's fantasy of an inhuman perfection for Desdemona, which paradoxically leads him to place complete confidence in the scoundrel Iago rather than his faithful and trusting wife. Cavell's argument that tragedy arises from a refusal to acknowledge one's own imperfection and from an unrealistic expectation of certainty about the inner lives of others, even those nearest to us, is part of his larger argument that skepticism arises from an unrealistic expectation of certainty, and a refusal to realize that the "presentness" of the world "to us cannot be a function of knowing. The world is to be *accepted*; as the presentness of other minds is not to be known, but acknowledged" (1987: 94). This is a lesson, he may suggest, that we can learn better from great narrative art than from philosophy, but it is in any case a lesson we must learn if we are to learn what to make of the representation of emotion in art and of emotion in our real lives.

Cavell thus rejects the most controversial part of the otherwise attractive general theory of art as a vehicle for the play of the imagination that has been developed by Kendall Walton, the position, namely, that because the events presented to us in a drama or film are "make-believe" or fictional our responses to them must also be make-believe or fictional emotions (Walton 1978; 1990; Walton's position on emotions has in turn generated a large literature on the enjoyment of horror and tragedy in art, such as Carroll 1990). In Cavell's view, I do not go to the theater to see an actress depict Desdemona, not even Mrs. Siddons: "I go to watch Desdemona" (1987: 99); and from watching Desdemona die, I do not feel fictional grief, but real powerlessness, from which in turn I can learn "my separateness" from others, and then both the real limits of my power to help others but also the real possibility of helping others before whom I am limited but not utterly powerless (p. 109). Cavell thus rejects the isolationist position that through "psychical distance" we acquire a distinct aesthetic emotion and the infectionist position that through a work of art certain emotions felt by the artist are simply communicated to us or we are simply seduced into feeling intended emotions. Instead, he deepens the recognition of Bosanquet, Collingwood, and many others that art clarifies our emotions by arguing that art specifically clarifies the conditions in which we have our emotions and both the possibility as well as limits on our action on our emotions. His distinctive work is thus part of the mainstream of twentieth-century aesthetics.[58]

Notes

1 See Halliwell 2002.
2 For a careful analysis of the restriction of the scope of Plato's attack upon the arts, see Alexander Nehamas, "Plato on imitation and poetry in *Republic* X," in Nehamas 1999: 251–78. Nehamas argues that Plato's attack upon mimesis applies only to poetry, and was aimed only at the educational pretenses of the poets and their interpreters.

3 See Baumgarten 1735: §CXVI and 1750–8: §1.

4 See Hutcheson 1725/1738, sect. I and VIII.

5 See Shaftesbury 1711 and Guyer 1993: ch. 2; and 2005b: ch. 1.

6 See Kant 1790, especially the General Remark following §29 and §59. See also Guyer 1993, especially chs. 1 and 3; and Guyer 2005b: ch. 7. On Kant's aesthetics generally, see also Crawford 1974; Savile 1987; and Allison 2001. On the relation between aesthetics and morality in Kant, see also Recki 2001. On the sublime, see Crowther 1989; Lyotard 1991; and Pries 1995.

7 See for example Davies 1991.

8 Kant always touched upon this topic in his lectures on anthropology, as well as in the *Critique of the Power of Judgment*; see Kant 1790: §§51, 53.

9 See Hegel 1975, especially vol. I: 25–55.

10 See Sartwell 1998.

11 See Wilcox 1953.

12 See Moritz 1785; Guyer 1992: ch. 4; and Bowman 1998.

13 "Reception aesthetics" is particularly associated with Wolfgang Iser and Hans Robert Jauss; see Iser 1978 and Jauss 1982.

14 For a trenchant analysis of Tolstoy's theory, see Bates 1989.

15 See Kant 1790: §§13–14.

16 See Alison 1790/1811. For further discussion of Santayana as well as of the relation of his view to Alison's as well as Kant's, see Guyer 2005b: ch. 7. For a monograph on Santayana's aesthetics, see Arnett 1955.

17 For the impact of Moore's thought on the Bloomsbury group, see Levy 1979: chs. 9 and 10.

18 See Kant 1790: §2.

19 See Hegel 1975, vol. I: 1–3.

20 Thus Arthur Danto's argument that Moore gave a pre-eminence to beauty that brought the twentieth-century de-emphasis of beauty in art or even its elimination as an almost inevitable consequence (Danto 2003: 30–7, 46–9) is only half the story. Moore could also have stood as godfather to at least some of the later movements that eliminated beauty precisely by making perfectly ordinary real objects into art. An example of a twentieth-century artist who attempted to efface the boundary between art and nature is Robert Smithson; see Shapiro 1995.

21 See Hume 1757 and Kant 1790: §§32-4, and the discussion of Sibley and Isenberg below.

22 Cézanne has been a seminal figure for many twentieth-century aestheticians, including R. G. Collingwood, who used Cézanne's work as an exemplar of the artist's expression of "total imaginative experience" (Collingwood 1938: 144–6), and Maurice Merleau-Ponty, who used him to illustrate his view that the phenomenology of perception includes a thick sense of objecthood (Merleau-Ponty 1945). For an interesting discussion of philosophers' use of Cézanne, see Schapiro 1999.

23 See Carroll 1989; Dean 1996; and Dickie 1965.

24 A well-known critique of Bullough's concept of psychical distance is Dickie 1974: ch. 4.

25 For an overview of Bosanquet's aesthetics, see Lang 1968.

26 For commentary on Dewey's aesthetics, see Alexander 1987; Haskins 1992; Shusterman 1992; Raters-Mohr 1994; Ryan 1995: ch. 10; Früchtl 1996: 86–92; Jackson 1998; Haskins and Seiple 1999; and Hinz 2002.

27 See Dewey's seminal article "The reflex arc concept in philosophy" (Dewey 1896).

28 In addition to *The Principles of Art*, Collingwood 1964 is a posthumous collection of essays in aesthetics. Clarendon Press has also announced a posthumous collection of writings on folktale, cultural criticism, and anthropology which will no doubt be relevant to the assessment of Collingwood's aesthetics. Most of the secondary literature on Collingwood concerns his philosophy of history, but on aesthetics see Donagan 1962; Jones 1972; Wollheim 1972 and 1980; Ridley 1997; and Johnson 1998: ch. 7.

29 Here Cassirer shared a theme that was fundamental to the contrast between natural sciences and historical sciences, the distinction between "nomothetic" and "idiographic" sciences, in the Heidelberg or Southwestern school of neo-Kantianism; see Rickert 1929.

30 For an earlier (1933) pregnant remark on whether there is anything "common to everything we call beautiful," see Wittgenstein 1980: 24e.

31 For commentary on Heidegger, see Kockelmans 1986; Bruns 1989; Ferry 1993; Schaeffer 2000; Harries and Jamme 1994; Young 2001; and Zuidevaart 2004; chs. 4 and 5.

32 The art critic Meyer Schapiro scorned Heidegger for not knowing that van Gogh had used his own shoes as the model for his painting (Schapiro 1994: 138). But even if this were true, it need make little difference to our interpretation of the painting unless the painting were supposed to be true in a very literal sense, which Heidegger certainly does not intend. The episode is discussed in Kelly 2003: ch. 1.

33 Heidegger's words here are *heimatliche Grunde*; I have rejected their translation as "homeland" by Young and Haynes because that seems misleadingly political. *The Origin of the Work of Art*, written during the years of Heidegger's engagement with Nazism, is no doubt a deeply political work, but its politics are not quite as close to the surface as the use of "homeland" would suggest.

34 For a Heideggerian interpretation of a wide range of architecture, see Harries 1997; for a less avowedly but still Heideggerian study focusing especially on siting and topography, see Leatherbarrow 2000.

35 See Fischer 1959; Arvon 1970; and Jameson 1971.

36 See Lenin 1967.

37 See Trotsky 1924.

38 See Bernstein 1984.

39 The literature on Benjamin has become extensive. For a few examples, see Buck-Morss 1989; Smith 1989; Wolin 1994; and Caygill 1998.

40 For reasons of space, this section will omit discussion of French figures who have influenced philosophical aesthetics and literary theory, the latter more than the former, from Sartre and Merleau-Ponty to Foucault, Derrida, and Bourdieu. See "French philosophy in the twentieth century," Chapter 19.

41 There are thus far only a few historical studies of this movement. See Lüdeking 1988 and Davies 1991. Two early and influential collections of papers in this movement were Elton 1954 and Barrett 1965. An extensive selection of important papers in analytical aesthetics from the larger period 1956 to 1999 is found in Lamarque and Olsen 2004. Two volumes of papers on Wittgenstein and aesthetics are Allen and Turvey 2001 and Lewis 2004.

42 For a few titles in the vast Wittgenstein literature that focus specifically on aesthetics, see Tilghman 1992; Hagberg 1994; and Hagberg 1995.

43 Dickie subsequently amplified his account of the artworld, making it clear that he meant the concept not purely extensionally, simply denoting certain groups of persons, but rather conventionally, denoting a variety of roles; but he still presupposed that we simply understand what makes a role count as an artworld role. See Dickie 1984: ch. v.

44 See Davies 1991 and Yanal 1994.

45 Attempts to get around this issue by defining the artworld historically, so that art at one time is what is made in connection with earlier traditions of art, have been offered by Jerrold Levinson in essays from 1979 to 1989 (Levinson 1990: Part I) and Noël Carroll in essays from 1993 (Carroll 2001: Part II). Dickie 1984 also suggests a more historical interpretation of his institutional theory than Dickie 1974.

46 Dickie recognizes this in Dickie 1984: ch. ii.

47 For discussions of Danto's philosophy of art, see Rollins 1993 and Kelly 2003: ch. 4.

48 One of the few discussions of Beardsley in later literature is Zuidevaart 2004: ch.1, but this discusses only Beardsley's account of metaphor and truth in literature.

49 In his attack upon the resemblance theory of representation Goodman appeals to the influential work of the art historian Ernst Gombrich; see Gombrich 1960.

50 See Zuidevaart 2004: ch. 8.

51 For this summary, see Margalit 1998: 322. For further development of Goodman's accounts of metaphor and exemplification, see Elgin 1983: chs. 4 and 5. For secondary literature on Goodman's aesthetics generally, see also Elgin 1997.

52 For commentary, see Bernstein 2001: ch. 2.

53 See Rose 1978; Jameson 1990; and Bernstein 2001: ch. 7.

54 For commentary on Adorno's aesthetics, see Recki 1986; Menke 1991; Zuidevaart 1991; Früchtl 1996; and Kelly 2003: ch. 2.

55 See also Brand 2000, a collection mostly by philosophers, and Beckley 1998, a collection by artists, critics, and a few philosophers . For discussion of Hickey and Scarry, see Nehamas 2000.

56 See Guyer 2005a: ch. 13.

57 For a valuable survey of at least the first phase of the recent debate, see Carroll 2000. An important collection of papers on this subject is Levinson 1998.

58 For commentary on Cavell, see Fischer 1989; Mulhall 1994; Gould 1998; and Hammer 2002.

For their helpful comments on an earlier version of this chapter, I owe special thanks to Alexander Nehamas, Michael Rohlf, and Bruce Kuklick.

References

Adorno, T. W. (1949) *Philosophy of Modern Music*. Translated by A. G. Mitchell and W. Blomster, London: Sheed & Ward, 1973.

—— (1958, 1965) *Notes to Literature*, 2 vols., Translated by S. W. Nicholsen, New York: Columbia University Press, 1991, 1992.

—— (1966) *Negative Dialectics* Translated by E. B. Ashton, London: Routledge & Kegan Paul, 1973.

—— (1970) *Aesthetic Theory*. Edited by G. Adorno and R. Tiedemann, translated by R. Hullot-Kentor, Minneapolis: University of Minnesota Press, 1997.

Adorno, T. W. and M. Horkheimer (1947) *Dialectic of Enlightenment*. Translated by J. Cumming, London: Verso, 1979.

Adorno, T. W., E. Frenkel-Brunswick, D. Levinson, and R. N. Sanford (1950) *The Authoritarian Personality*. New York: Harper & Brothers.

Alexander, T. M. (1987) *John Dewey's Theory of Art, Experience, and Nature: The Horizons of Feeling*. Albany: State University of New York Press.

Alison, A. (1790) *Essays on the Nature and Principles of Taste*. 2nd edn., 2 vols, Edinburgh: Bell & Bradfute et al., 1811.

Allen, R. and M. Turvey (eds.) (2001) *Wittgenstein, Theory and the Arts*. London: Routledge.

Allison, H. E. (2001) *Kant's Theory of Taste: A Reading of the Critique of Aesthetic Judgment*. Cambridge: Cambridge University Press.

Arnett, W. (1955) *Santayana and the Sense of Beauty*. Bloomington: Indiana University Press.

Arvon, H. (1970) *Marxist Esthetics*. Translated by H. Lane, Ithaca, NY: Cornell University Press, 1973.

Ayer, A. J. (1936) *Language, Truth and Logic*. London: Victor Gollancz. 2nd edn., 1946.

Barrett, C., SJ (ed.) (1965) *Collected Paper on Aesthetics*. Oxford: Blackwell.

Bates, S. (1989) "Tolstoy evaluated: Tolstoy's theory of art." In G. Dickie, R. Sclafani, and R. Roblin (eds.) *Aesthetics: A Critical Anthology*, 2nd edn., New York: St Martin's Press, pp. 64–72.

Baumgarten, A. G. (1735) *Meditationes philosophicae de nonnullis ad poema pertinentibus/Philosophische Betrachtungen über einige Bedingungen des Gedichtes*. Edited by H. Paetzold, Hamburg: Felix Meiner, 1983.

—— (1750–8) *Aesthetica*. Partial translation in Hans Rudolf Schweizer, *Ästhetik als Philosophie der sinnlichen Erkenntnis: Eine Interpretation der "Aesthetica" A. G. Baumgartens mit teilweise Wiedergabe des lateinischen Textes und deutscher Übersetzung*, Basel: Schwabe, 1973.

Beardsley, M. C. (1981) *Aesthetics: Problems in the Philosophy of Criticism*, 2nd edn. Indianapolis: Hackett. 1st edn., New York, Harcourt, Brace & World, 1958.

Beckley, B. (ed.) with D. Shapiro (1998) *Uncontrollable Beauty: Toward a New Aesthetics*. New York: Allworth Press.

Bell, C. (1914) *Art*. London: Chatto & Windus. Repr. New York: G. P. Putnam's Sons, 1958.

Benjamin, W. (1928) *The Origin of German Tragic Drama*. Translated by J. Osborne, London: Verso, 1977.

—— (1968) *Illuminations*, ed. H. Arendt, trans. H. Zohn. New York: Harcourt, Brace & World.

—— (1996–2003) *Selected Writings*, 4 vols., ed. H. Eiland and M. W. Jennings. Cambridge, MA: Harvard University Press. (Vol. 3 contains a new translation of "The work of art in the age of its technical reproducibility.")

—— (1999) *The Arcades Project*, trans. H. Eiland and K. J. McLaughlin. Cambridge, MA: Harvard University Press.

Berleant, A. (1992) *The Aesthetics of Environment*. Philadelphia: Temple University Press.

Bernstein, J. M. (1984) *The Philosophy of the Novel: Lukács, Marxism, and the Dialectics of Form*. Minneapolis: University of Minnesota Press.

—— (2001) *Adorno: Disenchantment and Ethics*. Cambridge: Cambridge University Press.

Bosanquet, B. (1892) *A History of Æsthetic*, 2nd edn. London: Allen & Unwin, 1904.

—— (1915) *Three Lectures on Aesthetic*. London: Macmillan.

Bowman, C. (1998) "Karl Philipp Moritz." In M. Kelly (ed.) *Encyclopedia of Aesthetics*, 4 vols., New York: Oxford University Press, vol. 3, pp. 295–6.

Brady, E. (1998) "Imagination and the aesthetic appreciation of nature." *Journal of Aesthetics and Art Criticism* 56: 137–48. Repr. in A. Carlson and A. Berleant (eds.) *The Aesthetics of Natural Environments*, Peterborough, Ont.: Broadview Press, 2004, pp. 156–69.

—— (2003) *Aesthetics of the Natural Environment*. Edinburgh: Edinburgh University Press.

Brady, E. and J. Levinson (eds.) (2001) *Aesthetic Concepts: Essays after Sibley*. Oxford: Clarendon Press.

Brand, P. Z. (ed.) (2000) *Beauty Matters*. Bloomington: Indiana University Press.

Bruns, G. L. (1989) *Heidegger's Estrangements: Language, Truth, and Poetry in the Later Writings*. New Haven, CT: Yale University Press.

Buck-Morss, S. (1989) *The Dialectics of Seeing: Walter Benjamin and the Arcades Project*. Cambridge, MA: MIT Press.

Budd, M. (1996) "The aesthetic appreciation of nature." *British Journal of Aesthetics* 36: 207–22. Repr. in *The Aesthetic Appreciation of Nature*. Oxford: Clarendon Press, 2002, pp. 1–23 and P. Lamarque and S. H. Olsen (eds.) *Aesthetics and the Philosophy of Art: The Analytic Tradition*, Oxford: Blackwell, 2004, pp. 543–69.

Budd, M. (2002) *The Aesthetic Appreciation of Nature*. Oxford: Clarendon Press.

Bullough, E. (1957) *Aesthetics: Lectures and Essays*, ed. E. M. Wilkinson. Stanford, CA: Stanford University Press.

Carlson, A. (1979) "Appreciation and the natural environment." *Journal of Aesthetics and Art Criticism* 37: 267–76. Repr. in *Aesthetics and the Environment: The Appreciation of Nature, Art and Architecture*, London: Routledge, 2000, pp. 41–53; A. Carlson and A. Berleant (eds.) *The Aesthetics of Natural Environments*, Peterborough, Ont.: Broadview Press, 2004, pp. 63–75; and P. Lamarque and S. H. Olsen (eds.) *Aesthetics and the Philosophy of Art: The Analytic Tradition*, Oxford: Blackwell, 2004, pp. 535–42.

—— (2000) *Aesthetics and the Environment: The Appreciation of Nature, Art and Architecture*. London: Routledge.

Carlson, A. and A. Berleant (eds.) (2004) *The Aesthetics of Natural Environments*. Peterborough, Ont.: Broadview Press.

Carroll, N. (1989) "Clive Bell's aesthetic hypothesis." In G. Dickie, R. Sclafani, and R. Roblin (eds.) *Aesthetics: A Critical Anthology*, 2nd edn., New York: St Martin's Press, pp. 84–95.

—— (1990) *The Philosophy of Horror, or Paradoxes of the Heart*. New York and London: Routledge.

—— (1996) "Moderate moralism." *British Journal of Aesthetics* 36: 223–38. Repr. in *Beyond Aesthetics: Philosophical Aesthetics*, Cambridge: Cambridge University Press, 2001, pp. 293–305.

—— (1997) "Art, narrative, and emotion." In M. Hjort and S. Laver (eds.) *Emotion and the Arts*, Oxford: Oxford University Press, pp. 190–211. Repr. in *Beyond Aesthetics: Philosophical Aesthetics*, Cambridge: Cambridge University Press, 2001, pp. 215–34.

—— (1998) "Art, narrative, and moral understanding." In J. Levinson (ed.) *Aesthetics and Ethics*, Cambridge: Cambridge University Press, pp. 126–60. Repr. in *Beyond Aesthetics: Philosophical Aesthetics*. Cambridge: Cambridge University Press, 2001, pp. 270–92.

—— (2000) "Art and ethical criticism." *Ethics* 110: 350–87.

—— (2001) *Beyond Aesthetics: Philosophical Aesthetics*. Cambridge: Cambridge University Press.

Cassirer, E. (1916) *Freiheit und Form: Studien zur deutschen Geistesgeschichte*. Repr. Darmstadt: Wissenschaftliche Buchgesellschaft, 1961.

—— (1932) *The Philosophy of the Enlightenment*. Translated by F. A. C. Koelln and J. P. Pettegrove, Princeton, NJ: Princeton University Press, 1951.

—— (1944) *An Essay on Man*. New Haven, CT: Yale University Press.

Cavell, S. (1969) *Must We Mean What We Say? A Book of Essays*. New York: Charles Scribner's Sons. Updated edn., Cambridge: Cambridge University Press, 2002.

—— (1979) *The Claim of Reason: Wittgenstein, Skepticism, Morality, and Tragedy*. New York: Oxford University Press.

—— (1981) *Pursuits of Happiness: The Hollywood Comedy of Remarriage*. Cambridge, MA: Harvard University Press.

—— (1987) *Disowning Knowledge in Six Plays of Shakespeare*. Cambridge: Cambridge University Press. Updated edn., *Disowning Knowledge in Seven Plays of Shakespeare*, 2003.

—— (1996) *Contesting Tears: The Hollywood Melodrama of the Unknown Woman*. Chicago: University of Chicago Press.

Caygill, H. (1998) *Walter Benjamin: The Colour of Experience*. London: Routledge.

Cohen, H. (1889) *Kants Begründung der Ästhetik*. Berlin: Ferdinand Dümmler.

—— (1912) *Ästhetik des reinen Gefühls*, 2 vols. Berlin: Bruno Cassirer.

Collingwood, R. G. (1924) *Speculum Mentis, or the Map of Knowledge*. Oxford: Clarendon Press.

—— (1925) *Outlines of a Philosophy of Art*. Oxford: Clarendon Press.

—— (1938) *The Principles of Art*. Oxford: Clarendon Press.

—— (1964) *Essays in the Philosophy of Art*, ed. A. Donagan. Bloomington: Indiana University Press.

—— (1989) *Essays in Political Philosophy*, ed. D. Boucher. Oxford: Clarendon Press.

Crawford, D. W. (1974) *Kant's Aesthetic Theory*. Madison: University of Wisconsin Press.

Croce, B. (1902) *Estetica come scienza dell'espressione e linguistica generale*. Milan: Sandron. Translated by C. Lyas as *The Aesthetic as the Science of Expression and of the Linguistic in General*, Cambridge: Cambridge University Press, 1992. (This translation omits Croce's history of aesthetics, which is included in the older translation: *Æsthetic: As Science of Expression and General Linguistic*, trans. D. Ainslie. Rev. edn., London: Macmillan, 1922.)

Crowther, P. (1989) *The Kantian Sublime: From Morality to Art*. Oxford: Clarendon Press.

Danto, A. C. (1964) "The artworld." *Journal of Philosophy* 61: 571–84. Repr. in G. Dickie, R. Sclafani, and R. Roblin (eds.) *Aesthetics: A Critical Anthology*, 2nd edn., New York: St Martin's Press, 1989, pp. 171–82.

—— (1981) *The Transfiguration of the Commonplace: A Philosophy of Art*. Cambridge, MA: Harvard University Press.

—— (1986) *The Philosophical Disenfranchisement of Art*. New York: Columbia University Press. 2nd edn., with a foreword by J. Gilmore, 2005.

—— (2003) *The Abuse of Beauty: Aesthetics and the Concept of Art*. Chicago and LaSalle, IL: Open Court.

Davies, S. (1991) *Definitions of Art*. Ithaca, NY: Cornell University Press.

Dean, J. T. (1996) "Clive Bell and G. E. Moore." *British Journal of Aesthetics* 36: 135–45.

Dewey, J. (1896) "The reflex arc concept in psychology." In *The Early Works of John Dewey*, ed. J. A. Boyston et al., Carbondale: Southern Illinois University Press, 1969–90, vol. 5, pp. 96–110.

—— (1925) *Experience and Nature*. Chicago and LaSalle, IL: Open Court. 2nd edn., 1929.

—— (1934) *Art as Experience*. New York: G. P. Putnam's Sons.

Dickie, G. (1965) "Clive Bell and the method of *Principia Ethica*." *British Journal of Aesthetics* 5: 139–43.

—— (1974) *Art and the Aesthetic: An Institutional Analysis*. Ithaca, NY: Cornell University Press.

—— (1984) *The Art Circle: A Theory of Art*. Repr. Evanston, IL: Chicago Spectrum Press, 1997.

Donagan, A. (1962) *The Later Philosophy of R. G. Collingwood*. Oxford: Clarendon Press. 2nd edn., Chicago: University of Chicago Press, 1985.

Elgin, C. Z. (1983) *With Reference to Reference*. Foreword by N. Goodman. Indianapolis and Cambridge: Hackett.

—— (ed.) (1997) *Nelson Goodman's Philosophy of Art*. New York: Garland.

Elton, W. R. (ed.) (1954) *Aesthetics and Language*. Oxford: Blackwell.

Ferry, L. (1993) [1990] *Homo Aestheticus: The Invention of Taste in the Democratic Age*, trans. R. de Loaiza. Chicago: University of Chicago Press.

Fischer, E. (1959) *The Necessity of Art: A Marxist Approach*. Translated by A. Bostock, Harmondsworth: Penguin, 1963.

Fischer, M. (1989) *Stanley Cavell and Literary Skepticism*. Chicago: University of Chicago Press.

Früchtl, J. (1996) *Ästhetische Erfahrung und moralisches Urteil*. Frankfurt am Main: Suhrkamp.

Fry, R. (1920) *Vision and Design*. London: Chatto & Windus. Repr. Oxford: Oxford University Press, 1981.

Gadamer, H.-G. (1960) *Truth and Method*. 2nd, revised edition, revised translation by J. Weinsheimer and D. G. Marshall, London and New York: Continuum, 2004.

—— (1977) *Die Aktualität des Schönen*. Stuttgart: Philipp Reclam Jr. Translated by N. Walker as *The Relevance of the Beautiful and Other Essays*, Cambridge: Cambridge University Press, 1986.

Gaut, B. (1998) "The ethical criticism of art." In J. Levinson (ed.) *Ethics and Aesthetics*, Cambridge: Cambridge University Press, pp. 182–203. Repr. in P. Lamarque and S. H. Olsen (eds.) *Aesthetics and the Philosophy of Art: The Analytic Tradition*. Oxford: Blackwell, 2004, pp. 283–94.

Gombrich, E. (1960) *Art and Illusion: A Study in the Psychology of Pictorial Representation*. Rev. edn., Princeton, NJ: Princeton University Press, 1969.

Goodman, N. (1968) *The Languages of Art*. Indianapolis: Bobbs-Merrill.

—— (1972) *Problems and Projects*. Indianapolis: Bobbs-Merrill.

—— (1978) *Ways of Worldmaking*. Indianapolis: Hackett.

—— (1984) *Of Mind and Other Matters*. Cambridge, MA: Harvard Univesity Press.

Gould, T. (1998) *Hearing Things: Voice and Method in the Writing of Stanley Cavell*. Chicago: University of Chicago Press.

Guyer, P. (1993) *Kant and the Experience of Freedom*. Cambridge: Cambridge University Press.

—— (2005a) *Kant's System of Nature and Freedom: Selected Essays*. Oxford: Clarendon Press.

—— (2005b) *Values of Beauty: Historical Essays in Aesthetics*. Cambridge: Cambridge University Press.

Hagberg, G. (1994) *Meaning and Interpretation: Wittgenstein, Henry James, and Literary Knowledge*. Ithaca, NY: Cornell University Press.

—— (1995) *Art as Language: Wittgenstein, Meaning, and Aesthetic Theory*. Ithaca, NY: Cornell University Press.

Halliwell, S. (2002) *The Aesthetics of Mimesis: Ancient Texts and Modern Problems*. Princeton, NJ: Princeton University Press.

Hammer, E. (2002) *Stanley Cavell: Skepticism, Subjectivity, and the Ordinary*. Cambridge: Polity Press.

Harries, K. (1997) *The Ethical Function of Architecture*. Cambridge, MA: MIT Press.

Harries, K. and C. Jamme (eds.) (1994) *Martin Heidegger: Politics, Art, and Technology*. New York: Holmes & Meier.

Haskins, C. (1992) "Dewey's *Art as Experience*: the tensions between aesthetics and aestheticism." *Transactions of the Charles S. Peirce Society* 28: 217–45.

Haskins, C. and D. I. Seiple (eds.) (1999) *Dewey Reconfigured: Essays on Deweyan Pragmatism*. Albany: State University of New York Press.

Hegel, G. W. F. (1975) *Aesthetics: Lectures on Fine Art*, 2 vols., trans. T. M. Knox. Oxford: Clarendon Press.

Heidegger, M. (1950) *Holzwege*. Frankfurt: Klostermann. Translated by J. Young and K. Haynes as *Off the Beaten Path*, Cambridge: Cambridge University Press, 2002. Contains "On the origin of the work of art" of 1934.

—— (1954) "Bauen Wohnen Denken." In *Vorträge und Aufsätze*. Pfüllingen: Gunter Neske. Translated by A. Hofstadter in Heidegger, *Poetry, Language, Thought*, ed. D. F. Krell, New York: Harper & Row, 1971.

Hepburn, R. W. (1966) "Contemporary aesthetics and the neglect of natural beauty." In B. Williams and A. Montefiore (eds.) *British Analytical Philosophy*, London: Routledge & Kegan Paul, pp. 285–310. Repr. in P. Lamarque and S. H. Olsen (eds.) *Aesthetics and the Philosophy of Art: The Analytic Tradition*, Oxford: Blackwell, 2004, pp. 521–34.

—— (2001) *The Reach of the Aesthetic: Collected Essays on Art and Nature*. Aldershot: Ashgate.

Hickey, D. (1993) *The Invisible Dragon: Four Essays on Beauty*. Los Angeles: Art Issues Press.

Hinz, R. (2002) "John Deweys pragmatistische Ästhetik und ihre Revitalizierung durch Richard Shusterman." In T. Hecken and A. Spree (eds.) *Nutzen und Klarheit: Anglo-amerikanische Aesthetik im 20. Jahrhundert*, Paderborn: Mentis, 2004, pp. 62–90.

Hume, D. (1757) "Of the standard of taste." In *Essays Moral, Political, and Literary*, ed. E. F. Miller, Indianapolis: Liberty Classics, 1989, pp. 226–49.

Hutcheson, F. (1725, 1738). *An Inquiry into the Original of Our Ideas of Beauty and Virtue*, 4th edn. London: D. Midwinter et al.

Isenberg, A. (1949) "Critical communication." *Philosophical Review* 58: 330–44. Repr. in *Aesthetics and the Theory of Criticism: Selected Essays of Arnold Isenberg*, ed. W. Callaghan, L. Caumann, C. Hempel, S.

Morgenbesser, M. Mothersill, E. Nagel, and T. Norman, Chicago: University of Chicago Press, 1973, pp. 156–71.

Iser, W. (1978) *The Act of Reading: A Theory of Aesthetic Response*. Baltimore: Johns Hopkins University Press.

Jackson, P. W. (1998) *John Dewey and the Lessons of Art*. New Haven, CT: Yale University Press.

Jacobson, D. (1997) "In praise of immoral art." *Philosophical Topics* 25: 155–99.

Jameson, F. (1971) *Marxism and Form: Twentieth-Century Dialectical Theories of Literature*. Princeton, NJ: Princeton University Press.

—— (1990) *Late Marxism: Adorno, or the Persistence of the Dialectic*. London: Verso.

Jauss, H. R. (1982) *Toward an Aesthetics of Reception*, trans. T. Bahti. Minneapolis: University of Minnesota Press.

Johnson, P. (1998) *R. G. Collingwood: An Introduction*. Bristol: Thoemmes.

Jones, P. (1972) "A critical outline of Collingwood's philosophy of art." In M. Krausz (ed.) *Critical Essays on the Philosophy of R. G. Collingwood*, Oxford: Clarendon Press.

Kant, I. (1790) *Critique of the Power of Judgment*. Edited by P. Guyer, translated by P. Guyer and E. Matthews, Cambridge: Cambridge University Press, 2000.

Kelly, M. (ed.) (1998) *Encyclopedia of Aesthetics*, 4 vols. New York: Oxford University Press.

—— (2003) *Iconoclasm in Aesthetics*. Cambridge: Cambridge University Press.

Kennick, W. E. (1958) "Does traditional aesthetics rest on a mistake?" *Mind* 67: 314–34.

Kockelmans, J. J. (1986) *Heidegger on Art and Art Works*. Dordrecht: Kluwer.

Lamarque, P. and S. H. Olsen (eds.) (2004) *Aesthetics and the Philosophy of Art: The Analytic Tradition*. Oxford: Blackwell.

Lang, B. (1968) "Bosanquet's aesthetic: a history and philosophy of the symbol." *Journal of Aesthetics and Art Criticism* 26: 377–87.

Langer, S. K. (1942) *Philosophy in a New Key: A Study in the Symbolism of Reason, Rite, and Art*. Cambridge, MA: Harvard University Press.

—— (1953) *Feeling and Form: A Theory of Art Developed from* Philosophy in a New Key. New York: Charles Scribner's Sons.

Leatherbarrow, D. (2000) *Uncommon Ground: Architecture, Technology, and Topography*. Cambridge, MA: MIT Press.

Lenin, V. I. (1967) *Lenin on Art and Literature*. Moscow: Progress Publishers.

Levinson, J. (1990) *Music, Art, and Metaphysics: Essays in Philosophical Aestetics*. Ithaca, NY: Cornell University Press.

—— (ed.) (1998) *Aesthetics and Ethics*. Cambridge: Cambridge University Press.

Levy, P. (1979) *Moore: G. E. Moore and the Cambridge Apostles*. New York: Holt, Rinehart, & Winston.

Lewis, P. B. (ed.) (2004) *Wittgenstein, Aesthetics and Philosophy*. Aldershot: Ashgate.

Lüdeking, K. (1988) *Analytische Philosopher der Kunst*. Frankfurt am Main: Athenäum.

Lukács, G. (1916) *The Theory of the Novel*. Translation by A. Bostock, Cambridge, MA: MIT Press, 1971.

Lyotard, J.-F. (1991) *Lessons on the Analytic of the Sublime*, trans. E. Rottenberg. Stanford: Stanford University Press, 1994.

McDowell, J. (1983) "Aesthetic value, objectivity, and the fabric of the world." In E. Schaper (ed.) *Pleasure, Preference and Value: Studies in Philosophical Aesthetics*, Cambridge: Cambridge University Press, pp. 1–17.

Mandelbaum, M. (1965) "Family resemblances and generalization concerning the arts." *American Philosophical Quarterly* 2: 219–28. Repr. in G. Dickie, R. Sclafani, and R. Roblin (eds.) *Aesthetics: A Critical Anthology*, 2nd edn., New York: St Martin's Press, 1989, pp. 138–51.

Marcuse, H. (1955) *Eros and Civilization*. Boston: Beacon Press.

—— (1964) *One-Dimensional Man*. Boston: Beacon Press.

—— (1978) *The Aesthetic Dimension: Toward a Critique of Marxist Aesthetics*. Boston: Beacon Press.

Margalit, A. (1998) "Goodman, Nelson: survey of thought." In M. Kelly (ed.) *Encyclopedia of Aesthetics*, 4 vols., New York: Oxford University Press, vol. 2, pp. 319–22.

Menke, C. (1991) *The Sovereignty of Art: Aesthetic Negativity in Adorno and Derrida*, trans. N. Solomon. Cambridge, MA: MIT Press.

Merleau-Ponty, M. (1945) "Cezanne's doubt." In G. A. Johnson (ed.) *The Merleau-Ponty Aesthetics Reader*, Evanston, IL: Northwestern University Press, 1993, pp. 59–75.

Moore, G. E. (1903) *Principia Ethica*, 2nd edn., with other papers, ed. T. Baldwin. Cambridge: Cambridge University Press, 1993.

Moritz, K. P. (1785) "Versuch einer Vereinigung aller schöner Künste und Wissenschaften unter dem Begriff des in sich selbst vollendeten. An Herrn Moses Mendelssohn." In *Karl Philipp Moritz, Werke*, 3 vols., ed. H. Günther, 2nd edn., Frankfurt am Main: Insel, 1981, vol. 2, pp. 543–8.

Mothersill, M. (1984) *Beauty Restored*. Oxford: Clarendon Press.

Mulhall, S. (1994) *Stanley Cavell: Philosophy's Recounting of the Ordinary*. Oxford: Clarendon Press.

Nehamas, A. (1999) *Virtues of Authenticity: Essays on Plato and Socrates*. Princeton, NJ: Princeton University Press.

—— (2000) "The return of the beautiful: morality, pleasure, and the value of uncertainty." *Journal of Aesthetics and Art Criticism* 58: 393–403.

—— (2002) "A promise of happiness: the place of beauty in a world of art." In G. B. Peterson (ed.) *The Tanner Lectures on Human Values* 23, Salt Lake City: University of Utah Press, pp. 187–231.

Nussbaum, M. C. (1986) *The Fragility of Goodness: Luck and Ethics in Greek Tragedy and Philosophy*. Cambridge: Cambridge University Press.

—— (1990) *Love's Knowledge: Essays on Philosophy and Literature*. New York: Oxford University Press.

—— (1995) *Poetic Justice: The Literary Imagination and Public Life*. Boston: Beacon Press.

—— (2001) *Upheavals of Thought: The Intelligence of Emotions*. Cambridge: Cambridge University Press.

Pries, C. (1995) *Übergänge ohne Brücken: Kants Erhabenes zwischen Kritik und Metaphysik*. Berlin: Akademie.

Raters-Mohr, M.-L. (1994) *Intensität und Widerstand: Metaphysik, Gesellschaftstheorie, und Ästhetik in John Deweys Art as Experience*. Bonn: Bouvier.

Recki, B. (1986) *Aura und Autonomie: Zur Subjektivität der Kunst bei Walter Benjamin und Theodor W. Adorno*. Würzburg: Kiepenhauer & Witsch.

—— (2001) *Ästhetik der Sitten: Die Affinität von ästhetischem Gefühl und praktischer Vernunft bei Kant*. Frankfurt am Main: Klostermann.

Rickert, H. (1929) *Die Grenzen der naturwissenschaftlichen Begriffsbildung*, 5th edn. Tübingen: Mohr. Abridged translation by G. Oakes, *The Limits of Concept Formation in Natural Science*, Cambridge: Cambridge University Press, 1986.

Ridley, A. (1997) *Collingwood*. London: Routledge.

Rollins, M. (ed.) (1993) *Danto and his Critics*. Oxford: Blackwell.

Rose, G. (1978) *The Melancholy Science: An Introduction to the Thought of Theodor W. Adorno*. London: Macmillan.

Ryan, A. (1995) *John Dewey and the High Tide of American Liberalism*. New York: W. W. Norton.

Santayana, G. (1896) *The Sense of Beauty*. New York: Charles Scribner's Sons.

Sartwell, C. (1998) "Art for art's sake." In M. Kelly (ed.) *Encyclopedia of Aesthetics*, 4 vols., New York: Oxford University Press, vol. 1, pp. 118–21.

Savile, A. (1982) *The Test of Time: An Essay in Philosophical Aesthetics*. Oxford: Clarendon Press.

—— (1987) *Aesthetic Reconstructions: The Seminal Writings of Lessing, Kant, and Schiller*. Oxford: Blackwell.

Scarry, E. (1999) *On Beauty and Being Just*. Princeton, NJ: Princeton University Press.

Schaeffer, J.-M. (2000) [1992] *Art of the Modern Age: Philosophy of Art from Kant to Heidegger*, trans. S. Rendell. Princeton, NJ: Princeton University Press.

Schapiro, M. (1994) *Theory and Philosophy of Art: Style, Artist, and Society*, Selected Papers, vol. IV. New York: George Braziller.

—— (1999) "Cézanne and the philosophers." In *Worldview in Painting:– Art and Society*. New York: George Braziller, pp. 75–105.

Scruton, R. (1974) *Art and Imagination: A Study in the Philosophy of Mind*. London: Methuen.

Shaftesbury, Third Earl of (Anthony Ashley Cooper) (1711) *Characteristics of Men, Manners, Opinions, Times*. Edited by P. Ayers, 2 vols., Oxford: Clarendon Press, 1999.

Shapiro, G. (1995) *Earthwards: Robert Smithson and Art after Babel*. Berkeley and Los Angeles: University of California Press.

Shusterman, R. (1992) *Pragmatist Aesthetics: Living Beauty, Rethinking Art.* Oxford: Blackwell.

Sibley, F. (1959) "Aesthetic concepts." *Philosophical Review* 68: 421–50. Repr. in *Approach to Aesthetics: Collected Papers on Philosophical Aesthetics*, ed. J. Benson, B. Redfern, and J. R. Cox, Oxford: Clarendon Press, 2001, pp. 1–23.

—— (1968) "Objectivity and aesthetics." *Proceedings of the Aristotelian Society, Supplementary Volume 42:* 31–54. Cited from *Approach to Aesthetics: Collected Papers on Philosophical Aesthetics*, ed. J. Benson, B. Redfern, and J. R. Cox, Oxford: Clarendon Press, 2001, pp. 71–87.

Smith, G. (ed.) (1989) *Benjamin: Philosophy, History, Aesthetics.* Chicago: University of Chicago Press.

Stevenson, C. L. (1944) *Language and Ethics.* New Haven, CT: Yale University Press.

Taylor, R. (ed.) (1977) *Aesthetics and Politics: The Key Texts of the Classic Debate within German Marxism.* London: Verso.

Tilghman, B. R. (1992) *Wittgenstein, Ethics, and Aesthetics: The View from Eternity.* Albany: State University of New York Press.

Tolstoy, L. (1898) *What is Art?* Translated by R. Pevear and L. Volokhonsky, Harmondsworth: Penguin, 1995.

Trotsky, L. (1924) *Literature and Revolution*, trans. R. Strunsky. Repr., London: RedWords, 1991.

Walton, K. L. (1970) "Categories of art." *Philosophical Review* 79: 334–67.

—— (1978) "Fearing fictions." *Journal of Philosophy* 75: 5–27.

—— (1990) *Mimesis as Make-Believe: On the Foundations of the Representational Arts.* Cambridge, MA: Harvard University Press.

Weitz, M. (1956) "The role of theory in aesthetics." *Journal of Aesthetics and Art Criticism* 15: 27–35.

—— (1977) *The Opening Mind: A Philosophical Study of Humanistic Concepts.* Chicago: University of Chicago Press. Cited from G. Dickie, R. Sclafani, and R. Roblin (eds.) *Aesthetics: A Critical Anthology*, 2nd edn., New York: St Martin's Press, 1989, pp. 152–9.

Wilcox, J. (1953) "The beginnings of *L'art pour l'art.*" *Journal of Aesthetics and Art Criticism* 11: 360–77.

Wittgenstein, L. (1953) *Philosophical Investigations*, trans. G. E. M. Anscombe. 2nd edn., Oxford: Blackwell, 1958.

—— (1967) *Lectures & Conversations on Aesthetics, Psychology and Religious Belief*, ed. C. Barrett. Berkeley and Los Angeles: University of California Press.

—— (1980) *Culture and Value*, ed. G. H. von Wright, trans. P. Winch. Oxford: Blackwell.

Wolin, R. (1994) *Walter Benjamin: An Aesthetic of Redemption*, rev. edn. Berkeley and Los Angeles: University of California Press.

Wollheim, R. (1960) *Art and its Objects.* New York: Harper & Row. 2nd, expanded edn., Cambridge: Cambridge University Press, 1980.

—— (1972) "On an alleged inconsistency in Collingwood's aesthetic." In M. Krausz (ed.) *Critical Essays on the Philosophy of R. G. Collingwood*, Oxford: Clarendon Press.

—— (1980) [1968] *Art and its Objects*, 2nd edn. Cambridge: Cambridge University Press.

—— (1987) *Painting as an Art.* The A. W. Mellon Lectures in the Fine Arts, 1984. Princeton, NJ: Princeton University Press.

Yanal, R. J. (ed.) (1994) *Institutions of Art: Reconsiderations of George Dickie's Philosophy.* University Park: Pennsylvania State University Press.

Young, J. (2001) *Heidegger's Philosophy of Art.* Cambridge: Cambridge University Press.

Zuidevaart, L. (1991) *Adorno's Aesthetic Theory.* Cambridge, MA: MIT Press.

—— (2004) *Artistic Truth: Aesthetics, Discourse, and Imaginative Disclosure.* Cambridge: Cambridge University Press.

Further reading

Several indispensable compendia for information about all aspects of aesthetics and its history, including the twentieth century, are:

Barck, K., M. Fontius, D. Schlenstedt, B. Steinwachs, and F. Wolfzettel (eds.) (2000–5) *Ästhetische Grundbegriffe*, 6 vols. Stuttgart: J. B. Metzler.

Gaut, B. and D. M. Lopes (eds.) (2001) *The Routledge Companion to Aesthetics.* London: Routledge.

Kelly, M. (ed.) (1998) *Encyclopedia of Aesthetics*, 4 vols. New York: Oxford University Press.

Levinson, J. (ed.) (2003) *The Oxford Handbook of Aesthetics*. Oxford: Oxford University Press.

Smith, P. and C. Wilde (eds.) (2002) *A Companion to Art Theory*. Oxford: Blackwell. (Twentieth-century coverage is more slanted toward European philosophy than the present chapter).

A voluminous sourcebook of texts by artists as well as philosophers and critics is:

Harrison, C. and P. Wood (eds.) (2003) *Art in Theory 1900–2000: An Anthology of Changing Ideas*. Oxford: Blackwell.

At the time of writing there is no history devoted exclusively to twentieth-century aesthetics, but the following more general histories contain useful discussions of figures and movements in the twentieth century up to the date of their publication:

Beardsley, M. C. (1966) *Aesthetics from Classical Greece to the Present: A Short History*. University, AL: University of Alabama Press.

Bernstein, J. M. (1992) *The Fate of Art: Aesthetic Alienation from Kant to Derrida and Adorno*. University Park: Pennsylvania State University Press. (Deals only with European figures).

Bowie, A. (1997) *From Romanticism to Critical Theory: The Philosophy of German Literary Theory*. London: Routledge. (As the title suggests, deals only with German authors).

Eagleton, T. (1990) *The Ideology of the Aesthetic*. Oxford: Blackwell.

Faas, E. (2002) *The Geneaology of Aesthetics*. Cambridge: Cambridge University Press. (In the twentieth century, deals only with European writers).

Ferry, L. (1993) [1990] *Homo Aestheticus: The Invention of Taste in the Democratic Age*, trans. R. de Loaiza. Chicago: University of Chicago Press.

Gethmann-Siefert, A. (1995) *Einführung in die Ästhetik*. Munich: Wilhelm Fink.

Gilbert, K. E. and G. Kuhn (1953) *A History of Esthetics*, 2nd edn. Bloomington: Indiana University Press.

Hammermeister, K. (2002) *The German Aesthetic Tradition*. Cambridge: Cambridge University Press.

Hecken, T. and A. Spree (eds.) (2004) *Nutzen und Klarheit: Anglo-amerikanische Ästhetik im 20. Jahrhundert*. Paderborn: Mentis.

Kultermann, U. (1987) *Kleine Geschichte der Kunsttheorie*. Darmstadt: Wissenschaftliche Buchgesellschaft.

Lüdeking, K. (1988) *Analytische Philosophie der Kunst*. Frankfurt am Main: Athenaüm.

Nida-Rümelin, J. and M. Betzler (eds.) (1998) *Ästhetik und Kunstphilosophie: Von der Antike bis zur Gegenwart in Einzeldarstellungen*. Stuttgart: Alfred Kröner.

Schaeffer, J.-M. (2000) [1992] *Art of the Modern Age: Philosophy of Art from Kant to Heidegger*, trans. S. Rendell. Princeton, NJ: Princeton University Press.

Scheer, B. (1997) *Einführung in die philosophische Ästhetik*. Darmstadt: Wissenschaftliche Buchgesellschaft.

Schneider, N. (1996) *Geschichte der Ästhetik von der Aufklärung bis zur Postmoderne*. Stuttgart: Philipp Reclam Jr.

GLOSSARY

Abduction: mode of reasoning which produces hypotheses such that, if true, they would explain certain phenomena. Peirce described it as the reasoning process which proceeds as follows: the surprising fact C is observed; but, if A were true, C would be a matter of course; hence, there is reason to suspect that A is true.

Acquaintance: A direct, unmediated, non-inferential relation between a person and a thing by means of which, according to Russell, the person acquires knowledge of the thing. Russell thought that every proposition I grasp is composed of elements with which I am acquainted (see **Knowledge by acquaintance** as opposed to *knowledge by description*).

Adicity: the number of terms of a property or relation. Thus the adicity of a binary relation is 2; that of a ternary relation is 3.

Adversarial style in philosophy: a term used to designate a particular form of philosophical dispute in which the aim is refutation of rival theorists. Some feminist philosophers indict adversarial philosophy as masculine and propose alternative collaborative and constructive forms of philosophical dialogue.

Aestheticism: the view, associated with late nineteenth-century artists and critics such as Walter Pater, J. M. Whistler, and Oscar Wilde, that art exists for the sake of its own distinctive pleasures and need not have any instrumental moral value. Art for art's sake.

Alienation (*Entfremdung*): term originally found in Hegel but now associated with Marxism, existentialism and Critical Theory, referring originally to the estrangement of the working class from society owing to their lack of control over the material forces controlling their existence, but broadening to encompass any profound sense of not belonging to society or a deep sense of lack of fulfillment of one's potential. Alienation is especially covered in Marx's 1844 *Economic and Philosophical Manuscripts*, an important source for twentieth-century Marxism (Lukács). For Marx, religion is one illusory way of coping with alienation. For Marxists, alienation can be overcome by restoring the truly human relationships in the labor process, whereby work becomes a fulfillment of one's own human nature rather than a means of survival. Alienation, then, is primarily a kind of self-alienation, the experience of humans who have been denied their self-realization.

Alterity: derived from the Latin word for "other" (*alter*) of two, alterity refers in particular to the "otherness" of other people, especially as used by European philosophers such as Levinas. It can also apply to the otherness or strangeness of situations or other cultures.

Analysis, conceptual: in a wide sense the explanation of concepts like knowledge or goodness either by providing an analytic definition or by describing the role the concept plays in statements or inferences. In a narrower sense the pursuit of such analysis in the spirit of linguistic philosophy, i.e. by examining the use and function of linguistic expressions that express the relevant concepts, notably in Wittgenstein and so-called ordinary-language philosophy.

Analysis, reductive versus connective: Reductive analysis explains concepts in terms of concepts thought to be simpler or more basic; connective analysis refrains from this ambition and seeks to explain the logical and conceptual connections between notions that need not form a hierarchical order.

Analytic definition: a definition which states conditions for the applicability of an expression or concept which are individually necessary and jointly sufficient, as in "drakes are male ducks." Contrasts with contextual definitions, explanations by way of family resemblances (see **Family resemblance**) and exemplifications.

Analytic philosophy: in a wide sense any philosophy which employs analysis or aspires to clarity and rational argument. In a narrow and more fruitful sense a historical movement which has its roots in Frege, but is associated primarily with the writings of Moore, Russell, and Wittgenstein. Part of the methodology of early analytic philosophy involved exposing the true logical form of a proposition that was often concealed by the superficial grammatical form of the sentence expressing that proposition. Later philosophers such as Davidson argued that discovery of logical form is the beginning but not the end of analysis.

Analytic/synthetic distinction: the much-disputed distinction between statements that are true purely in virtue of their meaning and those that are true or false in virtue of how the world happens to be. According to Kant, a judgment is analytic "if its predicate is already contained in the subject term." According to logical empiricism, a sentence is analytic if it is true solely by virtue of the meaning of its constituent terms. In his famous paper "Two dogmas of empiricism" (1951), Quine argued that the analytic/synthetic distinction cannot be upheld, and that empirical and non-empirical propositions differ only in degree.

Analyticity: Analytic propositions are thought to be true by virtue of the meaning of their constituent terms alone, e.g. "every bachelor is unmarried."

Anomalous monism: metaphysical view, advanced by Donald Davidson, according to which all mental events are physical events, but there are no strict laws linking mental and physical predicates.

Anxiety (Angst): literally "anxiety" or "dread," a term associated with Kierkegaard, Heidegger, and the existential tradition. In *The Concept of Anxiety*, Kierkegaard used the word *Angest* (Danish: "dread") to describe a profound and deep-seated spiritual condition of insecurity and despair. Both Kierkegaard and Heidegger distinguish between fear of something in particular and a more pervasive uneasiness and existential insecurity, an anxiety over nothing in particular and everything. Heidegger claims that one is anxious about one's **being-in-the-world** as a whole. Sartre sees anxiety as being essentially the experience of one's own limitless and ungrounded freedom.

967

Archaeology: term associated with Michel Foucault (e.g. *The Archaeology of Knowledge*) which refers to a synchronic technique for unearthing and comparing the deep structures of historical bodies of thought.

Atomism: the doctrine (deriving from the ancient Greeks) that the world is composed of atoms, i.e. indivisible entities. **Logical atomism** is the variant of this view which identifies indivisibility with logical simplicity.

Bad faith (*mauvaise foi*): a technical term found in Jean-Paul Sartre which means essentially a lie to oneself; in particular, the lie that my character and life have been determined by outside forces rather than by my own freedom.

Basic beliefs: beliefs that are justified without receiving any of their justification from other beliefs.

Behaviorism: the view that mental states can be analyzed in terms of observable behavior or the disposition to behave in certain observable ways. Behaviorism was maintained both in empirical psychology (Watson, Skinner) and in philosophy (Quine). It is often associated with the effort to reduce mental predicates to predicates relating to observable behavior. Behaviorism first emerged as a way of describing animal behavior (e.g. birds exhibit nest-building behavior in spring) avoiding anthropocentric explanations (e.g. "birds plan to build their nests in spring"), but it quickly was applied to human behavior.

Behaviorism, logical: the view, associated with Gilbert Ryle (and sometimes attributed to the later Wittgenstein), that assertions about mental processes or things can always be analyzed in behavioral terms.

Being (*Sein*): Traditionally, ontology studies being (the nature of ultimate entities, their mode of existence, and so on), but, in Heidegger, Being refers to the manner in which entities or beings have their own way or mode of being, their own way "to be," or as that which makes or allows things be the things they are. Heidegger speaks of the "Being" of beings and wants to reawaken the question of the "meaning of Being," which he maintains has been forgotten in contemporary thought although it was the motivating question for ancient Greek philosophy. In his later thought, Heidegger started to write the term "Being" in its Old German spelling *Seyn*.

Being-for-itself (*être pour soi*): The term "for itself" is associated with Hegel but is used especially by Sartre (also de Beauvoir and Merleau-Ponty) for the fundamental reality of consciousness, as something that exists and acts "for itself" to achieve its own fulfillment, self-completion, or self-realization.

Being-in-itself (*être en soi*): the fundamental reality of objects of consciousness, based on Hegel's concept of that which is "in itself" (*an sich*). Sartre uses it for the mode of all entities which do not have consciousness or "being-for-itself."

Being-in–the-world (*In-der-Welt-sein*): "World" as a technical term in phenomenology does not mean the set of physical objects in nature but refers to the indefinitely large set of backgrounds and contexts involved in any human conscious experience. When an object is perceived, one side presents itself, but there is an accompanying awareness of a "horizon" of other unseen sides, and of other contexts in which the thing might be perceived (a book could be seen *as* something to read or *as* a paperweight). The entire (ultimately unspecifiable) set of possible horizons is called "world." Building on Husserl's account, Heidegger (in *Being and Time*, 1927) introduces the technical term *Being-in-the-world* to express the indissoluble manner in which human existence (**Dasein**) is bound up with a set of contexts and concerns that make up the personal, social, cultural, historical *environment* (*Umwelt*), surroundings (*Umgebung*) or *milieu*. Traditional philosophy, by assuming the possibility of an isolated subject (e.g. Descartes), ignored this phenomenon of being-in-the-world, but there is no self without world. For Heidegger, inanimate objects do not have a world, and an animal's world is relatively impoverished, whereas being-in-the-world is constitutive of Dasein, and is communal, always including others: "The world of Dasein is a with-world" (Heidegger, *Being and Time*, §26). Different cultures may have different modes of being-in-the-world; leading to problems of relating "home" and "alien" worlds. For Ludwig Binswanger, understanding a manic patient requires understanding their particular mode of being-in-the-world.

Being-towards-death (*Sein zum Tode*): a concept in Kierkegaard and Heidegger, refers to the manner in which humans take cognisance of the fact that their existence involves radical finitude and will be cut short by death. For Heidegger, the challenge is how, given this finitude, it is possible for human existence (Dasein) to achieve wholeness. Death is not merely a biological or even theological phenomenon, but primarily an existential possibility, a challenge to our potential to become one, integrated person. Heidegger sees anxiety about death as essentially different from fear of losing one's life. Being-towards-death involves the attempt to achieve authenticity which does not deny finitude. "Death is a way to be which Dasein takes over as soon as it is" (Heidegger, *Being and Time*). There are also inauthentic responses to the possibility of death, e.g. hopelessness. We cannot experience another's death. Public discussion of death conceals the true nature of the phenomenon. Each individual must establish his or her own relation to the certain fact of one's demise. Existentialism and phenomenology emphasize that awareness of death is a structural feature of human existence. Freud's death instinct is another approach to the same phenomenon.

Brentano's thesis: Franz Brentano's proposal that intentionality (directedness, aboutness) is the exclusive mark of the mental (*Psychology from the Empirical Standpoint*, 1874). Intentionality, for Brentano, is that characteristic of our thought whereby it is directed at an object, and possesses a content that is other than itself.

Care (*Sorge*): term used by Heidegger in *Being and Time* to characterize the fundamental character of human existence (Dasein) that it cares about itself, is concerned for its survival, interests, well being, future, and so on.

Care ethics: a relational approach to moral theory initiated by theorists such as Nel Nodding (*Caring*, 1984) to replace moral sense, Kantian principle, and utilitarian calculation. In care ethics the quality of the relationship between parents and children, teachers and students, care-givers and patients determines the moral outcome.

Care of self: term used in the later Foucault to refer to the preoccupation of traditional philosophy with providing humans with a way of living that advanced their well-being or fulfillment. Pato ka refers similarly to "care of soul."

***Ceteris paribus* laws**: laws that hold under certain conditions, when other things are equal (or normal). The *ceteris paribus* clause is supposed to hedge the universal applicability (and exceptionless character) of the law.

Circle of intentional concepts: the view that any definition or explication of an intentional concept (e.g. belief, desire, intention, knowledge), must resort to further intentional concepts. As John Searle puts it: "It is not possible to give a logical analysis of the intentionality of the mental in terms of simpler notions, since intentionality is, so to speak, a ground floor property of the mind ... Any explanation of intentionality, therefore, takes place within the circle of intentional concepts" (Searle, *Intentionality*, 1983).

Class: an extensional entity, i.e. one whose identity is determined wholly by its members. The class of nineteenth-century British monarchs, for instance, is the very same thing as the class whose members are George III, George IV, William IV, and Victoria.

Closure, epistemic: According to the epistemic closure principle, knowledge is closed under known entailment. This means, roughly, that if one knows p, and also knows that p entails q, then one knows q or at least is in a position to know q[(Kp & K(p → q)) → Kq]. The principle's relevance arises from its use in skeptical reasoning. According to such reasoning, I cannot know that a given skeptical alternative (such as my being a brain-in-a-vat) is false [~K~q]. But I know that, say, my having hands entails that the alternative is false [K(p → ~q)]. Hence, appealing to epistemic closure, skeptics can argue that I don't know that I have hands [K~p].

Cognitivism/non-cognitivism (ethics): the view that moral judgments do or do not express genuine knowledge or, relatedly, that they are or are not truth-apt. Ordinary use (meaning): either the use made of a linguistic expression in everyday parlance (ordinary as opposed to technical or specialized), or the established use of a linguistic expression, whether it be in everyday parlance or in specialized disciplines (ordinary as opposed to extra-ordinary or deviant).

Cognitive turn: the turn away from **behaviorism** towards cognitive science in the last third of the twentieth century, spurred on by Chomsky's critique of behaviorist theories of language acquisition and by advances in computer science's modeling of mental activities.

Coherence theory of truth: theory, associated with Hegel and others, which takes beliefs or statements to be true insofar as they cohere or "fit" with one another (i.e. they exhibit no internal inconsistencies). On such a theory, truth derives from a truth-bearer's relationship to other bearers of truth, and not from a relationship to an extra-mental reality.

Coherentism: the view (in epistemology) that there are no basic beliefs because all beliefs receive at least part of their justification from other beliefs.

Communitarianism: a branch of contemporary political philosophy that stresses the importance of belonging and solidarity within a community for the successful formation of ethical individuals. Furthermore, any attempt to justify a particular community's ethics must give due notice to that community's self-understanding, traditions, and culture.

Completeness: the claim that a formal system is adequate to proving every sentence that is true in virtue of the subject matter in question.

Computational theory of mind: the view, defended by Jerry Fodor, according to which mental processes are computational processes operating on mental representations.

Conclusive reason: a reason, R, for p is conclusive if, and only if, one would not have R if p were false. Conclusive reasons, then, are truth-entailing.

Connectionism: According to the "classical" or symbol-manipulation view in cognitive psychology, thinking is computation, i.e. the manipulation of symbolic representations. By contrast, according to connectionism there is no separation between representations and processes operating over those representations. Rather, cognition is modeled as a network of interconnecting nodes, loosely inspired by neural networks, and information is distributed over the entire network.

Consensus theory of truth: Developed by Pierce, the consensus theory of truth holds that a proposition is true only if it would be accepted by all those who had sufficient relevant experiences for judging that proposition.

Consequentialism: the view that the rightness or wrongness of an action should be determined by the goodness or badness of its consequences or expected consequences.

Constructive empiricism: view about science according to which (1) science aims at empirically adequate theories and (2) acceptance of scientific theories involves belief only in their empirical adequacy (although acceptance involves *more* than belief, namely, commitment to a theory). It has been introduced and defended by van Fraassen.

Contextualism: the view that the truth-values of knowledge attributions are fixed by the standards of knowledge that govern the attributor's context. When we utter knowledge attributions we are either in a high-standards or a low-standards context, depending on what kind of error possibilities, if any, are salient to us. Sometimes error possibilities that our evidence cannot rule out, such as the brain-in-the-vat scenario, are the focus of our attention. As a result, the standards of knowledge will be very high, and we can no longer correctly attribute ordinary knowledge to anyone. When, on the other hand, skeptical alternatives of that kind are ignored, the standards of knowledge remain low, and attributions of ordinary knowledge will not be mistaken.

Continental philosophy: a misleading expression to signify either non-analytic philosophy in general, or philosophy from continental Europe or, least problematically, avant-garde movements in twentieth-century philosophy such as the work of Derrida, Deleuze, which derive from European thinkers (Hegel, Nietzsche, and Heidegger).

Conventionalism: the philosophical view that says of a certain kind of truths that they are truths by *convention* and not by dint of any kind of facts; the view that certain "truths" (e.g. some laws of nature) express not the nature of reality but our decision to accept them as true.

Conventionality (rule-governedness) of language: a cluster of ideas including: first, the idea that the connection between a linguistic expression and its meaning is conventional rather than natural or causal; second, the idea that speaking a language is a rule-governed activity; third, the idea that there is a normative dimension to meaning and language.

Correspondence theory of truth: The correspondence theory of truth (associated with Aristotle) holds that a thought, belief, proposition, or sentence is true if it corresponds to an actual state of affairs. The idea that truth consists in a certain relation of correspondence between the world and our words or thoughts. Often associated with the phrase "correspondence of the intellect with the matter" (*adequatio mentis ad rem*).

Creationism: the doctrine that each biological species, including human beings, was created separately by God, rather than being a product of biological evolution. Often associated with a fundamentalist or literal reading of a religious account of creation, e.g. Genesis.

Critical realism: a view of perceptual knowledge that represents a middle way between "direct (or naive) realism" and "indirect (or representative) realism." According to critical realism, the contents of our perceptual judgments are directly about or refer to the external physical objects themselves, but as mediated by sensory states of the perceiver such that some of the properties taken to characterize external objects (e.g. color) are in fact properties of sensory states of the perceivers themselves.

Critical Theory: an approach to social analysis pioneered in the early 1930s by theorists associated with the *Institut für Sozialforschung* (Institute for Social Research) in Frankfurt such as Theodor Adorno, Max Horkheimer, and Herbert Marcuse. Originally, Critical Theory sought to use Marxist-inspired analysis to resist the structures of totalitarianism and "instrumental reason" it took to be associated with capitalism. Since then, it has progressively moved away from an exclusively "Marxist" orientation to examine different forms of social and political domination and to offer a critique that is meant to contribute to the emancipation of those dominated. It is currently represented by figures such as Axel Honneth and Jürgen Habermas.

Dasein: German term meaning "existence" or "being there" but used as a technical term by Martin Heidegger in *Being and Time* (1927) to refer to the unique mode of being of humans. Dasein is characterized as **being-in-the-world**, as "mineness," as being essentially historical and concerned about the possibility of its own death. Furthermore, Dasein is essentially interpretive and self-interpretive; its own existence matters to it and it shapes its existence through its own self-understanding. For Heidegger the mistake of traditional **ontology** has been to treat human being as an entity among entities, thus obfuscating its unique mode of existing.

Deontology: represented paradigmatically by Kantian ethics, is the view that the rightness or wrongness of an action should be determined by whether or not the action conformed to proper principles of morality – principles which made explicit the duties of the agent.

Différance: a neologism coined by Jacques Derrida, derived from the French verb *différer*, which means both *to differ* and *to defer*. *Différance*, accordingly, expresses both the fact that there are irreducible *differences* between the structure of any phenomenon (a historical event, a text, a personality) and the dichotomies required to think or talk about it; and the consequent fact that efforts to impose the sharp distinction required by binary oppositions must always be "put off" (deferred) in the face of the recalcitrance of the phenomenon. The term is used by Derrida to gesture toward the limits of our concepts and language.

Difference: concept in contemporary Continental philosophy to refer to that which distinguishes one thing or person from another; the diversity, as opposed to unity, that Gilles Deleuze sees as ontologically primary. Various social movements often seek to "celebrate" difference over various forms of insistence of identity.

Duration (*la durée*): the lived experience of temporality (Bergson).

Eliminative induction: mode of induction based on the elimination of rival hypotheses. It is not so much concerned with how hypotheses are generated as with how they are justified once they become available. By eliminating all but one available hypothesis that stands in a certain relationship with the evidence (e.g. they entail the evidence, or they explain it, etc.), the one that remains is taken to be likely to be true.

Eliminative materialism: the view that beliefs, desires, and other mental states do not exist, and that explanations in terms of such states will be replaced by neurobiological explanations. In general terms eliminativism is a strategy which removes the obstacles that higher-level phenomena pose to naturalism (especially of an ontological kind) not by reducing them to lower-level phenomena, but by denying their existence. As regards mental phenomena, this strategy goes back to Feyerabend and Quine, but it also has affinities with Nietzschean nihilism, especially when applied to moral values and norms. Eliminative materialism claims that folk psychology is a radical false theory that does not admit of scientific refinement. Strictly speaking, there are no such things as beliefs, desires, or intentions, and an ideally completed physicalistic science of mind will no longer invoke these notions (Paul Churchland).

Emergentism: the view that some wholes exhibit novel features which are emergent, or not explicable in terms of the properties of the parts of the whole.

Empiricism: The epistemological view, opposed to **rationalism**, that sensory perception is the only source of knowledge (Locke: *nihil est in intellectu quod non prior fuerit in sensu*: nothing is in the intellect that was not first in the senses), or that sensory perception endows our language with its meaning or our concepts with their content (conceptual).

973

Endurantism: the view that, rather than persisting objects being composed of momentary temporal parts (as perdurantism contends), they are "wholly present" at every time at which they exist.

Enframing (Gestell): term used in the later Heidegger (especially in his essay, "The question concerning technology") to express the manner or process in which the encompassing technological rationale of modern industrial society and science has come to interpret the world in such a way that everything can be understood as some kind of useable or serviceable material (including human beings, e.g. as sources of organs for others, and so on). According to Heidegger this technological attitude of enframing is not a late product of modern science but is actually a consequence of the Greek metaphysical attitude towards nature and things.

Essentialism: the view, elaborated by Aristotle, that substances have essential as well as accidental properties. Essential properties define what specific kind the substance belongs to. A cat can lose its accidental properties while remaining a cat, but not its essential ones. Modern versions interpret essential properties as those that an entity possesses in every possible world in which it exists. These versions are based on advances in modal logic (Kripke, Barcan Marcus) and doctrines about the behavior of proper names and natural kind terms (the realist semantics of Kripke and Putnam). According to this essentialism, there are *natural kinds*; it is the business of empirical science to determine them.

Ethnocentrism: a philosophy, worldview, or body of knowledge from a particular limited ethnic perspective. Throughout the twentieth century the claim was often made by critical race theorists, feminists, and other groups that philosophy as practiced in Europe and North America expressed values and attitudes prejudicial to non-western cultures.

Evidentialism: regarding justification, the view that beliefs are justified to the degree they fit the subject's evidence. About knowledge, it is the view that knowing that p requires having evidence for p.

Evil demon problem: The problem, first posed by Descartes, of how one can know that one is not deceived by the evil demon (*malin genie*): a malevolent, omnipotent being who causes one to have perceptual experiences that are completely misleading. Arguably, one's evidence in the normal situation, and one's evidence while being deceived by an evil demon are indistinguishable. But if one's evidence is the same in either situation, how is one to know which situation one is in?

Existenz ("existence"): term associated with Jaspers and taken up by Heidegger and other existentialists to refer to the authentic experience of the unique mode of existing of human beings over and against other kinds of natural entities. Human existence is characterized first and foremost by freedom in the face of which humans experience **anxiety (Angst)**.

Explanation, deductive-nomological model of: According to this model, introduced by Hempel and Oppenheim, to offer an explanation of an event *e* is to construct a valid deductive argument of the following form:
    Antecedent/initial conditions
    Statements of laws
    Therefore, *e* (event/fact to be explained)

Explanation (*Erklären*) versus understanding (*Verstehen*): During the late nineteenth century, German philosophers (Dilthey) and historians (Droysen) argued for a methodological distinction between the natural sciences and the human or cultural sciences. As Dilthey put it: "We explain nature, but we understand mental life." This debate was later called the *explanation understanding* controversy. Explanation was understood to proceed in terms of the application of universally valid causal laws; understanding concerned the individual and his or her unique motivation. In the twentieth century, the methodological difference between hermeneutical or intentional understanding and (particularly nomological) scientific explanation was emphasized in the *reasons versus causes* debate in the 1960s. The opposite camp, led by Hempel, insisted on a unified scientific methodology, claiming that reasoned explanations of actions also exhibit a deductive-nomological structure.

Explication: analytical procedure, suggested by Carnap, by means of which an ordinary imprecise concept is made more precise. The *explicandum* is the concept to be explicated while the *explicatum* is the concept (or concepts) that sharpens the content of the *explicandum*.

Extensionality, extensional language: The extension of an expression is the class of objects that the expression applies to. The intension of an expression is its sense or meaning. A complex expression is called extensional if its extension is determined completely by the extensions of its constituent expressions. A statement is called extensional if no substitution of co-referential expressions within the statement changes its truth-value. An extensional language is a language that contains only extensional expressions. The extensionality *thesis* says that all language is extensional, or that intensional language is amenable to reductive analysis that lays bare its extensional logical structure.

Externalism: the view, associated primarily with philosophy of mind and philosophy of language (with Hilary Putnam in particular), that the contents of a thought depend at least in part on external events ("outside the head") such as social, linguistic, or physical contexts.

Externalism, epistemic: regarding justification, the view that what makes beliefs epistemically justified or unjustified need not be internal to the mind. Regarding knowledge, it is the view that internal justification (justification determined solely by what is internal to the mind) is not necessary for knowledge. What determines justification is internal to the mind if and only if (according to one approach) it qualifies as a mental state or (according to another approach) is recognizable on reflection.

Facticity (*Faktizität*): term that originates in German neo-Kantianism and is used by Husserl, Heidegger, and others, to express the contingent and factual character of human existence. For Heidegger, human existence is "factical" (*faktisch*), in that, despite its particularity and contingency, it is open to a range of *concrete* possibilities.

Fallibilism: the epistemological view that there is no guaranteed truth for humans, so that knowledge-claims are always defeasible. Even well-justified beliefs could be mistaken, so that they do not constitute knowledge. (The phrasing "All *knowledge* is fallible" is awkward, since knowledge implies truth.) The view that all statements are fallible, associated in particular with proponents of the Duhem–Quine hypothesis, C. S. Peirce, Popper, and many pragmatist philosophers contending that all our beliefs, even those which seem most certain at any given time, are in principle open to revision and replacement in light of future experience. Fallibilism, in stressing that knowledge does not require certainty, is an outlook opposed to skepticism in epistemology.

Falsificationism: the view, advocated by Popper, that scientific theories should be subjected to severe testing attempting to falsify them. It rests on the asymmetry between verification and falsification. The tests of scientific theories are attempts to refute a theory. Theories that survive severe testing are said to be corroborated. But, according to falsificationism, no amount of evidence can inductively support a theory.

Family resemblance: the view, explored by Ludwig Wittgenstein especially in his *Philosophical Investigations*, that concepts do not apply to objects in virtue of strictly definable necessary and sufficient conditions, but rather through overlapping networks of characteristics, none of which may be necessary or sufficient in all circumstances to ensure the application of the concept. The metaphor is drawn from the notion of members of a family, some of whom may resemble each other because of one characteristic (shape of nose), whereas others may resemble each other because of an entirely different characteristic (e.g. hair color, complexion). Wittgenstein uses the example of "games": there can be no essence of what a game is, there are only family resemblances between different kinds of game.

Feminism, French: a movement in French philosophy in the 1970s and 1980s influenced by post-structuralist theories of language and promoting "feminine" styles of reading, writing, and theorizing.

Feminist empiricism: the view that observance of logic and rigorous insistence on observational evidence is needed to eliminate bias and misogyny in scientific reasoning.

Feminist epistemology: a diverse body of work in epistemology produced by feminist philosophers critical of androcentrism and masculine bias in many areas of science, and who want to develop a more rigorous understanding of the relation between observation and theory and the role of values and metaphor in science.

Feminist standpoint epistemology: an approach to knowledge developed by Nancy Hartstock and other feminist philosophers in the 1980s and 1990s which is based on the argument that women, given their different situations and different perspectives on reality, are in a better position to develop adequate theories about that reality than men of privileged classes.

Fictionalism: the view that, in many cases, we can usefully replace a commitment to the real existence of metaphysically controversial entities by a pretence that they exist.

First philosophy: an intellectual discipline whose task it is to provide the general framework within which all more local pursuits of truth, as practiced by the special sciences, may be conducted. Term associated originally with Aristotle (*protē philosophia*) and Descartes (*prima philosophia*, *philosophie première*) but also used by Quine, Husserl, Levinas, and others. Levinas, for instance, wants to claim that ethics has

the status of first philosophy, whereas it was metaphysics for Aristotle and epistemology for Descartes.

Folk psychology: in its general sense, the everyday practice of explaining behavior in
terms of beliefs, desires, and other mental states. In a more restricted sense, a theory
positing beliefs, desires, and other mental states as interacting causes of behavior, grasp
of which underlies the everyday practice. The term is associated with Dennett (who
claims to have invented it), Paul Churchland, and others. The argument rages over
whether folk psychology offers a useful (even indispensable) practical means of interpreting human behavior (including one's own behaviour), or whether it is an outdated,
unscientific, and highly unreliable form of prediction, which will be progressively
replaced by science.

Form of life (*Lebensform*): a term that occurs very rarely in Wittgenstein's thought, but
has become popular for describing the overarching conception of a distinct way of life,
encompassing its historical, social, logical, and linguistic structures.

Formalism: the view that mathematics is just a game played with signs that have no
meaning beyond the role the rules of the game assign to them.

Foundationalism: the view that a person's justified beliefs are divided into two sets: basic
and non-basic beliefs. Basic beliefs are justified without receiving any of their justification from other beliefs. Non-basic beliefs receive at least part of their justification
from basic beliefs. According to foundationalism, all non-basic beliefs ultimately receive
their justification from basic beliefs.

Functionalism: the view that mental states can be analyzed in terms of their relationships
to sensory inputs, behavioral outputs, and other mental states. Thus pain is not identical
with a particular neuro-physiological state, but with any state which is caused by injury
and manifests itself in pain behavior. Functionalism treats the mind as analogous not to
the hardware of a digital computer, but to the software (program). Functionalism is the
orthodox view in contemporary philosophy of mind (going back to Putnam and Fodor).
It is often said that Aristotle is the founder of functionalism because of his view that the
function of an entity determines its form.

Genealogy: Michel Foucault's technique for exploring the inextricable relation between
knowledge (expressed in discourse) and power (expressed in non-discursive practices).

Gettier problem: In his paper "Is justified true belief knowledge?" Edmund Gettier showed
convincingly that justified true belief is not sufficient for knowledge. He showed this
by describing two examples of justified true belief that are not examples of knowledge.
In subsequent literature, many additional cases of that kind – typically referred to
as "Gettier cases" – have been devised. The problem they raise is that of finding a
condition that makes a proposed analysis of knowledge immune to refutation by appeal
to such cases.

Hermeneutics: Meaning "the art of interpretation," it is a movement associated with
Schleiemacher, Dilthey, Heidegger, and Gadamer. Hermenutics was originally a way of

interpreting difficult (often biblical) texts that Dilthey extended to the interpretation of history and human life in general. Hermenutics claims that, in order to interpret a text properly, one must contextualize it against the background of the text's language, the social history surrounding it, the details of the author's life, and so on. Today, it is generally taken to be a methodology for self-reflexively examining the presumptions and beliefs that an interpreter implicitly and perhaps unknowingly brings to the interpretation of a text.

Holism, confirmational: the view that theories are confirmed as wholes. Accordingly, when a theory is confirmed by the evidence, everything that the theory asserts or implies is confirmed.

Homunculus fallacy: The term was introduced by Anthony Kenny in 1971: "I shall call the reckless application of human-being predicates to insufficiently human-like objects the 'homunculus fallacy', since its most naïve form is tantamount to the postulation of a little man within a man to explain human experience and behaviour." The homunculus fallacy is committed when attributes are ascribed to parts of persons (e.g. to brains) which can be ascribed only to the person as a whole. Wittgensteinian philosophers such as Peter Hacker hold that this fallacy is widespread in the cognitive and the neurosciences.

Hume's principle: The number of Fs = the number of Gs if and only if there is a one-to-one correspondence between the Fs and the Gs. Used by Frege as a guiding principle in founding a theory of natural numbers (see **Numbers, natural**).

Hylomorphism: the union of form (Greek: *morphē*) and matter (Greek: *hyle*), especially associated with Aristotle's theory of the composition of material substances.

Ideal language philosophy: introduced by Gustav Bergmann to contrast with **ordinary-language philosophy**. A type of **linguistic philosophy** that seeks to resolve philosophical problems by constructing artificial languages in which these problems can no longer be formulated. Closely connected to logical construction.

Idealism: the label for a cluster of philosophical views which regard various sorts of things as mental or mind-dependent in some way; in contrast to a corresponding cluster of views labeled **realism**, which regard these things as non-mental. There are various forms of idealism. Berkeley's is usually regarded as a subjective idealism in that he held that everything is either a mind or an idea in the mind (ultimately all things are ideas in the mind of God). Kant is usually described as a transcendental idealist (see **Idealism, transcendental**) and Hegel is characterized as an Absolute Idealist.

Idealism, German: philosophical movement in Germany spanning from the late eighteenth century to the early nineteenth century (specifically including Kant, Hegel, Schelling, Fichte). Idealism in this form stressed that the perceptual properties of objects are not merely "imposed" on subjects by "things in themselves" apart from humans. Rather, how we encounter objects is dependent upon the way in which we, as subjects, always already perceive things in a particular way.

Idealism, transcendental: the view that things must be understood as objects (or what Kant termed "phenomena" or "appearances") correlated with human subjectivity rather than as "things in themselves." Sometimes, the doctrine is restricted specifically to Kant's claim that space and time are not properties of things in themselves but actually belong to the framework of human sensibility. The neo-Kantians and Husserl are responsible for advocating versions of transcendental idealism in the twentieth century. For Husserl, transcendental idealism is the view that all objectivity is a product of constituting subjectivity and that ultimately everything achieves its "being and meaning" from the activities of transcendental subjectivity. Transcendental idealism is often understood as form of "anti-realism" in that it denies that talk of a world in itself is meaningful.

Identity thesis: the thesis that mental phenomena (e.g. properties, states, events, processes) are (identical to) physical phenomena. The type identity thesis (also known as type physicalism) states that mental types (e.g. kinds, properties) are physical types. The token identity thesis (also known as token physicalism) states that mental particulars (e.g. events, instances of properties) are physical particulars.

Ideology: a succession of mythologies about human life that effectively articulated what was at stake in a way of life (a historical epoch defined by a type of economic productive activity) while at the same time obscuring what was really going on. Term associated with Marxism and with Critical Theory, but used more loosely in political philosophy generally to refer to an overall system of ideas motivating an individual or a group.

Impredicative definition: a definition which defines something in terms of a class to which it belongs, e.g. "the tallest man in the room."

Incompleteness theorem: The theorem of meta-mathematics which says that every consistent formal theory strong enough to be able to derive elementary arithmetic from it is incomplete, so that there are sentences expressible in the formal language which the theory neither proves nor refutes.

Indeterminacy of translation: the thesis, advanced by W. V. O. Quine, that different translation manuals could fit the same linguistic behavior equally well, and that hence there is no fact of the matter as to which gives the correct translation.

Inferentialist semantics: an approach that claims that the meaning of terms, at least those of interest to philosophy, can be satisfactorily explained by their inferential links to each other; or, a theory that claims that to know what a term means is to know what inferences one can make with it, to what other positions in the conceptual firmament one is entitled to move by virtue of undertaking the commitments that term brings with it.

Instrumentalism: view about science according to which theories should be seen as (useful) instruments for the organization, classification, and prediction of observable phenomena. The "cash value" of scientific theories is fully captured by what theories say about the observable world.

Intension: The intension of an expression is its sense or meaning as opposed to the class of objects (extension) to which the expression applies.

Intensionality: An intensional context is one in which substitution of co-referring terms does not preserve truth-value or in which substitutivity *salva veritate* fails, e.g. someone may believe that Peter is his boss and disbelieve that Mr Smith is his boss, not realizing that Peter *is* Mr Smith The truth-value of a sentence containing an intensional context depends not only on what is referred to, but also on how it is referred to. The linguistic expressions of the propositional attitudes (believing, desiring, intending that *p*) are intensional.

Intentionality: Intentionality is this property of *aboutness*: the property that mental states (as well as things like words and maps) can have of being about one thing or another, of having a particular *content*. The notion of intentionality was reintroduced to philosophy and psychology by Franz Brentano and is at the center of debate in philosophy of mind (reintroduced by Roderick Chisholm), specifically the question of whether intentionality can be naturalized (Dennett, Searle, et al.) or possibly even eliminated.

Internalism, epistemic: the view that the factors that determine whether or not a belief is justified must be internal to the mind. Depending on how internalism is construed, this constraint has the effect of limiting justification-determining factors either to mental states, or to things that are recognizable on reflection.

Interpretandum: the entity or subject matter which is to be interpreted

Intuition: a kind of immediate cognitive awareness of an object independently of any previous knowledge and without mediating reasoning or conception. Husserl, for instance, maintained that phenomenology proceeded through intuition rather than through argumentation. Bergson also maintained that certain experiences could only be intuited (such as the experience of lived time) and not rationally conceptualized.

Is/ought gap: the view, held by Hume, Kant, and Moore, that ought claims are logically autonomous, in that they cannot be derived from factual or descriptive statements (see **Open question argument, Naturalistic fallacy**)

Knowledge by acquaintance: term associated with Bertrand Russell, understood as a kind of knowledge that is non-propositional or non-descriptive and constitutes the grounds on which descriptive knowledge of external reality is based (see also **Acquaintance**).

Language of thought ("LOT"): term associated with Fodor to mean the language-like system of mental representation posited by the Representational Theory of Mind and Computational Theory of Mind. See also **Mentalese**.

Law of the excluded middle: the logical principle that, for any proposition *p*, either *p* is the case or not-*p* is the case; the law that for every sentence, either it or its negation is true.

Lebenswelt (life-world): a term used by Husserl (especially in his *Crisis of the European Sciences*, 1936) and by subsequent phenomenologists to describe the world as immediately experienced in everyday, pre-reflective, practical living as opposed to the world as explicated by the modern mathematical sciences. The life-world is always implicitly presupposed by humans in their actions and thoughts.

Liberalism: a branch of political philosophy that maintains that institutions and political structures are legitimated through making contributions to the interests of individuals. Liberalism seeks to articulate a framework of rules within which a plurality of individuals holding their own (often competing) interests can, through reasonable compromise, harmonize these interests to a greater degree than otherwise possible.

Linguistic philosophy: an approach to philosophical problems which detects their root in linguistic or conceptual confusions and seeks to resolve them either by replacing the relevant expressions (**ideal language philosophy, logical construction**) or by clarifying their use (**ordinary-language philosophy**).

Linguistic turn: the doctrine that any philosophical analysis of thought must proceed by means of an analysis of language. The term was coined by Gustav Bergmann in 1964 but brought to prominence by Richard Rorty.

Logic, inductive: a formal system based on probability calculus that aims to capture in a logical and quantitative way the notion of inductive support that evidence accrues to a hypothesis or theory.

Logic, monadic: that part of logic which restricts itself to forms of inference involving properties, not relations.

Logic, polyadic: logic which can handle nested quantification involving relations, and hence can express the difference between "Everyone loves someone" and "There is someone everyone loves."

Logic, syllogistic: Aristotle's logic, which deals with inferences involving simple predication.

Logical analysis: the process of identifying the components of a proposition, thought, fact, or sentence, and the way in which they are combined (its **logical form**).

Logical atomism: the view that logical analysis can, in principle, reveal elementary propositions whose logical forms reflect the ultimate constituents and structure of reality. Originally proposed by Bertrand Russell (initially in 1913) such that the world is made up of logical atoms, which for Russell meant "little patches of colour or sounds, momentary things ... predicates or relations and so on." Logical atoms are the ultimate simple subjects of predication.

Logical construction: a type of **logical analysis** in which philosophically troublesome expressions and sentences are paraphrased in a formal language, but without any aspiration that analysandum and analysans should be synonymous. The prime example is the "logical explication" pursued by Carnap and Quine.

Logical form: the structure of propositions as paraphrased by formal logic for the purpose of revealing those features which matter to the validity of arguments in which they occur. Logical form is a term associated with Russell. It is used in a somewhat different sense in contemporary linguistics.

Logical positivism or **logical empiricism**: a movement that flourished in Vienna (the "Vienna Circle") and Berlin in the 1920s. Tries to improve on traditional empiricism with the help of formal logic. Seeks to develop a consistent form of empiricism which acknowledges the existence of a priori knowledge in logic and mathematics, while insisting against Kant that all such knowledge is analytic.

Logicism: is the claim that mathematical truths are logical truths, provable by logical means (if provable at all), and so knowable in the same way as logic. The technical project (nowadays generally thought to have failed) of showing that arithmetic (Frege) or mathematics generally (Russell) is reducible to logic, so that the philosophical problems engendered by mathematics are subsumed within those of logic.

Materialism: the metaphysical view that only material things exist. Materialism maintains that all entities are reducible to and can ultimately be explained by matter, physical force, or complex physical processes as understood by science. Materialism denies the existence of any spiritual force, consciousness or mental state independent of these physical explanations. Marxists espouse dialectical materialism whereby history is generated by the interaction of opposing material forces.

Maximin: neologism which means "maximize the minimum" introduced by John Rawls in his *Theory of Justice* (1971). Rawls speaks of people adopting a maximin rule of choice: they would "rank the alternatives by their worst possible outcomes" and then adopt that alternative "the worst outcome of which is superior to the worst outcomes of the others."

Mentalese: neologism used by Jerry Fodor (as part of his **Language of thought** hypothesis) to refer to the kind of hypothesized internal, innate, language-like structure of the brain that must underlie thought and spoken language. Mentalese has to combine semantic parts into wholes, and account for propositional attitudes, etc.

Mentalism (about language, meaning, concepts): Mentalism treats meaning and concepts as psychic phenomena in the mind of individuals.

Mereology: From the Greek *meros* meaning "part," mereology is the formal study of part–whole relations, discussed by the students of Brentano, e.g. Carl Stumpf and notably by Edmund Husserl in the Third Logical Investigation, axiomatized by the Polish philosopher and logician Stanislaw Lesniewski and the American philosophers H. S. Leonard and Nelson Goodman.

Metaphysics (descriptive versus revisionary): a distinction drawn by Strawson: whereas revisionary metaphysics seeks to bring our conceptual scheme in line with the essential features of reality, descriptive metaphysics confines itself to describing the most funda-mental (pervasive and permanent) structures of the way we talk and think about reality.

Mimesis: Greek term meaning "imitation." Mimesis is used in aesthetics to express the relation between a literary text and the actions it purports to depict. Although it has some rather complex and ambiguous meanings as it was originally used by Plato and Aristotle, in the contemporary context mimesis is often used as "imitation" or "actualization." Mimesis denotes a certain indexing to more pure or perfect states of the past that must be recovered and restored to actualization (usually via artistic performance or aesthetic embodiment).

Modal logic: the branch of logic that deals with the modal notions of necessity, possibility, and contingency. Originally attributed to Aristotle who discussed the truth or falsity of assertions concerning the future ("there will be a sea-battle tomorrow") but broadened to include discussion of what must be the case or could possibly be the case. Considerably developed in the twentieth century, owing to advances in technical notation, by Ruth Barcan Marcus, Saul Kripke, David Lewis, and others.

Modal realism: the doctrine (associated with David Lewis) that, in addition to the concrete spatio-temporal universe which we inhabit, there are countless other equally real and equally concrete universes – all spatio-temporally and causally isolated from one another – which collectively constitute the totality of all possible worlds.

Modality: the language of necessity and possibility.

Myth of the given: the traditional view named and criticized by Wilfrid Sellars that some knowledge is allegedly just "given" directly in experience without presupposing any other knowledge or previously acquired cognitive capacities. In contrast to the myth of the given is the idea that knowledge is a normative standing in the "logical space of reasons," or the language-game of giving and asking for reasons.

Narrow content: mental content that depends solely on intrinsic properties of the thinker. See also **Wide content**.

Nativism: Nativists believe that the mind comes equipped with a great deal of innate (or a priori) structure and this innate structure plays an important role in explaining our mature cognitive capacities and abilities

Natural attitude: term used by Husserl (introduced in *Ideas* I, 1913) to refer to the tacit, realist belief in the existence of a mind-independent reality that pervades not only the positive sciences but also our daily pre-theoretical life.

Natural kind: class of entities that exhibit a certain kind of natural unity. Natural kind terms "carve nature at her joints," to borrow Plato's phrase. Since natural kinds are not creations of human cognition, they can exist without being recognized as such, or without their physical microstructure being known. *Water*, *gold*, and *tiger* are famous examples of natural kinds. Modern-day scientific **essentialism** holds that the stability of natural kinds is guaranteed by natural laws, and that discovering the "nature" or "essence" of a natural kind is the business of physical science.

Natural properties: G. E. Moore argued that "good" is not a natural property, while ethical naturalists propose that all real or genuine properties are natural. Moore himself made several attempts at explaining what the naturalness of a property consists in. One was that natural properties are properties "with which it is the business of the natural sciences or psychology to deal." Others proposed that all *empirical* properties should count as natural.

Naturalism: is the idea that there is no general method of inquiry in philosophy that is prior to, or foundational in relation to, the fallible but self-correcting explanatory methods that are characteristic of the empirical sciences. A movement going back to the nineteenth century. All naturalists are hostile to explanations that invoke phenomena beyond nature, such as God, abstract entities in a Platonic realm beyond space and time, or Cartesian soul-substances. But beyond this consensus, naturalism comes in various shapes and sizes. Meta-philosophical naturalism claims that philosophy is a branch of or continuous with natural science; epistemological naturalism is nothing other than scientism: it insists that there is no genuine knowledge outside natural science; ontological naturalism denies that there is any realm other than the natural world of matter, energy, and spatio-temporal objects or events.

Naturalism, analytical (semantical): Analytical or semantical naturalism holds that the project of naturalizing is an endeavor in conceptual analysis. It privileges a class of naturalistically acceptable properties or predicates and tries to show that other predicates are analyzable into predicates of this reference class. Various attempts at naturalizing the intentional in the philosophy of mind are exercises in analytical naturalism.

Naturalism, evolutionary: the view that evolutionary theory provides a powerful means of naturalizing man and his abilities. Sociobiology, evolutionary epistemology, evolutionary psychology, and evolutionary ethics are variants of evolutionary naturalism. They make the claim to explain cognitive, cultural, social, and moral accomplishments of mankind in the light of evolutionary history. Evolutionary naturalism is opposed to creationism, among other things.

Naturalism, meta-ethical: the view that the is/ought gap can be bridged, or that the naturalistic fallacy is not fallacious. Deemed infeasible by Moore.

Naturalistic fallacy: In his *Principia Ethica* (1903), G. E. Moore warned against "the fallacy which consists in identifying the simple notion which we mean by 'good' with some other notion." His criticism of this fallacy is closely connected with his **open question argument**. Since the notions of nature or the natural play no significant role in the fallacy, R. M. Hare has suggested replacing the term "naturalistic fallacy" (already considered unfortunate by Moore) by the term "descriptivistic fallacy." (See **Is/ought gap**.)

Naturalize, naturalization: The verb "to naturalize" was made popular by Quine's seminal paper "Epistemology naturalized." The verb emphasizes the *dynamical* aspect of naturalistic projects in philosophy. Naturalizing a phenomenon amounts to extending the area of application of the natural sciences to such phenomena that are not already covered beyond dispute. Husserl already used the verb "*naturalisieren*" (to naturalize) in his "Philosophy as a rigorous science" (1911).

Neutral monism: The view that mind and matter are complex constructions out of more basic elements which are *neutral*, neither mental nor material.

"New realism": In the early twentieth century a group of philosophers known as the "American new realists" defended **realism, direct (or naive)** in the theory of knowledge against the Hegelian Idealists in particular, in parallel with similar realist reactions by G. E. Moore and Russell in Britain.

Nihilation (*néantisation*): Sartre's neologism for the process whereby negation is introduced on the concrete level of immediate perception (as opposed to the reflective level of intellectual judgment). Correspondingly, *nothingness* denotes the reality of negation that is introduced by nihilation.

Nominalist: one who denies the existence of properties and relations, conceived as universals.

Numbers, natural: the finite counting numbers 0, 1, 2, etc.; **Cardinal numbers**: numbers which answer the question "How many?," whether finite (0, 1, 2, etc.) or infinite. The infinite numbers are represented as aleph numbers ($\aleph_0$, etc.), following the mathematician Georg Cantor, who defined the notion of cardinality and realized that infinite sets can have different cardinalities.

Observation, theory-ladenness of: the view that all observation is dependent on theories. It goes back to Duhem and his claim that observation in science is not just the act of reporting a phenomenon; it is the *interpretation* of a phenomenon in the light of some theory and other background beliefs.

Ockham's razor: Methodological principle attributed to William of Ockham and connected to the virtue of simplicity or parsimony: entities must not be multiplied without necessity (*Entia non sunt multiplicanda sine necessitate*).

Ontological commitment: term associated with Quine. The entities which a particular theory is committed to asserting as existent. Each science will have its own ontological commitment (zoology may be committed to the existence of tigers; physics may be committed to the existence of electrons; sociology to the existence of persons, and so on).

Ontological relativity: the view that the question of what there is can only be settled in relation to someone's preferred way of describing the world, not absolutely.

Ontology: that branch of metaphysics that seeks to identify the fundamental categories or kinds of being. The term "ontology" emerged in the eighteenth century and is often used interchangeably with the term "metaphysics." Aristotle's ontology was based on the concept of substance as primary. Other ontologies might assume that relations or events are fundamental. Ontology provides ways for distinguishing between different fundamental kinds of entity (concrete and abstract, real and ideal, essential, accidental, and so on).

Ontology, formal: term used by Husserl to refer to the study of the purely formal features of anything whatsoever, e.g. the nature of thing, property, or relation.

Ontology, fundamental: term introduced by Heidegger in *Being and Time*, to refer to the foundational science that explains how all others forms of entity and all other ontologies receive their characterization in relation to human existence or **Dasein**. Fundamental ontology, therefore, requires an antecedent consideration of human existence which Heidegger calls the existential analytic of Dasein.

Open question argument: G. E. Moore argued that any reductive definition of "good" in terms of natural properties is doomed to fail. His open question argument says that "good does not, by definition, mean anything that is natural; and it is therefore always an open question whether anything that is natural is good." (See **Is/ought gap**, **Naturalistic fallacy**.)

Ordinary-language philosophy: the view that philosophical questions are best addressed by investigating patterns of usage in everyday language. The label was originally introduced by Bergmann and was used mostly by enemies of conceptual analysis and. It signifies a type of **linguistic philosophy** which seeks to resolve philosophical problems by contrasting the philosophical use of the expressions that occur in them (e.g. "knowledge," "truth") with their use in non-philosophical discourse.

Other: term used in European philosophy, especially phenomenology, for persons other than myself, particularly in their fundamental ontological or ethical significance (in Sartre and Levinas). Husserl seeks to explain how the other is experienced as other from the vantage point of my own self. Levinas makes a distinction between *l'autre* (the other person) and *l'Autrui* (the Other). (See also **Alterity**.)

Particulars: a traditional term for objects that are not universals. Particulars are usually considered as instances of universals: this particular book is an instance of the universal *book*. Particulars can be concrete or abstract. Some (but not all) philosophers distinguish between particulars and individuals. Strawson for instance thinks that all particulars are individuals but not all individuals (e.g. numbers) are particulars.

Performative self-contradiction: term used by Apel and others, inspired by speech act theory of Austin and Searle. A performative contradiction is not strictly a logical contradiction, but rather a pragmatic contradiction between an utterance and the proposition which underlies that utterance. Speech act theory identifies certain kinds of utterances as *performatives* (statements that bring about or perform what they say, e.g. "I promise to marry you" uttered sincerely actually enacts that very promise of marriage). A performative contradiction occurs when the speaker contradict herself by denying something that the very performance of her speech act entails. The Cretan who says "all Cretans are liars" may be involved in such a performative contradiction (if he *intends* thereby to speak the truth). Similarly, if someone were to claim that he or she did not acknowledge the intersubjective validity contained in propositions, he or she would be committing a performative self-contradiction, as the very same argumentative speech act which he or she uses to utter that belief *presupposes* an implicit acknowledgment of intersubjective validity.

Phenomenological fallacy: term coined by U. T. Place to describe the (alleged) mistake of supposing that when we describe our experience – how things look, feel, and otherwise seem to us – we are describing the literal properties of inner mental objects.

Phenomenology: philosophical movement associated with Edmund Husserl and his students which sought to give an accurate descriptive account of the nature of experience precisely in the manner in which it is experienced (or given) while bracketing all attempts to explain that experience in terms of theories or concepts extraneous to the experience itself. Phenomenology is the science of phenomena, i.e. whatever appears to consciousness in the very manner in which it so appears. Husserl saw phenomenology as primarily descriptive and based on intuition, whereas Heidegger saw phenomenology as essentially hermeneutical in that it is mediated by language and by historical **understanding**.

Philosophical anthropology: movement in German philosophy where the comparison between human and animal was pivotal. Scheler, Plessner, and Gehlen were the dominant figures.

Philosophy of language: by contrast to linguistic philosophy not a philosophical method but a discipline, like philosophy of law or philosophy of science. Addresses philosophical problems connected to language, such as the nature of linguistic meaning, the functioning of singular terms and predicates, and the preconditions of linguistic understanding.

Physicalism: is an ontological thesis according to which the world consists of only those entities acknowledged by physics (or, by an ideally completed physics). Carnap proposed a different variant of physicalism. He did not take it to be an ontological position, but rather the thesis that all meaningful sentences are translatable into a universal language of science. Modern-day physicalism is often a thesis about the *explanatory* force of physics, and is a restricted form of **naturalism**. Physicalism is sometimes understood to be a redefined version of **materialism** but others argue that the entities recognized by physics may include non-material ones.

Platonism (about language, meaning, concepts): the claim that there are abstract entities that are neither mental nor physical but inhabit a realm beyond space and time.

Pluralism: a movement within the professional philosophical establishment in the United States in the latter part of the century in the American Philosophical Association that called for inclusion of diverse and innovative philosophical perspectives at professional meetings, in journal publications, and as course offerings. Examples include Continental philosophy, gay studies, race theory, and feminist philosophy.

Positivism: As originally formulated by thinkers such as Saint-Simon and Comte, positivism held that natural science is the highest form of knowledge. As such, all other sciences (philosophy, social sciences, etc.) were to be approached from the perspective of a single, unitary science that eschewed any "quasi-scientific" or metaphysical claims. Later, logical positivists took positivism to the next level by trying to use modal logic to express theoretical insights in purely observational terms.

Possible worlds: complete ways in which the whole of reality could be, including the actual world as the way in which everything actually is.

Post-analytic philosophy: an envisaged type of philosophy that transcends the alleged limitations of analytic philosophy with the help of **Continental philosophy**.

Post-conventional ethics: a way of talking about ethics that derives from Lawrence Kohlberg. In an attempt to expand on Piaget's work, Kohlberg sought to identify the stages of development involved in forming a moral consciousness. He identified six stages, falling into three categories: pre-conventional, conventional, and post-conventional. The developing moral consciousness passes through stages which are characterized by obedience, self-interest, conformity, and respect for law and order, before finally arriving at the post-conventional phases of moral consciousness which allow for moral concepts such as human rights and universal human ethics. Later, Habermas would rearticulate these categories in detail throughout his *Theory of Communicative Action* and *Communication and the Evolution of Society*.

Post-structuralism: a movement of the 1970s and 1980s (especially in France) that was both influenced by and reacted against structuralist social science.

Pragmatism: the "pragmatic maxim" was originally conceived by C. S. Peirce (1839–1914) as a method for exhaustively clarifying the conceptual meaning of any term by looking to its conceivable effects on practice, including in particular the practice of scientific inquiry. William James (1842–1910) and John Dewey (1859–1952) widened the scope of pragmatism to include "humanist" and "instrumentalist" approaches to truth in terms of good overall practical consequences of belief. Pragmatism in American philosophy has been characterized by anti-foundationalism (**fallibilism**, holistic empiricism) in epistemology and, in different ways, by both **naturalism** and **idealism** in **metaphysics**.

Praxis: Greek term for "action" but specifically used by philosophers to mean a kind of action which contributes to greater understanding. In common usage, praxis is simply the act of putting theoretical knowledge into practice. In its Marxist usage, praxis refers to the way in which theory and practice are unified in human agency.

Predicate calculus: the branch of formal logic which involves quantifiers (such as "some" and "all").

Present-at-hand (*Vorhanden*): term specifically associated with Heidegger (in *Being and Time*), but also found in Husserl, to express the "thereness" of entities which are simply available to be theoretically inspected by the knower or conscious subject. Heidegger criticizes Husserl for thinking that presence-at-hand is the primary mode in which everyday entities in the world are encountered rather than being "**ready-to-hand.**"

Presentism: the view that only the present moment and presently existing objects and events are real, as opposed to past or future moments, objects or events.

Problem/mystery: Gabriel Marcel's distinction between precisely formulable questions with answers based on clear public criteria (problems) and questions that involve an individual's deepest reality and so have no objective, universally valid answers (mysteries).

Proletariat: term used by Marxists and others to refer to those who work for a wage and who do not have any sort of ownership over the means of production (i.e. production plants, tools, raw materials, etc.)

Proposition: the content of a belief; what a sentence expresses.

Propositional attitudes: mental states which can be regarded as attitudes to propositions; they are ascribed by specifying a verb of attitude and a proposition, typically given by a "that-clause." For example, someone might believe, hope, or fear that there will be an egg for breakfast; these are different attitudes towards the same proposition.

Protocol sentences: sentences that were supposed to act as the foundation of all scientific knowledge. They were introduced by the logical positivists and the issue of their status and content embroiled them in a heated debate in the beginning of the 1930s, known as the protocol sentences debate. The expression "protocol sentences" was meant to capture the fact that they were registered in scientific *protocols*, which report the content of scientists' observations. Protocol sentences were understood in two different ways. They were taken either as expressible in a sense-data-language, or as expressible in a thing-language.

Psychologism: the view, widespread in the late nineteenth century (e.g. Mill), that logic is a branch of psychology which studies the laws of thought, and the laws of logic and mathematics are viewed as psychological laws governing our reasoning processes. Vigorously opposed by Frege, Husserl, and some neo-Kantians, for whom logic studies the laws of truth, not of thought. Frege summarized his criticism as follows: "an explanation of a mental process that ends in taking something to be true, can never take the place of proving what is taken to be true." Anti-psychologism in epistemology insists that questions of validity are independent from questions of the actual acquisition of knowledge.

Qualia: plural formed from the Latin *quale*, literally "how," "of what sort," to refer to the felt quality of experience. C. I. Lewis is considered to have introduced the term. The "felt" qualitative properties of (some) mental states, such as the painfulness of pains, the particular taste of wine, the distinctive visual character of sensations of color, and so on. There is a debate in the twentieth century about whether these phenomenal characteristics of consciousness add anything to our scientific knowledge.

Radical interpretation: the process of assigning meaning to a subject's words and content to the subject's attitudes on the basis of observation of the subject's behavior.

Ramsey sentences: are called thus because they were first introduced by Frank Ramsey in an article published in 1931 but they were explicitly named by Carl Hempel in 1958. In the lates 1950s Rudolf Carnap also realized he had re-discovered Ramsey sentences. The technique of replacing the theoretical terms of a theory with bound variables is known as Ramseyfication. The resulting Ramsey sentence can be used to define theoretical entities in terms of their relationships with one another and with other observables.

Rationalism: philosophical position that gives priority to the role of reason and understanding in knowledge over and against sense-experience (empiricism). Rationalism (in ethics) is also opposed to forms of explanation of moral behavior that are based on emotion, feeling, or moral sense. Rationalism is associated in the twentieth century with various ways of approaching the human mind emphasizing its innate capacity for processing knowledge.

Ready-to-hand (*Zuhanden*): term associated with Heidegger (especially *Being and Time*) to characterize the specific mode of being of entities when they are used pragmatically and unselfconsciously as tools or instruments, e.g. one simply grasps the door-handle in order to open the door. Readiness-to-hand is claimed by Heidegger to be a more basic mode of experiencing entities than ascertaining by theoretical inspection whether they are "**present-at-hand**."

Realism: the view that the truth of what we say and think is answerable to a mind-independent world of facts and objects. Realism is generally opposed to idealism or anti-realism.

Realism, direct (or naive): a commonsense view of perceptual knowledge holding that the sensory properties directly revealed in sense perception, such as the redness of an apple, are properties of the external physical objects themselves rather than of the perceiver's own sensory states. Among the challenges for direct realism is to explain the many perceptual appearances (e.g. hallucinations) that do not seem to be explainable in terms of properties of external physical objects.

Realism, indirect (or representative): a view of perceptual knowledge suggesting that perceivers are directly acquainted with properties of their own sensory states or representations, having only indirect or inferred knowledge of the corresponding (and perhaps very different) properties of the external physical objects themselves.

Realism, scientific: philosophical view about science that consists in three theses. *The metaphysical thesis*: the world has a definite and mind-independent structure. *The semantic thesis*: scientific theories should be taken at face value. They are truth-conditioned descriptions of their intended domain, both observable and unobservable. *The epistemic thesis*: mature and predictively successful scientific theories are well-confirmed and approximately true of the world.

Reasons, external versus internal: In his seminal paper "Internal and external reasons" (1980), Bernard Williams distinguishes two kinds of reasons for action: An agent has an *internal* reason to do only if he would be motivated to if he were to engage in deliberative reasoning. Such reasons are based on the agent's desires or aims, while *external* reasons are not. Williams argues that all reasons are internal, and that external reasons are disguised claims about what it would be good for someone to do, rather than claims about what he has reason to do.

Reduction (semantic, scientific): the attempt to show that certain "higher-level" phenomena (mind, meaning, morality) are in reality (when properly construed) nothing but lower-level (notably physical) phenomena, either because concepts and statements that seem to refer to higher-level phenomena can be analyzed as (shown to be synonymous with) concepts and statements that refer exclusively to lower-level phenomena (semantic reductionism.), or because there are scientific principles ("bridge laws") which allow the derivation of the laws governing higher-level phenomena from those of lower-level phenomena.

Reflection, primary versus secondary: Gabriel Marcel's distinction between thought that is abstract, objective, and distanced from the world (primary reflection) and thought that is concrete, personal, and implicated in the world (secondary reflection)

Reification: a development of Marx's "commodity fetishism," the process by which relations between agents and between agents and the world become relations between "things" or "objects" governed by impersonal laws. Capitalist modes of production, and in particular the division of labor, encapsulated reification and atomized individuals. More generally, reification means the objectification of social relations.

Relation, internal: A relation is internal if it is essential to the relata that they should stand in this relation; otherwise it is external. It may be thought, for instance, that I am internally related to my father by fatherhood, since I could not have had a different father from the one I actually had.

Reliabilism: regarding knowledge, the view that knowledge is true belief caused by, or originating in, a reliable source (in a way that excludes Gettier cases). About justification, reliabilism is the view that origination in a reliable source is both necessary and sufficient for justification. Some epistemologists advocate a weaker version of the view, according to which reliability is a necessary, not a sufficient, condition of knowledge.

Representational theory of mind: the view, advanced by Jerry Fodor, that propositional attitudes are relations to mental representations. To believe that snow is white is to stand in the appropriate relation to a mental representation with the content *snow is white*.

Rules, constitutive versus regulative: regulative rules specify how optimally to pursue an activity which can be explained independently of those rules (e.g. "Try to control the center" in chess); constitutive rules constitute the activity in that they are part of its explanation, e.g. "The king moves one square at a time." Violating the regulative rules of chess will (in standard cases) amount to playing chess badly, while violation of the constitutive rules no longer qualifies as playing chess at all.

Russell's paradox: Let K be the class of all classes which do not belong to themselves. Then K belongs to itself if and only if it does not belong to itself, which is absurd. So there cannot be any such class as K.

***Scientia mensura* principle**: shorthand expression for Wilfrid Sellars's dictum "In the dimension of describing and explaining the world, science is the measure of all things, of what is that it is, and of what is not that it is not." Sellars's formulation is a variation on the *homo mensura* doctrine from Plato's dialogue *Protagoras*.

Scientific image versus manifest image: distinction from Wilfrid Sellars concerning the clash between the world as ideally conceived by theoretical science, according to which nature is composed only of imperceptible impersonal entities, and the "manifest" world of perceptible objects and rational persons as conceived by sophisticated common sense. The philosopher, according to Sellars, seeks a "synoptic vision" in which the two "images" or conceptual frameworks could be harmonized.

Scientism: excessive deference to science and scientific method. Unlike naturalism, scientism is often regarded as a *practical* view about the *role* of science in society. All problem-solving shall be done by scientific methods, which answer to no higher authority. For scientism, science is the highest path not only to truth, but also to the solution of social and political problems. The term has a pejorative ring, so very few philosophers use it for self-characterization (quite unlike **naturalism**).

Second nature: acquired behavior that has become so habitual or deeply enrooted that it seems natural (i.e. innate or essential). In talk of second nature, "nature" is understood in the sense of "essence" or "real character," rather than in a biological sense. The notion of second nature deals with the nature of things, not with things of nature.

Self-actualization: the capacity to be the author of one's own unique identity amidst a struggle for recognition from other subjects. Term is used in Hegelian, Marxist, and existentialist philosophies to refer to the manner in which human beings bring about and fulfill their own condition. According to Honneth, self-actualization occurs through a successful negotiation of the three stages of demands within the struggle for recognition: (1) the demand for love which confirms one's own basic needs and sets the stage for cultivating self-confidence, (2) the demand for rights through which one learns to recognize others as similar to oneself, thus cultivating self-respect, and (3) the demand for recognition as a unique individual, thus creating self-esteem.

Sense-data: term used by Russell and Moore for items of immediate experience (such as patches of color in our visual field) which we sense directly, in contrast to the objects of everyday talk (such as tables and chairs) whose existence we only infer.

Sensibilia: objects of the same kind as **sense-data**, whether or not they are data to anyone's senses.

Sensory evidence: Quine's term: "By sensory evidence I mean stimulation of sensory receptors." According to Quine, the main question of epistemology reads: "Given only the evidence of our senses, how do we arrive at our theory of the world?," and he maintains that sensory evidence is the only kind of evidence we have. This view is criticized for leveling the difference between questions of fact and questions of justification, a difference that was important to traditional epistemology. How can stimulations of sensory receptors be *evidence* for our beliefs and theories? Davidson influentially retorted to his teacher: "No doubt meaning and knowledge depend on experience, and experience ultimately on sensation. But this is the 'depend' of causality, not of evidence or justification."

Significant form: the concept, most closely associated with Clive Bell, that art causes distinctive aesthetic emotion by purely formal elements, as opposed to any aspects of content or context. These formal elements are understood to exist in an object independentlyof the viewer and can also be instantiated in multiple instances.

Skepticism: the view that we know, in a certain area of knowledge, significantly less than we think we do. There is skepticism about our knowledge of the external world, the past, the future, and other minds. Skepticism is motivated by arguments that appeal to skeptical alternatives. Their structure is as follows. The first premise asserts that knowledge of an ordinary proposition, O, is possible only if one knows that a skeptical alternative, A, is false. The second premise asserts that one cannot know that A is false. From these two premises, the conclusion follows that O is not a proposition one can know.

Spiritualism: a primarily nineteenth-century French philosophical school that emphasized the autonomy of the free individual in opposition to the reductivist claims of positivism.

Supernaturalism: belief in forces, qualities, or entities beyond scientific or rational understanding.

Supervenience: an asymmetric relationship of determination between sets of properties or facts. If mental properties supervene on physical properties, then there is no variation in mental properties without a variation in physical properties. A special kind of dependence between "higher-level" and "lower-level" properties that does not allow conceptual reductions. A predicate or property F supervenes on some other predicate or property G if nothing can possess or lose F without possessing or losing G. Davidson submits that the mental supervenes on the physical, such that no mental change can occur without a physical change. In meta-ethics, it is proposed that "good" supervenes on non-moral or non-evaluational properties.

Teleofunctionalism: "Teleofunctionalist," "teleosemantical," or "biosemantical," theories of meaning and representation, as devised by Millikan, Papineau, Fodor and Dretske, try to explain the semantic content of mental representations with reference to biological functions. Since the mechanisms responsible for mental representation are products of biological evolution, representational contents must be traced back to "proper functions" (Millikan) of biological mechanisms or traits. Teleofunctional theories are *naturalized* theories of meaning.

Temporary intrinsics, problem of: the problem of explaining how the same object can possess mutually incompatible intrinsic properties, such as different shapes or colors, at different times, and thereby undergo qualitative change.

Theory of meaning: either an explanation or definition of the concept of linguistic meaning (e.g. the referential, the behaviorist, or the use theory), or, as in Davidson and Dummett, an axiomatic theory which allows the derivation of a meaning-stating ("interpretative") theorem for each sentence of a natural language.

Theory of mind (simulation theory): According to the simulation theory, humans and certain animals have to pretend or imagine what it is like to be the other mind they are trying to comprehend.

Theory of mind (theory theory): According to the *theory theory*, humans and certain other animals (e.g. chimpanzees) use a mentally represented theory of mind which includes general psychological laws to understand and infer what other minds are doing.

Token physicalism: See **Identity thesis**.

Transcendental pragmatics: according to Apel, an approach which takes argumentative discourse and its normative presuppositions as the foundation for all inquiry into justifiable validity claims. The foundational position of these presuppositions means that any attempt to relinquish them will lead to a "performative self-contradiction."

Turing machine: an idealized computing device defined by the British mathematician Alan Turing in order to make precise the notion of a computable function. The Turing machine has a head capable of moving along a potentially infinite tape, scanning and printing symbols on the tape as it goes. Where it moves and what it prints is dependent on the symbols it reads and its own internal state. The Turing machine table is the set of instructions which specifies the dependencies between input (symbol read), output (symbol printed and movement along the tape), and internal state.

Type physicalism: See **Identity thesis**.

Umwelt (environment, surrounding world): term used by Husserl, Heidegger, and others to express the manner in which human beings are integrated into a surrounding context which may in part be constituted by their language, social practices, conceptions of objectivity, and so on.

Universal pragmatics: In his *Theory of Communicative Action*, Habermas develops universal pragmatics as a reconstructive account of the basic structures of human linguistic competence. This account identifies normative presuppositions that form the basis of any speech act and the basis of a universalistic moral standpoint. However, Apel and Habermas disagree on the exact articulation of the presuppositions which provide the ultimate grounding of a universalistic moral standpoint. Apel thinks that Habermas fails to distinguish between the unconditional validity of argumentative presuppositions and empirically verifiable accounts of linguistic competence. These differences have led Apel to characterize his own theory as "transcendental pragmatics."

Understanding (Verstehen): term used by Dilthey, Weber, Heidegger, Gadamer, Apel, and Habermas, and the hermeneutic tradition generally, to refer to the kind of empathic understanding and interpretation required to understand the behavior of human subjects and social situations where the application of universal causal laws is not appropriate.

Universals: a traditional term for properties and relations (e.g. redness, adjacency); standardly contrasted with **particulars**. It is controversial how to characterize universals, whether there are any, or even whether there is a useful distinction between universals and particulars to be drawn.

Variable: a device used by logicians to link the argument places of expressions to the quantifiers that govern them. An occurrence of a variable is said to be "bound" by the quantifier to which it is linked; an occurrence not bound by any quantifier is said to be "free." In the expression $\forall xRxy$, for instance, the variable x is bound by the universal quantifier, whereas the variable y occurs free.

Veil of ignorance: A concept found in the work of John Rawls, associated with his conception of the "original position." The veil of ignorance is a thought-experiment designed to highlight issues of fairness in the distribution of roles in a society. Applying the veil of ignorance has the function of denying certain information to the choosers in Rawls's hypothetical state of nature, which he calls the "original position," the supposed starting point from which participants enter into a social contract. Being under the veil of ignorance in the original position, people do not have any knowledge of their particular situations: their place in society, gender, class position or social status, intelligence, and strength, etc. Moreover, each individual in the original position has to deliberate without knowledge of his or her own aims and values – "his conception of the good, the particulars of his rational plan of life" – and of the generation to which he or she belongs, and the particular details of his or her society ("its economic or political situation [and] the level of civilization and culture it has been able to achieve").

Verificationism: the view that the meaning of a statement depends on, or consists in, the method by which it could be either confirmed or refuted.

Verifiability: A statement is verifiable if its truth can be established in experience. Advocates of **logical positivism** took verifiability as a criterion of cognitive significance: those (non-analytic) statements are meaningful whose truth can be verified. In slogan form: meaning is the method of verification. The logical positivists mobilized this criterion to show that statements of metaphysics are meaningless.

Verisimilitude: concept introduced by Popper to capture the idea that false theories may nonetheless be close to the truth. In particular, existing scientific theories may be false but they may also be more verisimilar (i.e. closer to the truth) than their predecessors.

Virtue epistemology: An alternative to traditional epistemology, virtue epistemology aims at analyzing knowledge and justified belief by appeal to epistemic virtues: stable dispositions having a tendency to produce true beliefs. According to one approach, perception, introspection, memory, and rational intuition are examples of epistemic virtues. According to another approach, cognitive dispositions qualify as epistemic virtues only if they involve a kind of self-reflective awareness and control. According to this second view, primary examples of epistemic virtues are attentiveness, creativity, curiosity, intellectual honesty and objectivity, understanding, and wisdom. Cognitive faculties such as perception and memory qualify as epistemic virtues only inasmuch as their use exemplifies one of the aforementioned intellectual dispositions.

Wide content: mental content which depends in part on the thinker's environment or history.

Worldview (*Weltanschauung*): an individual's or group's grasp of the world and especially of the structures and values within which he, she, or they live. The term is associated with Dilthey and Jaspers but has become current to express the overall presupposed outlook of an individual or historical group. Recognition of the role played by language in providing the worldview of a people has been a persistent theme of twentieth-century philosophy.

INDEX

Index written by
  Gerard M-F Hill 2008